Essentials of Marketing

A Marketing Strategy Planning Approach

12
EDITION

Essentials of Marketing

A Marketing Strategy Planning Approach

William D. Perreault, Jr., Ph.D.
UNIVERSITY OF NORTH CAROLINA

Joseph P. Cannon, Ph.D.
COLORADO STATE UNIVERSITY

E. Jerome McCarthy, Ph.D.
MICHIGAN STATE UNIVERSITY

The McGraw-Hill Companies

McGraw-Hill
Irwin

ESSENTIALS OF MARKETING: A MARKETING STRATEGY PLANNING APPROACH

Published by McGraw-Hill/Irwin, a business unit of The McGraw-Hill Companies, Inc., 1221 Avenue of the Americas, New York, NY, 10020. Copyright © 2010, 2008, 2006, 2003, 2000, 1997, 1994, 1991, 1988, 1985, 1982, 1979 by The McGraw-Hill Companies, Inc. All rights reserved. No part of this publication may be reproduced or distributed in any form or by any means, or stored in a database or retrieval system, without the prior written consent of The McGraw-Hill Companies, Inc., including, but not limited to, in any network or other electronic storage or transmission, or broadcast for distance learning.

Some ancillaries, including electronic and print components, may not be available to customers outside the United States.

This book is printed on acid-free paper.

1 2 3 4 5 6 7 8 9 0 DOW/DOW 0 9

ISBN   978-0-07-340481-3
MHID   0-07-340481-0

Vice president and editor-in-chief: *Brent Gordon*
Publisher: *Paul Ducham*
Executive editor: *Doug Hughes*
Director of development: *Ann Torbert*
Coordinating editor: *Lin Davis*
Editorial coordinator: *Sean M. Pankuch*
Vice president and director of marketing: *Robin J. Zwettler*
Marketing manager: *Katie Mergen*
Vice president of editing, design and production: *Sesha Bolisetty*
Lead project manager: *Christine A. Vaughan*
Lead production supervisor: *Carol A. Bielski*
Lead designer: *Matthew Baldwin*
Senior photo research coordinator: *Lori Kramer*
Photo researcher: *Mike Hruby*
Senior media project manager: *Kerry Bowler*
Cover and interior design: *Keith McPherson*
Typeface: *10.5/12 Goudy*
Compositor: *Macmillan Publishing Solutions*
Printer: *R. R. Donnelley*

Library of Congress Cataloging-in-Publication Data

Perreault, William D.
    Essentials of marketing : a marketing strategy planning approach / William D. Perreault,
Joseph P. Cannon, E. Jerome McCarthy.—12th ed.
        p. cm.
    Includes index.
    ISBN-13: 978-0-07-340481-3 (alk. paper)
    ISBN-10: 0-07-340481-0 (alk. paper)
    1. Marketing.   I. Cannon, Joseph P., Ph. D. II. McCarthy, E. Jerome (Edmund Jerome)
III. Title.
HF5415.M378 2010
658.8—dc22
                                                                2009031814

www.mhhe.com

Essentials of Marketing Is Designed to Satisfy Your Needs

This book is about marketing and marketing strategy planning. And, at its essence, marketing strategy planning is about figuring out how to do a superior job of satisfying customers. We take that point of view seriously and believe in practicing what we preach. So you can trust that this new edition of *Essentials of Marketing*—and all of the other teaching and learning materials that accompany it—will satisfy your needs. We're excited about this 12th edition of *Essentials of Marketing,* and we hope that you will be as well.

In developing this edition, we've made hundreds of big and small additions, changes, and improvements in the text and all of the supporting materials that accompany it. We'll highlight some of those changes in this preface, but first it's useful to put this newest edition in a longer-term perspective.

Building on Pioneering Strengths

Essentials of Marketing pioneered an innovative structure—using the "four Ps" with a managerial approach—for the introductory marketing course. It quickly became one of the most widely used business textbooks ever published because it organized the best ideas about marketing so that readers could both understand and apply them. The unifying focus of these ideas is on how to make the marketing decisions that a manager must make in deciding what customers to target and how best to meet their needs.

Over many editions of *Essentials of Marketing,* there have been constant changes in marketing management and the marketing environment. Some of the changes have been dramatic, and others have been subtle. As a result, we have made ongoing changes to the text to reflect marketing's best practices and ideas. Throughout all of these changes, *Essentials of Marketing* and the supporting materials that accompany it have been more widely used than any other teaching materials for introductory marketing. It is gratifying that the four Ps framework has proved to be an organizing structure that has worked well for millions of students and teachers.

What's Different about Essentials of Marketing?

The success of *Essentials of Marketing* is not the result of a single strength—or one long-lasting innovation. Other textbooks have adopted our four Ps framework, and we have continuously improved the book. And the text's four Ps framework, managerial orientation, and strategy planning focus have proved to be foundation pillars that are remarkably robust for supporting new developments in the field and innovations in the text and package. Thus, with each new edition of *Essentials of Marketing* we have continued to innovate to better meet the needs of students and faculty. In fact, we have made ongoing changes in how we develop the logic of the four Ps and the marketing strategy planning process. As always, though, our objective is to provide a flexible, high-quality text and choices from comprehensive and reliable support materials—so that instructors and students can accomplish their learning objectives. At least four characteristics of *Essentials of Marketing* distinguish it from other texts: (1) we focus on developing analytical abilities and how-to-do-it skills, (2) we integrate special topics, (3) we provide a flexible teaching and learning package that allows instructors to teach and students to learn marketing *their* way, and (4) we have an unmatched attention to detail. These combine to deliver a proven product for instructors and students. Let us show you what we mean—and why and how instructors and students benefit from the *Essentials of Marketing* teaching and learning package.

Marketing operates in dynamic markets—today more than ever. Fast-changing global markets, challenges to our environment and sustainability, and

William D. Perreault, Jr.

William D. Perreault, Jr., is Kenan Professor of Business at the University of North Carolina. Dr. Perreault is the recipient of the two most prestigious awards in his field: the American Marketing Association Distinguished Educator Award and the Academy of Marketing Science Outstanding Educator Award. He also was selected for the Churchill Award, which honors career impact on marketing research. He was editor of the *Journal of Marketing Research* and has been on the review board of the *Journal of Marketing* and other journals.

The Decision Sciences Institute has recognized Dr. Perreault for innovations in marketing education, and at UNC he has received several awards for teaching excellence. His books include two other widely used texts: *Basic Marketing* and *The Marketing Game!*

Dr. Perreault is a past president of the American Marketing Association Academic Council and served as chair of an advisory committee to the U.S. Bureau of the Census and as a trustee of the Marketing Science Institute. He has also worked as a consultant to organizations that range from GE and IBM to the Federal Trade Commission and Venezuelan Ministry of Education.

Joseph P. Cannon

Joseph P. Cannon is associate professor of marketing at Colorado State University. He has also taught at the University of North Carolina at Chapel Hill, Emory University, Instituto de Empresa, INSEAD, and Thammasat University. He has received several teaching awards and honors.

Dr. Cannon's research has been published in the *Journal of Marketing, Journal of Marketing Research, Journal of the Academy of Marketing Science, Journal of Personal Selling and Sales Management, Journal of Public Policy and Marketing,* and *The Academy of Management Review* among others. He received the 2006 and 2008 Louis W. and Rhona L. Stern Awards for articles making a significant contribution to marketing and channels of distribution. He has written many teaching cases. He serves on the editorial review boards of the *Journal of Marketing,* where he received a distinguished reviewer award, the *Journal of the Academy of Marketing Sciences,* and the *Journal of Supply Chain Management.* For three years he served as chair of the American Marketing Association's Interorganizational Special Interest Group (IOSIG). Before entering academics, Dr. Cannon worked for six years in sales and marketing for Eastman Kodak Company.

E. Jerome McCarthy

E. Jerome McCarthy received his Ph.D. from the University of Minnesota and was a Ford Foundation Fellow at the Harvard Business School. He has taught at the Universities of Oregon, Notre Dame, and Michigan State. He was honored with the American Marketing Association's Trailblazer Award in 1987, and he was voted one of the "top five" leaders in marketing thought by marketing educators.

Besides publishing various articles, he is the author of books on data processing and social issues in marketing. He has been a frequent presenter at marketing conferences in the United States and internationally.

In addition to his academic interests, Dr. McCarthy has been involved in guiding the growth of organizations in the United States and overseas—both as a consultant and as a director. He has also been active in executive education. However, throughout his career, his primary interests have been in (1) "converting" students to marketing and effective marketing strategy planning and (2) preparing teaching materials to help others do the same. This is why he has spent a large part of his career developing and improving marketing texts to reflect the most current thinking in the field.

the blurring speed of advances in technology represent just a few of the dynamic trends confronting today's marketing manager. While some marketing texts attempt to describe this dynamic environment, *Essentials of Marketing* teaches students *analytical abilities and how-to-do-it skills* that prepare them for success. To move students in this direction, we deliberately include a variety of examples, explanations, frameworks, models, classification systems, cases, and how-to-do-it techniques that relate to our overall framework for marketing strategy planning. Similarly, the *Marketing Plan Coach* on the Student CD and the text website helps students see how to create marketing plans. Taken together, these items speed the development of "marketing sense" and enable the student to analyze marketing situations and develop marketing plans in a confident and meaningful way. They are practical and they work. And because they are interesting and understandable, they motivate students to see marketing as the challenging and rewarding area it is. In the end, the *Essentials of Marketing* teaching and learning package prepares students to analyze marketing situations and develop exceptional marketing strategies—not just recite endless sets of lists.

As opposed to many other marketing textbooks, we emphasize careful *integration of special topics.* Some textbooks treat "special" topics—like relationship marketing, international marketing, services marketing, marketing and the Internet, marketing for nonprofit organizations, marketing ethics, social issues, and business-to-business marketing—in separate chapters. We deliberately avoid doing that because we are convinced that treating such topics separately leads to an unfortunate compartmentalization of ideas. We think they are too important to be isolated in that way. For example, to simply tack on a new chapter on e-commerce or marketing applications on the Internet completely ignores the reality that these are not just isolated topics but rather must be considered broadly across the whole fabric of marketing decisions. Conversely, there is virtually no area of marketing decision making where it's safe to ignore the impact of e-commerce, the Internet, or information technology. The same is true with other topics. So they are interwoven and illustrated throughout the text to emphasize that marketing thinking is crucial in all aspects of our society and economy. Looking for the proof of how we integrate special topics across chapters? Check out the fold-out grid just inside the back cover.

The comprehensive package of materials gives you, the instructor, the *flexibility* to *teach marketing your way*—or you, the student, the ability to *learn marketing your way.* Marketing can be studied and used in many ways, and the *Essentials of Marketing* text material is only the central component of our *Professional Learning Units System (P.L.U.S.)* for students and teachers. Instructors and students can select from our units to develop their own personalized teaching and learning systems.

Our objective is to offer you a *P.L.U.S.* "menu" so that you can conveniently select units you want—and disregard what you do not want. Many combinations of units are possible depending on course and learning objectives. Later in this Preface we highlight each *P.L.U.S.* element—and the full details can be found in the discussion of the Instructor's Resource CD in the Instructor's Manual.

We take great pride in the *attention to detail* we put into revising each and every new edition of *Essentials of Marketing.* There are thousands of examples of this attention to detail throughout this edition of *Essentials of Marketing* and the rest of the learning package. In this edition of the book you will find we have extended, up-to-date case discussions of leading companies like Apple, Amazon, Cirque du Soleil, Nintendo, Under Armour, and Flip—with which students can relate. The photos and advertisements provide real examples and complement and extend concepts in each chapter. The electronic presentation slides feature scripts, print advertisements, exciting graphics, interactive exercises, and video clips—all updated with this and every edition of the book. Unlike other marketing plan software, our *Marketing Plan Coach* was developed by the authors to work with this book. And because we understand the importance of fair tests in the introductory marketing course, we have personally developed, evaluated, and refined a test question database with thousands of objective test questions. Instructors and students who use *Essentials of Marketing* know and appreciate this attention to detail.

Students only take the introductory marketing course once—and for many students it is their only marketing class. They deserve the benefits of a highly innovative yet *proven* set of learning materials. Our teaching and learning materials—from the textbook to the iPod videos to the test question bank to the online materials—have been constantly updated yet are proven to work for generations of students. Do you want to use an unproven textbook with your students?

What's New in This Edition of *Essentials of Marketing?*

There are several big changes to this edition of *Essentials of Marketing* and hundreds of smaller ones. *Essentials of Marketing* is quick to recognize the many dramatic changes in the marketing environment and marketing strategy.

One of the big changes has been the attention we have given to *sustainability and its implications for marketers. Essentials of Marketing* has long included discussions of the impact of marketing on the environment. Recently society has grown increasingly concerned with sustainability—the idea that it's important to meet present needs without compromising the ability of future generations to meet their own needs. Marketing managers are responding to customer concerns—and almost every chapter in this edition of *Essentials of Marketing* now includes some discussion of sustainability. As with other special topics, we do more than just describe sustainability; we explain how marketing managers take these concerns into account in their analysis—and screen opportunities on this criterion. Strategy decisions that take sustainability into account are not straightforward—and the approach used throughout the book helps students understand and address this challenge.

We have continued our efforts at making *Essentials of Marketing* the most readable and interesting textbook on the market. The entire text has been critically revised, updated, and rewritten. We have carefully consolidated and reorganized, and sometimes made the difficult decision to cut topics to make the book shorter and even more readable. Thus, most chapters in this edition are shorter than in the previous edition. You'll see that we discuss trends in the external market environment earlier in the text; further, we have moved the discussion of segmentation, targeting, and positioning so that it now leads directly into our discussion of customers in Chapters 5 and 6. All of the cases at the back of the book have also been updated, edited, revised, and/or replaced with new ones.

The aim of all this revising, refining, editing, and illustrating is to make the important concepts and points even clearer to students. We want to make sure that each student really does get a good feel for a market-directed system and how he or she can help it—and some company—run better. We believe marketing is important and interesting, and we want every student who reads *Essentials of Marketing* to share our enthusiasm. The result, we believe, is a book that is easier to read and more relevant for today's student.

There are hundreds of other changes spread throughout the book. Marketing is dynamic—the marketing environment and marketing practices are evolving quickly as technology, the economy, customers, and competition transform quickly in today's markets. Students want to read about the latest trends and marketing practices. Throughout every chapter, we have updated and added new discussions and examples of

- The evolution of advertising media including mobile advertising, blogs, social media like Facebook, and various forms of advertising on the Internet.
- The role and process of customers' search for information on the Internet—and its implications for marketing strategy.
- The influence of word-of-mouth and how it has changed in the era of the Internet and customer review sites.
- The needs of customers in emerging markets and developing countries—and how some organizations are meeting those customer needs.
- The use of innovation and idea generation for new products and marketing mix elements—and

how they've become key sources of competitive advantage.
- The evolving nature of retailing on the Internet—as firms better understand what works and what doesn't—and successful strategies that have emerged.
- Lifetime customer value and customer equity.
- Best practices in marketing, and how to avoid marketing mistakes (including errors and omissions all too common among many failed dot-com operators).
- Effective e-commerce innovations and changes in marketing over the Internet.
- The costs and benefits of different approaches for customer acquisition and retention.
- Relationship building in marketing.
- Customer service and customer retention.
- Ethical issues and the social impacts of marketing and macro-marketing.
- The importance of providing superior customer value as the means to achieve customer satisfaction and competitive advantage.
- The growing uses of technology in organizational buying.
- Low-cost methods for conducting marketing research and the use of specialized search engines.
- The increasing emphasis on design in product development.
- The circumstances when using direct channels of distribution make sense—and how to manage channel conflict that might come about when direct and indirect channels are used in combination.
- Promotional campaigns that use viral communications to generate "buzz" among consumers.
- New and emerging applications of customer relationship management databases and tools.

Updates have extended beyond the book to our entire learning package, including

- PowerPoint presentations that have been completely updated and revised—including the addition of short video clips in each chapter—thereby reducing instructor preparation and increasing student interest.
- A completely updated test bank of more than 5,000 questions—with more than 1,000 completely new questions—all written and edited *by the authors*.
- Eight new full-length videos and video cases for use in your classes—to increase student involvement. These are in addition to the more than 150 video clips and 27 full-length videos.
- An updated software interface for the computer-aided problems—to make them even easier for students to use.
- An updated *Marketing Plan Coach* that has been converted to html and moved online—in addition to its home on the Student CD.

Eighteen Chapters—with an Emphasis on Marketing Strategy Planning

The emphasis of *Essentials of Marketing* is on marketing strategy planning. Eighteen chapters introduce the important concepts in marketing and help the student see marketing through the eyes of the manager. The organization of the chapters and topics is carefully planned. But we took special care in writing so that

- It is possible to rearrange and use the chapters in many different sequences—to fit different needs.
- All of the topics and chapters fit together into a clear, overall framework for the marketing strategy planning process.

Broadly speaking, the chapters fall into two groupings. The first seven chapters introduce marketing and a broad view of the marketing strategy planning process. They cover topics such as the marketing environment, segmentation, differentiation, and buyer behavior, as well as how marketing information systems and research provide information about these forces to improve marketing decisions. The second half of the text goes into the details of planning the four Ps, with specific attention to the key strategy decisions in each area. Then we conclude with an integrative review and an assessment of marketing's challenges and opportunities.

The first chapter deals with the important role of marketing—focusing not only on how a marketing orientation guides a business or nonprofit organization in the process of providing superior value to customers but also on the role of macro-marketing and how a market-directed economy shapes choices and quality of life for consumers. Chapter 2 builds on these ideas with a focus on the marketing strategy planning process and why it involves narrowing down to the selection of a specific target market and blending the four Ps into a marketing mix to meet the needs of those customers. With that foundation in place, the chapter introduces an integrative model of the marketing strategy planning process that serves as an organizing framework for the rest of the text.

Chapter 3 introduces students to the importance of evaluating opportunities in the external environments affecting marketing. This chapter also highlights the critical role of screening criteria for narrowing down from possible opportunities to those that the firm will pursue. Then, Chapter 4 shows how analysis of the market relates to segmentation and differentiation decisions as well as the criteria for narrowing down to a specific target market and marketing mix.

You have to understand customers to segment markets and satisfy target market needs. So the next two chapters take a closer look at *customers*. Chapter 5 studies the behavioral aspects of the final consumer market. Chapter 6 looks at how business and organizational customers—like manufacturers, channel members, and government purchasers—are similar to and different from final consumers.

Chapter 7 is a contemporary view of getting information—from marketing information systems and marketing research—for marketing planning. This chapter includes discussion of how information technology—ranging from intranets to speedy collection of market research data—is transforming the marketing job. This sets the stage for discussions in later chapters about how research and marketing information improve each area of marketing strategy planning.

The next group of chapters—Chapters 8 through 17—is concerned with developing a marketing mix out of the four Ps: Product, Place (involving channels of distribution, logistics, and distribution customer service), Promotion, and Price. These chapters are concerned with developing the "right" Product and making it available at the "right" Place with the "right" Promotion and the "right" Price—to satisfy target customers and still meet the objectives of the business. These chapters are presented in an integrated, analytical way—as part of the overall framework for the marketing strategy planning process—so students' thinking about planning marketing strategies develops logically.

Chapters 8 and 9 focus on product planning for goods and services as well as managing product quality, new-product development, and the different strategy decisions that are required at different stages of the product life cycle. We emphasize the value of an organized new-product development process for developing really new products that propel a firm to profitable growth. This chapter also details how quality management approaches can improve implementation, including implementation of better service quality.

Chapters 10 through 12 focus on Place. Chapter 10 introduces decisions a manager must make about using direct distribution (for example, selling from the firm's own website) or working with other firms in a channel of distribution. We put special emphasis on the need for channel members to cooperate and coordinate to better meet the needs of customers. Chapter 11 focuses on the fast-changing arena of logistics and the strides that firms are making in using e-commerce to reduce the costs of storing, transporting, and handling products while improving the distribution service they provide customers. Chapter 12 provides a clear picture of retailers, wholesalers, and their strategy planning, including exchanges taking place via the Internet. This composite chapter helps students see why the big changes taking place in retailing are reshaping the channel systems for many consumer products.

Chapters 13 through 15 deal with Promotion. These chapters build on the concepts of integrated marketing communications, direct-response promotion, and customer-initiated digital communication, which are introduced in Chapter 13. Chapter 14 deals with the

ESSENTIALS OF MARKETING 12e   Perreault/Cannon/McCarthy

www.mhhe.com/fourps

roles of personal selling, customer service, and sales technology in the promotion blend. Chapter 15 covers advertising and sales promotion, including the ways that managers are taking advantage of the Internet and other highly targeted media to communicate more effectively and efficiently.

Chapters 16 and 17 deal with Price. Chapter 16 focuses on pricing objectives and policies, including use of information technology to implement flexible pricing, pricing in the channel, and the use of discounts, allowances, and other variations from a list price. Chapter 17 covers cost-oriented and demand-oriented pricing approaches and how they fit in today's competitive environments. The careful coverage of marketing costs helps equip students to deal with the renewed cost-consciousness of the firms they will join.

The final chapter considers how efficient the marketing process is. Here we evaluate the effectiveness of both micro- and macro-marketing—and we consider the competitive, technological, ethical, and social challenges facing marketing managers now and in the future. Chapter 18 also reinforces the integrative nature of marketing management and reviews the marketing strategy planning process that leads to creative marketing plans.

Three appendices can be used to supplement the main text material. Appendix A provides some traditional economic analysis of supply and demand that can be a useful tool in analyzing markets. Appendix B reviews some quantitative tools—or marketing arithmetic—which helps marketing managers who want to use accounting data in analyzing marketing problems. Appendix B also reviews forecasting as a way to predict market potential and sales for a company's product. Finally, many students like to look at Appendix C—which is about career opportunities in marketing.

The following sections include 44 cases. Eight of these written cases supplement video cases available to instructors in their video package and online to students. Almost all of the 36 short written cases have been updated with new information to make sure they reflect the realities of the current marketplace. The focus of these cases is on problem solving. They encourage students to apply, and really get involved with, the concepts developed in the text. At the end of each chapter, we recommend particular cases that best relate to that chapter's content.

Teaching and Learning Your Way—Elements of P.L.U.S.

Essentials of Marketing can be studied and used in many ways—the *Essentials of Marketing* text material is only the central component of our *Professional Learning Units System (P.L.U.S.)* for students and teachers. Instructors (and students) can select from our units to develop their own personalized systems. Many combinations of units are possible, depending on course objectives. As a quick overview, in addition to the *Essentials of Marketing* text,

the *P.L.U.S.* package includes a variety of new and updated supplements.

Most of the instructor resources may be found on the *Instructor's Resource CD.* McGraw-Hill has found that many instructors rely on electronic versions of the instructor's materials so, in order to save trees, print versions of these supplements are only produced on-demand. If you prefer to have hard copies of the *Multimedia Lecture Support Guide* or any of the Instructor's Manuals, request them through your McGraw-Hill sales representative.

Beyond the *Essentials of Marketing* textbook, the key components of *P.L.U.S.* include

Electronic Presentation Slides. Our "best in the business" multimedia lecture support package includes a variety of materials. For each chapter there is a set of PowerPoint presentations for a complete lecture that includes television commercials and short video clip examples, plus a set of archive slides with a high-quality selection of ads and photos. Many chapters have engaging interactive exercises as well.

Multimedia Lecture Support Guide. This guide supports the presentation slides and includes detailed lecture scripts, outlines, and archives.

Videos and Video Cases. The video package has been updated with 8 new videos—to give you 27 full-length videos. In addition, we have more than 150 short (1 to 4 minutes) video clips—many integrated into the PowerPoint presentation slides. See the Video Instructor's Manual for more ideas about how to use the videos in class.

Instructor's Manual to Accompany *Essentials of Marketing*. This manual includes an overview of all the teaching/learning units, as well as suggested answers to all questions, exercises, and assignments.

Test Bank. Our test bank includes thousands of objective test questions—*developed by the authors* to ensure they work really well with the text. McGraw-Hill's EZ-Test program facilitates the creation of tests. We take great pride in having a test bank that works for students and instructors.

Online Learning Center: www.mhhe.com/fourps. The website for the book provides access to a variety of student and instructor resources.

***Essentials of Marketing* Cartridges for Blackboard and WebCT.** Include *Essentials of Marketing* materials directly in your online course management program.

The Marketing Game! This simulation was designed to complement the strategy planning process in *Essentials of Marketing* and encourages students to compete and learn.

CPS (wireless Classroom Performance System) by eInstruction. Sometimes called "clicker" technology, this system allows for quick in-class online polls or quizzing. Ask your McGraw-Hill sales representative for more details.

Another set of resources is designed to be directly accessed by students. Optional book packages include the Student CD or access to the book's premium content website. These options allow motivated students to purchase access to additional resources that appeal to their learning style. Most of the student materials are available online, on a student CD, and/or in print. Look inside the front cover of this book for more details about how to obtain these learning resources. They include

Self-Test Quizzes and Bonus Quizzes. These help students prepare for tests and may be used with a computer or an iPod.

Online Applications in *Basic Marketing* and *Essentials of Marketing*. Links to current online articles, websites, podcasts, and videos are organized by content area and available at the book's website.

Marketing Plan Coach. This online software tool helps students build marketing plans using materials and concepts directly from the textbook. It was created by the authors specifically for use with *Essentials of Marketing*.

Computer-Aided Problems. This easy-to-use spreadsheet software program works with exercises at the end of each chapter in the text (and in the Learning Aid) to help develop analytical skills needed by today's managers.

Narrated Slide Shows. These provide overviews of key marketing concepts usually from a set of chapters. Eight in all, they are great to use before reading a new section in *Essentials of Marketing* or for help in studying for tests.

Learning with Ads. These are great for visual learners who can preview or study concepts from each chapter and examine applications in real print ads. About 10 to 15 ads per chapter.

Video Cases. Clips from video cases in the book are available for viewing on computers or iPods.

Learning Aid for Use with *Essentials of Marketing*. This study aid gives students something extra from your marketing class. It includes chapter summaries, access to more than 1,225 additional practice test questions, and over 75 application exercises. Check out the textbook's website to download sample chapters.

New with this Edition of *Essentials of Marketing!* McGraw-Hill Connect Marketing

Less Managing. More Teaching. Greater Learning. McGraw-Hill *Connect Marketing* for *Essentials of Marketing* is an online assignment and assessment solution that connects students with the tools and resources they'll need to achieve success.

McGraw-Hill *Connect Marketing* helps prepare students for their future by enabling faster learning, more efficient studying, and higher retention of knowledge.

McGraw-Hill *Connect Marketing* features. *Connect Marketing* offers a number of powerful tools and features to make managing assignments easier, so faculty can spend more time teaching. With *Connect Marketing*, students can engage with their coursework anytime and anywhere, making the learning process more accessible and efficient. *Connect Marketing* offers instructors the features described below.

Simple assignment management. With *Connect Marketing*, creating assignments is easier than ever, so faculty can spend more time teaching and less time managing. The assignment management function enables instructors to:

- Create and deliver assignments easily with selectable end-of-chapter questions and test bank items.
- Streamline lesson planning, student progress reporting, and assignment grading to make classroom management more efficient than ever.
- Go paperless with the eBook and online submission and grading of student assignments.

Smart grading. When it comes to studying, time is precious. *Connect Marketing* helps students learn more efficiently by providing feedback and practice material when they need it, where they need it. When it comes to teaching, an instructor's time also is precious. The grading function enables you to:

- Have assignments scored automatically, giving students immediate feedback on their work and side-by-side comparisons with correct answers.
- Access and review each response; manually change grades or leave comments for students to review.
- Reinforce classroom concepts with practice tests and instant quizzes.

Instructor library. The *Connect Marketing* Instructor Library is your repository for additional resources to improve student engagement in and out of class. You can select and use any asset that enhances your lecture. The *Connect Marketing* Instructor Library includes:

- *eBook*
- *PowerPoints*
- *Video Cases*
- *Marketing Plan Coach*
- *Video Instructor's Manual*
- *Learning with Ads*

Student study center. The *Connect Marketing* Student Study Center is the place for students to access additional resources. The Student Study Center:

- Offers students quick access to lectures, practice materials, eBooks, and more.
- Provides instant practice material and study questions, easily accessible on the go.
- Gives students access to the Personalized Learning Plan described below.

Diagnostic and adaptive learning of concepts: Learn-Smart. Students want to make the best use of their study time. The LearnSmart adaptive self-study technology within *Connect Marketing* provides students with a seamless combination of practice, assessment, and remediation for every concept in the textbook. LearnSmart's intelligent software adapts to every student response and automatically delivers concepts that advance the student's understanding while reducing time devoted to the concepts already mastered. The result for every student is the fastest path to mastery of the chapter concepts. LearnSmart:

- Applies an intelligent concept engine to identify the relationships between concepts and to serve new concepts to each student only when he or she is ready.
- Adapts automatically to each student, so students spend less time on the topics they understand and practice more those they have yet to master.
- Provides continual reinforcement and remediation, but gives only as much guidance as students need.
- Integrates diagnostics as part of the learning experience.
- Enables instructors to assess which concepts students have efficiently learned on their own, thus freeing class time for more applications and discussion.

Student progress tracking. *Connect Marketing* keeps instructors informed about how each student, section, and class is performing, allowing for more productive use of lecture and office hours. The progress-tracking function enables you to:

- View scored work immediately and track individual or group performance with assignment and grade reports.
- Access an instant view of student or class performance relative to learning objectives.
- Collect data and generate reports required by many accreditation organizations, such as AACSB.

Integrating eBooks—McGraw-Hill *Connect Plus Marketing*. McGraw-Hill reinvents the textbook learning experience for the modern student with *Connect Plus Marketing*. A seamless integration of an eBook and *Connect Marketing, Connect Plus Marketing*

provides all of the *Connect Marketing* features plus the following:

- An integrated eBook, allowing for anytime, anywhere access to the textbook.
- Dynamic links between the problems or questions that instructors assign to students and the location in the eBook where that problem or question is covered.
- A powerful search function to pinpoint and connect key concepts in a snap.

In short, *Connect Marketing* offers instructors and students powerful tools and features that optimize your time and energies, enabling instructors to focus on course content, teaching, and student learning. *Connect Marketing* also offers a wealth of content resources for both instructors and students. This state-of-the-art, thoroughly tested system supports instructors in preparing students for the world that awaits. For more information about *Connect*, go to **www.mcgrawhillconnect.com**, or contact your local McGraw-Hill sales representative.

Tegrity Campus: Lectures 24/7

Tegrity Campus is a service that makes class time available 24/7 by automatically capturing every lecture

 in a searchable format for students to review

when they study and complete assignments. With a simple one-click start-and-stop process, you capture all computer screens and corresponding audio. Students can replay any part of any class with easy-to-use browser-based viewing on a PC or Mac.

Educators know that the more students can see, hear, and experience class resources, the better they learn. In fact, studies prove it. With Tegrity Campus, students quickly recall key moments by using Tegrity Campus' unique search feature. This search helps students efficiently find what they need, when they need it, across an entire semester of class recordings. Help turn all your students' study time into learning moments immediately supported by your lecture.

To learn more about Tegrity watch a 2-minute Flash demo at **http://tegritycampus.mhhe.com**.

Lecture capture. Increase the attention paid to lecture discussion by decreasing the attention paid to note taking. For an additional charge Lecture Capture offers new ways for students to focus on the in-class discussion, knowing they can revisit important topics later. Lecture Capture enables an instructor to:

- Record and distribute your lecture with a click of button.

- Record and index PowerPoint presentations and anything shown on your computer so it is easily searchable, frame by frame.
- Offer access to lectures anytime and anywhere by computer, iPod, or mobile device.
- Increase intent listening and class participation by easing students' concerns about note-taking. Lecture Capture will make it more likely you will see students' faces, not the tops of their heads.

Learning Objectives, Assurance of Learning, and Accreditation

Assurance of learning is an important element of many accreditation standards. We designed the components of *Essentials of Marketing's P.L.U.S.* to support your teaching and learning objectives, so our *P.L.U.S.* provides excellent support for accreditation efforts. This topic is addressed in more detail in the *Instructor's Manual*. Briefly, however, each chapter in the book begins with a list of numbered learning objectives. Material related to these objectives is developed not only in the chapter but also in the exercises, questions, and problems for each chapter. Every test question is also classified by these objectives. In addition, questions are classified by level of difficulty, type of question (according to Bloom's Taxonomy), and skill areas specified by AACSB International, an accrediting group for business schools. EZ Test, McGraw-Hill's easy-to-use test bank software, can search the test bank by these and other categories, which helps with assurance of learning analysis and assessment.

Our publisher, the McGraw-Hill Companies, is a proud corporate member of AACSB International. This text and the accompanying supplements explicitly recognize and support the AACSB curriculum standards for business accreditation. For example, our Computer-Aided Problems help to develop analysis skills and our case studies and *Marketing Plan Coach* encourage development of integrated thinking, problem solving, and communication skills. We should be clear, however, that AACSB does not provide some sort of evaluation or certification of texts or their supporting materials. Rather, AACSB leaves content coverage and assessment decisions to an individual school, depending on the mission of the school and objectives of its faculty. Thus, the flex-ible *P.L.U.S.* package can help both faculty and students tailor a learning experience that meets objectives not only for the marketing course but also for the curriculum and accreditation.

McGraw-Hill Customer Care Contact Information

At McGraw-Hill, we understand that getting the most from new technology can be challenging. That's why our services don't stop after you purchase our products. You can e-mail our Product Specialists 24 hours a day to get product-training online. Or you can search our knowledge bank of Frequently Asked Questions on our support website. For Customer Support, call **800-331-5094**, e-mail **hmsupport@mcgraw-hill.com**, or visit **www. mhhe.com/support**. One of our Technical Support Analysts will be able to assist you in a timely fashion.

Responsibilities of Leadership

In closing, we return to a point raised at the beginning of this preface. *Essentials of Marketing* has been a leading textbook in marketing since its first edition. We take the responsibilities of that leadership seriously. We know that you want and deserve the very best teaching and learning materials possible. It is our commitment to bring you those materials—today with this edition and in the future with subsequent editions.

We recognize that fulfilling this commitment requires a process of continuous improvement. Revisions, updates, and development of new elements must be ongoing—because needs change. You are an important part of this evolution, of this leadership. We encourage your feedback. The most efficient way to get in touch with us is to send an e-mail message to Bill_Perreault@unc.edu or Joe.Cannon@colostate.edu. If you prefer the traditional approach, send a letter to 2104 N. Lakeshore Dr., Chapel Hill, NC, 27514. Thoughtful criticisms and suggestions from students and teachers alike have helped to make *Essentials of Marketing* what it is. We hope that you will help make it what it will be in the future.

William D. Perreault, Jr.
Joseph P. Cannon
E. Jerome McCarthy

Let's Walk through Your *Essentials of Marketing* Textbook . . .

At its essence, marketing strategy planning is about figuring out how to do a superior job of satisfying customers. With that in mind, the 12th edition of *Essentials of Marketing* was developed to satisfy your desire for knowledge and add value to your course experience. Not only will this text teach you about marketing and marketing strategy planning, but its design, pedagogy, and supplementary learning aids were developed to work well with the text and a variety of study situations.

Each person has a different approach to studying. Some may focus on reading that is covered during class, others prefer to prepare outside of the classroom and rely heavily on in-class interaction, and still others prefer more independence from the classroom. Some are more visual or more "hands on" in the way they learn, and others just want clear and interesting explanations. To address a variety of needs and course situations, many hours went into creating and designing the *Essentials of Marketing* textbook and other learning materials. We highlight how you can use these materials in the following section.

Take a moment now to learn more about all of the resources available to help you best prepare for this course and—whether you plan to work in marketing or not—for your future career.

Essentials of Marketing: An Innovative Marketing Experience

With 18 chapters that introduce the important concepts in marketing management, you will see all aspects of marketing through the eyes of the marketing manager. The first seven chapters introduce marketing and give you a framework for understanding marketing strategy planning in any type of organization, and then the second half of the text takes you into planning the four Ps of marketing (Product, Place, Promotion, and Price) with specific attention to the key strategy decisions in each area.

Essentials of Marketing pioneered the "four Ps" approach to organize and describe managerial marketing for introductory marketing courses. This new edition covers the dynamic changes taking place in marketing management and the marketing environment. Some of these changes have been dramatic, and others have been subtle. But the 12th edition helps you understand the changes taking place and reflects today's best marketing practices and ideas.

Start each chapter with an overview

Each chapter begins with an in-depth case study developed specifically to motivate your interest and highlight real-life examples of the learning objectives and specific marketing decision areas covered in that chapter. Each case study is accompanied by a list of learning objectives that will help you understand and identify important terms and concepts covered in the chapter. We recommend you read the opening case and learning objectives and then take just a few minutes to skim through the chapter, check out the exhibits, pictures, and headings before reading the conclusion. This preview gives you a picture of the chapter and how it fits together—and research shows that it helps increase your comprehension of the reading.

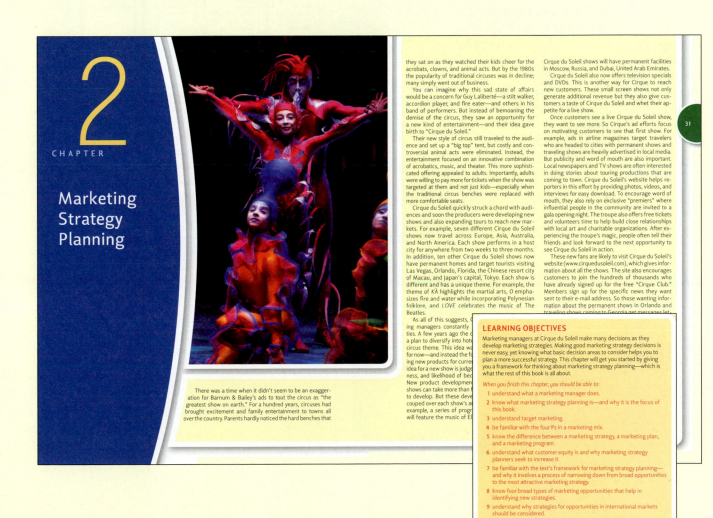

The exhibits, photos, and ads will help you understand the concepts . . .

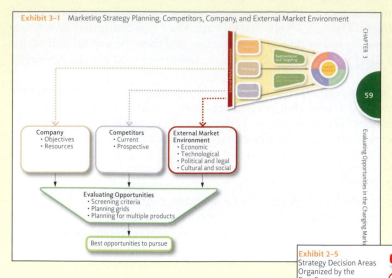

Exhibit 3–1 Marketing Strategy Planning, Competitors, Company, and External Market Environment

Company
• Objectives
• Resources

Competitors
• Current
• Prospective

External Market Environment
• Economic
• Technological
• Political and legal
• Cultural and social

Evaluating Opportunities
• Screening criteria
• Planning grids
• Planning for multiple products

Best opportunities to pursue

After introducing the Marketing Strategy Planning Process model in Chapter 2, we begin each chapter with an exhibit that clearly organizes the chapter's content. The exhibit does two things that you should notice. First, it shows how the topic in this chapter fits as a piece in the larger marketing strategy planning process—its fit with the rest of the content in the book. Second, the figure will show how that chapter's concepts fit together—another way to "preview" the chapter.

The four Ps are just one way we organize marketing concepts for you. We know that many students learn best with "conceptual organizers," figures, charts, and tables that help organize thinking and provide an easy way to remember key concepts. When you see these figures, study them for a minute and think about how they help you understand and learn new marketing concepts.

Exhibit 2–5 Strategy Decision Areas Organized by the Four Ps

Product	Place	Promotion	Price
• Physical good	• Objectives	• Objectives	• Objectives
• Service	• Channel type	• Promotion blend	• Flexibility
• Features	• Market exposure	• Salespeople Kind	• Level over product life cycle
• Benefits	• Kinds of intermediaries	Number Selection	• Geographic terms
• Quality level	• Kinds and locations of stores	Training Motivation	• Discounts
• Accessories		• Advertising Targets	• Allowances
• Installation	• How to handle transporting and storing	Kinds of ads Media type	
• Instructions	• Service levels	Copy thrust Prepared by whom	
• Warranty	• Recruiting intermediaries	• Sales promotion	
• Product lines	• Managing channels	• Publicity	
• Packaging			
• Branding			

Exhibit 4–3 Narrowing Down to Target Markets

All customer needs

Some generic market

One broad product-market

Narrowing down to specific product-market

Homogeneous (narrow) product-markets

Segmenting into possible target markets

| Single target market | Multiple target markets | Combined target markets |

Selecting target marketing approach

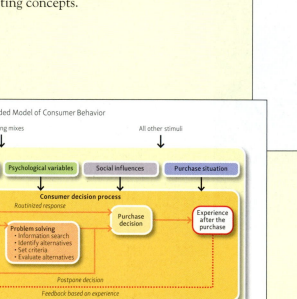

Exhibit 5–8 An Expanded Model of Consumer Behavior

Marketing mixes   All other stimuli

| Economic needs | Psychological variables | Social influences | Purchase situation |

Consumer decision process

Routinized response

Need awareness

Problem solving
• Information search
• Identify alternatives
• Set criteria
• Evaluate alternatives

Purchase decision

Experience after the purchase

Postpone decision

Feedback based on experience

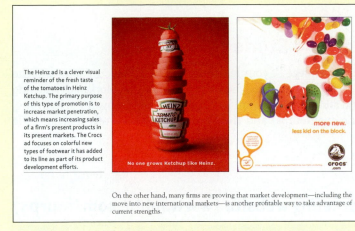

The Heinz ad is a clever visual reminder of the fresh taste of the tomatoes in Heinz Ketchup. The primary purpose of this type of promotion is to increase market penetration, which means increasing sales of a firm's present products in its present markets. The Crocs ad focuses on colorful new types of footwear it has added to its line as part of its product development efforts.

No one grows Ketchup like Heinz.

more new.
less kid on the block.

crocs.com

On the other hand, many firms are proving that market development—including the move into new international markets—is another profitable way to take advantage of current strengths.

Full-color photos and current ads are carefully placed in every chapter. They provide a visual demonstration of key concepts and emphasize important ideas discussed in the chapter.

Think critically about the issues facing marketing managers . . .

The book includes a variety of different opportunities for you to learn about the types of decisions facing real marketing managers. Stop and think about the Ethics Questions you confront in your reading. At the end of each chapter, we suggest some cases—which are interesting situations faced by real marketers. You can find the cases near the end of the book.

Ethics QUESTION

A marketing researcher conducts a study that reveals that a competing firm's brand-new marketing strategy is off to a very strong start in attracting new customers. He thinks that it will ultimately be so successful that it will increase the price of the competing firm's stock, so he decides to buy the stock before that happens. However, a friend suggests that the trade might not be ethical and perhaps could even be considered illegal insider trading. Does it seem unethical to you? Should it be illegal? Explain your thinking.

THE IMPORTANCE OF MARKETING STRATEGY PLANNING

SUGGESTED CASES

3. MANU Soccer Academy
4. Trusty Technology Services
5. PolyTech Products

12. DrRay.com
29. Specialized Castings, Inc.

Explore special topics . . .

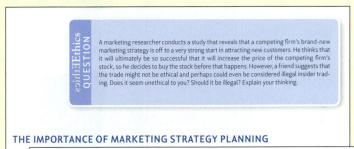

Internet EXERCISE

Go to the BuyerZone website (www.buyerzone.com). What types of products could be purchased by requesting a free quote on this site? From the home page click "Buying Advice> Furniture> Chairs> Chair Buyer's Guide," then look through this Buyer's Guide. Look at the Buyer's Guides for other products as well. What can be learned about buying different products from BuyerZone.com? For a marketing manager targeting smaller businesses, how could this site be helpful?

purchase and the level of uncertainty about what choice might be best. The time and expense of searching for information may not be justified for a minor purchase. But a major purchase often involves real detective work by the buyer.

New-task buying situations provide a good opportunity for a new supplier to make inroads with a customer. With a buyer actively searching for information, the seller's promotion has a much greater chance of being noticed and having an impact. Advertising, trade show exhibits, sales brochures, and salespeople can all help build the buyer's attention, but an informative website may be essential for

Follow a topic online with the Internet Exercises that let you see how firms can use the Web to enhance their marketing. And each chapter includes a boxed scenario to help you learn more about a particular marketing topic.

Warming Up to Sustainable Purchasing

With increased attention on global warming and the environment, managers in many organizations are wondering what their responsibility should be. It's true that the first focus of most organizational buying decisions is on green—dollars, that is. However, when purchasing managers consider sustainability as part of their vendor analysis, green choices often prove to be winners.

Attention to sustainability often identifies savings that previously were not obvious. Sometimes all that is involved is a simple change from what's routine. For example, when Falconbridge Limited's aluminum smelter changed to more efficient (but more expensive) lightbulbs, it saved almost $100,000 per year in energy bills. When the Fairmont Hotel in Vancouver searched for alternative chemicals to use in its pool, it found new ones that were healthier for guests and cut costs by $2,000. Hotels everywhere cleaned up when they stopped rewashing all of their linens every day. All it took was a card in the bath that says, "If you'd like us to replace a towel with a clean one, put it on the floor." The cards cost pennies, whereas the hot water, detergent, labor, and wear on linens cost millions.

fluorescent lightbulbs. Home Depot has more that 3,000 Eco Option products that promote energy conservation, sustainability, and clean water. Both retailers are building more energy-efficient stores and prodding their suppliers to think green by using less packaging. Cynics question their motives—because there's a benefit for retailers when packages take up less shelf space.

In California, some city governments are cooperating with energy firms to develop generators powered by ocean waves. Across the Atlantic, the mayor of London requires city agencies to buy recycled goods whenever possible. And federal agencies in the United States must buy energy-efficient PCs and monitors made without toxins that could later pollute landfills.

Some progressive firms make sustainability an essential buying criterion even if they don't see financial benefits. New Belgium Brewing Company puts sustainable values in its mission statement; that means its purchasing people select more

Beyond the Book—Walk through the
Essentials of Marketing Website and the Student CD

Think about your *Essentials of Marketing* textbook as the centerpiece of your learning experience. Computers and the Internet offer additional interactive learning opportunities. We have designed the *Essentials of Marketing* learning package to give you a variety of different ways to learn and study. So if you are looking for other pathways to learning, check out the *Essentials of Marketing* website (www.mhhe.com/fourps) and the Student CD, both of which include custom-developed programs.

Available for free at the *Essentials of Marketing* website (www.mhhe.com/fourps)

Help me study for my next test!

The *Essentials of Marketing* website has self-test quizzes—10 questions for each chapter. Buy the Student CD or pay for access to the premium website for even more quiz questions.

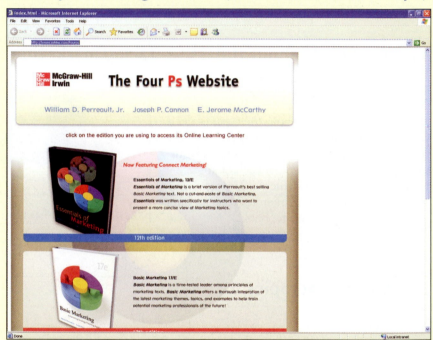

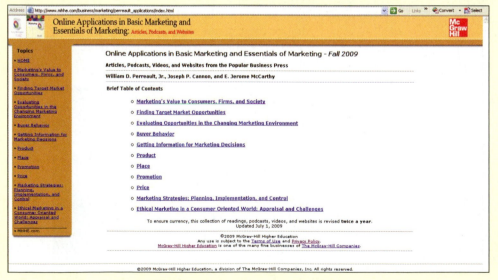

Read business articles, listen to podcasts, or watch videos online to learn more about marketing!

Check out the *Online Applications in Basic Marketing and Essentials of Marketing* at the book's website to find links to more than 100 sites where you can read, listen, or watch.

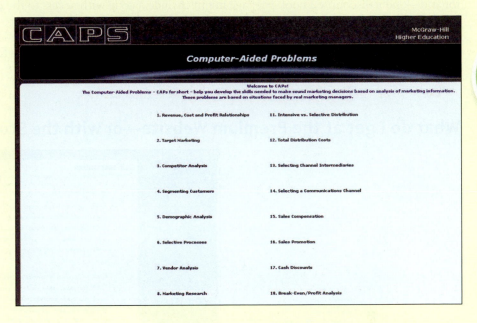

Learn how marketing managers use numbers and spreadsheets to analyze data and make marketing decisions!

Our Computer-Aided Problems (we call them CAPs) allow you to apply concepts from the book while you develop and hone analytical skills needed by today's marketing managers.

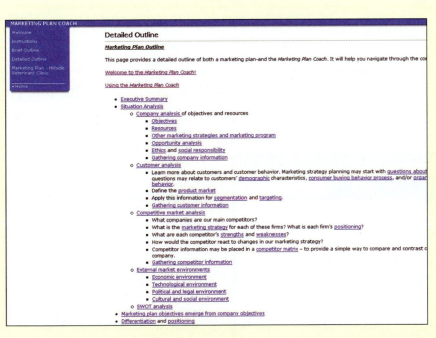

I want to write a marketing plan!

Check out the *Marketing Plan Coach*—it connects the concepts in your textbook with a real marketing plan. This website was designed by the authors of *Essentials of Marketing*—so it really works with your book.

The *Essentials of Marketing* Student CD and Premium Website—More Interactivity and More Ways to Learn!

We have even more ways to extend your marketing learning experience. Your instructor may have made these choices for you—and a discounted book package might include a code with access to the premium website or you might have received the Student CD with your new textbook. If the Internet is always easy to access, you might like the *Essentials of Marketing* Premium Website. Go to the site and for $10 you can access these additional learning experiences. If you prefer not to be tethered to the Web, you can ask your bookstore to get you the *Essentials of Marketing* Student CD.

What do I get at the Premium Website—or with the Student CD?

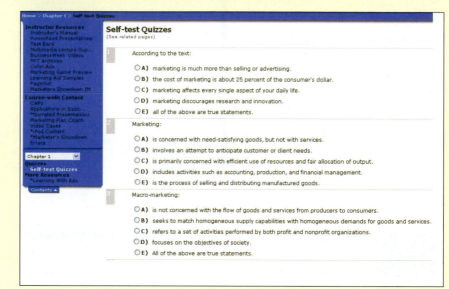

1. Bonus Quizzes—study for that next test with 20 multiple-choice questions per chapter.

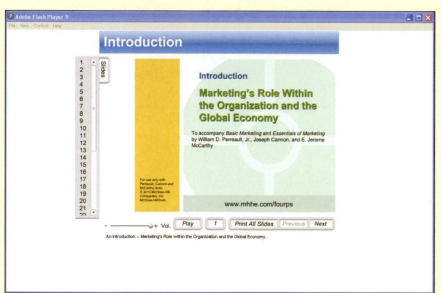

2. Narrated Slide Shows—provide an overview of key marketing concepts. Great to use before reading chapters for the first time or to help you study for tests. These can be downloaded to your iPod (or other MP3 device) if you want to take them with you.

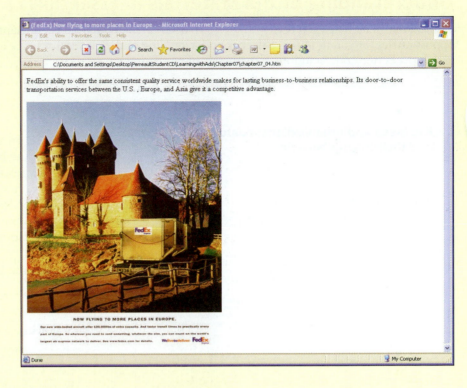

3. Learning with Ads—a great way to preview ideas from each chapter. You can look through print ads and read comments for ideas about how a chapter's concepts are applied by real companies. Great for visual learners.

4. Video Cases—get ready access to video clips from our video cases. Listen to and watch successful marketing in action.

The *Learning Aid*—One More Way to Get a Deeper Understanding of the Materials in *Essentials of Marketing*

The *Learning Aid* helps you review and test yourself on material from each chapter—while also providing opportunities for you to obtain a deeper understanding of the material. The *Learning Aid* offers a hands-on way to develop a better understanding of the basics of marketing.

Chapter 6

Business and organizational customers and their buying behavior

What This Chapter Is About

Chapter 6 discusses the buying behavior of the important business and organizational customers who buy for resale or for use in their own businesses. They buy more goods and services than final customers! There are many opportunities in marketing--to producers, to intermediaries, to government, and to nonprofit organizations--and it is important to understand how these organizational customers buy.

Organizations tend to be much more economic in their buying behavior than final consumers. Further, some must follow pre-set bidding and bargaining processes. Yet, they too have emotional needs. And sometimes a number of different people may influence the final purchase decision. Keep in mind that business and organizational customers are problem solvers too. Many of the ideas in Chapter 5 carry over, but with some adaptation.

This chapter deserves careful study because your past experience as a consumer is not as helpful here as it was in the last few chapters. Organizational customers are much less numerous. In some cases it is possible to create a separate marketing mix for each individual customer. Understanding these customers is necessary to plan marketing strategies for them. Try to see how they are both similar and different from final customers.

Important Terms

business and organizational customers, p. 140
purchasing specifications, p. 143
ISO 9000, p. 143
purchasing managers, p. 143
multiple buying influence, p. 144
buying center, p. 145
vendor analysis, p. 145
requisition, p. 147
new-task buying, p. 148
straight rebuy, p. 148

modified rebuy, p. 148
competitive bid, p. 150
just-in-time delivery, p. 154
negotiated contract buying, p. 154
outsource, p. 155
North American Industry Classification System (NAICS) codes, p. 156
open to buy, p. 160
resident buyers, p. 160
Foreign Corrupt Practices Act, p. 161

_____ 36. In international markets, it is legal to make small grease money payments--if they are customary in that country.

Answers to True-False Questions

1. F, p. 140	13. T, p. 148	25. T, p. 157
2. T, p. 142	14. T, p. 149	26. T, p. 158
3. T, p. 142	15. T, p. 150	27. F, p. 158
4. T, p. 143	16. T, p. 150	28. T, p. 159
5. T, p. 143	17. F, p. 151	29. T, p. 159
6. T, p. 145	18. T, p. 151	30. F, p. 159-160
7. F, p. 145	19. F, p. 151	31. F, p. 160
8. T, p. 145	20. F, p. 151	32. T, p. 160
9. T, p. 145-146	21. F, p. 154	33. F, p. 160
10. T, p. 147	22. F, p. 154	34. F, p. 160
11. T, p. 148	23. T, p. 155	35. F, p. 161
12. F, p. 148	24. T, p. 155-156	36. T, p. 161

Multiple-Choice Questions (Circle the correct response)

1. Which of the following is a business or organizational customer?
    a.   producers of goods and services.
    b.   a retailer.
    c.   a wholesaler.
    d.   a government agency.
    e.   All of the above are business and organizational customers.

2. In comparison to the buying of final consumers, the purchasing of organizational buyers:
    a.   is strictly economic and not at all emotional.
    b.   is always based on competitive bids from multiple suppliers.
    c.   leans basically toward economy, quality, and dependability.
    d.   is even less predictable.
    e.   Both a and c are true statements.

3. Today, many agricultural commodities and manufactured items are subject to rigid control or grading. As a result, organizational buyers often buy on the basis of:
    a.   purchasing specifications.
    b.   negotiated contracts.
    c.   competitive bids.

4. In a buying center, multiple buying influences can include:
    a.   users.
    b.   buyers.
    c.   gatekeepers.
    d.   deciders.
    e.   all of the above.

The *Learning Aid* provides a brief introduction to each chapter, a list of the important new terms (with page numbers for easy reference), true–false questions (with answers and page numbers) that cover all the important terms and concepts, and multiple-choice questions (with answers) that illustrate the kinds of questions that may appear in examinations.

Name: _____   Course & Section: _____

Exercise 6-3

Vendor analysis

This exercise is based on computer-aided problem number 6--Vendor Analysis. A complete description of the problem appears on page 163 of *Essentials of Marketing*, 12th edition.

1. Supplier 2 is thinking about adding U.S. wholesalers to its channel of distribution. The supplier would ship in large, economical quantities to the wholesaler and the wholesaler would keep a stock of chips on hand. The wholesaler would charge CompuTech a higher price--$1.90 a chip. But with the chips available from a reliable wholesaler CompuTech's inventory cost as a percent of its total order would only be 2 percent. In addition, the cost of transportation would only be $.01 per chip. Assuming CompuTech planned to buy 84,500 chips, what would its total costs be with and without the wholesaler? Should CompuTech encourage the supplier to add a wholesaler to the channel?

    Total Costs for Vendor Supplier 2, buying direct   _____

    Total Costs for Vendor Supplier 2, using wholesaler   _____

    _____

    _____

    _____

2. Supplier 2 has explored the idea of adding wholesalers to the channel, but has found that it will take at least another year to find suitable wholesalers and develop relationships. As a result, if CompuTech deals with Supplier 2 its inventory cost as a percent of the total order would remain at 5.4 percent, and transportation cost would remain at $.03 per chip. But the supplier is still interested in improving its marketing mix now--so it can develop a strong relationship with CompuTech. Based on an analysis of CompuTech's needs, Supplier 2 has developed a new design for the electronic memory chips.

    The redesigned chips will have a built-in connector, so CompuTech would not have to buy separate connectors. In addition, the new design would make it faster and easier to replace a defective chip. The supplier estimates that with the new design it would cost CompuTech only $1.00 to replace a bad chip.

    The supplier has not yet priced the new chip, but it would cost the supplier an additional $.06 to produce each chip. If the supplier set the price of the chip at $1.93 each (the old price of $1.87 plus the additional $.06), how much would the new design cost CompuTech on an order of 84,500 chips. (Hint: compute CompuTech's total cost for the current design based on an order quantity of 84,500 chips, and then compute the total cost assuming the new price, the reduced cost of replacing a defective chip, and no cost for a connector.)

The *Learning Aid* also incorporates cases, problems, and exercises, including ones that build on the end-of-chapter computer-aided problems—with clear instructions and worksheets for you to complete for additional practice.

The Marketing Game!

The Marketing Game! is a competitive marketing strategy simulation that allows you the opportunity to apply your marketing knowledge in a fun and interesting way. *The Marketing Game!* is applicable for all areas of marketing and all levels because the game is not based on just one simulation. Rather, it is based on several simulations with one integrated framework. *The Marketing Game!* is based on realistic marketing and realistic marketing relationships, and allows for maximum flexibility.

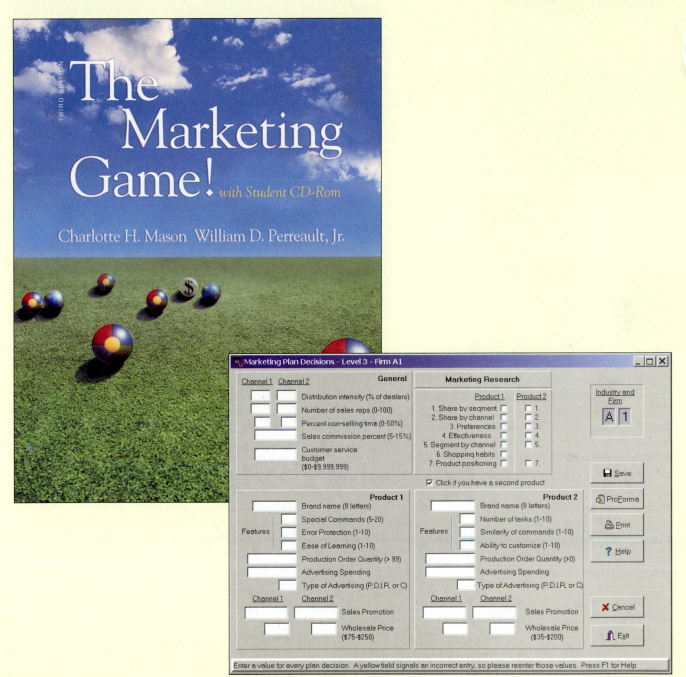

ESSENTIALS OF MARKETING 12e   Perreault/Cannon/McCarthy

Acknowledgments

Essentials of Marketing has been influenced and improved by the inputs of more people than it is possible to list. We do, however, want to express our appreciation to those who have played the most significant roles, especially in this edition.

We are especially grateful to our many students who have criticized and made comments about materials in *Essentials of Marketing*. Indeed, in many ways, our students have been our best teachers.

We owe our greatest debt of gratitude to Lin Davis. The book probably wouldn't exist if it weren't for her—because without her help it would have been just too overwhelming and we'd have quit! Lin has been part of this team for about 25 years. During that time, she has made contributions in every aspect of the text and package. For this edition, she spent countless hours researching photos and case histories, and she critiqued thousands of manuscript pages through countless revisions of the text and all the ac-companying materials. She has reviewed, edited, and critiqued every word we've written. Her hard work, positive attitude, and dedication to quality throughout the whole process is without match. We could not have asked for a better friend and colleague.

Many improvements in recent editions were stimulated by feedback from a number of colleagues around the country. Their feedback took many forms. In particular, we would like to recognize the helpful contributions of

Michele Adams, *Erie Community College South*
Thomas Ainscough, *University of South Florida*
Mary Albrecht, *Maryville University*
David Andrus, *Kansas State University at Manhattan*
April Atwood, *University of Washington*
Ainsworth Bailey, *University of Toledo*
Turina Bakker, *University of Wisconsin*
Jeff Bauer, *University of Cincinnati—Batavia*
Leta Beard, *University of Washington*
Amy Beattie, *Nichols College of Champlain*
Cathleen Behan, *Northern VA Community College*
Patty Bellamy, *Black Hills State University*
Suzeanne Benet, *Grand Valley State University*
Shahid Bhuian, *Louisiana Tech University*
John S. Bishop, Jr., *University of South Alabama*
David Blackmore, *University of Pittsburgh*
Jonathan Bohlman, *Purdue School of Management*
Laurie Brachman, *University of Wisconsin—Madison*
Kit Brenan, *Northland Community College*
John Brennan, *Florida State University*
Richard Brien, *De Anza College*
Elten Briggs, *University of Texas—Arlington*
Denny Bristow, *St. Cloud State University*
Kendrick W. Brunson, *Liberty University*
Derrell Bulls, *Texas Women's University*
Helen Burdenski, *Notre Dame College of Ohio*
Nancy Bush, *Wingate University*
Carmen Calabrese, *University of North Carolina—Pembroke*
Catherine Campbell, *University of Maryland University College*
James Carlson, *Manatee Community College*
Deborah Carter, *Coahoma Community College*
Donald Caudill, *Bluefield State College*
Kirti Celly, *California State University—Dominguez Hills*
Kenny Chan, *California State University—Chico*
E. Wayne Chandler, *Eastern Illinois University*
Chen Ho Chao, *Baruch College, City University of New York*
Valeri Chukhlomin, *Empire State College*
Margaret Clark, *Cincinnati State Technical and Community College*

Paris Cleanthous, *New York University—Stern School*
Thomas Cline, *St. Vincent College*
Gloria Cockerell, *Collin County Community College*
Linda Jane Coleman, *Salem State College*
Clare Comm, *University of Massachusetts—Lowell*
Brian Connett, *California State University—Northridge*
Craig Conrad, *Western Illinois University*
Sherry Cook, *Southwest Missouri State*
Matt Critcher, *University of Arkansas Community College—Batesville*
Tammy Crutchfield, *Mercer University*
Brent Cunningham, *Jacksonville State University*
Charles Davies, *Hillsdale College*
J. Charlene Davis, *Trinity University*
Scott Davis, *University of California at Davis*
Susan Higgins DeFago, *John Carroll University*
Les Dlabay, *Lake Forest College*
Glenna Dod, *Wesleyan College*
Gary Donnelly, *Casper College*
Paul Dowling, *University of Utah*
Laura Downey, *Purdue University*
Phillip Downs, *Florida State University*
Michael Drafke, *College of DuPage*
John Drea, *Western Illinois University*
Colleen Dunn, *Bucks Community College*
Sean Dwyer, *Louisiana Technical University*
Mary Edrington, *Drake University*
Steven Engel, *University of Colorado*
Keith Fabes, *Berkeley College*
Peter Fader, *University of Pennsylvania*
Ken Fairweather, *LeTourneau University*
Phyllis Fein, *Westchester Community College*
Lori S. Feldman, *Purdue University*
Mark Fenton, *University of Wisconsin—Stout*
Richard Kent Fields, *Carthage College*
Lou Firenze, *Northwood University*
Michael Fitzmorris, *Park University*
Richard Fogg, *Kansas State University*
Kim Folkers, *Wartburg College*
Renee Foster, *Delta State University*
Frank Franzak, *Virginia Commonwealth University*
John Gaffney, *Hiram College*
John Gaskins, *Longwood University*
Thomas Giese, *University of Richmond*
J. Lee Goen, *Oklahoma Baptist University*
David Good, *Central Missouri State University*
Pradeep Gopalakrishna, *Pace University*
Rahul Govind, *University of Mississippi*
Norman Govoni, *Babson College*
Gary Grandison, *Alabama State University*
Wade Graves, *Grayson Community College*
Mitch Griffin, *Bradley University*
Mike Griffith, *Cascade College*
Alice Griswold, *Clarke College*
Barbara Gross, *California State University, Northridge*
Susan Gupta, *University of Wisconsin at Milwaukee*
John Hadjmarcou, *University of Texas at El Paso*
Khalil Hairston, *Indiana Institute of Technology*
Adam Hall, *Western Kentucky University*
Bobby Hall, *Wayland Baptist University*
Joan Hall, *George Mason University*

Dorothy Harpool, *Wichita State University*
LeaAnna Harrah, *Marion Technical College*
James Harvey, *George Mason University*
Lewis Hershey, *University of North Carolina—Pembroke*
James Hess, *Ivy Tech Community College*
Wolfgang Hinck, *Louisiana State University—Shreveport*
Pamela Homer, *California State University—Long Beach*
Ronald Hoverstad, *University of the Pacific*
Deborah Baker Hulse, *University of Texas at Tyler*
Janet Hunter, *Northland Pioneer College*
Annette Jaiko, *Triton College/College of DuPage*
Carol Johanek, *Washington University*
Timothy Johnston, *University of Tennessee at Martin*
Keith Jones, *North Carolina A&T State University*
Fahri Karakaya, *University of Massachusetts*
Gary Karns, *Seattle Pacific University*
Pat Karush, *Thomas College*
Eileen Kearney, *Montgomery County Community College*
James Kellaris, *University of Cincinnati*
Robin Kelly, *Cuyahoga Community College*
Rob Kleine, *Ohio Northern University*
Kathleen Krentler, *San Diego State University*
Michael Kroff, *Montana State University—Bozeman*
Dmitri Kuksov, *Washington University*
Ann Kuzma, *Minnesota State University—Mankato*
Jean Laliberte, *Troy State University*
Linda Lamarca, *Tarleton State University*
Kevin Lambert, *Southeast Community College*
Richard LaRosa, *Indiana University of Pennsylvania*
Donald Larson, *The Ohio State University*
Debra Laverie, *Texas Tech University*
Marilyn Lavin, *University of Wisconsin—Whitewater*
David Levy, *Bellevue University*
Doug Livermore, *Morningside College*
Guy Lochiatto, *Massachusetts Bay Community College*
Lori Lohman, *Augsburg College*
Paul James Londrigan, *Mott Community College*
Terry Lowe, *Heartland Community College*
Harold Lucius, *Rowan University*
Richard Lutz, *University of Florida*
Andrew Lynch, *Southern New Hampshire University*
W. J. Mahony, *Southern Wesleyan University*
Patty Marco, *MATC Truax*
Rosalynn Martin, *MidSouth Community College*
Phyllis Mansfield, *Pennsylvania State University—Erie*
James McAloon, *Fitchburg State University*
Michele McCarren, *Southern State Community College*
Kevin McEvoy, *University of Connecticut—Stamford*
Rajiv Mehta, *New Jersey Institute of Technology*
Sanjay Mehta, *Sam Houston State University*
Matt Meuter, *California State University—Chico*
Michael Mezja, *University of Las Vegas*
Margaret Klayton Mi, *Mary Washington College*
Linda Mitchell, *Lindon State College*
Ted Mitchell, *University of Nevada, Reno*
Nichole Montgomery, *College of William & Mary*
Robert Montgomery, *University of Evansville*
Todd Mooradian, *College of William and Mary*
Kelvyn A. Moore, *Clark Atlanta University*
Marlene Morris, *Georgetown University*
Brenda Moscool, *California State University—Bakersfield*

Ed Mosher, *Laramie Community College*
Reza Motameni, *California State University—Fresno*
Steve Mumsford, *Gwynedd-Mercy College*
Clara Munson, *Albertus Magnus*
Suzanne Murray, *Piedmont Technical College*
Thomas Myers, *University of Richmond*
Cynthia Newman, *Rider University*
Philip S. Nitse, *Idaho State University at Pocatello*
J. R. Ogden, *Kutztown University*
David Oh, *California State University—Los Angeles*
Sam Okoroafo, *University of Toledo*
Jeannie O'Laughlin, *Dakota Wesleyan University*
Louis Osuki, *Chicago State University*
Esther S. Page-Wood, *Western Michigan University*
Karen Palumbo, *University of St. Francis*
Terry Paridon, *Cameron University*
Terry Paul, *Ohio State University—Columbus*
Sheila Petcavage, *Cuyahoga Community College*
Stephen Peters, *Walla Walla Community College*
Julie Pharr, *Tennessee Tech University*
Brenda Ponsford, *Clarion University*
Tracy Proulx, *Park University*
Anthony Racka, *Oakland Community College*
Kathleen Radionoff, *Cardinal Stritch University*
Daniel Rajaratnam, *Baylor University*
Catherine Rich-Duval, *Merrimack College*
Charles W. Richardson, Jr., *Clark Atlanta University*
Lee Richardson, *University of Baltimore*
Daniel Ricica, *Sinclair Community College*
Sandra Robertson, *Thomas Nelson Community College*
Kim Rocha, *Barton College*
Carlos Rodriguez, *Governors State University*
Robert Roe, *University of Wyoming*
Ann Root, *Florida Atlantic University—Boca Raton*
Mark Rosenbaum, *Northern Illinois University*
Tom Rossi, *Broome Community College*
Donald Roy, *Middle Tennessee State University*
Joel Saegert, *University of Texas at San Antonio*
C. M. Sashi, *Florida Atlantic University*
Erika Schlomer-Fischer, *California Lutheran University*
Lewis Schlossinger, *Community College of Aurora*
Charles Schwepker, *Central Missouri State University*
Murphy Sewell, *University of Connecticut—Storrs*
Kenneth Shamley, *Sinclair College*
Doris Shaw, *Kent State University*
Donald Shifter, *Fontbonne College*
Jeremy Sierra, *New Mexico State University*
Lisa Simon, *California Polytech—San Luis Obispo*
Rob Simon, *University of Nebraska—Lincoln*
James Simpson, *University of Alabama in Huntsville*
Aditya Singh, *Pennsylvania State University—McKeesport*
Mandeep Singh, *Western Illinois University*
Jill Slomski, *Mercyhurst College*
Kimberly Smith, *County College of Morris*
Robert Smoot, *Lees College*
Don Soucy, *University of North Carolina—Pembroke*
Roland Sparks, *Johnson C. Smith University*
Gene Steidinger, *Loras College*
Jim Stephens, *Emporia State University*
Tom Stevenson, *University of North Carolina*
Geoffrey Stewart, *University of Louisiana at Lafayette*

Karen Stewart, *The Richard Stockton College of New Jersey*
Charles Strain, Jr., *University of Houston—Downton*
Stephen Strange, *Henderson Community College*
Randy Stuart, *Kennesaw State University*
Rajneesh Suri, *Drexel University*
John Talbott, *Indiana University—Bloomington*
Uday Tate, *Marshall University*
A.J. Taylor, *Austin Peay State University*
Janice Taylor, *Miami University*
Kimberly Taylor, *Florida International University*
Jeff Thieme, *Syracuse University*
Scott Thompson, *University of Wisconsin—Oshkosh*
Dennis Tootelian, *California State University—Sacramento*
Gary Tschantz, *Walsh University*
Fran Ucci, *Triton College/College of DuPage*
Sue Umashankar, *University of Arizona*
David Urban, *Virginia Commonwealth University*
Peter Vantine, *Georgia Tech*
Steve Vitucci, *Tarleton State University*
Sharon Wagner, *Missouri Western State College*
Suzanne Walchli, *University of the Pacific*
Jane Wayland, *Eastern Illinois University*
Danny "Peter" Weathers, *Louisiana State University*
John Weiss, *Colorado State University*
M. G. M. Wetzeis, *Universiteit Maastrict, The Netherlands*
Fred Whitman, *Mary Washington College*
Judy Wilkinson, *Youngstown State University*
Phillip Wilson, *Midwestern State University*
Robert Witherspoon, *Triton College*
John Withey, *Indiana University—South Bend*
Jim Wong, *Shenandoah University*
Joyce H. Wood, *N. Virginia Community College*
Courtney Worsham, *University of South Carolina*
Newell Wright, *James Madison University*
Joseph Yasaian, *McIntosh College*
Gary Young, *Worcester State College*
Lin Zhang, *Truman State University*

We've always believed that the best way to build consistency and quality into the text and the other *P.L.U.S.* units is to do as much as possible ourselves. With the growth of multimedia technologies, it's darn hard to be an expert on them all. But we've had spectacular help in that regard.

We're indebted to Jay Carlson and Mandy Noelle Carlson for their creative work on the lecture-support PowerPoint presentation slides. David Urban, Milt Pressley, and Lewis Hershey participated in PowerPoint work on the previous editions and their influence is still felt. It's rare to find world-class marketing professors who also have their skill and experience with teaching technologies, so we are certainly fortunate that they've shared their brainwaves on this project.

Nick Childers at Shadows and Light Creative Services has been the guru behind the scenes in production work on the video package for many editions. He also worked with us in developing the first versions of our CDs. Nick Childers and Debra Childers continue to play an important role not only in the videos but in multimedia innovations.

For several editions, Judy Wilkinson has played a big role as producer of the video series for the book. In that capacity, she worked closely with us to come up with ideas, and she provided guidance to the talented group of marketing professors and managers who created or revised videos for this edition. Judy also is the author of several outstanding video segments. We express respect for and deep appreciation to Judy for her work on the video series. This edition of the book includes fantastic new videos authored by Linda Mothersbaugh, Debra Owens, Ron Tatham, Jeff Tanner, and Debra Childers.

Of course, like other aspects of *Essentials of Marketing*, the video series has evolved and improved over time, and its current strength is partly due to the insights of Phil Niffenegger, who served as producer for our early video efforts. The video series also continues to benefit from the contributions of colleagues who developed videos in earlier editions. They are

Gary R. Brockway	J. R. Montgomery
James Burley	Michael R. Mullen
David Burns	Phillip Niffenegger
Debra Childers	Deborah Owens
Martha O. Cooper	Thomas G. Ponzurick
Carolyn Costley	George Prough
W. Davis Folsom	Peter Rainsford
Douglas Hausknecht	Jane Reid
Scott Johnson	Roger Schoenfeldt
Bart Kittle	Thomas Sherer
Gene R. Lazniak	Jeanne M. Simmons
Bill Levy	Rollie O. Tillman
Don McBane	Robert Welsh
Charles S. Madden	Holt Wilson
W. Glynn Mangold	Poh-Lin Yeou
Robert Miller	

Faculty and students at our current and past academic institutions—Michigan State University, University of North Carolina, Colorado State University, Emory, Notre Dame, University of Georgia, Northwestern University, University of Oregon, University of Minnesota, and Stanford University—have significantly shaped the book. Professor Andrew A. Brogowicz of Western Michigan University contributed many fine ideas to early editions of the text and supplements. Neil Morgan, Charlotte Mason, Rich Gooner, Gary Hunter, John Workman, Nicholas Didow, Barry Bayus, Ken Manning, and Ajay Menon have provided a constant flow of helpful suggestions.

We also want to acknowledge the influence that the late Erin Anderson had on the authors. Erin made many important contributions to marketing thought and her insightful research had a great influence on the way we looked at marketing strategy planning. She was always generous with her time and ideas. We will miss her insights and her friendship.

We are also grateful to the colleagues with whom we collaborate to produce international adaptations of the text. In particular, Lindsey Meredith, Lynne Ricker, Stan Shapiro, Ken Wong, and Pascale G. Quester have all had a significant impact on *Essentials of Marketing*.

The designers, artists, editors, and production people at McGraw-Hill/Irwin who worked with us on this edition warrant special recognition. All of them have shared our commitment to excellence and brought their own individual creativity to the project. First, we should salute Christine Vaughan, who has done a great (and patient) job as production manager for the project. Without her adaptive problem solving, we could not have succeeded with a (very) rapid-response production schedule—which is exactly what it takes to be certain that teachers and students get the most current information possible.

We thank Devon Raemisch who worked as the editorial coordinator for most of the revision process in this edition. She turned the job over to Sean Pankuch and he has done a great job keeping us on task and on time. We owe a special debt of gratitude to our previous developmental editor Nancy Barbour. While Nancy has left McGraw-Hill, her work on many editions of this book have left a permanent, positive impression. Our executive editor, Doug Hughes, has provided a new and valued perspective on the *Essentials of Marketing* franchise. His ideas have had a great impact on the book.

Keith McPherson is a long-term, creative, and valuable contributor to the look and feel of *Essentials of Marketing*. He again took the creative lead in designing an attractive cover and inside for the book; he also put his personal touch on every piece of art and all of the illustrations in the text. These are enormously time-consuming efforts, but what a talent he is and what patience he exhibits in bringing it all together to create a book that not only discusses but really illustrates best practices in marketing! We also appreciate Mike Hruby, who again tracked down permissions for photos and ads we selected to use to illustrate important ideas.

Katie Mergen is our new marketing manager for the project. She has already jumped into the position with gusto and brought great ideas to the team. We also owe a debt of gratitude to Kerry Bowler who has taken the internal lead at McGraw-Hill in producing all of the *Essentials of Marketing* technology initiatives.

Our families have been patient and consistent supporters through all phases in developing *Essentials of Marketing*. The support has been direct and substantive. Pam Perreault and Chris Cannon have provided valuable assistance and more encouragement than you could imagine. Our kids—Suzanne, Will, Kelly, Ally, and Mallory—provide valuable suggestions and ideas as well as encouragement and support while their dads are too often consumed with a never-ending set of deadlines.

We are indebted to all the firms that allowed us to reproduce their proprietary materials here. Similarly, we are grateful to associates from our business experiences who have shared their perspectives and feedback and enhanced our sensitivity to the key challenges of marketing management. In that regard, we especially acknowledge Kevin Clancy, Peter Krieg, and their colleagues at Copernicus: The Marketing Investment Strategy Group. The combination of pragmatic experience and creative insight they bring to the table is very encouraging. If you want to see great marketing, watch them create it.

A textbook must capsulize existing knowledge while bringing new perspectives and organization to enhance it. Our thinking has been shaped by the writings of literally thousands of marketing scholars and practitioners. In some cases, it is impossible to give unique credit for a particular idea or concept because so many people have played important roles in anticipating, suggesting, shaping, and developing it. We gratefully acknowledge these contributors—from the early thought-leaders to contemporary authors and researchers—who have shared their creative ideas. We respect their impact on the development of marketing and more specifically this book.

To all of these persons—and to the many publishers who graciously granted permission to use their materials—we are deeply grateful. Responsibility for any errors or omissions is certainly ours, but the book would not have been possible without the assistance of many others. Our sincere appreciation goes to all who contributed.

William D. Perreault, Jr.
Joseph P. Cannon
E. Jerome McCarthy

Brief Contents

Contents

ESSENTIALS OF MARKETING 12e   Perreault/Cannon/McCarthy

www.mhhe.com/fourps

7

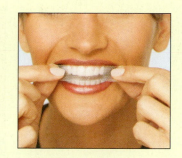

CHAPTER SEVEN

Improving Decisions with Marketing Information 164

8

CHAPTER EIGHT

Elements of Product Planning for Goods and Services 190

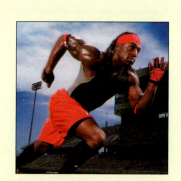

9

CHAPTER NINE

Product Management and New-Product Development 218

CHAPTER TWELVE

Retailers, Wholesalers, and Their Strategy Planning 292

CHAPTER THIRTEEN

Promotion—Introduction to Integrated Marketing Communications 320

CHAPTER FOURTEEN

Personal Selling and Customer Service 348

CHAPTER FIFTEEN

Advertising and Sales Promotion 376

16

CHAPTER SIXTEEN

Pricing Objectives and Policies 406

17

CHAPTER SEVENTEEN

Price Setting in the Business World 436

ESSENTIALS OF MARKETING 12e   Perreault/Cannon/McCarthy

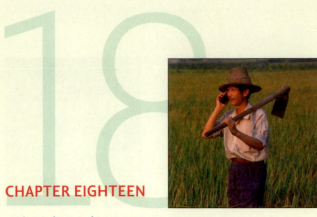

CHAPTER EIGHTEEN

Ethical Marketing in a Consumer-Oriented World: Appraisal and Challenges 462

Appendix A Economics Fundamentals 486

Appendix B Marketing Arithmetic 499

Appendix C Career Planning in Marketing 515

VIDEO CASES 529

CASES 544

xxxix

ESSENTIALS OF MARKETING 12e   Perreault/Cannon/McCarthy

www.mhhe.com/fourps

Essentials of Marketing

A Marketing Strategy Planning Approach

CHAPTER 1

Marketing's Value to Consumers, Firms, and Society

When it's time to roll out of bed in the morning, does the alarm ringtone on your Verizon cell phone wake you, or is it your Sony XM radio playing your favorite satellite station? Is the station playing hip-hop, classical, or country music—or perhaps a Red Cross ad asking you to contribute blood? Will you slip into your Levi's jeans, your shirt from Abercrombie and Fitch, and your Nikes, or does the day call for your Brooks Brothers interviewing suit? Will breakfast be Lender's Bagels with cream cheese or will you finish off that box of Kellogg's Frosted Mini-Wheats cereal made with whole grain wheat from America's heartland? Will you have some calcium-fortified Minute-Maid orange juice and brew a pot of Maxwell House coffee—or is this a day to meet a friend at the local Starbucks, where you'll pay someone else to fix you a Frappuccino while you use the Wi-Fi connection to log on to MSN.com to check your e-mail? Or perhaps if you're running late you can grab a ride to class in your friend's new Toyota Prius, swing by the McDonald's drive-thru for a McSkillet Burrito, a Vanilla Iced Coffee, and a smile from Ronald McDonald. What? Your

to Starbucks. What exactly is it about Starbucks that makes so many customers so satisfied with the experience? Why do they come back time and time again when they could get a cup of coffee almost anywhere, at half the price? Do loyal customers use the Starbucks card because it lets them participate in sweepstakes and get e-mail notices of in-store promotions and new products? Or is it because the card makes it fast and easy to order and pay? Why does Starbucks sell music CDs and offer Internet wireless hot spots at some locations? Twenty-five years ago Starbucks was a tiny company in Seattle; now it operates more than 15,000 coffee bars in 43 countries and is one of the best-known brand names in the world (even in Tokyo). Part of Starbucks' success comes from adapting its marketing strategy to changing market conditions—but not every change works. When a weaker economy caused some Starbucks' customers to trade down to lower-priced competitors like McDonald's or to brew their own coffee at home, Starbucks responded with new products. It added Perfect Oatmeal to the food menu, promoting it as a healthy breakfast choice; and offered it with a cup of coffee or tea at a value price. Starbucks hopes changes like these will win back customers.

Over the years McDonald's has also introduced many new products to meet changing customer needs. For example, the McSalad Shaker was a salad in a cup for convenient eating on the go. Customers, however, were looking for a more premium salad, which led to the introduction of the Premium Salad line. And the Snack Wrap satisfies McDonald's restaurant operations and its customers. The wrap can be quickly prepared using existing ingredients in McDonald's restaurants. And customers love that the wraps taste great, can be eaten on-the-go, and are a good value. McDonald's thought it was well positioned—as a brand that offers everyday value and convenience—to capture a larger portion of the opportunity in the multibillion dollar beverage industry. So, McDonald's dove into the high-end coffee market with its Premium Roast Coffee. The new blend was a hit, bringing new customers into restaurants, and boosting its coffee sales 40 percent in less than a year. Building on that success, McDonald's 14,000 U.S. restaurants added McCafé coffee bars selling Cappuccinos, Lattes, and Mochas.

As Starbucks, McDonald's, Dunkin' Donuts, and your local coffee shop battle it out, customers are the big winners. With all this choice, these companies have to work hard to meet customer needs and earn their business.[1]

friend decided that the new hybrid was too pricey for someone with only a part-time job? Well then, maybe you'll just have to take the bus that the city bought from General Motors. At least as you ride along you can watch videos on your iPhone.

When you think about it, you can't get very far into a day without bumping into marketing—and what the whole marketing system does for you. It affects every aspect of our lives—often in ways we don't even consider.

In other parts of the world, people wake up each day to different kinds of experiences. A family in rural China may have little choice about what food they will eat or where their clothing will come from. A consumer in a large city like Tokyo may have many choices but not be familiar with names like Lender's Bagels or Brooks Brothers.

What's more, each element in the descriptions above could be viewed in more detail and through a different lens. Consider, for example, that visit

MARKETING—WHAT'S IT ALL ABOUT?

Marketing is more than selling or advertising

Many people think that marketing means "selling" or "advertising." It's true that these are parts of marketing. But *marketing is much more than selling and advertising.*

How did all those bicycles get here?

To illustrate some of the other important things that are included in marketing, think about all the bicycles being pedaled with varying degrees of energy by bike riders around the world. Most of us don't make our own bicycles. Instead, they are made by firms like Trek, Performance, Huffy, and Murray.

Most bikes do the same thing—get the rider from one place to another. But a bike rider can choose from a wide assortment of models. They are designed in different sizes and with or without gears. Off-road bikes have large knobby tires. Kids and older people may want more wheels—to make balancing easier. Some bikes need baskets or even trailers for cargo. You can buy a basic bike for less than $50. Or you can spend more than $2,500 for a custom frame.

This variety of styles and features complicates the production and sale of bicycles. The following list shows some of the things a manager should do before and after deciding to produce and sell a bike.

"Life Comes at You Fast." Nationwide's trademarked phrase and "buildingscape" ad really get attention and remind consumers that Nationwide can help when things go awry. Creative advertising like this is an important part of marketing, but modern marketing involves much more. For example, Nationwide conducts research to understand customers' needs and then develops new policies and services to satisfy those needs at a price that represents a good value.

1. Analyze the needs of people who might buy a bike and decide if they want more or different models.
2. Predict what types of bikes—handlebar styles and types of wheels, brakes, and materials—different customers will want and decide which of these people the firm will try to satisfy.
3. Estimate how many of these people will want to buy bicycles, and when.
4. Determine where in the world these bike riders are and how to get the firm's bikes to them.
5. Estimate what price they are willing to pay for their bikes and if the firm can make a profit selling at that price.
6. Decide which kinds of promotion should be used to tell potential customers about the firm's bikes.
7. Estimate how many competing companies will be making bikes, what kind, and at what prices.
8. Figure out how to provide customer service if a customer has a problem after buying a bike.

The above activities are not part of **production**—actually making goods or performing services. Rather, they are part of a larger process—called *marketing*—that provides needed direction for production and helps make sure that the right goods and services are produced and find their way to consumers.

You'll learn much more about marketing activities in Chapter 2. For now, it's enough to see that marketing plays an essential role in providing consumers with need-satisfying goods and services and, more generally, in creating customer satisfaction. Simply put, **customer satisfaction** is the extent to which a firm fulfills a customer's needs, desires, and expectations.

MARKETING IS IMPORTANT TO YOU

Marketing is important to every consumer

Marketing affects almost every aspect of your daily life. The choices you have among the goods and services you buy, the stores where you shop, and the radio and TV programs you tune in to are all possible because of marketing. In the process of providing all these choices, marketing drives organizations to focus on what it takes to satisfy you, the customer. Most of the things you want or need are available conveniently *when* and *where* you want or need them.

Some courses are interesting when you take them but never relevant again once they're over. That's not so with marketing—you'll be a consumer dealing with marketing for the rest of your life regardless of what career you pursue. Moreover, as a consumer, you pay for the cost of marketing activities. In advanced economies, marketing costs about 50 cents of every consumer dollar. For some goods and services, the percentage is much higher. It makes sense to be an educated consumer and to understand what you get and don't get from all that spending.

Marketing will be important to your job

Another reason for studying marketing is that it offers many exciting and rewarding career opportunities. Throughout this book, you will find information about opportunities in different areas of marketing.

If you're aiming for a nonmarketing job, knowing about marketing will help you do your own job better. Throughout the book, we'll discuss ways that marketing relates to other functional areas. Further, marketing is important to the success of every organization. The same basic principles used to sell soap are also used to "sell" ideas, politicians, mass transportation, health care services, conservation, museums, and even colleges. Even your job résumé is part of a marketing campaign to sell yourself to some employer![2]

Marketing affects innovation and standard of living

An even more basic reason for studying marketing is that marketing plays a big part in economic growth and development. One key reason is that marketing encourages research and **innovation**—the development and spread of new ideas, goods, and services. As firms offer new and better ways of satisfying consumer needs, customers have more choices among products and this fosters competition for consumers' money. This competition drives down prices. Moreover, when firms develop products that really satisfy customers, fuller employment and higher incomes can result. The combination of these forces means that marketing has a big impact on consumers' standard of living—and it is important to the future of all nations.[3]

HOW SHOULD WE DEFINE MARKETING?

There are micro and macro views of marketing

In our bicycle example, we saw that a producer of bicycles has to perform many customer-related activities besides just making bikes. The same is true for an insurance company or an art museum. This supports the idea of marketing as a set of activities done by an individual organization to satisfy its customers.

On the other hand, people can't survive on bicycles and art museums alone! In advanced economies, it takes goods and services from thousands of organizations to satisfy the many needs of society. Further, a society needs some sort of marketing system to organize the efforts of all the producers, wholesalers, and retailers needed to satisfy the varied needs of all its citizens. So marketing is also an important social process.

We can view marketing in two ways: *from a micro view as a set of activities performed by organizations and also from a macro view as a social process.* Yet, in everyday use when people talk about marketing, they have the micro view in mind. So that is the way we will define marketing here. However, the broader macro view that looks at the whole production-distribution system is also important, so later we will provide a separate definition and discussion of macro-marketing.

Marketing defined

Marketing is the performance of activities that seek to accomplish an organization's objectives by anticipating customer or client needs and directing a flow of need-satisfying goods and services from producer to customer or client.

Let's look at this definition.[4]

Applies to profit and nonprofit organizations

Marketing applies to both profit and nonprofit organizations. Profit is the objective for most business firms. But other types of organizations may seek more members—or acceptance of an idea. Customers or clients may be individual consumers, business firms, nonprofit organizations, government agencies, or even foreign nations. While most customers and clients pay for the goods and services they receive, others may receive them free of charge or at a reduced cost through private or government support.

More than just persuading customers

Marketing isn't just selling and advertising. Unfortunately, some executives still think of it that way. They feel that the job of marketing is to "get rid of" whatever the company happens to produce. In fact, the aim of marketing is to identify customers' needs and meet those needs so well that the product almost "sells itself." This is true whether the product is a physical good, a service, or even an idea. If the whole marketing job has been done well, customers don't need much persuading. They should be ready to buy. And after they buy, they'll be satisfied and ready to buy the same way the next time.

Begins with customer needs

Marketing should begin with potential customer needs—not with the production process. Marketing should try to anticipate needs. And then marketing, rather than production, should determine what goods and services are to be developed—including decisions about product design and packaging; prices or fees; credit and collection policies; transporting and storing policies; advertising and sales policies; and, after the sale, installation, customer service, warranty, and perhaps even disposal and recycling policies.

Does not do it alone

This does not mean that marketing should try to take over production, accounting, and financial activities. Rather, it means that marketing—by interpreting customers' needs—should provide direction for these activities and try to coordinate them.

Marketing involves exchanges

The idea that marketing involves a flow of need-satisfying offerings from a producer to a customer implies that there is an exchange of the need-satisfying offering for something else, such as the customer's money. Marketing focuses on facilitating exchanges. In fact, *marketing doesn't occur unless two or more parties are willing to exchange something for something else*. For example, in a **pure subsistence economy**—when each family unit produces everything it consumes—there is no need to exchange goods and services and no marketing is involved. (Although each producer-consumer unit is totally self-sufficient in such a situation, the standard of living is typically relatively low.)

Builds a relationship with the customer

Keep in mind that a marketing exchange is often part of an ongoing relationship, not just a single transaction. When marketing helps everyone in a firm really meet the needs of a customer before and after a purchase, the firm doesn't just get a single sale. Rather, it has a sale and an ongoing *relationship* with the customer. Then, in the future, when the customer has the same need again—or some other need that the firm can meet—other sales will follow. Often, the marketing *flow* of need-satisfying goods and services is not just for a single transaction but rather is part of building a long-lasting relationship that benefits both the firm and the customer.

The focus of this text—management-oriented micro-marketing

Since you are probably preparing for a career in management, the main focus of this text will be on managerial marketing. We will see marketing through the eyes of the marketing manager.

The marketing ideas we will be discussing throughout this text apply to a wide variety of situations. They are important for new ventures started by one person as well as big corporations, in domestic and international markets, and regardless of whether the focus is on marketing physical goods, services, or an idea or cause. They are equally critical whether the relevant customers or clients are individual consumers, businesses, or some other type of organization. For editorial convenience, we will sometimes use the term *firm* as a shorthand way of referring to any type of organization, whether it is a political party, a religious organization, a government agency, or the like. However, to reinforce the point that the ideas apply to all types of organizations, throughout the book we will illustrate marketing concepts in a wide variety of situations.

Although marketing within individual firms is the primary focus of the text, marketing managers must remember that their organizations are just small parts of a larger macro-marketing system. Therefore, next we will briefly look at the macro view of marketing. Then, we will develop this idea more fully in later chapters.

MACRO-MARKETING

Macro-marketing is a social process that directs an economy's flow of goods and services from producers to consumers in a way that effectively matches supply and demand and accomplishes the objectives of society.[5]

Emphasis is on whole system

With macro-marketing we are still concerned with the flow of need-satisfying goods and services from producer to consumer. However, the emphasis with macro-marketing is not on the activities of individual organizations. Instead, the emphasis is on *how the whole marketing system works*. This includes looking at how marketing affects society and vice versa.

Every society needs a macro-marketing system to help match supply and demand. Different producers in a society have different objectives, resources, and skills. Likewise, not all consumers share the same needs, preferences, and wealth. In other words, within every society there are both heterogeneous (highly varied) supply capabilities and heterogeneous demands for goods and services. The role of a macro-marketing system is to effectively match this heterogeneous supply and demand *and* at the same time accomplish society's objectives.

An effective macro-marketing system delivers the goods and services that consumers want and need. It gets products to them at the right time, in the right place, and at a price they're willing to pay. It keeps consumers satisfied after the sale and brings them back to purchase again when they are ready. That's not an easy job—especially if you think about the variety of goods and services a highly developed economy can produce and the many kinds of goods and services consumers want.

Peruvian coffee farmers and their families provide coffee to Starbucks. But to overcome the spatial separation between growers and consumers, someone must first perform a variety of marketing functions, like standardizing and grading the coffee beans, transporting and storing them, and buying and selling them. When Starbucks sells consumers its branded coffee at one of its new "drive-thru" locations, it is providing the final activity of a process that began a continent away.

Exhibit 1–1 Marketing Facilitates Production and Consumption

Production Sector
Specialization and division of labor result in heterogeneous supply capabilities

Marketing needed to overcome discrepancies and separations

Discrepancies of Quantity. Producers prefer to produce and sell in large quantities. Consumers prefer to buy and consume in small quantities.

Discrepancies of Assortment. Producers specialize in producing a narrow assortment of goods and services. Consumers need a broad assortment.

Spatial Separation. Producers tend to locate where it is economical to produce, while consumers are located in many scattered places.

Separation in Time. Consumers may not want to consume goods and services at the time producers would prefer to produce them, and time may be required to transport goods from producer to consumer.

Separation of Information. Producers do not know who needs what, where, when, and at what price. Consumers do not know what is available from whom, where, when, and at what price.

Separation in Values. Producers value goods and services in terms of costs and competitive prices. Consumers value them in terms of satisfying needs and their ability to pay.

Separation of Ownership. Producers hold title to goods and services that they themselves do not want to consume. Consumers want goods and services that they do not own.

Consumption Sector
Heterogeneous demand for different goods and services and when and where they need to be to satisfy needs and wants

Separation between producers and consumers

Effective marketing in an advanced economy is difficult because producers and consumers are often separated in several ways. As Exhibit 1–1 shows, exchange between producers and consumers is hampered by spatial separation, separation in time, separation of information and values, and separation of ownership. You may love your MP3 player, but you probably don't know when or where it was produced or how it got to you. The people in the factory that produced it don't know about you or how you live.

In addition, most firms specialize in producing and selling large amounts of a narrow assortment of goods and services. This allows them to take advantage of mass production with its **economies of scale**—which means that as a company produces larger numbers of a particular product, the cost of each unit of the product goes down. Yet most consumers only want to buy a small quantity; they also want a wide assortment of different goods and services. These "discrepancies of quantity" and "discrepancies of assortment" further complicate exchange between producers and consumers (Exhibit 1–1). That is, each producer specializes in producing and selling large amounts of a narrow assortment of goods and services, but each consumer wants only small quantities of a wide assortment of goods and services.[6]

Marketing functions help narrow the gap

The purpose of a macro-marketing system is to overcome these separations and discrepancies. The "universal functions of marketing" help do this.

The **universal functions of marketing** are buying, selling, transporting, storing, standardization and grading, financing, risk taking, and market information. They must be performed in all macro-marketing systems. *How* these functions are performed—and *by whom*—may differ among nations and economic systems. But they are needed in any macro-marketing system. Let's take a closer look at them now.

Any kind of exchange usually involves buying and selling. The **buying function** means looking for and evaluating goods and services. The **selling function** involves promoting the product. It includes the use of personal selling, advertising, and other direct and mass selling methods. This is probably the most visible function of marketing.

The **transporting function** means the movement of goods from one place to another. The **storing function** involves holding goods until customers need them.

Standardization and grading involve sorting products according to size and quality. This makes buying and selling easier because it reduces the need for inspection and sampling. **Financing** provides the necessary cash and credit to produce, transport, store, promote, sell, and buy products. **Risk taking** involves bearing the uncertainties that are part of the marketing process. A firm can never be sure that customers will want to buy its products. Products can also be damaged, stolen, or outdated. The **market information function** involves the collection, analysis, and distribution of all the information needed to plan, carry out, and control marketing activities, whether in the firm's own neighborhood or in a market overseas.

Producers, consumers, and marketing specialists perform functions

Producers and consumers sometimes handle some of the marketing functions themselves. However, exchanges are often easier or less expensive when a marketing specialist performs some of the marketing functions. For example, both producers and consumers may benefit when an **intermediary**—someone who specializes in trade rather than production—plays a role in the exchange process. In Chapters 11 and 12 we'll cover the variety of marketing functions performed by the two basic types of intermediaries: retailers and wholesalers. Imagine what it would be like to shop at many different factories and farms for the wide variety of brands of packaged foods that you like rather than at a well-stocked local grocery store. While wholesalers and retailers must charge for services they provide, this charge is usually offset by the savings of time, effort, and expense that would be involved without them. So these intermediaries can help to make the whole macro-marketing system more efficient and effective.

Internet EXERCISE

Go to the Target home page (**www.target.com**) and click on a tab for one of the product categories. How many different manufacturers' products are shown? Would consumers be better off if each manufacturer just sold directly from its own website?

A wide variety of other marketing specialists may also help smooth exchanges between producers, consumers, or intermediaries. These specialists are **collaborators**—firms that facilitate or provide one or more of the marketing functions other than buying or selling. These collaborators include advertising agencies, marketing research firms, independent product-testing laboratories, Internet service providers, public warehouses, transporting firms, communications companies, and financial institutions (including banks).

Some marketing specialists perform all the functions. Others specialize in only one or two. Marketing research firms, for example, specialize only in the market information function. Further, technology may make a certain function easier to perform. For example, the buying process may require that a customer first identify relevant sellers and where they are. Even though that might be accomplished quickly and easily with an online search of the Internet, the function hasn't been cut out.

New specialists develop to fill market needs

As the Internet example suggests, new types of marketing specialists develop or evolve when new opportunities arise for someone to make exchanges between producers and consumers more efficient or effective. Such changes can come quickly, as is illustrated by the speed with which firms have adopted e-commerce. **E-commerce**

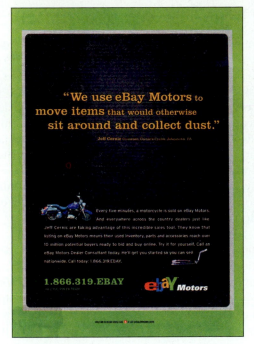

Intermediaries and collaborators develop and offer specialized services that facilitate exchange between producers and customers.

refers to exchanges between individuals or organizations—and activities that facilitate these exchanges—based on applications of information technology. New types of Internet-based intermediaries—like Amazon.com and eBay.com—are helping to cut the costs of many marketing functions. Similarly, Google.com and MSN.com make it easier for many firms to satisfy their customers with Web-based information searches or transactions. Collectively, these developments have had a significant impact on the efficiency of our macro-marketing system. At the same time, many individual firms take advantage of these innovations to improve profitability and customer satisfaction.[7]

Through innovation, specialization, or economies of scale, marketing intermediaries and collaborators are often able to perform the marketing functions better—and at a lower cost—than producers or consumers can. This allows producers and consumers to spend more time on production, consumption, or other activities—including leisure.

Functions can be shifted and shared

From a macro-marketing viewpoint, all of the marketing functions must be performed by someone—an individual producer or consumer, an intermediary, a marketing collaborator, or, in some cases, even a nation's government. No function can be completely eliminated. *However, from a micro viewpoint, not every firm must perform all of the functions. Rather, responsibility for performing the marketing functions can be shifted and shared in a variety of ways. Further, not all goods and services require all the functions at every level of their production.* "Pure services"—like a plane ride—don't need storing, for example. But storing is required in the production of the plane and while the plane is not in service.

Regardless of who performs the marketing functions, in general they must be performed effectively and efficiently or the performance of the whole macro-marketing system will suffer. With many different possible ways for marketing functions to be performed in a macro-marketing system, how can a society hope to arrive at a combination that best serves the needs of its citizens? To answer this question, we can look at the role of marketing in different types of economic systems.

THE ROLE OF MARKETING IN ECONOMIC SYSTEMS

All societies must provide for the needs of their members. Therefore, every society needs some sort of **economic system**—the way an economy organizes to use scarce resources to produce goods and services and distribute them for consumption by various people and groups in the society.

How an economic system operates depends on a society's objectives and the nature of its political institutions.[8] But regardless of what form these take, all economic systems must develop some method—along with appropriate economic institutions—to decide what and how much is to be produced and distributed by whom, when, to whom, and why.

There are two basic kinds of economic systems: command economies and market-directed economies. Actually, no economy is entirely command-oriented or market-directed. Most are a mixture of the two extremes.

Government officials may make the decisions

In a **command economy,** government officials decide what and how much is to be produced and distributed by whom, when, to whom, and why. These decisions are usually part of an overall government plan, so command economies are also called "planned" economies. It sounds good for a government to have a plan, but as a practical matter attempts by a government to dictate an economic plan often don't work out as intended.

Producers in a command economy generally have little choice about what goods and services to produce. Their main task is to meet the production quotas assigned in the plan. Prices are also set by government planners and tend to be very rigid—not changing according to supply and demand. Consumers usually have some freedom of choice—it's impossible to control every single detail! But the assortment of goods and services may be quite limited. Activities such as market research, branding, and advertising usually are neglected. Sometimes they aren't done at all.

Government planning in a command economy may work fairly well as long as an economy is simple and the variety of goods and services is small. It may even be necessary under certain conditions—during wartime, drought, or political instability, for example. However, as economies become more complex, government planning becomes more difficult and tends to break down. That's what happened to the economy in the former Soviet Union. Countries such as North Korea, Cuba, and Iran still rely on command-oriented economic systems. Even so, around the world there is a broad

Artists and craftsmen in developing economies often do not have a local market for their products, but Ten Thousand Villages, which operates a website and retail stores in the U.S., helps them reach customers and earn a profit. Their earnings in turn improve their quality of life and what they spend prompts economic development in their local communities.

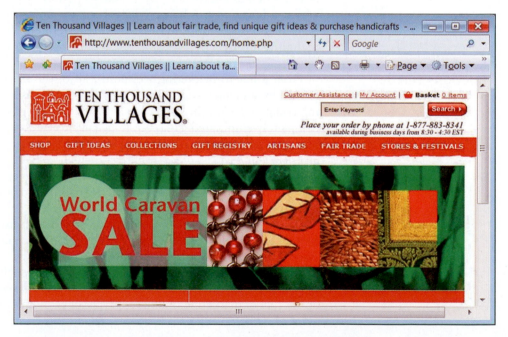

Marketing Helps India's Rural Poor

In recent decades India has experienced rapid economic growth. Many of its citizens have more income and enjoy a higher quality of life. That helps to explain why Unilever's Indian subsidiary, Hindustan Unilever Limited (HUL), has worked hard to build a 40 percent share of the Indian market with its product lines that include soaps, toothpaste, and packaged foods.

Previously, HUL focused primarily on India's urban areas. Yet, almost three-fourths of India's one *billion* plus people still live in rural areas. Only half of these rural villagers have access to electricity—and less than half have basic sanitation. Many of them have an income less than $2 a day. Conventional wisdom suggests that these poor rural villagers have too little money to be an attractive market. And it's expensive to distribute products to far-flung villages.

But now that is changing. HUL's marketing managers have decided that Indian villagers represent an opportunity for growth—and that villagers might benefit if they could purchase the soaps, toothpaste, and packaged food products that HUL is successfully selling in urban areas of India.

HUL has tailored a new marketing strategy to this target market. First, many products have been repackaged in "sachets"—small bags that contain a one- or two-day supply. HUL prices the small sachets so that villagers can afford them—and that in turn gives customers a chance to try quality products that were previously unavailable.

HUL has created its "Shakti Ammas" (women entrepreneurs) program to communicate the benefits of its products and distribute them in remote rural areas. The program sets rural women up as home-based distributors and sales agents. These women stock HUL products at their homes and go door-to-door to sell them. They also organize meetings in local schools and at village fairs to educate their fellow villagers on health and hygiene issues.

HUL now has more than 45,000 Shakti Ammas operating in over 135,000 villages across India. The Indian success spurred Unilever to adapt the model to developing countries across the globe. These women have a new source of income and are learning about business—while they bring the health benefits of improved hygiene to rural villages. And, of course, HUL hopes to clean up with a new source of growth.[9]

move toward market-directed economic systems—because they are more effective in meeting consumer needs.

A market-directed economy adjusts itself

In a **market-directed economy,** the individual decisions of the many producers and consumers make the macro-level decisions for the whole economy. In a pure market-directed economy, consumers make a society's production decisions when they make their choices in the marketplace. They decide what is to be produced and by whom—through their dollar "votes."

Price is a measure of value

Prices in the marketplace are a rough measure of how society values particular goods and services. If consumers are willing to pay the market prices, then apparently they feel they are getting at least their money's worth. Similarly, the cost of labor and materials is a rough measure of the value of the resources used in the production of goods and services to meet these needs. New consumer needs that can be served profitably—not just the needs of the majority—will probably be met by some profit-minded businesses.

Greatest freedom of choice

Consumers in a market-directed economy enjoy great freedom of choice. They are not forced to buy any goods or services, except those that must be provided for the good of society—things such as national defense, schools, police and fire protection, highway systems, and public-health services. These are provided by the community—and the citizens are taxed to pay for them.

Similarly, producers are free to do whatever they wish—provided that they stay within the rules of the game set by government *and* receive enough dollar "votes" from consumers. If they do their job well, they earn a profit and stay in business. But profit, survival, and growth are not guaranteed.

The role of government

The American economy and most other Western economies are mainly market-directed—but not completely. Society assigns supervision of the system to the government. For example, besides setting and enforcing the "rules of the game," government agencies are supposed to control interest rates and the supply of money. They also set import and export rules that affect international competition, regulate radio and TV broadcasting, sometimes control wages and prices, and so on. Government also tries to be sure that property is protected, contracts are enforced, individuals are not exploited, no group unfairly monopolizes markets, and firms deliver the kinds and quality of goods and services they claim to be offering. Clearly, as the current economic turmoil in the United States illustrates, a breakdown in regulation can cause problems in a market-directed economy.[10]

Is a macro-marketing system effective and fair?

The effectiveness and fairness of a particular macro-marketing system must be evaluated in terms of that society's objectives. Obviously, all nations don't share the same objectives. For example, Swedish citizens receive many "free" services—like health care and retirement benefits. Goods and services are fairly evenly distributed among the Swedish population. By contrast, North Korea places little emphasis on producing goods and services for individual consumers—and more on military spending. In India the distribution of goods and services is very uneven—with a big gap between the have-nots and the elite haves. Whether each of these systems is judged "fair" or "effective" depends on the objectives of the society.

So far, we have described how a market-directed macro-marketing system adjusts to become more effective and efficient by responding to customer needs. See Exhibit 1–2. As you read this book, you'll learn more about how marketing affects society and vice versa. You'll also learn more about specific marketing activities and be better informed

Exhibit 1–2
Model of a Market-Directed Macro-Marketing System

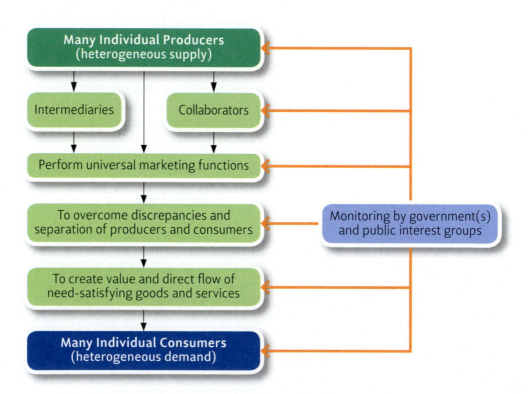

14

when drawing conclusions about how fair and effective the macro-marketing system is. For now, however, we'll return to our general emphasis on a managerial view of the role of marketing in individual organizations.

MARKETING'S ROLE HAS CHANGED A LOT OVER THE YEARS

It's clear that marketing decisions are very important to a firm's success. But marketing hasn't always been so complicated. In fact, understanding how marketing thinking has evolved makes the modern view clearer. So we will discuss five stages in marketing evolution: (1) the simple trade era, (2) the production era, (3) the sales era, (4) the marketing department era, and (5) the marketing company era. We'll talk about these eras as if they applied generally to all firms—but keep in mind that *some managers still have not made it to the final stages*. They are stuck in the past with old ways of thinking.

Specialization permitted trade—and distributors met the need

When societies first moved toward some specialization of production and away from a subsistence economy where each family raised and consumed everything it produced, traders played an important role. Early "producers for the market" made products that were needed by themselves and their neighbors. As bartering became more difficult, societies moved into the **simple trade era**—a time when families traded or sold their "surplus" output to local distributors. These specialists resold the goods to other consumers or other distributors. This was the early role of marketing—and it is still the focus of marketing in many of the less-developed areas of the world. In fact, even in the United States, the United Kingdom, and other more advanced economies, marketing didn't change much until the Industrial Revolution brought larger factories a little over a hundred years ago.

From the production to the sales era

From the Industrial Revolution until the 1920s, most companies were in the production era. The **production era** is a time when a company focuses on production of a few specific products—perhaps because few of these products are available in the market. "If we can make it, it will sell" is management thinking characteristic of the production era. Because of product shortages, many nations—including some of

Most railroads try to meet customer needs with convenient routes and on-time service. To make traveling more enjoyable, this French railroad offers service that includes door-to-door delivery of the passenger's luggage. The ad says "your luggage is big enough to travel by itself. It's up to us to ensure you'd rather go by train."

the post-communist republics of Eastern Europe—continue to operate with production era approaches.

By about 1930, most companies in the industrialized Western nations had more production capability than ever before. Now the problem wasn't just to produce—but to beat the competition and win customers. This led many firms to enter the sales era. The **sales era** is a time when a company emphasizes selling because of increased competition.

To the marketing department era

For most firms in advanced economies, the sales era continued until at least 1950. By then, sales were growing rapidly in most areas of the economy. The problem was deciding where to put the company's effort. Someone was needed to tie together the efforts of research, purchasing, production, shipping, and sales. As this situation became more common, the sales era was replaced by the marketing department era. The **marketing department era** is a time when all marketing activities are brought under the control of one department to improve short-run policy planning and to try to integrate the firm's activities.

To the marketing company era

Since 1960, most firms have developed at least some managers with a marketing management outlook. Many of these firms have even graduated from the marketing department era into the marketing company era. The **marketing company era** is a time when, in addition to short-run marketing planning, marketing people develop long-range plans—sometimes five or more years ahead—and the whole company effort is guided by the marketing concept.

WHAT DOES THE MARKETING CONCEPT MEAN?

The **marketing concept** means that an organization aims *all* its efforts at satisfying its *customers*—at a *profit*. The marketing concept is a simple but very important idea. See Exhibit 1–3.

The marketing concept is not a new idea—it's been around for a long time. But some managers show little interest in customers' needs. These managers still have a **production orientation**—making whatever products are easy to produce and

Exhibit 1–3
Organizations with a Marketing Orientation Carry Out the Marketing Concept

Customer satisfaction

Total company effort

The Marketing Concept

Profit (or another measure of long-term success) as an objective

then trying to sell them. They think of customers existing to buy the firm's output rather than of firms existing to serve customers and—more broadly—the needs of society.

Well-managed firms have replaced this production orientation with a marketing orientation. A **marketing orientation** means trying to carry out the marketing concept. Instead of just trying to get customers to buy what the firm has produced, a marketing-oriented firm tries to offer customers what they need.

Three basic ideas are included in the definition of the marketing concept: (1) customer satisfaction, (2) a total company effort, and (3) profit—not just sales—as an objective. These ideas deserve more discussion.

Customer satisfaction guides the whole system

"Give the customers what they need" seems so obvious that it may be hard for you to see why the marketing concept requires special attention. However, people don't always do the logical—especially when it means changing what they've done in the past. In a typical company 40 years ago, production managers thought mainly about getting out the product. Accountants were interested only in balancing the books. Financial people looked after the company's cash position. And salespeople were mainly concerned with getting orders for whatever product was in the warehouse. Each department thought of its own activity as the center of the business. Unfortunately, this is still true in many companies today.

Work together to do a better job

Ideally, all managers should work together as a team. Every department may directly or indirectly impact customer satisfaction. But some managers tend to build "fences" around their own departments. There may be meetings to try to get them to work together—but they come and go from the meetings worried only about protecting their own turf.

We use the term *production orientation* as a shorthand way to refer to this kind of narrow thinking—and lack of a central focus—in a business firm. But keep in mind that this problem may be seen in sales-oriented sales representatives, advertising-oriented agency people, finance-oriented finance people, directors of nonprofit organizations, and so on. It is not a criticism of people who manage production. They aren't necessarily any more guilty of narrow thinking than anyone else.

The fences come down in an organization that has accepted the marketing concept. There may still be departments because specialization often makes sense. But the total system's effort is guided by what customers want—instead of what each department would like to do. The marketing concept provides a guiding focus that *all* departments adopt. It should be a philosophy of the whole organization, not just an idea that applies to the marketing department.

Survival and success require a profit

Firms must satisfy customers. But keep in mind that it may cost more to satisfy some needs than any customers are willing to pay. Or it may be much more costly to try to attract new customers than it is to build a strong relationship with—and repeat purchases from—existing customers. So profit—the difference between a firm's revenue and its total costs—is the bottom-line measure of the firm's success and ability to survive. It is the balancing point that helps the firm determine what needs it will try to satisfy with its total (sometimes costly!) effort.

ADOPTION OF THE MARKETING CONCEPT HAS NOT BEEN EASY OR UNIVERSAL

The marketing concept was first accepted by consumer products companies such as General Electric and Procter & Gamble. Competition was intense in their markets—and trying to satisfy customers' needs more fully was a way to win in this competition. Widespread publicity about the success of the marketing concept at these companies helped spread the message to other firms.[11]

Producers of industrial commodities—steel, coal, paper, glass, and chemicals—have accepted the marketing concept slowly if at all. Similarly, many traditional retailers have been slow to accept the marketing concept.

Service industries are catching up

Service industries—including airlines, power and telephone companies, banks, investment firms, lawyers, physicians, accountants, and insurance companies—were slow to adopt the marketing concept, too. But in recent years this has changed dramatically.[12]

It's easy to slip into a production orientation

The marketing concept may seem obvious, but it's very easy to slip into a production-oriented way of thinking. For example, a company might rush a new product to market—rather than first finding out if it will fill an unsatisfied need. Many firms in high-technology businesses fall into this trap. Consider the thousands of new dot-com firms that failed. They may have had a vision of what the technology could do, but they didn't stop to figure out all that it would take to satisfy customers or make a profit. Imagine how parents felt when eToys.com failed to deliver online purchases of Christmas toys on time. If you had that experience, would you ever shop there again? What would you tell others?

Take a look at Exhibit 1–4. It shows some differences in outlook between adopters of the marketing concept and typical production-oriented managers. As the exhibit

Exhibit 1–4 Some Differences in Outlook between Adopters of the Marketing Concept and the Typical Production-Oriented Managers

Topic	Marketing Orientation	Production Orientation
Attitudes toward customers	Customer needs determine company plans.	They should be glad we exist, trying to cut costs and bringing out better products.
An Internet website	A new way to serve customers.	If we have a website customers will flock to us.
Product offering	Company makes what it can sell.	Company sells what it can make.
Role of marketing research	To determine customer needs and how well company is satisfying them.	To determine customer reaction, if used at all.
Interest in innovation	Focus is on locating new opportunities.	Focus is on technology and cost cutting.
Importance of profit	A critical objective.	A residual, what's left after all costs are covered.
Customer service	Satisfy customers after the sale and they'll come back again.	An activity required to reduce consumer complaints.
Inventory levels	Set with customer requirements and costs in mind.	Set to make production more convenient.
Focus of advertising	Need-satisfying benefits of goods and services.	Product features and how products are made.
Role of sales force	Help the customer to buy if the product fits customer's needs, while coordinating with rest of firm.	Sell the customer, don't worry about coordination with other promotion efforts or rest of firm.
Relationship with customer	Customer satisfaction before and after sale leads to a profitable long-run relationship.	Relationship ends when a sale is made.
Costs	Eliminate costs that do not give value to customer.	Keep costs as low as possible.

suggests, the marketing concept forces the company to think through what it is doing—and why. And it motivates the company to develop plans for accomplishing its objectives.

THE MARKETING CONCEPT AND CUSTOMER VALUE

Take the customer's point of view

A manager who adopts the marketing concept sees customer satisfaction as the path to profits. And to better understand what it takes to satisfy a customer, it's useful to take the customer's point of view.

A customer may look at a market offering from two views. One deals with the potential benefits of that offering; the other concerns what the customer has to give up to get those benefits. Consider a student who has just finished an exam and is thinking about getting a cup of mocha latte from Starbucks. Our coffee lover might see this as a great-tasting snack, a personal reward, a quick pick-me-up, and even as a way to get to know an attractive classmate. Clearly, different needs are associated with these different benefits. The cost of getting these benefits would include the price of the coffee and any tip, but there might be other nondollar costs. For example, how difficult it will be to park is a convenience cost. Slow service would be an aggravation. And you might worry about another kind of cost if the professor whose exam you have the next day sees you "wasting time" at Starbucks.

Customer value reflects benefits and costs

As this example suggests, both benefits and costs can take many different forms, perhaps ranging from economic to emotional. They also may vary depending on the situation. However, it is the customer's view of the various benefits and costs that is important. This leads us to the concept of **customer value**—the difference between the benefits a customer sees from a market offering and the costs of obtaining those benefits. A consumer is likely to be more satisfied when the customer value is higher—when benefits exceed costs by a larger margin. On the other hand, a consumer who sees the costs as greater than the benefits isn't likely to become a customer.

Some people think that low price and high customer value are the same thing. But that may not be the case at all. A good or service that doesn't meet a consumer's needs results in low customer value, even if the price is very low. Yet a high price may be more than acceptable when it obtains the desired benefits. Think again about our Starbucks example. You can get a cup of coffee for a much lower price, but Starbucks offers more than *just* a cup of coffee.

Customer may not think about it very much

It's useful for a manager to evaluate ways to improve the benefits, or reduce the costs, of what the firm offers customers. However, this doesn't mean that customers stop and compute some sort of customer value score before making each purchase. If they did, there wouldn't be much time in life for anything else. So a manager's objective and thorough analysis may not accurately reflect the customer's impressions. Yet it is the customer's view that matters—even when the customer has not thought about it.

Where does competition fit?

You can't afford to ignore competition. Consumers usually have choices about how they will meet their needs. So a firm that offers superior customer value is likely to win and keep customers. See Exhibit 1–5.

Often the best way to improve customer value, and beat the competition, is to be first to satisfy a need that others have not even considered.

The competition between Pepsi and Coke illustrates this. Coke and Pepsi were spending millions of dollars on promotion—fighting head-to-head for the same cola customers. They put so much emphasis on the cola competition that they missed other opportunities. That gave firms like Snapple the chance to enter the market and steal away customers. For these customers, the desired benefits—and the greatest customer value—came from the variety of a fruit-flavored drink, not from one more cola.

Exhibit 1–5
Customer Value and
Competition

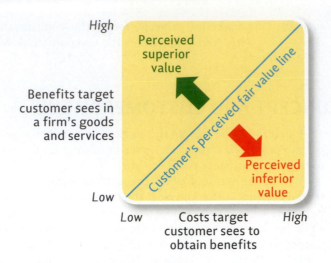

Build relationships with customer value

Firms that embrace the marketing concept seek ways to build a profitable long-term relationship with each customer. Even the most innovative firm faces competition sooner or later. And trying to get new customers by taking them away from a competitor is usually more costly than retaining current customers by really satisfying their needs. Satisfied customers buy again and again. This makes their buying job easier, and it also increases the selling firm's profits.

Building relationships with customers requires that everyone in a firm work together to provide customer value before and *after* each purchase. If there is a problem with a customer's bill, the accounting people can't just leave it to the salesperson to straighten it out or, even worse, act like it's "the customer's problem." The long-term relationship with the customer—and the lifetime value of the customer's future purchases—is threatened unless everyone works together to make things right for the customer. Similarly, the firm's advertising people can't just develop ads that try to convince a customer to buy once. If the firm doesn't deliver on the benefits promised in its ads, the customer is likely to go elsewhere the next time the need arises. And the same ideas apply whether the issue is meeting promised delivery dates, resolving warranty problems, giving a customer help on how to use a product, or even making it easy for the customer to return a purchase made in error.

In other words, any time the customer value is reduced—because the benefits to the customer decrease or the costs increase—the relationship is weakened.[13]

Exhibit 1–6 summarizes these ideas. In a firm that has adopted the marketing concept, everyone focuses on customer satisfaction. They look for ways to offer superior customer value. That helps attract customers in the first place—and keeps them satisfied after they buy. So when they are ready to make repeat purchases, the firm is able to keep them as customers. Sales may increase further because satisfied customers are likely to buy other products offered by the firm. In this way, the firm builds profitable relationships with its customers. In other words, when a firm adopts the marketing concept, it wins and so do its customers.

Curves' superior customer value satisfies customers

Curves fitness centers illustrate these ideas. They have been successful in building enduring relationships with their customers—women who are interested in a fast, regular workout. Research for Curves revealed that many women had simple fitness needs. They didn't want to work out with a lot of fancy training equipment; many didn't even want to shower at the workout center. Realizing this, Curves created smaller than normal fitness centers that fit in convenient strip malls. Smaller size and lower costs mean that Curves is able to open centers in small towns where larger fitness clubs could not survive. Its research also showed that many women preferred not to have men around when they exercise. Instead, they like the camaraderie of exercising with other women—which Curves enhances by arranging equipment in a circle. This arrangement

Exhibit 1–6
Satisfying Customers
with Superior Customer
Value to Build Profitable
Relationships

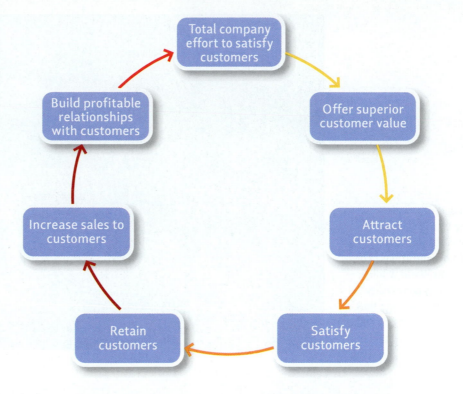

Internet
EXERCISE

What does Curves offer its customers at its website (**www.curves.com**)? How does this increase the value a customer receives from being a Curves member? What could Curves do with the website to further enhance its relationships with customers?

is coupled with simple exercises so a customer doesn't waste time waiting on machines—and she can count on finishing in just 30 minutes. Compared to competitors, Curves' fee is also attractive—less than $50 per month. Curves' overall approach works well for its members, which explains why they keep coming back. And because it provides superior customer value for its members Curves now has grown to 10,000 fitness centers worldwide.[14]

THE MARKETING CONCEPT APPLIES IN NONPROFIT ORGANIZATIONS

Newcomers to marketing thinking

The marketing concept is as important for nonprofit organizations as it is for business firms. In fact, marketing applies to all sorts of public and private nonprofit organizations—ranging from government agencies, health care organizations, educational institutions, and religious groups to charities, political parties, and fine arts organizations.

Support may not come from satisfied "customers"

As with any business firm, a nonprofit organization needs resources and support to survive and achieve its objectives. Yet support often does not come directly from those who receive the benefits the organization produces. For example, the World Wildlife Fund protects animals. If supporters of the World Wildlife Fund are not satisfied with its efforts—don't think the benefits are worth what it costs to provide them—they will put their time and money elsewhere.

Just as most firms face competition for customers, most nonprofits face competition for the resources and support they need. The Air Force faces a big problem if it can't attract new recruits. A shelter for the homeless may fail if supporters decide to focus on some other cause, such as AIDS education.

What is the "bottom line"?

As with a business, a nonprofit must take in as much money as it spends or it won't survive. However, a nonprofit organization does not measure "profit" in the same way as

Marketing is now widely accepted by many local, national, and international nonprofit organizations. For example, this World Wildlife Fund ad vividly conveys its environmental message that "a single tin of paint can pollute millions of litres of water."

a firm. And its key measures of long-term success are also different. The YMCA, colleges, symphony orchestras, and the United Way, for example, all seek to achieve different objectives and need different measures of success. When everyone in an organization agrees to *some* measure(s) of long-run success, it helps the organization focus its efforts.

May not be organized for marketing

Some nonprofits face other challenges in organizing to adopt the marketing concept. Often no one has overall responsibility for marketing activities. Even when some leaders do the marketing thinking, they may have trouble getting unpaid volunteers with many different interests to all agree with the marketing strategy. Volunteers tend to do what they feel like doing![15]

Nonprofits achieve objectives by satisfying needs

A simple example shows how marketing thinking helped a small town reduce robberies. Initially the chief of police asked the town manager for a larger budget—for more officers and patrol cars. Instead of a bigger budget, the town manager suggested a different approach. She put two officers in charge of a community watch program. They helped neighbors to organize and notify the police of any suspicious situations. They also set up a program to engrave ID numbers on belongings. And new signs warned thieves that a community watch was in effect. Break-ins all but stopped—without increasing the police budget. What the town *really* needed was more effective crime prevention—not just more police officers.

Throughout this book, we'll be discussing the marketing concept and related ideas as they apply in many different settings. Often we'll simply say "in a firm" or "in a business"—but remember that most of the ideas can be applied in *any* type of organization.

THE MARKETING CONCEPT, SOCIAL RESPONSIBILITY, AND MARKETING ETHICS

Society's needs must be considered

The marketing concept is so logical that it's hard to argue with it. Yet when a firm focuses its efforts on satisfying some consumers—to achieve its objectives—there may be negative effects on society. For example, producers and consumers making free choices can cause conflicts and difficulties. This is called the **micro-macro dilemma.** What is "good" for some firms and consumers may not be good for society as a whole.

For instance, many people in New York City buy bottled water because they like the convenience of easy-to-carry disposable bottles with spill-proof caps. On the other hand, the city already provides citizens with good tasting, safe tap water at a fraction of the cost. Is this just a matter of free choice by consumers? It's certainly a popular choice! On the other hand, critics point out that it is an inefficient use of resources to waste oil making and transporting millions of plastic bottles that end up in landfills where they leach chemicals into the soil. That kind of thinking, about the good of society as a whole, explains why New York City has run ads that encourage consumers to "get your fill" of free city water. What do you think? Should future generations pay the environmental price for today's consumer conveniences?[16]

Questions like these are not easy to answer. The basic reason is that many

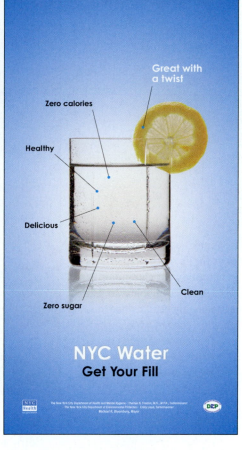

different people may have a stake in the outcomes—and social consequences—of the choices made by individual managers *and* consumers in a market-directed system. This means that marketing managers should be concerned with **social responsibility**—a firm's obligation to improve its positive effects on society and reduce its negative effects. As you read this book and learn more about marketing, you will also learn more about social responsibility in marketing—and why it must be taken seriously. You'll also see that being socially responsible sometimes requires difficult trade-offs.

Consider, for example, the environmental problems created by CFCs, chemicals that were used in hundreds of critical products, including fire extinguishers, cooling systems, and electronic circuit boards. When it was learned that CFCs deplete the earth's ozone layer, it was not possible to immediately stop producing and using all CFCs. For many products critical to society, there was no feasible short-term substitute. Du Pont and other producers of CFCs worked hard to balance these conflicting demands until substitute products could be found. Yet you can see that there are no easy answers for how such conflicts should be resolved.[17]

The issue of social responsibility in marketing also raises other important questions—for which there are no easy answers.

Should all consumer needs be satisfied?

Some consumers want products that may not be safe or good for them in the long run. Some critics argue that businesses should not offer high-heeled shoes, alcoholic beverages, or sugar-coated cereals because they aren't "good" for consumers in the long run.

Similarly, bicycles and roller blades are among the most dangerous products identified by the Consumer Product Safety Commission. Who should decide if these products will be offered to consumers?

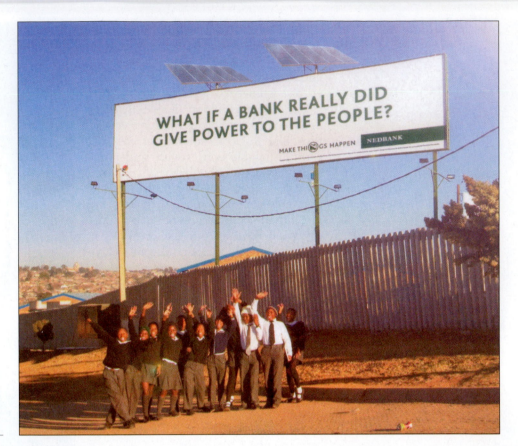

Nedbank has found creative ways for its marketing efforts to help the poor communities it serves in developing areas. Its solar-powered billboard converts the hot African sun to electricity that lights the ad and also powers the kitchen of the town's school, which feeds 1,100 children.

What if it cuts into profits?

Being more socially conscious often seems to lead to positive customer response. For example, many consumers praise Wal-Mart as a "safe haven" for kids to shop because it does not carry CDs that are not suitable for children, lewd videos, plastic guns that look authentic, and video games judged to be too violent. Toyota and Honda have had very good response to hybrid cars that produce less pollution (even though the price is higher). And some consumers buy only from firms that certify that their overseas factories pay a "fair wage" and don't rely on child labor.[18]

Yet as the examples above show, there are times when being socially responsible conflicts with a firm's profit objective. Concerns about such conflicts have prompted critics to raise the basic question: Is the marketing concept really desirable?

Many socially conscious marketing managers are trying to resolve this problem. Their definition of customer satisfaction includes long-range effects—as well as immediate customer satisfaction. They try to balance consumer, company, *and* social interests.

The marketing concept guides marketing ethics

Certainly some concerns about social responsibility and marketing arise because some individual firm or manager was intentionally unethical and cheated the market. Of course, a manager cannot be truly consumer-oriented and at the same time intentionally unethical. However, at times, problems and criticism may arise because a manager did not fully consider the ethical implications of a decision. In either case, there is no excuse for sloppiness when it comes to **marketing ethics**—the moral standards that guide marketing decisions and actions. Each individual develops moral standards based on his or her own values. That helps explain why opinions about what is right or wrong often vary from one person to another, from one society to another, and among different groups within a society. It is sometimes difficult to say whose opinions are "correct." Even so, such opinions may have a very real influence on whether an individual's (or a firm's) marketing decisions and actions are accepted or rejected. So marketing ethics are not only a philosophical issue, they are also a pragmatic concern.

Problems may arise when some individual manager does not share the same marketing ethics as others in the organization. One person operating alone can damage a firm's reputation and even survival. Of course, when a leader in an organization provides a bad role model, these problems can be magnified. For example, many critics argue that the meltdown of the mortgage market in 2008 and 2009 occurred because many executives in financial service firms failed to demonstrate basic ethical values such as fairness, responsibility, and honesty—and that regulators failed to do anything about it until it was too late.

To avoid these problems, and to be certain that standards for marketing ethics are as clear as possible, many organizations have developed their own written codes of ethics. These codes usually state—at least at a general level—the ethical standards that everyone in the firm should follow in dealing with customers and other people. Many professional societies also have such codes. For example, the American Marketing Association's code of ethics—see Exhibit 1–7—sets specific ethical standards for many aspects of marketing.[19]

Throughout the text, we will be discussing the types of ethical issues individual marketing managers face. But we won't be moralizing and trying to tell you how you should think on any given issue. Rather, by the end of the course we hope that *you* will have some firm personal opinions about what is and is not ethical in micromarketing activities.[20]

Exhibit 1–7   Summary of American Marketing Association Statement of Ethics

The American Marketing Association has developed a Statement of Ethics to guide its members' behavior. We have reproduced the preamble and parts of key sections of this document. The full document can be found at the association's website (www.marketingpower.com).

Preamble

The American Marketing Association commits itself to promoting the highest standard of professional ethical norms and values for its members. Norms are established standards of conduct that are expected and maintained by society and/or professional organizations. Values represent the collective conception of what people find desirable, important, and morally proper. Values serve as the criteria for evaluating the actions of others. Marketing practitioners must recognize that they not only serve their enterprises but also act as stewards of society in creating, facilitating, and executing the efficient and effective transactions that are part of the greater economy. In this role, marketers should embrace the highest ethical norms of practicing professionals and the ethical values implied by their responsibility toward stakeholders (e.g., customers, employees, investors, channel members, regulators, and the host community).

General Norms

- Marketers must do no harm.
- Marketers must foster trust in the marketing system.
- Marketers must embrace, communicate, and practice the fundamental ethical values that will improve consumer confidence in the integrity of the marketing exchange system.

Ethical Values

- Honesty—to be truthful and forthright in our dealings with customers and stakeholders.
- Responsibility—to try to balance justly the needs of the buyer with the interests of the seller.
- Fairness—to try to balance the needs of the buyer with the interests of the seller.
- Respect—to acknowledge the basic human dignity of all stakeholders.
- Openness—to create transparency in our marketing operations.
- Citizenship—to fulfill the economic, legal, philanthropic, and societal responsibilities that serve stakeholders in a strategic manner.

Ethics QUESTION

A customer purchases a Sony digital camera that comes with a 90-day manufacturer's warranty on parts and labor. The salesperson suggests that the customer consider the store's three-year extended service to cover any problems with the camera. The customer replies, "I'm getting a Sony because it's a reputable brand—and at $98 the service agreement is one-third the cost of the camera." Four months later, the customer returns to the store and complains that the camera no longer takes pictures and that "the store needs to make it right." If you were the store manager, what would you say? Would your response be any different if you knew that the customer was going to post his complaint on a consumer website?

Fortunately, the prevailing practice of most businesspeople is to be fair and honest. However, not all criticisms of marketing focus on ethical issues.

Marketing has its critics

We must admit that marketing—as it exists in the United States and other developed societies—has many critics. Marketing activity is especially open to criticism because it is the part of business most visible to the public.

A number of typical complaints about marketing are summarized in Exhibit 1–8. Think about these criticisms and whether you agree with them or not. What complaints do you have that are not covered by one of the categories in Exhibit 1–8?

Such complaints should not be taken lightly. They show that many people are unhappy with some parts of the marketing system. Certainly, the strong public support for consumer protection laws proves that not all consumers feel they are being treated like royalty.

As you consider the various criticisms of marketing, keep in mind that not all of them deal with the marketing practices of specific firms. Some of the complaints about marketing really focus on the basic idea of a market-directed macro-marketing system—and these criticisms often occur because people don't understand what marketing is—or how it works.[21] As you go through this book, we'll discuss some of these criticisms. Then in our final chapter, we will return to a more complete appraisal of marketing in our consumer-oriented society.

Exhibit 1–8
Sample Criticisms of Marketing

- Advertising is everywhere, and it's often annoying, misleading, or wasteful.
- The quality of products is poor and often they are not even safe.
- There are too many unnecessary products.
- Packaging and labeling are often confusing and deceptive.
- Retailers add too much to the cost of distribution and just raise prices without providing anything in return.
- Marketing serves the rich and exploits the poor.
- Service stinks, and when a consumer has a problem nobody cares.
- Marketing creates interest in products that pollute the environment.
- Private information about consumers is collected and used to sell them things they don't want.
- Marketing makes people too materialistic and motivates them toward "things" instead of social needs.
- Easy consumer credit makes people buy things they don't need and can't afford.

CONCLUSION

The basic purpose of this chapter is to introduce you to marketing and highlight its value for consumers, firms, and society. In Chapter 2, we introduce a marketing strategy planning process that is the framework for ideas developed throughout the rest of the text—and that will guide your marketing thinking in the future. This chapter sets the stage for that by introducing basic principles that guide marketing thinking.

You've learned about two views of marketing, both of which are important. One takes a micro view and focuses on marketing activities by an individual business (or other type of organization). This is what most people (including most business managers) have in mind when they talk about marketing. But it's important to understand that marketing also plays a more macro role. Macro-marketing is concerned with the way the whole marketing system works in a society or economy. It operates to make exchanges and relationships between producers and their customers more effective.

We discussed the functions of marketing and who performs them. This includes not only producers and their customers but also marketing specialists who serve as intermediaries between producers and consumers and other specialists (like product-testing labs and advertising agencies) who are collaborators and facilitate marketing functions.

We explained how a market-directed economy works, through the macro-marketing system, to provide consumers with choices. We introduced macro-marketing in this chapter, and we'll consider macro-marketing issues throughout the text. But the major focus of this book is on marketing by individual organizations. Someone in an organization must plan and manage its activities to make certain that customer needs are satisfied.

That's why understanding the marketing concept is another objective. The marketing concept is the basic philosophy that provides direction to a marketing-oriented firm. It stresses that the company's efforts should focus on satisfying some target customers—at a profit. Production-oriented firms tend to forget this. The various departments within a production-oriented firm let their natural conflicts of interest get in the way of customer satisfaction.

We also introduced the customer value concept. It is marketing's responsibility to make certain that what the firm offers customers really provides them with value that is greater than they can obtain somewhere else. In today's competitive markets, a firm must offer superior customer value if it wants to attract customers, satisfy them, and build beneficial long-term relationships with them.

A final objective was for you to see how social responsibility and marketing ethics relate to the marketing concept. The chapter ends by considering criticisms of marketing—both of the way individual firms work and of the whole macro system. When you have finished reading this book, you will be better able to evaluate these criticisms.

By learning more about marketing-oriented decision making, you will be able to make more efficient and socially responsible decisions. This will help improve the performance of individual firms and organizations (your employers). And eventually it will help our macro-marketing system work better.

KEY TERMS

QUESTIONS AND PROBLEMS

1. List your activities for the first two hours after you woke up this morning. Briefly indicate how marketing affected your activities.

2. If a producer creates a really revolutionary new product and consumers can learn about it and purchase it at a website, is any additional marketing effort really necessary? Explain your thinking.

3. Distinguish between the micro and macro views of marketing. Then explain how they are interrelated, if they are.

4. Refer to Exhibit 1–1, and give an example of a purchase you made recently that involved separation of information and separation in time between you and the producer. Briefly explain how these separations were overcome.

5. Describe a recent purchase you made. Indicate why that particular product was available at a store and, in particular, at the store where you bought it.

6. Define the functions of marketing in your own words. Using an example, explain how they can be shifted and shared.

7. Online computer shopping at websites makes it possible for individual consumers to get direct information from hundreds of companies they would not otherwise know about. Consumers can place an order for a purchase that is then shipped to them directly. Will growth of these services ultimately eliminate the need for retailers and wholesalers? Explain your thinking, giving specific attention to what marketing functions are involved in these "electronic purchases" and who performs them.

8. Explain why a small producer might want a marketing research firm to take over some of its information-gathering activities.

9. Distinguish between how economic decisions are made in a command economy and how they are made in a market-directed economy.

10. Would the functions that must be provided and the development of wholesaling and retailing systems be any different in a command economy from those in a market-directed economy?

11. Explain why a market-directed macro-marketing system encourages innovation. Give an example.

12. Define the marketing concept in your own words, and then explain why the notion of profit is usually included in this definition.

13. Define the marketing concept in your own words, and then suggest how acceptance of this concept might affect the organization and operation of your college.

14. Distinguish between production orientation and marketing orientation, illustrating with local examples.

15. Explain why a firm should view its internal activities as part of a total system. Illustrate your answer for (a) a large grocery products producer, (b) a plumbing wholesaler, (c) a department store chain, and (d) a cell phone service.

16. Give examples of some of the benefits and costs that might contribute to the customer value of each of the following products: (a) a wristwatch, (b) a weight-loss diet supplement, (c) a cruise on a luxury liner, and (d) a checking account from a bank.

17. Give an example of a recent purchase you made where the purchase wasn't just a single transaction but rather part of an ongoing relationship with the seller. Discuss what the seller has done (or could do better) to strengthen the relationship and increase the odds of you being a loyal customer in the future.

18. Discuss how the micro-macro dilemma relates to each of the following products: high-powered engines in cars, nuclear power, bank credit cards, and pesticides that improve farm production.

SUGGESTED CASES

1. McDonald's "Seniors" Restaurant   2. Harvest Farm Foods, Inc.   18. Whisper Valley Volunteer Fire Department

COMPUTER-AIDED PROBLEM

1. REVENUE, COST, AND PROFIT RELATIONSHIPS

This problem introduces you to the computer-aided problem (CAP) software—which is on the Online Learning Center for the text (www.mhhe.com/fourps) and on the optional Student CD—and gets you started with the use of spreadsheet analysis for marketing decision making. This problem is simple. In fact, you could work it without the software. But by starting with a simple problem, you will learn how to use the program more quickly and see how it will help you with more complicated problems. Instructions for the software are available at the end of this text.

Sue Cline, the business manager at Magna University Student Bookstore, is developing plans for the next academic year. The bookstore is one of the university's nonprofit activities, but any "surplus" (profit) it earns is used to support the student activities center.

Two popular products at the bookstore are the student academic calendar and notebooks with the school name. Sue Cline thinks that she can sell calendars to 90 percent of Magna's 3,000 students, so she has had 2,700 printed. The total cost, including artwork and printing, is $11,500. Last year the calendar sold for $5.00, but Sue is considering changing the price this year.

Sue thinks that the bookstore will be able to sell 6,000 notebooks if they are priced right. But she knows that many students will buy similar notebooks (without the school name) from stores in town if the bookstore price is too high.

Sue has entered the information about selling price, quantity, and costs for calendars and notebooks in the spreadsheet program so that it is easy to evaluate the effect of different decisions. The spreadsheet is also set up to calculate revenue and profit, based on

$$\text{Revenue} = (\text{Selling price}) \times (\text{Quantity sold})$$
$$\text{Profit} = (\text{Revenue}) - (\text{Total cost})$$

Use the program to answer the questions that follow. Record your answers on a separate sheet of paper.

a. From the Spreadsheet Screen, how much revenue does Sue expect from calendars? How much revenue from notebooks? How much profit will the store earn from calendars? From notebooks?

b. If Sue increases the price of her calendars to $6.00 and still sells the same quantity, what is the expected revenue? The expected profit? (Note: Change the price from $5.00 to $6.00 on the spreadsheet and the program will recompute revenue and profit.) On your sheet of paper, show the calculations that confirm that the program has given you the correct values.

c. Sue is interested in getting an overview of how a change in the price of notebooks would affect revenue and profit, assuming that she sells all 6,000 notebooks she is thinking of ordering. Prepare a table—on your sheet of paper—with column headings for three variables: selling price, revenue, and profit. Show the value for revenue and profit for different possible selling prices for a notebook—starting at a minimum price of $1.60 and adding 8 cents to the price until you reach a maximum of $2.40. At what price will selling 6,000 notebooks contribute $5,400.00 to profit? At what price would notebook sales contribute only $1,080.00? (Hint: Use the What If analysis feature to compute the new values. Start by selecting "selling price" for notebooks as the value to change, with a minimum value of $1.60 and a maximum value of $2.40. Select the revenue and profit for notebooks as the values to display.)

For additional questions related to this problem, see Exercise 1-5 in the *Learning Aid for Use with Essentials of Marketing*, 12th edition.

2
CHAPTER

Marketing Strategy Planning

There was a time when it didn't seem to be an exaggeration for Barnum & Bailey's ads to tout the circus as "the greatest show on earth." For a hundred years, circuses had brought excitement and family entertainment to towns all over the country. Parents hardly noticed the hard benches that they sat on as they watched their kids cheer for the acrobats, clowns, and animal acts. But by the 1980s the popularity of traditional circuses was in decline; many simply went out of business.

You can imagine why this sad state of affairs would be a concern for Guy Laliberté—a stilt walker, accordion player, and fire eater—and others in his band of performers. But instead of bemoaning the demise of the circus, they saw an opportunity for a new kind of entertainment—and their idea gave birth to "Cirque du Soleil."

Their new style of circus still traveled to the audience and set up a "big top" tent, but costly and controversial animal acts were eliminated. Instead, the entertainment focused on an innovative combination of acrobatics, music, and theater. This more sophisticated offering appealed to adults. Importantly, adults were willing to pay more for tickets when the show was targeted at them and not just kids—especially when the traditional circus benches were replaced with more comfortable seats.

Cirque du Soleil quickly struck a chord with audiences and soon the producers were developing new shows and also expanding tours to reach new markets. For example, seven different Cirque du Soleil shows now travel across Europe, Asia, Australia, and North America. Each show performs in a host city for anywhere from two weeks to three months. In addition, ten other Cirque du Soleil shows now have permanent homes and target tourists visiting Las Vegas, Orlando, Florida, the Chinese resort city of Macau, and Japan's capital, Tokyo. Each show is different and has a unique theme. For example, the theme of *KÀ* highlights the martial arts, *O* emphasizes fire and water while incorporating Polynesian folklore, and *LOVE* celebrates the music of The Beatles.

As all of this suggests, Cirque du Soleil's marketing managers constantly evaluate new opportunities. A few years ago the company even considered a plan to diversify into hotels and spas based on the circus theme. This idea was screened out—at least for now—and instead the focus has been on developing new products for current and new markets. Each idea for a new show is judged on its creativity, uniqueness, and likelihood of becoming a real blockbuster. New product development is very ambitious. New shows can take more than five years and $100 million to develop. But these development costs can be recouped over each show's anticipated 10-year run. For example, a series of programs now in development will feature the music of Elvis Presley and other new

Cirque du Soleil shows will have permanent facilities in Moscow, Russia, and Dubai, United Arab Emirates.

Cirque du Soleil also now offers television specials and DVDs. This is another way for Cirque to reach new customers. These small screen shows not only generate additional revenue but they also give customers a taste of Cirque du Soleil and whet their appetite for a live show.

Once customers see a live Cirque du Soleil show, they want to see more. So Cirque's ad efforts focus on motivating customers to see that first show. For example, ads in airline magazines target travelers who are headed to cities with permanent shows and traveling shows are heavily advertised in local media. But publicity and word of mouth are also important. Local newspapers and TV shows are often interested in doing stories about touring productions that are coming to town. Cirque du Soleil's website helps reporters in this effort by providing photos, videos, and interviews for easy download. To encourage word of mouth, they also rely on exclusive "premieres" where influential people in the community are invited to a gala opening night. The troupe also offers free tickets and volunteers time to help build close relationships with local art and charitable organizations. After experiencing the troupe's magic, people often tell their friends and look forward to the next opportunity to see Cirque du Soleil in action.

These new fans are likely to visit Cirque du Soleil's website (www.cirquedusoleil.com), which gives information about all the shows. The site also encourages customers to join the hundreds of thousands who have already signed up for the free "Cirque Club." Members sign up for the specific news they want sent to their e-mail address. So those wanting information about the permanent shows in Orlando and traveling shows coming to Georgia get messages letting them know of changes at the Orlando show and advance ticket sales to the Atlanta show.

Cirque du Soleil has been very successful, but it must continue to focus on ways to improve its customers' experiences. Imitators, like the Canadian Cirque Éloize and Le Rêve in Las Vegas, now try to offer similar entertainment fare. The reputation of the powerful Cirque du Soleil brand name gives the troupe a competitive advantage when it introduces new shows. It also allows Cirque to charge a premium price for tickets, which range from $40 to over $200 for the exclusive *Tapis Rouge* (red carpet) tickets. Cirque du Soleil's carefully crafted marketing mix generates ticket sales that exceed half a billion dollars each year.[1]

THE MANAGEMENT JOB IN MARKETING

In Chapter 1 you learned about the marketing concept—a philosophy to guide the whole firm toward satisfying customers at a profit. From the Cirque du Soleil case, it's clear that marketing decisions are very important to a firm's success. So let's look more closely at the marketing management process.

The **marketing management process** is the process of (1) *planning* marketing activities, (2) directing the *implementation* of the plans, and (3) *controlling* these plans. Planning, implementation, and control are basic jobs of all managers—but here we will emphasize what they mean to marketing managers.

Exhibit 2–1 shows the relationships among the three jobs in the marketing management process. The jobs are all connected to show that the marketing management process is continuous. In the planning job, managers set guidelines for the implementing job and specify expected results. They use these expected results in the control job to determine if everything has worked out as planned. The link from the control job to the planning job is especially important. This feedback often leads to changes in the plans or to new plans.

Exhibit 2–1
The Marketing
Management Process

Whole-company strategic management planning
Match resources to market opportunities

Marketing planning
• Set objectives
• Evaluate opportunities
• Create marketing strategies
• Prepare marketing plans
• Develop marketing program

Adjust plans
as needed

Control marketing plan(s) and program
• Measure results
• Evaluate progress

Implement marketing plan(s) and program

Managers should seek new opportunities

Smart managers are not satisfied just planning present activities. Markets are dynamic. Consumers' needs, competitors, and the environment keep changing. Consider Parker Brothers, a company that seemed to have a "Monopoly" in family games. While it continued selling board games, firms like Sega, Sony, and Nintendo zoomed in with video game competition. Of course, not every opportunity is good for every company. Really attractive opportunities are those that fit with what the whole company wants to do and is able to do well.

Strategic management planning concerns the whole firm

The job of planning strategies to guide a whole company is called **strategic (management) planning**—the managerial process of developing and maintaining a match between an organization's resources and its market opportunities. This is a top-management job. It includes planning not only for marketing but also for production, finance, human resources, and other areas.

Although marketing strategies are not whole-company plans, company plans should be market-oriented. And the marketing plan often sets the tone and direction for the whole company. So we will use *strategy planning* and *marketing strategy planning* to mean the same thing.[2]

WHAT IS A MARKETING STRATEGY?

Marketing strategy planning means finding attractive opportunities and developing profitable marketing strategies. But what is a "marketing strategy"? We have used these words rather casually so far. Now let's see what they really mean.

What is a marketing strategy?

A **marketing strategy** specifies a target market and a related marketing mix. It is a big picture of what a firm will do in some market. Two interrelated parts are needed:

1. A **target market**—a fairly homogeneous (similar) group of customers to whom a company wishes to appeal.
2. A **marketing mix**—the controllable variables the company puts together to satisfy this target group.

Exhibit 2–2
A Marketing Strategy

The importance of target customers in this process can be seen in Exhibit 2–2, where the target customer—the "C"—is at the center of the diagram. The customer is surrounded by the controllable variables that we call the "marketing mix." A typical marketing mix includes some product, offered at a price, with some promotion to tell potential customers about the product, and a way to reach the customer's place.

The marketing strategy for The Learning Company's software aims at a specific group of target customers: young parents who have a computer at home and want their kids to learn while playing. The strategy calls for a variety of educational software products—like *Reader Rabbit* and *Where in the World Is Carmen Sandiego?* The firm's software is designed with entertaining graphics and sound, and it's tested on kids to be certain that it is easy to use. To make it convenient for target customers to buy the software, it can be ordered from the firm's own website (www.learningcompany.com) or from other retailers like Toys "R" Us. Promotion has helped build customer interest in the software. For example, when marketing managers released *Where in Time Is Carmen Sandiego?* they not only placed ads in family-oriented magazines but also sent direct-mail flyers or e-mail to registered customers of the firm's other products. Some firms sell less-expensive games for kids, but parents are loyal to The Learning Company brand because it caters to their needs and offers first-class customer service—including a 90-day, no-questions-asked guarantee that assures the buyer of good customer value.[3]

SELECTING A MARKET-ORIENTED STRATEGY IS TARGET MARKETING

Target marketing is not mass marketing

Note that a marketing strategy specifies some *particular* target customers. This approach is called "target marketing" to distinguish it from "mass marketing." **Target marketing** says that a marketing mix is tailored to fit some specific target customers. In contrast, **mass marketing**—the typical production-oriented approach—vaguely aims at "everyone" with the same marketing mix. Mass marketing assumes that everyone is the same—and it considers everyone to be a potential customer. It may help to think of target marketing as the "rifle approach" and mass marketing as the "shotgun approach." See Exhibit 2–3.

Mass marketers may do target marketing

Commonly used terms can be confusing here. The terms *mass marketing* and *mass marketers* do not mean the same thing. Far from it! *Mass marketing* means trying to

Exhibit 2–3
Production-Oriented and Marketing-Oriented Managers Have Different Views of the Market

Production-oriented manager sees everyone as basically similar and practices "mass marketing"

Marketing-oriented manager sees everyone as different and practices "target marketing"

sell to "everyone," as we explained above. *Mass marketers* like Kraft Foods and Wal-Mart are aiming at clearly defined target markets. The confusion with mass marketing occurs because their target markets usually are large and spread out.

Target marketing can mean big markets and profits

Target marketing is not limited to small market segments—only to fairly homogeneous ones. A very large market—even what is sometimes called the "mass market"—may be fairly homogeneous, and a target marketer will deliberately aim at it. For example, a very large group of parents of young children are homogeneous on many dimensions, including their attitudes about changing baby diapers. In the United States alone, this group spends about $5 billion a year on disposable diapers—so it should be no surprise that it is a major target market for companies like Kimberly-Clark (Huggies) and Procter & Gamble (Pampers). On the other hand, babies and their parents are not the only ones who need disposable diapers. Many elderly people, especially those who are in nursing homes and have mobility problems, use diapers. Needless to say, the marketing mix that's right for babies isn't right for elder care. It's not just the sizes that are different, but also the forms. The elderly don't like the idea of needing "diapers"—so instead they wear disposable "pull ups."

The basic reason to focus on some specific target customers is so that you can develop a marketing mix that satisfies those customers' *specific* needs better than they are satisfied by some other firm. For example, E*trade uses an Internet site (www.etrade.com) to target knowledgeable investors who want a convenient, low-cost way to buy and sell stocks online without a lot of advice (or pressure) from a salesperson.

When a firm carefully targets its marketing mix, it is less likely to face direct competitors. So superior customer value is achieved with the benefits provided by the whole marketing mix rather than just by relying on a lower price. Whole Foods Market (WFM) is a good example. Most grocery stores sell the same brands—so they compete on price and profits tend to be weak. In contrast, WFM makes attractive profits with a differentiated marketing mix that delights its target customers. WFM sees itself as a buying agent for its customers and not the selling agent for manufacturers—so it evaluates the ingredients, freshness, safety, taste, nutritive value, and appearance of all the products it carries. It hires people who love food. They don't just sell food—but rather help their customers appreciate the difference natural and organic products can make in the quality of their lives. Service is attentive, friendly, and offered with some flair, which helps make the store fun and inviting. Customers often socialize while they shop. And they know that when they check out, WFM expects them to provide their own reusable shopping bags to carry food home—since that's better for the environment than having millions of disposable WFM grocery bags end up in the trash. Not everyone wants the marketing mix that WFM offers; but its target customers love shopping there—and they spread the word to others.[4]

DEVELOPING MARKETING MIXES FOR TARGET MARKETS

There are many marketing mix decisions

There are many possible ways to satisfy the needs of target customers. A product might have many different features. Customer service levels before or after the sale can be adjusted. The package, brand name, and warranty can be changed. Various advertising media—newspapers, magazines, cable, the Internet—may be used. A company's own sales force or other sales specialists can be used. The price can be changed, discounts can be given, and so on. With so many possible variables, is there any way to help organize all these decisions and simplify the selection of marketing mixes? The answer is yes.

The "four Ps" make up a marketing mix

It is useful to reduce all the variables in the marketing mix to four basic ones:

Product.
Place.

Product—the good or service for the target's needs

Place—reaching the target

Exhibit 2–5
Strategy Decision Areas
Organized by the
Four Ps

Promotion.
Price.

It helps to think of the four major parts of a marketing mix as the "four Ps."

Customer is not part of the marketing mix

The customer is shown surrounded by the four Ps in Exhibit 2–4. Some students assume that the customer is part of the marketing mix—but this is not so. The customer should be the *target* of all marketing efforts. The customer is placed in the center of the diagram to show this. The C stands for some specific customers—the target market.

Exhibit 2–5 shows some of the strategy decision variables organized by the four Ps. These will be discussed in later chapters. For now, let's just describe each P briefly.

The Product area is concerned with developing the right "product" for the target market. This offering may involve a physical good, a service, or a blend of both. Keep in mind that Product is not limited to physical goods. For example, the Product of H & R Block is a completed tax form. The Product of a political party are the policies it works to achieve. The important thing to remember is that your good or service should satisfy some customers' needs.

Along with other Product-area decisions like branding, packaging, and warranties, we will talk about developing and managing new products, product quality, and whole product lines.

Place is concerned with all the decisions involved in getting the "right" product to the target market's Place. A product isn't much good to a customer if it isn't available when and where it's wanted.

A product reaches customers through a channel of distribution. A **channel of distribution** is any series of firms (or individuals) that participate in the flow of products from producer to final user or consumer.

Sometimes a channel of distribution is short and runs directly from a producer to a final user or consumer. This is common in business markets and in the marketing of services. For example, Geico sells its insurance directly to final consumers. However,

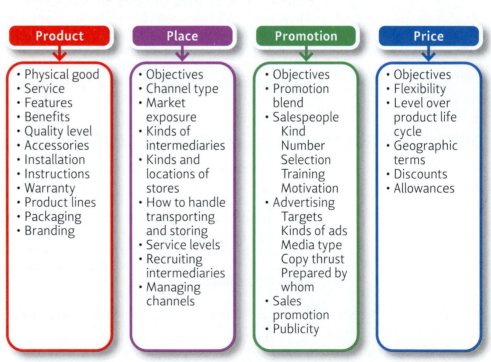

Product	Place	Promotion	Price
• Physical good • Service • Features • Benefits • Quality level • Accessories • Installation • Instructions • Warranty • Product lines • Packaging • Branding	• Objectives • Channel type • Market exposure • Kinds of intermediaries • Kinds and locations of stores • How to handle transporting and storing • Service levels • Recruiting intermediaries • Managing channels	• Objectives • Promotion blend • Salespeople Kind Number Selection Training Motivation • Advertising Targets Kinds of ads Media type Copy thrust Prepared by whom • Sales promotion • Publicity	• Objectives • Flexibility • Level over product life cycle • Geographic terms • Discounts • Allowances

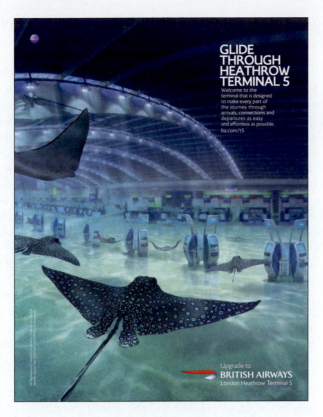

A firm's product may involve a physical good or a service or a combination of both. British Airways' planes provide the physical good part of its product and the quality of its equipment, including the special sleeper seats on its planes, help the firm do a superior job in meeting the needs of international travelers. But cutting-edge service is another part of British Airways' product. This ad emphasizes how easy it is to navigate the check-in process before reaching the gate.

as shown in Exhibit 2–6, channels are often more complex—as when Nestlé's food products are handled by wholesalers and retailers before reaching consumers. When a marketing manager has several different target markets, several different channels of distribution may be needed.

We will also see how physical distribution service levels and decisions concerning logistics (transporting, storing, and handling products) relate to the other Place decisions and the rest of the marketing mix.

Promotion—telling and selling the customer

The third P—Promotion—is concerned with telling the target market or others in the channel of distribution about the "right" product. Sometimes promotion is

Exhibit 2–6 Four Examples of Basic Channels of Distribution for Consumer Products

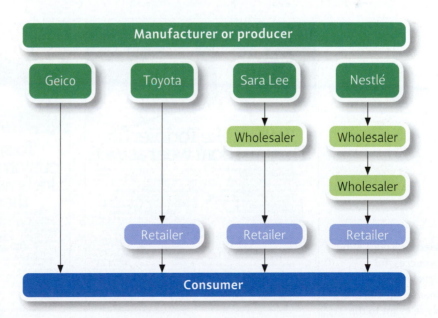

focused on acquiring new customers, and sometimes it's focused on retaining current customers. Promotion includes personal selling, mass selling, and sales promotion. It is the marketing manager's job to blend these methods of communication.

Personal selling involves direct spoken communication between sellers and potential customers. Personal selling may happen face-to-face, over the telephone or even via a videoconference over the Internet. Sometimes personal attention is required *after the sale*. **Customer service**—a personal communication between a seller and a customer who wants the seller to resolve a problem with a purchase—is often a key to building repeat business. Individual attention comes at a price; personal selling and customer service can be very expensive. Often this personal effort has to be blended with mass selling and sales promotion.

Mass selling is communicating with large numbers of customers at the same time. The main form of mass selling is **advertising**—any *paid* form of nonpersonal presentation of ideas, goods, or services by an identified sponsor. **Publicity**—any *unpaid* form of nonpersonal presentation of ideas, goods, or services—is another important form of mass selling. Mass selling may involve a wide variety of media, ranging from newspapers and billboards to the Internet.

Sales promotion refers to those promotion activities—other than advertising, publicity, and personal selling—that stimulate interest, trial, or purchase by final customers or others in the channel. This can involve use of coupons, point-of-purchase materials, samples, signs, contests, events, catalogs, novelties, and circulars.

Price—making it right

In addition to developing the right Product, Place, and Promotion, marketing managers must also decide the right Price. Price setting must consider the kind of competition in the target market and the cost of the whole marketing mix. A manager must also try to estimate customer reaction to possible prices. Besides this, the manager must know current practices as to markups, discounts, and other terms of sale. And if customers won't accept the Price, all of the planning effort is wasted.

Each of the four Ps contributes to the whole

All four Ps are needed in a marketing mix. In fact, they should all be tied together. But is any one more important than the others? Generally speaking, the answer is no—all contribute to one whole. When a marketing mix is being developed, all (final) decisions about the Ps should be made at the same time. That's why the four Ps are arranged around the customer (C) in a circle—to show that they all are equally important.

Let's sum up our discussion of marketing mix planning thus far. We develop a *Product* to satisfy the target customers. We find a way to reach our target customers' *Place*.

Toddler University's marketing strategy was successful because it developed a distinctive marketing mix that was precisely relevant to the needs of its target market.

38

Lifetime Value of Customers Can Be Very High—or Very Low

Investors lost millions when stock market values of dot-com firms collapsed after an initial, frenzied run up. But why did values get so high in the first place, especially when most dot-coms were not yet profitable? The stock went up because many investors expected that the firms would earn profits in the future as more consumers went online and the early dot-coms accumulated customers. These hopes were fueled by dot-coms that made optimistic predictions about the lifetime value of the customers they were acquiring. The lifetime value of the customer concept is not new. For decades Ford has known that a consumer who buys a Ford car and is satisfied is likely to buy another one the next time. If that happens again and again, over a lifetime the happy customer could spend $250,000 or more on Ford cars. Of course, this only works if the firm's marketing mix attracts the target customers and the relationship keeps them satisfied before, during, and after every purchase. If you don't satisfy and retain customers, they don't have high lifetime value and don't generate sales. Of course, sales revenue alone does not guarantee profits. For example, a firm can't give away products—or spend so much on promotion to acquire new customers (or keep the ones it has)—that the future revenue will never be able to offset the costs. Unfortunately, that is what happened with many of the dot-coms. They saw how the financial arithmetic might work—*assuming* that new customers kept buying and costs came under control. But without a sensible marketing strategy, that assumption was not realistic.[5]

We use *Promotion* to tell the target customers (and others in the channel) about the product that has been designed for them. And we set a *Price* after estimating expected customer reaction to the total offering and the costs of getting it to them.

Strategy jobs must be done together

It is important to stress—it cannot be overemphasized—that selecting a target market *and* developing a marketing mix are interrelated. Both parts of a marketing strategy must be decided together. It is *strategies* that must be evaluated against the company's objectives—not alternative target markets or alternative marketing mixes.

Understanding target markets leads to good strategies

The needs of a target market often virtually determine the nature of an appropriate marketing mix. So marketers must analyze their potential target markets with great care. This book will explore ways of identifying attractive market opportunities and developing appropriate strategies.

These ideas can be seen more clearly with a classic example from the children's fashion market.

Market-oriented strategy planning at Toddler University

The case of Jeff Silverman and Toddler University (TU), Inc., a shoe company he started, illustrates the strategy planning process. During high school and college, Silverman worked as a salesperson at local shoe stores. He also gained valuable experience during a year working for Nike. From these jobs he learned a lot about customers' needs and interests. He also realized that some parents were not satisfied when it came to finding shoes for their preschool children.

Silverman thought that there was a large, but hard to describe, mass market for general-purpose baby shoes—perhaps 60 or 70 percent of the potential for all kinds of baby shoes. Silverman did not focus on this market because it didn't make sense for his small company to compete head on with many other firms where he had no particular advantage. However, he identified four other markets that were quite different. In the following description of these markets, note that useful marketing mixes come to mind immediately.

The *Traditionalists* seemed to be satisfied with a well-manufactured shoe that was available from "quality" stores where they could seek help in selecting the right size and fit. They didn't mind if the design was old-fashioned and didn't change. They wanted a well-known brand that had a reputation for quality, even if it was a bit more expensive.

Many of the *Economy Oriented* parents were in the lower income group. They wanted a basic shoe at a low price. They saw baby shoes as all pretty much the same—so a "name" brand didn't have much appeal. They were willing to shop around to see what was on sale at local discount, department, or shoe stores.

The *Fashion Conscious* were interested in dressing up baby in shoes that looked like smaller versions of the latest styles that they bought for themselves. Fit was important, but beyond that a colorful design is what got their attention. They were more likely to look for baby-size shoes at the shop where they bought their own athletic shoes.

The *Attentive Parents* wanted shoes that met a variety of needs. They wanted shoes to be fun and fashionable and functional. They didn't want just a good fit but also design and materials that were really right for baby play and learning to walk. These well-informed, upscale shoppers were likely to buy from a store that specialized in baby items. They were willing to pay a premium price if they found the right product.

Silverman thought that Stride Rite and Buster Brown were meeting the needs of the Traditionalists quite well. The Economy Oriented and Fashion Conscious customers were satisfied with shoes from a variety of other companies, including Nike. But Silverman saw a way to get a toe up on the competition by targeting the Attentive Parents with a marketing mix that combined, in his words, "fit and function with fun and fashion." He developed a detailed marketing plan that attracted financial backers, and at age 24 his company came to life.

TU didn't have its own production facilities, so Silverman contracted with a producer in Taiwan to make shoes with his brand name and to his specs. And his specs were different—they improved the product for his target market. Unlike most rigid high-topped infant shoes, he designed softer shoes with more comfortable rubber soles. The shoes lasted longer because they are stitched rather than glued. An extra-wide opening made fitting easier on squirming feet. He also patented a special insert so parents could adjust the width. This change also helped win support from retailers. Since there are 11 sizes of children's shoes—and five widths—retailers usually need to stock 55 pairs of each model. TU's adjustable width reduced this stocking problem and made it more profitable for retailers to sell the line. It also made it possible for TU to resupply soldout inventory faster than competitors. Silverman's Product and Place decisions worked together well to provide customer value and also to give him a competitive advantage.

For promotion, Silverman developed print ads with close-up photos of babies wearing his shoes and informative details about their special benefits. Creative packaging also helped promote the shoe and attract customers in the store. For example, he put one athletic-style shoe in a box that looked like a gray gym locker. Silverman also provided the stores with "shoe rides"—electric-powered rocking replicas of its shoes. The rides not only attracted kids to the shoe department, but since they were coin-operated, they paid for themselves in a year.

TU priced most of its shoes at $35 to $40 a pair. This is a premium price, but with today's smaller families, the Attentive Parents are willing to spend more on each child.

In just four years, TU's sales jumped from $100,000 to over $40 million. To keep growth going, Silverman expanded distribution to reach new markets in Europe. To take advantage of TU's relationship with its satisfied target customers, he also added shoes for older kids to the Toddler University product assortment. Then Silverman made his biggest sale of all: He sold his company to Genesco, one of the biggest firms in the footwear business.[6]

THE MARKETING PLAN IS A GUIDE TO IMPLEMENTATION AND CONTROL

Marketing plan fills out marketing strategy

As the Toddler University case illustrates, a marketing strategy sets a target market and a marketing mix. It is a big picture of what a firm will do in some market. A marketing plan goes farther. A **marketing plan** is a written statement of a marketing strategy *and* the time-related details for carrying out the strategy. It should spell out the following in detail: (1) what marketing mix will be offered, to whom (that is, the target market), and for how long; (2) what company resources (shown as costs) will be needed at what rate (month by month perhaps); and (3) what results are expected (sales and profits perhaps monthly or quarterly, customer satisfaction levels, and the like). The plan should also include some control procedures—so that whoever is to carry out the plan will know if things are going wrong. This might be something as simple as comparing actual sales against expected sales—with a warning flag to be raised whenever total sales fall below a certain level.

The website for this text includes a feature called "Marketing Plan Coach." At the end of each chapter, there is a Marketing Plan Coach exercise that introduces you to aspects of a marketing plan that are related to the topics in that chapter. This gives you a step-by-step way to develop your plan-building skills as you progress through the text. In Chapter 18, we will review all of the elements in a marketing plan. At that point, you will have learned about all of the major strategy decision areas (Exhibit 2–5) and how to blend them into an innovative strategy.

Implementation puts plans into operation

After a marketing plan is developed, a marketing manager knows *what* needs to be done. Then the manager is concerned with **implementation**—putting marketing plans into operation. Strategies work out as planned only when they are effectively implemented. Many **operational decisions**—short-run decisions to help implement strategies—may be needed.

Managers should make operational decisions within the guidelines set down during strategy planning. They develop product policies, place policies, and so on as part of strategy planning. Then operational decisions within these policies probably will be necessary—while carrying out the basic strategy. Note, however, that as long as these operational decisions stay within the policy guidelines, managers are making no change in the basic strategy. If the controls show that operational decisions are not producing the desired results, however, the managers may have to reevaluate the whole strategy—rather than just working harder at implementing it.

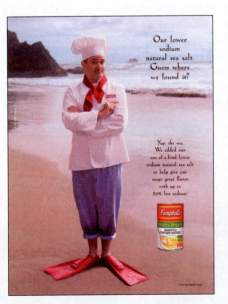

Campbell's has developed different soups (and related marketing mixes) that are targeted to the specific needs of different target markets. The marketing plan for each type of soup fits into Campbell's overall marketing program.

Exhibit 2–7   Relation of Strategy Policies to Operational Decisions for Baby Shoe Company

Marketing Mix Decision Area	Strategy Policies	Likely Operational Decisions
■ Product	Carry as limited a line of colors, styles, and sizes as will satisfy the target market.	Add, change, or drop colors, styles, and/or sizes as customer tastes dictate.
■ Place	Distribute through selected "baby-products" retailers that will carry the full line and provide good in-store sales support and promotion.	In market areas where sales potential is not achieved, add new retail outlets and/or drop retailers whose performance is poor.
■ Promotion	Promote the benefits and value of the special design and how it meets customer needs.	When a retailer hires a new salesperson, send current training package with details on product line; increase use of local newspaper print ads during peak demand periods (before holidays, etc.).
■ Price	Maintain a "premium" price, but encourage retailers to make large-volume orders by offering discounts on quantity purchases.	Offer short-term introductory price "deals" to retailers when a new style is first introduced.

It's easier to see the difference between strategy decisions and operational decisions if we illustrate these ideas using our Toddler University example. Possible four Ps or basic strategy policies are shown in the left-hand column in Exhibit 2–7, and examples of operational decisions are shown in the right-hand column.

Our focus in this text is on developing marketing strategies. But eventually marketing managers must control the marketing plans that they develop and implement. Thus, as we talk about each of the marketing decision areas, we will discuss some of the control problems. This will help you understand how control keeps the firm on course—or shows the need to plan a new course.[7]

Several plans make a whole marketing program

Most companies implement more than one marketing strategy—and related marketing plan—at the same time. Procter & Gamble targets users of laundry detergent with at least three different strategies. Some consumers want Tide's superior cleaning capabilities; others prefer the color protection of Cheer or the pleasant scents of Gain. Each detergent has a different formulation and a different approach for letting its target market know about its benefits. Yet P&G must implement each of these marketing strategies at the same time—along with strategies for Bounty, Olay, Charmin, and many other brands.

A **marketing program** blends all of the firm's marketing plans into one "big" plan. See Exhibit 2–8. This program, then, is the responsibility of the whole company.

Exhibit 2–8   Elements of a Firm's Marketing Program

Typically, the whole *marketing program* is an integrated part of the whole-company strategic plan we discussed earlier.

THE MARKETING PROGRAM SHOULD BUILD CUSTOMER EQUITY

Expected profits depend on customer equity

We've highlighted the benefit for target customers when the firm does effective strategy planning and offers them superior customer value. Now it's time to expand this thinking and consider how the marketing program should also benefit the firm—by increasing customer equity. **Customer equity** is the expected earnings stream (profitability) of a firm's current and prospective customers over some period of time. Top management expects marketing strategy planners to help identify *opportunities that will lead to an increase in the firm's customer equity*. Let's consider the logic for and implications of this important idea.

Owners expect financial returns

A firm may be owned by management or by stockholders and other types of investors. The owners are better off the greater the earnings (profit) from the money they invest in the firm. So, the financial value of a firm—for example, the value of its stock or what the firm would be worth if it were sold—is based mainly on the earnings (profit) that can be expected from its current and future operations. Top executives are ultimately responsible to the owners for *increasing* the financial value of a firm. In turn, top executives expect marketing managers to develop strategies that consider current and future profitability.

Profit growth comes from customers

Profit is the difference between the firm's revenues (total dollar sales) and the total costs it runs up to make those sales. Customers are key; they are the source of the revenue. The revenue comes from the prices they are willing to pay for the quantity of purchases they make. There are also costs associated with attracting and serving customers. If those costs are too great, even high levels of revenue won't be profitable.

Obviously, a marketing manager doesn't control all of a firm's costs; for example, General Motors faces huge pension costs for retired workers regardless of its current marketing strategies. Even so, the marketing manager selects opportunities and creates marketing strategies—and should make choices where the revenues from target customers are greater than the costs of acquiring those customers, retaining their business, and (hopefully) increasing it. In other words, the best way to increase customer equity is to find cost-effective ways to increase earnings from current customers while bringing profitable new customers into the fold.

To make this idea more concrete, let's look at what happens to customer equity at a new bank that has just gone into business. The bank's initial strategy focuses on acquiring *new* checking account customers. It offers personal attention and free checks—which are not available from the branches of big banks—and runs ads to tell potential customers about these benefits. Earnings increase as consumers sign on. At first, however, checking account earnings are a mere portion of what they could potentially be. That's because these customers will probably use more banking services if the bank meets their needs. For example, the bank might promote its helpful financial planning services to customers who have large checking account balances. Yet earnings, and customer equity, might grow even faster if the bank creates a strategy to attract *other* profitable customers. For example, it might encourage loan applications from owners of local businesses. Then, earnings from both consumers and business owners would contribute to growth and customer equity.

The parts of the marketing program must work as a whole

In Chapter 1 we introduced the idea that firms acquire new customers and retain the ones that they have by offering superior customer value. The customer equity idea shows how this translates to increased earnings over time—and why it determines the value of the firm and the return on investment it produces for the owners. So, a marketing manager needs to carefully consider what strategies will work well together—to produce an overall marketing program that increases customer equity—when seeking new opportunities.[8]

Planning for each strategy requires care

You can see that the success of the whole marketing program depends on the care that goes into planning individual strategies and how they will work together. Thus, in this text we will emphasize planning one marketing strategy at a time, rather than planning—or implementing—a whole marketing program. This is practical because it is important to plan each strategy carefully. Too many marketing managers fall into sloppy thinking. They try to develop too many strategies all at once—and don't develop any very carefully. However, when new strategies are evaluated, it makes sense to see how well they fit with the existing marketing program. So, throughout the book we'll discuss issues related to this fit as we cover the specific strategy decisions areas. Then, in Chapter 18 we'll summarize ideas about merging marketing plans into an overall marketing program.

Ethics QUESTION

A marketing researcher conducts a study that reveals that a competing firm's brand-new marketing strategy is off to a very strong start in attracting new customers. He thinks that it will ultimately be so successful that it will increase the price of the competing firm's stock, so he decides to buy the stock before that happens. However, a friend suggests that the trade might not be ethical and perhaps could even be considered illegal insider trading. Does it seem unethical to you? Should it be illegal? Explain your thinking.

THE IMPORTANCE OF MARKETING STRATEGY PLANNING

We emphasize the planning part of the marketing manager's job for a good reason. The "onetime" strategy decisions—the decisions that decide what business the company is in and the strategies it will follow—usually determine success, or failure. An extremely good plan might be carried out badly and still be profitable, while a poor but well-implemented plan can lose money. The case history that follows shows the importance of planning and why we emphasize marketing strategy planning throughout this text.

Time for new strategies in the watch industry

The conventional watchmakers—both domestic and foreign—had always aimed at customers who thought of watches as high-priced, high-quality symbols to mark special events, like graduations or retirement. Advertising was concentrated around Christmas and graduation time and stressed a watch's symbolic appeal. Expensive jewelry stores were the main retail outlets.

This commonly accepted strategy of the major watch companies ignored people in the target market that just wanted to tell the time and were interested in a reliable, low-priced watch. So the U.S. Time Company developed a successful strategy around its Timex watches and became the world's largest watch company. Timex completely upset the watch industry—both foreign and domestic—not only by offering a good product (with a one-year repair or replace guarantee) at a lower price, but also by using new, lower-cost channels of distribution. Its watches were widely available in drugstores, discount houses, and nearly any other retail stores that would carry them.

Marketing managers at Timex soon faced a new challenge. Texas Instruments, a new competitor in the watch market, took the industry by storm with its low-cost but very accurate electronic watches—using the same channels Timex had originally developed. But other firms quickly developed a watch that used a more stylish liquid crystal display for the digital readout. Texas Instruments could not change quickly enough to keep up, and the other companies took away its customers. The competition became so intense that Texas Instruments stopped marketing watches altogether.

While Timex and others were focusing on lower-priced watches, Japan's Seiko captured a commanding share of the high-priced gift market for its stylish and accurate quartz watches by obtaining strong distribution. All of this forced many traditional watchmakers—like some of the once-famous Swiss brands—to close their factories.

Then Switzerland's Swatch launched its colorful, affordable plastic watches and changed what consumers see when they

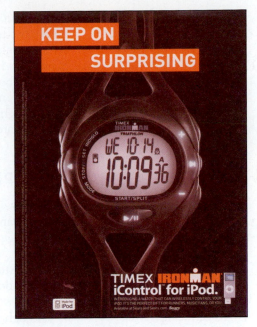

Timex has revised its strategy over the years and found new ways to meet consumer needs. Now it offers a watch in its Ironman line that makes it possible for runners and others who are music fans to wirelessly control their iPods.

look at their watches. Swatch promoted its watches as fashion accessories and set them apart from those of other firms, whose ads squabbled about whose watches were most accurate and dependable. Swatch was also able to attract new retailers by focusing its distribution on upscale fashion and department stores. The total size of the watch market increased because many consumers bought several watches to match different fashions.

The economic downturn in the early 1990s brought more changes. Consumers were more cost conscious and less interested in expensive watches like those made by Rolex that were the "in" status symbol a few years earlier. The reemergence of value-seeking customers prompted Timex to return to its famous advertising tagline of the 1960s: "It takes a licking and keeps on ticking." Its position as the inexpensive-but-durable choice helped it strengthen its distribution and gave it a leg up in getting shelf space for new products, such as its Indiglo line of watches.

By the turn of the century, the total market for watches was growing at only about 5 percent a year. To spark higher sales of its lines, Timex pushed to introduce more watches that combine time-telling and other needs. For example, Timex watches include heart-rate monitors, GPS systems to compute a runner's distance and speed, personal digital assistant functions (including data links to a computer), and Internet messenger capabilities so a watch can receive short text messages, like an alert from the wearer's stockbroker that it's time to sell. Of course, all of the new features can make a watch more complicated, so Timex developed technologies to make its watches easier to use. For example, watches with Timex's iControl can wirelessly sync with an iPod and control it. Innovations like these appeal to many customers. Yet, Timex now faces a different kind of competition. Many people carry gadgets—like smart phones—that perform the same functions and also display the time. The constant changes in consumers and competitors mean that marketing strategies at Timex must be updated and revised often if it is to continue to succeed in the market.[9]

Internet EXERCISE

WatchReport.com provides information about new offerings from different companies that sell watches. Go to the site (www.watchreport.com) and identify a watch from one of Timex's competitors that you think offers attractive new features or benefits. Do you think that Timex should offer a similar watch? Why or why not?

Dramatic shifts in strategy—like those described earlier—may surprise conventional, production-oriented managers. But such changes should be expected. Managers who embrace the marketing concept realize that they cannot just define their line of business in terms of the products they currently produce or sell. Rather, they have to think about the basic consumer needs they serve, how those needs may change in the future, and how they can improve the value they offer to customers. If they are too nearsighted, they may fail to see what's coming until too late. Marketing-oriented managers are always looking for attractive opportunities.

WHAT ARE ATTRACTIVE OPPORTUNITIES?

Effective marketing strategy planning matches opportunities to the firm's resources (what it can do) and its objectives (what top management wants to do). Successful strategies get their start when a creative manager spots an attractive market opportunity. Yet an opportunity that is attractive for one firm may not be attractive for another. Attractive opportunities for a particular firm are those that the firm has some chance of doing something about—given its resources and objectives.

Breakthrough opportunities are best

Throughout this book, we will emphasize finding **breakthrough opportunities**—opportunities that help innovators develop hard-to-copy marketing strategies that will be very profitable for a long time. That's important because there are always imitators who want to "share" the innovator's profits—if they can. It's hard to continuously provide *superior* value to target customers if competitors can easily copy your marketing mix.

Competitive advantage is needed—at least

Even if a manager can't find a breakthrough opportunity, the firm should try to obtain a competitive advantage to increase its chances for profit or survival. **Competitive advantage** means that a firm has a marketing mix that the target market sees as better than a competitor's mix. A competitive advantage may result from efforts in different areas of the firm—cost cutting in production, innovative R&D, more effective purchasing of needed components, or financing for a new distribution facility. Similarly, a strong sales force, a well-known brand name, or good dealers may give it a competitive advantage in pursuing an opportunity. Whatever the source, an advantage only succeeds if it allows the firm to provide superior value and satisfy customers better than some competitor.[10]

Avoid hit-or-miss marketing with a logical process

You can see why a manager *should* seek attractive opportunities. But that doesn't mean that everyone does—or that everyone can turn an opportunity into a successful strategy. It's all too easy for a well-intentioned manager to react in a piecemeal way to what appears to be an opportunity. Then by the time the problems are obvious, it's too late.

Developing a successful marketing strategy doesn't need to be a hit-or-miss proposition. And it won't be if you learn the marketing strategy planning process developed in this text. Exhibit 2–9 summarizes the marketing strategy planning process we'll be developing throughout the rest of the chapters.

MARKETING STRATEGY PLANNING PROCESS HIGHLIGHTS OPPORTUNITIES

We've emphasized that a marketing strategy requires decisions about the specific customers the firm will target and the marketing mix the firm will develop to appeal to that target market. We can organize the many marketing mix decisions (review Exhibit 2–5) in terms of the four Ps—Product, Place, Promotion, and Price. Thus, the "final" strategy decisions are represented by the target market surrounded by the

Exhibit 2–9
Overview of Marketing
Strategy Planning
Process

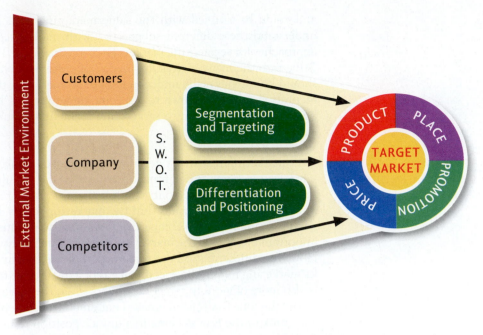

Note: Marketing manager narrows down from screening broad market opportunities to develop a focused marketing strategy.

four Ps. However, the idea isn't just to come up with *some* strategy. After all, there are hundreds or even thousands of combinations of marketing mix decisions and target markets (i.e., strategies) that a firm might try. Rather, the challenge is to zero in on the best strategy.

Process narrows down from broad opportunities to specific strategy

As Exhibit 2–9 suggests, it is useful to think of the marketing strategy planning process as a narrowing-down process. Later in this chapter and in Chapters 3 and 4 we will go into more detail about strategy decisions relevant to each of the terms in this figure. Then, throughout the rest of the book, we will present a variety of concepts and "how to" frameworks that will help you improve the way you make these strategy decisions. As a preview of what's coming, let's briefly overview the general logic of the process depicted in Exhibit 2–9.

The process starts with a broad look at a market—paying special attention to customer needs, the firm's objectives and resources, and competitors. This helps to identify new and unique opportunities that might be overlooked if the focus is narrowed too quickly.

Screening criteria make it clear why you select a strategy

There are usually more different opportunities—and strategy possibilities—than a firm can pursue. Each one has its own advantages and disadvantages. Trends in the external market environment may make a potential opportunity more or less attractive. These complications can make it difficult to zero in on the best target market and marketing mix. However, developing a set of specific qualitative and quantitative screening criteria can help a manager define what business and markets the firm wants to compete in. We will cover screening criteria in more detail in Chapter 3. For now, you should realize that the criteria you select in a specific situation grow out of an analysis of the company's objectives and resources.

Segmentation helps pinpoint the target

In the early stages of a search for opportunities we're looking for customers with needs that are not being satisfied as well as they might be. Of course, potential customers are not all alike. They don't all have the same needs—nor do they always want to meet needs in the same way. Part of the reason is that there are different possible types of customers with many different characteristics. In spite of the many possible differences, there often are subgroups (segments) of consumers who are similar and could be satisfied with the same marketing mix. Thus, we try to identify and understand these different subgroups—with market segmentation. We will explain approaches for segmenting markets later in Chapter 4. Then, in Chapters 5 and 6, we delve into the many interesting aspects of customer behavior. For now, however, you should know that really understanding customers is at the heart of using market segmentation to narrow down to a specific target market. In other words, segmentation helps a manager decide to serve some segment(s)—subgroup(s) of customers—and not others.

Narrow down to a superior marketing mix

A marketing mix won't get a competitive advantage if it *just* meets needs in the same way as some other firm. So in evaluating possible strategies, the marketing manager should think about whether there is a way to differentiate the marketing mix. **Differentiation** means that the marketing mix is distinct from and better than what is available from a competitor. Sometimes the difference is based mainly on one important element of the marketing mix—say, an improved product or faster delivery. However, differentiation often requires that the firm fine-tune all of the elements of its marketing mix to the specific needs of a distinctive target market. Differentiation is also more obvious to target customers when there is a consistent theme integrated across the four Ps decision areas. That emphasizes the difference so target customers will think of the firm as being in a unique position to meet their needs. For example, in Norway many auto buyers are particularly concerned about safety in the snow. So Audi offers a permanent four-wheel-drive system, called quattro, that helps the car to hold the road. Audi ads emphasize this differentiation. Rather than show the car, however, the ads feature things that are very sticky (like bubblegum!) and the only text is the headline "sticks like quattro" and the Audi brand name. Of course, handling is not Audi's only strength, but it is an important one in helping to position Audi as better than competing brands with this target market.

In Chapter 4, we'll introduce concepts relevant to this sort of positioning. Then, in Chapters 8 to 17, we'll cover the many ways in which the four Ps of the marketing mix can be differentiated. For now you can see that the thrust is to narrow down from all possible marketing mixes to one that is differentiated to meet target customers' needs particularly well. Of course, finding the best differentiation requires that we understand competitors as well as customers.

The natural colors available with Acuvue 2 Colours contact lenses help Johnson & Johnson differentiate its marketing mix as distinct from and better than what is available from its competitors.

S.W.O.T. analysis highlights advantages and disadvantages

A useful aid for identifying relevant screening criteria and for zeroing in on a feasible strategy is **S.W.O.T. analysis**—which identifies and lists the firm's strengths and weaknesses and its opportunities and threats. The name S.W.O.T. is simply an abbreviation for the first letters of the words strengths, weaknesses, opportunities, and threats. A good S.W.O.T. analysis helps the manager focus on a strategy that takes advantage of the firm's strengths and opportunities while avoiding its weaknesses and threats to its success.

The marketing strategy developed by Amilya Antonetti illustrates the basic ideas behind a S.W.O.T. analysis. Her son was allergic to the chemicals in standard detergents—and her research showed that many other children had the same problem. So she started SoapWorks and developed a line of hypoallergenic cleaning products to pursue this opportunity. Unlike the big firms, she didn't have relations with grocery chains or money for national TV ads. To get around these weaknesses, she used inexpensive radio ads in local markets and touted SoapWorks as a company created for moms by a mom who cared about kids. She had a credible claim that the big corporations couldn't make. Her ads also helped her get shelf space because they urged other mothers to ask for SoapWorks products and to tell friends about stores that carried them. This wasn't the fastest possible way to introduce a new product line, but her cash-strapped strategy played to her unique strengths with her specific target market.[11]

Exhibit 2–9 focuses on planning each strategy carefully. Of course, this same approach works well when several strategies are to be planned. Then, having an organized evaluation process is even more important. It forces everyone involved to think through how the various strategies fit together as part of an overall marketing program that increases customer equity.[12]

TYPES OF OPPORTUNITIES TO PURSUE

Many opportunities seem "obvious" only after someone else identifies them. So, early in the marketing strategy planning process it's useful for marketers to have a framework for thinking about the broad kinds of opportunities they may find. Exhibit 2–10 shows four broad possibilities: market penetration, market development, product development, and diversification. We will look at these separately to clarify the ideas. However, some firms pursue more than one type of opportunity at the same time.

Market penetration

Market penetration means trying to increase sales of a firm's present products in its present markets—probably through a more aggressive marketing mix. The firm may try to strengthen its relationship with customers to increase their rate of use or repeat purchases, or try to attract competitors' customers or current nonusers. Coleman got a 50 percent increase in sales of its outdoor equipment, like camping lanterns and coolers, by reaching its target market with special promotional displays at outdoor events like concerts, fishing tournaments, and NASCAR races. For example, about 250,000 auto racing fans camp on-site at NASCAR races each year—so a display at the campground is an effective way to reach customers when they have leisure time to browse through product displays and demos.[13]

New promotion appeals alone may not be effective. A firm may need to make it easier for customers to place repeat orders on the Internet. Or it may need to add more stores in present areas for greater convenience. Short-term price cuts or coupon offers may help.

Exhibit 2-10
Four Basic Types of
Opportunities

Many firms try to increase market penetration by developing closer relationships with customers so that they will be loyal. Frequent buyer clubs use this approach. Similarly, firms often analyze customer databases to identify "cross-selling" opportunities. For example, when a customer goes online to register Adobe's Acrobat Reader, the Web page promotes other related products, including its popular Photoshop software.

Market development

Market development means trying to increase sales by selling present products in new markets. This may involve searching for new uses for a product. E-Z-Go, a producer of golf carts, has done this. Its carts are now a quiet way for workers to get around malls, airports, and big factories. The large units are popular as utility vehicles on farms, at outdoor sports events, and at resorts. E-Z-Go even fits carts with ice compartments and cash drawers so they can be used for mobile food services.

Firms may also try advertising in different media to reach new target customers. Or they may add channels of distribution or new stores in new areas, including overseas. For example, to reach new customers, Dunkin' Donuts now sells its popular coffee at grocery stores and not just at its own outlets.[14]

Product development

Product development means offering new or improved products for present markets. By knowing the present market's needs, a firm may see new ways to satisfy customers. For example, in 2003 Campbell's came out with a line of soups with 25 percent less sodium than its regular product. That may seem like a minor change, but by 2008 it resulted in $650 million in sales because it was important to Campbell's health-conscious consumers. Ski resorts have developed trails for hiking and biking to bring their winter ski customers back in the summer. Nike moved beyond shoes and sportswear to offer its athletic target market a running watch, digital audio player, and even a portable heart-rate monitor. And of course Intel boosts sales by developing newer and faster chips.[15]

Diversification

Diversification means moving into totally different lines of business—perhaps entirely unfamiliar products, markets, or even levels in the production-marketing system. Products and customers that are very different from a firm's current base may look attractive to the optimists—but these opportunities are usually hard to evaluate. That's why diversification usually involves the biggest risk. McDonald's, for example, opened two hotels in Switzerland. The plan was to serve families on the weekend, but business travelers were the target during the week. Business travelers are not the group that McDonald's usually serves, and an upscale hotel is also very different from a fast-food restaurant. This helps to explain why operation of the Golden Arch hotels was taken over by a hospitality management company after two years. On the other hand, diversification can be successful—especially when the new strategy fits well with the firm's resources and marketing program.[16]

Which opportunities come first?

Usually firms find attractive opportunities fairly close to markets they already know. Most firms think first of greater market penetration. They want to increase profits and grow customer equity where they already have experience and strengths.

The Heinz ad is a clever visual reminder of the fresh taste of the tomatoes in Heinz Ketchup. The primary purpose of this type of promotion is to increase market penetration, which means increasing sales of a firm's present products in its present markets. The Crocs ad focuses on colorful new types of footwear it has added to its line as part of its product development efforts.

On the other hand, many firms are proving that market development—including the move into new international markets—is another profitable way to take advantage of current strengths.

INTERNATIONAL OPPORTUNITIES SHOULD BE CONSIDERED

It's easy for a marketing manager to fall into the trap of ignoring international markets, especially when the firm's domestic market is prosperous. Yet there are good reasons to go to the trouble of looking elsewhere for opportunities.

The world is getting smaller

International trade is increasing all around the world, and trade barriers are coming down. In addition, advances in e-commerce, transportation, and communications are making it easier and cheaper to reach international customers. With a website and e-mail, even the smallest firm can provide international customers with a great deal of information—and easy ways to order—at very little expense.

Develop a competitive advantage at home and abroad

If customers in other countries are interested in the products a firm offers—or could offer—serving them may improve economies of scale. Lower costs (and prices) may give a firm a competitive advantage both in its home markets *and* abroad. Black and Decker, for example, uses electric motors in many of its tools and appliances. By selling overseas as well as in the United States, it gets economies of scale and the cost per motor is very low.

Marketing managers who are only interested in the "convenient" customers in their own backyards may be rudely surprised to find that an aggressive, low-cost foreign producer is willing to pursue those customers. The owner of Purafil, a small firm in Atlanta that makes air purification equipment, puts it this way: "If I'm not [selling to an oil refinery] in Saudi Arabia, somebody else is going to solve their problem, then come attack me on my home turf."[17]

Get an early start in a new market

A company facing tough competition, thin profit margins, and slow sales growth at home may get a fresh start in another country where demand for its product is just beginning to grow. A marketing manager may be able to transfer marketing

Lipton is pursuing new customers and growth in over 100 countries. For example, its multilingual website in Belgium explains how to make exotic cocktails from Ice Tea, and in Asia it encourages consumer trial with free samples.

know-how—or some other competitive advantage—the firm has already developed. Consider JLG, a Pennsylvania-based producer of equipment used to lift workers and tools at construction sites. Faced with tough competition, JLG's profits all but evaporated. By cutting costs, the company improved its domestic sales. But it got an even bigger boost from expanding overseas. In the first five years, its international sales were greater than what its total sales had been before. Then, when JLG added distribution in China, international sales grew to be half of its business. Now JLG continues to enjoy growth, in spite of the home construction downturn in the United States, because JLG sales in Europe benefit from new safety rules that require workers to be on an aerial platform if they're working up high.[18]

Find better trends in variables

Unfavorable trends in the marketing environment at home—or favorable trends in other countries—may make international marketing particularly attractive. For example, population growth in the United States has slowed and income is leveling off. In other places in the world, population and income are increasing rapidly. Many U.S. firms can no longer rely on the constant market growth that once drove increased domestic sales. Growth—and perhaps even survival—will come only by aiming at more distant customers. It doesn't make sense to casually assume that all of the best opportunities exist "at home."[19]

Weigh the risks of going abroad

Marketing managers should consider international opportunities, but risks are often higher in foreign markets. Many firms fail because they don't know the foreign country's culture. Learning foreign regulations can be difficult and costly. Political or social unrest make it difficult to operate in some countries. Venezuela is a striking example. Current Venezuelan leaders have threatened to nationalize some international businesses that have located there. Careful planning can help reduce some of these risks, but ultimately managers must assess both the risks and opportunities that exist in each international market.

CONCLUSION

This chapter introduces you to the basic decision areas involved in marketing strategy planning and explains the logic for the marketing strategy planning process summarized in Exhibit 2–9. In the remainder of this book we'll rely on this exhibit as a way to highlight the organization of the topics we are discussing.

In this chapter, you learned that the marketing manager must constantly study the market environment—seeking attractive opportunities and planning new strategies. A marketing strategy specifies a target market and the marketing mix the firm will offer to provide that target market with superior customer value. A marketing mix has four major decision areas: the four Ps—Product, Place, Promotion, and Price.

There are usually more potential opportunities than a firm can pursue, so possible target markets must be matched with marketing mixes the firm can offer. This is a narrowing-down process. The most attractive strategies—really, marketing plans and whole marketing programs—are chosen for implementation.

A marketing program that is implemented well should increase the firm's customer equity. Customer equity refers to the expected earnings from a firm's current or prospective customers. This is a forward-looking idea and reinforces the need not only to acquire customers but to satisfy them with superior customer value so that, in the future, earnings from them will grow because of repeat business.

Controls are needed to be sure that the plans are carried out successfully. If anything goes wrong along the way, continual feedback should cause the process to be started over again—with the marketing manager planning more attractive marketing strategies. Thus, the job of marketing management is one of continuous planning, implementing, and control. Strategies are not permanent; changes should be expected as market conditions change.

Firms need effective strategy planning to survive in our increasingly competitive markets. The challenge isn't just to come up with some strategy, but to zero in on the strategy that is best for the firm given its objectives and resources—and taking into consideration its strengths and weaknesses and the opportunities and threats that it faces. To improve your ability in this area, this chapter introduces a framework for marketing strategy planning. The rest of this text is organized to deepen your understanding of this framework and how to use it to develop profitable marketing mixes for clearly defined target markets. After several chapters on analyzing target markets, we will discuss each of the four Ps in greater detail.

While market-oriented strategy planning is helpful to marketers, it is also needed by financial managers, accountants, production and personnel people, and all other specialists. A market-oriented plan lets everybody in the firm know what ballpark they are playing in and what they are trying to accomplish.

We will use the term *marketing manager* for editorial convenience, but really, when we talk about marketing strategy planning, we are talking about the planning that a market-oriented manager should do when developing a firm's strategic plans. This kind of thinking should be done—or at least understood—by everyone in the organization. And this includes even the entry-level salesperson, production supervisor, retail buyer, or human resources counselor.

KEY TERMS

marketing management process, 32
strategic (management) planning, 33
marketing strategy, 33
target market, 33
marketing mix, 33
target marketing, 34
mass marketing, 34
channel of distribution, 36
personal selling, 38

customer service, 38
mass selling, 38
advertising, 38
publicity, 38
sales promotion, 38
marketing plan, 41
implementation, 41
operational decisions, 41
marketing program, 42

customer equity, 43
breakthrough opportunities, 46
competitive advantage, 46
differentiation, 48
S.W.O.T. analysis, 49
market penetration, 49
market development, 50
product development, 50
diversification, 50

QUESTIONS AND PROBLEMS

1. Distinguish clearly between a marketing strategy and a marketing mix. Use an example.

2. Distinguish clearly between mass marketing and target marketing. Use an example.

3. Why is the target customer placed in the center of the four Ps in the text diagram of a marketing strategy (Exhibit 2–4)? Explain, using a specific example from your own experience.

4. If a company sells its products only from a website, which is accessible over the Internet to customers from all over the world, does it still need to worry about having a specific target market? Explain your thinking.

5. Explain, in your own words, what each of the four Ps involves.

6. Evaluate the text's statement, "A marketing strategy sets the details of implementation."

7. Distinguish between strategy decisions and operational decisions, illustrating for a local retailer.

8. In your own words, explain what customer equity means and why it is important.

9. Distinguish between a strategy, a marketing plan, and a marketing program, illustrating for a local retailer.

10. Outline a marketing strategy for each of the following new products: (*a*) a radically new design for a toothbrush, (*b*) a new fishing reel, (*c*) a new wonder drug, and (*d*) a new industrial stapling machine.

11. Provide a specific illustration of why marketing strategy planning is important for all businesspeople, not just for those in the marketing department.

12. Research has shown that only about three out of every four customers are, on average, satisfied by a firm's marketing programs. Give an example of a purchase you made where you were not satisfied and what the firm could have changed to satisfy you. If customer satisfaction is so important to firms, why don't they score better in this area?

13. Distinguish between an attractive opportunity and a breakthrough opportunity. Give an example.

14. Explain how new opportunities may be seen by defining a firm's markets more precisely. Illustrate for a situation where you feel there is an opportunity—namely, an unsatisfied market segment—even if it is not very large.

15. In your own words, explain why the book suggests that you should think of marketing strategy planning as a narrowing-down process.

16. Explain the major differences among the four basic types of growth opportunities discussed in the text and cite examples for two of these types of opportunities.

17. Explain why a firm may want to pursue a market penetration opportunity before pursuing one involving product development or diversification.

18. In your own words, explain several reasons why a marketing manager should consider international markets when evaluating possible opportunities.

19. Give an example of a foreign-made product (other than an automobile) that you personally have purchased. Give some reasons why you purchased that product. Do you think that there was a good opportunity for a domestic firm to get your business? Explain why or why not.

CREATING MARKETING PLANS

The Marketing Plan Coach software on the text website (and on the optional Student CD) includes a sample marketing plan for Hillside Veterinary Clinic. Skim through the different sections of the marketing plan. Look more closely at the "Marketing Strategy" section.

a. What is the target market for this marketing plan?

b. What is the strategy Hillside Veterinary Clinic intends to use?

c. What are your initial reactions to this strategy? Do you think it will be successful? Why or why not?

SUGGESTED CASES

3. MANU Soccer Academy
4. Trusty Technology Services
5. PolyTech Products

12. DrRay.com
29. Specialized Castings, Inc.

COMPUTER-AIDED PROBLEM

2. TARGET MARKETING

Marko, Inc.'s, managers are comparing the profitability of a target marketing strategy with a mass marketing "strategy." The spreadsheet gives information about both approaches.

The mass marketing strategy is aiming at a much bigger market. But a smaller percent of the consumers in the market will actually buy this product—because not everyone needs or can afford it. Moreover, because this marketing mix is not tailored to specific needs, Marko will get a smaller share of the business from those who do buy than it would with a more targeted marketing mix.

Just trying to reach the mass market will take more promotion and require more retail outlets in more locations—so

promotion costs and distribution costs are higher than with the target marketing strategy. On the other hand, the cost of producing each unit is higher with the target marketing strategy—to build in a more satisfying set of features. But because the more targeted marketing mix is trying to satisfy the needs of a specific target market, those customers will be willing to pay a higher price.

In the spreadsheet, "quantity sold" (by the firm) is equal to the number of people in the market who will actually buy one each of the product—multiplied by the share of those purchases won by the firm's marketing mix. Thus, a change in the size of the market, the percent of people who purchase, or the share captured by the firm will affect quantity sold. And a change in quantity sold will affect total revenue, total cost, and profit.

a. On a piece of paper, show the calculations that prove that the spreadsheet "total profit" value for the target marketing strategy is correct. (Hint: Remember to multiply unit production cost and unit distribution cost by the quantity sold.) Which approach seems better—target marketing or mass marketing? Why?

b. If the target marketer could find a way to reduce distribution cost per unit by $.25, how much would profit increase?

c. If Marko, Inc., decided to use the target marketing strategy and better marketing mix decisions increased its share of purchases from 50 to 60 percent—without increasing costs—what would happen to total profit? What does this analysis suggest about the importance of marketing managers knowing enough about their target markets to be effective target marketers?

For additional questions related to this problem, see Exercise 2–4 in the *Learning Aid for Use with Essentials of Marketing,* 12th edition.

3

CHAPTER

Evaluating Opportunities in the Changing Marketing Environment

The troubled global economy in 2009 destroyed the profits of many firms. With banks collapsing, government lawmakers struggled to identify new laws to attack the problems. With all this uncertainty, customers were putting off every purchase they could. Credit was also tight and that further reduced demand for big ticket items. Looking back, it seems obvious why automakers were in trouble—and why many consumers were so angry about politicians bailing out Wall Street but ignoring the loss of jobs, homes, and investment savings on Main Street.

Yet, in the midst of all this turmoil, Amazon.com reported strong profits and a positive growth outlook. The depressed economic environment actually gave Amazon a boost. Amazon's online approach, with wide selections of popular products at low prices, seemed to be exactly what penny-pinching consumers were looking for. Of course Amazon had also made online shopping more convenient. Further, in today's "greener" culture, consumers like the idea that buying online reduces trips to stores.

Even back in 1995, when Amazon.com first went online, it promised this sort of success. After all, Amazon's strategy took advantage of the trends in the external market, especially rapid consumer adoption of the World Wide Web. The economy was strong so early investors were patient while Amazon acquired customers. But Amazon wasn't just "lucky" to be in the right place at the right time. Jeff Bezos, founder of Amazon, pushed the firm to be innovative in improving every aspect of the customer experience online. For example, Amazon's one-click checkout technology made it fast and easy for customers to pay for purchases and arrange shipping.

In the early days, most consumers thought of Amazon as just another new online competitor for "bricks and mortar" bookstores. Publicity photos showing the huge Amazon warehouse and the youthful Bezos energetically pushing a cart full of books reinforced that positioning. But soon Bezos expanded into new product markets with offerings that initially included CDs, movies, games, electronics, home and garden, and later others ranging from health and beauty aids to industrial tools.

Amazon's proprietary e-commerce platform provided a competitive advantage in serving final consumers but also created another type of opportunity. By 2000, Amazon began to offer its platform for use by other retailers. Today, thousands of sellers leverage the power of Amazon's e-commerce abilities to reach new customers and offer their selections online. Partners such as Target Stores and Benefit Cosmetics work with Amazon to power their e-commerce offerings from end-to-end, including technology services, merchandising, customer service, and order fulfillment.

Amazon was equally quick to pursue global growth. By 1998, it had launched sites in both the United Kingdom and Germany. These markets were attractive initial targets because they were at a similar stage of economic development as the United States and there were many cultural similarities. Now, Amazon's emphasis is on emerging markets like China.

Amazon.com strives to be "Earth's most customer-centric company" where people can easily find virtually anything they want to buy online. Amazon is a leader in using customer relationship management systems to provide useful information that is customized to the interests and purchases of shoppers. For example, when a customer buys a book, Amazon analyzes the purchases of other people who bought that book and lists other titles that they considered. In addition, Amazon offers several community features—like customer reviews that help shoppers discover new products and make informed buying decisions.

Amazon endeavors to build on all aspects of its online advantages. Consider its packaging initiative where Amazon works with manufacturers to simplify product packaging. Gone are many of the annoying plastic "clamshell" cases commonly used in toy packaging. While useful for shelf displays in stores, they are not needed for selling online and instead run up costs. The new, smaller boxes reduce shipping costs and can be recycled.

Amazon's heritage was built on print books, but now digital e-books are important. Evidence of this includes the introduction of Amazon's own Kindle DX, a new generation wireless reading device. Its large 9.7-inch electronic paper display, built-in PDF reader, and storage for up to 3,500 books support a massive selection of content. Amazon offers more than 275,000 books for download from its Kindle Store. Consumers love the wide selection and Amazon's low price, which is typically only $9.99. Top magazines and newspapers plus more than 1,500 blogs are also available.

The Kindle and Amazon's push into downloadable media move Amazon into a new competitive environment where Apple is already established with popular offerings such as iPod, iTunes, and iPhone. Both Amazon and Apple are innovative firms with a portfolio of different business units, but as the digital revolution in media evolves they will increasingly find themselves in direct competition.[1]

THE MARKETING ENVIRONMENT

The marketing strategy planning process (see Exhibit 2–9) requires narrowing down to the best opportunities and developing a strategy that gives the firm a competitive advantage and provides target customers with superior customer value. This narrowing down should consider the important elements of the marketing environment and how they are shifting.

A large number of forces shapes the marketing environment. The direct environment includes customers, the company, and competitors. The external market environment is broader and includes four major areas:

1. Economic environment.
2. Technological environment.
3. Political and legal environment.
4. Cultural and social environment.

Managers can't alter the variables of the marketing environment. That's why it's useful to think of them as uncontrollable variables. On the other hand, a manager should analyze the environment when making decisions that can be controlled. For example, a manager can select a strategy that leads the firm into a market where competition is not yet strong.

Exhibit 3–1 Marketing Strategy Planning, Competitors, Company, and External Market Environment

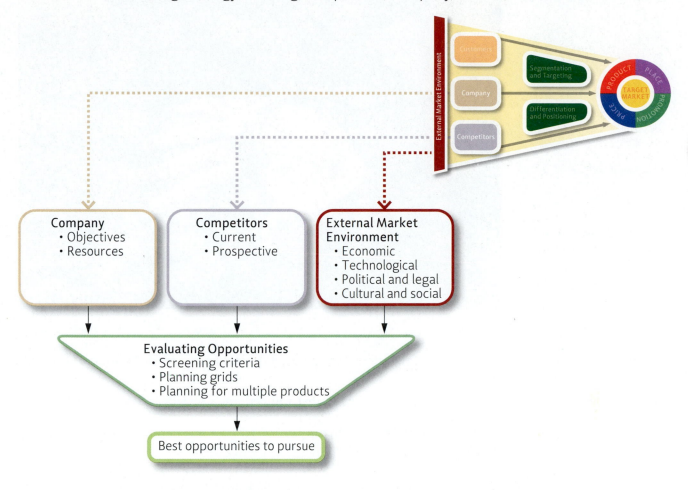

In this chapter, we'll look at the key marketing environment variables shown in Exhibit 3–1 in more detail. We'll see how they shape opportunities—limiting some possibilities but making others more attractive.

OBJECTIVES SHOULD SET FIRM'S COURSE

A company must decide where it's going, or it may fall into the trap expressed so well by the quotation: "Having lost sight of our objective, we redoubled our efforts." Company objectives should shape the direction and operation of the whole business.

It is difficult to set objectives that really guide the present and future development of a company. The marketing manager should be heard when the company is setting objectives. But setting whole-company objectives—within resource limits—is ultimately the responsibility of top management. Top management must look at the whole business, relate its present objectives and resources to the external environment, and then decide what the firm wants to accomplish in the future.

Three basic objectives provide guidelines

The following three objectives provide a useful starting point for setting a firm's objectives. They should be sought *together* because in the long run a failure

3M has introduced a super sticky version of its popular Post-It notes to stay ahead of competitors who try to imitate its original product.

in even one of the three areas can lead to total failure of the business. A business should

1. Engage in specific activities that will perform a socially and economically useful function.
2. Develop an organization to carry on the business and implement its strategies.
3. Earn enough profit to survive.[2]

A mission statement helps set the course

Our three general objectives provide guidelines, but a firm should develop its own objectives. This is important, but top executives often don't state their objectives clearly. If objectives aren't clear from the start, different managers may hold unspoken and conflicting objectives.

Many firms try to avoid this problem by developing a **mission statement**, which sets out the organization's basic purpose for being. For example, the mission of the Fort Smith Public Library (www.fspl.lib.ar.us) is "to serve the minds of the citizens in our community by providing easy access to resources that meet their informational and recreational needs." A good mission statement should focus on a few key goals rather than embracing everything. It should also supply guidelines when managers face difficult decisions. For example, if an employee of the library is trying to decide whether or not to write a proposal for the funding of a Spanish language story time or new computers that provide Internet access, it should be clear that these services are within the scope of the library's stated mission. A mission statement may need to be revised as new market needs arise or as the marketing environment changes. But this would be a fundamental change and not one that is made casually.[3]

The whole firm must work toward the same objectives

A mission statement is important, but it is not a substitute for more specific objectives that provide guidance in screening possible opportunities. For example, top management might set objectives such as "earn 25 percent annual return on investment" and "introduce at least three innovative and successful products in the next two years."

Of course, when there are a number of specific objectives stated by top management, it is critical that they be compatible. For example, the objective of introducing new products is reasonable. However, if the costs of developing and introducing the

60

Exhibit 3–2
A Hierarchy of
Objectives

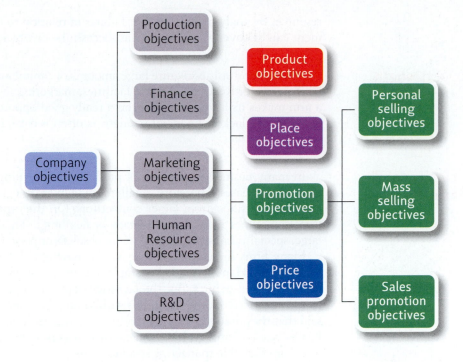

new products cannot be recouped within one year, the return on investment objective is impossible.[4]

Company objectives should lead to marketing objectives

To avoid such problems, the marketing manager should at least be involved in setting company objectives. Company objectives guide managers as they search for and evaluate opportunities—and later plan marketing strategies. Particular *marketing* objectives should be set within the framework of larger company objectives. As shown in Exhibit 3–2, firms need a hierarchy of objectives—moving from company objectives to marketing department objectives. For each marketing strategy, firms also need objectives for each of the four Ps—as well as more detailed objectives. For example, in the Promotion area, we need objectives for personal selling, mass selling, *and* sales promotion.

Toyota provides an example. One of its company objectives is to achieve high customer satisfaction. So the R&D people design vehicles to meet specific reliability objectives. Similarly, the production people work to cut manufacturing defects. The marketing department, in turn, sets specific customer satisfaction objectives for every product. That leads to specific promotion objectives to ensure that the sales and advertising people don't promise more than the company can deliver. Dealers and customer service people, in turn, work to quickly fix a problem the first time it's reported.

Both company objectives and marketing objectives should be realistic and achievable. Overly ambitious objectives are useless if the firm lacks the resources to achieve them.

COMPANY RESOURCES MAY LIMIT SEARCH FOR OPPORTUNITIES

Every firm has some resources—hopefully some unique ones—that set it apart. Breakthrough opportunities—or at least some competitive advantage—come from making use of these strengths while avoiding direct competition with firms having similar strengths.

To find its strengths, a firm must evaluate its functional areas (production, research and engineering, marketing, general management, and finance) as well as its present products and markets. The knowledge of people at the firm can also be a unique resource. By analyzing successes or failures in relation to the firm's resources, management can discover why the firm was successful—or why it failed—in the past.

Financial strength

Some opportunities require large amounts of capital just to get started. Money may be required for R&D, production facilities, marketing research, or advertising before a firm makes its first sale. And even a really good opportunity may not be profitable for years. So lack of financial strength is often a barrier to entry into an otherwise attractive market.

Producing capability and flexibility

In many businesses, the cost of producing and selling each unit decreases as the quantity increases. Therefore, smaller firms can be at a great cost disadvantage if they try to win business from larger competitors. On the other hand, new—or smaller—firms sometimes have the advantage of flexibility. They are not handicapped with large, special-purpose facilities that are obsolete or poorly located.

Many firms increase flexibility by not having any "in-house" manufacturing for their brands. Hanes is a good example. At one point, Hanes had U.S. factories for its underwear and t-shirts. But the factories were sold when most textile-related manufacturing moved to other countries with lower labor costs. Top managers for the brand said that they didn't have a competitive advantage in manufacturing anyway. Now, as Hanes' needs change, it has the flexibility to work with whatever suppliers around the world are best able to meet its specifications.

Marketing strengths

Our marketing strategy planning framework (Exhibit 2–9) helps in analyzing current marketing resources. In the product area, for example, a familiar brand can be a big strength. Starbucks is famous for its coffee beverages. When Starbucks introduced its Coffee Ice Cream, many people quickly tried it because they knew what Starbucks flavor meant.[5]

A new idea or process may be protected by a *patent*. A patent owner has a 20-year monopoly to develop and use its new product, process, or material. If one firm has a strong patent, competitors may be limited to second-rate offerings—and their efforts may be doomed to failure.[6]

Good relations with established wholesalers or retailers—or control of good locations—can be important resources. When marketing managers at Microsoft

Which opportunities a firm decides to pursue may depend on its resources and capabilities. For example, General Mills was already producing a key ingredient for its new Chocolate Chex Mix. Similarly, Nucor has become one of the largest steel producers in the United States by operating smaller steel mills in rural towns. Both General Mills and Nucor are innovative in other ways as well, which helps them to be flexible and responsive to changes in the market environment.

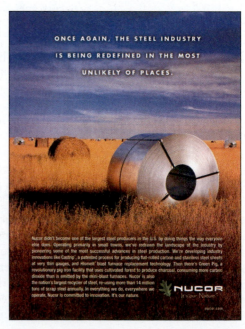

decided to introduce the Xbox game console, Microsoft software and computer accessories had already proved profitable for retailers like Best Buy that could reach the target market. So these retailers were willing to give the Xbox shelf space even if they were already carrying competing products from Nintendo or Sony.[7]

Promotion and price resources must be considered too. Fidelity Investments already has a skilled sales force. Marketing managers know these sales reps can handle new products and customers. And expertise to create an Internet website for online orders may enable a firm to expand its market.

Thorough understanding of a target market can give a company an edge. Many companies fail in new product-markets because they don't really understand the needs of the new customers or the new competitive environment.

ANALYZING COMPETITORS AND THE COMPETITIVE ENVIRONMENT

Choose opportunities that avoid head-on competition

The **competitive environment** affects the number and types of competitors the marketing manager must face and how they may behave. Although marketing managers usually can't control these factors, they can choose strategies that avoid head-on competition. And where competition is inevitable, they can plan for it.

Economists describe four basic kinds of market (competitive) situations: pure competition, oligopoly, monopolistic competition, and monopoly. Understanding the differences among these market situations is helpful in analyzing the competitive environment, and our discussion assumes some familiarity with these concepts. (For a review, see Exhibit A–11 and the related discussion in Appendix A, which follows Chapter 18.)

Most product-markets head toward pure competition—or oligopoly—over the long run. In these situations, competitors offer very similar products. Because customers see the different available products (marketing mixes) as close substitutes, managers just compete with lower and lower prices, and profit margins shrink. Sometimes managers cut prices much too quickly, without really thinking through the question of how to add more customer value.

Avoiding pure competition is sensible and certainly fits with our emphasis on the need to find a competitive advantage. Marketing managers can't just adopt the same "good" marketing strategy being used by other firms. That just leads to head-on competition and a downward spiral in prices and profits.

Most consumers don't know the technical differences between various products for finishing wood, so Minwax ads emphasize that Minwax Polyshades saves them time by combining a stain and final finish in one product. Dirt Devil wants to convince customers that its Scorpion Hand Vac has more power than competitors so its ad gives the specific amp and watt rating. However, a consumer who does not know the ratings for other brands may not know that this is an advantage.

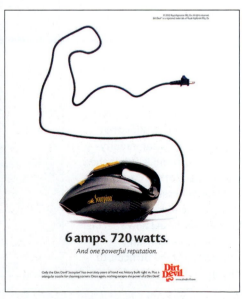

Competitor-free environments are rare

Monopoly situations, in which one firm completely controls a broad product-market, are rare in market-directed economies. Further, governments commonly regulate monopolies. For example, in many parts of the world prices set by utility companies must be approved by a government agency. Although most marketing managers can't expect to operate with complete control in an unregulated monopoly, they can move away from head-on competition.

Monopolistic competition is typical—and a challenge

In monopolistic competition, a number of different firms offer marketing mixes that at least some customers see as different. Each competitor tries to get control (a monopoly) in its "own" target market. But competition still exists because some customers see the various alternatives as substitutes. Most marketing managers in developed economies face monopolistic competition.

In monopolistic competition, marketing managers sometimes try to differentiate very similar products by relying on other elements of the marketing mix. For example, Clorox Bleach uses the same basic chemicals as other bleaches. But marketing managers for Clorox may help to set it apart from other bleaches by offering an improved pouring spout, by producing ads that demonstrate its stain-killing power, or by getting it better shelf positions in supermarkets. Yet such approaches may not work, especially if competitors can easily imitate each new idea.

Analyze competitors to find a competitive advantage

The best way for a marketing manager to avoid head-on competition is to find new or better ways to satisfy customers' needs and provide value. The search for a breakthrough opportunity—or some sort of competitive advantage—requires an understanding not only of customers but also of competitors. That's why marketing managers turn to **competitor analysis**—an organized approach for evaluating the strengths and weaknesses of current or potential competitors' marketing strategies.

The basic approach to competitor analysis is simple. You compare the strengths and weaknesses of your current (or planned) target market and marketing mix with what competitors are currently doing or are likely to do in response to your strategy.

The initial step in competitor analysis is to identify potential competitors. It's useful to start broadly and from the viewpoint of target customers. Companies may

Many consumers think that toilet paper is a commodity—where one brand is about the same as any other. Cashmere's bathroom tissue is softer and its ad campaign encourages consumers to see how special it is. However, consumer attitudes may be difficult to change.

offer quite different products to meet the same needs, but they are competitors if customers see them as offering close substitutes. For example, disposable diapers, cloth diapers, and diaper rental services all compete in the same broad market concerned with baby care. Identifying a broad set of potential competitors helps marketing managers understand the different ways customers are currently meeting needs and sometimes points to new opportunities. For example, even parents who usually prefer the economy of cloth diapers may be interested in the convenience of disposables when they travel.

Usually, however, marketing managers quickly narrow the focus of their analysis to the set of **competitive rivals**—firms that will be the closest competitors. Rivals offering similar products are usually easy to identify. However, with a really new and different product concept, the closest competitor may be a firm that is currently serving similar needs with a different type of product. Although such firms may not appear to be close competitors, they are likely to fight back—perhaps with a directly competitive product—if another firm starts to take away customers.

Anticipate competition that will come

A successful strategy attracts copycats who jump in for a share of the profit. Sometimes a creative imitator figures out a way to provide customers with superior value. Then sales may disappear before the pioneer even knows what's happened.

Finding a sustainable competitive advantage requires special attention to competitor strengths and weaknesses. For example, it is very difficult to dislodge a firm that is already a market leader simply by attacking with a similar strategy. The leader can usually defend its position by quickly copying the best parts of what a new competitor is trying to do. On the other hand, a competitor may not be able to defend quickly if it is attacked where it is weak. For example, Netflix's online DVD rental business initially grew by taking customers away from Blockbuster. Blockbuster quickly fought back with its own online service, but with a twist. A customer who ordered a DVD from Blockbuster online could view it and then immediately trade it for another at a local Blockbuster store. Netflix doesn't have stores, so it couldn't copy Blockbuster's approach.[8]

Internet EXERCISE

A marketing manager for Netflix may find it helpful to know more about how competitors advertise on search pages (like Google and Yahoo). The website KeywordSpy (**www.keywordspy.com**) offers that information and more. Go to this site and type "dvd rental" into its search bar. What competitors are identified? What information can you learn about Netflix and its competitors at this site? How could this information help Netflix's marketing manager?

Watch for competitive barriers

In a competitor analysis, you also consider **competitive barriers**—the conditions that may make it difficult, or even impossible, for a firm to compete in a market. Such barriers may limit your own plans or, alternatively, block competitors' responses to an innovative strategy.

For example, Exhibit 3–3 summarizes a competitor analysis in the Japanese market for disposable diapers. P&G was about to replace its original Pampers, which were selling poorly, with a new version that offered improved fit and absorbency. Kao and Uni-Charm, the two leading Japanese producers, both had better distribution networks. Kao also had a better computer system to handle reorders. Because most Japanese grocery stores and drugstores are very small, frequent restocking by wholesalers is critical. So getting cooperation in the channel was a potential competitive barrier for P&G. To overcome this problem, P&G changed its packaging to take up less space and offered wholesalers and retailers better markups.[9]

Seek information about competitors

A marketing manager should actively seek information about current or potential competitors. Although most firms try to keep the specifics of their plans secret, much public information may be available. Sources of competitor information include trade publications, alert sales reps, suppliers, and other industry experts. In business markets, customers may be quick to explain what competing suppliers are offering.

Exhibit 3-3 Competitor Analysis (summary): Disposable Diaper Competition in Japan

	P&G's Current and Planned Strategy	Kao's Strengths (+) and Weaknesses (−)	Uni-Charm's Strengths (+) and Weaknesses (−)
Target Market(s)	Upscale, modern parents who can afford disposable diapers	Same as for P&G	Same as for P&G, but also budget-conscious segment that includes cloth diaper users (+)
Product	Improved fit and absorbency (+); brand name imagery weak in Japan (−)	Brand familiarity (+), but no longer the best performance (−)	Two brands—for different market segments—and more convenient package with handles (+)
Place	Distribution through independent wholesalers to both food stores and drugstores (+), but handled by fewer retailers (−)	Close relations with and control over wholesalers who carry only Kao products (+); computerized inventory reorder system (+)	Distribution through 80% of food stores in best locations (+); shelf space for two brands (+)
Promotion	Heaviest spending on daytime TV, heavy sales promotion, including free samples (+); small sales force (−)	Large efficient sales force (+); lowest advertising spending (−) and out-of-date ad claims (−)	Advertising spending high (+); effective ads that appeal to Japanese mothers (+)
Price	High retail price (−), but lower unit price for larger quantities (+)	Highest retail price (−), but also best margins for wholesalers and retailers (+)	Lowest available retail price (+); price of premium brand comparable to P&G (−)
(Potential) Competitive Barriers	Patent protection (+), limits on access to retail shelf space (−)	Inferior product (−), excellent logistics support system (+)	Economies of scale and lower costs (+); loyal customers (+)
Likely Response(s)	Improve wholesaler and retailer margins; faster deliveries in channel; change package to require less shelf space	Press retailers to increase in-store promotion; change advertising and/or improve product	Increase short-term sales promotions; but if P&G takes customers, cut price on premium brand

A firm that puts all of its marketing information on a public website for customers also makes it readily available to competitors. Similarly, it's easy to schedule a regular online search through thousands of publications and databases for any mention of a competitor.

Ethical issues may arise   The search for information about competitors sometimes raises ethical issues. For example, people who change jobs and move to competing firms may have a great deal of information, but is it ethical for them to use it? Similarly, some firms have been criticized for going too far—like waiting at a landfill for competitors' trash to find copies of confidential company reports. And the high-tech version of that occurs when Internet "hackers" break into a competitor's computer network.

Beyond the moral issues, spying on competitors to obtain trade secrets is illegal. Damage awards can be huge. The courts ordered competing firms to pay Procter & Gamble about $125 million in damages for stealing secrets about its Duncan Hines soft cookies.[10]

THE ECONOMIC ENVIRONMENT

The **economic and technological environment** affects the way firms—and the whole economy—use resources. We will treat the economic and technological environments separately to emphasize that the technological environment provides a *base* for the economic environment. Technical skills and equipment affect the way companies convert an economy's resources into output. The economic environment, on the other hand, is affected by the way all of the parts of a macro-economic system interact. This then affects such things as national income, economic growth, and inflation. The economic environment may vary from one country to another, but economies around the world are linked.

Economic conditions change rapidly

The economic environment can, and does, change quite rapidly. The effects can be far-reaching and require changes in marketing strategy.

Even a well-planned marketing strategy may fail if a country or region goes through a rapid business decline. You can see how quickly this can occur by considering what happened in the U.S. housing market in the past few years. Earlier in the decade the economy was growing, household incomes were increasing, and interest rates were low. As a result, the housing market was hot. Manufacturers of building materials, home contractors, real estate firms, and mortgage companies all enjoyed strong profits as they scrambled to keep up with demand. However, by 2008 the economy was in recession and the housing market abruptly collapsed. Firms that had done so well a year earlier were suffering huge losses—and many went bankrupt. Worse, millions of people lost their homes when they could not afford rising payments for variable-rate mortgages. In a weak economy many consumers must really ratchet back on their spending—and do without products they would like to have. Many companies are not strong enough to survive such downturns.

Interest rates and inflation affect buying

Changes in the economy are often accompanied by changes in the interest rate— the charge for borrowing money. Interest rates directly affect the total price borrowers must pay for products. So the interest rate affects when, and if, they will buy. This is an especially important factor in some business markets. But it also affects consumer purchases of homes, cars, and other items usually bought on credit.

Interest rates usually increase during periods of inflation, and inflation is a fact of life in many economies. In some Latin American countries, inflation has exceeded 400 percent a year in recent years. In contrast, recent U.S. levels—3 to 20 percent— seem low. Still, inflation must be considered in strategy planning. When costs are rising rapidly and there are no more cost-cutting measures to take, a marketing manager may have to increase prices. For example, airlines and freight carriers raised prices sharply following the spiraling cost of fuel.

The global economy is connected

The economies of the world are connected—and changes in one economy quickly affect others. One reason for this is that the amount of international trade

The Smart car has been sold in Europe for a number of years. This European ad focuses on how easy it is to park. Now that the Smart car is being introduced in the U.S., the new market environment may require new promotion. For example, although the car is very small, advanced technology helps it meet tough U.S. safety regulations.

is increasing—and it is affected by changes in and between economies. For example, International Harvester (IH) was very successful selling its earth-moving equipment in Asia when construction was booming. However, when an economic downturn spread across Asia, many customers could no longer make payments and IH faced big losses.

Changes in the *exchange rate*—how much one country's money is worth in another country's money—have an important effect on international trade. When the dollar is strong, it's worth more in foreign countries. This sounds good—but it makes U.S. products more expensive overseas and foreign products cheaper in the United States. New domestic competition arises as foreign products gain a competitive edge with lower prices.

Marketing managers must watch the economic environment carefully. In contrast to the cultural and social environment, economic conditions can move rapidly and require immediate strategy changes.[11]

THE TECHNOLOGICAL ENVIRONMENT

Technology affects opportunities

Technology is the application of science to convert an economy's resources to output. Technology affects marketing in two basic ways: opportunities for new products and for new processes (ways of doing things). For example, advances in information technology make it possible for people in different parts of the world to communicate by satellite videoconferencing and to send complex design drawings over the Internet. Websites enable sophisticated e-commerce exchanges between remote firms. These process changes are accompanied by an exciting explosion of high-tech products—from genome-based medicines to cars that contact the police if they are stolen.

Technology transfer is rapid

New technologies have created important industries that didn't even exist a few years ago. A dozen years ago Google didn't exist. Now it's one of the best known firms in the world. With such big opportunities at stake, you can also see why there is such rapid transfer of technology from one part of the world to another. But technology transfer is not automatic. Someone—perhaps you—has to see the opportunity.

Internet technologies are reshaping marketing

Many of the big advances in business have come from early recognition of new ways to do things. There is perhaps no better example of this than the World Wide Web and the Internet. The **Internet** is a system for linking computers around the world. The idea of linking computers in a network was not new. Even so, the Internet expanded the network concept to include any computer anywhere and the World Wide Web made the exchange of information easy. As a result, this technology has changed just about every aspect of marketing.

New technology creates opportunities for new products. A wireless Bluetooth earpiece makes it easier to use a cell phone, but Aliph's Jawbone earpiece is stylish, small, light, and especially good at reducing background noise.

Consider the arena of promotion. The invention of TV changed marketing because it suddenly made it possible for a sponsor to broadcast a brief but vivid message to millions of people at the same time. Now, the Internet makes it possible for that sponsor to select any of millions of messages and to simultaneously narrowcast any of them to millions of different individuals. It is just as easy for customers to request the information in the first place, or to respond electronically once they have it. Thus, the Internet's capability changes our ideas about how firms communicate with customers, and vice versa. Similarly, the Internet has created totally different approaches to pricing. Airlines run online auctions of seats that might otherwise go unsold. To check out an online auction, go to www.ebay.com.

In hindsight, new approaches such as these seem obvious—given that the technology is available. But they are not obvious up front—unless you're really looking for them.[12]

Technology and ethical issues

Marketers often must help their firms decide what technological developments are ethically acceptable. For example, many firms track information about who "hits" the company Web page and what website they came from. The firm can then sell this information to whoever wants to use it to send promotional e-mail. Yet uninvited e-mail is just another form of invasion of privacy.

Some attractive technological developments may be rejected because of their long-run effects on the environment. Aseptic drink boxes, for example, are convenient but difficult to recycle. In a case like this, what's good for the firm and some customers may not be good for the cultural and social environment or acceptable in the political and legal environment. Being close to the market should give marketers a better feel for current trends and help firms avoid serious mistakes.[13]

THE POLITICAL ENVIRONMENT

The attitudes and reactions of people, social critics, and governments all affect the political environment. Consumers in the same country usually share a common political environment, but the political environment can also affect opportunities at a local or international level.

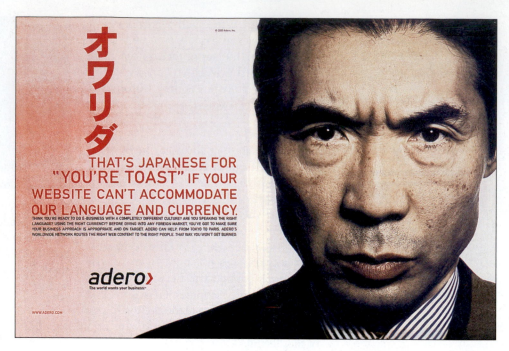

Adero wants marketers to keep in mind that a website that can attract prospects from all over the world won't be successful in turning them into customers if it ignores nationalism and cultural differences.

Nationalism can be limiting in international markets

Strong sentiments of **nationalism**—an emphasis on a country's interests before everything else—affect how macro-marketing systems work. They can affect how marketing managers work as well. Nationalistic feelings can reduce sales—or even block all marketing activity—in some international markets. For many years, China has made it difficult for outside firms to do business there—in spite of the fact that the Chinese economy has experienced explosive growth as its factories have turned out larger and larger portions of the goods sold in the United States, Europe, and other parts of the world.

The "Buy American" policy in many government contracts and business purchases reflects this same attitude in the United States. There is broad consumer support for protecting U.S. producers—and jobs—from foreign competition. That's why GM promotes its trucks in TV commercials to strains of "This Is Our Country" (even though some of its most popular models are produced in Mexico).[14]

Regional groupings are becoming more important

Important dimensions of the political environment are likely to be similar among nations that have banded together to have common regional economic boundaries. The move toward the unification of Europe and free trade among the nations of North America are examples of this sort of regional grouping.

The unification of European markets

Twenty years ago, each country in Europe had its own unique trade rules and regulations. These differences made it difficult and expensive to move products from one country to the others. Now, the countries of the European Union (EU) are reducing conflicting laws, taxes, and other obstacles to trade within Europe. This, in turn, is reducing costs and the prices European consumers pay.

Although Europe is becoming a large unified market, marketers will still encounter differences among European countries. What happened to Lands' End, the U.S.-based Internet and mail-order retailer, illustrates the issues. To better reach European consumers, Lands' End set up shop in England and Germany. As in the United States, its website touted the unconditional lifetime guarantee that is a key part of its strategy. However, German consumer protection rules prohibited promotion of the guarantee; the Germans argued that the promotion was misleading (on the logic that the cost of the guarantee was "hidden" in higher prices that consumers would pay). German officials wanted this ban to apply even if the German consumer purchased the product from a Lands' End website in England. Quirky local rules like this could erode some of the benefits that should come from more European unification.[15]

NAFTA is building trade cooperation

The international competition fostered by the moves to unify Europe provided impetus for other cooperative trade agreements, including the **North American Free Trade Agreement (NAFTA)** which lays out a plan to reshape the rules of trade among the United States, Canada, and Mexico. NAFTA basically enlarges the free-trade pact that had already knocked down most barriers to U.S.–Canada trade, and over a 15-year period it will eliminate most such barriers with Mexico. It also establishes a forum for resolving future trade disputes.

The changes that result from NAFTA may ultimately be as significant as those in Europe. Talks are under way to explore the concept of expanding NAFTA to create a free-trade zone for 34 countries across North, South, and Central America.

Of course, removal of some economic and political barriers—whether across all of the Americas or Europe—will not eliminate the need to adjust strategies to reach submarkets of consumers. Centuries of cultural differences will not disappear overnight. Some may never disappear.[16]

Some dramatic changes in the political environment—like the fall of communism in Eastern Europe—happen fast and are hard to predict. Yet many important political changes—both within and across nations—evolve more gradually.

THE LEGAL ENVIRONMENT

Changes in the political environment often lead to changes in the legal environment and in the way existing laws are enforced. The legal environment sets the basic rules for how a business can operate in society. The legal environment may severely limit some choices, but changes in laws and how they are interpreted also create new opportunities. To illustrate the effects of the legal environment, we will discuss how it has evolved in the United States. However, laws often vary from one country to another.

Trying to encourage competition

American economic and legislative thinking is based on the idea that competition among many small firms helps the economy. Therefore, attempts by business to limit competition are considered contrary to the public interest.

Starting in 1890, Congress passed a series of antimonopoly laws. Exhibit 3–4 shows the names and dates of these laws. Although the specific focus of each law is different, in general they are all intended to encourage competition.

Antimonopoly law and marketing mix planning

In later chapters, we will specifically apply antimonopoly law to the four Ps. Exhibit 3–4 provides a summary of the kind of proof the government must have to get a conviction under each of the major laws and which of the four Ps are most affected by each law.

Because of a change in regulations, some non-prescription drugs are no longer available on self-service retail shelves but rather are behind the pharmacy counter. With this change in the legal environment, marketers for Mucinex D want customers to know how to find the product in the store.

Exhibit 3–4   Focus (mostly prohibitions) of Federal Antimonopoly Laws on the Four Ps

Law	Product	Place	Promotion	Price
Sherman Act (1890) Monopoly or conspiracy in restraint of trade	Monopoly or conspiracy to control a product	Monopoly or conspiracy to control distribution channels		Monopoly or conspiracy to fix or control prices
Clayton Act (1914) Substantially lessens competition	Forcing sale of some products with others— tying contracts	Exclusive dealing contracts (limiting buyers' sources of supply)		Price discrimination by manufacturers
Federal Trade Commission Act (1914) Unfair methods of competition		Unfair policies	Deceptive ads or selling practices	Deceptive pricing
Robinson-Patman Act (1936) Tends to injure competition			Prohibits "fake" advertising allowances or discrimination in help offered	Prohibits price discrimination on goods of "like grade and quality" without cost justification, and limits quantity discounts
Wheeler-Lea Amendment (1938) Unfair or deceptive practices	Deceptive packaging or branding		Deceptive ads or selling claims	Deceptive pricing
Antimerger Act (1950) Lessens competition	Buying competitors	Buying producers or distributors		
Magnuson-Moss Act (1975) Unreasonable practices	Product warranties			

Prosecution is serious—you can go to jail

Businesses and *individual managers* are subject to both criminal and civil laws. Penalties for breaking civil laws are limited to blocking or forcing certain actions—along with fines. Where criminal law applies, jail sentences can be imposed. For example, several managers at Beech-Nut Nutrition Company were fined $100,000 each and sent to jail. In spite of ads claiming that Beech-Nut's apple juice was 100 percent natural, they tried to bolster profits by secretly using low-cost artificial ingredients.[17]

Consumer protection laws are not new

Although antimonopoly laws focus on protecting competition, the wording of the laws in Exhibit 3–4 has, over time, moved toward protecting consumers. Some consumer protections are also built into the English and U.S. common law systems. A seller has to tell the truth (if asked a direct question), meet contracts, and stand behind the firm's product (to some reasonable extent). Beyond this, it is expected that vigorous competition in the marketplace will protect consumers—*so long as they are careful.*

Yet focusing only on competition didn't protect consumers very well in some areas. So the government found it necessary to pass other laws. For example, various laws regulate packaging and labels, credit practices, telemarketing, and environmental issues. Usually, however, the laws focus on specific types of products.

Foods and drugs are controlled

Consumer protection laws in the United States go back to 1906 when Congress passed the Pure Food and Drug Act. Unsanitary meat-packing practices in the Chicago stockyards stirred consumer support for this act. Before the law, it was assumed that common law and the old warning "let the buyer beware" would take care of consumers.

Later acts corrected some loopholes in the law. The law now bans the shipment of unsanitary and poisonous products and requires much testing of drugs. The Food and Drug Administration (FDA) attempts to control manufacturers of these products. It can seize products that violate its rules—including regulations on branding and labeling.

Product safety is controlled

The Consumer Product Safety Act (of 1972), another important consumer protection law, set up the Consumer Product Safety Commission. This group has broad power to set safety standards and can impose penalties for failure to meet these standards. There is some question as to how much safety consumers really want—the commission found the bicycle the most hazardous product under its control!

But given that the commission has the power to *force* a product off the market—or require expensive recalls to correct problems—it is obvious that safety must be considered in product design. And safety must be treated seriously by marketing managers. There is no more tragic example of this than the recalls of Firestone tires used as original equipment on Ford's Explorer SUV. Hundreds of consumers were killed or seriously injured in accidents.[18]

State and local laws vary

Besides federal legislation—which affects interstate commerce—marketers must be aware of state and local laws. There are state and city laws regulating minimum prices and the setting of prices, regulations for starting up a business (licenses, examinations, and even tax payments), and in some communities, regulations prohibiting certain activities—such as telephone selling or selling on Sundays or during evenings.

Consumerists and the law say "let the seller beware"

The old rule about buyer–seller relations—*let the buyer beware*—has changed to *let the seller beware*. The shift to proconsumer laws and court decisions suggests that lawmakers are more interested in protecting consumers. This may upset production-oriented managers. But times have changed—and managers must adapt to this new political and legal environment.[19]

THE CULTURAL AND SOCIAL ENVIRONMENT

The **cultural and social environment** affects how and why people live and behave as they do—which affects customer buying behavior and eventually the economic, political, and legal environments. Many variables make up the cultural and social environment. Some examples are the languages people speak, the type of education they have, their religious beliefs, what type of food they eat, the style of clothing and housing they have, and how they view work, marriage, and family. Because the cultural and social environment has such broad effects, most people don't stop to think about it, or how it may be changing, or how it may differ for other people.

For example, over decades, the role of women has changed significantly. Just 50 years ago most people in the United States thought that a woman's primary role was in the home—as wife and mother. Now more than 70 percent of women age 35–44 work outside the home. Such changes have increased household income, changed shopping habits, and generated a greater need for many products including child care services and prepared take-out food.

Demographic data related to population and income provides a lot of insight about a society and its culture. Understanding the demographic dimensions is also important to marketing strategy planning so it's useful to look at some key demographic patterns and trends.

Marketing managers for eBay have found many opportunities for new growth in international markets.

Where people are around the world

Exhibit 3–5 summarizes data for a number of representative countries from different regions around the world. Even with a current population of over 309 million, the United States makes up less than 5 percent of the total world population, which is now over 6.6 billion. Marketing managers looking for growth may seek opportunities in other countries.

Although the size of a market is important, the population trend is also important. The world's population is growing fast, but that population growth varies dramatically from country to country. In general, less-developed countries experience the fastest rates. Haiti, Madagascar, Nigeria, Somalia, and Uganda, for example, are projected to increase their populations by more than 40 percent between 2010 and 2025. The U.S. population, on the other hand, will grow about 13 percent. During the same time frame, the growth of China's large population is expected to be less than 8 percent while Japan, Russia, and many European countries are projecting population declines. These trends have many marketing managers paying increased attention to developing countries.[20]

A shift from rural to urban areas

Just 50 years ago about two-thirds of the world's population lived in rural areas. Today about half live in urban areas as more people move to cities for better job opportunities. The extent of urbanization varies widely across countries. While about 80 percent of U.S. residents live in urban areas, more than 90 percent do in the United Kingdom, Kuwait, Australia, Israel, and Singapore (see Exhibit 3–5). By contrast, in Ethiopia, Nepal, and Uganda less than 16 percent of the people live in major urban areas.

For many firms, the concentration of people in major cities simplifies Place and Promotion decisions, especially for major cities in the wealthiest nations. Affluent, big-city consumers often have similar lifestyles and needs. Thus, many of the products successful in Toronto, New York, or Paris are likely to be successful in Caracas and Tokyo. The spread of the Internet, satellite TV, and other communication technologies has accelerated this trend.

There's no market when there's no income

Profitable markets require income—as well as people. The amount of money people can spend affects the products they are likely to buy. When considering international markets, firms must assume income is often one of the most important demographic

Exhibit 3–5 Demographic Dimensions for Representative Countries

Country	2010 Projected Population (000s)	2025 Projected Population (000s)	2010–2025 Projected Population Change (%)	2006 Population Density (per square mile)	2006 Percent of Population in Urban Areas	2006 GNI Per Capita ($U.S.)	2006 GDP (billions of $U.S.)	Estimated Literacy Percent
Algeria	34,555	40,255	16.5	36	58	3,030	114.7	69.9
Australia	20,925	23,023	10.0	7	91	35,990	768.2	99.0
Bangladesh	159,765	204,539	28.0	2,850	23	480	62.0	43.1
Brazil	195,580	217,822	11.4	58	81	4,730	1,068.0	88.6
Canada	34,253	38,165	11.4	9	81	36,170	1,251.5	99.0
China	1,347,563	1,453,000	7.8	365	44	2,010	2,668.1	90.9
Egypt	84,440	103,573	22.7	205	43	1,350	107.5	71.4
Ethiopia	81,754	107,804	31.9	173	16	180	13.3	42.7
Finland	5,255	5,251	−0.1	45	62	40,650	209.4	100.0
France	64,806	68,522	5.7	256	77	36,550	2,230.7	99.0
Germany	82,283	80,637	−2.0	611	75	36,620	2,906.7	99.0
Greece	10,750	10,671	−0.7	212	59	21,690	245.0	96.0
Haiti	9,386	13,254	41.2	799	36	480	5.0	52.9
Iceland	309	338	9.4	8	93	50,580	15.9	99.0
India	1,184,090	1,449,000	22.4	968	28	820	906.3	61.0
Israel	6,645	7,612	14.6	809	92	18,580	123.4	97.1
Italy	58,091	56,234	−3.2	512	68	32,020	1,844.7	98.4
Japan	126,804	117,816	−7.1	881	79	38,410	4,340.1	99.0
Kuwait	2,788	4,175	49.7	352	98	30,630	80.8	93.3
Madagascar	21,282	32,431	52.4	84	26	280	5.5	68.9
Mexico	112,469	130,199	15.8	145	75	7,870	839.2	91.0
Morocco	35,301	42,553	20.5	193	55	1,900	57.3	52.3
Mozambique	22,061	28,893	31.0	68	35	340	7.6	47.8
Nepal	30,758	39,918	29.8	512	14	290	8.1	48.6
Nigeria	145,032	206,166	42.2	375	44	640	114.7	68.0
Norway	4,676	4,917	5.2	39	78	66,530	311.0	100.0
Pakistan	173,814	218,496	25.7	538	34	770	128.8	49.9
Romania	22,181	21,260	−4.2	251	55	4,850	121.6	97.3
Russia	139,390	128,180	−8.0	22	73	5,780	986.9	99.4
Saudi Arabia	29,222	35,669	22.1	33	81	12,510	309.8	78.8
Singapore	4,701	5,101	8.5	17,060	100	29,320	132.2	92.5
Somalia	9,922	14,862	49.8	37	34	—	—	37.8
Spain	40,549	39,578	−2.4	209	77	27,570	1,244.0	97.9
Switzerland	7,623	7,774	2.0	490	68	57,230	379.8	99.0
Thailand	66,303	70,524	6.4	327	33	2,990	206.2	92.6
Uganda	33,399	56,745	69.9	379	12	300	9.3	66.8
U.K.	61,285	63,819	4.1	650	90	40,180	2,345.0	99.0
U.S.	309,163	349,666	13.1	84	79	44,970	13,201.8	99.0
Venezuela	27,223	33,189	21.9	75	88	6,070	181.9	93.0

dimensions. There are a variety of different measures of national income. One widely used measure is **gross domestic product (GDP)**—the total market value of all goods and services provided in a country's economy in a year by both residents and nonresidents of that country. *Gross national income (GNI)* is a measure that is similar to GDP, but GNI does not include income earned by foreigners who own resources in that nation. By contrast, GDP does include foreign income. (Note: until recently,

Most people would agree that a motorcycle is not a good way for a family of six to get around. But, most people in India don't have the money to afford cars that are common in the United States. That's why Tata Motors in India plans to produce a very basic "People's Car" that will sell for about $2,500.

GNI was called *gross national product* or *GNP*, so many government documents still include that label.)

When you compare countries with different patterns of international investment, the income measure you use can make a difference. For example, Ford has a factory in Thailand. The GDP measure for Thailand would include the profits from that factory because they were earned in that country. However, Ford is not a Thai firm and most of its profit will ultimately flow out of Thailand. Thus, the Thai GNI would not include those profits. You should see that using GDP income measures can give the impression that people in less-developed countries have more income than they really do. In addition, in a country with a large population the income of the whole nation must be spread over more people. So *GNI per capita* (per person) is a useful figure because it gives some idea of the income level of people in the country.

Exhibit 3–5 gives an estimate of GNI per capita and GDP for each country listed. You can see that the more developed industrial nations—including the United States, Japan, and Germany—account for the biggest share of the world's GDP. In these countries the GNI per capita is also quite high. This explains why so much trade takes place between these countries—and why many firms see them as the more important markets. In general, markets like these offer the best potential for products that are targeted at consumers with higher income levels. As a point of comparison, the GNI per capita in the United States is $44,970.[21]

Many managers, however, see great potential—and less competition—where GNI per capita is low. For example, Mars is making a big push to promote its candy in the countries of Eastern Europe. As with many other firms, it hopes to establish a relationship with consumers now, and then turn strong brand loyalty into profitable growth as consumer incomes increase.

Reading, writing, and marketing problems

The ability of a country's people to read and write has a direct influence on the development of its economy—and on marketing strategy planning. The degree of literacy affects the way information is delivered, which in marketing means promotion.

The Census Bureau estimates that 18 percent of adults (age 15 or older) in the world cannot read and write. Two-thirds of them are women. You may be surprised by the low literacy rates for some of the countries in Exhibit 3–5. Illiteracy creates challenges for product labels, instructions, and print advertising.[22]

POPULATION TRENDS IN THE U.S. CONSUMER MARKET

We've said that the U.S. population is not growing as quickly as in some other countries, but Exhibit 3–6 shows that current population and population growth vary a lot in different regions of the country. The states shaded blue and green are growing at the fastest rate. Note that the greatest growth is in western states like Nevada, Arizona, Idaho, and Utah. Growth will continue in the Sun Belt states as well. With growth over 20 percent, Florida leads the way. But Texas, Georgia, North Carolina, and Virginia are also growing rapidly.

These different rates of growth are important to marketers. Sudden growth in one area may create a demand for many new shopping centers—while retailers in declining areas face tougher competition for a smaller number of customers. In growing areas, demand can increase so rapidly that profits may be good even in poorly planned facilities.[23]

Local political boundaries don't define market areas

These continuing shifts—to and from urban and suburban areas—mean that the usual practice of reporting population by city and county boundaries can result in misleading descriptions of markets. Marketers are more interested in the size of homogeneous *marketing* areas than in the number of people within political boundaries. To meet this need, the U.S. Census Bureau also reports data by **Metropolitan Statistical Area (MSA)**,

Exhibit 3–6   2006 Population (in thousands) and Percent Change by State, 2000–2010

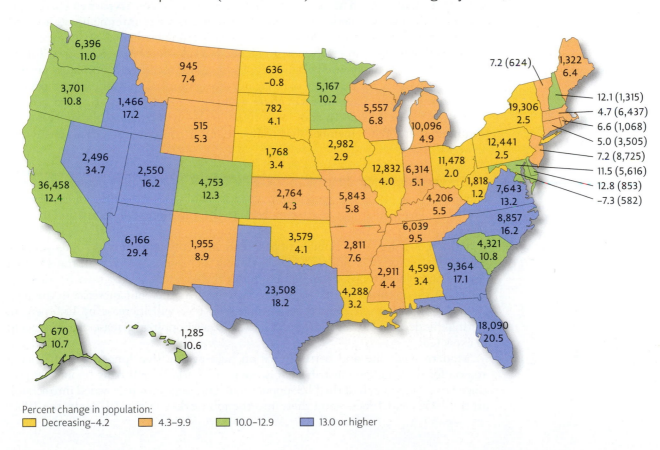

Percent change in population:
Decreasing–4.2   4.3–9.9   10.0–12.9   13.0 or higher

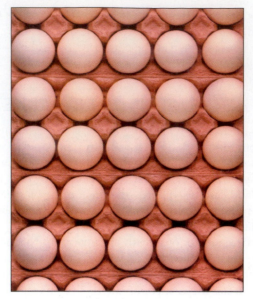

Purchasing power that's golden.

The average net worth of our viewers exceeds $2.7 million.

CNBC
cnbc.com

Highly targeted advertising media are proving especially effective at targeting messages to specific demographic groups. For example, CNBC targets high-income consumers whom it says have an average net worth over $2.7 million.

which is an integrated economic and social unit with a large population nucleus. Generally, an MSA centers on one city or urbanized area of 50,000 or more inhabitants and includes bordering urban areas.

The largest MSAs—basically those with a population of more than a million—are called Consolidated Metropolitan Statistical Areas. About 38 percent of all Americans live in the 20 largest CMSAs. More detailed data is available for areas within these sprawling, giant urban areas.

Some national marketers sell only in these metro areas because of their large, concentrated populations. They know that having so many customers packed into a small area can simplify the marketing effort. They can use fewer intermediaries and still offer products conveniently. One or two local advertising media—a city newspaper or cable TV channel—can reach most residents. If a sales force is needed, it will incur less travel time and expense because people are closer together. Metro areas are also attractive markets because they offer greater sales potential than their large population alone suggests. Consumers in these areas have more money to spend because wages tend to be higher. In addition, professionals—with higher salaries—are concentrated there. But remember that competition for consumer dollars is usually stiff in an MSA.[24]

The graying of America

Another important dimension of U.S. society is the age distribution. In 1980, the median age of the U.S. population was 30—but by 2010 the median age reached about 37. The median age is growing because the percentage of population in older age groups has increased.

Exhibit 3–7 shows the number of people in different age groups in 2000—and the expected sizes for 2010 and 2020. Note the big increases under way in the 45 to 64 and 65 and older groups. From 2000 to 2010, the 45 to 64 group grows by 30.8 percent, but then growth in that age group slows to a 3.3 percent increase in the next decade. The **senior citizen group**—people over 65—will increase by 15.0 percent during this decade. However, from 2010 to 2020, a whopping increase of 35.8 percent is expected!

Modern medicine and better nutrition help people live longer, but the major reason for the changing distribution is the post–World War II baby boom that produced over one-fourth of the U.S. population. This large group crowded into schools in the 1950s and 1960s—and then into the job market in the 1970s. In the 1980s

Exhibit 3–7 Population Distribution (and Percent Growth Rate) by Age Groups for Different 10-Year Periods

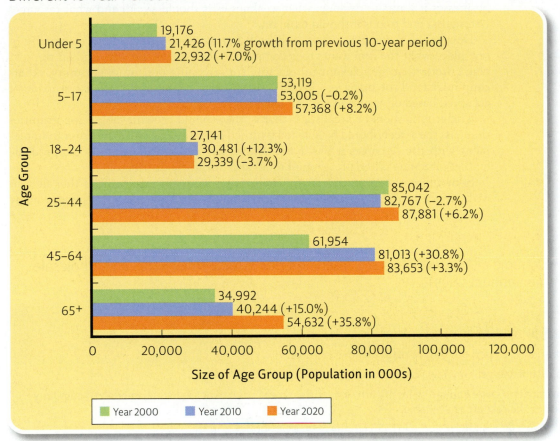

and 1990s, they swelled the middle-aged group. And early in the 21st century, they are now beginning to reach retirement and remain a dominant group in the total population.

Some of the effects of this big market are very apparent. For example, recording industry sales exploded—to the beat of rock-and-roll music and the Beatles—as the baby-boom group moved into their record-buying teens. Soon after, colleges added facilities and faculty to handle the surge, but then had to cope with excess capacity and loss of revenue when the student-age population dwindled. Now the baby boom group is creating new growth opportunities for such industries as tourism, health care, and financial services—all of which are important to the middle-aged and retired.[25]

Changes come slowly

The demographic data we've been reviewing show that changes in related cultural values and social attitudes come slowly. An individual firm should monitor and anticipate such changes and identify potential constraints and opportunities.

USING SCREENING CRITERIA TO NARROW DOWN TO STRATEGIES

Developing and applying screening criteria

After you analyze the firm's resources (for strengths and weaknesses), the environmental trends the firm faces, and the objectives of top management, you merge them all into a set of product-market screening criteria. These criteria should include both quantitative and qualitative components. The quantitative components summarize the firm's objectives: sales, profit, and return on investment (ROI) targets. (Note: ROI analysis is discussed briefly in Appendix B, which comes after Chapter 18.) The qualitative components summarize what kinds of businesses the firm wants to be in, what businesses it wants to exclude, what weaknesses it should avoid, and what resources (strengths) and trends it should build on.[26]

Developing screening criteria is difficult but worth the effort. They summarize in one place what the firm wants to accomplish. When a manager can explain the specific criteria that are relevant to selecting (or screening out) an opportunity, others can understand the manager's logic. Thus, marketing decisions are not just made or accepted based on intuition and gut feel.

The criteria should be realistic—that is, they should be achievable. Opportunities that pass the screen should be able to be turned into strategies that the firm can implement with the resources it has. For example, Exhibit 3–8 illustrates some product-market screening criteria for a small retail and wholesale distributor.

Sometimes screening criteria can help bring focus to opportunities that fit well with trends in the external market environment. For example, GE operates many

Exhibit 3–8 An Example of Product-Market Screening Criteria for a Small Retail and Wholesale Distributor ($10 million annual sales)

1. **Quantitative criteria**
   a. Increase sales by $1,500,000 per year for the next five years.
   b. Earn ROI of at least 25 percent before taxes on new ventures.
   c. Break even within one year on new ventures.
   d. Opportunity must be large enough to justify interest (to help meet objectives) but small enough so company can handle with the resources available.
   e. Several opportunities should be pursued to reach the objectives—to spread the risks.

2. **Qualitative criteria**
   a. Nature of business preferred.
      (1) Should take advantage of our Internet order system and website promotion.
      (2) New goods and services for present customers to strengthen relationships and customer equity.
      (3) "Quality" products that do not cannibalize sales of current products.
      (4) Competition should be weak and opportunity should be hard to copy for several years.
      (5) There should be strongly felt (even unsatisfied) needs—to reduce promotion costs and permit "high" prices.
   b. Constraints.
      (1) Nature of businesses to exclude.
         (a) Manufacturing.
         (b) Any requiring large fixed capital investments.
         (c) Any requiring many support people who must be "good" all the time and would require much supervision.
      (2) Geographic.
         (a) United States, Mexico, and Canada only.
      (3) General.
         (a) Make use of current strengths.
         (b) Attractiveness of market should be reinforced by more than one of the following basic trends: technological, demographic, social, economic, political.
         (c) Address environmental problems.

Marketing That Meets Earthly Needs

Twenty years ago, few managers worried about costs to the environment when evaluating market opportunities. And most consumers didn't see increased customer value in marketing strategies that were "planet friendly." Now that is changing. Problems like global warming and depletion of natural resources—even scarcity of drinking water for major urban areas—are receiving much attention. New federal and local laws push for conservation. The economics have changed as well; many firms are proving that it can be lucrative to solve ecological problems. There's also a cultural shift in consumers. Many seek "green" offerings and are even willing to pay a premium to get them.

Companies are finding a host of big and small ways to contribute solutions. For example, Unilever created a more concentrated version of its All liquid detergent and put it in a "small and mighty" bottle. In just two years, this simple change saved 1.3 million gallons of diesel fuel, 10 million pounds of plastic resin, and 80 million square feet of cardboard. Seeing results like that, P&G followed suit and converted all its liquid detergents to double concentration. Staples, the office supply retailer, has eco-modified 3,000 of its store-brand products—everything from sticky notes to cardboard boxes—to include 30 percent recycled paper. This isn't a choice that's left to Staples' customers. The recycled product is the only version available. Competing firms are now copying this approach.

Marketers have usually focused on encouraging people to consume. But now more firms are looking for opportunities that relate to what happens to products when consumers are through with them. Sony, for example, has a new program to recycle all used Sony electronic products—from PlayStation game consoles and Trinitron TVs to Vaio laptops and Walkman tape players. Dell, HP, and others already have recycling programs in place, but Sony plans for its approach to earn profits. This type of thinking is prompting some firms to design new products for easy *disassembly*. Parts snap together without fasteners or glue, lead-based solder and other biohazards are avoided, and pieces that can't be recycled are biodegradable. Automobile companies are making headway in this area as well.

We are a long way from solving some of our most pressing environmental problems. However, creative marketers know that finding solutions to these problems can be good for their firms as well as their customers, not only in the short term but long into the future.[27]

types of businesses, from jet aircraft engines and water treatment facilities to medical imaging and lightbulbs. Top management at GE believes that the really crucial needs of society relate to protecting the environment. They believe that efforts in this arena are so critical that they should be supported across all dimensions of the external environment. Thus, they want all GE managers to look for opportunities that fit what GE calls "ecomagination"—applying GE's creativity to solve problems related to ecology. GE is not alone in this kind of thinking. Many organizations now screen opportunities on **sustainability**—the idea that it's important to meet present needs without compromising the ability of future generations to meet their own needs. In many lines of business, that is a tall order. However, when managers begin to apply sustainability as a screening criteria, it leads them to better ways of meeting needs. At GE that means lightbulbs that use less energy, medical images with no toxic waste, jets that burn less fuel, and new ways to turn seawater into drinking water.[28]

Whole plans should be evaluated

You need to forecast the probable results of implementing a marketing strategy to apply the quantitative part of the screening criteria because only implemented plans generate sales, profits, and return on investment. For a rough screening, you only need to estimate the likely results of implementing each opportunity over a logical planning period. If a product's life is likely to be three years, for example, a good strategy may not produce profitable results for 6 to 12 months. But evaluated over the projected three-year life, the product may look like a winner. When evaluating the potential of

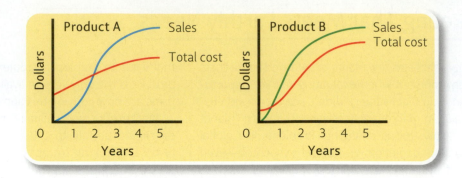

possible opportunities (product-market strategies), it is important to evaluate similar things—that is, *whole* plans.

Total profit approach can help evaluate possible plans

In the total profit approach, management forecasts potential sales and costs during the life of the plan to estimate likely profitability.

Managers may evaluate the prospects for each plan over a five-year planning period, using monthly and/or annual sales and cost estimates. This is shown graphically in Exhibit 3-9.

Managers often evaluate different marketing plans at the same time. Exhibit 3-9 compares a much improved product and product concept (Product A) with a "me-too" product (Product B) for the same target market. In the short run, the me-too product will make a profit sooner and might look like the better choice—if managers consider only one year's results. The improved product, on the other hand, will take a good deal of pioneering—but over its five-year life will be much more profitable.

PLANNING GRIDS HELP EVALUATE A PORTFOLIO OF OPPORTUNITIES

When a firm has many possibilities to evaluate, it usually has to compare quite different ones. This problem is easier to handle with graphical approaches—such as the nine-box strategic planning grid developed by General Electric and used by many other companies. Such grids can help evaluate a firm's whole portfolio of strategic plans or businesses.

General Electric looks for green positions

General Electric's (GE) strategic planning grid—see Exhibit 3-10—forces company managers to make three-part judgments (high, medium, and low) about the business strengths and industry attractiveness of all proposed or existing product-market plans.

Exhibit 3-10
General Electric's
Strategic Planning Grid

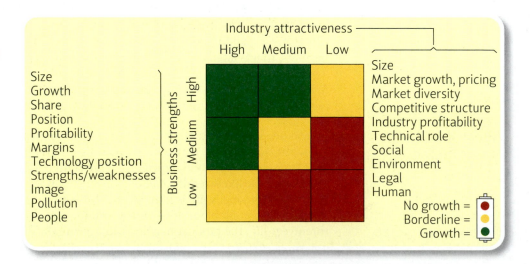

As you can see from Exhibit 3–10, this approach helps a manager organize information about the company's marketing environments (discussed earlier in this chapter) along with information about its strategy and translate it into relevant screening criteria.

The industry attractiveness dimension helps managers answer the question: Does this product-market plan look like a good idea? To answer that question, managers have to judge such factors (screening criteria) as the size of the market and its growth rate, the nature of competition, the plan's potential environmental or social impact, and how laws might affect it. Note that an opportunity may be attractive for *some* company—but not well suited to the strengths (and weaknesses) of a particular firm. That is why the GE grid also considers the business strengths dimension.

The business strengths dimension focuses on the ability of the company to pursue a product-market plan effectively. To make judgments along this dimension, a manager evaluates whether the firm has people with the right talents and skills to implement the plan, whether the plan is consistent with the firm's image and profit objectives, and whether the firm could establish a profitable market share given its technical capability, costs, and size. Here again, these factors suggest screening criteria specific to this firm and market situation.

GE feels opportunities that fall into the green boxes in the upper left-hand corner of the grid are its best growth opportunities. Managers give these opportunities high marks on both industry attractiveness and business strengths. The red boxes in the lower right-hand corner of the grid, on the other hand, suggest a no-growth policy. Existing red businesses may continue to generate earnings, but they no longer deserve much investment. Yellow businesses are borderline cases—they can go either way. GE may continue to support an existing yellow business but will probably reject a proposal for a new one. It simply wouldn't look good enough on the relevant screening criteria.

GE's "stoplight" evaluation method is a subjective, multiple-factor approach. It avoids the traps and possible errors of trying to use oversimplified, single-number criteria—like ROI or market share. Instead, top managers review detailed written summaries of many different screening criteria that help them make summary judgments. This approach helps everyone understand why the company supports some new opportunities and not others.[29]

General Electric considers factors that reflect its objectives. Another firm might modify the evaluation to emphasize other screening criteria—depending on its objectives and the type of product-market plans it is considering.

MULTIPRODUCT FIRMS HAVE A DIFFICULT STRATEGY-PLANNING JOB

Multiproduct firms, like General Electric, obviously have a more difficult strategic planning job than firms with only a few products or product lines aimed at the same target markets. Multiproduct firms have to develop strategic plans for very different businesses. And they have to balance plans and resources so the whole company reaches its objectives. This means they must approve plans that make sense for the whole company—even if it means getting needed resources by milking some businesses and eliminating others.

Details on how to manage a complicated multiproduct firm are beyond our scope. But you should be aware that the principles in this text are applicable—they just have to be extended. For example, some multiproduct firms form strategic business units (SBUs).

Strategic business units may help

A **strategic business unit (SBU)** is an organizational unit (within a larger company) that focuses on some product-markets and is treated as a separate profit center. By forming SBUs, a company formally acknowledges its very different activities. One SBU of Sara Lee, for example, produces baked goods for consumers and restaurants; another produces and markets Kiwi brand shoe-care products.

Some SBUs grow rapidly and require a great deal of attention and resources. Others produce only average profits and might be *milked*—that is, used to generate cash for the businesses with more potential. Product lines with poor market position, low profits, and slow growth should be dropped or sold.

EVALUATING OPPORTUNITIES IN INTERNATIONAL MARKETS

Evaluate the risks

The approaches we've discussed apply to international markets just as they do to domestic ones. But in international markets it is often harder to fully understand the marketing environment variables. This may make it more difficult to see the risks involved in particular opportunities. Some countries are politically unstable; their governments and constitutions come and go. An investment safe under one government might become a takeover target under another.

To reduce the risk of missing some basic variable that may help screen out a risky opportunity, marketing managers sometimes need a detailed analysis of the market environment they are considering entering. Such an analysis can reveal facts about an unfamiliar market that a manager in a distant country might otherwise overlook. Further, a local citizen who knows the marketing environment may be able to identify an "obvious" problem ignored even in a careful analysis. Thus, it is very useful for the analysis to include inputs from locals—perhaps cooperative distributors.[30]

Risks vary with environmental sensitivity

The farther you go from familiar territory, the greater the risk of making big mistakes. But not all products, or marketing mixes, involve the same risk. Think of the risks as running along a "continuum of environmental sensitivity." See Exhibit 3–11.

Some products are relatively insensitive to the economic and cultural environment they're placed in. These products may be accepted as is—or they may require just a little adaptation to make them suitable for local use. Most industrial products are near the insensitive end of this continuum.

Lamb Weston is successful in international markets because potatoes—in many different forms—are common in the diet of most cultures. Other products are much more sensitive to cultural differences.

Exhibit 3-11
Continuum of
Environmental
Sensitivity

Insensitive		Sensitive
Industrial products	Basic commodity-type consumer products	Consumer products that are linked to cultural variables

At the other end of the continuum, we find highly sensitive products that may be difficult or impossible to adapt to all international situations. Consumer products closely linked to other social or cultural variables are at this end. For example, some cultures view dieting as unhealthy; that explains why products like Diet Pepsi that are popular in the United States have done poorly there.

This continuum helps explain why many of the early successes in international marketing were basic commodities such as gasoline, soap, transportation vehicles, mining equipment, and agricultural machinery. It also helps explain why some consumer products firms have been successful with basically the same promotion and products in different parts of the globe.

Yet some managers don't understand the reason for these successes. They think they can develop a global marketing mix for just about *any* product. They fail to see that firms producing and/or selling products near the sensitive end of the continuum should carefully analyze how their products will be seen and used in new environments—and plan their strategies accordingly.[31]

What if risks are still hard to judge?

If the risks of an international opportunity are hard to judge, it may be wise to look first for opportunities that involve exporting. This gives managers a chance to build experience, know-how, and confidence over time. Then the firm will be in a better position to judge the prospects and risks of taking further steps.

CONCLUSION

Businesses need innovative strategy planning to survive in our increasingly competitive markets. In this chapter, we discussed the variables that shape the broad environment of marketing strategy planning and how they may affect opportunities. First we looked at how the firm's own resources and objectives may help guide or limit the search for opportunities. Then we went on to look at the need to understand competition and how to do a competitive analysis. Next we shifted our focus to the external market environments. They are important because changes in these environments present new opportunities, as well as problems, that a marketing manager must deal with in marketing strategy planning.

The economic environment—including chances of recession or inflation—also affects the choice of strategies. And the marketer must try to anticipate, understand, and deal with these changes—as well as changes in the technology underlying the economic environment.

The marketing manager must also be aware of legal restrictions and be sensitive to changing political climates. The acceptance of consumerism has already forced many changes.

The cultural and social environment affects how people behave and what marketing strategies will be successful.

Developing good marketing strategies within all these environments isn't easy. You can see that marketing planning is a challenging job that requires integration of information from many disciplines.

Eventually, managers need procedures for screening and evaluating opportunities. We explained an approach for developing qualitative and quantitative screening criteria—from an analysis of the strengths and weaknesses of the company's resources, the environmental trends it faces, and top management's objectives. We also discussed ways for evaluating and managing quite different opportunities—using the GE strategic planning grid and SBUs.

Now we can go on in the rest of the book to discuss how to turn opportunities into profitable marketing plans and programs.

KEY TERMS

QUESTIONS AND PROBLEMS

1. Do you think it makes sense for a firm to base its mission statement on the type of product it produces? For example, would it be good for a division that produces electric motors to have as its mission: "We want to make the best (from our customers' point of view) electric motors available anywhere in the world"?

2. Explain how a firm's objectives may affect its search for opportunities.

3. Specifically, how would various company objectives affect the development of a marketing mix for a new type of Internet browser software? If this company were just being formed by a former programmer with limited financial resources, list the objectives the programmer might have. Then discuss how they would affect the development of the programmer's marketing strategy.

4. Explain how a firm's resources may limit its search for opportunities. Cite a specific example for a specific resource.

5. In your own words, explain how a marketing manager might use a competitor analysis to avoid situations that involve head-on competition.

6. The owner of a small hardware store—the only one in a medium-sized town in the mountains—has just learned that a large home improvement chain plans to open a new store nearby. How difficult will it be for the owner to plan for this new competitive threat? Explain your answer.

7. Discuss the probable impact on your hometown if a major breakthrough in air transportation allowed foreign producers to ship into any U.S. market for about the same transportation cost that domestic producers incur.

8. Will the elimination of trade barriers between countries in Europe eliminate the need to consider submarkets of European consumers? Why or why not?

9. What and who is the U.S. government attempting to protect in its effort to preserve and regulate competition?

10. For each of the *major* laws discussed in the text, indicate whether in the long run the law will promote or restrict competition (see Exhibit 3–4). As a consumer without any financial interest in business, what is your reaction to each of these laws?

11. Drawing on data in Exhibit 3–5, do you think that Romania would be an attractive market for a firm that produces home appliances? What about Finland? Discuss your reasons.

12. Discuss how the worldwide trend toward urbanization is affecting opportunities for international marketing.

13. Discuss how slower population growth will affect businesses in your local community.

14. Discuss the impact of changes in the size of the 18–24 age group on marketing strategy planning in the United States.

15. Name three specific examples of firms that developed a marketing mix to appeal to senior citizens. Name three examples of firms that developed a marketing mix to appeal to teenagers.

16. Explain the product-market screening criteria that can be used to evaluate opportunities.

17. Explain General Electric's strategic planning grid approach to evaluating opportunities.

CREATING MARKETING PLANS

The Marketing Plan Coach software on the text website (and on the optional Student CD) includes a sample marketing plan for Hillside Veterinary Clinic. The situation analysis section of the marketing plan includes sections labeled "Competitors" and "External Market Environment." Review those sections and answer the following questions.

a. In the Competitors section, what dimensions were used to analyze competitors? What other dimensions might have been examined?

b. How was competitor information gathered? How else could Hillside have gathered information about its competitors?

c. What aspects of the External Market Environment are included in the marketing plan? What do you think is the most important information in this section?

SUGGESTED CASES

2. Harvest Farm Foods, Inc.
22. Bright Light Innovations

6. Global Steel Company
33. Mulligan & Starling

COMPUTER-AIDED PROBLEM

3. COMPETITOR ANALYSIS

Mediquip, Inc., produces medical equipment and uses its own sales force to sell the equipment to hospitals. Recently, several hospitals have asked Mediquip to develop a laser-beam "scalpel" for eye surgery. Mediquip has the needed resources, and 200 hospitals will probably buy the equipment. But Mediquip managers have heard that Laser Technologies—another quality producer—is thinking of competing for the same business. Mediquip has other good opportunities it could pursue—so it wants to see if it would have a competitive advantage over Laser Tech.

Mediquip and Laser Tech are similar in many ways, but there are important differences. Laser Technologies already produces key parts that are needed for the new laser product—so its production costs would be lower. It would cost Mediquip more to design the product—and getting parts from outside suppliers would result in higher production costs.

On the other hand, Mediquip has marketing strengths. It already has a good reputation with hospitals—and its sales force calls on only hospitals. Mediquip thinks that each of its current sales reps could spend some time selling the new product and that it could adjust sales territories so only four more sales reps would be needed for good coverage in the market. In contrast, Laser Tech's sales reps call on only industrial customers, so it would have to add 14 reps to cover the hospitals.

Hospitals have budget pressures—so the supplier with the lowest price is likely to get a larger share of the business. But Mediquip knows that either supplier's price will be set high enough to cover the added costs of designing, producing, and selling the new product—and leave something for profit.

Mediquip gathers information about its own likely costs and can estimate Laser Tech's costs from industry studies and Laser Tech's annual report. Mediquip has set up a spreadsheet to evaluate the proposed new product.

a. The initial spreadsheet results are based on the assumption that Mediquip and Laser Tech will split the business 50/50. If Mediquip can win at least 50 percent of the market, does Mediquip have a competitive advantage over Laser Tech? Explain.

b. Because of economies of scale, both suppliers' average cost per machine will vary depending on the quantity sold. If Mediquip had only 45 percent of the market and Laser Tech 55 percent, how would their costs (average total cost per machine) compare? What if Mediquip had 55 percent of the market and Laser Tech only 45 percent? What conclusion do you draw from these analyses?

c. It is possible that Laser Tech may not enter the market. If Mediquip has 100 percent of the market, and quantity purchases from its suppliers will reduce the cost of producing one unit to $6,500, what price would cover all its costs and contribute $1,125 to profit for every machine sold? What does this suggest about the desirability of finding your own unsatisfied target markets? Explain.

For additional questions related to this problem, see Exercise 3-4 in the *Learning Aid for Use with Essentials of Marketing*, 12th edition.

4

CHAPTER

Focusing Marketing Strategy with Segmentation and Positioning

These days Nintendo rides high in the video game world. Its DS handheld game, Wii (pronounced "we") console, and games with characters like Mario and Zelda sell millions of units. The key to Nintendo's success comes from meeting the entertainment needs of different groups of customers.

Back in the 1980s, Nintendo was a 100-year-old Japanese manufacturer of toys and playing cards. If Nintendo managers had continued to just think about the "toy market," the firm probably wouldn't even be around now. Instead, they saw profitable new opportunities in the broader "entertainment seekers market." In 1985, they released the Nintendo Entertainment System (NES) and interactive video games such as Super Mario Brothers. In those early days, video game consoles and software from different producers were quite similar. Even so, Nintendo's NES stood out as offering better value. And Nintendo's profits took off because once a household owned an NES console, it qualified as a prime target for new Nintendo games.

As the market evolved, Nintendo developed more new products focusing on the needs of different groups of customers. In the 1990s, its popular handheld system, Game Boy, successfully delivered portable fun to kids. Another group of customers, the "hard-core gamers," played complex and realistic games requiring consoles with high-speed processors and better graphics so Nintendo offered them its GameCube console. But Nintendo struggled to keep up with competitors like Sony's PlayStation and Microsoft's Xbox, which did a better job of meeting these customers' needs.

So planners at Nintendo looked for other customer groups whose needs were not being addressed; they thought that families, senior citizens, and teenage females might buy gaming systems if something met their needs. Together, these customers fit a category of "casual gamers" who wanted a different kind of gaming—a more interactive, fun, and social experience with easy-to-learn games, and, oh yeah, at an affordable price. So while these customers bought relatively few gaming products at the time, Nintendo thought the right marketing mix might change that.

Nintendo first appealed to these customers' needs with a new handheld game player called the DS (for Dual Screen). The DS responds to an intuitive touch panel and spoken commands. Casual gamers liked the simple rules and easy-to-learn controls; with a DS, they could play within minutes of picking it up. Further, the DS's Wi-Fi connection makes it easy for people to play together.

The games are also distinctive. Girls usually buy the pink DS and enjoy games like Nintendogs, where they teach virtual pets to play fetch or perform other tricks. Baby boomers prefer the clean look of the arctic white unit. Like the senior citizens, they find Brain Age engaging. It promises to "Train Your Brain in Minutes a Day" with a light mental workout of

Sudoku puzzles and word quizzes. Nintendo used print ads in magazines targeted at senior citizens to reach this segment. The ads showed gray-haired couples enjoying the Nintendo DS and promoted the idea that regular play aids memory. These combined efforts to attract first-time and casual gamers worked so well that the DS became the largest selling video game system of all time.

Building on its success with the casual gamers, Nintendo introduced the Wii. The Wii name emphasizes that the console is for everyone—and the $249 value price supports that position as well. The Wii's biggest innovation—a wireless, motion-sensitive controller—makes video game play easy and intuitive. The Wii's handheld controller guides onscreen actions when it is swung like a baseball bat, arced to simulate throwing a football, or tilted to steer a car or truck. Wii Sports, which comes packaged with the console, gets players off to a quick start with familiar games like tennis and bowling. Retirement communities even organize Wii bowling tournaments because they prompt senior citizens to socialize and exercise.

As this suggests, Wii is not for couch potatoes. Many games—like Madden Football, Rock Band, and Dance Dance Revolution—require players to get up and move. Parents appreciate that so much of Nintendo's promotion targets moms. For example, its Ambassadors program invited well-connected moms to luxury hotels where they sipped champagne, ate cookies, and played Wii. Many of these moms later threw their own parties and spread the word. Similarly, much of Wii's ad budget targeted women aged 25 to 49 on shows like "Dancing with the Stars."

New accessories for the Wii address casual gamers' needs. For example, the Wii Balance Board, a pressure sensitive platform the player stands on, controls the onscreen action with movements as a player leans from one side to another. Teens use the Balance Board with games like Skate City Heroes where they skateboard around a city—jumping from the top of skyscrapers and racing through factories. Many adults use the board to get in better shape—the Wii Fit game trains them in yoga, weight training, and aerobics while keeping a record of their progress.

Over the years, Nintendo's successes have come from identifying new ways to meet customers' needs. That's why NES, Gameboy, DS, and Wii have been smash hits. Now, Microsoft and Sony are developing similar offerings, and other innovators are coming on strong with different types of interactive entertainment from cell phone "apps" to multiplayer online games. Will Nintendo continue to compete with effective market segmentation? Stay tuned to find out. While you wait, Wii would like to play.[1]

SEARCH FOR OPPORTUNITIES CAN BEGIN BY UNDERSTANDING MARKETS

Strategy planning is a narrowing-down process

In Chapter 2 we provided a framework for a logical marketing strategy planning process. It involves careful evaluation of the market opportunities available before narrowing down to focus on the most attractive target market and marketing mix. In Chapter 3, we focused on approaches for analyzing how competitors and the external market environment shape the evaluation of opportunities. In this chapter we discuss concepts that can guide the selection of specific target customers. See Exhibit 4–1 for an overview.

In a broad sense, this chapter is about understanding and analyzing customers in a market. In Chapters 5 and 6 we will look more closely at specific influences on the behavior of both final consumers and organizational customers. However, this chapter sets the stage for that by explaining how marketing managers combine different types of information about customers to guide targeting decisions.

Since this chapter is about bringing focus to the search for market opportunities, a good place to start is by discussing what we really mean when we use the term *market*.

What is a company's market?

Identifying a company's market is an important but sticky issue. In general, a **market** is a group of potential customers with similar needs who are willing to exchange something of value with sellers offering various goods or services—that is, ways of satisfying those needs. However, within a general market, marketing-oriented managers develop marketing mixes for *specific* target markets. Getting the firm to focus on specific target markets is vital.

Don't just focus on the product

Some production-oriented managers don't understand this narrowing-down process. They get into trouble because they ignore the tough part of defining markets. To make the narrowing-down process easier, they just describe their markets in terms of

Exhibit 4–1 Focusing Marketing Strategy with Segmentation and Positioning

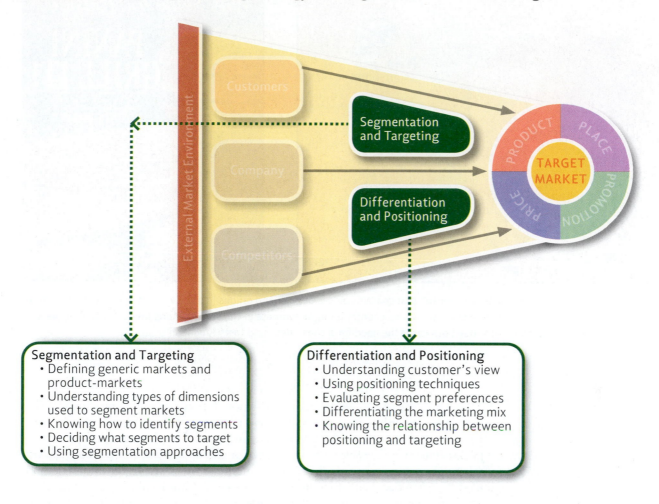

Segmentation and Targeting
- Defining generic markets and product-markets
- Understanding types of dimensions used to segment markets
- Knowing how to identify segments
- Deciding what segments to target
- Using segmentation approaches

Differentiation and Positioning
- Understanding customer's view
- Using positioning techniques
- Evaluating segment preferences
- Differentiating the marketing mix
- Knowing the relationship between positioning and targeting

products they sell. For example, producers and retailers of greeting cards might define their market as the "greeting card" market. But this production-oriented approach ignores customers—and customers make a market! This also leads to missed opportunities. Hallmark isn't missing these opportunities. Instead, Hallmark aims at the "personal-expression" market. Hallmark stores offer all kinds of products that can be sent as "memory makers"—to express one person's feelings toward another. And as opportunities related to these needs change, Hallmark changes too. For example, at the Hallmark website (www.hallmark.com) it is easy to get shopping suggestions from an online "gift assistant," to order flowers, or to personalize an electronic greeting card to send online.[2]

From generic markets to product-markets

To understand the narrowing-down process, it's useful to think of two basic types of markets. A **generic market** is a market with *broadly* similar needs—and sellers offering various, *often diverse*, ways of satisfying those needs. In contrast, a **product-market** is a market with *very* similar needs and sellers offering various *close substitute* ways of satisfying those needs.[3]

A generic market description looks at markets broadly and from a customer's viewpoint. Entertainment seekers, for example, have several very different ways to satisfy their needs. An entertainment seeker might buy a Blu-ray disc player and a high-definition TV (HDTV), sign up for a cruise on the Carnival Line, or reserve season tickets for the symphony. Any one of these *very different* products may satisfy this entertainment need. Sellers in this generic entertainment-seeker market have to focus

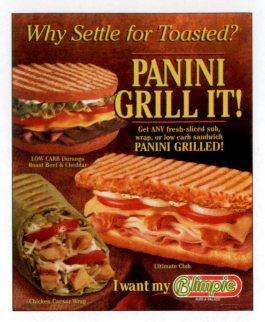

Flam is an eat-on-the-go French snack "in a wrap" that contains pieces of pork and onions in a thick sauce made with soft white cheese. It is not a sandwich, but if it were available in this country it might compete in the same generic market with Blimpie's Panini. The products are different, but they both serve the need for a convenient and tasty luncheon treat.

on the need(s) the customers want satisfied—not on how one seller's product (HDTV system, vacation, or live music) is better than that of another producer.

It is sometimes hard to understand and define generic markets because *quite different product types may compete with each other.* For example, a person on a business trip to Italy might want a convenient way to record memories of the trip. Minolta's digital camera, Sony's video camcorder, and even postcards from local shops may all compete to serve our traveler's needs. If customers see all these products as substitutes—as competitors in the same generic market—then marketers must deal with this complication.

Suppose, however, that our traveler decides to satisfy this need with a digital camera. Then—in this product-market—Minolta, Kodak, Panasonic, Nikon, and many other brands may compete with each other for the customer's dollars. In this *product-*market concerned with digital cameras *and* needs to conveniently record memories, consumers compare similar products to satisfy their image needs.

Broaden market definitions to find opportunities

Broader market definitions—including both generic market definitions and product-market definitions—can help firms find opportunities. But deciding *how* broad to go isn't easy. Too narrow a definition limits a firm's opportunities—but too broad a definition makes the company's efforts and resources seem insignificant. Consider, for example, the mighty Coca-Cola Company. It has great success and a huge market share in the U.S. cola-drinkers' market. On the other hand, its share of all beverage drinking worldwide is very small.

Here we try to match opportunities to a firm's resources and objectives. So the *relevant market for finding opportunities* should be bigger than the firm's present product-market—but not so big that the firm couldn't expand and be an important competitor. A small manufacturer of screwdrivers in Mexico, for example, shouldn't define its market as broadly as "the worldwide tool users market" or as narrowly as "our present screwdriver customers." But it may have the capabilities to consider "the handyman's hand-tool market in North America." Carefully naming your product-market can help you see possible opportunities.

Nestlé targets customers in many different geographic markets around the world, but often the product-markets in one country are different than in another. For example, Nestlé created banana-flavored milk ice on a stick to fit the local tastes and preferences of Chinese consumers. The same product would probably not have a following in other places.

NAMING PRODUCT-MARKETS AND GENERIC MARKETS

Some managers think about markets just in terms of the product they already produce and sell. But this approach can lead to missed opportunities. For example, think about how photographic film is being replaced with digital pictures, digital video recorders (DVRs) are replacing VCRs, and MP3 players have replaced portable CD players.

As this suggests, when evaluating opportunities, product-related terms do not—by themselves—adequately describe a market. A complete product-market definition includes a four-part description.

What:	1. Product type (type of good and type of service)
To meet what:	2. Customer (user) needs
For whom:	3. Customer types
Where:	4. Geographic area

We refer to these four-part descriptions as product-market "names" because most managers label their markets when they think, write, or talk about them. Such a four-part definition can be clumsy, however, so we often use a nickname. And the nickname should refer to people—not products—because, as we emphasize, people make markets!

Product type should meet customer needs

Product type describes the goods and/or services that customers want. Sometimes the product type is strictly a physical good or strictly a service. But marketing managers who ignore the possibility that *both* are important can miss opportunities.

Customer (user) needs refer to the needs the product type satisfies for the customer. At a very basic level, product types usually provide functional benefits such as nourishing, protecting, warming, cooling, transporting, cleaning, holding, and saving time. Although we need to identify such "basic" needs first, in advanced economies, we usually go on to emotional needs—such as needs for fun, excitement, pleasing appearance, or status. Correctly defining the need(s) relevant to a market is crucial and requires a good understanding of customers. We discuss these topics more fully in Chapters 5 and 6.

Customer type refers to the final consumer or user of a product type. Here we want to choose a name that describes all present (possible) types of customers. To define

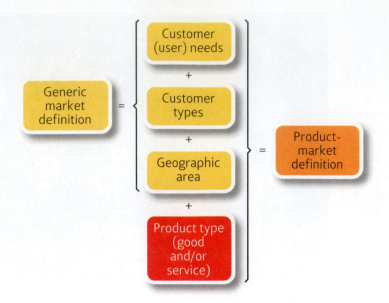

customer type, marketers should identify the final consumer or user of the product type, rather than the buyer—if they are different. For instance, producers should avoid treating intermediaries as a customer type—unless intermediaries actually use the product in their own business.

The *geographic area* is where a firm competes, or plans to compete, for customers. Naming the geographic area may seem trivial, but understanding the geographic boundaries of a market can suggest new opportunities. A firm aiming only at the domestic market, for example, may want to expand to other countries.

Product-market boundaries provide focus

This idea of making a decision about the boundaries of a market applies not just to geographic areas served but also to decisions about customer needs, product, and customer types. Thus, naming the market is not simply an exercise in assigning labels. Rather, the manager's market definition sets the limits of the market(s) in which the firm will compete. For example, both final consumers and business customers have a variety of "fastening" needs that might be met with products ranging from screws and glues to tapes and welding. However, if a marketing manager decides that the firm should focus on business customers and not on individual consumers, then that should be explicit in the market definition. That decision limits the scope of the market and, at the same time, sharpens the focus.

No product type in generic market names

A generic market description *doesn't include any product-type terms*. It consists of only three parts of the product-market definition—without the product type. This emphasizes that any product type that satisfies the customer's needs can compete in a generic market. Exhibit 4–2 shows the relationship between generic market and product-market definitions.

Later we'll study the many possible dimensions for segmenting markets. But for now you should see that defining markets only in terms of current products is not the best way to find new opportunities. Instead, the most effective way to find opportunities is to use market segmentation.

MARKET SEGMENTATION DEFINES POSSIBLE TARGET MARKETS

Market segmentation is a two-step process

Market segmentation is a two-step process of (1) *naming* broad product-markets and (2) *segmenting* these broad product-markets in order to select target markets and develop suitable marketing mixes.

Exhibit 4–3
Narrowing Down to
Target Markets

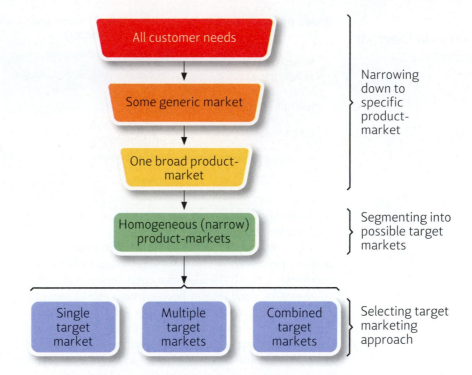

This two-step process isn't well understood. First-time market segmentation efforts often fail because beginners start with the whole mass market and try to find one or two demographic characteristics to divide up (segment) this market. Customer behavior is usually too complex to be explained in terms of just one or two demographic characteristics. For example, not all elderly men buy the same products or brands. Other dimensions usually must be considered—starting with customer needs.

Naming broad product-markets is disaggregating

The first step in effective market segmentation involves naming a broad product-market of interest to the firm. Marketers must break apart—disaggregate—all possible needs into some generic markets and broad product-markets in which the firm may be able to operate profitably. See Exhibit 4–3. No one firm can satisfy everyone's needs. So the naming—disaggregating—step involves brainstorming about very different solutions to various generic needs and selecting some broad areas—broad product-markets—where the firm has some resources and experience. This means that a car manufacturer would probably ignore all the possible opportunities in food and clothing markets and focus on the generic market, "transporting people in the world," and probably on the broad product-market, "cars, trucks, and utility vehicles for transporting people in the world."

Market grid is a visual aid to market segmentation

Assuming that any broad product-market (or generic market) may consist of submarkets, picture a market as a rectangle with boxes that represent the smaller, more homogeneous product-markets.

Exhibit 4–4, for example, represents the broad product-market of bicycle riders. The boxes show different submarkets. One submarket might focus on people who want basic transportation, another on people who want exercise, and so on. Alternatively, in the generic "transporting market" discussed earlier, we might see different product-markets of customers for bicycles, motorcycles, cars, airplanes, ships, buses, and "others."

Segmenting is an aggregating process

Marketing-oriented managers think of **segmenting** as an aggregating process—clustering people with similar needs into a "market segment." A **market segment** is

Exhibit 4–4
A Market Grid Diagram
with Submarkets

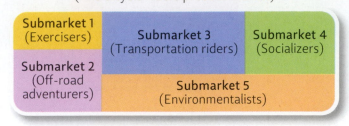

Broad product-market (or generic market) name goes here
(The bicycle-riders product-market)

| Submarket 1 (Exercisers) | Submarket 3 (Transportation riders) | Submarket 4 (Socializers) |
| Submarket 2 (Off-road adventurers) | Submarket 5 (Environmentalists) | |

a (relatively) homogeneous group of customers who will respond to a marketing mix in a similar way.

This part of the market segmentation process takes a different approach from the naming part. Here we look for similarities rather than basic differences in needs. Segmenters start with the idea that each person is one of a kind but that it may be possible to aggregate some similar people into a product-market.

Segmenters see each of these one-of-a-kind people as having a unique set of dimensions. Consider a product-market in which customers' needs differ on two important segmenting dimensions: need for status and need for dependability. In Exhibit 4–5A, each dot shows a person's position on the two dimensions. While each person's position is unique, many of these people are similar in terms of how much status and dependability they want. So a segmenter may aggregate them into three (an arbitrary number) relatively homogeneous submarkets—A, B, and C. Group A might be called "status-oriented" and Group C "dependability-oriented." Members of Group B want both and might be called the "demanders."

How far should the aggregating go?

The segmenter wants to aggregate individual customers into some workable number of relatively homogeneous target markets and then treat each target market differently.

Look again at Exhibit 4–5A. Remember we talked about three segments. But this was an arbitrary number. As Exhibit 4–5B shows, there may really be six segments. What do you think—does this broad product-market consist of three segments or six?

Another difficulty with segmenting is that some potential customers just don't fit neatly into market segments. For example, not everyone in Exhibit 4–5B was put into one of the groups. Forcing them into one of the groups would have made these segments more heterogeneous and harder to please. Further, forming additional segments for them probably wouldn't be profitable. They are too few and not very similar in terms of the two dimensions. These people are simply too unique to be catered

Exhibit 4–5
Every Individual Has His or Her Own Unique Position in a Market—Those with Similar Positions Can Be Aggregated into Potential Target Markets

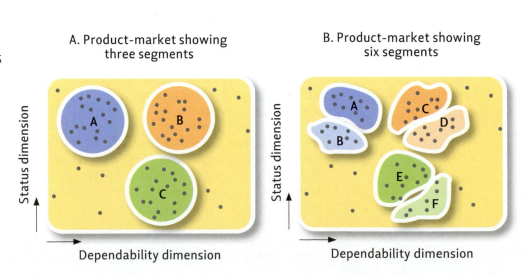

A. Product-market showing three segments

B. Product-market showing six segments

Status dimension

Dependability dimension

to and may have to be ignored—unless they are willing to pay a high price for special treatment.

The number of segments that should be formed depends more on judgment than on some scientific rule. But the following guidelines can help.

Criteria for segmenting a broad product-market

Ideally, "good" market segments meet the following criteria:

1. *Homogeneous (similar) within*—the customers in a market segment should be as similar as possible with respect to their likely responses to marketing mix variables *and* their segmenting dimensions.
2. *Heterogeneous (different) between*—the customers in different segments should be as different as possible with respect to their likely responses to marketing mix variables *and* their segmenting dimensions.
3. *Substantial*—the segment should be big enough to be profitable.
4. *Operational*—the segmenting dimensions should be useful for identifying customers and deciding on marketing mix variables.

It is especially important that segments be *operational*. This leads marketers to include demographic dimensions such as age, sex, income, location, and family size. In fact, it is difficult to make some Place and Promotion decisions without such information.

Target marketers aim at specific targets

Once you accept the idea that broad product-markets may have submarkets, you can see that target marketers usually have a choice among many possible target markets.

There are three basic ways to develop market-oriented strategies in a broad product-market.

1. The **single target market approach**—segmenting the market and picking one of the homogeneous segments as the firm's target market.
2. The **multiple target market approach**—segmenting the market and choosing two or more segments, and then treating each as a separate target market needing a different marketing mix.
3. The **combined target market approach**—combining two or more submarkets into one larger target market as a basis for one strategy.

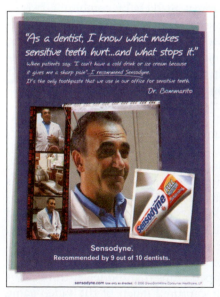

Firms that compete in the oral health care market have developed a variety of products that appeal to the needs of different customer segments. Sensodyne targets consumers who have sensitive teeth. Crest Pro-Health targets consumers, especially adults, who have a combined set of oral care concerns. Orajel targets parents of toddlers with a gentle, nonabrasive toothpaste and fun flavors that toddlers will love.

Exhibit 4–6
Segmenters and Combiners Aim at Specific Target Markets

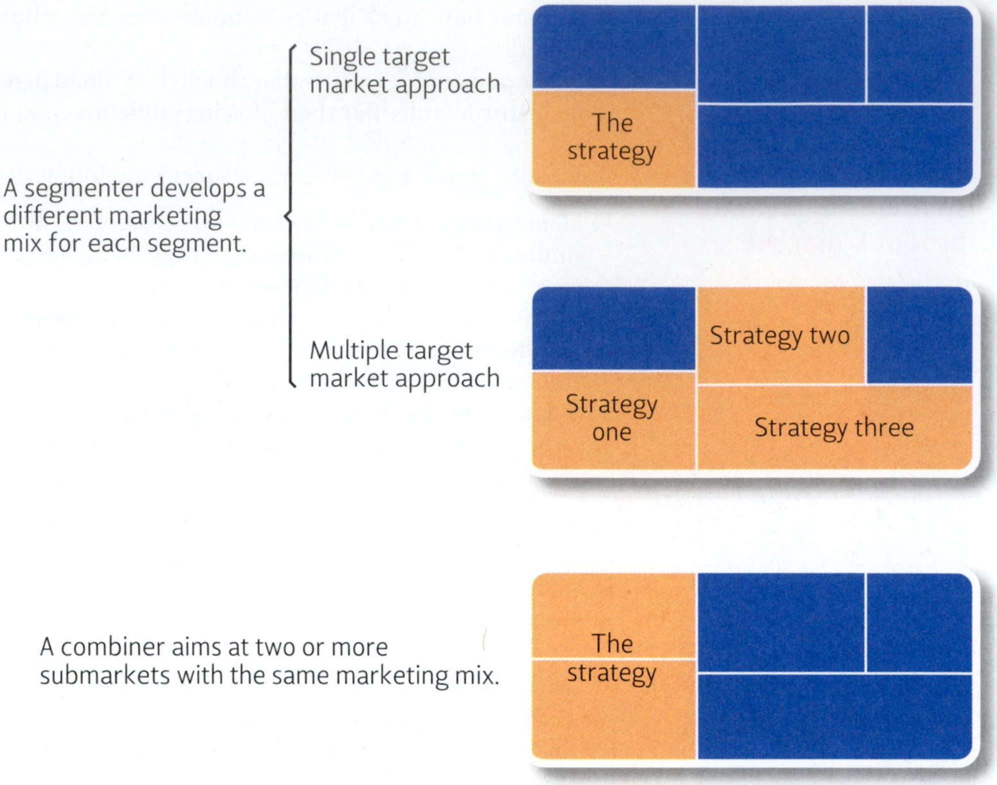

A segmenter develops a different marketing mix for each segment.

Single target market approach

The strategy

Multiple target market approach

Strategy one
Strategy two
Strategy three

A combiner aims at two or more submarkets with the same marketing mix.

The strategy

Note that all three approaches involve target marketing. They all aim at specific, clearly defined target markets. See Exhibit 4–6. For convenience, we call people who follow the first two approaches the "segmenters" and people who use the third approach the "combiners."

Combiners try to satisfy "pretty well"

Combiners try to increase the size of their target markets by combining two or more segments. Combiners look at various submarkets for similarities rather than differences. Then they try to extend or modify their basic offering to appeal to these "combined" customers with just one marketing mix.

A combined target market approach may help achieve some economies of scale. It may also require less investment than developing different marketing mixes for different segments—making it especially attractive for firms with limited resources.

Too much combining is risky

It is tempting to aim at larger combined markets instead of using different marketing mixes for smaller segmented markets. However, this makes it harder to develop marketing mixes that best satisfy potential customers. So a combiner faces the continual risk of innovative segmenters chipping away at the various segments of the combined target market—by offering more attractive marketing mixes to more homogeneous submarkets. ATI Technologies saw this happen. It produced high-quality graphics chips with features desired by a wide variety of computer users. But then ATI lost business to more specialized competitors like Nvidia Corp. Nvidia focused on the needs of video-game lovers who don't want to compromise when it comes to realistic special effects. Nvidia developed chips that did fewer things, but by doing those specialized things really well it captured much of the video-game lovers' business.[4]

Segmenters try to satisfy "very well"

Segmenters aim at one or more homogeneous segments and try to develop a different marketing mix for each segment. Segmenters usually fine-tune their marketing mixes for each target market—perhaps making basic changes in the product itself—because they want to satisfy each segment very well.

Instead of assuming that the whole market consists of a fairly similar set of customers (like the mass marketer does) or merging various submarkets together (like the combiner), segmenters believe that aiming at one, or some, of these smaller markets makes it possible to provide superior value and satisfy them better. This then provides greater profit potential for the firm.

Segmenting may produce bigger sales

Note that segmenters are not settling for a smaller sales potential or lower profits. Instead, they hope to increase sales by getting a much larger share of the business in the market(s) they target. A segmenter that really satisfies the target market can often build such a close relationship with customers that it faces no real competition. A segmenter that offers a marketing mix precisely matched to the needs of the target market can often charge a higher price that produces higher profits. Customers are willing to pay a higher price because the whole marketing mix provides better customer value.

Consider the success of the Aeron desk chair developed by Herman Miller (HM), an 80-year-old company that makes office furniture. Most firms that sell office furniture offered similar lines of executive desk chairs that were padded for comfort and conveyed the look of success. Marketing managers at HM realized that some customers felt that these traditional chairs were boring. Further, in an e-commerce world, even top executives sit at computers and want a chair that provides both good support and good looks. So to satisfy this upscale segment, HM designed a new type of chair from scratch. There's no fabric or padding, but everything about it adjusts to your body. It's so comfortable that HM positions it as "the chair you can wear." With a price tag close to $1,000, the Aeron chair became a status symbol for high-tech managers and has been as profitable as it is popular.[5]

Should you segment or combine?

Which approach should a firm use? This depends on the firm's resources, the nature of competition, and—most important—the similarity of customer needs, attitudes, and buying behavior.

In general, it's usually safer to be a segmenter—that is, to try to satisfy some customers *very* well instead of many just *fairly* well. That's why many firms use the single or multiple target market approach instead of the combined target market approach. Procter & Gamble, for example, offers many products that seem to compete directly with each other (e.g., Tide versus Cheer or Crest versus Gleem). However, P&G offers tailor-made marketing mixes to each submarket large and profitable enough to deserve a separate marketing mix. Though extremely effective, this approach may not be possible for a smaller firm with more limited resources. A smaller firm may have to use the single target market approach—focusing all its efforts at the one submarket niche where it sees the best opportunity.[6]

Kaepa, Inc., is a good example. Sales of its all-purpose sneakers plummeted as larger firms like Nike and Reebok stole customers with a multiple target market approach. They developed innovative products and aimed their promotion at specific needs—like jogging, aerobics, cross-training, and walking. Kaepa turned things around by catering to the needs of cheerleaders. Cheerleading squads can order Kaepa shoes with custom team logos and colors. The soles of the shoes feature finger grooves that make it easier for cheerleaders to build human pyramids. Kaepa also carefully targets its market research and promotion. Kaepa salespeople attend the cheerleading camps that each summer draw 40,000 enthusiasts. Kaepa even arranges for the cheering teams it sponsors to do demos at retail stores. This generates publicity and pulls in buyers, so retailers put more emphasis on the Kaepa line.[7]

Potential Target Market Dimensions	Effects on Strategy Decision Areas
1. Behavioral needs, attitudes, and how present and potential goods and services fit into customers' consumption patterns.	Affects *Product* (features, packaging, product line assortment, branding) and *Promotion* (what potential customers need and want to know about the firm's offering, and what appeals should be used).
2. Urgency to get need satisfied and desire and willingness to seek information, compare, and shop.	Affects *Place* (how directly products are distributed from producer to customer, how extensively they are made available, and the level of service needed) and *Price* (how much potential customers are willing to pay).
3. Geographic location and other demographic characteristics of potential customers.	Affects size of *Target Markets* (economic potential), *Place* (where products should be made available), and *Promotion* (where and to whom to target advertising and personal selling).

Profit is the balancing point

In practice, cost considerations probably encourage more aggregating—to obtain economies of scale—while demand (and revenue) considerations suggest less aggregating—to satisfy needs more exactly.

Profit is the balancing point. It determines how unique a marketing mix the firm can afford to offer to a particular group.

WHAT DIMENSIONS ARE USED TO SEGMENT MARKETS?

Segmenting dimensions guide marketing mix planning

Market segmentation forces a marketing manager to decide which product-market dimensions might be useful for planning marketing strategies. The dimensions should help guide marketing mix planning. Exhibit 4-7 shows the basic kinds of dimensions we'll be talking about in Chapter 5—and their probable effect on the four Ps. Ideally, we want to describe any potential product-market in terms of all three types of customer-related dimensions—plus a product type description—because these dimensions help us develop better marketing mixes.

People who are out in the sun should protect their skin. This safety need is a qualifying dimension of consumers in the marketing for sunblock products. However, parents may buy Banana Boat Baby and Kids Sunblock Lotion and Baby Sprays because they are easy on kids' eyes and don't cause tearing. For these parents this is a determining need. There are a variety of ways that Coffee-Mate is different from cream, but this ad focuses on the idea that it does not need to be refrigerated. For some consumers, that determines what they will buy.

Many segmenting dimensions may be considered

Customers can be described by many specific dimensions. Exhibit 4–8 shows some dimensions useful for segmenting consumer markets. A few are behavioral dimensions; others are geographic and demographic. We discuss these final consumer segmenting dimensions in Chapter 5. Exhibit 4–9 shows some additional dimensions for segmenting markets when the customers are businesses, government agencies, or other types of organizations. These dimensions for segmenting organizational customers are covered in Chapter 6. Regardless of whether customers are final consumers or organizations, segmenting a broad product-market *usually* requires using several different dimensions at the same time.[8]

What are the qualifying and determining dimensions?

To select the important segmenting dimensions, think about two different types of dimensions. **Qualifying dimensions** are those relevant to including a customer type in a product-market. **Determining dimensions** are those that actually affect the customer's purchase of a specific product or brand in a product-market.

A prospective car buyer, for example, has to have enough money—or credit—to buy a car and insure it. Our buyer also needs a driver's license. This still doesn't

Exhibit 4–8 Possible Segmenting Dimensions and Typical Breakdowns for Consumer Markets

Behavioral	
Needs	Economic, functional, physiological, psychological, social, and more detailed needs.
Benefits sought	Situation specific, but to satisfy specific or general needs.
Thoughts	Favorable or unfavorable attitudes, interests, opinions, beliefs.
Rate of use	Heavy, medium, light, nonusers.
Purchase relationship	Positive and ongoing, intermittent, no relationship, bad relationship.
Brand familiarity	Insistence, preference, recognition, nonrecognition, rejection.
Kind of shopping	Convenience, comparison shopping, specialty, none (unsought product).
Type of problem solving	Routinized response, limited, extensive.
Information required	Low, medium, high.
Geographic	
Region of world, country	North America (United States, Canada), Europe (France, Italy, Germany), and so on.
Region in country	(Examples in United States): Pacific, Mountain, West North Central, West South Central, East North Central, East South Central, South Atlantic, Middle Atlantic, New England.
Size of city	No city; population under 5,000; 5,000–19,999; 20,000–49,999; 50,000–99,999; 100,000–249,999; 250,000–499,999; 500,000–999,999; 1,000,000–3,999,999; 4,000,000 or over.
Demographic	
Income	Under $5,000; $5,000–9,999; $10,000–14,999; $15,000–19,999; $20,000–29,999; $30,000–39,999; $40,000–59,999; $60,000 and over.
Sex	Male, female.
Age	Infant; under 6; 6–11; 12–17; 18–24; 25–34; 35–49; 50–64; 65 or over.
Family size	1, 2, 3–4, 5 or more.
Family life cycle	Young, single; young, married, no children; young, married, youngest child under 6; young, married, youngest child over 6; older, married, with children; older, married, no children under 18; older, single; other variations for single parents, divorced, etc.
Occupation	Professional and technical; managers, officials, and proprietors; clerical sales; craftspeople; foremen; operatives; farmers; retired; students; housewives; unemployed.
Education	Grade school or less; some high school; high school graduate; some college; college graduate.
Ethnicity	Asian, Black, Hispanic, Native American, White, multiracial.
Social class	Lower-lower, upper-lower, lower-middle, upper-middle, lower-upper, upper-upper.

Note: Terms used in this table are explained in detail later in the text.

Exhibit 4–9
Possible Segmenting Dimensions for Business/Organizational Markets

Kind of relationship	Weak loyalty → strong loyalty to vendor Single source → multiple vendors "Arm's length" dealings → close partnership
Type of customer	Manufacturer, service producer, government agency, military, nonprofit, wholesaler or retailer (when end user), and so on.
Demographics	Geographic location (region of world, country, region within country, urban → rural); Size (number of employees, sales volume); Primary business or industry (North American Industry Classification System); Number of facilities
How customer will use product	Installations, components, accessories, raw materials, supplies, professional services
Type of buying situation	Decentralized → centralized Buyer → multiple buying influence Straight rebuy → modified rebuy → new-task buying
Purchasing methods	Vendor analysis, purchasing specifications, Internet bids, negotiated contracts, long-term contracts, e-commerce websites

Note: Terms used in this table are explained in detail later in the text.

guarantee a purchase. He or she must have a real need—like a job that requires "wheels" or kids who have to be carpooled. This need may motivate the purchase of *some* car. But these qualifying dimensions don't determine what specific brand or model car the person might buy. That depends on more specific interests—such as the kind of safety, performance, or appearance the customer wants. Determining dimensions related to these needs affect the specific car the customer purchases. If safety is a determining dimension for a customer, a Volvo wagon that offers side impact protection, air bags, and all-wheel drive might be the customer's first choice.

Determining dimensions may be very specific

How specific the determining dimensions are depends on whether you are concerned with a general product type or a specific brand. See Exhibit 4–10. The more specific you want to be, the more particular the determining dimensions may be. In a particular case, the determining dimensions may seem minor. But they are important because they *are* the determining dimensions.

Exhibit 4–10   Finding the Relevant Segmenting Dimensions

Segmenting dimensions become more specific to reasons why the target segment chooses to buy a particular brand of the product

All potential dimensions	Qualifying dimensions	Determining dimensions (product type)	Determining dimensions (brand specific)
Dimensions generally relevant to purchasing behavior	Dimensions relevant to including a customer type in the product-market	Dimensions that affect the customer's purchase of a specific type of product	Dimensions that affect the customer's choice of a specific brand

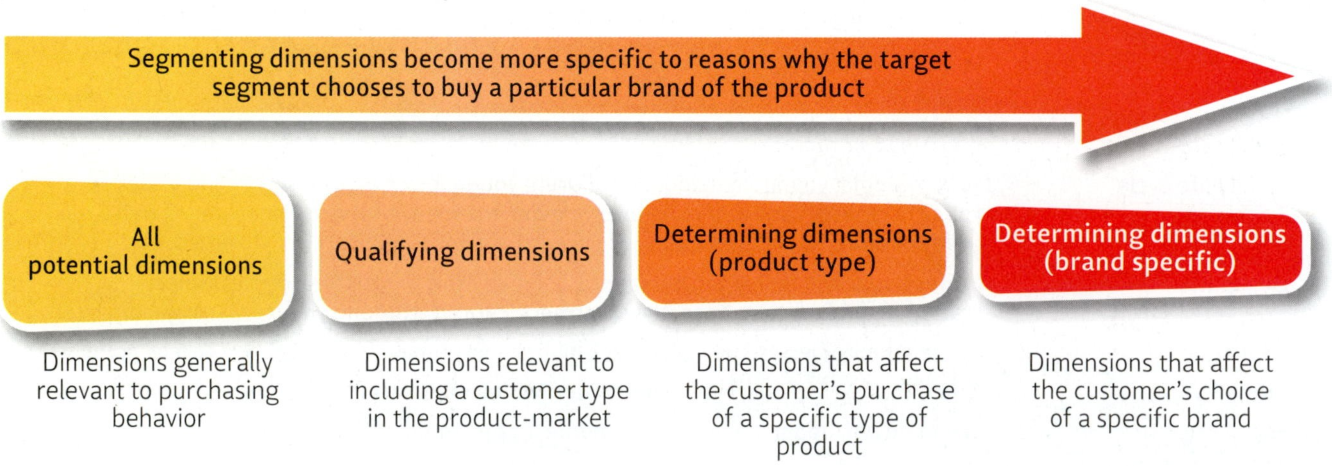

Marketers at General Mills know this. Lots of people try to text message or drive a car while eating breakfast or lunch. General Mills has figured out that for many of these target customers the real determining dimension in picking a snack is whether it can be eaten "one-handed."

Qualifying dimensions are important too

The qualifying dimensions help identify the "core benefits" that must be offered to everyone in a product-market. For example, people won't choose General Mills' one-handed snacks unless they qualify as being tasty. Qualifying and determining dimensions work together in marketing strategy planning.

Different dimensions needed for different submarkets

Note that each different submarket within a broad product-market may be motivated by a different set of dimensions. In the snack food market, for example, health food enthusiasts are interested in nutrition, dieters worry about calories, and economical shoppers with lots of kids may want volume to "fill them up."

Ethical issues in selecting segmenting dimensions

Marketing managers sometimes face ethical decisions when selecting segmenting dimensions. Problems may arise if a firm targets customers who are somehow at a disadvantage in dealing with the firm or who are unlikely to see the negative effects of their own choices. For example, some people criticize shoe companies for targeting poor, inner-city kids who see expensive athletic shoes as an important status symbol. Many firms, including producers of infant formula, have been criticized for targeting consumers in less-developed nations. Some nutritionists criticize firms that market soft drinks, candy, and snack foods to children.

Ethics QUESTION

A consumer group has criticized an encyclopedia publisher for targeting low-income parents. They respond well to sales appeals that focus on the low cost-per-day of encyclopedias that help kids enjoy learning. The critics say that the parents can't afford the books and don't understand the publisher's credit plan. In reply, the publisher cites a teacher group that touts the books as an excellent value. What do you think about this issue? If you were the marketing manager for the encyclopedia company, would you change its strategy?

Sometimes a marketing manager must decide whether a firm should serve customers it really doesn't want to serve. For example, banks sometimes offer marketing mixes that are attractive to wealthy customers but that basically drive off low-income consumers.

People often disagree about what segmenting dimensions are ethical in a given situation. A marketing manager needs to consider not only his or her own view but also the views of other groups in society. Even when there is no clear "right" answer, negative publicity may be very damaging. This is what Amazon.com encountered when it was revealed that it was charging some regular customers higher prices than new customers at its site.[9]

International marketing requires even more segmenting

Success in international marketing requires even more attention to segmenting. There are over 192 nations with their own unique cultures! And they differ greatly in language, customs (including business ethics), beliefs, religions, race, and income distribution patterns. (We discuss some of these differences in Chapters 3 and 5.) These additional differences can complicate the segmenting process. Even worse, critical data is often less available—and less dependable—as firms move into international markets. This is one reason why some firms insist that local operations and decisions be handled by natives. They, at least, have a feel for their markets.

There are more dimensions—but there is a way

Segmenting international markets may require more dimensions. But one practical method adds just one step to the approach discussed earlier. First, marketers segment by country or region—looking at demographic, cultural, and other characteristics, including stage of economic development. This may help them find regional or national submarkets that are fairly similar. Then—depending on whether the firm is aiming at final consumers or business markets—they apply the same basic approaches presented before.

MORE SOPHISTICATED TECHNIQUES MAY HELP IN SEGMENTING

Marketing researchers and managers often turn to computer-aided methods for help with the segmenting job. A detailed review of the possibilities is beyond the scope of this book. But a brief discussion will give you a flavor of how computer-aided methods work. In addition, the computer-aided problem for this chapter (4, Segmenting Customers) on the text website (and on the optional Student CD) gives you a hands-on feel for how managers use them.

Clustering usually requires a computer

Clustering techniques try to find similar patterns within sets of data. Clustering groups customers who are similar on their segmenting dimensions into homogeneous segments. Clustering approaches use computers to do what previously was done with much intuition and judgment.

The data to be clustered might include such dimensions as demographic characteristics, the importance of different needs, attitudes toward the product, and past buying behavior. The computer searches all the data for homogeneous groups of people. When it finds them, marketers study the dimensions of the people in the groups to see why the computer clustered them together. The results sometimes suggest new, or at least better, marketing strategies.[10]

A cluster analysis of the toothpaste market, for example, might show that some people buy toothpaste because it tastes good (the sensory segment), while others are concerned with the effect of clean teeth and fresh breath on their social image

Amazon.com sends e-mails to customers with recommendations based on their past purchases. Many customers find these messages, which inform them of new books, music, or movies that actually match their interests, useful.

CDW Targets the Small Business Segment with Uncommon Service

Sellers in business markets often rely on customer size as a key segmentation dimension. When potential profit from serving a big customer is high, the selling firm may even treat that customer as a "segment of one"—and develop a unique marketing mix targeted to win and keep its business. Even if a unique marketing mix isn't justified, big customers in these segments often get volume discounts, extra services, and personalized attention. By contrast, smaller customers are often left to get information and handle orders themselves—at a seller's website. This can be efficient, reduce costs for both the seller and customer, and serve the need. But that is not always the case.

CDW is a wholesaler that sells all sorts of computer gear produced by many manufacturers. There's a reason that *Fortune* magazine recognized it as one of "America's Most Admired Companies" in 2008. Most of its 360,000 business customers are too small to command much attention from equipment manufacturers. Yet they also have smaller IT departments and know less about buying IT equipment. CDW has enjoyed rapid growth because it offers a marketing mix that is atypical for these customers. Even the smallest customer gets a dedicated account manager (AM).

These salespeople don't just take orders; they go through months of CDW training so that they really understand a customer's needs and can help the buyer make the right purchases. The AM is a single point-of-contact with the account over time and is encouraged to act almost as an extension of the client's IT department. This relationship helps the AM anticipate client needs; the AM is also supported with customer relationship management databases that help predict when an upgrade is needed—rather than wait for the customer to ask. This is especially helpful to small customers who don't have backup systems in place to tide them over if something goes wrong. This is also why CDW fills orders fast—usually on the same day they are received. To provide that level of service with over 35,000 boxes shipped each day, CDW operates a 450,000-square-foot distribution center and keeps over $150 million in inventory on hand. CDW's "high-touch" strategy is costly, but high volume keeps its prices competitive. And CDW's sales volume is high because CDW delivers superior customer value that wins a large share of its target customers' business.[11]

(the sociables). Still others worry about decay or gum disease (the worriers), and some are just interested in the best value for their money (the value seekers). Each of these market segments calls for a different marketing mix—although some of the four Ps may be similar.

Customer database can focus the effort

A variation of the clustering approach is based on customer relationship management methods. With **customer relationship management (CRM)**, the seller fine-tunes the marketing effort with information from a detailed customer database. This usually includes data on a customer's past purchases as well as other segmenting information. For example, an auto-repair garage that keeps a database of customer oil changes can send a reminder postcard when it's time for the next oil change. Similarly, a florist that keeps a database of customers who have ordered flowers for Mother's Day or Valentine's Day can call them in advance with a special offer. Firms that operate over the Internet may have a special advantage with these database-focused approaches. They are able to communicate with customers via a website or e-mail, which means that the whole effort is not only targeted but also very inexpensive. Further, it's fast and easy for a customer to reply.[12]

Amazon.com takes this idea further. When a customer orders a book, the Amazon CRM system at the website recommends related books that have been purchased by other customers who bought that book.

DIFFERENTIATION AND POSITIONING TAKE THE CUSTOMER POINT OF VIEW

Differentiate the marketing mix—to serve customers better

As we've emphasized throughout, the reason for focusing on a specific target market—by using marketing segmentation approaches or tools such as cluster analysis or CRM—is so that you can fine-tune the whole marketing mix to provide some group of potential customers with superior value. By *differentiating* the marketing mix to do a better job meeting customers' needs, the firm builds a competitive advantage. When this happens, target customers view the firm's position in the market as uniquely suited to their preferences and needs. Further, because everyone in the firm is clear about what position it wants to achieve with customers, the Product, Promotion, and other marketing mix decisions can be blended better to achieve the desired objectives.

Although the marketing manager may want customers to see the firm's offering as unique, that is not always possible. Me-too imitators may come along and copy the firm's strategy. Further, even if a firm's marketing mix is different, consumers may not know or care. They're busy and, simply put, the firm's product may not be that important in their lives. Even so, in looking for opportunities it's important for the marketing manager to know how customers *do* view the firm's offering. It's also important for the marketing manager to have a clear idea about how he or she would like for customers to view the firm's offering. This is where another important concept, *positioning*, comes in.

AT&T has an ad campaign that helps to position AT&T as a provider of international communications—a benefit that differentiates it from other competitors.

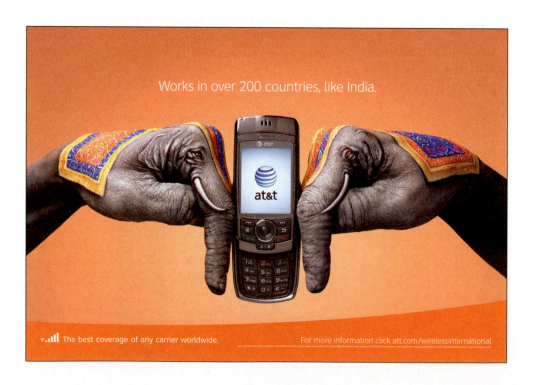

Positioning is based on customers' views

Positioning refers to how customers think about proposed or present brands in a market. A marketing manager needs a realistic view of how customers think about offerings in the market. Without that, it's hard to differentiate. At the same time, the manager should know how he or she *wants* target customers to think about the firm's marketing mix. Positioning issues are especially important when competitors in a market appear to be very similar. For example, many people think that there isn't much difference between one provider of home owner's insurance and another. But State Farm Insurance uses advertising to emphasize the value of the service and personal attention from its agents, who live right in the customer's neighborhood. Low-price insurers who sell from websites or toll-free numbers can't make that claim.

Once you know what customers think, then you can decide whether to leave the product (and marketing mix) alone or reposition it. This may mean *physical changes in the product* or simply *image changes based on promotion*. For example, most cola drinkers can't pick out their favorite brand in a blind test—so physical changes might not be necessary (and might not even work) to reposition a cola.

Figuring out what customers really think about competing products isn't easy, but there are approaches that help. Most of them require some formal marketing research. The results are usually plotted on graphs to help show how consumers view the competing products. Usually, the products' positions are related to two or three product features that are important to the target customers.

Managers make the graphs for positioning decisions by asking consumers to make judgments about different brands—including their "ideal" brand—and then use computer programs to summarize the ratings and plot the results. The details of positioning techniques—sometimes called *perceptual mapping*—are beyond the scope of this text. But Exhibit 4–11 shows the possibilities.[13]

Exhibit 4–11
"Product Space" Representing Consumers' Perceptions for Different Brands of Bar Soap

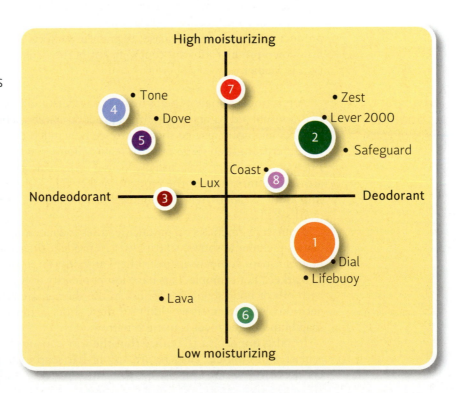

Exhibit 4–11 shows the "product space" for different brands of bar soap using two dimensions—the extent to which consumers think the soaps moisturize and deodorize their skin. For example, consumers see Dove as quite high on moisturizing but low on deodorizing. Dove and Tone are close together—implying that consumers think of them as similar on these characteristics. Dial is viewed as different and is further away on the graph. Remember that positioning maps are based on *customers' perceptions*—the actual characteristics of the products (as determined by a chemical test) might be different!

Each segment may have its own preferences

The circles in Exhibit 4–11 show different sets (submarkets) of consumers clustered near their ideal soap preferences. Groups of respondents with a similar ideal product are circled to show apparent customer concentrations. In this graph, the size of the circles suggests the size of the segments for the different ideals.

Ideal clusters 1 and 2 are the largest and are close to two popular brands—Dial and Lever 2000. It appears that customers in cluster 1 want more moisturizing than they see in Dial. However, exactly what this brand should do about this isn't clear. Perhaps Dial should leave its physical product alone—but emphasize moisturizing more in its promotion to make a stronger appeal to those who want moisturizers. A marketing manager talking about this approach might simply refer to it as "positioning the brand as a good moisturizer." Of course, whether the effort is successful depends on whether the whole marketing mix delivers on the promise of the positioning communication.

Note that ideal cluster 7 is not near any of the present brands. This may suggest an opportunity for introducing a new product—a strong moisturizer with some deodorizers. A firm that chooses to follow this approach would be making a segmenting effort.

Combining versus segmenting

Positioning analysis may lead a firm to combining—rather than segmenting—if managers think they can make several general appeals to different parts of a "combined" market. For example, by varying its promotion, Coast might try to appeal to segments 8, 1, and 2 with one product. These segments are all quite similar (close together) in what they want in an ideal brand. On the other hand, there may be clearly defined submarkets—and some parts of the market may be "owned" by one product or brand. In this case, segmenting efforts may be practical—moving the firm's own product into another segment of the general market area where competition is weaker.

Positioning as part of broader analysis

A positioning analysis helps managers understand how customers see their market. It is a visual aid to understanding a product-market. The first time such an analysis is done, managers may be shocked to see how much customers' perceptions of a market differ from their own. For this reason alone, positioning analysis may be crucial. But a positioning analysis usually focuses on specific product features and brands that are close competitors in the product-market. Thus, it is a product-oriented approach. Important *customer*-related dimensions—including needs and attitudes—may be overlooked.

Premature emphasis on product features is dangerous in other ways as well. As our bar soap example shows, starting with a product-oriented definition of a market and how bar soaps compete against other bar soaps can make a firm miss more basic shifts in markets. For example, bars have lost popularity to liquid soaps. Other products, like bath oils or body shampoos for use in the shower, are now part of the relevant competition also. Managers wouldn't see these shifts if they looked only at alternative bar soap brands—the focus is just too narrow.

It's also important to realize that the way consumers look at a product isn't just a matter of chance. Let's return to our bar soap example. While many consumers do think about soap in terms of moisturizing and deodorizing, other needs shouldn't be overlooked. For example, some consumers are especially concerned about wiping out germs. Marketers for Dial soap recognized this need and developed ads that positioned Dial as "the choice" for these target customers. This helped Dial win new customers, including those who switched from Lifebuoy—which was otherwise similar to Dial (see Exhibit 4–11). In fact, what happened to Lifebuoy highlights what happens if managers don't update their marketing strategy as customer needs and competition change. Lifebuoy was the first deodorant soap on the market; it was a leading brand for over 100 years. But it gradually lost sales to competitors with stronger marketing mixes (clearer differentiation, better positioning, and superior customer value) until 2002, when Lever stopped selling it.

As we emphasize throughout the text, you must understand potential needs and attitudes when planning marketing strategies. If customers treat different products as substitutes, then a firm has to position itself against those products too. Customers won't always be conscious of all of the detailed ways that a firm's marketing mix might be different, but careful positioning can help highlight a unifying theme or benefits that relate to the determining dimensions of the target market. Thus, it's useful to think of positioning as part of the broader strategy planning process—because the purpose is to ensure that the whole marketing mix is positioned for competitive advantage.

CONCLUSION

Chapters 2 and 3 introduced a framework for strategy planning that starts with analysis of the broad market and then narrows down to a specific target market and marketing mix. The basic purpose of this chapter is to show how marketing managers use market segmentation and positioning to guide that narrowing-down process.

Now that you've read this chapter you should understand how to carefully define generic markets and product-markets and how that can help in identifying and evaluating opportunities. We stressed the shortcomings of a too narrow, product-oriented view of markets and explained why it's better to take a broader view that also includes consideration of customer needs, the product type, the customer type, and the geographic area.

We also discussed approaches for market segmentation—the process of naming and then segmenting broad product-markets to find potentially attractive target markets. Some people try to segment markets by starting with the mass market and then dividing it into smaller submarkets based on a few demographic characteristics. But this can lead to poor results. Instead, market segmentation should first focus on a broad product-market and then group similar customers into homogeneous submarkets. The more similar the potential customers are, the larger the submarkets can be. Four criteria for evaluating possible product-market segments were presented.

Once a broad product-market is segmented, marketing managers can use one of three approaches to market-oriented strategy planning: (1) the single target market approach, (2) the multiple target market approach, or (3) the combined target market approach. In general, we encourage marketers to be segmenters rather than combiners.

Then we cover computer-aided approaches such as clustering techniques, CRM, and positioning. We emphasize the role of positioning in providing a focus or theme to the various elements of a differentiated marketing mix that fits the preferences of target customers.

In summary, good marketers should be experts on markets and likely segmenting dimensions. By creatively segmenting markets, they may spot opportunities—even breakthrough opportunities—and help their firms succeed against aggressive competitors offering similar products. Segmenting is basic to target marketing. And the more you practice segmenting, the more meaningful market segments you will see. In Chapters 5 and 6 you'll learn more about the buying behavior of final consumers and organizational customers. As you enrich your understanding of customers and how they behave, you will develop command of a broader set of dimensions that are important for segmentation and positioning.

KEY TERMS

market, 90

generic market, 91

product-market, 91

market segmentation, 94

segmenting, 95

market segment, 95

single target market approach, 97

multiple target market approach, 97

combined target market approach, 97

combiners, 98

segmenters, 98

qualifying dimensions, 101

determining dimensions, 101

clustering techniques, 104

customer relationship management (CRM), 105

positioning, 107

QUESTIONS AND PROBLEMS

1. Distinguish between a generic market and a product-market. Illustrate your answer.

2. Explain what market segmentation is.

3. List the types of potential segmenting dimensions, and explain which you would try to apply first, second, and third in a particular situation. If the nature of the situation would affect your answer, explain how.

4. Explain why segmentation efforts based on attempts to divide the mass market using a few demographic dimensions may be very disappointing.

5. Illustrate the concept that segmenting is an aggregating process by referring to the admissions policies of your own college and a nearby college or university.

6. Review the types of segmenting dimensions listed in Exhibits 4–8 and 4–9, and select the ones you think should be combined to fully explain the market segment you personally would be in if you were planning to buy a new watch today. List several dimensions and try to develop a shorthand name, like "fashion-oriented," to describe your own personal market segment. Then try to estimate what proportion of the total watch market would be in your market segment. Next, explain if there are any offerings

that come close to meeting the needs of your market. If not, what sort of a marketing mix is needed? Would it be economically attractive for anyone to try to satisfy your market segment? Why or why not?

7. Identify the determining dimension or dimensions that explain why you bought the specific brand you did in your most recent purchase of a (*a*) soft drink, (*b*) shampoo, (*c*) shirt or blouse, and (*d*) larger, more expensive item, such as a bicycle, camera, or boat. Try to express the determining dimension(s) in terms of your own personal characteristics rather than the product's characteristics. Estimate what share of the market would probably be motivated by the same determining dimension(s).

8. Consider the market for off-campus apartments in your city. Identify some submarkets that have different needs and determining dimensions. Then evaluate how well the needs in these market segments are being met in your geographic area. Is there an obvious breakthrough opportunity waiting for someone?

9. Explain how positioning analysis can help a marketing manager identify target market opportunities.

CREATING MARKETING PLANS

The Marketing Plan Coach software on the text website (and on the optional Student CD) includes a sample marketing plan for Hillside Veterinary Clinic. Look through the "Customers" section.

a. How does the marketing plan segment the market?

b. Can you think of other segmentation dimensions that could be used?

c. What do you think of the approach Hillside used to determine target markets? Are they using a single target market, multiple target market, or combined target market approach?

d. How does Hillside plan to differentiate and position its offering?

SUGGESTED CASES

3. MANU Soccer Academy   7. Waituiwa Lodge   10. Taffe's Ice Land

30. Eden Prairie Mills, Ltd.

COMPUTER-AIDED PROBLEM

4. SEGMENTING CUSTOMERS

The marketing manager for Audiotronics Software Company is seeking new market opportunities. He is focusing on the voice recognition market and has narrowed down to three segments: the Fearful Typists, the Power Users, and the Professional Specialists. The Fearful Typists don't know much about computers—they just want a fast way to create e-mail messages, letters, and simple reports without errors. They don't need a lot of special features. They want simple instructions and a program that's easy to learn. The Power Users know a lot about computers, use them often, and want a voice recognition program with many special features. All computer programs seem easy to them—so they aren't worried about learning to use the various features. The Professional Specialists have jobs that require a lot of writing. They don't know much about computers but are willing to learn. They want special features needed for their work—but only if they aren't too hard to learn and use.

The marketing manager prepared a table summarizing the importance of each of three key needs in the three segments (see first table below).

Audiotronics' sales staff conducted interviews with seven potential customers who were asked to rate how important each of these three needs were in their work. The manager prepared a spreadsheet to help him cluster (aggregate) each person into one of the segments—along with other similar people. Each person's ratings are entered in the spreadsheet, and the clustering procedure computes a similarity score that indicates how similar (a low score) or dissimilar (a high score)

the person is to the typical person in each of the segments. The manager can then "aggregate" potential customers into the segment that is most similar (that is, the one with the *lowest* similarity score).

a. The ratings for a potential customer appear on the first spreadsheet. Into which segment would you aggregate this person?

b. The responses for seven potential customers who were interviewed are listed in the second table below. Enter the ratings for a customer in the spreadsheet and then write down the similarity score for each segment. Repeat the process for each customer. Based on your analysis, indicate the segment into which you would aggregate each customer. Indicate the size (number of customers) of each segment.

c. In the interview, each potential customer was also asked what type of computer he or she would be using. The responses are shown in the second table along with the ratings. Group the responses based on the customer's segment. If you were targeting the Fearful Typists segment, what type of computer would you focus on when developing your software?

d. Based on your analysis, which customer would you say is least like any of the segments? Briefly explain the reason for your choice.

For additional questions related to this problem, see Exercise 4-4 in the *Learning Aid for Use with Essentials of Marketing*, 12th edition.

Market Segment	Importance of Need (1 = not important; 10 = very important)		
	Features	Easy to Use	Easy to Learn
Fearful typists	3	8	9
Power users	9	2	2
Professional specialists	7	5	6

Potential Customer	Importance of Need (1 = not important; 10 = very important)			
	Features	Easy to Use	Easy to Learn	Type of Computer
A.	8	1	2	Dell laptop
B.	6	6	5	HP desktop
C.	4	9	8	Apple
D.	2	6	7	Apple
E.	5	6	5	HP desktop
F.	8	3	1	Dell laptop
G.	4	6	8	Apple

5

CHAPTER

Final Consumers and Their Buying Behavior

When Sony introduced its Walkman in the late 1970s, it quickly became a popular way for on-the-go music lovers to play tapes of their favorite music—anywhere they went. Competing players quickly emerged, but Sony kept its lead by improving its Walkman and then offering models for CDs and digital audiotapes when those media came on the market.

In the late 1990s, the new MP3 format offered quality music from a small digital file that played on a computer or portable player. Diamond Multimedia's Rio was the first MP3 player. The Rio was innovative, but users had to download music from virus-ridden websites like Napster—or use special software to "rip" CDs to MP3 format. Many music buffs liked the idea of having songs at their fingertips but believed that getting the digital files was just too complicated. Further, lawsuits by music companies charged that sharing downloaded MP3 music files was illegal. All of this slowed down the initial adoption of MP3 players.

Creative Labs raised expectations in the market by promoting benefits like longer battery life, capacity for more songs, and lower prices. For some consumers, all of this choice required a more careful purchase decision. For example, some would search for information and reviews on the Internet or talk with salespeople in stores to figure out which model was best. Of course, some iPod fanatics didn't bother with that extra effort; they just upgraded to whatever improved models Apple brought to market.

Apple also promoted iPod versions to appeal to different market segments. For example, a Harry Potter iPod, complete with the Hogwarts crest, appealed to kids and a black and red U2 model targeted their parents. Apple offered the Shuffle for music lovers who wanted a small, bargain-priced player. And the iTunes store made it easy for consumers to download games and podcasts (online audio or video programs). New versions of the iPod added video and games to the user's experience and of course the iPhone did all that—and made phone calls.

Other cell phones that could play music were already on the market when Apple introduced the iPhone, but most consumers couldn't see the benefits. The iPhone changed that. The phone's colorful touch-screen display, websurfing, and cool handling of multimedia downloads wowed consumers. Soon iPhone owners could customize their phones by choosing from thousands of independently developed software applications ("apps") available for download at the iTunes store. Apps are small software programs that run on an iPhone and include games like Flight Control, a search tool from Google, a Facebook interface, and many more. Some of these are free, while others cost $10 or more. Initially, the iPhone was available only for use with AT&T's cellular service. To attract other customers, Apple introduced the iPod Touch, which has most of the phone's features but can't make calls.

Not all of Apple's marketing strategy decisions resonate with its customers. While Apple's most loyal customers stood in line to buy the first iPhones, many people balked at the $600 price tag and sales slowed. So, a couple of months later Apple cut the price $200. But, many early adopters of the iPhone felt betrayed and complained on online message boards and through e-mails to Apple's CEO Steve Jobs. He listened and Apple subsequently offered $100 store credits.

Apple's strategies have been very successful. Yet, in technology markets consumer attitudes and preferences can change quickly. So, to build on its successes, Apple will need to continue to identify new and better ways to meet customer needs.[1]

Attitudes quickly changed when Apple offered an innovative marketing mix that addressed the needs of these target customers. Its online iTunes.com store offered legal downloads of songs at a reasonable price and without the risk of viruses. Apple's free iTunes software made it easy to organize digital music on a computer and transfer it to Apple's iPod. The iPod was designed to be stylish and very easy to use in spite of its ability to play a huge number of songs. And Apple's ads made consumers aware of its new concept and motivated them with the promise of "a thousand songs in your pocket." Even skeptics who ignored the ads couldn't help but notice the distinctive white iPod cords dangling from the ears of a friend who was "in" on this cool new product. That prompted a lot of product conversations and persuasive on-the-spot iPod demos. Testimonials on blogs, website postings, and e-mails also helped spread the word.

Although most iPod owners were satisfied with their purchases, competitors like Dell, Sony, and

CONSUMER BEHAVIOR: WHY DO THEY BUY WHAT THEY BUY?

The Apple case shows that effective marketing strategy planning requires a real understanding of customers and why they buy as they do. Without that knowledge, it is difficult to zero in on the right target market, or to develop and adapt a marketing mix that will be the best value for those customers.

Understanding consumer behavior can be a challenge. Specific behaviors vary a great deal for different people, products, and purchase situations. In today's global markets the variations are countless. That makes it impractical to catalog all the possibilities. But there are general behavioral principles—frameworks—that marketing managers can apply to better understand their specific target markets. In this chapter our approach focuses on developing your skill in working with these frameworks by exploring thinking from economics, psychology, sociology, and other behavioral disciplines. We'll take a look at the topics overviewed in Exhibit 5–1, which includes a simplified model of consumer behavior.

We will begin with a discussion of influences on the consumer decision process: economic needs, psychological variables, social influences, and the purchase situation. Exhibit 5–2 provides an expanded look at these influences. Following our discussion of these different categories of influences, we will look more closely at the consumer decision process. We conclude the chapter with a discussion of consumer behavior in international markets.

ECONOMIC NEEDS AFFECT MOST BUYING DECISIONS

Economic buyers seek the best uses of their money

Most economists assume that consumers are **economic buyers**—people who know all the facts and logically compare choices to get the greatest satisfaction from spending their time and money. The economic-buyer theory says that consumers decide what to buy based on **economic needs** which are concerned with making the best use of a consumer's time and money—as the consumer judges it.

Exhibit 5-1   Consumer Behavior for Marketing Strategy Planning

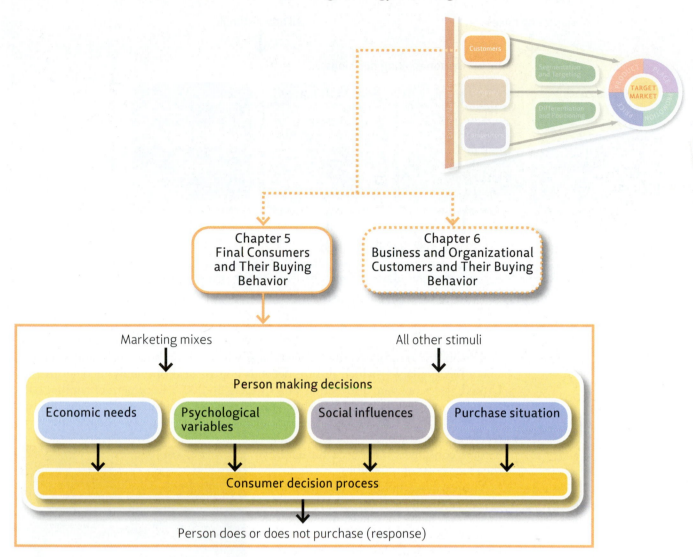

Some consumers look for the lowest price. Others will pay extra for convenience. And others may weigh price and quality for the best value. Some economic needs are

1. Economy of purchase or use.
2. Efficiency in operation or use.
3. Dependability in use.
4. Improvement of earnings.
5. Convenience.

Clearly, marketing managers must be alert to new ways to appeal to economic needs. Most consumers appreciate firms that offer them improved economic value for the money they spend. But improved value does not just mean offering lower and lower prices. For example, products can be designed to work better, require less service, or last longer. Promotion can inform consumers about product benefits in terms of measurable factors like operating costs, the length of the guarantee, or the time a product will save. Carefully planned Place decisions can make it easier and faster for customers who face a poverty of time to make a purchase.

Exhibit 5-2   A Model of Influences on Consumer Behavior

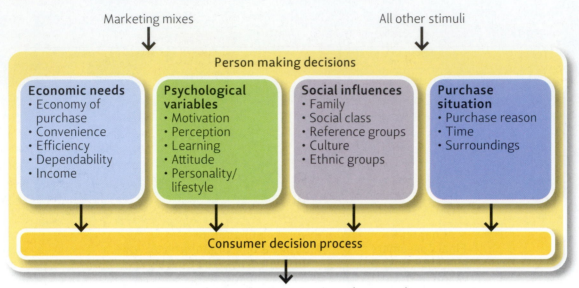

Marketing mixes

All other stimuli

Person making decisions

Economic needs
- Economy of purchase
- Convenience
- Efficiency
- Dependability
- Income

Psychological variables
- Motivation
- Perception
- Learning
- Attitude
- Personality/ lifestyle

Social influences
- Family
- Social class
- Reference groups
- Culture
- Ethnic groups

Purchase situation
- Purchase reason
- Time
- Surroundings

Consumer decision process

Person does or does not purchase (response)

Income affects needs

The ability to satisfy economic needs largely depends on how much money a consumer has available—which in turn depends a great deal on family income. In the United States, income distribution varies widely. In 2007, 40 percent of families had a total income less than $49,510 while only 20 percent of families had income greater than $112,638. While the median income of $61,355 may seem like a lot of money to a recent college graduate, America's middle-income consumers have been hit hard by the rising costs of necessities.

In most households, people don't have enough income to buy everything they want. For many products, these people can't be customers even if they want to be. For example, most families spend a good portion of their income on such necessities as food, rent or house payments, car and home furnishings, and insurance. A family's purchase of "luxuries" comes from **discretionary income**—what is left of income after paying taxes and paying for necessities.

Discretionary income is an elusive concept because the definition of necessities varies from family to family and over time. It depends on what they think is necessary for their lifestyle. High-speed Internet service purchased out of discretionary income by a lower-income family may be considered a necessity by a higher-income family.[2]

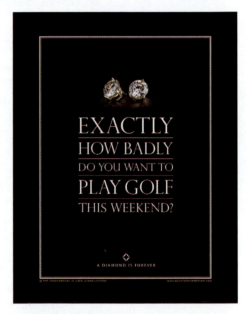

EXACTLY
HOW BADLY
DO YOU WANT TO
PLAY GOLF
THIS WEEKEND?

A DIAMOND IS FOREVER

Marketers for diamonds are very aware that spending varies with income and other demographic dimensions.

Economic conditions affect consumer confidence and spending

We discussed the broader economic environment in Chapter 3. Whether an economy is experiencing a downturn or prosperity can affect how consumers feel about the future. When consumers feel confident and secure in their jobs, they are more likely to borrow money to buy a larger house, a new car, or vacation in an exotic locale.

On the other hand, an economic recession can make consumers worried about job prospects—or they may be more careful with spending when their retirement savings have significantly declined. These changes affect consumer spending and how consumers perceive luxuries and necessities.

Economic value and income are important factors in many purchase decisions. But most marketing managers think that buyer behavior is not as simple as the economic-buyer model suggests. A product that one person sees as a good value—and has the income to buy—may be of little interest to someone else. So let's look more closely at the psychological variables that influence buying behavior.

PSYCHOLOGICAL INFLUENCES WITHIN AN INDIVIDUAL

Needs motivate consumers

Everybody is motivated by needs and wants. **Needs** are the basic forces that motivate a person to do something. Some needs involve a person's physical well-being, others the individual's self-view and relationship with others. Needs are more basic than wants. **Wants** are "needs" that are learned during a person's life. For example, everyone needs water or some kind of liquid, but some people also have learned to want Clearly Canadian's raspberry-flavored sparkling water on the rocks.

When a need is not satisfied, it may lead to a drive. The need for liquid, for example, leads to a thirst drive. A **drive** is a strong stimulus that encourages action to reduce a need. Drives are internal—they are the reasons behind certain behavior patterns. In marketing, a product purchase results from a drive to satisfy some need.

Some critics imply that marketers can somehow manipulate consumers to buy products against their will. But trying to get consumers to act against their will is a waste of time. Instead, a good marketing manager studies what consumer drives, needs, and wants already exist and how they can be satisfied better.

Consumers seek benefits to meet needs

We're all a bundle of needs and wants. Exhibit 5–3 lists some important needs that might motivate a person to some action. This list, of course, is not complete. But thinking about such needs can help you see what *benefits* consumers might seek from a marketing mix.

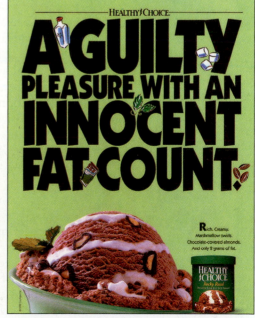

Economic needs affect many buying decisions, but for some purchases the behavioral influences on a consumer are more important.

Exhibit 5-3 Possible Needs Motivating a Person to Some Action

Types of Needs	Specific Examples			
Physiological needs	Food Sex Rest	Liquid Body elimination	Activity Self-preservation	Sleep Warmth/coolness
Psychological needs	Aggression Family preservation Nurturing Playing-relaxing Self-identification	Curiosity Imitation Order Power Tenderness	Being responsible Independence Personal fulfillment Pride	Dominance Love Playing-competition Self-expression
Desire for . . .	Acceptance Affiliation Comfort Esteem Knowledge Respect Status	Achievement Appreciation Leisure Fame Prestige Retaliation Sympathy	Acquisition Beauty Distance—"space" Happiness Pleasure Self-satisfaction Variety	Affection Companionship Distinctiveness Identification Recognition Sociability Fun
Freedom from . . .	Fear Pain Harm	Depression Stress Ridicule	Discomfort Loss Sadness	Anxiety Illness Pressure

When a marketing manager defines a product-market, the needs may be quite specific. For example, the food need might be as specific as wanting a Domino's thick-crust pepperoni pizza—delivered to your door hot and ready to eat.

Several needs at the same time

Consumer psychologists often argue that a person may have several reasons for buying—at the same time. Maslow is well known for his five-level hierarchy of needs. We will discuss a similar four-level hierarchy that is easier to apply to consumer behavior. Exhibit 5–4 illustrates the four levels along with an advertising slogan showing how a company has tried to appeal to each need. The lowest-level needs are physiological. Then come safety, social, and personal needs.[3]

Physiological needs are concerned with biological needs—food, liquid, rest, and sex. **Safety needs** are concerned with protection and physical well-being (perhaps involving health, security, medicine, and exercise). **Social needs** are concerned with love, friendship, status, and esteem—things that involve a person's interaction with others. **Personal needs**, on the other hand, are concerned with an individual's need for personal satisfaction—unrelated to what others think or do. Examples include self-esteem, accomplishment, fun, freedom, and relaxation.

Motivation theory suggests that we never reach a state of complete satisfaction. As soon as we get our lower-level needs reasonably satisfied, those at higher levels become more dominant. This explains why marketing efforts targeted at affluent consumers in advanced economies often focus on higher-level needs. It also explains why these approaches may be useless in parts of the world where consumers' basic needs are not being met.

A particular product may satisfy more than one need at the same time. In fact, most consumers try to fill a *set* of needs rather than just one need or another in sequence.

Discovering which needs to satisfy may require careful analysis. Consider, for example, the lowly vegetable peeler. Marketing managers for OXO International realized that many people, especially young children and senior citizens, have trouble gripping the handle of a typical peeler. OXO redesigned the peeler with a bigger handle that addressed this physical need. OXO also coated the handle with dishwasher-safe rubber. This makes cleanup more convenient—and the sharp peeler is safer to use when the

Exhibit 5–4   The PSSP Hierarchy of Needs

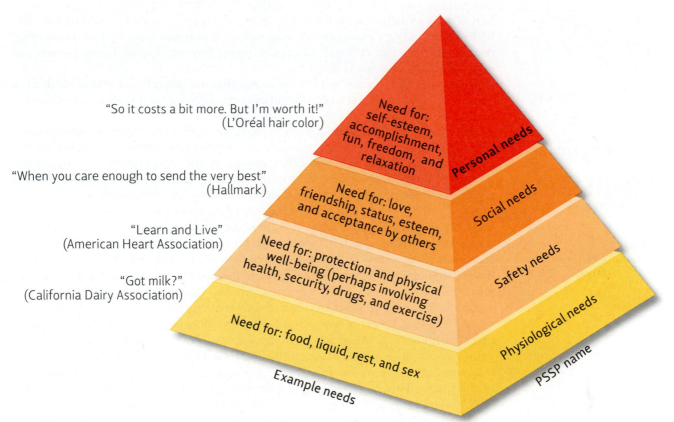

"So it costs a bit more. But I'm worth it!"
(L'Oréal hair color)

"When you care enough to send the very best"
(Hallmark)

"Learn and Live"
(American Heart Association)

"Got milk?"
(California Dairy Association)

Need for: self-esteem, accomplishment, fun, freedom, and relaxation — **Personal needs**

Need for: love, friendship, status, esteem, and acceptance by others — **Social needs**

Need for: protection and physical well-being (perhaps involving health, security, drugs, and exercise) — **Safety needs**

Need for: food, liquid, rest, and sex — **Physiological needs**

Example needs   **PSSP name**

grip is wet. The attractively designed grip also appeals to consumers who get personal satisfaction from cooking and who want to impress their guests. The premium-priced peeler has sold very well because it appeals to people with a variety of needs. Since that initial success, OXO has redesigned hundreds of everyday utensils, including its new Good Grip Convertible Colander. The colander's nonslip legs spring out and hold it securely in place over the sink for easy draining, but the legs fold down for use on a countertop.[4]

Perception determines what consumers see and feel

Consumers select varying ways to meet their needs sometimes because of differences in **perception**—how we gather and interpret information from the world around us.

We are constantly bombarded by stimuli—ads, products, stores—yet we may not hear or see anything. This is because we apply the following selective processes:

1. **Selective exposure**—our eyes and minds seek out and notice only information that interests us. How often have you closed a pop-up ad at a website without even noticing what it was for?
2. **Selective perception**—we screen out or modify ideas, messages, and information that conflict with previously learned attitudes and beliefs.
3. **Selective retention**—we remember only what we want to remember.

These selective processes help explain why some people are not affected by some advertising—even offensive advertising. They just don't see or remember it! Even if they do, they may dismiss it immediately.

Our needs affect these selective processes. And current needs receive more attention. For example, Goodyear tire retailers advertise some sale in the newspaper almost weekly. Most of the time we don't even notice these ads. Only when we need new tires do we tune in to Goodyear's ads.

**Learning determines
what response is likely**

Learning is a change in a person's thought processes caused by prior experience. Learning is often based on direct experience: A little girl tastes her first cone of Ben & Jerry's Cherry Garcia flavor ice cream, and learning occurs! Learning may also be based on indirect experience or associations. If you watch an ad that shows other people enjoying Ben & Jerry's Chocolate Fudge Brownie low-fat frozen yogurt, you might conclude that you'd like it too.

Consumer learning may result from things that marketers do, or it may result from stimuli that have nothing to do with marketing. Either way, almost all consumer behavior is learned.[5]

Experts describe a number of steps in the learning process. We've already discussed the idea of a drive as a strong stimulus that encourages action. Depending on the **cues**—products, signs, ads, and other stimuli in the environment—an individual chooses some specific response. A **response** is an effort to satisfy a drive. The specific response chosen depends on the cues and the person's past experience.

Reinforcement of the learning process occurs when the response is followed by satisfaction—that is, reduction in the drive. Reinforcement strengthens the relationship between the cue and the response. And it may lead to a similar response the next time the drive occurs. Repeated reinforcement leads to development of a habit—making the individual's decision process routine. Exhibit 5–5 shows the relationships of the important variables in the learning process.

The learning process can be illustrated by a thirsty person. The thirst *drive* could be satisfied in a variety of ways. But if the person happened to walk past a vending machine and saw a Mountain Dew sign—a *cue*—then he might satisfy the drive with a *response*—buying a Mountain Dew. If the experience is satisfactory, positive *reinforcement* occurs, and our friend may be quicker to satisfy this drive in the same way in the future. This emphasizes the importance of developing good products that live up to the promises of the firm's advertising. People can learn to like or dislike Mountain Dew—reinforcement and learning work both ways. Unless marketers satisfy their customers, they must constantly try to attract new ones to replace the dissatisfied ones who don't come back.

Exhibit 5–5
The Learning Process

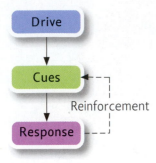

**Positive cues help
a marketing mix**

Sometimes marketers try to identify cues or images that have positive associations from some other situation and relate them to their marketing mix. Many people associate the smell of lemons with a fresh, natural cleanliness. So companies often add lemon scent to household cleaning products—Clorox bleach and Pledge furniture

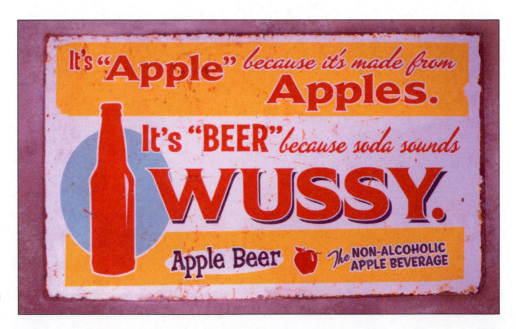

Most consumers don't know what Apple Beer is, but as this ad suggests they may still form an attitude based on the name.

120

polish, for example—because it has these associations. Similarly, firms like Calvin Klein use ads suggesting that people who use their products have more appeal to the opposite sex. Simple cues may even be important for a big purchase. Luxury-car makers try for a "new car smell" with an aroma of leather and wood, even though the car would really smell more like metal and adhesives as it comes off the production line in a factory.[6]

Many needs are culturally learned

Many needs are culturally (or socially) learned. The need for food, for instance, may lead to many specific food wants. Many Japanese enjoy sushi (raw fish), and their children learn to like it. Fewer Americans, however, have learned to enjoy it.

Some critics argue that marketing efforts encourage people to spend money on learned wants totally unrelated to any basic need. For example, Germans are less concerned about perspiration, and many don't buy or use antiperspirants. Yet Americans spend millions of dollars on such products. Advertising says that using Ban deodorant "takes the worry out of being close." But is marketing activity the cause of the difference in the two cultures? Most research says that advertising can't convince buyers of something contrary to their basic attitudes.

Attitudes relate to buying

An **attitude** is a person's point of view toward something. The "something" may be a product, an advertisement, a salesperson, a firm, or an idea. Attitudes are an important topic because they affect the selective processes, learning, and buying decisions.

Because attitudes are usually thought of as involving liking or disliking, they have some action implications. Beliefs are not so action-oriented. A **belief** is a person's opinion about something. Beliefs may help shape a consumer's attitudes but don't necessarily involve any liking or disliking. It is possible to have a belief—say, that Listerine PocketPak strips have a medicinal taste—without really caring what they taste like. On the other hand, beliefs about a product may have a positive or negative effect in shaping consumers' attitudes. For example, promotion for Splenda, a no-cal sweetener in a yellow packet, informs consumers that it's "made from sugar so it tastes like sugar." A dieter who believes that Splenda will taste better because it is made from sugar might try it instead of just routinely rebuying another brand, like Equal. On the other hand, a person with diabetes might believe that he should avoid Splenda—like he avoids other products made from sugar—even though Splenda is actually suitable for people with diabetes.[7]

Consumer beliefs, whether correct or incorrect, often influence consumer attitudes and choices.

In an attempt to relate attitude more closely to purchase behavior, some marketers stretch the attitude concept to include consumer "preferences" or "intention to buy." Managers who must forecast how much of their brand customers will buy are particularly interested in the intention to buy. Forecasts would be easier if attitudes were good predictors of intentions to buy. Unfortunately, the relationships usually are not that simple. A person may have positive attitudes toward GPS navigation systems for cars, but no intention of buying one.

"Green" attitudes and beliefs change marketing mixes

A growing number of consumers believe that they can have a positive effect on the environment if they buy from companies that can help them make "greener" choices. Marketing managers have responded by developing marketing mixes to address these ecological interests. Subway sandwich shops have added recycling bins. Both UPS and Enterprise Rent-A-Car have fleets of alternative fuel vehicles. General Mills changed Hamburger Helper from curly to straight noodles; that helped shrink package sizes by 20 percent and resulted in 500 fewer distribution trucks on the road each year. And Nike makes its Trash Talk basketball shoes from manufacturing waste—literally turning garbage into shoes. It is unclear how these changes will affect consumer attitudes. Some experts think that too many "green" claims will confuse customers or even prompt a backlash of negative attitudes.[8]

Internet EXERCISE

Climate Counts provides information to help consumers make choices that have a positive impact on the planet. Go to the Climate Counts website (**www.climatecounts.org**), click on the "Climate Scores" link, choose a scoreboard sector, and compare the different companies. Select one company and view its efforts. How do you think this information might affect how *consumers* behave? Do you think the information will affect how *companies* behave?

Most marketers work with existing attitudes

Marketers generally try to understand the attitudes of their potential customers and work with them. Because attitudes tend to be enduring, it's usually more economical to work with consumer attitudes than to try to change them. Changing negative attitudes probably is the most difficult job that marketers face.[9]

Ethical issues may arise

Part of the marketing job is to inform and persuade consumers about a firm's offering. An ethical issue sometimes arises, however, if consumers have *inaccurate* beliefs. For example, promotion of a "children's cold formula" may play off parents' fears that adult medicines are too strong—even though the basic ingredients in the children's formula are the same and only the dosage is different.

Marketers must also be careful about promotion that might encourage false beliefs, even if the advertising is not explicitly misleading. For example, ads for Ultra Slim-Fast low-fat beverage don't claim that anyone who buys the product will lose weight and look like the slim models in the ads—but some critics argue that the advertising gives that impression.

Ethics QUESTION

You are a marketing assistant for a large firm that recently ran a test market for Tastee DeeLites, a new brand of cookies that have less fat than your company's regular cookies. Tastee DeeLites were developed to comply with government rules for what could be called "low fat," so the ads and package used in the test market highlighted that benefit. Test-market sales were very promising. However, now a consumer activist group is sending out a chain e-mail that denounces Tastee DeeLites and your company for encouraging obesity. The e-mail complains that high calories make Tastee DeeLites even more fattening than regular cookies and that the product's name and "low fat" claim are misleading. Your boss has asked you to recommend how the firm should handle this situation. Drawing on what you've learned about consumer behavior, do you think consumers would be misled? Does your company have any responsibility to respond to these charges? Should changes be made to the product, package, or promotion?

Salud! For Better Health, Spaniards Drink Bacteria for Breakfast

During the 1990s, many European consumers began to change their relaxed approach to meals. A bustling economy led to busier lifestyles, which prompted more interest in eat-on-the-go foods. This was even true of breakfast, which for many Europeans traditionally had meant a leisurely cup of coffee and croissant. And, with more consumers entering the older age groups, there was also increased attention to healthy eating.

Marketing managers for France's Danone spotted these trends and thought the firm's Actimel yogurt might address some of these needs. Indeed, scientists had already shown that consumers who regularly drink Actimel were healthier. Yet, there were challenges. Actimel is healthy because each serving contains over 10 billion live bacteria, like the "friendly" ones in the human body, that aid digestion. Yet, most consumers didn't understand that—and drinking bacteria doesn't sound like an appealing idea. To make things worse, marketing research revealed that consumers thought that yogurts were either tasty *or* healthy—but not both! They believed that healthy yogurts had an undesirable medicinal taste.

To help change this perception, Danone developed new Actimel flavors that would delight consumers once they tried the product. Even so, some consumers lost interest when they learned that the cost of Actimel was double that of regular yogurts. On the other hand, Actimel's higher price helped to pay for heavy introductory advertising to inform more consumers about its valuable health benefits. Actimel's attention-getting ads used appeals such as "Fight the cold. Practice self-defense." Still, many doubters remained unconvinced that Actimel could either improve their health or taste good. Danone was finally able to gain more trial and change attitudes with the "Actimel Challenge." With this challenge Danone promised to give consumers their money back if they didn't like Actimel and feel better after drinking it for two weeks.

Selling Actimel at health food stores might have reinforced its premium health positioning and provided more initial sales support. But Danone wanted customers to be able to find and buy Actimel easily. So distribution focused on placing four packs in regular supermarkets and single-serve packages in convenience stores.

Over time, favorable consumer experience with this marketing mix has grown Actimel into a brand that many Europeans routinely purchase. In Spain it even outsells Coca-Cola. It has also sold well in other parts of the world, including Asia. Danone has had trouble selling its bacteria-based products in the United States. But it keeps trying. Actimel was recently launched across the United States with the name DanActive. Danone's marketers hope American culture is now ready to accept the idea of drinking "bugs" as a tasty way to be healthy.[10]

Meeting expectations is important

Attitudes and beliefs sometimes combine to form an **expectation**—an outcome or event that a person anticipates or looks forward to. Consumer expectations often focus on the benefits or value that the consumer expects from a firm's marketing mix. This is an important issue for marketers because a consumer is likely to be dissatisfied if his or her expectations are not met. Promotion that overpromises can create this problem. Finding the right balance, however, can be difficult. A few years ago, Van Heusen came up with a new way to treat its wash-and-wear shirts so that they look better when they come out of the wash. Van Heusen promoted these shirts as "wrinkle-free." The new shirt is an improvement, but consumers who expect it to look as if it had been ironed are disappointed.[11]

Personality affects how people see things

Many researchers study how personality affects people's behavior, but the results have generally been disappointing to marketers. A trait like neatness can be associated with users of certain types of products—like cleaning materials. But marketing

Dimension	Examples		
Activities	Work Hobbies Social events	Vacation Entertainment Club membership	Surfing Web Shopping Sports
Interests	Family Home Job	Community Recreation Fashion	Food Media Achievements
Opinions	Themselves Social issues Politics	Business Economics Education	Products Future Culture
Demographics	Income Age Family life cycle	Geographic area Ethnicity Dwelling	Occupation Family size Education

managers have not found a way to use personality in marketing strategy planning.[12] As a result, they've stopped focusing on personality measures borrowed from psychologists and instead developed lifestyle analysis.

Psychographics focus on activities, interests, and opinions

Psychographics or **lifestyle analysis** is the analysis of a person's day-to-day pattern of living as expressed in that person's Activities, Interests, and Opinions—sometimes referred to as AIOs. Exhibit 5–6 shows a number of variables for each of the AIO dimensions—along with some demographics used to add detail to the lifestyle profile of a target market.

Understanding the lifestyle of target customers has been especially helpful in providing ideas for advertising themes. Let's see how it adds to a typical demographic description. It may not help Toyota marketing managers much to know that an average member of the target market for a Highlander SUV is 34.8 years old, married, lives in a three-bedroom home, and has 2.3 children. Lifestyles help marketers paint a more human portrait of the target market. For example, lifestyle analysis might show that the 34.8-year-old is also a community-oriented consumer with traditional values who especially enjoys spectator sports and spends much time in other family activities. An ad might show the Highlander being used by a happy family at a ball game so the target market could really identify with the ad. And the ad might be placed on an ESPN show whose viewers match the target lifestyle profile.[13]

Marketing managers for consumer products firms who are interested in learning more about the lifestyle of a target market sometimes turn to outside specialists for help. For example, SRI Consulting Business Intelligence (SRIC-BI), a research firm, offers a service called geoVALS (VALS is an abbreviation for values, attitudes, and lifestyles). GeoVALS uses psychographics to show where customers live and why they behave as they do; it is especially useful for targeting direct-mail ad campaigns.[14]

SOCIAL INFLUENCES AFFECT CONSUMER BEHAVIOR

We've been discussing some of the ways needs, attitudes, and other psychological variables influence the buying process. Now we'll look at how a consumer's family, social class, reference groups, culture, and ethnic groups influence the consumer decision process.

Family life cycle influences needs

Relationships with other family members influence many aspects of consumer behavior. Family members may share many attitudes and values, consider each other's opinions, and divide various buying tasks. Marital status, age, and the age of any

Schwan's uses catalogs and a website (www.schwans.com) to promote food products and complete meals which it delivers directly to a consumer's home. A service like this is especially valuable to dual-career families and professionals who face a poverty of time.

children in the family have an especially important effect on how people spend their income. Put together, these dimensions tell us about the life-cycle stage of a family. Exhibit 5–7 shows a summary of stages in the family life cycle.[15]

Young people and families accept new ideas

Singles and young couples seem to be more willing to try new products and brands—and they are careful, price-conscious shoppers. Although many young people are waiting longer to marry, most tie the knot eventually. These younger families—especially those with no children—are still accumulating durable goods, such as automobiles and home furnishings. Only as children arrive and grow does family spending shift to soft goods and services, such as education, medical, and personal care. This usually happens when the family head reaches the 35–49 age group. To meet expenses, people in this age group often make more purchases on credit, and they save less of their income.

Exhibit 5–7   Stages in Modern Family Life Cycles

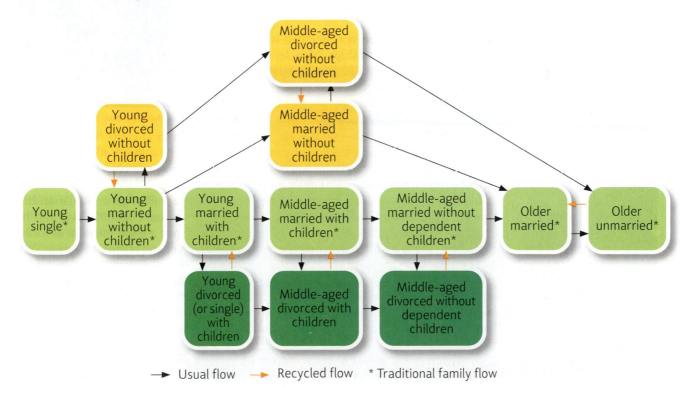

We can think of the American culture, the French culture, or the Latin American culture. People within these cultural groupings tend to be more similar in outlook and behavior. But often it is useful to think of subcultures within such groupings. For example, within the American culture, there are various religious, ethnic, and regional subcultures.

Failure to consider cultural differences, even subtle ones, can result in problems. To promote their product and get people to try it, marketers for Pepto-Bismol often provide free samples at festivals and street fairs. Their idea is that people tend to overindulge at such events. However, when they distributed sample packets at a festival in San Francisco's Chinatown, they insulted many of the people they wanted to influence. Booths with Chinese delicacies lined the streets, and many of the participants interpreted the sample packets (which featured the word "Nauseous" in large letters) as suggesting that Chinese delicacies were nauseating. The possibility of this misinterpretation may seem obvious in hindsight, but if it had been that obvious in advance the whole promotion would have been handled differently.[22]

Do ethnic groups buy differently?

America may be called the melting pot, but ethnic groups deserve special attention when analyzing markets. One basic reason is that people from different ethnic groups may be influenced by very different cultural variables. They may have quite varied needs and their own ways of thinking. Moreover, Americans value diversity and the United States is becoming a multicultural market. As a result, rather than disappearing in a melting pot, some important cultural and ethnic dimensions are being preserved and highlighted. This creates both opportunities and challenges for marketers.

Some important ethnic differences are obvious. For example, about one out of five families in the United States speaks a language other than English at home. Some areas have a much higher rate. In Miami and San Antonio, for example, about one out of three families speaks Spanish. This obviously affects promotion planning.

Stereotypes are common—and misleading

A marketer needs to study ethnic dimensions very carefully because they can be subtle and fast-changing. This is also an area where stereotyped thinking is the most common—and misleading. Many firms make the mistake of treating all consumers in a particular ethnic group as homogeneous. For example, some marketing managers treat all 40.5 million African American consumers as "the black market," ignoring the great variability among African American households on other segmenting dimensions.

Ethnic markets are becoming more important

More marketers pay attention to ethnic groups now because the number of ethnic consumers is growing at a much faster rate than the overall society. Much of this growth results from immigration. In addition, however, the median age of Asian Americans, African Americans, and Hispanics is much lower than that of whites—and the birthrate is higher. In combination, these factors have a dramatic effect.

Hispanic market is growing

Let's take a closer look at Hispanic Americans—now the largest and fastest growing ethnic group in the United States—with a median family income of $37,867. Recently, their numbers have increased at the rate of about 1 million per year. In 2010, the Hispanic population will be about 48 million and make up 15.5 percent of the total population. To put this in perspective, the Hispanic population in the United States will be almost 20 percent greater than the population of Spain and almost 40 percent greater than the population of Canada. Hispanics also provide marketing opportunities for the future because they tend to be younger than the U.S. population as a whole.

Many companies are responding to this trend. For example, many Wells Fargo branches in the Southwest have added Latin-style decor, bicultural tellers, and Spanish-language promotion, including free coloring books for Hispanic kids. Efforts such as these have significantly increased Wells Fargo's business.

Within the American culture, there are various religious, ethnic, and regional subcultures. For example, Univision's network appeals to the fast-growing Hispanic subculture, so Univision wants advertisers to know about the buying power of the Hispanic market.

Asian American market grows fast too

While there are fewer Asian Americans (about 14.2 million people and 4.2 percent of the U.S. population in 2010), the number has more than tripled since 1980. Asian Americans have the highest median family income ($68,957) of the major ethnic groups. Because of this growth and income, companies as varied as Kraft, Wal-Mart, and Allstate are targeting these consumers, especially in specific local markets where the Asian American population is concentrated.

Income and population create ethnic market buying power

The buying power of ethnic submarkets is also increasing rapidly. Estimates indicate that by the end of the decade Hispanics and African Americans will each spend nearly $1 trillion a year and Asian Americans over $500 billion a year. It's also important to marketers that much of this buying power is often concentrated in certain cities and states, which makes targeted promotion and distribution more efficient. For example, over 20 percent of San Francisco residents are Asians.

These ethnic shifts are changing the face of the American market. Already more than 36 percent of American children are African American, Hispanic, or Asian. Longer term, whites are expected to become a minority by 2050.[23]

Culture varies in international markets

Planning strategies that consider cultural differences in international markets can be even harder—and such cultures usually vary more. Each foreign market may need to be treated as a separate market with its own submarkets. Ignoring cultural differences—or assuming that they are not important—almost guarantees failure in international markets.

Consider the situation faced by marketers as they introduced Swiffer, the fast-selling wet mop, in Italy. Research showed that Italian women wash their floors four times more often than Americans. Based on that, you might predict a big success for Swiffer in Italy. Yet, many new cleaning products flop there. Fortunately, the research suggested a reason. Many Italians have negative attitudes about ad claims that a product makes cleaning *easier*. This is a popular appeal in the United States, but many Italian women doubt that something that works easily will meet their standards for cleanliness. So, for the Italian market Swiffer was modified and beeswax was added to polish floors after they have been mopped. The strategy for Cif, a popular cleaner, had a similar twist. Rather than tout the convenience of Cif as an all-purpose spray cleaner, different versions were tailored for specific cleaning tasks and the ads were changed to promote the cleaner's strength. Now both Swiffer and Cif are top sellers in Italy.[24]

INDIVIDUALS ARE AFFECTED BY THE PURCHASE SITUATION

Purchase reason can vary

Why a consumer makes a purchase can affect buying behavior. For example, a student buying a pen to take notes might pick up an inexpensive Bic. But the same student might choose a Cross pen as a gift for a friend. And a gadget-lover with some free time on his hands might buy a digital pen that transfers handwritten notes to a tablet computer—just for the fun of trying it.

Time affects what happens

Time influences a purchase situation. *When* consumers make a purchase—and the time they have available for shopping—will influence their behavior. Socializing with friends at a Starbucks induces different behavior than grabbing a quick cup of 7-Eleven coffee on the way to work.

The urgency of the need is another time-related factor. A sports buff who needs a digital video recorder with an "instant replay" feature in time for the Super Bowl—that evening—might spend an hour driving across town in heavy traffic to get the right unit. In a different circumstance, the same person might order a unit online from a website and figure that the extra time for it to be shipped is well worth the money saved.

From another point of view, how long something takes may be relative. Our online shopper might be frustrated by a Web page that takes two minutes to load and abandon his virtual shopping cart after the digital video recorder is already selected. This happens all of the time online. In contrast, you don't often see a consumer walk away from a shopping cart because of a two-minute wait in a checkout line at a store.

Surroundings affect buying too

Surroundings can affect buying behavior. The excitement at an on-site auction may stimulate impulse buying. Checking out an auction online might lead to a different response.

Surroundings may discourage buying too. For example, some people don't like to stand in a checkout line where others can see what they're buying—even if the other shoppers are complete strangers.[25]

Needs, benefits sought, attitudes, motivation, and even how a consumer selects certain products all vary depending on the purchase situation. So different purchase situations may require different marketing mixes—even when the same target market is involved.

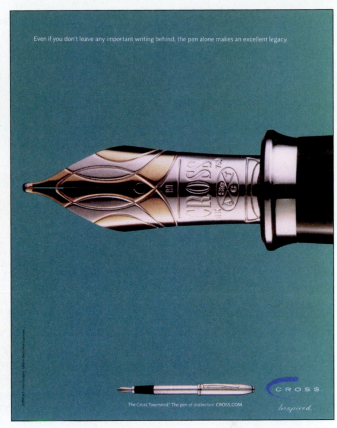

Consumer behavior varies in different situations. As the Expedia ad suggests, some people who are frugal most of the time think differently—and spend freely—while on vacation. As reflected in the ad for the Cross pen, consumers who are shopping for a gift often make different choices than they would for an everyday pen.

THE CONSUMER DECISION PROCESS

The model in Exhibit 5–2 organizes the many different influences on consumer behavior. It helps explain *why* consumers make the decisions they make. Now, we'll expand that model with a closer look at the steps in the consumer decision process and a focus on *how* consumers make decisions.[26] See Exhibit 5–8.

Recognizing a need creates a problem for the consumer

The consumer decision process begins when a consumer becomes aware of an unmet need. The consumer's problem-solving process then focuses on how best to meet that need. Problem recognition often happens quickly. A student on the way to class, for example, may realize that she's thirsty and wants something to drink. Or problem recognition may take shape over time. For example, a recent grad with a new apartment might want a comfortable place to sit while watching TV in the evening. These situations present problems that may be solved with a purchase. But what purchase should it be?

Three levels of problem solving are useful

How a consumer solves the problem depends on the situation. Exhibit 5–9 highlights the basic problem-solving steps a consumer may go through to satisfy a need. A consumer may search for information, identify alternatives and decide what factors (criteria) are important, and then evaluate one or more alternative products that might meet the need. How long this process takes or how much conscious thought a consumer gives to each step varies from product to product. It is helpful, therefore,

Exhibit 5–8 An Expanded Model of Consumer Behavior

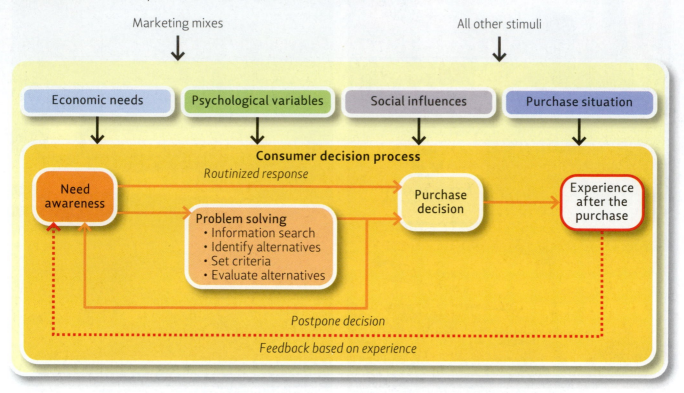

Exhibit 5–9
Consumer Problem
Solving

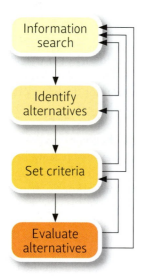

to recognize three levels of problem solving that consumers may use for any kind of product. See Exhibit 5–10.

Consumers use **extensive problem solving** when they put much effort into deciding how to satisfy a need—as is likely for a completely new purchase or to satisfy an important need. For example, an avid computer "gamer" may put a great deal of effort into buying a new gaming computer. Our gamer might solicit friends' opinions about the graphics speed and audio quality for different models before going online to compare options and prices and read technical reviews. Then, the gamer might visit a local store for a hands-on demo of a favorite game on a few computers.

Limited problem solving is used by consumers when *some* effort is required in deciding the best way to satisfy a need. This is typical when the consumer has some previous experience with a product but isn't quite sure which choice to make at the moment. A seasoned computer gamer, for instance, may already know that he likes sports games and what store has the newest releases. At the store he might get the salesperson's advice and check out the video quality on a few games before deciding which to buy. This is a deliberate purchase, but only a limited amount of effort is expended before making the decision.

A consumer uses **routinized response behavior** when he or she regularly selects a particular way of satisfying a need when it occurs. Routinized response is typical when a consumer has considerable experience in how to meet a specific need and requires no new information. For example, our gamer might automatically buy the latest version of "Madden NFL" as soon as EA Sports makes it available.

Routine response behavior is also typical for **low-involvement purchases**—purchases that have little importance or relevance for the customer. Let's face it, buying a box of salt is probably not one of the burning issues in your life.[27]

Buying isn't always rational

The idea of a decision process does *not* imply that consumers always apply *rational* processes in their buying decisions. To the contrary, consumers don't always seek

Exhibit 5-10   Problem-Solving Continuum

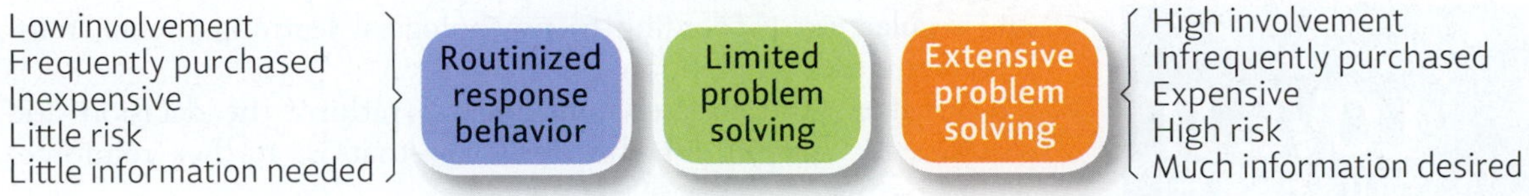

Low involvement
Frequently purchased
Inexpensive
Little risk
Little information needed
} **Routinized response behavior**   **Limited problem solving**   **Extensive problem solving** {
High involvement
Infrequently purchased
Expensive
High risk
Much information desired

accurate information or make smart choices that provide the best economic value. This is often because of the influences on consumer behavior that we discussed earlier in the chapter.

Consumers can have second thoughts after a purchase

After making a purchase, buyers often have second thoughts and wonder if they made the right choice. The resulting tension is called **dissonance**—a feeling of uncertainty about whether the correct decision was made. This may lead a customer to seek additional information to confirm the wisdom of the purchase.

Post-purchase regret is a bigger problem

Sometimes uncertainty isn't the issue. Rather the consumer is certain about being unhappy with a purchase. The disappointment of a new pair of shoes that don't fit quite right can be experienced for a long time. A consumer may regret making a purchase for a variety of reasons. But, whatever the reason, regret is not likely to lead to the same decision in the future.

Some consumers spread the word after they buy

Many consumers talk about their purchases and share opinions about their good and bad experiences. Recommendations from friends can have a big influence on whether we try a new restaurant, buy a hybrid car, or choose a different dentist. Consumers are even more likely to share stories about being dissatisfied than satisfied.

Internet EXERCISE

Go to the Best Buy website (**www.bestbuy.com**) and assume you are thinking about buying a netbook computer. Enter "netbook" into the Best Buy search tool. Look at the various resources and available netbooks. What features from Best Buy's website help guide customers through the stages of the consumer decision process in Exhibit 5–8?

The Internet gives people a forum to share their opinions with a large audience. Many people rely on such information in making purchase choices. For example, online audiobook retailer Audible.com's customers often use reviews by other listeners to help make selections. A recent study revealed that more than a fourth of Google search results on the top 20 brands link to consumer opinions. However, sometimes information posted by consumers isn't accurate—and that can be a real headache for marketers.[28]

New concepts require an adoption process

When consumers face a really new concept, their previous experience may not be relevant. These situations involve the **adoption process**—the steps individuals go through on the way to accepting or rejecting a new idea. Although the adoption process is similar to the decision-making process, learning plays a clearer role and promotion's contribution to a marketing mix is more visible.

In the adoption process, an individual moves through some fairly definite steps:

1. *Awareness*—the potential customer comes to know about the product but lacks details. The consumer may not even know how it works or what it will do.
2. *Interest*—if the consumer becomes interested, he or she will gather general information and facts about the product.
3. *Evaluation*—a consumer begins to give the product a mental trial, applying it to his or her personal situation.
4. *Trial*—the consumer may buy the product to experiment with it in use. A product that is either too expensive to try or isn't available for trial may never be adopted.

A new pomegranate and blueberry juice is probably a less familiar product for most people, so Minute Maid offers a free trial to speed the adoption process.

5. *Decision*—the consumer decides on either adoption or rejection. A satisfactory evaluation and trial may lead to adoption of the product and regular use. According to psychological learning theory, reinforcement leads to adoption.
6. *Confirmation*—the adopter continues to rethink the decision and searches for support for the decision—that is, further reinforcement.[29]

PepsiCo had to work with the adoption process when it introduced Pepsi One, a low-calorie cola. Many consumers are interested in staying trim, but diet sodas have an image of bad taste. In light of that, Pepsi's initial ads didn't directly say that Pepsi One was a diet drink. Rather, they used the slogan "True Cola Taste. One Calorie." But that confused a lot of consumers who couldn't tell what made it different from Diet Pepsi. Because awareness and interest were low among consumers, retailers didn't devote much shelf space to Pepsi One, so it often wasn't even there for a consumer to consider. Even after a year on the market, trial was low. To help more consumers through the adoption process, Pepsi made changes. New ads explained that Pepsi One used a new sweetener, that tasted better than the ones used in other diet drinks. The ads showed consumers drinking Pepsi One and not being able to taste the difference from a regular cola; they used the tagline "Too good to be one calorie, but it is." To generate more trial, Pepsi provided free samples on campuses, in office cafeterias, and at movie theaters.[30]

CONSUMER BEHAVIOR IN INTERNATIONAL MARKETS

All the influences interact—often in subtle ways

You're a consumer, so you probably have very good intuition about the many influences on consumer behavior that we've been discussing. That's good, but it's also a potential trap—especially when developing marketing mixes for consumers in international markets. The less a marketing manager knows about the *specific* social and intrapersonal variables that shape the behavior of target customers, the more likely it is that relying on intuition or personal experience will be misleading. Many specific influences do not generalize from one culture to another.

Cadbury's effort to develop a Japanese market for its Dairy Milk Chocolate candy bar illustrates the point. In marketing research, Japanese consumers said that they didn't like the high milk-fat content of Cadbury's bar. But Cadbury's managers reasoned that this was because they were not accustomed to the candy. After all, in most other countries it's the rich taste of the candy that turns consumers into "chocoholics." When Cadbury introduced the bar in Japan, it was a real flop. Taste preferences in other countries simply didn't generalize to Japan.[31]

Sometimes an understanding of local cultural influences points to new ways to blend the four Ps. For example, Nestlé knew that free samples would be a good way to kick start the adoption process when it wanted to introduce a new line of food flavorings in Brazil. In the United States, it's common to distribute samples at stores. But local Nestlé managers knew a more effective approach. In Brazil, cooks rely on stoves that run on gas rather than electricity, so local deliverymen regularly bring canisters of gas into consumers' kitchens. Nestlé paid the deliverymen to offer their customers samples of the flavoring and explain how to use them. Consumers showed more interest in the samples when the conversation usually took place right by the stove where the flavorings would be used.[32]

Watch out for stereotypes, and change

Consumers in a foreign culture may be bound by some similar cultural forces, but that doesn't mean that they are all the same. So it's important to watch out for

 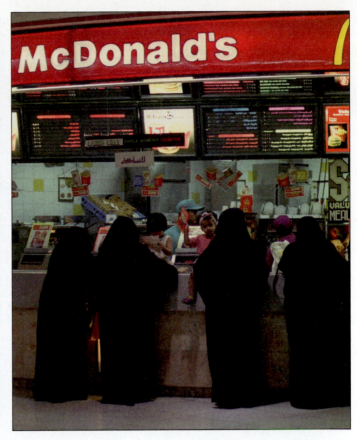

In Saudi Arabia, McDonald's modifies its marketing mix to adapt to the local culture. For example, the McDonald's in Riyadh is segregated by sex with a separate section for women and children.

oversimplifying stereotypes. Further, changes in the underlying social forces may make outdated views irrelevant.

Developing a marketing mix that really satisfies the needs of a target market takes a real understanding of consumer behavior and the varied forces that shape it. So when planning strategies for international markets, it's best to involve locals who have a better chance of understanding the experiences, attitudes, and interests of your customers.

CONCLUSION

In this chapter, we analyzed the individual consumer as a problem solver who is influenced by economic needs, psychological variables, social influences, and the purchase situation. We showed how these variables influence the consumer decision process, what the steps in that process are, and why it is important to consider these steps when planning a marketing strategy. For example, we discussed three levels of problem solving that you can use to evaluate how consumers approach different types of purchase decisions. We also discussed how the consumer's experience after the purchase impacts what that consumer will do in the future.

From a broader perspective, this chapter makes it clear that each consumer and purchase decision is somewhat unique. So, it isn't possible to catalog all of the individual possibilities. Rather, the overall focus of this chapter is to provide you with general frameworks that you can use to analyze consumers regardless of what the particular product or decision may be. This also helps you to identify the dimensions of consumer behavior that are most important for segmenting the market and developing a targeted marketing mix.

By now it should be clear that expensive marketing errors can be made when you assume that other consumers will behave in the same manner as you or your family and friends. That's why we rely on the social and behavioral sciences for insight about consumer behavior in general and why marketing research is so important to marketing managers when they are developing a marketing strategy for a particular target market. When managers understand how and why consumers behave the way they do, they are better able to develop effective marketing mixes that really meet the needs of their target market.

KEY TERMS

economic buyers, 114
economic needs, 114
discretionary income, 116
needs, 117
wants, 117
drive, 117
physiological needs, 118
safety needs, 118
social needs, 118
personal needs, 118
perception, 119
selective exposure, 119

selective perception, 119
selective retention, 119
learning, 120
cues, 120
response, 120
reinforcement, 120
attitude, 121
belief, 121
expectation, 123
psychographics, 124
lifestyle analysis, 124
empty nesters, 126

social class, 126
reference group, 127
opinion leader, 127
culture, 127
extensive problem solving, 132
limited problem solving, 132
routinized response behavior, 132
low-involvement purchases, 132
dissonance, 133
adoption process, 133

QUESTIONS AND PROBLEMS

1. In your own words, explain economic needs and how they relate to the economic-buyer model of consumer behavior. Give an example of a purchase you recently made that is consistent with the economic-buyer model. Give another that is not explained by the economic-buyer model. Explain your thinking.

2. Explain what is meant by a hierarchy of needs and provide examples of one or more products that enable you to satisfy each of the four levels of need.

3. Cut out or photocopy two recent advertisements: one full-page color ad from a magazine and one large display from a newspaper. In each case, indicate which needs the ads are appealing to.

4. Explain how an understanding of consumers' learning processes might affect marketing strategy planning. Give an example.

5. Briefly describe your own *beliefs* about the potential value of low-energy compact fluorescent lightbulbs, your *attitude* toward them, and your *intention* about buying one the next time you need to replace a bulb.

6. Give an example of a recent purchase experience in which you were dissatisfied because a firm's marketing mix did not meet your expectations. Indicate how the purchase fell short of your expectations—and also explain whether your expectations were formed based on the firm's promotion or on something else.

7. Explain psychographics and lifestyle analysis. Explain how they might be useful for planning marketing strategies to reach college students, as opposed to average consumers.

8. A supermarket chain is planning to open a number of new stores to appeal to Hispanics in southern California. Give some examples that indicate how the four Ps might be adjusted to appeal to the Hispanic subculture.

9. How should social class influences affect the planning of a new restaurant in a large city? How might the four Ps be adjusted?

10. Illustrate how the reference group concept may apply in practice by explaining how you personally are influenced by some reference group for some product. What are the implications of such behavior for marketing managers?

11. Give two examples of recent purchases where the specific purchase situation influenced your purchase decision. Briefly explain how your decision was affected.

12. Give an example of a recent purchase in which you used extensive problem solving. What sources of information did you use in making the decision?

13. On the basis of the data and analysis presented in Chapters 3 and 5, what kind of buying behavior would you expect to find for the following products: (*a*) a haircut, (*b*) a shampoo, (*c*) a digital camera, (*d*) a tennis racket, (*e*) a dress belt, (*f*) a cell phone, (*g*) life insurance, (*h*) an ice cream cone, and (*i*) a new checking account? Set up a chart for your answer with products along the left-hand margin as the row headings and the following factors as headings for the columns: (*a*) how consumers would shop

for these products, (b) how far they would travel to buy the product, (c) whether they would buy by brand, (d) whether they would compare with other products, and (e) any other factors they should consider. Insert short answers—words or phrases are satisfactory—in the various boxes. Be prepared to discuss how the answers you put in the chart would affect each product's marketing mix.

14. Review the model in Exhibit 5–2 and then reread the Apple case at the beginning of this chapter. List and briefly describe specific points in the case that illustrate the model.

15. Interview a friend or family member about two recent purchase decisions. One decision should be an important purchase, perhaps the choice of an automobile, a place to live, or a college. The second purchase should be more routine, such as a meal from a fast-food restaurant or a regularly purchased grocery item. For each purchase, ask your friend questions that will help you understand how the decision was made. Use the model in Exhibit 5–8 to guide your questions. Describe the similarities and differences between the two purchase decisions.

CREATING MARKETING PLANS

The Marketing Plan Coach software on the text website (and the optional Student CD) includes a sample marketing plan for Hillside Veterinary Clinic. Look through the "Customers" section and consider the following questions.

a. Based on the marketing plan, what do we know about the consumer behavior of the target market?

b. What additional information do you think would be helpful before developing a marketing strategy for Hillside?

SUGGESTED CASES

1. McDonald's "Seniors" Restaurant
9. Sweetest Dreams Inn
30. Eden Prairie Mills, Ltd.
3. MANU Soccer Academy
10. Taffe's Ice Land
8. Lombardi's Italian Grill
11. The Next Step

COMPUTER-AIDED PROBLEM

5. SELECTIVE PROCESSES

Submag, Inc., uses direct-mail promotion to sell magazine subscriptions. Magazine publishers pay Submag $3.12 for each new subscription. Submag's costs include the expenses of printing, addressing, and mailing each direct-mail advertisement plus the cost of using a mailing list. There are many suppliers of mailing lists, and the cost and quality of different lists vary.

Submag's marketing manager, Shandra Debose, is trying to choose between two possible mailing lists. One list has been generated from phone directories. It is less expensive than the other list, but the supplier acknowledges that about 10 percent of the names are out-of-date (addresses where people have moved away). A competing supplier offers a list of active members of professional associations. This list costs 4 cents per name more than the phone list, but only 8 percent of the addresses are out-of-date.

In addition to concerns about out-of-date names, not every consumer who receives a mailing buys a subscription. For example, *selective exposure* is a problem. Some target customers never see the offer—they just toss out junk mail without even opening the envelope. Industry studies show that this wastes about 10 percent of each mailing—although the precise percentage varies from one mailing list to another.

Selective perception influences some consumers who do open the mailing. Some are simply not interested. Others don't want to deal with a subscription service. Although the price is good,

these consumers worry that they'll never get the magazines. Submag's previous experience is that selective perception causes more than half of those who read the offer to reject it.

Of those who perceive the message as intended, many are interested. But *selective retention* can be a problem. Some people set the information aside and then forget to send in the subscription order.

Submag can mail about 25,000 pieces per week. Shandra Debose has set up a spreadsheet to help her study effects of the various relationships discussed earlier and to choose between the two mailing lists.

a. If you were Debose, which of the two lists would you buy based on the initial spreadsheet? Why?

b. For the most profitable list, what is the minimum number of items that Submag will have to mail to earn a profit of at least $3,500?

c. For an additional cost of $.01 per mailing, Submag can include a reply card that will reduce the percent of consumers who forget to send in an order (Percent Lost— Selective Retention) to 45 percent. If Submag mails 25,000 items, is it worth the additional cost to include the reply card? Explain your logic.

For additional questions related to this problem, see Exercise 5-5 in the *Learning Aid for Use with Essentials of Marketing*, 12th edition.

6

Business and Organizational Customers and Their Buying Behavior

MetoKote Corp. specializes in protective coating applications, like powder-coat and liquid paint, that other manufacturers need for the parts and equipment they make. For example, when you see John Deere agricultural, construction, or lawn and grounds-care equipment, many of the components have likely been coated (painted) in a MetoKote facility. In fact, Deere & Company and MetoKote have a close buyer–seller relationship. While Deere uses a variety of methods to identify suppliers and get competitive bids for many items it needs, it's different with MetoKote. Deere isn't going to switch to some other supplier just because other options provide cheaper coatings. MetoKote not only provides protective coatings for many John Deere products, it has built facilities right next to some Deere plants. When it's time for a component to be coated, a conveyer belt moves the part out of the John Deere plant and into the MetoKote facility. A short time later it's back—and it's green or yellow.

Deere favors this type of arrangement. It lets MetoKote's experts keep up with all of the environmental regulations and new technologies for coatings.

For a manufacturer, this type of relationship allows its facilities to be smaller and less costly to build and maintain, as the space isn't required for large spray booths. With MetoKote's facilities located nearby, newly coated parts for Deere do not have to be shipped, resulting in fewer scratches and dents—which results in higher-quality parts with less rework required.

Many people were involved in the decision to purchase coating services in this way. The responsibility for choosing vendors didn't just rest with the purchasing department but involved input from people in finance, quality control, and in some cases even the production employees.

John Deere needs high-quality protective finishes because its customers want durable, long-lasting equipment. Like John Deere, they want good value. Upholding Deere & Company's long reputation for quality service is equally as important as the company's reputation for a quality product.

For example, if a huge commercial farm in Brazil needs a repair part, workers can contact the local John Deere dealer or at any hour visit the company's website (www.deere.com) to access its online service that allows customers to learn which dealers have a needed part in inventory, check the price, and place an order for fast delivery. But helping John Deere customers and dealers earn better profits doesn't stop there.

For example, some John Deere farm equipment includes a global positioning device that tracks exactly where the equipment goes when it is plowing, seeding, or cutting. The company's GreenStar system, which can easily be moved from machine to machine, uses advanced technology to measure average farm and field yields and to facilitate documentation

of tillage practices, planting, spraying, weather, and more. For example, Deere's new cotton harvester inserts a radio frequency ID (RFID) tag as it spools a 4,750 pound bale of cotton fiber and then automatically wraps it in a plastic film. The RFID chip, combined with global positioning system (GPS) data, lets cotton processors trace the precise origin of each bale. They know, for instance, if the cotton was grown without pesticides and qualifies to be sold as organic. The plastic film eliminates the 20 percent drop in the quality of the cotton fiber that can result from water damage. Deere innovations like these can help a farmer make better management decisions, increase productivity, and provide better value to the entire operation.

To give farmers and other equipment customers better service, Deere is streamlining distribution. It is dropping dealers who don't measure up to its goals on measures such as customer satisfaction—and encouraging the dealers that remain to consolidate so that they will have economies of scale in purchasing, be able to afford more specialists in important areas like e-commerce, and be able to share inventory among multiple locations. Of course, this changes Deere's relationship with its dealers. Now Deere views them as members of a high-performance team rather than as members of the Deere family.

John Deere recognizes that different customers have different needs. For example, golf courses buy Deere equipment to maintain their fairways, roughs, greens, and sand traps. Golf course managers value the reliability and durability of Deere equipment. However, they also need a variety of operating supplies—ranging from grass seed and irrigation equipment to ball washers and chemicals. Golf course managers have many responsibilities besides purchasing, and it's time-consuming for them to have to work with many different suppliers. So, John Deere introduced its One Source service which provides golf course managers with a "one-stop shop" for the things they need—all backed by the trusted Deere name. One Source strengthens Deere's relationships with both its dealers and their golf course customers. Of course, it creates new challenges for John Deere's purchasing department. It must identify, evaluate, monitor, and recommend the suppliers for the products that golf courses need. Deere's dealers and golf course customers rely on Deere's purchasing specialists to make the right decisions, and that's part of the customer value that Deere provides. Innovative approaches to delivering customer value, such as One Source for golf courses, make Deere the supplier of choice for many business customers.[1]

BUSINESS AND ORGANIZATIONAL CUSTOMERS—A BIG OPPORTUNITY

Most people think about an individual final consumer when they hear the term *customer*. But many marketing managers aim at customers who are not final consumers. In fact, more purchases are made by businesses and other organizations than by final consumers.

Business and organizational customers are any buyers who buy for resale or to produce other goods and services. There are many different types of organizational customers, including

- *Producers of goods and services*—including manufacturers, farmers, real estate developers, hotels, banks, even doctors and lawyers.
- *Intermediaries*—wholesalers and retailers.
- *Government units*—federal agencies in the United States and other countries as well as state and local governments.
- *Nonprofit organizations*—national organizations like the Red Cross and Girl Scouts as well as local organizations like museums and churches.

As this suggests, not all organizational customers are business firms. Even so, they are sometimes loosely referred to as *business buyers, intermediate buyers,* or *industrial buyers*—and marketing managers often refer to organizational customers collectively as the "business-to-business" market, or simply, the *B2B market*.

In this chapter, we'll focus on organizational customers and their buying behavior. See Exhibit 6–1. In Chapter 5 we focused on buying by final consumers, so here we'll start by covering important ways that organizational buying tends to be different from buying by final consumers. Then, later in the chapter, we'll focus on some key differences among the specific types of organizational customers.

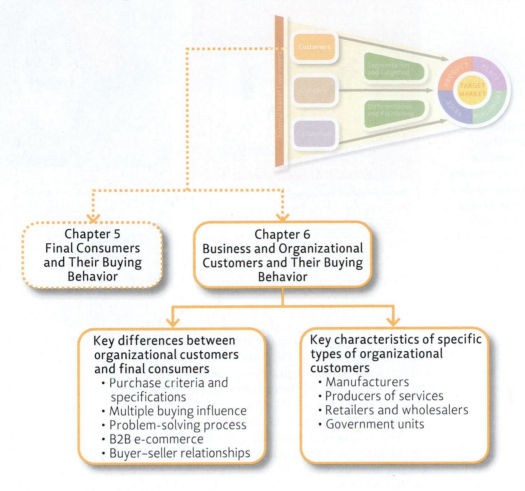

So, keep in mind that, for many firms, marketing strategy planning is about meeting the needs of organizational customers, not final consumers. A firm can target both final consumers and organizations, but different marketing mixes may be needed. As you learn about the buying behavior of organizations, think about how a firm's marketing mix may need to be different and how it may be adjusted.

ORGANIZATIONAL CUSTOMERS ARE DIFFERENT

Organizations buy for a basic purpose

Like final consumers, organizations make purchases to satisfy needs. But it's often easier to understand an organization's needs because most organizations make purchases for the same basic reason. They buy goods and services that will help them meet the demand for the goods and services that they in turn supply to their markets. In other words, their basic need is to satisfy their own customers and clients. A producer buys because it wants to earn a profit by making and selling goods or services. A wholesaler or retailer buys products it can profitably resell to its customers. A town government wants to meet its legal and social obligations to citizens.

Basic purchasing needs are economic

Organizations typically focus on economic factors when they make purchase decisions and are usually less emotional in their buying than final consumers.

Promotion to organizational buyers often focuses on economic factors. Kyocera's ad, targeted at office and information technology managers, promotes the long life and lower operating costs of its business printers. Michelin's ad, from a trade magazine for commercial trucking firms, focuses on the fuel and weight savings of its X One wide single tire.

Buyers try to consider the total cost of selecting a supplier and its particular marketing mix, not just the initial price of the product. For example, a hospital that needs a new type of digital X-ray equipment might look at both the original cost and ongoing costs, how it would affect doctor productivity, and, of course, the quality of the images it produces. The hospital might also consider the seller's reliability and its ability to provide speedy maintenance and repair.

The matter of dependability deserves further emphasis. An organization may not be able to function if purchases don't arrive when they're expected. For example, there's nothing worse to a manufacturer than shutting down a production line because sellers haven't delivered the goods. Dependable product quality is important too. For example, a bug in e-commerce software purchased by a firm might cause the firm's on-line order system to shut down. The costs of finding and correcting the problem—to say nothing about the cost of the lost business—could be much greater than the original cost of the software.

Even small differences are important

Understanding how the buying behavior of a particular organization differs from others can be very important. Even seemingly trivial differences in buying behavior may be important because success often hinges on fine-tuning the marketing mix.

Sellers often approach each organizational customer directly, usually through a sales representative. This gives the seller more chance to adjust the marketing mix for each individual customer. A seller may even develop a unique strategy for each individual customer. This approach carries target marketing to its extreme. But sellers often need unique strategies to compete for large-volume purchases.

Serving customers in international markets

Many marketers discover that there are good opportunities to serve business customers in different countries around the world. The basic approaches marketers use to deal with business customers in different parts of the world are much less varied than those required to reach individual consumers. This is probably why the shift to a global economy has been so rapid for many firms. Their business customers in different countries tend to buy in similar ways and can usually be reached with similar marketing mixes. Moreover, business customers are often willing to work with distant suppliers who have developed superior marketing mixes.

Specifications describe the need

Organizational buyers often buy on the basis of a set of **purchasing specifications**—a written (or electronic) description of what the firm wants to buy. When quality is highly standardized, as is often the case with manufactured items, the specification may simply consist of a brand name or part number. Often, however, the purchase requirements are more complicated; then the specifications may set out detailed information about the performance standards the product must meet. Purchase specifications for services tend to be detailed because services are less standardized and usually are not performed until after they're purchased.

Customers may expect quality certification

Organizational customers considering a new supplier or one from overseas may be concerned about product quality. However, this is becoming less of an obstacle because of ISO 9000. **ISO 9000** is a way for a supplier to document its quality procedures according to internationally recognized standards.

ISO 9000 assures a customer that the supplier has effective quality checks in place, without the customer having to conduct its own costly and time-consuming audit. Some customers won't buy from any supplier who doesn't have it. To get ISO 9000 certified, a company must prove to outside auditors that it documents how the company operates and who is responsible for quality every step of the way.[2]

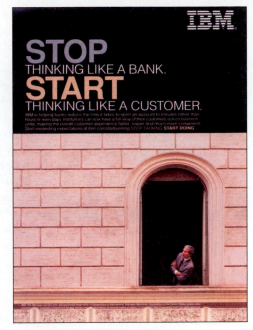

In business-to-business markets, information technology, including the Internet, is making it faster, easier, and less expensive for firms to connect with suppliers and customers. IBM is an important supplier in this area. For example, with its systems banks can open a new account in minutes rather than the hours or even days it took in the past.

MANY DIFFERENT PEOPLE MAY INFLUENCE A DECISION

Purchasing managers are specialists

Many organizations rely on specialists to ensure that purchases are handled sensibly. These specialists have different titles in different firms (such as procurement officer, supply manager, purchasing agent, or buyer), but basically they are all **purchasing managers**—buying specialists for their employers. In large organizations, they usually specialize by product area and are real experts.

Most firms look to their procurement departments to help cut costs and provide competitive advantage. In this environment, purchasing people have a lot of clout. And there are good job opportunities in purchasing for capable business graduates.

Salespeople often have to see a purchasing manager first—before they contact any other employee. These buyers hold important positions and take a dim view of sales reps who try to go around them. Rather than being "sold," these buyers want salespeople to provide accurate information that will help them buy wisely. They like information on new goods and services, and tips on potential price changes, supply shortages, and other changes in market conditions. Sometimes all it takes for a sales rep to keep a buyer up-to-date is to send an occasional e-mail. But a buyer can tell when a sales rep has the customer firm's interest at heart.

Although purchasing managers usually coordinate relationships with suppliers, other people may also play important roles in influencing the purchase decision.[3]

Multiple buying influence in a buying center

Multiple buying influence means that several people—perhaps even top management—play a part in making a purchase decision. Possible buying influences include

1. *Users*—perhaps production line workers or their supervisors.
2. *Influencers*—perhaps engineering or R&D people who help write specifications or supply information for evaluating alternatives.
3. *Buyers*—the purchasing managers who have the responsibility for working with suppliers and arranging the terms of the sale.
4. *Deciders*—the people in the organization who have the power to select or approve the supplier—often a purchasing manager but perhaps top management for larger purchases.
5. *Gatekeepers*—people who control the flow of information within the organization—perhaps a purchasing manager who shields users or other deciders. Gatekeepers can also include receptionists, secretaries, research assistants, and others who influence the flow of information about potential purchases.

An example shows how the different buying influences work. Suppose Electrolux, the Swedish firm that produces vacuum cleaners, wants to buy a machine to stamp out the various metal parts it needs. An assistant to the purchasing manager does an Internet search to identify possible vendors. However, the list that the assistant (a gatekeeper) prepares for the manager excludes a few vendors on the basis of an initial evaluation of information from their websites. The manager e-mails a description of the problem to vendors on the list. It turns out that each of them is eager to get the business and submits a proposal. Several people (influencers) at Electrolux help to evaluate the vendors' proposals. A finance manager worries about the high cost and suggests leasing the machine. The quality control people want a machine that will do a more accurate job—although it's more expensive. The production manager is interested in speed of operation. The production line workers want the machine that is easiest to use so workers can continue to rotate jobs.

The company president (the decider) asks the purchasing department to assemble all the information but retains the power to select and approve the supplier. The purchasing manager's assistant schedules visits with salespeople. After

A person who works on a utility firm's high-power wires needs safe, durable climbing gear. A number of different people may influence the decision about which gear the firm should buy.

Exhibit 6–2
Multiple Influence and
Roles in the Buying
Center

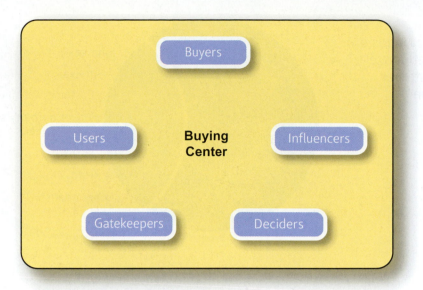

all these buying influences are considered, one of the purchasing agents for the firm (the buyer) will be responsible for making recommendations and arranging the terms of the sale.

It is helpful to think of a **buying center** as all the people who participate in or influence a purchase. Because different people may make up a buying center from one decision to the next, the salesperson must study each case carefully. Just learning who to talk with may be hard, but thinking about the various roles in the buying center can help. See Exhibit 6–2.

The salesperson may have to talk to every member of the buying center—stressing different topics for each. This not only complicates the promotion job but also lengthens it. Approval of a routine order may take anywhere from a day to several months. On very important purchases—a new building, major equipment, or a new information system—the selling period may take a year or more.[4]

Vendor analysis considers all of the influences

Considering all of the factors relevant to a purchase decision can be very complex. A supplier or product that is best in one way may not be best in others. To try to deal with these situations, many firms use **vendor analysis**—a formal rating of suppliers on all relevant areas of performance. The purpose isn't just to get a low price from the supplier on a given part or service. Rather, the goal is to lower the *total costs* associated with purchases. Analysis might show that the best vendor is the one that helps the customer reduce costs of excess inventory, retooling of equipment, or defective parts.[5]

Behavioral needs are relevant too

Vendor analysis tries to focus on economic factors, but purchasing in organizations may also involve many of the

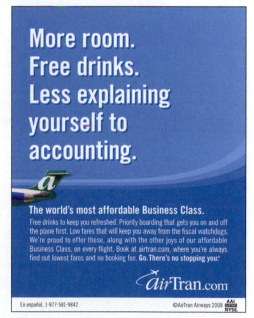

A seller's marketing mix may need to consider both the needs of the customer company as well as the needs of individuals who influence the purchase decision.

Exhibit 6–3
Overlapping Needs of Individual Influencers and the Customer Organization

Risk
Job security
Comfort
Individual's needs
Career advancement
Money/Rewards
Other needs

Overlap in needs

Innovation
Survival
Customer satisfaction
Company's needs
Growth
Profit
Other needs

same behavioral dimensions we discussed in Chapter 5. Purchasing managers and others involved in buying decisions are human, and they want friendly relationships with suppliers.

The purchasing people in some firms are eager to imitate progressive competitors or even to be the first to try new products. Such "innovators" deserve special attention when new products are being introduced.

The different people involved in purchase decisions are also human with respect to protecting their own interests and their own position in the company. That's one reason people from different departments may have different priorities in trying to influence what is purchased. Similarly, purchasing managers may want to avoid taking risks that might reflect badly on their decisions. If a new source delivers late or quality is poor, you can guess who will be blamed. Marketers who can help the buyer avoid risk have a definite appeal. In fact, this may make the difference between a successful and unsuccessful marketing mix.

A seller's marketing mix should satisfy *both* the needs of the customer company as well as the needs of individuals who influence the purchase. Therefore, sellers need to find an overlapping area where both can be satisfied. See Exhibit 6–3 for a summary of this idea.

Ethical conflicts may arise

Although organizational buyers are influenced by their own needs, most are serious professionals who are careful to avoid a conflict between their own self-interest and company outcomes. Marketers must be careful here. A salesperson who offers one of his company pens to a prospect may view the giveaway as part of the promotion effort—but the customer firm may have a policy against any employee accepting *any* gift from a supplier.

Most organizational buyers do their work ethically and expect marketers to do the same. Yet there have been highly publicized abuses. For example, the telephone company that serves New York found out that some of its buyers were giving contracts to suppliers who offered them vacation trips and other personal favors. Abuses of this sort have prompted many organizations to set up policies that prohibit a buyer or other employees from accepting anything from a potential supplier.

Marketers need to take concerns about conflict of interest very seriously. Part of the promotion job is to persuade different individuals who may influence an organization's purchase. Yet the whole marketing effort may be tainted if it even *appears* that a marketer has encouraged a person who influences a decision to put personal gain ahead of company interest.[6]

Purchasing may be centralized

If a large organization has facilities at many locations, much of the purchasing work may be done at a central location. With centralized buying, a sales rep may be able to sell to facilities all over a country—or even across several countries—without leaving a base city. Wal-Mart handles most of the purchase decisions for stores in its retail chain from its headquarters in Arkansas. Many purchasing decisions for agencies of the U.S. government are handled in Washington, D.C.

Many firms also have centralized controls on who can make purchases. A person who needs to purchase something usually completes a **requisition**—a request to buy something. This is frequently handled online to cut time and paper shuffling. Even so, there may be delays before a supervisor authorizes the requisition and a purchasing manager can select the "best" seller and turn the authorization into a purchase order. The process may take a few hours for a simple purchase—but it may turn into months for a complex purchase.

Spend management systems control purchasing

Some firms use "spend management" systems to track every single purchase. In large firms this helps the purchasing department analyze the details of who is buying what and how. Sometimes this leads to cost-cutting opportunities or better purchasing policies. Computer purchases by a college illustrate the idea. Colleges buy hundreds of computers each year, but often they're purchased one at a time by different departments. If the college documents the total spending, it can contract for better terms from preferred vendors. The college might also change its policies so that any department can quickly order a standard computer from these vendors without approval from a purchasing manager.

Eastman Chemical Co. developed Eastman Tritan, an innovative copolyester (plastic-like) material. Tritan is durable, heat resistant, and offers design flexibility and ease of processing. For example, it is ideal for the molded parts needed by kitchen appliance manufacturers. Yet, Eastman still faces a challenge. A customer firm that is making straight rebuys from a supplier it has worked with in the past may not be seeking new materials or suppliers.

From innovation blooms innovative design.

Eastman Tritan™ copolyester can empower designers and engineers with a new level of design freedom. It lets you open your mind to shapes, colors, dimensions and functional integrity that weren't possible — or practical — until now. Tritan and an open mind are sure to open new market opportunities for you.

Your challenge: Separate your products from the rest of the bunch.

Tritan is a powerful tool for enhancing existing products — or creating dramatic new solutions. Clarity, toughness, chemical resistance, easy processing, higher heat resistance and much more all help you produce superior products with lasting value.

Whatever shape your innovations take in the future, you can count on Eastman Chemical Company, a world leader in polymer technology, to help apply Tritan in the most creative and effective ways.

To see recent product applications and the latest regulatory approvals for Tritan, visit www.eastman.com/tritan or call (1) 888-321-1021 (U.S.), (31) 10 2402 888 (Europe). How will you use Tritan to transform the future?

Exhibit 6–4
Organizational Buying
Processes

Characteristics	Type of Process		
	New-Task Buying	Modified Rebuy	Straight Rebuy
Time Required	Much	Medium	Little
Multiple Influence	Much	Some	Little
Review of Suppliers	Much	Some	None
Information Needed	Much	Some	Little

ORGANIZATIONAL BUYERS ARE PROBLEM SOLVERS

Three kinds of buying processes are useful

In Chapter 5, we discussed problem solving by consumers and how it might vary from extensive problem solving to routine buying. In organizational markets, we can adapt these concepts slightly and work with three similar buying processes: a new-task buying process, a modified rebuy process, or a straight rebuy.[7] See Exhibit 6–4.

New-task buying occurs when a customer organization has a new need and wants a great deal of information. New-task buying can involve setting product specifications, evaluating sources of supply, and establishing an order routine that can be followed in the future if results are satisfactory. Multiple buying influence is common in new-task buying.

A **straight rebuy** is a routine repurchase that may have been made many times before. Buyers probably don't bother looking for new information or new sources of supply. Most of a company's small or recurring purchases are of this type—but they take only a small part of an organized buyer's time. Important purchases may be made this way too—but only after the firm has decided what procedure will be "routine."

The **modified rebuy** is the in-between process where some review of the buying situation is done—though not as much as in new-task buying. Sometimes a competitor will get lazy enjoying a straight rebuy situation. An alert marketer can turn these situations into opportunities by providing more information or a better marketing mix.

Straight rebuys often use e-commerce order systems

E-commerce computer systems *automatically* handle a large portion of straight rebuys. Buyers program decision rules that tell the computer how to order and leave the details of following through to the computer. For example, when an order comes in

Exhibit 6–5
Major Sources of
Information Used by
Organizational Buyers

	Marketing sources	Nonmarketing sources
Personal sources	• Salespeople • Others from supplier firms • Trade shows	• Buying center members • Outside business associates • Consultants and outside experts
Impersonal sources	• Advertising in trade publications • Sales literature • Sales catalogs • Web page	• Rating services • Trade associations • News publications • Product directories • Internet

Warming Up to Sustainable Purchasing

With increased attention on global warming and the environment, managers in many organizations are wondering what their responsibility should be. It's true that the first focus of most organizational buying decisions is on green—dollars, that is. However, when purchasing managers consider sustainability as part of their vendor analysis, green choices often prove to be winners.

Attention to sustainability often identifies savings that previously were not obvious. Sometimes all that is involved is a simple change from what's routine. For example, when Falconbridge Limited's aluminum smelter changed to more efficient (but more expensive) lightbulbs, it saved almost $100,000 per year in energy bills. When the Fairmont Hotel in Vancouver searched for alternative chemicals to use in its pool, it found new ones that were healthier for guests and cut costs by $2,000. Hotels everywhere cleaned up when they stopped rewashing all of their linens every day. All it took was a card in the bath that says, "If you'd like us to replace a towel with a clean one, put it on the floor." The cards cost pennies, whereas the hot water, detergent, labor, and wear on linens cost millions.

Retailers and wholesalers must be guided by what customers want; putting green products on their shelves will just rack up losses unless there's customer demand. But firms like Wal-Mart and Home Depot are advertising their sustainable choices because many consumers want them. Wal-Mart took note when in one year its customers bought 100 million eco-friendly fluorescent lightbulbs. Home Depot has more that 3,000 Eco Option products that promote energy conservation, sustainability, and clean water. Both retailers are building more energy-efficient stores and prodding their suppliers to think green by using less packaging. Cynics question their motives—because there's a benefit for retailers when packages take up less shelf space.

In California, some city governments are cooperating with energy firms to develop generators powered by ocean waves. Across the Atlantic, the mayor of London requires city agencies to buy recycled goods whenever possible. And federal agencies in the United States must buy energy-efficient PCs and monitors made without toxins that could later pollute landfills.

Some progressive firms make sustainability an essential buying criterion even if they don't see financial benefits. New Belgium Brewing Company puts sustainable values in its mission statement; that means its purchasing people select more energy efficient (but higher-priced) brew kettles, use wind-powered electricity, and build facilities that are more costly but use the latest green ideas. Many nonprofit organizations take this altruistic approach as well. It's hard to imagine the Sierra Club not having sustainability as a value when it's time to make purchases.[8]

---

that requires certain materials or parts, the computer information system automatically orders them from the appropriate suppliers, sets the delivery date, and schedules production.

When economic conditions change, buyers modify the computer instructions. If nothing unusual happens, however, the computer system continues to routinely rebuy as needs develop—electronically sending purchase orders to the regular supplier.

Obviously, it's a big deal to be selected as the major supplier that routinely receives all of a customer's electronic orders for the products you sell. Often this type of customer will be more impressed by an attractive marketing mix for a whole line of products than just a lower price for a particular order.

New-task buying requires information

Customers in a new-task buying situation are likely to seek information from a variety of sources. See Exhibit 6–5. Many of the impersonal sources are readily available online. How much information a customer collects depends on the importance of the purchase and the level of uncertainty about what choice might be best. The time and expense of searching for information may not be justified for a minor purchase. But a major purchase often involves real detective work by the buyer.

New-task buying situations provide a good opportunity for a new supplier to make inroads with a customer. With a buyer actively searching for information, the seller's promotion has a much greater chance of being noticed and having an impact. Advertising, trade show exhibits, sales brochures, and salespeople can all help build the buyer's attention, but an informative website may be essential for getting attention in the first place.[9]

Search engines—a first step to gathering information

Most purchasing managers start with an Internet search when they need to identify new suppliers, better ways to meet needs, or information to improve decisions. Buyers often rely on highly specialized search engines—like one that finds all types of steel that meet certain technical specifications and then compares delivered prices. But buyers also use general-purpose search engines like Google. A search across the whole Web can often locate off-the-shelf products that eliminate the need to buy expensive, custom-made items. For example, a firm in Saudi Arabia ordered $1,000 worth of tiny rubber grommets from Allstates Rubber & Tool, a small firm in the suburbs of Chicago. If the buyer's search hadn't located the Allstates website, the only alternative would have been to pay much more for custom-made grommets—and Allstates wouldn't have picked up a new customer.[10]

Marketing managers know that it is critical to have a website that buyers can find. That's why suppliers often pay for a sponsored link (an ad) that appears when certain keywords are included in a search. A supplier might also change its website so that it is more likely to appear high on a list of searches.

Online marketplaces connect buyers and sellers in particular industries

Online marketplace websites are another source of information that are usually specific to particular industries. At VertMarkets (www.vertmarkets.com), there are links to 68 distinct online marketplaces that cover businesses ranging from semiconductor manufacturing to food service. Online marketplaces provide some organizational buyers with "one-stop shopping"; they can keep up with industry news, identify suppliers, gather information relevant to purchases, and place orders. For sellers, marketplaces are a good way to generate new sales leads.

Buyers ask for competitive bids to compare offerings

When buyers in B2B markets have identified potential suppliers, they sometimes ask them to submit a **competitive bid**—the terms of sale offered by the supplier in response to the purchase specifications posted by a buyer. If different suppliers' quality, dependability, and delivery schedules all meet the specs, the buyer will select the low-price bid. But a creative marketer needs to look carefully at the buyer's specs—and the need—to see if other elements of the marketing mix could provide a competitive advantage.

Rather than search for suppliers, buyers sometimes post their requirements and invite qualified suppliers to submit a bid. Some firms set up or participate in a procurement website that directs suppliers to companies (or divisions of a company) that need to make purchases. These sites make it easy for suppliers to find out about the purchase needs of the organizations that sponsor the sites. This helps increase the number of suppliers competing for the business and that can drive down prices or provide more beneficial terms of sale.

For example, when the California Department of Transportation was planning $4 billion in new construction projects, it established a procurement site so that potential suppliers knew each project's requirements for submitting a competitive bid.

Reverse auctions foster price competition among suppliers

Competitive bidding has been around for a long time. However, before the Internet it was slow and inconvenient. Now, a buyer can go though multiple rounds of bidding very quickly with an online reverse auction. First, suppliers are invited to place a bid for specific goods or services. Usually the bidding focuses on price, but sometimes other terms of sale (like warranty or delivery time) are considered as well. Typically, each bid, and the supplier who made it, will be visible to all potential bidders on the auction website. An auction takes place over a period of several hours—making it fast, cost effective, and convenient for buyers looking for the lowest price. Reverse auctions work best for undifferentiated products, including products such as plastic resin, personal computers, or transportation services. Reverse auctions are less effective when the value provided to the customer comes from a complete marketing mix, not just a low price.

While reverse auctions can help buyers get lower prices, suppliers have to carefully decide how to respond. A seller who gets caught up in trying to "win" a reverse auction may bid at a price that loses money. This is what happened with stationery supplier Gartner Studios. Its competitive strength was product design, but when many of its regular customers switched to reverse auctions, suppliers with lower bid prices were getting the business. Gartner was faced with losing customers or losing money to keep them. To win with low bids and still make profits, Gartner worked to cut its own supply costs and switched production to Asia. Now, when planning a bid, Gartner has lower costs but also knows how low a bid is still profitable for the company. Gartner also pays attention to whom else is bidding. That impacts how low Gartner's bid needs to be. Many of its customers won't choose the lowest bidder if it is a supplier that has a reputation for poor quality or late delivery.[11]

What buying procedure becomes routine is critical

From the discussion above, you can see that buyers make important decisions about how to deal with one or more suppliers. At one extreme, a buyer might want to rely on competition among all available vendors to get the best price on each and every order it places. At the other extreme, it might just routinely buy from one vendor with whom it already has a good relationship. In practice, there are many important and common variations between these extremes. To better understand the variations, let's take a closer look at the benefits and limitations of different types of buyer–seller relationships.

In today's business markets, suppliers of both goods and services are working to build closer relationships with their business customers—to meet needs better and create a competitive advantage. AFLAC provides cost-effective insurance products that help companies attract and retain employees.

BUYER–SELLER RELATIONSHIPS IN BUSINESS MARKETS

Close relationships may produce mutual benefits

There are often significant benefits of a close working relationship between a supplier and a customer firm. And such relationships are becoming common. Many firms are reducing the number of suppliers with whom they work— expecting more in return from the suppliers that remain. The best relationships involve real partnerships where there's mutual trust and a long-term outlook. Closely tied firms often share tasks at lower total cost than would be possible working at arm's length.

The partnership between AlliedSignal and Betz Laboratories, for example, shows the benefits of a good relationship. A while back, Betz was just one of several suppliers that sold Allied chemicals to keep the water in its plants from gunking up pipes and rusting machinery. But Betz didn't stop at selling commodity powders. Teams of Betz experts and Allied engineers studied each plant to find places where water was being wasted. In less than a year, a team in one plant found $2.5 million in potential cost reductions. For example, by adding a few valves to recycle the water in a cooling tower, Betz was able to save 300 gallons of water a minute, which resulted in savings of over $100,000 a year and reduced environmental impact. Because of ideas like this, Allied's overall use of water treatment chemicals decreased. However, Betz sales to Allied doubled because it became Allied's sole supplier.[12]

Relationships may not make sense

Although close relationships can produce benefits, they are not always best. A long-term commitment to a partner may reduce flexibility. When competition drives down prices and spurs innovation, the customer may be better off letting suppliers compete for the business. It may not be worth the customer's investment to build a relationship for purchases that are not particularly important or made that frequently.

It may at first appear that a seller would *always* prefer to have a closer relationship with a customer, but that is not so. Some customers may place orders that are too small or require so much special attention that the relationship would never be profitable for the seller. Also, in situations where a customer doesn't want a relationship, trying to build one may cost more than it's worth.[13]

Relationships have many dimensions

Relationships are not "all or nothing" arrangements. Many firms may have a close relationship in some ways and not in others. Thus, it's useful to think about five key dimensions that help characterize most buyer–seller relationships: cooperation, information sharing, operational linkages, legal bonds, and relationship-specific adaptations. Purchasing managers for the buying firm and salespeople for the supplier usually coordinate the different dimensions of a relationship. However, as shown in Exhibit 6–6, close relationships often involve direct contacts between a number of people from other areas in both firms.[14]

Cooperation treats problems as joint responsibilities

In cooperative relationships, the buyer and seller work together to achieve both mutual and individual objectives. The two firms treat problems that arise as a joint responsibility. National Semiconductor (NS) and Siltec, a supplier of silicon wafers,

Exhibit 6–6
Key Dimensions of Relationships in Business Markets

152

CDW is a wholesaler that offers its business customers a full array of computing and technology products. CDW has an ongoing, cooperative relationship with many of its customers, but its relationship with most customers is not structured with a long-term legal bond. Rather, CDW earns the customer's trust and business by sharing information and helping the customer solve problems.

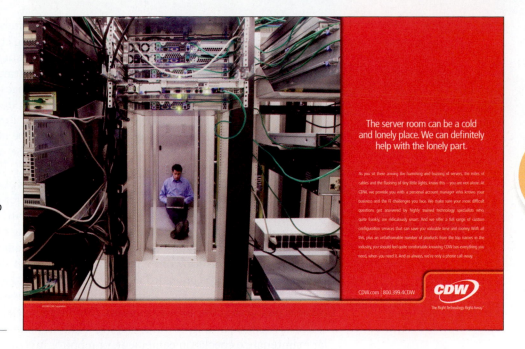

The server room can be a cold and lonely place. We can definitely help with the lonely part.

CDW.com | 800.399.4CDW

CDW
The Right Technology. Right Away.

found clever ways to cooperate and cut costs. Workers at the NS plant used to throw away the expensive plastic cassettes that Siltec uses to ship the silicon wafers. Now Siltec and NS cooperate to recycle the cassettes. This helps the environment and also saves more than $300,000 a year. Siltec passes along most of that to NS as lower prices.[15]

Shared information is useful but may be risky

Some relationships involve open sharing of information. This might include the exchange of proprietary cost data, discussion of demand forecasts, and joint work on new product designs. Information might be shared through information systems or over the Internet. This is often a key facet of relationships that involve e-commerce.

Many firms provide relationship partners with access to password-protected websites. One big advantage of this approach is that it is fast and easy to update the information. It also saves time. A customer can check detailed product specs or the status of a job on the production line without having to wait for someone to respond.

Information sharing can lead to better decisions, reduced uncertainty about the future, and better planning. However, firms don't want to share information if there's a risk that a partner might misuse it. For example, some suppliers claim that a former General Motors' purchasing chief showed blueprints of their secret technology to competing suppliers. Violations of trust in a relationship are an ethical matter and should be taken seriously.

Suppliers are sometimes reluctant to give customers bad news, but when a supplier tells a buying firm about a problem, it is possible to plan ahead—or even address the problem immediately. Edscha, a German firm that supplies sunroofs for BMW, ran into financial trouble when the economy slowed. BMW couldn't wait six months to get another supplier so it offered to help Edscha. Now BMW closely monitors the financial health of all important suppliers. That way it won't be surprised even if a supplier chooses not to share information.[16]

Marketers who ask for feedback from customers can learn how to improve and increase the value of the relationship. Good buying organizations provide regular feedback to their suppliers without being asked—and smart suppliers listen closely and respond to them. Honda, for example, provides a monthly report card that details the supplier's performance in five areas: quality, delivery, quantity delivered, performance history, and any special incidents. The report fosters an ongoing dialogue between Honda and its suppliers and makes sure both parties know how things are going.[17]

Operational linkages share functions between firms

Operational linkages are direct ties between the internal operations of the buyer and seller firms. These linkages usually involve ongoing coordination of activities between the firms. Shared activities are especially important when neither firm, working on its own, can perform a function as well as the two firms can working together.

Business customers often require operational linkages to reduce total inventory costs, maintain adequate inventory levels, and keep production lines moving. On the other hand, keeping too much inventory is expensive. Providing a customer with inventory when it's needed may require that a supplier be able to provide **just-in-time delivery**—reliably getting products there *just* before the customer needs them. We'll discuss just-in-time systems in more detail in Chapter 11. For now, it's enough to know that closer relationships between buyers and sellers involve operational linkages that lower costs and increase efficiency. Vertex Fasteners, for example, makes corrosion-resistant fasteners that are used by manufacturers in many different industries. Vertex creates value for its cost-conscious customers by working closely with a network of expert distributors. Distributors know each customer's specific needs so they can carefully label and pack orders for Vertex products in a way that saves the customer time and money when a truck is unloaded and shelves are stocked at the customer's factory.[18]

Operational linkages may also involve the routine activities of individuals who almost become part of the customer's operations. Design engineers, salespeople, and service representatives may participate in developing solutions to ongoing problems, conduct regular maintenance checks on equipment, or monitor inventory and coordinate orders.

Contracts spell out obligations

Many purchases in business markets are simple transactions. The seller's responsibility is to transfer title to goods or perform services, and the buyer's responsibility is to pay the agreed price. However, more complex relationships may be spelled out in detailed legal contracts. An agreement may apply only for a short period, but long-term contracts are also common.

For example, a customer might ask a supplier to guarantee a 6 percent price reduction for a particular part for each of the next three years and pledge to virtually eliminate defects. In return, the customer might offer to double its orders and help the supplier boost productivity.

Sometimes the buyer and seller know roughly what is needed but can't fix all the details in advance. For example, specifications or total requirements may change over time. Then the relationship may involve **negotiated contract buying**, which means agreeing to contracts that allow for changes in the purchase arrangements. In such cases, the general project and basic price is described but with provision for changes and price adjustments up or down.

Some managers figure that even a detailed contract isn't a good substitute for regular, good-faith reviews to make sure that neither party gets hurt by changing business conditions. Harley-Davidson used this approach when it moved toward closer relationships with a smaller number of suppliers. Purchasing executives tossed out detailed contracts and replaced them with a short statement of principles to guide relationships between Harley and its suppliers.

Specific adaptations invest in the relationship

Relationship-specific adaptations involve changes in a firm's product or procedures that are unique to the needs or capabilities of a relationship partner. Industrial suppliers often custom design a new product for just one customer; this may require investments in R&D or new manufacturing technologies. MetoKote, in its relationship with John Deere described at the beginning of this chapter, made a specific adaptation by building its coating plant right next door to Deere's factory.

Buying firms may also adapt to a particular supplier; Lenovo designed its ultra-mobile IdeaPad notebook to work with Intel's new Atom N270 processor. However, buyers are often hesitant about making big investments that increase dependence on a specific supplier. Typically, they do it only when there isn't a good alternative—perhaps because only one or a few suppliers are available to meet a need—or if the benefits of the investment are clear before it's made.

Specific adaptations are usually made when the buying organization chooses to **outsource**—contract with an outside firm to produce goods or services rather than to produce them internally. Many firms have turned to outsourcing to cut costs— and that's why much outsourcing is handled by suppliers in countries where labor costs are lower. For example, many American companies are outsourcing part of their customer service operations to firms in India.[19]

Powerful customer may control the relationship

Although a marketing manager may want to work in a cooperative partnership, that may be impossible with large customers who have the power to dictate how the relationship will work. For example, Duall/Wind was a supplier of small plastic parts for Polaroid. But when Duall/Wind wanted to raise its prices to cover increasing costs, Polaroid balked. Polaroid's purchasing manager demanded that Duall/Wind show a breakdown of all its costs, from materials to labor to profit. As Duall/Wind's president said, "I had a tough time getting through my head that Polaroid wanted to come right in here and have us divulge all that." But Polaroid is a big account—and it got the information it wanted. Polaroid buyers agreed to a price increase only after they were confident that Duall/Wind was doing everything possible to control costs.[20]

Buyers may still use several sources to spread their risk

Even if a marketing manager develops the best marketing mix possible and cultivates a close relationship with the customer, the customer may not give *all* of its business to one supplier. Buyers often look for several dependable sources of supply to protect themselves from unpredictable events such as strikes, fires, or floods in one of their suppliers' plants. A good marketing mix is still likely to win a larger share of the total business— which can prove to be very important. From a buyer's point of view, it may not seem like a big deal to give a particular supplier a 30 percent share of the orders rather than a 20 percent share. But for the seller that's a 50 percent increase in sales![21]

Variations in buying by customer type

We've been discussing aspects of relationships and buying approaches that generally apply with different types of customer organizations—in both the United States and internationally. However, it's also useful to have more detail about specific types of customers.

MANUFACTURERS ARE IMPORTANT CUSTOMERS

There are not many big ones

One of the most striking facts about manufacturers is how few there are compared to final consumers. This is true in every country. In the United States, for example, there are about 339,100 factories. Exhibit 6–7 shows that the majority of these are

Exhibit 6–7 Size Distribution of Manufacturing Establishments

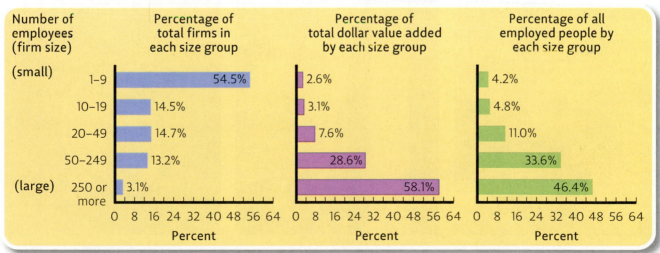

Number of employees (firm size)	Percentage of total firms in each size group	Percentage of total dollar value added by each size group	Percentage of all employed people by each size group
(small) 1–9	54.5%	2.6%	4.2%
10–19	14.5%	3.1%	4.8%
20–49	14.7%	7.6%	11.0%
50–249	13.2%	28.6%	33.6%
(large) 250 or more	3.1%	58.1%	46.4%

quite small—over half have less than 10 workers. But output from these small firms accounts for less than 3 percent of manufacturing value. In small plants, the owners often do the buying. And they buy less formally than buyers in the relatively few large manufacturing plants—which employ most of the workers and produce a large share of the value added by manufacturing. For example, only about 3 percent of all plants have 250 or more employees, yet they employ nearly half of the production workers and produce about 60 percent of the value added by manufacturers.

In other countries, the size distribution of manufacturers varies. But across different countries, the same general conclusion holds: Marketers often segment industrial markets on the basis of customer size because large firms do so much of the buying.

Customers cluster in geographic areas

In addition to concentration by company size, industrial markets are concentrated in certain geographic areas. Internationally, industrial customers are concentrated in countries that are at the more advanced stages of economic development. From all the talk in the news about the United States shifting from an industrial economy to a service and information economy, you might conclude that the United States is an exception—that the industrial market in this country is shrinking. It is true that the number of people employed in manufacturing has been shrinking, but U.S. manufacturing output is higher than at any other time in the nation's history. The rate of growth, however, is fastest in countries where labor is cheap.[22]

Within a country, there is often further concentration of manufacturing in specific areas. In the United States, many factories are concentrated in big metropolitan areas—especially in New York, Pennsylvania, Ohio, Illinois, Texas, and California. There is also concentration by industry. In Germany, for example, the steel industry is concentrated in the Ruhr Valley. Similarly, U.S. manufacturers of high-tech electronics are concentrated in California's famous Silicon Valley near San Francisco and also along Boston's Route 128.

Business data often classifies industries

The products an industrial customer needs to buy depend on the business it is in. Because of this, sales of a product are often concentrated among customers in similar businesses. For example, apparel manufacturers are the main customers for zippers. Marketing managers must focus their marketing mixes on prospective customers who exhibit characteristics similar to their current customers.

Detailed information is often available to help a marketing manager learn more about customers in different lines of business. The U.S. government collects and publishes data by the **North American Industry Classification System (NAICS) codes**—groups of firms in similar lines of business. (NAICS is pronounced like "nakes.") The number of establishments, sales volumes, and number of employees—broken down

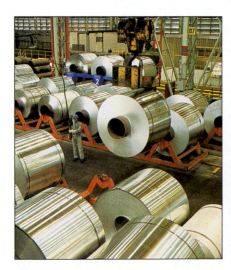  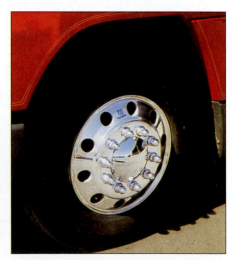

A firm like Alcoa Aluminum is likely to find that the majority of its customers are concentrated within a few industries that it can identify by North American Industry Classification System code number.

Exhibit 6–8   Illustrative NAICS Code Breakdown for Apparel Manufacturers

by geographic areas—are given for each NAICS code. A number of other countries collect similar data, and some of them try to coordinate their efforts with an international variation of the NAICS system. However, in many countries data on business customers is incomplete or inaccurate.

So let's take a closer look at how the NAICS codes work. The NAICS code breakdowns start with broad industry categories such as construction (23), manufacturing (31), retail trade (44), finance and insurance (52), and so on. See Exhibit 6–8. Within each two-digit industry breakdown, much more detailed data may be available for three-digit industries (that is, subindustries of the two-digit industries). For example, within the two-digit manufacturing industry (code 31) there are manufacturers of food (311), leather (316), and others, including apparel manufacturers (315). Then each three-digit group of firms is further subdivided into more detailed four-, five-, and six-digit classifications. For instance, within the three-digit (315) apparel manufacturers there are four-digit subgroups for knitting mills (3151), cut and sew firms (3152), and producers of apparel accessories (3159). Exhibit 6–8 illustrates that breakdowns are more detailed as you move to codes with more digits. However, detailed data (say, broken down at the four-digit level) isn't available for all industries in every geographic area. The government does not provide detail when only one or two plants are located in an area.

Many firms find their *current* customers' NAICS codes and then look at NAICS-coded lists for similar companies that may need the same goods and services. Other companies look at which NAICS categories are growing or declining to discover new opportunities.[23]

PRODUCERS OF SERVICES—SMALLER AND MORE SPREAD OUT

The service side of the U.S. economy is large and has been growing fast. Service operations are also growing in some other countries. There are many good opportunities to provide these service companies with the products they need to support their operations. But there are also challenges.

The United States has about 4.6 million service firms—over 13 times as many as it has manufacturers. Some of these are big companies with international operations. Examples include AT&T, Hilton Hotels, Prudential Insurance, and Accenture. These firms have purchasing departments that are like those in large manufacturing organizations. But as you might guess given the large number of service firms, most of them are small. They're also more spread out around the country than manufacturing concerns. Factories often locate where transportation facilities are good, raw materials are available, and it is less costly to produce goods in quantity. Service operations, in contrast, often have to be close to their customers.

Buying may not be as formal

Purchases by small service firms are often handled by whoever is in charge (or an administrative assistant). This may be a doctor, lawyer, owner of a local insurance agency, or manager of a hotel. Suppliers who usually deal with purchasing specialists in large organizations may have trouble adjusting to this market. Personal selling is still an important part of promotion, but reaching these customers in the first place often requires more advertising. And small service firms may need much more help in buying than a large corporation.

In a smaller service organization, purchases may be made by the person who is in charge rather than a person with full-time responsibility for purchasing.

Small service customers like Internet buying

Small service companies that don't attract much personal attention from salespeople often rely on e-commerce for many of their purchases. Purchases by small customers can add up—so for many suppliers these customers are an important target market. Increasingly suppliers cater to the needs of these customers with specially designed websites. A well-designed website can be efficient for both customers and suppliers. Customers can get information, place orders, or follow up with a call or e-mail for personal attention from a salesperson or customer service rep when it's needed.

RETAILERS AND WHOLESALERS BUY FOR THEIR CUSTOMERS

Most retail and wholesale buyers see themselves as purchasing agents for their target customers—remembering the old saying that "Goods well bought are half sold." Typically, retailers do *not* see themselves as sales agents for particular manufacturers. They buy what they think they can profitably sell. For example, the buying specialist at Walgreens Drugstores who handles products targeted at ethnic consumers is a real expert. He knows what ethnic customers want and won't be persuaded by a sales rep for a manufacturer who can't provide it. Of course, there is a place for collaboration, as when the Walgreens buyer works with people at Soft Sheen Products to develop a new product for the African American target market. That's profitable for both firms.

Committee buying is impersonal

Space in retail stores is limited, and buyers for retail chains simply are not interested in carrying every product that some salesperson wants them to sell. In an average week, 150 to 250 new items are offered to the buying offices of a large chain like Safeway. If the chain accepted all of them, it would add 10,000 new items during a single year! Obviously, these firms need a way to deal with this overload.

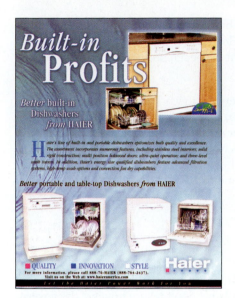

Firms that partner with retailers to reach final consumers often must work with retail buying specialists. Retail buying specialists for Lowe's buy Haier products because they think the retailer can profitably resell them to its customers.

The entrepreneurs who started PenAgain, for example, had to have more than a unique product to get shelf space at Wal-Mart. Their presentation to Wal-Mart had to include hard data that showed their marketing mix was already working well in other retail stores and evidence of their ability to supply the large quantities a retailer the size of Wal-Mart would need.[24]

Decisions to add or drop lines or change buying policies may be handled by a *buying committee*. The seller still calls on and gives a pitch to a buyer—but the buyer does not have final responsibility. Instead, the buyer prepares forms summarizing proposals for new products and passes them on to the committee for evaluation. The seller may not get to present her story to the buying committee in person. This rational, almost cold-blooded approach certainly reduces the impact of a persuasive salesperson. On the other hand, it may favor a firm that has hard data on how its whole marketing mix will help the retailer to attract and keep customers.

Buyers watch computer output closely

Most firms use computerized inventory replenishment systems. Scanners at retail checkout counters keep track of what goes out the door—and computers use this data to update the records. Even small retailers and wholesalers use automated control systems that create daily reports showing sales of every product. Buyers with this kind of information know, in detail, the profitability of the different competing products. If a product isn't moving, the retailer isn't likely to be impressed by a salesperson's request for more in-store attention or added shelf space.

Reorders are straight rebuys

Retailers and wholesalers usually carry a large number of products. A drug wholesaler, for example, may carry up to 125,000 products. Because they deal with so many products, most intermediaries buy their products on a routine, automatic reorder basis—straight rebuys—once they make the initial decision to stock specific items. Automatic computer ordering is a natural outgrowth of computerized checkout systems. Sellers to these markets must understand the size of the buyer's job and have something useful to say and do when they call.

Some are not "open to buy"

Retail buyers are sometimes controlled by a miniature profit and loss statement for each department or merchandise line. In an effort to make a profit, the buyer tries to forecast sales, merchandise costs, and expenses. The figure for "cost of merchandise" is the amount buyers have budgeted to spend over the budget period. If the money has not yet been spent, buyers are **open to buy**—that is, the buyers have budgeted funds that can be spent during the current period. However, if the budget has been spent, they are no longer in the market and no amount of special promotion or price-cutting is likely to induce them to buy.

Resident buyers may help a firm's buyers

Resident buyers are independent buying agents who work in central markets (New York City, Paris, Rome, Hong Kong, Chicago, Los Angeles) for several retailer or wholesaler customers based in outlying areas or other countries. They buy new styles and fashions and fill-in items as their customers run out of stock during the year.

Resident buying organizations fill a need. They help small channel members (producers and intermediaries) reach each other inexpensively. Resident buyers usually are paid an annual fee based on their purchases.

THE GOVERNMENT MARKET

Size and diversity

Some marketers ignore the government market because they think that government red tape is more trouble than it's worth. They probably don't realize how big the government market really is. Government is the largest customer group in many countries—including the United States. About 30 percent of the U.S. gross domestic product is spent by various government units; the figure is much higher in some economies. Different government units in the United States buy almost every kind of product. They run not only schools, police departments, and military organizations, but also supermarkets, public utilities, research laboratories, offices, hospitals, and even liquor stores. These huge government expenditures cannot be ignored by an aggressive marketing manager.

Competitive bids may be required

Government buyers in the United States are expected to spend money wisely—in the public interest—so their purchases are usually subject to much public review. To avoid charges of favoritism, most government customers buy by specification using a mandatory bidding procedure. Often the government buyer must accept the lowest bid that meets the specifications. You can see how important it is for the buyer to write precise and complete specifications. Otherwise, sellers may submit a bid that fits the specs but doesn't really match what is needed. By law, a government unit might have to accept the lowest bid—even for an unwanted product.

Writing specifications is not easy—and buyers usually appreciate the help of well-informed salespeople. Salespeople *want* to have input on the specifications so their product can be considered or even have an advantage. A contract can be landed without the lowest bid when lower bids don't meet minimum or requested specifications.

Rigged specs are an ethical concern

At the extreme, a government customer who wants a specific brand or supplier may try to write the description so that no other supplier can meet all the specs. The buyer may have good reasons for such preferences—a more reliable product, prompt delivery, or better service after the sale. This kind of loyalty sounds great, but marketers must be sensitive to the ethical issues involved. Laws that require government customers to get bids are intended to increase competition among suppliers, not reduce it. Specs that are written primarily to defeat the purpose of these laws may be viewed as illegal bid rigging.

The approved supplier list

Specification and bidding difficulties aren't problems in all government orders. Items that are bought frequently—or for which there are widely accepted standards—are purchased routinely. The government unit simply places an order at a previously approved price. To share in this business, a supplier must be on the list of approved suppliers and agree on a price that will stay the same for a specific period—perhaps a year.

Negotiated contracts are common too

Negotiation is often necessary when there are many intangible factors. Unfortunately, this is exactly where favoritism and influence can slip in. And such influence is not unknown—especially in city and state government. Nevertheless, negotiation is an important buying method in government sales—so a marketing mix should emphasize more than just low price.[25]

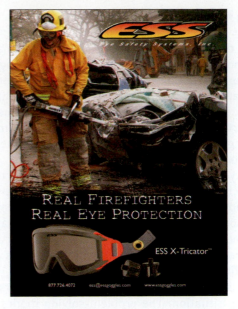

Government agencies are important customers for a wide variety of products.

Learning what government wants

In the United States, there are more than 87,575 local government units (school districts, cities, counties, and states) as well as many federal agencies that make purchases. Keeping on top of all of them is nearly impossible. Potential suppliers should focus on the government units they want to cater to and learn the bidding methods of those units. Then it's easier to stay informed since most government contracts are advertised. Target marketing can make a big contribution here—making sure the marketing mixes are well matched with the different bid procedures.

A marketer can learn a lot about potential government target markets from various government publications and by using the Internet. For example, the General Services Administration handles vendor contracts for off-the-shelf goods and services; information for vendors is available at www.gsa.gov. There is an online resource center for government contracting at www.govcon.com. The Small Business Administration (www.sba.gov) offers many resources, including the U.S. *Purchasing, Specifications, and Sales Directory*. It explains government procedures to encourage competition for such business. Various state and local governments also offer guidance, as do government units in many other countries.

Dealing with foreign governments

Selling to government units in foreign countries can be a real challenge. In many cases, a firm must get permission from the government in its own country to sell to a foreign government. Moreover, most government contracts favor domestic suppliers if they are available. Even if such favoritism is not explicit, public sentiment may make it very difficult for a foreign competitor to get a contract. Or the government bureaucracy may simply bury a foreign supplier in so much red tape that there's no way to win.

Is it unethical to "buy help"?

In some countries, government officials expect small payments (grease money) just to speed up processing of routine paperwork, inspections, or decisions from the local bureaucracy. Outright influence peddling—where government officials or their friends request bribe money to sway a purchase decision—is common in some markets. In the past, marketers from some countries have looked at such bribes as a cost of doing business. However, the **Foreign Corrupt Practices Act**, passed by the U.S. Congress in 1977, prohibits U.S. firms from paying bribes to foreign officials. A person who pays bribes, or authorizes an agent to pay them, can face stiff penalties. However, the law was amended in 1988 to allow small grease money payments if they are customary in a local culture. Further, a manager isn't held responsible if an agent in the foreign country secretly pays bribes. More recently, the Sarbanes-Oxley Act of 2002 makes individual executives responsible for their company's financial disclosures; and a bribe mischaracterized as a legitimate expense may violate the law. Managers need to be careful and up-front about such payments or risk being on the wrong side of these laws.[26]

CONCLUSION

In this chapter, we examined organizational buying and how it differs from final consumer buying. We saw that organizational buyers rely heavily on economic factors and cost–benefit analysis to make purchase decisions. The chapter showed how multiple influences are important in buying decisions—and how marketing managers must recognize and attend to the needs of all members of the buying center.

Buying behavior—and marketing opportunities—may change when there's a close relationship between a supplier and a customer. However, close relationships are not all or nothing. There are different ways that a supplier can build close relationships with its customers. We identified key dimensions of relationships and their benefits and limitations.

This chapter also showed how buying differs with the buying situation. The problem-solving modes used by final consumers and discussed in Chapter 5 also apply here—with some modification.

E-commerce plays a key role in organizational buying and B2B marketing. We discussed some of the different ways that these technologies are being used.

We saw that organizational buyers buy for resale or to produce other goods and services—and include manufacturers, farms, distributors, retailers, government agencies, and nonprofit organizations. There are many similarities in how these organizations buy—but also differences. The chapter concludes by providing insights about buying practices particular to manufacturers, service firms, and governments.

Understanding how organizations buy can help marketing managers identify logical dimensions for segmenting markets and developing marketing mixes. But the nature of products being offered may require further adjustments in the mix. Different product classes are discussed in Chapter 8. Variations by product may provide additional segmenting dimensions to help a marketing manager fine-tune a marketing strategy.

KEY TERMS

business and organizational customers, 140
purchasing specifications, 143
ISO 9000, 143
purchasing managers, 143
multiple buying influence, 144
buying center, 145

vendor analysis, 145
requisition, 147
new-task buying, 148
straight rebuy, 148
modified rebuy, 148
competitive bid, 150
just-in-time delivery, 154

negotiated contract buying, 154
outsource, 155
North American Industry Classification System (NAICS) codes, 156
open to buy, 160
resident buyers, 160
Foreign Corrupt Practices Act, 161

QUESTIONS AND PROBLEMS

1. In your own words, explain how buying behavior of business customers in different countries may have been a factor in speeding the spread of international marketing.

2. Compare and contrast the buying behavior of final consumers and organizational buyers. In what ways are they most similar and in what ways are they most different?

3. Briefly discuss why a marketing manager should think about who is likely to be involved in the buying center for a particular purchase. Is the buying center idea useful in consumer buying? Explain your answer.

4. If a nonprofit hospital were planning to buy expensive MRI scanning equipment (to detect tumors), who might be involved in the buying center? Explain your answer and describe the types of influence that different people might have.

5. Describe the situations that would lead to the use of the three different buying processes for a particular product—lightweight bumpers for a pickup truck.

6. Why would an organizational buyer want to get competitive bids? What are some of the situations when competitive bidding can't be used?

7. How likely would each of the following be to use competitive bids? (a) a small town that needed a road resurfaced, (b) a scouting organization that needed a printer to print its scouting handbook, (c) a hardware retailer that wants to add a new lawn mower line, (d) a grocery store chain that wants to install new checkout scanners, and (e) a sorority that wants to buy a computer to keep track of member dues. Explain your answers.

8. Discuss the advantages and disadvantages of just-in-time supply relationships from an organizational buyer's point of view. Are the advantages and disadvantages merely reversed from the seller's point of view?

9. Explain why a customer might be willing to work more cooperatively with a small number of suppliers rather than pitting suppliers in a competition against each other. Give an example that illustrates your points.

10. Would a tool manufacturer need a different marketing strategy for a big retail chain like Home Depot than for a single hardware store run by its owner? Discuss your answer.

11. How do you think a furniture manufacturer's buying habits and practices would be affected by the specific type of product to be purchased? Consider fabric for upholstered furniture, a lathe for the production line, cardboard for shipping cartons, and lubricants for production machinery.

12. Discuss the importance of target marketing when analyzing organizational markets. How easy is it to isolate homogeneous market segments in these markets?

13. Explain how NAICS codes might be helpful in evaluating and understanding business markets. Give an example.

14. Considering the nature of retail buying, outline the basic ingredients of promotion to retail buyers. Does it make any difference what kinds of products are involved? Are any other factors relevant?

15. The government market is obviously an extremely large one, yet it is often slighted or even ignored by many firms. Red tape is certainly one reason, but there are others. Discuss the situation and be sure to include the possibility of segmenting in your analysis.

16. Some critics argue that the Foreign Corrupt Practices Act puts U.S. businesses at a disadvantage when competing in foreign markets with suppliers from other countries that do not have similar laws. Do you think that this is a reasonable criticism? Explain your answer.

CREATING MARKETING PLANS

The Marketing Plan Coach software on the text website (and on the optional Student CD) includes a sample marketing plan for Hillside Veterinary Clinic. Hillside decided to focus on final consumers and their pets rather than include organizational customers that might need veterinary care for animals. Such customers might range from dog breeders and farmers to animal protection shelters and law enforcement agencies that work with dogs. Would it be easy or hard for Hillside to expand its focus to serve customers who are not final consumers? Explain your thinking.

SUGGESTED CASES   5. PolyTech Products   6. Global Steel Company

COMPUTER-AIDED PROBLEM

6. VENDOR ANALYSIS

CompuTech, Inc., makes circuit boards for microcomputers. It is evaluating two possible suppliers of electronic memory chips.

The chips do the same job. Although manufacturing quality has been improving, some chips are always defective. Both suppliers will replace defective chips. But the only practical way to test for a defective chip is to assemble a circuit board and "burn it in"—run it and see if it works. When one chip on a board is defective at that point, it costs $2.00 for the extra labor time to replace it. Supplier 1 guarantees a chip failure rate of not more than 1 per 100 (that is, a defect rate of 1 percent). The second supplier's 2 percent defective rate is higher, but its price is lower.

Supplier 1 has been able to improve its quality because it uses a heavier plastic case to hold the chip. The only disadvantage of the heavier case is that it requires CompuTech to use a connector that is somewhat more expensive.

Transportation costs are added to the price quoted by either supplier, but Supplier 2 is further away so transportation costs are higher. And because of the distance, delays in supplies reaching CompuTech are sometimes a problem. To ensure that a sufficient supply is on hand to keep production going, CompuTech must maintain a backup inventory—and this increases inventory costs. CompuTech figures inventory costs—the expenses of finance and storage—as a percentage of the total order cost.

To make its vendor analysis easier, CompuTech's purchasing agent has entered data about the two suppliers on a spreadsheet. He based his estimates on the quantity he thinks he will need over a full year.

a. Based on the results shown in the initial spreadsheet, which supplier do you think CompuTech should select? Why?

b. CompuTech estimates it will need 100,000 chips a year if sales go as expected. But if sales are slow, fewer chips will be needed. This isn't an issue with Supplier 2; its price is the same at any quantity. However, Supplier 1's price per chip will be $1.95 if CompuTech buys less than 90,000 during the year. If CompuTech only needs 84,500 chips, which supplier would be more economical? Why?

c. If the actual purchase quantity will be 84,500 and Supplier 1's price is $1.95, what is the highest price at which Supplier 2 will still be the lower-cost vendor for CompuTech? (Hint: You can enter various prices for Supplier 2 in the spreadsheet—or use the analysis feature to vary Supplier 2's price and display the total costs for both vendors.)

For additional questions related to this problem, see Exercise 6-3 in the *Learning Aid for Use with Essentials of Marketing*, 12th edition.

7

CHAPTER

Improving Decisions with Marketing Information

When you see the array of products—strips, gels, swabs, and more—on drugstore shelves to make your smile whiter and brighter, it's easy to forget that just a few years ago this category of products—for a combination of oral care and beauty needs—didn't exist. Movie stars would pay Hollywood dentists thousands of dollars for special whitening treatments, but the rest of us would just envy their pearly smiles.

That changed after research convinced marketing managers for Crest oral care products that this unmet need was a big opportunity. A variety of marketing research firms, including National Opinion Research and Semaphore, helped with the research. For example, focus group interviews suggested that consumers would be excited about a do-it-yourself whitening treatment that was effective, simple to use, and affordable. Responses by representative samples of consumers to survey questionnaires confirmed that this was a large market. Online product concept tests revealed that there would be demand even at a price around $50, which would cover development and introductory promotion costs. On the other hand, research also revealed that dentists, who are influential in recommending oral care products, were concerned that the product might eat into their business.

When the R&D people came up with the idea of using a clear, tape-like strip that works by sticking to the teeth, product effectiveness tests confirmed that consumers could see a difference in whiteness. Research also showed that 30 minutes was the consumer limit for wearing the strips. Research even helped in selecting a brand name, Crest Whitestrips, and in focusing the positioning with advertising copy on "easy to use" and "superior whitening versus toothpaste" benefits.

Rather than work with traditional test markets in retail stores, marketing managers used infomercials and ads in consumer magazines to explain the product and direct consumers to a website (www.whitestrips.com) where they could buy Whitestrips. That approach not only produced sales quickly but also showed retailers that there was strong demand, even at a $44 retail price. Moreover, by doing studies on the Internet, researchers were able to deliver consumer test market input to marketing managers within days. For example, when researchers found that 80 percent of customers were female rather than the 50/50 split of men and women that was expected, the ad agency refined the focus of the advertising media.

When Whitestrips went into national distribution, the new product launch was one of the most successful in 20 years. Within a year, sales of Whitestrips surpassed $200 million and the product became the category leader. A professional version of Whitestrips for dentists to sell contributed to this success. Some dentists reported that the strips even helped increase interest in other types of cosmetic dentistry.

Crest soon faced competition from entries such as Mentadent's Tooth Whitening System and Colgate's Simply White, which was half the price of Whitestrips. Although more consumers were buying whiteners, data from Information Resources, Inc., showed that Whitestrips' market share was slipping. Consumer research also showed that customers wanted more convenience, so Crest fought back with new products. One was a premium version of Whitestrips that works in half the time. Another was Crest Night Effects—a lower-price product that is dabbed on the teeth and worn while sleeping. Many retailers took shelf space away from Mentadent to stock all three of Crest's whitening products. They could see in their routine sales analysis reports that Mentadent was losing sales to both Colgate and Crest.

Crest also switched its promotion to attract new customers. Although early adopters had wanted scientific evidence of the effectiveness of whiteners, research revealed that consumers adopting the product later were more focused on what other people thought. So Crest developed advertising that urged consumers to try Whitestrips for special social occasions, like a wedding or college reunion.

Efforts such as these were successful in generating sales growth for Crest—and competitors had successes of their own. But, when the marketing information system showed that sales of Whitestrips were falling again—as were sales of competing whitening products—marketing managers knew that it was time to work on a different problem—how to attract different segments of customers than those who had been the first to adopt whiteners. Research on different segments of the oral care market identified one segment of busy customers who liked the idea of whiter teeth, but didn't want to spend the 30 minutes needed to use the product. For these customers Crest developed Whitestrips Daily Multicare. It only takes a single five-minute a day application. Research also uncovered a segment of women who were not persuaded by previous Whitestrips promotion that used a vanity appeal. These women were interested as much in health benefits as appearance benefits. For this segment Crest created Whitestrips Daily Whitening Plus Tartar Protection and emphasized both benefits in its promotion to this target group. These new strategies reinvigorated Whitestrips sales in the U.S. market—and sales are again growing at more than 10 percent per year. Crest has even greater hopes for Whitestrips in the fast-growing Chinese market, where it already has a 25 percent share of toothpaste sales.[1]

EFFECTIVE MARKETING REQUIRES GOOD INFORMATION

Information is a bridge to the market

To make good marketing decisions, managers need accurate information about what is happening in the market. They usually can't get all of the information that they'd like, but part of their job is to find cost-effective ways to get the information that they really must have.

In this chapter, we'll focus on the two key sources that marketing managers turn to for information to make better decisions. One source is **marketing research**—procedures that develop and analyze new information about a market. Marketing research may involve use of questionnaires, interviews with customers, experiments, and many other approaches. But most marketing managers have some information needs that would take too long, or cost too much, to address with one-at-a-time marketing research projects. So, in many companies, marketing managers also routinely get help from a **marketing information system (MIS)**—which is an organized way of continually gathering, accessing, and analyzing information that marketing managers need to make ongoing decisions.

Marketing managers may need marketing research, an MIS, or a combination of both to get the information they need to make decisions during any step in the marketing strategy planning process—or to improve implementation and control. See Exhibit 7–1. In this chapter, we'll discuss ways to make marketing research and an MIS more useful, and the key issues that marketing managers face in using them.

Success requires cooperation with specialists

Most large companies have a separate marketing research department to plan and manage research projects. People in these departments usually rely on outside specialists—like interviewing and tabulating services—to carry out the work on particular projects. Further, they may call in specialized marketing consultants and marketing research organizations to take charge of a whole project.

Smaller companies usually don't have separate marketing research departments. They often depend on their salespeople or managers to conduct what research they do.

Exhibit 7–1   Marketing Information Inputs to Marketing Strategy Planning Decisions

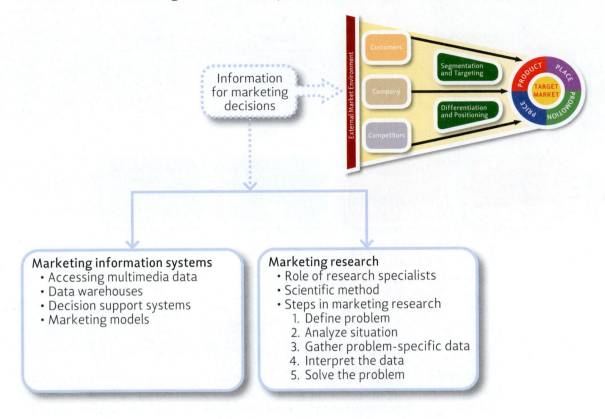

Marketing information systems
- Accessing multimedia data
- Data warehouses
- Decision support systems
- Marketing models

Marketing research
- Role of research specialists
- Scientific method
- Steps in marketing research
  1. Define problem
  2. Analyze situation
  3. Gather problem-specific data
  4. Interpret the data
  5. Solve the problem

Some nonprofit organizations have begun to use marketing research—usually with the help of outside specialists. For example, there are research firms that specialize in conducting marketing research for colleges, museums, and politicians.

Most companies also have a separate department with information technology specialists to help set up and maintain an MIS. Even small firms may have a person who handles all of the technical work on its computer systems. Increasingly, both small and large firms are turning to outside consultants and service providers for help with information systems. As we will discuss, collaboration and good communication between the marketing manager and these internal and external technical specialists is sometimes a challenge.

CHANGES ARE UNDER WAY IN MARKETING INFORMATION SYSTEMS

Marketing managers for some companies make decisions based almost totally on their own judgment—with very little hard data. The manager may not even know that he or she is about to make the same mistake that the previous person in that job already made! When it's time to make a decision, they may wish they had more information. But by then it's too late, so they do without.

MIS makes information available and accessible

Many firms realize that it doesn't pay to wait until you have important questions you can't answer. They anticipate the information they will need. They work to develop a *continual flow of information* that is available and quickly accessible from an MIS when it's needed.

We won't cover all of the technical details of planning for an MIS. But you should understand what an MIS is so you know some of the possibilities. We'll be discussing the elements of a complete MIS as shown in Exhibit 7–2. As part of that review, we'll highlight how technology is changing MIS use.

Exhibit 7-2 Elements of a Complete Marketing Information System

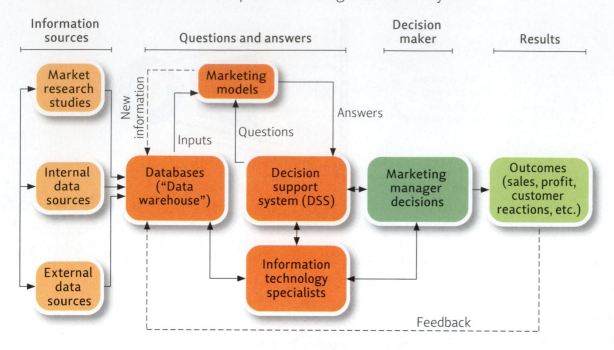

Information sources | Questions and answers | Decision maker | Results

- Market research studies
- Internal data sources
- External data sources

New information

Inputs → Databases ("Data warehouse")

Marketing models

Questions / Answers

Decision support system (DSS)

Marketing manager decisions

Outcomes (sales, profit, customer reactions, etc.)

Information technology specialists

Feedback

Get more information—faster and easier

Advances in information technology have ushered in *radical* improvements in marketing information systems. Now it's easy to set up and use an MIS and exchange data among remote computers. Managers have access to much more information. It's instantly available, and often just a mouse click away.

The *type* of information available is also changing dramatically. Until recently, marketing managers relied on computers mainly for number crunching. The multimedia revolution in computing lifted that limitation. Now it doesn't matter whether marketing information takes the form of a report, spreadsheet, database, presentation, photo, graphic, video, or table of statistics. It is all being created on computer. So it can be easily stored and accessed by computer. When we talk about a "database" of marketing information, it may include all types of information, not just numbers.

An intranet is easy to update

Many firms, even very small ones, have their own **intranet**—a system for linking computers within a company. An intranet works like the Internet. However, to maintain security, access to websites or data on an intranet is usually limited to employees. Even so, information is available on demand. Further, it's a simple matter to "publish" new information to a website as soon as it becomes available.

You seldom have all the information you need. Both customers and competitors can be unpredictable. Getting the precise information you want may cost too much or take too long. For example,

Development of powerful intranets and computer software makes it easier and less expensive for companies to gather and analyze marketing information.

data on international markets is often incomplete, outdated, or difficult to obtain. So a manager often must decide what information is really critical and how to get it.

Marketing managers must help develop an MIS

In some companies, an MIS is set up by a person or group that provides *all* departments in the firm with information technology support. Or it may be set up by marketing specialists.

These specialists are important, but the marketing manager should play an important role, too. Marketing managers know what data they've routinely used or needed in the past. They can also foresee what types of data might be useful. They should communicate these needs to the specialists so the information will be there when they want it and in the form they want it.

Decision support systems put managers online

An MIS system organizes incoming information into a **data warehouse**—a place where databases are stored so that they are available when needed. You can think of a data warehouse as an electronic library, where all of the information is indexed extremely well. Firms with an MIS often have information technology specialists who help managers get specialized reports and output from the warehouse. However, to get better decisions, most MIS systems now provide marketing managers with a decision support system. A **decision support system (DSS)** is a computer program that makes it easy for a marketing manager to get and use information *as he or she is making decisions*.

A decision support system usually involves some sort of **search engine**—a computer program that helps a marketing manager find information that is needed. For example, a manager who wants sales data for the previous week or day might search for any database or computer file that references the term *unit sales* as well as the relevant data. The search engine would identify any files where that term appeared. If there were many, the manager could narrow the search further (say by specifying the product of interest).

When the search is focused on numerical data, simply finding the information may not go far enough. Thus, a DSS typically helps change raw data—like product sales for the previous day—into more *useful information*. For example, it may draw graphs to show relationships in data—perhaps comparing yesterday's sales to the sales on the same day in the last four weeks.

Marketing dashboards monitor the market

At Verizon Communications, marketing managers' computers display a "marketing dashboard." Like the speedometer and fuel gauge on a car, a **marketing dashboard** displays up-to-the-minute marketing data in an easy-to-read format. A marketing dashboard is usually customized to a manager's areas of responsibility. A Verizon dashboard might show the percentage of customer calls dropped by cell towers, the number and location of repair trucks in the field, or the number of callers "on hold" waiting for customer service help. With early warning about potential problems, the manager can quickly make corrections. For example, a manager might call in extra customer service help if too many customers are "on hold."

Some decision support systems go even further. They allow a manager to see how answers to questions might change in various situations. For example, a manager at Home Depot may want to decide whether to use radio advertising or newspaper inserts to stimulate paint sales in a particular store or market area. The Home Depot MIS has data on sales by product and store over time, as well as data on spending for different types of promotion by market. Drawing on data showing how a promotion worked in the past, the DSS will make sale estimates using a marketing model. A **marketing model** is a statement of relationships among marketing variables. The manager can look at the sales (and costs) expected with different types of promotion and select the marketing mix that is best for that target market.[2]

In short, the decision support system puts managers online so they can study available data and make better marketing decisions—faster.[3]

If marketing managers don't plan ahead, they often don't have the information they need to make good decisions. Even with advance planning, it takes collaboration and good communication between the research specialist and the marketing manager to be certain that information is cost effective and on target.

Information for planning, implementation, and control

Once marketing managers use an MIS—and perhaps a DSS—they are eager for more information. They realize that they can improve all aspects of their planning—blending individual Ps, combining the four Ps into mixes, and developing and selecting plans. Further, they can monitor the implementation of current plans, comparing results against plans and making necessary changes more quickly. For example, LensCrafters is the sales leader in optical retailing. Each of its 890 North American stores carries a very large selection of frame styles, lenses, and sunglasses tailored not only to the age, gender, and ethnic makeup of the local market but also to what is selling at that particular store. Shifts in eyewear fashions can come fast. So managers at LensCrafters routinely analyze sales data available in the firm's marketing information system. By breaking down sales by product, store, and time period, they can spot buying trends early and plan for them. Sales analysis is helping in a different way in China. Since 2006 LensCrafters has opened 166 stores—and used different types of promotion to attract customers. LensCrafters analyzed the sales levels achieved with each type of promotion, so now when it opens a new store it can concentrate on what works best.[4]

Managers often use an MIS to conduct a **sales analysis**—a detailed breakdown of a company's sales records. For example, a sales manager might compare sales data for different salespeople, products, types of customers, or channels of distribution. Of course, a manager may be interested in aspects of performance other than sales. Other marketing "metrics"—including costs, profitability, market share, and the like—can also be examined.

Managers for Staples, the big office supplies chain, used these types of analyses to help make better decisions on everything from where to locate new stores to how to organize display space. One analysis, which considered sales and costs in detail, led to the conclusion that the chain's basic emphasis on furniture lines (like desks and file cabinets) was a mistake. While these high-ticket furniture lines provided better gross margins than everyday office supplies (like Bic pens and Scotch tape) they took up much more floor space and required more time from salespeople. So Staples shrunk or eliminated the furniture department in most of its stores—and sales and profits improved.[5]

Many firms are not there yet

Of course, not every firm has a complete MIS system. And in some firms that do, managers don't know how to use what's there. A major problem is that many managers are used to doing it the old way—and they don't think through what information they need.

One sales manager thought he was progressive when he asked his assistant for a report listing each sales rep's sales for the previous month and the current month. The assistant quickly found the relevant information on the firm's intranet, put it into an Excel spreadsheet, and printed out the report. Later, however, she was surprised to see the sales manager working on the list with a calculator. He was figuring the percentage change in sales for the month and ranking the reps from largest increase in sales to smallest. The spreadsheet software could have done all of that—instantly—but the sales manager got what he *asked for,* not what he really needed. An MIS can provide information—but only the marketing manager knows what problem needs solving. It's the job of the manager—not the computer or the MIS specialist—to ask for the right information in the right form.[6]

THE SCIENTIFIC METHOD AND MARKETING RESEARCH

Marketing research—combined with the strategy planning framework we discussed in Chapter 2—can also help marketing managers make better decisions.

Marketing research is guided by the **scientific method**, a decision-making approach that focuses on being objective and orderly in *testing* ideas before accepting them. With the scientific method, managers don't just *assume* that their intuition is correct. Instead, they use their intuition and observations to develop **hypotheses**—educated guesses about the relationships between things or about what will happen in the future. Then they test their hypotheses before making final decisions.

A manager who relies only on intuition might introduce a new product without testing consumer response. But a manager who uses the scientific method might say, "I think (hypothesize) that consumers currently using the most popular brand will prefer our new product. Let's run some consumer tests. If at least 60 percent of the consumers prefer our product, we can introduce it in a regional test market. If it doesn't pass the consumer test there, we can make some changes and try again." With this approach, decisions are based on evidence, not just hunches.

The scientific method forces an orderly research process. Some managers don't carefully specify what information they need. They blindly move ahead—hoping that research will provide "the answer." Other managers may have a clearly defined problem or question but lose their way after that. These hit-or-miss approaches waste both time and money.

FIVE-STEP APPROACH TO MARKETING RESEARCH

The **marketing research process** is a five-step application of the scientific method that includes:

1. Defining the problem.
2. Analyzing the situation.
3. Getting problem-specific data.
4. Interpreting the data.
5. Solving the problem.

Exhibit 7–3 shows the five steps in the process. Note that the process may lead to a solution before all of the steps are completed. Or as the feedback arrows show, researchers may return to an earlier step if needed. For example, the interpreting step may point to a new question—or reveal the need for additional information—before a final decision can be made.

Good marketing research requires cooperation between researchers and marketing managers. Researchers must be sure their research focuses on real problems.

Marketing managers must be able to explain what their problems are and what kinds of information they need. They should be able to communicate with specialists in the specialists' language. Marketing managers may only be "consumers" of research. But they should be informed consumers—able to explain exactly what they want from the research. They should also know about some of the basic decisions made during the research process so they know the limitations of the findings.

For this reason, our discussion of marketing research won't emphasize mechanics but rather how to plan and evaluate the work of marketing researchers.[7]

Exhibit 7–3 Five-Step Scientific Approach to Marketing Research Process

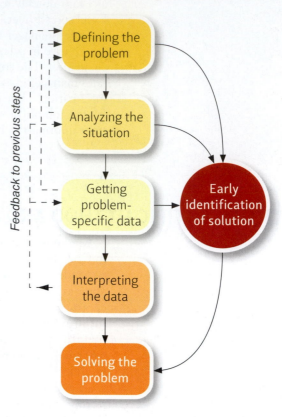

DEFINING THE PROBLEM—STEP 1

Defining the problem is often the most difficult step in the marketing research process. But it's important for the objectives of the research to be clearly defined. The best research job on the wrong problem is wasted effort.

Our strategy planning framework is useful for guiding the problem definition step. It can help the researcher identify the real problem area and what information is needed. Do we really know enough about our target markets to work out all of the four Ps? Before deciding how to position our product, do we understand our competitor's strengths and weaknesses? Do we know enough to decide what celebrity to use in an ad or how to handle the price war in New York City or Tokyo? If not, we may want to do research rather than rely on intuition.

The problem definition step sounds simple—and that's the danger. It's easy to confuse problems with symptoms. Marketers at Kiwi, known for shoe polish, jumped to conclusions about their problems. When sales slowed, they initially figured they needed new polishing products. But when they conducted research to determine what foot care needs were not being met, they found women placed a priority on fresh smelling shoes. This led to the development of Kiwi Fresh'ins. These lightly scented disposable inserts keep feet feeling fresh and comfortable all day and have been a great success.[8]

Sometimes the research objectives are very clear. A manager wants to know if the targeted households have tried a new product and what percent of them bought it a second time. But research objectives aren't always so simple. The manager might also want to know *why* some didn't buy or whether they had even heard of the product. Companies rarely have enough time and money to study everything. A manager must narrow the research objectives. One good way is to develop a list of research questions that includes all the possible problem areas. Then the manager can consider the items on the list more completely—in the situation analysis step—before narrowing down to final research objectives.

ANALYZING THE SITUATION—STEP 2

What information do we already have?

When the marketing manager thinks the real problem has begun to surface, a situation analysis is useful. A **situation analysis** is an informal study of what information is already available in the problem area. It can help define the problem and specify what additional information, if any, is needed.

The situation analysis may begin with quick research—perhaps an Internet search; a closer look at information in an MIS; and phone calls or informal talks with people familiar with the industry, problem, or situation.

Situation analysis helps educate a researcher

The situation analysis is especially important if the marketing manager is dealing with unfamiliar areas or if the researcher is a specialist who doesn't know much about the management decisions to be made. They *both* must be sure they understand the problem area—including the nature of the target market, the marketing mix, competition, and other external factors. Otherwise, the researcher may rush ahead and make costly mistakes or simply discover facts that management already knows. The following case illustrates this danger.

A marketing manager at the home office of a large retail chain hired a research firm to do in-store interviews to learn what customers liked most, and least, about some of its stores in other cities. Interviewers diligently filled out their questionnaires. When the results came in, it was apparent that neither the marketing manager nor the researcher had done their homework. No one had even talked with the local store managers! Several of the stores were in the middle of some messy remodeling—so all the customers' responses concerned the noise and dust from the construction. The research was a waste of money.

Secondary data may provide the answers— or some background

The situation analysis should also find relevant **secondary data**—information that has been collected or published already. Later, in Step 3, we will cover **primary data**—information specifically collected to solve a current problem. Too often researchers rush to gather primary data when much relevant secondary information is already available—at little or no cost! See Exhibit 7–4.

Much secondary data is available

Ideally, much secondary data is already available from the firm's MIS. Data that has not been organized in an MIS may be available from the company's files and reports. Secondary data also is available from libraries, trade associations, government agencies, and private research organizations; increasingly, these organizations put their information online. So one of the first places a researcher should look for secondary data is on the Internet.

Search the Internet for information

Marketing managers can find a treasure trove of useful information on the Internet. It's all readily accessible from a computer (or even by wireless smart phone). But available is not the same as reliable. Anyone can post anything on the Internet. So, as with any other research source, you should carefully evaluate the accuracy of Internet sources.

The key to the Internet is finding what's needed. Internet subject directories that categorize websites by topic are a good place to start. Yahoo.com has a popular directory, but libraries and other organizations have created many more. Two good directory resources are the Librarians' Index to the Internet (www.lii.org) and INFOMINE (http://infomine.ucr.edu). Powerful Internet search engines, like the ones at Google.com and Ask.com, provide lists of links to websites that include words or phrases specified by the researcher. A problem is that searches often identify too many irrelevant sources.

Exhibit 7-4   Sources of Secondary and Primary Data

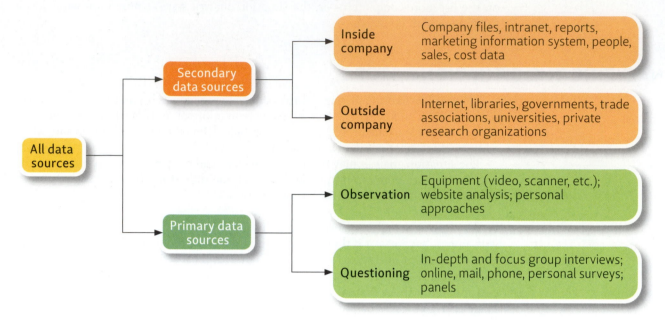

Search engines miss important databases

Many managers don't realize that much of the information stored on the Internet is in database formats that standard website search engines can't find. To search for information in those databases you must first locate the website with the relevant database and then use software at the site to search inside the database. Directories that describe database sites help with the first step. The directory at the website www.completeplanet.com, for example, provides an organized listing of more than 70,000 searchable databases.

Special-interest groups on the Web

Many marketing managers join discussion groups or newsgroups that share information on topics of specific interest. Belonging to these groups is like subscribing to an electronic newsletter. Similarly, some websites provide automatic e-mail notifications when information is updated. This service can be valuable for information you need to come to you automatically—before you even know it's available. Indeed, it may be available at the website of a competing firm. A competitor's press releases or job listings sometimes provide important information about future plans. Microsoft, for example, was alerted to a competitor's plans by looking at its online job postings.

Some marketing managers take a more hands-on approach. They log in to blogs or online discussion groups to "eavesdrop" or ask questions as customers chat about companies or brands of interest. Specialized search engines like Blogdex and Google Groups locate this type of site.[9]

Internet EXERCISE

Blogs provide a place for people to write about what interests them and post it on the Internet for all to read. One way to learn more about trends in Internet word-of-mouth is to track the frequency with which certain words are used in blogs. BlogPulse automates this process. Go to **www.blogpulse.com** and click on "Tools" and then "Trend Search." You'll compare three digital camera brands: type the names "Canon," "Kodak," and "Nikon" in the trend search terms edit box. Choose 6 months for the date range and then click "Get Trend." Which brand name appears most frequently in blogs? What do you think causes the sudden spikes in the charts? How could this information be helpful to a marketing manager at Canon?

A firm's own data on customers' past purchases, if properly analyzed, can be an important source of information for evaluating new opportunities.

Government data is inexpensive

Federal and state governments publish data on many subjects. Government data is often useful in estimating the size of markets. Almost all government data is available in inexpensive print and digital publications, on websites, and in downloads ready for further analysis.

Sometimes it's more practical to use summary publications for leads to more detailed reports. For the U.S. market, one of the most useful summary references is the *Statistical Abstract of the United States*. Like an almanac, it is issued in print form each year and gives 1,500 summary tables from more than 200 published sources. Detailed footnotes guide readers to more specific information on a topic. The abstract and much of the source material on which it is based are available online at www.census.gov. Similarly, the *United Nations Statistical Yearbook* is one of the best summaries of worldwide data; like many other international statistical references, it is available on CD-ROM and online (www.un.org/depts/unsd).

Secondary data is very limited on some international markets. However, most countries with advanced economies have government agencies that help researchers get the data they need. For example, Statistics Canada (www.statcan.gc.ca) compiles a great deal of information on the Canadian market. Eurostat (epp.eurostat.ec.europa.eu), the statistical office for the European Union countries, and the Organization for Economic Cooperation (in Paris) offer many publications packed with data on Europe. In the United States, the Department of Commerce (www.commerce.gov) distributes statistics compiled by all other federal departments. Some city and state governments have similar agencies for local data. The Yahoo website (www.yahoo.com) provides an index to a large amount of information about different governments.

Private sources are useful, too

Many private research organizations—as well as advertising agencies, newspapers, and magazines—regularly compile and publish data. A good business library is valuable for sources such as *Sales & Marketing Management*, *Advertising Age*, *Journal of Marketing*, and the publications of the National Industrial Conference Board.

The *Encyclopedia of Associations* lists 75,000 U.S. and international trade and professional associations that can be a good source of information. For example, the American Marketing Association (www.marketingpower.org) has an information center with many marketing publications.

Situation analysis yields a lot—for very little

The virtue of a good situation analysis is that it can be very informative but takes little time. And it's inexpensive compared with more formal research efforts—like a large-scale survey. A phone, access to the Internet, and time might be all a marketing manager needs to gather a lot of insight. Situation analysis can help focus further research or even eliminate the need for it entirely. The situation analyst is really trying to determine the exact nature of the situation and the problem.

Determine what else is needed

At the end of the situation analysis, you can see which research questions—from the list developed during the problem definition step—remain unanswered. Then you have to decide exactly what information you need to answer those questions and how to get it. This may require discussion between technical experts and the marketing manager. Often companies use a written **research proposal**—a plan that specifies what information will be obtained and how—to be sure no misunderstandings occur later. The research plan may include information about costs, what data will be collected, how it will be collected, who will analyze it and how, and how long the process will take.

GETTING PROBLEM-SPECIFIC DATA—STEP 3

Gathering primary data

There are different methods for collecting primary data. Which approach to use depends on the nature of the problem and how much time and money are available.

In most primary data collection, the researcher tries to learn what customers think about some topic or how they behave under some conditions. There are two basic methods for obtaining information about customers: *questioning* and *observing*. Questioning can range from qualitative to quantitative research. And many kinds of observing are possible.

Qualitative questioning— open-ended with a hidden purpose

Qualitative research seeks in-depth, open-ended responses, not yes or no answers. The researcher tries to get people to share their thoughts on a topic—without giving them many directions or guidelines about what to say.

A researcher might ask different consumers, "What do you think about when you decide where to shop for food?" One person may talk about convenient location, another about service, and others about the quality of the fresh produce. The real advantage of this approach is *depth*. Each person can be asked follow-up questions so the researcher really understands what *that* respondent is thinking. The depth of the qualitative approach gets at the details—even if the researcher needs a lot of judgment to summarize it all.

Focus groups stimulate discussion

The most widely used form of qualitative questioning in marketing research is the **focus group interview**, which involves interviewing 6 to 10 people in an informal group setting. The focus group also uses open-ended questions, but here the interviewer wants to get group interaction—to stimulate thinking and get immediate reactions.

A skilled focus group leader can learn a lot from this approach. A typical session may last an hour, so participants can cover a lot of ground. Sessions are often recorded (or broadcast over the Internet or by satellite) so different managers can form their own impressions of what happened. Some research firms create electronic focus groups in which participants log onto a specified website and with others participate in a chat session; each person types in comments that are shared on the computer screen of each of the other participants. What they type is the record of the session.[10]

Online focus groups can offset some of the limitations of traditional focus groups. Participants who meet online feel freer to express their honest thoughts—and an aggressive individual is less likely to dominate the group. For example, AOL found that men were often embarrassed to admit to others in a traditional focus group that they had trouble controlling spam on their computers. In online groups, they revealed their real concerns. The online groups' inputs helped in AOL's revamp of its spam blocker system and its ads to explain the benefits of using AOL.[11]

Regardless of how a focus group is conducted, conclusions reached from a session usually vary depending on who watches it. A typical problem—and serious limitation—with qualitative research is that it's hard to measure the results objectively. The results seem to depend largely on the viewpoint of the researcher. In addition, people willing to participate in a focus group—especially those who talk the most—may not be representative of the broader target market.

Focus groups can be conducted quickly and at relatively low cost—an average of about $4,000 each. This is part of their appeal. But focus groups are probably being overused. It's easy to fall into the trap of treating an idea arising from a focus group as a "fact" that applies to a broad target market.

To avoid this trap, some researchers use qualitative research to prepare for quantitative research. For example, the Jacksonville Symphony Orchestra wanted to broaden its base of support and increase ticket sales. It hired a marketing research firm to conduct focus group interviews. These interviews helped the marketing managers refine their ideas about what these target "customers" liked and did not like about the

Focus groups are popular, and well-run groups can provide useful information. Similarly, online interview sessions can be conducted quickly and affordably. As with any type of marketing research, a marketing manager should be aware of both the advantages and limitations of the specific approach used when drawing conclusions and making decisions.

orchestra. The ideas were then tested with a larger, more representative sample. When the managers planned their promotion and the orchestra's program on the basis of the research, ticket sales nearly doubled.[12]

Qualitative research can provide good ideas—hypotheses. But we need other approaches—perhaps based on more representative samples and objective measures—to *test* the hypotheses.

Structured questioning gives more objective results

When researchers use identical questions and response alternatives, they can summarize the information quantitatively. Samples can be larger and more representative, and various statistics can be used to draw conclusions. For these reasons, most survey research is **quantitative research**—which seeks structured responses that can be summarized in numbers, like percentages, averages, or other statistics. For example, a marketing researcher might calculate what percentage of respondents have tried a new product and then figure an average score for how satisfied they were.

Fixed responses speed answering and analysis

Survey questionnaires usually provide fixed responses to questions to simplify analysis of the replies. This multiple-choice approach also makes it easier and faster for respondents to reply. Simple fill-in-a-number questions are also widely used in quantitative research. Fixed responses are also more convenient for computer analysis, which is how most surveys are analyzed.

Surveys come in many forms

Decisions about what specific questions to ask and how to ask them usually depend on how respondents will be contacted—by mail (or electronic mail), via a website, on the phone, or in person. What question and response approach is used may also affect the survey. There are many possibilities. For example, whether the survey is self-administered or handled by an interviewer, the questionnaire may be on paper or in an interactive computer format (perhaps distributed on a CD or disk or displayed on a website). The computer can be programmed to skip certain questions, depending on answers given. Computerized questionnaires also allow the research to show pictures or play audio/video clips (for example, to get reactions to an advertising jingle). In an automated telephone interview, questions may be prerecorded on an audio tape or computer and the subject responds by pushing touch-tone buttons on the phone.

Mail and online surveys are common and convenient

A questionnaire distributed by mail, e-mail, or online is useful when extensive questioning is necessary. Respondents can complete the questions at their convenience. They may be more willing to provide personal information—since a questionnaire can be completed anonymously. But the questions must be simple and easy to follow since no interviewer is there to help. If the respondent is likely to be a computer user, a questionnaire on a website can include a help feature with additional directions for people who need them.

A big problem with questionnaires is that many people don't complete them. The **response rate**—the percentage of people contacted who complete the questionnaire—is often low and respondents may not be representative. Mail, e-mail, and online surveys are economical if a large number of people respond. But they may be quite expensive if the response rate is low. Worse, the results may be misleading if the respondents are not representative. For example, people who complete online questionnaires tend to be younger, better educated, or different in other ways that impact how they answer.

Distributing questionnaires by e-mail, or at a website, is popular. It is quick, and the responses come back in computer form. Surveys sent by regular mail usually take a lot longer.

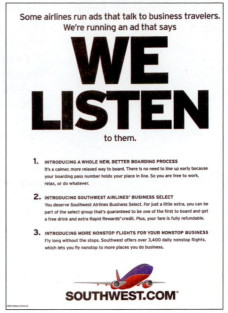

Southwest uses surveys and other types of research to "listen" to customer inputs, but it also has a blog at www.blogsouthwest.com where it encourages customers and employees to share their opinions.

Regardless of how quickly a questionnaire is distributed, it often takes a month or more to get the data back. That is too slow for some decisions. Moreover, it is difficult to get respondents to expand on particular points. In markets where illiteracy is a problem, it may not be possible to get any response. In spite of these limitations, the convenience and economy of self-administered surveys makes them popular.

Telephone surveys—fast and effective

Telephone interviews are also popular. They are effective for getting quick answers to simple questions. Telephone interviews allow the interviewer to probe and really learn what the respondent is thinking. In addition, with computer-aided telephone interviewing, answers are immediately recorded on a computer, resulting in fast data analysis. On the other hand, many consumers find calls intrusive—and about a third refuse to answer any questions. Moreover, respondents can't be certain who is calling or how personal information might be used.

Personal interview surveys—can be in-depth

A personal interview survey is usually much more expensive per interview than e-mail, mail, or telephone surveys. But it's easier to get and keep the respondent's attention when the interviewer is right there. The interviewer can also help explain complicated directions and perhaps get better responses. For these reasons, personal interviews are commonly used for research on business customers. To reduce the cost of locating consumer respondents, interviews are sometimes done at a store or shopping mall. This is called a mall intercept interview because the interviewer stops a shopper and asks for responses to the survey.

Researchers have to be careful that having an interviewer involved doesn't affect the respondent's answers. Sometimes people won't give an answer they consider embarrassing. Or they may try to impress or please the interviewer. Further, in some cultures people don't want to give any information. For example, many people in Africa, Latin America, and Eastern Europe are reluctant to be interviewed. This is also a problem in many low-income, inner-city areas in the United States; even Census Bureau interviewers have trouble getting cooperation.[13]

Sometimes questioning has limitations. Then observing may be more accurate or economical.

Observing—what you see is what you get

Observing—as a method of collecting data—focuses on a well-defined problem. Here we are not talking about the casual observations that may stimulate ideas in the early steps of a research project. With the observation method, researchers try to see or record what the subject does naturally. They don't want the observing to *influence* the subject's behavior.

A museum director wanted to know which of the many exhibits was most popular. A survey didn't help. Visitors seemed to want to please the interviewer and usually said that all of the exhibits were interesting. Putting observers near exhibits—to record how long visitors spent at each one—didn't help either. The curious visitors stood around to see what the observer was recording, and that messed up the measures. Finally, the museum floors were waxed to a glossy shine. Several weeks later, the floors around the exhibits were inspected. It was easy to tell which exhibits were most popular—based on how much wax had worn off the floor!

In some situations, consumers are recorded on video. This may be in a store, at home, or out with friends. Later, researchers can study the tape by running the film at very slow speed or actually analyzing each frame. Researchers use this technique to study the routes consumers follow through a store or how they select products. A dog food manufacturer put video cameras on the pet food aisle in supermarkets to learn more about how people choose dog food and treats. The videos showed that kids often picked the treats, but that the kids' parents chose the food. The videos also revealed that kids couldn't reach treats when they were on higher shelves. Sales immediately increased when the treats were moved to lower shelves.[14]

Many franchise companies use the observation method to check how well a franchisee is performing. Krispy Kreme hires people to go to its stores and act like normal customers. Then these "secret shoppers" report back to Krispy Kreme on the quality of the food, how they were treated, and the cleanliness of the store. The report may include digital pictures or videos that are instantly sent over the Internet from a laptop computer.

Marketers sometimes can find ways to improve products by observing customers as they use them. For example, product developers at Microsoft watch customers try new software products so that they can change features that are confusing or hard to learn. This sort of usability testing is a good idea when changes are made to a website. In fact, firms that have online shopping sites often use software to "watch" how consumers use the website, how much time they spend at each display, and the like.[15]

Observing is common in advertising research

Observation methods are common in advertising research. For example, Nielsen Media Research (www.nielsenmedia.com) uses a device called the "people meter" that adapts the observation method to television audience research. This device is attached to the TV set in the homes of selected families. It records when the set is on and what station is tuned in. Similarly, Arbitron developed its Portable People Meter (PPM) to automatically measure radio listening habits.

Observing website visitors

Website analysis software allows marketing managers to observe customer behavior at a firm's website. For example, there are tools that help marketing managers understand how a customer came to a website—was it the keyword used in a Google search, a response to an e-mail promotion, or a link from an online review site? Reports show the series of clicks made by visitors and how long they stayed on each page. This information can help marketing managers make changes to the site so that it attracts the right customers and offers useful information so they stay and make purchases.

Online retailer Shipwreck Beads wanted to promote a summer sale of fire-polished beads, so it e-mailed 76,000 customers and placed banner ads on the websites for *Bead-Style* and *Bead and Button* magazines. Web analysis tools showed which promotions and which keywords generated the most leads. Because the answers were available very quickly, the firm revised the advertising copy to include more instances of the phrase "fire-polished beads." This simple change improved placement on search pages and, within a month, hits to its website increased fourfold.[16]

Checkout scanners see a lot

Computerized scanners at retail checkout counters help researchers collect very specific, and useful, information. Often this type of data feeds directly into a firm's MIS. Managers of a large chain of stores can see exactly what products have sold each day and how much money each department in each store has earned. But the scanner also has wider applications for marketing research.

Information Resources, Inc. (www.infores.com), and ACNielsen (www.acnielsen. com) use **consumer panels**—a group of consumers who provide information on a continuing basis. Whenever a panel member shops for groceries, he or she gives an ID card to the clerk, who scans the number. Then the scanner records every purchase—including brands, sizes, prices, and any coupons used. In a variation of this approach, consumers use a handheld scanner to record purchases once they get home. Sometimes members of a panel answer questions and the answers are merged with the scanner data.

Analysis of panel data revealed that Ocean Spray was seeing sales slip to competitors. Households with kids are the heaviest purchasers of juice; yet they were purchas-

It's the less tart taste kids have a hard time putting into words.

Ocean Spray® White Cranberry® has the unique taste your whole family will love. So they'll never have a hard time asking you for more. Better make room in the fridge for all the taste-bud-loving varieties.

White Cranberry Juice Drinks. ©2001 Ocean Spray Cranberries, Inc.

ing Ocean Spray on a less frequent basis. Further research with these panel members revealed this was due to its "too tart" taste and tendency to stain. To combat this, the company focused its energies on developing White Cranberry Juice Drinks by harvesting the berries before they develop their traditional red color and pungent taste. An ad for the new product depicted a mom and her small son enjoying the taste of the new White Cranberry juice. When the boy accidentally spills it on the floor, it's also clear that it doesn't stain. Now that the "no stain" message has sunk in, Ocean Spray's ads put more emphasis on the idea that kids love the taste.[17]

Data captured by electronic scanners is equally important to e-commerce in business-to-business markets. Increasingly, firms mark their shipping cartons and packages with computer-readable bar codes that make it fast and easy to track inventory, shipments, orders, and the like. As information about product sales or shipments becomes available, it is instantly included in the MIS and accessible over the Internet.[18]

Experimental method controls conditions

A marketing manager can get a different kind of information—with either questioning or observing—using the experimental method. With the **experimental method**, researchers compare the responses of two (or more) groups that are similar except on the characteristic being tested. Researchers want to learn if the specific characteristic—which varies among groups—*causes* differences in some response among the groups. For example, a researcher might be interested in comparing responses of consumers who had seen an ad for a new product with consumers who had not seen the ad. The "response" might be an observed behavior—like the purchase of a product—or the answer to a specific question—like "How interested are you in this new product?" See Exhibit 7–5.

Marketing managers for Mars—the company that makes Snickers candy bars—used the experimental method to help solve a problem. They wanted to know if making their candy bar bigger would increase sales enough to offset the higher cost. To decide, they conducted a marketing experiment in which the company carefully varied the size of candy bars sold in *different* markets. Otherwise, the marketing mix stayed the same. Then researchers tracked sales in each market area to see the effect of the different sizes. They saw a big difference immediately; the added sales more than offset the cost of a bigger candy bar.

Test-marketing of new products is another type of marketing experiment. In a typical approach, a company tries variations on its planned marketing mix in a few geographic market areas. The results of the tests help to identify problems or refine the

Exhibit 7–5   Illustration of Experimental Method in Comparing Effectiveness of Two Ads

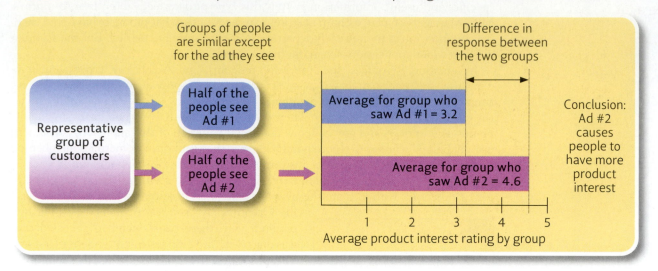

marketing mix—before the decision is made to go to broader distribution. However, alert competitors may disrupt such tests—perhaps by increasing promotion or offering retailers extra discounts.[19]

Syndicated research shares data collection costs

Some private research firms specialize in collecting data and then sell it to managers in many different client firms. Often the marketing manager subscribes to the research service and gets regular updates. About 40 percent of marketing research spending is for syndicated research, and this helps explain why it can be an economical approach when marketing managers from many different firms need the same type of data. For example, many different auto producers use J. D. Power's (www.jdpower.com) surveys of customer satisfaction—often as the basis for advertising claims. Subscription data services are available for many different industries—ranging from food services to prescription drugs to micro electronic devices.[20]

A combination of research methods may be needed

Using one research method to solve an initial problem may identify new questions that are best answered with different research methods. Consider WD-40, a popular all-purpose lubricant sold in a blue-and-yellow spray can. To find potential new uses of WD-40, researchers visited mechanics and watched them as they worked. These observers realized that even small cans of WD-40 were difficult for mechanics to handle in tight spaces. In addition, the spray created drips and messes because it was difficult to control the amount being applied.

To address these problems, the new-product team developed a prototype for the No Mess Pen, a small marker that delivers a precise amount of the lubricant. Then, researchers held focus groups to get reactions from mechanics. They weren't encouraging. Mechanics didn't think that the small unit would handle their large application needs. Yet, many thought their spouses might like the pen for small household lubrication jobs. To follow up on this idea, WD-40 conducted online surveys. More than two-thirds of the women respondents said they would buy the product. To fine-tune targeting and promotion, WD-40 then conducted more than 40 in-home studies to learn how families actually used the No Mess Pen. This research confirmed that women were the primary target market, but that men used the pens as well. Moreover, the pen didn't replace the can of WD-40 already found in most households; rather, pens were stored in desk drawers, cars, and toolboxes so they'd be handy. WD-40 used different research methods to address different problems, but in combination they contributed to making the No Mess Pen a great success.[21]

Understand the costs and benefits

Whether collecting secondary data for a situation analysis or primary data from a focus group or survey, marketing research takes time and money. A good marketing

Low-Cost Research

When millions are at stake, Kraft General Foods doesn't blink at spending $100,000 or more for a single market research project. Managers in small companies can only dream of having the research budgets to do that. But, ironically, not having good information may pose an even greater risk for small companies. While a big firm with deeper pockets can survive a marketing misstep or two, a mistake in an important marketing strategy decision can put a small firm out of business.

With a little creativity a good marketing manager can generate a lot of information using relatively little cash. For example, if you were thinking about starting a soccer training academy for kids, you might start by asking a lot of questions. Ask your friends for ideas about what to do and where to advertise. Go out to local soccer fields and question parents. Are they interested? When would they want the training to be available? How much are they willing to pay? Talk to kids, too. What could make soccer camp more fun?

If a firm's target market is accessible via the Internet, online surveys can be an economical way for running ideas and questions past a larger group. Greenfield Online (www.greenfieldonline.com), for instance, recruits people to respond to the online surveys it hosts for clients. For about $6,000, Greenfield can get responses to a 12-question survey from a representative sample of 150 people—and do it within a week. Look for other, do-it-yourself approaches. For example, Waterpik offers new customers a $5 coupon to encourage them to fill out its online survey.

Managers at small companies can learn a lot by studying competitors' promotion material, monitoring their websites, and shopping in their stores. Get on competitors' e-mail lists and study their advertising, products, and pricing on a regular basis. Firms that compete in business markets can also check each other out at trade shows. And trade magazines have articles, ads, and even letters to the editor that can alert you to new developments.

Make everyone in your company a researcher. Let them know you want them to be aware of important information that they see and to share useful ideas that they hear from a customer, similar business in a different market, or the like. Above all, keep an eye on your current customers. Be sincere and regular about asking them, "Is there anything we can do better?" Be sure to listen when they answer. Set up internal monitoring systems that alert you to the loss of a customer—and then be conscientious about calling to find out what happened. What you learn may help you prevent another customer from defecting—and it may even get the old customer back.

Finally, don't be unnecessarily frugal. Marketing managers should remember the scientific method and be wary of shortcuts that can result in misleading information and bad decisions. For example, don't skip the step of pretesting a questionnaire; that may save some money or a few hours of work, but waste the total amount spent on a real study with a "bad" questionnaire. Samples should still represent the target market, and that includes focus groups. A focus group with a group of employees may be convenient, but it isn't the same as using real customers.[22]

manager knows that the value of additional information lies in the ability to design more effective marketing strategies. Similarly, different research methods provide different insights—and come at different costs. There are also benefits to getting information quickly—particularly in some markets.

INTERPRETING THE DATA—STEP 4

What does it really mean?

After someone collects the data, it has to be analyzed to decide what it all means. In quantitative research, this step usually involves statistics. **Statistical packages**—easy-to-use computer programs that analyze data—have made this step easier. As we

Exhibit 7–6 Cross-Tabulation Breakdown of Responses to an Internet Service Provider Consumer Survey

		\multicolumn{5}{c}{What is your household income?}				
		Less than $30,000	$30,000 to 50,000	$50,000 to $75,000	More than $75,000	Total Sample
Does your home	Yes	23.7%	46.2%	52.3%	72.4%	47.1%
have broadband	No	76.3	53.8	47.7	27.6	52.9
Internet service?	Total	100.0%	100.0%	100.0%	100.0%	100.0%

Interpretation: In the survey 47.1 percent of people said that they had broadband Internet service in their homes. However, the adoption of broadband Internet service was higher at higher income levels. For example, 72.4 percent of households with over $75,000 income have broadband but only 23.7 percent have it among homes with income less than $30,000.

noted earlier, some firms provide *decision support systems* so managers can use a statistical package to interpret data themselves. More often, however, technical specialists are involved at the interpretation step.

Cross-tabulation is one of the most frequently used approaches for analyzing and interpreting marketing research data. It shows the relationship of answers to two different questions. Exhibit 7–6 is an example. The cross-tab analysis shows that households with higher incomes are much more likely to have broadband Internet service.

There are many other approaches for statistical analysis—the best one depends on the situation. The details of statistical analysis are beyond the scope of this book. But a good manager should know enough to understand what a research project can and can't do.[23]

Is your sample really representative?

It's usually impossible for marketing managers to collect all the information they want about everyone in a **population**—the total group they are interested in. Marketing researchers typically study only a **sample**, a part of the relevant population. How well a sample *represents* the total population affects the results. Results from a sample that is not representative may not give a true picture.

The manager of a retail store might want a phone survey to learn what consumers think about the store's hours. If interviewers make all of the calls during the day, consumers who work outside the home during the day won't be represented. Those interviewed might say the limited store hours are "satisfactory." Yet it would be a mistake to assume that *all* consumers are satisfied.

Research results are not exact

An estimate from a sample, even a representative one, usually varies somewhat from the true value for a total population. Managers sometimes forget this. They assume that survey results are exact. Instead, when interpreting sample estimates, managers should think of them as *suggesting* the approximate value.

If random selection is used to develop the sample, researchers can use various methods to help determine the likely accuracy of the sample value. This is done in terms of **confidence intervals**—the range on either side of an estimate that is likely to contain the true value for the whole population. Some managers are surprised to learn how wide that range can be.

Consider a wholesaler who has 2,000 retail customers and wants to learn how many of these retailers carry a product from a competing supplier. If the wholesaler randomly samples 100 retailers and 20 say yes, then the sample estimate is 20 percent. But with that information the wholesaler can only be 95 percent confident that the percentage of all retailers is in the confidence interval between 12 and 28 percent. The larger the sample size, the greater the accuracy of estimates from a random sample. With a larger sample, a few unusual responses are less likely to make a big difference.[24]

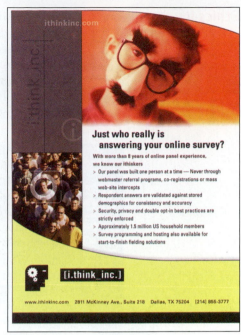

Survey Sampling Inc., and i.think_inc. help marketing researchers develop samples that are really representative of the target market.

Validity problems can destroy research

Even if the sampling is carefully planned, it is also important to evaluate the quality of the research data itself.

Managers and researchers should be sure that research data really measures what it is supposed to measure. Many of the variables marketing managers are interested in are difficult to measure accurately. Questionnaires may let us assign numbers to consumer responses, but that still doesn't mean that the result is precise. An interviewer might ask, "How much did you spend on soft drinks last week?" A respondent may be perfectly willing to cooperate—and be part of the representative sample—but just not be able to remember.

Validity concerns the extent to which data measures what it is intended to measure. Validity problems are important in marketing research because many people will try to answer even when they don't know what they're talking about. Further, a poorly worded question can mean different things to different people and invalidate the results. Often, pretests of a research project are required to evaluate the quality of the questions and measures and to ensure that potential problems have been identified.

Poor interpretation can destroy research

Besides sampling and validity problems, a marketing manager must consider whether the analysis of the data supports the *conclusions* drawn in the interpretation step. Sometimes technical specialists pick the right statistical procedure—their calculations are exact—but they misinterpret the data because they don't understand the management problem. In one survey, car buyers were asked to rank five cars in order from "most preferred" to "least preferred." One car was ranked first by slightly more respondents than any other car, so the researcher reported it as the "most liked car." That interpretation, however, ignored the fact that 70 percent of the respondents ranked the car *last*!

Interpretation problems like this can be subtle but crucial. Some people draw misleading conclusions on purpose to get the results they want. Marketing managers must decide whether *all* of the results support the interpretation and are relevant to their problem.

Marketing manager and researcher should work together

Marketing research involves many technical details. But the marketing researcher and the marketing manager must work together to be sure that they really do solve the problem facing the firm. If the whole research process has been a joint effort, then the interpretation step can move quickly to solving the problem.

Ethics involved in interpreting and presenting results

Marketing managers want information they can trust when they make marketing decisions. But research often involves many hidden details. A person who wants to misuse research to pursue a personal agenda can often do so.

Perhaps the most common ethical issues concern decisions to withhold certain information about the research. For example, a manager might selectively share only those results that support his or her viewpoint. Others involved in a decision might never know that they are getting only partial truths. [25]

SOLVING THE PROBLEM—STEP 5

The last step is solving the problem

In the problem solution step, managers use the research results to make marketing decisions.

Some researchers, and some managers, are fascinated by the interesting tidbits of information that come from the research process. They are excited if the research reveals something they didn't know before. But if research doesn't have action implications, it has little value and suggests poor planning by the researcher and the manager.

When the research process is finished, the marketing manager should be able to apply the findings in marketing strategy planning—the choice of a target market or the mix of the four Ps. If the research doesn't provide information to help guide these decisions, the company has wasted research time and money.

We emphasize this step because it is the reason for and logical conclusion to the whole research process. This final step must be anticipated at each of the earlier steps.

INTERNATIONAL MARKETING RESEARCH

Research contributes to international success

Marketing research on overseas markets is often a major contributor toward international marketing success. Conversely, export failures are often due to a lack of home office expertise concerning customer interests, needs, and other segmenting dimensions as well as environmental factors such as competitors' prices and products. Effective marketing research can help to overcome these problems.

Accurate data may be hard to find

In many countries, it is difficult—especially for a foreigner—to gather accurate information. Let's look at the challenge in China. Because the economy is growing so rapidly, secondary data that is out of date may be much more inaccurate than would be the case in a country with slow growth. Some important secondary data (such as the *China Statistical Yearbook*) is now available in an English language version, but that is often not the case. There are other problems, such as no explanation of the methods used to collect the data. That's important because the Chinese market is both large and complicated. Imagine how you would try to do a competitor analysis when there are over 1,000 Chinese firms that brew beer! Collecting primary data is difficult too. Western researchers feel that Chinese managers and consumers are not very receptive to direct questioning. Those who agree to cooperate may be hesitant to say anything

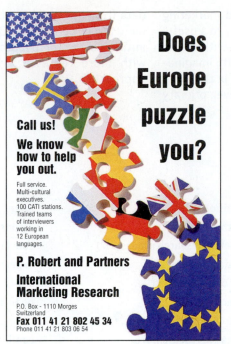

There are a large number of international marketing research firms that offer specialized services to marketing managers.

negative about their own companies or anything favorable about competitors. So, it takes experienced interviewers to carefully interpret responses.[26]

Avoid mistakes with local researchers

Whether a firm is small and entering overseas markets for the first time or already large and well established internationally, there are often advantages to working with local marketing research firms. They know the local situation and are less likely to make mistakes based on misunderstanding the customs, language, or circumstances of the customers they study.

Many large research firms have a network of local offices around the world to help with such efforts. Similarly, multinational or local advertising agencies and intermediaries can often provide leads on identifying the best research suppliers.

Some coordination and standardization makes sense

When a firm is doing similar research projects in different markets around the world, it makes sense for the marketing manager to coordinate the efforts. The manager should try to standardize research procedures, measures, and the marketing information system across international marketing operations. Without these precautions, it may be impossible for managers to go into much depth in comparing and contrasting data from different markets.[27]

CONCLUSION

Marketing managers face difficult decisions in selecting target markets and managing marketing mixes, but they rarely have all the information they would like to have before making those decisions. Even less information may be available in international markets. This doesn't mean that managers have to rely solely on intuition; they can usually obtain some good information that will improve the quality of their decisions. Both large and small firms can take advantage of Internet and intranet capabilities to develop marketing information systems (MIS) that help to ensure routinely needed data is available and quickly accessible.

Some questions can only be answered with marketing research. Marketing research should be guided by the scientific method. This approach to solving marketing problems involves five steps: (1) defining the problem, (2) analyzing the situation, (3) obtaining data, (4) interpreting data, and (5) developing and implementing a solution. This objective and organized approach helps to keep problem solving on task. It reduces the risk of doing costly and unnecessary research that doesn't achieve the desired end—solving the marketing problem.

Our strategy planning framework can be very helpful in evaluating marketing research. By finding and focusing on real problems, researchers and marketing managers may be able to move more quickly to a useful solution during the situation analysis stage—without the costs and risks of gathering primary data. With imagination, they may even be able to find answers in their MIS or in readily available secondary data. However, primary data from questioning, observing, or conducting experiments may be needed. Qualitative data often provides initial insights or hypotheses—which might be tested with more representative samples and quantitative approaches.

KEY TERMS

marketing research, 166

marketing information system (MIS), 166

intranet, 168

data warehouse, 169

decision support system (DSS), 169

search engine, 169

marketing dashboard, 169

marketing model, 169

sales analysis, 170

scientific method, 171

hypotheses, 171

marketing research process, 171

situation analysis, 173

secondary data, 173

primary data, 173

research proposal, 176

qualitative research, 176

focus group interview, 176

quantitative research, 178

response rate, 178

consumer panels, 181

experimental method, 181

statistical packages, 183

population, 184

sample, 184

confidence intervals, 184

validity, 185

QUESTIONS AND PROBLEMS

1. Discuss the concept of a marketing information system and why it is important for marketing managers to be involved in planning the system.

2. In your own words, explain why a decision support system (DSS) can add to the value of a marketing information system. Give an example of how a decision support system might help.

3. If a firm's intranet and marketing decision support system do not include a search engine, would they still be useful to a marketing manager? Why?

4. Discuss how output from a marketing information system (MIS) might differ from the output of a typical marketing research department.

5. Discuss some of the likely problems facing the marketing manager in a small firm who plans to search the Internet for information on competitors' marketing plans.

6. Explain the key characteristics of the scientific method and show why these are important to managers concerned with research.

7. How is the situation analysis different from the data collection step? Can both these steps be done at the same time to obtain answers sooner? Is this wise?

8. Distinguish between primary data and secondary data and illustrate your answer.

9. With so much secondary information now available free or at low cost over the Internet, why would a firm ever want to spend the money to do primary research?

10. If a firm were interested in estimating the distribution of income in the state of California, how could it proceed? Be specific.

11. If a firm were interested in estimating sand and clay production in Georgia, how could it proceed? Be specific.

12. Go to the library (or get on the Internet) and find (in some government publication or website) three marketing-oriented "facts" on international markets that you did not know existed or were available. Record on one page and show sources.

13. Explain why a company might want to do focus group interviews rather than individual interviews with the same people.

14. Distinguish between qualitative and quantitative approaches to research—and give some of the key advantages and limitations of each approach.

15. Define response rate and discuss why a marketing manager might be concerned about the response rate achieved in a particular survey. Give an example.

16. Prepare a table that summarizes some of the key advantages and limitations of mail, e-mail, telephone, and personal interview approaches for administering questionnaires.

17. Would a firm want to subscribe to a shared cost data service if the same data were going to be available to competitors? Discuss your reasoning.

18. Explain how you might use different types of research (focus groups, observation, survey, and experiment) to

forecast market reaction to a new kind of disposable baby diaper, which is to receive no promotion other than what the retailer will give it. Further, assume that the new diaper's name will not be associated with other known products. The product will be offered at competitive prices.

19. Marketing research involves expense—sometimes considerable expense. Why does the text recommend the use of marketing research even though a highly experienced marketing executive is available?

20. A marketing manager is considering opportunities to export her firm's current consumer products to several

different countries. She is interested in getting secondary data that will help her narrow down choices to countries that offer the best potential. The manager then plans to do more detailed primary research with consumers in those markets. What suggestions would you give her about how to proceed?

21. Discuss the concept that some information may be too expensive to obtain in relation to its value. Illustrate.

CREATING MARKETING PLANS

The Marketing Plan Coach software on the text website (and on the optional Student CD) includes a sample marketing plan for Hillside Veterinary Clinic. Look through the "Customers" and "Competitors" sections in the Situation Analysis and consider the following questions.

a.   What different types of marketing research were conducted to fill out these sections of the marketing plan?

b.   What are the strengths of the research conducted? What are the weaknesses?

c.   Keeping in mind probable cost and time to complete, what additional research would you recommend?

SUGGESTED CASES   3. MANU Soccer Academy 8. Lombardi's Italian Grill 9. Sweetest Dreams Inn

COMPUTER-AIDED PROBLEM

7. MARKETING RESEARCH

Texmac, Inc., has an idea for a new type of weaving machine that could replace the machines now used by many textile manufacturers. Texmac has done a telephone survey to estimate how many of the old-style machines are now in use. Respondents using the present machines were also asked if they would buy the improved machine at a price of $10,000.

Texmac researchers identified a population of about 5,000 textile factories as potential customers. A sample of these were surveyed, and Texmac received 500 responses. Researchers think the total potential market is about 10 times larger than the sample of respondents. Two hundred twenty of the respondents indicated that their firms used old machines like the one the new machine was intended to replace. Forty percent of those firms said that they would be interested in buying the new Texmac machine.

Texmac thinks the sample respondents are representative of the total population, but the marketing manager realizes that estimates based on a sample may not be exact when applied to the whole population. He wants to see how sampling error would affect profit estimates. Data for this problem appears in the spreadsheet. Quantity estimates for the whole market are computed from the sample estimates. These quantity estimates are used in computing likely sales, costs, and profit contribution.

a.   An article in a trade magazine reports that there are about 5,200 textile factories that use the old-style machine. If

the total market is really 5,200 customers—not 5,000 as Texmac originally thought—how does that affect the total quantity estimate and profit contribution?

b.   Some of the people who responded to the survey didn't know much about different types of machines. If the actual number of old machines in the market is really 200 per 500 firms—not 220 as estimated from survey responses—how much would this affect the expected profit contribution (for 5,200 factories)?

c.   The marketing manager knows that the percentage of textile factories that would actually buy the new machine might be different from the 40 percent who said they would in the survey. He estimates that the proportion that will replace the old machine might be as low as 36 and as high as 44 percent—depending on business conditions. Use the analysis feature to prepare a table that shows how expected quantity and profit contribution change when the sample percent varies between a minimum of 36 and a maximum of 44 percent. What does this analysis suggest about the use of estimates from marketing research samples? (Note: Use 5,200 for the number of potential customers and use 220 as the estimate of the number of old machines in the sample.)

For additional questions related to this problem, see Exercise 7-4 in the Learning Aid for Use with Essentials of Marketing, 12th edition.

CHAPTER

8

Elements of Product Planning for Goods and Services

Kevin Plank was a business major and football player at the University of Maryland when he spotted an opportunity. He and his teammates wore cotton T-shirts under their football pads, but the T-shirts quickly became sweat-soaked, heavy, and uncomfortable during practices and games. When Plank began looking for a product that would perform better than a T-shirt, he learned about new types of fabrics and performance clothing for bicyclists and hikers.

In New York City's garment district, Plank learned about a polyester-Lycra blend fabric that didn't trap moisture. He worked with a tailor to develop several prototype shirts and then asked friends who were players in the National Football League to try them. The players really liked the skintight, compression shirts. They fit comfortably under football gear and wicked away sweat—keeping the players cooler, drier, and lighter. When Plank's friends clamored for more shirts, he knew he had a good start. However, he couldn't afford a big ad campaign to tout the benefits of his product, and he didn't have relationships with retailers who could help build demand with final consumers. So Plank moved to commercialization with a focus on a target market he knew: college football teams.

Plank went back to New York and ordered 500 shirts, the first products with the Under Armour brand name and the start of what became the Heat-Gear warm weather product line. Then he loaded his shirts in his SUV and traveled to colleges across the Southeast. He tried to persuade coaches, players, and equipment managers about the benefits of his unique shirts. Many were not initially convinced of the value—especially since the price was three to five times the price of a T-shirt. But its advantage was clear after a player would try one for a football practice—and praise for the product spread quickly.

Success with college and professional athletes helped the company build credibility. It also led to relationships with specialty-sports retailers who could reach the larger and more profitable consumer market. Under Armour's well-known brand helped it gain exclusive display space in sports retailers like Dick's Sporting Goods. The "store within a store" highlights the Under Armour brand—and draws customers who buy other high-margin Under Armour products.

Under Armour's success attracted Nike and Adidas—and later store brands like Kohl's Tek Gear and JCPenney's Simply for Sports—to the performance clothing market. To fight back, Under Armour put more emphasis on creative promotion to build customer preference for the Under Armour brand. For example, Under Armour got a prominent product placement in the football movie *Any Given Sunday*. Similarly, Under Armour ran TV and print ads featuring professional

athletes like football players San Francisco 49er Vernon Davis and Dallas Cowboy (and former Plank teammate) Eric Ogbogu. When the muscular Ogbogu barked the firm's tag line, "Protect This House," it instantly became a part of popular sports culture and a rallying cry of players and fans in football stadiums across the country.

Under Armour continued to look for growth through new product ideas. One successful idea came from a coach who wanted a cold weather version of the popular T-shirt that would keep players warm as well as dry. Under Armour responded with the first products in its ColdGear line. New products for a variety of other athletic markets have followed, including leggings that are popular with skiers and polo shirts that are a hit with golfers.

It's tough to quickly steal away a large share of customers in a mature product-market, but that is just what Under Armour accomplished with its new design for football cleats. The new-product development team researched playing surfaces, player movements, and body types to design cleats that were more durable, lighter, and more breathable. Developers relied on 3-D design software to build virtual versions of shoes—and then rapidly prototyped models to be

tested. Player feedback led to more refinements. Of course, it also took an innovative ad campaign and point-of-purchase promotion for the cleats to capture a 20 percent share of sales in this highly competitive market.

This success motivated moves into running shoes and other footwear. Its line of cross-training shoes includes three different models. Under Armour used a shoe box with a see-through top to attract attention and highlight the new technology used in the shoes' design. A point-of-purchase display inside the box helps a customer decide which model is best. The approach aids consumers in self-service stores.

In less than 15 years, Under Armour has grown from a start-up into a firm with more than $725 million in annual sales. Of course, growth in the performance clothing market is slowing and competition from big-name firms like Nike and a growing number of store brands is increasing. But Kevin Plank is used to taking on bigger competitors. Once during his college football days, the 5-foot 11-inch, 229-pound Plank was assigned to block his 6-foot 4-inch, 269-pound buddy Ogbogu, and the bigger man ended up on his back with a concussion. Watch out Nike![1]

THE PRODUCT AREA INVOLVES MANY STRATEGY DECISIONS

The Under Armour case highlights some of the important topics and strategy decision areas that we'll discuss in this chapter and Chapter 9. As shown in Exhibit 8–1, there are many strategy decisions in the Product area. They're the focus of this chapter. Then, in Chapter 9, we'll take a "how to" look at developing new products and also explain how strategy usually changes as products move through their life in the market.

We'll start here by looking at Product through the eyes of the customer. This focuses attention on the total benefits provided by the Product—regardless of whether it is a physical good, a service, or both. Then we'll review strategy decisions for three important Product areas: branding, packaging, and warranties. We'll conclude by considering product classes, which are based on how customers think about and shop for products. They help show how strategy decisions for Product relate to decisions for Place, Promotion, and Price.

WHAT IS A PRODUCT?

Customers buy satisfaction, not parts

When Kodak sells an EasyShare digital camera, is it just selling a certain number of switches and buttons, a plastic case, a lens, and megapixels of memory?

When Air Jamaica sells a ticket for a flight to the Caribbean, is it just selling so much wear and tear on an airplane and so much pilot fatigue?

The answer to these questions is *no*. Instead, what these companies are really selling is the satisfaction, use, or benefit the customer wants.

Consumers care that their EasyShare camera makes it easy to take great pictures *and* share them. They care that with the EasyShare's software they can organize or e-mail their photos, or send them to the EasyShare website when they want prints. Retailers who sell cameras add their own needs. They would like for customers to

Exhibit 8-1   Product Decisions for Marketing Strategy Planning

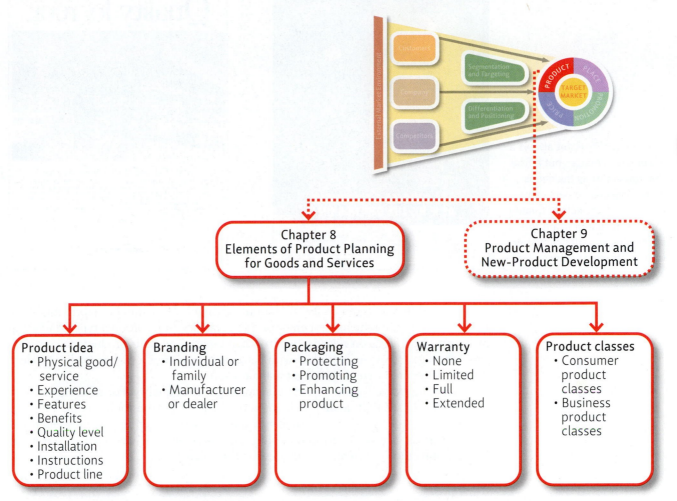

Product idea	Branding	Packaging	Warranty	Product classes
• Physical good/ service • Experience • Features • Benefits • Quality level • Installation • Instructions • Product line	• Individual or family • Manufacturer or dealer	• Protecting • Promoting • Enhancing product	• None • Limited • Full • Extended	• Consumer product classes • Business product classes

come into the store asking for the camera by name—so that it's easy to sell. And they want an attractive package that calls attention to all of these benefits.

Similarly, Air Jamaica's customers want a safe, comfortable flight—but they also want quick and accurate reservations, smooth check-in at the airport, and luggage that arrives undamaged and on time. In other words, marketing managers deliver the highest level of satisfaction when the customer's *entire experience* with the product meets the customer's needs.

Product means the need-satisfying offering of a firm. The idea of "Product" as potential customer satisfaction or benefits is very important. Many business managers get wrapped up in the technical details involved in producing a product. But most customers think about a product in terms of the total satisfaction it provides. That satisfaction may require a "total" product offering that is really a combination of excellent service, a physical good with the right features, useful instructions, a convenient package, a trustworthy warranty, and perhaps even a familiar name that has satisfied the consumer in the past.

Product quality and customer needs

Product quality should also be determined by how customers view the product. From a marketing perspective, **quality** means a product's ability to satisfy a customer's needs or requirements. This definition focuses on the customer—and how the customer thinks a product will fit some purpose. For example, the "best" satellite TV service may not be the one with the highest number of channels but the one that includes a local channel that a consumer wants to watch. Similarly, the best-quality clothing for casual wear on campus may be a pair of jeans, not a pair of dress slacks made of a higher-grade fabric.

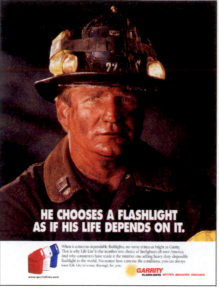

Product quality is not always a life or death matter, but a firm that understands the needs of its target customers can focus on the aspects of quality that are most important for developing superior customer value in its goods and services.

Among different types of jeans, the one with the most durable fabric might be thought of as having the highest grade or *relative quality* for its product type. Marketing managers often focus on relative quality when comparing their products to competitors' offerings. However, a product with better features is not a higher-quality product if the features aren't what the target market wants.

In Chapter 9, we'll look at ways to manage product quality. For now, however, it is important to see that quality and satisfaction depend on the total product offering. If potato chips get stale on the shelf because of poor packaging, the consumer will be dissatisfied. A broken button on a shirt will disappoint the customer—even if the laundry did a nice job cleaning and pressing the collar.[2]

Goods and/or services are the product

A product may be a physical *good* or a *service*, or a *blend of both*. Exhibit 8–2 shows that a product can range from a 100 percent emphasis on a physical good—for a commodity like steel pipe—to a 100 percent emphasis on service—for a product like satellite radio from Sirius. Many products include a combination of goods and services. When you eat out, you are buying food (a physical good) that is prepared and served by a restaurant's staff (a service).

When competitors focus only on physical goods, a firm can sometimes differentiate its offering by blending in a service that the target market values. Many companies make high-quality HDTVs, but Panasonic's research revealed that some consumers

Exhibit 8-2   Examples of Possible Blends of Physical Goods and Services in a Product

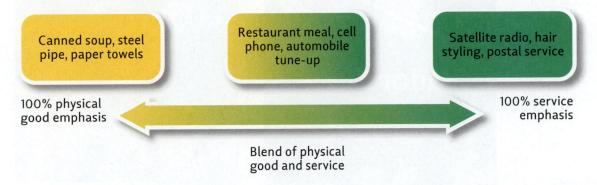

Canned soup, steel pipe, paper towels

Restaurant meal, cell phone, automobile tune-up

Satellite radio, hair styling, postal service

100% physical good emphasis

100% service emphasis

Blend of physical good and service

worry about how to set up a new unit. So Panasonic added Plasma Concierge service to support its HDTV customers with well-trained advisors and priority in-home service. This idea also works when the emphasis is on services. Luxury hotels compete to take care of their guests with excellent service, but sometimes differentiate by also offering the softest linens or an extra-comfy bed.

Regardless of the blend of goods and services involved, the marketing manager must consider most of the same elements in planning products and marketing mixes. Given this, we usually won't make a distinction between goods and services but will call all of them *Products*. However, understanding key differences in goods and services can help fine-tune marketing strategy planning. So, let's look at some of these differences next.

DIFFERENCES IN GOODS AND SERVICES

How tangible is the product?

Because a good is a physical thing, it can be seen and touched. You can try on a pair of Timberland shoes, smell Starbucks beans as they roast, and page through the latest issue of *People* magazine. A good is a *tangible* item. It's usually easy to know exactly what you will get before you decide to buy it. And once you've bought it, you own it.

In contrast, services are not physical—they are *intangible*. When you provide a customer with a service, the customer can't keep it. Rather, a service is experienced, used, or consumed. You go to a DreamWorks Pictures movie, but afterward all you have is a memory. You can buy a pass to ski at Vail and enjoy the experience, but you don't own the ski lift. Sometimes it's a challenge that customers can't see, feel, or smell a service before they buy it. For example, a person who wants advice from an accountant doesn't know in advance how good the advice will be.

To reduce this uncertainty, service customers often seek referrals from friends or advice from online reviews. They may also look for cues to help them judge the quality of a service before they buy. That's why some service providers emphasize physical evidence of quality. A lawyer is likely to have diplomas on the wall, shelves loaded with books, and furnishings that suggest success.

Where the product is produced

Goods are typically mass-produced in a factory far away from the customer. A service is usually produced in person—where the customer is located—*after* the customer has committed to buy. It is often difficult to achieve economies of scale with personal services. One reason is that service suppliers often need duplicate equipment and staff at places where the service is actually provided. Merrill Lynch sells investment advice along with financial products worldwide. That advice could, perhaps, be produced more economically in a single building in New York City and made available only on its website. But Merrill Lynch has offices all over the world because many customers want a personal touch from their stockbroker.

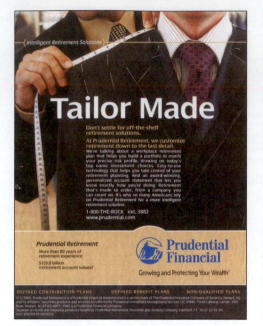

A consumer can't hold a service and look at it before purchasing, so service firms often use messages and images in their promotion that help make the benefits of the service experience more vivid.

Quality consistency

A worker in a factory that makes Whirlpool appliances can be in a bad mood and customers will never know. Even if there are production problems, quality controls are likely to catch defective goods before they leave the factory. Service quality often isn't that consistent; one reason is that it's hard to separate the service experience from the person who provides it. A rude teller in a bank can drive customers away. Service providers also vary in their ability, and problems with the service they deliver are usually obvious to customers. In addition, when many people must all work well together—as in a hospital or on a cruise ship—it's even more of a challenge to deliver consistent service quality.

Services cannot be stored

Services are perishable. They can't be produced and then stored to sell at some future time when more customers want to buy. This makes it difficult to balance supply and demand, especially if demand varies a lot. At Thanksgiving, Southwest Airlines has to turn away customers because most of its flights are fully booked; other airlines may get that business. Perhaps Southwest could buy more planes and hire more pilots, but most of the time that would result in costly excess capacity—planes flying with empty seats. The revenue that could have come from any empty seats is lost forever.

Because of problems like this, airlines, doctors, hotels, and other service firms sometimes charge fees to clients who don't show up when they say they will. Service organizations also use a variety of approaches to shift customer demand to less busy times. Movie tickets are cheaper for afternoon shows, restaurants offer early-bird specials, and hotels that cater to business travelers promote weekend getaways. Firms also try to reduce the dissatisfaction that customers may feel if they must wait for service. Golf courses provide practice greens, and some doctors' offices provide comfortable seating and magazines.[4]

WHOLE PRODUCT LINES MUST BE DEVELOPED TOO

A **product assortment** is the set of all product lines and individual products that a firm sells. A **product line** is a set of individual products that are closely related. The seller may see the products in a line as related because they're produced or operate in a similar way, sold to the same target market, sold through the same types of outlets, or priced at about the same level. Sara Lee, for example, has many product lines in its product assortment—including beverages, luncheon meats, desserts, insecticides, body care, air care, and shoe care. But Enterprise has one product line—different types of vehicles to rent. An **individual product** is a particular product within a product line. It usually is differentiated by brand, level of service offered, price, or some other characteristic. For example, each size and flavor of a brand of soap is an individual product. Intermediaries usually think of each separate product as a stock-keeping unit (SKU) and assign it a unique SKU number.

Each individual product and target market may require a separate strategy. For example, Sara Lee's strategy for selling its Café Pilão coffee in Brazil is different from its strategy for selling Endust cleaning spray in the United States. We'll focus mainly on developing one marketing strategy at a time. But remember that a marketing manager may have to plan *several* strategies to develop an effective marketing program for a whole company.

BRANDING IS A STRATEGY DECISION

There are so many brands—and we're so used to seeing them—that we take them for granted. But branding is an important decision area, so we will treat it in some detail.

What is branding?

Branding means the use of a name, term, symbol, or design—or a combination of these—to identify a product. It includes the use of brand names, trademarks, and practically all other means of product identification.

Brand name has a narrower meaning. A **brand name** is a word, letter, or a group of words or letters. Examples include America Online (AOL), WD-40, 3M Post-its, and PT Cruiser.

Trademark is a legal term. A **trademark** includes only those words, symbols, or marks that are legally registered for use by a single company. A **service mark** is the same as a trademark except that it refers to a service offering.

The word *FedEx* can be used to explain these differences. The FedEx overnight delivery service is branded under the brand name FedEx (whether it's spoken or printed in any manner). When "FedEx" is printed in a certain kind of script, however, it becomes a trademark. A trademark need not be attached to the product. It need not even be a word—it can be a symbol. Exhibit 8–3 shows some common trademarks.

These differences may seem technical. But they are very important to business firms that spend a lot of money to protect and promote their brands. Sometimes a firm's brand name is the only element in its marketing mix that a competitor can't copy.

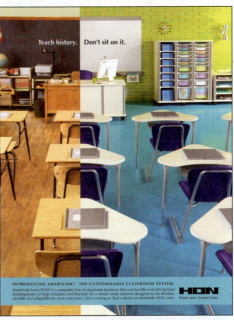

The Tostitos product line includes several types of chips as well as dips. In addition to its full-line of office furniture, the HON Company also offers classroom furniture.

Exhibit 8-3 Recognized Trademarks and Symbols Help in Promotion

Brands meet needs

Well-recognized brands make shopping easier. Think of trying to buy groceries, for example, if you had to evaluate each of 25,000 items every time you went to a supermarket. Many customers are willing to buy new things—but having gambled and won, they like to buy a sure thing the next time. Brand names connect a product with the benefits a customer can expect. The connection may be learned from past consumer experience, from the firm's promotion, or in other ways. *Certified Angus Beef* stands for "tender, high-quality meat," and *Jiffy Lube* means "fast and convenient oil change." Consumers know what they will get when they buy these branded products.

Brand promotion has advantages for branders as well as customers. A good brand reduces the marketer's selling time and effort. Good brands can also improve the company's image—speeding acceptance of new products marketed under the same name. For example, many consumers quickly tried Listerine PocketPaks breath fresheners when they appeared because they already knew they trusted Listerine mouthwash.[5]

CONDITIONS FAVORABLE TO BRANDING

Can you recall a brand name for file folders, bed frames, electric extension cords, or nails? As these examples suggest, it's not always easy to establish a respected brand.
The following conditions are favorable to successful branding:

1. The product is easy to label and identify by brand or trademark.
2. The product quality is easy to maintain and the best value for the price.
3. Dependable and widespread availability is possible. When customers start using a brand, they want to be able to continue using it.
4. Demand is strong enough that the market price can be high enough to make the branding effort profitable.
5. There are economies of scale. If the branding is really successful, costs should drop and profits should increase.
6. Favorable shelf locations or display space in stores will help. This is something retailers can control when they brand their own products.

In general, these conditions are less common in less-developed economies, and that may explain why efforts to build brands in less-developed nations often fail. For example, one study found Chinese consumers willing to pay a premium of only 2 percent for branded products they regularly purchase—as compared to premiums of 20 percent or more in developed countries.[6]

ACHIEVING BRAND FAMILIARITY IS NOT EASY

Today, familiar brands exist for most product categories, ranging from crayons (Crayola) to real estate services (RE/MAX).

Brand acceptance must be earned with a good product and regular promotion. **Brand familiarity** means how well customers recognize and accept a company's brand. The degree of brand familiarity affects the planning for the rest of the marketing mix—especially where the product should be offered and what promotion is needed.

Five levels of brand familiarity

Five levels of brand familiarity are useful for strategy planning: (1) rejection, (2) non-recognition, (3) recognition, (4) preference, and (5) insistence.

Some brands have been tried and found wanting. **Brand rejection** means that potential customers won't buy a brand unless its image is changed. Rejection may suggest a change in the product or perhaps only a shift to target customers who have a better image of the brand. Overcoming a negative image is difficult and can be very expensive.

Brand rejection is a big concern for service-oriented businesses because it's hard to control the quality of service. A business traveler who gets a dirty room in a Hilton Hotel in Caracas, Venezuela, might not return to a Hilton anywhere. Yet it's difficult for Hilton to ensure that every maid does a good job every time.

Some products are seen as basically the same. **Brand nonrecognition** means final consumers don't recognize a brand at all—even though intermediaries may use the brand name for identification and inventory control. Examples include school supplies, inexpensive dinnerware, many of the items that you'd find in a hardware store, and thousands of dot-coms on the Internet.

Brand recognition means that customers remember the brand. This may not seem like much, but it can be a big advantage if there are many "nothing" brands on the market. Even if consumers can't recall the brand without help, they may be reminded when they see it in a store among other less familiar brands.

Most branders would like to win **brand preference**—which means that target customers usually choose the brand over other brands, perhaps because of habit or favorable past experience. **Brand insistence** means customers insist on a firm's branded product and are willing to search for it.

It takes time and money to build brand awareness. The benefits of that investment can sometimes be extended to new products, even ones in related product categories. Dove has introduced moisturizing shampoos and conditioners. While a well-known brand name is an advantage, a firm must protect its brand if it falls into use as a general name for a product category. That's why Dow reminds people that Styrofoam is its registered brand name for insulating board—and not a general name for foam cups.

Take Your Coffee Black and Your STYROFOAM™ Brand Insulation Blue™.

Exhibit 8–4
Characteristics of a
Good Brand Name

• Short and simple	• Suggestive of product benefits
• Easy to spell and read	• Adaptable to packaging/labeling needs
• Easy to recognize and remember	• No undesirable imagery
• Easy to pronounce	• Always timely (does not go out-of-date)
• Can be pronounced in only one way	• Adaptable to any advertising medium
• Can be pronounced in all languages (for international markets)	• Legally available for use (not in use by another firm)

The right brand name can help

A good brand name can help build brand familiarity. It can help tell something important about the company or its product. Exhibit 8–4 lists some characteristics of a good brand name.

Companies that compete in international markets face a special problem in selecting brand names. A name that conveys a positive image in one language may be meaningless in another. Or, worse, it may have unintended meanings. GM's Nova car is a classic example. GM stuck with the Nova name when it introduced the car in South America. It seemed like a sensible decision because *nova* is the Spanish word for star. However, Nova also sounds the same as the Spanish words for "no go." Consumers weren't interested in a no-go car, and sales didn't pick up until GM changed the name.[7]

A respected name builds brand equity

Because it's costly to build brand recognition, some firms prefer to acquire established brands rather than try to build their own. The value of a brand to its current owner or to a firm that wants to buy it is sometimes called **brand equity**—the value of a brand's overall strength in the market. For example, brand equity is likely to be higher if many satisfied customers insist on buying the brand and if retailers are eager to stock it. That almost guarantees ongoing profits.

The financial value of the Yahoo! brand name illustrates the brand equity idea. In 1994, Yahoo! was just a tiny start-up trying to make it with a directory site on the Internet. Most people had never heard the name, and few even knew what the Internet was or why you'd need a directory site. As interest in the Internet grew, Yahoo! promoted its brand name with quirky TV and magazine ads. At a time when many people were just getting to know the Web, Yahoo! came across as an approachable and fun place to go on the Internet. Within a few years, Yahoo! attracted more than 100 million unique customer visits. Yahoo! wants its brand to become just as well known in places like Taiwan, China, and France. Because Yahoo! charges fees to advertisers eager to reach these users, the familiarity of its brand translates directly into ad revenues. And, in 2008, Microsoft offered to buy Yahoo! for more than $40 million.[8]

PROTECTING BRAND NAMES AND TRADEMARKS

U.S. common law and civil law protect the rights of trademark and brand name owners. The **Lanham Act** (of 1946) spells out what kinds of marks (including brand names) can be protected and the exact method of protecting them. The law applies to goods shipped in interstate or foreign commerce.

The Lanham Act does not force registration. But registering under the Lanham Act is often a first step toward protecting a trademark to be used in international markets. That's because some nations require that a trademark be registered in its home country before they will register or protect it.

You must protect your own

A brand can be a real asset to a company. Each firm should try to see that its brand doesn't become a common descriptive term for its kind of product. When this happens, the brand name or trademark becomes public property—and the owner loses

Differentiation by Design

Today, many companies are finding that they can get a competitive advantage by having designers involved in basic decisions about product features and functions—rather than just having them there to finalize the look. Designers now help with decisions about what benefits a product will offer, including the right look and feel to achieve ease of use.

Office equipment and furniture manufacturer Herman Miller has redesigned many common products to appeal to customers who value sustainability. Its design for the Leaf personal desk lamp uses light-emitting diodes (LEDs) that allow the user to choose the color and intensity of the light. The LEDs last for 60,000 hours—much longer than the traditional fluorescent lightbulbs they replace—yet use only 40 percent as much electricity. Leaf also contains 37 percent recycled materials. The sustainable features, combined with an artistic and functional design, differentiate the lamp and help it sell well, even at a price of almost $500.

Kaiser Permanente, the health care giant, did research that revealed that its facilities were alienating many patients. Most patients already had health concerns when they arrived, so the stark waiting rooms made them anxious, the poor signage was confusing, and small exam rooms were lonely. Kaiser turned to designers for help. They expanded the exam rooms, added privacy curtains, and invited patients to have a friend wait with them. After the redesign, Kaiser's patients reported more satisfaction with the health care they received. The health care was actually the same, but the facilities were improved.

In Europe, the circulation of newspapers steadily declined for years. Young adults with fast-paced lifestyles had little time and weren't reading them. However, Metro attracted many new customers from this demographic group after changing the morning newspaper experience. Switching to a tabloid design and short-article format did the trick.

A decade ago, discount retailer Target relied on TV and magazine ads to try to build a cool image. But the products it carried were mostly the same stuff sold by rival Wal-Mart. To differentiate itself, Target put more emphasis on products with affordable, attractive, and functional designs. Target recruited designers like Michael Graves to create new lines of housewares, office supplies, furniture, toys, and games—all of which helped to reposition Target's image. Today, Target's design-centered differentiation helps it reduce direct price competition.[9]

all rights to it. This happened with the names cellophane, aspirin, shredded wheat, and kerosene.[10]

Counterfeiting is accepted in some cultures

Even when products are properly registered, counterfeiters may make unauthorized copies. Counterfeit products cause a brand to lose sales and jeopardize its reputation. Many well-known brands—ranging from Levi's jeans to Rolex watches to Zantax medicine—face this problem. International trade in counterfeit and pirated goods may exceed $500 billion annually. Counterfeiting continues to grow and is especially common in developing countries where regulation is weak or cultural values differ. In China for example, many DVDs, CDs, and software programs are bootleg copies. And counterfeiters are increasingly brazen. In Azerbaijan and Bulgaria, BP discovered counterfeit BP service stations—with low-quality fuel.[11]

WHAT KIND OF BRAND TO USE?

Keep it in the family

Branders of more than one product must decide whether they are going to use a **family brand**—the same brand name for several products—or individual brands for each product. Examples of family brands are Keebler snack food products and Sears' Kenmore appliances.

General Mills owns the Cascadian Farm brand name, but uses the separate name to reinforce the positioning of its organic line of cereals. Both General Mills cereals and Cascadian Farm cereals may have to compete for shelf space—and consumer attention—against similar store (dealer) brands of cereal which often sell at lower prices.

The use of the same brand for many products makes sense if all are similar in type and quality. The main benefit is that the goodwill attached to one or two products may help the others. Money spent to promote the brand name benefits more than one product, which cuts promotion costs for each product.

A special kind of family brand is a **licensed brand**—a well-known brand that sellers pay a fee to use. For example, the familiar Sunkist brand name has been licensed to many companies for use on more than 400 products in 30 countries.[12]

Individual brands for outside and inside competition

A company uses **individual brands**—separate brand names for each product—when it's important for the products to each have a separate identity, as when products vary in quality or type.

Internet EXERCISE

Go to the Procter & Gamble website (**www.pg.com**) and click on "Products," then "View All Brands," and then "Hair Care" so you can see all of the different shampoos that P&G makes. How are the different brands positioned? To what target markets do they appeal?

If the products are really different, such as Elmer's glue and Borden's ice cream, individual brands can avoid confusion. Some firms use individual brands with similar products to make segmentation and positioning efforts easier. For example, when General Mills introduced a line of organic cereals, it used the Cascadian Farm name and the Big G logo was not on the box. The rationale was that consumers who try to avoid additives might not trust a big corporate brand.[13]

Generic "brands"

Products that some consumers see as commodities may be difficult or expensive to brand. Some manufacturers and intermediaries have responded to this problem with **generic products**—products that have no brand at all other than identification of their contents and the manufacturer or intermediary. Generic products are usually offered in plain packages at lower prices. They are quite common in less-developed nations.[14]

WHO SHOULD DO THE BRANDING?

Manufacturer brands versus dealer brands

Manufacturer brands are brands created by producers. These are sometimes called *national brands* because the brand is promoted all across the country or in large regions. Note, however, that many manufacturer brands are now distributed globally. Such brands include Nabisco, Campbell's, Whirlpool, Ford, and IBM. Many creators of service-oriented firms—like McDonald's, Orkin Pest Control, and Bank of America—promote their brands this way too.

Dealer brands, also called **private brands**, are brands created by intermediaries. Examples of dealer brands include the brands of Kroger, Ace Hardware, Radio Shack, Wal-Mart, and Sears. Some of these are advertised and distributed more

The package for Grillero beef looks different from the way most beef is packaged and also provides a way to tell French consumers that the product is organic.

widely than many national brands. For example, national TV ads helped Original Arizona Jeans (by JCPenney) and Canyon River Blues (by Sears) compete with Levi's and Wrangler.

From the intermediary's perspective, the major advantage of selling a popular manufacturer brand is that the product is already presold to some target customers. The major disadvantage is that manufacturers normally offer lower gross margins than the intermediary might be able to earn with a dealer brand.

Who's winning the battle of the brands?

The **battle of the brands**, the competition between dealer brands and manufacturer brands, is just a question of whose brands will be more popular and who will be in control.

At one time, manufacturer brands were much more popular than dealer brands. Now sales of both kinds of brands are about equal—but sales of dealer brands are expected to continue growing. Intermediaries have some advantages in this battle. With the number of large retail chains growing, they are better able to arrange reliable sources of supply at low cost. They can also give the dealer brand special shelf position or promotion. The lower prices typical for dealer brands make them even more attractive in an economic downturn.[15]

The Brand People Stick With.

Del Monte wants retailers to remember that many consumers already know and trust its brand name. Establishing successful brand names in the produce section is no easy feat.

THE STRATEGIC IMPORTANCE OF PACKAGING

Packaging involves promoting, protecting, and enhancing the product. Packaging can be important to both sellers and customers. See Exhibit 8–5. It can make a product more convenient to use or store. It can prevent spoiling or damage. Good packaging makes products easier to identify and promotes the brand at the point of purchase and even in use.

Exhibit 8–5   Some Ways Packaging Benefits Consumers and Marketers

Opportunity to Add Value	Some Decision Factors	Examples
Promoting	Link product to promotion	The bunny on the Energizer battery package is a reminder that it "keeps going and going."
	Branding at point of purchase or consumption	Coke's logo greets almost everyone each time the refrigerator is opened.
	Product information	Nabisco's nutrition label helps consumers decide which cookie to buy, and a UPC code reduces checkout time and errors.
Protecting	For shipping and storing	Sony's MP3 player is kept safe by Styrofoam inserts.
	From tampering	Tylenol's safety seal prevents tampering.
	From shoplifting	Cardboard hang-tag on Gillette razor blades is too large to hide in hand.
	From spoiling	Kraft's shredded cheese has a resealable zipper package to keep it fresh.
Enhancing product	The environment	Tide detergent bottle can be recycled.
	Convenience in use	Squeezable tube of Yoplait Go-Gurt is easy to eat on the go and in new situations.
	Added product functions	Plastic tub is useful for refrigerator leftovers after the Cool Whip is gone.

Packaging can enhance the product

A new package can make *the* important difference in a new marketing strategy—by meeting customers' needs better. Sometimes a new package makes the product easier or safer to use. For example, most drug and food products now have special seals to prevent product tampering. And clever packaging is an important part of a new effort by Campbell's Soup to pump new life into an old product—soup. Campbell's developed its Soup at Hand with a package that doesn't require a can opener or a stirring pot and instead is microwavable. Soup at Hand is just right for today's on-the-go consumers who want a portable meal solution, so it also helps Campbell's get distribution in convenience stores and vending machines. Consumers value convenience, so the Soup at Hand price of $1.49 (versus $0.79 for a traditional can of soup) also produces attractive profits.[16]

Packaging sends a message

Packaging can tie the product to the rest of the marketing strategy. Packaging for Energizer batteries features the pink bunny seen in attention-getting TV ads and reminds consumers that the batteries are durable. A good package sometimes gives a firm more promotional effect than it could get with advertising. Customers see the package in stores, when they're actually buying. A consumer who needs a new showerhead is likely to pick the brand and style by comparing alternatives at a retail store. Waterpik's package makes it easy for the consumer to see and evaluate the product and the curved design helps to focus attention on the flexible hose.

Packaging may lower distribution costs

Better protective packaging is very important to manufacturers and wholesalers. They sometimes have to pay the cost of goods damaged in shipment. Retailers need protective packaging too. It can reduce storing costs by cutting breakage, spoilage, and theft. Good packages also save space and weight so they are easier to transport, handle, and display—and better for the environment.[17]

Universal product codes speed handling

To speed handling of fast-selling products, government and industry representatives have developed a **universal product code (UPC)** that identifies each product with marks readable by electronic scanners. A computer then matches each code to the product and its price. These codes speed the checkout process and reduce the need to mark the price on every item. They also reduce errors by cashiers and make it easy to control inventory and track sales of specific products.[18]

WHAT IS SOCIALLY RESPONSIBLE PACKAGING?

Customers benefit from many of the advances that have been made in packaging. However, packaging is an area where managers face issues of social responsibility, including concerns about the role of packaging in pollution, global warming, and resource use.

Packaging excesses can hurt the environment

There have been several times when a crisis has brought attention to the environmental impact of packaging. For example, when scientists revealed that chemicals used in spray cans (for hairspray, deodorant, and other products) were damaging the earth's atmosphere, firms scrambled to find alternatives. However, it turns out that what we view as "normal" is actually a bigger problem. U.S. shoppers generate much more trash per person than anywhere else on earth. Much of what is tossed out is packaging. It overloads landfills, litters our streets, and pollutes the environment. For years plastic seemed to be the perfect packaging material because it is clean, light, and durable; now the consequence is that discarded plastic is everywhere and lasts forever. Even colorful package graphics are troublesome. The ink to print them often has toxins that later creep into the soil and water. Firms should try to give consumers what they want, but in applying that logic to packaging many people have been short-sighted. And both managers and consumers have often acted as if there was nothing an *individual* could do to reduce environment problems. Now that attitude is changing.

Many firms are taking steps to preserve the environment. Timberland makes its shoe boxes with 100 percent recycled materials, soy-based inks, and water-based glues. Music groups like Pearl Jam have eliminated plastic jewel cases from their CDs; of course, downloads from iTunes don't use CDs or packages. Whole Foods Market uses salad-bar containers made from sugar-cane waste; they safely turn into compost within about 90 days. It makes sense for firms to publicize such efforts to attract like-minded consumers. Publicity also calls attention to the idea that even small changes can add up to big improvements, especially when many people are involved. The recycling

Stonyfield Farm wants its customers to know that it is sensitive to the environment. It communicates how it is trying to improve the environmental performance of its packaging with messages on the lids of its yogurt containers and at the company's website.

programs that thrive in many communities illustrate this point. The total cost of the programs are often covered by selling mounds of cans, bottles, and other package materials that would otherwise be in dumps.

Can consumers evaluate eco impacts?

The benefits of recycling now seem obvious. However, consumers often don't know if a particular product and package is an eco-friendly choice. Some firms are beginning to provide such information. Tesco, the largest retail chain in Britain, posts a "carbon rating" on all 70,000 products it carries. These ratings remind consumers that what they buy impacts global warming. With ratings displayed at the point of purchase, producers have an incentive to improve. Clearly, producers are trying to appeal to green consumers in a variety of ways. For example, Canon created its Generation Green brand of printer cartridges that can be recycled and that come in a biodegradable package.

Efforts like these also highlight challenges. Some critics think that the environmental claims that firms make will be misleading or confusing if they are not standardized and regulated. It's hard to know, for example, how the environmental impact of Generation Green print cartridges compares to competitors' products. Similarly, Tesco's carbon rating plan is innovative, but measuring carbon usage is imprecise and many consumers don't know how to use the ratings. Despite such difficulties, more effort to protect the environment is needed.[19]

Laws reduce confusion

The **Federal Fair Packaging and Labeling Act** (of 1966) requires that consumer goods be clearly labeled in easy-to-understand terms to give consumers more information. The law also calls on industry to try to reduce the confusing number of package sizes and make labels more useful. Since then, there have been further guidelines. The most far-reaching are based on the Nutrition Labeling and Education Act of 1990. It requires food manufacturers to use a uniform format that allows consumers to compare the nutritional value of different products. Recently there

have been more changes, including requirements to clearly show the fat content of food and ingredients that trigger common food allergies.[20]

Ethical decisions remain

Although various laws provide guidance on many packaging issues, many areas still require marketing managers to make ethical choices. For example, some firms have been criticized for designing packages that conceal a downsized product, giving consumers less for their money. Similarly, some retailers design packages and labels for their dealer products that look just like, and are easily confused with, manufacturer brands. Are efforts such as these unethical, or are they simply an attempt to make packaging a more effective part of a marketing mix? Different people will answer differently.

Many critics think that labeling information is too often incomplete or misleading. For example, what does it really mean if a label says a food product is "organic" or "low fat"? But how far should a marketing manager go in putting potentially negative information on a package? For example, should Häagen-Dazs affix a label that says "this product will clog your arteries"? That sounds extreme, but what type of information *is* appropriate?

Many consumers like the convenience that accompanies the myriad product and packaging choices available.

Is it unethical for a marketing manager to give consumers with different preferences a choice? Some critics argue that it is. Others praise firms that give consumers choices.[21]

WARRANTY POLICIES ARE A PART OF STRATEGY PLANNING

Warranty puts promises in writing

A **warranty** explains what the seller promises about its product. A marketing manager should decide whether to offer a specific warranty, and if so what the warranty will cover and how it will be communicated to target customers. This is an area where the legal environment—as well as customer needs and competitive offerings—must be considered.

U.S. common law says that producers must stand behind their products—even if they don't offer a specific warranty. A written warranty provided by the seller may promise more than the common law provides. However, it may actually *reduce* the responsibility a producer would have under common law.

The federal **Magnuson-Moss Act** (of 1975) says that producers must provide a clearly written warranty if they choose to offer any warranty. The warranty does not have to be strong. However, Federal Trade Commission (FTC) guidelines try to ensure that warranties are clear and definite and not deceptive or unfair. A warranty must also be available for inspection before the purchase.

A company has to make it clear whether it's offering a full or limited warranty—and the law defines what *full* means. Most firms offer a limited warranty if they offer one at all. In recent years, many firms have reduced the period of warranty coverage. Apple's popular iPod music player, for example, only has a 90-day warranty.

Warranty may improve the marketing mix

Some firms use warranties to improve the appeal of their marketing mix. They design more quality into their goods or services and offer refunds or replacement, not just repair, if there is a problem. Warranties lessen consumer risk. A strong warranty can send consumers a signal about brand quality. A few years ago, Hyundai, the South Korean car maker, pushed to improve quality. Yet among consumers its old reputation lingered. That changed after Hyundai put a 10-year warranty on its cars and used TV ads to tout it as "America's best warranty."

In a competitive market, a product's warranty or guarantee can be the critical difference in a firm's marketing mix.

Service guarantees

Service guarantees are becoming more common as a way to attract, and keep, customers. Some Pizza Hut locations guarantee a luncheon pizza in five minutes or it's free. General Motors set up a fast-oil-change guarantee to compete with fast-lube specialists who were taking customers away from dealers. If the dealer doesn't get the job done in 29 minutes or less, the next oil change is free.

There's more risk in offering a service guarantee than a warranty on a physical product. A lazy employee or a service breakdown can create a big expense. However, without the guarantee, dissatisfied customers may just go away mad without ever complaining.

Warranty support can be costly

The cost of warranty support ultimately must be covered by the price that consumers pay. This has led some firms to offer warranty choices. The basic price for a product may include a warranty that covers a short time period or that covers parts but not labor. Consumers who want more or better protection pay extra for an extended warranty or a service contract.[22]

PRODUCT CLASSES HELP PLAN MARKETING STRATEGIES

So far in this chapter, we've focused on key strategy decisions for Product (see Exhibit 8–1). Managers usually try to blend those decisions in a unique way to differentiate the firm's offering and create superior customer value. However, you don't have to treat *every* product as unique when planning strategies. Rather, some classes of products require similar marketing mixes. So, now we'll introduce these product classes and show why they are a useful starting point for developing marketing mixes for new products and for evaluating present mixes.

Product classes start with type of customer

All products fit into one of two broad groups—based on the type of customer that will use them. **Consumer products** are products meant for the final consumer. **Business products** are products meant for use in producing other products.

The same product—like Bertolli Olive Oil—*might* be both a consumer product and a business product. Consumers buy it to use in their own kitchens, but food processing companies and restaurants buy it in large quantities as an ingredient in the products they sell. Selling the same product to both final consumers and business customers requires (at least) two different strategies.

There are product classes within each group. Consumer product classes are based on *how consumers think about and shop for products*. Business product classes are based on *how buyers think about products and how they'll be used*.

CONSUMER PRODUCT CLASSES

Consumer product classes divide into four groups: (1) convenience, (2) shopping, (3) specialty, and (4) unsought. *Each class is based on the way people buy products.* See Exhibit 8–6 for a summary of how these product classes relate to marketing mixes.[23]

Convenience products—purchased quickly with little effort

Convenience products are products a consumer needs but isn't willing to spend much time or effort shopping for. These products are bought often, require little service or selling, don't cost much, and may even be bought by habit. A convenience product may be a staple, impulse product, or emergency product.

Staples are products that are bought often, routinely, and without much thought—like breakfast cereal, canned soup, and most other packaged foods used almost every day in almost every household.

Impulse products are products that are bought quickly—as *unplanned* purchases—because of a strongly felt need. True impulse products are items that the customer

Exhibit 8-6 Consumer Product Classes and Marketing Mix Planning

Consumer Product Class	Marketing Mix Considerations	Consumer Behavior
Convenience products		
Staples	Maximum exposure with widespread, low-cost distribution; mass selling by producer; usually low price; branding is important.	Routinized (habitual), low effort, frequent purchases; low involvement.
Impulse	Widespread distribution with display at point of purchase.	Unplanned purchases bought quickly.
Emergency	Need widespread distribution near probable point of need; price sensitivity low.	Purchase made with time pressure when a need is great.
Shopping products		
Homogeneous	Need enough exposure to facilitate price comparison; price sensitivity high.	Customers see little difference among alternatives, seek lowest price.
Heterogeneous	Need distribution near similar products; promotion (including personal selling) to highlight product advantages; less price sensitivity.	Extensive problem solving; consumer may need help in making a decision (salesperson, website, etc.).
Specialty products	Price sensitivity is likely to be low; limited distribution may be acceptable, but should be treated as a convenience or shopping product (in whichever category product would typically be included) to reach persons not yet sold on its specialty product status.	Willing to expend effort to get specific product, even if not necessary; strong preferences make it an important purchase; Internet becoming important information source.
Unsought products		
New unsought	Must be available in places where similar (or related) products are sought; needs attention-getting promotion.	Need for product not strongly felt; unaware of benefits or not yet gone through adoption process.
Regularly unsought	Requires very aggressive promotion, usually personal selling.	Aware of product but not interested; attitude toward product may even be negative.

hadn't planned to buy, decides to buy on sight, may have bought the same way many times before, and wants right now. If the buyer doesn't see an impulse product at the right time, the sale may be lost.[24]

Emergency products are products that are purchased immediately when the need is great. The customer doesn't have time to shop around when a traffic accident occurs, a thunderstorm begins, or an impromptu party starts. The price of the ambulance service, raincoat, or ice cubes won't be important.

Shopping products— are compared

Shopping products are products that a customer feels are worth the time and effort to compare with competing products. Shopping products can be divided into two types, depending on what customers are comparing: (1) homogeneous or (2) heterogeneous shopping products.

Homogeneous shopping products are shopping products the customer sees as basically the same and wants at the lowest price. Some consumers feel that certain sizes and types of computers, television sets, washing machines, and even cars are very similar. So they shop for the best price. For some products, the Internet has become the fast way to do that.

Firms may try to emphasize and promote their product differences to avoid head-to-head price competition. For example, Rustoleum says that its spray paint goes on smoother and does a better job of preventing rust. But if consumers don't think the differences are real or important in terms of the value they seek, they'll just look at price.

Heterogeneous shopping products are shopping products the customer sees as different and wants to inspect for quality and suitability. Furniture, clothing, and membership in a spa are good examples. Often the consumer expects help from a knowledgeable salesperson. Quality and style matter more than price. In fact, once the customer finds the right product, price may not matter as long as it's reasonable. For example, you may have asked a friend to recommend a good dentist without even asking what the dentist charges.

Branding may be less important for heterogeneous shopping products. The more carefully consumers compare price and quality, the less they rely on brand names or labels. Some retailers carry competing brands so consumers won't go to a competitor to compare items.

Specialty products—no substitutes please!

Specialty products are consumer products that the customer really wants and makes a special effort to find. Shopping for a specialty product doesn't mean comparing—the buyer wants that special product and is willing to search for it. It's the customer's *willingness to search*—not the extent of searching—that makes it a specialty product.

Any branded product that consumers insist on by name is a specialty product. Marketing managers want customers to see their products as specialty products and ask for them over and over again. Building that kind of relationship isn't easy. It means satisfying the customer every time. However, that's easier and a lot less costly than trying to win back dissatisfied customers or attract new customers who are not seeking the product at all.

Unsought products—need promotion

Unsought products are products that potential customers don't yet want or know they can buy. So they don't search for them at all. In fact, consumers probably won't buy these products if they see them—unless promotion can show their value.

There are two types of unsought products. **New unsought products** are products offering really new ideas that potential customers don't know about yet. Informative

For consumers who have never heard of Joint Juice, it is a new unsought product. Effective promotion, and its catchy brand name, will help to end its unsought status, especially among target consumers who want healthy joints. In contrast, most people hate to wash dishes and know the benefits of having a dishwasher. Still, many consumers see dishwashers as homogeneous products and shop by price. But Bosch wants its target customers to see its distinctively quiet dishwashers as heterogeneous shopping products, or perhaps even specialty items.

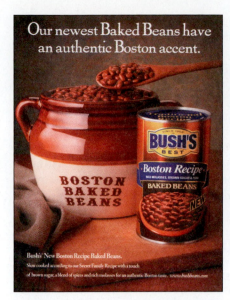 

Many items in Bush's Best line of food products sell as both consumer and business products, and different marketing mixes are required to reach the different target markets.

promotion can help convince customers to accept the product, ending its unsought status. Dannon's yogurt, Litton's microwave ovens, and AOL's Netscape browser are all popular items now, but initially they were new unsought products.

Regularly unsought products are products—like gravestones, life insurance, and encyclopedias—that stay unsought but not unbought forever. There may be a need, but potential customers aren't motivated to satisfy it. For this kind of product, personal selling is *very* important.

Many nonprofit organizations try to "sell" their unsought products. For example, the Red Cross regularly holds blood drives to remind prospective donors of how important it is to give blood.

One product may be seen in several ways

The same product might be seen in different ways by different target markets at the same time. For example, a product viewed as a staple by most consumers in the United States, Canada, or some similar affluent country might be seen as a heterogeneous shopping product by consumers in another country. The price might be much higher when considered as a proportion of the consumer's budget, and the available choices might be very different. Similarly, for some people salsa is seen as a staple; for others—who, for example, think it is worth tracking down W. B. Williams Georgia Style Peach Salsa on the Internet—it is a specialty product.

BUSINESS PRODUCTS ARE DIFFERENT

Business product classes are different from the consumer product classes—because they relate to how and why business firms make purchases. Thus, knowing the specific classes of business products helps in strategy planning. First, however, it's useful to note some important ways that the market for business products is different from the market for consumer products.

One demand derived from another

The big difference between the consumer products market and the business products market is **derived demand**—the demand for business products derives from the demand for final consumer products. For example, car manufacturers buy about one-fifth of all steel products. But if demand for cars drops, they'll buy less steel. Then even the steel supplier with the best marketing mix is likely to lose sales.[25]

Total *industry* demand for business products is fairly inelastic. Business firms must buy what they need to produce their own products. Even if the cost of basic silicon doubles, for example, Intel needs it to make computer chips. However, sharp business buyers try to buy as economically as possible. So the demand facing *individual sellers* may be extremely elastic—if similar products are available at a lower price.

How a firm's accountants—and the tax laws—treat a purchase is also important to business customers. An **expense item** is a product whose total cost is treated as a business expense in the year it's purchased. A **capital item** is a long-lasting product that can be used and depreciated for many years. Often it's very expensive. Customers pay for the capital item when they buy it, but for tax purposes the cost is spread over a number of years. This may reduce the cash available for other purchases.

BUSINESS PRODUCT CLASSES—HOW THEY ARE DEFINED

Business product classes are based on how buyers think about products and how the products will be used. The classes of business products are (1) installations, (2) accessories, (3) raw materials, (4) components, (5) supplies, and (6) professional services. Exhibit 8–7 relates these product classes to marketing mix planning.

Exhibit 8–7   Business Product Classes and Marketing Mix Planning

Business Product Classes	Marketing Mix Considerations	Buying Behavior
Installations	Usually requires skillful personal selling by producer, including technical contacts, or understanding of applications; leasing and specialized support services may be required.	Multiple buying influence (including top management) and new-task buying are common; infrequent purchase, long decision period, and boom-or-bust demand are typical.
Accessory equipment	Need fairly widespread distribution and numerous contacts by experienced and sometimes technically trained personnel; price competition is often intense, but quality is important.	Purchasing and operating personnel typically make decisions; shorter decision period than for installations; Internet sourcing.
Raw materials	Grading is important, and transportation and storing can be crucial because of seasonal production and/or perishable products; markets tend to be very competitive.	Long-term contract may be required to ensure supply; online auctions.
Component parts and materials	Product quality and delivery reliability are usually extremely important; negotiation and technical selling typical on less-standardized items; replacement after market may require different strategies.	Multiple buying influence is common; online competitive bids used to encourage competitive pricing.
Maintenance, repair, and operating (MRO) supplies	Typically require widespread distribution or fast delivery (repair items); arrangements with appropriate intermediaries may be crucial.	Often handled as straight rebuys, except important operating supplies may be treated much more seriously and involve multiple buying influence.
Professional services	Services customized to buyer's need; personal selling very important; inelastic demand often supports high prices.	Customer may compare outside service with what internal people could provide; needs may be very specialized.

Installations—a boom-or-bust business

Installations—such as buildings, land rights, and major equipment—are important capital items. One-of-a-kind installations—like office buildings and custom-made machines—generally require special negotiations for each sale. Negotiations often involve top management and can stretch over months or even years. Standardized major equipment is treated more routinely.

Installations are a boom-or-bust business. During growth periods, firms may buy installations to increase capacity. But during a downswing, sales fall off sharply.[26]

Specialized services are needed as part of the product

Suppliers sometimes include special services with an installation at no extra cost. A firm that sells (or leases) equipment to dentists, for example, may install it and help the dentist learn to use it.

Accessories— important but short-lived capital items

Accessories are short-lived capital items—tools and equipment used in production or office activities—like Canon's small copy machines, Rockwell's portable drills, and Steelcase's filing cabinets. Accessories are more standardized than installations and they're usually needed by more customers.

Since these products cost less and last a shorter time than installations, multiple buying influence is less important. Operating people and purchasing agents, rather than top managers, may make the purchase decision. As with installations, some customers may wish to lease or rent—to expense the cost.

Raw materials become part of a physical good

Raw materials are unprocessed expense items—such as logs, iron ore, and wheat—that are moved to the next production process with little handling. Unlike installations and accessories, *raw materials become part of a physical good and are expense items*.

There are two types of raw materials: (1) farm products and (2) natural products. **Farm products** are grown by farmers—examples are oranges, sugar cane, and cattle. **Natural products** are products that occur in nature—such as timber, iron ore, oil, and coal.

The need for grading is one of the important differences between raw materials and other business products. Nature produces what it will—and someone must sort and grade raw materials to satisfy various market segments.

Most buyers of raw materials want ample supplies in the right grades for specific uses—fresh vegetables for Green Giant's production lines or logs for Weyerhaeuser's paper mills. To ensure steady quantities, raw materials customers often sign long-term contracts, sometimes at guaranteed prices.

Component parts and materials must meet specifications

Components are processed expense items that become part of a finished product. Component *parts* are finished (or nearly finished) items that are ready for assembly into the final product. Intel's microprocessors included in personal computers and TRW's air bags in cars are examples. Component *materials* are items such as wire, plastic, or textiles. They have already been processed but must be processed further before becoming part of the final product. Quality is important with components because they become part of the firm's own product.

Some components are custom-made. Then teamwork between the buyer and seller may be needed to arrive at the right specifications. So a buyer may develop a close partnership with a dependable supplier. In contrast, standardized component materials are more likely to be purchased online using a competitive bidding system.

Since component parts go into finished products, a replacement market often develops. Car tires are components originally sold in the OEM (*original equipment market*) that become consumer products in the *after market*.[27]

Supplies for maintenance, repair, and operations

Supplies are expense items that do not become part of a finished product. Supplies can be divided into three types: (1) maintenance, (2) repair, and (3) operating supplies—giving them their common name: MRO supplies.

Maintenance and small operating supplies are like convenience products. The item will be ordered because it is needed—but buyers won't spend much time on it. For such "nuisance" purchases branding is important, and so are breadth of assortment and the seller's dependability. Intermediaries usually handle the many supply items. They are often purchased via online catalog sites.[28]

Important operating supplies, like coal and fuel oil, receive special treatment. Usually there are several sources for such commodity products—and large volumes may be purchased at global exchanges on the Internet.

Professional services— pay to get it done

Professional services are specialized services that support a firm's operations. They are usually expense items. Management consulting services can improve the company's efficiency. Information technology services can maintain a company's networks and websites. Advertising agencies can help promote the firm's products. And food services can improve morale.

Managers compare the cost of buying professional services outside the firm (*outsourcing*) to the cost of having company people do them. Work that was previously done by an employee is now often purchased from an independent specialist. Clearly, the number of service specialists is growing in our complex economy.

CONCLUSION

In this chapter, we looked at Product broadly— which is the right vantage point for marketing strategy planning. We saw that a product may be a good or a service, or some combination of both. And we saw that a firm's Product is what it offers to *satisfy the needs of its target market*—which may include the customer's experience both before and after the purchase. We also described some key marketing differences between goods and services.

We reviewed the Product area strategy decisions required for branding and packaging—and saw how the right decisions can add value for customers and give a product a competitive edge. Customers view a brand as a guarantee of quality, which leads to repeat purchases, lower promotion costs, higher sales figures, and greater customer equity. Packaging offers promotional opportunities and informs customers. Variations in packaging can also help a product appeal to different segments of the market. And packaging can help protect the product anywhere in the channel of distribution. We also saw how warranties can play an important role in strategy planning—by reducing buying risk. Customers see warranties as a signal of quality.

The brand familiarity a product earns is a measure of the marketing manager's ability to carve out a separate market. Therefore, ultimately, brand familiarity affects place, price, and promotion decisions. Strategy planning for the marketing mix will vary across product classes. We introduced both consumer product classes (based on *how consumers think about and shop for products*) and business product classes (based on *how buyers think about products and how they'll be used*). In addition, we showed how the product classes affect planning marketing mixes.

KEY TERMS

product, 193

quality, 193

product assortment, 196

product line, 196

individual product, 197

branding, 197

brand name, 197

trademark, 197

service mark, 197

brand familiarity, 199

brand rejection, 199

brand nonrecognition, 199

QUESTIONS AND PROBLEMS

1. Define, in your own words, what a Product is.

2. Discuss several ways in which physical goods are different from pure services. Give an example of a good and then an example of a service that illustrates each of the differences.

3. What products are being offered by a shop that specializes in bicycles? By a travel agent? By a supermarket? By a new car dealer?

4. Consumer services tend to be intangible, and goods tend to be tangible. Use an example to explain how the lack of a physical good in a pure service might affect efforts to promote the service.

5. Explain some of the different aspects of the customer experience that could be managed to improve customer satisfaction if you were the marketing manager for: (a) an airport branch of a rental car agency, (b) a fast-food restaurant, (c) an online firm selling software directly to consumers from a website, and (d) a hardware store selling lawn mowers.

6. Is there any difference between a brand name and a trademark? If so, why is this difference important?

7. Is a well-known brand valuable only to the owner of the brand?

8. Suggest an example of a product and a competitive situation where it would not be profitable for a firm to spend large sums of money to establish a brand.

9. List five brand names and indicate what product is associated with the brand name. Evaluate the strengths and weaknesses of the brand name.

10. Explain family brands. Should Best Buy carry its own dealer brands to compete with some of the popular manufacturer brands it carries? Explain your reasons.

11. In the past, Sears emphasized its own dealer brands. Now it is carrying more well-known manufacturer brands. What are the benefits to Sears of carrying more manufacturer brands?

12. What does the degree of brand familiarity imply about previous and future promotion efforts? How does the degree of brand familiarity affect the Place and Price variables?

13. You operate a small hardware store with emphasis on manufacturer brands and have barely been breaking even. Evaluate the proposal of a large wholesaler who offers a full line of dealer-branded hardware items at substantially lower prices. Specify any assumptions necessary to obtain a definite answer.

14. Give an example where packaging costs probably (a) lower total distribution costs and (b) raise total distribution costs.

15. Is it more difficult to support a warranty for a service than for a physical good? Explain your reasons.

16. How would the marketing mix for a staple convenience product differ from the one for a homogeneous shopping product? How would the mix for a specialty product differ from the mix for a heterogeneous shopping product? Use examples.

17. Give an example of a product that is a new unsought product for most people. Briefly explain why it is an unsought product.

18. In what types of stores would you expect to find (a) convenience products, (b) shopping products, (c) specialty products, and (d) unsought products?

19. What kinds of consumer products are the following: (a) watches, (b) automobiles, and (c) toothpastes? Explain your reasoning.

20. Cite two examples of business products that require a substantial amount of service in order to be useful.

21. Explain why a new law office might want to lease furniture rather than buy it.

22. Would you expect to find any wholesalers selling the various types of business products? Are retail stores required (or something like retail stores)?

23. What kinds of business products are the following: (a) lubricating oil, (b) electric motors, and (c) a firm that provides landscaping and grass mowing for an apartment complex? Explain your reasoning.

24. How do raw materials differ from other business products? Do the differences have any impact on their marketing mixes? If so, what specifically?

25. For the kinds of business products described in this chapter, complete the following table (use one or a few well-chosen words).

    1. *Kind of distribution facility(ies) needed and functions they will provide.*
    2. *Caliber of salespeople required.*
    3. *Kind of advertising required.*

Products	1	2	3
Installations			
Buildings and land rights			
Major equipment			
Standard			
Custom-made			
Accessories			
Raw materials			
Farm products			
Natural products			
Components			
Supplies			
Maintenance and small operating supplies			
Important operating supplies			
Professional services			

CREATING MARKETING PLANS

The Marketing Plan Coach software on the text website (and on the optional Student CD) includes a sample marketing plan for Hillside Veterinary Clinic. Look through the "Marketing Strategy" section.

a. What goods does Hillside Veterinary Clinic sell?

b. What services does Hillside Veterinary Clinic sell?

c. What consumer product classes are offered by Hillside Veterinary Clinic?

d. The discussion of product classes in this chapter indicates what marketing mix is typical for different classes of products. Does the marketing strategy recommended in the marketing plan fit with those considerations? Why or why not?

SUGGESTED CASES

1. McDonald's "Seniors" Restaurant
3. MANU Soccer Academy
13. File-It Supplies, Inc.
31. At-Home Health Services, Inc.

COMPUTER-AIDED PROBLEM

8. BRANDING DECISION

Wholesteen Dairy, Inc., produces and sells Wholesteen brand condensed milk to grocery retailers. The overall market for condensed milk is fairly flat, and there's sharp competition among dairies for retailers' business. Wholesteen's regular price to retailers is $8.88 a case (24 cans). FoodWorld—a fast-growing supermarket chain and Wholesteen's largest customer—buys 20,000 cases of Wholesteen's condensed milk a year. That's 20 percent of Wholesteen's total sales volume of 100,000 cases per year.

FoodWorld is proposing that Wholesteen produce private-label condensed milk to be sold with the FoodWorld brand name. FoodWorld proposes to buy the same total quantity as it does now, but it wants half (10,000 cases) with the Wholesteen brand and half with the FoodWorld brand. FoodWorld wants Wholesteen to reduce costs by using a lower-quality can for the FoodWorld brand. That change will cost Wholesteen $.01 less per can than it costs for the cans that Wholesteen uses for its own brand. FoodWorld will also provide preprinted labels with its brand name—which will save Wholesteen an additional $.02 a can.

Wholesteen spends $70,000 a year on promotion to increase familiarity with the Wholesteen brand. In addition, Wholesteen gives retailers an allowance of $.25 per case for their local advertising, which features the Wholesteen brand. FoodWorld has agreed to give up the advertising allowance for its own brand, but it is only willing to pay $7.40 a case for the milk that will be sold with the FoodWorld brand name. It will continue under the old terms for the rest of its purchases.

Sue Glick, Wholesteen's marketing manager, is considering the FoodWorld proposal. She has entered cost and revenue data on a spreadsheet—so she can see more clearly how the proposal might affect revenue and profits.

a. Based on the data in the initial spreadsheet, how will Wholesteen profits be affected if Glick accepts the Food-World proposal?

b. Glick is worried that FoodWorld will find another producer for the FoodWorld private label milk if Wholesteen rejects the proposal. This would immediately reduce Wholesteen's annual sales by 10,000 cases. FoodWorld might even stop buying from Wholesteen altogether. What would happen to profits in these two situations?

c. FoodWorld is rapidly opening new stores and sells milk in every store. The FoodWorld buyer says that next year's purchases could be up to 25,000 cases of Wholesteen's condensed milk. But Sue Glick knows that FoodWorld may stop buying the Wholesteen brand and want all 25,000 cases to carry the FoodWorld private label brand. How will this affect profit? (Hint: enter the new quantities in the "proposal" column of the spreadsheet.)

d. What should Wholesteen do? Why?

For additional questions related to this problem, see Exercise 8-5 in the *Learning Aid for Use with Essentials of Marketing*, 12th edition.

CHAPTER

9

Product Management and New-Product Development

The founders of iRobot didn't know that their company would become the world leader in home robots. However, from the start they didn't intend to just imitate other firms' products. Instead they wanted to create totally new product concepts that would change society. That is where they're headed, with products like Roomba, Scooba, Verro, Looj, and Packbot. The Packbot is a business and military product. This nimble but rugged computer-controlled equipment shoots audio and video in places that are too dangerous for humans. It helps soldiers clear roadside bombs in Iraq and search caves in Afghanistan. It can even work underwater or climb stairs in a factory.

When iRobot started, the company focused on just military and business products. One project with S.C. Johnson involved industrial cleaning robots. iRobot later entered the consumer market, developing concepts for robotic toys for Hasbro. Here they learned the importance of cost control; for two years many toy ideas iRobot pitched to Hasbro were rejected. They were technically elegant but too expensive. These experiences helped iRobot focus on an idea for a low-priced robotic vacuum cleaner—later named *the Roomba*.

Roomba's new-product developers—including some brilliant scientists—knew the importance of looking at the Roomba from the customer's perspective. So early prototypes of the Roomba went home with iRobot employees where their spouses, friends, and neighbors tested them out. The developers gained valuable feedback and quickly learned that not everyone was technically savvy. So when design engineers talked about how best to train customers to use the Roomba, the team realized that was backwards. Instead of training customers, they designed Roomba's software to figure out what to do when a customer pushed the start button. The owner's manual is available in many languages, but because the Roomba is so simple to use, it is only a few pages long and most people won't need it.

The original idea was for Roomba to just have sweeper brushes. However, in focus groups consumers said that the Roomba also needed a vacuum. Responding to this consumer input added extra expense late in the project, but iRobot was ready because of the cost control lessons learned from working with Hasbro. With Roomba, developers had controlled every penny from the outset, and were able to add the vacuum and value consumers wanted.

Before iRobot introduced the Roomba in 2002, the vacuum cleaner market was mature, with few breakthrough product ideas. Then came Roomba. It's a slick-looking, 15-inch disk, less than 4 inches tall. It's a robot but it requires no programming. You simply place it on the floor, press a button to turn it on, and Roomba automatically wanders around the room doing its job. It can scoot under the sofa, scurry around the furniture, and return to the battery charger when the job is done.

Marketing managers were concerned the Roomba's appeal might be limited to a small market of gadget-loving techies. But they wanted to sell Roomba to a larger market

segment—people who hate to vacuum. To offset consumer concerns about the complexity of the technology, introductory promotion described the Roomba as an intelligent vacuum cleaner, not as a robot. For the first three years, the word *robot* didn't even appear on the package (except in the iRobot company name).

For its launch, iRobot worked with specialty retailers including Sharper Image, Hammacher Schlemmer, and Brookstone. These retailers were willing to show videos of Roomba in action and train their salespeople to explain and demonstrate Roomba in their stores. The extra promotion push was important because initially customers didn't know the brand name and were not looking for this sort of product. However, iRobot quickly generated publicity for the Roomba—with everything from appearances on the "Today" show and videos on MySpace to reviews in magazines, newspapers, and CNET.com. All of this media attention—and some traditional ads—propelled sales and quickly made Roomba a familiar brand. After production caught up with demand, iRobot expanded distribution to include Bed Bath and Beyond, Linens and Things, and Target.

By controlling costs, iRobot was able to offer Roomba at $200. A higher price might have been acceptable to some customers, but that low price helped fend off potential competitors, at least for a while. Soon other competitors, including Electrolux, P3, iTouchless, and Infinuvo, jumped into the market. Roomba's established brand identity kept it ahead of the pack.

Roomba sales grew quickly and it is now a well-known brand with more than 2.5 million units sold. iRobot's product managers have responded with more specialized Roomba models for different target markets. Pet owners appreciate the special features of the Roomba Pet Series, men like that the Dirt Dog sweeps workshops, and small business owners buy the Professional Series Roomba. The differentiation helps iRobot generate higher margins and better return on investment with models priced up to $600.

The now familiar iRobot brand name helps it sell related products that wash floors (Scooba), clear leaves from gutters (Looj), and clean pools (Verro). iRobot's creative product development, along with the strategies designed to reach its target markets, have resulted in remarkable growth—with sales increasing from $54 million in 2003 to $308 million in 2008. iRobot has shown that it has the technical skills to create innovative and reliable new products while being guided by the voices of its customers. It may encounter some more bumps along the way—few firms can completely avoid problems with new products. Even so, iRobot is likely to enjoy more success as the product-market it has pioneered experiences rapid growth in the next decade.[1]

LEARNING OBJECTIVES

Developing new products and managing them for profitable growth are keys to success for most firms. Yet, many new products fail. Even products that succeed face new challenges as competition becomes more intense. So, the marketing strategy that supported the product's initial success usually needs to change as the market evolves. This chapter will help you understand this evolution and how it relates to effective new-product development and creative strategy changes for existing products—both of which are crucial to attracting and retaining target customers.

When you finish this chapter you should be able to:

1 understand how product life cycles affect strategy planning.

2 know what is involved in designing new products and what "new products" really are.

3 understand the new-product development process.

4 see why product liability must be considered in screening new products.

5 understand the need for product or brand managers.

6 understand how total quality management can improve goods and services.

7 understand important new terms (shown in red).

INNOVATION AND MARKET CHANGES CREATE OPPORTUNITIES

Successful new products, like those in the iRobot case, are critical in driving profitable growth for both new and established companies. iRobot pioneered a fast-growing new product-market—and "computer-controlled cleaning tools" are meeting customer needs in new ways. Similarly, in Chapter 5, we looked at how the iPod and other innovations in digital media are changing personal entertainment. In fact, all around us there is a constant life-and-death struggle where old products are replaced by new products. Digital video recorders are quickly making videotapes obsolete, just as cell phones have replaced shortwave radios and phone booths and made it possible for people to communicate from places where it was previously impossible. Really new product ideas disrupt the old ways of doing things—not only for marketers, but also for consumers.

These innovations show that products, customer behavior, and competition change over time. These changes create opportunities for marketing managers and pose challenges as well. Developing new products and managing existing products to meet changing conditions is important to the success of every firm. In Chapter 8 we looked at important strategy planning decisions that need to be made for new products and sometimes changed for existing products. In this chapter, we'll look at how successful new products are developed in the first place—and what marketing managers need to know and do to manage their growth. We'll start by explaining the cycle of growth and decline that new product innovations go through. When you understand the stages in this cycle, you can see *why* it is so critical for a firm to have an effective new-product development process—and why the challenges of managing a product change as it matures. See Exhibit 9–1.

Exhibit 9–1   The Role of Product Management and New-Product Development in Marketing Strategy

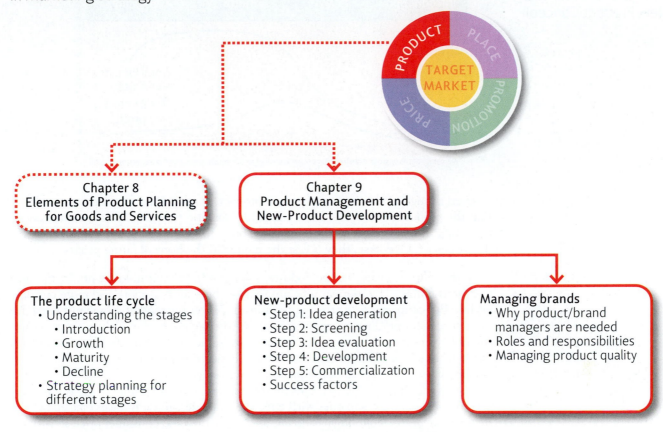

MANAGING PRODUCTS OVER THEIR LIFE CYCLES

Revolutionary products create new product-markets. But competitors are always developing and copying new ideas and products—making existing products out-of-date more quickly than ever. Products, like consumers, go through life cycles.

Product life cycle has four major stages

The **product life cycle** describes the stages a really new product idea goes through from beginning to end. The product life cycle is divided into four major stages: (1) market introduction, (2) market growth, (3) market maturity, and (4) sales decline. The product life cycle is concerned with new types (or categories) of products in the market, not just what happens to an individual brand.

A particular firm's marketing mix usually must change during the product life cycle. There are several reasons why customers' attitudes and needs may change over the product life cycle. The product may be aimed at entirely different target markets at different stages. And the nature of competition moves toward pure competition or oligopoly.

Further, total sales of the product—by all competitors in the industry—vary in each of its four stages. They move from very low in the market introduction stage to high at market maturity and then back to low in the sales decline stage. More important, the profit picture changes too. These general relationships can be seen in Exhibit 9–2. Note that sales and profits do not move together over time. *Industry profits decline while industry sales are still rising.*[2]

Market introduction— investing in the future

In the **market introduction** stage, sales are low as a new idea is first introduced to a market. Customers aren't looking for the product. Even if the product offers superior value, customers don't even know about it. Informative promotion is needed to tell potential customers about the advantages and uses of the new product concept.

Exhibit 9-2
Typical Life Cycle of a
New Product Concept

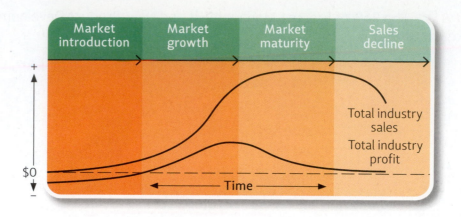

Market introduction	Market growth	Market maturity	Sales decline

Total industry sales

Total industry profit

Time

Even though a firm promotes its new product, it takes time for customers to learn that the product is available. Most companies experience losses during the introduction stage because they spend so much money for Product, Place, and Promotion development. Of course, they invest the money in the hope of future profits.

Market growth—profits go up and down

In the **market growth** stage, industry sales grow fast—but industry profits rise and then start falling. The innovator begins to make big profits as more and more customers buy. But competitors see the opportunity and enter the market. Some just copy the most successful product or try to improve it to compete better. Others try to refine their offerings to do a better job of appealing to some target markets. The new entries result in much product variety. So monopolistic competition—with down-sloping demand curves—is typical of the market growth stage.

This is the time of biggest profits *for the industry*. It is also a time of rapid sales and earnings growth for companies with effective strategies. *But it is toward the end of this stage when industry profits begin to decline* as competition and consumer price sensitivity increase. See Exhibit 9-2.

Some firms make big strategy planning mistakes at this stage by not understanding the product life cycle. They see the big sales and profit opportunities of the early market growth stage but ignore the competition that will soon follow. When they realize their mistake, it may be too late. This happened with many dot-coms during the late 1990s. Marketing managers who understand the cycle and pay attention to competitor analysis are less likely to encounter this problem.

Now that GPS devices are in the market growth stage of the product life cycle, competition is intense between a number of firms who offer a variety of models with different features. To stay ahead, Magellan continues to innovate. For example, its Maestro targets people who want a thin, portable unit with advanced features like voice command and live traffic reporting.

**Market maturity—
sales level off, profits
continue down**

The **market maturity** stage occurs when industry sales level off and competition gets tougher. Many aggressive competitors have entered the race for profits—except in oligopoly situations. Industry profits go down throughout the market maturity stage because promotion costs rise and some competitors cut prices to attract business. Less efficient firms can't compete with this pressure—and they drop out of the market. There is a long-run downward pressure on prices.

New firms may still enter the market at this stage—increasing competition even more. Note that late entries skip the early life-cycle stages, including the profitable market growth stage. And they must try to take a share of the saturated market from established firms, which is difficult and expensive. The market leaders have a lot at stake, so they fight hard to defend their share. Customers who are happy with their current relationship won't switch to a new brand. So late entrants usually have a tough battle.

Persuasive promotion becomes even more important during the market maturity stage. Products may differ only slightly. Most competitors have discovered effective appeals or just copied the leaders. As the various products become almost the same in the minds of potential consumers, price sensitivity is a real factor.[3]

In the United States, the markets for most cars, boats, and many household appliances are in market maturity. This stage may continue for many years—until a basically new product idea comes along—even though individual brands or models come and go. For example, high-definition digital TV (HDTV) is coming on now, so it is making obsolete not only the old-style TVs but also the broadcast systems on which they rely.

**Sales decline—a time
of replacement**

During the **sales decline** stage, new products replace the old. Price competition from dying products becomes more vigorous—but firms with strong brands may make profits until the end because they have successfully differentiated their products.

As the new products go through their introduction stage, the old ones may keep some sales by appealing to their most loyal customers or those who are slow to try new ideas. These conservative buyers might switch later—smoothing the sales decline.

PRODUCT LIFE CYCLES SHOULD BE RELATED TO SPECIFIC MARKETS

Remember that product life cycles describe industry sales and profits for a *product idea* within a particular product-market. The sales and profits of an individual brand may not, and often do not, follow the life-cycle pattern. They may vary up and down

In the market maturity stage of the product life cycle, product improvements usually don't result in big increases in the size of the overall market but rather help the improved brand take a larger market share. For example, Colgate's new brush for sensitive teeth may win a larger share of business from segments with that need. Similarly, Dawn may become even more popular with an air freshener built into the base.

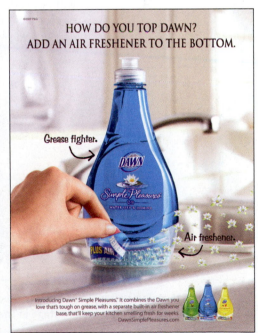

throughout the life cycle—sometimes moving in the opposite direction of industry sales and profits. Further, a product idea may be in a different life-cycle stage in different markets.

Individual brands may not follow the pattern

A given firm may introduce or drop a specific product during *any* stage of the product life cycle. A "me-too" brand introduced during the market growth stage, for example, may never get sales at all and suffer a quick death. For instance, Wal-Mart tried to rent DVDs by mail—but the innovator, Netflix, was already established as the market leader. When customers did not see Wal-Mart's marketing mix as better, it failed to attract enough customers and closed operations.

Strategy planners who naively expect sales of an individual product to follow the general product life-cycle pattern are likely to be rudely surprised. In fact, it might be more sensible to think in terms of "product-market life cycles" rather than product life cycles—but we will use the term *product life cycle* because it is commonly accepted and widely used.

Each market should be carefully defined

How we see product life cycles depends on how broadly we define a product-market. For example, milk is a mature product in the United States. U.S. consumers drink about 18 times more milk than consumers in Asia. Milk is a good source of calcium in diets, so higher milk consumption there could help reduce Asia's high level of osteoporosis, a bone disease related to low calcium levels. To get sales growth in Asia, milk producers promote this benefit—but they've also added ginger and honey flavors to appeal to Asian palates.[4] As this example suggests, a firm with a mature product can sometimes find new growth in international markets.

If a market is defined broadly, there may be many competitors—and the market may appear to be in market maturity. On the other hand, if we focus on a narrow submarket—and a particular way of satisfying specific needs—then we may see much shorter product life cycles as improved product ideas come along to replace the old.

PRODUCT LIFE CYCLES VARY IN LENGTH

How long a whole product life cycle takes—and the length of each stage—varies a lot across products. The cycle may vary from 90 days—in the case of toys like the *Incredibles* movie line—to possibly 100 years for gas-powered cars.

The product life-cycle concept does not tell a manager precisely *how long* the cycle will last. But a manager can often make a good guess based on the life cycle for similar products. Sometimes marketing research can help too. However, it is more important to expect and plan for the different stages than to know the precise length of each cycle.

New products that do a better job of meeting the needs of specific target customers are more likely to move quickly and successfully through the introductory stage of the product life cycle.

Some products move fast

A new-product idea will move through the early stages of the life cycle more quickly when it has certain characteristics. For example, the greater the *comparative advantage* of a new product over those already on the market, the more rapidly its sales will grow. Sales growth is also faster when the product is *easy to use* and if its advantages are *easy to communicate*. If the product *can be tried* on a limited basis—without a lot of risk to the customer—it can usually be introduced more quickly. Finally, if the product is *compatible* with the values and experiences of target customers, they are likely to buy it more quickly.

The fast adoption of DVD players is a good example. The idea of renting or buying movies to view at home was already compatible with consumer lifestyles, but many consumers hesitated before buying a DVD player. They wanted to see if DVD movies would be readily available. As movies appeared, DVD player sales took off because they had advantages over VHS tape players. Consumers could tell that the picture and audio quality were better from a store demo—without buying anything. Further, ads highlighted DVD extras such as deleted scenes and interviews with directors. DVD players also worked with music CDs. Now that the price of DVD recorders (and digital video recorders) have fallen, they have driven VHS recorders into the market decline stage of the product life cycle. Note, however, that DVD player adoption has not been as fast in less-developed countries where TV penetration is still low, movies are not available, and the costs are higher relative to consumer income.[5]

Internet EXERCISE

A number of software, hardware, and programming firms are working on products that deliver Internet information via TV. Explore the MSN TV website (**www.msntv.com**) to find out about one aspect of this idea and try the demos. How does MSN TV stack up when you consider the characteristics that help a new product move through the life cycle more quickly?

Product life cycles are getting shorter

Although the life of different products varies, in general product life cycles are getting shorter. This is partly due to rapidly changing technology. One new invention may make possible many new products that replace old ones. Tiny electronic microchips led to thousands of new products—from Texas Instruments calculators in the early days to microchip-controlled heart valves now.

The XO Laptop is another interesting case. It is a stripped-down unit with a sunlight-friendly screen that was developed by a professor at MIT. He created it as a way to help kids in the developing world, and he hoped a low $150 price would encourage governments to buy in bulk. Some people thought he was just an idealist, but the XO created such a stir that it prodded Microsoft and Intel to figure out what they should do for this market.[6]

Although life cycles keep moving in the developed economies, many advances bypass most consumers in less-developed economies. These consumers struggle at the subsistence level, without an effective macro-marketing system to stimulate innovation. However, some of the innovations and economies of scale made possible in the advanced societies do trickle down to benefit these consumers. Inexpensive antibiotics and drought-resistant plants, for example, are making a life-or-death difference.

The early bird usually makes the profits

The product life cycle means that firms must be developing new products all the time. Further, they must try to use marketing mixes that will make the most of the market growth stage—when profits are highest.

During the growth stage, competitors are likely to rapidly introduce product improvements. Fast changes in marketing strategy may be required here because profits don't necessarily go to the innovator. Sometimes fast copiers of the basic idea win in the market growth stage. General Motors' electric car, the EV1, was the first zero-emission vehicle on the market when it was first sold in California. However, Toyota and Honda leapfrogged past GM when they introduced hybrid vehicles powered by a combination of gas engine and electric motor. Their hybrids did not eliminate all emissions, but they met other needs better. They have more power and are less expensive. The market for low-emission hybrids is growing rapidly, yet GM is still playing catch-up. Marketers need to be innovative, but at the same time they must be flexible in adapting to the needs and attitudes of their target markets.[7]

The short happy life of fashions and fads

The sales of some products are influenced by **fashion**—the currently accepted or popular style. Fashion-related products tend to have short life cycles. What is currently popular can shift rapidly. A certain color or style of clothing—baggy jeans, miniskirts, or four-inch-wide ties—may be in fashion one season and outdated the next. Marketing managers who work with fashions often have to make really fast product changes.

How fast is fast enough? Zara, a women's fashion retailer based in Spain, takes only about two weeks to go from a new fashion concept to having items on the racks of its stores. At headquarters, sales managers sit at computers monitoring sales at every store around the world. When a garment is hot, more is produced and shipped. Otherwise, it's dropped. And then Zara's market-watching designers, who are sitting nearby, get the order to whip up fresh designs. The designers get a constant flow of new fashion ideas from music videos, fashion shows, and magazines. Zara quickly produces just enough of a design to test the waters and then sends it out for overnight delivery to some of its stores around the world. Stores are stocked with new designs, not just new orders, about twice a week. Shipping labels identify the newest collections so they can be rushed to the sales floor on their plastic shipping hangers, and only later are they switched to Zara's normal wood hangers. Zara regulars know to search out the black plastic hangers for the latest looks. Store managers use handheld computers that show how garments rank by sales, so clerks can reorder best-sellers in less than an hour. These orders arrive, together with new pieces, two days later. With this system, items are rarely on the shelves of Zara stores for more than a few weeks, but that helps to convey an air of exclusivity.[8]

A certain color or style may be in fashion one season and outdated the next. Zara, a fashion retailer, puts its catalog on its website (www.zara.com) so it can be updated quickly each season.

A **fad** is an idea that is fashionable only to certain groups who are enthusiastic about it. But these groups are so fickle that a fad is even more short lived than a regular fashion. Low-carbohydrate diets were very popular for a while, for example. Many toys—whether it's a Hasbro *Lord of the Rings* plastic figure or a Toymax Paintball pack—are fads but do well during a short-lived cycle.[9]

PLANNING FOR DIFFERENT STAGES OF THE PRODUCT LIFE CYCLE

Length of cycle affects strategy planning

Where a product is in its life cycle—and how fast it's moving to the next stage—should affect marketing strategy planning. Marketing managers must make realistic plans for the later stages. Exhibit 9–3 shows the relationship of the product life cycle to the marketing mix variables. The technical terms in this figure are discussed later in the book.

Introducing new products

Exhibit 9–3 shows that a marketing manager has to do a lot of strategy planning to introduce a really new product. Money must be spent developing the new product. Even if the product is unique, this doesn't mean that everyone will immediately come

Exhibit 9–3
Typical Changes in Marketing Variables over the Product Life Cycle

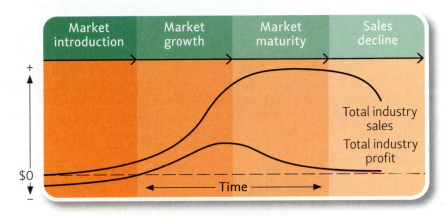

Product	One or few	Variety—try to find best product	All "same"	Some drop out
		Build brand familiarity	Battle of brands	
Place	Build channels	Move toward more intensive distribution		
	Maybe selective distribution			
Promotion	Build primary demand	Build selective demand		
	Pioneering-informing	Informing/Persuading ⟶ Persuading/Reminding (frantically competitive)		
Price	Skimming or penetration	Meet competition (especially in oligopoly) or Price dealing and price cutting		
Competitive situation	Monopoly or monopolistic competition	Monopolistic competition or oligopoly	Monopolistic competition or oligopoly heading toward pure competition	

running to the producer's door. The firm will have to build channels of distribution—perhaps offering special incentives to win cooperation. Promotion is needed to build demand *for the whole idea* not just to sell a specific brand. Because all this is expensive, it may lead the marketing manager to try to "skim" the market—charging a relatively high price to help pay for the introductory costs.

The correct strategy, however, depends on how quickly the new idea will be accepted by customers—and how quickly competitors will follow with their own versions of the product. When the early stages of the cycle will be fast, a low initial (penetration) price may make sense to help develop loyal customers early and keep competitors out.

Pioneer may need help from competitors

Sometimes it's not in the best interest of the market pioneer for competitors to stay out of the market. Building customer interest in a really new product idea—and obtaining distribution to make the product available—can be too big a job for a single company. Two or more companies investing in promotion to build demand may help to stimulate the growth of the whole product-market. Sony worked with Samsung and Philips (among others) to help Blu-ray beat out rival HD-DVD and create a new standard for high-definition video.[10]

New product sales may not take off

Not all new-product ideas catch on. Customers or intermediaries may not be satisfied with the marketing mix, or other new products may meet the same need better. But the success that eludes a firm with its initial strategy can sometimes be achieved by modifying the strategy. David Mintz invented a soy-based frozen dessert and started Tofutti Brands, Inc., to sell it. Tofutti was especially appealing to people who could not eat dairy products. Mintz's strategy was to offer a limited number of flavors and partner with a big company that already had national distribution in supermarkets. Häagen-Dazs agreed to the plan but wanted exclusive distribution rights. Sales grew quickly at first but then plummeted when conflicts between Mintz and Häagen-Dazs ended the relationship. To keep consumers interested in Tofutti while he slowly rebuilt distribution through a dozen specialized wholesalers, Mintz had to constantly offer new flavors.[11]

Managing maturing products

It's important for a firm to have some competitive advantage as it moves into market maturity. Even a small advantage can make a big difference—and some firms do very well by carefully managing their maturing products. They are able to capitalize on a slightly better product or perhaps lower production or marketing costs. Or they

Some companies continue to do well in market maturity by improving their products or by finding new uses and applications. As shown in this ad, DuPont International's Lycra has expanded from personal apparel to furniture upholstery.

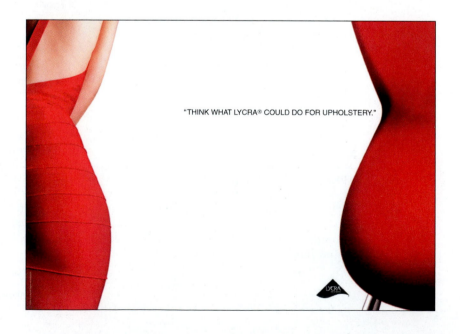

"THINK WHAT LYCRA® COULD DO FOR UPHOLSTERY."

228

are simply more successful at promotion—allowing them to differentiate their more or less homogeneous product from competitors. For example, graham crackers were competing in a mature market and sales were flat. Nabisco used the same ingredients to create bite-sized Teddy Grahams and then promoted them heavily. These changes captured new sales and profits for Nabisco.[12]

Industry profits are declining in market maturity. Top managers must see this, or they will expect the attractive profits that are no longer possible. If top managers don't understand the situation, they may place impossible burdens on the marketing department—causing marketing managers to think about deceptive advertising or some other desperate attempt to reach impossible objectives.

Product life cycles keep moving. But that doesn't mean a firm should just sit by as its sales decline. There are other choices. A firm can improve its product or develop an innovative new product for the same market. Or it can develop a new strategy targeted at a new market where the life cycle is not so far along. That approach is working for InSinkErator. It has an 80 percent share of all garbage disposals, but in the mature U.S. market, disposals are already in half of all homes. In contrast, garbage disposals are in only about 10 percent of homes in many areas of Europe. While many households there can afford a disposal, most cities prohibited them on environmental grounds. When research showed that garbage disposals actually provide environmental benefits, InSinkErator adapted its strategy and sales in Europe have grown quickly.[13]

Improve the product or develop a new one

When a firm's product has won loyal customers, it can be successful for a long time—even in a mature or declining market. However, continued improvements may be needed as customers' needs shift. An outstanding example is Procter & Gamble's Tide. Introduced in 1947, Tide led to a whole new generation of powdered laundry products that cleaned better with fewer suds. But Tide continues to change because of new washing machines and fabrics. The Tide sold today has had at least 55 modifications.

Do product modifications—like those made with powdered Tide—create a wholly new product that should have its own product life cycle? Or are they technical adjustments of the original product idea? We will take the latter position—focusing on the product idea rather than changes in features. This means that some of these Tide changes were made in the market maturity stage. But this type of product improvement can help to extend the product life cycle.

On the other hand, a firm that develops an innovative new product may move to a new product life cycle. For example, by 1985 new liquid detergents like Wisk were

Tide detergent has been improved many times over the years, and currently there are 37 different versions of Tide, including the new 2X Ultra Tide. However, some innovations, like Tide's convenient Rapid Action Tablets, that were introduced in the market maturity stage of the product life cycle are no longer on the market. On the other hand, the handy Tide to Go stain remover extends the brand name to a new product category.

moving into the growth stage, and sales of powdered detergents were declining. To share in the growth-stage profits for liquid detergents and to offset the loss of customers from powdered Tide, Procter & Gamble introduced Liquid Tide.

Even though regular powdered detergents are in the decline stage, traditional powdered Tide continues to sell well because it still does the job for some consumers. But sales growth is likely to come from liquid detergents and the newer low-suds detergents.[14]

Develop new strategies for different markets

In a mature market, a firm may be fighting to keep or increase its market share. But if the firm finds a new use for the product, it may stimulate overall demand. DuPont's Teflon fluorocarbon resin is a good example. It was developed more than 50 years ago and has enjoyed sales growth as a nonstick coating for cookware and as a lining for chemically resistant equipment. But marketing managers for Teflon are not waiting to be stuck with declining profits in those mature markets. They are constantly developing strategies for new markets. For example, Teflon is now selling well as a special coating for the wires used in high-speed communications between computers and as a lightweight film that offers greater output power for photovoltaic solar panels.[15]

Phasing out dying products

Not all strategies are exciting growth strategies. If prospects are poor in a product-market, a phase-out strategy may be needed. The need for phasing out becomes more obvious as the sales decline stage arrives. But even in market maturity, it may be clear that a particular product is not going to be profitable enough to reach the company's objectives. In any case, it is wise to remember that marketing plans are implemented as ongoing strategies. Salespeople make calls, inventory moves in the channel, advertising is scheduled for several months into the future, and so on. So the firm usually experiences losses if managers end a plan too abruptly. Because of this, it's sometimes better to phase out the product gradually.

Phasing out a product may involve some difficult implementation problems. But phase-out is also a *strategy*—and it must be market-oriented to cut losses. In fact, it is possible to milk a dying product for some time if competitors move out more quickly and there is ongoing (though declining) demand. Some customers are willing to pay attractive prices to get their old favorite.

NEW-PRODUCT PLANNING

In most markets, progress marches on. So it is essential for a firm to develop new products or modify its current products to meet changing customer needs and competitors' actions. Not having an active new-product development process means that consciously, or subconsciously, the firm has decided to milk its current products and go out of business. New-product planning is not an optional matter. It has to be done just to survive in today's dynamic markets. Consider something as basic as a Bic lighter. It's always been a reliable product and a good value. For years, most of them were used to light cigarettes. But in response to changes in the cultural environment, Bic is coming out with new products for other needs. The Luminere lighter, for example, has a long stem that can move into several positions that make it ideal for lighting candles in hard-to-reach places.

What is a new product?

In discussing the introductory stage of product life cycles, we focused on the types of really new product innovations that tend to disrupt old ways of doing things. However, each year firms introduce many products that are basically refinements of existing products. So a **new product** is one that is new *in any way* for the company concerned.

A product can become "new" in many ways. A fresh idea can be turned into a new product and start a new product life cycle. For example, Alza Corporation's time-release skin patches are replacing pills and injections for some medications.

Variations on an existing product idea can also make a product new. For example, Logitech has improved the lowly computer mouse by making it wireless and Gatorade has made its bottle easier to grip. Even small changes in an existing product can make it new.[16]

FTC says product is "new" only six months

A firm can call its product new for only a limited time. Six months is the limit according to the **Federal Trade Commission (FTC)**—the federal government agency that polices antimonopoly laws. To be called new, says the FTC, a product must be entirely new or changed in a "functionally significant or substantial respect."[17]

Ethical issues in new-product planning

New-product decisions—and decisions to abandon old products—often involve ethical considerations. For example, some firms (including firms that develop drugs) have been criticized for holding back important new-product innovations until patents run out, or sales slow down, on their existing products.

At the same time, others have been criticized for "planned obsolescence"—releasing new products that the company plans to soon replace with improved new versions. Similarly, wholesalers and retailers complain that producers too often keep their new-product introduction plans a secret and leave intermediaries with dated inventory that they can sell only at a loss.

Companies also face ethical dilemmas when they decide to stop supplying a product or the service and replacement parts to keep it useful. An old model of a Cuisinart food processor, for example, might be in perfect shape except for a crack in the plastic mixing bowl. It's sensible for the company to improve the design if the crack is a frequent problem, but if consumers can't get a replacement part for the model they already own, they're left holding the bag.

Different marketing managers might have very different reactions to such criticisms. However, product management decisions often have a significant effect on customers and intermediaries. A too-casual decision may lead to a negative backlash that affects the firm's strategy or reputation.[18]

AN ORGANIZED NEW-PRODUCT DEVELOPMENT PROCESS IS CRITICAL

Identifying and developing new-product ideas—and effective strategies to go with them—is often the key to a firm's success and survival. But the costs of new-product development and the risks of failure are high. Experts estimate that consumer packaged-goods companies spend more than $20 million to introduce a new brand—and 80 to 95 percent of those new brands flop. That's a big expense—and a waste. In the service sector, the front-end cost of a failed effort may not be as high, but it can have a devastating long-term effect if dissatisfied consumers turn elsewhere for help.[19]

A new product may fail for many reasons. Most often, companies fail to offer a unique benefit or underestimate the competition. Sometimes the idea is good but the company has design problems—or the product costs much more to produce than was expected. Some companies rush to get a product on the market without developing a complete marketing plan.[20]

But moving too slowly can be a problem too. With the fast pace of change for many products, speedy entry into the market can be a key to competitive advantage. Marketing managers at Xerox learned this the hard way. Japanese competitors were taking market share with innovative new models of copiers. It turned out that the competitors were developing new models twice as fast as Xerox and at half the cost. For Xerox to compete, it had to slash its five-year product development cycle.[21]

Exhibit 9-4   New-Product Development Process

Idea generation	Screening	Idea evaluation	Development	Commercialization
Ideas from: Customers and users Marketing research Competitors Other markets Company people Intermediaries, etc.	Strengths and weaknesses Fit with objectives Market trends Rough ROI estimate	Concept testing Reactions from customers Rough estimates of costs, sales, and profits	R&D Develop model or service prototype Test marketing mix Revise plans as needed ROI estimate	Finalize product and marketing plan Start production and marketing "Roll out" in select markets Final ROI estimate

The longer new-product development takes, the more likely it is that customer needs will be different when the product is actually introduced. Back in 2005, consumer interest in trucks and SUVs was high. General Motors expected that popularity to continue when planning new models. But, by the time those vehicles were on the market in 2008, gasoline prices had skyrocketed—and consumer preferences were switching to smaller cars. In contrast, Toyota's new-product planning had focused on more fuel efficiency, and its new 2008 hybrid models were in hot demand.

To move quickly and also avoid expensive new-product failures, companies should follow an organized new-product development process. The following pages describe such a process, which moves logically through five steps: (1) idea generation, (2) screening, (3) idea evaluation, (4) development (of product and marketing mix), and (5) commercialization.[22] See Exhibit 9-4.

The general process is similar for both consumer and business markets—and for both goods and services. There are some significant differences, but we will emphasize the similarities in the following discussion.

Process tries to kill new ideas—economically

An important element in the new-product development process is continued evaluation of a new idea's likely profitability and return on investment. The hypothesis tested is that the new idea will *not* be profitable. This puts the burden on the new idea—to prove itself or be rejected. Such a process may seem harsh, but experience shows that most new ideas have some flaw. Marketers try to discover those flaws early, and either find a remedy or reject the idea completely. Applying this process requires much analysis of the idea *before* the company spends money to develop and market a product. This is a major departure from the usual production-oriented approach—in which a company develops a product first and then asks sales to "get rid of it."

Step 1: Idea generation

Finding new-product ideas can't be left to chance. Instead, firms need a formal procedure to generate a continuous flow of ideas. New ideas can come from a company's own sales or production staff, wholesalers or retailers, competitors, consumer surveys, or other sources such as trade associations, advertising agencies, or government agencies. By analyzing new and different views of the company's markets, studying present consumer behavior, and anticipating future trends, a marketing manager can spot opportunities that have not yet occurred to competitors or even to potential customers. For example, ideas for new service concepts may come directly from analysis of consumer complaints.

No one firm can always be first with the best new ideas. So companies should pay attention to what competitors are doing. Some firms use what's called *reverse engineering*. For example, new-product specialists at Ford Motor Company buy other firms' cars as soon as

Customers Help Brew New Products

To generate better new products, marketing managers need to be vigilant in looking for new ideas. And customers can be one great source of new-product ideas. Sometimes you just need to remember to ask them. When Jim McCann, CEO of online gift shop 1-800-Flowers.com, gives a talk, he always asks for new-product idaeas. One customer answered his question by sending him a photo of a flower arrangement in an oversized martini glass. Soon afterwards, the "Happy Hour Bouquet" became the company's biggest new-product introduction ever.

Starbucks asks for customer input online at mystarbucksidea.com. Customers go to the site to share ideas they have for Starbucks, vote (thumbs up or down), and discuss or comment on ideas from others. Starbucks employees monitor the site and write about progress they are making toward implementing particular ideas. In its first year, fans shared more than 70,000 ideas—and Starbucks put 94 into action. Ideas range from "splash sticks" which minimize spills by plugging the drinking hole in lids to new breakfast sandwich suggestions. Other companies, including Best Buy, Dell, and General Mills also have "crowd-sourcing" sites where customers are asked to submit new ideas.

T-shirt maker Threadless' customers go a couple steps further. They provide designs for shirts, evaluate submissions, and then buy what the company sells. Threadless community members submit t-shirt designs as part of a contest. Winning designs are chosen based on ratings and comments from other members. Threadless produces the winners and sells them on its website—and because community members tell them which shirts to make, every product sells out.

Toy manufacturer Lego tapped some of its most enthusiastic users to develop the latest version of Mindstorms programmable bricks. The Mindstorms User Panel, which eventually grew to 14 citizen members, got involved on the ground floor of the latest incarnation of the popular robot-based product. After signing non-disclosure agreements, the four original members found out that Lego wanted them to work with Lego employees to completely make over the already successful Mindstorms. These dedicated customers regularly communicated with each other and the "paid" Mindstorms NXT development team by e-mail, offering engineers ideas and regular feedback.

The lifeblood of new-product development is ideas. Today, many smart companies realize that ideas can come from anywhere—but customers are one important source. Successful companies get more ideas from customers by asking for their input, providing opportunities for them to share their thoughts, and listening to what they say.[23]

they're available. Then they take the cars apart to look for new ideas or improvements. British Airways talks to travel agents to learn about new services offered by competitors.[24]

Other firms "shop" in international markets for new ideas. For instance, food companies in Europe are experimenting with an innovation from Japan—a clear, odorless, natural film for wrapping food. Consumers don't have to unwrap it; when they put the product in boiling water or a microwave, the wrapper vanishes.[25]

Step 2: Screening

Screening involves evaluating the new ideas with the type of S.W.O.T analysis described in Chapter 2 and the product-market screening criteria described in Chapter 3. Recall that these criteria include the combined output of a resources (strengths and weaknesses) analysis, a long-run trends analysis, and a thorough understanding of the company's objectives. See Exhibit 2–9 and Exhibit 3–8. A "good" new idea should eventually lead to a product (and marketing mix) that will give the firm a competitive advantage—hopefully, a lasting one.

The life-cycle stage at which a firm's new product enters the market has a direct bearing on its prospects for growth. So screening should consider how the strategy for a new product will hold up over the whole product life cycle.

Exhibit 9–5
Types of New-Product
Opportunities

		Immediate satisfaction	
		High	Low
Long-run consumer welfare	High	Desirable products	Salutary products
	Low	Pleasing products	Deficient products

Thinking about the strengths and weaknesses of a new-product idea from both a short- and long-term perspective can be a challenge. However, decisions about how the firm brings a new product to market often shape future market opportunities (and threats). A classic example is IBM's decision to license the operating system for the IBM PC when it was introduced. At that time, designing a PC to use an existing operating system (like the one then available from Microsoft) was a fast and low-cost way to get to market. However, the operating system ultimately produced more profit for Microsoft than the hardware did for IBM.

Some companies screen based on consumer welfare

Screening should also consider how a new product will affect consumers over time. Ideally, the product should increase consumer welfare, not just satisfy a whim. Exhibit 9–5 shows different kinds of new-product opportunities. Obviously, a socially responsible firm tries to find desirable opportunities rather than deficient ones. This may not be as easy as it sounds, however. Some consumers want pleasing products and give little thought to their own long-term welfare.

A consumer in the United States may conclude that a new product with a low price is a good value and purchase it. If the product's low price was possible because it was produced in China—where there are fewer costly pollution controls—the real value may not be what it seems. Even if the product itself is satisfactory right now, unchecked pollution from Chinese factories is contributing to global climate change. Over time that will reduce the welfare of the product's customers—and all other people. This story isn't about some fictional shopper or product. Rather, many of us can't judge the impact on consumer welfare of the products we buy. However, thinking through such issues is part of the challenge that managers face in trying to develop socially responsible new products.[26]

Safety must be considered

Real acceptance of the marketing concept prompts managers to screen new products on the basis of how safe they are. Safety is not a casual matter. The U.S. **Consumer Product Safety Act** (of 1972) set up the Consumer Product Safety Commission to encourage safety in product design and better quality control. The commission has a great deal of power. It can set safety standards for products. It can order costly repairs or return of unsafe products. And it can back up its orders with fines and jail sentences. The Food and Drug Administration has similar powers for foods and drugs.

Product safety complicates strategy planning because not all customers—even those who want better safety features—are willing to pay more for safer products. Some features cost a lot to add and increase prices considerably. These safety concerns must be considered at the screening step because a firm can later be held liable for unsafe products.

Outsourcing of production to factories in China has caused problems for a number of well-known brands, including toys that were recalled due to safety problems such as lead poisoning.

Products can turn to liabilities

Product liability means the legal obligation of sellers to pay damages to individuals who are injured by defective or unsafe products. Product liability is a serious matter. Liability settlements may exceed not only a company's insurance coverage but its total assets!

Relative to most other countries, U.S. courts enforce a very strict product liability standard. Sellers may be held responsible for injuries related to their products no matter how the items are used or how well they're designed. In one widely publicized judgment, McDonald's paid a huge settlement to a woman who was burned when her coffee spilled. The court concluded that there was not enough warning about how hot the coffee was.

Product liability is a serious ethical and legal matter. Many countries are attempting to change their laws so that they will be fair to both firms and consumers. But until product liability questions are resolved, marketing managers must be even more sensitive when screening new-product ideas.[27]

ROI is a crucial screening criterion

Getting by the initial screening criteria doesn't guarantee success for the new idea. But it does show that at least the new idea is in the right ballpark *for this firm*. If many ideas pass the screening criteria, a firm must set priorities to determine which ones go on to the next step in the process. This can be done by comparing the ROI (return on investment) for each idea—assuming the firm is ROI-oriented. The most attractive alternatives are pursued first.

Step 3: Idea evaluation

When an idea moves past the screening step, it is evaluated more carefully. Note that an actual product has not yet been developed—and this can handicap the firm in getting feedback from customers. For help in idea evaluation, firms use **concept testing**—getting reactions from customers about how well a new-product idea fits their needs. Concept testing uses market research—ranging from informal focus groups to formal surveys of potential customers.

Companies can often estimate likely costs, revenue, and profitability at this stage. And marketing research can help identify the size of potential markets. Even informal focus groups are useful—especially if they show that potential users are not excited about the new idea. If results are discouraging, it may be best to kill the idea at this stage. Remember, in this hypothesis-testing process, we're looking for any evidence that an idea is *not* a good opportunity for this firm and should be rejected.

Product planners must think about wholesaler and retailer customers as well as final consumers. Intermediaries may have special concerns about handling a proposed product. A Utah ice-cream maker was considering a new line of ice-cream novelty products—and he had visions of a hot market in California. But he had to drop his idea when he learned that grocery store chains wanted payments of $20,000 each just to stock his frozen novelties in their freezers.[28]

Idea evaluation is often more precise in business markets. Potential customers are more informed—and their needs focus on the economic reasons for buying rather than emotional factors. Further, given the derived nature of demand in business markets, most needs are already being satisfied in some way. So new products just substitute for existing ones. This means that product planners can compare the cost advantages and limitations of a new product with those currently being used. And by interviewing well-informed people, they can determine the range of product requirements and decide whether there is an opportunity.

Whatever research methods are used, the idea evaluation step should gather enough information to help decide whether there is an opportunity, whether it fits with the firm's resources, *and* whether there is a basis for developing a competitive advantage. With such information, the firm can estimate likely ROI in the various market segments and decide whether to continue the new-product development process.[29]

Step 4: Development

Product ideas that survive the screening and idea evaluation steps must now be analyzed further. Usually, this involves some research and development (R&D) and engineering to design and develop the physical part of the product. In the case of a new service offering, the firm will work out the details of what training, equipment, staff, and so on will be needed to deliver on the idea. Input from a firm's earlier efforts helps guide this technical work.

With computer-aided design (CAD) systems, designers can develop lifelike 3-D color drawings of packages and products. Changes can be made almost instantly. They can be sent by e-mail to managers all over the world for immediate review. They can even be put on a website for marketing research with remote customers. Then once the designs are finalized, they feed directly into computer-controlled manufacturing systems. Companies like Motorola and Timex have found that these systems cut their new-product development time in half—giving them a leg up on many competitors.

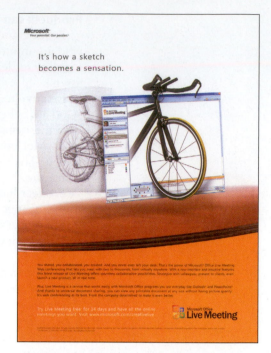

Microsoft Office Live Meeting makes it easy for managers to collaborate and share information without leaving their desks even if they are in different locations. Capabilities such as this are helping to make new-product development efforts faster and easier.

Even so, it is still useful to test models and early versions of the product in the market. This process may have several cycles. A manufacturer may build a model of a physical product or produce limited quantities; a service firm may try to train a small group of service providers. Product tests with customers may lead to revisions—*before* the firm commits to full-scale efforts.

With actual goods or services, potential customers can react to how well the product meets their needs. Focus groups, panels, and larger surveys can react to specific features and to the whole product idea. Sometimes that reaction kills the idea. For example, Coca-Cola Foods believed it had a great idea with Minute Maid Squeeze-Fresh, frozen orange juice concentrate in a squeeze bottle. In tests, however, Squeeze-Fresh bombed. Consumers loved the idea but hated the product. It was messy to use, and no one knew how much concentrate to squeeze in the glass.[30]

Firms often use full-scale market testing to get reactions in real-market conditions or to test variations in the marketing mix. For example, a firm may test alternative brands, prices, or advertising copy in different test cities. Note that the firm is testing the whole marketing mix, not just the product. For example, a hotel chain might test a new service offering at one location to see how it goes over.

Running market tests is costly, but *not* testing is risky. Frito-Lay was so sure it understood consumers' snack preferences that it introduced a three-item cracker line without market testing. Even with network TV ad support, MaxSnax met with overwhelming consumer indifference. By the time Frito-Lay pulled the product from store shelves, it had lost $52 million.[31]

Step 5: Commercialization

A product idea that survives this far can finally be placed on the market. Putting a product on the market is expensive, and success usually requires cooperation of the whole company. Manufacturing or service facilities have to be set up. Goods have to be produced to fill the channels of distribution, or people must be hired and trained to provide services. Further, introductory promotion is costly—especially if the company is entering a very competitive market.

Because of the size of the job, some firms introduce their products city by city or region by region—in a gradual "rollout"—until they have complete market coverage. Rollouts also permit more market testing, but the main purpose is to do a good job implementing the marketing plan. Marketing managers also need to pay close attention to control—to ensure that the implementation effort is working and that the strategy is on target.

NEW-PRODUCT DEVELOPMENT: A TOTAL COMPANY EFFORT

We've been discussing the steps in a logical, new-product development process. However, as shown in Exhibit 9–6, many factors can impact the success of the effort.

Top-level support is vital

Companies that are particularly successful at developing new goods and services seem to have one key trait in common: enthusiastic top-management support for new-product development. New products tend to upset old routines that managers of established products often try in subtle but effective ways to maintain. So someone with top-level support, and authority to get things done, needs to be responsible for new-product development.[32]

When Schick developed its new Quattro shaving system, it also developed a marketing plan that included a special end-of-aisle display (like this one created by Weyerhaeuser) that showcases the new razor, blades, and packaging.

Exhibit 9–6 New-Product Development Success Factors

A culture of innovation

A culture that supports innovation can generate more ideas. For example, Google allows its employees the freedom to spend 20 percent of their time working on new ideas, even if the ideas are unrelated to their job description. When people don't see the incentive to push for new ideas, they are likely to get distracted by other priorities that seem more pressing. For many years 3M has had an objective that 30 percent of sales should come from products that didn't exist four years earlier. Consistent with that goal, 3M's innovative culture produced breakthrough products like Scotch Stretchy Tape, Post-it Note Cards, Scotch Brite Tub & Tile Scrubber, and Vikuiti brand films for video screens. However, when the company moved toward more emphasis on cost cutting, the new-product pipeline began to dry up. To regain its innovative edge, 3M is going back to a better balance of efficiency *and* innovation.[33]

Put someone in charge

Rather than leaving new-product development to someone in engineering, R&D, or sales who happens to be interested in taking the initiative, successful companies *put* someone in charge. It may be a person, department, or team. But it's not a casual thing. It's a major responsibility of the job.

A new-product development team with people from different departments helps ensure that new ideas are carefully evaluated and profitable ones are quickly brought to market. It's important to choose the right people for the job. Overly conservative managers may kill too many, or even all, new ideas. Or committees may create bureaucratic delays that make the difference between a product's success or failure.

Market needs guide R&D effort

From the idea generation stage to the commercialization stage, the R&D specialists, the operations people, and the marketing people must work together to evaluate the feasibility of new ideas. They may meet in person, or communicate with e-mail or intranet sites, or perhaps via teleconferencing or some other technology. There are many ways to share ideas. So it isn't sensible for a marketing manager to develop elaborate marketing plans for goods or services that the firm simply can't produce—or produce profitably. It also doesn't make sense for R&D people to develop a technology or product that does not have potential for the firm and its markets. Clearly, a balancing act is involved here. But the critical point is the basic one we've been emphasizing throughout the whole book: Marketing-oriented firms seek to satisfy customer needs at a profit with an integrated, whole company effort.

Steps should not be skipped

Because speed can be important, it's always tempting to skip needed steps when some part of the process seems to indicate that the company has a "really good idea." But the process moves in steps—gathering different kinds of information along the way. By skipping steps, a firm may miss an important aspect that could make a whole strategy less profitable or actually cause it to fail.

NEED FOR PRODUCT MANAGERS

Product variety leads to product managers

When a firm has only one or a few related products, everyone is interested in them. But when a firm has products in several different product categories, management may decide to put someone in charge of each category, or each brand, to be sure that attention to these products is not lost in the rush of everyday business. **Product managers** or **brand managers** manage specific products—often taking over the jobs formerly handled by an advertising manager. That gives a clue to what is often their major responsibility—Promotion—since the products have already been developed by the new-product people. However, some brand managers start at the new-product development stage and carry on from there.

Product managers are especially common in large companies that produce many kinds of products. Several product managers may serve under a marketing manager. Sometimes these product managers are responsible for the profitable operation of a particular product's whole marketing effort. Then they have to coordinate their efforts with others, including the sales manager, advertising agencies, production and research people, and even channel members. This is likely to lead to difficulties if product managers have no control over the marketing strategy for other related brands or authority over other functional areas whose efforts they are expected to direct and coordinate.

To avoid these problems, in some companies the product manager serves mainly as a "product champion"—concerned with planning and getting the promotion effort implemented. A higher-level marketing manager with more authority coordinates the efforts and integrates the marketing strategies for different products into an overall plan.

The activities of product managers vary a lot depending on their experience and aggressiveness and the company's organizational philosophy. Today, companies are emphasizing marketing *experience*—because this important job takes more than academic training and enthusiasm. But it is clear that someone must be responsible for developing and implementing product-related plans, especially when a company has many products.[34]

MANAGING PRODUCT QUALITY

Total quality management meets customer requirements

In Chapter 8 we explained that product quality means the ability of a product to satisfy a customer's needs or requirements. Now we'll expand that idea and discuss some ways a manager can improve the quality of a firm's goods and services. We'll develop these ideas from the perspective of **total quality management (TQM)**, the philosophy that everyone in the organization is concerned about quality, throughout all of the firm's activities, to better serve customer needs.

The cost of poor quality is lost customers

Most of the early attention in quality management focused on reducing defects in goods produced in factories. At one time most firms assumed defects were an inevitable part of mass production. They saw the cost of replacing defective parts or goods as just a cost of doing business—an insignificant one compared to the advantages of mass production. However, many firms were forced to rethink this assumption when Japanese producers of cars, electronics, and cameras showed that defects weren't inevitable. Much to the surprise of some production-oriented managers, the Japanese experience showed that it is less expensive to do something right the first time than it is to pay to do it poorly and *then* pay again to fix problems. And their success in taking customers away from established competitors made it clear that the cost of defects wasn't just the cost of replacement!

From the customer's point of view, getting a defective product and having to complain about it is a big headache. The customer can't use the defective product and suffers the inconvenience of waiting for someone to fix the problem—if *someone* gets around to it. It certainly doesn't deliver superior value. Rather, it erodes goodwill and leaves customers dissatisfied. The big cost of poor quality is the cost of lost customers.

Firms that adopted TQM methods to reduce manufacturing defects soon used the same approaches to overcome many other problems. Their success brought attention to what is possible with TQM—whether the problem concerns poor customer service, flimsy packaging, or salespeople who can't answer customers' questions.

Getting a handle on doing things right the first time

The idea of identifying customer needs and doing things right the first time seems obvious, but it's easier said than done. Problems always come up, and it's not always clear what isn't being done as well as it could be. People tend to ignore problems that don't pose an immediate crisis. But firms that adopt TQM always look for ways to improve implementation with **continuous improvement**—a commitment to constantly make things better one step at a time. Once you accept the idea that there *may* be a better way to do something and you look for it, you

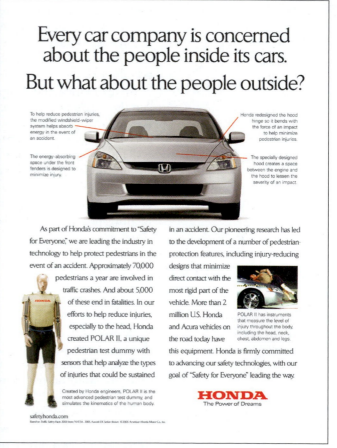

Independent product testing labs, like the Canadian Standards Association (CSA), give Canadian consumers added confidence that products are safe. Similar organizations operate in other countries. Honda is committed to developing new vehicles that provide "safety for everyone"—and that includes pedestrians who might be involved in an accident.

may just find it! The place to start is to clearly define "defects" from the customer's point of view.

Things gone right and things gone wrong

Managers who use the TQM approach think of quality improvement as a sorting process—a sorting out of things gone right and things gone wrong. The sorting process calls for detailed measurements related to a problem. Then managers use a set of statistical tools to analyze the measurements and identify the problem areas that are the best candidates for fixing. The statistical details are beyond our focus here, but it's useful to get a feel for how managers use the tools.

Starting with customer needs

Let's consider the case of a restaurant that does well during the evening hours but wants to improve its lunch business. The restaurant develops a strategy that targets local businesspeople with an attractive luncheon buffet. The restaurant decides on a buffet because research shows that target customers want a choice of good healthy food and are willing to pay reasonable prices for it—as long as they can eat quickly and get back to work on time.

As the restaurant implements its new strategy, the manager wants a measure of how things are going. So she encourages customers to fill out comment cards that ask "How did we do today?" After several months of operation, things seem to be going reasonably well—although business is not as brisk as it was at first. The manager reads the comment cards and divides the ones with complaints into categories—to count up different reasons why customers weren't satisfied.

Slay the dragons first

Then the manager creates a graph (see Exhibit 9–7) showing a frequency distribution for the different types of complaints. Quality people call this a **Pareto chart**—a graph that shows the number of times a problem cause occurs, with problem causes ordered from most frequent to least frequent. The manager's Pareto chart reveals that customers complain most frequently that they have to wait for a seat. There were other common complaints—the buffet was not well organized, the table was not clean, and so on. However, the first complaint is much more common than the next most frequent one.

This is typical. The worst problems often occur over and over again. This focuses the manager's attention on which quality problem to fix first. A rule of quality management is to slay the dragons first—which simply means start with the biggest problem. After removing that problem, the battle moves on to the next most frequent problem. If you do this *continuously,* you solve a lot of problems—and you don't just satisfy customers, you delight them.

Exhibit 9–7
Pareto Chart Showing Frequency of Different Complaints

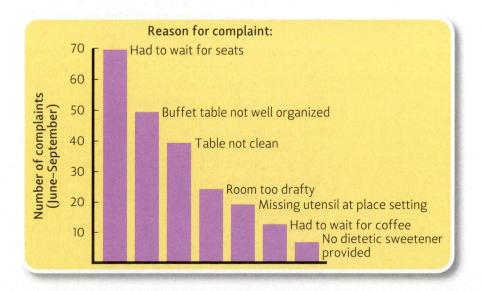

Exhibit 9–8 Fishbone Diagram Showing Cause and Effect for "Why Tables Are Not Cleared Quickly"

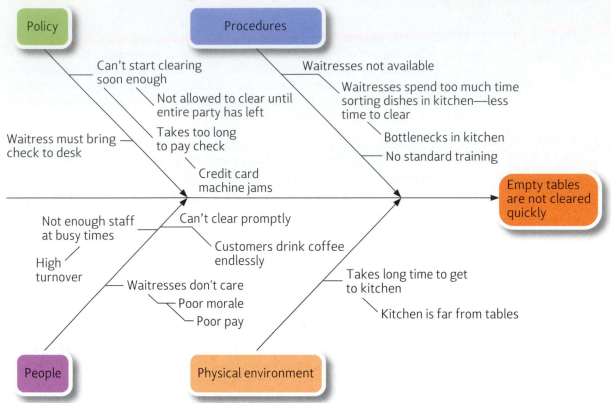

Figure out why things go wrong

So far, our manager has only identified the problem. To solve it, she creates a **fishbone diagram**—a visual aid that helps organize cause-and-effect relationships for "things gone wrong." See Exhibit 9–8. With this diagram, our restaurant manager discovers that customers wait to be seated because tables aren't cleared soon enough. In fact, the Pareto chart (Exhibit 9–7) shows that customers also complain frequently about tables not being clean. So the two implementation problems may be related.

The manager's fishbone diagram also summarizes other causes for tables not being cleaned quickly. There are different basic categories of causes—restaurant policy, procedures, people problems, and the physical environment. With this overview of different ways the service operation is going wrong, the manager can decide what to fix. She establishes different formal measures. For example, she counts how frequently different causes delay customers from being seated. She finds that the cashier's faulty credit card scanning machine holds up check processing. About half the time the cashier has to stop and enter the credit card information by hand. The fishbone diagram shows that restaurant policy is to clear the table after the entire party leaves. But customers have to wait at their tables while the staff deals with the faulty credit card machine, and cleaning is delayed. With the credit card machine replaced, the staff can clear the tables sooner—and because they're not so hurried they do a better cleaning job. Two dragons are on the way to being slayed!

Our case shows that people in different areas of the restaurant affect customer satisfaction. The waitperson couldn't do what was needed to satisfy customers because the cashier had trouble with the credit card machine. The TQM approach helps everyone see and understand how their job affects what others do and the customer's satisfaction.[35]

Building quality into services

The restaurant case illustrates how a firm can improve product quality with TQM approaches. We used a service example because providing customer service is often a difficult area, regardless of whether a firm's product is primarily a service, primarily a physical good, or a blend of both. For example, a manufacturer of ball bearings isn't just providing wholesalers or producers with round pieces of steel. Customers need information about deliveries, they need orders filled properly, and they may have questions to ask the firm's accountant or engineers. Because almost every firm must manage the service it provides customers, let's focus on some of the special concerns of managing service quality.

Train people and empower them to serve

It's difficult to maintain consistent quality in services because the server is inseparable from the service. A person doing a specific service job may perform one specific task correctly but still annoy the customer in a host of other ways. So two keys to improving service quality are: (1) training and (2) empowerment.

All employees who have any contact with customers need training—many firms see 40 hours a year of training as a minimum. Good training usually includes role-playing on handling different types of customer requests and problems. A rental car attendant who is rude when a customer is trying to turn in a car may leave the customer dissatisfied—even if the rental car was perfect.

Companies can't afford an army of managers to inspect how each employee implements a strategy—and such a system usually doesn't work anyway. Quality cannot be "inspected in." It must come from the people who do the service jobs. So firms that commit to service quality empower employees to satisfy customers' needs. **Empowerment** means giving employees the authority to correct a problem without first checking with management. At a hotel, for instance, an empowered room-service employee knows it's OK to run across the street to buy the specific brand of bottled water a guest requests.

Managers lead the quality effort

Managers must show that they are committed to doing things right to satisfy customers and that quality is everyone's job. Without top-level support, some people won't get beyond their business-as-usual attitude—and TQM won't work.

Specify jobs and measure performance

Managers who develop successful quality programs clearly specify and write out exactly what tasks need to be done, how, and by whom. This may seem unnecessary. After all, most people know, in general, what they're supposed to do. However, if the tasks are clearly specified, it's easier to see what criteria should be used to measure performance.

Once criteria are established, there needs to be some basis on which to evaluate the job being done. In our restaurant example, one part of the job specification for the cashier is to process credit card payments. In that case, relevant criteria might include the amount of time that it takes and the number of people waiting in line to pay. If the restaurant manager had seen a record of how long it was taking to process credit cards, she would have known that for many customers it was taking too long. Without the measure, the precise nature of the problem was hidden.

Getting a return on quality is important

While the cost of poor quality is lost customers, the type of quality efforts we've been discussing also result in costs. It's easy to fall into the trap of running up *unnecessary costs* trying to improve some facet of quality that really isn't that important to customer satisfaction or customer retention. When that happens, customers may still be satisfied, but the firm can't make a profit because of the extra costs. In other words, there isn't a financial return on the money spent to improve quality. A manager should focus on quality efforts that really provide the customer with superior value—quality that costs no more to provide than customers will ultimately be willing to pay.[36]

CONCLUSION

This chapter introduced the product life-cycle concept and showed how life cycles affect marketing strategy planning. The product life-cycle concept shows why new products are so important to growth in markets and also helps to explain why different strategies—including strategies for new improved products—need to be developed over time. Innovators—or fast copiers—that successfully bring new products to market are usually the ones who achieve the greatest growth in customer equity.

In today's highly competitive marketplace it is no longer profitable to simply sell "me-too" products. Markets, competition, and product life cycles are changing at a fast pace. New products help a company appeal to new target markets by appealing to unmet needs. New products can also encourage current customers to purchase more. In addition, they can help retain customers by adapting to changing customer needs.

Just because a product is new to a company doesn't mean that it is a really new innovation and starts a new-product life cycle. However, from a marketing manager's perspective, a product is new to the firm if it is new in any way or to any target market. Firms don't just develop and introduce new products; they do so within the context of the whole marketing strategy.

Many new products fail. But we presented an organized new-product development process that helps to prevent that fate. The process makes it clear that new-product success isn't just the responsibility of people from R&D or marketing but rather requires a total company effort.

We also described product and brand management. To help a product or brand grow, managers in these positions usually recommend ways to adjust all of the elements of the marketing mix, but the emphasis is often on Promotion.

Poor product quality results in dissatisfied customers. So alert marketers look for ways to design better quality into new products and to improve the quality of ones they already have. Approaches developed in the total quality management (TQM) movement can be a big help in this regard. Ultimately, the challenge is for the manager to focus on aspects of quality that really matter to the target customer. Otherwise, the cost of the quality offered may be higher than what target customers are willing to pay.

In combination, this chapter and Chapter 8 introduce strategy decision areas for Product and important frameworks that help you see how Product fits within an overall strategy. These chapters also start you down the path to a deeper understanding of the 4Ps. In Chapter 10, we expand on that base by focusing on the role of Place in the marketing mix.

KEY TERMS

product life cycle, 221

market introduction, 221

market growth, 222

market maturity, 223

sales decline, 223

fashion, 226

fad, 227

new product, 231

Federal Trade Commission (FTC), 231

Consumer Product Safety Act, 234

product liability, 235

concept testing, 235

product managers, 239

brand managers, 239

total quality management (TQM), 239

continuous improvement, 240

Pareto chart, 241

fishbone diagram, 242

empowerment, 243

QUESTIONS AND PROBLEMS

1. Explain how industry sales and industry profits behave over the product life cycle.

2. Cite two examples of products that you think are currently in each of the product life-cycle stages. Consider services as well as physical goods.

3. Explain how you might reach different conclusions about the correct product life-cycle stage(s) in the worldwide automobile market.

4. Explain why individual brands may not follow the product life-cycle pattern. Give an example of a new brand that is not entering the life cycle at the market introduction stage.

5. Discuss the life cycle of a product in terms of its probable impact on a manufacturer's marketing mix. Illustrate using personal computers.

6. What characteristics of a new product will help it to move through the early stages of the product life cycle more quickly? Briefly discuss each characteristic—illustrating with a product of your choice. Indicate how each characteristic might be viewed in some other country.

7. What is a new product? Illustrate your answer.

8. Explain the importance of an organized new-product development process and illustrate how it might be used

for (a) a new hair care product, (b) a new children's toy, and (c) a new subscribers-only cable television channel.

9. Discuss how you might use the new-product development process if you were thinking about offering some kind of summer service to residents in a beach resort town.

10. Explain the role of product or brand managers. When would it make sense for one of a company's current brand managers to be in charge of the new-product development process? Explain your thinking.

11. If a firm offers one of its brands in a number of different countries, would it make sense for one brand manager to be in charge, or would each country require its own brand manager? Explain your thinking.

12. Discuss the social value of new-product development activities that seem to encourage people to discard products that are not all worn out. Is this an economic waste? How worn out is all worn out? Must a shirt have holes in it? How big?

13. What are the major advantages of total quality management as an approach for improving the quality of goods and services? What limitations can you think of?

CREATING MARKETING PLANS

The Marketing Plan Coach software on the text website (and on the optional Student CD) includes a sample marketing plan for Hillside Veterinary Clinic. Look through the "Marketing Strategy" section.

a. Hillside offers many different products. Identify several of these products and indicate where you think each of them is in its product life cycle.

b. Exhibit 9–3 summarizes some marketing mix characteristics based on where a product fits in the product life cycle. Is Hillside's marketing plan consistent with what this exhibit suggests? Why or why not?

SUGGESTED CASES

6. Global Steel Company
22. Bright Light Innovations

20. Recreation Supplies Unlimited

COMPUTER-AIDED PROBLEM

9. GROWTH STAGE COMPETITION

AgriChem, Inc., has introduced an innovative new product—a combination fertilizer, weed killer, and insecticide that makes it much easier for soybean farmers to produce a profitable crop. The product introduction was quite successful, with 1 million units sold in the year of introduction. And AgriChem's profits are increasing. Total market demand is expected to grow at a rate of 200,000 units a year for the next five years. Even so, AgriChem's marketing managers are concerned about what will happen to sales and profits during this period.

Based on past experience with similar situations, they expect one new competitor to enter the market during each of the next five years. They think this competitive pressure will drive prices down about 6 percent a year. Further, although the total market is growing, they know that new competitors will chip away at AgriChem's market share—even with the 10 percent a year increase planned for the promotion budget. In spite of the competitive pressure, the marketing managers are sure that familiarity with AgriChem's brand will help it hold a large share of the total market and give AgriChem greater economies of scale than competitors. In fact, they expect that the ratio of profit to dollar sales for AgriChem should be about 10 percent higher than for competitors.

AgriChem's marketing managers have decided the best way to get a handle on the situation is to organize the data in a spreadsheet. They have set up the spreadsheet so they can change the "years in the future" value and see what is likely to happen to AgriChem and the rest of the industry. The starting spreadsheet shows the current situation with data from the first full year of production.

a. Compare AgriChem's market share and profit for this year with what is expected next year—given the marketing managers' current assumptions. What are they expecting? (Hint: Set number of years in the future to 1.)

b. Prepare a table showing AgriChem's expected profit, and the expected industry revenue and profit, for the current year and the next five years. Briefly explain what happens to industry sales and profits and why. (Hint: Do an analysis to vary the number of years in the future value in the spreadsheet from a minimum of 0—the current year—to a maximum of 5. Display the three values requested.)

c. If market demand grows faster than expected—say, at 280,000 units a year—what will happen to AgriChem's profits and the expected industry revenues and profits over the next five years? What are the implications of this analysis?

For additional questions related to this problem, see Exercise 9-4 in the *Learning Aid for Use with Essentials of Marketing*, 12th edition.

CHAPTER 10

Place and Development of Channel Systems

In the 1970s the early "microcomputers" were hard to set up and difficult to use—so few people wanted them. That also explains why there were no computer stores. Altair, one of the first brands, initially sold mainly at "electronics fairs." Most of these gatherings were in California; often buyers and sellers just met in an open market on Saturday mornings. Then Heath introduced its more powerful H89 computer through mail order catalogs as a build-it-yourself kit. Heath added value with good telephone technical support.

Soon after that, Xerox used its competitive advantage in distribution to introduce its 820 model. Business customers liked buying computers from the same wholesalers that regularly handled their Xerox copiers. By 1980, Radio Shack's large retail store network helped the easy-to-use TRS-80 become the best-selling computer. Customers appreciated the accessibility of Radio Shack's in-store staff and tech support specialists.

As you read this, it probably occurs to you that most of the firms mentioned no longer sell computers. These early firms didn't adjust quickly enough when IBM introduced its first PC. IBM's familiar brand gave more customers the confidence to buy. Sales of PCs surged as IBM established a chain of its own retail stores and worked closely with select dealers who promised to pay special attention to the IBM brand. Big-business customers bought in quantity directly from IBM's aggressive sales force. After IBM's design became an industry standard, firms like Compaq, HP, and Toshiba, quickly jumped in with PC models of their own—often selling through independent computer dealers.

Soon after, Michael Dell, then just a freshman in college, started buying and reselling computers from his dorm room. Dell figured a target market of price-conscious customers would respond to a different marketing mix. He used direct-response advertising in computer magazines; customers called a toll-free number to order a computer with the exact features they wanted. Then Dell used UPS to ship directly to the customer. Prices were low, too, because the direct channel eliminated retailer markup and the build-to-order approach reduced inventory costs. Dell also built reliable machines and delivered superior customer service. It would have been tough to centralize all of this if he had been working with thousands of retailers.

Dell's advertising positioned the company in consumers' minds as an aggressive, value-oriented source of computers. At the same time, Dell added a direct-sales force to call on big government and corporate buyers—because they expected in-person selling and a relationship, not just a telephone contact. And when these important customers said they wanted Dell to offer high-powered servers to run their corporate networks, Dell put money into R&D to create what they needed.

Dell also saw the prospect for international growth. Many computer firms had moved into Europe by exporting. But Dell made direct investments in the company's own operations there. Dell knew it would be tough to win over skeptical European buyers. They had never bought such big-ticket items as PCs over the phone. On the other hand, there were fewer big retail chains with low prices there, which gave Dell a significant price advantage. In less than five years, sales in Europe grew to 40 percent of Dell's total revenue.

Back home in the United States, IBM and other firms tried to imitate Dell's successful direct-order approach. However, this move created conflict with the retailers already selling the bulk of IBM's PCs; the retailers were not happy with competition from their own supplier! When these retailers responded by pushing other brands, IBM discovered it couldn't simply copy Dell's strategy without losing the distribution it already had.

As competition drove down profit margins, Dell saw the Internet as an opportunity to extend the direct model to a website (www.dell.com). The site provides a low-cost method for giving customers information and advice and makes ordering a custom PC even easier for the average customer. Sales and profits boomed—although competitors soon found ways to leverage the Internet as well.

Dell continued to adapt its marketing mix in response to evolving competition and customer needs. But new advertising campaigns had mixed results and some new product lines were either unsuccessful (TVs and MP3 players) or late to market (stylish laptops and netbook computers). So Dell again looked at distribution options. When Dell found that some customer segments preferred to purchase "in person" from a local retail store, Dell began selling preconfigured desktop and laptop computers through retailers like Wal-Mart and Staples. To better serve small business customers that wanted more technical support and training, Dell added wholesalers like Ingram Micro and Tech Data to its channel of distribution. Dell now embraces a multichannel distribution approach.

In its mature market, Dell needs to continue to adjust its marketing program to succeed against tough competitors. And it is likely that an important part of the competitive environment will relate to how Dell and other firms handle strategy decisions for Place.[1]

MARKETING STRATEGY PLANNING DECISIONS FOR PLACE

Managers must think about **Place**—making goods and services available in the right quantities and locations, when customers want them. And when different target markets have different needs, a number of Place variations may be required. Our opening case makes it clear that new Place arrangements can dramatically change the competition in a product-market. This is especially important in business today because information technology, including websites and e-commerce, makes it easier for firms to work together more efficiently and also to reach customers directly.

In this chapter and the two that follow, we'll deal with the many important marketing strategy decisions that a marketing manager must make concerning Place. Exhibit 10–1 gives an overview. We'll start here with a discussion of Place objectives and how they relate to product classes and the product life cycle—ideas introduced in the Product chapters (8 and 9). We'll then discuss the type of channel that's needed to meet customers' needs. We'll show why specialists are often involved and how they come together to form a **channel of distribution**—any series of firms or individuals who participate in the flow of products from producer to final user or consumer. We'll also consider how to manage relations among channel members to reduce conflict and improve cooperation. This chapter concludes by considering the desired level of market exposure (and how many channel outlets are needed) as well as approaches for reaching customers in international markets.

In Chapter 11, we'll expand the Place discussion to decisions that a marketing manager makes about physical distribution, including customer service level, transporting, and storing. Then, in Chapter 12, we'll take a closer look at the many different types

Exhibit 10–1 Marketing Strategy Planning Decisions for Place

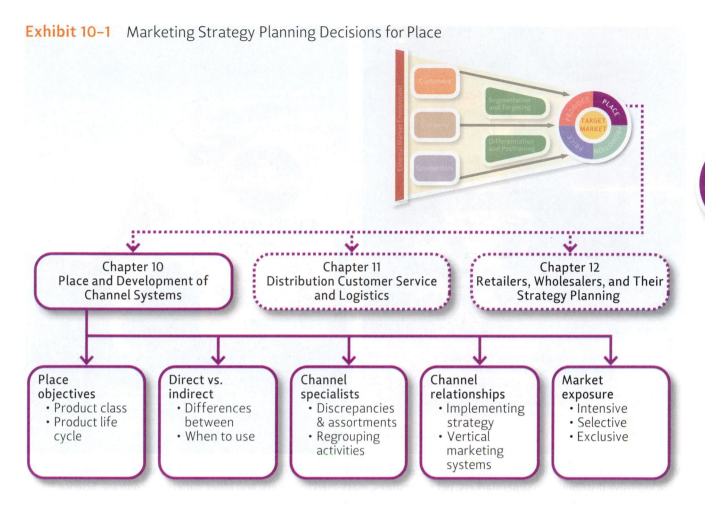

of retailing and wholesaling firms. We'll consider their role in channels as well as the strategy decisions they make to satisfy their own customers.

PLACE DECISIONS ARE GUIDED BY "IDEAL" PLACE OBJECTIVES

All marketing managers want to be sure that their goods and services are available in the right quantities and locations—when customers want them. But customers may have different needs in these areas as they make different purchases.

Product classes suggest Place objectives

In Chapter 8 we introduced the product classes, which summarize consumers' urgency to have needs satisfied and willingness to seek information, shop, and compare. Now you should be able to use the product classes to handle Place decisions.

Exhibit 8–6 shows the relationship between consumer product classes and ideal Place objectives. Similarly, Exhibit 8–7 shows the business product classes and how they relate to customer needs. Study these exhibits carefully. They set the framework for making Place decisions. In particular, the product classes help us decide how much market exposure we'll need in each geographic area.

Place system is not automatic

Several different product classes may be involved if different market segments view a product in different ways. Thus, marketing managers may need to develop several strategies, each with its own Place arrangements. There may not be one Place arrangement that is best.

Place decisions have long-run effects

The marketing manager must also consider Place objectives in relation to the product life cycle; see Exhibit 9–3. Place decisions often have long-run effects. They're

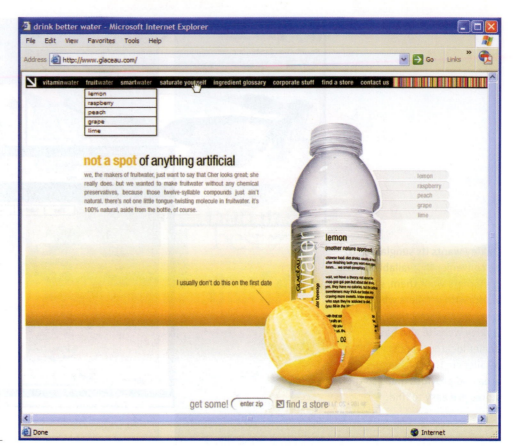

As a small company trying to obtain distribution, Glacéau focused on putting freestanding coolers for its Vitaminwater in stores, like Bed Bath & Beyond, that had not carried beverages in the past. Thus, Glacéau didn't just compete for the same shelf space but rather expanded the distribution outlets available for beverages.

Suitable intermediaries are not available

A firm may have to go direct if suitable intermediaries are not available or will not cooperate. For example, when Glacéau began selling its now popular Vitaminwater, wholesale distributors had no interest in carrying it. So the owner of the company delivered the bottled water directly to small retailers in New York City. Once he proved his product would sell, distributor interest grew. On the other hand, to enter the California market, Glacéau gave distribution rights to just one distributor. As a result, it was in this distributor's interest to work closely with Glacéau to build the market. Eventually Coca-Cola purchased Glacéau; at that point Coke added many of its own distributors. Glacéau became a success by slowly building support from retailers and wholesalers, but many new products fail because the producer can't find willing channel partners and doesn't have the resources to handle direct distribution.[2]

Common with business customers and services

Many business products are sold direct-to-customer. Alcan sells aluminum to General Motors direct. And Honda sells its motors direct to lawn mower producers. This is understandable since in business markets there are fewer transactions, orders are larger, and customers may be concentrated in one geographic area. Further, once relationships are established, e-commerce systems can efficiently handle orders.

Service firms often use direct channels. If the service must be produced in the presence of customers, there may be little need for intermediaries. An accounting firm like PricewaterhouseCoopers, for example, must deal directly with its customers.

However, many firms that produce physical goods turn to channel specialists to help provide the services customers expect. GE may hope that its authorized appliance dealers don't get many repair calls, but the service is available when customers need it. Here the intermediary produces the service.[3]

Some consumer products are sold direct

Many companies that produce consumer products have websites where a consumer can place a direct order. But for most consumer products this is still a small part of total sales. Most consumer products are sold through intermediaries.

Of course, some consumer products are sold direct to consumers where they live or work. Mary Kay and Avon cosmetics, Electrolux vacuum cleaners, Quixtar-Amway household products, and Tupperware are examples. These firms and many others are finding that this is a good way to crack open international markets ranging from India and China to Brazil and the U.K. Most of these firms rely on direct selling, which involves personal sales contact between a representative of the company and an individual consumer. However, most of these "salespeople" are *not* company employees. Rather, they usually work independently and the companies that they sell for refer to them as *dealers, distributors, agents,* or some similar term. So in a strict technical sense, this is not really direct producer-to-consumer distribution.[4]

Don't be confused by the term *direct marketing*

Even though most consumer products are sold through intermediaries, an increasing number of firms rely on **direct marketing**—direct communication between a seller and an individual customer using a promotion method other than face-to-face personal selling. Sometimes direct marketing promotion is coupled with direct distribution from a producer to consumers. Park Seed Company, for example, sells the seeds it grows directly to consumers with a mail catalog and website. However, many firms that use direct marketing promotion distribute their products through intermediaries. So the term *direct marketing* is primarily concerned with the Promotion area, not Place decisions. We'll talk about direct marketing promotion in more detail in Chapter 13.[5]

When indirect channels are best

Even if a producer wants to handle the whole distribution job, sometimes it's simply not possible. Customers often have established buying patterns. For example, Square D, a producer of electrical supplies, might want to sell directly to electrical contractors. It can certainly set up a website for online orders or even open sales offices in key markets. But if contractors like to make all of their purchases in one convenient stop—at a local electrical wholesaler—the only practical way to reach them is through a wholesaler.

Similarly, consumers are spread throughout many geographic areas and often prefer to shop for certain products at specific places. Some consumers, for instance, see Sears as *the* place to shop for tires, so they'll only buy the brands that Sears carries. This is one reason most firms that produce consumer products rely so heavily on indirect channels (see Exhibit 2–6).[6]

Direct distribution usually requires a significant investment in facilities, people, and information technology. A company that has limited financial resources or that wants to retain flexibility may want to avoid that investment by working with established intermediaries.

Intermediaries may further reduce a producer's need for working capital by buying the producer's output and carrying it in inventory until it's sold. If customers want a good "right now," there must be inventory available to make the

For many years, Levi Strauss did not distribute its jeans through Wal-Mart. Rather, it worked with fashion shops to project a more selective image. However, as Wal-Mart and other mass-merchandisers attracted a larger and larger share of jeans shoppers, Levi Strauss created its Signature line to reach this segment. Signature jeans feature lighter-weight denim and less detailing, and they are now available at Wal-Mart, Target, and Kmart.

sale. And if customers are spread over a large area, it will probably be necessary to have widespread distribution.

Some wholesalers play a critical role by providing credit to customers at the end of the channel. A wholesaler who knows local customers can help reduce credit risks. As sales via the Internet grow, sellers are looking for faster and better ways to check the credit ratings of distant customers. It's an unhappy day when the marketing manager learns that a customer who was shipped goods based on an online order can't pay the invoice.

The most important reason for using an indirect channel of distribution is that an intermediary can often help producers serve customer needs better and at lower cost. Remember that we discussed this briefly in Chapter 1. Now we'll go into more detail.

CHANNEL SPECIALISTS MAY REDUCE DISCREPANCIES AND SEPARATIONS

The assortment and quantity of products customers want may be different from the assortment and quantity of products companies produce. Producers are often located far from their customers and may not know how best to reach them. Customers in turn may not know about their choices. Specialists develop to adjust these discrepancies and separations.[7]

Intermediaries may supply needed information

Specialists often help provide information to bring buyers and sellers together. For example, most consumers don't know much about the wide variety of home and auto insurance policies available. A local independent insurance agent may help them decide which policy, and which insurance company, best fits their needs.

Intermediaries who are close to their customers are often able to anticipate customer needs and forecast demand more accurately. This information can help reduce inventory costs in the whole channel—and it may help the producer smooth out production.

Most producers seek help from specialists when they first enter international markets. Specialists can provide crucial information about customer needs and insights into differences in the marketing environment.

Discrepancies of quantity and assortment

Discrepancy of quantity means the difference between the quantity of products it is economical for a producer to make and the quantity final users or consumers normally want. For example, most manufacturers of golf balls produce large quantities—perhaps 200,000 to 500,000 in a given time period. The average golfer, however, wants only a few balls at a time. Adjusting for this discrepancy usually requires intermediaries—wholesalers and retailers.

Producers typically specialize by product—and therefore another discrepancy develops. **Discrepancy of assortment** means the difference between the lines a typical producer makes and the assortment final consumers or users want. Most golfers, for example, need more than golf balls. They want golf shoes, gloves, clubs, a bag, and, of course, a golf course to play on. And they usually don't want to shop for each item separately. So, again, there is a need for wholesalers and retailers to adjust these discrepancies.

Channel specialists adjust discrepancies with regrouping activities

Regrouping activities adjust the quantities or assortments of products handled at each level in a channel of distribution.

There are four regrouping activities: accumulating, bulk-breaking, sorting, and assorting. When one or more of these activities is needed, a marketing specialist may develop to fill this need.

Adjusting quantity discrepancies by accumulating and bulk-breaking

Accumulating involves collecting products from many small producers. Much of the coffee that comes from Colombia is grown on small farms in the mountains. Accumulating the small crops into larger quantities is a way of getting the lowest transporting rate and making it more convenient for distant food processing companies to buy and handle it. Accumulating is especially important in less-developed

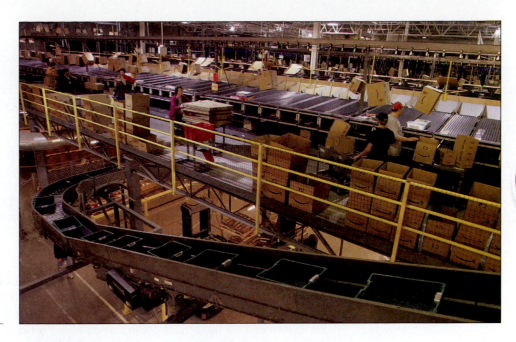

Amazon, the large online retailer, helps to match supply and demand when it fills Internet orders from its warehouse in Nevada. It accumulates large quantities of the most popular books from thousands of publishers, and then breaks bulk when it takes orders and ships them—often a single book at a time—to millions of individual consumers.

countries and in other situations, like agricultural markets, where there are many small producers.

Accumulating is also important with professional services because they often involve the combined work of a number of individuals, each of whom is a specialized producer. A hospital makes it easier for patients by accumulating the services of a number of health care specialists, many of whom may not actually work for the hospital.

Many wholesalers and retailers who operate from Internet websites focus on accumulating. Specialized sites for everything from Chinese art to Dutch flower bulbs bring together the output of many producers.

Bulk-breaking involves dividing larger quantities into smaller quantities as products get closer to the final market. The bulk-breaking may involve several levels in the channel. Wholesalers may sell smaller quantities to other wholesalers or directly to retailers. Retailers continue breaking bulk as they sell individual items to their customers.

Adjusting assortment discrepancies by sorting and assorting

Different types of specialists adjust assortment discrepancies. They perform two types of regrouping activities: sorting and assorting.

Sorting means separating products into grades and qualities desired by different target markets. For example, an investment firm might offer its customers shares in a mutual fund made up only of stocks for companies that pay regular dividends. Similarly, a wholesaler that specializes in serving convenience stores may focus on smaller packages of frequently used products.

Assorting means putting together a variety of products to give a target market what it wants. This usually is done by those closest to the final consumer or user—retailers or wholesalers who try to supply a wide assortment of products for the convenience of their customers. Thus, a wholesaler selling Yazoo tractors and mowers to golf courses might also carry Pennington grass seed and Scott fertilizer.

Watch for changes

Specialists should develop to adjust discrepancies *if they must be adjusted*. But there is no point in having intermediaries just because that's the way it's been done in the past. Sometimes a breakthrough opportunity can come from finding a better way to reduce discrepancies. Some manufacturers of business products can now reach more customers in distant markets with an Internet website than it was previously possible for them to reach with independent manufacturers' reps who sold on commission (but otherwise left distribution to the firm). The website cost advantage can translate to lower prices and a marketing mix that is a better value for some target segments.[8]

CHANNEL RELATIONSHIP MUST BE MANAGED

Marketing manager must choose type of channel relationship

Intermediary specialists can help make a channel more efficient. But there may be problems getting the different firms in a channel to work together well. How well they work together depends on the type of relationship they have. This should be carefully considered since marketing managers usually have choices about what type of channel system to join or develop.

The whole channel should have a product-market commitment

Ideally, all of the members of a channel system should have a shared *product-market commitment*—with all members focusing on the same target market at the end of the channel and sharing the various marketing functions in appropriate ways. When members of a channel do this, they are better able to compete effectively for the customer's business. Unfortunately, many marketing managers overlook this idea because it's not the way their firms have traditionally handled channel relationships.

Traditional channel systems involve weak relationships

In **traditional channel systems**, the various channel members make little or no effort to cooperate with each other. They buy and sell from each other—and that's the extent of their relationship. Each channel member does only what it considers to be in its own best interest. It doesn't worry about other members of the channel. This is shortsighted, but it's easy to see how it can happen. The objectives of the various channel members may be different. For example, Cooper Industries wants a wholesaler

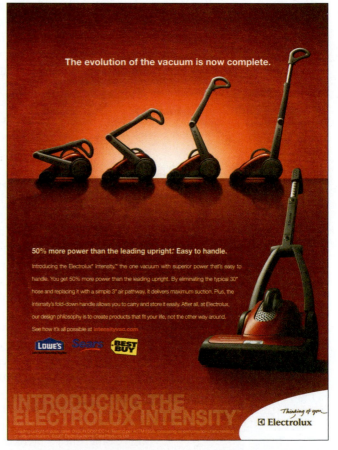

Acting as channel captains in their respective channels, both Peterson and Electrolux are able to get cooperation from many independent wholesalers and retailers (as well as big chains like Lowe's) because they develop marketing strategies that help the whole channel compete more effectively and that also help everyone in the channel do a better job of meeting the needs of target customers at the end of the channel.

of electrical building supplies to sell Cooper products. But a wholesaler who works with different producers may not care whose products get sold. The wholesaler just wants happy customers and a good profit margin.[9]

Conflict gets in the way

Specialization can make a channel more efficient—but not if the specialists are so independent that the channel doesn't work smoothly. Because members of traditional channel systems often have different objectives—and different ideas about how things should be done—conflict is common.

There are two basic types of conflict in channels of distribution. *Vertical conflicts* occur between firms at different levels in the channel of distribution. A vertical conflict may occur if a producer and a retailer disagree about how much shelf space or promotion effort the retailer should give the producer's product. For example, when Wherehouse Entertainment (a large retail music chain) started to sell used CDs—at about half the price of new ones—several recording companies said that they would halt cooperative advertising payments to any retailer that sold used CDs. The recording companies felt that the used CDs hurt their sales.[10]

Horizontal conflicts occur between firms at the same level in the channel of distribution. For example, a bicycle store that keeps a complete line of bikes on display, has a knowledgeable sales staff, and lets customers take test rides, isn't happy to find out that an online store with little inventory offers customers lower prices on the same items. The online retailer gets a free ride from the competing store's investment in inventory.

Managing channel conflict

Some level of conflict may be inevitable—or even useful if that is what it takes for customers at the end of the channel to receive better value. However, most marketing managers try to avoid conflicts that harm relationships with channel partners. To mollify channel partners, manufacturers often try to serve different market segments through each channel. For example, convenience stores like 7-11 and membership stores like Costco both sell Coke—but one offers it cold in individual servings and the other offers it warm and 24 cans at a time. Each offers a different marketing mix to a different target market.

In general, treating channel partners fairly—even when one partner is more powerful—tends to build trust, promote cooperation, and reduce conflict. The goal is to better satisfy the needs of target customers at the end of the channel. [11]

Internet EXERCISE

Avon Products, Inc., has created a separate "mark" line of cosmetics and other beauty products that is targeted at young women. Avon sells mark at a website and through independent sales reps (agents), including college students who sell to their friends. Review the mark website (**www.meetmark.com**). Do you think that mark reps view the website as competing for their customers' purchases and a source of conflict, or do they think that it helps them promote mark and identify new prospects? Explain your thinking.

Channel captain can guide channel relationships

While each channel system should act as a unit, some firms are in a better position to take the lead in the relationship and in coordinating the whole channel effort. This situation calls for a **channel captain**—a manager who helps direct the activities of a whole channel and tries to avoid or solve channel conflicts.

For example, when Harley-Davidson wanted to expand sales of fashion accessories, it was difficult for motorcycle dealers to devote enough space to all of the different styles. Harley considered selling the items directly from its own website, but that would take sales away from dealers who were working hard to help Harley sell both cycles and fashions. So Harley's president asked a group of dealers and Harley managers to work together to come up with a plan they all liked. The result was a website that sells Harley products through the dealer that is closest to the customer.[12]

The concept of a single channel captain is logical. But most traditional channels don't have a recognized captain. The various firms don't act as a coordinated system. Yet firms are interrelated, even if poorly, by their policies. So it makes

Exhibit 10–2 How Channel Functions May Be Shifted and Shared in Different Channel Systems

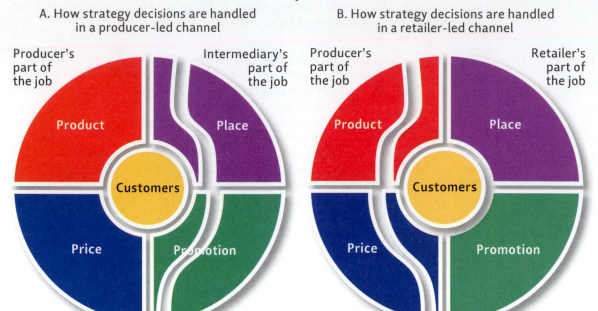

A. How strategy decisions are handled in a producer-led channel

Producer's part of the job — Product, Price

Intermediary's part of the job — Place, Promotion

Customers

B. How strategy decisions are handled in a retailer-led channel

Producer's part of the job — Product, Price

Retailer's part of the job — Place, Promotion

Customers

sense to try to avoid channel conflicts by planning for channel relations. The channel captain arranges for the necessary functions to be performed in the most effective way.[13]

Some producers lead their channels

In the United States, producers frequently take the lead in channel relations. Intermediaries often wait to see what the producer intends to do and wants them to do. Then they decide whether their roles will be profitable and whether they want to join in the channel effort.

Exhibit 10–2A shows this type of producer-led channel system. Here the producer has selected the target market and developed the Product, set the Price structure, done some consumer and channel Promotion, and developed the Place setup. Intermediaries are then expected to finish the Promotion job in their respective places. Of course, in a retailer-dominated channel system, the marketing jobs would be handled in a different way.

Some intermediaries are channel captains

Sometimes wholesalers or retailers do take the lead. They are closer to the final user or consumer and are in an ideal position to assume the channel captain role. These firms analyze their customers' needs and then seek out producers who can provide these products at reasonable prices. With the growth of powerful chains, like Wal-Mart and Toys "R" Us, retailers now dominate the channel systems for many products in the United States and Europe. Large retailers often use their power. During a recent economic recession, the Belgian grocery chain Delhaize decided that 300 Unilever products were priced too high and removed them from its shelves. This hurt the channel relationship, but the grocer came across as a champion of the consumer and made its point with Unilever.[14] In Japan, very large wholesalers (trading companies) are often the channel captains.

Retailers like Sears and wholesalers like Ace Hardware who develop their own dealer brands in effect act like producers. They specify the whole marketing mix for a product and merely delegate production to a factory. Exhibit 10–2B shows how marketing strategy might be handled in this sort of retailer-led channel system.[15]

VERTICAL MARKETING SYSTEMS FOCUS ON FINAL CUSTOMERS

Many marketing managers accept the view that a coordinated channel system can help everyone in the channel. These managers are moving their firms away from traditional channel systems and instead developing or joining vertical marketing systems. **Vertical marketing systems** are channel systems in which the whole channel focuses on the same target market at the end of the channel. Such systems make sense, and are growing, because if the final customer doesn't buy the product, the whole channel suffers. There are three types of vertical marketing systems—corporate, administered, and contractual. Exhibit 10–3 summarizes some characteristics of these systems and compares them with traditional systems.

Inspired by the success of self-serve ticketing kiosks at airports, Apple is supplementing its own retail stores and distribution through other retailers with special vending machines that sell iPods in airports and high-traffic areas.

Corporate channel systems shorten channels

Some corporations develop their own vertical marketing systems by internal expansion or by buying other firms, or both. With **corporate channel systems**—corporate ownership all along the channel—we might say the firm is going "direct." But actually the firm may be handling manufacturing, wholesaling, *and* retailing—so it's more accurate to think of the firm as a vertical marketing system.

Corporate channel systems may develop by **vertical integration**—acquiring firms at different levels of channel activity. For example, in England, most of the quaint local pubs are now actually owned and operated by the large beer breweries.

Vertical integration has potential advantages—stable sources of supplies, better control of distribution and quality, greater buying power, and lower executive overhead. Provided that the discrepancies of quantity and assortment are not too great at each level in a channel, vertical integration can be profitable. However, many managers have found that it's hard to be really good at running manufacturing, wholesaling, and retailing businesses that are very different from each other. Instead, they try to be more efficient at what they do best and focus on ways to get cooperation in the channel for the other activities.[16]

Exhibit 10–3 Characteristics of Traditional and Vertical Marketing Systems

		Type of Channel		
		Vertical Marketing Systems		
Characteristics	Traditional	Administered	Contractual	Corporate
Amount of cooperation	Little or none	Some to good	Fairly good to good	Complete
Control maintained by	None	Economic power and leadership	Contracts	Ownership by one company
Examples	Typical channel of "independents"	General Electric, Miller Beer, Scotts Miracle Grow	McDonald's, Holiday Inn, Ace Hardware, Super Valu, Coca-Cola, Chevrolet	Florsheim Shoes, Sherwin-Williams, Mothers Work

Mothers Work is a good example of a corporate channel system started by a retailer. It began as a mail-order catalog specializing in maternity clothes. Now it sells more than a third of all maternity clothes in the United States. Vertical integration has been a key factor in its ability to give its customers what they want. It has over 700 company-run stores, its own designers, fabric-cutting operations, warehouses, and information systems to tie them all together.

Administered and contractual systems may work well

Firms can often gain the advantages of vertical integration without building a costly corporate channel. A manager can develop administered or contractual channel systems instead. In **administered channel systems**, the channel members informally agree to cooperate with each other. They can agree to routinize ordering, share inventory and sales information over computer networks, standardize accounting, and coordinate promotion efforts. In **contractual channel systems**, the channel members agree by contract to cooperate with each other. With both of these systems, the members retain some of the flexibility of a traditional channel system.

The opportunities to reduce costs and provide customers with superior value are growing in these systems because of help from information technology. For example, like many retailers, Costco has a system that it calls "vendor managed inventory" in which key suppliers take over responsibility for managing a set of products, often a

STIHL uses selective distribution and sells its high-quality chain saws through 8,000 independent STIHL servicing dealers nationwide. They give product demonstrations, good advice, and expert on-site service. These dealers know that the STIHL brand is not available at home-improvement warehouses that put more emphasis on price competition and less on service.

Can I Download Some Popcorn with That Movie?

The market for entertainment is changing rapidly—and Hollywood has responded with new channels of distribution. For a long time, movie studios carefully managed how their films proceeded through tightly controlled channels. Movies took years to trickle down from theaters to premium cable TV channels like HBO and eventually to network television. This approach maximized the studios' revenue from each channel—and kept channel conflict at a minimum. But those days are gone and movie studios are scrambling to get revenue faster from more channels of distribution.

Each new outlet for movies has provided more convenience or a different consumer experience. In the late 1970s, the first video stores started renting movies for $10 a day. Studios also began selling movies. Disney's animated classics were especially popular at first because kids would watch the same movie many times. However, sales did not really take off until prices dropped below $25. As sales grew, distribution became more intense and retailers like Wal-Mart and Kmart were added to the mix. Blockbuster and other big rental chains also took off.

Now, if you don't feel like driving to pick up a flick, your cable channel or satellite television provider probably offers pay-per-view. Or, if you prefer, Netflix offers movie downloads or mails DVDs to your home and you can return them whenever you want. Illegal channels have developed, too. Pirates often post movies on the Internet before they're even available in theaters, and some consumers copy DVDs on home computers and pass them around. However, new movie download services that are legal are also coming online, and smaller digital file formats make movies portable with a video cell phone or iPod. You may not care about portability if you've got your own comfy home theater setup. And bricks-and-mortar theaters, the traditional channel, are fighting to get customers back with stadium seating, bar and table service, and giant IMAX screens.

Concerns about movie piracy eroding sales have prompted movie studios to speed up the timing of movie distribution across channels. This has increased competition and conflict across channels. Some studios are releasing movies to theaters and on DVD at the same time—or skipping the theater channel altogether.

So where will you watch your next movie? At an IMAX theater, in your home theater, or on your cell phone in a seat on a train—you can decide. These changes give you the power to choose—and movie studios hope all these channels get more people watching more movies.[17]

whole product category. Costco uses this approach with Kimberly-Clark (KC), the firm that makes Huggies. Every day, an analyst at KC's headquarters reviews Costco's online data that details Huggies' sales and inventory at every Costco store. If inventory is getting low, a new order is placed and shipping is scheduled. This system reduces buying and selling costs, inventory management, lost sales from inventory stock-outs, and consumer frustration when products aren't available. Because KC does this job well, it makes more money and so does Costco.[18]

Vertical marketing systems—dominant force in the marketplace

Vertical systems in the consumer products area have a healthy majority of retail sales and should continue to increase their share in the future. Vertical marketing systems are becoming the major competitive units in the U.S. distribution system—and they are growing rapidly in other parts of the world as well.[19]

THE BEST CHANNEL SYSTEM SHOULD ACHIEVE IDEAL MARKET EXPOSURE

You may think that all marketing managers want their products to have maximum exposure to potential customers. This isn't true. Some product classes require much less market exposure than others. **Ideal market exposure** makes a product available widely enough to satisfy target customers' needs but not exceed them. Too much exposure only increases the total cost of marketing.

Ideal exposure may be intensive, selective, or exclusive

Intensive distribution is selling a product through all responsible and suitable wholesalers or retailers who will stock or sell the product. **Selective distribution** is selling through only those intermediaries who will give the product special attention. **Exclusive distribution** is selling through only one intermediary in a particular geographic area. As we move from intensive to exclusive distribution, we give up exposure in return for some other advantage—including, but not limited to, lower cost.

Intensive distribution—sell it where they buy it

Intensive distribution is commonly needed for convenience products and business supplies—such as laser printer cartridges, ring binders, and copier paper—used by all offices. Customers want such products nearby. For example, Rayovac batteries were not selling well even though their performance was very similar to other batteries. Part of that was due to heavier advertising for Duracell and Energizer. But consumers usually don't go shopping for batteries. They're purchased on impulse 83 percent of the time. To get a larger share of purchases, Rayovac had to be in more stores. It offered retailers a marketing mix with less advertising and a lower price. In three years, the brand moved from being available in 36,000 stores to 82,000 stores—and that increase gave sales a big charge.[20]

As demand for premium coffee increased, Dunkin' Donuts took advantage of its brand reputation and the quality of its product to obtain distribution in supermarkets.

Selective distribution—sell it where it sells best

Selective distribution covers the broad area of market exposure between intensive and exclusive distribution. It may be suitable for all categories of products. Only the better intermediaries are used here. Companies commonly use selective distribution to gain some of the advantages of exclusive distribution—while still achieving fairly widespread market coverage.

Reduce costs and get better partners

A selective policy might be used to avoid selling to wholesalers or retailers that (1) place orders that are too small to justify making calls, (2) make too many returns or request too much service, (3) have a poor credit rating, or (4) are not in a position to do a satisfactory job.

Selective distribution is becoming more popular than intensive distribution as firms see that they don't need 100 percent coverage of a market to support national advertising. Often the majority of sales come from relatively few customers—and the others buy too little compared to the cost of working with them. This is called the 80/20 rule—80 percent of a company's sales often come from only 20 percent of its customers *until it becomes more selective in choosing customers*.

Esprit—a producer of women's clothing—was selling through about 4,000 department stores and specialty shops in the United States. But Esprit's sales analysis showed that sales in Esprit's own stores were about four times better than sales in other outlets. Profits increased when Esprit cut back to about half as many outlets and opened more of its own stores and a website.[21]

Get special effort from channel members

Selective distribution can produce greater profits not only for the producer but for all channel members. Wholesalers and retailers are more willing to promote products aggressively if they know they're going to obtain the majority of sales through their own efforts. They may carry wider lines, do more promotion, and provide more service—all of which lead to more sales.

Selective often moves to intensive as market grows

In the early part of the life cycle of a new unsought good, a producer may have to use selective distribution. Well-known wholesalers and retailers may have the power to get such a product introduced, but sometimes on their own terms. That often means limiting the number of competing wholesalers and retailers. The producer may be happy with such an arrangement at first but dislike it later when more retailers want to carry the product.

Exclusive distribution sometimes makes sense

Exclusive distribution is just an extreme case of selective distribution—the firm selects only one wholesaler or retailer in each geographic area. Besides the various advantages of selective distribution, producers may want to use exclusive distribution to help control prices and the service offered in a channel. Franchisors like McDonald's and 1-800-GOT-JUNK? offer franchisees exclusive territories.

Is limiting market exposure legal?

Exclusive distribution is an area considered under U.S. antimonopoly laws. Courts currently focus on whether an exclusive distribution arrangement hurts competition.

Horizontal arrangements among competitors are illegal

Horizontal arrangements—among *competing* retailers, wholesalers, or producers—to limit sales by customer or territory have consistently been ruled illegal by the U.S. Supreme Court. Courts consider such arrangements obvious collusion that reduces competition and harms customers.

Vertical arrangements may or may not be legal

The legality of vertical arrangements—between producers and intermediaries—is not as clear-cut. A 1977 Supreme Court decision (involving Sylvania and the distribution of TV sets) reversed an earlier ruling that it was always illegal to set up vertical relationships limiting territories or customers. Now courts can weigh the possible good effects against the possible restrictions on competition. They look at competition between whole channels rather than just focusing on competition at one level of distribution.

The Sylvania decision does not mean that all vertical arrangements are legal. Rather, it says that a firm has to be able to legally justify any exclusive arrangements.

Thus, firms should be extremely cautious about entering into *any* exclusive distribution arrangement. The courts can force a change in relationships that were expensive to develop. And even worse, the courts can award triple damages if they rule that competition has been hurt.

The same cautions apply to selective distribution. Here, however, less formal arrangements are typical—and the possible impact on competition is more remote. It is now more acceptable to carefully select channel members when building a channel system. Refusing to sell to some intermediaries, however, should be part of a logical plan with long-term benefits to consumers.[22]

CHANNEL SYSTEMS CAN BE COMPLEX

Trying to achieve the desired degree of market exposure can lead to complex channels of distribution. Firms may need different channels to reach different segments of a broad product-market or to be sure they reach each segment. Sometimes this results in competition between different channels.

Consider the different channels used by a company that publishes computer books. See Exhibit 10–4. This publisher sells through a general book wholesaler who in turn sells to Internet book retailers and independent book retailers. The publisher may have some direct sales of its best-selling books to a large chain or even to consumers who

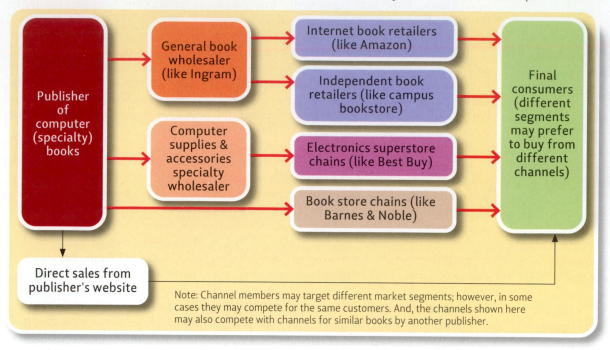

Note: Channel members may target different market segments; however, in some cases they may compete for the same customers. And, the channels shown here may also compete with channels for similar books by another publisher.

order directly from its website. However, it might also sell through a computer supplies wholesaler that serves electronics superstores like Best Buy. This can cause problems because different wholesalers and retailers want different markups. It also increases competition, including price competition. And the competition among different intermediaries may lead to conflicts between the intermediaries and the publisher.

Multichannel distribution systems may be needed

Multichannel distribution occurs when a producer uses several competing channels to reach the same target market—perhaps using several intermediaries in addition to selling directly. Multichannel distribution is becoming more common. For instance, big retail chains want large quantities and low prices. A producer may sell directly to retail chains and rely on wholesalers to sell to smaller accounts. Some established intermediaries resent this because they don't appreciate *any* competition—especially price competition set up by their own suppliers.

Other times, producers are forced to use multichannel distribution because their present channels are doing a poor job or aren't reaching some potential customers. For example, Reebok International had been relying on local sporting goods stores to sell its shoes to high school and college athletic teams. But Reebok wasn't getting much of the business. When it set up its own team-sales department to sell directly to the schools, it got a 30,000-unit increase in sales.[23]

Ethical decisions may be required

If competition changes or customers' Place requirements shift, the current channel system may not be effective. The changes required to serve customer needs may hurt one or more members of the channel. Ethical dilemmas in the channels area arise in situations like this—because not everyone in the channel can win.

For example, wholesalers and the independent retailers that they serve in a channel of distribution may trust a producer channel-captain to develop marketing strategies that will work for the whole channel. However, the producer may decide that consumers, and its own business, are best served by a change (say, dropping current wholesalers and selling directly to big retail chains). A move of this sort, if implemented immediately, may not give current wholesaler-partners a chance to make adjustments of their own. The more dependent they are on the producer, the more severe the impact is likely to be. It's not easy to determine the best or most ethical solution in these situations. However, marketing managers must think carefully about the consequences of Place strategy changes for other channel members. In channels, as in any business dealing, relationships of trust must be treated with care.[24]

Reverse channels are important too

Most firms focus on getting products to their customers. But some marketing managers must also plan for **reverse channels**—channels used to retrieve products that customers no longer want. The need for reverse channels may arise in a variety of different situations. Toy companies, automobile firms, drug companies, and others sometimes have to recall products because of safety problems. A firm that makes an error in completing an order may have to take returns. If a Viewsonic computer monitor breaks while it's still under warranty, someone needs to get it to the repair center. Soft-drink companies may need to recycle empty bottles. And, of course, consumers sometimes buy something in error and want to return it. This is common with online purchases where consumers can't see, touch, or try the product before purchasing it.[25]

New laws require reverse channels in some industries

Some firms have developed reverse channels only after being forced to by new laws designed to help the environment. For example, some "take back" laws require manufacturers to recycle or reuse hazardous materials or products at the end of their useful life—at no additional cost to the customer. In Europe, auto makers must take back and recycle or reuse 85 percent of any vehicle made after 2004, and the European Community's Waste Electrical and Electronic Equipment (WEEE) Directive has firms taking back products like computers and televisions. Similar laws are cropping up in the United States.

Reverse channels support sustainability and profitability

Reverse channels that help the environment can also be profitable. In rural China, for example, it's cheaper for Coke to reuse glass bottles than to rely on plastic packages or cans. Recycling has been even more important to Xerox. Customers responded well to Xerox's offer to dispose of old copy machines with the purchase of new models. But in the first year of the program, Xerox discovered that by refurbishing parts that were still in use with new models it could save $50 million. Similarly, by helping consumers recycle electronics, firms like Sony, Office Depot, and Best Buy are seen as green corporate citizens.

Reverse channels are also a way to give customers environmentally friendly choices. For example, new Ecoworx carpet tiles from Shaw Floors are manufactured using recycled carpets. Shaw also promises that when the time comes it will pick up and recycle the tiles at no cost to the customer. To make it easy for the customer to follow up, Shaw's telephone number is on the back of each tile.[26]

Plan for reverse channels

When marketing managers don't plan for reverse channels, the firm's customers may be left to solve "their" problem. That usually doesn't make sense. So a complete plan for Place may need to consider an efficient way to return products—with policies that different channel members agree on. It may also require specialists who were not involved in getting the product to the consumer. But if that's what it takes to satisfy customers, it should be part of marketing strategy planning.[27]

ENTERING INTERNATIONAL MARKETS

All of the strategy decisions for Place (see Exhibit 10–1) apply whether a firm is just focused on its domestic market or is also trying to reach target customers in international markets. However, when marketing managers plan for international markets, additional choices may be required. The external market environment, including culture and laws, are almost always different from what the marketing manager knows. Developing countries with less stable economies and political environments involve even more risk. So we'll briefly discuss five basic ways to enter international markets. See Exhibit 10–5. As a rule, the more control marketing managers have over the marketing mix being used in an international market, the greater the risk and the larger the investment for their firm.

Exporting often comes first

Some companies get into international marketing just by **exporting**—selling some of what the firm produces to foreign markets. Some firms start exporting just to take advantage of excess capacity—or even to get rid of surplus inventory. Some firms decide to change little if anything about the product, the label, or even the instructions. This explains why some early efforts at exporting are not very satisfactory. Other firms work closely with intermediaries who develop appropriate marketing mix changes and handle problems such as customs, import and export taxes, shipping, exchange rates, and recruiting or working with foreign wholesalers and retailers in the foreign country.

Licensing is often an easy way

Licensing means selling the right to use some process, trademark, patent, or other right for a fee or royalty. The licensee in the foreign market takes most of the risk, because it must make some initial investment to get started. The licensee also does most of the marketing strategy planning for the markets it is licensed to serve. If good partners are available, this can be an effective way to enter a market. Gerber entered the Japanese baby food market this way, but exports to other countries.

Management contracting sells know-how

Management contracting means that the seller provides only management and marketing skills—others own the production and distribution facilities. Some mines and oil refineries are operated this way—and Hilton operates hotels all over the world for local owners using this method. This is another relatively low risk approach to international marketing. The low level of commitment to fixed

Exhibit 10–5 Basic Approaches for Entering International Markets

| Exporting | Licensing | Management contracting | Joint venture | Direct investment |

Generally increasing investment, risk, and control of marketing →

Mercedes-Benz manufactures Axor Tractor Trucks in Turkey according to European standards so that they are both powerful and economical. That combination makes Axor a leader in both domestic and export sales.

facilities makes the approach attractive in developing nations or ones where the government is less stable.

Joint venturing increases involvement

In a **joint venture** a domestic firm enters into a partnership with a foreign firm. As with any partnership, there can be honest disagreements over objectives—for example, how much profit is desired and how fast should it be paid out—as well as operating policies. Where a close working relationship can be developed—perhaps based on one firm's technical and marketing know-how and the foreign partner's knowledge of the market and political connections—this approach can be very attractive to both parties. Typically the two partners must make significant investments and agree on the marketing strategy. Once a joint venture is formed, it can be difficult to end if things aren't working out. J.P. Morgan used this approach to enter China, where stiff regulations prohibited a foreign firm from owning a controlling share of a Chinese investment bank or money management firm.

Direct investment involves ownership

When a foreign market looks really promising, a firm may want to take a bigger step with a direct investment. **Direct investment** means that a parent firm has a division (or owns a separate subsidiary firm) in a foreign market. This gives the parent firm complete control of marketing strategy planning. Direct investment is a big commitment and usually entails greater risks. If a local market has economic or political problems, the firm cannot easily leave. On the other hand, by providing local jobs, a company builds a strong presence in a new market. This helps the firm build a good reputation with the government and customers in the host country. And the firm does not have to share profits with a partner.[28]

CONCLUSION

In this chapter we discussed the role of Place in marketing strategy. Place decisions are especially important because they may be difficult and expensive to change. So marketing managers must make Place decisions very carefully.

We discussed how product classes and the product life cycle are related to Place objectives. This helps us determine how much a firm should rely on indirect channel systems with intermediaries or direct systems.

Marketing specialists and channel systems develop to adjust discrepancies of quantity and assortment. Their regrouping activities are basic in any economic system. And adjusting discrepancies provides opportunities for creative marketers.

Channels of distribution tend to work best when there is cooperation among the members of a channel—and conflict is avoided. So we discussed the importance of planning channel systems and the role of a channel captain. We stressed that channel systems compete with each other and that vertical marketing systems seem to be winning.

Channel planning also requires firms to decide on the degree of market exposure they want. The ideal level of exposure may be intensive, selective, or exclusive. We discussed the legal issues marketing managers must consider in developing channel systems. Finally, we examined different approaches for entering international markets.

KEY TERMS

place, 248
channel of distribution, 248
direct marketing, 253
discrepancy of quantity, 254
discrepancy of assortment, 254
regrouping activities, 254
accumulating, 254
bulk-breaking, 255
sorting, 255
assorting, 255

traditional channel systems, 256
channel captain, 257
vertical marketing systems, 259
corporate channel systems, 259
vertical integration, 259
administered channel systems, 260
contractual channel systems, 260
ideal market exposure, 261
intensive distribution, 262

selective distribution, 262
exclusive distribution, 262
multichannel distribution, 264
reverse channels, 265
exporting, 266
licensing, 266
management contracting, 266
joint venture, 267
direct investment, 267

QUESTIONS AND PROBLEMS

1. Review the Dell case at the beginning of the chapter and then discuss the competitive advantages that Barnes & Noble would have over a small bookshop. What advantages does a small bookshop have?

2. Give two examples of service firms that work with other channel specialists to sell their products to final consumers. What marketing functions is the specialist providing in each case?

3. Discuss some reasons why a firm that produces installations might use direct distribution in its domestic market but use intermediaries to reach overseas customers.

4. Explain discrepancies of quantity and assortment using the clothing business as an example. How does the application of these concepts change when selling steel to the automobile industry? What impact does this have on the number and kinds of marketing specialists required?

5. Explain the four regrouping activities with an example from the building supply industry (nails, paint, flooring, plumbing fixtures, etc.). Do you think that many specialists develop in this industry, or do producers handle the job themselves? What kinds of marketing channels would you expect to find in this industry, and what functions would various channel members provide?

6. Insurance agents are intermediaries who help other members of the channel by providing information and handling the selling function. Does it make sense for an insurance agent to specialize and work exclusively with one insurance provider? Why or why not?

7. Discuss the Place objectives and distribution arrangements that are appropriate for the following products (indicate any special assumptions you have to make to obtain an answer):
   a. A postal scale for products weighing up to 2 pounds.
   b. Children's toys: (1) radio-controlled model airplanes costing $80 or more, (2) small rubber balls.
   c. Heavy-duty, rechargeable, battery-powered nut tighteners for factory production lines.
   d. Fiberglass fabric used in making roofing shingles.

8. Give an example of a producer that uses two or more different channels of distribution. Briefly discuss what problems this might cause.

9. Explain how a channel captain can help traditional independent firms compete with a corporate (integrated) channel system.

10. Find an example of vertical integration within your city. Are there any particular advantages to this vertical integration? If so, what are they? If there are no such advantages, how do you explain the integration?

11. What would happen if retailer-organized channels (either formally integrated or administered) dominated consumer products marketing?

12. How does the nature of the product relate to the degree of market exposure desired?

13. Why would intermediaries want to be exclusive distributors for a product? Why would producers want exclusive distribution? Would intermediaries be equally anxious to get exclusive distribution for any type of product? Why or why not? Explain with reference to the following products: candy bars, batteries, golf clubs, golf balls, steak knives, televisions, and industrial woodworking machinery.

14. Explain the present legal status of exclusive distribution. Describe a situation where exclusive distribution is almost sure to be legal. Describe the nature and size of competitors and the industry, as well as the nature of the exclusive arrangement. Would this exclusive arrangement be of any value to the producer or intermediary?

15. Discuss the promotion a new grocery products producer would need in order to develop appropriate channels and move products through those channels. Would the nature of this job change for a new producer of dresses? How about for a new, small producer of installations?

16. Describe the advantages and disadvantages of the approaches to international market entry discussed in this chapter.

CREATING MARKETING PLANS

The Marketing Plan Coach software on the text website (and on the optional Student CD) includes a sample marketing plan for Hillside Veterinary Clinic. Look through the "Marketing Strategy" section.

a. Why does Hillside sell its product directly instead of indirectly?

b. Hillside has a small selection of pet supplies that it sells to people who bring in their pets. What products does it resell at retail? What channel functions does it provide, and what channel functions are performed by its suppliers?

SUGGESTED CASES

13. File-It Supplies, Inc.
15. The Trujillo Group
16. Bunyan Lumber

32. Lever, Ltd.
34. Innovative Aluminum Products, Inc.

COMPUTER-AIDED PROBLEM

10. INTENSIVE VERSUS SELECTIVE DISTRIBUTION

Hydropump, Inc., produces and sells high-quality pumps to business customers. Its marketing research shows a growing market for a similar type of pump aimed at final consumers—for use with Jacuzzi-style tubs in home remodeling jobs. Hydropump will have to develop new channels of distribution to reach this target market because most consumers rely on a retailer for advice about the combination of tub, pump, heater, and related plumbing fixtures they need. Hydropump's marketing manager, Robert Black, is trying to decide between intensive and selective distribution. With intensive distribution, he would try to sell through all the plumbing supply, bathroom fixture, and hot-tub retailers who will carry the pump. He estimates that about 5,600 suitable retailers would be willing to carry a new pump. With selective distribution, he would focus on about 280 of the best hot-tub dealers (2 or 3 in the 100 largest metropolitan areas).

Intensive distribution would require Hydropump to do more mass selling—primarily advertising in home renovation magazines—to help stimulate consumer familiarity with the brand and convince retailers that Hydropump equipment will sell. The price to the retailer might have to be lower too (to permit a bigger markup) so they will be motivated to sell Hydropump rather than some other brand offering a smaller markup.

With intensive distribution, each Hydropump sales rep could probably handle about 300 retailers effectively. With selective distribution, each sales rep could handle only about 70 retailers because more merchandising help would be necessary. Managing the smaller sales force and fewer retailers, with the selective approach, would require less manager overhead cost.

Going to all suitable and available retailers would make the pump available through about 20 times as many retailers and have the potential of reaching more customers. However, many customers shop at more than one retailer before making a final choice—so selective distribution would reach almost as many potential customers. Further, if Hydropump is using selective distribution, it would get more in-store sales attention for its pump and a larger share of pump purchases at each retailer.

Black has decided to use a spreadsheet to analyze the benefits and costs of intensive versus selective distribution.

a. Based on the initial spreadsheet, which approach seems to be the most sensible for Hydropump? Why?

b. A consultant points out that even selective distribution needs national promotion. If Black has to increase advertising and spend a total of $100,000 on mass selling to be able to recruit the retailers he wants for selective distribution, would selective or intensive distribution be more profitable?

c. With intensive distribution, how large a share (percent) of the retailers' total unit sales would Hydropump have to capture to sell enough pumps to earn $200,000 profit?

For additional questions related to this problem, see Exercise 10-3 in the *Learning Aid for Use with Essentials of Marketing*, 12th edition.

CHAPTER 11

Distribution Customer Service and Logistics

If you want a Coca-Cola, there's usually one close by—no matter where you might be in the world. And that's no accident. An executive for the best-known brand name in the world stated the objective simply: "Make Coca-Cola available within an arm's reach of desire." To achieve that objective, Coke works with many different channels of distribution. But that's just the start. Think about what it takes for a bottle, can, or cup of Coke to be there whenever you're thirsty. In warehouses and distribution centers, on trucks, in gyms and sports arenas, and thousands of other retail outlets, Coke handles, stores, and transports more than 400 billion servings of the soft drink a year. Getting all of that product to consumers could be a logistical nightmare, but Coke does it effectively and at a low cost.

Fast information about market needs helps keep Coke's distribution on target. Coke uses an Internet-based data system that links about one million retailers and other sellers to Coke and its bottlers. The system lets Coke bottlers and retailers exchange orders, invoices, and pricing information online. Orders are processed instantly—so sales to consumers at the end of the channel aren't lost because of stock-outs. Similarly, computer systems show Coke managers exactly what's selling in each market; they can even estimate the effects of promotions as they plan inventories and deliveries. And Coke products move efficiently through the channel. In Cincinnati, for example, Coke built the beverage industry's first fully automated distribution center. And when Coke's truck drivers get to the retail store, they knowingly stock the shelves with the correct mix of products.

Coke's strategies in international markets rely on many of the same ideas. But the stage of market development varies in different countries, so Coke's emphasis varies as well. To increase sales in France, for example, Coke installed thousands of soft-drink coolers in French supermarkets. In Great Britain, Coke emphasizes multipacks because it wants to have more inventory at the point of consumption—in consumers' homes. And, in Australia, some Coke vending machines have built-in cell phone systems; a press of a button makes a call so customers can charge the Coke to their cell phone accounts. Most U.S. firms face sanctions from doing business in Iran, but there is a loophole for foodstuffs. So, for several years Coke's Irish subsidiary has been shipping thousands of gallons of concentrate into Iran. Coke has quickly grabbed a large share of the national soft-drink market there.

Fortune magazine recently put the spotlight on Coca-Cola's commitment to sustainability, and decisions in the logistics area can have big environmental effects. For example, Coke is helping to develop vending machines that

are HFC-free and up to 50 percent more energy efficient. Similarly, in the U.S., Coke is adding diesel hybrid delivery trucks that cut emissions and fuel consumption by a third; in Uruguay, Coke's Montevideo Refrescos subsidiary uses electric trucks for deliveries in congested urban areas. In spite of positive steps like these, Coke still faces some challenges concerning sustainability and logistics. For example, critics argue that in a society where there is already a safe supply of tap water it doesn't make sense to bottle water, transport it in trucks that consume fuel and contribute to pollution, and then add worry about how best to dispose of the empty bottles.

In less-developed areas, the focus may be on different challenges—especially if the limitations of the Place system can make Coke products hard to find or costly. Until recently, retail stores in Afghanistan received Coke products shipped in from neighboring Pakistan—and a can of Coke sold for 40 cents. This priced many potential customers out of the market. So Coke built a local bottling plant and set up recycling systems; Coke's share rose when the price fell to about 13 cents.

Coke is also working to increase fountain-drink sales in domestic and international markets. As part of that effort, Coke equips restaurants and food outlets with Coke dispensers. Once a Coke dispenser is installed, the retailer usually doesn't have room for a competitor's dispenser. The number of fountain outlets has grown so rapidly that one Coke account rep serves as many as 1,000 retail customers in a geographic area. That means that the little guys could get lost in the shuffle. However, to give them the service they need at a reasonable cost, Coke launched Coke.net, a password-protected Web portal where fountain customers can access account managers online, track syrup orders, request equipment repairs, or download marketing support materials.

Of course, Pepsi is a tough competitor and isn't taking all of this sitting down. It has added more noncola products, and its edgy ads for Propel Fitness Water and other products have helped it gain market share and more shelf space in retail stores. Smaller players like Red Bull Energy Drink and Hansen's Natural Sodas also compete for distributors' attention and retail shelf space. Coke is pushing on new fronts as well. Who wins customers and profits in this broader competition will depend on overall marketing programs—but clearly Place has an important role to play.[1]

Choosing the right distribution channels is crucial in getting products to the target market's Place. But, as the Coca-Cola case shows, that alone doesn't ensure that products are placed "within an arm's reach of desire"—when, where, in the quantities that customers want them, and at a price they're willing to pay. In this chapter we discuss how marketing managers ensure that they also have physical distribution systems that meet their customers' needs—at both an acceptable service level and an affordable cost.

When you finish this chapter you should be able to:

1 understand why logistics (physical distribution) is such an important part of Place and marketing strategy planning.

2 understand why the physical distribution customer service level is a key marketing strategy variable.

3 understand the physical distribution concept and why the coordination of storing, transporting, and related activities is so important.

4 see how firms can cooperate and share logistics activities that will provide added value to their customers.

5 know about the advantages and disadvantages of various transportation methods.

6 know how inventory and storage decisions affect marketing strategy.

7 understand the distribution center concept.

8 understand important new terms (shown in red).

PHYSICAL DISTRIBUTION GETS IT TO CUSTOMERS

Whenever Product includes a physical good, Place requires logistics decisions. **Logistics** is the transporting, storing, and handling of goods in ways that match target customers' needs with a firm's marketing mix—both within individual firms and along a channel of distribution. **Physical distribution (PD)** is another common name for logistics.

There are many different combinations of logistics decisions. Each combination can result in a different level of distribution service and different costs. So, firms must determine the best way to provide the level of distribution service that customers want and are willing to pay for. We start this chapter by considering these critical logistics decisions. See Exhibit 11–1. Next, we describe the choice among different modes of transportation: Each has its own costs and benefits. We conclude with decisions about inventory and the use of distribution centers.

Logistics costs are very important to both firms and consumers. These costs vary from firm to firm and, from a macro-marketing perspective, from country to country. For some products, a firm may spend half or more of its total marketing dollars on physical distribution activities. The amounts involved are often so large that even small improvements in this area can have a big effect on a whole macro-marketing system and consumers' quality of life. For example, many supermarket chains worked with suppliers and producers to create a system called Efficient Consumer Response (ECR). In the United States alone, the collaboration saved more than $30 billion per year by coordinating shipments and delivery, cutting down on out-of-stock problems, and reducing inventory.[2]

Exhibit 11–1   The Role of Logistics and Physical Distribution Customer Service in Marketing Strategy

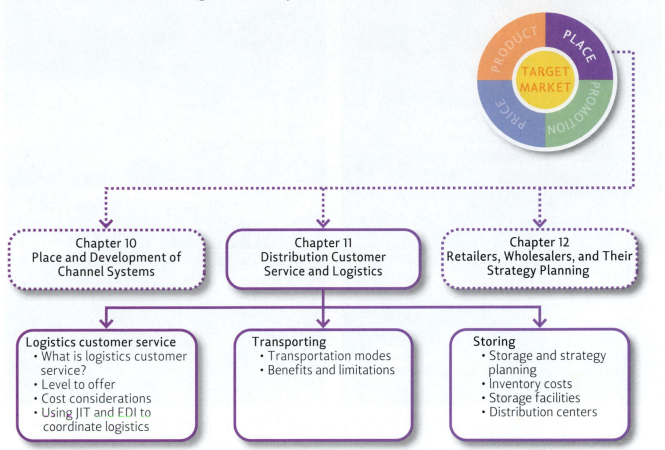

PHYSICAL DISTRIBUTION CUSTOMER SERVICE

From the beginning, we've emphasized that marketing strategy planning is based on meeting customers' needs. Planning for logistics and Place is no exception. So let's start by looking at logistics through a customer's eyes.

Customers want products, not excuses

Customers don't care how a product was moved or stored or what some channel member had to do to provide it. Rather, customers think in terms of the physical distribution **customer service level**—how rapidly and dependably a firm can deliver what they, the customers, want.

What does this really mean? It means that Toyota wants to have enough windshields delivered to make cars *that* day—not late so production stops *or* early so there are a lot of extras to move around or store. It means that business executives who rent cars from Hertz want them to be ready when they get off their planes. It means that when you order a blue shirt at the Lands' End website you receive blue, not pink. It means you want your Tostitos to be whole when you buy a bag at the snack bar—not crushed into crumbs from rough handling in a warehouse.

Physical distribution is invisible to most consumers

PD is, and should be, a part of marketing that is "invisible" to most consumers. It only gets their attention when something goes wrong. At that point, it may be too late to do anything that will keep them happy.

In countries where physical distribution systems are inefficient, consumers face shortages of the products they need. By contrast, most consumers in the United States and Canada don't think much about physical distribution. This probably means that

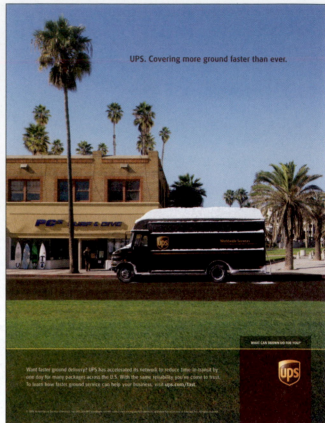

The physical distribution customer service level—including fast and reliable delivery of whatever assortment is needed—is critical to many business customers.

these market-directed macro-marketing systems work pretty well—that a lot of individual marketing managers have made good decisions in this area. But it doesn't mean that the decisions are always clear-cut or simple. In fact, many trade-offs may be required.

Trade-offs of costs, service, and sales

Most customers would prefer very good service at a very low price. But that combination is hard to provide because it usually costs more to provide higher levels of service. So most physical distribution decisions involve trade-offs between costs, the customer service level, and sales.

If you want a new HP computer and the Best Buy store where you would like to buy it doesn't have it on hand, you're likely to buy it elsewhere; or if that model HP is hard to get, you might just switch to some other brand. Perhaps the Best Buy store could keep your business by guaranteeing two-day delivery of your computer—by using airfreight from HP's factory. In this case, the manager is trading the cost of storing inventory for the extra cost of speedy delivery—assuming that the computer is available in inventory *somewhere* in the channel. In this example, missing one sale may not seem that important, but it all adds up. A few years ago a computer company lost over $500 million in sales because its computers weren't available when and where customers were ready to buy them.

Exhibit 11–2 illustrates trade-off relationships like those highlighted in the HP example. For example, faster but more expensive transportation may reduce the need for a costly inventory of computers. If the service level is too low, customers will buy elsewhere and sales will be lost. Alternatively, the supplier may hope that a higher service level will attract more customers. But if the service level is higher than customers want or are willing to pay for, sales will be lost to competitors.

Exhibit 11–2
Trade-Offs among
Physical Distribution
Costs, Customer Service
Level, and Sales

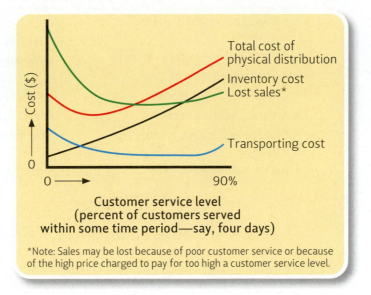

*Note: Sales may be lost because of poor customer service or because of the high price charged to pay for too high a customer service level.

The trade-offs that must be made in the PD area can be complicated. The lowest-cost approach may not be best—if customers aren't satisfied. If different target markets want different customer service levels, several different strategies may be needed.[3]

Many firms are trying to address these complications with e-commerce. Information technology can sometimes improve service levels *and* cut costs at the same time. Better information flows make it easier to coordinate activities, improve efficiency, and add value for the customer.

PHYSICAL DISTRIBUTION CONCEPT FOCUSES ON THE WHOLE DISTRIBUTION SYSTEM

The physical distribution concept

The **physical distribution (PD) concept** says that all transporting, storing, and product-handling activities of a business and a whole channel system should be coordinated as one system that seeks to minimize the cost of distribution for a given customer service level. Both lower costs and better service help to increase customer value. This seems like common sense, but until recently most companies treated physical distribution functions as separate and unrelated activities.

Within a firm, responsibility for different logistics activities was spread among various departments—production, shipping, sales, warehousing, purchasing, and others. No one person was responsible for coordinating storing and shipping decisions or customer service levels. It was even rarer for different firms in the channel to collaborate. Each just did its own thing. Unfortunately, in too many firms these old-fashioned ways persist—with a focus on individual functional activities rather than the whole physical distribution system.[4]

Decide what service level to offer

With broader adoption of the physical distribution concept, this is changing. Firms work together to decide what aspects of service are most important to customers at the end of the channel. Then they focus on finding the least expensive way to achieve the target level of service.

Exhibit 11–3 shows a variety of factors that may influence the customer service level (at each level in the channel). The most important aspects of customer service depend on target market needs. Xerox might focus on how long it takes to deliver copy machine repair parts once it receives an order. When a copier breaks down, customers want the repair "yesterday." The service level might be stated as "we will deliver 90 percent of all emergency repair parts within 24 hours." This might require that commonly

Exhibit 11–3
Examples of Factors
That Affect PD Service
Levels

- Advance information on product availability
- Time to enter and process orders
- Backorder procedures
- Where inventory is stored
- Accuracy in filling orders
- Damage in shipping, storing, and handling
- Online status information

- Advance information on delays
- Time needed to deliver an order
- Reliability in meeting delivery date
- Complying with customer's instructions
- Defect-free deliveries
- How needed adjustments are handled
- Procedures for handling returns

needed parts be available on the service truck, that order processing be very fast, and that parts not available locally be sent by airfreight. Obviously, supplying this service level will affect the total cost of the PD system. But it may also beat competitors.

Fast PD service can be critical for retailers that appeal to consumers who are eager to get a new product that is in hot demand—the latest CD or DVD release, a bestselling book, or a popular toy or video game.[5]

Find the lowest total cost for the right service level

In selecting a PD system, the **total cost approach** involves evaluating each possible PD system and identifying *all* of the costs of each alternative. This approach uses the tools of cost accounting and economics. Costs that otherwise might be ignored—like inventory carrying costs—are considered. The possible costs of lost sales due to a lower customer service level may also be considered.

For example, Vegpro Kenya compared different PD systems for shipping ready-to-eat fresh produce from fields in Kenya to grocery stores in major European cities. The analysis showed that the costs of airfreight transportation were significantly higher than using trucks and ships. But the firm also found that costs of spoilage and inventory could be much lower when airfreight is used. The faster airfreight-based PD system brought customers fresher produce at about the same total cost. So Vegpro cleans, chops, and packages vegetables in its 27,000-square-foot, air-conditioned facility at the Nairobi airport—using low-cost African labor. And the next day, fresh beans, baby carrots, and other vegetables are on store shelves in Madrid, London, and Paris.[6]

Sauder tries to help customer firms do a better job of tracking the status of orders and making certain that products are where they are needed at the right time.

COORDINATING LOGISTICS ACTIVITIES AMONG FIRMS

Functions can be shifted and shared in the channel

As a marketing manager develops the Place part of a strategy, it is important to decide how physical distribution functions can and should be divided within the channel. Who will store, handle, and transport the goods—and who will pay for these services? Who will coordinate all of the PD activities?

Disaster Relief Is No Logistics Picnic

Hurricanes, tsunamis, and earthquakes create immediate needs for emergency relief supplies. And the logistics involved in delivering them include many of the same activities found in the physical delivery of other goods. However, in a disaster situation, life and death often hinge upon the speed with which food, water, and medical supplies can be delivered. Yet, when bridges, roads, and airports are destroyed, local transportation can be complicated, if not impossible. And, even worse, there is no advance warning when or where aid will be needed. Imagine what it would be like for one business to be instantly ready to distribute millions of products to a target market that usually doesn't exist, moves around the world, and then without notice pops up somewhere with insatiable needs.

People in advanced societies have high expectations that help will be immediate when disaster strikes. Yet, it's nearly impossible for relief agencies to meet those expectations. Still, improved performance is on the way from both disaster relief agencies and private businesses, which have learned from recent efforts. For example, instead of stockpiling drugs, tents, and blankets, agencies are learning to rely on outsourcing. Agencies arrange open orders with suppliers who must be prepared to instantly ship supplies whenever and wherever they are needed.

Organizations with logistics expertise also lend a helping hand. As soon as Wal-Mart's emergency operation center learned that Hurricane Katrina was coming, it prestocked stores in the Gulf region with extra water, flashlights, and batteries as well as canned soup and meats. Residents survived with these crucial supplies before government aid arrived. Immediately following disasters in all parts of the world, transportation giants like FedEx, DHL, and China Southern Airlines have responded quickly with planes and trucks that facilitate delivery of needed supplies. The Fritz Institute analyzes past relief efforts and consults with agencies to help them better prepare for future responses.

When chaos hits, coordination of relief efforts is possible only if there is good information. Agencies need to know what supplies are available, where they're located, what needs are greatest, and where and how quickly deliveries can be made. Having one central communication hub—to collect and share this type of information—and IT systems specifically dedicated to the task, are key. A new system called Suma allows relief workers to manage incoming donations, put them in the right storage places, and establish shipping priorities.

Other physical distribution solutions are decidedly low-tech, but equally important. For example, boxes need to be color coded so it's obvious which ones contain critical medical supplies and perishable food. And donated goods must be packed in cartons light enough to be carried manually in locations that have no power or equipment.[7]

There is no right sharing arrangement. Physical distribution can be varied endlessly in a marketing mix and in a channel system. And competitors may share these functions in different ways—with different costs and results.

How PD is shared affects the rest of a strategy

How the PD functions are shared affects the other three Ps—especially Price. The sharing arrangement can also make (or break) a strategy. Consider Channel Master, a firm that wanted to take advantage of the growing market for the dishlike antennas used to receive TV signals from satellites. The product looked like it could be a big success, but the small company didn't have the money to invest in a large inventory. So Channel Master decided to work only with wholesalers who were willing to buy (and pay for) several units—to be used for demonstrations and to ensure that buyers got immediate delivery.

In the first few months Channel Master earned $2 million in revenues—just by providing inventory for the channel. And the wholesalers paid the interest cost of carrying inventory—over $300,000 the first year. Here the wholesalers shared the risk of the new venture, but it was a good decision for them, too. They won many sales from a competing channel whose customers had to wait several months for delivery. And by getting off to a strong start, Channel Master became a market leader.

A coordinated effort reduces conflict

If firms in the channel do not plan and coordinate how they will share PD activities, PD is likely to be a source of conflict rather than a basis for competitive advantage. Let's consider this point by taking a closer look at just-in-time (JIT) delivery systems (which we introduced in Chapter 6).

JIT requires a close, cooperative relationship

A key advantage of JIT for business customers is that it reduces their PD costs—especially storing and handling costs. However, if the customer doesn't have any backup inventory, there's no security blanket if a supplier's delivery truck gets stuck in traffic, there's an error in what's shipped, or there are any quality problems. Thus, a JIT system requires that a supplier have extremely high quality control in every PD activity.

A JIT system usually requires that a supplier respond to very short order lead times and the customer's production schedule. Thus, e-commerce order systems and information sharing over computer networks are often required. JIT suppliers often locate their facilities close to important customers. Trucks may make smaller and more frequent deliveries—perhaps even several times a day.

A JIT system shifts greater responsibility for PD activities backward in the channel. If the supplier can be more efficient than the customer could be in controlling PD costs—and still provide the customer with the service level required—this approach can work well for everyone in the channel. However, JIT is not always the best approach. It may be better for a supplier to produce and ship in larger, more economical quantities—if the savings offset the distribution system's total inventory and handling costs.[8]

Supply chain may involve even more firms

In our discussion, we have taken the point of view of a marketing manager. This focuses on how logistics should be coordinated to meet the needs of customers at the end of the channel of distribution. Now, however, we should broaden the picture somewhat because the relationships within the distribution channel are sometimes part of a broader network of relationships in the **supply chain**—the complete set of firms and facilities and logistics activities that are involved in procuring materials, transforming them into intermediate or finished products, and distributing them to customers.

For example, Manitowoc is one of the world's largest manufacturers of cranes. Its huge mobile cranes are used at construction sites all around the world. Robert Ward, who is in charge of purchasing for Manitowoc, must ensure an unbroken flow of parts and materials so that Manitowoc can keep its promises to customers about when cranes will be delivered. This is difficult because each crane has component parts from many suppliers around the globe. Further, any supplier may be held up by problems with its own suppliers.

In one case, Manitowoc's German factory was having trouble getting key chassis parts from two suppliers in Poland. Ward traced the problem back to a Scandinavian steel mill that was behind on shipments to the Polish firms. Manitowoc buys a lot of steel and has a lot of leverage with steel distributors, so Ward scoured Europe for distributors

Boom: steel iron source fabricated in Belgium & U.S.

Manitowoc Mobile Crane

Counterweights: Poland & France

Cable: U.S.

Hook: Netherlands & Belgium

Chasis: steel from Sweden & Germany, fabricated in Poland

Tires: France, Japan & China

Cabs: Germany

Steel rims: Germany & China

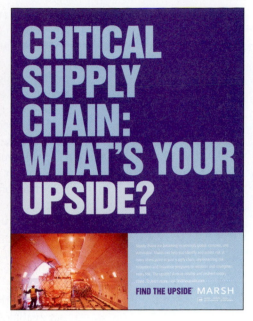

Firms often seek help from outside specialists to improve the efficiency and effectiveness of their domestic and international supply chains.

who had extra inventory of steel plate. The steel he found was more expensive than buying the steel directly from the mill, but the mill couldn't keep supplies flowing and the distributors could. By helping to coordinate the whole supply chain, Manitowoc was able to keep its promises and deliver cranes to its customers on schedule.[9]

Ideally, all of the firms in the supply chain should work together to meet the needs of the customer at the very end of the chain. That way, at each link along the chain the shifting and sharing of logistics functions and costs are handled to result in the most value for the final customer. This also helps all of the firms do a better job of competing against other supply chains.[10]

Better information helps coordinate PD

Coordinating all of the elements of PD has always been a challenge—even in a single firm. Trying to coordinate orders, inventory, and transportation throughout the whole supply chain is even tougher. But information shared over the Internet and at websites has been important in finding solutions to these challenges. Physical distribution decisions will continue to improve as more firms are able to have their computers "talk to each other" directly and as websites help managers get access to up-to-date information whenever they need it.

Internet EXERCISE

Managers who are members of the Council of Supply Chain Management Professionals usually have responsibilities in purchasing, logistics, or materials management. The website of this organization (**http://cscmp.org**) provides many useful resources to both members and nonmembers. Under "Education and Awards," choose "Awards" and then find the "Supply Chain Innovation Award." Choose one of the nominees of this award (older winners can be viewed free), and read how the nominee addressed a logistics challenge. Explain how other companies might learn from this firm's experience.

Electronic data interchange sets a standard

Until recently, differences in computer systems from one firm to another hampered the flow of information. Many firms attacked this problem by adopting **electronic data interchange (EDI)**—an approach that puts information in a standardized format easily shared between different computer systems. In many firms, purchase orders, shipping reports, and other paper documents were replaced with computerized EDI. With EDI, a customer transmits its order information directly to the supplier's computer. The supplier's computer immediately processes the order and schedules production, order assembly, and transportation. Inventory information is automatically updated, and status reports are available instantly. The supplier might then use EDI to send the updated information to the transportation provider's computer. In fact, most international transportation firms rely on EDI links with their customers.[11]

Improved information flow and better coordination of PD activities is a key reason for the success of Pepperidge Farm's line of premium cookies. Most of the company's delivery truck drivers use hand-held computers to record the inventory at each stop along their routes. They use a wireless Internet connection to instantly transmit the information into a computer at the bakeries, and cookies in short supply are produced. The right assortment of fresh cookies is quickly shipped to local markets, and delivery trucks are loaded with what retailers need that day. Pepperidge Farm moves cookies from its bakeries to store shelves in about three days; most cookie producers take about 10 days. That means fresher cookies for consumers and helps to support Pepperidge Farm's high-quality positioning and premium price.[12]

Ethical issues may arise

Some ethical issues that arise in the PD area concern communications about product availability. For example, some critics say that Internet sellers too often take orders for products that are not available or which they cannot deliver as quickly as customers expect. Yet a marketing manager can't always know precisely how long it will take before a product will be available. It doesn't make sense for the marketer to lose a customer if it appears that he or she can satisfy the customer's needs. But the customer may be inconvenienced or face added cost if the marketer's best guess isn't accurate. Similarly, some critics say that stores too often run out of products that they promote to attract consumers to the store. Yet it may not be possible for the marketer to predict demand, or to know when placing an ad that deliveries won't arrive. Different people have different views about how a firm should handle such situations. Some retailers just offer rain checks.

> **Ethics QUESTION**
>
> Many major firms, ranging from Nike and Starbucks to Wal-Mart and IKEA, have been criticized for selling products from overseas suppliers whose workers toil in bad conditions for long hours and at low pay. Defenders of the companies point out that overseas sourcing provides jobs that are better than what workers would have without it. Critics think that companies that sell products in wealthy countries have a social responsibility to see that suppliers in less-developed nations pay a fair wage and provide healthy working conditions. What do you think? Should U.S. firms be required to monitor the employment practices of suppliers in their supply chains? Should all suppliers be held to Western legal or moral standards? What solutions or compromises might be offered?[13]

THE TRANSPORTING FUNCTION ADDS VALUE TO A MARKETING STRATEGY

Transporting aids economic development and exchange

Transporting is the marketing function of moving goods. Transportation makes products available when and where they need to be—at a cost. But the cost is less than the value added to products by moving them or there is little reason to ship in the first place.

Transporting can help achieve economies of scale in production. If production costs can be reduced by producing larger quantities in one location, these savings may more than offset the added cost of transporting the finished products to customers. Without low-cost transportation, both within countries and internationally, there would be no mass distribution as we know it today.

The cost of transportation adds little to the total cost of products—like pharmaceuticals—that are already valuable relative to their size and weight. But transporting costs can be a large part of the total cost for heavy products that are low in value, like sheet aluminum.

Transporting can be costly

Transporting costs limit the target markets a marketing manager can serve. Shipping costs increase delivered cost—and that's what really interests customers. Transport costs add little to the cost of products that are already valuable relative to their size and weight. A case of medicine, for example, might be shipped to a drugstore at low cost. But transporting costs can be a large part of the total cost for heavy products of low value—like many minerals and raw materials. You can imagine that shipping a massive roll of aluminum to a producer of soft-drink cans is an expensive proposition. Exhibit 11–4 shows transporting costs as a percent of total sales dollars for several products.[14]

Governments may influence transportation

Government often plays an important role in the development of a country's transportation system, including its roads, harbors, railroads, and airports. And different countries regulate transportation differently, although regulation has in general been decreasing.

For example, as part of their move toward unification, most European countries are reducing their transporting regulations. The construction of the tunnel under the English Channel is a dramatic example of the changes taking place. The "chunnel" allows trains to speed between England and the rest of Europe.

As regulations decreased in the United States, competition in the transportation industry increased. As a result, a marketing manager generally has many carriers in one or more modes competing for the firm's transporting business. Or a firm can do its own transporting. So knowing about the different modes is important.[15]

Exhibit 11–4
Transporting Costs as a Percent of Selling Price for Different Products

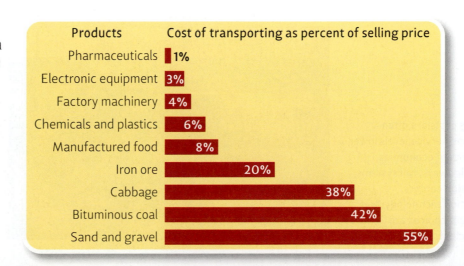

Products	Cost of transporting as percent of selling price
Pharmaceuticals	1%
Electronic equipment	3%
Factory machinery	4%
Chemicals and plastics	6%
Manufactured food	8%
Iron ore	20%
Cabbage	38%
Bituminous coal	42%
Sand and gravel	55%

Exhibit 11–5 Benefits and Limitations of Different Transport Modes

			Transporting Features			
Mode	Cost	Delivery Speed	Number of Locations Served	Ability to Handle a Variety of Goods	Frequency of Scheduled Shipments	Dependability in Meeting Schedules
Truck	High	Fast	Very extensive	High	High	High
Rail	Medium	Average	Extensive	High	Low	Medium
Water	Very low	Very slow	Limited	Very high	Very low	Medium
Air	Very high	Very fast	Extensive	Limited	High	High
Pipeline	Low	Slow	Very limited	Very limited	Medium	High

WHICH TRANSPORTING ALTERNATIVE IS BEST?

Transporting function must fit the whole strategy

The transporting function should fit into the whole marketing strategy. But picking the best transporting alternative depends on the product, other physical distribution decisions, and what service level the company wants to offer. The best alternative should provide the level of service (for example, speed and dependability) required at as low a cost as possible. Exhibit 11–5 shows that different modes of transportation have different strengths and weaknesses. Low transporting cost is *not* the only criterion for selecting the best mode.[16]

Railroads—large loads moved at low cost

Railroads are still the workhorse of the U.S. transportation system. They carry more freight over more miles than any other mode. However, they account for less than 10 percent of transport revenues. They carry heavy and bulky goods—such as coal, steel, and chemicals—over long distances at relatively low cost. Because railroad freight usually moves more slowly than truck shipments, it is not as well suited for perishable items or those in urgent demand. Railroads are most efficient at handling full carloads of goods. Less-than-carload (LCL) shipments take a lot of handling, which means they usually move more slowly and at a higher price per pound than carload shipments.[17]

Trucks are more expensive, but flexible and essential

The flexibility and speed of trucks make them better at moving small quantities of goods for shorter distances. They can travel on almost any road. They go where the rails can't. They are also reliable in meeting delivery schedules, which is an essential requirement for logistics systems that provide rapid replenishment of inventory after a sale. In combination these factors explain why at least 75 percent of U.S. consumer products travel at least part of the way from producer to consumer by truck. And in countries with

Logistics costs are often higher and service levels lower in developing economies, where highways, rail systems, distribution centers, information technology, and equipment choices are limited or inefficient.

THINK 18-wheel air freshener

Ultra low sulfur diesel and advanced engines will mean 90% less emissions

THE *people* OF AMERICA'S OIL AND NATURAL GAS INDUSTRY

Critics say that increased reliance on truck freight is bad for the environment, but the trade association that represents America's oil and natural gas industry says that engineers are at work on new "ultra low sulfur and advanced engines that will result in 90 percent less emissions."

good highway systems, trucks can give extremely fast service. Trucks compete for high-value items.[18]

Ship it overseas, but slowly

Water transportation is the slowest shipping mode, but it is usually the lowest-cost way of shipping heavy freight. Water transportation is very important for international shipments and often the only practical approach. This explains why port cities like Boston, New York City, Rotterdam, Osaka, and Singapore are important centers for international trade.

Inland waterways are important too

Inland waterways (such as the Mississippi River and Great Lakes in the United States and the Rhine and Danube in Europe) are also important, especially for bulky, nonperishable products such as iron ore, grain, and gravel. However, when winter ice closes freshwater harbors, alternate transportation must be used.

Pipelines move oil and gas

Pipelines are used primarily to move oil and natural gas. So pipelines are important both in the oil-producing and oil-consuming countries. Only a few major cities in the United States, Canada, Mexico, and Latin America are more than 200 miles from a major pipeline system. However, the majority of the pipelines in the United States are located in the Southwest, connecting oil fields and refineries.

Internet EXERCISE

Shipping by sea can be a less costly mode of transportation. But with more than 100 carriers operating ships, it can be difficult to get a handle on all the options. OceanSchedules.com (**www.oceanschedules.com**) aims to change this. Go to the website and do a "port to port" search, with "Hong Kong" as the origin and "Vancouver, British Columbia" as the destination. Next select "by departure" and enter today's date and 1 week out. Finally, click "Get Schedules." How many different boats could take your shipment? Now change the longest transit time to 28 days and check what difference that makes in the number of available boats. What happens if you change the arrival date? How could this website be useful to a company shipping light fixtures from Hong Kong to Canada?

Airfreight is expensive, but fast and growing

The most expensive cargo transporting mode is airplane—but it is fast! Airfreight rates are on average three times higher than trucking rates—but the greater speed may offset the added cost.

High-value, low-weight goods—like high-fashion clothing and parts for the electronics industry—are often shipped by air. Perishable products that previously could not be shipped are now being flown across continents and oceans. Flowers and bulbs from Holland, for example, now are jet-flown to points all over the world. And airfreight has become very important for small emergency deliveries, like repair parts, special orders, and business documents that must be somewhere the next day.

But airplanes may cut the total cost of distribution

Using planes may reduce the cost of packing, unpacking, and preparing goods for sale and may help a firm reduce inventory costs by eliminating outlying warehouses. Valuable benefits of airfreight's speed are less spoilage, theft, and damage. Although the *transporting* cost of air shipments may be higher, the *total* cost of distribution may be lower. As more firms realize this, airfreight firms—like DHL Worldwide Express, FedEx, and Emery Air Freight—have enjoyed rapid growth.[19]

Put it in a container— and move between modes easily

Products often move by several different modes and carriers during their journey. This is especially common for international shipments. Japanese firms, like Sony, ship stereos to the United States, Canada, and Europe by boat. When they arrive at the dock, they are loaded on trains and sent across the country. Then the units are delivered to a wholesaler by truck or rail.

To better coordinate the flow of products between modes, transportation companies like CSX offer customers a complete choice of different transportation modes. Then CSX, not the customer, figures out the best and lowest-cost way to shift and share transporting functions between the modes.[20]

Loading and unloading goods several times used to be a real problem. Parts of a shipment would become separated, damaged, or even stolen. And handling the goods, perhaps many times, raised costs and slowed delivery. Many of these problems are reduced with **containerization**—grouping individual items into an economical shipping quantity and sealing them in protective containers for transit to the final destination. This protects the products and simplifies handling during shipping. Some containers are as large as truck bodies.

Piggyback—a ride on two or more modes

Piggyback service means loading truck trailers—or flatbed trailers carrying containers—on railcars to provide both speed and flexibility. Railroads now pick up truck trailers at the producer's location, load them onto specially designed rail flatcars, and haul them as close to the customer as rail lines run. The trailers are then hooked up to a truck tractor and delivered to the buyer's door. Similar services are offered on oceangoing ships—allowing door-to-door service between cities around the world.

Transportation in developing countries can cost more

Transportation choices are usually not so good in developing countries. Roads are often poor, rail systems may be limited, and ports may be undeveloped. Local firms that specialize in logistics services may not exist at all. Even so, firms that are willing to invest the effort can reap benefits and help their customers overcome the effects of these problems.

Metro AG, a firm based in Germany that has opened wholesale facilities in Bangalore and several other major cities in India, illustrates this point. Metro focuses on selling food products and other supplies to the thousands of restaurants, hotels, and other small businesses in the markets it serves. When Metro started in India, 40 percent of the fruits and vegetables it purchased from farmers were spoiled, damaged, or lost by the time they got to Metro. These problems piled up because the produce traveled from the fields over rough roads and was handled by as many as seven intermediaries along the way. To overcome these problems, Metro gave farmers crates to protect freshly picked crops from damage and to keep them away from dirt and bacteria that would shorten their shelf life. Further, crates were loaded and unloaded only once because Metro bought its own refrigerated trucks—to pick up produce and bring it directly to its outlets. Metro used the same ideas to speed fresh seafood from fishermen's boats. Many of Metro's restaurant customers previously bought what they needed from a variety of small suppliers, many of whom would run out of stock. Now the restaurant owners save time and money with one-stop shopping at Metro. Metro is growing fast in India because it has quality products that are in stock when they're needed, and it's bringing down food costs for its customers.[21]

Transportation choices have environmental costs too

Marketing managers must be sensitive to the environmental effects of transportation decisions. Trucks, trains, airplanes, and ships contribute to air pollution and global warming; estimates suggest that on average more than half of a firm's total carbon emissions come from transportation. There are other problems as well. For example, a damaged pipeline or oil tanker can spew thousands of gallons of oil before it can be repaired.

Many firms are taking steps to reduce such problems. FedEx and UPS are revamping their fleets to use more electric and alternative fuel vehicles. Rail is usually the cleanest way to move land freight a long distance, but General Electric's recently introduced Evolution locomotives have 5 percent better fuel economy and 40 percent lower emissions compared to previous models. GE is already working on a hybrid locomotive that will improve fuel economy another 10 percent. Truck manufacturers are also working to improve fuel efficiency and environmental impact. Peterbilt

When Metro set up its cash-and-carry wholesale operations in India, it could not rely on the same logistics systems it used in Germany. Rather, Metro had to create its own fleet of refrigerated trucks to pick up produce directly from farmers. However, this reduced stock-outs and helped Metro offer customers better-quality produce at lower prices.

and International are among firms working to build diesel-hybrid 18-wheelers. The U.S. government supports these initiatives through the Environmental Protection Agency's SmartWay program. It helps freight carriers, shippers, and logistics companies improve fuel efficiency and reduce environmental impact. Both trucking and railroad firms have procedures to ensure that transporting toxic cargo is safer. Today the public *expects* companies to manufacture, transport, sell, and dispose of products in an environmentally sound manner.[22]

THE STORING FUNCTION AND MARKETING STRATEGY

Store it and smooth out sales, increase profits and consumer satisfaction

Storing is the marketing function of holding goods so they're available when they're needed. **Inventory** is the amount of goods being stored.

Maintaining the right inventory level is difficult when it's hard to foresee likely demand. Consider what happened when Frito-Lay introduced Tostitos Gold, a thicker version of Tostitos tortilla snack chips that was developed to work well with dips and salsa. Marketing managers did not know if consumers would be willing to pay a premium price, normally reserved for low-fat or organic chips, for Tostitos Gold. To fuel demand, they ran a pair of celebrity ads on the Tostitos Fiesta Bowl national championship football game. In the ads, Jay Leno and Little Richard liven up parties with Tostitos Gold. The ads show how serving the chip "that's extra thick for hearty dips" can inject life into otherwise boring situations. The ads did a better job than expected in stirring interest, and chip lovers were so enthusiastic about Tostitos Gold that the chips were quickly out-of-stock at most supermarkets. The stock-outs resulted in lost sales of about $500,000 a week.[23]

A firm that stocks out when customers are ready to buy may not only lose the sale but also damage the relationship and the possibility of future sales. This problem contributed to Kmart's bankruptcy. Many consumers decided it was no longer a convenient place to shop when stores repeatedly ran out of basic staples that consumers expected to find.

Storing is necessary when production of goods doesn't match consumption. This is common with mass production. Nippon Steel, for example, might produce thousands of steel bars of one size before changing the machines to produce another size. It's often cheaper to produce large quantities of one size, and store the unsold quantity, than to have shorter production runs. Thus, storing goods allows the producer to achieve economies of scale in production.

Storing varies the channel system

Storing allows producers and intermediaries to keep stocks at convenient locations, ready to meet customers' needs. In fact, storing is one of the major activities of some intermediaries.

Most channel members provide the storing function for some length of time. Even final consumers store some things for their future needs. Which channel members store the product, and for how long, affects the behavior of all channel members. For example, the producer of Snapper lawn mowers tries to get wholesalers to inventory a wide selection of its machines. That way, retailers can carry smaller inventories since they can be sure of dependable local supplies from wholesalers. And the retailers might decide to sell Snapper—rather than Toro or some other brand that they would have to store at their own expense.

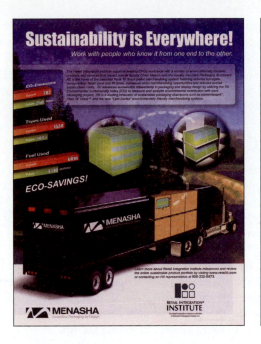

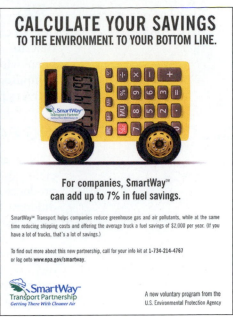

Menasha, a supplier of innovative packaging, wants its client firms to realize that its package designs can help to reduce both logistics costs and environmental impact. The Environmental Protection Agency's voluntary SmartWay Transport Partnership is another approach to achieve environmental goals by reducing fuel costs as well as air pollution.

If consumers "store" the product, more of it may be used or consumed. That's why Breyer's likes customers to buy its half-gallon packages. The "inventory" is right there in the freezer—and ready to be eaten—whenever the impulse hits.

Goods are stored at a cost

Storing can increase the value of goods, but *storing always involves costs* too. Different kinds of cost are involved. See Exhibit 11–6. Car dealers, for example, must store cars on their lots—waiting for the right customer. The interest expense of money tied up in the inventory is a major cost. In addition, if a new car on the lot is dented or scratched, there is a repair cost. If a car isn't sold before the new models come out, its value drops. There is also a risk of fire or theft—so the retailer must carry insurance. And, of course, dealers incur the cost of leasing or owning the display lot where they store the cars.

In today's competitive markets, most firms watch their inventories closely. They try to cut unnecessary inventory because it can make the difference between a profitable strategy and a loser. On the other hand, a marketing manager must be very careful in making the distinction between unnecessary inventory and inventory needed to provide the distribution service level customers expect.[24]

Exhibit 11–6 Many Expenses Contribute to Total Inventory Cost

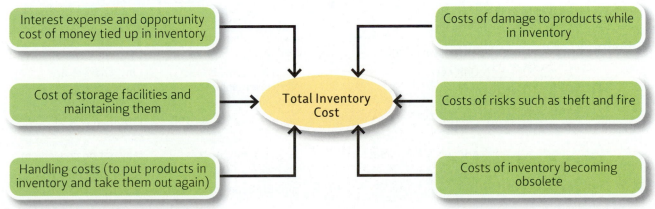

Many firms are finding that they can cut inventory costs and still provide the desired customer service level—if they can reduce the time it takes to replace items that are sold. This is one important reason that the JIT and ECR approaches have been widely adopted. The firms involved use EDI, the Internet, and similar computerized approaches to share information and speed up the order cycle and delivery process.

SPECIALIZED STORING FACILITIES MAY BE REQUIRED

New cars can be stored outside on the dealer's lot. Fuel oil can be stored in a specially designed tank. Coal and other raw materials can be stored in open pits. But most products must be stored inside protective buildings. Often, firms can choose among different types of specialized storing facilities. The right choice may reduce costs and serve customers better.

**Private warehouses
are common**

Private warehouses are storing facilities owned or leased by companies for their own use. Most manufacturers, wholesalers, and retailers have some storing facilities either in their main buildings or in a separate location. A sales manager often is responsible for managing a manufacturer's finished-goods warehouse, especially if regional sales branches aren't near the factory.

Firms use private warehouses when a large volume of goods must be stored regularly. Yet private warehouses can be expensive. If the need changes, the extra space may be hard, or impossible, to rent to others.

**Public warehouses fill
special needs**

Public warehouses are independent storing facilities. They can provide all the services that a company's own warehouse can provide. A company might choose a public warehouse if it doesn't have a regular need for space. For example, Tonka Toys uses public warehouses because its business is seasonal. Tonka pays for the space only when it is used. Public warehouses are also useful for manufacturers that must maintain stocks in many locations, including foreign countries. See Exhibit 11–7 for a comparison of private and public warehouses.[25]

**Warehousing facilities
cut handling costs too**

The cost of physical handling is a major storing cost. Goods must be handled once when put into storage and again when removed to be sold. To reduce these costs, modern one-story buildings away from downtown traffic have replaced most old multistory warehouses. They eliminate the need for elevators and permit the use of power-operated lift trucks, battery-operated motor scooters, roller-skating order pickers, electric hoists for heavy items, and hydraulic ramps to speed loading and unloading. Bar codes, universal product code (UPC) numbers, and electronic radio frequency identification (RFID) tags make it easy for computers to monitor inventory, order needed stock, and track storing and shipping costs. For example, a warehouse worker may wear

Exhibit 11–7
A Comparison of Private
Warehouses and Public
Warehouses

Characteristics	Type of Warehouse	
	Private	Public
Fixed investment	Very high	No fixed investment
Unit cost	High if volume is low Very low if volume is very high	Low: charges are made only for space needed
Control	High	Low managerial control
Adequacy for product line	Highly adequate	May not be convenient
Flexibility	Low: fixed costs have already been committed	High: easy to end arrangement

Zappos.com says that "we are a service company that happens to sell." In practice, that means it has a warehouse that's as big as 17 football fields to support transactions from its website at the needed customer service level. Further, Zappos.com's storing, transporting, and handling must be efficient for the firm to compete with "free shipping" and "110% price protection."

a tiny scanner ring when removing cartons from a shelf so that information in the bar codes can be instantly read and transmitted via a Bluetooth wireless network to the firm's information system. Similarly, RFID tags may transmit detailed information about the contents of a carton as it moves along a conveyor system. Some warehouses also have computer-controlled order-picking systems or conveyor belts that speed the process of locating and assembling the assortment required to fill an order.[26]

THE DISTRIBUTION CENTER—A DIFFERENT KIND OF WAREHOUSE

Is storing really needed?

Discrepancies of assortment or quantity between one channel level and another are often adjusted at the place where goods are stored. It reduces handling costs to regroup and store at the same place—*if both functions are required*. But sometimes regrouping is required when storing isn't.

Don't store it, distribute it

A **distribution center** is a special kind of warehouse designed to speed the flow of goods and avoid unnecessary storing costs. Anchor Hocking moves over a million pounds of its housewares products through its distribution center each day. Faster inventory turnover and easier bulk-breaking reduce the cost of carrying inventory.

Today, the distribution center concept is widely used by firms at all channel levels. Many products buzz through a distribution center without ever tarrying on a shelf; workers and equipment immediately sort the products as they come in and then move them to an outgoing loading dock and the vehicle that will take them to their next stop.

Direct store delivery skips the distribution center

Some firms prefer to skip the distribution center altogether and ship products directly from where they are manufactured to retail stores. This may move products more quickly, but usually at a higher cost. Frito-Lay uses this approach. It handles more than 10,000 direct delivery routes to more than 200,000 small-store customers. The route drivers build close relationships with the many small retailers. That helps Frito-Lay better understand end consumers and adapt product mixes to particular stores. These extra services result in more shelf space and higher prices at the small stores.[27]

Managers must be innovative to provide customers with superior value

More competitive markets, improved technology, coordination among firms, and efficient new distribution centers are bringing big improvements to the PD area. Yet the biggest challenges may be more basic. As we've emphasized here, physical distribution activities transcend departmental, corporate, and even national boundaries. So taking advantage of ways to improve often requires cooperation all along the channel system. Too often, such cooperation doesn't exist—and changing ingrained ways of doing things is hard. But marketing managers who push for innovations in these areas are likely to win customers away from firms and whole channel systems that are stuck doing things in the old way.[28]

CONCLUSION

This chapter explained the major logistics activities and how they contribute to the value of products by getting them to the place that customers want or need them. *If* the distribution customer service level meets their needs and can be provided at a reasonable cost, customers may not even think about the logistics activities that occur behind the scenes. But if products are not available when and where they need to be, a strategy will fail. So decisions in these areas are an important part of Place and marketing strategy planning.

We emphasized the relation between customer service level, transporting, and storing. The physical distribution concept focuses on coordinating all the storing, transporting, and product-handling activities into a smoothly working system—to deliver the desired service level and customer value at the lowest total cost.

Marketing managers often want to improve service and may select a higher-cost alternative to improve their marketing mix. The total cost approach might reveal that it is possible both to reduce costs and to improve customer service—perhaps by working closely with other members of the supply chain.

We discussed various modes of transporting and their advantages and disadvantages. We also discussed ways to reduce inventory costs. For example, distribution centers are an important way to cut storing and handling costs, and computerized information links—within firms and among firms in the channel—are increasingly important in blending all of the logistics activities into a smooth-running system.

Effective marketing managers make important strategy decisions about physical distribution. Creative strategy decisions may result in lower PD costs while maintaining or improving the customer service level. And production-oriented competitors may not even understand what is happening.

KEY TERMS

logistics, 272

physical distribution (PD), 272

customer service level, 273

physical distribution (PD) concept, 275

total cost approach, 276

supply chain, 278

electronic data interchange (EDI), 279

transporting, 280

containerization, 284

piggyback service, 284

storing, 286

inventory, 286

private warehouses, 288

public warehouses, 288

distribution center, 289

QUESTIONS AND PROBLEMS

1. Explain how adjusting the customer service level could improve a marketing mix. Illustrate.

2. Briefly explain which aspects of customer service you think would be most important for a producer that sells fabric to a firm that manufactures furniture.

3. Briefly describe a purchase you made where the customer service level had an effect on the product you selected or where you purchased it.

4. Discuss the types of trade-offs involved in PD costs, service levels, and sales.

5. Give an example of why it is important for different firms in the supply chain to coordinate logistics activities.

6. Discuss some of the ways computers are being used to improve PD decisions.

7. Explain why a just-in-time delivery system would require a supplier to pay attention to quality control. Give an example to illustrate your points.

8. Discuss the problems a supplier might encounter in using a just-in-time delivery system with a customer in a foreign country.

9. Review the list of factors that affect PD service levels in Exhibit 11-3. Indicate which ones are most likely to be improved by EDI links between a supplier and its customers.

10. Explain the total cost approach and why it may cause conflicts in some firms. Give examples of how conflicts might occur between different departments.

11. Discuss the relative advantages and disadvantages of railroads, trucks, and airlines as transporting methods.

12. Discuss why economies of scale in transportation might encourage a producer to include a regional merchant wholesaler in the channel of distribution for its consumer product.

13. Discuss some of the ways that air transportation can change other aspects of a Place system.

14. Explain which transportation mode would probably be most suitable for shipping the following goods to a large Los Angeles department store:

    a. 300 pounds of Maine lobster.

    b. 15 pounds of screwdrivers from Ohio.

    c. Three dining room tables from High Point, North Carolina.

    d. 500 high-fashion dresses from the fashion district in Paris.

e. A 10,000-pound shipment of exercise equipment from Germany.

f. 600,000 pounds of various appliances from Evansville, Indiana.

15. Indicate the nearest location where you would expect to find large storage facilities. What kinds of products would be stored there? Why are they stored there instead of some other place?

16. When would a producer or intermediary find it desirable to use a public warehouse rather than a private warehouse? Illustrate, using a specific product or situation.

17. Discuss the distribution center concept. Is this likely to eliminate the storing function of conventional wholesalers? Is it applicable to all products? If not, cite several examples.

18. Clearly differentiate between a warehouse and a distribution center. Explain how a specific product would be handled differently by each.

19. If a retailer operates only from a website and ships all orders by UPS, is it freed from the logistics issues that face traditional retailers? Explain your thinking.

CREATING MARKETING PLANS

The Marketing Plan Coach software on the text website (and on the optional Student CD) includes a sample marketing plan for Hillside Veterinary Clinic. Look through the "Marketing Strategy" section. To provide veterinary care to pets, Hillside needs to have a variety of medical supplies on hand. To handle that, it relies on deliveries from suppliers and its own inventory decisions. It also sells some retail pet products to customers, and that requires a separate set of decisions about how it will handle inventory.

a. What logistics issues related to medical supplies should Hillside consider? Can you think of ways in which delivery from its suppliers or its own inventory decisions will be important in its ability to help its patients?

b. With respect to the retail pet products that Hillside sells, what level of customer service should customers expect?

c. What issues are involved in storage of pet supplies?

SUGGESTED CASES   16. Bunyan Lumber   26. Best Way Canning, Inc.

COMPUTER-AIDED PROBLEM

11. TOTAL DISTRIBUTION COST

Proto Company has been producing various items made of plastic. It recently added a line of plain plastic cards that other firms (such as banks and retail stores) will imprint to produce credit cards. Proto offers its customers the plastic cards in different colors, but they all sell for $40 per box of 1,000. Tom Phillips, Proto's product manager for this line, is considering two possible physical distribution systems. He estimates that if Proto uses airfreight, transportation costs will be $7.50 a box, and its cost of carrying inventory will be 5 percent of total annual sales dollars. Alternatively, Proto could ship by rail for $2 a box. But rail transport will require renting space at four regional warehouses—at $26,000 a year each. Inventory carrying cost with this system will be 10 percent of total annual sales dollars. Phillips prepared a spreadsheet to compare the cost of the two alternative physical distribution systems.

a. If Proto Company expects to sell 20,000 boxes a year, what are the total physical distribution costs for each of the systems?

b. If Phillips can negotiate cheaper warehouse space for the rail option so that each warehouse costs only $20,000 per year, which physical distribution system has the lowest overall cost?

c. Proto's finance manager predicts that interest rates are likely to be lower during the next marketing plan year and suggests that Tom Phillips use inventory carrying costs of 4 percent for airfreight and 7.5 percent for railroads (with warehouse cost at $20,000 each). If interest rates are in fact lower, which alternative would you suggest? Why?

For additional questions related to this problem, see Exercise 11-3 in the *Learning Aid for Use with Essentials of Marketing*, 12th edition.

12

CHAPTER

Retailers, Wholesalers, and Their Strategy Planning

When it comes to buying consumer electronics, are you a demon or an angel? If you don't know the answer, Best Buy probably does. Best Buy constantly evaluates its portfolio of customers to do a better job of segmenting the angels—customers who buy high-margin items like HDTVs at full price and then add accessories, an extended service contract, and perhaps Geek Squad installation help. Best Buy is cutting free from its demons, the 20 percent of its customers who are unprofitable. Some demons are just aggressive bargain hunters. They clip competitors' ads and demand price matches or "cherry pick" and buy only deeply discounted sale products. But an unscrupulous demon might go further and buy a video camera, use it on a vacation, send in for its rebate, and then return it for a refund. Best Buy's customer relationship management (CRM) system identifies demons and takes them off its mail promotion list. It also charges a 15 percent restocking fee on returns and sells returned products on the Internet (thwarting demons from rebuying their own returns at the lower, open-box price).

On a more positive (and profitable) note, Best Buy targets five key segments among its angel customers: upscale suburban moms, affluent professional males, teenage entertainment/gaming enthusiasts, budget-conscious families who are practical technology adopters, and small businesses. Best Buy analyzes each store's sales data and demographics to identify the most significant segments. Then it converts stores, or creates a store-within-a-store, to better meet the needs of those segments.

For example, Best Buy's research showed that while female shoppers buy 55 percent of electronic items, they didn't like the Best Buy shopping experience. Now Best Buy focuses on the most lucrative subset of women shoppers—busy moms in suburban areas. The retailer has a nickname for a woman in this segment. She's "Jill." In the past, sales staff either didn't explain things enough or talked down to and insulted Jill. So now a store that appeals to Jill offers "personal shopping assistants." They help Jill find what she wants in less time. Rather than ask, "How many megapixels do you need?" retrained salespeople ask Jill, "What do you want to photograph?"—and then they suggest what will best suit her needs. And, rather than organize cameras by brand on the shelf, models with similar features are displayed together so that Jill can compare them more easily. Stores that target Jill know she is a great candidate for small appliances, so they carry a broader assortment and place them in the regular aisles on easy-to-reach shelves—not off in a corner with the stoves.

Segmented stores differ depending on the target market. Stores that target the affluent male professional ("Barry"), for instance, have a private in-store home theater demo room, complete with comfy leather viewing chairs and popcorn. Barry likes the newest DVDs. So, on days when hot DVDs are released, home theater specialists roam the aisles, look for Barry, and steer him to preview DVDs in the demo room. You know you're an angel—and probably a Barry—if a $12,000 home theater setup is an impulse buy after a visit to the demo room.

Best Buy first tested the targeted stores concept in California. Test stores showed significant increases in sales, profits, and the percentage of customers who made a purchase. The reasons for these successes were measured and analyzed and then rolled out to other similar stores.

Best Buy's marketing strategy planning has not always been so sophisticated. Rather, it started in 1966 as Sound of Music, which was a conventional, limited-line retail store that sold a few select brands of hi-fi equipment. Since then, Best Buy's strategies for growth mirror some of the important trends that have emerged in retailing. It was one of the first stores to adopt the mass-merchandising approach in selling consumer electronics; it focused on lower prices and faster turnover—rather than high markups—to draw customers and increase revenues and profits. The approach helped Best Buy achieve economies of scale in areas such as buying, promotion, and management. Over time it has scrambled its product line toward innovative and profitable new products—not just stereo equipment but also categories such as digital cameras and camcorders, video systems including HDTV, home appliances, and now its full line of Geek Squad in-home technical services. Similarly, Best Buy was an innovator among bricks-and-mortar retailers when it quickly took advantage of Internet retailing with a website that complements its stores' offerings. It also developed state-of-the-art distribution centers and logistics systems, which reduced its reliance on traditional merchant wholesalers and helped to cut costs. On the other hand, some progressive wholesalers have benefited from these changes. For example, Best Buy uses Internet-based brokers to find construction firms that help it cut costs when building new stores.

Best Buy does a lot right—which is why *Forbes* magazine named Best Buy a "company of the year" and *Fortune* ranked it #4 on its list of most admired companies. Further, Circuit City, a major competitor, is now out of business. Yet, Wal-Mart is pushing deeper into the electronics market and other strong competitors abound. To continue this run of success, Best Buy must stay ahead of retailing trends. For example, it has opened a number of small 3,000-square-foot Best Buy Mobile stores—some as a store-within-a-store and others as independent stores in malls. Keeping an eye on customers and competitors helps to keep Best Buy in the lead.[1]

RETAILERS AND WHOLESALERS PLAN THEIR OWN STRATEGIES

In Chapter 10, we discussed the vital role that retailers and wholesalers perform in channel systems. Now we'll look at the decisions that retailers and wholesalers make in developing their own strategies. See Exhibit 12–1. The chapter begins with a discussion of strategy planning for retailers. Retailers must create a marketing mix that provides value for a target market. We also discuss how retailing has evolved and where it stands today, including some important international differences. The chapter concludes by considering strategy planning by different types of wholesalers.

Understand how retailing and wholesaling are evolving

Understanding the how and why of past changes in retailing and wholesaling will help you know what to expect in the future. It will also make it clear that it is the whole strategy, not just one aspect of it, that ultimately is a success or failure. This may seem obvious, but it's a point that many people have ignored—at great cost.

Consider the dramatic changes prompted by the Internet. A few years ago many people were proclaiming that it would quickly change everything we thought about successful retailing. Yet many creative ideas for online retailing bombed precisely because managers of dot-coms failed to understand why retailing has evolved as it has. For many consumers and many types of purchases, it won't matter that an online

Exhibit 12-1 Marketing Strategy Planning for Retailers and Wholesalers

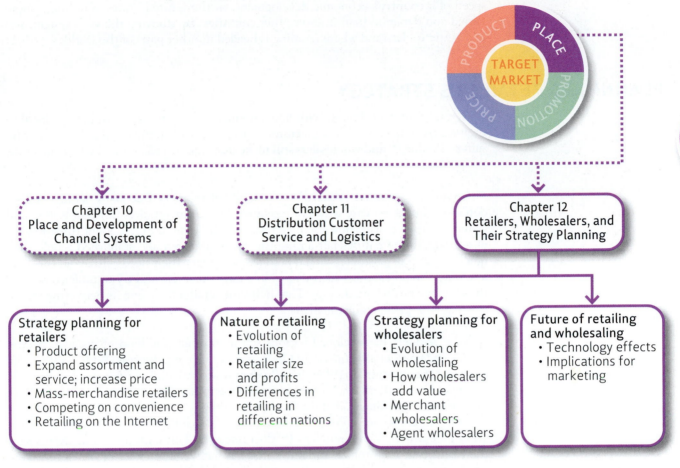

retailer posts low prices for an incredible assortment if there's no way to get customer service, products are not actually available, or it's a hassle to return a green shirt that looked blue on the website. *You* want to avoid the trap of this sort of incomplete thinking!

So in this chapter we'll focus on decisions that apply to all retailers and wholesalers, while highlighting how their strategies are changing.

THE NATURE OF RETAILING

Retailing covers all of the activities involved in the sale of products to final consumers. Retailers range from large chains of specialized stores, like Best Buy, to individual merchants like the woman who sells baskets from an open stall in the central market in Ibadan, Nigeria. Some retailers operate from stores and others operate without a store—by selling online, on TV, with a printed catalog, from vending machines, or even in consumers' homes. Most retailers sell physical goods produced by someone else. But in the case of service retailing—like dry cleaning, fast food, tourist attractions, online bank accounts, or one-hour photo processing—the retailer is also the producer. Because they serve individual consumers, even the largest retailers face the challenge of handling small transactions. And the total number of transactions with consumers is much greater than at other channel levels.

Retailing is crucial to consumers in every macro-marketing system. For example, consumers spend more than $4.5 *trillion* (that's $4,500,000,000,000!) a year buying goods and services from U.S. retailers.

The nature of retailing and its rate of change are generally related to the stage and speed of a country's economic development. In the United States, retailing is more varied and dynamic than in most other countries. By studying the U.S. system, you will better understand where retailing is headed in other parts of the world.

PLANNING A RETAILER'S STRATEGY

Retailers interact directly with final consumers—so strategy planning is critical to their survival. If a retailer loses a customer to a competitor, the retailer is the one who suffers. Producers and wholesalers still make *their* sale regardless of which retailer sells the product.

Consumers have reasons for buying from particular retailers

Different consumers prefer different kinds of retailers. But many retailers either don't know or don't care why. All too often, beginning retailers just rent a store and assume customers will show up. As a result, in the United States about three-fourths of new retailing ventures fail during the first year. Even an established retailer will quickly lose if its customers find a better way to meet their needs. To avoid this fate, a retailer should carefully identify possible target markets and try to understand why these people buy where they do. That helps the retailer fine-tune its marketing mix to the needs of specific target markets.[2]

Retailer's whole offering is its Product

Most retailers in developed nations sell more than one kind of product. So the brands and product assortment they carry can be critical to success. Yet it's best to take a broader view in thinking about the Product strategy decisions for a retailer's marketing mix. The retailer's *whole* offering—assortment of goods and services, advice from salesclerks, convenience, and the like—is its "Product."

Different consumers have different needs—and needs vary from one purchase situation to another. Which retailer's Product offers the best customer value depends on the needs that a customer wants to satisfy. Whatever the effect of other consumer needs, economic needs are usually very important in shaping the choice of a retailer. Social and individual needs may also come into play. Our discussion of consumer behavior in Chapter 5 applies here.

It's best to think of a retailer's Product as its whole offering—including its assortment of goods and services, advice from salespeople or a website, the convenience of shopping, and hours it is available.

Features of offering relate to needs

Features of a retailer's offering that relate to economic needs include

- *Convenience* (available hours, finding needed products, fast checkout, location, parking).
- *Product selection* (width and depth of assortment, brands, quality).
- *Special services* (special orders, home delivery, gift wrap, entertainment).
- *Fairness in dealings* (honesty, correcting problems, return privileges, purchase risks).
- *Helpful information* (courteous sales help, displays, demonstrations, product information).
- *Prices* (value, credit, special discounts, taxes or extra charges).

Some features that relate to social and emotional needs include

- *Social image* (status, prestige, "fitting in" with other shoppers).
- *Shopping atmosphere* (comfort, safety, excitement, relaxation, sounds, smells).

In later chapters we'll go into much more detail on the promotion and price decisions that all firms, including retailers and wholesalers, make.

Strategy requires carefully set policies

In developing a strategy a retailer should consciously make decisions that set policies on *all* of the preceding issues. Each of them can impact a customer's view of the costs and benefits of choosing that retailer. And in combination they differentiate one retailer's offering and strategy from another. If the combination doesn't provide superior value to some target market, the retailer will fail.

Consumer needs relate to segmentation and positioning

Segmentation and positioning decisions are important to retailers. And ignoring either economic or social and emotional needs in those decisions can lead to serious errors in a retailer's strategy planning.

Consider, for example, how the shopping atmosphere may have an emotional effect on a consumer's view of a retailer. How merchandise is displayed, what decorations, colors, and finishes are used, and even the temperature, sounds, and smell of a store all contribute to its store image and the shopping experience. Tiffany's, for example, offers luxury surroundings and inventive displays to attract upscale consumers—or ones who get an ego boost from Tiffany's prestige image. Of course, interesting surroundings are usually costly, and the prices that consumers pay must cover that expense. An online jewelry retailer offers a completely different shopping experience and deals with a different set of needs. So a retailer's atmosphere and image may be a plus or a minus, depending on the target market. And there's no single right answer about which target market is best. Like Tiffany's, Dollar General has been very profitable. But it has a "budget" image and atmosphere that appeals to working-class customers, many of whom just prefer to shop where they don't feel out of place.[3]

Different types of retailers emphasize different strategies

Retailers have an almost unlimited number of ways in which to alter their offerings—their marketing mixes—to appeal to a target market. Because of all the variations, it's oversimplified to classify retailers and their strategies on the basis of a single characteristic—such as merchandise, services, sales volume, or even whether they operate in cyberspace. But a good place to start is by considering basic types of retailers and some differences in their strategies.

CONVENTIONAL RETAILERS—TRY TO AVOID PRICE COMPETITION

Single-line, limited-line retailers specialize by product

About 150 years ago, **general stores**—which carried anything they could sell in reasonable volume—were the main retailers in the United States. But with the growing number of consumer products after the Civil War, general stores couldn't offer enough variety in all their traditional lines. So some stores began specializing in dry goods, apparel, furniture, or groceries.

Exhibit 12–2 Types of Retailers and the Nature of Their Offerings (*with examples*)

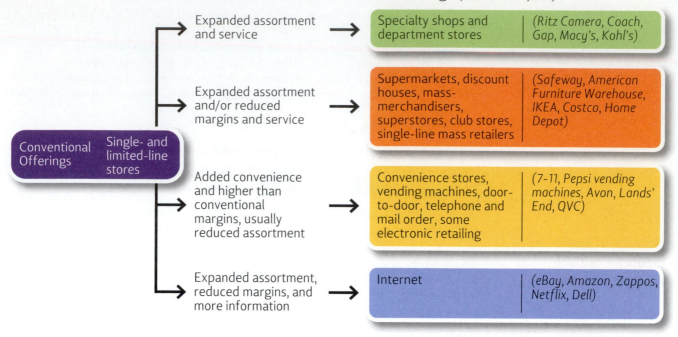

Now most *conventional* retailers are **single-line** or **limited-line stores**—stores that specialize in certain lines of related products rather than a wide assortment. Many specialize not only in a single line, such as clothing, but also in a *limited line* within the broader line. Within the clothing line, a retailer might carry *only* shoes, formal wear, or even neckties but offer depth in that limited line.

Single-line, limited-line stores are being squeezed

The main advantage of limited-line retailers is that they can satisfy some target markets better. Perhaps some are just more conveniently located. But most adjust to suit specific customers. They build a relationship with their customers and earn a position as *the* place to shop for a certain type of product. But these retailers face the costly problem of having to stock some slow-moving items in order to satisfy their target markets. Many of these stores are small—with high expenses relative to sales. So they try to keep their prices up by avoiding competition on identical products.

Conventional retailers like this have been around for a long time and are still found in every community. They are a durable lot and clearly satisfy some people's needs. In fact, in most countries conventional retailers still handle the vast majority of all retailing sales. However, this situation is changing fast. Nowhere is the change clearer than in the United States. Conventional retailers are being squeezed by retailers who modify their mixes in the various ways suggested in Exhibit 12–2. Let's look closer at some of these other types of retailers.

EXPAND ASSORTMENT AND SERVICE—TO COMPETE AT A HIGH PRICE

Specialty shops usually sell shopping products

A **specialty shop**—a type of conventional limited-line store—is usually small and has a distinct "personality." Specialty shops sell special types of shopping products, such as high-quality sporting goods, exclusive clothing, cameras, or even antiques. They aim at a carefully defined target market by offering a unique product assortment, knowledgeable salesclerks, and better service.

Catering to certain types of customers whom the management and salespeople know well simplifies buying, speeds turnover, and cuts costs due to obsolescence and style changes. Specialty shops probably will continue to be a part of the retailing scene as long as customers have varied tastes and the money to satisfy them.[4]

Department stores combine many limited-line stores and specialty shops

Department stores are larger stores that are organized into many separate departments and offer many product lines. Each department is like a separate limited-line store and handles a wide variety of a shopping product, such as men's wear or housewares. They are usually strong in customer services, including credit, merchandise return, delivery, and sales help.

Department stores are still a major force in some cities. But in the United States, the number of department stores, the average sales per store, and their share of retail business has declined continuously since the 1970s. Well-run limited-line stores compete with good service and often carry the same brands. In the United States and many other countries, mass-merchandising retailers have posed an even bigger threat.[5]

EVOLUTION OF MASS-MERCHANDISING RETAILERS

Mass-merchandising is different from conventional retailing

The conventional retailers just discussed think that demand in their area is fixed—and they have a "buy low and sell high" philosophy. Many modern retailers reject these ideas. Instead, they accept the **mass-merchandising concept**—which says that retailers should offer low prices to get faster turnover and greater sales volumes—by appealing to larger markets. The mass-merchandising concept applies to many types of retailers, including both those that operate stores and those that sell online. But to understand mass-merchandising better, let's look at its evolution from the development of supermarkets and discounters to modern mass-merchandisers like Wal-Mart in the United States, Tesco in the U.K., and Amazon.com on the Internet.

Supermarkets started the move to mass-merchandising

From a world view, most food stores are relatively small limited-line operations. Shopping for food is inconvenient and expensive. Many Italians, for example, still go to one shop for pasta, another for meat, and yet another for milk. This may seem outdated, but many of the world's consumers don't have access to **supermarkets**—large stores specializing in groceries with self-service and wide assortments.

The basic idea for supermarkets developed in the United States during the 1930s Depression. Some innovators introduced self-service to cut costs but provided a broad assortment in large bare-bones stores. Profits came from large-volume sales, not from high traditional markups.[6]

Modern supermarkets carry 45,000 product items and stores average around 47,500 square feet. To be called a supermarket, a store must have annual sales of at least $2 million, but the average supermarket sells about $20 million a year. In the United States, there are about 35,000 supermarkets, and in most areas they are at the saturation level and competition is intense. In many other countries, however, they are just becoming a force.[7]

Supermarkets are planned for maximum efficiency. Scanners at checkout make it possible to carefully analyze the sales of each item and allocate more shelf space to faster-moving and higher-profit items. *Survival* depends on efficiency. Net profits in supermarkets usually run a thin 1 percent of sales *or less!*

Some supermarket operators have opened "super warehouse" stores. These 50,000- to 100,000-square-foot stores carry more items than supermarkets. These efficiently run, warehouse-like facilities can sell groceries at up to 25 percent less than the typical supermarket price.[8]

Discount houses upset some conventional retailers

After World War II, some retailers started to focus on discount prices. These **discount houses** offered "hard goods" (cameras, TVs, and appliances) at substantial price cuts to customers who would go to the discounter's low-rent store, pay cash, and take care of any service or repair problems themselves. These retailers sold at 20 to 30 percent off the list price being charged by conventional retailers.

In the early 1950s, with war shortages finally over, manufacturer brands became more available. The discount houses were able to get any brands they wanted and to offer wider assortments. At this stage, many discounters turned respectable—moving

Although U.S. supermarkets were the first mass-merchandisers, the mass-merchandising concept is now used by many retailers. Single-line mass-merchandisers like Office Depot offer selections and prices that make it difficult for conventional retailers to compete.

to better locations and offering more services and guarantees. It was from these origins that today's mass-merchandisers developed.

Mass-merchandisers are more than discounters

Mass-merchandisers are large, self-service stores with many departments that emphasize "soft goods" (housewares, clothing, and fabrics) and staples (like health and beauty aids) but still follow the discount house's emphasis on lower margins to get faster turnover. Mass-merchandisers, like Wal-Mart and Target, have checkout counters in the front of the store and little sales help on the floor. Today, the average mass-merchandiser has nearly 60,000 square feet of floor space, but many new stores are 100,000 square feet or more. Mass-merchandisers grew rapidly—and they've become the primary place to shop for many frequently purchased consumer products.

By itself, Wal-Mart handles 30 percent or more of the total national sales for whole categories of products. Even if you don't shop at Wal-Mart, Sam Walton (who started the company) has had a big impact on your life. He pioneered the use of high-tech systems to create electronic links with suppliers and take inefficiencies out of retailing logistics. That brought down costs *and* prices and attracted more customers, which gave Wal-Mart even more clout in pressuring manufacturers to lower prices. Other retailers are still scrambling to catch up. It was competition from Wal-Mart on most staples such as health and beauty aids and household cleaning products that prompted firms in the supermarket supply chain to start the Efficient Consumer Response movement we discussed in Chapter 11.[9]

Supercenters meet all routine needs

Some supermarkets and mass-merchandisers have moved toward becoming **supercenters (hypermarkets)**—very large stores that try to carry not only food and drug items but all goods and services that the consumer purchases *routinely*. These superstores look a lot like a combination of the supermarkets, drugstores, and mass-merchandisers from which they have evolved, but the concept is different. A supercenter is trying to meet *all* the customer's routine needs at a low price. Supercenter operators include Meijer, Fred Meyer, Target, and Wal-Mart. In fact, Wal-Mart's supercenters have turned it into the largest food retailer in the United States.

Supercenters average more than 150,000 square feet and carry about 50,000 items. Their assortment in one place is convenient, but many time-pressured consumers think that the crowds, lines, and "wandering around" time in the store are not.[10]

New mass-merchandising formats keep coming

The warehouse club is another retailing format that quickly gained popularity. Sam's Club and Costco are two of the largest. Consumers usually pay an annual membership fee to shop in these large, no-frills facilities. Among the 3,500 items per store, they carry food, appliances, yard tools, tires, and other items that many consumers see as homogeneous shopping items and want at the lowest possible price. The growth of these clubs has also been fueled by sales to small-business customers. That's why some people refer to these outlets as wholesale clubs. However, when half or more of a firm's sales are to final consumers, it is classified as a retailer, not a wholesaler.[11]

Single-line mass-merchandisers are coming on strong

Since 1980, many retailers focusing on single product lines have adopted the mass-merchandisers' approach with great success. Toys "R" Us pioneered this trend. Similarly, IKEA (furniture), Home Depot (home improvements), Best Buy (electronics), and Staples (office supplies) attract large numbers of customers with their large assortment and low prices in a specific product category. These stores are called *category killers* because it's so hard for less specialized retailers to compete.[12]

SOME RETAILERS FOCUS ON ADDED CONVENIENCE

Convenience (food) stores must have the right assortment

Convenience (food) stores are a convenience-oriented variation of the conventional limited-line food stores. Instead of expanding their assortment, however, convenience stores limit their stock to pickup or fill-in items like bread, milk, beer, and eat-on-the-go snacks. Many also sell gas. Stores such as 7-Eleven and Stop-N-Go aim to fill consumers' needs between trips to a supermarket, and many of them are competing with fast-food outlets. They offer convenience, not assortment, and often charge prices 10 to 20 percent higher than nearby supermarkets. However, as many other retailers have expanded their hours, intense competition is driving down convenience store prices and profits.[13]

Some retailers are trying to speed up the checkout process—and avoid the need to check IDs or confirm a customer's age—with a fingerprint reader that also replaces the need for a credit card. Systems like this may become popular in the future, but some consumers have concerns about how biometric information might be used.

Vending machines are convenient

Automatic vending is selling and delivering products through vending machines. Vending machine sales account for only about 1.5 percent of total U.S. retail sales. Yet for some target markets this retailing method can't be ignored.

While vending machines can be costly to operate, consumers like their convenience. Traditionally, soft drinks, candy bars, and snack foods have been sold by vending machines. Now some higher-margin products are beginning to use this channel. RedBox rents DVD movies from vending machines at some McDonald's restaurants. In Japan, it's common to find digital cameras in vending machines.[14]

Shop at home, in a variety of ways

In-home shopping in the United States started in the pioneer days with **door-to-door selling**—a salesperson going directly to the consumer's home. Variations on this approach are still important for firms like Quixtar-Amway and Mary Kay. It meets some consumers' need for convenient personal attention. It is also growing in popularity in some international markets, like China, where it provides salespeople with a good income. In the United States, it now accounts for less than 1 percent of retail sales. It's getting harder to find someone at home during the day.

On the other hand, time-pressured, dual-career families are a prime target market for **telephone and direct-mail retailing** that allow consumers to shop at home—usually placing orders by mail or a toll-free long-distance telephone call and charging the purchase to a credit card. Typically, catalogs and ads on TV let customers see the offerings, and purchases are delivered by UPS. Some consumers really like this convenience, especially for products not available in local stores.

This approach reduces costs by using mailing lists to target specific customers and by using warehouse-type buildings and limited sales help. And shoplifting—a big expense for most retailers—isn't a problem. In recent years, many of these firms have faced increased competition, slower sales growth, and lower profits. As we will discuss, however, the Internet is opening up new growth opportunities for many of them.[15]

Put the catalog on cable TV or computer

QVC, Home Shopping Network, and others are succeeding by devoting cable TV channels to home shopping. The explosion in the number of available cable channels and new interactive cable services have helped sales from this approach grow even faster. In addition, QVC has opened a major website on the Internet. However, selling on the Internet is much more than just a variation of selling on TV or from a catalog.[16]

RETAILING ON THE INTERNET

It's in the growth stage

Internet retailing is still in the growth stage. On the one hand, Internet usage continues to rise and consumer e-commerce purchases have grown at a fast rate. In 1997, consumers spent about $2.7 billion on the Internet. To put that in perspective, it took about 3 percent of Wal-Mart's stores to rack up the same sales. By 2007 that number topped $200 billion—not including travel services. While that's only about 7 percent of all retail sales, the share is much larger in some categories. About half of all computer hardware and software and a quarter of all books are sold online. And retailing on the Internet continues to grow quickly—at more than 20 percent a year. So it is useful to consider what is different about it today and how it will evolve.

Moving information versus moving goods

Stripped to its essence, the Internet dramatically lowers the cost of communication and makes it faster. The Internet produces the biggest gains in businesses where better information flows result in more efficiency. That's what happens in much online B2B e-commerce. On the other hand, Place decisions for consumer markets need to deal with the challenge of getting many small purchases to the *consumer's* place. To date, much of the investment in Internet retailing systems has been directed toward moving information (like orders), not physical goods. It takes, for example, about $25 million to build a world-class website for consumer e-commerce. But it costs about $150 million to build a distribution center and systems to support a large-scale consumer Web operation. Therefore, much of the attention so far has been on the "front door" of the Internet "store" and not on the back end of retailing operations where more of the big costs accumulate. The failure to understand "back door" costs has led to the downfall of many online retailers.

Convenience takes on new meanings

Traditional thinking about retail stores looked at shopping convenience from the perspective of product assortments and location. On the Internet, by contrast, a

Some consumers look on the Internet for low prices on products that they need, but buying sight-unseen is sometimes a problem. For example, some U.S. consumers order low-price drugs over the Internet from Canada, but as the GlaxoSmithKline ad suggests, the customer doesn't really know where the drugs come from when they're ordered this way. On the other hand, many people have confidence in the brand name medicines that they buy for their pets at discount prices from www.1800PetMeds.com.

consumer can get to a very wide assortment, perhaps from different sellers, by clicking from one website to another. The assortment moves toward being unlimited.

But the Internet makes shopping inconvenient in other ways. You have to plan ahead. You can't touch a product. When you buy something, you've actually just ordered it and you don't have it to use. Someone else has to deliver it, and that involves delays and costs.

More and less information at the same time

On the Internet a consumer can't really inspect a product. Many consumers see that as a disadvantage. On the other hand, in a retail store it's often hard to get good information. At a website detailed product information is just a mouse-click away.

Better information available on the Internet makes many consumers better shoppers, even if they buy in a store rather than online. That's what many Web surfers do now. That reduces the risk of buying the wrong thing and the hassles of returning it if there's a problem.

More powerful computers and broadband Internet connections are also opening up many more possibilities for multimedia information—pictures, product-demo videos, and audio explanations. The Internet is also a good medium for messaging and videoconferencing. It is becoming easier for consumers to get help from a real person while at a website. Many failed dot-com retailers figured out too late that cutting costs by dropping human customer service support was a big mistake. They ignored the lessons learned by mass-merchandisers when they tried to do the same thing in their early days.

The costs are sometimes misleading

The Internet makes it easy to compare products and prices from different sellers. That has put price pressure on Internet sellers who have not figured out how else to differentiate what they offer. For more expensive items, a discount price may offset delivery costs. That often isn't the case with less-expensive items. Low-cost ways of handling post-purchase deliveries need to be developed for the Internet to be really practical for everyday purchases. However, some firms are making this work. For example, Tesco in England sells groceries from a website and delivers them within 24 hours.

Another cost occurs if a product must be returned. That, of course, assumes you get what you order. The Internet is the ultimate weapon for fly-by-night operators. Fraud is already a big problem.

Retailers are refining their online efforts

At least four distinct approaches are used by different online retailers. Retailers that have bricks-and-mortar stores at many locations often use a website to *supplement* their stores and other promotion—and to test the online retail format. For example, when Target and Home Depot first offered products online, they used their websites primarily to promote items that had the highest profit margins and to drive traffic into their stores. For instance, Target's site originally emphasized bedding and apparel rather than household supplies. Both Target and Home Depot now use their websites to offer a broad range of products.

In contrast, some retailers take a strong multichannel approach and use their websites to *complement* their stores or catalogs. This is more common among retailers who have higher profit margins on the lines they sell. For example, Williams-Sonoma sells upscale housewares. It closely coordinates its online, catalog, and store outlets so that they focus on different benefits. At its stores customers are free to handle items and see how they look next to each other, while the website provides more detailed product information and convenient ordering.

Among online-only retailers, some try to differentiate their offering primarily by being *more efficient* than competitors. They focus on offering consumers low prices on

Where to Go to Buy an Unpopular Product

A local Borders bookstore that carries 100,000 book titles seems overwhelming. Yet, at Amazon.com online shoppers can choose from over 7 million. A local Wal-Mart stocks about 4,000 best-selling CD titles, but the iTunes store has more than 10 million for download. Does it really make sense for online stores to offer assortments that are so much larger?

Part of the answer to the assortment decision concerns the cost of shelf space. Retailers who have fancy facilities in high-traffic locations with ample parking have a high cost per square foot of shelf space. Even if the retailer sells products at low prices, the store will draw customers from a limited geographic area. With these limits, it makes sense for the store to carry only the products that are the most in demand (popular) with the local target market. Stocking less-popular products would be risky because most of them would just sit there running up inventory costs with little likelihood of increased sales.

The cost to store inventory is usually a lot lower for an online retailer with a warehouse somewhere off the beaten path. If the retailer can sell some of the less-popular items, the added revenue from them may offset the added inventory costs—and increase profits. When an online seller can draw customers from just about everywhere, it is likely to generate at least some sales of even the most "unpopular" products. After all, when customers who want an "unpopular" choice can't find it at a local retail store, they are likely to look for it online. So, the online retailer's ability to offer a greater assortment is often a key source of competitive advantage. Further, for some online sellers, occasional sales of a large number of unpopular products can add up to be even more than the sales of a few very popular ones. We can see this at Amazon.com where more than 30 percent of total book sales come from books that are not even among the top 100,000 most popular. Similarly, more than 25 percent of Netflix DVD rentals are titles outside the top 3,000 found at your local Blockbuster.

To get extra sales from the "unpopular" products, the trick for many online retailers is to help consumers find what they want among the endless "aisles" of choices. For example, ScannerWarehouse.com has more than 200 models of flatbed scanners, but for many customers that much choice is just confusing. To simplify the choice, the site might offer customers a simple way to "filter" the list to show only the scanners that are priced under $100 and that have a document feeder. Smart search engines are also helpful. When a customer types "George Foreman grill" into the search bar at Amazon.com, a list with more than 100 products—sorted by relevance—appears. When the searcher clicks on a specific model, the page automatically generates possible alternatives— "customers who viewed this item also viewed . . ." The page may also include links to reviews, customer ratings, an animated demo, video clips, warranty details, and many other types of information.

In the early days of the Internet many people predicted that online stores would compete primarily on price. Certainly that is true of many. However, some successful online sellers attract customers with wide product selections, tools that help figure out the best choices, and service that encourages customer loyalty.[17]

products that are in very competitive product-markets—like books, computers, and shoes—that have lower profit margins. These online sellers, including Amazon and Zappos, need high sales volume to offset the large investments they must make in their e-commerce and logistics systems.

The essence of the fourth online approach is to differentiate by being very *focused* on the specific needs of target customers, many of whom don't have similar offerings available in their local market. Good examples include outdoor-gear seller L.L. Bean and jeweler Ross-Simons. Retailers in this category typically use the Web to supplement a catalog operation or a limited number of stores. Smaller companies who can't afford expensive brand-building advertising campaigns often use this approach also. They rely on targeted direct mail (or e-mail) promotions to acquire new customers and provide exceptional customer service to retain customers they already have.[18]

Many retail chains, like Best Buy, are combining "clicks and mortar" to meet consumers' needs better than would be possible with only an online website. Some Best Buy stores have a special Magnolia section to demo large-screen HDTVs and sound systems. However, specialty retailers, like Home Theater Direct, compete primarily for online customers by offering a focused product line and useful product information that is not conveniently available at stores in the customers' local market.

WHY RETAILERS EVOLVE AND CHANGE

The wheel of retailing keeps rolling

The **wheel of retailing theory** says that new types of retailers enter the market as low-status, low-margin, low-price operators and then, if successful, evolve into more conventional retailers offering more services with higher operating costs and higher prices. Then they're threatened by new low-status, low-margin, low-price retailers—and the wheel turns again. Department stores, supermarkets, and mass-merchandisers went through this cycle. Some Internet sellers are on this path.

The wheel of retailing theory, however, doesn't explain all major retailing developments. Vending machines entered as high-cost, high-margin operations. Convenience food stores are high-priced. Suburban shopping centers don't emphasize low price.

Scrambled merchandising— mixing product lines for higher profits

Conventional retailers tend to specialize by product line. But many modern retailers are moving toward **scrambled merchandising**—carrying any product lines they think they can sell profitably. Supermarkets and drugstores sell anything they can move in volume—panty hose, phone cards, one-hour photo processing, motor oil, potted plants, and computer software. Mass-merchandisers don't just sell everyday items but also cell phones, computer printers, and jewelry.[19]

Product life-cycle concept applies to retailer types too

A retailer with a new idea may have big profits—for a while. But if it's a really good idea, the retailer can count on speedy imitation and a squeeze on profits. Other retailers will copy the new format or scramble their product mix to sell products that offer them higher margins or faster turnover. That puts pressure on the original firm to change or lose its market.

Some conventional retailers are in decline as these life and death cycles continue. Recent innovators, like the Internet merchants, are still in the market growth stage. See Exhibit 12–3. Some retailing formats that are mature in the United States are only now beginning to grow in other countries.

Ethical issues may arise

Most retailers face intense competitive pressure. The desperation that comes with such pressure has pushed some retailers toward questionable marketing practices.

Critics argue, for example, that retailers too often advertise special sale items to bring price-sensitive shoppers into the store or to a website but then don't stock

Exhibit 12-3   Retailer Life Cycles—Timing and Years to Market Maturity

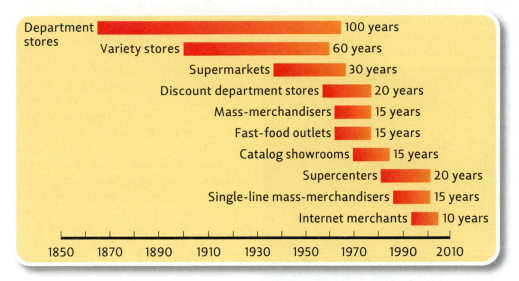

enough to meet demand. Other retailers are criticized for pushing consumers to trade up to more expensive items. What is ethical and unethical in situations like these, however, is subject to debate. Retailers can't always anticipate demand perfectly, and deliveries may not arrive on time. Similarly, trading up may be a sensible part of a strategy—if it's done honestly.

The marketing concept should guide firms away from unethical treatment of customers. However, a retailer on the edge of going out of business may lose perspective on the need to satisfy customers in both the short and the long term.[20]

Ethics QUESTION

Farmers in poor countries get very little money for crops—such as coffee, cocoa, and bananas—that they grow for export. Some consumers in prosperous nations are willing to pay retailers higher prices for "fair trade" goods so that the farmers receive greater compensation. But critics question whether fair trade works as it should. For example, Sainsbury's is a popular British food retailer. It was charging $2.74 per pound for "fair trade" bananas versus only $.69 per pound for regular bananas. Farmers, however, only got $.16 extra from that $2.05 price premium. Critics charge that Sainsbury's makes more from the "fair trade" promotion than the farmers it is supposed to help. Many retailers have similar programs. Do you think that Sainsbury's is acting ethically? What do you think Sainsbury's and other similar retailers should do? Why?[21]

RETAILER SIZE AND PROFITS

A few big retailers do most of the business

The large number of retailers (1,119,850) might suggest that retailing is a field of small businesses. To some extent this is true. When the last census of retailers was published, over 56 percent of all the retail stores in the United States had annual sales of less than $1 million. But that's only part of the story. Those same retailers accounted for less than 8 cents of every $1 in retail sales!

The larger retail stores—those selling more than $5 million annually—do most of the business. Only about 11 percent of the retail stores are this big, yet they account for almost 70 percent of all retail sales. Many small retailers are being squeezed out of business.[22]

Big chains are building market clout

Many independent retail stores are finding it difficult to compete with the large retail chains that now account for the majority of all retail sales in the United States. However, some independents are working together to compete more effectively. For example, Ace Hardware is a wholesaler-sponsored voluntary chain that provides store owners with some of the advantages of a corporate chain operation—without having to give up their independence.

Independents form chains too

The main way for a retailer to achieve economies of scale is with a corporate chain. A **corporate chain** is a firm that owns and manages more than one store—and often it's many. Chains have grown rapidly and now account for about half of all retail sales. You can expect chains to continue to grow and take business from independent stores.

Good advice is the best tool.

ACE
The helpful place.

Large chains use central buying for different stores. They take advantage of quantity discounts and develop their own efficient distribution centers. They can use computer networks to control inventory costs and stock-outs. They may also spread promotion, information technology, and management costs to many stores. Retail chains also have their own dealer brands. Many of these chains are becoming powerful members, or channel captains, in their channel systems. In fact, the most successful of these big chains, like Home Depot and Wal-Mart, control access to so many consumers that they have the clout to dictate almost every detail of relationships with their suppliers.[23]

Competitive pressure from corporate chains encouraged the development of both cooperative chains and voluntary chains. **Cooperative chains** are retailer-sponsored groups—formed by independent retailers—that run their own buying organizations and conduct joint promotion efforts. Cooperative chains face a tough battle. Some, like True Value Hardware, are still adapting as they identify the weaknesses of corporate chains. For example, ads remind consumers that they don't need to waste a half-hour lost in a big store to pick up some simple item.

Voluntary chains are wholesaler-sponsored groups that work with "independent" retailers. Some are linked by contracts stating common operating procedures and requiring the use of common storefront designs, store names, and joint promotion efforts. Examples include SuperValu in groceries and Ace in hardware.

Franchisors form chains too

In a **franchise operation,** the franchisor develops a good marketing strategy, and the retail franchise holders carry out the strategy in their own units. Each franchise holder benefits from its relationship with the larger company and its experience, buying power, promotion, and image. In return, the franchise holder usually signs a contract to pay fees and commissions and to strictly follow franchise rules designed to continue the successful strategy.

Franchise holders' sales account for about a third of all retail sales. One reason is that franchising is especially popular with service retailers, a fast-growing sector of the economy.[24]

DIFFERENCES IN RETAILING IN DIFFERENT NATIONS

New ideas spread across countries

New retailing approaches that succeed in one part of the world are often quickly adapted to other countries. Self-service approaches that started with supermarkets in the United States are now found in retail operations worldwide. The supercenter concept, on the other hand, initially developed in Europe.

Mass-merchandising requires mass markets

The low prices, selections, and efficient operations offered by mass-merchandisers might be attractive to consumers everywhere. But consumers in less-developed nations often don't have the income to support mass distribution. The small shops that survive in these economies sell in very small quantities, often to a small number of consumers.

Some countries block change

The political and legal environment severely limits the evolution of retailing in some nations. Japan is a prime example. For years its Large Store Law—aimed at protecting the country's politically powerful small shopkeepers—has been a real barrier to retail change. The law restricts development of large stores by requiring special permits, which are routinely denied.

Japan is taking steps to change the Large Store Law. One such change allowed Toys "R" Us to move into the Japanese market. Even so, most experts believe that it will be years before Japan moves away from its system of small, limited-line shops. Many countries in other parts of Asia and South America impose similar restrictions. On the other hand, the European Union is prompting member countries to drop such rules.[25]

Retailers moving to international markets must adapt marketing strategies

Slow growth at home has prompted some large retail chains to move into international markets. They think that the competitive advantages that worked well in one market can provide a similar advantage in another country. But legal and cultural differences in international markets can make success difficult. Despite success in Latin America and Canada, Wal-Mart has struggled in Germany and Japan. Similarly, French mass-merchandiser Carrefour expanded in Europe and South America, but its U.S. stores failed and it experienced legal problems in Indonesia.

Other retailers, like California-based My Dollarstore, have seen quick international growth. My Dollarstore franchises the "dollar store" concept worldwide, and it adapts its marketing strategy to the local market. In India, the price of each product is 99 rupees or about two dollars. Dollar stores in the United States target lower-income consumers, but in India the "Made in America" label attracts many higher-income consumers. Initially the merchandise in the Indian stores was the same as in U.S. stores. However, My Dollarstore quickly discovered what sold (Hershey's syrup is a hit) and what didn't (papaya and carrot juice). It also offered money-back guarantees, an unusual practice in India. Adaptations like these helped entice consumers into My Dollarstore's Indian franchises.[26]

WHAT IS A WHOLESALER?

It's hard to define what a wholesaler is because there are so many different wholesalers doing different jobs. Some of their activities may even seem like manufacturing. As a result, some wholesalers describe themselves as "manufacturer and dealer." Some like to identify themselves with such general terms as *merchant*, *agent*, *dealer*, or *distributor*. And others just take the name commonly used in their trade—without really thinking about what it means.

To avoid a long technical discussion on the nature of wholesaling, we'll use the U.S. Bureau of the Census definition:

Wholesaling is concerned with the *activities* of those persons or establishments that sell to retailers and other merchants, or to industrial, institutional, and commercial users, but that do not sell in large amounts to final consumers.

So **wholesalers** are firms whose main function is providing wholesaling activities. Wholesalers sell to all of the different types of organizational customers described in Chapter 6.

Wholesaling activities are just variations of the basic marketing functions—gathering and providing information, buying and selling, grading, storing, transporting, financing, and risk taking—we discussed in Chapter 1. You can understand wholesalers' strategies better if you look at them as members of channels. They add value by doing jobs for their customers and for their suppliers.

WHOLESALING IS CHANGING WITH THE TIMES

A hundred years ago wholesalers dominated distribution channels in the United States and most other countries. The many small producers and small retailers needed their services. This situation still exists in less-developed economies. However, in the developed nations, as producers became larger many bypassed the wholesalers. Similarly, large retail chains often take control of functions that had been handled by wholesalers. Now e-commerce is making it easier for producers and consumers to "connect" without having a wholesaler in the middle of the exchange.

In light of these changes, many people have predicted a gloomy future for wholesalers. In the 1980s that seemed to be the pattern. Now, however, there are 429,500 wholesalers in the United States and they are adapting rapidly and finding new ways to add value in the channel. For example, some of the biggest B2B e-commerce sites on the Internet are wholesaler operations, and many wholesalers are enjoying significant growth.

Producing value and profits, not chasing orders

Progressive wholesalers are becoming more concerned with their customers and with channel systems. Many are using technology to offer better service. Others develop voluntary chains that bind them more closely to their customers.

Frieda's, Inc., is a good example; it is a wholesaler that each year supplies supermarkets and food-service distributors with $30 million worth of exotic fruits and vegetables. It was started by Frieda Caplan in 1962; now, her daughters Karen and Jackie run the company. It is a sign of the marketing savvy of these women that artichokes, Chinese donut peaches, alfalfa sprouts, and spaghetti squash no longer seem very exotic. All of these crops were once viewed as unusual. Few farmers grew them, supermarkets didn't handle them, and consumers didn't know about them. Caplan helped to change all of that. She realized that some supermarkets wanted to attract less price-sensitive consumers who preferred more interesting choices in the hard-to-manage produce department. So she looked for products that would help her retailer-

customers meet this need. For example, the funny looking kiwi fruit with its fuzzy brown skin was popular in New Zealand but virtually unknown to U.S. consumers. Caplan worked with small farmer-producers to ensure that she could provide her retailer-customers with a steady supply. She packaged kiwi with interesting recipes and promoted it to consumers. Because of her efforts, demand has grown and most supermarkets now carry kiwi. That has attracted competition from larger wholesalers. But that doesn't bother the Caplans. When one of their specialty items becomes a commodity with low profit margins, another novel item replaces it. In a typical year, Frieda's

introduces about 40 new products—like Asian pears, kiwano melons, sun-dried yellow tomatoes, and hot Asian chiles.

Frieda's also has an advantage because of the special services it provides. It was the first wholesaler to routinely use airfreight for orders and send produce managers a weekly "hot sheet" about the best sellers. The Caplans also use seminars and press releases to inform produce buyers about how to improve sales. For example, one attention-getting story about Frieda's "El Mercado de Frieda" line helped retailers do a better job serving Hispanic customers. Similarly, Frieda's website attracts final consumers with helpful tips and recipes. And now that more consumers are eating out, Frieda's has established a separate division to serve the special needs of food-service distributors.[27]

Perhaps good-bye to some

Not all wholesalers are progressive, and less efficient ones will fail. Some wholesalers will disappear as the functions they provided in the past are shifted and shared in different ways in the channel. Cost-conscious buyers for Wal-Mart, Lowe's, and other chains are refusing to deal with some of the wholesalers who represent small producers. They want to negotiate directly with the producer. Similarly, producers see advantages in having closer direct relationships with fewer suppliers—and they're paring out weaker vendors. Efficient delivery services like UPS and Federal Express are also making it easy for many producers to ship directly to their customers, even ones in foreign markets. The Internet is putting pressure on wholesalers whose primary role is providing information to bring buyers and sellers together.[28]

Is it an ethical issue?

All of this is squeezing some wholesalers out of business. Some critics, including many of the wounded wholesalers, argue that it's unethical for powerful suppliers or customers to simply cut out wholesalers who spend money and time, perhaps decades, developing markets. Contracts between channel members and laws sometimes define what is or is not legal. But the ethical issues are often more ambiguous.

For example, Amana notified Cooper Distributing Co. that it intended to cancel their distribution agreement in 10 days. Cooper had handled Amana appliances for 30 years, and Amana products represented 85 percent of Cooper's sales. Amana's explanation to Cooper? "We just think we can do it better."

Situations like this arise often. They may be cold-hearted, but are they unethical? We argue that it isn't fair to cut off the relationship with such short notice. But most wholesalers realize that their business is *always* at risk—if they don't perform channel functions better or cheaper than their suppliers or customers can do themselves.[29]

Survivors will need effective strategies

The wholesalers who do survive will need to be efficient, but that doesn't mean they'll all have low costs. Some wholesalers' higher operating expenses result from the strategies they select, including the special services they offer to *some* customers.

WHOLESALERS ADD VALUE IN DIFFERENT WAYS

Exhibit 12–4 compares the number, sales volume, and operating expenses of some major types of wholesalers. The differences in operating expenses suggest that each of these types performs, or does not perform, certain wholesaling functions. But which ones and why? And why do manufacturers use merchant wholesalers—costing 13.1 percent of sales—when agent wholesalers cost only 3.7 percent?

To answer these questions, we must understand what these wholesalers do and don't do. Exhibit 12–5 gives a big-picture view of the major types of wholesalers we'll be discussing. There are lots more specialized types, but our discussion will give you a sense of the diversity. Note that a major difference between merchant and agent wholesalers is whether they *own* the products they sell. Before discussing these wholesalers, we'll briefly consider producers who handle their own wholesaling activities.

Exhibit 12–4
U.S. Wholesale Trade by Type of Wholesale Operation

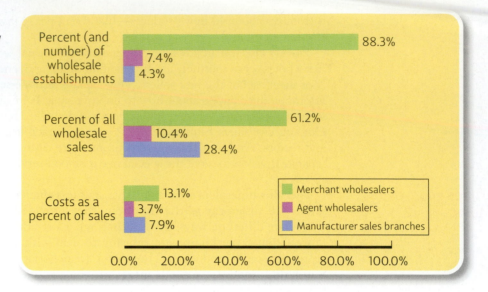

Percent (and number) of wholesale establishments: 88.3% / 7.4% / 4.3%

Percent of all wholesale sales: 61.2% / 10.4% / 28.4%

Costs as a percent of sales: 13.1% / 3.7% / 7.9%

Merchant wholesalers
Agent wholesalers
Manufacturer sales branches

0.0% 20.0% 40.0% 60.0% 80.0% 100.0%

Manufacturers' sales branches are considered wholesalers

Manufacturers who just take over some wholesaling activities are not considered wholesalers. However, when they have **manufacturers' sales branches**—warehouses that producers set up at separate locations away from their factories—they're classified as wholesalers by the U.S. Census Bureau and by government agencies in many other countries.

In the United States, these manufacturer-owned branch operations account for about 4.3 percent of wholesale facilities—but they handle 28.4 percent of total wholesale sales. One reason sales per branch are so high is that the branches are usually placed in the best market areas. This also helps explain why their operating costs, as a percent of sales, are often lower. It's also easier for a manufacturer to coordinate information and logistics functions with its own branch operations than with independent wholesalers.[30]

Exhibit 12–5 Types of Wholesalers

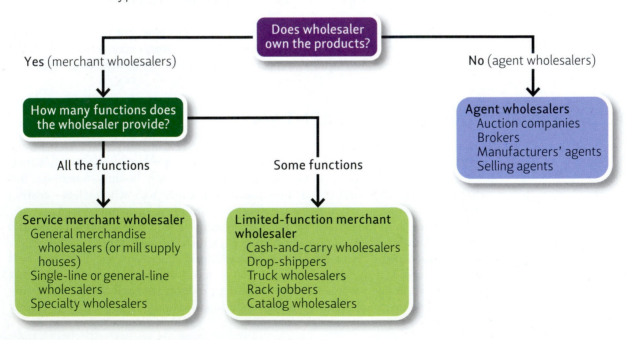

Does wholesaler own the products?

Yes (merchant wholesalers)

No (agent wholesalers)

How many functions does the wholesaler provide?

All the functions

Some functions

Agent wholesalers
Auction companies
Brokers
Manufacturers' agents
Selling agents

Service merchant wholesaler
General merchandise wholesalers (or mill supply houses)
Single-line or general-line wholesalers
Specialty wholesalers

Limited-function merchant wholesaler
Cash-and-carry wholesalers
Drop-shippers
Truck wholesalers
Rack jobbers
Catalog wholesalers

MERCHANT WHOLESALERS ARE THE MOST NUMEROUS

Merchant wholesalers own (take title to) the products they sell. They often specialize by certain types of products or customers. For example, Fastenal is a wholesaler that specializes in distributing threaded fasteners used by a variety of manufacturers. It owns (takes title to) the fasteners for some period before selling to its customers. If you think all merchant wholesalers are fading away, Fastenal is proof that they can serve a needed role. In the last decade Fastenal's profits have grown at about the same pace as Microsoft's.[31]

Exhibit 12–4 shows that almost 90 percent of the wholesaling establishments in the United States are merchant wholesalers—and they handle over 61 percent of wholesale sales. Merchant wholesalers are even more common in other countries. Japan is an extreme example. Products are often bought and sold by a series of merchant wholesalers on their way to the business user or retailer.[32]

Service wholesalers provide all the functions

Service wholesalers are merchant wholesalers that provide all the wholesaling functions. Within this basic group are three types: (1) general merchandise, (2) single-line, and (3) specialty.

General merchandise wholesalers are service wholesalers that carry a wide variety of nonperishable items such as hardware, electrical supplies, furniture, drugs, cosmetics, and automobile equipment. With their broad line of convenience and shopping products, they serve hardware stores, drugstores, and small department stores. *Mill supply houses* operate in a similar way, but they carry a broad variety of accessories and supplies to serve the needs of manufacturers.

Single-line (or general-line) wholesalers are service wholesalers that carry a narrower line of merchandise than general merchandise wholesalers. For example, they might carry only food, apparel, or certain types of industrial tools or supplies. In consumer products, they serve the single-and limited-line stores. In business products, they cover a wider geographic area and offer more specialized service.

Specialty wholesalers are service wholesalers that carry a very narrow range of products and offer more information and service than other service wholesalers. For example, a firm that produces specialized lights for vehicles might rely on specialty wholesalers to help reach auto makers in different countries. A consumer products specialty wholesaler might carry only health foods instead of a full line of groceries. Some limited-line and specialty wholesalers are growing by helping independent retailer-customers compete with mass-merchandisers. But in general, many consumer-products wholesalers have been hit hard by the growth of retail chains that set up their own distribution centers and deal directly with producers.

A specialty wholesaler of business products might limit itself to fields requiring special technical knowledge or service. Richardson Electronics is an interesting example. It specializes in distributing replacement parts, such as electron tubes, for old equipment that many manufacturers still use on the factory floor. Richardson describes itself as "on the trailing edge of technology," but many of its customers operate in countries where new technologies are not yet common. Richardson gives them easy access to information from its website (www.rell.com) and makes its products available quickly by stocking them in locations around the world.[33]

3M produces about 1,600 products that are used by auto body repair shops in the United States, Europe, Japan, and other countries. To reach this target market, 3M works with hundreds of specialty wholesalers.

Limited-function wholesalers provide some functions

Cash-and-carry wholesalers want cash

Drop-shippers do not handle the products

Truck wholesalers deliver—at a cost

Rack jobbers sell hard-to-handle assortments

Catalog wholesalers reach outlying areas

Limited-function wholesalers provide only *some* wholesaling functions. In the following paragraphs, we briefly discuss the main features of these wholesalers. Although less numerous in some countries, these wholesalers are very important for some products.

Cash-and-carry wholesalers operate like service wholesalers—except that the customer must pay cash. In the United States, big warehouse clubs have taken much of this business. But cash-and-carry operators are common in less-developed nations where very small retailers handle the bulk of retail transactions. Full-service wholesalers often refuse to grant credit to small businesses that may have trouble paying their bills.

Drop-shippers own (take title to) the products they sell—but they do *not* actually handle, stock, or deliver them. These wholesalers are mainly involved in selling. They get orders and pass them on to producers. Then the producer ships the order directly to the customer. Drop-shippers commonly sell bulky products (like lumber) for which additional handling would be expensive and possibly damaging. Drop-shippers in the United States are already feeling the squeeze from buyers and sellers connecting directly via the Internet. But the progressive ones are fighting back by setting up their own websites and getting fees for referrals.

Truck wholesalers specialize in delivering products that they stock in their own trucks. Their big advantage is that they promptly deliver perishable products that regular wholesalers prefer not to carry. A 7-Eleven store that runs out of potato chips on a busy Friday night doesn't want to be out of stock all weekend! They help retailers keep a tight rein on inventory, and they seem to meet a need.

Rack jobbers specialize in hard-to-handle assortments of products that a retailer doesn't want to manage—and rack jobbers usually display the products on their own wire racks. For example, a grocery store or mass-merchandiser might rely on a rack jobber to decide which paperback books or magazines it sells. The wholesaler knows which titles sell in the local area and applies that knowledge in many stores.

Catalog wholesalers sell out of catalogs that may be distributed widely to smaller industrial customers or retailers that might not be called on by other wholesalers. Customers place orders at a website or by mail, e-mail, fax, or telephone. These wholesalers sell lines such as hardware, jewelry, sporting goods, and computers. For example, Inmac uses a catalog that is printed in six languages and a website (www.inmac.com) to sell a complete line of computer accessories. Many of its customers don't have a local wholesaler, but they can place orders from anywhere in the world. Most catalog wholesalers quickly adapted to the Internet. It fits what they were already doing and makes it easier. But they're facing more competition too; the Internet allows customers to compare prices from more sources of supply.[34]

AGENTS ARE STRONG ON SELLING

They don't own the products

Agent wholesalers are wholesalers who do *not* own the products they sell. Their main purpose is to help in buying and selling. Agent wholesalers normally specialize by customer type and by product or product line. But they usually provide even fewer functions than the limited-function wholesalers. They operate at relatively low cost—sometimes 2 to 6 percent of their selling price—or less in the case of website-based agents who simply bring buyers and sellers together. Worldwide, the role of agents is rapidly being transformed by the Internet. Those who didn't get on board this fast-moving train were left behind.

They are important in international trade

Agents are common in international trade. Many markets have only a few well-financed merchant wholesalers. The best many producers can do is get local representation through agents and then arrange financing through banks that specialize in international trade.

Agent wholesalers are usually experts on local business customs and regulations in their own countries. Sometimes a marketing manager can't work through a foreign government's red tape without the help of a local agent.

Manufacturers' agents—freewheeling sales reps

A **manufacturers' agent** sells similar products for several noncompeting producers—for a commission on what is actually sold. Such agents work almost as members of each company's sales force, but they're really independent wholesalers. More than half of all agent wholesalers are manufacturers' agents. Their big plus is that they already call on some customers and can add another product line at relatively low cost—and at no cost to the producer until something sells! If an area's sales potential is low, a company may use a manufacturers' agent because the agent can do the job at low cost. Small producers often use agents everywhere because their sales volume is too small to justify their own sales force.

Agents can be especially useful for introducing new products. For this service, they may earn 10 to 15 percent commission. (In contrast, their commission on large-volume established products may be quite low—perhaps only 2 percent.) A 10 to 15 percent commission rate may seem small for a new product with low sales. Once a product sells well, however, a producer may think the rate is high and begin using its own sales reps.

Export or import agents are basically manufacturers' agents who specialize in international trade. These agent wholesalers operate in every country and help international firms adjust to unfamiliar market conditions in foreign markets.

Manufacturers' reps will continue to play an important role in businesses that need an agent to perform order-getting tasks. But manufacturers' reps everywhere are feeling pressure when it comes to routine business contacts. More producers are turning to telephone selling, websites, e-mail, teleconferencing, and faxes to contact customers directly.[35]

Brokers provide information

Brokers bring buyers and sellers together. Brokers usually have a *temporary* relationship with the buyer and seller while a particular deal is negotiated. They are especially useful when buyers and sellers don't come into the market very often. The broker's product is information about what buyers need and what supplies are available. If the transaction is completed, they earn a commission from whichever party hired them. **Export and import brokers** operate like other brokers, but they specialize in bringing together buyers and sellers from different countries. Smart brokers quickly saw new opportunities to expand their reach by using the Internet. As the Internet causes consolidation, it will also provide more value. A smaller number of cyberbrokers will cut costs and dominate the business with larger databases of buyers and sellers.

Selling agents—almost marketing managers

Selling agents take over the whole marketing job of producers—not just the selling function. A selling agent may handle the entire output of one or more producers, even competing producers, with almost complete control of pricing, selling, and advertising. In effect, the agent becomes each producer's marketing manager.

A few years ago, auctions were used for only a few specialized product categories. But now online services like eBay are making auctions a convenient and popular approach for buying and selling many different types of products.

Financial trouble is one of the main reasons a producer calls in a selling agent. The selling agent may provide working capital but may also take over the affairs of the business. But selling agents also work internationally. A **combination export manager** is a blend of manufacturers' agent and selling agent—handling the entire export function for several producers of similar but noncompeting lines.

Auction companies speed up the sale

Auction companies provide a place where buyers and sellers can come together and bid to complete a transaction. Traditionally they were important in certain lines—such as livestock, fur, tobacco, and used cars—where demand and supply conditions change rapidly.

WHAT WILL HAPPEN TO RETAILERS AND WHOLESALERS IN THE FUTURE?

A common theme in this chapter—and Chapters 10 and 11—is that channels of distribution are in the midst of dynamic changes. One key factor is the growth and success of large chains of retail stores. They are shifting power in channels of distribution and leading to dramatic improvements in logistics and e-commerce. But before all of this, the evolution of retailing and wholesaling was ongoing. Intermediaries that find new and better ways to add value prosper.

In time, more revolutionary change may come. Imagine, for example, what it would take for you—and everyone you know—to do most of your routine shopping on the Internet. What new marketing functions would be needed, and who would provide them?[36]

Let's admit it. You can only speculate about where retailing and wholesaling will lead. But perhaps it's good to speculate a little. The way markets work in the future will depend on creative innovations that people like you imagine, analyze, and ultimately turn into profitable marketing strategies.

CONCLUSION

Modern retailing is scrambled—and we'll probably see more changes in the future. In such a dynamic environment, a producer's marketing manager must choose very carefully among the available kinds of retailers. And retailers must plan their marketing mixes with their target customers' needs in mind—while at the same time becoming part of an effective channel system.

In this chapter we described many different types of retailers, each offering different marketing mixes that appeal to different target customers. Lower margins and faster turnover are the modern philosophy for mass-merchandisers, but this is no guarantee of success as retailers' life cycles move on.

Retailing tends to evolve in predictable patterns—and we discussed the wheel of retailing theory to help understand this. But the growth of chains and scrambled merchandising will continue as retailing evolves to meet changing consumer demands. Important breakthroughs are possible—perhaps with the Internet—and consumers probably will continue to move away from conventional retailers.

Wholesalers can provide functions for those both above and below them in a channel of distribution. These services are closely related to the basic marketing functions. There are many types of wholesalers. Some provide all the wholesaling functions—while others specialize in only a few. Eliminating wholesalers does not eliminate the need for the functions they now provide, but technology is helping firms to perform these functions in more efficient ways.

Merchant wholesalers are the most numerous and account for the majority of wholesale sales. Their distinguishing characteristic is that they take title to (own) products. Agent wholesalers, on the other hand, act more like sales representatives for sellers or buyers—and they do not take title.

Despite dire predictions, wholesalers continue to exist. The more progressive ones are adapting to a changing environment. But some less-progressive wholesalers will fail. The Internet is already taking its toll. On the other hand, new types of intermediaries are evolving. Some are creating new ways of helping producers and their customers achieve their objectives by finding new ways to add value.

KEY TERMS

QUESTIONS AND PROBLEMS

1. What sort of a "product" are specialty shops offering? What are the prospects for organizing a chain of specialty shops?

2. Distinguish among discount houses, price-cutting by conventional retailers, and mass-merchandising. Forecast the future of low-price selling in food, clothing, and appliances. How will the Internet affect that future?

3. Discuss a few changes in the marketing environment that you think help to explain why telephone, mail-order, and Internet retailing have been growing so rapidly.

4. What are some advantages and disadvantages to using the Internet for shopping?

5. Apply the wheel of retailing theory to your local community. What changes seem likely? Will established retailers see the need for change, or will entirely new firms have to develop?

6. What advantages does a retail chain have over a retailer who operates with a single store? Does a small retailer have any advantages in competing against a chain? Explain your answer.

7. Many producers are now seeking new opportunities in international markets. Are the opportunities for international expansion equally good for retailers? Explain your answer.

8. Discuss how computer systems affect wholesalers' and retailers' operations.

9. Consider the evolution of wholesaling in relation to the evolution of retailing. List several changes that are similar, and several that are fundamentally different.

10. Do wholesalers and retailers need to worry about new-product planning just as a producer needs to have an organized new-product development process? Explain your answer.

11. How do you think a retailer of Maytag washing machines would react if Maytag set up a website, sold direct to

consumers, and shipped direct from its distribution center? Explain your thinking.

12. What risks do merchant wholesalers assume by taking title to goods? Is the size of this risk about constant for all merchant wholesalers?

13. Why would a manufacturer set up its own sales branches if established wholesalers were already available?

14. What is an agent wholesaler's marketing mix?

15. Why do you think that many merchant wholesalers handle competing products from different producers, while manufacturers' agents usually handle only noncompeting products from different producers?

16. What alternatives does a producer have if it is trying to expand distribution in a foreign market and finds that the best existing merchant wholesalers won't handle imported products?

17. Discuss the future growth and nature of wholesaling if chains, scrambled merchandising, and the Internet continue to become more important. How will wholesalers have to adjust their mixes? Will wholesalers be eliminated? If not, what wholesaling functions will be most important? Are there any particular lines of trade where wholesalers may have increasing difficulty?

CREATING MARKETING PLANS

The Marketing Plan Coach software on the text website (and on the optional Student CD) includes a sample marketing plan for Hillside Veterinary Clinic. Look through the "Marketing Strategy" section.

a. What kind of retail operation is the vet clinic? Does it fit any of the types described in this chapter?

b. How could Hillside make use of a website?

c. The marketing plan notes future plans to offer kennel (boarding) services and pet supplies. How will this change Hillside's current strategy? Does the marketing plan provide a good sense of what needs to be done? Do you have other recommendations for Hillside?

SUGGESTED CASES

11. The Next Step
12. DrRay.com
14. Express Multimedia

15. The Trujillo Group
16. Bunyan Lumber

COMPUTER-AIDED PROBLEM

12. SELECTING CHANNEL INTERMEDIARIES

Art Glass Productions, a producer of decorative glass gift items, wants to expand into a new territory. Managers at Art Glass know that unit sales in the new territory will be affected by consumer response to the products. But sales will also be affected by which combination of wholesalers and retailers Art Glass selects. There is a choice between two wholesalers. One wholesaler, Giftware Distributing, is a merchant wholesaler

that specializes in gift items; it sells to gift shops, department stores, and some mass-merchandisers. The other wholesaler, Margaret Degan & Associates, is a manufacturers' agent that calls on many of the gift shops in the territory.

Art Glass makes a variety of glass items, but the cost of making an item is usually about the same—$5.20 a unit. The items would sell to Giftware Distributing at $12.00 each—and in turn the merchant wholesaler's price to retailers would be $14.00—

leaving Giftware with a $2.00 markup to cover costs and profit. Giftware Distributing is the only reputable merchant wholesaler in the territory, and it has agreed to carry the line only if Art Glass is willing to advertise in a trade magazine aimed at retail buyers for gift items. These ads will cost $8,000 a year.

As a manufacturers' agent, Margaret Degan would cover all of her own expenses and would earn 8 percent of the $14.00 price per unit charged the gift shops. Individual orders would be shipped directly to the retail gift shops by Art Glass, using United Parcel Service (UPS). Art Glass would pay the UPS charges at an average cost of $2.00 per item. In contrast, Giftware Distributing would anticipate demand and place larger orders in advance. This would reduce the shipping costs, which Art Glass would pay, to about $.60 a unit.

Art Glass' marketing manager thinks that Degan would only be able to sell about 75 percent as many items as Giftware Distributing—since she doesn't have time to call on all of the smaller shops and doesn't call on any department stores. On the other hand, the merchant wholesaler's demand for $8,000 worth of supporting advertising requires a significant outlay.

The marketing manager at Art Glass decided to use a spreadsheet to determine how large sales would have to be to make it more profitable to work with Giftware and to see how the different channel arrangements would contribute to profits at different sales levels.

a. Given the estimated unit sales and other values shown on the initial spreadsheet, which type of wholesaler would contribute the most profit to Art Glass Productions?

b. If sales in the new territory are slower than expected, so that the merchant wholesaler was able to sell only 3,000 units—or the agent 2,250 units—which wholesaler would contribute the most to Art Glass' profits? (*Note:* Assume that the merchant wholesaler only buys what it can sell; that is, it doesn't carry extra inventory beyond what is needed to meet demand.)

c. Prepare a table showing how the two wholesalers' contributions to profit compare as the quantity sold varies from 3,500 units to 4,500 units for the merchant wholesaler and 75 percent of these numbers for the manufacturers' agent. Discuss these results. (*Note:* Use the analysis feature to vary the quantity sold by the merchant wholesaler, and the program will compute 75 percent of that quantity as the estimate of what the agent will sell.)

For additional questions related to this problem, see Exercise 12-4 in the *Learning Aid for Use with Essentials of Marketing*, 12th edition.

13

Promotion— Introduction to Integrated Marketing Communications

Back in the 1930s, in the heart of the Depression, Leo and Lillian Goodwin started the Government Employees Insurance Company—Geico. Geico kept operating costs low by only selling auto insurance to two low-risk target markets, federal employees and military officers. Geico passed the savings on in the form of lower premiums—and sales steadily grew for decades. In 1996, investor Warren Buffet's Berkshire Hathaway bought Geico.

Geico's new management was eager to accelerate earnings growth by targeting new markets. However, getting growth in the mature auto insurance market meant that Geico would need to take customers away from better-known competitors such as Allstate and State Farm. If that were not already difficult enough, many prospects didn't even know about Geico and those who did often didn't know how to pronounce the name. Ted Ward, Geico's vice president of marketing, discussed this situation with representatives of the firm's ad agency, the Martin Agency of Richmond, Virginia. Together they decided that an aggressive advertising campaign could increase awareness of Geico, bring in new customers, and result in profitable growth.

The key idea for the Geico campaign was to use an animated, talking gecko to help get attention and communicate the firm's message. In the first commercial, the charming reptile with the British accent stated, "I'm the gecko, not to be confused with Geico that can save you hundreds on car insurance. So please stop calling me." The humorous ads quickly generated awareness and interest among target customers, many of whom had never heard of Geico. The original plan was for the gecko campaign to run for a short time, but customers loved the gecko and he continues to be an important part of Geico's image and promotions.

Geico wants customers to know it offers good value—great car insurance at low prices. But to prove this, customers must get a price quote. It's quick and easy to get a quote at Geico's website, so to spur the target audience to action Geico ads remind them that "15 minutes could save you 15 percent or more on your car insurance." Many people responded to the appeal of saving money, but others didn't. Research revealed that many in the hesitant group assumed that requesting an online quote would be difficult.

To overcome this resistance, Geico came up with a clever advertising campaign to convince people that getting a quote from the website is "so easy a caveman can do it." The print and TV ads feature refined cavemen living in the modern world who are offended that the ads imply they are not intelligent. The funny spots attract attention—and a short-lived television show about the cavemen also reminded viewers of Geico's message. The caveman character generated publicity for Geico in other ways, too. He was featured on a pre-Super Bowl TV special playing golf with NFL legend Phil Simms; on another occasion he interviewed stars on the red carpet at the Academy Awards. There's also a funny website, iheartcavemen.com, that helps people connect with the popular icon, and many people e-mail a link to the site to friends.

To communicate with many different target markets, Geico uses a variety of media and messages. Along with targeted direct-response mail, Geico's ads also appear on bumper cars at amusement parks and turnstiles at train stations. In addition, Geico sponsors a variety of motorsports and water sports teams, including NASCAR driver Max Papis and powerboat racers Marc Granet and Scott Begovich. The gecko icon appears on the cars, boats, and motorcycles Geico sponsors—and fans can learn more about all the teams at geicogarage.com. Geico also uses Internet search advertising. When someone types "car insurance" into the search engine at Google or Yahoo!, a sponsored link to Geico's website appears at the top of the page.

Geico's humorous ads help make Geico a familiar name, but for most people car insurance is a serious matter and they want to talk to a real person before deciding what to do. These customers can visit with a Geico salesperson at one of its local offices or call Geico's toll-free number and talk on the phone with an inside sales rep. Geico selects capable salespeople who want to be helpful—and then trains them to develop an understanding of each customer's needs and concerns so that they can then explain the benefits of Geico to the customer in a persuasive way.

Of course, Geico seeks to build an ongoing relationship with customers after they sign up for a policy. Regular contacts and updates are handled with promotional e-mails. Similarly, salespeople sometimes call customers to let them know about other Geico products, such as less-familiar umbrella insurance policies, that may benefit customers. Later, if a customer who purchases a policy has a problem, Geico's highly rated customer service team works to resolve it quickly.

While Geico is the fourth largest insurer in the United States, it is the industry's largest advertiser. Emphasizing advertising in its promotion blend has generated very good returns for Geico. In the past five years, it has acquired more new customers than any other insurance company. It has also achieved an average annual growth rate of more than 10 percent—the highest among major insurers. To catch up, competitors have increased their own promotion budgets and are trying to woo back the customers they've lost. So, to keep its growth going, Geico will need to continue to satisfy the clients who already have its policies while at the same time developing integrative marketing communications to reach new generations of car owners and offering them policies and service experiences that will convert them to customers for life.[1]

Chick-fil-A introduced its trickster cows with this "Eat Mor Chickin" graffiti billboard in Dallas in 1995, but over the years the campaign's message has become familiar to a broader target audience as its marketing communications have expanded to include TV, radio, print, and in-store point-of-purchase materials as well as merchandise such as "cow calendars."

the use of traditional media like magazines, newspapers, radio and TV, signs, and direct mail as well as new media such as the Internet. While advertising must be paid for, another form of mass selling—publicity—is "free."

Publicity avoids media costs

Publicity is any *unpaid* form of nonpersonal presentation of ideas, goods, or services. Of course, publicity people are paid. But they try to attract attention to the firm and its offerings *without having to pay media costs*. For example, movie studios try to get celebrities on TV talk shows because this generates a lot of interest and sells tickets to new movies without the studio paying for TV time.

Many companies write press releases hoping to generate publicity in newspapers, magazines, or on television. Southwest Airlines, for example, wanted its press releases to help promote special fares and new routes. So, its public relations (PR) staff used a targeted approach to get attention from news reporters. Many reporters research story ideas on specialized search engines like Yahoo! News, so the PR staff at Southwest wanted its press releases to appear at the top of the reporters' search lists. Southwest's PR staff researched what keywords reporters used most frequently on these search engines—and then put those words in press releases. For example, PR used the phrase "cheap airfare" because it was in four times as many search requests as "cheap airline tickets." Southwest also put a hot link to its special promotion fare Web page at the very start of each press release. The link allowed Southwest PR staff to track which press release worked best; then it used that information to fine-tune other messages. These extra efforts paid off. Southwest generated $1.5 million in online ticket sales with just four press releases.[2]

If a firm has a really new message, publicity may be more effective than advertising. Trade magazines, for example, may carry articles featuring the newsworthy products of regular advertisers—in part because they *are* regular advertisers. The firm's publicity people write the basic copy and then try to convince magazine editors to print it. A consumer might carefully read a long magazine story but ignore an ad with the same information.

Some companies prepare videos designed to get free publicity for their products on TV news shows. For example, after learning that Seattle Mariner baseball player Jay Buhner loves Cheerios, a General Mills marketing manager had 162 boxes of the cereal stuffed into his spring-training locker and recorded Buhner's surprise on opening his locker. TV news programs in 12 major markets showed the video. It would have cost hundreds of thousands of dollars to get as much attention with advertising.[3]

One problem with publicity is that the media don't always say or show what the firm intends. When Segway got an order from the vice president of the United States, it seemed like a perfect opportunity for publicity. It looked even better at the White House when President Bush got on to take a ride—until he fell off the Segway with photographers snapping pictures.[4]

CHAPTER 13

Exhibit 13–2
Example of Sales
Promotion Activities

Aimed at final consumers or users	Aimed at wholesalers or retailers	Aimed at company's own sales force
Contests	Price deals	Contests
Coupons	Promotion allowances	Bonuses
Aisle displays	Sales contests	Meetings
Samples	Calendars	Portfolios
Trade shows	Gifts	Displays
Point-of-purchase materials	Trade shows	Sales aids
Banners and streamers	Meetings	Training materials
Frequent buyer programs	Catalogs	
Sponsored events	Merchandising aids	
	Videos	

325

Sometimes customers pass publicity on

People have always been able to tell friends about an interesting ad, story, or product, but customers can instantly spread Internet messages to many people at once, almost as if the message were a virus. Firms often try to spark this sort of "viral" publicity by creating a message or website that is so appealing to target customers that they'll want to pass it along. In one case, Fox Entertainment wanted its target market of youthful males to know it had released DVDs of its "American Dad!" TV show. To draw their attention, Fox developed an online fighting game that pitted animated characters from the show against characters from another show, "The Family Guy." Fox publicized its game (www.americandadvsfamilyguy.com) by sending the link to bloggers and fan sites interested in the shows. Fans quickly checked out the site, played the game, and forwarded the link to friends. Within a month, the game was played 2.8 million times, and many players bought the new DVDs right at the website.[5]

Sales promotion tries to spark immediate interest

Sales promotion refers to promotion activities—other than advertising, publicity, and personal selling—that stimulate interest, trial, or purchase by final customers or others in the channel. Sales promotion may be aimed at consumers, at intermediaries, or at a firm's own employees. Examples are listed in Exhibit 13–2. Relative to other promotion methods, sales promotion can usually be implemented quickly and get results sooner. In fact, most sales promotion efforts are designed to produce immediate results.

Less is spent on advertising than personal selling or sales promotion

Many people incorrectly think that promotion money gets spent primarily on advertising—because advertising is all around them. But all the special sales promotions—coupons, sweepstakes, trade shows, and the like—add up to even more money. Similarly, much personal selling goes on in the channels and in other business markets. In total, firms spend less money on advertising than on personal selling or sales promotion.

SOMEONE MUST PLAN, INTEGRATE, AND MANAGE THE PROMOTION BLEND

Each promotion method has its own strengths and weaknesses. In combination, they complement each other. Each method also involves its own distinct activities and requires different types of expertise. As a result, it's usually the responsibility of specialists—such as sales managers, advertising managers, and promotion managers—to develop and implement the detailed plans for the various parts of the overall promotion blend.

Sales managers manage salespeople

Sales managers are concerned with managing personal selling. Often the sales manager is responsible for building good distribution channels and implementing Place policies. In smaller companies, the sales manager may also act as the marketing manager and be responsible for advertising and sales promotion.

Advertising managers work with ads and agencies

Advertising managers manage their company's mass-selling effort—in television, newspapers, magazines, and other media. Their job is choosing the right media and developing the ads. Advertising departments within their own firms may help in these efforts—or they may use outside advertising agencies. The advertising manager may handle publicity too. Or it may be handled by an outside agency or by whoever handles **public relations**—communication with noncustomers, including labor, public interest groups, stockholders, and the government.

Sales promotion managers need many talents

Sales promotion managers manage their company's sales promotion effort. In some companies, a sales promotion manager has independent status and reports directly to the marketing manager. If a firm's sales promotion spending is substantial, it probably *should* have a specific sales promotion manager. Sometimes, however, the sales or advertising departments handle sales promotion efforts—or sales promotion is left as a responsibility of individual brand managers. Regardless of who the manager is, sales promotion activities vary so much that many firms use both inside and outside specialists.

Marketing manager talks to all, blends all

Although many specialists may be involved in planning for and implementing specific promotion methods, determining the blend of promotion methods is a strategy decision—and it is the responsibility of the marketing manager.

The various promotion specialists tend to focus on what they know best and their own areas of responsibility. A creative Web page designer or advertising copywriter in New York may have no idea what a salesperson does during a call on a wholesaler. In addition, because of differences in outlook and experience, the advertising, sales, and sales promotion managers often have trouble working with each other as partners. Too often they just view other promotion methods as using up budget money they want.

The marketing manager must weigh the pros and cons of the various promotion methods and then devise an effective promotion blend—fitting in the various departments and personalities and coordinating their efforts. Then the advertising, sales, and sales promotion managers should develop the details consistent with what the marketing manager wants to accomplish.

Send a consistent and complete message with integrated marketing communications

Effective blending of all of the firm's promotion efforts should produce **integrated marketing communications**—the intentional coordination of every communication from a firm to a target customer to convey a consistent and complete message.

The Geico case at the start of this chapter is a good example of integrated marketing communications. Different promotion methods handle different parts of the job. Yet the methods are coordinated so that the sum is greater than the parts. The separate messages are complementary, but also consistent.

It seems obvious that a firm's different communications to a target market should be consistent. However, when a number of different people are working on different promotion elements, they are likely to see the same big picture only if a marketing manager ensures that it happens. Getting consistency is harder when different firms in the channel handle different aspects of the promotion effort, especially if they have conflicting objectives.

To get effective coordination, everyone involved with the promotion effort must clearly understand the plan for the overall marketing strategy. They all need to understand how each promotion method will contribute to achieve specific promotion objectives.[6]

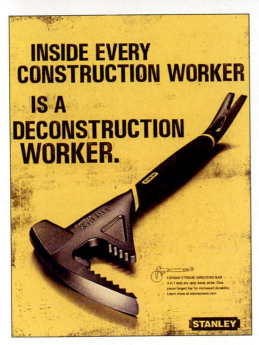

Stanley Works depends on a blend of integrated marketing communications, including sales presentations and product demonstration tours, trade ads focused on retailers, ads targeted at end users, and a website that provides information on the whole line.

WHICH METHODS TO USE DEPENDS ON PROMOTION OBJECTIVES

Overall objective is to affect behavior

A marketing manager usually has to set priorities for the promotion objectives. The ultimate objective is to encourage customers to choose a *specific* product. However, what promotion objectives are the current priority will depend on the market situation and target market. For example, if people in a target market have already had positive experiences with a firm's brand, then the promotion objective would probably be different from the objectives if target customers have no knowledge of a firm—or even a negative attitude toward it. So, in this section we describe some specific objectives and how different promotion methods can help achieve them.

Informing, persuading, and reminding are basic promotion objectives

Promotion objectives must be clearly defined—because the right promotion blend depends on what the firm wants to accomplish. It's helpful to think of three basic promotion objectives: *informing, persuading,* and *reminding* target customers about the company and its marketing mix. All try to affect buyer behavior by providing more information.

It's also useful to set more specific promotion objectives that state *exactly who* you want to inform, persuade, or remind, and *why.* This is unique to each company's strategy—and specific objectives vary by promotion method. We'll talk about more specific promotion objectives in Chapters 14 and 15. Here we'll focus on the three basic promotion objectives and how you can reach them.

Informing is educating

Potential customers must know something about a product if they are to buy at all. A firm with a really new product may not have to do anything but inform consumers about it. An *informing* objective can show that it meets consumer needs better than other products. Sometimes consumers try to become better educated before buying. A consumer who wants a digital camera, for example, can go to Best Buy's website to learn about digital cameras, find technical specifications, and read reviews by other customers.

Persuading usually becomes necessary

When competitors offer similar products, the firm must not only inform customers that its product is available but also persuade them to buy it. A *persuading* objective means the firm will try to develop a favorable set of attitudes so customers will buy, and keep buying, its product. A persuading objective often tries to demonstrate how one brand is better than others. To convince consumers to buy Brawny paper towels, ads show Brawny as the towel that's best for tough cleanup jobs. Spray 'n Wash convinces customers firsthand with in-store demonstrations that show how the product removes stains caused by spaghetti sauce or red wine.[7]

Reminding may be enough, sometimes

If target customers already have positive attitudes about a firm's marketing mix—or a good relationship with a firm—a *reminding* objective might be suitable. Customers who have been attracted and sold once are still targets for competitors' appeals. Reminding them of their past satisfaction may keep them from shifting to a competitor. Campbell's realizes that most people know about its soup—so much of its advertising is intended to remind.

Promotion objectives relate to adoption process

In Chapter 5, we looked at consumer buying as a problem-solving process in which buyers go through steps on the way to adopting (or rejecting) an idea or product. The three basic promotion objectives relate to these steps. See Exhibit 13–3. *Informing* and *persuading* may be needed to affect the potential customer's knowledge and attitudes about a product and then bring about its adoption. Later promotion can simply *remind* the customer about that favorable experience and confirm the adoption decision.

Exhibit 13-3
Relation of Promotion Objectives, Adoption Process, and AIDA Model

Promotion Objectives	Adoption Process	AIDA Model
Informing	Awareness	Attention
	Interest	Interest
Persuading	Evaluation	Desire
	Trial	
Reminding	Decision	Action
	Confirmation	

This Yahoo! ad reminds Internet advertisers that consumers indicate what they are interested in when they search for information on the Internet, so firms that sponsor search links can expect to attract more customers to their websites.

The AIDA model is a practical approach

The basic promotion objectives and adoption process fit very neatly with another action-oriented model—called AIDA—that we will use in this chapter and in Chapters 14 and 15 to guide some of our discussion.

The **AIDA model** consists of four promotion jobs: (1) to get *Attention*, (2) to hold *Interest*, (3) to arouse *Desire*, and (4) to obtain *Action*. (As a memory aid, note that the first letters of the four key words spell AIDA, the well-known opera.)

Exhibit 13–3 shows the relationship of the adoption process to the AIDA jobs. Getting attention is necessary to make consumers aware of the company's offering. Holding interest gives the communication a chance to build the consumer's interest in the product. Arousing desire affects the evaluation process, perhaps building preference. And obtaining action includes gaining trial, which may lead to a purchase decision. Continuing promotion is needed to confirm the decision and encourage an ongoing relationship and additional purchases.

British marketers for Pampers diapers generated interest and awareness with TV ads that showed the world from a baby's perspective. To encourage desire and action, they used creative in-store and point-of-purchase advertising. For example, on the doors of restrooms with baby-changing facilities, fake door knobs were placed unreachably high, with the message: "Babies have to stretch for things. That's why they like the extra stretchiness of Pampers Active fit." And on store shelves, in a play on babies' disobedient nature, pull-out Pampers information cards were marked "Do Not Pull."[8]

PROMOTION REQUIRES EFFECTIVE COMMUNICATION

Communication can break down

Promotion is wasted when it doesn't communicate effectively. There are many reasons why a promotion message can be misunderstood or not heard at all. To understand this, it's useful to think about a whole **communication process**—which means a source trying to reach a receiver with a message. Exhibit 13–4 shows the elements of the communication process. Here we see that a **source**—the sender of a message—is trying to deliver a message to a **receiver**—a potential customer. Customers evaluate both the message and the source of the message in terms of trustworthiness and

Exhibit 13–4 The Traditional Communication Process

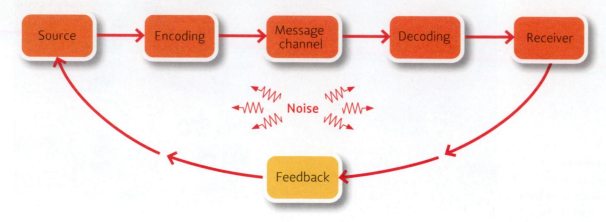

credibility. For example, American Dental Association (ADA) studies show that Listerine mouthwash helps reduce plaque buildup on teeth. Listerine mentions the ADA endorsement in its promotion to help make the promotion message credible.

A major advantage of personal selling is that the source—the seller—can get immediate feedback from the receiver. It's easier to judge how the message is being received and to change it if necessary. Mass sellers usually must depend on marketing research or total sales figures for feedback—and that can take too long. Many marketers include toll-free telephone numbers and website addresses as ways of building direct-response feedback from consumers into their mass-selling efforts.

The **noise**—shown in Exhibit 13–4—is any distraction that reduces the effectiveness of the communication process. Conversations and snack-getting during TV ads are noise. The clutter of competing ads on the Internet is noise. Advertisers who plan messages must recognize that many possible distractions—noise—can interfere with communications.

This German ad for an innovative rolling paint ball shows how a kid might decorate a wall. The target customer's frame of reference might be important in interpreting this ad. An uptight parent might see the ad and worry about kids making a mess of their bedroom walls. A different parent might see it as a way to stimulate a kid's artistic creativity.

Encoding and decoding depend on a common frame of reference

The basic difficulty in the communication process occurs during encoding and decoding. **Encoding** is the source deciding what it wants to say and translating it into words or symbols that will have the same meaning to the receiver. **Decoding** is the receiver translating the message. This process can be very tricky. The meanings of various words and symbols may differ depending on the attitudes and experiences of the two groups. People need a common frame of reference to communicate effectively. See Exhibit 13–5. Maidenform encountered this problem with its promotion aimed at working women. The company ran a series of ads depicting women stockbrokers and doctors wearing Maidenform lingerie. The men in the ads were fully dressed. Maidenform was trying to show women in positions of authority, but some women felt the ads presented them as sex objects. In this case, the promotion people who encoded the message didn't understand the attitudes of the target market and how they would decode the message.[9]

The same message may be interpreted differently

Different audiences may interpret a message differently. Such differences are common in international marketing when cultural differences or translation are problems. In Taiwan, the translation of the Pepsi slogan "Come alive with the Pepsi Generation" came out as "Pepsi will bring your ancestors back from the dead." Worse, a campaign for Schweppes Tonic Water in Italy translated the name into Schweppes Toilet Water. Many firms run into problems like this.[10]

Exhibit 13–5
This Same Message May Be Interpreted Differently

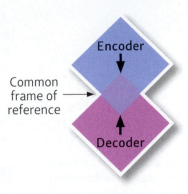

Encoder

Common frame of reference

Decoder

Message channel is important too

The communication process is complicated even more because the message is coming from a source through some **message channel**—the carrier of the message. A source can use many message channels to deliver a message. The salesperson does it in person with voice and action. Advertising must do it with media such as magazines, TV, e-mail, or Internet websites. A particular message channel may enhance or detract from a message. A TV ad, for example, can *show* that Dawn dishwashing detergent "takes the grease away"; the same claim might not be convincing if it arrived in a consumer's e-mail.

Ethical issues in marketing communications

Promotion is one of the most often criticized areas of marketing. Many criticisms focus on whether communications are honest and fair. Marketers must sometimes make ethical judgments in considering these charges and in planning their promotion.

For example, when a TV news program broadcasts a video publicity release, consumers don't know it was prepared to achieve marketing objectives. They think the news staff is the source. That may make the message more credible, but is it fair? Many say yes—as long as the publicity information is truthful. But gray areas still remain.

Critics raise similar concerns about the use of celebrities in advertisements. A person who plays the role of an honest and trustworthy person on a popular TV series may be a credible message source in an ad, but is using such a person misleading to consumers? Some critics believe it is. Others argue that consumers recognize advertising when they see it and know celebrities are paid for their endorsements.

The most common criticisms of promotion relate to exaggerated claims. If an ad or a salesperson claims that a product is the "best available," is that just a personal opinion or should every statement be backed up by proof? What type of proof should be required? Some promotions do misrepresent the benefits of a product. However, most marketing managers want relationships with, and repeat purchases from, their customers. They realize that customers won't come back if the marketing mix doesn't deliver what the promotion promises. Further, many consumers are skeptical about all the claims they hear and see. As a result, most marketing managers work to make promotion claims specific and believable.[11]

INTEGRATED DIRECT-RESPONSE PROMOTION IS VERY TARGETED

The challenge of developing promotions that reach *specific* target customers has prompted many firms to turn to direct marketing—direct communication between a seller and an individual customer using a promotion method other than face-to-face personal selling. Most direct marketing communications are designed to prompt immediate feedback—a direct response—by customers. That's why this type of communication is often called *direct-response promotion*.

Early efforts in the direct-response area focused on direct-mail advertising. A carefully selected mailing list—perhaps from the firm's customer relationship management (CRM) database—allowed advertisers to reach customers with specific interests. And direct-mail advertising proved to be very effective when the objective was to get a direct response from the customer.

Now it's more than direct-mail advertising

Taco Bell created a clever, direct-response Valentine promotion. Ads invited consumers to go to the Taco Bell website. There they could fill in a form to compose an e-mail love letter. The site said that love is like Taco Bell's Beefy Melts . . . the cheesier the better. Many people who received a love letter clicked on a Taco Bell link so they could send their own letters—getting Taco Bell's cheesy message to millions of consumers.

Achieving a measurable, direct response from specific target customers is still the heart of direct promotion. But direct-response media now include telephone, print, e-mail, a website, broadcast, and even interactive video. The customer's response may

be a purchase (or donation), a question, or a request for more information. At a website, the response may be a simple mouse-click to link to more information, put an item in a virtual shopping cart, or make a purchase.

Often the customer responds by calling a toll-free telephone number or, in the case of business markets, by sending a fax or an e-mail. Then a salesperson calls and follows up. That might involve filling an order or scheduling a personal visit with a prospect. There are many variations on this approach, and direct-response promotion is often an important component of integrated marketing communications programs. What distinguishes this general approach is that the marketer targets more of its promotion effort at specific individuals who respond directly.[12]

Target customer directly with a CRM database

Direct-response promotion usually relies on a CRM database to target specific prospects. The database includes customers' names and their home and e-mail addresses—as well as past purchases and other segmenting characteristics. Marketing managers like to be in regular contact with customers to stimulate customer interest or a call for action. Greenpeace and the Cousteau Society mail newsletters to people interested in environmental issues—keeping them informed of the cause or asking for donations.

CRM databases are also useful for business customers. For example, Forrester Research conducts market research on many industries and then sells its research reports. Customers register at the Forrester site and indicate specific industries and topics they want to follow. Forrester sends regular e-mails with the updates they request. Similarly, HP sends customized e-newsletters to its business customers to announce new products and to give advice on frequently asked service questions. These newsletters have increased sales of HP's new products and reduced calls to its service center. Effective e-mail programs give customers targeted information they find timely and useful.[13]

However, marketing managers should be careful they don't create ill will by bombarding customers with "spam"—e-mail messages they don't want. Growing concerns about spam have led many businesses and individuals to use filters that screen it out. But spam filters often delete useful messages—including requested e-newsletters. So marketing managers can't rely too heavily on e-mail because they can't be sure their target customers are even getting the message.[14]

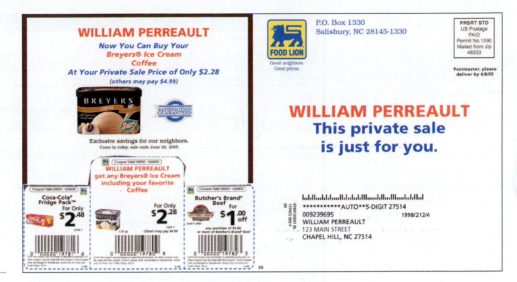

Food Lion, a popular supermarket, uses a CRM database to target coupons to individual customers. It can forecast likely sales based on past purchases.

Direct-response methods raise ethical concerns

Direct-response promotion and CRM database targeting have become an important part of many marketing mixes. But critics argue that thousands of acres of trees are consumed each week just to make the paper for direct-response "junk mail" that consumers don't want. In addition, many consumers don't like getting direct-promotion telephone solicitations at any time, but especially during evening meal times when these calls are particularly frequent. Similarly, most e-mail users resent that they need to spend time dealing with the constant flow of spam that floods their e-mail boxes; there's so much spam that it slows down the whole Internet. There are many other privacy issues related to how a direct-response database might be used, especially if it includes details of a consumer's purchases.

Most firms that use direct-response promotion are very sensitive to these concerns and take steps to address them. However, many people feel that solutions to these problems require other steps and laws in these areas are changing. For example, most states have passed laws prohibiting automatic calling systems that use prerecorded messages rather than a live salesperson. Many states have their own "do not call" laws, and federal laws are under review. A host of new regulations concerning consumer privacy are also being considered by lawmakers. So marketers who do not heed warnings about consumer concerns in this area may find themselves in trouble—not only with customers but in the courts.[15]

THE CUSTOMER MAY INITIATE THE COMMUNICATION PROCESS

Traditional thinking about promotion—and for that matter about the communication process—has usually been based on the idea that it's the seller ("source") who initiates the communication. Of course, for decades consumers have been looking in the Yellow Pages for information or asking retail salespeople for help. Similarly, it's not news that organizational buyers contact potential vendors to ask questions or request bids.

In the past, a marketer usually viewed the buyer as a passive message receiver—at least until the marketer has done something to stimulate attention, interest, and desire. That's one reason that targeting is so important—so that the promotion expense isn't wasted on someone who isn't interested. Moreover, most mass-selling messages are based on the idea that you can get a customer's attention and interest for only a minute or two. Even with direct-response promotion, the marketer typically has taken the first step.

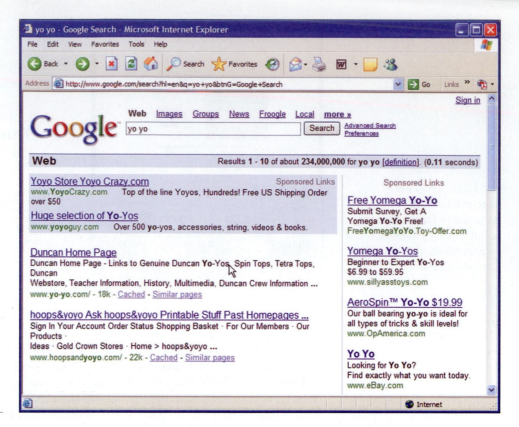

Internet search engines have reduced the time it takes for customers to search for information about products and stores. Some marketing managers have tried to understand how search engines work so that their sites show up early in the list of results. Another approach is to pay a search engine firm for a sponsored link (ad) on the first page of results. See the sponsored links on the Google results screen produced by a search for "yo yo."

New electronic media enable interactive communication

However, this is changing. Buyers can now access a great deal of information (including pictures, video, and audio, as well as text) and place an order without the seller having been directly involved at all. The interactive technologies enabling this change take many different forms. Some of the most important are websites, e-mail list-servers, caller-controlled fax-on-demand, computerized telephone voice-messaging systems, video kiosks in malls, CD and DVD disks on personal computers, and MSN TV.

For example, England has had interactive cable TV for over a decade. Consumers can use a standard TV and remote control to get information that ranges from local weather to specials at the local supermarket. Similar systems are becoming more available in other countries as government regulations change and as cable companies upgrade their equipment.

Work is under way on interactive cable systems in which icons will appear on-screen as consumers watch a program or movie. For example, an icon might appear on a jacket worn by a talk show guest. A consumer who is interested in the product will be able to press a button on a remote control to pause the show and get more information about the product and where to buy it—or even to place an order. The same concept is already implemented on DVDs for some movies. When this type of system is available via cable (or with streaming video over the Internet), it will reshape the way many marketing communications are handled.

Consider the simple model of customer ("receiver") initiated interactive communication shown in Exhibit 13–6. At first it doesn't seem very different from the traditional communication model we considered earlier (Exhibit 13–4). However, the differences are significant.

Consumer initiates communication with a search process

In the model in Exhibit 13–6, a customer initiates the communication process with a decision to search for information in a particular message channel. The most far-reaching message channel to search is the Internet. The message channel is still

Exhibit 13-6
A Model of Customer-Initiated Interactive Communication

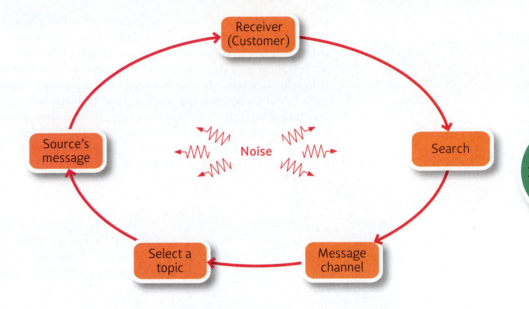

the carrier of the message, as was the case before, but "searchable" message channels usually feature an archive of existing messages on a number of topics. There may be many available topics—even millions.

In the next step, the consumer selects one specific topic on which to receive a message. Selecting a topic might be done in one of a variety of ways, depending on the message channel. The most typical approaches involve using a mouse, remote control device, or keypad to highlight a selection from an initial list (like a table of contents or index). Of course, other approaches are common. Many dial-up telephone systems use voice-recognition.

Many consumers initiate communication when they enter search keywords into a search engine like Google or Yahoo!. What does this mean for a marketer? An online retailer that sells golf gear wants to appear near the top of the search results when someone searches for "Big Bertha golf," Callaway's popular line of golf clubs. In this case, the retailer might pay a search engine company to put a sponsored (advertising) link near the top of the list. Or, there are other technical approaches that make it more likely that a seller's website will appear near the top of the search results. Either way, the marketer wants to be sure that when customers "look" that its business is "seen"—or the firm's message won't be communicated.

Consumer decides how much information to get

Once a specific topic is selected, the message for that topic is displayed. Typically, the message is brief. But it may include a simple way to get more detailed information, select another related topic, return to the original selection process, or quit the search. Thus, after each message the consumer can decide whether to search further (say, to get more detail). This interactive approach makes it easy for the consumer to get as much information as desired. However, noise may still be a problem. For example, a consumer may waste time and still not find what is needed—because it is not available or is too hard to find. Of course, an online seller doesn't want to lose a customer who has made it to the website but then encountered some problem. So, many online sellers have a live person who is ready to help if a customer needs it. At the Lands' End site, a customer can click a button to have a salesperson call on the phone and give help or alternatively give online help in an instant-messaging chat session.

Some messages are outside the firm's control

When customers search, they often find messages that the firm can't control. For example, a gadget lover might go to CNET.com to check the features of a product but in the process see a critical review written by an objective expert. Marketing managers can't afford to ignore websites or other places where customers post comments or get information. Complaints highlight unmet customer needs, and often the manager can do something about them. Online retailer Petco Animal Supplies, for instance, asks its suppliers to redesign products that repeatedly get poor reviews. It also makes sense for firms to encourage satisfied customers to post reviews. The owner of a California spa was horrified to learn her spa had only a two-and-a-half star rating on Yelp.com, a review site. To turn things around, she immediately sent e-mails to try to make things right with the unhappy reviewers, but she also encouraged her satisfied customers to post reviews. Soon the spa had an acceptable four-star rating at Yelp, and rather than scaring off prospects it was spurring them to action.[16]

Custom communications will be more personalized

The traditional principles of communication discussed earlier in the chapter are still important in customer-initiated interactive communication. At the same time, the interactive approach allows the marketer to customize communication to the needs and responses of the consumer. As new approaches develop in this arena, we are seeing more promotion targeted at single-person "segments." For example, many websites place "cookies" on a customer's computer so that when the customer revisits their sites the system can "remember" the customer and automatically recall past purchase activity. For example, when a customer returns to Amazon.com, the site recommends books based on that customer's purchase history.[17]

HOW TYPICAL PROMOTION PLANS ARE BLENDED AND INTEGRATED

There is no one right blend

There is no one *right* promotion blend for all situations. Each one must be developed as part of a marketing mix and should be designed to achieve the firm's promotion objectives in each marketing strategy. So let's take a closer look at typical promotion blends in different situations.

Get a push in the channel with promotion to intermediaries

When a channel of distribution involves intermediaries, their cooperation can be crucial to the success of the overall marketing strategy. **Pushing** (a product through a channel) means using normal promotion effort—personal selling, advertising, and sales promotion—to help sell the whole marketing mix to possible channel members. This approach emphasizes the importance of securing the wholehearted cooperation of channel members to promote the product in the channel and to the final user.

Producers usually take on much of the responsibility for the pushing effort in the channel. However, wholesalers often handle at least some of the promotion to retailers. Similarly, retailers often handle promotion in their local markets. The overall effort is most likely to be effective when all of the individual messages are carefully integrated.

The Hanes ad (on the left) is targeted at parents and kids and designed to stimulate demand and help pull Hanes' popular products through the channel of distribution. The Hanes trade ad (on the right) is targeted at retailers and designed to inform them about the consumer promotion and encourage them to carry Hanes brand products.

Promotion to intermediaries emphasizes personal selling

Salespeople handle most of the important communication with wholesalers and retailers. They don't want empty promises. They want to know what they can expect in return for their cooperation and help. A salesperson can answer questions about what promotion will be directed toward the final consumer, each channel member's part in marketing the product, and important details on pricing, markups, promotion assistance, and allowances. A salesperson can also help the firm determine when it should adjust its marketing mix from one intermediary to another.

When suppliers offer similar products and compete for attention and shelf space, intermediaries usually pay attention to the one with the best profit potential. So sales promotions targeted at intermediaries usually focus on short-term arrangements that will improve the intermediary's profits. For example, a soft-drink bottler might offer a convenience store a free case of drinks with each two cases it buys. The free case improves the store's profit margin on the whole purchase.

Firms run ads in trade magazines to recruit new intermediaries or to inform channel members about a new offering. Trade ads usually encourage intermediaries to contact the supplier for more information, and then a salesperson takes over.

Push within a firm—with promotion to employees

Some firms emphasize promotion to their own employees—especially salespeople or others in contact with customers. This type of *internal marketing* effort is basically a variation on the pushing approach. One objective of an annual sales meeting is to inform reps about important elements of the marketing strategy—so they'll work together as a team to implement it. Some firms use promotion to motivate employees to provide better customer service or achieve higher sales. This is typical in services where the quality of the employees' efforts is a big part of the product. For example, at one time, advertising for McDonald's used the theme "We love to see you smile." The ads communicate to customers, but also remind employees that the service they provide is crucial to customer satisfaction.

Pulling policy—customer demand pulls the product through the channel

Most producers focus a significant amount of promotion on customers at the end of the channel. This helps to stimulate demand and pull the product through the channel of distribution. **Pulling** means getting customers to ask intermediaries for the product.

Pulling and pushing are usually used in combination. See Exhibit 13–7. However, if intermediaries won't work with a producer—perhaps because they're already carrying a competing brand—a producer may try to use a pulling approach by itself. This

Exhibit 13–7 Promotion May Encourage Pushing in the Channel, Pulling by Customers, or Both

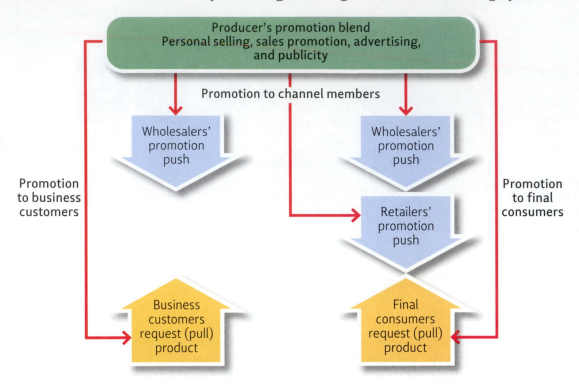

involves highly aggressive promotion to final consumers or users—perhaps using coupons or samples—temporarily bypassing intermediaries. If the promotion works, the intermediaries are forced to carry the product to satisfy customer requests. However, this approach is risky. Customers may lose interest before reluctant intermediaries make the product available. At minimum, intermediaries should be told about the planned pulling effort—so they can be ready if the promotion succeeds.

Who handles promotion to final customers at the end of the channel varies in different channel systems, depending on the mix of pushing and pulling. Further, the promotion blend typically varies depending on whether customers are final consumers or business users.[18]

Promotion to final consumers

The large number of consumers almost forces producers of consumer products and retailers to emphasize advertising and sales promotion. Sales promotion—such as coupons, contests, or free samples—builds consumer interest and short-term sales of a product. Effective mass selling may build enough brand familiarity so that little personal selling is needed, as in self-service and discount operations.[19]

Personal selling can be effective too. But aggressive personal selling to final consumers usually is found in channel systems for expensive products, such as those for financial services, furniture, consumer electronics, designer clothing, and automobiles.

Promotion to business customers

Producers and wholesalers that target business customers often emphasize personal selling. This is practical because there are fewer of these customers and their purchases are typically larger. Sales reps can be more flexible in adjusting their companies' appeals to suit each customer—and personal contact is usually required to close a sale. A salesperson is also able to call back later to follow up, resolve any problems, and nurture the relationship with the customer.

While personal selling dominates in business markets, mass selling is necessary too. A typical sales call on a business customer costs about $500.[20] That's because salespeople spend less than half their time actually selling. The rest is consumed by such tasks as traveling, paperwork, sales meetings, and strictly service calls. So it's seldom practical for salespeople to carry the whole promotion load.

Ads in trade magazines or at a B2B e-commerce website, for instance, can inform potential customers that a product is available. Most trade ads give a toll-free telephone number, fax number, or website address to stimulate direct inquiries. Domestic and international trade shows also help identify prospects. Even so, most sellers who target business customers spend only a small percentage of their promotion budget on mass selling and sales promotion.

Each market segment may need a unique blend

Knowing what type of promotion is typically emphasized with different targets is useful in planning the promotion blend. But each unique market segment may need a separate marketing mix and a different promotion blend. You should be careful not to slip into a shotgun approach when what you really need is a rifle approach—with a more careful aim.

ADOPTION PROCESSES CAN GUIDE PROMOTION PLANNING

The AIDA and adoption processes look at individuals. This emphasis on individuals helps us understand how promotion affects the way that people behave. But it's also useful to look at markets as a whole. Different segments of customers within a market may behave differently—with some taking the lead in trying new products and, in turn, influencing others.

Promotion must vary for different adopter groups

Research on how markets accept new ideas has led to the adoption curve model. The **adoption curve** shows when different groups accept ideas. It emphasizes the relations among groups and shows that individuals in some groups act as leaders in accepting a new idea. Promotion efforts usually need to change over time to adjust to differences among the adopter groups.

Exhibit 13–8 shows the adoption curve for a typical successful product. Some of the important characteristics of each of these customer groups are discussed next. Which one are you? Does your group change for different products?

Innovators don't mind taking some risks

The **innovators** are the first to adopt. They are eager to try a new idea and willing to take risks. Innovators tend to be young and well educated. They are likely to be

Exhibit 13–8   The Adoption Curve

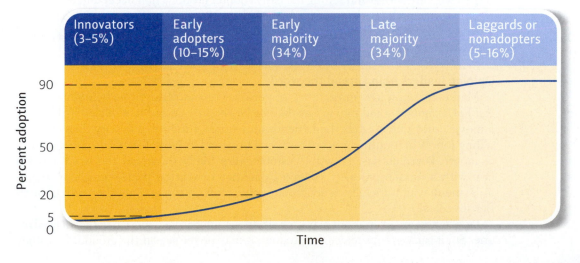

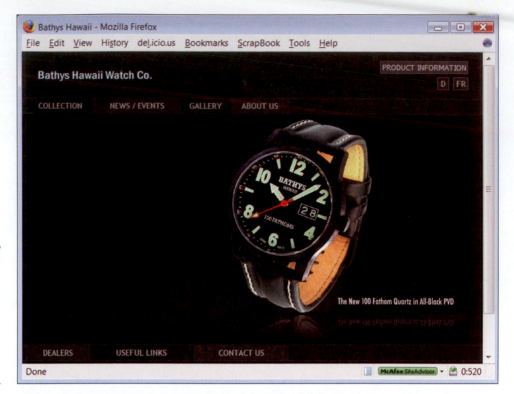

The website for Bathys Hawaii Watch Co. was getting about 60 hits a day until Gizmodo.com, a blog on new consumer technology that appeals to technology opinion leaders, wrote about the Bathys watch designed especially for surfers. After that, website hits jumped to 1,800 per day and sales increased by 300 percent.

mobile and have many contacts outside their local social group and community. Business firms in the innovator group are often specialized and willing to take the risk of doing something new.

Innovators tend to rely on impersonal and scientific information sources, or other innovators, rather than salespeople. They often search for information on the Internet, read articles in technical publications, or look for informative ads in special-interest magazines.

Early adopters are often opinion leaders

Early adopters are well respected by their peers and often are opinion leaders. They tend to be younger, more mobile, and more creative than later adopters. But unlike innovators, they have fewer contacts outside their own social group or community. Business firms in this category also tend to be specialized.

Of all the groups, this one tends to have the greatest contact with salespeople. Mass media are important information sources too. Marketers should be very concerned with attracting and selling the early adopter group. Their acceptance is crucial. The next group, the early majority, look to the early adopters for guidance. The early adopters can help the promotion effort by spreading *word-of-mouth* information and advice among other consumers.

Opinion leaders help spread the word

Marketers know the importance of personal recommendations by opinion leaders. For example, some movie fans like to be the first to see new flicks. If they like a movie, they quickly tell their friends and word-of-mouth publicity does the real selling job. When online grocer FreshDirect opened in New York City, positive word of mouth keyed its fast growth. Customers are likely to spread the word about a firm with a unique product; Voodoo Doughnut benefitted from buzz about its unusual menu which includes a doughnut with bacon on top and another with Crunch Berries cereal.

Consumers are even more likely to talk about a negative experience than a positive one. So, if early groups reject the product, it may never get off the ground. In a study

Marketers Are Wading into the Blogosphere

Many marketers are adding a new dimension to their promotion blend by using blogs. A *blog*, short for *Web log*, is a website that provides a running stream of messages, links, and comments. Blogs are usually created by an individual to express personal opinions about some topic. But many marketers like the first-person, conversational style that is typical of blogs. As with other types of personal communication, including personal selling, blogs can help make a connection with customers and enhance the relationship with them, but at a low cost.

Kodak employees write about photography—not Kodak cameras—at the "1000 Words" blog. By promoting photography, and providing a forum for photo buffs to share ideas about taking pictures, Kodak hopes its blog will change readers into customers. Similarly, yogurt maker Stonyfield Farm uses blogs to reinforce the healthy and wholesome positioning of its foods. Its "Baby Babble" blog targets new parents, and "The Bovine Bugle" tells about daily activities at a farm that supplies Stonyfield with milk.

Most blogs rely on and reflect the passions of their creators. Ed Brill is a global sales executive for IBM's Lotus Notes software. Each day about 13,000 Lotus users check what he's thinking at his blog (www. edbrill.com). One reason is that Brill provides important news fast. For example, when the general manager of Lotus was replaced, Brill posted the news within hours and explained what it would mean for customers. But Brill's site isn't strictly business. It includes photos of Brill and his friends and comments on personal matters, like the fancy watch he received as a Valentine's gift. IBM is a big company and Lotus is a huge brand, but Brill's personal blog helps to humanize them and build relationships with customers.

Marketers for GourmetStation, a Web-based retailer of high-end food, wanted to generate a little buzz. They thought a blog "written" by the website's fictional connoisseur of fine food and wine, T. Alexander, would be just the ticket. Soon Alexander was blogging away, recommending foods and wines. However, some bloggers are very protective of "their" media—and don't like the idea of any blog that appears too commercial. Some of these critics quickly blogged their criticism of GourmetStation's blog for not being authentic—and one gave it a "Beyond Lame Award." In this case, the criticisms didn't seem to matter to customers—and instead all the attention generated more hits for the website. However, marketers need to be aware that creative promotion on the Web can draw critics. Still, firms that keep their focus on the target market are likely to win in the long run.[21]

of consumers, 64 percent said they would not shop at a store after being told about someone else's negative experience there.[22]

The popularity of blogs, online review sites, and similar Web media give "word of mouse" far-reaching impact. When Hot Hot Hot, a retailer that specializes in hot sauces for food, established its website, it urged customers to click a link and e-mail its Web address to their friends. Very quickly, largely because of these referrals, 1,500 people were visiting the website each day.

When consumers are not motivated to spread the word, a company called BzzAgent helps marketing managers get conversations started. BzzAgent works with about 125,000 "agents." Agents who sign up to help with a particular campaign receive product samples and information. If they like the product, they are urged to pass the word. But BzzAgent encourages them to be ethical and disclose their status as "buzz agents." Kraft Foods, General Mills, and Dockers have run campaigns like this.[23]

Internet EXERCISE

BzzAgent has a code of conduct for its agents, but even so it has received some negative publicity that questions the ethics of its agents. Go to the BzzAgent site (www.BzzAgent.com) and click on "Join BzzAgent" and then on "Code of Conduct" to read through the code. If a BzzAgent follows the guidelines in the code, do you think the practice is ethical? In your opinion, what actions would make a BzzAgent's behavior unethical?

The **early majority** avoid risk and wait to consider a new idea after many early adopters have tried it—and liked it. Average-sized business firms that are less specialized often fit in this category. If successful companies in their industry adopt the new idea, they will too.

The early majority have a great deal of contact with mass media, salespeople, and early adopter opinion leaders. Members usually aren't opinion leaders themselves.

Late majority is cautious

The **late majority** are cautious about new ideas. Often they are older and more set in their ways, so they are less likely to follow early adopters. In fact, strong social pressure from their own peer group may be needed before they adopt a new product. Business firms in this group tend to be conservative, smaller-sized firms with little specialization.

The late majority make little use of marketing sources of information—mass media and salespeople. They tend to be oriented more toward other late adopters rather than outside sources they don't trust.

Laggards or nonadopters hang on to tradition

Laggards or **nonadopters** prefer to do things the way they've been done in the past and are very suspicious of new ideas. They tend to be older and less well educated. The smallest businesses with the least specialization often fit this category. They cling to the status quo and think it's the safe way.

The main source of information for laggards is other laggards. This certainly is bad news for marketers. In fact, it may not pay to bother with this group.[24]

PROMOTION BLENDS VARY OVER THE LIFE CYCLE

Stage of product in its life cycle

The adoption curve helps explain why a new product goes through the product life-cycle stages described in Chapter 9. Promotion blends usually have to change to achieve different promotion objectives at different life-cycle stages.

Market introduction stage—"this new idea is good"

During market introduction, the basic promotion objective is informing. If the product is a really new idea, the promotion must build **primary demand**—demand for the general product idea—not just for the company's own brand. Video phone

The ad sponsored by the American Academy of Dermatology gives reasons to see a dermatologist and focuses on building primary demand for the services of dermatologists (rather than for a particular doctor). By contrast, the ad for Bawls Guarana high caffeine beverage seeks to build selective demand for the Bawls brand.

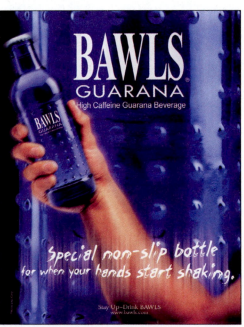

service and "smart" appliances (that connect to the Internet) are good examples of product concepts where primary demand is just beginning to grow. There may be few potential innovators during the introduction stage, and personal selling can help find them. Firms also need salespeople to find good channel members and persuade them to carry the new product. Sales promotion may be targeted at salespeople or channel members to get them interested in selling the new product. And sales promotion may also encourage customers to try it.

Market growth stage— "our brand is best"

In the market growth stage, more competitors enter the market, and promotion emphasis shifts from building primary demand to stimulating **selective demand**— demand for a company's own brand. The main job is to persuade customers to buy, and keep buying, the company's product.

Now that there are more potential customers, mass selling becomes more economical. But salespeople and personal selling must still work in the channels, expanding the number of outlets and cementing relationships with channel members.

Banquet Homestyle Bakes illustrates this stage. When ConAgra Foods introduced Homestyle Bakes, it was the first shelf-stable meal kit with the meat already in the package. ConAgra, also the producer of Armour processed meats, had the expertise to create a tasty product that a consumer could prepare in a few minutes and then just stick in the oven. When Homestyle Bakes came out, there was no direct competition. The sales force used market research data to convince retailers to give the product shelf space, and ads used humor to highlight that the package was so heavy because it already included meat. However, over time promotion shifted to emphasize that Homestyle Bakes was adding a variety of new flavors and 10 percent more meat. Similarly, the sales force shifted its efforts to get retailers to participate in Homestyle Bakes' "Super Meals/Super Moms" contests, which offered harried moms prizes such as a visit to a spa, to keep them interested in the Homestyle brand.[25]

Market maturity stage—"our brand is better, really"

In the market maturity stage, mass selling and sales promotion may dominate the promotion blends of consumer products firms. Business products may require more aggressive personal selling—perhaps supplemented by more advertising. The total dollars allocated to promotion may rise as competition increases.

The best thing since sliced bread

Your complete source for Marketing at Retail

· Displays – Temporary and Permanent
· Concept and Design
· Pallet Programs
· Assembly and Fulfillment

Special end-of-aisle displays, like this one for Wonder bread, and other point-of-purchase sales promotion materials are especially important for consumer staples in the highly competitive market maturity stage of the product life cycle.

If a firm already has high sales—relative to competitors—it may have a real advantage in promotion at this stage. For example, sales of Tylenol tablets are about four times the sales of Motrin competing tablets. If both Tylenol and Motrin spend the same percentage of sales (say 35 percent) on promotion, Tylenol will spend four times as much as its smaller competitor and will probably communicate to more people.

Firms that have differentiated their marketing mixes may favor mass selling because they have something to talk about. For instance, a firm with a strong brand may use reminder-type advertising or target frequent-buyer promotions at current customers to strengthen the relationship and keep customers loyal. This may be more effective than costly efforts to win customers away from competitors.

However, as a market drifts toward pure competition, some companies resort to price-cutting. This may temporarily increase the number of units sold, but it is also likely to reduce total revenue and the money available for promotion. The temporary sales gains disappear and prices are dragged down even lower when competitors retaliate with their own short-term sales promotions, like price-off coupons. As cash flowing into the business declines, spending may have to be cut back.[26]

Sales decline stage— "let's tell those who still want our product"

During the sales decline stage, the total amount spent on promotion usually decreases as firms try to cut costs to remain profitable. Since some people may still want the product, firms need more targeted promotion to reach these customers.

On the other hand, some firms may increase promotion to try to slow the cycle, at least temporarily. Crayola had almost all of the market for children's crayons, but sales were slowly declining as new kinds of markers came along. Crayola increased ad spending to urge parents to buy their kids a "fresh box."

SETTING THE PROMOTION BUDGET

Size of budget affects promotion efficiency and blend

There are some economies of scale in promotion. An ad on national TV might cost less *per person* reached than an ad on local TV. Similarly, citywide radio, TV, and newspapers may be cheaper than neighborhood newspapers or direct personal contact. But the *total cost* for some mass media may force small firms, or those with small promotion budgets, to use promotion alternatives that are more expensive per contact. For example, a small retailer might want to use local television but find that there is only enough money for a Web page, an ad in the Yellow Pages, and an occasional newspaper ad.

Find the task, budget for it

The most common method of budgeting for promotion expenditures is to compute a percentage of either past sales or sales expected in the future. The virtue of this method is its simplicity. However, just because this mechanical approach is common doesn't mean that it's smart. It leads to expanding marketing expenditures when business is good and cutting back when business is poor. When business is poor, this approach may just make the problem worse—if weak promotion is the reason for declining sales.

In the light of our continuing focus on planning marketing strategies to reach objectives, the most sensible approach to budgeting promotion expenditures is the **task method**—basing the budget on the job to be done. It helps you to set priorities so that the money you spend produces specific results. In fact, this approach makes sense for *any* marketing expenditure, but here we'll focus on promotion.

A practical approach is to determine which promotion objectives are most important and which promotion methods are most economical and effective for the communication tasks relevant to each objective. The costs of these tasks are then totaled—to determine how much should be budgeted for promotion (just as money is allocated for other marketing activities required by the strategy). In other words, the firm can assemble its total promotion budget directly from detailed plans rather than by simply relying on historical patterns or ratios.

This method also helps to eliminate budget fights between managers responsible for different promotion methods who see themselves as pitted against each other for limited budget dollars. The specialists may still make their own suggestions about how to perform tasks. But then the budget allocations are based on the most effective ways of getting things done, not on what the firm did last year, what some competitor does, or even on internal politics. With this approach, different promotion specialists are also more likely to recognize that they must all work together to achieve truly integrated marketing communications.[27]

CONCLUSION

Promotion is an important part of any marketing mix. Most consumers and intermediate customers can choose from among many products. To be successful, a producer must not only offer a good product at a reasonable price but also inform potential customers about the product and where they can buy it. Further, producers must tell wholesalers and retailers in the channel about their product and marketing mix. These intermediaries, in turn, must use promotion to reach their customers. And the promotion blend must fit with the rest of the marketing mix and the target market.

In this chapter, we introduced different promotion methods and we discussed the advantages and disadvantages of each method. We also discussed the integrated marketing communications concept and explained why most firms use a blend of different promotion methods. While the overall promotion objective is to affect buying behavior, the basic promotion objectives are informing, persuading, and reminding. These objectives help guide the marketing manager's decisions about the promotion blend.

Models from the behavioral sciences help us understand the communication process and how it can break down. These models recognize different ways to communicate. We discussed direct-response promotion for developing more targeted promotion blends. And we described an approach where customers initiate and interact with the marketer's communications. It provides new and different challenges for marketing managers.

This chapter also recognized other factors that influence decisions about promotion blends. Marketing managers must make decisions about how to split promotion that is directed at final consumers or business customers—and at channel members. Promotion blends are also influenced by the adoption curve and the product life-cycle stages. Finally, we described how promotion budgets are set and influence promotion decisions.

In this chapter, we considered some basic concepts that apply to all areas of promotion. In Chapters 14 and 15, we'll discuss personal selling, customer service, advertising, and sales promotion in more detail.

KEY TERMS

promotion, 322

personal selling, 323

mass selling, 323

advertising, 323

publicity, 324

sales promotion, 325

sales managers, 326

advertising managers, 326

public relations, 326

sales promotion
    managers, 326

integrated marketing
    communications, 326

AIDA model, 329

communication process, 329

source, 329

receiver, 329

noise, 330

encoding, 330

decoding, 330

message channel, 331

pushing, 336

pulling, 337

adoption curve, 339

innovators, 339

early adopters, 340

early majority, 342

late majority, 342

laggards, 342

nonadopters, 342

primary demand, 342

selective demand, 343

task method, 344

QUESTIONS AND PROBLEMS

1. Briefly explain the nature of the three basic promotion methods available to a marketing manager. What are the main strengths and limitations of each?

2. In your own words, discuss the integrated marketing communications concept. Explain what its emphasis on "consistent" and "complete" messages implies with respect to promotion blends.

3. Relate the three basic promotion objectives to the four jobs (AIDA) of promotion using a specific example.

4. Discuss the communication process in relation to a producer's promotion of an accessory product—say, a new

electronic security system businesses use to limit access to areas where they store confidential records.

5. If a company wants its promotion to appeal to a new group of target customers in a foreign country, how can it protect against its communications being misinterpreted?

6. Promotion has been the target of considerable criticism. What specific types of promotion are probably the object of this criticism? Give a particular example that illustrates your thinking.

7. With direct-response promotion, customers provide feedback to marketing communications. How can a marketing

manager use this feedback to improve the effectiveness of the overall promotion blend?

8. How can a promotion manager target a message to a certain target market with electronic media (like the Internet) when the customer initiates the communication? Give an example.

9. What promotion blend would be most appropriate for producers of the following established products? Assume average- to large-sized firms in each case and support your answer.

   a. Chocolate candy bar.
   b. Car batteries.
   c. Panty hose.
   d. Castings for truck engines.
   e. A special computer used by manufacturers for control of production equipment.
   f. Inexpensive plastic rainhats.
   g. A digital tape recorder that has achieved specialty-product status.

10. A small company has developed an innovative new spray-on glass cleaner that prevents the buildup of electrostatic dust on computer screens and TVs. Give examples of some low-cost ways the firm might effectively promote its product. Be certain to consider both push and pull approaches.

11. Would promotion be successful in expanding the general demand for: (a) almonds, (b) air travel, (c) golf clubs, (d) walking shoes, (e) high-octane unleaded gasoline, (f) single-serving, frozen gourmet dinners, and (g) bricks? Explain why or why not in each case.

12. Explain how an understanding of the adoption process would help you develop a promotion blend for digital tape recorders, a new consumer electronics product that produces high-quality recordings. Explain why you might change the promotion blend during the course of the adoption process.

13. Explain how opinion leaders affect a firm's promotion planning.

14. Discuss how the adoption curve should be used to plan the promotion blend(s) for a new automobile accessory—an electronic radar system that alerts a driver if he or she is about to change lanes into the path of a car that is passing through a blind spot in the driver's mirrors.

15. If a marketing manager uses the task method to budget for marketing promotions, are competitors' promotion spending levels ignored? Explain your thinking and give an example that supports your point of view.

16. Discuss the potential conflict among the various promotion managers. How could this be reduced?

CREATING MARKETING PLANS

The Marketing Plan Coach software on the text website (and on the optional Student CD) includes a sample marketing plan for Hillside Veterinary Clinic. Look through the "Marketing Strategy" section.

a. What are Hillside's promotion objectives? How do they differ for the various goods and services the company offers?

b. Do the promotion activities recommended in the plan fit with the promotion objectives? Create a table to compare them. Label the columns: good/service, promotion objective, and promotion activities.

c. Based on the situation analysis, target market, and intended positioning, recommend other (low-cost) promotion activities for Hillside?

SUGGESTED CASES

18. Whisper Valley Volunteer Fire Department   19. OurPerfectWedding.com

COMPUTER-AIDED PROBLEM

13. SELECTING A COMMUNICATIONS CHANNEL

Helen Troy, owner of three Sound Haus stereo equipment stores, is deciding what message channel (advertising medium) to use to promote her newest store. Her current promotion blend includes direct-mail ads that are effective for reaching her current customers. She also has knowledgeable salespeople who work well with consumers once they're in the store. However, a key objective in opening a new store is to attract new customers. Her best prospects are professionals in the 25–44 age range with incomes over $38,000 a year. But only some of the people in this group are audiophiles who want the top-of-the-line brands she carries. Troy has decided to use local advertising to reach new customers.

Troy narrowed her choice to two advertising media: an FM radio station and a biweekly magazine that focuses on entertainment in her city. Many of the magazine's readers are out-of-town visitors interested in concerts, plays, and restaurants. They usually buy stereo equipment at home. But the magazine's audience research shows that many local professionals do subscribe to the magazine. Troy doesn't think that the objective can be achieved with a single ad. However, she believes that ads in six issues will generate good local awareness with her target market. In addition, the magazine's color format will let her present the prestige image she wants to convey in an ad. She thinks that will help convert aware prospects to buyers. Specialists at a local advertising agency will prepare a high-impact ad for $2,000, and then Troy will pay for the magazine space.

The FM radio station targets an audience similar to Troy's own target market. She knows repeated ads will be needed to be sure that most of her target audience is exposed to her ads. Troy thinks it will take daily ads for several months to create adequate awareness among her target market. The FM station will provide an announcer and prepare a tape of Troy's ad for a one-time fee of $200. All she has to do is tell the station what the message content for the ad should say.

Both the radio station and the magazine gave Troy reports summarizing recent audience research. She decides that comparing the two media in a spreadsheet will help her make a better decision.

a. Based on the data displayed on the initial spreadsheet, which message channel (advertising medium) would you recommend to Troy? Why?

b. The agency that offered to prepare Troy's magazine ad will prepare a fully produced radio ad—including a musical jingle—for $2,500. The agency claims that its musical ad will have much more impact than the ad the radio station will create. The agency says its ad should produce the same results as the station ad with 20 percent fewer insertions. If the agency claim is correct, would it be wise for Troy to pay the agency to produce the ad?

c. The agency will not guarantee that its custom-produced radio ad will reach Troy's objective—making 80 percent of the prospects aware of the new store. Troy wants to see how lower levels of awareness—between 50 percent and 70 percent—would affect the advertising cost per buyer and the cost per aware prospect. Use the analysis feature to vary the percent of prospects who become aware. Prepare a table showing the effect on the two kinds of costs. What are the implications of your analysis?

For additional questions related to this problem, see Exercise 13-3 in the *Learning Aid for Use with Essentials of Marketing,* 12th edition.

14

Personal Selling and Customer Service

As a student in the College of Business at the University of Illinois, Pooja Gupta wanted a job that would offer interesting challenges, give opportunities for professional growth, and value her enthusiasm. She found what she wanted with Ferguson. Ferguson was actively recruiting on college campuses to find the brightest and best candidates for its sales jobs—so, in a way, the job found her.

Gupta knew that motivated young people often find the best opportunities in fast-growing companies. She didn't expect, however, that her fast-growing company would be a wholesaler of plumbing supplies, pipes, valves, and fittings. To the contrary, she'd heard that many wholesalers were declining. But that didn't apply to Ferguson. For decades it has doubled in size about every five years—and now it's the largest distributor of plumbing products in the United States. And in a business that serves such a wide variety of customer types—large industrial firms, city waterworks, commercial builders and subcontractors, kitchen and bath dealers, and final consumers—you don't get that kind of growth without an effective sales force.

It's Ferguson's sales force that gets the initial orders with new customers, builds the relationships that instill customer loyalty, and provides the customer service support that Ferguson emphasizes. What's more, salespeople at Ferguson are real experts. They understand their customers' business problems and how Ferguson's products, e-commerce, and state-of-the-art logistics systems can help solve them. An effective sales force like the one at Ferguson doesn't just happen. Someone needs to figure out the promotion jobs that require personal selling and then get the right people on the job. As the president of the company put it, "In a time when computer interfaces often replace face-to-face contact and a handshake, and quality is sacrificed for convenience, Ferguson remains committed to our long-standing philosophy. We never settle for less than the best in products, in customer service provided, and in the associates who are the Ferguson team." Ferguson's growth is a tribute to that philosophy.

The strength of Ferguson's parent company, Wolseley PLC, also contributes to the overall success of Ferguson's sales force. Wolseley is an international business that operates in 27 countries, has 63,000 employees, and recently had annual sales over $33 billion. Wolseley focuses on distribution of construction products, so approaches that prove successful in one of its businesses are transferred to others.

Ferguson carries over a million products, provides service centers at almost 1,400 locations, and has divisions that specialize by different customer segments. It would be futile for sales reps to try to be expert in everything. Instead, sales managers carefully match each salesperson to particular

territories, customers, and product lines. Gupta, for example, helps contractors in the Virginia market figure out how to satisfy the needs of final consumers for whom they are building or remodeling homes. She knows the current fashions for kitchen and bath renovations, how to reduce "behind-the-wall" plumbing installation costs for a big new apartment building, and the advantages and limitations of hundreds of brands from companies like Kohler, Elkay, Moen, and Jacuzzi. Other Ferguson salespeople work with cities and huge waterworks contractors on infrastructure projects such as updating water purification facilities. And salespeople for Ferguson's Integrated Systems Division (ISD) are really selling a big business idea rather than "pipe." They show top executives at customer firms why they should invest millions of dollars in a full-service supply relationship where Ferguson does all of the purchasing and warehousing for entire manufacturing facilities. In stark contrast, the main sales job in one of Ferguson's new self-service Xpress outlets is to ring up sales when hurried plumbers need repair parts.

To recruit talented people for these varied jobs, Ferguson's sales managers use a wide variety of methods. For example, the careers section of Ferguson's website collects job applicant profiles on an ongoing basis. When a position opens up, qualified candidates are notified. And Ferguson actively recruits on college campuses, hiring about 700 graduates every year. After a pre-interview on campus, candidates go to a regional office and meet a number of managers from that area. After the best people are selected, Ferguson provides the sales training to make them even better. Of course, the training is different for different people. For example, most new college recruits work for a short time in a Ferguson warehouse, which helps them understand the company's logistics system, its products, and its industry as well as the company's "can-do" culture. Other training methods range from self-study computer modules to role playing to working in the field with experienced managers who help them build professional problem-solving skills as well as technical knowledge. Even experienced sales reps need ongoing training on new strategies or policies.

To be sure that each salesperson is highly motivated, Ferguson's sales managers must make certain that sales compensation arrangements and benefits reward salespeople for producing needed results. For example, the evaluation considers how well individuals work with others on a team—because in the customer-service culture at Ferguson great teamwork is critical.[1]

Producers who rely on merchant wholesalers or e-commerce to obtain widespread distribution often use missionary salespeople. The sales rep can give a promotion boost to a product that otherwise wouldn't get much attention because it's just one of many. A missionary salesperson for Vicks' cold remedy products, for example, might visit pharmacists during the cold season and encourage them to use a special end-of-aisle display for Vicks' cough syrup—and then help set it up. The wholesaler that supplies the drugstore would benefit from any increased sales but might not take the time to urge use of the special display.

An imaginative missionary salesperson can double or triple sales for a company. Naturally, this doesn't go unnoticed. Missionary sales jobs are often a route to order-oriented jobs.

Technical specialists are experts who know product applications

Technical specialists are supporting salespeople who provide technical assistance to order-oriented salespeople. Technical specialists are often science or engineering graduates with the know-how to understand the customer's applications and explain the advantages of the company's product. They are usually more skilled in showing the technical details of their product than in trying to persuade customers to buy it. Before the specialist's visit, an order getter probably has stimulated interest. The technical specialist provides the details.

Customer service reps solve problems after a purchase

Customer service reps work with customers to resolve problems that arise with a purchase, usually after the purchase has been made. Unlike other supporting sales activities, which are needed only in certain selling situations, *every* marketing-oriented company needs good people to handle customer service. Customer service is important to both business customers and final consumers. There are times when a customer's problem simply can't be resolved without a personal touch.

In general, all types of personal selling help to win customers, but effective customer service is especially critical in keeping them. It is often the key to building repeat business. It's useful to think of customer service reps as *the salespeople who promote a customer's next purchase—by being sure that the customer is satisfied with a previous purchase*. In this chapter, you'll see that the strategy decisions for customer service reps are the same as for others involved in personal selling. In spite of this, some firms don't view customer service as a personal selling activity—or as part of the firm's integrated marketing communications. They manage it as a production operation where output consists of responses to questions from "problem customers." That approach is one reason that customer service is often a problem area for firms. So, it's useful to take a closer look at why customer service activities are so important and why firms should manage them as part of the personal selling effort.

La vida es móvil. Móvil es Vodafone.

Llegó la hora de llamar a Mi País por sólo 18 cént./min.

vodafone

Spain has one of Europe's fastest-growing immigrant populations, with more than 600,000 foreigners arriving annually. To help increase its share of this fast-growing target market, cell-phone operator Vodafone has set up customer service hotlines with representatives who can communicate in 11 languages, from Arabic to Romanian.

Another successful store opening.

See you bright and early.

From ground breaking to grand opening, we're there for you. In fact, we pretty much camp out, working with store designers, construction crews, electricians and your staff to make sure that on your big opening day, everything works. To put us to work for you, call 1-800-960-1190.

HOBART

Solid equipment. Sound advice.

When a customer firm, like a supermarket chain, buys Hobart equipment for a new store, Hobart people are there every step of the way to be certain that the customer's needs are met.

CUSTOMER SERVICE PROMOTES THE NEXT PURCHASE

Customer service is not the product

People sometimes use the term *customer service* as a catch-all expression for anything that helps customers. Our focus here is on the service that is required *to solve a problem that a customer encounters with a purchase*. In that regard, it is useful to think about the difference between customer service and the service (or support) that is part of the product that a customer buys.

In Chapter 8, we discussed the idea that a firm's product is its need-satisfying offering, and that it may be a physical good, a service, or a combination of the two. See Exhibit 8–2. Wells Fargo offers consumers credit card services for a fee. Wolf Camera makes prints from customers' digital images. Dell sells computer hardware and software that is supported with telephone or website technical support for some period of time after the purchase. In all of these situations, customers see service as an important aspect of what they are purchasing.

However, from a customer's perspective, that kind of service is different from the customer service that is required to fix a problem when something doesn't work as the customer hopes or expects. For example, our customer doesn't expect the Wells Fargo ATM to eat her credit card when she's on a trip, doesn't want Wolf to charge more than the advertised price for her pictures, and isn't planning on Dell sending the wrong computer. These problems are breakdowns in the firms' marketing mixes. What the customer expected from the seller is not what the customer got.

When a customer service rep works to solve a customer's problem, it often involves taking steps to remedy what went wrong. But repairing a negative experience is fundamentally different from providing a positive experience in the first place. No matter how effective the customer service solution, the problem is an inconvenience or involves other types of costs to the customer. Thus, the customer value from the firm's marketing mix is lower than what the customer bargained for. Often it's also less than the value the firm *intended* to provide.

Why customer service is part of promotion

We mentioned before that customers weigh negative experiences more heavily than positive experiences when they decide whether to buy the same product (or from the same company) again. They are also more likely to tell other people about bad experiences with a company than about good ones. The practical matter is that customer service interactions arise because the customer is unhappy. So, if the firm doesn't have an effective way to provide customer service, it is, consciously or unconsciously, making a decision to kiss that customer good-bye. In today's highly competitive markets, that can be a big mistake, especially in situations where it's costly to acquire new customers or when the lifetime value of a customer is significant. Poor customer service reduces the firm's customer equity.

This is why firms should view customer service reps as a key part of personal selling. They are not just fixing the customer's problem, but rather fixing the company's problem, which is the risk of losing customers.

Customer service reps are customer advocates

A breakdown in any element of the marketing mix can result in a requirement for customer service. Ideally, a firm should deliver what it promises, but marketing is a human process and mistakes do happen. Consider, for example, a customer who decides to use Verizon cell phone service because its ad—or the salesperson at the Radio Shack who sold the phone—said that the first month of service would be free. If Verizon bills the customer for the first month, is it a pricing problem, a promotion problem, or a lack of coordination in the channel? From the customer's perspective, it really doesn't matter. What does matter is that expectations have been dashed. The customer doesn't need explanations or excuses but instead needs an advocate to make things right.

Sometimes the marketing mix is fine, but the customer makes a purchase that is a mistake. Or customers may simply change their minds. Either way, customers usually expect sellers to help fix purchasing errors. Firms need policies about how customer service reps should deal with customer errors. But, most firms simply can't afford to alienate customers, even ones who have made an error, if they expect them to come back in the future. Sometimes the toughest sales job is figuring out how to keep a customer who is unhappy.

Regardless of whether the firm or customer causes the problem, customer service reps need to be effective communicators, have good judgment, and realize that they are advocates not only for their firm but also for its customers. As that implies, the rest of the company needs to be organized to provide the support reps need to fix problems.

THE RIGHT STRUCTURE HELPS ASSIGN RESPONSIBILITY

We have described three sales tasks—order-getting, order-taking, and supporting. A sales manager must organize the sales force so that all the necessary tasks are done well. In many situations, a particular salesperson might be given two, or all three, of these tasks. For example, 10 percent of a particular job may be order-getting, 80 percent order-taking, and the additional 10 percent customer service. On the other hand, organizations are often structured to have different salespeople specializing by different sales tasks and by the target markets they serve.

Sales tasks may be handled by a team

If different people handle different sales tasks, firms often rely on **team selling**—when different people work together on a specific account. Sometimes members of a sales team are not from the sales department at all. If improving the relationship with the customer calls for input from the quality control manager, then that person becomes a part of the team, at least temporarily. Producers of big-ticket items often use team selling. IBM uses team selling to sell information technology solutions for a whole business. Different specialists handle different parts of the job—but the whole team coordinates its efforts to achieve the desired result.

Different target markets need different sales tasks

Sales managers often divide sales force responsibilities based on the type of customer involved. For example, Bigelow—a company that makes quality carpet for homes and office buildings—divided its sales force into groups of specialists. Some Bigelow salespeople call only on architects to help them choose the best type of carpet for new office buildings. These reps know all the technical details, such as how well a certain carpet fiber will wear or its effectiveness in reducing noise from office equipment. Often no sale is involved because the architect only suggests specifications and doesn't actually buy the carpet. Other Bigelow salespeople call on retail carpet

Companies Have Customer Service Nightmares, Too

Not long ago, customers who experienced poor customer service usually had little recourse. They could scream a few curse words at the customer service rep on the other end of the line, complain to some of their friends, or simply suffer in silence and stop buying from the offending firm. Perhaps this was therapeutic for some customers, but that doesn't mean that it helped them resolve the problem. Now, frustrated customers are frequently taking matters into their own hands. In today's wired world, there are a lot of ways for angry customers who have had service nightmares to give the offending company a wake-up call.

Take Mona Shaw. She bought Comcast's Triple Play package of phone, Internet, and cable television service. However, the installer showed up two days late and then didn't even finish the job. Worse, two days later Comcast cut off all her services. Mona went to her local Manassas, Virginia, Comcast office where she waited two hours to speak to a customer service manager before being told the manager had gone home for the day. After stewing about this all weekend—hey, she couldn't watch TV—Shaw returned to Comcast's office on Monday with a hammer, which she used to smash a keyboard and a telephone, before asking, "Have I got your attention now?" Shaw was arrested, though the charges were later dropped. This incident got major play from national media, which certainly didn't help improve Comcast's already bad reputation for customer service.

Even without the benefit of coverage by news media, the Internet gives a motivated customer a way to quickly spread all of the gory details of a bad customer service experience. Michael Whitford used the Consumerist blog and YouTube to tell more than 340,000 people how he felt about Apple's customer service. Apple had refused to fix his under-warranty MacBook computer.

Customer service reps said that liquid had been spilled on it, which Whitford denied. In response to this exchange, Whitford created a homemade video where he explained his problem and then used a sledgehammer to smash his Mac-Book. Four days after posting the video online, Apple contacted him and gave him a brand new computer—after he took down the video.

Dell Computer had a blogger of its own to contend with. Jeff Jarvis wrote about his difficulties with a new Dell laptop on his personal blog, BuzzMachine. He proclaimed to his readers that the computer was a "lemon" and that Dell wasn't doing a good job fixing it. Hundreds of other frustrated Dell customers commented on his blog about similar stories of their own. In light of this outpouring, Jarvis wrote an open letter to Michael Dell encouraging him to read blogs, write blogs, and ask for more customer input. Jarvis must have hit a nerve because Dell acted on Jarvis' suggestions and created a new Direct2Dell site where chief blogger Lionel Menchaca started giving the company a personal face. That improved communications and helped to smooth customer relations—even after some Dell laptops burst into flames because of subpar batteries from a Dell supplier.

Customers love to share their customer service nightmares. So, the best approach is for firms to make sure customers have only "sweet dream" experiences and don't need to contact customer service. But, the reality is that even the best companies sometimes make customer service mistakes. Now these firms have to make extra sure customer service responds well—or they may have their own nightmare after they see their failures documented on a blog or plastered all over the nightly news.[6]

---

stores. These reps encourage the store manager to keep a variety of Bigelow carpets in stock. They also introduce new products, help train the store's salespeople, and try to solve any problems that occur. Bigelow also has a group of customer service reps who are available via a toll-free number. They help final consumers who have purchased carpet but have a problem that the carpet store can't resolve.

Big accounts get special treatment

Very large customers often require special sales efforts—and relationships with them are treated differently. Moen, a maker of plumbing fixtures, has a regular sales force to call on building material wholesalers and an elite **major accounts sales force** that sells directly to large accounts—like Lowe's or other major retail chains that carry plumbing fixtures.

The Clorox sales team responsible for the launch of liquid bleach in the Brazilian market drew on people from R&D, marketing, and sales.

You can see why this sort of special attention is justified when you consider Procter & Gamble's relationship with Wal-Mart. Wal-Mart accounts for one-fourth or more of the total national sales in many of the product categories in which P&G competes. For instance, Wal-Mart sells about one-third of the toothpaste in the United States. If P&G wants to grow its share of the toothpaste market, it has to make certain that it stimulates an effective sales effort with Wal-Mart.

Some salespeople specialize in telephone selling

Some firms have a group of salespeople who specialize in **telemarketing**—using the telephone to "call" on customers or prospects. In Chapter 13, we highlighted the consumer backlash to the use of cold call telemarketing for prospecting. However, the reception to telephone selling in business markets is often quite different.

In business markets, an "inside" sales force can often build profitable relationships with small or hard-to-reach customers the firm might otherwise have to ignore. Telephone selling is also used to extend personal selling efforts to new target markets or increase the frequency of contact with current customers. The big advantage of telephone selling by an inside sales group in these situations is that it saves time and money for the seller, and it gives customers a fast and easy way to solve a purchasing problem. For example, many firms use toll-free incoming telephone lines to make it convenient for customers to call the inside sales force for assistance or to place an order. Telephone contact may supplement a good website; the website provides standard information and an inside salesperson answers specific questions on the phone.

Companies that produce goods and services for final consumers also rely heavily on toll-free telephone lines to give final consumers easy access to customer service reps. In most cases, there is no other practical way for the producer to be sure that retailers are taking care of customers or their problems. A customer service call center provides a way for the producer to get direct feedback from customers—and perhaps find solutions to potential problems.[7]

Sales tasks are done in sales territories

Often companies organize selling tasks on the basis of a **sales territory**—a geographic area that is the responsibility of one salesperson or several working together. A territory might be a region of a country, a state, or part of a city, depending on the market potential. An airplane manufacturer like Boeing might consider a whole country as *part* of a sales territory for one salesperson.

Carefully set territories can reduce travel time and the cost of sales calls. Assigning territories can also help reduce confusion about who has responsibility for a set of sales tasks. Consider the Hyatt Hotel chain. At one time, each hotel had its own salespeople to get bookings for big conferences and business meetings. That meant that people who had responsibility for selecting meeting locations might be called on by sales reps from 20 or 30 different Hyatt hotels. Now, the Hyatt central office divides up responsibility for working with specific accounts; one rep calls on an account and then tries to sell space in the Hyatt facility that best meets the customer's needs.

Sometimes simple geographic division isn't easy. A company may have different products that require very different knowledge or selling skills—even if products sell in the same territory or to the same customer. For example, Du Pont makes special films for hospital X-ray departments as well as chemicals used in laboratory blood tests.

Size of sales force depends on workload

Once the important sales tasks are specified and the responsibilities divided, the sales manager must decide how many salespeople are needed. The first step is estimating how much work can be done by one person in some time period. Then the sales manager can make an educated guess about how many people are required in total, as the following example shows.

For many years, the Parker Jewelry Company was very successful selling its silver jewelry to department and jewelry stores in the southwestern region of the United States. But top managers wanted to expand into the big urban markets in the northeastern states. They realized that most of the work for the first few years would require order getters. They felt that a salesperson would need to call on each account at least once a month to get a share of this competitive business. They estimated that a salesperson could make only five calls a day on prospective buyers and still allow time for travel, waiting, and follow-up on orders that came in. This meant that a sales rep who made calls 20 days a month could handle about 100 stores (5 a day × 20 days).

The managers used a CD-ROM database that included all of the telephone Yellow Pages listings for the country. Then they simply divided the total number of stores by 100 to estimate the number of salespeople needed. This also helped them set up territories—by defining areas that included about 100 stores for each salesperson. Obviously, managers might want to fine-tune this estimate for differences in territories—such as travel time. But the basic approach can be adapted to many different situations.[8]

Some managers forget that over time the right number of salespeople may change as sales tasks change. Then when a problem becomes obvious, they try to change everything in a hurry—a big mistake. Consideration of what type of salespeople and how many should be ongoing. If the sales force needs to be reduced, it doesn't make sense to let a lot of people go all at once, especially when that could be avoided with some planning.

Sometimes technology can substitute for personal selling

Some sales tasks that have traditionally been handled by a person can now be handled effectively and at lower cost by an e-commerce system or other technology. The situation that the firm faces may influence which approach makes the most sense and how many salespeople are really needed. See Exhibit 14–2.

Exhibit 14–2
Examples of Possible Personal Selling Emphasis in Some Different Business-Market Selling Situations

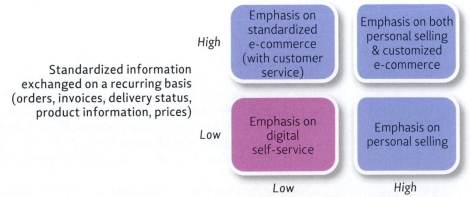

Firms like Avaya are always seeking new ways to help their sales reps stay in touch with customers, even when they are on the road. Sears wants consumers to know that its HomeCentral appliance repairs are provided by qualified service people.

A salesperson is required in important selling situations where there is a need to create and build relationships. Here the salesperson (or customer service rep) focuses on tasks like creative problem solving, persuading, coordinating among people who do different jobs, and finding ways to support the customer. On the other hand, information technology is cost effective for handling needs related to the recurring exchange of standardized information (such as inventory, orders, and delivery status). Similarly, details of product specifications and prices can be organized at a website. Of course, there should be some way to provide good customer service when needs arise. In a complex relationship, using technology for standard information frees the sales rep to spend time on value-added communication.

Digital self-service is not a cure-all

When relationship building by a sales rep is not required, a firm may be able to meet customers' needs best by providing digital self-service. This is the role of ATMs for banks. If the customer needs money at an airport in the middle of the night, the ATM provides better support than the customer could get with a real person at the bank. Many firms provide self-service at websites. A computer shopper at the CompUSA website can answer a few simple questions about how she expects to use a computer, and then software at the website recommends which features are most important and what brands have those features. Similarly, a wholesaler's website might forecast the likely demand for a new product based on responses from retailers to a few questions about their local market areas.

While digital self-service works well in many situations, it has risks when it's used for customer service problems. A customer service rep can be a customer's advocate, but technology can't. The more serious the customer's problem, the less likely it is that digital self-service can resolve it; and a problem can easily escalate when the customer can't get help. For example, it may appear cost-efficient to rely on a telephone menu system that offers customers a series of choices to categorize their problem, but if the process wastes time or doesn't work, customers will be even more frustrated. Worse, the company won't know there's a problem to fix. Personal communication is expensive, but so is the cost of angry ex-customers who couldn't get help when they needed it.

We've focused on technology that substitutes for personal contact by a salesperson. But marketing managers also need to make decisions about providing sales technology support to help salespeople communicate more effectively.

Videoconferencing technology like the TelePresence system from Cisco allows a salesperson (or sales team) to make a sales presentation anywhere in the world.

INFORMATION TECHNOLOGY PROVIDES TOOLS TO DO THE JOB

Changes in how sales tasks are handled

How sales tasks and responsibilities are planned and handled is changing in many companies because of the new sales technology tools that are available. It is usually the sales manager's job—perhaps with help from specialists in technology—to decide what types of tools are needed and how they will be used.

To get a sense of what is involved, consider a day in the life of a sales rep for a large consumer packaged goods firm. Over a hasty breakfast, she plans the day's sales calls on her laptop's organizer, logs onto the company network, and sorts through a dozen e-mail messages she finds there. One is from a buyer for a supermarket chain. Sales in the chain's paper towel category are off 10 percent, and he wants to know if the rep can help. The rep downloads sales trend data for the chain and its competitors from her firm's intranet. A spreadsheet analysis of the data reveals that the sales decline is due to new competition from warehouse clubs. After a videoconference with a brand manager and a company sales promotion specialist to seek advice, she prepares a Power-Point presentation, complete with a proposed shelf-space plan, that recommends that the buyer promote larger-size packages of both her company's and competitors' brands. Before leaving home, the rep e-mails an advance copy of the report to the buyer and her manager. In her car, she calls the buyer to schedule an appointment.[9]

New software and hardware provide a competitive advantage

The sales rep in this example relies on support from an array of software and hardware that wasn't available a decade ago. Software for CRM, spreadsheet sales

Information technology is making the modern sales force more efficient and giving salespeople new ways to meet the needs of their customers while achieving the objectives of their jobs. Salesforce.com is an online solution to sales force automation.

analysis, digital presentations, time management, sales forecasting, customer contact, and shelf-space management is at the salesperson's fingertips. Commonplace hardware includes everything from PDAs with wireless Internet access to personal videoconferencing systems. In many situations, these technologies give sales reps new ways to meet customers' needs while achieving the objectives of their jobs.

These tools change how well the job is done. Yet this is not simply a matter that is best left to individual sales reps. Use of these tools may be necessary just to compete effectively. For example, if a customer expects a sales rep to access data on past sales and provide an updated sales forecast, a sales organization that does not have this capability will be at a real disadvantage in keeping that customer's business.

On the other hand, these tools have costs. There is an obvious expense of buying the technology. But there is also the training cost of keeping everyone up-to-date. Often that is not an easy matter. Some salespeople who have done the sales job well for a long time "the old-fashioned way" resent being told that they have to change what they are doing, even if it's what customers expect. So if a firm expects salespeople to be able to use these technologies, that requirement needs to be included in selecting and training people for the job.[10]

SOUND SELECTION AND TRAINING TO BUILD A SALES FORCE

Selecting good salespeople takes judgment, plus

It is important to hire *well-qualified* salespeople who will do a good job. But selection in many companies is done without serious thought about exactly what kind of person the firm needs. Managers may hire friends and relations, or whoever is available, because they feel that the only qualification for a sales job is a friendly personality. This approach leads to poor sales, lost customers, and costly sales force turnover.

Progressive companies are more careful. They constantly update a list of possible job candidates. They invite applications at the company's website. They schedule candidates for multiple interviews with various executives and do thorough background

Many firms turn to outside specialists, like Caliper, who can help sales managers improve the selection, training, and motivation of their sales reps.

Customers who rent heavy construction equipment want to deal with a knowledgeable salesperson. So CAT selects salespeople who have experience with the applications for which the equipment will be used and gives them training on CAT products and new developments in the market.

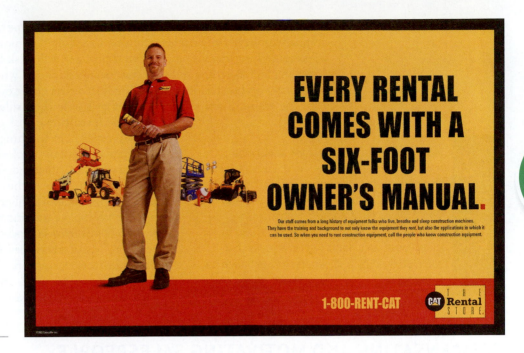

checks. Unfortunately, such techniques don't guarantee success. But a systematic approach based on several different inputs results in a better sales force.

One problem in selecting salespeople is that two different sales jobs with identical titles may involve very different selling or supporting tasks and require different skills. A carefully prepared job description helps avoid this problem.

Job descriptions should be in writing and specific

A **job description** is a written statement of what a salesperson is expected to do. It might list 10 to 20 specific tasks—as well as routine prospecting and sales report writing. Each company must write its own job specifications. And it should provide clear guidelines about what selling tasks the job involves. This is critical to determine the kind of salespeople who should be selected—and later it provides a basis for seeing how they should be trained, how well they are performing, and how they should be paid.

Good salespeople are trained, not born

The idea that good salespeople are born that way may have some truth—but it isn't the whole story. A salesperson needs to be taught about the company and its products, about giving effective sales presentations, and about building relationships with customers. But this isn't always done. Many salespeople do a poor job because they haven't had good training. Firms often hire new salespeople and immediately send them out on the road, or the retail selling floor, with no grounding in the basic selling steps and no information about the product or the customer. They just get a price list and a pat on the back. This isn't enough!

All salespeople need some training

It's up to sales and marketing management to be sure that salespeople know what they're supposed to do and how to do it. Hewlett-Packard Co. recently faced this problem. For years the company was organized into divisions based on different product lines—printers, network servers, and the like. However, sales reps who specialized in the products of one division often couldn't compete well against firms that could offer customers total solutions to computing problems. When a new top executive came in and reorganized the company, all sales reps needed training in their new responsibilities, how they would be organized, and what they should say to their customers about the benefits of the reorganization.

Sales training should be modified based on the experience and skills of the group involved. But the company's sales training program should cover at least the following areas: (1) company policies and practices, (2) product information, (3) building relationships with customer firms, and (4) professional selling skills.

Many companies spend the bulk of their training time on product information and company policy. They neglect training in selling techniques because they think selling is something anyone can do. But training in selling skills can pay off. Estée Lauder, for example, has selling skills for the "beauty advisors" who sell its cosmetics down to a fine art—and its training manual and seminars cover every detail. Its advisors who take the training seriously immediately double their sales.[11] Training can also help salespeople learn how to be more effective in cold calls on new prospects, in listening carefully to identify a customer's real objections, in closing the sale, and in working with customers in difficult customer service situations.

Training often starts in the classroom with lectures, case studies, and videotaped trial presentations and demonstrations. But a complete training program adds on-the-job observation of effective salespeople and coaching from sales supervisors. Many companies also use Web-based training, weekly sales meetings or work sessions, annual conventions, and regular e-mail messages and newsletters, as well as ongoing training sessions, to keep salespeople up-to-date.[12]

Sales managers need to think about what training their salespeople need, but sales reps also need to take the initiative and stay up-to-date on what is happening in the sales profession. *Selling Power* magazine maintains a website at **www.sellingpower.com**. Go to the website and identify several ideas that could be used by a salesperson to enhance his or her skills.

COMPENSATING AND MOTIVATING SALESPEOPLE

To recruit, motivate, and keep good salespeople, a firm has to develop an effective compensation plan. Ideally, sales reps should be paid in such a way that what they want to do—for personal interest and gain—is in the company's interest too. Most companies focus on financial motivation—but public recognition, sales contests, and simple personal recognition for a job well done can be highly effective in encouraging greater sales effort.[13] Our main emphasis here, however, will be on financial motivation.[14]

Two basic decisions must be made in developing a compensation plan: (1) the level of compensation and (2) the method of payment.

To build a competitive sales force, a company must pay at least the going market wage for different kinds of salespeople. To be sure it can afford a specific type of salesperson, the company should estimate—when the job description is written—how valuable such a salesperson will be. A good order getter may be worth $100,000 to one company but only $15,000 to $25,000 to another—just because the second firm doesn't have enough to sell! In such a case, the second company should rethink its job specifications, or completely change its promotion plans, because the going rate for order getters is much higher than $15,000 a year.

If a job requires extensive travel, aggressive pioneering, or customer service contacts with troublesome customers, the pay may have to be higher. But the salesperson's compensation level should compare, at least roughly, with the pay scale of the rest of the firm. Normally, salespeople earn more than the office or production force but less than top management.

Given some competitive level of compensation, there are three basic methods of payment: (1) straight salary, (2) straight commission (incentive), or (3) a combination plan. A straight salary offers the most security for the salesperson. Commission pay, in contrast, offers the most incentive and is tied to results actually achieved. A commission is often based on a percentage of dollar sales, but it may be a financial incentive based on other outcomes—such as the number of new accounts, customer satisfaction ratings, or customer service problems resolved in some time period. Most salespeople want some security, and most companies want salespeople to have some incentive to do better work, so the most popular method is a combination plan that includes some salary and some commission. Bonuses, profit sharing, pensions, stock plans, insurance, and other fringe benefits may be included, too.

Salary gives control—if there is close supervision

A salesperson on straight salary earns the same amount regardless of how he or she spends time. So the salaried salesperson is expected to do what the sales manager asks—whether it is order-taking, supporting sales activities, solving customer service problems, or completing sales call reports. However, the sales manager maintains control *only* by close supervision. As a result, straight salary or a large salary element in the compensation plan increases the amount of sales supervision needed.

Commissions can both motivate and direct

If personal supervision would be difficult, a firm may get better control with a compensation plan that includes some commission, or even a straight commission plan, with built-in direction. One trucking company, for example, has a sales incentive plan that pays higher commissions on business needed to balance freight shipments—depending on how heavily traffic has been moving in one direction or another. Another company that wants to motivate its salespeople to devote more time to developing new accounts could pay higher commissions on shipments to a new customer. However, a salesperson on a straight commission tends to be his or her own boss. The sales manager is less likely to get help on sales activities that won't increase the salesperson's earnings.

An incentive compensation plan can help motivate salespeople, but incentives must be carefully aligned with the firm's objectives. For example, IBM at one time had a sales commission plan that resulted in IBM salespeople pushing customers to buy expensive computers that were more powerful than they needed. The sales reps got sales and increased their income, but later many customers were dissatisfied and switched to other suppliers. Now most IBM sales reps receive incentive pay that is in part based on satisfaction ratings they earn from their customers. Many firms use variations of this approach—because incentives that just focus on short-term sales objectives may not motivate sales reps to develop long-term, need-satisfying relationships with their customers.

Incentives should link efforts to results

The incentive portion of a sales rep's compensation should be large only if there is a direct relationship between the salesperson's efforts and results. Otherwise, a salesperson in a growing territory might have rapidly increasing earnings, while the sales rep in a poor area will have little to show for the same amount of work. Such a situation isn't fair, and it can lead to high turnover and much dissatisfaction. A sales manager can take such differences into consideration when setting a salesperson's **sales quota**—the specific sales or profit objective a salesperson is expected to achieve.

Commissions reduce need for working capital

Small companies that have limited working capital or uncertain markets often prefer straight commission, or combination plans with a large commission element. When sales drop off, costs do too. Such flexibility is similar to using manufacturers' agents who get paid only if they deliver sales. This advantage often dominates in selecting a sales compensation method. Exhibit 14–3 shows the general relation between personal selling expense and sales volume for each of the basic compensation alternatives.

Exhibit 14–3
Relation between Personal Selling Expenses and Sales Volume—for Three Basic Personal Selling Compensation Alternatives

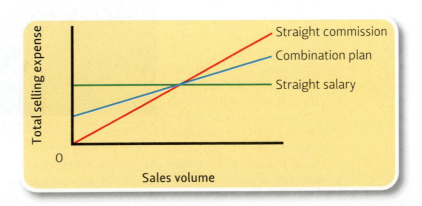

Compensation plans should be clear

Salespeople are likely to be dissatisfied if they can't see the relationship between the results they produce and their pay. A compensation plan that includes different commissions for different products or types of customers can become quite complicated. Simplicity is best achieved with straight salary. But in practice, it's usually better to sacrifice some simplicity to gain some incentive, flexibility, and control. The best combination of these factors depends on the job description and the company's objectives.

To make it easier for a sales rep to see the relationship between effort and compensation, some firms provide the rep with that information online. For example, sales reps at Oracle, a company that sells database systems, can check a website and see how they are doing. As new sales results come in, the report at the website is updated. Sales managers can also make changes quickly—for example, by putting a higher commission on a product or more weight on customer satisfaction scores.[15]

Sales managers must plan, implement, and control

Managers must regularly evaluate each salesperson's performance and be certain that all the needed tasks are being done well. The compensation plan may have to be changed if the pay and work are out of line. And by evaluating performance, firms can also identify areas that need more attention—by the salesperson or management.[16]

PERSONAL SELLING TECHNIQUES—PROSPECTING AND PRESENTING

We've stressed the importance of training in selling techniques. Now let's discuss these ideas in more detail so you understand the basic steps each salesperson should follow—including prospecting and selecting target customers, planning sales presentations, making sales presentations, and following up after the sale. Exhibit 14–4 shows the steps we'll consider. You can see that the salesperson is just carrying out a planned communication process, as we discussed in Chapter 13.[17]

Prospecting—narrowing down to the right target

Narrowing the personal selling effort down to the right target requires constant, detailed analysis of markets and much prospecting. Basically, **prospecting** involves following all the leads in the target market to identify potential customers.

Finding live prospects who will help make the buying decision isn't as easy as it sounds. In business markets, for example, the salesperson may need to do some hard detective work to find the real purchase decision makers.

Some companies provide prospect lists or a customer relationship management (CRM) database to make this part of the selling job

Salespeople are constantly looking for ways to be more efficient in identifying sales leads and prospects.

Exhibit 14–4
Key Steps in the
Personal Selling Process

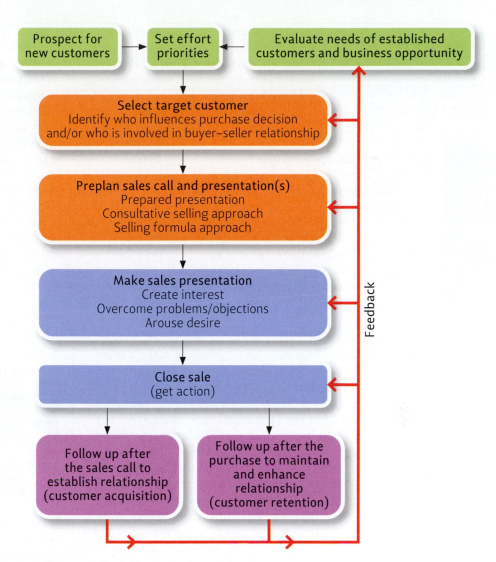

easier. The CRM database may be integrated with other marketing communication tools to help salespeople spend more time working on the best prospects. Thought-Lava, a website design firm, uses its CRM database to initially contact prospects by e-mail. It uses software that tracks which prospects open the e-mail, which click through to the firm's website, and even which pages they visit. Given this information, ThoughtLava's salespeople know in advance which of the firm's services interest each prospect, and that helps them decide which prospects to focus on.[18]

All customers are not equal

While prospecting focuses on identifying new customers, established customers require attention too. It's often time-consuming and expensive to establish a relationship with a customer, so once established it makes sense to keep the relationship healthy. That requires the rep to routinely review active accounts, rethink customers' needs, and reevaluate each customer's long-term business potential. Some small accounts may have the potential to become big accounts, and some accounts that previously required a lot of costly attention may no longer warrant it. So a sales rep may need to set priorities both for new prospects and existing customers.

How long to spend with whom?

Once a set of prospects and customers who need attention have been identified, the salesperson must decide how much time to spend with each one. A sales rep must qualify customers—to see if they deserve more effort. The salesperson usually makes these decisions by weighing the potential sales volume as well as the likelihood of a sale. This requires judgment. But well-organized salespeople usually develop some system because they have too many demands on their time.[19]

Many firms provide their reps with CRM systems to help with this process also. Most of them use some grading scheme. A sales rep might estimate how much each prospect is likely to purchase and the probability of getting and keeping the business given the competition. The computer then combines this information and grades each prospect. Attractive accounts may be labeled A—and the salesperson may plan to call on them weekly until the sale is made, the relationship is in good shape, or the customer is moved into a lower category. B customers might offer somewhat lower potential and be called on monthly. C accounts might be called on only once a year—unless they happen to contact the salesperson. And D accounts might be transferred to a telemarketing group.[20]

Three kinds of sales presentations may be useful

Once the salesperson selects a target customer, it's necessary to make a **sales presentation**—a salesperson's effort to make a sale or address a customer's problem. But someone has to plan what kind of sales presentation to make. This is a strategy decision. The kind of presentation should be set before the sales rep goes calling. And in situations where the customer comes to the salesperson—in a retail store, for instance—planners have to make sure that prospects are brought together with salespeople.

A marketing manager can choose two basically different approaches to making sales presentations: the prepared approach or the consultative selling approach. Another approach, the selling formula approach, is a combination of the two. Each of these has its place.

IT'S TIME TO GET HUMAN AGAIN!

Electronic communication is a great way to conduct business BUT RELATIONSHIPS DRIVE BUSINESS RESULTS.

Learn to connect with your fellow humans with Dale Carnegie Training— the original and still the best resource for developing the people side of business.

To find your nearest Dale Carnegie Training office, please call: 800-231-5800 ext. 202 or visit us online at: www.dalecarnegie.com

DALE CARNEGIE® TRAINING

Many firms turn to outside training specialists, like Dale Carnegie Training, for programs that can help salespeople learn how to connect with customers.

The prepared sales presentation

The **prepared sales presentation** approach uses a memorized presentation that is not adapted to each individual customer. This approach says that a customer faced with a particular stimulus will give the desired response—in this case, a yes answer to the salesperson's prepared statement, which includes a **close**, the salesperson's request for an order.

If one trial close doesn't work, the sales rep tries another prepared presentation and attempts another closing. This can go on for some time—until the salesperson runs out of material or the customer either buys or decides to leave. Exhibit 14–5 shows the relative participation of the salesperson and customer in the prepared approach. Note that the salesperson does most of the talking.

Firms may rely on this canned approach when only a short presentation is practical. It's also sensible when salespeople aren't very skilled. The company can control what they say and in what order. For example, Novartis uses missionary salespeople to tell doctors about new drugs when they're introduced. Doctors are busy, so they only give

Exhibit 14–5
Prepared Approach to
Sales Presentation

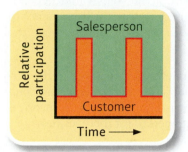

Exhibit 14–6
Consultative Selling
Approach to Sales
Presentation

Exhibit 14–7
Selling Formula
Approach to Sales
Presentation

the rep a minute or two. That's just enough time to give a short, prepared pitch and leave some samples. To get the most out of the presentation, Novartis refines it based on feedback from doctors whom it pays to participate in focus groups.[21]

But a canned approach has a weakness. It treats all potential customers alike. It may work for some and not for others. A prepared approach may be suitable for simple order-taking—but it is no longer considered good selling for complicated situations.

Consultative selling—builds on the marketing concept

The **consultative selling approach** involves developing a good understanding of the individual customer's needs before trying to close the sale. This name is used because the salesperson is almost acting as a consultant to help identify and solve the customer's problem. With this approach, the sales rep makes some general benefit statements to get the customer's attention and interest. Then the salesperson asks questions and *listens carefully* to understand the customer's needs. Once they agree on needs, the seller tries to show the customer how the product fills those needs and to close the sale. This is a problem-solving approach—in which the customer and salesperson work together to satisfy the customer's needs. That's why it's sometimes called the need-satisfaction approach. Exhibit 14–6 shows the participation of the customer and the salesperson during such a sales presentation.

The consultative selling approach takes skill and time. The salesperson must be able to analyze what motivates a particular customer and show how the company's offering would help the customer satisfy those needs. The sales rep may even conclude that the customer's problem is really better solved with someone else's product. That might result in one lost sale, but it also is likely to build real trust and more sales opportunities over the life of the relationship with the customer. That's why this kind of selling is typical in business markets when a salesperson already has established a close relationship with a customer.

Selling formula approach—some of both

The **selling formula approach** starts with a prepared presentation outline—much like the prepared approach—and leads the customer through some logical steps to a final close. The prepared steps are logical because we assume that we know something about the target customer's needs and attitudes.

Exhibit 14–7 shows the selling formula approach. The salesperson does most of the talking at the beginning of the presentation—to communicate key points early. This part of the presentation may even have been prepared as part of the marketing strategy. As the sales presentation moves along, however, the salesperson brings the customer into the discussion to help clarify just what needs this customer has. The salesperson's job is to discover the needs of a particular customer to know how to proceed. Once it is clear what kind of customer this is, the salesperson comes back to show how the product satisfies this specific customer's needs and to close the sale.

AIDA helps plan sales presentations

AIDA—Attention, Interest, Desire, Action: Most sales presentations follow this AIDA sequence. The time a sales rep spends on each of the steps varies depending on the situation and the selling approach being used. But it is still necessary to begin a presentation by getting the prospect's *attention* and, hopefully, to move the customer to *action*.[22]

Ethical issues may arise

As in every other area of marketing communications, ethical issues arise in the personal selling area. The most basic issue, plain and simple, is whether a salesperson's presentation is honest and truthful. But addressing that issue is a no-brainer. No company is served well by a salesperson who lies or manipulates customers to get their business.

Ethics QUESTION

Assume that you are a sales rep and sell costly electronic systems used in automated factories. You made a sales presentation to a customer, but he didn't place an order—and then wouldn't take your calls when you tried to inform him that your company was coming out with a more reliable model at the same price. Months later, he faxes a purchase order for immediate delivery on the model you originally discussed. You have the old model in stock, and it will be difficult to sell once the new model arrives in two weeks. Do you try to contact the customer again to tell him about the new model, or do you do what he has requested and immediately fill the order with the old model? Either way, if you make the sale, the commission will pay for your upcoming vacation to the Caribbean. Explain what you would do and why.

On the other hand, most sales reps sooner or later face a sales situation in which they must make more difficult ethical decisions about how to balance company interests, customer interests, and personal interests. Conflicts are less likely to arise if the firm's marketing mix really meets the needs of its target market. Similarly, they are less likely to occur when the firm sees the value of developing a longer-term relationship with the customer. Then the salesperson is arranging a happy marriage. By contrast, ethical conflicts are more likely when the sales rep's personal outcomes (such as commission income) or the selling firm's profits hinge on making sales to customers whose needs are only partially met by the firm's offering. A number of financial services firms, for example, have garnered bad publicity—and even legal problems—from situations like this.

Ideally, companies can avoid the whole problem by supporting their salespeople with a marketing mix that really offers target customers unique benefits. Moreover, top executives, marketing managers, and sales managers set the tone for the ethical climate in which a salesperson operates. If they set impossible goals or project a "do-what-you-need-to-do" attitude, a desperate salesperson may yield to the pressure of the moment. When a firm clearly advocates ethical selling behavior and makes it clear that manipulative selling techniques are not acceptable, the salesperson is not left trying to swim "against the flow."[23]

CONCLUSION

In this chapter, we discussed the importance and nature of personal selling. Selling is much more than just getting rid of the product. In fact, a salesperson who is not given strategy guidelines may have to become the strategy planner for the market he or she serves. Ideally, however, the sales manager and marketing manager work together to set some strategy guidelines: the kind and number of salespeople needed, what sales technology support will be provided, the kind of sales presentation desired, and selection, training, and motivation approaches.

We discussed the three basic sales tasks: (1) order-getting, (2) order-taking, and (3) supporting. Most sales jobs combine at least two of these three tasks. We also consider the role of customer service and why it is so important to a firm and its customers. Once a firm specifies the important tasks, it can decide on the structure of its sales organization and the number of salespeople it needs. The nature of the job and the level and method of compensation also depend on the blend of these tasks. Firms should develop a job description for each sales job. This, in turn, provides guidelines for selecting, training, and compensating salespeople.

Once the marketing manager agrees to the basic plan and sets the budget, the sales manager must implement the plan, including directing and controlling the sales force. This includes assigning sales territories and control-

ling performance. You can see that the sales manager has more to do than jet around the country sipping martinis and entertaining customers. A sales manager is deeply involved with the basic management tasks of planning and control—as well as ongoing implementation of the personal selling effort.

We also reviewed some basic selling techniques and identified three kinds of sales presentations. Each has its place—but the consultative selling approach seems best for higher-level sales jobs. In these kinds of jobs, personal selling is achieving a new, professional status because of the competence and level of personal responsibility required of the salesperson. The day of the old-time glad-hander is passing in favor of the specialist who is creative, industrious, persuasive, knowledgeable, highly trained, and therefore able to help the buyer. This type of salesperson always has been, and probably always will be, in short supply. And the demand for high-level salespeople is growing.

KEY TERMS

basic sales tasks, 353

order getters, 353

order-getting, 353

order takers, 354

order-taking, 354

supporting salespeople, 355

missionary salespeople, 355

technical specialists, 356

customer service reps, 356

team selling, 358

major accounts sales force, 359

telemarketing, 360

sales territory, 360

job description, 365

sales quota, 367

prospecting, 368

sales presentation, 370

prepared sales presentation, 370

close, 370

consultative selling approach, 371

selling formula approach, 371

QUESTIONS AND PROBLEMS

1. What strategy decisions are needed in the personal selling area? Why should the marketing manager make these strategy decisions?

2. What kind of salesperson (or what blend of the basic sales tasks) is required to sell the following products? If there are several selling jobs in the channel for each product, indicate the kinds of salespeople required. Specify any assumptions necessary to give definite answers.
   a. Laundry detergent.
   b. Costume jewelry.
   c. Office furniture.
   d. Men's underwear.
   e. Mattresses.
   f. Corn.
   g. Life insurance.

3. Distinguish among the jobs of producers', wholesalers', and retailers' order-getting salespeople. If one order getter is needed, must all the salespeople in a channel be order getters? Illustrate.

4. Discuss the role of the manufacturers' agent in a marketing manager's promotion plans. What kind of salesperson is a manufacturers' agent? What type of compensation plan is used for a manufacturers' agent?

5. Discuss the future of the specialty shop if producers place greater emphasis on mass selling because of the inadequacy of retail order-taking.

6. Compare and contrast missionary salespeople and technical specialists.

7. Think about a situation when you or a friend or family member encountered a problem with a purchase and tried

to get help from a firm's customer service representative. Briefly describe the problem, how the firm handled it, and what you think about the firm's response. How could it have been improved?

8. Would it make sense for your school to have a person or group whose main job is to handle "customer service" problems? Explain your thinking.

9. A firm that produces mixes for cakes, cookies, and other baked items has an incoming toll-free line for customer service calls. The manager of the customer service reps has decided to base about a third of their pay on the number of calls they handle per month and on the average amount of time on the phone with each customer. What do you think are the benefits and limitations of this incentive pay system? What would you recommend to improve it?

10. Explain how a compensation plan could be developed to provide incentives for experienced salespeople and

yet make some provision for trainees who have not yet learned the job.

11. Cite an actual local example of each of the three kinds of sales presentations discussed in the chapter. Explain for each situation whether a different type of presentation would have been better.

12. Are the benefits and limitations of a canned presentation any different if it is supported with a PowerPoint presentation or DVD than if it is just a person talking? Why or why not?

13. Describe a consultative selling sales presentation that you experienced recently. How could it have been improved by fuller use of the AIDA framework?

14. How would our economy operate if personal salespeople were outlawed? Could the economy work? If so, how? If not, what is the minimum personal selling effort necessary? Could this minimum personal selling effort be controlled by law?

CREATING MARKETING PLANS

The Marketing Plan Coach software on the text website (and on the optional Student CD) includes a sample marketing plan for Hillside Veterinary Clinic. Look through the "Marketing Strategy" section.

a. What personal selling tasks are performed at Hillside Veterinary Clinic and who does them?

b. If Hillside wanted to put more emphasis on "order-getting" to promote growth, what ideas do you have for how to do it?

c. Based on the situation analysis, target market, and intended positioning, recommend some ways that Hillside could actively work to improve its reputation for customer service.

SUGGESTED CASES

12. DrRay.com   21. Advanced Materials, Inc.   23. West Side Furniture   28. PCT, Inc.

COMPUTER-AIDED PROBLEM

14. SALES COMPENSATION

Franco Welles, sales manager for Nanek, Inc., is trying to decide whether to pay a sales rep for a new territory with straight commission or a combination plan. He wants to evaluate possible plans—to compare the compensation costs and profitability of each. Welles knows that sales reps in similar jobs at other firms make about $36,000 a year.

The sales rep will sell two products. Welles is planning a higher commission for Product B—because he wants it to get extra effort. From experience with similar products, he has some rough estimates of expected sales volume under the different plans and various ideas about commission rates. The details are found in the spreadsheet. The program computes compensation and how much the sales rep will contribute to profit. "Profit contribution" is equal to the total revenue

generated by the sales rep minus sales compensation costs and the costs of producing the units.

a. For the initial values shown in the spreadsheet, which plan—commission or combination—would give the rep the highest compensation, and which plan would give the greatest profit contribution to Nanek, Inc.?

b. Welles thinks a sales rep might be motivated to work harder and sell 1,100 units of Product B if the commission rate (under the commission plan) were increased to 10 percent. If Welles is right (and everything else stays the same), would the higher commission rate be a good deal for Nanek? Explain your thinking.

c. A sales rep interested in the job is worried about making payments on her new car. She asks if Welles would consider paying her with a combination plan but with more guaranteed income (an $18,000 base salary) in return for taking a 3 percent commission on Products B and A. If this arrangement results in the same unit sales as Welles originally estimated for the combination plan, would Nanek, Inc., be better off or worse off under this arrangement?

d. Do you think the rep's proposal will meet Welles' goals for Product B? Explain your thinking.

For additional questions related to this problem, see Exercise 14-3 in the *Learning Aid for Use with Essentials of Marketing*, 12th edition.

15
CHAPTER

Advertising and Sales Promotion

In the summer of 1965, 17-year-old Fred DeLuca was trying to figure out how to pay for college. A family friend suggested that Fred open a sandwich shop—and then the friend invested $1,000 to help get it started. Within a month, they opened their first sandwich shop. From that humble start grew the Subway franchise chain with over 29,000 outlets in 86 countries.

Targeted advertising and sales promotion have been important to Subway's growth. For 10 years, memorable Subway ads featured Jared Fogle, a college student who was overweight but lost 245 pounds by only eating Subway's low-fat sandwiches, like the "Veggie Delite." Jared says it was a fluke that he ended up in Subway's ads. After all, he was recruited to do the ads because of good publicity that Subway got after national media picked up a story that Jared's friend wrote about him in a college newspaper. On the other hand, Subway's strategy at that time focused on its line of seven different sandwiches with under 6 grams of fat. The objective was to set Subway apart from other fast food, position it to appeal to health-conscious eaters, and spark new sales growth. Jared already knew he liked Subway sandwiches, but the "7 under 6" promotion inspired him to incorporate them into his diet.

As soon as Jared's ads began to run, word of his inspiring story spread and consumer awareness of Subway and its healthy fare increased. It's always hard to isolate the exact impact of ads on sales, but sales grew more than 18 percent that year. Another benefit was that the ads attracted attention from potential franchisees. Many of them followed up by requesting the franchise brochure, which explains how Subway's strategy works and why it is profitable for franchisees. For instance, it describes how franchisees elect a group to help manage advertising and media buying decisions—so that Subway outlets get the most return from their advertising dollars. Subway headquarters also supports franchisees by providing materials and guidance for the local advertising and sales promotion they do to reach their own target customers.

Local franchisees often work together to develop their own promotions. For example, groups in Buffalo, New York, and Seattle developed a text messaging promotion. Signs in stores promise a free six-inch sub—and messages about sandwich deals—to customers who sign up at MySubwayMobile.com. Thousands of customers registered and now receive text message offers on their mobile phones. This program helps generate business at otherwise slow times for sub shops. For example, to bring customers in on days with bad weather, Subway sends out a text message with a "buy one get one free" offer.

Subway tries to balance its menu and promotion to appeal to two different segments: customers interested in low fat *and* those most concerned about taste. Subway counters high-end fare from Panera Bread and Quiznos Sub with its "Subway Selects" line of sandwiches made with zesty sauces and special breads. They were introduced with a bilingual campaign developed by the Messner Vetere ad agency. The ads' "Eat fresh" theme and images provided a copy thrust that appealed to both target markets. Subway also gets cooperative promotional support from Coca-Cola now that it has taken over as the exclusive soft-drink supplier for all Subway outlets.

Subway recognizes that it needs to vary its creative approaches to get its message out to different target markets. For example, young men age 18 to 34 are heavy purchasers of fast food and they appreciate bargains. Many guys in this group are big on video games. So Subway placed ads promoting its $2.49 daily specials on a virtual billboard in a popular online action game. Subway also teamed with the TV show "Family Guy," which also targets this segment, to develop an online game and television ads using characters from the popular animated show.

Subway includes many other elements in its promotion blend. For example, Subway made Jared available to help people keep New Year's resolutions to lose weight. Dieters who signed up at Subway's website received recorded phone calls from Jared that encouraged them to eat healthy and stay active. The website also provides tips on dieting and exercise as well as nutritional details about Subway sandwiches. These details help consumers who want all the health-related facts. The available information makes sense in light of the scrutiny the Federal Trade Commission gives to firms that make promotional claims related to weight loss and health.

Subway also leveraged its healthy fast-food positioning and stepped up efforts to combat childhood obesity and increase sales to kids and teens.

Subway's F.R.E.S.H. Steps promotion encourages kids and their parents to "Feel Responsible, Energized, Satisfied, and Happy." A television advertising campaign let parents and kids know how to make healthy eating choices and live a more active lifestyle. As a national sponsor of Little League Baseball and Softball, Subway advertises in *Little League* magazine and targets little leaguers and their parents via direct mail and with point-of-sale materials. Subway also teamed up with Discovery Kids cable TV where it told kids 6 to 12 years old to "play hard and fresh." This promotion included tie-ins with the network's *Endurance* show, where kids compete in outdoor activities. Subway developed an online Endurance game, a sweepstakes to win extreme sports vacation trips, and a Kids Pack meal that includes toys promoting outdoor activities.

Subway is in a very competitive, dynamic market. More change is sure to come. But so far, Subway has achieved profitable growth with a targeted strategy that includes effective use of promotion.[1]

ADVERTISING, SALES PROMOTION, AND MARKETING STRATEGY PLANNING

Advertising and sales promotion can play a central role in the promotion blend. On a per-contact basis, these promotion methods provide a relatively low-cost way to inform, persuade, and activate customers. Advertising and sales promotion can position a firm's marketing mix as the one that meets customer needs. They can help motivate channel members or a firm's own employees, as well as final customers.

Unfortunately the results that marketers *actually achieve* with advertising and sales promotion are very uneven. It's often said that half of the money spent on these activities is wasted—but that most managers don't know which half. Mass selling can be exciting and involving, or it can be downright obnoxious. Sometimes it's based on careful research, yet much of it is based on someone's pet idea. A creative idea may produce great results or be a colossal waste of money. Ads may stir emotions or go unnoticed.

This chapter explains approaches to help you understand how successful advertising and sales promotion works. See Exhibit 15–1. After a brief overview of the cost of advertising, we look at the different decisions marketing managers—and the advertising agencies they may work with—have to make: (1) advertising objectives and what they want to achieve, (2) who the target audience is, (3) what kind of advertising to use, (4) which media to use to reach target customers, (5) what to say (the copy thrust), and (6) who will do the work—the firm's own marketing or advertising people or outside agencies. We also discuss legal issues in advertising.

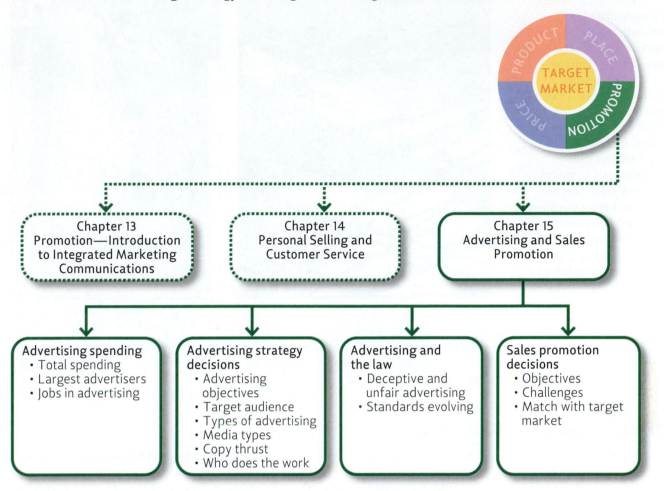

There are challenges in managing sales promotion, but it offers advantages over advertising for some objectives. So, this chapter also presents decisions that must be made with respect to different types of sales promotion for different targets.

International dimensions are important

The basic strategy planning decisions for advertising and sales promotion are the same regardless of where in the world the target market is located. However, the look and feel of advertising and sales promotion vary a lot in different countries. The choices available to a marketing manager within each of the decision areas may also vary dramatically from one country to another.

Commercial television may not be available. If it is, government rules may limit the type of advertising permitted or when ads can be shown. Radio broadcasts in a market area may not be in the target market's language. The target audience may not be able to read. Access to interactive media like the Internet may be nonexistent. Cultural influences may limit ad messages. Ad agencies who already know a nation's unique advertising environment may not be available.

International dimensions also impact sales promotion. Trade promotion may be difficult, or even impossible, to manage. A typical Japanese grocery retailer with only 250 square feet of space, for example, doesn't have room for *any* special end-of-aisle displays. Consumer promotions may be affected, too. In some developing nations, samples can't be distributed through the mail, because they're routinely stolen before they get to target customers. And some countries ban consumer sweepstakes because they see them as a form of gambling.

Traditional media choices are more limited in some international markets, so marketers like Procter & Gamble (P&G) must be creative to communicate their messages. In Thailand, P&G used a large green comb installed near the top of a 13-foot-high utility pole to promote its Rejoice conditioners. The tagline on the comb says, "Tangles? Switch to Rejoice conditioners." Air New Zealand developed an eye-catching 3-D wallscape featuring a kayak going over a waterfall to promote its travel services.

In this chapter we'll consider a number of these international issues, but we'll focus on the array of choices available in the United States and other advanced economies.[2]

ADVERTISING IS BIG BUSINESS

Total spending is big—and growing internationally

As an economy grows, advertising becomes more important—because more consumers have income and advertising can get results. But good advertising results cost money. And spending on advertising is significant. In 1946, U.S. advertising spending was slightly more than $3 billion. By 2008, it was about $271 billion. Ad spending has dropped some since then because of the downturn in the economy, but as the economy recovers more growth in ad spending is likely.

Over the last decade, the rate of advertising spending has increased even more rapidly in other countries. However, advertising in the United States still accounts for over 43 percent of worldwide ad spending. Europe accounts for about 35 percent, and Asia about 15 percent though spending in Asia is growing rapidly, especially in China. For most countries in other regions, advertising spending has traditionally been quite low.[3]

Most advertisers aren't really spending that much

While total spending on advertising seems high, U.S. corporations spend an average of only about 2.5 percent of their sales dollars on advertising. Worldwide, the percentage is even smaller. Exhibit 15–2 shows, however, that advertising spending as a percent of sales dollars varies significantly across product categories. Producers of consumer products generally spend a larger percent than firms that produce business products. For example, U.S. companies that make perfume and cosmetics spend about 19.2 percent. However, companies that sell plastics to manufacturers spend only about 1.8 percent on advertising. Some business products companies—those that depend on e-commerce or personal selling—may spend less than $1/_{10}$ of 1 percent.

In general, the percent is smaller for retailers and wholesalers than for producers. While some large chains like Kohl's, Macy's, and JCPenney spend over 5 percent, other retailers and wholesalers spend 2 percent or less. Individual firms may spend more or less than others in the industry, depending on the role of advertising in their promotion blend.[4]

Exhibit 15–2   Advertising Spending as Percent of Sales for Illustrative Product Categories

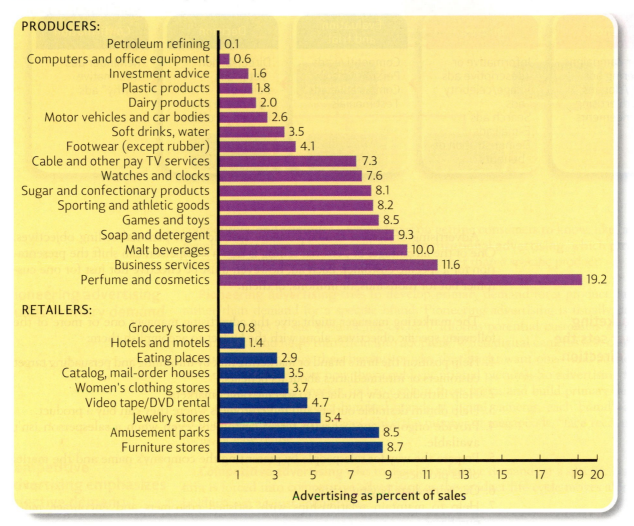

PRODUCERS:

Petroleum refining	0.1
Computers and office equipment	0.6
Investment advice	1.6
Plastic products	1.8
Dairy products	2.0
Motor vehicles and car bodies	2.6
Soft drinks, water	3.5
Footwear (except rubber)	4.1
Cable and other pay TV services	7.3
Watches and clocks	7.6
Sugar and confectionary products	8.1
Sporting and athletic goods	8.2
Games and toys	8.5
Soap and detergent	9.3
Malt beverages	10.0
Business services	11.6
Perfume and cosmetics	19.2

RETAILERS:

Grocery stores	0.8
Hotels and motels	1.4
Eating places	2.9
Catalog, mail-order houses	3.5
Women's clothing stores	3.7
Video tape/DVD rental	4.7
Jewelry stores	5.4
Amusement parks	8.5
Furniture stores	8.7

Advertising as percent of sales

Advertising doesn't employ that many people

While total advertising expenditures are large, the advertising industry itself employs relatively few people. The major expense is for media time and space. In the United States, the largest share of this—24 percent—goes for television (including cable). Direct mail takes about 22 percent of the total and newspapers about 14 percent. The shares for radio (6 percent), the Yellow Pages (5 percent), magazines (5 percent), the Internet (4 percent) and outdoor (1 percent) are much smaller.[5]

Many students hope for a glamorous job in advertising, but there are fewer jobs in advertising than you might think. In the United States, only about 460,000 people work directly in the advertising industry. Advertising agencies employ only about half of all these people.[6]

ADVERTISING OBJECTIVES ARE A STRATEGY DECISION

Advertising objectives must be specific

Every ad and every advertising campaign should have clearly defined objectives. These should grow out of the firm's overall marketing strategy and the promotion jobs assigned to advertising. It isn't enough for the marketing manager to say, "Promote the product." The marketing manager must decide exactly what advertising should do.

Competitive advertising may be either direct or indirect. The **direct type** aims for immediate buying action. The **indirect type** points out product advantages to affect future buying decisions.

Most of Delta Airlines' advertising is of the competitive variety. Much of it tries for immediate sales—so the ads are the direct type with prices, timetables, and phone numbers to call for reservations. Some of its ads are the indirect type. They focus on the quality of service and suggest you check Delta's website the next time you travel.

NOT ALL CEREAL BARS ARE CREATED EQUAL.

You want your kids to have all the advantages. So give them a cereal bar that has plenty of them. A Milk 'n cereal bar, only from General Mills. For real cereal nutrition, all you have to do is look for the 🅶.

50% larger, twice the calcium, and three times the iron of Kellogg's bars.

General Mills used a comparative ad that made direct comparisons with other brands to highlight the advantages of its Milk 'n Cereal bars (50 percent larger, twice the calcium, and three times the iron of Kellogg's bars).

Comparative advertising is even rougher. **Comparative advertising** means making specific brand comparisons—using actual product names. A recent comparative ad for Clorox Disinfecting Wipes, for example, claimed that a competing wipe from Windex didn't disinfect as well.

Many countries forbid comparative advertising, but that situation is changing. In the United States, the Federal Trade Commission decided to encourage comparative ads because it thought they would increase competition and provide consumers with more useful information. Superiority claims are supposed to be supported by research evidence—but the guidelines aren't clear. When P&G's Dryel did not fare well in independent test comparisons with stain removal by professional dry cleaners, P&G changed its ad claims. However, some firms just keep running tests until they get the results they want. Others talk about minor differences that don't reflect a product's overall benefits.

Comparative ads can also backfire by calling attention to competing products that consumers had not previously considered.[8]

Reminder advertising reinforces a favorable relationship

Reminder advertising tries to keep the product's name before the public. It may be useful when the product has achieved brand preference or insistence, perhaps in the market maturity or sales decline stages. It is used primarily to reinforce previous promotion. Here the advertiser may use soft-sell ads that just mention or show the name—as a reminder. Hallmark, for example, often relies on reminder ads because most consumers already know the brand name and, after years of promotion, associate it with high-quality cards and gifts.

Institutional advertising— remember our name

Institutional advertising usually focuses on the name and prestige of an organization or industry. It may seek to inform, persuade, or remind. Its basic objective is to develop goodwill or improve an organization's relations with various groups—not only customers but also current and prospective channel members, suppliers, shareholders, employees, and the general public. The British government, for instance, uses institutional advertising to promote England as a place to do business. Many Japanese firms, like Hitachi, emphasize institutional advertising, in part because they often use the company name as a brand name.

Some organizations use institutional advertising to advocate a specific cause or idea. Insurance companies and organizations like Mothers Against Drunk Driving, for example, use these advocacy ads to encourage people not to drink and drive.[9]

COORDINATING ADVERTISING EFFORTS WITH COOPERATIVE RELATIONSHIPS

Vertical cooperation—advertising allowances, cooperative advertising

Sometimes a producer knows that an advertising job can be done more effectively or more economically by someone further along in the channel. Alternatively, a retail chain like Best Buy may approach a manufacturer like Panasonic with an ad program and tell them how much it will cost to participate. In either case, the producer may offer **advertising allowances**—price reductions to firms further along in the channel to encourage them to advertise or otherwise promote the firm's products locally.

Cooperative advertising involves producers sharing in the cost of ads with wholesalers or retailers. This helps the intermediaries compete in their local markets. It also helps the producer get more promotion for the advertising dollar because media usually give local advertisers lower rates than national or international firms. In addition, a retailer or wholesaler who is paying a share of the cost is more likely to follow through.

Integrated communications from cooperative relationships

Coordination and integration of ad messages in the channel is another reason for cooperative advertising. One big, well-planned, integrated advertising effort is often better than many different, perhaps inconsistent, local efforts.

To get this coordination, producers often provide a master of an ad on a DVD, CD, website, or printed sheets. The intermediaries add their identification before turning the ad over to local media.

However, allowances and support materials alone don't ensure cooperation. When channel members don't agree with the advertising strategy, it can be a serious source of conflict. For example, Wendy's strategy includes an objective to be the late-night, quick-serve restaurant of choice for its target market. This requires staying open late at night and advertising the longer hours. However, some Wendy's restaurants are franchise operations rather than company-owned. A franchise operator who does not think that late-night hours will be profitable in his or her local market may not want to stay open for the longer hours or pay franchise fees to support the national ad campaign.[10]

Ethical concerns may arise

Ethical issues sometimes arise concerning advertising allowance programs. For example, a retailer may run one producer's ad to draw customers to the store but then sell them another brand. Is this unethical? Some producers think it is. A different view is that retailers are obligated to the producer to run the ad but obligated to consumers to sell them what they want, no matter whose brand it may be. A producer can often avoid the problem by setting the allowance amount as a percent of the retailer's *actual purchases*. Smart producers also insist on proof that the advertising was really done. That way, a retailer who doesn't produce sales—or even run the ads—doesn't get the allowance.[11]

CHOOSING THE "BEST" MEDIUM—HOW TO DELIVER THE MESSAGE

What is the best advertising medium? There is no simple answer to this question. Effectiveness depends on how well the medium fits with the rest of a marketing strategy—that is, it depends on (1) your promotion objectives, (2) what target markets you want to reach, (3) the funds available for advertising, and (4) the nature of the media, including who they *reach*, with what *frequency*, with what *impact*, and at what *cost*.

Exhibit 15–5 shows estimated ad spending, percent growth, and some pros and cons of major kinds of media. However, some of the advantages noted in this table may not apply in all markets. For example, direct mail may not be a flexible choice in a country with a weak postal system. Internet ads might be worthless if a firm's target customers don't have access to the Internet. Similarly, TV audiences are often less selective and targeted, but a special-interest cable TV show may reach a very specific audience.[12]

Exhibit 15–5 Estimated Ad Spending, Percent Growth, and Advantages and Disadvantages of Major Media

Kinds of Media	Ad Spending 2008 ($ in billions)	Percent Growth 2007 to 2008	Advantages	Disadvantages
Television and cable	$70.0	5.7%	Demonstrations, good attention, wide reach, cable can be selective	Expensive in total, "clutter"
Direct mail	63.7	4.5	Selected audience, flexible, can personalize	Relatively expensive per contact, "junk mail," hard to retain attention
Newspaper	42.1	−1.8	Flexible, timely, local market	May be expensive, short life, no "pass along"
Radio	18.6	0.2	Wide reach, segmented audience, inexpensive	Weak attention, many different rates, short exposure
Yellow Pages	14.7	1.1	Reaches local customers seeking purchase information	Many other competitors listed in same place, hard to differentiate
Magazine	14.1	3.0	Very targeted, good detail, good "pass along"	Inflexible, long lead times
Internet	12.7	16.5	Ads link to more detailed website, some "pay for results," easier to track results	Hard to compare costs with other media
Outdoor	6.6	6.1	Flexible, repeat exposure, inexpensive	"Mass market," very short exposure

Medium should fit promotion objectives

The medium should support the promotion objectives. If the objective requires demonstrating product benefits, TV may be the best alternative. If the objective is to inform, telling a detailed story and using precise pictures, then Internet advertising might be right. Alternatively, with a broad target market, print media like magazines and newspapers may be better. For example, Jockey switched its advertising to magazines from television when it decided to show the variety of styles of its men's briefs. Jockey worried that there were problems with modeling men's underwear on television. However, Jockey might have stayed with TV if it had been targeting consumers in France or Brazil, where nudity in TV ads is common.[13]

Match your market with the media

To guarantee good media selection, the advertiser first must *clearly* specify its target market. Then the advertiser can choose media that reach those target customers. Most media firms use marketing research to develop profiles of their audiences. Generally, this research focuses on demographic characteristics rather than the segmenting dimensions specific to the planning needs of *each* different advertiser.

Advertisers pay for the whole audience

The audience for media that *do* reach your target market may also include people who are *not* in the target group. But *advertisers pay for the whole audience the media delivers*, including those who aren't potential customers. For example, Delta Faucet, a faucet manufacturer that wanted its ads to reach plumbers, placed ads on ESPN's Saturday college football telecasts. Research showed that many plumbers watched the ESPN games. Yet plumbers are only a very small portion of the total college football audience—and the size of the total audience determined the cost of the advertising time.[14]

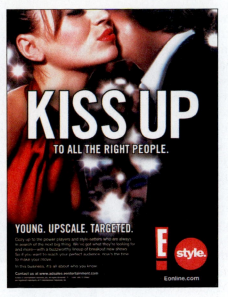

Highly targeted advertising media are proving especially effective at targeting messages to specific demographic, social, and cultural groups.

Because it's hard to pick the best media, media analysts often focus on cost per thousand of audience size. This may seem an objective approach, but advertisers preoccupied with keeping these costs down may ignore the relevant segmenting dimensions and slip into mass marketing.

Some media help zero in on specific target markets

Today, advertisers direct more attention to reaching smaller, more defined target markets. The most obvious evidence of this is in the growth of spending on direct-mail advertising to consumers in databases. For example, Germany's Otto Versand, the world's largest mail-order company, maintains CRM databases that track each customer's past purchases and responses to previous mailings. These data help the firm to accurately predict whether a customer will respond to a particular mailing. Such data also help mail-order firms segment customers, develop better messages, and increase the efficiency of their direct-mail campaigns.[15]

Traditional media are also becoming more targeted. TV is a good example. Cable TV channels—like CNN, Nickelodeon, ESPN, and MTV—are taking advertisers away from the networks because they target specific audiences. ESPN, for example, has an audience heavily weighted toward affluent, male viewers. Moreover, being specialized doesn't necessarily mean that the target market is small. MTV appeals most strongly to young viewers, but its programming is seen in about 400 million homes worldwide—more than any other programmer.

Radio has also become a more specialized medium. Some stations cater to particular ethnic and racial groups, such as Hispanics, African Americans, or French Canadians. Others aim at specific target markets with rock, country, or classical music. Satellite and Internet radio stations reach a larger number of consumers, so expect even more targeting.

Many magazines serve only special-interest groups, such as cooks, new parents, and personal computer users. In fact, the most profitable magazines seem to be the ones aimed at clearly defined markets. Many specialty magazines also have international editions that help marketers reach consumers with similar interests in different parts of the world.

There are also trade magazines in many fields, such as chemical engineering, furniture retailing, electrical wholesaling, farming, and the aerospace market. *Standard Rate and Data* provides a guide to the thousands of magazines now available in the United States. Similar guides exist in most other countries.

Specialized media are small, but gaining

The advertising media listed in Exhibit 15–5 are attracting the vast majority of advertising media budgets. But advertising specialists always look for cost-effective new media that will help advertisers reach their target markets. For example, one company successfully sells space for signs on bike racks that it places in front of 7-Eleven stores. A new generation of ATMs show video ads while customers wait to get their money.[16] Purina has created podcasts—downloadable files that can be listened to on an MP3 player or computer—that offer pet owners advice on issues ranging from helping pets lose weight to pet health insurance.[17]

ITT is a global engineering company with a wide variety of products—such as fluid control systems. ITT wanted to project a more integrated position as the leading water equipment provider. The industry's annual international trade show was an opportunity to communicate to customers, prospects, investors, employees, and other influencers all at the same time. So ITT marketers used unique media placements— such as outdoor ads

near the convention center and huge billboards in the main transportation center leading into the convention center—to present its message. Research before and after the show revealed a 20 percent increase in show attendees who viewed ITT as a market leader.

There's a call from your ad

In many countries there are about as many cell phones as adults, and people carry them everywhere. This has a lot of advertisers wishing their ads could give their customers a call. Now they're getting help with this wish. In the United Kingdom, for instance, the leading cellular service provider signs up subscribers to receive once-a-week text-message offers, such as half-price movie tickets. Some firms are even experimenting with ads that target customers based on the customer's location at a particular moment. Imagine walking down a city street on a hot day and suddenly getting a text-message offer for a discount on a cold Frappuccino at the Starbucks across the street. There are still some technical hurdles before this scene becomes common, but it illustrates the pinpoint targeting that will be possible.[18]

"Must buys" may use up available funds

Some media are obvious "must buys," like the local newspaper for a retailer in a small town. Most firms serving local markets view a Yellow Pages listing as a must buy. Website advertising is increasingly seen as a must buy. It may be the only medium for firms trying to reach business buyers in overseas markets. Must buy ads may even use up the available funds.

ADVERTISING AND THE INTERNET—NEW OPPORTUNITIES AND NEW CHALLENGES

The Internet influences many purchases

Internet use is growing fast as more people head to the Web for news, e-mail, information, and entertainment. About 50 percent of U.S. households have broadband Internet service; viewed more broadly, 90 percent of the people in the United States have some sort of Internet access—they can connect by some means and know how to do it. Internet access is not yet as high in most other countries (see

Does Advertising That's Everywhere Get Us Anywhere?

There's no holiday from advertising. You get to the beach, look down, and huge versions of the Skippy peanut butter logo are embossed in the sand. You roll your eyes in dismay and catch a view of a plane pulling a 100-foot-long banner ad with Catherine Zeta-Jones urging you to "Sign up for T-Mobile's free Friday minutes." You walk down the street and try to ignore the billboards and bus stop shelter ads. But it's hard not to notice trucks whose trailers are billboards—and there are even ads on the trucks' mud flaps. A bus drives by wrapped in an ad for McDonald's—and you see a cab with hubcaps advertising Taco Bell. You *are* getting hungry, but you packed a lunch and seek refuge in a nearby park. Not quite an escape from ads—the bench you sit on is an ad for a check-cashing service—and just for good measure the banana you pull out of your lunch bag has a sticker advertising Florida oranges. A couple of girls walk by wearing T-shirts emblazoned with "Abercrombie and Fitch" and "Old Navy." Then you hear a deep voice—but it's just a cell phone—the ring tone of the guy sitting next to you is promoting Stephen King's new movie with the author's voice. Then your cell phone displays a text message which offers you a discounted admission at a nearby club—how do they know where you are?

You need to get away from this commercial overload, so you head back to your condo to kick back, watch a movie, play computer games, and maybe read e-mail. But this is no escape! An ad and discount for the local Hard Rock Café are printed on the key to your rented condo. The "ad-free" pay-per-view movie—*National Treasure: Book of Secrets*—has product placements from Red Bull, Blackberry, MSN, and Mercedes. You pull out your laptop and load up Tony Hawk's American Wasteland video game—but you can't miss all the Jeep Wranglers, Cherokees, and Liberties driving around in the game—not a coincidence. So you close the game and check your e-mail. Getting onto a wireless Internet connection, your pop-up blocker stops many ads, but some still worm through. You sort through your e-mails—half of which are uninvited spam messages. Ugh. Is there no place to hide?

There are certainly many cases where promotion benefits both the consumer and the firm, and after all it is revenues from advertising that cover the cost of lots of great stuff consumers get for free. Yet sometimes you can't help but wish that you—and your wallet—were not the targets that so many companies are aiming at![19]

Exhibit 15–6). Yet it is a force among target markets that do use the Internet. For instance, in the United States, Internet users average 65 hours a month online. Many of them spend more time surfing the Web than they do watching television, listening to the radio, or reading newspapers and magazines. This helps to explain why 10 percent of consumer purchases are made online, and another 40 percent of purchases

Exhibit 15–6

Number of Internet Users In Different Parts of the World

Region	Population (000s)	Internet Usage (000s)	Population Penetration (%)
Africa	941,249	44,361	4.7
Asia	3,733,783	510,479	13.7
Europe	801,821	348,126	43.4
Middle East	192,755	33,511	17.4
North America	334,660	238,015	71.1
Latin America/Caribbean	569,133	126,204	22.2
Oceania/Australia	33,568	19,175	57.1
World total	6,606,970	1,319,872	20.0

Source: Internet World Stats (www.internetworldstats.com), based on Internet usage for December 2007. Data from Nielsen/NetRatings and International Telecommunications Union.

are influenced by what consumers see and learn online. This is an important shift in consumer behavior. So, let's explore some of the challenges and opportunities for marketing managers as they try to target specific customers or segments through Internet advertising.[20]

Most Internet ads seek a direct response

Advertising on the Internet takes a variety of forms, but the purpose is usually to attract the interest of people in the advertiser's target market so they'll click through to the firm's website. Many people try to ignore any advertising—and on the Internet they may even use software that eliminates some types of ads. However, to get the attention of Web surfers, Internet advertisers have created many different types of ads.

Banner ads are small rectangular boxes that usually include text, graphics, and sometimes video to create interest. Because banner ads can be easy to ignore, advertisers turned to *pop-up ads* that open in a new browser window (and block what the Web user is trying to view—until they're closed). A variation is the *pop-under ad,* which opens under the Web page being viewed, so it usually isn't noticed until after the Web browser is closed. Most people find these ads very annoying and many use software to block them. Yet some advertisers still use them because they do get responses. Some firms that *sell* Internet advertising will probably continue to look for ways around ad blocking software in an effort to try to force consumers to view an ad. But that approach probably doesn't make much sense for a marketing-oriented firm. Rather, it is better to try to reach target customers who are actually interested in what the firm has to communicate.

Sites often target specific customers

Target marketers try to place ads on websites that are designed to appeal to the firm's target market. For example, Morningstar's website attracts many investors who want current financial information about the stock market, so Ameritrade posts its online brokerage ads there. And Electric Cyclery, a retailer of electric bikes and scooters, runs ads at the TreeHugger blog because it attracts environmentalists.

Advertisers who seek exposure to a broader target market can place an ad at a popular Web portal like Yahoo! or MSN. These sites get 20 to 25 million visits a day. But they are expensive—up to $500,000 per day for a banner ad on the main page.

Search ads know what customers are looking for

Google and other search engine sites know customers' interests based on the keywords they use in a search. Many consumers conduct searches to get information for buying decisions. So REI might pay a search engine firm for a sponsored search ad that appears with the search results when specific search terms, like *hiking boots,* are entered.

Some ads know where customers have been on the Web

Behavioral targeting delivers ads to consumers based on previous websites the customer has visited. Some websites place a small file called a cookie on the computer of people who visit the site. These cookies give an advertiser some information about the consumer. For example, cookies could indicate whether a Web surfer has been to the company's website before, made a purchase on the last visit, or perhaps abandoned a partially full shopping cart. Or, based on what other sites a customer has visited, it is sometimes possible to determine likely interest in an offering. For example, a California theme park wanted to increase vacation package sales at its website. Special ads were delivered to Web surfers whose computers had cookies to indicate that they lived in specific western states and had also visited a travel site in the previous two weeks. This proved to be a cost-effective way to target ads and boost online sales.

Some advertisers only pay if ads deliver

Many websites charge advertisers a fee based on how frequently or how long an ad is shown. However, competition for advertisers has prompted *pay-per-click* advertising, where advertisers only pay when a customer clicks on the ad and links to the advertiser's website. For example, Omaha Steaks, which sells frozen meat by mail order, uses Google search ads. Its ads appear when any of about 1,600 keywords, including *Omaha steaks* or *filet mignon,* are entered at Google. Omaha Steaks pays about 70 cents for each click-through.[22]

Pay-per-click advertising is a big shift from traditional media where firms have to pay for their ads whether they work or not. A lot more firms will put ads on websites if there is a direct relationship between costs and results. Moreover, this arrangement gives a website more incentive to attract an audience that some specific advertiser wants to reach.

Websites need to maintain interest and create desire

After a customer clicks to a company's website, that site has to provide something of interest or the customer will immediately click away. Some ads or searches simply link customers to the firm's home page. However, a customized "landing page" helps keep customers at the site by increasing their interest and desire. For example, Autobytel uses search ads to target car buyers at MSN. The landing page at the Autobytel website depends on the search term the customer enters. For example, a customer who searches on the phrase *used Ford Focus* would land on a page with information about the Ford Focus and a photo.

Once customers get to a company's website, the site can provide much more interactivity than traditional advertising. For example, sites often provide a link so that visitors can see a different language. MSN uses this approach. Increasingly, content moves beyond the text and pictures typical of print ads and instead includes videos, sound, a product database, customer reviews or forums, and order-entry shopping carts. The website can also offer a great deal more information than advertising and allow customers to self-direct to pages that are of the greatest interest. In addition, a website can provide links to outside sources of information. Or a Web page can invite the viewer to sign up for more information via e-mail or even start a chat session with a salesperson.[23]

Advertising on social network sites

Social network websites allow people with shared interests to interact. The most popular of these sites, YouTube, MySpace, and Facebook, attract millions of visitors each day—primarily teens and young adults. Different sites are popular in other countries. For example, Orkut has about the same number of users as MySpace, but most live in Brazil or India. Because of this high level of interest, firms are trying to use these sites for advertising.

The marketing manager for Febreze Fabric Refresher, a spray bottle that eliminates odors from fabrics, thought college students would appreciate that Febreze can be used to delay washing clothes. So, to reach college students, he placed a website, WhatStinks.com, in Facebook. To get the target market's attention and interest, Facebook banner ads used taglines like "Febreze . . . Because surprise! Your parents are visiting" and "Febreze . . . Because the laundry room is soooooo far away!" The site also included a game where players use bottles of Febreze to shoot at dirty socks and underwear. This creative approach got the attention of college students in ways that advertising in other media might not.[24]

PLANNING THE "BEST" MESSAGE—WHAT TO COMMUNICATE

Specifying the copy thrust

Once you decide *how* the messages will reach the target audience, you have to decide on the **copy thrust**—what the words and illustrations should communicate.

Carrying out the copy thrust is the job of advertising specialists. But the advertising manager and the marketing manager need to understand the process to be sure that the job is done well.

Let AIDA help guide message planning

Basically, the overall marketing strategy should determine *what* the message should say. Then management judgment, perhaps aided by marketing research, can help decide how to encode this content so it will be decoded as intended.

As a guide to message planning, we can use the AIDA concept: getting Attention, holding Interest, arousing Desire, and obtaining Action.

Getting attention

Getting attention is an ad's first job. Many readers leaf through magazines without paying attention to any of the ads, and viewers get snacks during TV commercials. When watching a program on TiVo, they may zip past the commercial with a flick of a button. On the Internet, they may use a pop-up blocker or click on the next website before the ad message finishes loading onto the screen.

Many attention-getting devices are available. A large headline, computer animations, shocking statements, attractive models, animals, online games, special effects—anything different or eye-catching—may do the trick. However, the attention-getting device can't detract from, and hopefully should lead to, the next step, holding interest.

Holding interest

Holding interest is more difficult. A humorous ad, an unusual video effect, or a clever photo may get your attention—but once you've seen it, then what? If there is no relation between what got your attention and the marketing mix or your needs, you'll move

Levi's capitalized on the tagline "Live unbuttoned" when it created this 3-D billboard wearing 501 jeans.

on. To hold interest, the tone and language of the ad must fit with the experiences and attitudes of the target customers and their reference groups. As a result, many advertisers develop ads that relate to specific emotions. They hope that the good feeling about the ad will stick, even if its details are forgotten.

To hold interest, informative ads need to speak the target customer's language. Persuasive ads must provide evidence that convinces the customer. For example, TV ads often demonstrate a product's benefits.

Layouts for print ads should be arranged to encourage the eye to move smoothly through the ad—perhaps from a headline that starts in the upper left-hand corner to the illustration or body copy in the middle and finally to the lower right corner where the ad's "signature" usually gives the company or brand name,

The owner of Oklahoma Truck Supply used an upside-down 8-ton semi to promote his truck repair shop on Oklahoma's Interstate 35. The truck is held erect by poured concrete buried 14 feet deep. The ad not only gets attention but also prompts the reader to think about its distinctive selling proposition.

toll-free number, and website address. If all of the elements of the ad work together as a whole, they will help to hold interest and build recall.[25]

Arousing desire

Arousing desire to buy a particular product is one of an ad's most difficult jobs. The ad must convince customers that the product can meet their needs. Testimonials may persuade a consumer that other people with similar needs like the product. Product comparisons may highlight the advantages of a particular brand.

Although products may satisfy certain emotional needs, many consumers find it necessary to justify their purchases on some logical basis. Snickers candy bar ads helped ease the guilt of calorie-conscious snackers by assuring them that "Snickers satisfies you when you need an afternoon energy break."

An ad should usually focus on a *unique selling proposition* that aims at an important unsatisfied need. This can help differentiate the firm's marketing mix and position its brand as offering superior value to the target market. For example, Altoids has used humor in its ads to highlight the "curiously strong" flavor of its mints. Too many advertisers ignore the idea of a unique selling proposition. Rather than using an integrated blend of communications to tell the whole story, they cram too much into each ad—and then none of it has any impact.

Obtaining action

Getting action is the final requirement—and not an easy one. From communication research, we now know that prospective customers must be led beyond considering how the product *might* fit into their lives to actually trying it.

Direct-response ads can sometimes help promote action by encouraging interested consumers to do *something* even if they are not ready to make a purchase. For example, Fidelity Investments has run TV ads featuring colorful graphs, a sign with "Wow!," and the company's phone number and website address. And just in case viewers don't "get it," Blondie's song "Call Me" plays in the background. Fidelity wants to encourage interested consumers to make the first step in building a relationship.

Careful research on attitudes in the target market may help uncover strongly felt *unsatisfied* needs. Appealing to important needs can get more action and also provide the kind of information buyers need to confirm the correctness of their decisions. Some customers seem to read more advertising *after* a purchase than before.

Can global messages work?

Many international consumer products firms try to use one global advertising message all around the world. Of course, they translate the message or make other minor adjustments—but the focus is one global copy thrust. Some do it to cut the cost of developing different ads for each country. Others feel their customers' basic needs are the same, even in different countries. Some just do it because it's fashionable to "go global."

This approach works for some firms. Coca-Cola and IBM, for example, believe that the needs their products serve are very similar for customers around the world. They focus on the similarities among customers who make up their target market rather than the differences. However, most firms who use this approach experience terrible results. They may save money by developing fewer ads, but they lose sales because they don't develop advertising messages, and whole marketing mixes, aimed at specific target markets. They just try to appeal to a global "mass market."[26]

ADVERTISING AGENCIES OFTEN DO THE WORK

An advertising manager manages a company's advertising effort. Many advertising managers, especially those working for large retailers, have their own advertising departments that plan specific advertising campaigns and carry out the details. Others turn over much of the advertising work to specialists—the advertising agencies.

Ad agencies are specialists

Advertising agencies are specialists in planning and handling mass-selling details for advertisers. Agencies play a useful role. They are independent of the advertiser and have an outside viewpoint. They bring experience to an individual client's problems

Adforum.com is a website that provides information about more than 70,000 ad agencies as well as examples of ads that they create.

Exhibit 15–7 Top Eight Advertising Agency Supergroups

Organization	Largest Agencies	Headquarters Location	2007 Revenue ($ in billions)	Select Clients
Omnicom Group	BBDO Worldwide, DDB Worldwide, TBWA Worldwide	New York	$12.69	Apple, Bud, ExxonMobil, FedEx, GE, Pepsi
WPP Group	Grey Worldwide, JWT, Ogilvy & Mather Worldwide, Y&R	London	12.38	Altria, American Express, Ford, GlaxoSmithKline, IBM, P&G
Interpublic	DraftFCB, Lowe Worldwide, McCann Erickson Worldwide	New York	6.55	GM, Johnson & Johnson, Microsoft, Unilever, UPS, Verizon
Publicis Groupe	Leo Burnett Worldwide, Publicis Worldwide, Saatchi & Saatchi	Paris	6.38	British Airways, Coca-Cola, Disney, Kellogg, L'Oreal, McDonald's
Dentsu	Colby & Partners, Dentsu	Tokyo	2.93	Canon, Hitachi, International Olympic Committee, Kao, Matsushita, Toshiba
Aegis Group	Aegis Media, Isobar, Synovate	London	2.21	AT&T, Cablevision, Columbia House, Comcast, Green Mountain Energy, Qwest
Havas	Arnold Worldwide, Euro RSCG 4D, MPG	Suresnes, France	2.09	Air France, Danone, Nokia, Sony, Tesco, Volvo
Hakuhodo DY Holdings	Daiko, Hakuhodo, Yomiko	Tokyo	1.39	Adidas, American Tobacco Company, Konica, NEC, Nissan, Sapporo

because they work for many other clients. They can often do the job more economically than a company's own department. And if an agency isn't doing a good job, the client can select another. However, ending a relationship with an agency is a serious decision. Too many marketing managers just use their advertising agency as a scapegoat. Whenever anything goes wrong, they blame the agency.

Some full-service agencies handle any activities related to advertising, publicity, or sales promotion. They may even handle overall marketing strategy planning as well as marketing research, product and package development, and sales promotion. Other agencies are more specialized. For example, in recent years there has been rapid growth of firms that specialize in developing websites and Internet ads.

The biggest agencies handle much of the advertising

The vast majority of advertising agencies are small, with 10 or fewer employees. But the largest agencies account for most of the billings. Over the past two decades many of the big agencies merged, creating mega-agencies with worldwide networks. Exhibit 15–7 shows a list of eight of the largest agency networks and examples of some of their clients. Although their headquarters are located in different nations, they have offices worldwide. The move toward international marketing is a key reason behind the mergers and advertisers have responded as expected. For example, the "Big Four" organizations at the top of Exhibit 15–7 get about 54 percent of all advertising/media agency revenue.

The mega-agency can offer varied services, wherever in the world a marketing manager needs them. This may be especially important for managers in large corporations—like Toyota, Renault, Unilever, NEC, and PepsiCo—that advertise worldwide.[27]

The really big agencies are less interested in smaller accounts. Smaller agencies will continue to appeal to customers who want more personal attention and a close relationship that is more attuned to their marketing needs.

Are they paid too much?

Traditionally, U.S. advertising agencies have been paid a commission of about 15 percent on media and production costs. This arrangement evolved because media usually have two prices: one for national advertisers and a lower rate for local advertisers, such as local retailers. The advertising agency gets a 15 percent commission on national rates but not on local rates. This makes it worthwhile for producers and national intermediaries to use agencies. National advertisers have to pay the full media rate anyway, so it makes sense to let the agency experts do the work and earn their commission. Local retailers—allowed the lower media rate—seldom use agencies.

Some firms pay the agency based on results

A number of advertisers now grade the work done by their agencies—and the agencies' pay depends on the grade. General Foods was the first to do this. It lowered its basic commission to about 13 percent. However, it paid the agency a bonus of about 3 percent on campaigns that earned an A rating. If the agency only earned a B, it lost the bonus. If it earned a C, it had to improve fast or GF removed the account. Variations on this approach are common. For example, Carnation directly links its agency's compensation with how well its ads score in market research tests. This approach forces the advertiser and agency to agree on very specific objectives for their ads and what they expect to achieve. It also reduces the likelihood of the creative people in an agency focusing on ads that will win artistic approval in their industry rather than ads that do what the firm needs done.[28]

MEASURING ADVERTISING EFFECTIVENESS IS NOT EASY

Success depends on the total marketing mix

It would be convenient if we could measure the results of advertising by looking at sales. Some breakthrough ads do have a very direct effect on a company's sales—and the advertising literature is filled with success stories that "prove" advertising increases sales. Similarly, market research firms like Information Resources can sometimes compare sales levels before and after the period of an ad campaign. Yet we usually can't measure advertising success just by looking at sales. The total marketing mix—not just advertising—is responsible for the sales result. Sales results are also affected by what competitors do and by other changes in the external marketing environment.

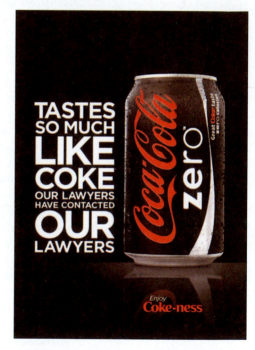

The idea for Coke Zero came from research that showed that younger men wanted the taste of Coke without the calories, but didn't like the word "diet." After the initial launch of Coke Zero fizzled, Coke switched to aggressive spending on a creative new ad campaign. Coke Zero sales took hold. Was it the new ads that saved the product or the increased budget, black packaging, and sampling program that accompanied the ads?

Research and testing can improve the odds

Ideally, advertisers should pretest advertising before it runs rather than relying solely on their own guesses about how good an ad will be. The judgment of creative people or advertising experts may not help much. They often judge only on the basis of originality or cleverness of the copy and illustrations.

Many progressive advertisers now demand laboratory or market tests to evaluate an ad's effectiveness. For example, split runs on cable TV systems in test markets are an important approach for testing ads in a normal viewing environment. Scanner sales data from retailers in those test markets can provide an estimate of how an ad is likely to affect sales. This approach will become even more powerful in the future as more cable systems allow viewers to provide immediate feedback to an ad as it appears on TV or on the Internet.

Hindsight may lead to foresight

After ads run, researchers may try to measure how much consumers recall about specific products or ads. The response to radio or television commercials or magazine readership can be estimated using various survey methods to check the size and composition of audiences (the Nielsen and Starch reports are examples). Similarly, most Internet advertisers keep track of how many "hits" on the firm's website come from ads placed at other websites.[29]

HOW TO AVOID UNFAIR ADVERTISING

Government agencies may say what is fair

In most countries, the government takes an active role in deciding what kinds of advertising are allowable, fair, and appropriate. For example, France and Japan limit the use of cartoon characters in advertising to children, and Canada bans *any* advertising targeted directly at children. In Switzerland, an advertiser cannot use an actor to represent a consumer. New Zealand limits political ads on TV. In the United States, print ads must be identified so they aren't confused with editorial matter; in other countries ads and editorial copy can be intermixed. Most countries limit the number and length of commercials on broadcast media.

What is seen as positioning in one country may be viewed as unfair or deceptive in another. For example, when Pepsi was advertising its cola as "the choice of the new generation" in most countries, Japan's Fair Trade Committee didn't allow it—because in Japan Pepsi was not "the choice."[30]

Differences in rules mean that a marketing manager may face very specific limits in different countries, and local experts may be required to ensure that a firm doesn't waste money developing ads that will never be shown or which consumers will think are deceptive.

FTC controls unfair practices in the United States

In the United States, the Federal Trade Commission (FTC) has the power to control unfair or deceptive business practices, including deceptive advertising. The FTC has been policing deceptive advertising for many years. And it may be getting results now that advertising agencies as well as advertisers must share equal responsibility for false, misleading, or unfair ads.

This is a serious matter. If the FTC decides that a particular practice is unfair or deceptive, it has the power to require affirmative disclosures—such as the health warnings on cigarettes—or **corrective advertising** —ads to correct deceptive advertising. Years ago the FTC forced Listerine to spend millions of dollars on advertising to "correct" earlier ads that claimed the mouthwash helped prevent colds. Advertisers still remember that lesson. The possibility of large financial penalties or the need to pay for corrective ads has caused more agencies and advertisers to stay well within the law.

However, sometimes ad claims seem to get out of hand anyway. For example, there have been many ads and infomercials that tout various gadgets and dietary supplements as effective for weight loss. For most of these products there is no evidence that they work (unless used while training to compete in a marathon). Given the heightened concerns about obesity, the FTC has started to crack down on claims related to weight loss and health. For example, KFC quickly stopped running several of its TV ads after the FTC objected to the ads and opened an investigation. KFC's ads positioned fried chicken as a healthy choice in fast food, but there was also lots of small print at the bottom of the screen to qualify the claims.[31]

"Green" claims must be backed by evidence

To appeal to consumers who want environmentally friendly products and packaging, firms often advertise their green benefits. Because these green claims are difficult for consumers to verify, the FTC wants to make certain that they are not deceptive. As a result, the FTC developed guidelines for environmental claims used in brand names and logos as well as in labels, ads, and other promotional materials. At the heart of the guidelines is the idea that claims should be verified in a reasonable way, and that typically means using scientific evidence as support.[32]

What is unfair or deceptive is changing

What constitutes unfair and deceptive advertising is a difficult question. The law provides some guidelines, but the marketing manager must make personal judgments as well. The social and political environment is changing worldwide. Practices considered acceptable some years ago are now questioned or considered deceptive. Saying or even implying that your product is best may be viewed as deceptive. And a 1988 revision of the Lanham Act protects firms whose brand names are unfairly tarnished in comparative ads.

Supporting ad claims is a fuzzy area

It's really not hard to figure out how to avoid criticisms of being unfair and deceptive. A little puffing is acceptable, and probably always will be. But marketing managers need to put a stop to the typical production-oriented approach of trying to use advertising to differentiate me-too products that are not different and don't offer customers better value.[33]

SALES PROMOTION—DO SOMETHING DIFFERENT TO STIMULATE CHANGE

The nature of sales promotion

Sales promotion refers to those promotion activities—other than advertising, publicity, and personal selling—that stimulate interest, trial, or purchase by final customers or others in the channel. Exhibit 13–2 shows examples of typical sales promotions targeted at final customers, channel members, or a firm's own employees.

Sales promotion is generally used to complement the other promotion methods. While advertising campaigns and sales force strategy decisions tend to have longer-term effects, a particular sales promotion activity usually lasts for only a limited time period. But sales promotion can often be implemented quickly and get sales results sooner than advertising. Further, sales promotion objectives usually focus on prompting some short-term action. For an intermediary, such an action might be a decision to stock a product, provide a special display space, or give the product extra sales emphasis. For a consumer, the desired action might be to try a new product, switch from another brand, or buy more of a product. The desired action by an employee might be a special effort to satisfy customers.

Retailers are using digital signs as key marketing tools right at the point of purchase.

Exhibit 15–8   Some Possible Effects of a Sales Promotion on Sales

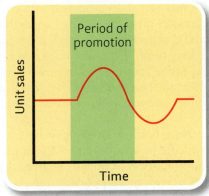

Sales temporarily increase, then decrease, then return to regular level

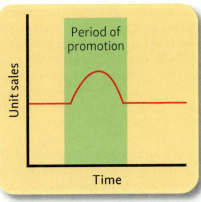

Sales temporarily increase and then return to regular level

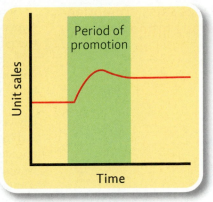

Sales increase and then remain at higher level

Sales promotion objectives and situation should influence decision

There are many different types of sales promotion, but what type is appropriate depends on the situation and objectives. For example, Exhibit 15–8 shows some possible ways that a short-term promotion might affect sales. The sales pattern in the graph on the left might occur if Hellmann's issues coupons to help clear its excess mayonnaise inventory. Some consumers might buy earlier to take advantage of the coupon, but unless they use extra mayonnaise their next purchase will be delayed. In the center graph, kids might convince parents to eat more Big Macs while McDonald's has a *Lord of the Rings* promotion, but when it ends things go back to normal. The graph on the right shows a Burger King marketer's dream come true: Free samples of a new style of french fries quickly pull in new customers who like what they try and keep coming back after the promotion ends. From these examples, you can see that the situation and the objective of the promotion should determine what specific type is best.

Sales promotion spending has grown in mature markets

Sales promotion involves so many different types of activities that it is difficult to estimate accurately how much is spent in total. There is general consensus, however, that the total spending on sales promotion exceeds spending on advertising.[34]

One reason for increased use of sales promotion by many consumer products firms is that they are generally competing in mature markets. There's only so much soap that consumers want to buy, regardless of how many brands there are vying for their dollars. There's also only so much shelf space that retailers will allocate to a particular product category.

The competitive situation is intensified by the growth of large, powerful retail chains. They have put more emphasis on their own dealer brands and also demanded more sales promotion support for the manufacturer brands they do carry.

Perhaps in part because of this competition, many consumers have become more price sensitive. Many sales promotions, like coupons, have the effect of lowering the prices consumers pay. So sales promotion has been used as a tool to overcome consumer price resistance.

The growth of sales promotion has also been fostered by the availability of more ad agencies and specialists who plan and implement sales promotion programs. Of course, the most basic reason for the growth of spending on sales promotion is that it can be very effective if it is done properly. But there are problems in the sales promotion area.

PROBLEMS IN MANAGING SALES PROMOTION

Does sales promotion erode brand loyalty?

Some experts think that marketing managers—especially those who deal with consumer packaged goods—put too much emphasis on sales promotion. They argue that the effect of most sales promotion is temporary and that money spent on advertising and personal selling helps the firm more over the long term. When the market is not growing, sales promotion may just encourage "deal-prone" customers (and intermediaries) to switch back and forth among brands. Here, all the expense of the sales promotion simply contributes to lower profits. It also increases the prices that consumers pay because it increases selling costs.

However, once a marketing manager is in this situation there may be little choice other than to continue. In mature markets, frequent sales promotions may be needed just to offset the effects of competitors' promotions. One escape from this competitive rat race is for the marketing manager to seek new opportunities—with a strategy that doesn't rely solely on short-term sales promotions for competitive advantage.

There are alternatives

Procter & Gamble is a company that changed its strategy, and promotion blend, to decrease its reliance on sales promotion targeted at intermediaries. It is offering intermediaries lower prices on many of its products and supporting those products with more advertising and promotion to final consumers. P&G believes that this approach builds its brand equity, serves consumers better, and leads to smoother-running relationships in its channels. Not all retailers are happy with P&G's changes. However, many other producers are following P&G's lead.[35]

Sales promotion is hard to manage

Another problem in the sales promotion area is that it is easy to make big, costly mistakes. Because sales promotion includes such a wide variety of activities, it's difficult for the typical company to develop skill in managing all of them. Even large firms and agencies that specialize in sales promotion run into difficulties because each promotion is typically custom-designed and then used only once. Yet mistakes caused by lack of experience can be costly or hurt relationships with customers.

In a promotion for Pampers diapers that was designed to reward loyal buyers and steal customers away from competing Huggies, marketing managers offered parents Fisher-Price toys if they collected points printed on Pampers' packages. At first the promotion seemed to be a big success because so many parents were collecting points. But that turned into a problem when Fisher-Price couldn't produce enough toys to redeem all the points. Pampers had to add 50 toll-free phone lines to handle all the complaints, and a lot of angry parents stopped buying Pampers for good. Problems like this are common.[36]

Most M&M's are sold as consumer products, but M&M's printed with special messages or brand logos are a sweet way to remind business customers about a firm.

Not a sideline for amateurs

Sales promotion mistakes are likely to be worse when a company has no sales promotion manager. If the personal selling or advertising managers are responsible for sales promotion, they often treat it as a "stepchild." They allocate money to sales promotion if there is any "left over" or if a crisis develops.

Making sales promotion work is a learned skill, not a sideline for amateurs. That's why specialists in sales promotion have developed, both inside larger firms and as outside consultants. Some of these people are real experts. But it's the marketing manager's responsibility to set sales promotion objectives and policies that will fit in with the rest of each marketing strategy.[37]

DIFFERENT TYPES OF SALES PROMOTION FOR DIFFERENT TARGETS

Sales promotion for final consumers or users

Much of the sales promotion aimed at final consumers or users tries to increase demand, perhaps temporarily, or speed up the time of purchase. Such promotion might involve developing materials to be displayed in retailers' stores, including banners, sample packages, calendars, and various point-of-purchase materials. It might include sweepstakes contests as well as coupons designed to get customers to buy a product by a certain date. Coupon distribution has dropped off some in recent years but still averages about 650 coupons for every man, woman, and child in America! However, only about 1 percent of all coupons are redeemed.[38]

All of these sales promotion efforts are aimed at specific objectives. For example, if customers already have a favorite brand, it may be hard to get them to try anything new. A free trial-sized bottle of mouthwash might be just what it takes to get cautious consumers to try the new product. Samples might be distributed house to house, by mail, at stores, or attached to other products sold by the firm. In this type of situation, sales of the product might start to pick up as soon as customers try the product and find out that they like it. And sales will continue at the higher level after the promotion is over if satisfied customers make repeat purchases. Thus, the cost of the sales promotion in this situation might be viewed as a long-term investment.

Once a product is established, consumer sales promotion usually focuses on short-term sales increases. For example, after a price-off coupon for a soft drink is distributed, sales might temporarily pick up as customers take advantage of buying at a lower price. When the objective of the promotion is focused primarily on producing a short-term increase in sales, it's sensible for the marketing manager to evaluate the cost of the promotion relative to the extra sales expected. If the increase in sales won't at least cover the cost of the promotion, it probably doesn't make sense to do it. Otherwise, the firm is "buying sales" at the cost of reduced profit.

Sales promotion directed at industrial customers might use the same kinds of ideas. In addition, the sales promotion people might set up and staff trade show exhibits. For example, Epson uses trade show exhibits to reach German business customers. Sometimes trade show exhibitors use attractive models to encourage buyers to look at a firm's product, especially when it is displayed near other similar products in a circuslike atmosphere. Trade shows are a cost-effective way to reach target customers and generate a list of "live" prospects for sales rep follow-up. However, many firms handle these leads badly. One study indicated that 85 percent of leads never got followed up by anybody.

Some sellers give promotion items—pen sets, watches, or clothing (perhaps with the firm's brand name on them)—to remind business customers of their products. This

402

is common, but it can be a problem. Some companies do not allow buyers to accept any gifts.[39]

Sales promotion for intermediaries

Sales promotion aimed at intermediaries—sometimes called *trade promotion*—emphasizes price-related matters. The objective may be to encourage intermediaries to stock new items, buy in larger quantity, buy early, or stress a product in their own promotion efforts.

The tools used here include merchandise allowances, promotion allowances, and perhaps sales contests to encourage retailers or wholesalers to sell specific items or the company's whole line. Offering to send contest winners to Hawaii, for example, may increase sales.

About half of the sales promotion spending targeted at intermediaries has the effect of reducing the price that they pay for merchandise. So we'll go into more detail on different types of trade discounts and allowances in Chapter 16.

Sales promotion for own employees

Sales promotion aimed at the company's own sales force might try to encourage providing better service, getting new customers, selling a new product, or selling the company's whole line. Depending on the objectives, the tools might be contests, bonuses on sales or number of new accounts, and holding sales meetings at fancy resorts to raise everyone's spirits.

Ongoing sales promotion work might also be aimed at the sales force—to help sales management. Sales promotion might be responsible for preparing sales portfolios, digital videos, PowerPoint presentations, displays, and other sales aids, as well as sales training materials.

Service-oriented firms such as hotels and restaurants use sales promotions targeted at their employees. Some, for example, give a monthly cash prize for the employee who provides the "best service." And the employee's picture is displayed to give recognition.[40]

CONCLUSION

It may seem simple to develop an advertising campaign. Just pick the medium and develop a message. But it's not that easy.

This chapter discussed why marketing managers should set specific objectives to guide the entire advertising effort. Knowing what they want to achieve, marketing managers can determine what kind of advertising—product or institutional—to use. We also discussed three basic types of product advertising: pioneering, competitive (direct and indirect), and reminder.

Marketing managers must also choose from various media—so we discussed their advantages and disadvantages. Because the Internet offers new advertising opportunities and challenges we discussed how it is similar to and different from other media. And, of course, marketing managers must determine the message—or copy thrust—that will appear in ads.

Many technical details are involved in mass selling. Advertising agencies often handle these jobs. But specific objectives must be set for agencies, or their advertising may have little direction and be almost impossible to evaluate. This chapter also discussed how to make sure that advertising is done legally.

Sales promotion spending is big and growing. This approach is especially important in prompting action—by customers, intermediaries, or salespeople. There are many different types of sales promotion, and it is a problem area in many firms because it is difficult for a firm to develop expertise with all of the possibilities.

Advertising and sales promotion are often important parts of a promotion blend, but in most blends personal selling also plays an important role. Further, promotion is only a part of the total marketing mix a marketing manager must develop to satisfy target customers. So to broaden your understanding of the four Ps and how they fit together, in Chapters 16 and 17 we'll go into more detail on the role of Price in strategy decisions.

KEY TERMS

product advertising, 382
institutional advertising, 383
pioneering advertising, 383
competitive advertising, 383
direct type advertising, 384

indirect type advertising, 384
comparative advertising, 384
reminder advertising, 384
advertising allowances, 385

cooperative advertising, 385
copy thrust, 392
advertising agencies, 394
corrective advertising, 397

QUESTIONS AND PROBLEMS

1. Identify the strategy decisions a marketing manager must make in the advertising area.

2. Discuss the relation of advertising objectives to marketing strategy planning and the kinds of advertising actually needed. Illustrate.

3. List several media that might be effective for reaching consumers in a developing nation with low per capita income and a high level of illiteracy. Briefly discuss the limitations and advantages of each medium you suggest.

4. Give three examples where advertising to intermediaries might be necessary. What are the objective(s) of such advertising?

5. What does it mean to say that "money is invested in advertising"? Is all advertising an investment? Illustrate.

6. Find advertisements to final consumers that illustrate the following types of advertising: (*a*) institutional, (*b*) pioneering, (*c*) competitive, and (*d*) reminder. What objective(s) does each of these ads have? List the needs each ad appeals to.

7. Describe the type of media that might be most suitable for promoting: (*a*) tomato soup, (*b*) greeting cards, (*c*) a business component material, and (*d*) playground equipment. Specify any assumptions necessary to obtain a definite answer.

8. Briefly discuss some of the pros and cons an advertising manager for a producer of sports equipment might want to think about in deciding whether to advertise on the Internet.

9. Discuss the use of testimonials in advertising. Which of the four AIDA steps might testimonials accomplish? Are they suitable for all types of products? If not, for which types are they most suitable?

10. Find a magazine ad that you think does a particularly good job of communicating to the target audience. Would the ad communicate well to an audience in another country? Explain your thinking.

11. Johnson & Johnson sells its baby shampoo in many different countries. Do you think baby shampoo would be a good product for Johnson & Johnson to advertise with a single global message? Explain your thinking.

12. Discuss the future of smaller advertising agencies now that many of the largest are merging to form mega-agencies.

13. Does advertising cost too much? How can this be measured?

14. How would your local newspaper be affected if local supermarkets switched their weekly advertising and instead used a service that delivered weekly, freestanding ads directly to each home?

15. Is it unfair to criticize a competitor's product in an ad? Explain your thinking.

16. Explain why P&G and other consumer packaged goods firms are trying to cut back on some types of sales promotion like coupons for consumers and short-term trade promotions such as "buy a case and get a case free."

17. Discuss some ways that a firm can link its sales promotion activities to its advertising and personal selling efforts—

so that all of its promotion efforts result in an integrated effort.

18. Indicate the type of sales promotion that a producer might use in each of the following situations and briefly explain your reasons:

a. A firm has developed an improved razor blade and obtained distribution, but customers are not motivated to buy it.

b. A competitor is about to do a test market for a new brand and wants to track sales in test market areas to fine-tune its marketing mix.

c. A big grocery chain won't stock a firm's new popcorn-based snack product because it doesn't think there will be much consumer demand.

19. Why wouldn't a producer of toothpaste just lower the price of its product rather than offer consumers a price-off coupon?

20. If sales promotion spending continues to grow—often at the expense of media advertising—how do you think this might affect the rates charged by mass media for advertising time or space? How do you think it might affect advertising agencies?

CREATING MARKETING PLANS

The Marketing Plan Coach software on the text website (and on the optional Student CD) includes a sample marketing plan for Hillside Veterinary Clinic. Look through the "Marketing Strategy" section.

a. What are Hillside's advertising objectives?

b. What types of advertising and media are being proposed? Why are these types used and not others?

c. What type of copy thrust is recommended? Why?

d. What sales promotion activities are being planned? What are the goals of sales promotion?

SUGGESTED CASES

18. Whisper Valley Volunteer Fire Department   20. Recreation Supplies Unlimited
36. Sorenson Builders

COMPUTER-AIDED PROBLEM

15. SALES PROMOTION

As a community service, disc jockeys from radio station WMKT formed a basketball team to help raise money for local nonprofit organizations. The host organization finds or fields a competing team and charges $5 admission to the game. Money from ticket sales goes to the nonprofit organization.

Ticket sales were disappointing at recent games, averaging only about 300 people per game. When WMKT's marketing manager, Bruce Miller, heard about the problem, he suggested using sales promotion to improve ticket sales. The PTA for the local high school—the sponsor for the next game—is interested in the idea but is concerned that its budget doesn't include any promotion money. Miller tries to help them by reviewing his idea in more detail.

Specifically, he proposes that the PTA give a free T-shirt (printed with the school name and date of the game) to the first 500 ticket buyers. He thinks the T-shirt giveaway will create a lot of interest. In fact, he says he is almost certain the promotion would help the PTA sell 600 tickets, double the usual number. He speculates that the PTA might even have a sellout of all 900 seats in the school gym. Further, he notes that the T-shirts will more than pay for themselves if the PTA sells 600 tickets.

A local firm that specializes in sales promotion items agrees to supply the shirts and do the printing for $2.40 a shirt if the PTA places an order for at least 400 shirts. The PTA thinks the idea is interesting but wants to look at it more closely to see what will happen if the promotion doesn't increase ticket sales. To help the PTA evaluate the alternatives, Miller sets up a spreadsheet with the relevant information.

a. Based on the data from the initial spreadsheet, does the T-shirt promotion look like a good idea? Explain your thinking.

b. The PTA treasurer worries about the up-front cost of printing the T-shirts and wants to know where they would stand if they ordered the T-shirts and still sold only 300 tickets. He suggests it might be safer to order the minimum number of T-shirts (400). Evaluate his suggestion.

c. The president of the PTA thinks the T-shirt promotion will increase sales but wonders if it wouldn't be better just to lower the price. She suggests $2.60 a ticket, which she arrives at by subtracting the $2.40 T-shirt cost from the usual $5.00 ticket price. How many tickets would the PTA have to sell at the lower price to match the money it would make if it used the T-shirt promotion and actually sold 600 tickets? (Hint: Change the selling price in the spreadsheet and then vary the quantity using the analysis feature.)

For additional questions related to this problem, see Exercise 15-3 in the *Learning Aid for Use with Essentials of Marketing,* 12th edition.

Pricing Objectives and Policies

In a YouTube world, homemade videos are everywhere. But getting from the first "moving pictures" to widespread *home* movie-making took almost a century. The film for early movies was flammable and dangerous to handle—not exactly ideal for recording family memories. By 1960, safe film with good color and audio was readily available, but the prices for cameras, film, processing, and projectors limited home movie-making to the very wealthy. A turning point came in 1983 when Sony's Betamovie videotape combination camera-recorder-player hit the consumer market. It eliminated film and processing and used a regular TV screen to show movies. Still, its $1,500 sticker was high for the average consumer so adoption was slow. Before long RCA and Panasonic and other firms using the VHS format entered the market, and the competition brought down prices and prompted market growth.

By 2000, prices were way down and home videos of special events—like kids' soccer games, birthday parties, and choir performances—were more common. Yet movie-making was complicated by a new generation of camcorders with many advanced features that consumers didn't know how to use. And once a movie was recorded, it was a big challenge to edit it or show it to others. Making home movies seemed hard, so many families left their camcorder in a closet.

A startup company, Pure Digital Technologies (PDT), saw opportunities in this market situation. PDT's first products were one-time-use digital cameras for retailers like Ritz Camera and Walgreens. The retailers sold the cameras for $10.99 and printed the 25 pictures for another $10.99, which offered good profit margins. Prompted by this, the CVS drugstore chain asked PDT for a one-time-use camcorder. Unfortunately, not many CVS customers saw value in paying $29.95 for a camcorder and $12.99 more to transfer video clips to a DVD, so sales were slow.

PDT's marketing managers noticed the CVS camcorder generated plenty of online buzz. Users liked its portability and simplicity—some even "hacked" the camcorders to make them reusable. PDT's marketing managers thought there was an opportunity to develop a new marketing mix. So they designed a new camcorder. It was small (4" × 2.5" × 1"), ran on two AA batteries, included a 1.5 inch color playback screen, had built-in memory to hold 30 minutes of video, and needed just a few buttons to operate. Its flip-out USB connector made it easy to download videos to a computer and the included software made it easy to edit, save, organize, and e-mail videos. To keep costs low, manufacturing was outsourced to China.

In May 2006, PDT's Point and Shoot Video Camcorder launched at Target Stores. Later it was available at Amazon.com, Wal-Mart, and other retailers. PDT thought a

low manufacturer's suggested retail price of $129.99 would quickly grow sales and build market share. To help differentiate the camcorder, PDT changed the brand name to Flip.

In 2007, PDT added the Flip Ultra to the product line. For only $30 more than Flip, Flip Ultra offered better quality sound and video, and five different colors. FlipShare software was built right into the Flip Ultra so it was even easier to upload movies to YouTube or other video sharing websites.

While gadget lovers were the earliest adopters, Flip primarily appeals to two target markets. Moms toss the camera into their handbags and capture spontaneous family memories. They love how easy it is to send video clips to relatives. And teenagers enjoy posting videos of themselves and their friends to YouTube and MySpace.

With a limited budget for promotion, Flip relied heavily on publicity to get the word out. Favorable reviews from influential technology writers like Walt Mossberg of *The Wall Street Journal* drew attention for Flip. Positive customer reviews of Flip posted at Amazon.com also touted how easy it was to take and share videos. It generated even more buzz when stars like Tyra Banks, Jessica Alba, and Ellen Degeneres were photographed with a Flip or publicly sang its praises. Even Oprah Winfrey proclaimed it as one of her favorite things.

In 2008 the Flip Mino ("minnow") and high definition Flip Mino*HD* replaced the original Flip. The new models were 40 percent smaller, sleeker in design, included a rechargeable battery, and had manufacturer suggested retail prices of $179.99 and $229.99. However, retailers often sold them for $20-$30 less. At TheFlip.com, an online customer could buy a Mino and for no extra charge customize it with a unique design or uploaded photo.

Flip found a marketing mix that delivered customer value. In less than two years PDT sold over 1.5 million camcorders and its 24 percent market share trailed only Sony! PDT's success caught the attention of Cisco Systems, which bought it in 2009. Cisco's financial resources will help fend off strong competitors, which is important because Kodak, Sony, and Creative are among those now selling small, low-priced Web-sharing camcorders. Of course, many cell phones and cameras also take video clips. So even though Flip's first-mover advantage built brand awareness, PDT will need to continue adapting Flip's marketing strategy to enjoy continued success.[1]

PRICE HAS MANY STRATEGY DIMENSIONS

Price is one of the four major strategy decision variables that a marketing manager controls. Pricing decisions affect both the number of sales a firm makes and how much money it earns. Price is what a customer must give up to get the benefits offered by the rest of a firm's marketing mix, so it plays a direct role in shaping customer value.

Guided by the company's objectives, marketing managers develop specific pricing objectives. These objectives drive decisions about key pricing policies: (1) how flexible prices will be, (2) the level of prices over the product life cycle, (3) to whom and when discounts and allowances will be given, and (4) how transportation costs will be handled. See Exhibit 16–1. After we've looked at these specific areas, we will discuss how they combine to impact customer value as well as laws that are relevant. In Chapter 17, we will discuss how prices are set.

It's not easy to define price in real-life situations because price reflects many dimensions. People who don't realize this can make big mistakes.

Suppose you've been saving to buy a new car and you see in an ad that, after a $1,000 rebate, the base price for the new-year model is $16,494—5 percent lower than the previous year. At first this might seem like a real bargain. However, your view of this deal might change if you found out you also had to pay a $400 transportation charge and an extra $480 for an extended service warranty. The price might look even less attractive if you discovered that the navigation system, side air bags, and moonroof that were standard the previous year are now options that cost $1,900. The cost of the higher interest rate on the car loan and the sales tax on all of this might come as an unpleasant surprise too. Further, how would you feel if you bought the car anyway and then learned that a friend who just bought the exact same model got a much lower price from the dealer by using a broker he found on the Internet?[2]

Exhibit 16–1 Strategy Planning and Pricing Objectives and Policies

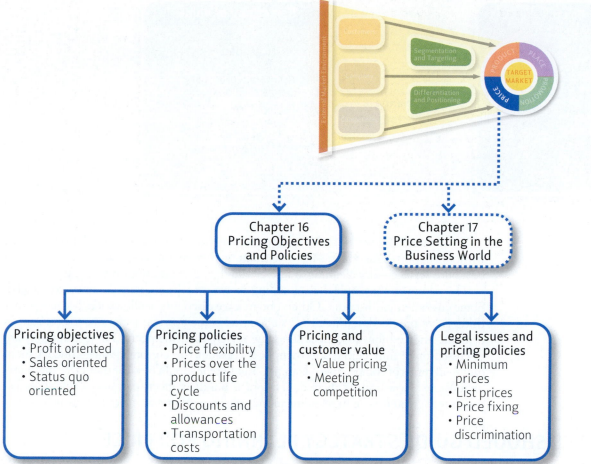

Chapter 16
Pricing Objectives
and Policies

Chapter 17
Price Setting in the
Business World

Pricing objectives
• Profit oriented
• Sales oriented
• Status quo
  oriented

Pricing policies
• Price flexibility
• Prices over the
  product life
  cycle
• Discounts and
  allowances
• Transportation
  costs

**Pricing and
customer value**
• Value pricing
• Meeting
  competition

**Legal issues and
pricing policies**
• Minimum
  prices
• List prices
• Price fixing
• Price
  discrimination

The price equation: Price equals something of value

This example emphasizes that when a seller quotes a price, it is related to *some* assortment of goods and services. So **Price** is the amount of money that is charged for "something" of value. Of course, price may be called different things in different settings. Colleges charge tuition. Landlords collect rent. Motels post a room rate. Country clubs get dues. Banks ask for interest when they loan money. Airlines have fares. Doctors set fees. Employees want a wage. People may call it different things, but *almost every business transaction in our modern economy involves an exchange of money— the Price—for something.*

IKEA's clever—and carefully located—promotional signs remind customers that its price is a good value compared to what they pay for other everyday goods and services.

Exhibit 16–2 Price Exchanged for Something of Value (as seen by consumers or users)

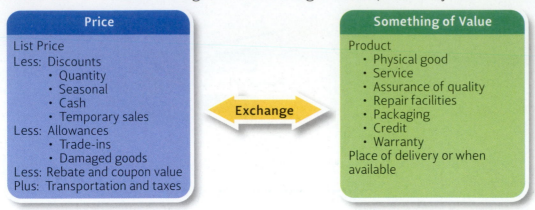

Price		Something of Value

List Price
Less: Discounts
    • Quantity
    • Seasonal
    • Cash
    • Temporary sales
Less: Allowances
    • Trade-ins
    • Damaged goods
Less: Rebate and coupon value
Plus: Transportation and taxes
	Exchange	Product
		    • Physical good
		    • Service
		    • Assurance of quality
		    • Repair facilities
		    • Packaging
		    • Credit
		    • Warranty
		Place of delivery or when available

The something can be a physical product in various stages of completion, with or without supporting services, with or without quality guarantees, and so on. Or it could be a pure service—dry cleaning, a lawyer's advice, or insurance on your car.

The nature and extent of this something determines the amount of money exchanged. Some customers pay list price. Others obtain large discounts or allowances because something is *not* provided. Exhibit 16–2 summarizes some possible variations for consumers or users, and Exhibit 16–3 does the same for channel members. These variations are discussed more fully below, and then we'll consider the customer value concept more fully—in terms of competitive advantage. But here it should be clear that Price has many dimensions. How each of these dimensions is handled affects customer value. If a customer sees greater value in spending money in some other way, no exchange will occur.

OBJECTIVES SHOULD GUIDE STRATEGY PLANNING FOR PRICE

Pricing objectives should flow from, and fit in with, company-level and marketing objectives. Pricing objectives should be *explicitly stated* because they have a direct effect on pricing policies as well as the methods used to set prices. Exhibit 16–4 shows the various types of pricing objectives we'll discuss.

Exhibit 16–3 Price Exchanged for Something of Value (as seen by channel members)

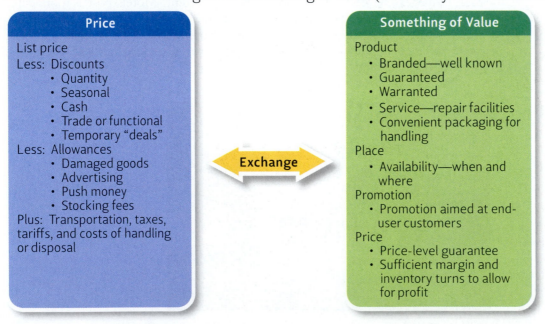

Price		Something of Value

List price
Less: Discounts
    • Quantity
    • Seasonal
    • Cash
    • Trade or functional
    • Temporary "deals"
Less: Allowances
    • Damaged goods
    • Advertising
    • Push money
    • Stocking fees
Plus: Transportation, taxes, tariffs, and costs of handling or disposal
	Exchange	Product
		    • Branded—well known
		    • Guaranteed
		    • Warranted
		    • Service—repair facilities
		    • Convenient packaging for handling
		Place
		    • Availability—when and where
		Promotion
		    • Promotion aimed at end-user customers
		Price
		    • Price-level guarantee
		    • Sufficient margin and inventory turns to allow for profit

Exhibit 16–4
Possible Pricing
Objectives

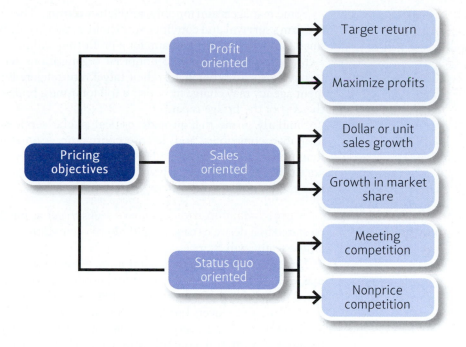

PROFIT-ORIENTED OBJECTIVES

Target returns provide specific guidelines

A **target return objective** sets a specific level of profit as an objective. Often this amount is stated as a percentage of sales or of capital investment. A large manufacturer like Motorola might aim for a 15 percent return on investment. The target for Safeway and other supermarket chains might be a 1 percent return on sales.

A target return objective has administrative advantages in a large company. Performance can be compared against the target. Some companies eliminate divisions, or drop products, that aren't yielding the target rate of return. For example, General Electric sold its small appliance division to Black & Decker because it felt it could earn higher returns in other product-markets.

Barnes & Noble offers free delivery on some Internet orders and that helps it to compete against local retailers or other online sellers who add a delivery charge to the price of a book.

Some just want satisfactory profits

Some managers aim for only satisfactory returns. They just want returns that ensure the firm's survival and convince stockholders they're doing a good job. Similarly, some small family-run businesses aim for a profit that will provide a comfortable lifestyle.[3]

Many private and public nonprofit organizations set a price level that will just recover costs. In other words, their target return figure is zero. For example, a government agency may charge motorists a toll for using a bridge but then drop the toll when the cost of the bridge is paid.

Similarly, firms that provide critical public services—including many utilities, insurance companies, and defense contractors—sometimes pursue only satisfactory long-run targets. They are well aware that the public expects them to set prices that are in the public interest. They may also have to face public or government agencies that review and approve prices.[4]

Profit maximization can be socially responsible

A **profit maximization objective** seeks to get as much profit as possible. It might be stated as a desire to earn a rapid return on investment—or, more bluntly, to charge all the traffic will bear.

Pricing to achieve profit maximization doesn't always lead to high prices. Low prices may expand the size of the market and result in greater sales and profits. For example, when prices of cell phones were very high, only businesses and wealthy people bought them. When producers lowered prices, nearly everyone bought one.

If a firm is earning a very large profit, other firms will try to copy or improve on what the company offers. Frequently, this leads to lower prices.

SALES-ORIENTED OBJECTIVES

A **sales-oriented objective** seeks some level of unit sales, dollar sales, or share of market—*without referring to profit*.

Sales growth doesn't necessarily mean big profits

Some managers are more concerned about sales growth than profits. They think sales growth always leads to more profits. This kind of thinking causes problems when a firm's costs are growing faster than sales. Some major corporations have had declining profits in spite of growth in sales. At the extreme, Pets.com had growing sales but racked up losses until it burned through investors' money and went bankrupt. Generally, however, business managers now pay more attention to profits, not just sales.[5]

Breyers wants customers to know that the value of its ice cream is greater, even if the price is a little higher than a competing ice cream, because of the purity of the ingredients it uses. Mars and other firms that sell snack foods have had success with 100-calorie packages; sometimes the idea of "all of the pleasure and none of the regret" is worth a higher price to the customer even if the portion (and cost to the firm) is smaller.

Some nonprofit organizations set prices to increase market share—precisely because they are *not* trying to earn a profit. For example, many cities set low fares to fill up their buses, reduce traffic, and help the environment. Buses cost the same to run empty or full, and there's more benefit when they're full even if the total revenue is no greater.

Market share objectives are popular

Many firms seek to gain a specified share (percent) of a market. If a company has a large market share, it may have better economies of scale than its competitors. In addition, it's usually easier to measure a firm's market share than to determine if profits are being maximized.

A company with a longer-run view may aim for increased market share when the market is growing. The hope is that future volume will justify sacrificing some profit in the short run. Companies as diverse as 3M and Coca-Cola look at opportunities in Eastern Europe and Southeast Asia this way.

Of course, market share objectives have the same limitations as straight sales growth objectives. A larger market share, if gained at too low a price, may lead to profitless "success."

STATUS QUO PRICING OBJECTIVES

Don't-rock-the-boat objectives

Managers satisfied with their current market share and profits sometimes adopt **status quo objectives**—don't-rock-the-*pricing*-boat objectives. Managers may say that they want to stabilize prices, or meet competition, or even avoid competition. This don't-rock-the-boat thinking is most common when the total market is not growing.

Or stress nonprice competition instead

A status quo pricing objective may be part of an aggressive overall marketing strategy focusing on **nonprice competition**—aggressive action on one or more of the Ps other than Price. Some Internet firms originally thought that they'd compete with low prices and still earn high profits from volume. However, when they didn't get the sales volume they hoped for, they realized that there were also some nonprice ways to compete. For example, Zappos.com offers free shipping and guarantees that it will meet local shoe store prices. But it wins customers with its enormous selection of shoes, a website that makes it easy for customers to find what they want, and excellent customer service before and after the sale.

MOST FIRMS SET SPECIFIC PRICING POLICIES—TO REACH OBJECTIVES

Administered prices help achieve objectives

Price policies usually lead to **administered prices**—consciously set prices. In other words, instead of letting daily market forces (or auctions) decide their prices, most firms set their own prices. They may hold prices steady for long periods of time or change them more frequently if that's what's required to meet objectives.

If a firm doesn't sell directly to final customers, it usually wants to administer both the price it receives from intermediaries and the price final customers pay. After all, the price final customers pay will ultimately affect the quantity it sells.

Yet it is often difficult to administer prices throughout the channel. Other channel members may also wish to administer prices to achieve their own objectives. This is what happened to Alcoa, one of the largest aluminum producers. To reduce its excess inventory, Alcoa offered its wholesalers a 30 percent discount off its normal price. Alcoa expected the wholesalers to pass most of the discount along to their customers to stimulate sales throughout the channel. Instead, wholesalers bought *their* aluminum at the lower price but passed on only a small discount to customers. As a result, the quantity Alcoa sold didn't increase much, and it still had excess inventory, while the wholesalers made much more profit on the aluminum they did sell.[6]

Marketing managers for Trico Winter Wiper Blades consciously set prices so that consumers receive a good value at a price that will yield attractive profits for both the producer and the retailer. Carnival's managers use flexible pricing—including discounts for retired people.

Some firms don't even try to administer prices. They just meet competition—or worse, mark up their costs with little thought to demand. They act as if they have no choice in selecting a price policy.

Remember that Price has many dimensions. Managers usually *do* have many choices. They *should* administer their prices. And they should do it carefully because, ultimately, customers must be willing to pay these prices before a whole marketing mix succeeds. In the rest of this chapter, we'll talk about policies a marketing manager must set to do an effective job of administering Price.[7]

PRICE FLEXIBILITY POLICIES

**One-price policy—
the same price for
everyone**

One of the first decisions a marketing manager has to make is whether to use a one-price or a flexible-price policy. A **one-price policy** means offering the same price to all customers who purchase products under essentially the same conditions and in the same quantities. The majority of U.S. firms use a one-price policy—mainly for administrative convenience and to maintain goodwill among customers.

A one-price policy makes pricing easier. But a marketing manager must be careful to avoid a rigid one-price policy. This can amount to broadcasting a price that competitors can undercut, especially if the price is somewhat high. One reason for the growth of mass-merchandisers is that conventional retailers rigidly applied traditional margins and stuck to them.

**Flexible-price policy—
different prices for
different customers**

A **flexible-price policy** means offering the same product and quantities to different customers at different prices. When computers are used to implement flexible pricing, the decisions focus more on what type of customer will get a price break.

**Pricing databases
make flexible
pricing easier**

Various forms of flexible pricing are more common now that most prices are maintained in a central computer database. Frequent changes are easier. You see this when supermarket chains give frequent-shopper club members reduced prices on weekly specials. The checkout scanner reads the code on the package, and then the computer looks up the club price or the regular price depending on whether a club card has been scanned.

Some marketing managers have set up relationships with Internet companies whose ads invite customers to "set your own price." For example, at www.priceline.com, visitors specify the desired schedule for an airline flight and what price they're willing to pay. Priceline electronically forwards the information to airlines and if one accepts the offer the consumer is notified.

It may appear that these marketing managers have given up on administering prices. Just the opposite is true. They are carefully administering a flexible price. Most airlines, for example, set a very high list price. Not many people pay it. Travelers who plan ahead or who accept nonpeak flights get a discount. Business travelers who want high-demand flights on short notice pay the higher prices. However, it doesn't make sense to stick to a high price and fly the plane half empty. So the airline continuously adjusts the price on the basis of how many seats are left to fill. If seats are still empty at the last minute, the website offers a rock-bottom fare. Other firms, especially service businesses, use this approach when they have excess capacity.[8]

Salespeople can adjust prices to the situation

Flexible pricing is most common in the channels, in direct sales of business products, and at retail for expensive shopping products. Retail shopkeepers in less-developed economies typically use flexible pricing. These situations usually involve personal selling, not mass selling. The advantage of flexible pricing is that the salesperson can adjust price—considering prices charged by competitors, the relationship with the customer, and the customer's bargaining ability. Flexible-price policies often specify a *range* in which the actual price charged must fall.[9]

Too much price-cutting erodes profits

Some sales reps let price-cutting become a habit. This can lead to a lower price level and lower profit. A small price cut may not seem like much; but keep in mind that all of the revenue that is lost would go to profit. If salespeople for a producer that usually earns profits equal to 20 percent of its sales cut prices by an average of about 10 percent, profits would drop by half! See Exhibit 16–5.

Disadvantages of flexible pricing

Flexible pricing does have disadvantages. A customer who finds that others paid lower prices for the same marketing mix will be unhappy. This can cause real conflict in channels. For example, the Winn-Dixie supermarket chain stopped carrying products of some suppliers who refused to give Winn-Dixie the same prices available to chains in other regions of the country. Similarly, companies that post different prices for different segments on a website that all can see often get complaints.

If buyers learn that negotiating is in their interest, the time needed for bargaining will increase. This can increase selling costs and reduce profits. It can also frustrate customers. For example, most auto dealers use flexible pricing and bargain for what

Exhibit 16–5
Impact of Price Cut on Profit

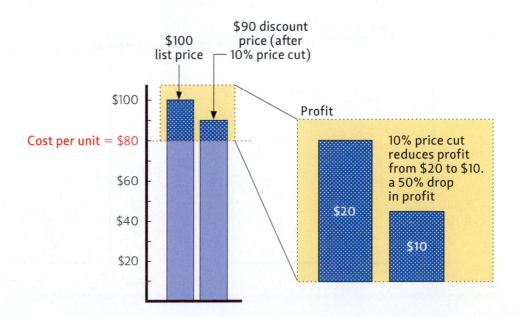

they can get. Inexperienced consumers, reluctant to bargain, often pay hundreds of dollars more than the dealer is willing to accept. By contrast, CarMax has earned high customer-satisfaction ratings by offering haggle-weary consumers a one-price policy.[10]

PRICE-LEVEL POLICIES—OVER THE PRODUCT LIFE CYCLE

Marketing managers who administer prices must consciously set a price-level policy. As they enter the market, they have to set introductory prices that may have long-run effects. They must consider where the product life cycle is and how fast it's moving. And they must decide if their prices should be above, below, or somewhere in between relative to the market.

Skimming pricing— feeling out demand at a high price

A **skimming price policy** tries to sell the top (skim the cream) of a market—the top of the demand curve—at a high price before aiming at more price-sensitive customers. Skimming may maximize profits in the market introduction stage for an innovation, especially if there are few substitutes or if some customers are not price sensitive. Skimming is also useful when you don't know very much about the shape of the demand curve. It's sometimes safer to start with a high price that can be reduced if customers balk.

Skimming has critics

Some critics argue that firms should not try to maximize profits by using a skimming policy on new products that have important social consequences—a patent-protected, life-saving drug or a technique that increases crop yields, for example. Many of those who need the product may not have the money to buy it. This is a serious concern. However, it's also a serious problem if firms don't have any incentive to take risks and develop new products.[11]

Price moves down the demand curve

A skimming policy usually involves a slow reduction in price over time. See Exhibit 16–6. Note that as price is reduced, new target markets are probably being sought. So as the price level steps down the demand curve, new Place, Product, and Promotion policies may be needed too.

Exhibit 16–6   Alternative Introductory Pricing Policies

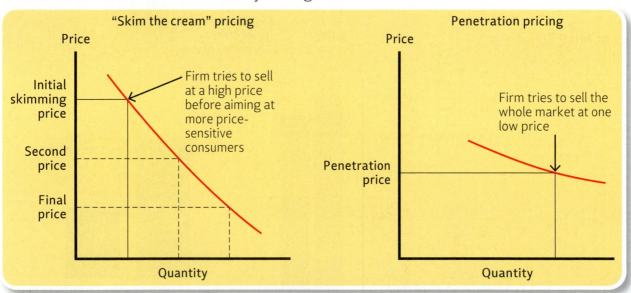

DuPont Corian, a solid countertop material, was costly to develop. When Corian was introduced, there was little direct competition and a premium price helped to recover development costs. Now that there is more competition, discounted prices are sometimes available.

When McCaw Cellular Communications—the firm that pioneered cellular phone service and was later bought out by AT&T—first came on the market, it set a high price. Each wireless minute cost about $1, and customers had to pay about $675 for a large, clunky phone. McCaw used dealers to sell the premium-priced packages because they could explain the value of the system and get orders. They mainly targeted firms that gave phones to their on-the-go executives and salespeople. Many of these customers were not price sensitive because no good substitute was available. However, that changed as other cellular providers came into the market. To improve the value of its offering, McCaw bought large quantities of phones from Motorola at low cost and then packaged them with a service contract at a high discount. As the market grew, economies of scale kicked in and McCaw cut prices even more. McCaw also did more advertising and started to sell cellular services through a variety of retail outlets, including mass-merchandisers. These Promotion and Place changes cut selling costs and helped reach the growing number of families who wanted cell service. Free weekend and evening minutes for consumers when demand from business customers was low sweetened the deal. In addition, prices on phones had come down so much that retailers gave away a phone with a one-year service contract—and offered family plans where additional family members were added to a contract for about $10 each. By then, AT&T was relying more heavily on television advertising that encouraged customers to sign up at an AT&T store or at the AT&T website—which helped cut channel markups from the selling price. Promotion and discounting became even more aggressive as cell phone services merged, but AT&T was able to build its share because it was the exclusive service provider for Apple's hot iPhone. However, Sprint didn't just roll over and let AT&T win the competition for the growing number of smart-phone users. Rather, it slashed the total costs of using smart phones with its "Simply Everything" plan. For $99 a month it offered customers unlimited talking, Web browsing, text, picture and video messaging, music downloads, and even 150 radio stations. As this example suggests, as the skimming price in the market is reduced, it is often accompanied by a series of changes in marketing strategy.[12]

Penetration pricing—get volume at a low price

A **penetration pricing policy** tries to sell the whole market at one low price. This approach might be wise when the elite market—those willing to pay a high price—is small. This is the case when the whole demand curve is fairly elastic. See Exhibit 16–6. A penetration policy is even more attractive if selling larger quantities results in lower costs because of economies of scale. Penetration pricing may be wise if the firm expects strong competition very soon after introduction.

Sony relied on penetration pricing when it battled with Toshiba to introduce a next-generation optical disc player. Sony's Blu-ray format and Toshiba's HD-DVD format were incompatible formats. Sony had to win market acceptance quickly. If Toshiba's HD-DVD format became the standard, Sony's investment to develop and promote Blu-ray would go down the drain.

To motivate buyers, Sony cut the price on its Blu-ray players to the bone. Getting adoptions quickly was critical because studios would distribute movies in the format most popular with consumers. Sony saw an opportunity to kick-start its efforts by including a Blu-ray disc drive in its PS3 third-generation game console. When

it came out in late 2006, the PS3 was more expensive than competing consoles because it had more power and a Blu-ray drive. However, Sony priced it below its current production cost. This move was part of Sony's penetration pricing plan for Blu-ray. All the PS3 consoles that Sony sold that Christmas contributed to economies of scale and lower prices on the regular Blu-ray players. In addition, all of the excited people who clamored to buy PS3s for their favorite games also used them for their Blu-ray movies. This added to Sony's Blu-ray market share with consumers and gave it an advantage with studios. By spring of 2008, Sony had a clear lead and Toshiba threw in the towel on its HD-DVD format.

Of course, even a low penetration price doesn't keep competitors out of a market permanently. Product life cycles do march on. However, a firm that gets a head start in a new market can often maintain its advantage.[13]

Introductory price dealing—temporary price cuts

Low prices do attract customers. Therefore, marketers often use **introductory price dealing**—temporary price cuts—to speed new products into a market and get customers to try them. However, don't confuse these *temporary* price cuts with low penetration prices. The plan here is to raise prices as soon as the introductory offer is over. By then, hopefully, target customers will have decided it is worth buying again at the regular price.

Established competitors often choose not to meet introductory price dealing—as long as the introductory period is not too long or too successful. However, some competitors match introductory price deals with their own short-term sale prices to discourage customers from shopping around.

Different price-level policies through the channel

The price of a product sold to channel members should be set so that channel members can cover their costs and make a profit. For example, a producer of a slightly

Marketers often use introductory price dealing—in the form of temporary price cuts or introductory coupons—to speed new products into a market.

better product might set a price level that is low relative to competitors when selling to retailers but suggest an above-the-market retail price. This encourages retailers to emphasize the product because it yields higher profits for them.

The price of money may affect the price level

We've been talking about the price level of a firm's product. But a nation's money also has a price level—what it is worth in some other currency. For example, on April 16, 2008, one U.S. dollar was worth 0.50 British pounds. In other words, the exchange rate for the British pound against the U.S. dollar was 0.50. Exhibit 16–7 lists exchange rates for money from several countries over a number of years. From this exhibit you can see that exchange rates change over time—and sometimes the changes are significant. For example, on April 16, 2005, a U.S. dollar was worth 42.89 Thai baht; just three years later the U.S. dollar was worth 27 percent less—only 31.44 Thai baht.

As the following example shows, exchange rate changes can have a significant effect on international trade and how a firm's price is viewed by customers in an overseas market. Jacquelyn Tran started BeautyEncounter.com, an online retail

Exhibit 16–7
Exchange Rates for Various Currencies against the U.S. Dollar over Time

Base Currency	Number of Units of Base Currency per U.S. Dollar*			
	1999	2002	2005	2008
British pound	0.62	0.69	0.64	0.50
Thai baht	37.40	43.48	42.89	31.44
Japanese yen	117.86	131.19	120.04	101.40
Australian dollar	1.55	1.88	1.64	1.06
Canadian dollar	1.49	1.58	1.46	1.00
Euro	1.07	1.13	0.92	0.63

*Units shown are for April 16 in each year.

The price that a customer actually pays for a British Airways flight depends on the currency used to buy the ticket and the exchange rate between that currency and the British pound.

cosmetics website, in 1999. Before long, her domestic business was doing well and she was also attracting some sales from the United Kingdom, France, Germany, Japan, Canada, and Latin America. Her sales to international customers grew at an even faster rate after 2005 as the U.S. dollar weakened against other currencies (see Exhibit 16–7). You can see why this would happen by looking at the change in the exchange rate of the euro against the dollar. In April of 2005, the exchange rate for the euro against the dollar was 0.92, so a customer living in Europe paid 92 euros to purchase $100 worth of beauty supplies. Three years later, the exchange rate had dropped to 0.63, so at that point it cost the customer only 63 euros to purchase the same $100 worth of supplies. So, from the perspective of a European customer, the change in the exchange rate over that time period had the same effect as a price cut. Yet, many of those customers didn't just buy the same beauty supplies and pocket the extra 29 euros. Instead, they continued to spend the same amount in their home currency (92 euros), which in 2008 was equal to $146. In effect, these customers increased the size of their orders from Beauty Encounter by 46 percent (from $100 to $146). The shift in exchange rates also made the firm's cosmetics cheaper relative to competing cosmetics retailers in Europe, and that attracted new overseas customers.

Beauty Encounter's export business benefited from exchange rate changes from 2005 to 2008. But exchange rates can move in the opposite direction. If exchange rates return to the 2005 level, or even to the 2002 level, Beauty Encounter's export sales are likely to drop.[14]

Internet EXERCISE

There is a website (**www.x-rates.com**) that converts one country's currency to another. Go to the website, click on "Currency Calculator," and determine how much $100 U.S. is worth in Thai bahts, British pounds, and euros. How do those numbers compare with April 2008 (see Exhibit 16–7)?

DISCOUNT POLICIES—REDUCTIONS FROM LIST PRICES

Prices start with a list price

Most price structures are built around a base price schedule or list price. **Basic list prices** are the prices final customers or users are normally asked to pay for products. In this book, unless noted otherwise, list price refers to basic list price.

In Chapter 17, we discuss how firms set these list prices. For now, however, we'll consider variations from list price and why they are made.

Discounts are reductions from list price given by a seller to buyers who either give up some marketing function or provide the function themselves. Discounts can be useful in marketing strategy planning. In the following discussion, think about what function the buyers are giving up, or providing, when they get each of these discounts.

Quantity discounts encourage volume buying

Quantity discounts are discounts offered to encourage customers to buy in larger amounts. This lets a seller get more of a buyer's business, or shifts some of the storing function to the buyer, or reduces shipping and selling costs—or all of these. There are two kinds of quantity discounts: cumulative and noncumulative.

Cumulative quantity discounts apply to purchases over a given period— such as a year—and the discount usually increases as the amount purchased increases. Cumulative discounts encourage *repeat* buying by reducing the customer's cost for additional purchases. This is a way to develop loyalty and ongoing relationships with customers. For example, a Lowe's lumberyard might give a cumulative quantity discount to a building contractor who is not able to buy all of the needed materials at once. Lowe's wants to reward the contractor's patronage and discourage shopping around.

A cumulative quantity discount is often attractive to business customers who don't want to run up their inventory costs. They are rewarded for buying large quantities, even though individual orders may be smaller.

Noncumulative quantity discounts apply only to individual orders. Such discounts encourage larger orders but

Customers who buy six applications of Frontline Plus flea protection get two more for free. This is basically a quantity discount that results in a 33 percent savings for the customer.

do not tie a buyer to the seller after that one purchase. Lowe's lumberyard may resell insulation products made by several competing producers. Owens-Corning might try to encourage Lowe's to stock larger quantities of its pink insulation by offering a noncumulative quantity discount.

Seasonal discounts— buy sooner

Seasonal discounts are discounts offered to encourage buyers to buy earlier than present demand requires. If used by a manufacturer, this discount tends to shift the storing function further along in the channel. It also tends to even out sales over the year. For example, Kyota offers wholesalers a lower price on its garden tillers if they buy in the fall, when sales are slow.

Service firms that face irregular demand or excess capacity often use seasonal discounts. For example, some tourist attractions, like ski resorts, offer lower weekday rates when attendance would otherwise be down.

Payment terms and cash discounts set payment dates

Most sales to businesses are made on credit. The seller sends a bill (invoice) by mail or electronically, and the buyer's accounting department processes it for payment. Some firms depend on their suppliers for temporary working capital (credit). Therefore, it is very important for both sides to clearly state the terms of payment— including the availability of cash discounts—and to understand the commonly used payment terms.

Net means that payment for the face value of the invoice is due immediately. These terms are sometimes changed to net 10 or net 30, which means payment is due within 10 or 30 days of the date on the invoice.

Cash discounts are reductions in price to encourage buyers to pay their bills quickly. The terms for a cash discount usually modify the net terms.

2/10, net 30 means the buyer can take a 2 percent discount off the face value of the invoice if the invoice is paid within 10 days. Otherwise, the full face value is due within 30 days. And it usually is stated or understood that an interest charge will be added after the 30-day free-credit period.

Why cash discounts are given and should be evaluated

Smart buyers carefully evaluate cash discounts. A discount of 2/10, net 30 may not look like much at first. But the buyer earns a 2 percent discount for paying the invoice just 20 days sooner than it should be paid anyway. By not taking the discount, the company in effect is borrowing at an annual rate of 36 percent. That is, assuming a 360-day year and dividing by 20 days, there are 18 periods during which the company could earn 2 percent—and 18 times 2 equals 36 percent a year.

Consumers say "charge it"

Credit sales are also important to retailers. Retailers usually accept credit cards from services such as Visa or MasterCard and pay a percent of the revenue from each credit sale for the service. Some retailers also have aggressive promotions to sign up customers for their own credit cards because customers that carry a store's credit card may spend more money at the store. Generous credit terms, such as "no interest or payments for one full year" do stimulate sales. However, credit that is too easy exposes retailers to the risk of losses when the economy turns down. There are also ethical concerns about credit card companies and retailers that make it too easy for consumers to buy things they really can't afford. The problem becomes worse when an unpaid balance on a credit card carries a very high interest rate. This can significantly increase a customer's total costs for purchases. Even worse, it leaves many low-income consumers trapped in debt.

Sale prices encourage consumers to purchase products immediately. To get the sale price, customers give up the convenience of buying when they want to buy and instead buy when the seller wants to sell.

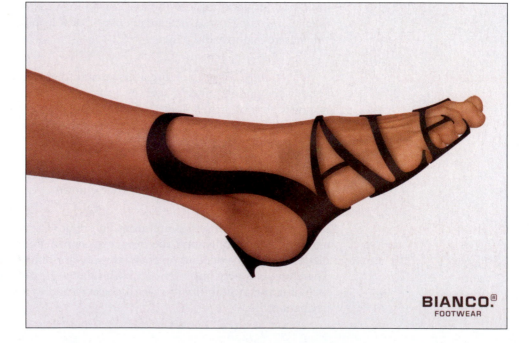

BIANCO.®
FOOTWEAR

Trade discounts often are set by tradition

A **trade (functional) discount** is a list price reduction given to channel members for the job they are going to do. A manufacturer, for example, might allow retailers a 30 percent trade discount from the suggested retail list price to cover the cost of the retailing function and their profit. Similarly, the manufacturer might allow wholesalers a *chain* discount of 30 percent and 10 percent off the suggested retail price. In this case, the wholesalers would be expected to pass the 30 percent discount on to retailers.[15]

Special sales reduce list prices—temporarily

A **sale price** is a temporary discount from the list price. Sale price discounts encourage immediate buying. In other words, to get the sale price, customers give up the convenience of buying when they want to buy and instead buy when the seller wants to sell.

Special sales provide a marketing manager with a quick way to respond to changing market conditions without changing the basic marketing strategy. For example, a retailer might use a sale to help clear extra inventory or to meet a competing store's price.

In recent years, sale prices and deals have become much more common. Some retailers have sales so often that consumers just wait to purchase when there's a sale. Others check out a website like www.fatwallet.com to figure out where the product they want is already on sale.

To avoid these problems, some firms that sell consumer convenience products offer **everyday low pricing**—setting a low list price rather than relying on frequent sales, discounts, or allowances. Many supermarkets use this approach.

Sale prices should be used carefully, consistent with well-thought-out pricing objectives and policies. A marketing manager who constantly uses temporary sales to adjust the price level probably has not done a good job setting the normal price.[16]

ALLOWANCE POLICIES—OFF LIST PRICES

Allowances, like discounts, are given to final consumers, customers, or channel members for doing something or accepting less of something.

Advertising allowances—something for something

Advertising allowances are price reductions given to firms in the channel to encourage them to advertise or otherwise promote the supplier's products locally. For example, Sony might give an allowance (3 percent of sales) to its retailers. They, in turn, are expected to spend the allowance on local advertising.

Stocking allowances—get attention and shelf space

Stocking allowances—sometimes called *slotting allowances*—are given to an intermediary to get shelf space for a product. For example, a producer might offer a retailer cash or free merchandise to stock a new item. Stocking allowances are used mainly to get supermarket chains to handle new products. Supermarkets are more willing to give space to a new product if the supplier will offset their handling costs and risks. With a big stocking allowance, the intermediary makes extra profit—even if a new product fails and the producer loses money.

Are stocking allowances ethical?

Critics say that retailer demands for big stocking allowances slow new product introductions and make it hard for small producers to compete. Some producers feel that retailers' demands are unethical—just a different form of extortion. Retailers, on the other hand, point out that the fees protect them from producers that simply want to push more and more me-too products onto their shelves. Perhaps the best way for a producer to cope with the problem is to develop new products that really do offer consumers superior value. Then it benefits everyone in the channel, including retailers, to get the products to the target market.[17]

Many consumers go to Subway primarily because it offers a wide selection of healthy fare at a reasonable price. Even so, some consumers are very price sensitive, so Subway promotes a reduced price for a "Daily Special" sandwich and also distributes a coupon for a "Free Sub" when other requirements are met.

PMs—push for cash

Push money (or prize money) allowances—sometimes called *PMs* or *spiffs*—are given to retailers by manufacturers or wholesalers to pass on to the retailers' salesclerks for aggressively selling certain items. PM allowances are used for new items, slower-moving items, or higher-margin items. They are often used for pushing furniture, clothing, consumer electronics, and cosmetics. A salesclerk, for example, might earn an additional $5 for each new model Panasonic DVD player sold.

Bring in the old, ring up the new—with trade-ins

A **trade-in allowance** is a price reduction given for used products when similar new products are bought. Trade-ins give the marketing manager an easy way to lower the effective price without reducing list price. Proper handling of trade-ins is important when selling durable products.

SOME CUSTOMERS GET SOMETHING EXTRA

Clipping coupons— more for less

Many producers and retailers offer discounts (or free items) through coupons distributed in packages, mailings, print ads, or at the store. By presenting a coupon to a retailer, the consumer is given a discount off list price. This is especially common in the consumer packaged goods business—but the use of price-off coupons is also growing in other lines of business.

Retailers are willing to redeem producers' coupons because it increases their sales—and they usually are paid for the trouble of handling the coupons. For example, a retailer that redeems a 50 cents off coupon might be repaid 75 cents.[18]

Internet EXERCISE

FatWallet (**www.fatwallet.com**) is one of many websites that can help consumers find good deals. To see how it works, assume that you are interested in buying a new printer for your personal computer. Start by selecting a specific model that you like at the HP website (**www.hpshopping.com**). Then, search at www.fatwallet.com to see what you can learn about buying that printer. For example, check for advice in the consumer forums and see if there are any coupons. Identify different retailers that sell the printer, and read the ratings of those retailers. Where would you buy the printer, and why did you choose that retailer?

Cash rebates when you buy

Some firms offer **rebates**—refunds paid to consumers after a purchase. Sometimes the rebate is very large. Some automakers offer rebates of $500 to $6,000 to promote sales of slow-moving models. Rebates are also used on lower-priced items, ranging from Duracell batteries and Memorex CD-Rs to Logitech webcams and Paul Masson wines. Rebates give a producer a way to be certain that final consumers actually get the price reduction. If the rebate amount were just taken off the price charged intermediaries, they might not pass the savings along to consumers.

But rebates have their critics. While rebates prompt many consumers to make a purchase, many rebates—even high-value rebates—are never redeemed. A few years ago TiVo offered a $100 holiday season rebate, but half of the consumers eligible failed to even request their rebate. For many customers the paperwork and hassle deter them; others simply forget after they leave the store. The growing consumer backlash against rebates and the threat of government regulation have prompted many firms to drop rebates from their marketing strategies.[19]

A pricing consultant has suggested that your firm set a premium price for the paper-shredding machines it sells through office equipment stores—but that there be a $20 mail-in rebate with each unit. The consultant says his research shows that, when an office shredder wears out, it's usually the administrative assistant who is sent to buy a replacement. The consultant says that many of these buyers will pick your firm's shredder, in spite of the higher price, so that they can pocket the rebate. At the end of his report he says, "This is an accepted way to motivate the decision maker. Think about all those executives who rack up frequent-flier miles on business trips and then use the free tickets they get for family vacations." Your boss has left the decision up to you. Would you follow the consultant's advice? Why or why not?

LIST PRICE MAY DEPEND ON GEOGRAPHIC PRICING POLICIES

Retail list prices sometimes include free delivery. Or free delivery may be offered to some customers as an aid to closing the sale. But deciding who pays the freight charge is more important on sales to business customers than to final consumers because more money is involved. Purchase orders usually specify place, time, method of delivery, freight costs, insurance, handling, and other charges. There are many possible variations for an imaginative marketing manager, and some specialized terms have developed.

F.O.B. pricing is easy

A commonly used transportation term is **F.O.B.**—which means free on board some vehicle at some place. Typically, F.O.B. pricing names the place—often the location of the seller's factory or warehouse—as in F.O.B. Taiwan or F.O.B. mill. This means that the seller pays the cost of loading the products onto some vehicle, then title to the products passes to the buyer. The buyer pays the freight and takes responsibility for damage in transit.

If a firm wants to pay the freight for the convenience of customers, it can use F.O.B. delivered or F.O.B. buyer's factory. In this case, title does not pass until the products are delivered. If the seller wants title to pass immediately but is willing to prepay freight (and then include it in the invoice), F.O.B. seller's factory-freight prepaid can be used.

F.O.B. shipping point pricing simplifies the seller's pricing—but it may narrow the market. Since the delivered cost varies depending on the buyer's location, a customer located farther from the seller must pay more and might buy from closer suppliers.

Zone pricing smooths delivered prices

Zone pricing means making an average freight charge to all buyers within specific geographic areas. The seller pays the actual freight charges and bills each customer for an average charge. For example, a company in Canada might divide the United States into seven zones, then bill all customers in the same zone the same amount for freight even though actual shipping costs might vary.

Zone pricing reduces the wide variation in delivered prices that results from an F.O.B. shipping point pricing policy. It also simplifies transportation charges.

Uniform delivered pricing—one price to all

Uniform delivered pricing means making an average freight charge to all buyers. It is a kind of zone pricing—an entire country may be considered as one zone— that includes the average cost of delivery in the price. Uniform delivered pricing is most often used when (1) transportation costs are relatively low and (2) the seller wishes to sell in all geographic areas at one price, perhaps a nationally advertised price.

Freight-absorption pricing—competing on equal grounds in another territory

When all firms in an industry use F.O.B. shipping point pricing, a firm usually competes well near its shipping point but not farther away. As sales reps look for business farther away, delivered prices rise and the firm finds itself priced out of the market.

This problem can be reduced with **freight-absorption pricing**—which means absorbing freight cost so that a firm's delivered price meets that of the nearest competitor. This amounts to cutting list price to appeal to new market segments. Some firms look at international markets this way; they just figure that any profit from export sales is a bonus.

PRICING POLICIES COMBINE TO IMPACT CUSTOMER VALUE

Look at Price from the customer's viewpoint

We've discussed pricing policies separately so far, but from the customer's view they all combine to impact customer value. So when we talk about Price we are really talking about the whole set of price policies that define the real price level. On the other hand, superior value isn't just based on having a lower price than some competitor but rather on the whole marketing mix.

In today's competitive markets, a marketing manager must look for ways to improve the marketing mix so that it attracts customers with superior customer value. For example, Haggar uses higher-quality buttons, even though it increases Haggar's costs, because customers expect good buttons. Hyundai creates high value by offering "America's Best Warranty" on a full-featured vehicle at a very low price.

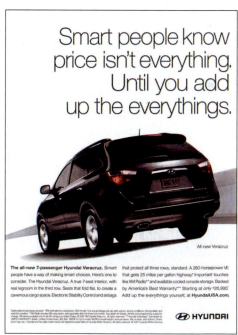

Value pricing leads to superior customer value

Smart marketers look for the combination of Price decisions that result in value pricing. **Value pricing** means setting a fair price level for a marketing mix that really gives the target market superior customer value.

Value pricing doesn't necessarily mean cheap if cheap means bare-bones or low-grade. It doesn't mean high prestige either if the prestige is not accompanied by the right quality goods and services. Rather, the focus is on the customer's requirements and how the whole marketing mix meets those needs.

Toyota is a firm that has been effective with value pricing. It has different marketing mixes for different target markets. But from the $10,000 Echo to the $60,000 Land Cruiser, the Japanese automaker consistently offers better quality and lower prices than its competitors. Among fast-food restaurants, Wendy's has a good reputation for value pricing.

Companies that use value pricing deliver on their promises. They try to give the consumer pleasant surprises—like an unexpected service—because it increases value and builds customer loyalty. They return the price if the customer isn't completely satisfied. They avoid unrealistic price levels—prices that are high only because consumers already know the brand name. They build relationships so customers will come back time and again.

There are Price choices in most markets

Some marketing managers miss the advantages of value pricing. They've heard economists say that in perfect competition it's foolish to offer products above or below the market price. But most firms *don't* operate in perfect competition where what firms offer is exactly the same.

Most operate in monopolistic competition, where products and whole marketing mixes are *not* exactly the same. This means that there are pricing options. At one extreme, some firms are clearly above the market—they may even brag about it. Tiffany's is well known as one of the most expensive jewelry stores in the world. Other firms emphasize below-the-market prices in their marketing mixes. Prices offered by discounters and mass-merchandisers, such as Wal-Mart and Tesco, illustrate this approach. They may even promote their pricing policy with catchy slogans like "guaranteed lowest prices."

Value pricers define the target market and the competition

In making price decisions and using value pricing, it is important to clearly define the *relevant target market* and *competitors* when making price comparisons.

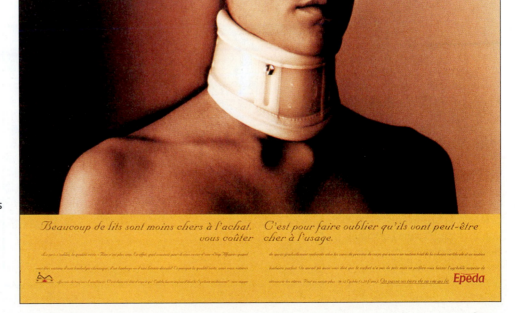

Epeda sells high-quality mattresses. It wants customers to know that its higher price is worth it. This ad says, "Lots of mattresses are cheap to buy, the reason is to make you forget how much sleeping on them is going to cost you."

Consider Wal-Mart prices again from this view. Wal-Mart may have lower prices on electronics products like flat-panel televisions, but it offers less expertise from the store's sales staff, less selection, and no help installing or setting up a new television. Wal-Mart may appeal to budget-oriented shoppers who compare prices *and* value among different mass-merchandisers. But a specialty electronics store appeals to different customers and may not even be a direct competitor!

A producer of flat-panel televisions with this point of view may offer the specialty electronics store models that are not available to Wal-Mart—to ensure that customers don't view price as the only difference between the two stores. Further, the specialty store needs to clearly communicate to its target market *how* it offers superior value. Wal-Mart is certainly going to communicate that it offers low prices. If that's all customers hear, they will see no differences between retailers except for price. The specialty retailer must emphasize its expertise, selection, or the superior performance of its product line—so that target customers who value these differences know where to find them.

Meeting competitors' prices may be necessary

In a mature market there is downward pressure on both prices and profit margins. Moreover, differentiating the value a firm offers may not be easy when competitors can quickly copy new ideas. Extending our flat-panel example, if our speciality store is in a city with a number of similar stores with the same products, there may not be a way to convince consumers that one beats all of the others. In such circumstances there may be no real pricing choice other than to "meet the competition." With profit margins already thin, they would quickly disappear or turn into losses at a lower price. And a higher price would simply prompt competitors to promote their price advantage.[20]

Similarly, a B2B supplier may have a better marketing mix than competitors; but if buyers have decided to use a procurement website and reverse auction as the only way to buy, the supplier may not have any choice but to decide what the lowest price is that it will bid to get the business. Winning the bid at a profit-losing price doesn't help.

Even though competition can be intense, too many marketers give up too easily. They often can find a way to differentiate, even if it's something that competitors dismiss as less important. For example, Kellogg was facing soggy sales and tough competition in the dry cereal category. Dealer brands made price competition even tougher. However, when Kellogg added freeze-dried fruit to create Special K Red Berries, it

Consumers often use websites like mySimon.com that search for the best prices on particular items. When it's easy for customers to compare prices, marketers must clearly communicate to the customer how the rest of the marketing mix is better and why it justifies a higher price.

428

attracted many customers away from competing brands. The berries did increase costs, but Kellogg's profits still improved. In Europe, where price sensitivity was greatest, Kellogg kept the price the same but reduced the size of the Red Berries box. In the United States, the size of the box is standard but the price was increased enough to provide profit margins. Even though General Mills later copied the idea, Kellogg had a head start and quickly came out with other fruit-added cereals. And both producers benefited by having a way to differentiate from the low-price store brands in their category.[21]

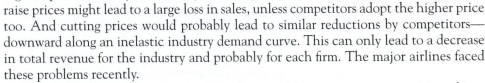

There may be little choice about Price in oligopoly situations. Pricing at the market—that is, meeting competition—may be the only sensible policy. To raise prices might lead to a large loss in sales, unless competitors adopt the higher price too. And cutting prices would probably lead to similar reductions by competitors—downward along an inelastic industry demand curve. This can only lead to a decrease in total revenue for the industry and probably for each firm. The major airlines faced these problems recently.

To avoid these problems, each oligopolist may choose a status quo pricing objective and set its price at the competitive level. Some critics call this pricing behavior conscious parallel action, implying it is unethical and the same as intentional conspiracy among firms. As a practical matter, however, that criticism seems overly harsh. It obviously isn't sensible for firms to ignore their competitors.

Value pricing fits with market-oriented strategy planning

There are times when the marketing manager's hands are tied and there is little that can be done to differentiate the marketing mix. However, most marketing managers do have choices—many choices. They can vary strategy decisions with respect to all of the marketing mix variables, not just Price, to offer target customers superior value. And when a marketer's hands are really tied, it's time to look for new opportunities that offer more promise.

LEGALITY OF PRICING POLICIES

This chapter discusses the many pricing decisions that must be made. However, some pricing decisions are limited by government legislation. The first step to understanding pricing legislation is to know the thinking of legislators and the courts. To get a better idea of the "why" of legislation, we'll focus on U.S. legislation here, but many other countries have similar pricing laws.[22]

Minimum prices are sometimes controlled

Unfair trade practice acts put a lower limit on prices, especially at the wholesale and retail levels. They have been passed in more than half the states in the United States. Selling below cost in these states is illegal. Wholesalers and retailers are usually required to take a certain minimum percentage markup over their merchandise-plus-transportation costs. The practical effect of these laws is to protect certain limited-line food retailers—such as dairy stores—from the kind of "ruinous" competition supermarkets might offer if they sold milk as a leader, offering it below cost for a long time.

The United States and most other countries control the minimum price of imported products with antidumping laws. **Dumping** is pricing a product sold in a foreign market below the cost of producing it or at a price lower than in its domestic market. These laws are usually designed to protect the country's domestic producers and jobs. But there is debate about how well they work.

Consider what happened when U.S. steel producers pushed for tariffs because overseas steel mills, many of which are subsidized by their own governments, were selling at a lower price in the United States than at home. Most U.S. steel producers suffered losses and were forced to cut jobs. After the tariffs went into place, U.S. steel producers increased their profits by raising prices. But, as a result, other U.S. firms that needed to buy steel faced higher costs. Yet these firms couldn't raise *their* prices because they still had global competitors in their own product-markets. Some critics argued that U.S. steel companies were inefficient and that the tariffs protected them by sacrificing their customers. Less than two years later, the United States dropped the steel tariffs. However, by then other countries seized the excuse to impose tariffs of their own, which made it harder for U.S. companies to get export business. Dumping can have big macro-marketing effects, but it is a difficult problem to fix.[23]

Even very high prices may be OK

Generally speaking, firms can charge high prices—even outrageously high prices—as long as they don't conspire with their competitors to fix prices, discriminate against some of their customers, or lie.

Of course, there are exceptions. Firms in regulated businesses may need to seek approval for their prices. For example, in the United States, most states regulate automobile insurance rates. Some countries impose more general price controls—to reduce inflation or try to control markets. However, most countries have followed the move toward a market-directed economy. That doesn't mean, however, that there aren't important regulations in the pricing area.

You can't lie about prices

Phony list prices are prices customers are shown to suggest that the price has been discounted from list. Some customers seem more interested in the supposed discount than in the actual price. Most businesses, trade associations, and government agencies consider the use of phony list prices unethical. In the United States, the FTC tries to stop such pricing—using the **Wheeler Lea Amendment**, which bans "unfair or deceptive acts in commerce."[24]

A few years ago, some electronics retailers were criticized on these grounds. They'd advertise a $300 discount on a computer when the customer signed up for an Internet service provider, but it might not be clear to the consumer that a three-year commitment—costing over $700—was required.

Price fixing is illegal— you can go to jail

Difficulties with pricing—and violations of pricing legislation—usually occur when competing marketing mixes are quite similar. When the success of an entire marketing strategy depends on price, there is pressure (and temptation) to make agreements with competitors (conspire). And **price fixing**—competitors getting together to raise, lower, or stabilize prices—is common and relatively easy. *But it is also completely illegal in the United States.* It is considered "conspiracy" under the Sherman Act and the Federal Trade Commission Act. To discourage price fixing, both companies and individual managers are held responsible. In a recent case, an executive at Archer Daniels Midland (ADM) Company was sentenced to three years in jail and the company was fined $100 million.

Federal price-fixing laws in the United States focus on protecting customers who purchase directly from a supplier. For example, a wholesaler could bring action against a producer-supplier for fixing prices. However, retailers or consumers who bought the producer's products from the wholesaler could not bring action. In contrast, many state laws now allow "indirect customers" in the channel to sue the price fixer.[25]

Different countries have different rules concerning price fixing, and this has created problems in international trade. Japan, for example, allows price fixing, especially if it strengthens the position of Japanese producers in world markets.

Producers may set minimum retail prices

Manufacturers usually suggest a retail list price and then leave it up to retailers to decide what to charge in their local markets. In fact, until recently the courts prohibited manufacturers from imposing a minimum price at which their goods could be

A Brighter Way to Save

Compact fluorescent light (CFL) bulbs have quickly become a popular way for consumers to save money, energy, and planet Earth—if quickly means 35 years or so. General Electric (GE) invented the modern CFL in response to the 1973 oil crisis, but the project was put on hold before GE finished the new-product development process. It didn't appear that there was enough consumer interest for GE to earn its target return on the $25 million investment required to build a new CFL factory. So GE didn't pursue the opportunity. Nevertheless, its design ultimately leaked out and the first CFL bulbs came on the market in the 1980s. These early bulbs were bulky and didn't even fit traditional light sockets; they also had an orange hue that made the light harsh. And in case customers were not bothered by these disadvantages, each bulb cost over $20. Needless to say, few consumers were beating down retailers' doors to buy CFLs.

Since then, the value equation has changed a lot. Current technology allows CFLs to screw into existing incandescent light fixtures—so consumers don't face extra costs and hassles to switch bulbs. The quality of the light is also very similar to that of incandescent bulbs (which CFL bulbs are designed to replace). Even so, consumers may still get sticker shock when they see the $3.00 price tag. That's about six times what they expect to pay for a traditional incandescent bulb. Yet, CFL bulbs are a better buy because they last 10 times longer. That doesn't even factor in the energy savings: a consumer who replaces just the five most frequently used bulbs in a home can save up to $60 a year in electric bills.

Because CFL bulbs use less electricity, each CFL bulb reduces carbon dioxide emissions by about 180 pounds a year.

There are still some drawbacks. Compared to incandescent bulbs, CFLs don't get to full brightness as quickly, don't dim as well, and contain small amounts of mercury—an environmental hazard that requires special handling. Yet, most consumers who learn about the pros and cons of CFL bulbs see buying them as a no-brainer. Utility companies see them that way too. Because the bulbs reduce the overall demand for electricity, there's less need to build expensive new power plants. In light of that, some utilities subsidize half of the price that consumers pay for CFLs.

Retailers like Wal-Mart and Home Depot actively promote CFLs because they are in demand and because the bulbs help to highlight their environmental images. Wal-Mart, for example, dropped incandescents and now sells only CFLs. Home Depot gave away a million CFL bulbs to celebrate Earth Day (and pull consumers into its stores).

Environmentalists around the world salute efforts like these and are also pressing for new laws to support CFLs or limit incandescents. More than a dozen countries, including the United States, Finland, and Pakistan, have passed such laws. U.S. regulations call for a phase out of incandescents between 2012 and 2020, but 20 percent of all incandescents have already been replaced with CFLs—and that percentage is growing rapidly as more people understand the value they get when they purchase them.[26]

sold. This was viewed as a form of price fixing and a violation of the Sherman Antitrust Act. However, the ruling in a recent Supreme Court case changes that. The case involved Leegin Creative Leather Products and Kay's Kloset, a retailer that had been discounting Leegin's handbags. To prevent the discounting, Leegin stopped selling to Kay's Kloset. Kay's Kloset brought suit and said that retailers should be free to set their own prices—which, in turn, would keep prices lower for consumers. However, Leegin argued that its strategy focused on building the reputation of its brand with excellent service and advertising. Its retailers coudn't provide that level of service and promotion if they didn't charge a price that offered a sufficient profit margin. Leegin also argued that if one retailer ignored the strategy and cut its price on Leegin products, other retailers would follow suit—and soon the retailers wouldn't be able to provide the backing Leegin bags needed to compete. The court ruling, which supported

Leegin, marks an important change because it gives manufacturers more power to control retail pricing. [27]

Price level and price flexibility policies can lead to price discrimination. The **Robinson-Patman Act** (of 1936) makes illegal any **price discrimination**—selling the same products to different buyers at different prices—*if it injures competition*. The law does permit some price differences—but they must be based on (1) cost differences or (2) the need to meet competition. Both buyers and sellers are considered guilty if they know they're entering into discriminatory agreements.

Firms in businesses as varied as transportation services, book publishing, and auto parts have been charged with violations of the Robinson-Patman Act in recent, nationally publicized cases. Competitors who have been injured by a violation of the law have incentive to go to court because they can receive a settlement that is three times larger than the damage suffered.

The Robinson-Patman Act allows a marketing manager to charge different prices for similar products if they are *not* of "like grade and quality." But the FTC says that if the physical characteristics of a product are similar, then they are of like grade and quality. A landmark U.S. Supreme Court ruling against the Borden Company upheld the FTC's view that a well-known label *alone* does not make a product different from one with an unknown label. The company agreed that the canned milk it sold at different prices under different labels was basically the same.

But the FTC's victory in the Borden case was not complete. The U.S. Court of Appeals found no evidence of injury to competition and further noted that there could be no injury unless Borden's price differential exceeded the "recognized consumer appeal of the Borden label." How to measure "consumer appeal" was not spelled out, so producers who want to sell several brands—or dealer brands at lower prices than their main brand—probably should offer physical differences, and differences that are really useful.[28]

The Robinson-Patman Act allows price differences if there are cost differences—say, for larger quantity shipments or because intermediaries take over some of the physical distribution functions. But justifying cost differences is a difficult job. And the justification must be developed *before* different prices are set. The seller can't wait until a competitor, disgruntled customer, or the FTC brings a charge. At that point, it's too late.[29]

Under the Robinson-Patman Act, meeting a competitor's price is permitted as a defense in price discrimination cases. A major objective of antimonopoly laws is to protect competition, not competitors. And "meeting competition in good faith" still seems to be legal.

Some firms violate the Robinson-Patman Act by providing push money, advertising allowances, and other promotion aids to some customers and not others. The act prohibits such special allowances, *unless they are made available to all customers on "proportionately equal" terms.*[30]

Because price discrimination laws are complicated and penalties for violations heavy, many business managers follow the safest course by offering few or no quantity discounts and the same cost-based prices to *all* customers. This is *too* conservative a reaction. But when firms consider price differences, they may need a lawyer involved in the discussion!

CONCLUSION

The Price variable offers an alert marketing manager many possibilities for varying marketing mixes. This chapter began by discussing how a firm's pricing objectives may be oriented toward profit, sales, or maintaining the status quo. Clear pricing objectives help in making decisions about the firm's important pricing policies.

This chapter discussed the pros and cons of flexible pricing and some of the approaches that firms use to implement it. It also considered the initial price level decision—skim the cream or penetration—that the marketing manager must make with new products at the introductory stage of their life cycle. We also discussed a variety of ways that marketing managers adjust the basic list price under different circumstances—by using different types of discounts, allowances, and transportation costs. These policies need to be clearly defined by the marketing manager.

The chapter described how the different components of price are traded off against the other marketing mix variables to create something of value for the customer. We also discuss value pricing and how to create a competitive advantage by offering customers superior value—which isn't the same as just offering lower and lower prices.

Pricing comes under greater scrutiny from the law than some other marketing mix variables. So it is important to understand key legal constraints that influence pricing decisions.

This chapter provided a foundation for understanding the objectives and policies that guide pricing decisions. This information provides input into the price setting process, which we describe in greater detail in the following chapter when we look at both cost and demand-oriented approaches to pricing.

KEY TERMS

price, 409

target return objective, 411

profit maximization objective, 412

sales-oriented objective, 412

status quo objectives, 413

nonprice competition, 413

administered prices, 413

one-price policy, 414

flexible-price policy, 414

skimming price policy, 416

penetration pricing policy, 418

introductory price dealing, 418

basic list prices, 420

discounts, 420

quantity discounts, 421

cumulative quantity discounts, 421

noncumulative quantity discounts, 421

seasonal discounts, 421

net, 422

cash discounts, 422

2/10, net 30, 422

trade (functional) discount, 423

sale price, 423

everyday low pricing, 423

allowances, 423

advertising allowances, 423

stocking allowances, 423

push money (or prize money)
   allowances, 424

trade-in allowance, 424

rebates, 425

F.O.B., 425

zone pricing, 426

uniform delivered pricing, 426

freight-absorption pricing, 426

value pricing, 427

unfair trade practice acts, 429

dumping, 429

phony list prices, 430

Wheeler Lea Amendment, 430

price fixing, 430

Robinson-Patman Act, 432

price discrimination, 432

QUESTIONS AND PROBLEMS

1. Identify the strategy decisions a marketing manager must make in the Price area. Illustrate your answer for a local retailer.

2. How should the acceptance of a profit-oriented, a sales-oriented, or a status quo–oriented pricing objective affect the development of a company's marketing strategy? Illustrate for each.

3. Distinguish between one-price and flexible-price policies. Which is most appropriate for a hardware store? Why?

4. What pricing objective(s) is a skimming pricing policy most likely implementing? Is the same true for a penetration pricing policy? Which policy is probably most appropriate for each of the following products: (*a*) a new type of home lawn-sprinkling system, (*b*) a skin patch drug to help smokers quit, (*c*) a DVD of a best-selling movie, and (*d*) a new children's toy?

5. How would differences in exchange rates between different countries affect a firm's decisions concerning

the use of flexible-price policies in different foreign markets?

6. Are seasonal discounts appropriate in agricultural businesses (which are certainly seasonal)?

7. What are the effective annual interest rates for the following cash discount terms: (*a*) 1/10, net 20; (*b*) 1/5, net 10; and (*c*) net 25?

8. Do stocking allowances increase or reduce conflict in a channel of distribution? Explain your thinking.

9. Why would a manufacturer offer a rebate instead of lowering the suggested list price?

10. How can a marketing manager change a firm's F.O.B. terms to make an otherwise competitive marketing mix more attractive?

11. What type of geographic pricing policy is most appropriate for the following products (specify any assumptions necessary to obtain a definite answer): (*a*) a chemical by-product, (*b*) nationally advertised candy bars, (*c*) rebuilt auto parts, and (*d*) tricycles?

12. How would a ban on freight absorption (that is, requiring F.O.B. factory pricing) affect a producer with substantial economies of scale in production?

13. Give an example of a marketing mix that has a high price level but that you see as a good value. Briefly explain what makes it a good value.

14. Think about a business from which you regularly make purchases even though there are competing firms with similar prices. Explain what the firm offers that improves value and keeps you coming back.

15. Cite two examples of continuously selling above the market price. Describe the situations.

16. Explain the types of competitive situations that might lead to a meeting-competition pricing policy.

17. Would consumers be better off if all nations dropped their antidumping laws? Explain your thinking.

18. How would our marketing system change if manufacturers were required to set fixed prices on *all* products sold at retail and *all* retailers were required to use these prices? Would a manufacturer's marketing mix be easier to develop? What kind of an operation would retailing be in this situation? Would consumers receive more or less service?

19. Is price discrimination involved if a large oil company sells gasoline to taxicab associations for resale to individual taxicab operators for $2\frac{1}{2}$ cents a gallon less than the price charged to retail service stations? What happens if the cab associations resell gasoline not only to taxicab operators but to the general public as well?

CREATING MARKETING PLANS

The Marketing Plan Coach software on the text website (and on the optional Student CD) includes a sample marketing plan for Hillside Veterinary Clinic. Look through the "Marketing Strategy" section.

a. A veterinary clinic located in another town gives its customers a 10 percent discount on their next vet bill if they refer a new pet owner to the clinic. Do you think that this would be a good idea for Hillside? Does it fit with Hillside's strategy?

b. The same clinic offered customers a sort of cumulative discount—an end-of-year refund if their total spending at the clinic exceeded a certain level. That clinic sees it as a way of being nice to people whose pets have had a lot of problems. Do you think that this is a good idea for Hillside? Why or why not?

SUGGESTED CASES   13. File-It Supplies, Inc.   25. United Plastics Mfg., Inc.

COMPUTER-AIDED PROBLEM

16. CASH DISCOUNTS

Joe Tulkin owns Tulkin Wholesale Co. He sells paper, tape, file folders, and other office supplies to about 120 retailers in nearby cities. His average retailer-customer spends about $900 a month. When Tulkin started business in 1991, competing wholesalers were giving retailers invoice terms of 3/10, net 30. Tulkin never gave the issue much thought—he just used the same invoice terms when he billed customers. At that time, about half of his customers took the discount. Recently, he noticed a change in the way his customers were paying their bills. Checking his records, he found that 90 percent of the retailers

were taking the cash discount. With so many retailers taking the cash discount, it seems to have become a price reduction. In addition, Tulkin learned that other wholesalers were changing their invoice terms.

Tulkin decides he should rethink his invoice terms. He knows he could change the percent rate on the cash discount, the number of days the discount is offered, or the number of days before the face amount is due. Changing any of these, or any combination, will change the interest rate at which a buyer is, in effect, borrowing money if he does not take the discount. Tulkin decides that it will be easier to evaluate the effect of different invoice terms if he sets up a spreadsheet to let him change the terms and quickly see the effective interest rate for each change.

a. With 90 percent of Tulkin's customers now taking the discount, what is the total monthly cash discount amount?

b. If Tulkin changes his invoice terms to 1/5, net 20, what interest rate is each buyer paying by not taking the cash discount? With these terms, would fewer buyers be likely to take the discount? Why?

c. Tulkin thinks 10 customers will switch to other wholesalers if he changes his invoice terms to 2/10, net 30, while 60 percent of the remaining customers will take the discount. What interest rate does a buyer pay by not taking this cash discount? For this situation, what will the total gross sales (total invoice) amount be? The total cash discount? The total net sales receipts after the total cash discount? Compare Tulkin's current situation with what will happen if he changes his invoice terms to 2/10, net 30.

For additional questions related to this problem, see Exercise 16-3 in the *Learning Aid for Use with Essentials of Marketing*, 12th edition.

17

CHAPTER

Price Setting in the Business World

Not long ago, Sony's strategy for its Bravia line of large-screen, flat-panel televisions seemed clear-cut. As with its other product lines, Sony's new-product teams coupled cutting-edge technology with stylish designs to give consumers a superior home entertainment experience. For each popular size of TV, Sony offered two or three models at different price points. The low-end model was a basic TV that was similar to other brands on the market, but with a few special features and a price premium that reflected Sony's reputation for reliability and picture clarity. Its strength, though, was at the high end. Those models offered higher screen resolution with more contrast, more connections for different types of accessory equipment, a learning remote control, and displays with richer color. Although many consumers don't know how to judge these features, Sony trained retailer salespeople to demonstrate Sony's benefits. While Sony's prices were often higher than competitors, retailers liked the high profit margins on Sony products, and Sony's promotion and brand name helped bring in customers.

For the past few years, however, Sony has scrambled to adjust its strategy. Let's look at how this market has evolved and how it has influenced Sony's strategy and pricing.

In 2001, the average price of flat-panel TVs was about $10,000. Demand was limited, so flat screens were distributed mainly by commercial audio-video suppliers who sold them to business customers. However, as prices came down over the next few years, consumer demand grew and Sony started to distribute its flat panels through electronics chains such as Best Buy and Circuit City. That helped to bring down selling costs, but an even larger factor in the rapid drop in prices was that economies of scale in production began to kick in.

Suppliers of LCD panels invested billions of dollars in new factories to make panels large enough for TVs. Soon, competing suppliers were cutting prices to get a larger share and to get the sales volume needed to break even on their investments. Because about 60 percent of the cost of an LCD TV was for the panel, TV makers started to cut their prices too. By 2004, a 32-inch high-definition Sony LCD was about $3,999. At that price the size of the consumer market was limited, but retailers' profits looked good with the 30 percent margins they earned on large LCD TVs.

Sony was holding its own against its traditional competitors—firms like Sharp and Panasonic—but, by 2004, Sony suddenly experienced competition from almost 100 new upstart TV makers. Vizio has proved to be one of the most successful. It handled design and marketing itself, but left production to contract manufacturers in China. As a result, its overhead costs were less than 1 percent of sales, compared to Sony's overhead costs of 10 to 20 percent of sales. To gain

market share, Vizio settled for slim profit margins of just 2 percent, much lower than Sony. Vizio didn't try to offer a TV that had the most advanced video standards or technology. Rather it just tried to have a TV in its product line at each of the most popular sizes. This strategy gave Vizio a significant price advantage on the retail floor and helped it get distribution in discount stores like Wal-Mart and Costco. Vizio did virtually no advertising. That job was left to retailers.

Vizio's sales grew rapidly, but most of the upstart firms that offered undifferentiated no-name brands and did no consumer promotion suffered a different fate. By late summer of 2006 these firms were fighting to get retail distribution—not only at electronics stores but also at outlets like Office Depot, Kohl's, and Home Depot that had not previously handled TVs. These retailers wanted to share in the profits of this growth market, but they carried limited selections and offered no service or support. While these TVs were low-priced, few saw them as a good value. Even so, the focus on rock-bottom prices started a price war. The war increased unit sales, but it cut into retail margins of all retailers and many of the new outlets simply stopped carrying TVs. When that happened, most of the no-name brands went out of business.

However, retailers were not the only ones hit by price competition because they, in turn, pressured TV makers, like Sony, to cut prices too. That was a serious matter. After the war, the price of LCD flat screens continued to tumble and dropped 40 percent in less than a year. As Sony's premium prices disappeared, its profits got ravaged. There was simply too much supply relative to demand. Sony's expensive strategy called for a high price.

The ongoing focus on price in this market is turning LCD TVs into a commodity. Sony is fighting this trend by refocusing its product line on larger sizes and developing new technology. For example, in 2008 about 68 percent of its line consisted of TVs that are larger than 40 inches. Prices and profit margins in that range have not been hit as hard as smaller TVs, and at larger sizes more shoppers can see the differences in Sony's quality. Even so, these changes have only helped Sony to hold on to its market share—while it has been attacked from the low end by firms like Vizio and from the high end by competitors like Samsung (which has taken advantage of its excellent supply chain to keep its costs low). Moving forward, Sony must continue to adapts its marketing strategy to deliver value to its target customers.[1]

PRICE SETTING IS A KEY STRATEGY DECISION

In Chapter 16 we discussed the idea that pricing objectives and policies should guide pricing decisions. We described different dimensions of the pricing decision and how they combine to create value for customers. This chapter builds on those concepts—all of which influence price setting—and gives you additional frameworks that will help you understand how marketing managers set prices. See Exhibit 17–1.

There are many ways to set prices. But, for simplicity, they can be reduced to two basic approaches—*cost-oriented* and *demand-oriented* price setting. We will discuss cost-oriented approaches first because they are most common. Also, understanding the problems of relying on a cost-oriented approach shows why a marketing manager must consider customer demand and price sensitivity to make good Price decisions. We conclude the chapter with a discussion of some special price setting issues—pricing full lines of products, bid pricing, and negotiated pricing.

SOME FIRMS JUST USE MARKUPS

Markups guide pricing by intermediaries

Some firms, including most retailers and wholesalers, set prices by using a **markup**—a dollar amount added to the cost of products to get the selling price. For example, suppose that a CVS drugstore buys a bottle of Pert Plus shampoo and conditioner for $2.40. To make a profit, the drugstore obviously must sell Pert Plus for more than $2.40. If it adds $1.20 to cover operating expenses and provide a profit, we say that the store is marking up the item $1.20.

Exhibit 17–1 Price Setting and Strategy Planning

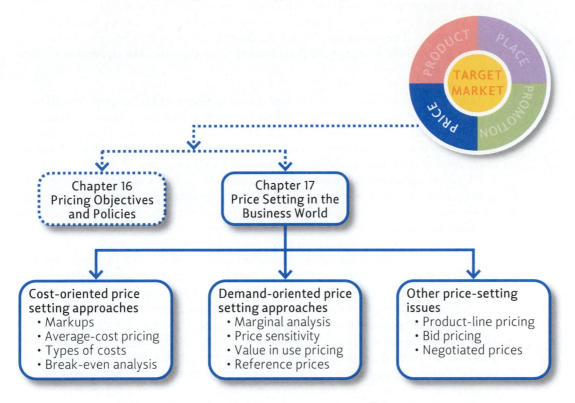

Markups, however, usually are stated as percentages rather than dollar amounts. And this is where confusion sometimes arises. Is a markup of $1.20 on a cost of $2.40 a markup of 50 percent? Or should the markup be figured as a percentage of the selling price—$3.60—and therefore be 33⅓ percent? A clear definition is necessary.

Markup percent is based on selling price— a convenient rule

Unless otherwise stated, **markup (percent)** means percentage of selling price that is added to the cost to get the selling price. So the $1.20 markup on the $3.60 selling price is a markup of 33⅓ percent. Markups are related to selling price for convenience.

Kohler is an example of a specialized product that relies on selective distribution and sells in smaller volumes usually offering retailers higher markups, in part to offset the retailer's higher carrying costs and marketing expenses. Splenda, the low-cal sweetener, faced tough competition from Equal and Sweet 'n Low, when it came out. It built distribution as it became more popular with consumers, and then targeted food makers to use Splenda as an ingredient in their products because a large base of established Splenda fans would help with sales.

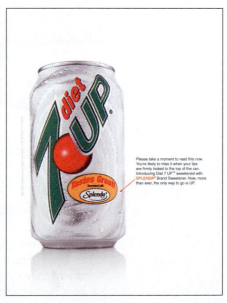

There's nothing wrong with the idea of markup on cost. However, to avoid confusion, it's important to state clearly which markup percent you're using.

A manager may want to change a markup on selling price to one based on cost, or vice versa. The calculations used to do this are simple. (See the section on markup conversion in Appendix B on marketing arithmetic. The appendixes follow Chapter 18.)[2]

Many use a standard markup percent

Many intermediaries select a standard markup percent and then apply it to all their products. This makes pricing easier. When you think of the large number of items the average retailer and wholesaler carry—and the small sales volume of any one item—this approach may make sense. Spending the time to find the best price to charge on every item in stock (day to day or week to week) might not pay.

Moreover, different companies in the same line of business often use the same markup percent. There is a reason for this: Their operating expenses are usually similar. So they see a standard markup as acceptable as long as it's large enough to cover the firm's operating expenses and provide a reasonable profit.

Markups are related to gross margins

How does a manager decide on a standard markup in the first place? A standard markup is often set close to the firm's *gross margin*. Managers regularly see gross margins on their operating (profit and loss) statements. The gross margin is the amount left—after subtracting the cost of sales (cost of goods sold) from net sales—to cover the expenses of selling products and operating the business. (See Appendix B on marketing arithmetic if you are unfamiliar with these ideas.) Our CVS manager knows that there won't be any profit if the gross margin is not large enough. For this reason, CVS might accept a markup percent on Pert Plus that is close to the store's usual gross margin percent.

Smart producers pay attention to the gross margins and standard markups of intermediaries in their channel. They usually allow trade (functional) discounts similar to the standard markups these intermediaries expect.

Markup chain may be used in channel pricing

Different firms in a channel often use different markups. A **markup chain**—the sequence of markups firms use at different levels in a channel—determines the price structure in the whole channel. The markup is figured on the *selling price* at each level of the channel.

For example, Black & Decker's selling price for a cordless electric drill becomes the cost the Ace Hardware wholesaler pays. The wholesaler's selling price becomes the hardware retailer's cost. And this cost plus a retail markup becomes the retail selling price. Each markup should cover the costs of running the business and leave a profit.

Exhibit 17–2 illustrates the markup chain for a cordless electric drill at each level of the channel system. The production (factory) cost of the drill is $43.20. In this case, the producer takes a 10 percent markup and sells the product for $48. The markup is 10 percent of $48 or $4.80. The producer's selling price now becomes the wholesaler's cost—$48. If the wholesaler is used to taking a 20 percent markup on selling price, the markup is $12—and the wholesaler's selling price becomes $60. The $60 now becomes the cost for the hardware retailer. And a retailer who is used to a 40 percent markup adds $40, and the retail selling price becomes $100.

High markups don't always mean big profits

Some people, including many conventional retailers, think high markups mean big profits. Often this isn't true. A high markup may result in a price that's too high—a price at which few customers will buy. You can't earn much if you don't sell much, no matter how high your markup on a single item. So high markups may lead to low profits.

Exhibit 17–2   Example of a Markup Chain and Channel Pricing

Lower markups can speed turnover and the stockturn rate

Some retailers and wholesalers, however, try to speed turnover to increase profit—even if this means reducing their markups. They realize that a business runs up costs over time. If they can sell a much greater amount in the same time period, they may be able to take a lower markup and still earn higher profits at the end of the period.

An important idea here is the **stockturn rate**—the number of times the average inventory is sold in a year. Various methods of figuring stockturn rates can be used (see the section "Computing the Stockturn Rate" in Appendix B). A low stockturn rate may be bad for profits.

At the very least, a low stockturn increases inventory carrying cost and ties up working capital. If a firm with a stockturn of 1 (once per year) sells products that cost it $100,000, it has that much tied up in inventory all the time. But a stockturn of 5 requires only $20,000 worth of inventory ($100,000 cost ÷ 5 turnovers a year). If annual inventory carrying cost is about 20 percent of the inventory value, that reduces costs by $16,000 a year. That's a big difference on $100,000 in sales!

Whether a stockturn rate is high or low depends on the industry and the product involved. An electrical parts wholesaler may expect an annual rate of 2—while a supermarket might expect 8 stockturns on average but 20 stockturns for soaps and 70 stockturns for fresh fruits and vegetables.

Mass-merchandisers run in fast company

Although some intermediaries use the same standard markup percent on all their products, this policy ignores the importance of fast turnover. Mass-merchandisers know this. They put low markups on fast-selling items and higher markups on items that sell less frequently. For example, Wal-Mart may put a small markup on fast-selling health and beauty aids (like toothpaste or shampoo) but higher markups on appliances and clothing.

Where does the markup chain start?

Some markups eventually become standard in a trade. Most channel members tend to follow a similar process—adding a certain percentage to the previous price. But who sets price in the first place? The firm that brands a product is usually the one that sets its basic list price. It may be a large retailer, a large wholesaler, or most often, the producer.

Some producers just start with a cost per unit figure and add a markup—perhaps a standard markup—to obtain their selling price. Or they may use some rule-of-thumb formula such as:

$$\text{Selling price} = \text{Average production cost per unit} \times 3$$

Marketing managers need to be aware of the costs associated with offering a marketing mix.

A producer who uses this approach might develop rules and markups related to its own costs and objectives. Yet even the first step—selecting the appropriate cost per unit to build on—isn't easy. Let's discuss several approaches to see how cost-oriented price setting really works.

AVERAGE-COST PRICING IS COMMON AND CAN BE DANGEROUS

Average-cost pricing means adding a reasonable markup to the average cost of a product. A manager usually finds the average cost per unit by studying past records. Dividing the total cost for the last year by all the units produced and sold in that period gives an estimate of the average cost per unit for the next year. If the cost was $32,000 for all labor and materials and $30,000 for fixed overhead expenses—such as selling expenses, rent, and manager salaries—then the total cost is $62,000. See Exhibit 17–3A. If the company produced 40,000 items in that time period, the average cost is $62,000 divided by 40,000 units, or $1.55 per unit. To get the price, the producer decides how much profit per unit to add to the average cost per unit. If the company considers 45 cents a reasonable profit for each unit, it sets the new price at $2.00. Exhibit 17–3A shows that this approach produces the desired profit if the company sells 40,000 units.

It does not make allowances for cost variations as output changes

It's always a useful input to pricing decisions to understand how costs operate at different levels of output. Further, average-cost pricing is simple. But it can also be dangerous. It's easy to lose money with average-cost pricing. To see why, let's follow this example further.

First, remember that the average price of $2.00 per unit was based on output of 40,000 units. But if the firm is only able to produce and sell 20,000 units in the next year, it may be in trouble. See Exhibit 17–3B. Twenty thousand units sold at $2.00 each ($1.55 cost plus 45 cents for expected profit) yield a total revenue of only $40,000. The overhead is still fixed at $30,000, and the variable material and labor cost drops by half to $16,000—for a total cost of $46,000. This means a loss of $6,000, or 30 cents a unit. The method that was supposed to allow a profit of 45 cents a unit actually causes a loss of 30 cents a unit!

The basic problem with the average-cost approach is that it doesn't consider cost variations at different levels of output. In a typical situation, costs are high with low

Exhibit 17–3   Results of Average-Cost Pricing

A. Calculation of Planned Profit if 40,000 Items Are Sold		B. Calculation of Actual Profit if Only 20,000 Items Are Sold	
Calculation of Costs:		**Calculation of Costs:**	
Fixed overhead expenses	$30,000	Fixed overhead expenses	$30,000
Labor and materials ($.80 a unit)	32,000	Labor and materials ($.80 a unit)	16,000
Total costs	$62,000	Total costs	$46,000
"Planned" profit	18,000		
Total costs and planned profit	$80,000		
Calculation of Profit (or Loss):		**Calculation of Profit (or Loss):**	
Actual unit sales × price ($2.00*)	$80,000	Actual unit sales price × ($2.00*)	$40,000
Minus: total costs	62,000	Minus: total costs	46,000
Profit (loss)	$18,000	Profit (loss)	($6,000)
Result:		**Result:**	
Planned profit of $18,000 is earned if 40,000 items are sold at $2.00 each.		Planned profit of $18,000 is not earned. Instead, $6,000 loss results if 20,000 items are sold at $2.00 each.	

*Calculation of "reasonable" price: $\dfrac{\text{Expected total costs and planned profit}}{\text{Planned number of items to be sold}} = \dfrac{\$80,000}{40,000} = \$2.00$

output, and then economies of scale set in—the average cost per unit drops as the quantity produced increases. This is why mass production and mass distribution often make sense. It's also why it's important to develop a better understanding of the different types of costs a marketing manager should consider when setting a price.

MARKETING MANAGERS MUST CONSIDER VARIOUS KINDS OF COSTS

Average-cost pricing may lead to losses because there are a variety of costs—and each changes in a *different* way as output changes. Any pricing method that uses cost must consider these changes. To understand why, we need to define six types of cost.

There are three kinds of total cost

1. **Total fixed cost** is the sum of those costs that are fixed in total—no matter how much is produced. Among these fixed costs are rent, depreciation, managers' salaries, property taxes, and insurance. Such costs stay the same even if production stops temporarily.
2. **Total variable cost**, on the other hand, is the sum of those changing expenses that are closely related to output—expenses for parts, wages, packaging materials, outgoing freight, and sales commissions.

At zero output, total variable cost is zero. As output increases, so do variable costs. If Levi's doubles its output of jeans in a year, its total cost for denim cloth also (roughly) doubles.

3. **Total cost** is the sum of total fixed and total variable costs. Changes in total cost depend on variations in total variable cost, since total fixed cost stays the same.

There are three kinds of average cost

The pricing manager usually is more interested in cost per unit than total cost because prices are usually quoted per unit.

1. **Average cost (per unit)** is obtained by dividing total cost by the related quantity (that is, the total quantity that causes the total cost).

Exhibit 17–4 Cost Structure of a Firm

Quantity (Q)	Total Fixed Costs (TFC)	Average Fixed Costs (AFC)	Average Variable Costs (AVC)	Total Variable Costs (TVC)	Total Cost (TC)	Average Cost (AC)
0	$30,000	—	—	—	$30,000	—
10,000	30,000	$3.00	$0.80	$8,000	38,000	$3.80
20,000	30,000	1.50	0.80	16,000	46,000	2.30
30,000	30,000	1.00	0.80	24,000	54,000	1.80
40,000	**30,000**	**0.75**	**0.80**	**32,000**	**62,000**	**1.55**
50,000	30,000	0.60	0.80	40,000	70,000	1.40
60,000	30,000	0.50	0.80	48,000	78,000	1.30
70,000	30,000	0.43	0.80	56,000	86,000	1.23
80,000	30,000	0.38	0.80	64,000	94,000	1.18
90,000	30,000	0.33	0.80	72,000	102,000	1.13
100,000	30,000	0.30	0.80	80,000	110,000	1.10

$$\begin{bmatrix} 110,000 \ (TC) \\ -80,000 \ (TVC) \\ \hline 30,000 \ (TFC) \end{bmatrix}$$

$$\frac{0.30 \ (AFC)}{(Q) \ 100,000 \ \lvert 30,000 \ (TFC)}$$

$$\begin{bmatrix} 100,000 \ (Q) \\ \times 0.80 \ (AVC) \\ \hline 80,000 \ (TVC) \end{bmatrix} \begin{bmatrix} 30,000 \ (TFC) \\ +80,000 \ (TVC) \\ \hline 110,000 \ (TC) \end{bmatrix}$$

$$\frac{1.10 \ (AC)}{(Q) \ 100,000 \ \lvert 110,000 \ (TC)}$$

2. **Average fixed cost (per unit)** is obtained by dividing total fixed cost by the related quantity.
3. **Average variable cost (per unit)** is obtained by dividing total variable cost by the related quantity.

An example shows cost relations

A good way to get a feel for these different types of costs is to extend our average-cost pricing example (Exhibit 17–3A). Exhibit 17–4 shows the six types of cost and how they vary at different levels of output. The line for 40,000 units is highlighted because that was the expected level of sales in our average-cost pricing example. For simplicity, we assume that average variable cost is the same for each unit. Notice, however, that total variable cost increases when quantity increases.

Exhibit 17–5 shows the three average cost curves from Exhibit 17–4. Notice that average fixed cost goes down steadily as the quantity increases. Although the average

Exhibit 17–5
Typical Shape of Cost (per unit) Curves When Average Variable Cost per Unit Is Constant

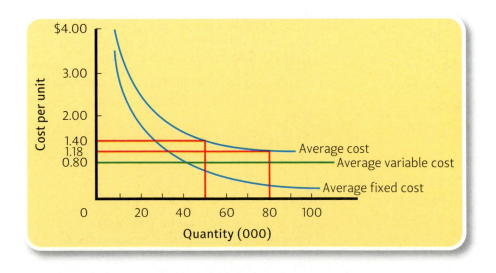

variable cost remains the same, average cost decreases continually too. This is because average fixed cost is decreasing. With these relations in mind, let's reconsider the problem with average-cost pricing.

Ignoring demand is the major weakness of average-cost pricing

Average-cost pricing works well if the firm actually sells the quantity it used to set the average-cost price. Losses may result, however, if actual sales are much lower than expected. On the other hand, if sales are much higher than expected, then profits may be very good. But this will only happen by luck—because the firm's demand is much larger than expected.

To use average-cost pricing, a marketing manager must make *some* estimate of the quantity to be sold in the coming period. Without a quantity estimate, it isn't possible to compute average cost. But unless this quantity is related to price—that is, unless the firm's demand curve is considered—the marketing manager may set a price that doesn't even cover a firm's total cost! You saw this happen in Exhibit 17–3B, when the firm's price of $2.00 resulted in demand for only 20,000 units and a loss of $6,000.

The demand curve is still important even if a manager has not taken time to think about it. For example, Exhibit 17–6 shows the demand curve for the firm we're discussing. This demand curve shows *why* the firm lost money when it tried to use average-cost pricing. At the $2.00 price, quantity demanded is only 20,000. With this demand curve and the costs in Exhibit 17–4, the firm will incur a loss whether management sets the price at a high $3 or a low $1.20. At $3, the firm will sell only 10,000 units for a total revenue of $30,000. But total cost will be $38,000—for a loss of $8,000. At the $1.20 price, it will sell 60,000 units—at a loss of $6,000. However, the curve suggests that at a price of $1.65 consumers will demand about 40,000 units, producing a profit of about $4,000.

In short, average-cost pricing is simple in theory but often fails in practice. In stable situations, prices set by this method may yield profits but not necessarily *maximum* profits. And note that such cost-based prices may be higher than a price that would be more profitable for the firm, as shown in Exhibit 17–6. When demand conditions are changing, average-cost pricing is even more risky.

Exhibit 17–7 summarizes the relationships just discussed. Cost-oriented pricing requires an estimate of the total number of units to be sold. That estimate determines the *average* fixed cost per unit and thus the average total cost. Then the firm

Exhibit 17–6

Evaluation of Various Prices along a Firm's Demand Curve

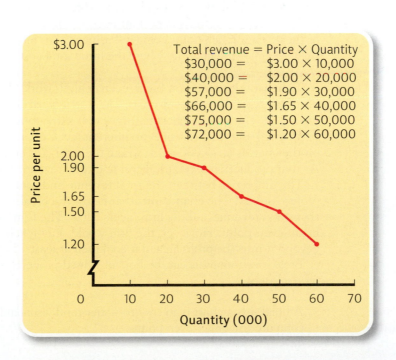

Total revenue	=	Price × Quantity
$30,000	=	$3.00 × 10,000
$40,000	=	$2.00 × 20,000
$57,000	=	$1.90 × 30,000
$66,000	=	$1.65 × 40,000
$75,000	=	$1.50 × 50,000
$72,000	=	$1.20 × 60,000

Exhibit 17–7
Summary of Relationships among Quantity, Cost, and Price Using Cost-Oriented Pricing

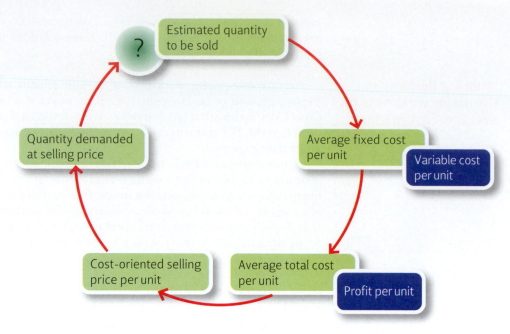

adds the desired profit per unit to the average total cost to get the cost-oriented selling price. How customers react to that price determines the actual quantity the firm will be able to sell. But that quantity may not be the quantity used to compute the average cost![3]

Don't ignore competitors' costs

Another danger of average-cost pricing is that it ignores competitors' costs and prices. Just as the price of a firm's own product influences demand, the price of available substitutes may impact demand. By finding ways to cut costs, a firm may be able to offer prices lower than competitors and still make an attractive profit.

BREAK-EVEN ANALYSIS CAN EVALUATE POSSIBLE PRICES

Some price setters use break-even analysis in their pricing. **Break-even analysis** evaluates whether the firm will be able to break even—that is, cover all its costs—with a particular price. This is important because a firm must cover all costs in the long run or there is not much point being in business. This method focuses on the **break-even point (BEP)**—the quantity where the firm's total cost will just equal its total revenue.

Break-even charts help find the BEP

To help understand how break-even analysis works, look at Exhibit 17–8, an example of the typical break-even chart. *The chart is based on a particular selling price*—in this case $1.20 a unit. The chart has lines that show total costs (total variable plus total fixed costs) and total revenues at different levels of production. The break-even point on the chart is at 75,000 units, where the total cost and total revenue lines intersect. At that production level, total cost and total revenue are the same—$90,000.

The difference between the total revenue and total cost at a given quantity is the profit—or loss! The chart shows that below the break-even point, total cost is higher than total revenue and the firm incurs a loss. The firm would make a profit above the break-even point. However, the firm would only reach the break-even point, or get beyond it into the profit area, *if* it could sell at least 75,000 units at the $1.20 price.

Break-even analysis can be helpful if used properly, so let's look at this approach more closely.

How to compute a break-even point

A break-even chart is an easy-to-understand visual aid, but it's also useful to be able to compute the break-even point.

Exhibit 17–8
Break-Even Chart for
a Particular Situation

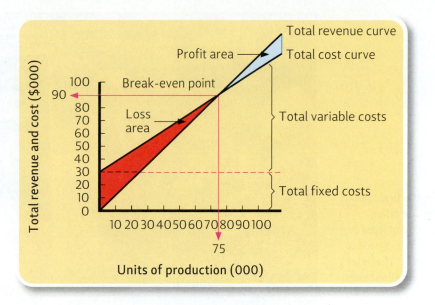

The BEP, in units, can be found by dividing total fixed costs (TFC) by the **fixed-cost (FC) contribution per unit**—the assumed selling price per unit minus the variable cost per unit. This can be stated as a simple formula:

$$\text{BEP (in units)} = \frac{\text{Total fixed cost}}{\text{Fixed cost contribution per unit}}$$

This formula makes sense when we think about it. To break even, we must cover total fixed costs. Therefore, we must figure the contribution each unit will make to covering the total fixed costs (after paying for the variable costs to produce the item). When we divide this per-unit contribution into the total fixed costs that must be covered, we have the BEP (in units).

To illustrate the formula, let's use the cost and price information in Exhibit 17–8. The price per unit is $1.20. The average variable cost per unit is 80 cents. So the FC contribution per unit is 40 cents ($1.20 − 80 cents). The total fixed cost is $30,000 (see Exhibit 17–8). Substituting in the formula:

$$\text{BEP} = \frac{\$30,000}{.40} = 75,000 \text{ units}$$

From this you can see that if this firm sells 75,000 units, it will exactly cover all its fixed and variable costs. If it sells even one more unit, it will begin to show a profit—in this case, 40 cents per unit. Note that once the fixed costs are covered, the part of revenue formerly going to cover fixed costs is now *all profit*.

BEP can be stated in dollars too

The BEP can also be figured in dollars. The easiest way is to compute the BEP in units and then multiply by the assumed per-unit price. If you multiply the selling price ($1.20) by the BEP in units (75,000) you get $90,000—the BEP in dollars.

Each possible price has its own break-even point

Often it's useful to compute the break-even point for each of several possible prices and then compare the BEP for each price to likely demand at that price. The marketing manager can quickly reject some price possibilities when the expected quantity demanded at a given price is way below the break-even point for that price.

Break-even analysis is helpful—but not a pricing solution

Break-even analysis is helpful for evaluating alternatives. It is also popular because it's easy to use. Yet break-even analysis is too often misunderstood. Beyond the BEP, profits seem to be growing continually. And the graph—with its straight-line total

The money that a firm spends on marketing and other expenses must be at least covered by a firm's price if it is to make a profit. That's why Gillette enjoys big economies of scale by selling the same razors in many markets around the world.

revenue curve—makes it seem that any quantity can be sold at the assumed price. But this usually isn't true. It is the same as assuming a perfectly horizontal demand curve at that price. In fact, most managers face down-sloping demand situations. And their total revenue curves do *not* keep going straight up.

Break-even analysis is a useful tool for analyzing costs and evaluating what might happen to profits in different market environments. But it is a cost-oriented approach. Like other cost-oriented approaches, it does not consider the effect of price on the quantity that consumers will want—that is, the demand curve.

So to really zero in on the most profitable price, marketers are better off estimating the demand curve itself and then using marginal analysis, which we'll discuss next.[4]

MARGINAL ANALYSIS CONSIDERS BOTH COSTS AND DEMAND

Marginal analysis helps find the right price

The best pricing tool marketers have for looking at costs and revenue (demand) at the same time is marginal analysis. **Marginal analysis** focuses on the changes in total revenue and total cost from selling one more unit to find the most profitable price and quantity. Marginal analysis shows how costs, revenue, and profit change at different prices. The price that maximizes profit is the one that results in the greatest difference between total revenue and total cost.[5]

Demand estimates involve "if-then" thinking

Since the price determines what quantity will be sold, a manager needs an estimate of the demand curve to compute total revenue. A practical approach here is for managers to think about a price that appears to be too high and one that is too low. Then, for a number of prices between these two extremes, the manager estimates what quantity it might be possible to sell. You can think of this as a summary of the answers to a series of what-if questions—*What* quantity will be sold *if* a particular price is selected?

Profit is the difference between total revenue and total cost

The first two columns in Exhibit 17–9 give quantity and price combinations (demand) for an example firm. Total revenue in column 3 of Exhibit 17–9 is equal to a price multiplied by its related quantity. Costs at the different quantities are also shown. The profit at each quantity and price is the difference between total revenue and total cost. In this example, the best price is $79 (and a quantity of six units sold) because that combination results in the highest profit ($106). Now let's look at this example in more detail.

Exhibit 17–9
Revenue, Cost, and Profit at Different Prices for a Firm

(1) Quantity (Q)	(2) Price (P)	(3) Total Revenue (TR)	(4) Total Variable Cost (TVC)	(5) Total Cost (TC)	(6) Profit (TR − TC)
0	$150	$ 0	$ 0	$200	$ − 200
1	140	140	96	296	− 156
2	130	260	116	316	− 56
3	117	351	131	331	+ 20
4	105	420	144	344	+ 76
5	92	460	155	355	+ 105
6	79	474	168	368	+ 106
7	66	462	183	383	+ 79
8	53	424	223	423	+ 1
9	42	378	307	507	− 129
10	31	310	510	710	− 400

Profit maximization with total revenue and total cost curves

Exhibit 17–10 graphs the total revenue, total cost, and total profit relationships for the numbers we've been working with in Exhibit 17–9. The highest point on the total profit curve is at a quantity of six units. This is also the quantity where we find the greatest vertical distance between the total revenue curve and the total cost curve. Exhibit 17–9 shows that it is the $79 price that results in selling six units, so $79 is the price that leads to the highest profit. A price lower than $79 would result in a higher sales volume. But you can see that the total profit curve declines beyond a quantity of six units. So a profit-maximizing marketing manager would not be interested in setting a lower price.

A profit range is reassuring

Marginal analysis focuses on the price that earns the *highest* profit. But a slight miss doesn't mean failure because demand estimates don't have to be exact. There is

Exhibit 17–10
Graphic Determination of the Price Giving the Greatest Total Profit for a Firm

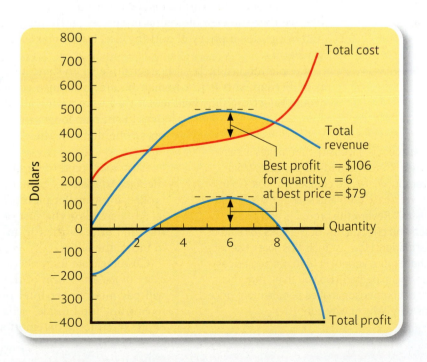

usually a range of profitable prices. You can see this in Exhibit 17–9 and in the section of Exhibit 17–10 shown in yellow. Although the price that would result in the highest profit is $79, the firm's strategy would be profitable all the way from a price of $53 to $117. So the effort of trying to estimate demand will probably lead to being some place in the profitable range. In contrast, mechanical use of average-cost pricing could lead to a price that is much too high—or much too low.

A rough demand estimate is better than none

Some managers don't take advantage of marginal analysis because they think they can't determine the exact shape of the demand curve. But that view misses the point of marginal analysis. Marginal analysis encourages managers to think carefully about what they *do know* about costs and demand. Only rarely is either type of information exact. So in practice, the focus of marginal analysis is not on finding the precise price that will maximize profit. Rather, the focus is on getting an estimate of how profit might vary across a *range of relevant prices*. Further, a number of practical demand-oriented approaches can help a marketing manager do a better job of understanding the likely shape of the demand curve for a target market. We'll discuss these approaches next.

MORE DEMAND-ORIENTED APPROACHES FOR SETTING PRICES

Evaluating the customer's price sensitivity

A manager who knows what influences target customers' price sensitivity can do a better job estimating the demand curve that the firm faces. Marketing researchers have identified a number of factors that influence price sensitivity across many different market situations.

The first is the most basic. When customers have *substitute ways* of meeting a need, they are likely to be more price sensitive. A cook who wants a cappuccino maker to be able to serve something distinctive to guests at a dinner party may be willing to pay a high price. However, if different machines are available and our cook sees them as pretty similar, price sensitivity will be greater. It's important not to ignore dissimilar alternatives if the customer sees them as substitutes. If a machine for espresso were much less expensive than one for cappuccino, our cook might decide that an espresso machine would meet her needs just as well.

The impact of substitutes on price sensitivity is greatest when it is easy for customers to *compare prices*. For example, unit prices make it easier for our cook to compare the prices of espresso and cappuccino grinds on the grocery store shelf. Many people believe that the ease of comparing prices on the Internet increases price sensitivity and brings down prices. If nothing else, it may make sellers more aware of competing prices.

People tend to be less price sensitive when someone else pays the bill or *shares the cost*. Perhaps this is just human nature. Insurance companies think that consumers would reject high medical fees if they were paying all of their own bills. And executives might plan longer in advance to get better discounts on airline flights if their companies weren't footing the bills.

Customers tend to be more price sensitive the greater the *total expenditure*. Sometimes a big expenditure can be broken into smaller pieces. Mercedes knows this. When its ads focused on the cost of a monthly lease rather than the total price of the car, more consumers got interested in biting the bullet.

Customers are less price sensitive the greater the *significance of the end benefit* of the purchase. Computer makers will pay more to get Intel processors if they believe that having an "Intel inside" sells more machines. Positioning efforts often focus on emotional benefits of a purchase to

Business customers may be less sensitive to the additional cost of color printing when they realize that business documents attract 82 percent more attention when they are in color.

increase the significance of a benefit. Ads for L'Oréal hair color, for example, show close-ups of beautiful hair while popular celebrities tell women to buy it "because you're worth it." A consumer who cares about the price of a bottle of hair color might still have no question that she's worth the difference in price.

Customers are sometimes less price sensitive if there are *switching costs*—costs that a customer faces when buying a product that is different from what has been purchased or used in the past. Switching costs can be quite high for some business customers. For example, once a firm's employees know how to use Microsoft Excel, the company would not want to incur the financial cost and time it would take to train employees in a new software package. But switching costs can apply to final consumers as well. For example, if a hair salon raises its prices, many customers will not switch to a new salon. The hassles of looking for a new stylist—and the risk of ending up with a bad hair day—usually make it easier to simply pay the higher price.

These factors apply in many different purchase situations, so it makes sense for a marketing manager to consider each of them in refining estimates of how customers might respond at different prices.[6]

Ethics QUESTION

You are a pricing specialist for a large grocery store chain that has always charged the same prices in all of its stores. However, average operating costs are higher for its inner-city stores. In addition, having the store nearby is very important to low-income, inner-city consumers who have to rely on public transportation. It's hard for them to shop around, and thus they are less price sensitive. Research indicates that these stores can charge prices that are 5 percent higher on average with little effect on sales volume. This would significantly increase profitability. Do you think the chain should charge higher prices at its inner-city stores? If the manager of the store decided to set higher prices on some products and leave others unchanged—to result in an overall average increase of 5 percent—what products would you recommend for higher prices? Why? If prices were increased and antipoverty activists got TV coverage by picketing the chain, how would you respond to a TV reporter covering the story?

Competitor analysis and price sensitivity

Customer demand depends on available alternatives. So a marketing manager can often improve pricing decisions and profitability by considering customer price sensitivity as part of a competitor analysis. The new CEO of Parker Hannifin (PH), a large industrial parts maker, realized this. Before he arrived, PH managers usually set the price for a part by summing all the costs that were involved in making it and then adding a 35 percent markup. Managers liked this approach; it was easy and also left some room for haggling. Yet, the new CEO saw that they could improve what they were doing. First, he asked them to classify every product—and there were thousands—into categories. At one extreme, there was a new category for PH parts that were basically commodities and just like what competitors offered. At the other extreme, there was a category for PH parts that were important to customers and that were only available from PH. This category included a high-pressure valve that was used on airplane doors; no other supplier had a valve that worked as well for this critical application. Prices on parts in this category were raised by 5 percent or more—as long as the price still represented a good value. On commodity parts, prices were reduced by 5 percent to beat competitors. And, of course, there were a number of other levels of price adjustment for categories between the extremes. Fine-tuning PH prices to consider competition was simple, but it increased profits by 25 percent.[7]

Value in use pricing—how much will the customer save?

Organizational buyers think about how a purchase will affect their total costs. Many marketers who aim at business markets keep this in mind when estimating demand and setting prices. They use **value in use pricing**—which means setting prices that will capture some of what customers will save by substituting the firm's product for the one currently being used.

For example, a producer of computer-controlled machines used to assemble cars knows that the machine doesn't just replace a standard machine. It also reduces labor costs, quality control costs, and—after the car is sold—costs of warranty repairs. The

Value in use pricing considers what a customer will save by buying a product. Grasshopper's ad touts the savings realized by switching to its diesel-fueled products.

marketer can estimate what each auto producer will save by using the machine—and then set a price that makes it less expensive for the auto producer to buy the computerized machine than to stick with the old methods. The number of customers who have different levels of potential savings also provides some idea about the shape of the demand curve.

Creating a superior product that could save customers money doesn't guarantee that customers will be willing to pay a higher price. To capture the value created, the seller must convince buyers of the savings—and buyers are likely to be skeptical. A salesperson needs to be able to show proof of the claims.[8]

Auctions show what a customer will pay

Auctions have always been a way to determine exactly what some group of potential customers would pay, or not pay, for a product. However, the use of online auctions has dramatically broadened the use of this approach for both consumer and business products. Millions of auctions are on eBay each day. And some firms are setting up their own auctions, especially for products in short supply. The U.S. government is using online auctions as well. For example, the Federal Communications Commission (FCC) auctions rights to use airwaves for cell phones and other wireless devices. Count on more growth in online auctions.[9]

Some sellers use sequential price reductions

Some sellers are taking the auction approach and adapting it by using sequential price reductions over time. The basic idea is that the seller starts with a relatively high price and sells as much of the product as possible at that price, but plans from the start on a series of step-by-step price reductions until the product is sold out. This approach is most commonly used with products that have a short life or are in short supply, but which would just run up inventory costs if they are not sold. Retailers like TJ Maxx use this approach with women's fashions, and grocery stores use it with perishable food like fruits and vegetables. Cruise lines sell space this way; they don't want the ship to sail with empty cabins. Some people may think of this as a "clearance" sale. But the difference here is that the plan from the outset is to work down the demand curve in steps—appealing to segments who are least price sensitive first—until all of a product is sold. However, sellers hope that if they offer the right products they'll never get to price reductions (which earn lower margins). Rather, they prefer to be bringing in the next round of products to start the process over again.

Customers may have reference prices

Some people don't devote much thought to what they pay for the products they buy, including some frequently purchased goods and services. But consumers often have a **reference price**—the price they expect to pay—for many of the products they purchase. And different customers may have different reference prices for the same basic type of purchase. For example, a person who really enjoys reading might have a higher reference price for a popular paperback book than another person who is only an occasional reader.[10]

If a firm's price is lower than a customer's reference price, customers may view the product as a better value and demand may increase. See Exhibit 17–11. Sometimes a firm will try to position the benefits of its

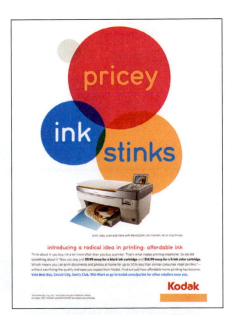

If the price of a product is lower than the target market's reference price, it is likely to be viewed as offering better customer value. The reference price for Kodak's cartridges is simple: Its cartridges cost about half what the cartridges for similar inkjet printers cost.

Exhibit 17–11   How Customer's Reference Price Influences Perceived Value (for a marketing mix with a given set of benefits and costs)

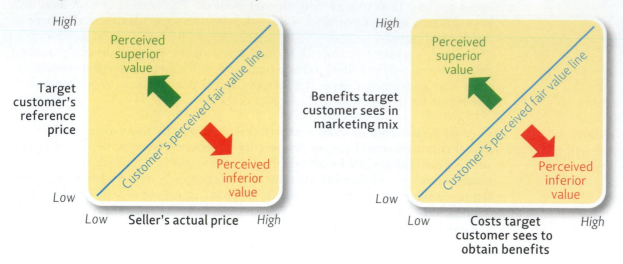

product in such a way that consumers compare it with a product that has a higher reference price. Public Broadcasting System TV stations do this when they ask viewers to make donations that match what they pay for "just one month of cable service." Insurance companies frame the price of premiums for homeowners' coverage in terms of the price to repair flood damage—and advertising makes the damage very vivid. Some retailers just want consumers to use the manufacturer's list price as the reference price, even if no one anywhere actually pays that list price.

Leader pricing—make it low to attract customers

Leader pricing means setting some very low prices—real bargains—to get customers into retail stores. The idea is not only to sell large quantities of the leader items but also to get customers into the store to buy other products. Certain products are picked for their promotion value and priced low but above cost. In food stores, the leader prices are the "specials" that are advertised regularly to give an image of low

Even in 2002 when this ad was published, Porsche targeted customers to frame the price of its exciting sports car relative to the thrill of each mile driven, not just relative to some other car. "A dollar a mile for the first 42,600 miles. Free after that."

A dollar a mile for the first 42,600 miles. Free after that.

It's every bit the sports car you've heard it is. It's more attainable than you might think. $42,600 secures you a mid-mounted flat-six engine, timeless Porsche lines, and the kind of balance and control you simply cannot put a price on. Porsche. There is no substitute.

PORSCHE

prices. Leader pricing is normally used with products for which consumers do have a specific reference price.

Leader pricing can backfire if customers buy only the low-priced leaders. To avoid hurting profits, managers often select leader items that aren't directly competitive with major lines—as when bargain-priced blank CDs are a leader for an electronics store.[11]

Bait pricing—offer a steal, but sell under protest

Bait pricing is setting some very low prices to attract customers but trying to sell more expensive models or brands once the customer is in the store. For example, a furniture store may advertise a color TV for $199. But once bargain hunters come to the store, salespeople point out the disadvantages of the low-priced TV and try to convince them to trade up to a better, and more expensive, set. Bait pricing is something like leader pricing. But here the seller *doesn't* plan to sell many at the low price.

If bait pricing is successful, the demand for higher-quality products expands. This approach may be a sensible part of a strategy to trade up customers. And customers may be well served if—once in the store—they find a higher-priced product offers features better suited to their needs. But bait pricing is also criticized as unethical.

Is bait pricing ethical?

Extremely aggressive and sometimes dishonest bait-pricing advertising has given this method a bad reputation. Some stores make it very difficult to buy the bait item. The Federal Trade Commission considers this type of bait pricing a deceptive act and has banned its use in interstate commerce. Even well-known chains like Sears have been criticized for bait-and-switch pricing.

Psychological pricing— some prices just seem right

Psychological pricing means setting prices that have special appeal to target customers. Some people think there are whole ranges of prices that potential customers see as the same. So price cuts in these ranges do not increase the quantity sold. But just below this range, customers may buy more. Then, at even lower prices, the quantity demanded stays the same again—and so on. Exhibit 17–12 shows the kind of demand curve that leads to psychological pricing. Vertical drops mark the price ranges that customers see as the same. Pricing research shows that there *are* such demand curves.[12]

Exhibit 17–12
Demand Curve When Psychological Pricing Is Appropriate

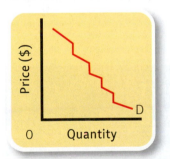

Odd-even pricing is setting prices that end in certain numbers. For example, products selling below $50 often end in the number 5 or the number 9—such as 49 cents or $24.95. Prices for higher-priced products are often $1 or $2 below the next even dollar figure—such as $99 rather than $100.

Some marketers use odd-even pricing because they think consumers react better to these prices—perhaps seeing them as "substantially" lower than the next highest even price. Marketers using these prices seem to assume that they have a rather jagged demand curve—that slightly higher prices will substantially reduce the quantity demanded. Long ago, some retailers used odd-even prices to force their clerks to make change. Then the clerks had to record the sale and could not pocket the money.[13]

Price lining—a few prices cover the field

Price lining is setting a few price levels for a product line and then marking all items at these prices. This approach assumes that customers have a certain reference price in mind that they expect to pay for a product. For example, many neckties are priced between $20 and $50. In price lining, there are only a few prices within this range. Ties will not be priced at $20, $21, $22, $23, and so on. They might be priced at four levels—$20, $30, $40, and $50.

Price lining has advantages other than just matching prices to what consumers expect to pay. The main advantage is simplicity—for both salespeople and customers. It is less confusing than having many prices. Some customers may consider items in only one price class. Their big decision, then, is which item(s) to choose at that price.

For retailers, price lining has several advantages. Sales may increase because (1) they can offer a bigger variety in each price class and (2) it's easier to get customers to make decisions within one price class. Stock planning is simpler because demand is larger at the relatively few prices. Price lining can also reduce costs because inventory needs are lower.

Demand-backward pricing and prestige pricing

Demand-backward pricing is setting an acceptable final consumer price and working backward to what a producer can charge. It is commonly used by producers of consumer products, especially shopping products such as women's clothing and appliances. It is also used with gift items for which customers will spend a specific amount—because they are seeking a $10 or a $15 gift. Here a reverse cost-plus pricing process is used. This method has been called market-minus pricing.

The producer starts with the retail (reference) price for a particular item and then works backward—subtracting the typical margins that channel members expect. This gives the approximate price the producer can charge. Then the average or planned marketing expenses can be subtracted from this price to find how much can be spent producing the item. Candy companies do this. They alter the size of the candy bar to keep the bar at the expected price.

Prestige pricing is setting a rather high price to suggest high quality or high status. Some target customers want the best, so they will buy at a high price. But if the price seems cheap, they worry about quality and don't buy. Prestige pricing is most common for luxury products such as furs, jewelry, and perfume.

Exhibit 17–13
Demand Curve Showing a Prestige Pricing Situation

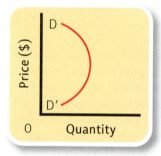

It is also common in service industries, where the customer can't see the product in advance and relies on price to judge its quality. Target customers who respond to prestige pricing give the marketing manager an unusual demand curve. Instead of a normal down-sloping curve, the curve goes down for a while and then bends back to the left again.[14] See Exhibit 17–13.

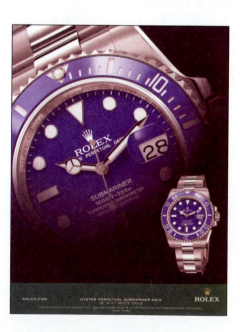

Prestige pricing is often used with luxury products like Rolex watches and high-end consumer electronics to suggest high quality. But Paradigm wants consumers to view its low price as a sign of good quality and good value, not as a signal of low quality.

How to Make Money by Giving Your Products Away

One way to generate customer demand is to give your product away. This not-so-new approach to pricing is gaining popularity. There are a few reasons for this trend. First, technology, the Internet, and advances in manufacturing have significantly reduced the marginal costs for many products. It costs close to nothing for Facebook to add another user or for one more customer to download Google's Picasa photo organizing and editing software. Second, offering something for free generates buzz and the promotional benefit can easily outweigh the costs. Further, in many product categories, consumers expect the price to be free. For example, most readers of online newspapers and magazines refuse to pay when publishers try to charge for subscriptions.

How do firms give something away and still make money? One approach relies on cross-subsidies, where a customer gets something for free but pays for something else. After King Gillette invented the safety razor in 1903, he had a hard time getting widespread adoption of his shaving innovation. But when he gave away the razors and sold replacement blades, sales and profits skyrocketed! Banks offer some customers 0 percent interest (a free loan) for a year when they transfer a credit card balance. This works best when customers need to experience the good value of the firm's offering to recognize the benefits.

Another approach counts on advertisers to provide the revenue. "Free" attracts customer eyeballs, and advertisers pay for access to eyeballs. For example, Japanese photo copy shop Tadacopy offers college students free photocopies—with advertising on the back of each page. *Time* magazine's website and Fox television are free, which draws a larger audience. The larger audience is attractive to advertisers who pay fees.

Sometimes one customer segment pays and covers the costs of a "freeloader" segment. Many websites and software firms offer a free basic service but make their money by charging for a premium service. For example, Flickr offers free online photo sharing, but some customers pay $24.95 a year to get the additional features of Flickr Pro. The revenue from paying customers allows Flickr to cover the freeloaders. The Brazilian band, Banda Calypso, uses a variation of this approach. It gives street vendors masters of its CDs and CD liner art at no charge. The street vendors' sales of high-quality, low-priced CDs bring in new fans and Banda Calypso benefits when many of these fans pay for tickets to the band's live performances.

Of course, many companies use a combination of these approaches. For example, RyanAir's planes have advertising inside and out and RyanAir has given away more than 1.5 million promotional airfare tickets. It makes money, instead, by charging for "extras" like food and drinks in flight, handling your baggage, or booking your hotel and rental car. It also has customers who pay for the convenience of a last minute purchase or a guaranteed seat.

Once customers get something for free, they may be reluctant to pay for it later. So, before a firm offers something for nothing, it's important to think through what the firm will get in return—and how that relates to the firm's pricing objectives.[15]

PRICING A FULL LINE

Our emphasis has been, and will continue to be, on the problem of pricing an individual product mainly because this makes our discussion clearer. But most marketing managers are responsible for more than one product. In fact, their "product" may be the whole company line! So we'll discuss this matter briefly.

Full-line pricing—market- or firm-oriented

Full-line pricing is setting prices for a whole line of products. How to do this depends on which of two basic situations a firm is facing.

In one case, all products in the company's line are aimed at the same general target market, which makes it important for all prices and value to be logically related. This is a common approach with shopping products. A producer of TV sets might offer several models with different features at different prices to give its target customers some choice. The difference among the prices and benefits should appear reasonable when the target customers are evaluating them. Customer perceptions can be important here. A low-priced item, even one that is a good value at that price, may drag down the image of the higher end of the line. Alternatively, one item that consumers do not see as a good value may spill over to how they judge other products in the line.

In other cases, the different products in the line are aimed at entirely different target markets so there doesn't have to be any relation between the various prices. A chemical producer of a wide variety of products with several target markets, for example, probably should price each product separately.

Costs are complicated in full-line pricing

The marketing manager must try to recover all costs on the whole line—perhaps by pricing quite low on more competitive items and much higher on ones with unique benefits. However, estimating costs for each product is a challenge because there is no single right way to assign a company's fixed costs to each of the products. Regardless of how costs are allocated, any cost-oriented pricing method that doesn't consider demand can lead to very unrealistic prices. To avoid mistakes, the marketing manager should judge demand for the whole line as well as demand for each individual product in each target market.

Complementary product pricing

Complementary product pricing is setting prices on several products as a group. This may lead to one product being priced very low so that the profits from another product will increase, thus increasing the product group's total profits. When Gillette introduced the M3Power battery-powered wet-shaving system, the shaver, two blade cartridges, and a Duracell battery had a relatively low suggested retail price of $14.99. However, the blade refill cartridges, which must be replaced frequently, come in a package of four at a hefty price of $10.99.

Complementary product pricing differs from full-line pricing because different production facilities may be involved—so there's no cost allocation problem. Instead, the problem is really understanding the target market and the demand curves for each of the complementary products. Then various combinations of prices can be tried to see what set will be best for reaching the company's pricing objectives.

Product-bundle pricing—one price for several products

A firm that offers its target market several different products may use **product-bundle pricing**—setting one price for a set of products. Firms that use product-bundle pricing usually set the overall price so that it's cheaper for the customer to buy the products at the same time than separately. A bank may offer a product-bundle price for a safe-deposit box, traveler's checks, and a savings account. AT&T bundles voice mail, caller ID, and call forwarding. Bundling encourages customers to spend more and buy products that they might not otherwise buy—because the added cost of the extras is not as high as it would normally be, so the value is better.

Most firms that use product-bundle pricing also set individual prices for the unbundled products. This may increase demand by attracting customers who want one item in a product assortment but don't want the extras. Many firms treat services this way. A software company may have a product-bundle price for its software and access to a toll-free telephone assistance service. However, customers who don't need help can pay a lower price and get just the software.[16]

BID PRICING AND NEGOTIATED PRICING DEPEND HEAVILY ON COSTS

A new price for every job

We introduced the issue of competitive bidding and reverse auctions in Chapter 6. But now let's take a closer look at bid pricing. **Bid pricing** means offering a specific price for each possible job rather than setting a price that applies for all customers. In an e-commerce reverse auction for a standardized product, this may just require that the manager decide the firm's lowest acceptable selling price. But in many situations bid pricing is more complicated. For example, building contractors usually must bid on possible projects. And many companies selling services (like cleaning or data processing) must submit bids for jobs they would like to have.

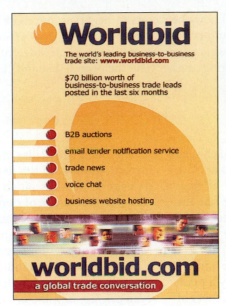

The Internet is making it fast and easy for customers to communicate their needs to a larger number of suppliers to solicit competitively based bid prices.

A big problem in bid pricing on a complicated job is estimating all the costs that will apply. This may sound easy, but a complicated bid may involve thousands of cost components. Further, management must include an overhead charge and a charge for profit.

Because many firms use an e-mail distribution list or website to solicit bids, the process is fast and easy for the buyer. But a seller has to be geared up to set a price and respond quickly. However, this system does allow the seller to set a price based on the precise situation and what costs and revenue are involved.

Bids are usually based on purchase specifications provided by the customer. The specs may be sent by e-mail or posted on a website. Sometimes the seller can win the business, even with a higher bid price, by suggesting changes in the specs that save the customer money.

At times it isn't possible to figure out specs or costs in advance. This may lead to a negotiated contract where the customer agrees to pay the supplier's total cost plus an agreed-on profit figure (say, 10 percent of costs or a dollar amount)—after the job is finished.

Ethical issues in cost-plus bid pricing

Some unethical sellers give bid prices based on cost-plus contracts a bad reputation by faking their records to make costs seem higher than they really are. In other cases, there may be honest debate about what costs should be allowed. We've already considered, for instance, the difficulties in allocating fixed costs.

Demand must be considered too

Competition must be considered when adding in overhead and profit for a bid price. Usually, the customer will get several bids and accept the lowest one. So unthinking addition of typical overhead and profit rates should be avoided. Some bidders use the same overhead and profit rates on all jobs, regardless of competition, and then are surprised when they don't get some jobs.[17]

Negotiated prices— what will a specific customer pay?

Sometimes the customer asks for bids and then singles out the company that submits the *most attractive* bid, not necessarily the lowest, for further bargaining. What a customer will buy—if the customer buys at all—depends on the **negotiated price**, a price set based on bargaining between the buyer and seller. As with simple bid pricing, negotiated pricing is most common in situations where the marketing mix is adjusted for each customer—so bargaining may involve the whole marketing mix, not just the price level. Through the bargaining process, the seller tries to determine what aspects of the marketing mix are most important—and worth the most—to the customer.

CONCLUSION

In this chapter, we discussed various approaches to price setting. Generally, retailers and wholesalers use markups. Some just use the same markups for all their items because it is simpler, but this is usually not the best approach. It's more effective to consider customer demand, competition, and how markups relate to turnover and profit.

It's important for marketing managers to understand costs; if customers are not willing to pay a price that is at least high enough to cover all of the costs of the marketing mix, the firm won't be profitable. So, we describe the different types of cost that a marketing manager needs to understand and how average-cost pricing is used to set prices. But, we note that this approach can fail because it ignores demand. We look at break-even analysis, which is a variation of the cost-oriented approach. It is useful for analyzing possible prices. However, managers must estimate demand to evaluate the chance of reaching these possible break-even points.

The major difficulty with demand-oriented pricing involves estimating the demand curve. But experienced managers, perhaps aided by marketing research, can estimate the nature of demand for their products. Even if estimates are not exact, they can help to get prices in the right ballpark . . . and there's usually a profitable range around the most profitable price. So marketers should consider demand when setting prices. We see this with value in use pricing, psychological pricing, odd-even pricing, full-line pricing, and even bid pricing. Understanding the factors that influence customer price sensitivity can make these approaches more effective.

While we do not recommend that cost-oriented approaches be used by themselves, they do help the marketing manager understand the firm's profitability. Pricing decisions should consider the cost of offering the whole marketing mix. But smart marketers do not accept cost as a given—target marketers always look for ways to be more efficient—to reduce cost while improving the value that they offer customers.

KEY TERMS

markup, 438

markup (percent), 439

markup chain, 440

stockturn rate, 441

average-cost pricing, 442

total fixed cost, 443

total variable cost, 443

total cost, 443

average cost (per unit), 443

average fixed cost (per unit), 444

average variable cost (per unit), 444

break-even analysis, 446

break-even point (BEP), 446

fixed-cost (FC) contribution per unit, 447

marginal analysis, 448

value in use pricing, 452

reference price, 453

leader pricing, 454

bait pricing, 455

psychological pricing, 455

odd-even pricing, 455

price lining, 455

demand-backward pricing, 456

prestige pricing, 456

full-line pricing, 457

complementary product pricing, 458

product-bundle pricing, 458

bid pricing, 458

negotiated price, 459

QUESTIONS AND PROBLEMS

1. Why do many department stores seek a markup of about 30 percent when some discount houses operate on a 20 percent markup?

2. A producer distributed its riding lawn mowers through wholesalers and retailers. The retail selling price was $800, and the manufacturing cost to the company was $312. The retail markup was 35 percent and the wholesale markup 20 percent. (*a*) What was the cost to the whole-

saler? To the retailer? (*b*) What percentage markup did the producer take?

3. Relate the concept of stock turnover to the growth of mass-merchandising. Use a simple example in your answer.

4. If total fixed costs are $200,000 and total variable costs are $100,000 at the output of 20,000 units, what are the probable total fixed costs and total variable costs at an

Sellers must know their costs to negotiate prices effectively. However, negotiated pricing is a demand-oriented approach. Here the seller analyzes very carefully a particular customer's position on a demand curve, or on different possible demand curves based on different offerings, rather than the overall demand curve for a group of customers.

output of 10,000 units? What are the average fixed costs, average variable costs, and average costs at these two output levels? Explain what additional information you would want to determine what price should be charged.

5. Construct an example showing that mechanical use of a very large or a very small markup might still lead to un- profitable operation while some intermediate price would be profitable. Draw a graph and show the break-even point(s).

6. The Davis Company's fixed costs for the year are es- timated at $200,000. Its product sells for $250. The variable cost per unit is $200. Sales for the coming year are expected to reach $1,250,000. What is the break- even point? Expected profit? If sales are forecast at only $875,000, should the Davis Company shut down opera- tions? Why?

7. Discuss the idea of drawing separate demand curves for different market segments. It seems logical because each target market should have its own marketing mix. But won't this lead to many demand curves and possible prices? And what will this mean with respect to functional discounts and varying prices in the marketplace? Will it be legal? Will it be practical?

8. Distinguish between leader pricing and bait pricing. What do they have in common? How can their use affect a mar- keting mix?

9. Cite a local example of psychological pricing and evaluate whether it makes sense.

10. Cite a local example of odd-even pricing and evaluate whether it makes sense.

11. How does a prestige pricing policy fit into a marketing mix? Would exclusive distribution be necessary?

12. Is a full-line pricing policy available only to producers? Cite local examples of full-line pricing. Why is full-line pricing important?

CREATING MARKETING PLANS

The Marketing Plan Coach software on the text website (and on the optional Student CD) includes a sample marketing plan for Hillside Veterinary Clinic. Look through the "Marketing Strategy" section.

a. A veterinary clinic must have some system for dealing with emergencies that occur on weekends and at night when the clinic is closed. Individual vets usually rotate so that someone is always on call to handle emergencies. The price for emergency care is usually 50 percent higher than the price for care during normal hours. Do you think that Hillside should charge higher prices for emergency care? Does it fit with Hillside's strategy?

b. Some customers have expensive pedigree dogs and cats and are less price sensitive than others about fees for veterinary care. Do you think that it would be possible for Hillside to charge higher prices in caring for expensive pets? Why or why not?

SUGGESTED CASES

17. Oh So Pure Water, Inc.   24. Lone Star Wire, Inc.
27. Superior Molding, Inc.   35. Mama Rossi's Pizza

COMPUTER-AIDED PROBLEM

17. BREAK-EVEN/PROFIT ANALYSIS

This problem lets you see the dynamics of break-even anal- ysis. The starting values (costs, revenues, etc.) for this prob- lem are from the break-even analysis example in this chapter (see Exhibit 17–8).

The first column computes a break-even point. You can change costs and prices to figure new break-even points (in units and dollars). The second column goes further. There you can specify target profit level, and the unit and dollar sales needed to achieve your target profit level will be computed. You can also estimate possible sales quantities, and the pro- gram will compute costs, sales, and profits. Use this spread- sheet to address the following issues.

a. Vary the selling price between $1.00 and $1.40. Prepare a table showing how the break-even point (in units and dollars) changes at the different price levels.

b. If you hope to earn a target profit of $15,000, how many units would you have to sell? What would total cost be? Total sales dollars? (Note: Use the right-hand ["profit analysis"] column in the spreadsheet.)

c. Using the "profit analysis" column (column 2), allow your estimate of the sales quantity to vary between 64,000 and 96,000. Prepare a table that shows, for each quantity level, what happens to average cost per unit and profit. Explain why average cost changes as it does over the dif- ferent quantity values.

For additional questions related to this problem, see Exercise 17-4 in the Learning Aid for Use with Essentials of Marketing, 12th edition.

www.mhhe.com/fourps

Ethical Marketing in a Consumer-Oriented World: Appraisal and Challenges

The worldwide drive toward market-directed economies is dramatic evidence that consumer-citizens want freedom and choices not only in politics but in markets. Command economies simply weren't able to meet needs. Even in China, government officials have softened their hard line on central planning and now allow Western firms to market products, many of which will improve the life of Chinese consumers.

Although there's much talk about the world as a global village, we're not there yet. Someone in a real village in Uganda may be able to get a glimpse of the quality of life that consumers in the advanced Western economies enjoy, but for that person it doesn't seem real. What is real is the struggle of everyday life—living without electricity or running water—and, in fact, worrying about malnutrition, disease, and hunger. A rice farmer in China who lives a primitive life but communicates by cell phone may not feel like he's in a time warp, but those of us in developed economies might see it that way. The plight of consumers doesn't seem quite as severe in the emerging democracies, like those in Eastern Europe. But the vast majority of citizen-consumers in those societies can still only wonder if they'll ever have choices among a wide variety of goods and services—and the income to buy them—that most consumers take for granted in the United States, Canada, England, most countries in Western Europe, Australia, and a few other advanced economies.

Even in the face of a serious global economic downturn the challenges faced by consumers, and marketing managers, in the advanced economies seem minor by contrast. In England, for example, some consumers who live in villages that are off the beaten path may worry, instead, that they are not included in the 96 percent of the British population served by Tesco delivery vans. Tesco, the largest supermarket chain in England, created its online shopping service for groceries (and hundreds of other products) just a few years ago, but now its fleet of vans make over 250,000 deliveries a week.

If online shopping for groceries has had a slower start in the United States, it just may be because many Americans are more interested in instant gratification. We expect the corner convenience store to have a nice selection of frozen gourmet dinners that we can prepare in minutes in a microwave oven. Or perhaps that's too much hassle. After all, Domino's will deliver a hot pizza in less than 30 minutes. And McDonald's has our McGriddles ready when we pull up at the drive-thru at 7 in the morning. In a relative sense, few of the world's consumers can expect so much and get so much of what they expect.

But is it a good thing that firms give us what we want? Think about how automakers offered SUVs to appeal to consumers. They do satisfy many of the needs of suburban lifestyles. But most SUVs are gas guzzlers. Some critics even charge that the U.S. has jumped into wars in the Middle East because of such over-reliance on oil. On the other hand, as gas prices and consumer environmental sensitivity have increased, producers have responded with hybrid technologies. Clean hydrogen vehicles may even be in our future. Of course, such adjustments take time.

As another example, much national attention is now directed toward problems of obesity, especially among children. In the United States, 37 percent of children weigh too much. However, that surge of obesity among children is a global trend. Nutritionists say that in the United States and elsewhere, a key culprit is too much fat, starch, and sugar in diets. World Health Organization experts say that today's levels of childhood obesity will later lead to an explosion of illnesses (like heart disease, diabetes, and hypertension) that will drain economies, create enormous suffering, and cause premature deaths. Many nutritionists and public-health officials point the finger of blame at food processors and fast food. When a group of obese teenagers sued McDonald's, claiming that it made them fat, the widely publicized case was fodder for jokes on late-night TV shows. But fast-food companies are not laughing. The judge threw out the case but left open the door for future suits. Some legal experts say that this is just the beginning of legal actions—and they draw the parallel with suits against tobacco companies 30 years ago. Many fast-food companies are scrambling to add salads, fruit, and other low-fat fare to their menus. But should consumers have the right to choose high-fat foods if that is what they want?

When you think about the contrast between problems of starvation and too much fast food, it's not hard to decide which consumers are better off. But is that just a straw man comparison? Is the situation in the less-developed nations one extreme, with the system in the United States and similar societies just as extreme—only in a different way?

Would we be better off if we didn't put quite so much emphasis on marketing?

Do we need so many brands of products? Does all the money spent on advertising really help consumers? Should we expect to be able to get fast food any hour of the day—or order groceries over the Internet and have a van deliver them to the front door? Or, conversely, do all of these choices just increase the prices consumers pay without really adding anything of value? More generally, does marketing serve society well?

These questions are what this chapter is about. Now that you have a better understanding of what marketing is all about, and how the marketing manager contributes to the macro-marketing process, you should be able to decide whether marketing costs too much.[1]

HOW SHOULD MARKETING BE EVALUATED?

We must evaluate at two levels

We've stressed the need for marketing to satisfy customers at a cost that customers consider a good value. So, in this final chapter we'll focus on both customer satisfaction and the costs of marketing as we evaluate marketing's impact on society (see Exhibit 18–1). As we discussed in Chapter 1, it's useful to distinguish between two levels of marketing. Managerial (micro) marketing concerns the marketing activities of an individual firm, whereas macro-marketing concerns how the whole marketing system works. Some complaints against marketing are aimed at only one of these levels at a time. In other cases, the criticisms seem to be directed to one level but actually are aimed at the other. Some critics of specific ads, for example, probably would not be satisfied with any advertising. When evaluating marketing, we must treat each of these levels separately.

Nation's objectives affect evaluation

Different nations have different social and economic objectives. Dictatorships, for example, may be mainly concerned with satisfying the needs of society as seen by the political elite. In a socialist state, the objective might be to satisfy society's needs as defined by government planners. In some societies, the objectives are defined by religious leaders. In others, it's whoever controls the military.

Consumer satisfaction is the objective in the United States

In the United States, *the basic objective of our market-directed economic system has been to satisfy consumer needs as they, the consumers, see them.* This objective implies that political freedom and economic freedom go hand in hand and that citizens in a free society have the right to live as they choose. The majority of American consumers would be unwilling to give up the freedom of choice they now enjoy. The same can be said for Canada, Great Britain, and most other countries in the

Exhibit 18–1 Ethical Marketing in a Consumer-Oriented World

External Market Environment

Customers

Company

Competitors

Segmentation and Targeting

Differentiation and Positioning

PRODUCT · PLACE · TARGET · PROMOTION · PRICE

Marketing's Impact on Society: Micro and Macro Views

Evaluating marketing
- Micro versus macro criteria
- Measuring consumer satisfaction
- Micro-marketing often costs too much
- Macro-marketing does not cost too much

Putting together innovative marketing plans
- Strategy planning process
- Understanding customers
- Blending marketing mix
- Content of the marketing plan

Challenges facing marketers
- Opportunities for improvement
- Marketing managers and social responsibility
- How far should the marketing concept go?

European Union. However, for focus we will concentrate on marketing as it exists in American society.

Therefore, let's try to evaluate the operation of marketing in the American economy—where the present objective is to satisfy consumer needs *as consumers see them*. This is the essence of our system.

This upscale food store in Iran looks similar to those in Western economies, but prices of many consumer products have risen dramatically as the government has clashed with the West. The President of Iran pledged to use oil revenue to ease poverty, but so far that objective has not received much attention.

CAN CONSUMER SATISFACTION BE MEASURED?

Since consumer satisfaction is our objective, marketing's effectiveness must be measured by *how well* it satisfies consumers. There have been various efforts to measure overall consumer satisfaction not only in the United States but also in other countries. For example, a team of researchers at the University of Michigan has created the American Customer Satisfaction Index based on regular interviews with thousands of customers of about 200 companies in 39 industries. Similar studies are available for the European Union.

Satisfaction depends on individual aspirations

This sort of index makes it possible to track changes in consumer satisfaction measures over time and even allows comparison among countries. That's potentially useful. Yet there are limits to interpreting any measure of consumer satisfaction when we try to evaluate macro-marketing effectiveness in any absolute sense. One basic issue is that satisfaction depends on and is *relative to* your level of aspiration or expectation. Less prosperous consumers begin to expect more out of an economy as they see the higher living standards of others. Also, aspiration levels tend to rise with repeated successes and fall with failures. Products considered satisfactory one day may not be satisfactory the next day, or vice versa. Twenty-five years ago, most people were satisfied with a 21-inch color TV that pulled in three or four channels. But once you become accustomed to a large-screen HD model and enjoy all the options possible with a digital satellite receiver, on-demand programs, and a DVR, that old TV is never the same again.

In addition, consumer satisfaction is a highly personal concept. Thus, looking at the "average" satisfaction of a whole society does not provide a complete picture for evaluating macro-marketing effectiveness. At a minimum, some consumers are more satisfied than others. So although efforts to measure satisfaction are useful, any evaluation of macro-marketing effectiveness has to be in part subjective.

Probably the supreme test is whether the macro-marketing system satisfies enough individual consumer-citizens so that they vote—in the ballot box—to keep it running. So far, we've done so in the United States.[2]

There are many measures of micro-marketing effectiveness

Measuring the marketing effectiveness of an individual firm is also difficult, but it can be done. Expectations may change just as other aspects of the marketing environment change—so firms have to do a good job of coping with the change. Individual business firms can and should try to measure how well their marketing mixes satisfy their customers (or why they fail). In fact, most large firms now have some type of ongoing effort to determine whether they're satisfying their target markets. For example, the J.D. Power and Associates marketing research firm is well known for its studies of consumer satisfaction with different makes of automobiles and computers. And the American Customer Satisfaction Index is also used to rate individual companies.

Many large and small firms measure customer satisfaction with

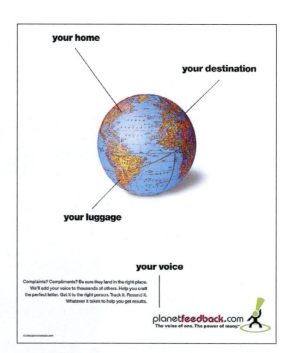

Planetfeedback.com is a website that makes it easy for consumers to give feedback to companies.

Let's take a closer look at the American Customer Satisfaction Index (ACSI). Go to the organization's website (**www.theacsi.org**). Click on "ACSI Scores" and look at "Scores by Industry." In some industries, ACSI has been measuring customer satisfaction since 1994. What industries have shown the greatest improvement since that time? What industries have declined in customer satisfaction? Why do you think some industries have moved up, while others have moved down?

Internet
EXERCISE

attitude research studies. Other widely used methods include comment cards, e-mail response features on websites, unsolicited consumer responses (usually complaints), opinions of intermediaries and salespeople, market test results, and profits. Of course, customers may be very satisfied about some aspects of what a firm is doing but dissatisfied about other dimensions of performance.[3]

In our market-directed system, it's up to each customer to decide how effectively individual firms satisfy his or her needs. Usually, customers will buy more of the products that satisfy them—and they'll do it repeatedly. That's why firms that develop really satisfying marketing mixes are able to develop profitable long-term relationships with the customers that they serve. Because efficient marketing plans can increase profits, profits can be used as a rough measure of a firm's efficiency in satisfying customers. Nonprofit organizations have a different bottom line, but they too will fail if they don't satisfy supporters and get the resources they need to continue to operate.

Evaluating marketing effectiveness is difficult, but not impossible

It's easy to see why opinions differ concerning the effectiveness of micro- and macro-marketing. If the objective of the economy is clearly defined, however—and the argument is stripped of emotion—the big questions about marketing effectiveness probably *can* be answered.

In this chapter, we argue that micro-marketing (how individual firms and channels operate) frequently *does* cost too much but that macro-marketing (how the whole marketing system operates) *does not* cost too much, *given the present objective of the American economy—consumer satisfaction*. Don't accept this position as *the* answer but rather as a point of view. In the end, you'll have to make your own judgment.[4]

MICRO-MARKETING OFTEN DOES COST TOO MUCH

Throughout the text, we've explored what marketing managers could or should do to help their firms do a better job of satisfying customers—while achieving company objectives. Many firms implement highly successful marketing programs, but others are still too production-oriented and inefficient. For customers of these latter firms, micro-marketing often does cost too much.

Coke spent many millions of dollars to develop and promote Blak, a fusion of cola and coffee that was sold in the energy drink category. After more than a year of investments to build the brand, Coke finally abandoned the effort. Even companies with outstanding marketing talents sometimes make expensive marketing mistakes.

Research shows that many consumers are not satisfied. But you know that already. All of us have had experiences when we weren't satisfied—when some firm didn't deliver on its promises. And the problem is much bigger than some marketers want to believe. Research suggests that the majority of consumer complaints are never reported. Worse, many complaints that are reported never get fully resolved.

The failure rate is high

Further evidence that too many firms are too production-oriented—and not nearly as efficient as they could be—is the fact that so many new products fail. New and old businesses—even ones that in the past were leaders in their markets—fail regularly too.

Generally speaking, marketing inefficiencies are due to one or more of three reasons:

1. Lack of interest in or understanding of the sometimes fickle customer.
2. Improper blending of the four Ps—caused in part by overemphasis on internal problems as contrasted with a customer orientation.
3. Lack of understanding of or adjustment to the marketing environment, especially what competitors do.

Any of these problems can easily be a fatal flaw—the sort of thing that leads to business failures. A firm can't create value if it doesn't have a clue what customers think or say. Even if a firm listens to the "voice of the customer," there's no incentive for the customer to buy if the benefits of the marketing mix don't exceed the costs. And if the firm succeeds in coming up with a marketing mix with benefits greater than costs, it still won't be a superior value unless it's better than what competitors offer.

The high cost of missed opportunities

Another sign of failure is the inability of firms to identify new target markets and new opportunities. A new marketing mix that isn't offered doesn't fail—but the lost opportunity can be significant for both a firm and society. Too many managers seize on whatever strategy seems easiest rather than seeking really new ways to satisfy customers. Too many companies stifle really innovative thinking. Layers of bureaucracy and a "that's not the way we do things" mentality just snuff it out.

On the other hand, not every new idea is a good idea for every company. Many firms have lost millions of dollars with failed efforts to jump on the "what's new" bandwagon—without stopping to figure out how it is going to really satisfy the customer and result in profit for the firm. That is as much a ticket for failure as being too slow or bureaucratic.

Ethics QUESTION

Your firm has a new strategy that will make its established product obsolete. However, it will take a year before you are ready to implement the new strategy. If you announce your plan in advance, profits will disappear because many customers and intermediaries will delay purchases until the new product is released. If you don't announce the new plan, customers and intermediaries will continue to buy the established product as their needs dictate, but some will be stuck owning the inferior product and won't do business with you again in the future. How would you decide what to do?

Micro-marketing does cost too much, but things are changing

For reasons like these, marketing does cost too much in many firms. Despite much publicity, the marketing concept is not applied in many places.

But not all firms and marketers deserve criticism. More of them *are* becoming customer-oriented. And many are paying more attention to market-oriented planning to carry out the marketing concept more effectively. Throughout the text, we've highlighted firms and strategies that are making a difference. The successes of innovative firms—like Cirque du Soleil, Amazon.com, Nintendo, Apple, Under Armour, iRobot, Best Buy, and Geico—do not go unnoticed. Yes, they make some mistakes. That's human—and marketing is a human enterprise. But they have also shown the results that market-oriented strategy planning can produce.

Another encouraging sign is that more companies are recognizing that they need a diverse set of backgrounds and talents to meet the increasingly varied needs of their increasingly global customers. They're shedding "not-invented-here" biases and embracing new technologies, comparing what they do with the best practices of firms in totally different industries, and teaming up with outside specialists who can bring a fresh perspective.

Managers who adopt the marketing concept as a way of business life do a better job. They look for target market opportunities and carefully blend the elements of the marketing mix to meet their customers' needs. As more of these managers rise in business, we can look forward to much lower micro-marketing costs and strategies that do a better job of satisfying customer needs.

MACRO-MARKETING DOES NOT COST TOO MUCH

Some critics of marketing take aim at the macro-marketing system. They typically argue that the macro-marketing system causes a poor use of resources and leads to an unfair distribution of income. Most of these complaints imply that some marketing activities by individual firms should not be permitted—and because they are, our macro-marketing system does a less-than-satisfactory job. Let's look at some of these positions to help you form your own opinion.

Micro-efforts help the economy grow

Some critics feel that marketing helps create a monopoly or at least monopolistic competition. Further, they think this leads to higher prices, restricted output, and reduction in national income and employment.

It's true that firms in a market-directed economy try to carve out separate monopolistic markets for themselves with new products. But consumers do have a choice. They don't *have* to buy the new product unless they think it's a better value. The old products are still available. In fact, to meet the new competition, prices of the old products usually drop. And that makes them even more affordable.

Over several years, the innovator's profits may rise—but rising profits also encourage further innovation by competitors. This leads to new investments, which contribute to economic growth and higher levels of national income and employment. Around the world, many countries failed to achieve their potential for economic growth under command systems because this type of profit incentive didn't exist.

Even in mature product categories marketing stimulates innovation and the development of new ways to meet customers' needs. For example, greater interest in healthy eating has prompted Sara Lee to develop a whole-grain bread that tastes like regular white bread, and Marie's salad dressing achieves its straight-from-the-garden taste with no preservatives or trans fat.

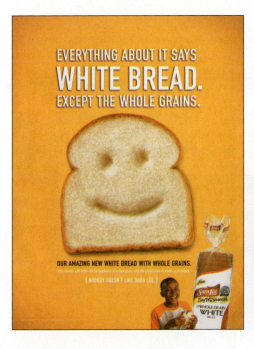

Increased profits also attract competition. Profits and prices then begin to drop as new competitors enter the market and begin producing somewhat similar products. (Recall the rise and fall of industry profit during the product life cycle.)

Is advertising a waste of resources?

Advertising is the most criticized of all micro-marketing activities. Indeed, many ads *are* annoying, insulting, misleading, and downright ineffective. This is one reason why micro-marketing often does cost too much. However, advertising can also make both the micro- and macro-marketing processes work better.

Advertising is an economical way to inform large numbers of potential customers about a firm's products. Provided that a product satisfies customer needs, advertising can increase demand for the product—resulting in economies of scale in manufacturing, distribution, and sales. Because these economies may more than offset advertising costs, advertising can actually *lower* prices to the consumer.[5]

Consumers are not puppets

The idea that firms can manipulate consumers to buy anything the company chooses to produce simply isn't true. A consumer who buys a soft drink that tastes terrible won't buy another can of that brand, regardless of how much it's advertised. In fact, many new products fail the test of the market. Not even large corporations are assured of success every time they launch a new product. Consider, for example, the dismal fate of Pets.com and eToys.com, Ford's Edsel, Sony's beta format VCRs, Xerox's personal computers, and half of the TV programs put on the air in recent years. And if powerful corporations know some way to get people to buy products against their will, would huge companies like Chrysler, Eastern Airlines, Morgan Stanley, and Wachovia ever have racked up billions of dollars in losses?

Needs and wants change

Consumer needs and wants change constantly. Few of us would care to live the way our grandparents lived when they were our age. Marketing's job is not just to satisfy consumer wants as they exist at any particular point in time. Rather, marketing must keep looking for new *and* better ways to create value and serve consumers.[6]

Does marketing make people materialistic?

There is no doubt that marketing caters to materialistic values. However, people disagree as to whether marketing creates these values or simply appeals to values already there.

Even in the most primitive societies, people want to accumulate possessions. The tendency for ancient pharaohs to surround themselves with wealth and treasures can hardly be attributed to the persuasive powers of advertising agencies!

Products do improve the quality of life

Clearly, the quality of life can't be measured just in terms of quantities of material goods. But when we view products as the means to an end rather than the end itself, they *do* make it possible to satisfy higher-level needs. The Internet, for example, empowers people with information in ways that few of us could have even imagined a decade ago.

Marketing reflects our own values

Critics say that advertising elevates the wrong values—for example, by relying on sex appeal to get attention—and generally sending the signal that what really matters most is self-gratification. For example, GoDaddy.com sells Internet domain names and related services. Its stated objective for a Super Bowl ad was to create the most talked about ad ever, and it figured that a risqué ad was the way to go. The ad that it ultimately aired (after trying another dozen or so ideas that were rejected as inappropriate for TV) was a spoof on Janet Jackson's "wardrobe malfunction" during the Super Bowl halftime show the previous year. The

sexy woman dancing around in the commercial doesn't have anything to do with GoDaddy.com, but she did get a lot of attention and GoDaddy's awareness levels went up significantly. A survey showed that it was one of the four most liked commercials during the Super Bowl and the year, but also one of the four most disliked. There are thousands of other ads that rely on something related to sex to get attention. But, is it advertising that creates interest in sex or something else? Experts who study values seem to agree that, in the short run, marketing reflects social values, while in the long run it enhances and reinforces them. Further, many companies work hard to figure out their customers' beliefs and values. Then they refuse to use ads that would be offensive to their target customers.[7]

Not all needs are met

Some critics argue that our macro-marketing system is flawed because it does not provide solutions to important problems, such as questions about how to help the homeless, the uneducated, dependent children, minorities who have suffered discrimination, the elderly poor, and the sick. Many of these people do live in dire circumstances. But is that the result of a market-directed system?

There is no doubt that many firms focus their effort on people who can pay for what they have to offer. But as the forces of competition drive down prices, more people should be able to afford more of what they need. Problems in the financial markets hurt everyone—and millions have lost their homes because of the mortgage crisis. Yet, marketing will play a crucial role in recovering from these problems. The matching of supply and demand will again stimulate economic growth, create jobs, and spread income among more people. In other words, a market-directed economy makes efficient use of resources. However, it can't guarantee that government aid programs are effective. It doesn't ensure that all voters and politicians agree on which problems should be solved first—or how taxes should be set and allocated. It can't eliminate the possibility of a child being ignored.

These are important societal issues. Citizen-consumers in a democratic society assign some responsibilities to business and some to government. Ultimately, consumer-citizens vote in the ballot box for how they want governments to deal with these concerns—just as they vote with their dollars for which firms to support. As more managers in the public sector understand and apply marketing concepts, we should be able to do a better job meeting the needs of all people.

MARKETING STRATEGY PLANNING PROCESS REQUIRES LOGIC AND CREATIVITY

We've said that our macro-marketing system *does not* cost too much, given that customer satisfaction is the present objective of our economy. But we admit that the performance of many business firms leaves a lot to be desired. This presents a challenge to serious-minded students and marketers—and raises the question: What needs to be done?

We hope that this book has convinced you that a large part of the answer to that question is that the effectiveness and *value of marketing efforts in individual firms is improved significantly when managers take the marketing concept seriously—and when they apply the marketing strategy planning process we've presented*. So, let's briefly review these ideas and show how they can be integrated into a marketing plan.

Marketing strategy planning process brings focus to efforts

Developing a good marketing strategy and turning the strategy into a marketing plan requires creative blending of the ideas we've discussed throughout this text. Exhibit 18–2 provides a broad overview of the major areas we've been talking about. You first saw this exhibit in Chapter 2—before you learned what's really involved in each idea. Now we must integrate ideas about these different areas to narrow down to a specific target market and marketing mix that represents a real opportunity. This

Dove created *Evolution*, a time-lapse film of an attractive, but slightly frumpy, young woman who sits for hours as a team of hair dressers, make-up artists, and photo-retouchers transform her into a beautiful billboard model. At the end the kicker is, "No wonder our perception of beauty is distorted." Millions sent their friends a link to the film (www.campaignforrealbeauty.com). Part of Dove's "campaign for real beauty," *Evolution* shows what is possible when a firm applies creative marketing thinking to take a stand on an important social issue. It not only supports a cause but also supports the positioning of Dove products—all without the expense of advertising in traditional media.

narrowing-down process requires a thorough understanding of the market. That understanding is enhanced by careful analysis of customers' needs, current or prospective competitors, and the firm's own objectives and resources. Similarly, trends in the external marketing environment may make a potential opportunity more or less attractive.

There are usually more different strategy possibilities than a firm can pursue. Each possible strategy usually has a number of different potential advantages and disadvantages. This can make it difficult to zero in on the best target market and marketing mix. However, as we discussed in Chapter 3, developing a set of specific qualitative and quantitative screening criteria—to define what business and market(s) the firm wants to compete in—can help eliminate potential strategies that are not well suited to the firm.

Careful analysis helps the manager focus on a strategy that takes advantage of the firm's strengths and opportunities while avoiding its weaknesses and threats to its success. These strengths and weaknesses can be compared with the pros and cons of strategies that are considered. For example, if a firm is considering a strategy that focuses on a target market that is already satisfied by a competitor's offering, finding a competitive advantage might require an innovative new product, improved distribution, more effective promotion, or a better price. Just offering a marketing mix that

Exhibit 18-2
Overview of Marketing Strategy Planning Process

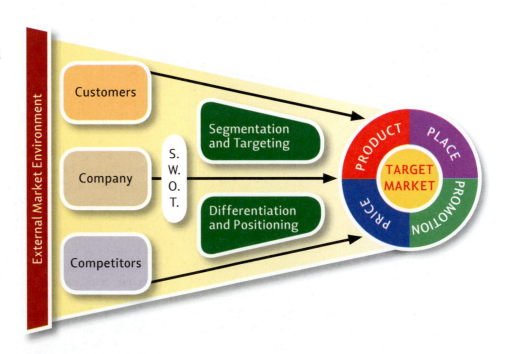

Exhibit 18–3
Strategy Decision Areas Organized by the Four Ps

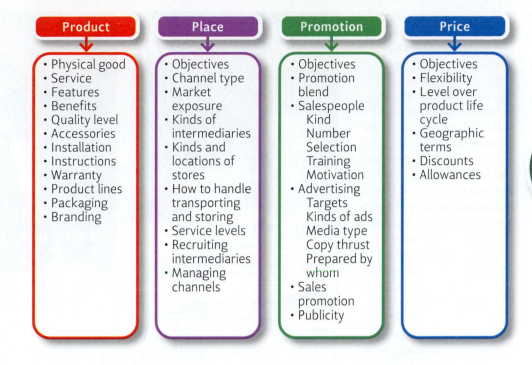

Product	Place	Promotion	Price

• Physical good
• Service
• Features
• Benefits
• Quality level
• Accessories
• Installation
• Instructions
• Warranty
• Product lines
• Packaging
• Branding
	• Objectives
	• Channel type
	• Market exposure
	• Kinds of intermediaries
	• Kinds and locations of stores
	• How to handle transporting and storing
	• Service levels
	• Recruiting intermediaries
	• Managing channels
		• Objectives
		• Promotion blend
		• Salespeople
		  Kind
		  Number
		  Selection
		  Training
		  Motivation
		• Advertising
		  Targets
		  Kinds of ads
		  Media type
		  Copy thrust
		  Prepared by whom
		• Sales promotion
		• Publicity
			• Objectives
			• Flexibility
			• Level over product life cycle
			• Geographic terms
			• Discounts
			• Allowances

is like what is available from competitors usually doesn't provide any real basis for the firm to position or differentiate its marketing mix as offering superior customer value.

Marketing manager must blend the four Ps

Exhibit 18–3 reviews the major marketing strategy decision areas organized by the four Ps. Each of these requires careful decision making. Yet marketing planning involves much more than just independent decisions and assembling the parts into a marketing mix. The four Ps must be creatively *blended*—so the firm develops the best mix for its target market. In other words, each decision must work well with all of the others to make a logical whole.

In our discussion, we've given the job of integrating the four Ps strategy decisions to the marketing manager. Now you should see the need for this integrating role. It is easy for specialists to focus on their own areas and expect the rest of the company to work for or around them. This is especially true in larger firms where the size of the whole marketing job is too big for one person. Yet the ideas of the product manager, the advertising manager, the sales manager, the logistics manager, and whoever makes pricing decisions may have to be adjusted to improve the whole mix. It's critical that each marketing mix decision work well with all of the others. A breakdown in any one decision area may doom the whole strategy to failure.

THE MARKETING PLAN BRINGS ALL THE DETAILS TOGETHER

Marketing plan provides a blueprint for implementation

Once the manager has selected the target market, decided on the (integrated) marketing mix to meet that target market's needs, and developed estimates of the costs and revenues for that strategy, it's time to put it all together in the marketing plan. As we explained in Chapter 2, a marketing plan includes the time-related details—including costs and revenues—for a marketing strategy. Thus, the plan basically serves as a blueprint for what the firm will do.

Exhibit 18–4 provides a summary outline of the different sections of a complete marketing plan. You can see that this outline is basically an abridged overview of the topics we've covered throughout the text. Thus, you can flesh out your thinking for any portion of a marketing plan by reviewing the section of the book where that topic

Treif's marketing mix, targeted at firms that process meat, includes this ad for its high-quality slicing equipment, which uses the brand name Zebra-CE. The brand name and the picture of zebras with thick and thin stripes are intended to highlight the thick and thin cutting technology of the equipment but a potential customer might miss the point and instead be distracted with thoughts of sliced zebra meat. Gardenburger's ad takes a humorous approach, which might appeal to consumers who are cynical about advertiser's sales pitches. On the other hand, Hindu consumers (who would logically be potential customers for Gardenburger products) might find it offensive that the ad alludes to Hindu religious beliefs.

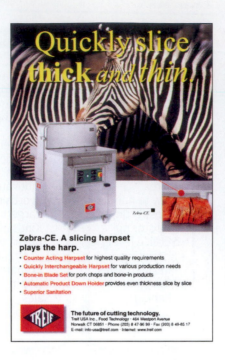

is discussed in more detail. Further, the Hillside Veterinary Clinic case in the Marketing Plan Coach on the text website (and on the optional Student CD) gives you a real example of the types of thinking and detail that are included.

Marketing plan spells out the timing of the strategy

Some time schedule is implicit in any strategy. A marketing plan simply spells out this time period and the time-related details. Usually, we think in terms of some reasonable length of time—such as six months, a year, or a few years. But it might be only a month or two in some cases, especially when rapid changes in fashion or technology are important. Or a strategy might be implemented over several years, perhaps the length of the early stages of the product's life.

Although the outline in Exhibit 18–4 does not explicitly show a place for the time frame for the plan or the specific costs for each decision area, these should be included in the plan—along with expected estimates of sales and profit—so that the plan can be compared with *actual performance* in the future. In other words, the plan not only makes it clear to everyone what is to be accomplished and how—it also provides a basis for the control process after the plan is implemented.[8]

A complete plan spells out the reasons for decisions

The plan outline shown in Exhibit 18–4 is quite complete. It doesn't just provide information about marketing mix decisions—it also includes information about customers (including segmenting dimensions), competitors' strategies, other aspects of the marketing environment, and the company's objectives and resources. This material provides important background information relevant to the "why" of the marketing mix and target market decisions.

Too often, managers do not include this information; their plans just lay out the details of the target market and the marketing mix strategy decisions. This shortcut approach is more common when the plan is really just an update of a strategy that has been in place for some time. However, that approach can be risky.

Managers too often make the mistake of casually updating plans in minor ways—perhaps just changing some costs or sales forecasts—but otherwise sticking with what was done in the past. A big problem with this approach is that it's easy to lose sight of why those strategy decisions were made in the first place. When the market situation changes, the original reasons may no longer apply. Yet if the logic for those strategy decisions is not retained, it's easy to miss changes taking place that should result in a plan being reconsidered. For example, a plan that was established in the growth stage of the product life cycle may have been very successful for a number of years. But a marketing manager can't be complacent and assume that success will continue forever. When market maturity hits, the firm may be in for big trouble—unless the basic strategy and plan are modified. If a plan spells out the details of the market analysis and logic for the marketing mix and target market selected, then it is a simple matter to routinely check and update it. Remember: The idea is for all of the analysis and strategy decisions to fit together as an integrated whole. Thus, as some of the elements of the plan or marketing environment change, the whole plan may need a fresh approach.

CHALLENGES FACING MARKETERS

Marketers face the challenge of preparing creative and innovative marketing plans, but that in itself will not improve the value of marketing to society. We need to face up to other basic challenges that require new ways of thinking.

Change is the only thing that's constant

We need better marketing performance at the firm level. Progressive firms pay attention to changes in the market—including trends in the marketing environment—and how marketing strategies need to be improved to consider these changes. Exhibit 18–5 lists some of the important trends and changes we've discussed throughout this text.

Most of the changes and trends summarized in Exhibit 18–5 are having a positive effect on how marketers serve society. And this ongoing improvement is self-directing. As consumers shift their support to firms that do meet their needs, laggard businesses are forced to either improve or get out of the way.

If it ain't broke, improve it

Marketing managers must constantly evaluate their strategies to be sure they're not being left in the dust by competitors who see new and better ways of doing things. It's crazy for a marketing manager to constantly change a strategy that's working well. But too many managers fail to see or plan for needed changes. They're afraid to do anything different and adhere to the idea that "if it ain't broke, don't fix it." But a firm can't always wait until a problem becomes completely obvious to do something about it. When customers move on and profits disappear, it may be too late to fix the problem. Marketing managers who take the lead in finding innovative new markets and approaches get a competitive advantage.

We need to welcome international competition

Marketers can't afford to bury their heads in the sand and hope that international competition will go away. Rather, they must realize that it is part of today's marketing environment. It creates even more pressure on marketing managers to figure out what it takes to gain a competitive advantage—both at home and in foreign markets. But with the challenge comes opportunities. The forces of competition in and among market-directed economies will help speed the diffusion of marketing advances to consumers everywhere. As macro-marketing systems improve worldwide, more consumers will have income to buy products—from wherever in the world those products come.

We need to use technology wisely

We live in a time of dramatic new technologies. Many marketers hate the idea that what they've learned from years of on-the-job experience may no longer apply when a technology like the Internet comes along. Or they feel that it's the job of the technical specialist to figure out how a new technology can help the firm serve its customers. But marketers can't just pawn that responsibility off on "somebody else." If that means learning about new technologies, then that is just part of the marketing job.

At a broader level, firms face the challenge of determining what technologies are acceptable and which are not. For example, gene research has opened the door to

Exhibit 18-4   Summary Outline of Different Sections of Marketing Plan

<u>Situation Analysis</u>

Company Analysis
  Company objectives and overall marketing objectives
  Company resources (marketing, production, financial, human, etc.)
  Other marketing plans (marketing program)
  Previous marketing strategy
  Major screening criteria relevant to product-market opportunity selected
      Quantitative (ROI, profitability, risk level, etc.)
      Qualitative (nature of business preferred, social responsibility, environment, etc.)
  Major constraints
  Marketing collaborators (current and potential)

Customer Analysis (organizational customers and/or final consumers)
  Product-market
  Possible segmenting dimensions (customer needs, other characteristics)
      Qualifying dimensions and determining dimensions
  Identify target market(s) (one or more specific segments)
      Operational characteristics (demographics, geographic locations, etc.)
  Potential size (number of people, dollar purchase potential, etc.) and likely growth
  Key economic, psychological, and social influences on buying
  Type of buying situation
  Nature of relationship with customers

Competitor Analysis
  Nature of current/likely competition
  Current and prospective competitors (or rivals)
      Current strategies and likely responses to plan
  Competitive barriers to overcome and sources of potential competitive advantage

Analysis of the Market Context—External Market Environment
  Economic environment
  Technological environment
  Political and legal environment
  Cultural and social environment

Key Factors from Situation Analysis
  S.W.O.T.: Strengths, weaknesses, opportunities, and threats from situation analysis

<u>Marketing Plan Objectives</u>
  Specific objectives to be achieved with the marketing strategy

<u>Differentiation and Positioning</u>
  How will marketing mix be differentiated from the competition?
  How will the market offering be positioned?

<u>Marketing Strategy</u>
Overview of the Marketing Strategy
  General direction for the marketing strategy
  Description of how the four Ps fit together

Target Market(s)
  Summary of characteristics of the target market(s) to be approached

Product
  Product class (type of consumer or business product)
  Current product life-cycle stage
  New-product development requirements (people, dollars, time, etc.)
  Product liability, safety, and social responsibility considerations
  Specification of core physical good or service
      Features, quality, etc.
  Supporting service(s) needed
  Warranty (what is covered, timing, who will support, etc.)
  Branding (manufacturer versus dealer, family versus individual, etc.)

Packaging
    Promotion and labeling needs
    Protection needs
Cultural sensitivity of product
Fit with product line

Place
Objectives
    Degree of market exposure required
    Distribution customer service level required
Type of channel (direct, indirect)
    Other channel members or collaborators required
    Type /number of wholesalers (agent, merchant, etc.)
    Type/number of retailers
    How discrepancies and separations will be handled
    How marketing functions will be shared
Coordination needed in company, channel, and supply chain
    Information requirements (EDI, the Internet, e-mail, etc.)
Transportation requirements
Inventory product-handling requirements
Facilities required (warehousing, distribution centers, etc.)
Reverse channels (for returns, recalls, etc.)

Promotion
Objectives
Major message theme(s) (for integrated marketing communications/positioning)
Promotion blend
    Advertising (type, media, copy thrust, etc.)
    Personal selling (type and number of salespeople, compensation, effort allocation, etc.)
    Sales promotion (for customers, channel members, employees)
    Publicity
    Interactive media
Mix of push and pull required
Who will do the work?

Price
Nature of demand (price sensitivity, price of substitutes)
Demand and cost analyses (marginal analysis)
Markup chain in channel
Price flexibility
Price level(s) (under what conditions) and impact on customer value
Adjustments to list price (geographic terms, discounts, allowances, etc.)

Marketing Information Requirements
Marketing research needs (with respect to customers, 4Ps, external environment, etc.)
Secondary and primary data needs
Marketing information system needs, models to be used, etc.

Implementation and Control
Special Implementation Problems to Overcome
People required
Manufacturing, financial, and other resources needed

Control
Marketing information systems and data needed
Criterion measures/comparison with objectives (customer satisfaction, sales, cost, performance analysis, etc.)

Budget, Sales Forecasts, and Estimates of Profit
Costs (all elements in plan, over time)
Sales (by market, over time, etc.)
Estimated operating statement (pro forma)

Timing
Specific sequence of activities and events, etc.
Likely changes over the product life cycle

Risk Factors and Contingency Plans

life-saving medicines, genetically altered crops that resist drought or disease, and even cloning of human beings. Yet in all of these arenas there is intense conflict among different groups about what is appropriate. How should these decisions be made? There is no simple answer to this question, but it's clear that old production-oriented views are *not* the answer. Perhaps we will move toward developing answers if some of the marketing ideas that have been applied to understanding individual needs can be extended to better understand the needs of society as a whole.

We must consider *long-run* consumer welfare

Throughout this book we have emphasized the importance of the marketing concept—satisfying customers through a total company effort at a profit. Unfortunately, some firms take too short-run a view. They satisfy customers in the short-run and take their profits, without worrying about longer-term problems. For example, some banks, mortgage brokers, and credit card companies made credit too easy to get. Some customers enjoyed this for a while, but many purchased homes or built up credit card debt that they couldn't afford. While this helped companies earn high profits in the short term, many customers later defaulted on loans. Eventually, such activities harmed customers—and wreaked havoc on our global economy. Marketing managers must have a long-run view of customer satisfaction and recognize their social responsibility.

We may need more social responsibility

Good business managers put themselves in the consumer's position. A useful rule to follow might be: Do unto others as you would have others do unto you. In practice, this means developing satisfying marketing mixes for specific target markets. While trying to serve the needs of some target market, does the marketing strategy disregard the rights and needs of other consumers or create problems that will be left for future generations?[9]

The environment is everyone's need

Marketers need to work harder and smarter at finding ways to satisfy consumer needs without sacrificing the environment. All consumers need the environment, whether they realize it yet or not. We are only beginning to understand the consequences of the environmental damage that's already been done. Acid rain, depletion of the ozone layer, global warming, and toxic waste in water supplies—to mention but a few current environmental problems—have catastrophic effects.

Environmental problems pose a major challenge to society, but they're also an opportunity for innovative firms—because there will be rewards for firms that develop better ways of addressing them.

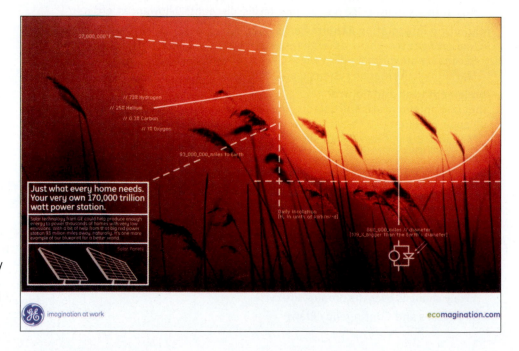

Exhibit 18–5   Some Important Changes and Trends Affecting Marketing Strategy Planning

Communication Technologies
The Internet and intranets
Satellite communications and Wi-Fi
HTML e-mail and instant messaging
Video conferencing and Internet phones
Smart phones

Role of Computerization
E-commerce, websites
Computers and PDAs
Spreadsheet analysis
Wireless networks
Scanners, bar codes, and RFID for tracking
Multimedia integration

Marketing Research
Search engines and web analytics
Growth of marketing information systems
Decision support systems
XML data exchange
Single source data (and scanner panels)
Data warehouses and data mining
Multimedia data and questionnaires
Customer relationship management (CRM) systems

Demographic Patterns
"Wired" households
Explosion in senior and ethnic submarkets
Aging of the baby boomers
Population growth slowdown in U.S.
Geographic shifts in population
Slower real income growth in U.S.

Business and Organizational Customers
Closer relationships and single sourcing
Just-in-time inventory systems/EDI
Web portals and Internet sourcing
Interactive bidding and proposal requests
Shift to NAICS
ISO 9000
E-commerce and supply chain management

Product
More attention to "really new" products
Faster new-product development
Computer-aided design (CAD)
R&D teams with market-driven focus
More attention to quality
More attention to service technologies
More attention to sustainable design
Category management

Channels and Logistics
Internet selling (wholesale and retail)
More vertical marketing systems
Clicks and bricks (multichannel)
Larger, more powerful retail chains
More attention to distribution service
Real-time inventory replenishment
Rapid response, JIT, and ECR
Automated warehousing and handling
Cross-docking at distribution centers
Logistics outsourcing
Cross-channel logistics coordination
Growth of mass-merchandising

Sales Promotion
Database-directed promotion
Point-of-purchase promotion
Trade promotion becoming more sensible
Event sponsorships
Product placement
Better support from agencies
Customer loyalty programs
Customer acquisition cost analysis

Personal Selling
Post-sale customer service
Sales technology
Use of laptop computers
Major accounts specialization
More telemarketing and team selling
Use of e-mail, fax, and voice mail

Mass Selling
Interactive media (Internet ads, etc.)
Integrated marketing communications
More targeted media
    Blogs
    Specialty publications
    Specialty radio and TV (cable, satellite)
    Point-of-purchase
Growth of interactive agencies
Consolidation of global agencies
Consolidation of media companies
Changing agency compensation
Direct-response advertising
Shrinking media budgets

Pricing
Electronic bid pricing and auctions
Value pricing
Overuse of sales and deals
Bigger differences in functional discounts
More attention to exchange rate effects
Lower markups on higher stockturn items
Spreadsheets for marginal analysis

International Marketing
More international market development
Global competitors—at home and abroad
Global communication over Internet
New trade rules (NAFTA, WTO, EU, etc.)
More attention to exporting by small firms
International expansion by retailers
Impact of "pop" culture on traditional cultures
Tensions between "have" and "have-not" cultures
Growing role of airfreight

General
Economic decline
S.W.O.T. analysis
Privacy issues
Benchmarking and total quality management
More attention to positioning and differentiation
Less regulation of business
Increased use of alliances
Shift away from diversification
More attention to profitability, not just sales
Greater attention to superior value
Addressing environmental concerns

In the past, most firms didn't pass the cost of environmental damage on to consumers in the prices that they paid. Pollution was a hidden and unmeasured cost for most companies. That is changing rapidly. Firms are already paying billions of dollars to correct problems, including problems created years ago. The government isn't accepting the excuse that "nobody knew it was a big problem."[10]

We need the truth

Promotion provides powerful ways to communicate with customers. Yet, too many firms lapse into telling only half the truth. This is most obvious when there is a shift in consumer interest. For example, a firm's ad may accurately proclaim that its food product has no "trans fat"—but do consumers think that means it's healthy, low calorie, or even low in fat? Today we're also seeing a lot of incomplete or misleading "greenwashing" claims about firms' environmental practices and eco-friendly products. It's good for a firm to create a biodegradable package and promote it, but the cleaning product in the package shouldn't contain chemicals that will be harmful once they're in the sewer system.

Growing consumer cynicism about promotion is also a problem. As it gets worse, both firms and consumers suffer. Regulations say that marketing communications shouldn't be false or misleading, but managers need to take seriously the responsibility to be truthful to their customers. Marketing communications should be helpful—not just legal. Managers who don't get this message are likely to learn a hard lesson—from activists who spread criticisms of their firms across the Web and other media. The potential harm to a brand's reputation from this sort of negative publicity has many firms cautious about overstating their claims, including ones related to sustainability efforts.[11]

Consumer privacy needs to be protected

Marketers must also be sensitive to consumers' rights and privacy. Today, sophisticated marketing research methods, the Internet, and other technologies make it easier to abuse these rights. For example, credit card records—which reveal much about consumers' purchases and private lives—are routinely sold to anybody who pays for the computer file.

Most consumers don't realize how much data about their personal lives—some of it incorrect but treated as fact—is collected and available. A simple computer billing error may land consumers on a bad-credit list without their knowledge. Worse, poor security can result in identity theft. Marketing managers should use technology responsibly to improve the quality of life, not disrupt it. If you don't think privacy is a serious matter, enter your social security number in an Internet search engine and see what pops up. You may be surprised.[12]

May need to change laws and how they are enforced

One of the advantages of a market-directed economic system is that it operates automatically. But in our version of this system, consumer-citizens provide certain constraints (laws), which can be modified at any time. Managers who ignore consumer attitudes must realize that their actions may cause new restraints.

Before piling on too many new rules, however, some of the ones we have may need to be revised—and others may need to be enforced more carefully. Antitrust laws, for example, are often applied to protect competitors from each other—but they were originally intended to encourage competition.

Specifically, U.S. antitrust laws were developed so that all firms in a market would compete on a level playing field. But in many markets, that level playing field no longer exists. In our global economy, individual U.S. firms now compete with foreign firms whose governments urge them to cooperate with each other. Such foreign firms don't see each other as competitors; rather they see U.S. firms, as a group, as the competitors.

Laws should affect top managers

Strict enforcement of present laws could have far-reaching results if more price fixers, fraudulent or deceptive advertisers, and others who violate existing laws—thus affecting the performance of the macro-marketing system—were sent to jail

Marketers Learn New Rules for Schools

For many years, schools have been a targeted place for youth-oriented marketers to promote their products to the United States' 51 million elementary and secondary students. Coke and Pepsi have been eager to contribute scoreboards (or is that billboards?) for high school sports fields. In school cafeterias, which serve over 34 million meals a day, Kellogg's cereal and Dannon's yogurt have sponsored programs to motivate learning (and increase consumption). McDonald's put its logo and a picture of Ronald McDonald on elementary school report cards in Florida. A school district in Colorado got national attention for selling advertising space on the sides of its school buses. Targeting students who are captive at school is not a new idea. The National Dairy Council has promoted dairy products in the schools since 1915.

In spite of a long history of promotion in the schools, it has been a controversial topic. The controversy heated up years ago after the launch of the Channel One television network—with ads and programming for schools—drew a great deal of attention. Many critics saw it as a crass attempt to exploit classroom students. However, other people liked the idea, among other reasons because the schools got benefits. Channel One provides excellent news programs, and schools also get video equipment and chances to win support for Internet access. Over time, sponsors have provided schools with other types of teaching materials—or even direct financial support. Although the focus of critics in the past was on the question of whether any type of promotion in schools was acceptable, now the criticisms have solidified around the issues of what foods and beverages can be promoted and available in schools. Two major events are relevant to this issue.

First, prompted by international concerns about childhood obesity, McDonald's, PepsiCo, Kraft Foods, General Mills, and a half-dozen other major food and beverage companies have vowed to obey a self-imposed set of limits on advertising to kids, especially those under 12. For example, the participating companies say that half of their advertising directed to kids will promote healthier dietary choices and lifestyles. More central here, they have also said that they won't advertise food or drinks in elementary schools at all. Second, the Institute of Medicine, which advises Congress on health, recently issued new guidelines that recommend that schools stop offering soft drinks, candy, cookies, cakes, and other high-fat, high-calorie foods and beverages. In combination, these changes could have sweeping effects. However, there are still a lot of questions. For example, it is not clear how promotion of food products in high schools will be handled—and what, if anything, will be different about promotion of nonfood products in elementary schools.

Some budget-strapped schools say that they won't give up the support provided by promotions unless new laws require them to comply. Their position isn't just about the money. Some educators believe that the teaching materials that come with the promotions are excellent.

What is clear from the public debate is that promotions targeted at students raise sensitive issues of educational standards, ethics, and taste. Because of that, Kraft and some other firms have stopped all promotions in schools. But self-control doesn't go far enough for many critics. Some state legislatures have already passed stricter regulations on what foods and drinks can be sold in schools. Marketers who are not attentive to concerns such as these may get caught up in a public backlash.[13]

or given heavy fines. A quick change in attitudes might occur if unethical top managers—those who plan strategy—were prosecuted, instead of the salespeople or advertisers expected to deliver on weak or undifferentiated strategies.

Laws merely define minimal ethical standards

Whether a marketer is operating in his or her own country or in a foreign nation, the legal environment sets the *minimal* standards of ethical behavior as defined by a society. In addition, the American Marketing Association's Statement of Ethics

The Utah Transit Authority (UTA) thought that more university students would ride the bus long-term if they were motivated by personal benefit rather than environmental or social conscience. For most people, the pros and cons of riding the bus, like other product choices, are more a personal matter. So UTA decided it should offer an answer to the question, "What's in it for me?" The answer in this particular UTA ad is "social opportunities." Although public transit is not exactly a sexy product, the ad employs a "sex sells" approach. What do you think? Is this a good idea? Why?

You can learn a lot on the bus.

University of Utah students ride free with student I.D. **U T A**

(Exhibit 1–7) provides basic guidelines that a marketing manager should observe. But marketing managers constantly face ethical issues where there are no clearly defined answers. Every marketing manager should make a personal commitment to carefully evaluate the ethical consequences of marketing strategy decisions.

On the other hand, innovative new marketing strategies *do* sometimes cause problems for those who have a vested interest in the old ways. Some people try to portray anything that disrupts their own personal interest as unethical. But that is not an appropriate ethical standard. The basic ethical charge to marketers is to find new *and* better ways to serve society's needs.

Need socially responsible consumers

We've stressed that marketers should act responsibly—but consumers have responsibilities too. Some consumers abuse policies about returning goods, change price tags in self-service stores, and are downright abusive to salespeople. Others think nothing of ripping off businesses because "they're rich." Shoplifting is a major problem for most traditional retailers, averaging almost 2 percent of sales nationally. In supermarkets, losses to shoplifters are on average greater than profits. Online retailers, in turn, must fight the use of stolen or fraudulent credit cards. Honest consumers pay for the cost of this theft in higher prices.[14]

Americans tend to perform their dual role of consumer-citizens with a split personality. We often behave differently at the cash register than we do on our soap box. For example, we say that we want to protect the environment, but when it comes to making our own purchase decisions, we're likely to pick the product that is more convenient or lower priced rather than the one that is the sustainable choice. We protest sex and violence in the media, but some of the most profitable websites on the Internet are purveyors of pornography. Parents complain about advertising aimed at children but use TV as a Saturday morning baby-sitter.

Unethical or illegal behavior is widespread. In a major survey of workers, managers, and executives from a wide range of industries, 48 percent admitted to taking unethical or illegal actions in the past year. Offenses included things like cheating on expense accounts, paying or accepting kickbacks, trading sex for sales, lying to

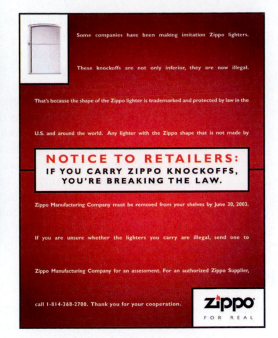

In today's competitive marketplace, both consumers and businesses have social responsibilities.

customers, leaking company secrets, and looking the other way when environmental laws are violated. Think about it—we're talking about half of the workforce.[15]

As consumer-citizens, each of us shares the responsibility for preserving an effective macro-marketing system. And we should take this responsibility seriously. That even includes the responsibility to be smarter customers. Let's face it, a majority of consumers ignore most of the available information that could help them spend money (and guide the marketing process) more wisely. Consumerism has encouraged nutritional labeling, open dating, unit pricing, truth-in-lending, plain-language contracts and warranties, and so on. Many companies provide extensive information at their websites or in brochures. Government agencies publish many consumer buying guides on everything from tires to appliances, as do organizations such as Consumers Union. Most of this information is available from home, over the Internet. It makes sense to use it.

> **Internet EXERCISE**
>
> One of the most widely read blogs, the Consumerist (**www.consumerist.com**), operates as a consumer watchdog and monitors corporate behavior. Go to this blog and read a posting critical of some firm's behavior; click through to the original source if necessary. What do you think of this story? Does it change your attitude toward the firm? How could sites like these influence consumers? How could they influence firms?

HOW FAR SHOULD THE MARKETING CONCEPT GO?

Should marketing managers limit consumers' freedom of choice?

Achieving a better macro-marketing system is certainly a desirable objective. But what part should a marketer play in deciding what products to offer?

This is extremely important, because some marketing managers, especially those in large corporations, can have an impact far larger than they do in their roles as consumer-citizens. For example, should they refuse to produce hazardous products, like skis or motorcycles, even though such products are in strong demand? Should they install safety devices that increase costs but that customers don't want?

These are difficult questions to answer. Some things marketing managers do clearly benefit both the firm and consumers because they lower costs or improve consumers' options. But other decisions may actually reduce consumer choice and conflict with a desire to improve the effectiveness of our macro-marketing system.

Consumer-citizens should vote on the changes

It seems fair to suggest, therefore, that marketing managers should be expected to improve and expand the range of goods and services they make available—always trying to add value and better satisfy consumers' needs and preferences. This is the job we've assigned to business.

If pursuing this objective makes excessive demands on scarce resources or has an unacceptable ecological effect, then consumer-citizens have the responsibility to vote for laws restricting individual firms that are trying to satisfy consumers' needs. This is the role that we, as consumers, have assigned to the government—to ensure that the macro-marketing system works effectively.

It is important to recognize that some *seemingly minor* modifications in our present system *might* result in very big, unintended problems. Allowing some government agency to prohibit the sale of products for seemingly good reasons could lead to major changes we never expected and could seriously reduce consumers' present rights to freedom of choice, including "bad" choices.

CONCLUSION

Macro-marketing does *not* cost too much. Consumers have assigned business the role of satisfying their needs. Customers find it satisfactory and even desirable to permit businesses to cater to them and even to stimulate wants. As long as consumers are satisfied, macro-marketing will not cost too much—and business firms will be permitted to continue as profit-making entities.

But business exists at the consumer's discretion. It's mainly by satisfying the consumer that a particular firm—and *our* economic system—can justify its existence and hope to keep operating.

In carrying out this role—granted by consumers—business firms are not always as effective as they could be. Many business managers don't understand the marketing concept or the role that marketing plays in our way of life. They seem to feel that business has a God-given right to operate as it chooses. And they proceed in their typical production-oriented ways. Further, many managers have had little or no training in business management and are not as competent as they should be. Others fail to adjust to the changes taking place around them. And a few dishonest or unethical managers can do a great deal of damage before consumer-citizens take steps to stop them. As a result, marketing by individual firms often *does* cost too much. But the situation is improving. More business training is now available, and more competent people are being

attracted to marketing and business generally. Clearly, *you* have a role to play in improving marketing activities in the future.

The marketing strategy planning process presented in this book provides a framework that will guide you to more effective marketing decisions—and marketing that really does deliver superior value to customers. It also benefits the firm, through profits and growth. It's truly a "win-win" situation. And in our competitive, market-driven economy, managers and firms that lead the way in creating these successes will not go unnoticed. As effective marketing management spreads to more companies, the whole macro-marketing system will be more efficient and effective.

To keep our system working effectively, individual firms should implement the marketing concept in a more efficient, ethical, and socially responsible way. At the same time, we—as consumers—should consume goods and services in an intelligent and socially responsible way. Further, we have the responsibility to vote and ensure that we get the kind of macro-marketing system we want. What kind do you want? What should you do to ensure that fellow consumer-citizens will vote for your system? Is your system likely to satisfy you as well as another macro-marketing system? You don't have to answer these questions right now—but your answers will affect the future you'll live in and how satisfied you'll be.

QUESTIONS AND PROBLEMS

1. Explain why marketing must be evaluated at two levels. What criteria should be used to evaluate each level of marketing? Defend your answer. Explain why your criteria are better than alternative criteria.

2. Discuss the merits of various economic system objectives. Is the objective of the American economic system sensible? Could it achieve more consumer satisfaction if

sociologists or public officials determined how to satisfy the needs of lower-income or less-educated consumers? If so, what education or income level should be required before an individual is granted free choice?

3. Should the objective of our economy be maximum efficiency? If your answer is yes, efficiency in what? If not, what should the objective be?

4. Discuss the conflict of interests among production, finance, accounting, and marketing executives. How does this conflict affect the operation of an individual firm? The economic system? Why does this conflict exist?

5. Why does adoption of the marketing concept encourage a firm to operate more efficiently? Be specific about the impact of the marketing concept on the various departments of a firm.

6. In the short run, competition sometimes leads to inefficiency in the operation of our economic system. Many people argue for monopoly in order to eliminate this inefficiency. Discuss this solution.

7. How would officially granted monopolies affect the operation of our economic system? Consider the effect on allocation of resources, the level of income and employment, and the distribution of income. Is the effect any different if a firm obtains a monopoly by winning out in a competitive market?

8. Comment on the following statement: "Ultimately, the high cost of marketing is due only to consumers."

9. Distinguish clearly between a marketing strategy and a marketing plan. If a firm has a really good strategy, does it need to worry about developing a written plan?

10. How far should the marketing concept go? How should we decide this issue?

11. Should marketing managers, or business managers in general, refrain from producing profitable products that some target customers want but that may not be in their long-run best interest? Should firms be expected to produce "good" but less profitable products? What if such products break even? What if they are unprofitable but the company makes other profitable products—so on balance it still makes some profit? What criteria are you using for each of your answers?

12. Should a marketing manager or a business refuse to produce an "energy-gobbling" appliance that some consumers are demanding? Should a firm install an expensive safety device that will increase costs but that customers don't want? Are the same principles involved in both these questions? Explain.

13. Discuss how one or more of the trends or changes shown in Exhibit 18–5 are affecting marketing strategy planning for a specific firm that serves the market where you live.

14. Discuss how slower economic growth or no economic growth would affect your college community—in particular, its marketing institutions.

CREATING MARKETING PLANS

The Marketing Plan Coach software on the text website (and on the optional Student CD) includes a sample marketing plan for Hillside Veterinary Clinic. Review the entire marketing plan.

a. How do the pieces fit together?

b. Does the marketing strategy logically follow from the target market dimensions?

c. Does the marketing strategy logically follow from the differentiation and positioning?

d. Does the plan appear reasonable given the stated objectives?

SUGGESTED CASES

17. Oh So Pure Water, Inc.
30. Eden Prairie Mills, Ltd.
34. Innovative Aluminum Products, Inc.

22. Bright Light Innovations
31. At-Home Health Services, Inc.

27. Superior Molding, Inc.
32. Lever, Ltd.

28. PCT, Inc.

A

Economics Fundamentals

LEARNING OBJECTIVES

The economist's traditional analysis of supply and demand is a useful tool for analyzing markets. In particular, you should master the concepts of a demand curve and demand elasticity. A firm's demand curve shows how target customers view the firm's Product—really its whole marketing mix. And the interaction of demand and supply curves helps set the size of a market and the market price. The interaction of supply and demand also determines the nature of the competitive environment, which has an important effect on strategy planning. The learning objectives and following sections of this appendix discuss these ideas more fully.

When you finish this appendix, you should be able to:

1 understand the "law of diminishing demand."

2 understand demand and supply curves and how they set the size of a market and its price level.

3 know about elasticity of demand and supply.

4 know why demand elasticity can be affected by availability of substitutes.

5 know the different kinds of competitive situations and understand why they are important to marketing managers.

6 understand important new terms (shown in red).

PRODUCTS AND MARKETS AS SEEN BY CUSTOMERS AND POTENTIAL CUSTOMERS

Economists see individual customers choosing among alternatives

A basic idea from economics is that most customers have a limited income and simply cannot buy everything they want. They must balance their needs and the prices of various products. Economists usually assume that customers have a fairly definite set of preferences and that they evaluate alternatives in terms of whether the alternatives will make them feel better or in some way improve their situation.

But what exactly is the nature of a customer's desire for a particular product?

Usually economists answer this question in terms of the extra utility the customer can obtain by buying more of a particular product—or how much utility would be lost if the customer had less of the product. It is easier to understand the idea of utility if we look at what happens when the price of one of the customer's usual purchases changes.

The law of diminishing demand

Suppose that consumers buy potatoes in 10-pound bags at the same time they buy other foods such as bread and rice. If the consumers are mainly interested in buying a certain amount of food and the price of the potatoes drops, it seems reasonable to expect that they will switch some of their food money to potatoes and away from some other foods. But if the price of potatoes rises, you expect our consumers to buy fewer potatoes and more of other foods.

The general relationship between price and quantity demanded illustrated by this food example is called the **law of diminishing demand**—which says that if the price of a product is raised, a smaller quantity will be demanded and if the price of a product is lowered, a greater quantity will be demanded. Experience supports this relationship between price and total demand in a market, especially for broad product categories or commodities such as potatoes.

The relationship between price and quantity demanded in a market is what economists call a "demand schedule." An example is shown in Exhibit A–1. For each row in the table, column 2 shows the quantity consumers will want (demand) if they have to pay the price given in column 1. The third column shows that the total revenue (sales) in the potato market is equal to the quantity demanded at a given price times that price. Note that as prices drop, the total *unit* quantity increases, yet the total *revenue* decreases. Fill in the blank lines in the third column and observe the behavior of total revenue, an important number for the marketing manager. We will explain what you should have noticed, and why, a little later.

The demand curve—usually down-sloping

If your only interest is seeing at which price the company will earn the greatest total revenue, the demand schedule may be adequate. But a demand curve shows more. A **demand curve** is a graph of the relationship between price and quantity demanded in a market, assuming that all other things stay the same. Exhibit A–2 shows the demand curve for potatoes—really just a plotting of the demand schedule in Exhibit A–1. It shows how many potatoes potential customers will demand at various possible prices. This is a "down-sloping demand curve."

Most demand curves are down-sloping. This just means that if prices are decreased, the quantity customers demand will increase.

Exhibit A–1
Demand Schedule for Potatoes (10-pound bags)

Point	(1) Price of Potatoes per Bag (P)	(2) Quantity Demanded (bags per month) (Q)	(3) Total Revenue per Month (P × Q = TR)
A	$1.60	8,000,000	$12,800,000
B	1.30	9,000,000	——————
C	1.00	11,000,000	11,000,000
D	0.70	14,000,000	——————
E	0.40	19,000,000	——————

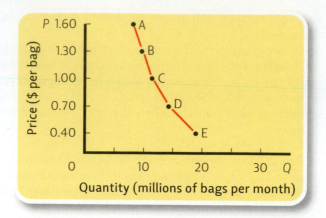

Demand curves always show the price on the vertical axis and the quantity demanded on the horizontal axis. In Exhibit A–2, we have shown the price in dollars. For consistency, we will use dollars in other examples. However, keep in mind that these same ideas hold regardless of what money unit (dollars, yen, francs, pounds, etc.) is used to represent price. Even at this early point, you should keep in mind that markets are not necessarily limited by national boundaries—or by one type of money.

Note that the demand curve only shows how customers will react to various possible prices. In a market, we see only one price at a time, not all of these prices. The curve, however, shows what quantities will be demanded, depending on what price is set.

Microwave oven demand curve looks different

To get a more complete picture of demand-curve analysis, let's consider another product that has a different demand schedule and curve. A demand schedule for standard 1-cubic-foot microwave ovens is shown in Exhibit A–3. Column (3) shows the total revenue that will be obtained at various possible prices and quantities. Again, as the price goes down, the quantity demanded goes up. But here, unlike the potato example, total revenue increases as prices go down—at least until the price drops to $150.

Every market has a demand curve, for some time period

These general demand relationships are typical for all products. But each product has its own demand schedule and curve in each potential market, no matter how small the market. In other words, a particular demand curve has meaning only for a particular market. We can think of demand curves for individuals, groups of individuals who form a target market, regions, and even countries. And the time period covered really should be specified, although this is often neglected because we usually think of monthly or yearly periods.

Exhibit A–3
Demand Schedule for
1-Cubic-Foot Microwave
Ovens

Point	(1) Price per Microwave Oven (P)	(2) Quantity Demanded per Year (Q)	(3) Total Revenue (TR) per Year (P × Q = TR)
A	$300	20,000	$ 6,000,000
B	250	70,000	15,500,000
C	200	130,000	26,000,000
D	150	210,000	31,500,000
E	100	310,000	31,000,000

Exhibit A–4
Demand Curve for
1-Cubic-Foot
Microwave Ovens

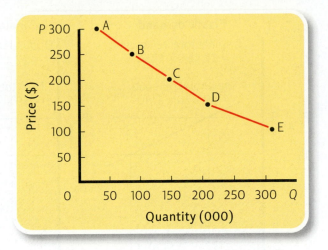

The difference between elastic and inelastic

The demand curve for microwave ovens (see Exhibit A–4) is down-sloping—but note that it is flatter than the curve for potatoes. It is important to understand what this flatness means.

We will consider the flatness in terms of total revenue, since this is what interests business managers.*

When you filled in the total revenue column for potatoes, you should have noticed that total revenue drops continually if the price is reduced. This looks undesirable for sellers and illustrates inelastic demand. **Inelastic demand** means that although the quantity demanded increases if the price is decreased, the quantity demanded will not "stretch" enough—that is, it is not elastic enough—to avoid a decrease in total revenue.

In contrast, **elastic demand** means that if prices are dropped, the quantity demanded will stretch (increase) enough to increase total revenue. The upper part of the microwave oven demand curve is an example of elastic demand.

But note that if the microwave oven price is dropped from $150 to $100, total revenue will decrease. We can say, therefore, that between $150 and $100, demand is inelastic—that is, total revenue will decrease if price is lowered from $150 to $100.

Thus, elasticity can be defined in terms of changes in total revenue. *If total revenue will increase if price is lowered, then demand is elastic. If total revenue will decrease if price is lowered, then demand is inelastic.* (Note: A special case known as "unitary elasticity of demand" occurs if total revenue stays the same when prices change.)

Total revenue may increase if price is raised

A point often missed in discussions of demand is what happens when prices are raised instead of lowered. With elastic demand, total revenue will *decrease* if the price is *raised*. With inelastic demand, however, total revenue will *increase* if the price is *raised*.

The possibility of raising price and increasing dollar sales (total revenue) at the same time is attractive to managers. This only occurs if the demand curve is inelastic. Here total revenue will increase if price is raised, but total costs probably will not increase—and may actually go down—with smaller quantities. Keep in mind that profit is equal to total revenue minus total costs. So when demand is inelastic, profit will increase as price is increased!

The ways total revenue changes as prices are raised are shown in Exhibit A–5. Here total revenue is the rectangular area formed by a price and its related quantity. The larger the rectangular area, the greater the total revenue.

---

*Strictly speaking, two curves should not be compared for flatness if the graph scales are different, but for our purposes now we will do so to illustrate the idea of "elasticity of demand." Actually, it would be more accurate to compare two curves for one product on the same graph. Then both the shape of the demand curve and its position on the graph would be important.

Exhibit A–5

Changes in Total Revenue as Prices Increase

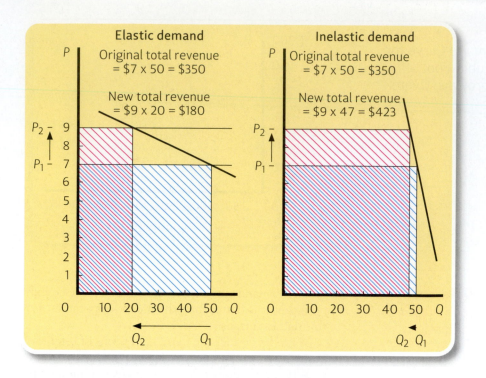

P_1 is the original price here, and the total potential revenue with this original price is shown by the area with blue shading. The area with red shading shows the total revenue with the new price, P_2. There is some overlap in the total revenue areas, so the important areas are those with only one color. Note that in the left-hand figure—where demand is elastic—the revenue added (the red-only area) when the price is increased is less than the revenue lost (the blue-only area). Now let's contrast this to the right-hand figure, when demand is inelastic. Only a small blue revenue area is given up for a much larger (red) one when price is raised.

An entire curve is not elastic or inelastic

It is important to see that it is *wrong to refer to a whole demand curve as elastic or inelastic*. Rather, elasticity for a particular demand curve refers to the change in total revenue between two points on the curve, not along the whole curve. You saw the change from elastic to inelastic in the microwave oven example. Generally, however, nearby points are either elastic or inelastic—so it is common to refer to a whole curve by the degree of elasticity in the price range that normally is of interest—the *relevant range*.

Demand elasticities affected by availability of substitutes and urgency of need

At first, it may be difficult to see why one product has an elastic demand and another an inelastic demand. Many factors affect elasticity, such as the availability of substitutes, the importance of the item in the customer's budget, and the urgency of the customer's need and its relation to other needs. By looking more closely at one of these factors—the availability of substitutes—you will better understand why demand elasticities vary.

Substitutes are products that offer the buyer a choice. For example, many consumers see grapefruit as a substitute for oranges and hot dogs as a substitute for hamburgers. The greater the number of "good" substitutes available, the greater will be the elasticity of demand. From the consumer's perspective, products are "good" substitutes if they are very similar (homogeneous). If consumers see products as extremely different, or heterogeneous, then a particular need cannot easily be satisfied by substitutes. And the demand for the most satisfactory product may be quite inelastic.

As an example, if the price of hamburger is lowered (and other prices stay the same), the quantity demanded will increase a lot, as will total revenue. The reason is

Exhibit A–6
Demand Curve for
Hamburger (a product
with many substitutes)

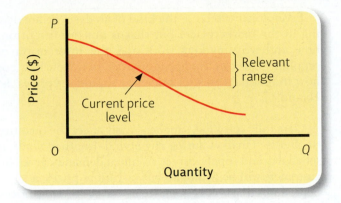

that not only will regular hamburger users buy more hamburger, but some consumers who formerly bought hot dogs or steaks probably will buy hamburger too. But if the price of hamburger is raised, the quantity demanded will decrease, perhaps sharply. Still, consumers will buy some hamburger, depending on how much the price has risen, their individual tastes, and what their guests expect (see Exhibit A–6).

In contrast to a product with many "substitutes"—such as hamburger—consider a product with few or no substitutes. Its demand curve will tend to be inelastic. Motor oil is a good example. Motor oil is needed to keep cars running. Yet no one person or family uses great quantities of motor oil. So it is not likely that the quantity of motor oil purchased will change much as long as price changes are *within a reasonable range*. Of course, if the price is raised to a staggering figure, many people will buy less oil (change their oil less frequently). If the price is dropped to an extremely low level, manufacturers may buy more—say, as a lower-cost substitute for other chemicals typically used in making plastic (Exhibit A–7). But these extremes are outside the relevant range.

Demand curves are introduced here because the degree of elasticity of demand shows how potential customers feel about a product—and especially whether they see substitutes for the product. But to get a better understanding of markets, we must extend this economic analysis.

MARKETS AS SEEN BY SUPPLIERS

Customers may want some product—but if suppliers are not willing to supply it, then there is no market. So we'll study the economist's analysis of supply. And then we'll bring supply and demand together for a more complete understanding of markets.

Exhibit A–7
Demand Curve for
Motor Oil (a product
with few substitutes)

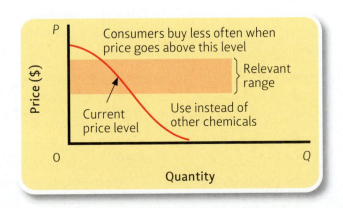

Economists often use the kind of analysis we are discussing here to explain pricing in the marketplace. But that is not our intention. Here we are interested in how and why markets work and the interaction of customers and potential suppliers. Later in this appendix we will review how competition affects prices, but how individual firms set prices, or should set prices, is discussed fully in Chapters 16 and 17.

Supply curves reflect supplier thinking

Generally speaking, suppliers' costs affect the quantity of products they are willing to offer in a market during any period. In other words, their costs affect their supply schedules and supply curves. While a demand curve shows the quantity of products customers will be willing to buy at various prices, a **supply curve** shows the quantity of products that will be supplied at various possible prices. Eventually, only one quantity will be offered and purchased. So a supply curve is really a hypothetical (what-if) description of what will be offered at various prices. It is, however, a very important curve. Together with a demand curve, it summarizes the attitudes and probable behavior of buyers and sellers about a particular product in a particular market—that is, in a product-market.

Some supply curves are vertical

We usually assume that supply curves tend to slope upward—that is, suppliers will be willing to offer greater quantities at higher prices. If a product's market price is very high, it seems only reasonable that producers will be anxious to produce more of the product and even put workers on overtime or perhaps hire more workers to increase the quantity they can offer. Going further, it seems likely that producers of other products will switch their resources (farms, factories, labor, or retail facilities) to the product that is in great demand.

On the other hand, if consumers are only willing to pay a very low price for a particular product, it's reasonable to expect that producers will switch to other products, thus reducing supply. A supply schedule (Exhibit A–8) and a supply curve (Exhibit A–9) for potatoes illustrate these ideas. This supply curve shows how many potatoes would be produced and offered for sale at each possible market price in a given month.

In the very short run (say, over a few hours, a day, or a week), a supplier may not be able to change the supply at all. In this situation, we would see a vertical supply curve. This situation is often relevant in the market for fresh produce. Fresh strawberries, for example, continue to ripen, and a supplier wants to sell them quickly—preferably at a higher price—but in any case, they must be sold.

If the product is a service, it may not be easy to expand the supply in the short run. Additional barbers or medical doctors are not quickly trained and licensed, and they only have so much time to give each day. Further, the prospect of much higher prices in the near future cannot easily expand the supply of many services. For example, a hit play or an "in" restaurant or nightclub is limited in the amount of product it can offer at a particular time.

Exhibit A–8
Supply Schedule for Potatoes (10-pound bags)

Point	Possible Market Price per 10-lb. Bag	Number of Bags Sellers Will Supply per Month at Each Possible Market Price
A	$1.60	17,000,000
B	1.30	14,000,000
C	1.00	11,000,000
D	0.70	8,000,000
E	0.40	3,000,000

Note: This supply curve is for a month to emphasize that farmers might have some control over when they deliver their potatoes. There would be a different curve for each month.

Exhibit A–9
Supply Curve for
Potatoes (10-pound
bags)

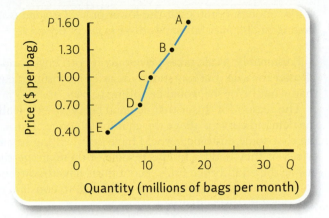

Elasticity of supply

The term *elasticity* also is used to describe supply curves. An extremely steep or almost vertical supply curve, often found in the short run, is called **inelastic supply** because the quantity supplied does not stretch much (if at all) if the price is raised. A flatter curve is called **elastic supply** because the quantity supplied does stretch more if the price is raised. A slightly up-sloping supply curve is typical in longer-run market situations. Given more time, suppliers have a chance to adjust their offerings, and competitors may enter or leave the market.

DEMAND AND SUPPLY INTERACT TO DETERMINE THE SIZE OF THE MARKET AND PRICE LEVEL

We have treated market demand and supply forces separately. Now we must bring them together to show their interaction. The *intersection* of these two forces determines the size of the market and the market price—at which point (price and quantity) the market is said to be in *equilibrium*.

The intersection of demand and supply is shown for the potato data discussed earlier. In Exhibit A–10, the demand curve for potatoes is now graphed against the supply curve in Exhibit A–9.

In this potato market, demand is inelastic—the total revenue of all the potato producers would be greater at higher prices. But the market price is at the **equilibrium point**—where the quantity and the price sellers are willing to offer are equal to the quantity and price that buyers are willing to accept. The $1.00 equilibrium price for potatoes yields a smaller *total revenue* to potato producers than a higher price would. This lower equilibrium price comes about because the many producers are willing to

Exhibit A–10
Equilibrium of Supply
and Demand for
Potatoes (10-pound
bags)

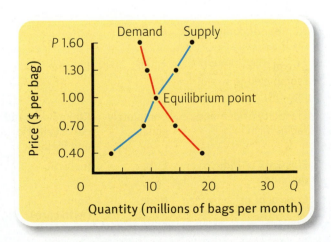

supply enough potatoes at the lower price. *Demand is not the only determiner of price level. Cost also must be considered—via the supply curve.*

Some consumers get a surplus

Presumably, a sale takes place only if both buyer and seller feel they will be better off after the sale. But sometimes the price a consumer pays in a sales transaction is less than what he or she would be willing to pay.

The reason for this is that demand curves are typically down-sloping, and some of the demand curve is above the equilibrium price. This is simply another way of showing that some customers would have been willing to pay more than the equilibrium price—if they had to. In effect, some of them are getting a bargain by being able to buy at the equilibrium price. Economists have traditionally called these bargains the **consumer surplus**—that is, the difference to consumers between the value of a purchase and the price they pay.

Some business critics assume that consumers do badly in any business transaction. In fact, sales take place only if consumers feel they are at least getting their money's worth. As we can see here, some are willing to pay much more than the market price.

DEMAND AND SUPPLY HELP US UNDERSTAND THE NATURE OF COMPETITION

The elasticity of demand and supply curves and their interaction help predict the nature of competition a marketing manager is likely to face. For example, an extremely inelastic demand curve means that the manager will have much choice in strategy planning, especially price setting. Apparently customers like the product and see few substitutes. They are willing to pay higher prices before cutting back much on their purchases.

The elasticity of a firm's demand curve is not the only factor that affects the nature of competition. Other factors are the number and size of competitors and the uniqueness of each firm's marketing mix. Understanding these market situations is important because the freedom of a marketing manager, especially control over price, is greatly reduced in some situations.

A marketing manager operates in one of four kinds of market situations. We'll discuss three kinds: pure competition, oligopoly, and monopolistic competition. The fourth kind, monopoly, isn't found very often and is like monopolistic competition. The important dimensions of these situations are shown in Exhibit A–11.

Exhibit A–11
Some Important Dimensions Regarding Market Situations

Important Dimensions	Types of Situations			
	Pure Competition	Oligopoly	Monopolistic Competition	Monopoly
Uniqueness of each firm's product	None	None	Some	Unique
Number of competitors	Many	Few	Few to many	None
Size of competitors (compared to size of market)	Small	Large	Large to small	None
Elasticity of demand facing firm	Completely elastic	Kinked demand curve (elastic and inelastic)	Either	Either
Elasticity of industry demand	Either	Inelastic	Either	Either
Control of price by firm	None	Some (with care)	Some	Complete

When competition is pure

Many competitors offer about the same thing

Pure competition is a market situation that develops when a market has

1. Homogeneous (similar) products.
2. Many buyers and sellers who have full knowledge of the market.
3. Ease of entry for buyers and sellers; that is, new firms have little difficulty starting in business—and new customers can easily come into the market.

More or less pure competition is found in many agricultural markets. In the potato market, for example, there are thousands of small producers—and they are in pure competition. Let's look more closely at these producers.

Although the potato market as a whole has a down-sloping demand curve, each of the many small producers in the industry is in pure competition, and each of them faces a flat demand curve at the equilibrium price. This is shown in Exhibit A–12.

As shown at the right of Exhibit A–12, an individual producer can sell as many bags of potatoes as he chooses at $1—the market equilibrium price. The equilibrium price is determined by the quantity that all producers choose to sell given the demand curve they face.

But a small producer has little effect on overall supply (or on the equilibrium price). If this individual farmer raises 1/10,000th of the quantity offered in the market, for example, you can see that there will be little effect if the farmer goes out of business—or doubles production.

The reason an individual producer's demand curve is flat is that the farmer probably couldn't sell any potatoes above the market price. And there is no point in selling below the market price! So in effect, the individual producer has no control over price.

Markets tend to become more competitive

Not many markets are *purely* competitive. But many are close enough so we can talk about "almost" pure competition situations—those in which the marketing manager has to accept the going price.

Such highly competitive situations aren't limited to agriculture. Wherever *many* competitors sell *homogeneous* products—such as textiles, lumber, coal, printing, and laundry services—the demand curve seen by *each producer* tends to be flat.

Markets tend to become more competitive, moving toward pure competition (except in oligopolies—see later). On the way to pure competition, prices and profits are pushed down until some competitors are forced out of business. Eventually, in

Exhibit A–12 Interaction of Demand and Supply in the Potato Industry and the Resulting Demand Curve Facing Individual Potato Producers

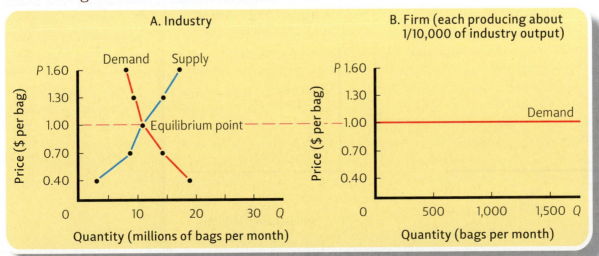

long-run equilibrium, the price level is only high enough to keep the survivors in business. No one makes any profit—they just cover costs. It's tough to be a marketing manager in this situation!

When competition is oligopolistic

A few competitors offer similar things

Not all markets move toward pure competition. Some become oligopolies. **Oligopoly** situations are special market situations that develop when a market has

1. Essentially homogeneous products—such as basic industrial chemicals or gasoline.
2. Relatively few sellers—or a few large firms and many smaller ones who follow the lead of the larger ones.
3. Fairly inelastic industry demand curves.

The demand curve facing each firm is unusual in an oligopoly situation. Although the industry demand curve is inelastic throughout the relevant range, the demand curve facing each competitor looks "kinked." See Exhibit A–13. The current market price is at the kink.

There is a market price because the competing firms watch each other carefully—and they know it's wise to be at the kink. Each firm must expect that raising its own price above the market price will cause a big loss in sales. Few, if any, competitors will follow the price increase. So the firm's demand curve is relatively flat above the market price. If the firm lowers its price, it must expect competitors to follow. Given inelastic industry demand, the firm's own demand curve is inelastic at lower prices, assuming it keeps its share of this market at lower prices. Since lowering prices along such a curve will drop total revenue, the firm should leave its price at the kink—the market price.

Sometimes there are price fluctuations in oligopolistic markets. This can be caused by firms that don't understand the market situation and cut their prices to try to get business. In other cases, big increases in demand or supply change the basic nature of the situation and lead to price cutting. Price cuts can be drastic, such as Du Pont's price cut of 25 percent for Dacron. This happened when Du Pont decided that industry production capacity already exceeded demand, and more plants were due to start production.

It's important to keep in mind that oligopoly situations don't just apply to whole industries and national markets. Competitors who are focusing on the same local target market often face oligopoly situations. A suburban community might have several gas stations, all of which provide essentially the same product. In this case, the "industry" consists of the gas stations competing with each other in the local product-market.

Exhibit A–13   Oligopoly—Kinked Demand Curve—Situation

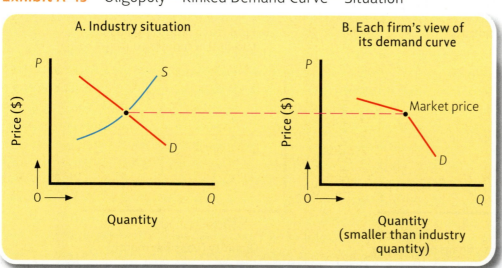

As in pure competition, oligopolists face a long-run trend toward an equilibrium level, with profits driven toward zero. This may not happen immediately—and a marketing manager may try to delay price competition by relying more on other elements in the marketing mix.

When competition is monopolistic

A price must be set

You can see why marketing managers want to avoid pure competition or oligopoly situations. They prefer a market in which they have more control. **Monopolistic competition** is a market situation that develops when a market has

1. Different (heterogeneous) products—in the eyes of some customers.
2. Sellers who feel they do have some competition in this market.

The word *monopolistic* means that each firm is trying to get control in its own little market. But the word *competition* means that there are still substitutes. The vigorous competition of a purely competitive market is reduced. Each firm has its own down-sloping demand curve. But the shape of the curve depends on the similarity of competitors' products and marketing mixes. Each monopolistic competitor has freedom—but not complete freedom—in its own market.

Judging elasticity will help set the price

Since a firm in monopolistic competition has its own down-sloping demand curve, it must make a decision about price level as part of its marketing strategy planning. Here, estimating the elasticity of the firm's own demand curve is helpful. If it is highly inelastic, the firm may decide to raise prices to increase total revenue. But if demand is highly elastic, this may mean there are many competitors with acceptable substitutes. Then the price may have to be set near that of the competition. And the marketing manager probably should try to develop a better marketing mix.

CONCLUSION

The economist's traditional demand and supply analysis provides a useful tool for analyzing the nature of demand and competition. It is especially important that you master the concepts of a demand curve and demand elasticity. How demand and supply interact helps determine the size of a market and its price level. The interaction of supply and demand also helps explain the nature of competition in different market situations. We discuss three competitive situations: pure competition, oligopoly, and monopolistic competition. The fourth kind, monopoly, isn't found very often and is like monopolistic competition.

The nature of supply and demand—and competition—is very important in marketing strategy planning. We discuss these topics more fully in Chapters 3 and 4 and then build on them throughout the text. This appendix provides a good foundation on these topics.

KEY TERMS

law of diminishing demand, 487

demand curve, 487

inelastic demand, 489

elastic demand, 489

substitutes, 490

supply curve, 492

inelastic supply, 493

elastic supply, 493

equilibrium point, 493

consumer surplus, 494

pure competition, 495

oligopoly, 496

monopolistic competition, 497

QUESTIONS AND PROBLEMS

1. Explain in your own words how economists look at markets and arrive at the "law of diminishing demand."

2. Explain what a demand curve is and why it is usually down-sloping. Then give an example of a product for which the demand curve might not be down-sloping over some possible price ranges. Explain the reason for your choice.

3. What is the length of life of the typical demand curve? Illustrate your answer.

4. If the general market demand for men's shoes is fairly elastic, how does the demand for men's dress shoes compare to it? How does the demand curve for women's shoes compare to the demand curve for men's shoes?

5. If the demand for perfume is inelastic above and below the present price, should the price be raised? Why or why not?

6. If the demand for shrimp is highly elastic below the present price, should the price be lowered?

7. Discuss what factors lead to inelastic demand and supply curves. Are they likely to be found together in the same situation?

8. Why would a marketing manager prefer to sell a product that has no close substitutes? Are high profits almost guaranteed?

9. If a manufacturer's well-known product is sold at the same price by many retailers in the same community, is this an example of pure competition? When a community has many small grocery stores, are they in pure competition? What characteristics are needed to have a purely competitive market?

10. List three products that are sold in purely competitive markets and three that are sold in monopolistically competitive markets. Do any of these products have anything in common? Can any generalizations be made about competitive situations and marketing mix planning?

11. Cite a local example of an oligopoly, explaining why it is an oligopoly.

Marketing Arithmetic

LEARNING OBJECTIVES

Marketing students must become familiar with the essentials of the language of business. Businesspeople commonly use accounting terms when talking about costs, prices, and profit. And using accounting data is a practical tool in analyzing marketing problems. The objectives of this appendix and the sections that follow will help you understand these concepts and how they are used by marketing managers.

When you finish this appendix, you should be able to:

1 understand the components of an operating statement (profit and loss statement).

2 know how to compute the stockturn rate.

3 understand how operating ratios can help analyze a business.

4 understand how to calculate markups and markdowns.

5 understand how to calculate a return on investment (ROI) and return on assets (ROA).

6 understand the basic forecasting approaches and why they are used.

7 understand important new terms (shown in red).

THE OPERATING STATEMENT

An **operating statement** is a simple summary of the financial results of a company's operations over a specified period of time. Some beginning students may feel that the operating statement is complex, but as we'll soon see, this really isn't true. *The main purpose of the operating statement is determining the net profit figure and presenting data to support that figure.* This is why the operating statement is often referred to as the *profit and loss statement.*

Exhibit B–1 shows an operating statement for a wholesale or retail business. The statement is complete and detailed so you will see the framework throughout the discussion, but the amount of detail on an operating statement is *not* standardized. Many companies use financial statements with much less detail than this one. They emphasize clarity and readability rather than detail. To really understand an operating statement, however, you must know about its components.

Only three basic components

The basic components of an operating statement are *sales*—which come from the sale of goods and services; *costs*—which come from the producing and selling process; and the balance—called *profit or loss*—which is just the difference between sales and costs. So there are only three basic components in the statement: sales, costs, and profit (or loss). Other items on an operating statement are there only to provide supporting details.

Time period covered may vary

There is no one time period an operating statement covers. Rather, statements are prepared to satisfy the needs of a particular business. This may be at the end of each day or at the end of each week. Usually, however, an operating statement summarizes results for one month, three months, six months, or a full year. Since the time period does vary, this information is included in the heading of the statement as follows:

> **Perry Company**
> **Operating Statement**
> **For the (Period) Ended (Date)**

Also see Exhibit B–1.

Management uses of operating statements

Before going on to a more detailed discussion of the components of our operating statement, let's think about some of the uses for such a statement. Exhibit B–1 shows that a lot of information is presented in a clear and concise manner. With this information, a manager can easily find the relation of net sales to the cost of sales, the gross margin, expenses, and net profit. Opening and closing inventory figures are available—as is the amount spent during the period for the purchase of goods for resale. Total expenses are listed to make it easier to compare them with previous statements and to help control these expenses.

All this information is important to a company's managers. Assume that a particular company prepares monthly operating statements. A series of these statements is a valuable tool for directing and controlling the business. By comparing results from one month to the next, managers can uncover unfavorable trends in the sales, costs, or profit areas of the business and take any needed action.

A skeleton statement gets down to essential details

Let's refer to Exhibit B–1 and begin to analyze this seemingly detailed statement to get first-hand knowledge of the components of the operating statement.

As a first step, suppose we take all the items that have dollar amounts extended to the third, or right-hand, column. Using these items only, the operating statement looks like this:

Gross sales	$540,000
Less: Returns and allowances	40,000
Net sales	500,000
Less: Cost of sales	300,000
Gross margin	200,000
Less: Total expenses	160,000
Net profit (loss)	$ 40,000

Exhibit B–1
An Operating Statement (profit and loss statement)

Perry Company Operating Statement For the Year Ended December 31, 200X			
Gross sales			$540,000
Less: Returns and allowances			40,000
Net sales			$500,000
Cost of sales:			
Beginning inventory at cost		$80,000	
Purchases at billed cost	$310,000		
Less: Purchase discounts	40,000		
Purchases at net cost	270,000		
Plus: freight-in	20,000		
Net cost of delivered purchases		290,000	
Cost of goods available for sale		370,000	
Less: Ending inventory at cost		70,000	
Cost of sales			300,000
Gross margin (gross profit)			200,000
Expenses:			
Selling expenses:			
Sales salaries	60,000		
Advertising expense	20,000		
Website updates	10,000		
Delivery expense	10,000		
Total selling expense		100,000	
Administrative expense:			
Office salaries	30,000		
Office supplies	10,000		
Miscellaneous administrative expense	5,000		
Total administrative expense		45,000	
General expense:			
Rent expense	10,000		
Miscellaneous general expenses	5,000		
Total general expense		15,000	
Total expenses			160,000
Net profit from operation			$ 40,000

Is this a complete operating statement? The answer is *yes*. This skeleton statement differs from Exhibit B–1 only in supporting detail. All the basic components are included. In fact, the only items we must list to have a complete operating statement are

Net sales	$500,000
Less: Costs	460,000
Net profit (loss)	$ 40,000

These three items are the essentials of an operating statement. All other subdivisions or details are just useful additions.

Meaning of sales

Now let's define the meaning of the terms in the skeleton statement.

The first item is sales. What do we mean by sales? The term **gross sales** is the total amount charged to all customers during some time period. However, there is always some customer dissatisfaction or just plain errors in ordering and shipping goods. This results in returns and allowances, which reduce gross sales.

A **return** occurs when a customer sends back purchased products. The company either refunds the purchase price or allows the customer dollar credit on other purchases.

An **allowance** usually occurs when a customer is not satisfied with a purchase for some reason. The company gives a price reduction on the original invoice (bill), but the customer keeps the goods and services.

These refunds and price reductions must be considered when the firm computes its net sales figure for the period. Really, we're only interested in the revenue the company manages to keep. This is **net sales**—the actual sales dollars the company receives. Therefore, all reductions, refunds, cancellations, and so forth made because of returns and allowances are deducted from the original total (gross sales) to get net sales. This is shown below.

Gross sales	$540,000
Less: Returns and allowances	40,000
Net sales	$500,000

Meaning of cost of sales

The next item in the operating statement—**cost of sales**—is the total value (at cost) of the sales during the period. We'll discuss this computation later. Meanwhile, note that after we obtain the cost of sales figure, we subtract it from the net sales figure to get the gross margin.

Meaning of gross margin and expenses

Gross margin (gross profit) is the money left to cover the expenses of selling the products and operating the business. Firms hope that a profit will be left after subtracting these expenses.

Selling expense is commonly the major expense below the gross margin. Note that in Exhibit B–1, **expenses** are all the remaining costs subtracted from the gross margin to get the net profit. The expenses in this case are the selling, administrative, and general expenses. (Note that the cost of purchases and cost of sales are not included in this total expense figure—they were subtracted from net sales earlier to get the gross margin. Note, also, that some accountants refer to cost of sales as cost of goods sold.)

Net profit—at the bottom of the statement—is what the company earned from its operations during a particular period. It is the amount left after the cost of sales and the expenses are subtracted from net sales. *Net sales and net profit are not the same.* Many firms have large sales and no profits—they may even have losses! That's why understanding costs, and controlling them, is important.

DETAILED ANALYSIS OF SECTIONS OF THE OPERATING STATEMENT

Cost of sales for a wholesale or retail company

The cost of sales section includes details that are used to find the cost of sales ($300,000 in our example).

In Exhibit B–1, you can see that beginning and ending inventory, purchases, purchase discounts, and freight-in are all necessary to calculate cost of sales. If we pull the cost of sales section from the operating statement, it looks like this:

Cost of sales:		
Beginning inventory at cost		$80,000
Purchases at billed cost.	$310,000	
Less: Purchase discounts	40,000	
Purchases at net cost.	270,000	
Plus: freight-in	20,000	
Net cost of delivered purchases		290,000
Cost of goods available for sale		370,000
Less: Ending inventory at cost.		70,000
Cost of sales.		$300,000

Cost of sales is the cost value of what is *sold,* not the cost of goods on hand at any given time.

Inventory figures merely show the cost of goods on hand at the beginning and end of the period the statement covers. These figures may be obtained by physically count-ing goods on hand on these dates or estimated from perpetual inventory records that show the inventory balance at any given time. The methods used to determine the inventory should be as accurate as possible because these figures affect the cost of sales during the period and net profit.

The net cost of delivered purchases must include freight charges and purchase dis-counts received since these items affect the money actually spent to buy goods and bring them to the place of business. A **purchase discount** is a reduction of the origi-nal invoice amount for some business reason. For example, a cash discount may be given for prompt payment of the amount due. We subtract the total of such discounts from the original invoice cost of purchases to get the *net* cost of purchases. To this figure we add the freight charges for bringing the goods to the place of business. This gives the net cost of *delivered* purchases. When we add the net cost of delivered pur-chases to the beginning inventory at cost, we have the total cost of goods available for sale during the period. If we now subtract the ending inventory at cost from the cost of the goods available for sale, we get the cost of sales.

One important point should be noted about cost of sales. The way the value of inventory is calculated varies from one company to another—and it can cause big dif-ferences in the cost of sales and the operating statement. (See any basic accounting textbook for how the various inventory valuation methods work.)

Exhibit B–1 shows the way the manager of a wholesale or retail business arrives at her cost of sales. Such a business *purchases* finished products and resells them. In a manufacturing company, the purchases section of this operating statement is replaced by a section called cost of production. This section includes purchases of raw materi-als and parts, direct and indirect labor costs, and factory overhead charges (such as heat, light, and power) that are necessary to produce finished products. The cost of production is added to the beginning finished products inventory to arrive at the cost of products available for sale. Often, a separate cost of production statement is pre-pared, and only the total cost of production is shown in the operating statement. See Exhibit B–2 for an illustration of the cost of sales section of an operating statement for a manufacturing company.

Expenses

Expenses go below the gross margin. They usually include the costs of selling and the costs of administering the business. They do not include the cost of sales, either purchased or produced.

There is no right method for classifying the expense accounts or arranging them on the operating statement. They can just as easily be arranged alphabetically or

Exhibit B-2

Cost of Sales Section of
an Operating Statement
for a Manufacturing
Firm

Cost of sales:			
Finished products inventory (beginning)		$ 20,000	
Cost of production (Schedule 1)		100,000	
Total cost of finished products available for sale		120,000	
Less: Finished products inventory (ending) . .		30,000	
Cost of sales			$ 90,000

Schedule 1, Schedule of cost of production

Beginning work in process inventory			15,000
Raw materials:			
Beginning raw materials inventory		10,000	
Net cost of delivered purchases		80,000	
Total cost of materials available for use		90,000	
Less: Ending raw materials inventory		15,000	
Cost of materials placed in production		75,000	
Direct labor		20,000	
Manufacturing expenses:			
Indirect labor	$4,000		
Maintenance and repairs	3,000		
Factory supplies	1,000		
Heat, light, and power	2,000		
Total manufacturing expenses		10,000	
Total manufacturing costs			105,000
Total work in process during period			120,000
Less: Ending work in process inventory			20,000
Cost of production			$100,000

according to amount, with the largest placed at the top and so on down the line.
In a business of any size, though, it is clearer to group the expenses in some way
and use subtotals by groups for analysis and control purposes. This was done in
Exhibit B–1.

Summary on operating statements

The statement presented in Exhibit B–1 contains all the major categories in an
operating statement—together with a normal amount of supporting detail. Further
detail can be added to the statement under any of the major categories without
changing the nature of the statement. The amount of detail normally is determined
by how the statement will be used. A stockholder may be given a sketchy operating
statement—while the one prepared for internal company use may have a lot of
detail.

COMPUTING THE STOCKTURN RATE

A detailed operating statement can provide the data needed to compute the
stockturn rate—a measure of the number of times the average inventory is sold during a year. Note that the stockturn rate is related to the *turnover during a year*, not the
length of time covered by a particular operating statement.

The stockturn rate is a very important measure because it shows how rapidly the
firm's inventory is moving. Some businesses typically have slower turnover than others. But a drop in turnover in a particular business can be very alarming. It may mean
that the firm's assortment of products is no longer as attractive as it was. Also, it may

mean that the firm will need more working capital to handle the same volume of sales. Most businesses pay a lot of attention to the stockturn rate, trying to get faster turnover (and lower inventory costs).

Three methods, all basically similar, can be used to compute the stockturn rate. Which method is used depends on the data available. These three methods, which usually give approximately the same results, are shown below.*

$$(1) \qquad \frac{\text{Cost of sales}}{\text{Average inventory at cost}}$$

$$(2) \qquad \frac{\text{Net sales}}{\text{Average inventory at selling price}}$$

$$(3) \qquad \frac{\text{Sales in units}}{\text{Average inventory in units}}$$

Computing the stockturn rate will be illustrated only for Formula 1, since all are similar. The only difference is that the cost figures used in Formula 1 are changed to a selling price or numerical count basis in Formulas 2 and 3. (*Note:* Regardless of the method used, you must have both the numerator and denominator of the formula in the same terms.)

If the inventory level varies a lot during the year, you may need detailed information about the inventory level at different times to compute the average inventory. If it stays at about the same level during the year, however, it's easy to get an estimate. For example, using Formula 1, the average inventory at cost is computed by adding the beginning and ending inventories at cost and dividing by 2. This average inventory figure is then divided into the cost of sales (in cost terms) to get the stockturn rate.

For example, suppose that the cost of sales for one year was $1,000,000. Beginning inventory was $250,000 and ending inventory $150,000. Adding the two inventory figures and dividing by 2, we get an average inventory of $200,000. We next divide the cost of sales by the average inventory ($1,000,000 ÷ $200,000) and get a stockturn rate of 5. The stockturn rate is covered further in Chapter 17.

OPERATING RATIOS HELP ANALYZE THE BUSINESS

Many businesspeople use the operating statement to calculate **operating ratios**—the ratio of items on the operating statement to net sales—and to compare these ratios from one time period to another. They can also compare their own operating ratios with those of competitors. Such competitive data is often available through trade associations. Each firm may report its results to a trade association, which then distributes summary results to its members. These ratios help managers control their operations. If some expense ratios are rising, for example, those particular costs are singled out for special attention.

Operating ratios are computed by dividing net sales into the various operating statement items that appear below the net sales level in the operating statement. The net sales is used as the denominator in the operating ratio because it shows the sales the firm actually won.

We can see the relation of operating ratios to the operating statement if we think of there being another column to the right of the dollar figures in an operating

---

*Differences occur because of varied markups and nonhomogeneous product assortments. In an assortment of tires, for example, those with low markups might have sold much better than those with high markups. But with Formula 3, all tires would be treated equally.

statement. This column contains percentage figures, using net sales as 100 percent. This approach can be seen below.

Gross sales...	$540,000	
Less: Returns and allowances	40,000	
Net sales	500,000	100%
Less: Cost of sales..................................	300,000	60
Gross margin	200,000	40
Less: Total expenses................................	160,000	32
Net profit...	$ 40,000	8%

The 40 percent ratio of gross margin to net sales in the preceding example shows that 40 percent of the net sales dollar is available to cover selling and administrative expenses and provide a profit. Note that the ratio of expenses to sales added to the ratio of profit to sales equals the 40 percent gross margin ratio. The net profit ratio of 8 percent shows that 8 percent of the net sales dollar is left for profit.

The value of percentage ratios should be obvious. The percentages are easily figured and much easier to compare than large dollar figures.

Note that because these operating statement categories are interrelated, only a few pieces of information are needed to figure the others. In this case, for example, knowing the gross margin percent and net profit percent makes it possible to figure the expenses and cost of sales percentages. Further, knowing just one dollar amount and the percentages lets you figure all the other dollar amounts.

MARKUPS

A **markup** is the dollar amount added to the cost of sales to get the selling price. The markup usually is similar to the firm's gross margin because the markup amount added onto the unit cost of a product by a retailer or wholesaler is expected to cover the selling and administrative expenses and to provide a profit.

The markup approach to pricing is discussed in Chapter 17, so it will not be discussed at length here. But a simple example illustrates the idea. If a retailer buys an article that costs $1 when delivered to his store, he must sell it for more than this cost if he hopes to make a profit. So he might add 50 cents onto the cost of the article to cover his selling and other costs and, hopefully, to provide a profit. The 50 cents is the markup.

The 50 cents is also the gross margin or gross profit from that item *if* it is sold. But note that it is *not* the net profit. Selling expenses may amount to 35 cents, 45 cents, or even 55 cents. In other words, there is no guarantee the markup will cover costs. Further, there is no guarantee customers will buy at the marked-up price. This may require markdowns, which are discussed later in this appendix.

Markup conversions

Often it is convenient to use markups as percentages rather than focusing on the actual dollar amounts. But markups can be figured as a percent of cost or selling price. To have some agreement, *markup (percent)* will mean percentage of selling price unless stated otherwise. So the 50-cent markup on the $1.50 selling price is a markup of 33⅓ percent. On the other hand, the 50-cent markup is a 50 percent markup on cost.

Some retailers and wholesalers use markup conversion tables or spreadsheets to easily convert from cost to selling price, depending on the markup on selling price they want. To see the interrelation, look at the two formulas below. They can be used to convert either type of markup to the other.

$$(4) \qquad \text{Percent markup} \atop \text{on selling price} = \frac{\text{Percent markup on cost}}{100\% + \text{Percent markup on cost}}$$

$$(5) \qquad \text{Percent markup on cost} = \frac{\text{Percent markup on selling price}}{100\% - \text{Percent markup on selling price}}$$

In the previous example, we had a cost of $1, a markup of 50 cents, and a selling price of $1.50. We saw that the markup on selling price was 33⅓ percent—and on cost, it was 50 percent. Let's substitute these percentage figures—in Formulas 4 and 5—to see how to convert from one basis to the other. Assume first of all that we only know the markup on selling price and want to convert to markup on cost. Using Formula 5, we get

$$\text{Percent markup on cost} = \frac{33\frac{1}{3}\%}{100\% - 33\frac{1}{3}\%} = \frac{33\frac{1}{3}\%}{66\frac{2}{3}\%} = 50\%$$

On the other hand, if we know only the percent markup on cost, we can convert to markup on selling price as follows:

$$\text{Percent markup on selling price} = \frac{50\%}{100\% + 50\%} = \frac{50\%}{150\%} = 33\frac{1}{3}\%$$

These results can be proved and summarized as follows:

Markup $0.50 = 50% of cost, or 33⅓% of selling price

+ Cost $1.00 = 100% of cost, or 66⅔% of selling price

Selling price $1.50 = 150% of cost, or 100% of selling price

Note that when the selling price ($1.50) is the base for a markup calculation, the markup percent (33⅓ percent = $.50/$1.50) must be less than 100 percent. As you can see, that's because the markup percent and the cost percent (66⅔ percent = $1.00/$1.50) sum to exactly 100 percent. So if you see a reference to a markup percent that is greater than 100 percent, it could not be based on the selling price and instead must be based on cost.

MARKDOWN RATIOS HELP CONTROL RETAIL OPERATIONS

The ratios we discussed above were concerned with figures on the operating statement. Another important ratio, the **markdown ratio**, is a tool many retailers use to measure the efficiency of various departments and their whole business. But note that it is *not directly related to the operating statement*. It requires special calculations.

A **markdown** is a retail price reduction required because customers won't buy some item at the originally marked-up price. This refusal to buy may be due to a variety of reasons—soiling, style changes, fading, damage caused by handling, or an original price that was too high. To get rid of these products, the retailer offers them at a lower price.

Markdowns are generally considered to be due to business errors, perhaps because of poor buying, original markups that are too high, and other reasons. (Note, however, that some retailers use markdowns as a way of doing business rather than a way to correct errors. For example, a store that buys overstocked fashions from other retailers may start by marking each item with a high price and then reduce the price each week until it sells.) Regardless of the reason, however, markdowns are reductions in the original price—and they are important to managers who want to measure the effectiveness of their operations.

Markdowns are similar to allowances because price reductions are made. Thus, in computing a markdown ratio, markdowns and allowances are usually added together and then divided by net sales. The markdown ratio is computed as follows:

$$\text{Markdown \%} = \frac{\$ \text{ Markdowns} + \$ \text{ Allowances}}{\$ \text{ Net sales}} \times 100$$

The 100 is multiplied by the fraction to get rid of decimal points.

Returns are *not* included when figuring the markdown ratio. Returns are treated as consumer errors, not business errors, and therefore are not included in this measure of business efficiency.

Retailers who use markdown ratios usually keep a record of the amount of markdowns and allowances in each department and then divide the total by the net sales in each department. Over a period of time, these ratios give management one measure of the efficiency of buyers and salespeople in various departments.

It should be stressed again that the markdown ratio is not calculated directly from data on the operating statement since the markdowns take place before the products are sold. In fact, some products may be marked down and still not sold. Even if the marked-down items are not sold, the markdowns—that is, the reevaluations of their value—are included in the calculations in the time period when they are taken.

The markdown ratio is calculated for a whole department (or profit center), *not* individual items. What we are seeking is a measure of the effectiveness of a whole department, not how well the department did on individual items.

RETURN ON INVESTMENT (ROI) REFLECTS ASSET USE

Another off-the-operating-statement ratio is **return on investment (ROI)**—the ratio of net profit (after taxes) to the investment used to make the net profit, multiplied by 100 to get rid of decimals. Investment is not shown on the operating statement. But it is shown on the **balance sheet** (statement of financial condition), which is another accounting statement that shows a company's assets, liabilities, and net worth. It may take some digging or special analysis, however, to find the right investment number.

Investment means the dollar resources the firm has invested in a project or business. For example, a new product may require $4 million in new money—for inventory, accounts receivable, promotion, and so on—and its attractiveness may be judged by its likely ROI. If the net profit (after taxes) for this new product is expected to be $1 million in the first year, then the ROI is 25 percent—that is, ($1 million ÷ $4 million) × 100.

There are two ways to figure ROI. The *direct* way is

$$\text{ROI (in \%)} = \frac{\text{Net profit (after taxes)}}{\text{Investment}} \times 100$$

The *indirect* way is

$$\text{ROI (in \%)} = \frac{\text{Net profit (after taxes)}}{\text{Sales}} = \frac{\text{Sales}}{\text{Investment}} \times 100$$

This way is concerned with net profit margin and turnover—that is,

$$\text{ROI (in \%)} = \text{Net profit margin} \times \text{Turnover} \times 100$$

This indirect way makes it clearer how to *increase* ROI. There are three ways:

1. Increase profit margin (with lower costs or a higher price).
2. Increase sales.
3. Decrease investment.

Effective marketing strategy planning and implementation can increase profit margins or sales, or both. And careful asset management can decrease investment.

ROI is a revealing measure of how well managers are doing. Most companies have alternative uses for their funds. If the returns in a business aren't at least as high as outside uses, then the money probably should be shifted to more profitable uses.

Some firms borrow more than others to make investments. In other words, they invest less of their own money to acquire assets—what we called *investments*. If ROI calculations use only the firm's own investment, this gives higher ROI figures to those who borrow a lot—which is called *leveraging*. To adjust for different borrowing proportions—to make comparisons among projects, departments, divisions, and companies easier—another ratio has come into use. **Return on assets (ROA)** is the ratio of net profit (after taxes) to the assets used to make the net profit—times 100. Both ROI and ROA measures are trying to get at the same thing—how effectively the company is using resources. These measures became increasingly popular as profit rates dropped and it became more obvious that increasing sales volume doesn't necessarily lead to higher profits—or ROI or ROA. Inflation and higher costs for borrowed funds also force more concern for ROI and ROA. Marketers must include these measures in their thinking or top managers are likely to ignore their plans and requests for financial resources.

FORECASTING TARGET MARKET POTENTIAL AND SALES

Effective strategy planning and developing a marketing plan require estimates of future sales, costs, and profits. Without such information, it's hard to know if a strategy is potentially profitable.

The marketing manager's estimates of sales, costs, and profits are usually based on a forecast (estimate) of target **market potential**—what a whole market segment might buy—and a **sales forecast**—an estimate of how much an industry or firm hopes to sell to a market segment. Usually we must first try to judge market potential before we can estimate what share a particular firm may be able to win with its particular marketing mix.

Three levels of forecasts are useful

We're interested in forecasting the potential in specific market segments. To do this, it helps to make three levels of forecasts.

Some economic conditions affect the entire global economy. Others may influence only one country or a particular industry. And some may affect only one company or

SunLite maintains a large domestic inventory of its casual outdoor furniture so it can quickly resupply its retailer-customers. A number of firms, like Third Wave Research Group, now offer marketers software or databases to help them more accurately forecast sales for specific market areas, products, or segments.

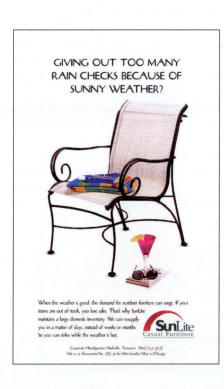

one product's sales potential. For this reason, a common top-down approach to forecasting is to

1. Develop a *national income forecast* (for each country in which the firm operates) and use this to
2. Develop an *industry sales forecast*, which then is used to
3. Develop forecasts for a *specific company*, its *specific products*, and the *segments* it targets.

Generally, a marketing manager doesn't have to make forecasts for a national economy or the broad industry. This kind of forecasting—basically trend projecting—is a specialty in itself. Such forecasts are available in business and government publications, and large companies often have their own technical specialists. Managers can use just one source's forecast or combine several. Unfortunately, however, the more targeted the marketing manager's earlier segmenting efforts have been, the less likely that industry forecasts will match the firm's product-markets. So managers have to move directly to estimating potential for their own companies and for their specific products.

Two approaches to forecasting

Many methods are used to forecast market potential and sales, but they can all be grouped into two basic approaches: (1) extending past behavior and (2) predicting future behavior. The large number of methods may seem confusing at first, but this variety has an advantage. Forecasts are so important that managers often develop forecasts in two or three different ways and then compare the differences before preparing a final forecast.

Extending past behavior can miss important turning points

When we forecast for existing products, we usually have some past data to go on. The basic approach, called **trend extension**, extends past experience into the future. With existing products, for example, the past trend of actual sales may be extended into the future. See Exhibit B–3.

Ideally, when extending past sales behavior, we should decide why sales vary. This is the difficult and time-consuming part of sales forecasting. Usually we can gather a lot of data about the product or market or about changes in the marketing environment. But unless we know the *reason* for past sales variations, it's hard to predict in what direction, and by how much, sales will move. Graphing the data and statistical techniques—including correlation and regression analysis—can be useful here. (These techniques, which are beyond our scope, are discussed in beginning statistics courses.)

Once we know why sales vary, we can usually develop a specific forecast. Sales may be moving directly up as population grows in a specific market segment, for example. So we can just estimate how population is expected to grow and project the impact on sales.

The weakness of the trend extension method is that it assumes past conditions will continue unchanged into the future. In fact, the future isn't always like the past. An agent wholesaler's business may have been on a steady path, but the development of the Internet may have added a totally new factor. The past trend for the agent's sales has changed because now the agent can quickly reach a broader market.

As another example, for years the trend in sales of disposable diapers moved closely with the number of new births. However, as the number of women in the workforce

Exhibit B-3
Straight-Line Trend Projection—Extends Past Sales into the Future

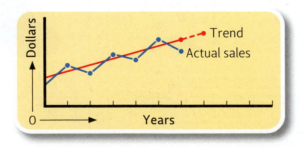

increased and as more women returned to jobs after babies were born, use of disposable diapers increased, and the trend changed. As in these examples, trend extension estimates will be wrong whenever big changes occur. For this reason—although they may extend past behavior for one estimate—most managers look for another way to help them forecast sharp market changes.

Predicting future behavior takes judgment

When we try to predict what will happen in the future, instead of just extending the past, we have to use other methods and add more judgment. Some of these methods (to be discussed later) include juries of executive opinion, salespeople's estimates, surveys, panels, and market tests.

FORECASTING COMPANY AND PRODUCT SALES BY EXTENDING PAST BEHAVIOR

Past sales can be extended

At the very least, a marketing manager ought to know what the firm's present markets look like and what it has sold to them in the past. A detailed sales analysis for products and geographic areas helps to project future results.

Just extending past sales into the future may not seem like much of a forecasting method. But it's better than just assuming that next year's total sales will be the same as this year's.

Factor method includes more than time

A simple extension of past sales gives one forecast. But it's usually desirable to tie future sales to something more than the passage of time.

The factor method tries to do this. The **factor method** tries to forecast sales by finding a relation between the company's sales and some other factor (or factors). The basic formula is: Something (past sales, industry sales, etc.) *times* some factor *equals* sales forecast. A **factor** is a variable that shows the relation of some other variable to the item being forecast. For instance, in the preceding example, both the birthrate and the number of working mothers are factors related to sales of disposable diapers.

A bread producer example

The following example, about a bread producer, shows how firms can make forecasts for many geographic market segments using the factor method and available data. This general approach can be useful for any firm—producer, wholesaler, or retailer.

Analysis of past sales relationships showed that the bread manufacturer regularly sold one-tenth of 1 percent (0.001) of the total retail food sales in its various target markets. This is a single factor. By using this single factor, a manager could estimate the producer's sales in a new market for the coming period by multiplying a forecast of expected retail food sales by 0.001.

Sales & Marketing Management magazine makes retail food sales estimates each year. Exhibit B–4 shows the kind of geographically detailed data available.

Let's carry this bread example further—using the data in Exhibit B–4 for the Denver, Colorado, metro area. Denver's food sales were $4,700,116,000 for the previous year. By simply accepting last year's food sales as an estimate of next year's sales and multiplying the food sales estimate for Denver by the 0.001 factor (the firm's usual share of food purchases in such markets), the manager would have an estimate of next year's bread sales in Denver. That is, last year's food sales estimate ($4,700,116,000) times 0.001 equals this year's bread sales estimate of $4,700,116.

Factor method can use several factors

The factor method is not limited to just one factor; several factors can be used together. For example, *Sales & Marketing Management* regularly gives a "buying power index" (BPI) as a measure of the potential in different geographic areas. See Exhibit B–4. This index considers (1) the population in a market, (2) the retail sales in that market, and (3) income in that market. The BPI for the Denver, Colorado, metro area, for

Exhibit B-4 Illustrative Page from *Sales & Marketing Management's Survey of Buying Power: Metro and County Totals*

COLORADO

METRO AREA County City	Population Total Population (000s)	% Population by Age Group 18-24	25-34	35-49	50+	Households (000s)	Retail Sales by Store Group ($000) Total Retail Sales	Food & Beverage Stores	Food Service & Drinking Establishments	General Merchandise	Furniture & Home Furnish. & Electron. & Appliances	Motor Vehicle & Parts Dealers	Total EBI ($000)	Effective Buying Income Median Hsld. EBI	A $20,000-$34,999	B $35,000-$49,999	C $50,000 & Over	Buying Power Index
BOULDER-LONGMONT	303.7	13.6	15.5	25.6	22.4	119.6	5,081,227	1,001,555	556,377	448,453	247,484	1,220,087	7,716,546	51,714	17.8	17.1	51.6	0.1360
BOULDER	303.7	13.6	15.5	25.6	22.4	119.6	5,081,227	1,001,555	556,377	448,453	247,484	1,220,087	7,716,546	51,714	17.8	17.1	51.6	0.1360
•Boulder	97.1	26.4	18.8	20.0	20.1	40.7	2,147,663	439,133	267,970	121,357	117,520	447,464	2,480,204	43,427	21.5	15.8	43.1	0.0479
•Longmont	74.6	8.7	14.6	25.3	23.6	28.0	1,126,804	250,483	122,965	125,103	40,068	272,449	1,531,271	47,526	19.4	20.1	46.8	0.0290
COLORADO SPRINGS	537.3	10.7	14.4	24.7	22.6	200.1	7,883,675	819,826	647,101	984,753	465,488	2,031,112	10,259,019	42,082	24.7	21.0	38.7	0.1994
EL PASO	537.3	10.7	14.4	24.7	22.6	200.1	7,883,675	819,826	647,101	984,753	465,488	2,031,112	10,259,019	42,082	24.7	21.0	38.7	0.1994
•Colorado Springs	373.1	10.5	14.8	24.5	23.7	146.5	6,786,693	628,690	549,107	858,048	443,063	1,848,219	7,353,670	41,212	24.9	20.9	37.5	0.1515
DENVER	2,199.5	9.2	16.2	25.0	23.8	858.0	33,750,880	4,700,116	3,232,590	3,615,646	2,518,616	9,368,057	52,585,220	49,109	18.8	19.0	48.9	0.9282
ADAMS	382.9	10.5	16.7	23.3	21.1	134.3	4,558,882	670,017	371,810	416,956	385,657	1,466,781	6,459,840	42,802	22.5	22.4	38.7	0.1253
Thornton	87.3	9.7	17.5	24.9	18.0	30.6	707,386	152,812	68,679	122,478	40,099	150,769	1,594,293	48,053	19.4	22.4	46.8	0.0270
Westminster	105.4	9.9	17.1	26.0	20.3	40.1	1,052,771	153,993	114,177	292,678	100,304	88,416	2,368,971	51,512	17.0	21.6	51.9	0.0384
ARAPAHOE	505.4	8.8	15.1	25.7	23.9	197.5	9,846,119	1,160,676	872,314	963,885	595,477	4,049,257	13,314,002	52,887	18.2	18.6	53.1	0.2422
Aurora	286.8	10.4	17.2	24.0	21.0	109.0	3,889,713	531,245	378,269	566,166	225,882	1,236,463	5,874,943	47,398	20.7	21.5	46.0	0.1076
DENVER	568.5	11.1	19.9	22.1	25.1	243.7	9,287,630	1,235,129	1,270,413	730,810	755,362	1,701,220	13,899,851	42,540	21.6	18.4	41.0	0.2474
•Denver	568.5	11.1	19.9	22.1	25.1	243.7	9,275,551	1,224,988	1,269,426	730,810	755,362	1,700,815	13,899,851	42,540	21.6	18.4	41.0	0.2474
DOUGLAS	200.7	4.9	15.9	29.6	18.0	69.6	2,725,601	517,182	250,871	294,714	289,389	355,394	5,147,699	59,715	10.9	18.2	64.7	0.0851
JEFFERSON	542.0	8.3	13.2	26.8	26.5	212.9	7,332,648	1,117,112	467,182	1,209,281	492,731	1,795,405	13,763,828	54,470	16.4	18.6	55.1	0.2282
Arvada	104.0	8.0	11.9	25.9	28.1	40.0	1,007,245	224,707	79,597	133,524	60,181	74,965	2,332,241	51,557	18.1	19.3	51.8	0.0376
Lakewood	148.0	9.9	15.2	24.1	28.8	62.3	2,065,827	297,529	149,068	292,832	124,879	567,796	3,451,207	46,782	20.8	21.1	45.2	0.0599
DENVER-BOULDER-GREELEY CONSOLIDATED AREA	2,695.8	10.0	15.9	24.9	23.6	1,044.7	40,882,936	5,939,206	3,929,714	4,267,775	2,809,610	11,246,398	63,170,157	48,397	19.2	19.0	47.9	1.1216

example, is 0.9282—that is, Denver accounts for 0.9282 percent of the total U.S. buying power. This means that consumers who live in Denver have higher than average buying power. We know this because Denver accounts for about 0.77 percent of the U.S. population.

Using several factors rather than only one uses more information. And in the case of the BPI, it gives a single measure of a market's potential. Rather than falling back on using population only, or income only, or trying to develop a special index, the BPI can be used in the same way that we used the 0.001 factor in the bread example.

PREDICTING FUTURE BEHAVIOR CALLS FOR MORE JUDGMENT AND SOME OPINIONS

These past-extending methods use quantitative data—projecting past experience into the future and assuming that the future will be like the past. But this is risky in competitive markets. Usually, it's desirable to add some judgment to other forecasts before making the final forecast yourself.

Jury of executive opinion adds judgment

One of the oldest and simplest methods of forecasting—the **jury of executive opinion**—combines the opinions of experienced executives, perhaps from marketing, production, finance, purchasing, and top management. Each executive estimates market potential and sales for the *coming years*. Then they try to work out a consensus.

The main advantage of the jury approach is that it can be done quickly and easily. On the other hand, the results may not be very good. There may be too much extending of the past. Some of the executives may have little contact with outside market influences. But their estimates could point to major shifts in customer demand or competition.

Estimates from salespeople can help too

Using salespeople's estimates to forecast is like the jury approach. But salespeople are more likely than home office managers to be familiar with customer reactions and what competitors are doing. Their estimates are especially useful in some business markets where the few customers may be well known to the salespeople. But this approach can be useful in any type of market.

However, managers who use estimates from salespeople should be aware of the limitations. For example, new salespeople may not know much about their markets. Even experienced salespeople may not be aware of possible changes in the economic climate or the firm's other environments. And if salespeople think the manager is going to use the estimates to set sales quotas, the estimates may be low!

Surveys, panels, and market tests

Special surveys of final buyers, retailers, or wholesalers can show what's happening in different market segments. Some firms use panels of stores—or final consumers—to keep track of buying behavior and to decide when just extending past behavior isn't enough.

Surveys are sometimes combined with market tests when the company wants to estimate customers' reactions to possible changes in its marketing mix. A market test might show that a product increased its share of the market by 10 percent when its price was dropped 1 cent below competition. But this extra business might be quickly lost if the price were increased 1 cent above competition. Such market experiments help the marketing manager make good estimates of future sales when one or more of the four Ps is changed.

Accuracy depends on the marketing mix

Forecasting can help a marketing manager estimate the size of possible market opportunities. But the accuracy of any sales forecast depends on whether the firm selects and implements a marketing mix that turns these opportunities into sales and profits.

KEY TERMS

QUESTIONS AND PROBLEMS

1. Distinguish between the following pairs of items that appear on operating statements: (*a*) gross sales and net sales, and (*b*) purchases at billed cost and purchases at net cost.

2. How does gross margin differ from gross profit? From net profit?

3. Explain the similarity between markups and gross margin. What connection do markdowns have with the operating statement?

4. Compute the net profit for a company with the following data:

Beginning inventory (cost)	$ 150,000
Purchases at billed cost	330,000
Sales returns and allowances	250,000
Rent.....................................	60,000
Salaries.................................	400,000
Heat and light..........................	180,000
Ending inventory (cost)	250,000
Freight cost (inbound)	80,000
Gross sales.............................	1,300,000

5. Construct an operating statement from the following data:

Returns and allowances...............	$ 150,000
Expenses	20%
Closing inventory at cost	600,000
Markdowns............................	2%
Inward transportation	30,000
Purchases	1,000,000
Net profit (5%)........................	300,000

6. Compute net sales and percent of markdowns for the following data:

Markdowns	$ 40,000
Gross sales..........................	400,000
Returns..............................	32,000
Allowances	48,000

7. (*a*) What percentage markups on cost are equivalent to the following percentage markups on selling price: 20, $37^1/_2$, 50, and $66^2/_3$? (*b*) What percentage markups on selling price are equivalent to the following percentage markups on cost: $33^1/_3$, 20, 40, and 50?

8. What net sales volume is required to obtain a stockturn rate of 20 times a year on an average inventory at cost of $100,000 with a gross margin of 25 percent?

9. Explain how the general manager of a department store might use the markdown ratios computed for her various departments. Is this a fair measure? Of what?

10. Compare and contrast return on investment (ROI) and return on assets (ROA) measures. Which would be best for a retailer with no bank borrowing or other outside sources of funds (that is, the retailer has put up all the money that the business needs)?

11. Explain the difference between a forecast of market potential and a sales forecast.

12. Suggest a plausible explanation for sales fluctuations for (*a*) computers, (*b*) ice cream, (*c*) washing machines, (*d*) tennis rackets, (*e*) oats, (*f*) disposable diapers, and (*g*) latex for rubber-based paint.

13. Explain the factor method of forecasting. Illustrate your answer.

14. Based on data in Exhibit B–4, discuss the relative market potential of the city of Boulder, Colorado, and the city of Lakewood, Colorado, for (*a*) prepared cereals, (*b*) automobiles, and (*c*) furniture.

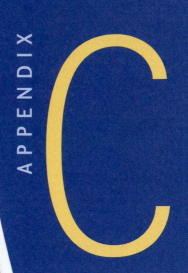

Career Planning in Marketing

THERE'S A PLACE IN MARKETING FOR YOU

We're happy to tell you that many opportunities are available in marketing. There's a place in marketing for everyone, from a service provider in a fast-food restaurant to a vice president of marketing in a large company such as Microsoft or Procter & Gamble. The opportunities range widely, so it will help to be more specific. In the following pages, we'll discuss (1) the typical pay for different marketing jobs, (2) setting your own objectives and evaluating your interests and abilities, and (3) the kinds of jobs available in marketing. We'll also provide some ideas about using the Internet to get more information and perhaps apply for a job or post your own information; this material is in the box with the title "Getting Wired for a Career in Marketing."

THERE ARE MANY MARKETING JOBS, AND THEY CAN PAY WELL

There are many interesting and challenging jobs for those with marketing training. You may not know it, but 60 percent of graduating college students take their initial job in a sales, marketing, or customer service position regardless of their stated major. So you'll have a head start because you've been studying marketing, and companies are always looking for people who already have skills in place. In terms of upward mobility, more CEOs have come from the sales and marketing side than all other fields combined. The sky is the limit for those who enter the sales and marketing profession prepared for the future!

Further, marketing jobs open to college-level students do pay well. According to the most recent salary surveys from the National Association of Colleges and Employers at the time this book went to press, marketing graduates were being offered starting salaries around $40,000, with a range from $25,000 to more than $60,000. Students with a master's in marketing averaged about $60,000; those with an MBA averaged about $75,000. Starting salaries can vary considerably, depending on your background, experience, and location.

Starting salaries in marketing compare favorably with many other fields. They are lower than those in such fields as computer science and electrical engineering where college graduates are currently in demand. But there is even better opportunity for personal growth, variety, and income in many marketing positions. The *American Almanac of Jobs and Salaries* ranks the median income of marketers number 10 in a list of 125 professions. Marketing also supplies about 50 percent of the people who achieve senior management ranks.

How far and fast your career and income rise above the starting level, however, depends on many factors, including your willingness to work, how well you get along with people, and your individual abilities. But most of all, it depends on *getting results*—individually and through other people. And this is where many marketing jobs offer the newcomer great opportunities. It is possible to show initiative, ability, creativity, and judgment in marketing jobs. And some young people move up very rapidly in marketing. Some even end up at the top in large companies or as owners of their own businesses.

Marketing is often the route to the top

Marketing is where the action is! In the final analysis, a firm's success or failure depends on the effectiveness of its marketing program. This doesn't mean the other functional areas aren't important. It merely reflects the fact that a firm won't have much need for accountants, finance people, production managers, and so on if it can't successfully meet customers' needs and sell its products.

Because marketing is so vital to a firm's survival, many companies look for people with training and experience in marketing when filling key executive positions. In general, chief executive officers for the nation's largest corporations are more likely to have backgrounds in marketing and distribution than in other fields such as production, finance, and engineering.

DEVELOP YOUR OWN PERSONAL MARKETING STRATEGY

Now that you know there are many opportunities in marketing, your problem is matching the opportunities to your own personal objectives and strengths. Basically the problem is a marketing problem: developing a marketing strategy to sell a product—yourself—to potential employers. Just as in planning strategies for products, developing your own strategy takes careful thought. Exhibit C–1 shows how you can organize your own strategy planning. This exhibit shows that you should evaluate yourself first—a personal analysis—and then analyze the environment for opportunities. This will help you sharpen your own long- and short-run objectives, which will lead to developing a strategy. Finally, you should start implementing your own personal marketing strategy. These ideas are explained more fully below.

Exhibit C–1
Organizing Your Own
Personal Marketing
Strategy Planning

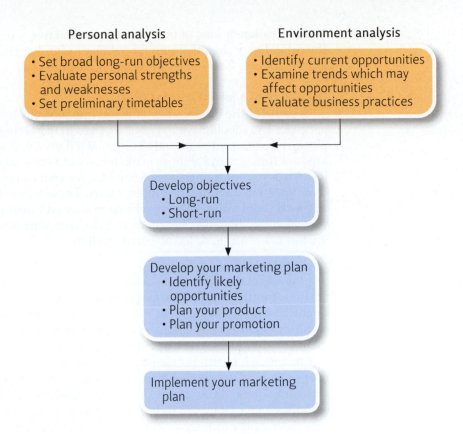

Personal analysis
- Set broad long-run objectives
- Evaluate personal strengths and weaknesses
- Set preliminary timetables

Environment analysis
- Identify current opportunities
- Examine trends which may affect opportunities
- Evaluate business practices

Develop objectives
- Long-run
- Short-run

Develop your marketing plan
- Identify likely opportunities
- Plan your product
- Plan your promotion

Implement your marketing plan

CONDUCT YOUR OWN PERSONAL ANALYSIS

You are the Product you are going to include in your own marketing plan. So first you have to decide what your long-run objectives are—what you want to do, how hard you want to work, and how quickly you want to reach your objectives. Be honest with yourself—or you will eventually face frustration. Evaluate your own personal strengths and weaknesses—and decide what factors may become the key to your success. Finally, as part of your personal analysis, set some preliminary timetables to guide your strategy planning and implementation efforts. Let's spell this out in detail.

Set broad long-run objectives

Your strategy planning may require some trial-and-error decision making. But at the very beginning, you should make some tentative decisions about your own objectives—what you want out of a job and out of life. At the very least, you should decide whether you are just looking for a job or whether you want to build a career. Beyond this, do you want the position to be personally satisfying—or is the financial return enough? And just how much financial return do you need? Some people work only to support themselves (and their families) and their leisure-time activities. These people try to find job opportunities that provide adequate financial returns but aren't too demanding of their time or effort.

Other people look first for satisfaction in their job—and they seek opportunities for career advancement. Financial rewards may be important too, but these are used mainly as measures of success. In the extreme, the career-oriented individual may be willing to sacrifice a lot, including leisure and social activities, to achieve success in a career.

Once you've tentatively decided these matters, then you can get more serious about whether you should seek a job or a career in marketing. If you decide to pursue a career, you should set your broad long-run objectives to achieve it. For example, one long-run objective might be to pursue a career in marketing management (or marketing research). This might require more academic training than you planned, as well as a different kind of training. If your objective is to get a job that pays well, on the other hand, then this calls for a different kind of training and different kinds of job experiences before completing your academic work.

What kind of a job is right for you?

Because of the great variety of marketing jobs, it's hard to generalize about what aptitudes you should have to pursue a career in marketing. Different jobs attract people with various interests and abilities. We'll give you some guidelines about what kinds of interests and abilities marketers should have. However, if you're completely lost about your own interests and abilities, see your campus career counselor and take some vocational aptitude and interest tests. These tests will help you to compare yourself with people who are now working in various career positions. They will *not* tell you what you should do, but they can help, especially in eliminating possibilities you are less interested in or less able to do well in.

One useful approach is to decide whether you are basically "people-oriented" or "thing-oriented." This is a very important decision. A people-oriented person might be very unhappy in an inventory management job, for example, whereas a thing-oriented person might be miserable in a personal selling or retail management job that involves a lot of customer contact.

Marketing has both people-oriented and thing-oriented jobs. People-oriented jobs are primarily in the promotion area—where company representatives must make contact with potential customers. This may be direct personal selling or customer service activities—for example, in technical service or installation and repair. Thing-oriented jobs focus more on creative activities and analyzing data—as in advertising and marketing research—or on organizing and scheduling work—as in operating warehouses, transportation agencies, or the back-end of retailers.

People-oriented jobs tend to pay more, in part because such jobs are more likely to affect sales, the lifeblood of any business. Thing-oriented jobs, on the other hand, are often seen as cost generators rather than sales generators. Taking a big view of the whole company's operations, the thing-oriented jobs are certainly necessary—but without sales, no one is needed to do them.

Thing-oriented jobs are usually done at a company's facilities. Further, especially in lower-level jobs, the amount of work to be done and even the nature of the work may be spelled out quite clearly. The time it takes to design questionnaires and tabulate results, for example, can be estimated with reasonable accuracy. Similarly, running a warehouse, analyzing inventory reports, scheduling outgoing shipments, and so on are more like production operations. It's fairly easy to measure an employee's effectiveness and productivity in a thing-oriented job. At the least, time spent can be used to measure an employee's contribution.

A sales rep, on the other hand, might spend all weekend thinking and planning how to make a half-hour sales presentation on Monday. For what should the sales rep be compensated—the half-hour presentation, all of the planning and thinking that went into it, or the results? Typically, sales reps are rewarded for results—and this helps account for the sometimes extremely high salaries paid to effective order getters. At the same time, some people-oriented jobs can be routinized and are lower paid. For example, salespeople in some retail stores are paid at or near the minimum wage.

Here we have oversimplified deliberately to emphasize the differences among types of jobs. Actually, of course, there are many variations between the two extremes. Some sales reps must do a great deal of analytical work before they make a presentation. Similarly, some marketing researchers must be extremely people-sensitive to get potential customers to reveal their true feelings. But the division is still useful because it focuses on the primary emphasis in different kinds of jobs.

Evaluate personal strengths and weaknesses

Are you people-oriented or thing-oriented?

Managers needed for both kinds of jobs

Getting Wired for a Career in Marketing

The Internet is a great resource at every stage of career planning and job hunting. It can help you learn: how to do a self-assessment, the outlook for different industries and jobs, what firms have jobs open, how to improve a résumé and post it online for free, and just about anything else you can imagine. Here we'll highlight just a few ideas and websites that can help you get started. However, if you start with some of these suggestions, each website you visit will provide links to other relevant sites that will give you new ideas.

One good place to start is at Yahoo (www.yahoo.com). Select "HotJobs" and take a look at all of the information and services that are available when you select the "Career Tools" link. For example, you can browse résumé tools and salary information, look at job listings, and much more. You may also want to study the similar information at www.monster.com.

Another website to check is at www.marketing-jobs.com. It has listings of marketing jobs, links to a number of companies with openings, a résumé center with ideas for preparing a résumé and posting it on the Internet, and lists of helpful periodicals. You might also go to www.careerjournal.com. There are job listings, job-hunting advice, career articles from *The Wall Street Journal*, and more. You can create and post a résumé there as well. Professional associations are another great resource. For example, the American Marketing Association website is at www.marketingpower.com, and the Sales and Marketing Executives International website is at www.smei.org. The Council of Supply Chain Management Professionals website is at http://cscmp.org.

Another potentially useful website address is www.collegegrad.com. It has links for posting a résumé, information on writing cover letters and getting references, and ideas about how to find a company with job openings. To get a sample of what's possible in tracking down jobs, visit the website at www.thejobresource.com and experiment with its search engine, which lets you look at what's available by state. For example, you might want to search through job listings that mention terms such as *entry level*, *marketing*, *advertising*, and *sales*.

This should get you started. Remember, however, that in Chapter 7 we gave addresses for a number of websites with search engines. You can use one of them to help find more detail on any topic that interests you. For example, you might go to www.google.com and search on terms such as *marketing jobs*, *salary surveys*, *post a résumé*, or *entry level position*.

Managers are needed for the people in both kinds of jobs. Managing others requires a blend of both people and analytical skills—but people skills may be the more important of the two. Therefore, people-oriented individuals are often promoted into managerial positions more quickly.

What will differentiate your product?

After deciding whether you're generally people-oriented or thing-oriented, you're ready for the next step—trying to identify your specific strengths (to be built on) and weaknesses (to be avoided or remedied). It is important to be as specific as possible so you can develop a better marketing plan. For example, if you decide you are more people-oriented, are you more skilled in verbal or written communication? Or if you are more thing-oriented, what specific analytical or technical skills do you have? Are you good at working with numbers, using a computer, solving complex problems, or coming to the root of a problem? Other possible strengths include past experience (career-related or otherwise), academic performance, an outgoing personality, enthusiasm, drive, and motivation.

It is important to see that your plan should build on your strengths. An employer will be hiring you to do something—so promote yourself as someone who is able to do something *well*. In other words, find your competitive advantage in your unique strengths—and then communicate these unique things about *you* and what you can do. Give an employer a reason to pick you over other candidates by showing that you'll add superior value to the company.

While trying to identify strengths, you also must realize that you may have some important weaknesses, depending on your objectives. If you are seeking a career that requires technical skills, for example, then you need to get those skills. Or if you are seeking a career that requires independence and self-confidence, then you should try to develop those characteristics in yourself—or change your objectives.

Set some timetables

At this point in your strategy planning process, set some timetables to organize your thinking and the rest of your planning. You need to make some decisions at this point to be sure you see where you're going. You might simply focus on getting your first job, or you might decide to work on two marketing plans: (1) a short-run plan to get your first job and (2) a longer-run plan—perhaps a five-year plan—to show how you're going to accomplish your long-run objectives. People who are basically job-oriented may get away with only a short-run plan, just drifting from one opportunity to another as their own objectives and opportunities change. But those interested in careers need a longer-run plan. Otherwise, they may find themselves pursuing attractive first-job opportunities that satisfy short-run objectives but quickly leave them frustrated when they realize that they can't achieve their long-run objectives without additional training or other experiences that require starting over again on a new career path.

ENVIRONMENT ANALYSIS

Strategy planning is a matching process. For your own strategy planning, this means matching yourself to career opportunities. So let's look at opportunities available in the marketing environment. (The same approach applies, of course, in the whole business area.) Exhibit C–2 shows some of the possibilities and salary ranges. The exhibit is assembled from salary data at www.salary.com. The salary ranges reflect the 25th percentile to the 75th percentile in the spring of 2008. For more information, look at Salary.com, where you can find job descriptions and data adjusted to different parts of the country. You can also find information about other career paths common to marketing majors—including logistics and purchasing/procurement management.

Keep in mind that the salary ranges in Exhibit C–2 are rough estimates. Salaries for a particular job often vary depending on a variety of factors, including company size, industry, and geographic area. People in some firms also get big bonuses that are not counted in their salary. There are many other sources of salary information. For example, *Advertising Age* publishes an annual survey of salary levels for different marketing and advertising jobs, with breakdowns by company size and other factors. Many trade associations, across a variety of different industries, also publish surveys, and the U.S. government's Bureau of Labor Statistics (www.bls.gov) includes salary data. If you use the search engine at www.google.com and do a search on *salary survey*, you will find hundreds of such surveys for a number of different industries.

Identifying current opportunities in marketing

Because of the wide range of opportunities in marketing, it's helpful to narrow your possibilities. After deciding on your own objectives, strengths, and weaknesses, think about where in the marketing system you might like to work. Would you like to work for manufacturers, or wholesalers, or retailers? Or does it really matter? Do you want to be involved with consumer products or business products? By analyzing your feelings about these possibilities, you can begin to zero in on the kind of job and the functional area that might interest you most.

One simple way to get a better idea of the kinds of jobs available in marketing is to review the chapters of this text—this time with an eye for job opportunities rather than new concepts. The following paragraphs contain brief descriptions of job areas that marketing graduates are often interested in with references to specific chapters in the text. Some, as noted, offer good starting opportunities, while others do not. While reading these paragraphs, keep your own objectives, interests, and strengths in mind.

Exhibit C–2 Some Career Paths and Salary Ranges*

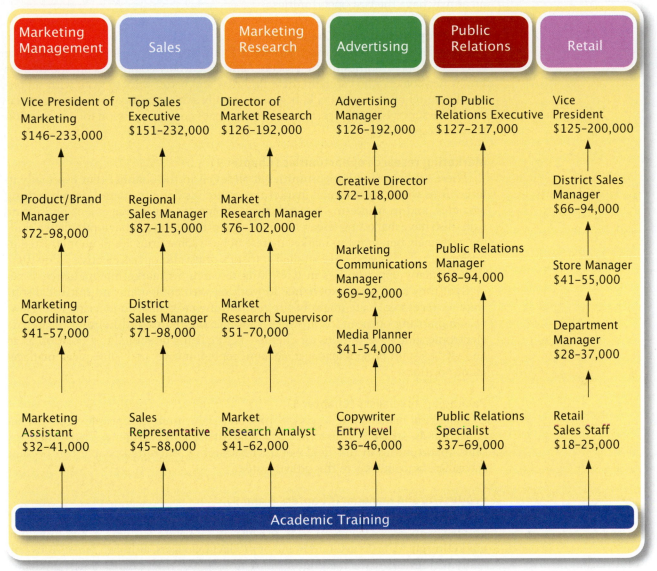

Marketing Management	Sales	Marketing Research	Advertising	Public Relations	Retail
Vice President of Marketing $146–233,000	Top Sales Executive $151–232,000	Director of Market Research $126–192,000	Advertising Manager $126–192,000	Top Public Relations Executive $127–217,000	Vice President $125–200,000
			Creative Director $72–118,000		District Sales Manager $66–94,000
Product/Brand Manager $72–98,000	Regional Sales Manager $87–115,000	Market Research Manager $76–102,000		Public Relations Manager $68–94,000	
			Marketing Communications Manager $69–92,000		Store Manager $41–55,000
Marketing Coordinator $41–57,000	District Sales Manager $71–98,000	Market Research Supervisor $51–70,000			
			Media Planner $41–54,000		Department Manager $28–37,000
Marketing Assistant $32–41,000	Sales Representative $45–88,000	Market Research Analyst $41–62,000	Copywriter Entry level $36–46,000	Public Relations Specialist $37–69,000	Retail Sales Staff $18–25,000

Academic Training

*Salaries are based on data from Salary.com and represent the range from the 25th to the 75th percentile as of May 2008, rounded to the nearest 1,000. Salary for retail vice president estimated.

Marketing manager (Chapter 2)

This is usually not an entry-level job, although aggressive students may move quickly into this role in smaller companies.

Customer or market analyst (Chapters 3 through 5)

Opportunities as consumer analysts and market analysts are commonly found in large companies, marketing research organizations, advertising agencies, and some consulting firms. Investment banking firms also hire entry-level analysts; they want to know what the market for a new business is like before investing. Beginning market analysts start in thing-oriented jobs until their judgment and people-oriented skills are tested. The job may involve collecting or analyzing secondary data or preparation of reports and plans. Because knowledge of statistics, computer software, Internet search techniques, or behavioral sciences is very important, marketing graduates often find themselves competing with majors from statistics, sociology, computer science, and economics. Graduates who have courses in marketing *and* one or more of these areas may have the best opportunities.

Purchasing agent/buyer (Chapter 6)

Entry-level opportunities are commonly found in large companies, and there are often good opportunities in the procurement area. Many companies are looking for bright newcomers who can help them find new and better ways to work with suppliers. To get off on the right track, beginners usually start as trainees or assistant buyers under the supervision of experienced buyers. That's good preparation for a promotion to more responsibility.

Marketing research opportunities (Chapter 7)

There are entry-level opportunities at all levels in the channel (but especially in large firms where more formal marketing research is done in-house), in advertising agencies, and in marketing research firms. Some general management consulting firms also have marketing research groups. Quantitative and behavioral science skills are extremely important in marketing research, so some firms are more interested in business graduates who have studied statistics or psychology as electives. But there still are many opportunities in marketing research for marketing graduates, especially if they have some experience in working with computers and statistical software. A recent graduate might begin in a training program—conducting interviews or summarizing open-ended answers from questionnaires and helping to prepare electronic slide presentations for clients—before being promoted to a position as an analyst, assistant project manager, account representative, and subsequent management positions.

Packaging specialists (Chapter 8)

Packaging manufacturers tend to hire and train interested people from various backgrounds—there is little formal academic training in packaging. There are many sales opportunities in this field—and with training, interested people can become specialists fairly quickly in this growing area.

Product/brand manager (Chapters 8 and 9)

Many multiproduct firms have brand or product managers handling individual products—in effect, managing each product as a separate business. Some firms hire marketing graduates as assistant brand or product managers, although larger firms typically recruit MBAs for these jobs. Many firms prefer that recent college graduates spend some time in the field doing sales work or working with an ad agency or sales promotion agency before moving into brand or product management positions.

Product planner (Chapter 9)

This is usually not an entry-level position. Instead, people with experience on the technical side of the business or in sales might be moved onto a new-product development team as they demonstrate judgment and analytical skills. However, new employees with winning ideas for new products don't go unnoticed—and they sometimes have the opportunity to grow fast with ideas they spearhead. Having a job that puts you in contact with customers is often a good way to spot new needs.

Distribution channel management (Chapter 10)

This work is typically handled or directed by sales managers and therefore is not an entry-level position. However, many firms form teams of specialists who work closely with their counterparts in other firms in the channel to strengthen coordination and relationships. Such a team often includes new people in sales or purchasing because it gives them exposure to a different part of the firm's activities. It's also not unusual for people to start working in a particular industry and then take a different job at a different level in the channel. For example, a graduate who has trained to be a store manager for a chain of sporting goods stores might go to work for a manufacturers' representative that handles a variety of sports equipment.

Logistics opportunities (Chapter 11)

There are many sales opportunities with physical distribution specialists—but there are also many thing-oriented jobs involving traffic management, warehousing, and materials handling. Here training in accounting, finance, and computer methods could be very useful. These kinds of jobs are available at all levels in channels of distribution.

Retailing opportunities (Chapter 12)

Not long ago, most entry-level marketing positions in retailing involved some kind of sales work. That has changed rapidly in recent years because the number of large retail chains is expanding and they often recruit graduates for their management training programs. Retailing positions tend to offer lower-than-average starting salaries—but they often provide opportunities for very rapid advancement. In a fast-growing chain, results-oriented people can move up very quickly. Most retailers require new employees to have some selling experience before managing others—or buying. A typical marketing graduate can expect to work as an assistant manager or do some sales work and manage one or several departments before advancing to a store management position—or to a staff position that might involve buying, advertising, location analysis, and so on.

Wholesaling opportunities (Chapter 12)

Entry-level jobs with merchant wholesalers typically fall into one of two categories. The first is in the logistics area—working with transportation management, inventory control, distribution customer service, and related activities. The other category usually involves personal selling and customer support. Agent wholesalers typically focus on selling, and entry-level jobs often start out with order-taking responsibilities that grow into order-getting responsibilities. Many wholesalers are moving much of their information to the Internet, so marketing students with skills and knowledge in this arena may find especially interesting opportunities.

Personal selling opportunities (Chapter 14)

Because there are so many different types of sales jobs and so many people are employed in sales, there are many good entry-level opportunities in personal selling. This might be order-getting, order-taking, customer service, or missionary selling. Many sales jobs now rely on sales technology, so some of the most challenging opportunities will go to students who know how to prepare spreadsheets and presentation materials using software programs like Microsoft Office. Many students are reluctant to get into personal selling—but this field offers benefits that are hard to match in any other field. These include the opportunity to earn high salaries and commissions quickly, a chance to develop your self-confidence and resourcefulness, an opportunity to work with minimal supervision—almost to the point of being your own boss—and a chance to acquire product and customer knowledge that many firms consider necessary for a successful career in product/brand management, sales management, and marketing management. On the other hand, many salespeople prefer to spend their entire careers in selling. They like the freedom and earning potential that go with a sales job over the headaches and sometimes lower salaries of sales management positions.

Customer service opportunities (Chapter 14)

As this book points out, marketing managers are recognizing the growing importance in providing customers with service after the sale. There are a number of different opportunities in customer service. Many firms need qualified customer service representatives who work with customers to fulfill their needs and help ensure customer satisfaction. Customer service reps may interact with customers on the phone, by online chat, or via e-mail. But other service representatives help customers at their businesses with installations or equipment repair. While some of the entry level positions that require only high school education are being outsourced to other countries, positions requiring strong communication skills and a good education provide an opportunity for marketing majors. There are also management positions that develop customer service strategies, control costs, and focus on hiring, training, and retaining customer service reps and enhancing customer satisfaction.

Advertising opportunities (Chapters 13 and 15)

Job opportunities in this area are varied and highly competitive. And because the ability to communicate and a knowledge of the behavioral sciences are important, marketing and advertising graduates often find themselves competing with majors from fields such as English, communication, psychology, and sociology. There are thing-oriented jobs such as copywriting, media buying, art, computer graphics, and so on. Competition for these jobs is very strong—and they go to people with a track record. So the entry-level positions are as assistant to a copywriter, media buyer, or art director. There are also people-oriented positions involving work with clients, which are probably of more interest to marketing graduates. This is a glamorous but small and extremely competitive industry where young people can rise very rapidly—but they can also be as easily displaced by new bright young people. Entry-level salaries in advertising are typically low. There are sometimes good opportunities to get started in advertising with a retail chain that prepares its advertising internally. Another way to get more experience with advertising is to take a job with one of the media, perhaps in sales or as a customer consultant. Selling advertising space on a website or cable TV station or newspaper may not seem as glamorous as developing TV ads, but media salespeople help their customers solve promotion problems and get experience dealing with both the business and creative side of advertising.

Sales promotion opportunities (Chapters 13 and 15)

The number of entry-level positions in the sales promotion area is growing because the number of specialists in this area is growing. For example, specialists might help a company plan a special event for employees, figure out procedures to distribute free samples, or perhaps set up a database to send customers a newsletter. Because clients' needs are often different, creativity and judgment are required. It is usually difficult for an inexperienced person to show evidence of these skills right out of school, so entry-level people often work with a project manager until they learn the ropes. In companies that handle their own sales promotion work, a beginner usually starts by getting some experience in sales or advertising.

Pricing opportunities (Chapters 16 and 17)

Pricing decisions are usually handled by experienced executives. However, in some large companies and consulting firms there are opportunities as pricing analysts for marketing graduates who have quantitative skills. These people work as assistants to higher-level executives and collect and analyze information about competitors' prices and costs, as well as the firm's own costs. Thus, being able to work with accounting numbers and computer spreadsheets is often important in these jobs. However, sometimes the route to these jobs is through experience in marketing research or product management.

Credit management opportunities

Specialists in credit have a continuing need for employees who are interested in evaluating customers' credit ratings and ensuring that money gets collected. Both people skills and thing skills can be useful here. Entry-level positions normally involve a training program and then working under the supervision of others until your judgment and abilities are tested.

International marketing opportunities

Many marketing students are intrigued with the adventure and foreign travel promised by careers in international marketing. Some firms hire recent college graduates for positions in international marketing, but more often these positions go to MBA graduates. However, that is changing as more and more firms are pursuing international markets. It's an advantage in seeking an international marketing job to know a second language and to know about the culture of countries where you would like to work. Your college may have courses or international exchange programs that would help in these areas. Graduates aiming for a career in international marketing usually must spend time mastering the firm's domestic marketing operations before being sent abroad. So a good way to start is to focus on firms that are already involved in international marketing, or who are planning to move in that direction soon. On the other hand, there are many websites with listings of international jobs. For example, you might want to visit www.overseasjobs.com.

Customer relations/consumer affairs opportunities (Chapters 13 and 18)

Most firms are becoming more concerned about their relations with customers and the general public. Employees in this kind of work, however, usually have held various positions with the firm before doing customer relations.

A strategy planner should always be evaluating the future because it's easier to go along with trends than to buck them. This means you should watch for political, technical, or economic changes that might open, or close, career opportunities.

Study trends that may affect your opportunities

If you can spot a trend early, you may be able to prepare yourself to take advantage of it as part of your long-run strategy planning. Other trends might mean you should avoid certain career options. For example, technological changes in computers and communications, including the Internet, are leading to major changes in retailing and advertising, as well as in personal selling. Cable television, telephone selling, and direct-mail selling may reduce the need for routine order takers, while increasing the need for higher-level order getters. More targeted and imaginative sales presentations for delivery by mail, e-mail, phone, or Internet websites may be needed. The retailers that prosper will have a better understanding of their target markets. And they may need to be supported by wholesalers and manufacturers that can plan targeted promotions that make economic sense. This will require a better understanding of the production and physical distribution side of business, as well as the financial side. And this means better training in accounting, finance, inventory control, and so on. So plan your personal strategy with such trends in mind.

This humorous ad on the side of a vending machine says, "Life's too short for the wrong job!" Planning for the right job—like planning a marketing strategy—pays off.

One good way to get more detailed analysis is to go to the U.S. Bureau of Labor Statistics website at http://stats.bls.gov and use the search procedure to look for the term *occupational outlook.* The Bureau provides detailed comments about the outlook for employment and growth in different types of jobs, industries, and regions.

Evaluate business practices

Finally, you need to know how businesses really operate and the kind of training required for various jobs. We've already seen that there are many opportunities in marketing—but not all jobs are open to everyone, and not all jobs are entry-level jobs. Positions such as marketing manager, brand manager, and sales manager are higher rungs on the marketing career ladder. They become available only when you have a few years of experience and have shown leadership and judgment. Some positions require more education than others. So take a hard look at your long-run objectives—and then see what degree you may need for the kinds of opportunities you might like.

DEVELOP OBJECTIVES

Once you've done a personal analysis and environment analysis—identifying your personal interests, your strengths and weaknesses, and the opportunities in the environment—define your short-run and long-run objectives more specifically.

Develop long-run objectives

Your long-run objectives should clearly state what you want to do and what you will do for potential employers. You might be as specific as indicating the exact career area you want to pursue over the next 5 to 10 years. For example, your long-run objective might be to apply a set of marketing research and marketing management tools to the food manufacturing industry, with the objective of becoming director of marketing research in a small food manufacturing company.

Your long-run objectives should be realistic and attainable. They should be objectives you have thought about and for which you think you have the necessary skills (or the capabilities to develop those skills) as well as the motivation to reach the objectives.

Develop short-run objectives

To achieve your long-run objective(s), you should develop one or more short-run objectives. These should spell out what is needed to reach your long-run objective(s). For example, you might need to develop a variety of marketing research skills *and* marketing management skills—because both are needed to reach the longer-run objective. Or you might need an entry-level position in marketing research for a large food manufacturer to gain experience and background. An even shorter-run objective might be to take the academic courses that are necessary to get that desired entry-level job. In this example, you would probably need a minimum of an undergraduate

Your long-run objectives should clearly state what you want to do and what you will do for potential employers.

526

degree in marketing, with an emphasis on marketing research. (Note that, given the longer-run objective of managerial responsibility, a business degree would probably be better than a degree in statistics or psychology.)

DEVELOPING YOUR MARKETING PLAN

Now that you've developed your objectives, move on to developing your own personal marketing plan. This means zeroing in on likely opportunities and developing a specific marketing strategy for these opportunities. Let's talk about that now.

Identify likely opportunities

An important step in strategy planning is identifying potentially attractive opportunities. Depending on where you are in your academic training, this can vary all the way from preliminary exploration to making detailed lists of companies that offer the kinds of jobs that interest you. If you're just getting started, talk to your school's career counselors and placement officers about the kinds of jobs being offered to your school's graduates. Your marketing instructors can help you be realistic about ways you can match your training, abilities, and interests to job opportunities. Also, it helps to read business publications such as *BusinessWeek, Fortune, The Wall Street Journal,* and *Advertising Age*. If you are interested in opportunities in a particular industry, check at your library or on the Internet to see if there are trade publications or websites that can bring you up to speed on the marketing issues in that area. Your library or college may also have an online service to make it easier to search for articles about specific companies or industries. And many companies have their own websites that can be a very useful source of information.

Don't overlook the business sections of your local newspapers to keep in touch with marketing developments in your area. And take advantage of any opportunity to talk with marketers directly. Ask them what they're doing and what satisfactions they find in their jobs. Also, if your college has a marketing club, join it and participate actively in the club's programs. It will help you meet marketers and students with serious interest in the field. Some may have had interesting job experiences and can provide you with leads on part-time jobs or exciting career opportunities.

If you're far along in your present academic training, list companies that you know something about or are willing to investigate, trying to match your skills and interests with possible opportunities. Narrow your list to a few companies you might like to work for.

If you have trouble narrowing down to specific companies, make a list of your personal interest areas—sports, travel, reading, music, or whatever. Think about the companies that compete in markets related to these interests. Often your own knowledge about these areas and interest in them can give you a competitive advantage in getting a job. This helps you focus on companies that serve needs you think are important or interesting. A related approach is to do a search on the Internet for websites related to your areas of interest. Websites often display ads or links to firms that are involved in that specific interest area. Further, many companies post job openings on their own websites or at websites that specialize in promoting job searches by many companies.

Then do some research on these companies. Find out how they are organized, their product lines, and their overall strategies. Try to get clear job descriptions for the kinds of positions you're seeking. Match these job descriptions against your understanding of these jobs and your objectives. Jobs with similar titles may offer very different opportunities. By researching job positions and companies in depth, you should begin to have a feel for where you would be comfortable as an employee. This will help you narrow your target market of possible employers to perhaps five firms. For example, you may decide that your target market for an entry-level position consists of large corporations with (1) in-depth training programs, (2) a wide product line, and (3) a wide variety of marketing jobs that will enable you to get a range of experiences and responsibilities within the same company.

Planning your product

Just like any strategy planner, you must decide what Product features are necessary to appeal to your target market. Identify which credentials are mandatory and which are optional. For example, is your present academic program enough, or will you need more training? Also, identify what technical skills are needed, such as computer programming or accounting. Further, are there any business experiences or extracurricular activities that might help make your Product more attractive to employers? This might involve active participation in college organizations or work experience, either on the job or in internships.

Planning your promotion

Once you identify target companies and develop a Product you hope will be attractive to them, you have to tell these potential customers about your Product. You can write directly to prospective employers, sending a carefully developed résumé that reflects your strategy planning. Or you can visit them in person (with your résumé). Many colleges run well-organized interviewing services. Seek their advice early in your strategy planning effort.

IMPLEMENTING YOUR MARKETING PLAN

When you complete your personal marketing plan, you have to implement it, starting with working to accomplish your short-run objectives. If, as part of your plan, you decide that you need specific outside experience, then arrange to get it. This may mean taking a low-paying job or even volunteering to work in political organizations or volunteer organizations where you can get that kind of experience. If you decide that you need skills you can learn in academic courses, plan to take these courses. Similarly, if you don't have a good understanding of your opportunities, then learn as much as you can about possible jobs by talking to professors, taking advanced courses, and talking to businesspeople. Of course, trends and opportunities can change—so continue to read business publications, talk with professionals in your areas of interest, and be sure that the planning you've done still makes sense.

Strategy planning must adapt to the environment. If the environment changes or your personal objectives change, you have to develop a new plan. This is an ongoing process—and you may never be completely satisfied with your strategy planning. But even trying will make you look much more impressive when you begin your job interviews. Remember, while all employers would like to hire a Superman or a Wonder Woman, they are also impressed with candidates who know what they want to do and are looking for a place where they can fit in and make a contribution. So planning a personal strategy and implementing it almost guarantee you'll do a better job of career planning, and this will help ensure that you reach your own objectives, whatever they are.

Whether or not you decide to pursue a marketing career, the authors wish you the best of luck in your search for a challenging and rewarding career, wherever your interests and abilities may take you.

Essentials of Marketing includes two different types of marketing cases: the 8 special video cases in this section and the 36 traditional cases in the next section. All of the cases offer you the opportunity to evaluate marketing concepts at work in a variety of real-world situations. However, the video cases add a multimedia dimension because we have produced a special video to accompany each of the written cases. The videos are available to professors who adopt *Essentials of Marketing* for use in their course. (These case-based videos are in addition to the teaching videos we have custom produced and made available to instructors for possible use with other parts of the text.)

The videos bring to life many of the issues considered in each case. However, you can read and analyze the written case descriptions even if there is no time or opportunity to view the video. Either way, you'll find the case interesting and closely tied to the important concepts you've studied in the text.

The set of questions at the end of each case will get you started in thinking about the marketing issues in the case. Further, we provide instructors with a number of suggestions on using the video cases—both for group discussion in class or individual assignments. Thus, as is also true with the traditional cases in the next section, the video cases can be used in many different ways and sequences. You can analyze all of the cases, or only a subset. In fact, the same case can be analyzed several times for different purposes. As your understanding of marketing deepens throughout the course, you'll "see" many more of the marketing issues considered in each case.

Video Cases

1. Chick-fil-A: "Eat Mor Chikin" (Except on Sunday)*

There aren't many companies like Chick-fil-A. Most U.S. companies struggle to balance ambitious financial objectives with the desire to be ethical in business dealings and demonstrate a social conscience. Chick-fil-A easily surpasses industry norms for financial performance and eagerly embraces and protects a corporate culture rich with religious values and charity. The contrast is striking to most observers. Yet the Chick-fil-A phenomenon is easily understood when you study its entrepreneurial heritage.

S. Truett Cathy, founder, chairman, and CEO of Chick-fil-A, started his restaurant career in 1946 when he and his brother Ben opened a restaurant in Atlanta called the Dwarf Grill (renamed the Dwarf House two years later). It was not until 1967 that Cathy opened the first Chick-fil-A restaurant in Atlanta's Greenbriar Shopping Center. He is credited with introducing the original boneless breast of chicken sandwich and pioneering the placement of fast-food restaurants in shopping malls. Today, Chick-fil-A is the second-largest quick-service chicken restaurant chain in the United States, based on sales ($1.975 billion in 2005). It operates more than 1,250 restaurants in 37 states and Washington, D.C.

Chick-fil-A's unique corporate culture derives from Cathy's Christian background and his desire to inspire and influence people. The company's official statement of corporate purpose is "to glorify God by being a faithful steward of all that is entrusted to us and to have a positive influence on all who come in contact with Chick-fil-A." This level of commitment to religious values is reflected in a number of ways. For example, all Chick-fil-A locations, in a mall or stand-alone, are closed on Sundays. Cathy has been quoted on numerous occasions as saying, "Our decision to close on Sunday (starting in 1946) was our way of honoring God and directing our attention to things more important than our business. If it took seven days to make a living with a restaurant, then we needed to be in some other line of work. Through the years, I have never wavered from that position."

Chick-fil-A also has an extensive corporate giving program. The company has helped thousands of restaurant employees, foster children, and other young people through the WinShape Foundation that Cathy established in 1984 to help "shape winners." The foundation sponsors WinShape Homes, which currently operates 14 homes in Georgia, Tennessee, Alabama, and Brazil. The WinShape College Program at Berry College in Rome, Georgia, is a co-op program offering joint four-year scholarship funding to incoming freshmen of up to $32,000. In addition to the WinShape scholarships, Chick-fil-A offers $1,000 college scholarships to its restaurant team members. Camp WinShape is a summer camp for boys and girls. WinShape Marriage provides development, education, and encouragement for married couples on the campus of WinShape Retreat, a multiuse conference and retreat facility located on the Mountain Campus of Berry College.

Chick-fil-A's unique corporate culture is matched by its equally unique marketing efforts, especially in the advertising and promotion areas. Its "Eat Mor Chikin" campaign is one of the longest-running advertising campaigns in the United

States. Started in June 1995 when the first Chick-fil-A billboard was erected in Atlanta, the Eat Mor Chikin cows have become cult figures, convincing diners to stray from the herd of beef-burger eateries and to "eat mor chikin"—particularly in Chick-fil-A restaurants. In focus groups, respondents rate the cows as one of the three things they like best about the Chick-fil-A brand—the other two being the food and the company's policy of being closed on Sundays.

The Eat Mor Chikin theme, created by Dallas-based ad agency the Richards Group, was first introduced in 1995 as a three-dimensional billboard concept depicting a black-and-white cow sitting atop the back of another cow painting the words "Eat-Mor-Chikin" on the billboard. Since then, the theme has been used as the basis of an integrated marketing campaign, which encompasses billboards, in-store point-of-purchase materials, promotions, radio and TV advertising, clothing and merchandise (e.g., plush cows, bobble-head cows), and calendars. Introduced in 1998, Chick-fil-A's cow calendars have been a marketer's dream come true. The calendar is produced annually by the Richards Group. Sales have sharply increased—from 337,000 for the first printed calendar to 1.5 million for the 2006 renaissance-themed calendar entitled "Cows in Shining Armor," featuring "famous" medieval cows named Angus Kahn, Charbroilemagne, Boldhoof, Lady Guineveal, and Moolius Caesar. The calendars sell for $5 and contain Chick-fil-A food and beverage coupon offers.

Sponsorship of collegiate sports such as the Chick-fil-A Peach Bowl (renamed the Chick-fil-A Bowl in 2006) are another way in which Chick-fil-A builds its brand. A local promotion emphasis at the market and restaurant level completes Chick-fil-A's integrated marketing approach.

In 1998, the Eat Mor Chikin campaign won a national silver EFFIE award in the Fast Food/Restaurants category for creativity and effectiveness in advertising. The outdoor Advertising Association of America recognized Chick-fil-A and its renegade cows with the organization's OBIE Hall of Fame Award in 2006.

Chick-fil-A is growing rapidly through store openings and menu additions. Menu additions include Chick-fil-A Chick-n Strips in 1995, Chick-fil-A Cool Wraps in 2001, Chick-fil-A Southwest chargrilled salad in 2003, fruit cup in 2004, and a breakfast menu featuring Chick-fil-A Chick-n Minis, a chicken or sausage breakfast burrito, and a chicken, egg, and cheese bagel in 2004. The chain introduced the industry's first premium two-blend coffee line in 2005 with Café Blends and the complementary Cinnamon Cluster. Hand-Spun milkshakes were launched in 2006.

The company had sales of $1.975 billion in 2005 and forecasts sales of $3 billion by 2010. Also by 2010, the company looks to double its current size in terms of new locations, primarily through stand-alone restaurants and aggressive expansion into the western United States. Chick-fil-A also has licensed restaurants in nontraditional locations such as airports, corporate offices, hospitals, and college campuses.

Dan Cathy, the son of S. Truett Cathy and Chick-fil-A's current president and COO, takes restaurant openings seriously. The openings are not simple ribbon-cuttings. Cathy

---

*This case was prepared by Dr. J. B. Wilkinson, professor emeritus, Youngstown State University.

holds a dedication dinner during which he and other company leaders wait on newly hired employees. He also "camps out" the night before a store opening with Chick-fil-A raving fans and customers. Beginning in 2003, Chick-fil-A offered the first 100 customers in line at its new stores a free combo meal each week for a year. People lined up hours in advance, setting up tents and lawn chairs overnight in the parking lot to ensure a place in line. Observing this, Cathy decided to join them and since then, camping out with Chick-fil-A fans and customers at store openings has become a tradition for him.

Dan Cathy takes his role as a leader seriously and defines his role through his interaction with customers and employees.

He frequently visits Chick-fil-A restaurants and often pitches in to help. Like his father, Dan Cathy is on a mission to meet customers, franchisees, and employees face to face and spread the Chick-fil-A business philosophy of "Second Mile" service, great food, and influencing others.

1. What types of marketing strategies is Chick-fil-A following?
2. How would you describe Chick-fil-A's positioning strategy?
3. Is Sunday closing a competitive advantage for Chick-fil-A? Explain.
4. Should other retailers consider closing on Sunday? Why? Why not?

2. Bass Pro Shops (Outdoor World)*

Have you ever seen an elk, an antelope, or a buffalo? What about a largemouth bass? Don't fret—you don't have to go to Montana to see what wildlife looks like! You can visit your nearest Bass Pro Shops Outdoor World and experience merchandising at its best, participate in workshops that teach outdoor skills (e.g., safe boating and hunting, beginning fishing, outdoor cooking, fly tying, nature photography, and GPS navigation), and take advantage of in-store amusements like an indoor trout stream, shooting arcades, or a live mermaid show (in the Las Vegas store). Better yet, you can visit the original Outdoor World store referred to as the "Grand Daddy," located in Springfield, Missouri, and spend your vacation at the largest hunting, boating, camping, and fishing outlet in the country—330,000 square feet of experiential retailing!

Bass Pro Shops are part of a larger trend in retailing called "destination development"—a trend in retail development that blends goods and services with theater and entertainment. Destination retailers offer shoppers more than just merchandise; each offers a unique environment in which customers enjoy a quality personal experience. The idea that a store is more than just a "big box filled with merchandise" has spawned a number of destination developments that function as open-air centers with exciting landscapes and architecture. Each store within the development operates as a stage for fresh and engaging experiences for shoppers (e.g., the Bass Pro Shops stock-car-racing simulations, snowboarding, or natural rock-climbing walls) and offers unusual attractions, activities, learning opportunities, theme restaurants, and entertainment. These types of developments act as "tourism districts," attracting visitors from 200 to 300 miles away.

Bass Pro Shops have successfully implemented the concept of destination development. Operating about 50 large retail stores in the United States and one in Canada, Bass Pro Shops has become the nation's leading retailer of outdoor gear. Its stores rank among the top tourist destinations in their respective states. Over 100 million people visit its stores annually and spend an estimated $1.9 billion to experience one of the most exciting store environments in retailing today!

Industry analysts agree that Bass Pro stores are unlike any other in terms of customer service, awesome displays

and visual imagery, exciting activities, and deep merchandise assortments in fishing, boating, hunting, outdoor gear, and camping. All stores have several common features including: taxidermy mounts, indoor water displays that showcase fish species, Outdoor Skills Workshops, artwork, and activity areas (e.g., archery and firing ranges, fishing tournaments). In addition, each store is uniquely designed to pick up the local flavor of the area's outdoor heritage and to include historical pictures, indigenous wildlife exhibits, and artifacts from local hunters and fishers. Several stores are spectacular in this regard. For example, the Denham Springs, Louisiana, store (near Baton Rouge) opened to crowds of shoppers (65,000 in the first four days). The store features an artistic replication of a Louisiana swamp complete with towering cypress trees draped in Spanish moss. Another example is the Bass Pro Shops Sportsman's Center in Miami, Florida. It is designed to make visitors feel like they are walking through a sunken ship, complete with barnacle-encrusted trusses. Suspended ceiling dioramas portray underwater scenes, and colorful fish appear to swim overhead. The Bass Pro Shops store located along the western shore of Lake Ray Hubbard (in Dallas, Texas) has a panoramic view of the lake through floor-to-ceiling windows that extend the entire Eastern exposure of the building. As shoppers progress toward this enticing feature, they have an equally panoramic view of a vast indoor boat showroom that can be reached by descending twin staircases that circle past waterfalls and around a swimming pool–size aquarium. The store also features a 365-seat World Famous Islamorada Fish Company Restaurant overlooking the lake. The recently opened Independence, Missouri, store features an indoor mill with a working wheel plus a 30-acre park complete with a lake stocked with bass and bluegill where customers can try out their new purchases.

Bass Pro stores have been difficult for competitors to emulate. They are large, expensive, and labor intensive. For example, the new 150,000-square-foot store in Rossford, Ohio (near Toledo) will employ 250 to 300 associates, many of whom are highly skilled in outdoor activities like fly-fishing, boating, and hunting. To make each Bass Pro store look different, an in-house group located in Nixa, Missouri, designs the interior and exterior of stores. An eclectic group of artisans and craftspeople—blacksmiths, metalworkers, welders,

---

*This case was prepared by Dr. J. B. Wilkinson, professor emeritus, Youngstown State University.

woodcarvers, and fabricators—handmake the chandeliers, lights, lanterns, wood carvings, ironwork, murals, mounted animals, displays, and special features that go into the stores. About 30 percent of each store's retail space is devoted to aquariums, waterfalls, murals, metalwork, museum-quality dioramas, and fireplaces. Bass Pro Shops' philosophy on merchandising also ups the ante. In-store displays aren't just fixtures—they are marketing tools designed to reflect local traditions and attract customers. For example, in the Lake Ray Hubbard store, canoes serve as shelving for apparel. In-store digital networks entertain and educate shoppers (how-to spots, technical features, PSAs for fishing, hunting, and conservation) and provide targeted advertising at the point of sale (vendor-sponsored ads and in-store promotions). The programming also includes vivid scenes of the outdoors and highlights its NASCAR team. Six to seven 42-inch plasma-screen displays are located in key departments of each Bass Pro store. Some of the programming content is common across all stores, and some of it is customized to fit an individual store (targeted marketing). In addition, the level of customer service has become legendary. Bass Pro Shops has been recognized many times for its conservation efforts and outdoor education programs. The company supports a wide range of environmental, habitat conservation, and youth education programs through philanthropic efforts.

Bass Pro Shops can trace its roots to a small fishing department started by founder John Morris in 1972 to sell homemade bait and worms. Located in the back of his dad's liquor store in Springfield, Missouri (on the road to Table Rock Lake and Branson), the business was popular enough that Morris launched a catalog in 1974 to sell homemade bait. Soon, it became the world's largest mail-order sporting goods store. The flagship Springfield store has been improved over the years to become the tourist mecca that it is today. Along the way, other businesses were added: American Rod and Gun in 1975 (a wholesaling entity serving independently owned retailers), Tracker Marine in 1978 (a producer of recreational boats for Tracker dealerships and independent marine dealers under various brands, including Tracker Boats), Big Cedar Lodge in 1988 (a resort on Table Rock Lake), and the Islamorada Fish Company Restaurant chain. Other endeavors include Bass Pro Shops Outdoor World Television (on the Outdoor Channel), Bass Pro Shops Outdoor World Radio, Outdoor World Tips (written for newspapers and magazines), and Bass Pro Shops NASCAR participation. Beginning in 1995, the company began adding stores, beginning with the Bass Pro Shops Sportsman's Warehouse in Atlanta, Georgia. Since then, more than 48 stores have been added to the chain. Bass Pro Shops is regarded as the nation's leading retailer of outdoor gear, selling through massive stores, catalogs, and a website (www.basspro.com).

However, industry analysts have posed the question, "Are there limits to growth in the sporting and outdoor goods retail category?" Competition is intense. Competitors include: large-format sporting goods stores, traditional and specialty sporting goods stores, mass-merchandisers, and catalog and Internet-based retailers. The most direct competitor to Bass Pro Shops is Cabela's—a chain of retail stores that has similar but less distinctive décor and merchandise. Other important competitors include Sports Authority, Dick's Sporting Goods, Academy Sports and Outdoors, Gander Mountain, Sportsman's Warehouse, and Wal-Mart. All are growing rapidly despite the fact that the industry is declining in terms of active participants in outdoor activities like hunting, fishing, and camping. Some markets such as Denver, Kansas City, Dallas, and Milwaukee seem "overstuffed" with outdoor chains. But some experts are predicting renewed growth in outdoor sales as consumers experience Bass Pro's destination stores. They point to Home Depot's ability to "grow its customer base" (increasing the number of "do-it-yourself" consumers) through how-to clinics and quality construction materials and tools. In addition, U.S. demographics favor increased sales of outdoor goods as the baby-boom generation retires and takes up new leisure-time activities.

Pessimists argue that large-format stores are risky in economic downturns. To build a Bass Pro Shop Outdoor World requires a big initial investment. Once open, high overhead and low inventory turnover are common in some merchandise categories. As a consequence, break-even sales must draw customers from a large trading area. Recessions and adverse weather conditions may also hurt sales, especially in overstocked markets.

Despite concerns by industry experts, recent Bass Pro store openings have attracted hordes of customers. It's been estimated that the average customer travels two hours to reach the store and shops for more than three hours! Shoppers also seem blind to pricing differences for identical products between Bass Pro stores and discounters like Wal-Mart. All of this suggests that destination retailing works and that the marriage between retailing and entertainment is here to stay!

1. Prepare a S.W.O.T. analysis for Bass Pro Shops. What types of strategies do you recommend based on your analysis?
2. Can you think of retailers in other categories that might successfully emulate the format and execution of Bass Pro Shops?

Toyota Prius: The Power of Excellence in Product Innovation and Marketing*

Prius (Latin for "to go before") was introduced to the Japanese market in 1997 amid much publicity and extravaganza.

*This case was prepared by Dr. J. B. Wilkinson, professor emeritus, Youngstown State University.

It was the world's first mass-produced car powered by a combination of gasoline and electricity. For the Toyota Motor Corporation, the Prius product launch represented a major strategic commitment and a long-term financial gamble.

The Prius story began in the early 1990s when Toyota released its first Earth Charter, setting the goal of minimizing its overall environmental impact. In September 1993, the company began to plan for the development of a car for the next century. Called Globe 21st Century, or G21, the plan was to produce a car with better fuel economy and lower emissions than existing automobiles.

Alternative ideas were considered before deciding to press ahead with a gas-electric hybrid system; these included direct-injection diesel engines, electric motors, hydrogen-powered fuel cells, and solar-powered vehicles. Mass production of gasoline-electric hybrids was not possible until recently. Improved technology with respect to batteries and powerful control electronics to coordinate the two propulsion systems made the idea more attractive.

GM (as well as Ford, Honda, and Toyota) failed to successfully market electric cars in the 1990s. Although GM's EV1 was a technical triumph, consumers were scared off by its limited battery life. All three American carmakers developed diesel-electric hybrid cars in the 1990s, but none were deemed acceptable to the market. A diesel engine is more expensive than a gasoline engine, so a diesel hybrid required a higher price premium. Development of a hydrogen-powered fuel cell vehicle was simply not technically feasible within the time frame that Toyota had set for its goal.

The hybrid technology chosen to power the Prius combines a gasoline engine with an integrated electric-drive system. Like conventional cars and trucks, the hybrid system relies on a gasoline-fueled engine to generate power; the electric motor system provides a second power channel. These two complementary systems work together to create a more efficient powertrain.

At start-up, only the electric motor is used, and it powers the vehicle at low- to mid-range speeds. Under normal driving conditions, the gas engine is engaged and power is allocated between the two engines to maximize efficiency during operations such as acceleration, deceleration, coasting, and stopping. In the city, with its stop-and-go traffic, the Prius relies more on the electric engine, whereas for highway driving, the gas engine is the primary power producer. The benefits of this powertrain combination are greater fuel efficiency and low exhaust emissions. Compared to electric cars, the hybrid system offers a high level of convenience since the battery is recharged from surplus engine power.

The Prius development effort took four years. The biggest challenges Toyota engineers faced were handling the powerful voltage between the battery and the electric motor and determining how to fit the gas engine, the electric motor, and a jumbo battery into a compact car frame. Solving these problems involved adapting the heavy-duty transistors used in Japan's bullet trains and shrinking the parts through computer modeling. A prototype car was shown to the public in 1995 and in December 1997, the first production car rolled out of Toyota's Takaoka factory in Toyota City near Nagoya. For the next two years, Toyota sold Prius only in Japan. First-year sales were around 12,000 units due to limited production capability. Toyota elected to defer capital investment in manufacturing facilities and to produce the Prius on existing assembly lines: a "hedging" strategy in case the hybrid "flopped." The initial price was just $16,929, which industry analysts say was below the estimated cost of building a

Prius. However, even at that price, buyers paid a premium of several thousand dollars for a Prius compared to similar-size conventional cars. Industry analysts speculated that Toyota would have to sell around 250,000 Priuses a year to make a profit.

Prius was introduced to the U.S. market in 2000. The Honda Insight, a two-seater gas-electric hybrid, had been in the U.S. market for a year with first-year sales of about 3,500. Toyota limited U.S. sales of the Prius to 17,000 units during the introductory year. Base price for the Prius was $19,995 (roughly the same as for a Honda Insight). Both the Prius and the Insight were priced below cost but several thousand dollars higher than similar-sized conventional cars. However, the higher price was partially offset by better gasoline mileage (52 m.p.g. in city driving for the first-generation Prius).

The advertising campaign that launched the Prius into the U.S. market used "Prius Genius" as its tagline and courted leading-edge buyers of the technological generation. Celebrity buyers like Cameron Diaz heightened Toyota's publicity efforts, which included an "Engine of Change" tour—a 15-city circuit where the Prius was shown to leaders in government, media, and environmental groups. In addition, the Prius was seen by millions of Academy Award viewers as an "alternative limo" used by environmentally friendly Hollywood celebrities.

Toyota enjoyed a dramatic jump in Prius sales after its U.S. debut. Sales were so strong that demand outstripped production capability. It was not uncommon for buyers to wait up to six months to receive their new Prius. By 2004, global sales totaled 250,000, and Toyota was earning a modest profit per vehicle. The second-generation Prius (Prius II) hit U.S. showrooms in October 2003. As other car manufacturers (Ford, GM) entered the market with hybrid vehicles and Honda increased its number of hybrid models (Civic), Toyota changed its marketing strategy to emphasize its Hybrid Synergy Drive in Prius II as the powertrain of choice—a classic selective demand-building strategy, suitable for the growth stage in a product's life cycle. The objective of this strategy was to differentiate Toyota's hybrid technology from other hybrid systems emerging in the market. Unlike competitive systems on the market in 2004, the new high-voltage/high-power Hybrid Synergy Drive powertrain was capable of operating in either gas or electric modes, as well as a mode in which both the gas engine and electric motor are in operation. Compared to the original Toyota Hybrid System (THS) in Prius I, the new Hybrid Synergy Drive system delivered significantly more power and performance, best-in-class fuel economy, and best-in-market emissions performance. Toyota also worked to reduce the cost of its hybrids. Because gasoline-electric hybrids employ two motors under the hood, hybrids are more expensive to produce than conventional gas-powered vehicles (about $3,000 more). Cost reductions would lead to price reductions, making Toyota's hybrid cars more affordable.

The 2004 second-generation Prius was designed to appeal to a broader market. It was larger, more powerful, with numerous technical improvements and aerodynamic styling (plus a four-door, lift-back configuration), and loaded with high-tech options like the Smart Entry/Smart Start, which allows the driver to open and start the vehicle without inserting a key.

Other options included a hands-free cell phone system and a navigation system. Base price was held at $19,995, the same as the first Prius cost during its introductory year in the United States. This second-generation car won some of the industry's most prestigious awards and was named European Car of the Year 2005.

The success of the Prius has provided Toyota with numerous product opportunities, including hybrid technology extension and licensing strategies. Toyota recently introduced a hybrid Lexus RX400h (2004) and Highlander (2005). A hybrid Camry and Lexus GS sedan were planned for 2006.

Toyota expects that a quarter of its unit sales in the United States will use gasoline-electric technology by 2010. To achieve that goal, virtually all Toyota vehicles including trucks will offer hybrid power systems.

1. *In what stage of the product life cycle is the Toyota Prius? Explain.*
2. *Describe the marketing strategies being followed by Toyota for the Prius.*
3. *Do you think Toyota should convert all of its cars to hybrids? Why? Why not?*

4. Potbelly Sandwich Works Grows through "Quirky" Marketing*

Want an inexpensive gourmet sandwich served in a fun and funky place by friendly young people? Lots of people do, including celebrities Will Ferrell, Sandra Bullock, and Keanu Reaves. In fact, Potbelly Sandwich Works was ranked as one of the top fastest-growing chains in the restaurant industry.[1]

Chances are you have never eaten at a Potbelly, but you probably will in the near future. Under the leadership of Bryant Keil, chairman and CEO, Chicago-based Potbelly Sandwich Works is expanding rapidly (see Table 1). Keil bought the original Potbelly in 1996. Prior to that, it was a very successful neighborhood sandwich shop run by a couple who had originally started the business as an antique store in 1977. They added homemade sandwiches and desserts to bolster the business and soon the food became more popular than the antiques. As time went on, booths were added along with ovens for toasting the sandwiches and the antiques became "décor" rather than merchandise for sale. A prominently placed antique potbelly stove provided inspiration for the sandwich shop's name.

Although Potbelly has many sandwich shop rivals and competition in the fierce quick-serve segment of the restaurant industry, Potbelly has more than held its own. Billed as "a unique and quirky sandwich joint," it has a unique appeal. Potbelly's core strategy elements include *product, place, promotion,* and *price.*

Product

According to Keil, "Anyone can sell a sandwich. You need to sell an experience." Industry observers point to several aspects of the Potbelly experience that make it the first choice for young professionals on a quick lunch break. First is the menu, which features made-to-order toasted sandwiches, soups, homemade desserts, malts, shakes, and yogurt smoothies. Toasting is part of what makes Potbelly's sandwiches distinctive. Quality ingredients, including a freshly baked Italian sub roll and freshly sliced meats and cheese also contribute

to superior value. Friendly service and an upbeat atmosphere, live music, antique fixtures, real books for customers to read or borrow, and vintage memorabilia create a homey environment for customers. The idea behind Potbelly is simple: superior value, fun-filled atmosphere, warm, comfy décor, and quick, friendly service.

Place

Potbelly stores average 2,200 square feet but can top 4,000 square feet. Most units have indoor seating for more than 50 and outdoor seating during warmer months. Geographic locations are selected carefully. Keil looks for cities that are not saturated with sandwich chains and have an urban/suburban density of core customers—young professionals less than 35 years old. Locations must be convenient for them since Potbelly stores rely on high repeat business. All units are corporate owned and operated.

Promotion

Historically, Potbelly Sandwich Works has not had an ad budget. Promotions are keyed to events like store openings and National Sandwich Day. For example, on National Sandwich Day, Potbelly hosts a "Belly Buster" sandwich-eating contest at Potbelly stores. Prizes are awarded to winners and runners-up. Diners randomly receive free meals. Other event promotions raise money for local charities such as food banks, and community-based reading and music appreciation programs.

Price

Potbelly sandwiches sell for $3.79. Sheila's Dream Bar, made of oatmeal, caramel and chocolate, is $1.29, while homemade chocolate chip or sugar cookies go for only 99 cents. Checks average about $6.50. Pricing is an integral part of the value Potbelly offers customers and can be summed up as, "Just good food at good prices!"

Considered separately, any one of Potbelly's marketing strategy elements may not seem overly powerful as a competitive weapon, but combined and implemented with zeal, they are a significant competitive threat to national, regional, and local competitors. Brands like Subway, Quiznos, Cosi, Panera,

---

*This case was prepared by Dr. J. B. Wilkinson, professor emeritus, Youngstown State University.
[1]"Way to Grow: A Tight Real Estate Market Doesn't Deter Top Chains' Expansion Plans," *Restaurants and Institutions,* July 2005, p. 121.

Table 1 Potbelly Store Openings by Year and City, 1997–2005

Market	1997	1998	1999	2000	2001	2002	2003	2004	2005	Total
Chicago	1	1	1	2	3	8	11	9	11	48*
Washington D.C.						8	3	4	3	18
Michigan							4	2	1	7
Minnesota							1	3	2	6
Wisconsin							2		2	4
Indiana								1	1	2
Texas								3	8	11
Ohio									6	6
Total	1	1	1	2	3	16	21	22	34	102

*Includes the original Potbelly opened in 1977 and bought by Keil in 1996.

Jimmy John's, and Schlotzsky's Deli are wary that Potbelly will become a major national competitor. The Potbelly experience appears to be difficult to duplicate. For example, Quiznos may have similar food quality but not similar atmosphere; Cosi may have the hangout ambience down but not the food! Subway is especially vulnerable since it has neither the food nor the warm and comfy fun store environment.

Yet Potbelly has a tough road ahead. It requires management to maintain the superior performance of current units while creating new Potbelly units in new markets. Each Potbelly is special in terms of location, décor, and staff. The unit must be tailored to its neighborhood and community. Attentive, enthusiastic workers must be found. Food quality and a fun atmosphere must become an integral part of the store culture. Not an easy task!

1. Identify and describe Potbelly's strategy in terms of product (present or new) and market (present or new).
2. How would you describe Potbelly's positioning strategy?
3. What types of environmental opportunities and threats do you see in Potbelly's external environment? How might they affect Potbelly's current strategy?

5. Suburban Regional Shopping Malls: Can the Magic Be Restored?*

The suburban regional shopping mall is regarded by many as the "crown jewel" of shopping experiences. In a single location, shoppers can visit over a hundred stores, go to a movie, eat, walk, and lounge for an entire day in a secure, pleasant atmosphere sheltered from undesirable weather and the demands of everyday life. Most Americans at one time or another have escaped for the day to such a mall and felt "uplifted" in spirit by the experience. So pervasive is the suburban regional shopping mall that William Kowinski in the *The Malling of America* (1985) claims that in the United States alone there are more enclosed malls than cities, four-year colleges, or television stations! Indeed, few of us can remember a time when shopping was a trip to "downtown," or the central business district (CBD) of a large city.

Many suburban regional shopping malls are over one million square feet in size, contain over a hundred stores, and offer shoppers free parking, restaurants, play facilities, lounge facilities, restrooms, and movie theaters. Some centers even provide amusement rides and other entertainment opportunities. One of the dominant features of these large shopping complexes is the presence of multiple department stores that "anchor" the extreme points of the mall's layout and "pull" shoppers to the mall from surrounding suburban areas. Department stores also encourage shoppers to walk through the mall. In fact, department stores were the driving force behind the original development of suburban regional shopping malls and have played a critical role in their continuing success.

The movement of traditional department stores from CBD locations to the suburbs, complete with large "full-line" departments, contributed greatly to the explosive growth of suburban regional shopping malls during the post–World War II era. At its inception, the suburban regional shopping mall was designed to be a substitute, or even a replacement, for a city's CBD, but without the usual congestion or parking difficulties. This strategy was particularly attractive after the opening of Southdale Center in suburban Minneapolis in 1956 (www.southdale.com), which demonstrated the viability of a regional shopping mall with multiple anchors.

*This case and the script for the accompanying video were prepared by Dr. J. B. Wilkinson, professor emeritus, Youngstown State University, and Dr. David J. Burns, Xavier University.

In 2002 there were a total of 46,336 shopping centers in the United States, of which about 1,200 could be considered regional or superregional malls (www.icsc.org). In addition to regional and superregional malls, numerous types of shopping centers have evolved since the 1950s. The International Council of Shopping Centers has defined eight principal shopping center types: neighborhood, community, regional, superregional, fashion/specialty, power, theme/festival, and outlet.

The suburban regional shopping malls and their department store anchors enjoyed great success for almost 50 years and seemed virtually invincible to threats until the final decade of the twentieth century. During that era, several chinks developed in the competitive armor of this type of retail institution, and the problems seem to be getting worse. Shopper activity is declining: the number of tenant vacancies is increasing; and the delinquency rate on mall mortgages is disturbing. Increasingly larger percentages of consumer discretionary income are being spent elsewhere. To make matters worse, many of the older malls need renovating to remain attractive to shoppers. Renovation of an older mall can cost tens of millions of dollars.

Changes in consumers and in their wants and needs appear to be the major factor that underlies the woes of suburban regional shopping malls. Since the first multi-anchor center opened in 1956, the lifestyles of American families have changed significantly. In 1950, for instance, only 24 percent of wives worked outside the home; today, that percentage exceeds 60 percent. Women between the ages of 18 and 45, the mainstay of mall shoppers, simply do not have the time to shop like they once had. As a result, shopping has become much more purpose-driven. Shopping statistics bear this out. Shoppers are visiting suburban regional shopping malls less frequently, visiting fewer stores when they do shop, and also spending less time at the mall when they do shop. Shoppers, however, are more likely to make a purchase when they do visit a mall. Yet the typical suburban regional shopping mall was designed for a "shop-all-day" or a "shop-'til-you drop" philosophy.

Another consumer trend that spells trouble for suburban regional shopping malls is increased shopper price sensitivity. A wider selection of shopping alternatives from which to choose and the desire to make the family income go further (which, in essence, is equal to a pay increase) have proven to be strong forces pushing shoppers to comparison shop between retail establishments—something that most malls are not designed to facilitate. Despite the large number of stores contained within a regional suburban shopping mall, comparison shopping between stores is not an easy task. Most malls are laid out to cater to a leisure-oriented shopper. Similar stores are located in different wings of the shopping mall to encourage shoppers to walk through the entire center. Shoppers may walk upwards to a quarter-mile in their quest to compare products! This is not consistent with the desire for shopping convenience and efficiency on the part of most consumers.

Competition also has played a role in the problems that plague suburban regional shopping malls. High levels of competition characterize most mature industries, and the shopping center industry is no exception. Regional malls have both direct and indirect competitors. Direct competitors are nearby shopping centers with either similar or dissimilar formats. Indirect competitors comprise other types of retail store sites like freestanding or clustered sites and nonstore retailing sites. Nonstore retailing includes online shopping, catalog shopping, home TV shopping, telemarketing, and other forms of direct marketing, all of which have made considerable inroads into retail store sales. Suburban regional shopping malls have been especially vulnerable to both forms of competition.

Many of the more successful retailers (e.g., Kohl's, Home Depot) are located on freestanding sites or in large open-air centers—locations that have greater appeal to time-pressed, purpose-driven shoppers than mall locations. Similarly, many outlet malls, which cater to price-sensitive shoppers, are typically open-air centers to facilitate store access. In addition, some of the newer small shopping centers cater to a focused lifestyle (teen or professional woman) or have an organizing theme (home decor, hobby) that satisfies the specific needs of a market niche by offering a more focused product assortment than what can be found in a suburban regional shopping mall.

Oversupply of retail space has posed considerable problems to all shopping centers. The United States has 20 square feet for every man, woman, and child, compared to 1.4 square feet per person in Great Britain. Sales per square foot of retail space is declining in the United States. In fact, revenue from retail sales is contracting. It grew an average of 2.5 percent in the 1970s; 1.3 percent in the 1980s; and only 0.8 percent in the 1990s, adjusted for inflation. The result has been retail consolidation, store closings, and bankruptcies, leaving shopping centers fighting for a shrinking base of retail tenants.

Finally, department stores, the primary traffic generators for suburban regional shopping malls, are experiencing serious competitive problems. Over the past two decades, department stores have lost half of their market share to discounters and specialty stores. They also have suffered a significant sales revenue decline, causing store closings and consolidation. Given the role department stores have played as traffic generators for shopping malls, the problems of department stores have added to the problems of suburban regional shopping malls. Quite simply, fewer department store shoppers have meant fewer shoppers in the mall. To make matters worse, an empty department store space in a mall gives shoppers less reason to visit that portion of the mall and often leads to the closure of nearby stores. Besides being unproductive, the resulting empty retail space is unsightly, projecting the same image that empty storefronts in the CBDs of cities do—decay and decline.

The predictable outcome of all these changes is that construction of new suburban regional shopping malls has virtually come to a halt. Furthermore, a significant number of existing centers are being "decommissioned"—converted into alternative uses such as office space, learning centers, and telemarketing call centers, or torn down to be replaced by other forms of retail centers. Over 300 malls have been decommissioned since the mid-1990s, a trend which is expected to continue.

The dim outlook for suburban regional shopping malls has stimulated much creative thought about turnaround strategies for those still in operation. One turnaround strategy that has been suggested deals with the way suburban regional shopping malls are traditionally configured and involves changing the way stores in the center are arranged with respect to one another. The traditional layout locates similar stores in different wings or corridors of the center to encourage shoppers to travel through the entire center in their quest to locate and compare products. This type of layout maximizes customer interchange between stores but does not address shopping efficiency. Zonal merchandising represents a different approach to a center's layout. Under zonal merchandising, similar tenants are located in close proximity to one another. This reduces shopping time for shoppers who come to the mall to purchase a specific product. It also creates opportunities for differentiating mall areas in terms of decor, music, amenities, and special events to suit the tastes of shoppers who are most likely to be visiting stores in those areas.

Zonal merchandising has been used most commonly for fast food. Called "food courts," these clusters of fast-food providers have been very successful. Food court tenants have experienced higher levels of sales than under traditional layouts. Food courts also have shown that they are able to draw shoppers from other locations in the mall, similar to the traffic-generating role of a traditional anchor store.

Based on the success of the food court, several attempts to implement zonal merchandising on a wider scale have been made. Beginning with Bridgewater Commons in New Jersey (www.bridgewatercommons.com), several new projects have incorporated zonal merchandising principles, including Rivertown Crossings in Grand Rapids, Michigan (www.rivertowncrossings.com), which has grouped some categories of stores by product line carried, and Park Meadows in Denver, Colorado (www.parkmeadows.com), which has grouped stores by customer lifestyle. The results of these endeavors have been promising, and General Growth (www.generalgrowth.com), the developer of Rivertown Crossings, plans to implement some form of clustering at all of its future projects. Attempts to reconfigure existing centers around zonal merchandising ideas, such as the changes at Glendale Galleria in Glendale, California (www.glendalegalleria.com), seem to be successful as well.

An alternative strategy, which has been proposed for turning around traditional suburban regional shopping malls, is the incorporation of entertainment within the center. The idea behind this strategy is quite simple: add value to the shopper's visit to a mall and give shoppers additional reasons to shop in the mall rather than at home. Entertainment can run the gamut from simple play areas or a carousel for children to video arcades and virtual golf courses to a full-scale amusement park, such as the Mall of America (www.mallofamerica.com). However, adding entertainment offerings to suburban regional shopping malls does not guarantee success. The entertainment must be something that will attract shoppers and keep their interest for a lengthy period of time—not something which shoppers tire of easily. Also the effect of the entertainment activities on a center's retailing activities must be considered. Entertainment centers in suburban regional malls often attract people with social goals instead of shopping goals, which does not benefit a center's merchandise-based stores.

Some industry analysts suggest that the key to revitalizing the suburban regional shopping mall is to make the shopping experience itself more exciting. Even at Mall of America, the home of the largest mall-based entertainment facility in the United States, the primary attraction of the center is the entertainment and excitement provided by the shopping experience itself; shoppers find stores and products which they cannot find elsewhere in the region.

Most suburban regional shopping malls are unexciting. They offer shoppers a relatively nondescript homogeneous shopping experience. They look alike, possess the same stores, and sell the same products. What has been forgotten by mall managers is that entertainment, in a mall sense, is not necessarily what activities can be added to the center, but what entertainment is provided by the shopping experience. Shoppers are searching for shopping experiences that are fresh, different, and fun. To provide this experience, suburban regional shopping malls need to attract stores and sell products that are unique, interesting, and ever-changing. The recent addition of the Build-a-Bear Workshop to the offerings of several suburban regional shopping malls is one such example. The Build-a-Bear Workshop (www.buildabear.com) is a novel retail concept that provides a playful, creative environment. The challenge for mall managers is to find new and exciting retailing concepts like Build-a-Bear Workshop on a continual basis.

The Easton Town Center in Columbus, Ohio (www.eastontowncenter.com) is an example of a suburban regional shopping center that was explicitly designed to provide shoppers with a fun, exciting, entertaining place to shop. Easton Town Center was designed as an open-air center that mimics small-town America over 50 years ago. The center possesses an entertainment-oriented product mix with numerous restaurants, 30 movie theaters, spas, a comedy club, a cabaret, specialty stores, and Nordstrom and Lazarus as anchor department stores. The center has a "town square" and special event areas. It is considered to be one of the most successful retail centers in the region.

The challenge to mall developers and managers is clear. Since the opening of Southdale Center in 1956, changes in competition, retailing, and consumer shopping behavior have resulted in significant threats and opportunities. If suburban regional shopping malls are to enjoy continued success, they must creatively adapt to the new industry and shopping environment. Managers and owners of suburban regional shopping malls must determine the change strategy that is best for them. A number of considerations should guide their thinking—the competition, the needs of shoppers in their area, the opportunities available, and the center's resources. Just as one size does not fit all, the same turnaround strategy will not suit all suburban regional shopping malls.

1. *Imagine yourself as the manager of a struggling local suburban regional shopping mall. What do you think the mall should do to improve its performance?*
2. *What shopping trends do you foresee over the next 10 years? How might these trends affect suburban regional shopping malls?*
3. *What new retail concepts can you identify? How might you learn about more? What strategies do you suggest for learning about new retail concepts?*

6. Girl Scouts*

Girl Scouting is dedicated to and available to all girls age 5 to 17. Today there are approximately 3.6 million Girl Scouts in the United States, including over 2.7 million girls and nearly 900,000 adult members, most of whom are volunteers. Membership categories for the girls are

Category	Age	Grade
Daisy	5–6	K, 1
Brownie	6, 7, 8	1, 2, 3
Junior Girl Scout	8, 9, 10, 11	3, 4, 5, 6
Cadette Girl Scout	11, 12, 13, 14	6, 7, 8, 9
Senior Girl Scout	14–17	9–12

Membership is at an all-time high. In 1999, as a result of specific target market initiatives, growth was especially strong among Hispanic (a 6.3 percent increase) and African American (a 5.9 percent increase) girls. And membership is not just limited to the United States. Through its membership in the World Association of Girl Guides and Girl Scouts, Girl Scouts of the U.S.A. (GSUSA) is part of a larger entity of over 10 million girls in 140 countries. Although some programs for overseas travel and adventure exist, the international link is still being developed and is not nearly as strong as the link between GSUSA and the local councils.

As is true for many nonprofit organizations, the Girl Scouts organization operates on two levels. At the corporate or headquarters level is Girl Scouts of the U.S.A., located in New York. A board of directors, a national president, and a national executive director run GSUSA. From these offices, plans are made for the national parent and for the local councils. These local councils may be thought of as strategic business units (SBUs) for the Girl Scouts. Over 300 local councils serve to direct the activities of the more than 226,000 troops in the United States and overseas. A local board of directors and an executive director manages each of these local councils. To become a part of GSUSA, each of these local councils must go through a type of accreditation review by the national organization. Every four years each council is reviewed, and if it continues to meet the established criteria, it will be rechartered. This chartering process provides GSUSA with a strong weapon to maintain some level of consistency for the strategies and actions of the member Girl Scout councils.

Strategic marketing planning clearly is necessary to run such a large organization. GSUSA does extensive corporate-level planning and also provides the local councils with assistance for their own formulation and execution of plans.

Strategic marketing planning at the corporate level is the responsibility of the president and the board, with input from board committees, board task groups, community leaders, and community groups. Four steps are involved. The first step is a S.W.O.T. analysis, a review of internal strengths and external trends. This includes using the database maintained by GSUSA that details membership, program attendance, financial and development data, and similar benchmarks. The study of external trends results in the *Environmental Scanning Report*, which uses social, economic, political, and technological data from a variety of sources. This document is then made available to corporate- and council-level planners. One result of this S.W.O.T. analysis is the identification of a set of critical issues facing GSUSA. These issues are then used in the second step: to develop corporate goals covering a six-year period. These goals are reviewed at the midpoint of the planning period. In the third step, the group develops strategic guidelines, strategies, and long-range projects. Finally, the group develops long-range resource strategies that are needed to support the projects identified in the third step.

Staff and volunteers involved in implementing the strategic plans are responsible for the development of one-year plans (tactical planning). At this fourth step, priorities are established; specific operational goals are set; action plans are developed, including decisions about who, how, what, and when; and the operational budget is determined.

The completed corporate plan shapes all efforts and programs at the national level. However, local planners can exercise some discretion in planning for their markets. To accomplish local planning, some councils hold planning retreats with local board and community experts; some hold planning sessions for just staff; and some limit the efforts to a committee of the board. Whatever the process, the council board develops a set of five-year goals that it reviews annually. While these usually mirror national goals, each local council has the opportunity to change priorities or to add other goals peculiar to their local efforts. Using these goals, the staff develops proposals for specific objectives and action steps for board approval. These approved objectives and action steps form the basis for the local council's annual operating plan.

During the year, results are measured, compared to objectives, and subjected to corrective actions. Also during the year, the staff has the opportunity to reevaluate the goals that have been set by the board for the coming year and may provide suggestions to the board. The board then meets again early in the following year to plan for that year and to add goals for the fifth year in the current plan. Thus, the local council board always has a plan that looks five years ahead.

Marketing plans and efforts must be directed at three distinct groups. First, plans must be developed for recruiting and marketing efforts directed to the target market for Scouting: girls and their families. In addition, marketing plans also must target volunteers. Scouting could not function nearly as effectively without its giant network of volunteers, both at the local and national levels. There are over 880,000 adult members of Girl Scouting and most of them are volunteers. Many

---

*This case and accompanying video script were prepared by Dr. George Prough, the University of Akron, with assistance from Lori Arguelles, Communications Director, GSUSA, and Mary Kintz, Director of Member Services, Western Reserve Girl Scouts Council.

of these volunteers were involved in scouting when they were young. Others are parents of current scouts.

Finally, the community at large represents an important stakeholder group. This group includes donors, both corporate and individual, who provide financial and other resources; schools and school counselors; church organizations and the like. During the S.W.O.T. analysis, all three groups are studied, and this provides input for recruitment plans and for the ongoing marketing efforts.

Quite clearly, young girls in the target demographic are the first and most important marketing target. Marketing efforts aimed at this group include recruitment efforts as well as retention efforts (keeping existing Scouts delighted with their experiences).

Plans of both types must consider the competition faced by Girl Scouting. All organizations face competition of various sorts, but Girl Scouts planners face an unusual situation. Essentially, the competition for Scouting is other activities that compete for a girl's time. This includes school clubs and other school-related activities; sports; private lessons such as piano, ballet, and music; church; and other social activities, including dating boys. However, the thinking about competition at Girl Scouts is different. Girl Scouting does not attempt to defeat the competition. Instead, Scouting embraces many of these competing activities and offers them as part of their product mix. If it finds that a certain activity is becoming more important to young girls, then Scouting looks at the possibility of incorporating that activity into its product mix of activities.

As girls mature, this kind of competition grows more intense. Older girls have more choices, making retention in these categories more difficult. As a result, there has been a growing concern that the programs and offerings of Girl Scouting, especially in the older age categories, is not sufficiently contemporary. Retention of these older girls is a problem. For instance, analysis of the U.S. membership shows the following data regarding the number of girls served by the Girl Scouts in each membership category:

Category	Girls Served in the Category
Daisy	1 of every 8
Brownie	1 of every 4
Junior Girl Scout	1 of every 7
Cadette Girl Scout	1 of every 25
Senior Girl Scout	1 of every 73

To better understand customers and the competing demands on their lives, Girl Scouts USA is beginning to do extensive market and customer research among young girls. During the fall of 2000, GSUSA launched the Girl Scout Research Institute, a research and public policy information center focusing on the healthy development of girls. Through this Institute, the GSUSA hopes to develop a large database of information on girls, with the additional goal of positioning itself as an information resource and expert on girls.

Within this competitive market, the GSUSA uses a variety of plans and strategies in order to attract new girls. The national website offers an overview for interested girls; however, it is not very interactive and has limited recruiting value. Nationally prepared brochures and literature are also available. Often these can be useful as stuffers in store, mall, and other point-of-sale display units. But many councils choose to localize and personalize these efforts. For these councils, most of the recruitment and marketing efforts are planned and developed at the local level. Local websites, school visits, locally prepared fliers, recruiting efforts at malls, churches, and other similar local activities lend a more personal touch to their recruiting.

Specific to certain types of competition, GSUSA has responded with a changing product mix. Each year, Girl Scouts adds to its diversity of activities and merit badges, all awarded for participation and mastery of particular tasks. With the increase in girls participating in sporting activities, Girl Scouts developed *GirlSports*, a program offering senior Girl Scouts from around the country a chance to spend a week during the summer developing certain sporting skills. During the 2000 version, 26 girls met in Oakland, California, with local athletes and trainers, learned 13 extreme sports, and studied with ESPN fitness experts and Olympic athletes. An expanded version of *GirlSports* is being developed to include over 100,000 girls competing in nearly 2,300 different sporting events in over 300 councils.

Another trend identified was the increasing interest of girls in the sciences. As a result, the *Girl at the Center* program was developed. This is a science and technology program in which local councils can take advantage of partnerships between the Girl Scouts and over 31 science museums, encouraging families and girls to explore and learn more about the sciences. *Girl at the Center* and the *GirlSports* program are examples of how the Girl Scouts organization is forming partnerships with others to make its programs relevant and successful.

Girl Scouting uses several methods to appeal to its second target, its volunteers—both to attract them and to keep them motivated and involved. To attract volunteers at the national level, the website offers valuable insight as do the nationally prepared brochures highlighting the benefits of volunteering and the many ways of doing so. But again, the local councils often develop their own marketing efforts. Parents are targeted by maintaining a parents' network and involving parents in meetings and events. When the local council has events at malls or churches, the council staff involved makes every attempt to sell volunteering to adults as much as they do scouting to young girls. Additionally, many local councils work with area organizations in an attempt to generate volunteers. Universities, schools, the local housing authority, and other volunteer-based organizations have proven to be excellent sources of interns or other types of volunteers.

To keep volunteers motivated and involved, GSUSA national offers a variety of adult development and training opportunities. These include programs at the corporate training center, a number of online training offerings, and certification programs that support and enable the volunteers to improve their abilities to perform their functions.

Girl Scouting's third target, its stakeholder group, consists of the community at large. Efforts to interact with this stakeholder group can be planned, and suggestions are made at the national level; however, many of these efforts involve personal contacts and one-on-one relationships with donors or other partnership targets. As a result, many of these efforts are developed and conducted by people at the local council level.

1. *Compare strategic marketing planning by the Girl Scouts with planning by for-profit organizations. What are the similarities? What are the differences?*
2. *What changes would you suggest to improve the planning process in the Girl Scouts?*

7. The GM HUMMER: Brand Equity, Positioning, and Development*

Few brands have the cachet, exotic heritage, and unique identity that GM's HUMMER exudes. It has a brand image and equity that sets it apart from most automobiles in the industry. Within General Motors Corp., it represents an important growth opportunity in a highly competitive and dynamic market.

The HUMMER can trace its roots to AM General (formerly Willys-Overland Motors, Inc.) and the year 1979 when the U.S. Army issued a draft specification for a new light tactical vehicle that could replace light civilian trucks and various other specially designed Army vehicles. The specifications indicated that the Army wanted a versatile, cross-country vehicle capable of performing both combat and combat-support roles. Other required attributes and characteristics included durability, mobility, and reliability; diesel-power and automatic transmission; and the capability of being modified to carry communications and weapons systems (missiles, automatic weapons). Thus, the concept for a High-Mobility Multipurpose Wheeled Vehicle (HMMWV), nicknamed HUMVEE, was conceived. AM General became one of three contenders awarded an Army contract for the design and construction of 11 prototype HMMWVs—six weapons carriers and five utility vehicles. These prototypes were tested in various off-road conditions in combat environments—rocky hills, sand, mud and water, desert heat, and Arctic cold. In March 1983, AM General was awarded a five-year contract for 55,000 HMMWVs in 15 different configurations. Most were to be used in the Army, but some were allocated to the Marine Corps, Air Force, and Navy. By mid-1991, more than 72,000 vehicles had been produced. The total as of 2006 is more than 190,000, including international sales.

Civilians learned about the HUMVEE during the 1991 Gulf War (Operation: Desert Storm). Photographs and video broadcasts from Kuwait spawned a great deal of interest in the HUMVEE from the American public. Arnold Schwarzenegger was so taken with the vehicle that he persuaded AM General to sell him one and to make them available to civilians under the brand name HUMMER. In 1992, AM General began selling the HUMMER H1. In 2002, AM General began producing the HUMMER H2, which was marketed and sold by General Motors.

HUMMER H1 was essentially a civilian version of the military HUMVEE—a large, heavy vehicle (over 8,500 lbs.) with a large diesel engine and complex driveline. It got about 10 mpg, but was excellent off-road—an icon of strength,

durability, and rugged individualism. It originally cost about $50,000 ($140,000 in 2006) and attracted off-road enthusiasts, celebrities, and men who wanted to make a "tough-guy" statement. H1 buyers are 95 percent male, and sales have been about 700 a year. There are about 12,000 of these macho-mobiles on the road today. The last HUMMER H1 for commercial sale rolled off the assembly line in 2006. In a statement issued by HUMMER General Manager Martin Walsh, the reason for dropping the HUMMER H1 from the line was to focus on models with broader appeal instead of the small niche market attracted to H1.

In 1999, AM General sold the marketing rights to the HUMMER brand name to General Motors. Under this agreement, AM General continued to produce the HUMMER H1. In 2002, AM General opened a new plant to produce the HUMMER H2 SUV and later in 2005 an SUT sport utility truck variant. However, GM has exclusive ownership of the HUMMER brand name and has been very active in licensing it for use on colognes, flashlights, bicycles, laptops, apparel, jewelry, CD players, and other items.

HUMMER H2 was positioned as a kinder, gentler vehicle, while maintaining the macho mystique of the brand. Many of the print ads for the H2 showed it sitting still in a vast outdoor setting, which made it look petite. One of the original commercials featured a well-dressed woman behind the wheel. However, one of the ads bragged, "In a world where SUVs have begun to look like their owners, with love handles and mushy seats, the H2 proves that there is still one out there that can drop and give you 20." In fact, the H2 was only slightly smaller and lighter than the H1 with tires as high as a kitchen table and side mirrors as big as manila folders. Yet, it performed more like a well-mannered SUV. It also came in bright colors (e.g., bright yellow and red) with cup-holders, heated seats, and other comforts. At a price of around $50,000, it competed with luxury SUVs like the Range Rover, Lincoln Navigator, and Cadillac Escalade. Buyers for the H2 were "successful achievers" and "rugged individualists." A large percentage of buyers for the H2 are women (about 25 percent). Celebrity owners of the H2 include Arnold Schwarzenegger, LeBron James, and Patti Labelle.

HUMMER H3 was introduced in spring 2005. Configured as a midsize SUV and priced around $30,000 to $40,000, the H3 looked a lot like the HUMMER H2 but was much smaller and got an EPA estimated 20 mpg highway. The lower price made the H3 affordable for a younger demographic. Standard features included full power equipment and door locks with lockout protection; electric rear-window defogger; exterior power-adjustable, manually folding rear-view mirrors; three

*This case was prepared by Dr. J. B. Wilkinson, professor emeritus, Youngstown State University.

12-volt covered auxiliary power outlets; instrument cluster and center stack with a brushed finish in the interior; and other items. Options included a DVD-based navigation radio, a large power sunroof, and accessories to personalize the vehicle. However, the H3 had the same off-road prowess as the larger H2 and was infused with the same militaristic styling and take-the-hill attitude.

The commercials for HUMMER H3 were designed for mass-market appeal to connect with a wider cross section of consumers than the HUMMER brand had sought out in the past. In one commercial, a group of exasperated HUMMER executives stand around a boardroom table, trying to come up with the next hot product—something new. Ed the Courier, a very short guy, comes in and says, "Why not make a smaller one?" In another commercial, the camera focuses on an empty parking spot. As music from the Richard Strauss symphony "Also Sprach Zarathustra" plays, a HUMMER H3 pulls up to the spot and parallel parks effortlessly. To prove the H3 still has the "right stuff," another commercial has the H3 plowing through mountain roads and scaling boulders, much like the H2 did in its commercials. More recently, a 2006 Super Bowl ad called "Monsters" showed a Godzilla clone squaring off against a giant robot. Instead of fighting, they fall in love. When the female monster gives birth, a red H3 is born.

GM is counting on the HUMMER H3 to increase the volume and accessibility of the brand to more customers through its 172 HUMMER dealers. As part of its brand recognition strategy, GM now sells HUMMERS through separate dealerships that all have a distinctive design—sort of a militaristic steel, glass, and concrete Quonset hut look.

Possible future plans for the brand include a diesel and a hybrid-electric engine for the H2. A prototype called the HUMMER H2H, powered by a hydrogen fuel cell, is on loan to Governor Arnold Schwarzenegger. Opportunities in international markets are strong. Beginning in 2006, GM will be assembling HUMMERS at a plant in Port Elizabeth, South Africa, for local South African consumption and for export to other markets.

1. How would you describe the brand image and positioning of the original HUMMER H1?
2. How has the brand image and positioning changed with the HUMMER H2 and HUMMER H3?
3. What is the major risk in GM's repositioning strategy for the HUMMER brand?

8. Segway Finds Niche Markets for Its Human Transporter Technology*

Amid heavy media coverage and much speculation, "Ginger" made its debut on ABC's *Good Morning America* on December 3, 2001. It thrilled some and disappointed others, but the technology was breathtaking to all.

Now known as the Segway Human Transporter (HT), Ginger was the brainchild of inventor and entrepreneur Dean Kamen, who is best known for his inventions in the medical field. While in college, Kamen invented the first wearable drug-infusion pump. In the following years, he invented the first portable insulin pump, the first portable dialysis machine, and an array of heart stents. This string of successes established Kamen's reputation and turned DEKA Research and Development Corp., the R&D lab he founded, into a premier company for medical-device design.

The inspiration for Ginger occurred during the development of the IBOT wheelchair at DEKA. Developed for and funded by Johnson & Johnson, the IBOT wheelchair is a gyro-stabilized, microprocessor-controlled wheelchair that gives disabled people the same kind of mobility the rest of us take for granted. Officially called the Independence IBOT mobility system, this six-wheel machine can go up and down curbs, cruise effortlessly through sand or gravel, climb stairs, and rise up on its wheels to lift its occupant to eye level while maintaining balance and maneuverability with such stability that it can't be knocked over. The IBOT wheelchair has been likened to a sophisticated robot.

As Kamen and his team at DEKA were working on the IBOT, it dawned on them that they could build a device using similar technology for pedestrians—one that could go farther, move more quickly, and carry more. The IBOT was also the source of the "Ginger" code name for the Segway HT during its development stage. Watching the IBOT "dance up the stairs," Kamen's team likened it to Fred Astaire—hence the name Ginger for its smaller partner with only two wheels!

Segway's breakthrough technology is based on dynamic stabilization. A self-balancing, electric-powered transport device, the Segway HT contains gyroscopes and sensors that monitor a user's center of gravity and respond to subtle shifts in weight. Lean forward, go forward; lean back, go back; lean back a bit more and you go in reverse; turn by twisting your wrist; arch your back a tad and you slow to a halt. Exactly how the Segway achieves this is difficult to explain, but in every Segway, there are gyroscopes that act like your inner ear, a computer that acts like your brain, motors that act like your muscles, and wheels that act like your feet. You step aboard and it "oscillates" for a few seconds, getting the feel of you, and then it's fully cruiseable at 6 mph in "learning mode," and 12.5 miles per hour "flat-out." It has a range of about 17 to 25 miles per battery charge and can support weights of 80 pounds. It has no brakes, no engine, no throttle, no gearshift, no steering wheel, and gives off no emissions. It is much cleaner than a car and faster than a bike. It is more pedestrian-friendly than bikes or scooters and safer than a skateboard.

The commercial potential for Segway is enormous. For this reason, Kamen decided to move development and manufacturing of the Segway HT to a new company with

*This case was prepared by Dr. J. B. Wilkinson, professor emeritus, Youngstown State University.

the vision to develop highly efficient, zero-emission transportation solutions using dynamic stabilization technology. The new company, Segway LLC (changed to Segway, Inc., in 2005) is headquartered in Bedford, New Hampshire, and construction of a manufacturing and assembly plant was completed in 2001.

Kamen has openly stated that the Segway "will be to the car what the car was to the horse and buggy!" He imagines them everywhere: in parks, on battlefields, on factory floors, zipping around distribution centers, and especially on downtown sidewalks. But market acceptance and penetration has been slow for this engineering marvel.

The Segway HT was initially marketed to major corporations and government agencies. Kamen personally demonstrated the Segway to the postmaster general who was keen to put letter carriers on Segways and to the head of the National Park Service who wanted to do the same with park rangers. Both were among Segway's first customers. The Pentagon's research agency, DARPA, bought Segways to give to robotics labs. The objective was to use Segway bases in the development of robots to do menial tasks (cleaning, picking crops), specialized jobs (nurses aids), and dangerous missions (bomb removal or rescue work in earthquake debris). Amazon.com, GE Plastics, and Delphi Automotive Systems purchased Segways for use in warehouses and manufacturing plants. Police departments, cities, and airports bought Segways for use by foot patrols, security personnel, and meter readers. Customer studies by these early buyers showed double-digit productivity gains and reduced reliance on motorized transport. For postal workers, the Segway has increased their carrying capacity and delivery speed. Test studies with police officers and security personnel have shown faster response times and better sightlines from being higher in the air than pedestrians.

In 2002, Segways went on sale to the public for the first time on Amazon.com at a price of around $5,000. In 2003, the retail store Brookstone became the first retailer to sell the Segway HT. By January 2004, it was estimated by industry observers that about 6,000 Segways had been sold. Given Kamen's stated ambition of replacing automobiles and other forms of personal transport alternatives, initial consumer sales were disappointing.

However, the Segway HT is still in the early stages of its product life cycle. According to product life-cycle theories and related empirical studies on diffusion of innovations, products move through their life cycles in different ways and the length of any particular stage varies according to many factors. In general, the speed with which a product moves through its introduction and growth stages varies according to product characteristics, market characteristics, competition, and environmental factors. The initial marketing strategy for a product will also affect market acceptance (adoption). A product will move quickly through the introduction and growth stages when it has high relative advantage—cost and benefits—compared to alternative products and is highly compatible with a buyer's current attitudes, lifestyle, and usage situation. The more complex a product is to understand and use, the slower will be its rate of adoption. In addition, if the product can be tried in small amounts, potential buyers perceive less risk associated with initial trial and this will speed adoption. Communication of the new product will affect market acceptance since buyers must first learn about a new product before the buying process can be initiated. Thus, a company's communication strategies and the degree to which favorable word-of-mouth opinion occurs will impact sales. Finally, new products will have higher rates of market acceptance if market conditions, competition, and environmental trends are favorable.

Industrial and government applications for the Segway HT continue to be positive. It's ideally suited for use in large-scale manufacturing plants and warehousing operations, for use by the police and security personnel in certain types of situations, for meter reading, for corporate and university campus transportation, and for package and mail delivery. And it has found a number of new niches in recent years. For example, tour groups are using Segways to move tourists between attractions in cities where tour buses and cars have operational difficulties. For example, Bill and Emily Neuenschwander's tours use Segways equipped with a radio on the handlebars that provide a running commentary to guide customers through tours of the Minneapolis, Minnesota, riverfront and surrounding historic landmarks. Visitors to theme parks, museums, and islands (e.g., Amelia Island Plantation Resort) use them. Some lawyers use them between offices and courtrooms. Some medics use them to reach injured people faster.

However, in the consumer market, the Segway HT is still an unsought product for many people. Industry observers believe that the automobile is a preferred alternative for a number of reasons, including the infrastructure of cities, commuting distances, weather, and the American family lifestyle. Most people agree that the use of a Segway HT on highways and busy streets is dangerous. Also, many commuters live more than 5 miles from work. The need to recharge Segways raises the question of public sources of electricity. Issues related to public safety also have slowed consumer sales. Although the Segway HT is approved in most states for use on sidewalks, restrictions have been placed on speed, helmet use, minimum operating age, and use on streets and highways. At the local level, additional regulations apply. For example, San Francisco banned their use on city sidewalks, and they are outlawed in subways in Washington, D.C. Many see the mix of pedestrians, bicycles, skateboards, roller skates, ATVs, scooters, and Segways as a dangerous mix on sidewalks, hiking trails, and other public areas.

On the other hand, the Segway HT has obvious advantages to walking and other types of personal transport in some types of situations where people need to get from one place to another quickly and efficiently using a clean, quiet, and environmental-friendly transport device. The market potential for the product has barely been tapped. Early consumer buyers were mostly "techies" who like to own new, high-tech products, and they have played an important role in communicating the benefits and fun of owning a Segway HT. They have established local clubs across America and have started a number of websites devoted to Segway. In 2003, owners and enthusiasts held the first SegwayFest to celebrate all things Segway. The Fest has been held every year since.

In 2004, Segway launched a repositioning campaign to change the image of the Segway HT from "staid," "high-tech," and "serious" to "fun, smart transportation." The new and more traditional marketing campaign included new customer materials, dealer displays, and cable TV advertising with the tagline "Get Moving." Segway also has been increasing the number of dealerships and distributors worldwide. The new distribution strategy allows potential buyers to see the different models and to try them out before buying. The dealer network increases the visibility of the product and lowers buyers' perceived risk associated with servicing. Publicity, media appearances, and product placement on television shows such as *Frasier*, *Arrested Development*, and *The Simpsons* continue to provide important market exposure.

The new positioning strategy emphasizes the leisure aspect of the Segway HT. New models aimed at the recreation market have been introduced. For example, the Segway GT is geared toward golf enthusiasts and includes a golf bag carrier. The Segway XT is the company's off-road vehicle which can perform well in a variety of environments. The Centaur is a four-wheeled ATV-like vehicle that can pick up its wheels to climb over obstacles or simply glide on two wheels at 25 mph.

To further develop the market for the Segway technology, the company has started to market Segway Smart Motion Technology through licensing and partnering with third parties to codevelop new products. Under this program, any number of specialized products could emerge.

The future for Segway is ultimately unlimited. America's commitment to end its dependence on petroleum and reduce harmful emissions is not likely to change. Segway technology has part of the answer to how this can occur. The consumer market for Segway has developed slowly, but the future is assured. For this "new-to-the-world" product, the life cycle will be long and classically configured. Its impact on all sectors of the economy will be profound. How we work, play, and get around will radically change in the 21st century. From the company's perspective, this is just dandy! Its ultimate goal is to "be to the car what the car was to the horse and buggy!"

1. *How might Segway, Inc., further develop the market for Segway technology? Hint: What types of marketing strategies are associated with sales growth?*
2. *What would be some advantages and disadvantages of using a Segway HT to get around on campus?*
3. *What types of applications and usage situations are there for Segway HTs in your area?*
4. *What kinds of problems would the use of Segway HTs create in your area? What are some possible solutions for these problems? Explain.*

543

Video Cases

Cases

Guide to the use of these cases

Cases can be used in many ways. And the same case can be analyzed several times for different purposes.

"Suggested cases" are listed at the end of most chapters, but these cases can also be used later in the text. The main criterion for the order of these cases is the amount of technical vocabulary—or text principles—that are needed to read the case meaningfully. The first cases are "easiest" in this regard. This is why an early case can easily be used two or three times—with different emphasis. Some early cases might require some consideration of Product and Price, for example, and might be used twice, perhaps regarding product planning and later pricing. In contrast, later cases, which focus more on Price, might be treated more effectively *after* the Price chapters are covered.

In some of the cases, we have disguised certain information—such as names or proprietary financial data—at the request of the people or firms involved in the case. However, such changes do not alter the basic substantive problems you will be analyzing in a case.

1. McDonald's "Seniors" Restaurant

Quinn McMahon is manager of a McDonald's restaurant in a city with many "seniors." She has noticed that some senior citizens have become not just regular patrons—but patrons who come for breakfast and stay on until about 3 P.M. Many of these older customers were attracted initially by a monthly breakfast special for people aged 55 and older. The meal costs $1.99, and refills of coffee are free. Every fourth Monday, between 100 and 150 seniors jam Quinn's McDonald's for the special offer. But now almost as many of them are coming every day—turning the fast-food restaurant into a meeting place. They sit for hours with a cup of coffee, chatting with friends. On most days, as many as 100 will stay from one to four hours.

Quinn's employees have been very friendly to the seniors, calling them by their first names and visiting with them each day. In fact, Quinn's McDonald's is a happy place—with her employees developing close relationships with the seniors. Some employees have even visited customers who have been hospitalized. "You know," Quinn says, "I really get attached to the customers. They're like my family. I really care about these people." They are all "friends," and it is part of McDonald's corporate philosophy (as reflected in its website, www.mcdonalds.com) to be friendly with its customers and to give back to the communities it serves.

These older customers are an orderly group and very friendly to anyone who comes in. Further, they are neater than most customers and carefully clean up their tables before they leave. Nevertheless, Quinn is beginning to wonder if anything should be done about her growing "non-fast-food" clientele. There's no crowding problem yet, during the time when the seniors like to come. But if the size of the senior citizen group continues to grow, crowding could become a problem. Further, Quinn is concerned that her restaurant might come to be known as an "old people's" restaurant—which might discour-

age some younger customers. And if customers felt the restaurant was crowded, some might feel that they wouldn't get fast service. On the other hand, a place that seems busy might be seen as a "good place to go" and a "friendly place."

Quinn also worries about the image she is projecting. McDonald's is a fast-food restaurant (there are over 32,000 of them in 132 countries), and normally customers are expected to eat and run. Will allowing people to stay and visit change the whole concept? In the extreme, Quinn's McDonald's might become more like a European-style restaurant where the customers are never rushed and feel very comfortable about lingering over coffee for an hour or two! Quinn knows that the amount her senior customers spend is similar to the average customer's purchase—but the seniors do use the facilities for a much longer time. However, most of the older customers leave McDonald's by 11:30, before the noon crowd comes in.

Quinn is also concerned about another possibility. If catering to seniors is OK, then should she do even more with this age group? In particular, she is considering offering bingo games during the slow morning hours—9 A.M. to 11 A.M. Bingo is popular with some seniors, and this could be a new revenue source—beyond the extra food and drink purchases that probably would result. She figures she could charge $5 per person for the two-hour period and run it with two underutilized employees. The prizes would be coupons for purchases at her store (to keep it legal) and would amount to about two-thirds of the bingo receipts (at retail prices). The party room area of her McDonald's would be perfect for this use and could hold up to 150 persons.

Evaluate Quinn McMahon's current strategy regarding senior citizens. Does this strategy improve this McDonald's image? What should she do about the senior citizen market—that is, should she encourage, ignore, or discourage her seniors? What should she do about the bingo idea? Explain.

2. Harvest Farm Foods, Inc.

It is 2008, and Patrick Webb, newly elected president of Harvest Farm Foods, Inc., faces a severe decline in profits. Harvest Farm Foods, Inc., is a 127-year-old California-based food processor. Its multiproduct lines are widely accepted under the Harvest Farm Foods brand. The company and its subsidiaries prepare, package, and sell canned and frozen foods, including fruits, vegetables, pickles, and condiments. Harvest Farm Foods, which operates more than 30 processing plants in the United States, is one of the larger U.S. food processors—with annual sales of about $650 million.

Until 2006, Harvest Farm Foods was a subsidiary of a major midwestern food processor, and many of the present managers came from the parent company. Harvest Farm Foods' last president recently said:

> The influence of our old parent company is still with us. As long as new products look like they will increase the company's sales volume, they are introduced. Traditionally,

there has been little, if any, attention paid to margins. We are well aware that profits will come through good products produced in large volume.

Ji-Sung Park, a 25-year employee and now production manager, agrees with the multiproduct-line policy. As he puts it: "Volume comes from satisfying needs. We will can or freeze any vegetable or fruit we think consumers might want." Ji-Sung Park also admits that much of the expansion in product lines was encouraged by economics. The typical plants in the industry are not fully used. By adding new products to use this excess capacity, costs are spread over greater volume. So the production department is always looking for new ways to make more effective use of its present facilities.

Harvest Farm Foods has a line-forcing policy, which requires that any store wanting to carry its brand name must be willing to carry most of the 65 items in the Harvest Farm Foods line. This policy, coupled with its wide expansion of product lines, has resulted in 88 percent of the firm's sales coming from major supermarket chain stores, such as Safeway, Kroger, and A&P.

Smaller stores are generally not willing to accept the Harvest Farm Foods policy. Ji-Sung Park explains, "We know that only large stores can afford to stock all our products. But the large stores are the volume! We give consumers the choice of any Harvest Farm Foods product they want, and the result is maximum sales." Many small retailers have complained about Harvest Farm Foods' policy, but they have been ignored because they are considered too small in potential sales volume per store to be of any significance.

In late 2008, a stockholders' revolt over low profits (in 2008, they were only $500,000) resulted in Harvest Farm Foods' president and two of its five directors being removed. Patrick Webb, an accountant from the company's outside auditing firm, was brought in as president. One of the first things he focused on was the variable and low levels of profits in the past several years. A comparison of Harvest Farm Foods' results with comparable operations of some large competitors supported his concern. In the past 13 years, Harvest Farm Foods' closest competitors had an average profit return on shareholders' investment of 5 to 9 percent, while Harvest Farm Foods averaged only 1.5 percent. Further, Harvest Farm Foods' sales volume has not increased much from the 1987 level (after adjusting for inflation)—while operating costs have soared upward. Profits for the firm were about $8 million in 1987. The closest Harvest Farm Foods has come since then is about $6 million—in 1995. The outgoing president blamed his failure on an inefficient sales department. He said, "Our sales department has deteriorated. I can't exactly put my finger on it, but the overall quality of salespeople has dropped, and morale is bad. The team just didn't perform." When Patrick Webb e-mailed Carolyn Birdsong, the vice president of sales, with this charge, her reply was,

It's not our fault. I think the company made a key mistake in the early 80s. It expanded horizontally—by increasing its number of product offerings—while major competitors were expanding vertically, growing their own raw materials and making all of their packing materials. They can control quality and make profits in manufacturing that can be used in promotion. I lost some of my best people from frustration. We just aren't competitive enough to reach the market the way we should with a comparable product and price.

In a lengthy e-mail from Carolyn Birdsong, Patrick Webb learned more about the nature of Harvest Farm Foods' market. Although all the firms in the food-processing industry advertise heavily, the size of the market for most processed foods hasn't grown much for many years. Further, most consumers are pressed for time and aren't very selective. If they can't find the brand of food they are looking for, they'll pick up another brand rather than go to some other store. No company in the industry has much effect on the price at which its products are sold. Chain store buyers are very knowledgeable about prices and special promotions available from all the competing suppliers, and they are quick to play one supplier against another to keep the price low. Basically, they have a price they are willing to pay—and they won't exceed it. However, the chains will charge any price they wish on a given brand sold at retail. (That is, a 48-can case of beans might be purchased from any supplier for $23.10, no matter whose product it is. Generally, the shelf price for each is no more than a few pennies different, but chain stores occasionally attract customers by placing a well-known brand on sale.)

Besides insisting that processors meet price points, like for the canned beans, some chains require price allowances if special locations or displays are desired. They also carry nonadvertised brands and/or their own brands at a lower price—to offer better value to their customers. And most will willingly accept producers' cents-off coupons, which are offered by Harvest Farm Foods as well as most of the other major producers of full lines.

At this point, Patrick Webb is trying to decide why Harvest Farm Foods, Inc., isn't as profitable as it once was. And he is puzzled about why some competitors are putting products on the market with low potential sales volume. (For example, one major competitor recently introduced a line of exotic foreign vegetables with gourmet sauces.) And others have been offering frozen dinners or entrees with vegetables for several years. Apparently, Harvest Farm Foods' managers considered trying such products several years ago but decided against it because of the small potential sales volumes and the likely high costs of new-product development and promotion.

Evaluate Harvest Farm Foods' present situation. What would you advise Patrick Webb to do to improve Harvest Farm Foods' profits? Explain why.

3. MANU Soccer Academy

Tom Owen came to the United States from the U.K. in 1998 on a soccer scholarship. Tom grew up playing soccer on many competitive teams through high school and had a brief professional career in England. When St. Albans College recruited him to play soccer, he thought it would open his life to a grand adventure. That adventure changed his life.

While at St. Albans, Owen met his future wife, Randy Simpson, who also played soccer there. She graduated a year ahead of him and went to Fort Collins, Colorado, where she played on the semiprofessional Fort Collins Force women's soccer team. When Owen finished college, he followed Simpson to northern Colorado. Simpson was captain of the Force and worked for the sports marketing company that owned the team.

Owen got a job at a local meat packing plant, but soccer was his passion. He made the practice squad for the Colorado Rapids Major League Soccer team, but injuries cut his professional career short. Another passion for Owen became teaching soccer to kids. He has a natural talent for coaching. Owen is charismatic, kids enjoy his easy-going demeanor and British accent, and he really knows soccer and how to teach the game to youngsters.

In 2004, Owen founded the MANU Soccer Academy—a tribute to Manchester United, his favorite team from back home. At first he trained small groups of young players aged 7 to 14. He grouped them by age, gender, and skill and conducted training sessions for small groups of five to seven at a local park. The first kids he attracted came by word of mouth as they quickly told friends and teammates about "this British guy who teaches soccer and makes it fun." His small after-school camps quickly grew to include more than 50 kids. Word continued to get around, and by the following summer Owen conducted 10 different camps—and quit his job at the meat packing plant. He also trained 11 different MANU 3v3 soccer teams that competed in tournaments across the state and nation during the summer. All of his players had bright blue jerseys with the MANU name across the front, and the success of these teams made the jerseys a great promotion vehicle. In 2006, four of his teams competed in the national 3v3 soccer tournament, with one winning a national championship.

To keep up with the rapid growth, Owen brought a few friends over from England to assist with training. Jakub Kuszczak moved to the United States to become Owen's assistant director of coaching. Owen and Kuszczak planned to work year-round as trainers and hire a couple of local coaches to help them conduct training sessions. During the summer he added a couple of local college soccer players and a few former teammates from England. The summer season works nice for his British mates, because that is the off-season for those still playing professionally. Owen is confident he can hire and train more coaches if he needs them to handle future growth.

Youth soccer is big in Colorado and across much of the United States. It is the largest participation sport for kids. Fort Collins is a soccer hotbed, and this has helped Owen's business grow. He now trains about 600 kids per year. But he has even greater ambitions. For example, he would like to build a training facility; the space he currently rents is not always well-suited to soccer. However, he figures he would need to double his business to justify the cost of the soccer complex he wants to build. So he is now wondering how to grow his business.

About 90 percent of his current customers live in Fort Collins, which has a population of about 110,000 people. Owen believes awareness of his program is close to 100 percent among competitive soccer players ages 11 to 14—and is probably at about 40 percent among families with soccer-playing kids ages 6 to 10. Most of his customers are 10 to 13 years old and enroll in two to three MANU programs per year. He has

also run a few camps in Boulder and Northglenn, which are about 50 miles from Fort Collins. These have been successful but are currently limited.

There are several small cities within 25 miles of Fort Collins. Loveland, a city of about 60,000, borders Fort Collins on the south. Greeley and Longmont, each with about 80,000 people, are about 25 miles away by interstate highway. These areas have very limited soccer training programs except for their competitive teams, and awareness of MANU is not very high. Those who have heard of his academy are often not familiar with its philosophy and programs. Owen is not sure if parents in these communities would be willing to drive their kids to Fort Collins for training. If not, he would have to run his programs there.

Owen knows that he wants to grow his business, but wonders how he can accomplish his goal. He currently sees a few options:

1. His current customer retention rate is pretty high: about 80 percent. However, when the kids reach 14 or 15 years old, other high school sports and activities make them less interested in extra soccer training. One option is to try to increase retention by developing programs targeted at kids over 14.

2. Another option is to develop a marketing strategy that would encourage his current customers to buy more. He wonders if they have other needs that he might be able to serve.

3. Owen could try to grow the business by entering new markets and acquiring new customers. His market penetration with kids 6 to 9 years old is still quite modest. He might develop new programs to better meet this group's needs.

4. Another new market option would be to serve more kids from Loveland, Longmont, and Greeley.

Evaluate Owen's different options for growing MANU's customer equity. Develop a set of marketing strategy ideas for each of the options. What could Owen do for market research to better assess his options?

4. Trusty Technology Services

Maribel Mendez is getting desperate about her new business. She's not sure she can make a go of it—and she really wants to stay in her hometown of Petoskey, Michigan, a beautiful summer resort area along the eastern shore of Lake Michigan. The area's permanent population of 10,000 more than triples in the summer months and doubles at times during the winter skiing and snowmobiling season.

Maribel spent four years in the Navy after college graduation, returning home in June 2007. When she couldn't find a good job in the Petoskey area, she decided to go into business for herself and set up Trusty Technology Services. Maribel's plan was to work by herself and basically serve as a "for hire" computer consultant and troubleshooter for her customers. She knew that many of the upscale summer residents relied on a home computer to keep in touch with business dealings and

friends at home, and it seemed that someone was always asking her for computer advice. She was optimistic that she could keep busy with a variety of on-site services—setting up a customer's new computer, repairing hardware problems, installing software or upgrades, creating a wireless network, correcting problems created by viruses, and the like.

Maribel thought that her savings would allow her to start the business without borrowing any money. Her estimates of required expenditures were: $7,000 for a used SUV; $1,125 for tools, diagnostic equipment, and reference books; $1,700 for a laptop computer, software, and accessories; $350 for an initial supply of fittings and cables; and $500 for insurance and other incidental expenses. This total of $10,675 still left Maribel with about $5,000 in savings to cover living expenses while getting started.

Maribel chose the technology services business because of her previous work experience. She worked at a computer "help desk" in college and spent her last year in the Navy trouble-shooting computer network problems. In addition, from the time Maribel was 16 years old until she finished college, she had also worked during the summer for Fletch Truman. Fletch operates the only successful computer services company in Petoskey. (There was one other local computer store that also did some on-location service work when the customer bought equipment at the store, but that store recently went out of business.)

Fletch prides himself on quality work and has been able to build up a good business with repeat customers. Specializing in services to residential, small business, and professional offices, Fletch has built a strong customer franchise. For 20 years, Fletch's major source of new business has been satisfied customers who tell friends or coworkers about his quality service. He is highly regarded as a capable person who always treats clients fairly and honestly. For example, seasonal residents often give Fletch the keys to their vacation homes so that he can do upgrades or maintenance while they are away for months at a time. Fletch's customers are so loyal, in fact, that Fix-A-Bug—a national computer service franchise—found it impossible to compete with him. Even price-cutting was not an effective weapon against Fletch.

From having worked with Fletch, Maribel thought that she knew the computer service business as well as he did; in fact, she had sometimes been able to solve technical problems that left him stumped. Maribel was anxious to reach her $60,000-per-year sales objective because she thought this would provide her with a comfortable living in Petoskey. While aware of opportunities to do computer consulting for larger businesses, Maribel felt that the sales volume available there was limited because many firms had their own computer specialists or even IT departments. As Maribel saw it, her only attractive opportunity was direct competition with Fletch.

To get started, Maribel spent $1,400 to advertise her business in the local newspaper and on an Internet website. With this money she bought two large announcement ads and 52 weeks of daily ads in the classified section, listed under "Miscellaneous Residential and Business Services." The website simply listed businesses in the Petoskey area and gave a telephone number, e-mail address, and brief description. She also listed her business under "Computer Services" at Craigslist for Northern Michigan—updating this notice and information once a month. She put magnetic sign boards on her SUV and waited for business to take off.

Maribel had a few customers, but much of the time she wasn't busy and she was able to gross only about $200 a week. Of course, she had expected much more. Many of the people who did call were regular Fletch customers who had some sort of crisis when he was already busy. While these people agreed that Maribel's work was of the same quality as Fletch's, they preferred Fletch's "quality-care" image and they liked the fact that they had an ongoing relationship with him.

Sometimes Maribel did get more work than she could handle. This happened during April and May, when seasonal businesses were preparing for summer openings and owners of summer homes and condos were ready to "open the cottage." The same rush occurred in September and October, as many of these places were being closed for the winter; those customers often wanted help backing up computer files or packing up computer equipment so they could take it with them. During these months, Maribel was able to gross about $150 to $200 a day.

Toward the end of her discouraging first year in business, Maribel Mendez is thinking about quitting. While she hates to think about leaving Petoskey, she can't see any way of making a living there with her independent technology services business. Fletch seems to dominate the market, except in the rush seasons and for people who need emergency help. And the resort market is not growing very rapidly, so there is little hope of a big influx of new businesses and homeowners to spur demand.

Evaluate Maribel Mendez's strategy planning for her new business. Why isn't she able to reach her objective of $60,000? What should Maribel do now? Explain.

5. PolyTech Products

Melissa Raymond, a chemist in PolyTech Products' resins laboratory, is trying to decide how hard to fight for the new product she has developed. Raymond's job is to find new, more profitable applications for the company's present resin products—and her current efforts are running into unexpected problems.

During the last four years, Raymond has been under heavy pressure from her managers to come up with an idea that will open up new markets for the company's foamed polystyrene.

Two years ago, Raymond developed the "foamed-dome concept"—a method of using foamed polystyrene to make dome-shaped roofs and other structures. She described the procedure for making domes as follows: The construction of a foamed dome involves the use of a specially designed machine that bends, places, and bonds pieces of plastic foam together into a predetermined dome shape. In forming a dome, the machine head is mounted on a boom, which swings around a pivot like the hands of a clock, laying and bonding layer upon layer of foam board in a rising spherical form.

According to Raymond, polystyrene foamed boards have several advantages:

1. Foam board is stiff—but can be formed or bonded to itself by heat alone.
2. Foam board is extremely lightweight and easy to handle. It has good structural rigidity.
3. Foam board has excellent and permanent insulating characteristics. (In fact, the major use for foam board is as an insulator.)
4. Foam board provides an excellent base on which to apply a variety of surface finishes, such as a readily available concrete-based stucco that is durable and inexpensive.

Using her good selling abilities, Raymond easily convinced her managers that her idea had potential.

According to a preliminary study by the marketing research department, the following were areas of construction that could be served by the domes:

1. Bulk storage.
2. Cold storage.
3. Educational construction.
4. Covers for industrial tanks.
5. Light commercial construction.
6. Planetariums.
7. Recreational construction (such as a golf-course starter house).

The marketing research study focused on uses for existing dome structures. Most of the existing domes are made of cement-based materials. The study showed that large savings would result from using foam boards, due to the reduction of construction time.

Because of the new technology involved, the company decided to do its own contracting (at least for the first four to five years). Raymond thought this was necessary to make sure that no mistakes were made by inexperienced contractor crews. (For example, if not applied properly, the plastic may burn.)

After building a few domes in the United States to demonstrate the concept, Raymond contacted some leading U.S. architects. Reactions were as follows:

"It's very interesting, but we're not sure the fire marshal of Chicago would ever give his OK."

"Your tests show that foamed domes can be protected against fires, but there are no *good* tests for unconventional building materials as far as I am concerned."

"I like the idea, but foam board does not have the impact resistance of cement."

"We design a lot of recreational facilities, and kids will find a way to poke holes in the foam."

"Building codes in our area are written for wood and cement structures. Maybe we'd be interested if the codes change."

After this unexpected reaction, management didn't know what to do. Raymond still thinks they should go ahead with the project. She wants to build several more demonstration projects in the United States and at least three each in Europe and Japan to expose the concept in the global market. She thinks architects outside the United States may be more receptive to really new ideas. Further, she says, it takes time for potential users to "see" and accept new ideas. She is sure that more exposure to more people will speed acceptance. And she is convinced that a few reports of well-constructed domes in leading trade papers and magazines will go a long way toward selling the idea. She is working on getting such reports right now. But her managers aren't sure they want to OK spending more money on "her" project. Her immediate boss is supportive, but the rest of the review board is less sure about more demonstration projects or going ahead at all—just in the United States or in global markets.

Evaluate how PolyTech Products got into the present situation. What should Melissa Raymond do? What should Raymond's managers do? Explain.

6. Global Steel Company

Global Steel Company is one of two major producers of wide-flange beams in the United States. The other producer is USX. A number of small firms also compete, but they tend to compete mainly on price in nearby markets where they can keep transport costs low. Typically, all interested competitors charge the same delivered price, which varies some depending on how far the customer is from either of the two major producers. In other words, local prices are higher in more remote geographic markets.

Wide-flange beams are one of the principal steel products used in construction. They are the modern version of what are commonly known as I-beams. USX rolls a full range of wide flanges from 6 to 36 inches. Global entered the field about 30 years ago, when it converted an existing mill to produce this product. Global's mill is limited to flanges up to 24 inches, however. At the time of the conversion, Global felt that customer usage of sizes over 24 inches was likely to be small. In recent years, however, there has been a definite trend toward the larger and heavier sections.

The beams produced by the various competitors are almost identical—since customers buy according to standard dimensional and physical-property specifications. In the smaller size range, there are a number of competitors. But above 14 inches, only USX and Global compete. Above 24 inches, USX has no competition.

All the steel companies sell these beams through their own sales forces. The customer for these beams is called a structural fabricator. This fabricator typically buys unshaped beams and other steel products from the mills and shapes them according to the specifications of each customer. The fabricator sells to the contractor or owner of the structure being built.

The structural fabricator usually must sell on a competitive-bid basis. The bidding is done on the plans and specifications prepared by an architectural or structural engineering firm and forwarded to the fabricator by the contractor who wants the bid. Although thousands of structural fabricators compete in the United States, relatively few account for the majority of wide-flange tonnage in the various geographical regions. Since the price is the same from all producers, they typically buy beams on the basis of availability (i.e., availability to meet production schedules) and performance (i.e., reliability in meeting the promised delivery schedule).

Several years ago, Global's production schedulers saw that they were going to have an excess of hot-rolled plate capacity in the near future. At the same time, development of a new production technology allowed Global to weld three plates together into a section with the same dimensional and physical properties and almost the same cross section as a rolled wide-flange beam. This development appeared to offer two key advantages to Global: (1) It would enable Global to use some of the excess plate capacity, and (2) larger sizes of wide-flange beams could be offered. Cost analysts showed that by using a fully depreciated plate mill and the new welding process it would be possible to produce and sell larger wide-flange beams at competitive prices—that is, at the same price charged by USX.

Global's managers were excited about the possibilities, because customers usually appreciate having a second source of supply. Also, the new approach would allow the production of up to a 60-inch flange. With a little imagination, these larger sizes might offer a significant breakthrough for the construction industry.

Global decided to go ahead with the new project. As the production capacity was converted, the salespeople were kept well informed of the progress. They, in turn, promoted this new capability to their customers, emphasizing that soon they would be able to offer a full range of beam products. Global sent several general information letters to a broad mailing list but did not advertise. The market development section of the sales department was very busy explaining the new possibilities of the process to fabricators at engineering trade associations and shows.

When the new production line was finally ready to go, the market reaction was disappointing. No orders came in and none were expected. In general, customers were wary of the new product. The structural fabricators felt they couldn't use it without the approval of their customers, because it would involve deviating from the specified rolled sections. And as long as they could still get the rolled section, why make the extra effort for something unfamiliar, especially with no price advantage. The salespeople were also bothered with a very common question: How can you take plate that you sell for about $460 per ton and make a product that you can sell for $470? This question came up frequently and tended to divert the whole discussion to the cost of production rather than to the way the new product might be used or its value in the construction process.

Evaluate Global's situation. What should Global do?

7. Waituiwa Lodge

Nestled in the high country of New Zealand's South Island is a getaway adventure playground aimed unashamedly at the world's very wealthy. Presidents, playboys, and other such globe-trotters are the prime targets of this fledgling tourism business developed by Waituiwa Lodge. The lodge offers this exclusive niche the opportunity of a secluded holiday in a little-known paradise. Guests, commonly under public scrutiny in their everyday lives, can escape such pressures at a hunting retreat designed specifically with their needs in mind.

A chance meeting between a New Zealand Department of Conservation investigator and the son of the former Indonesian president marked the beginning of this specialty tourist operation. Recognizing that "filthy rich" public figures are constantly surrounded by security and seldom have the luxury of going anywhere incognito, the New Zealander, Scott Baldwin, suggested that he and his new friend purchase a high-country station and hunting-guide company that was for sale. Baldwin believed that the facilities, and their secluded and peaceful environment, would make an ideal holiday haven for this elite group. His Indonesian partner concurred.

Baldwin, who was by now the company's managing director, developed a carefully tailored package of goods and services for the property. Architecturally designed accommodations, including a game trophy room and eight guest rooms, were constructed using high-quality South Island furniture and fittings, to create the ambience necessary to attract and satisfy the demands of their special clientele.

Although New Zealand had an international reputation for being sparsely populated and green, Baldwin knew that rich travelers frequently complained that local accommodations were below overseas standards. Since the price (NZ$700 a night) was not a significant variable for this target market, sumptuous guest facilities were built. These were designed to be twice the normal size of most hotel rooms, with double-glazed windows that revealed breathtaking views. Ten full-time staff and two seasonal guides were recruited to ensure that visitors received superior customized service, in fitting with the restrained opulence of the lodge.

The 28,000 hectares of original farmland that made up the retreat and backed onto the South Island's Mount Cook National Park were converted into a big-game reserve. All merino sheep on the land were sold, and deer, elk, chamois, and wapiti were brought in and released. This was a carefully considered plan. Baldwin, the former conservationist, believed that financially and environmentally this was the correct decision. Not only do tourists, each staying for one week and taking part in safari shooting, inject as much cash into the business as the station's annual wool clip used to fetch, but the game does less harm to the environment than sheep. Cattle, however, once part of the original station, were left to graze on lower river-flat areas.

For those high-flying customers seeking less bloodthirsty leisure activities, Waituiwa developed photographic "safaris" and other product-line extensions. Horse-trekking, golfing on a nearby rural course (with no need for hordes of security forces), helicopter trips around nearby Lake Tekapo, nature walks, and other such activities formed part of the exclusive package.

While still in the early stages of operation, this retreat has already attracted a steady stream of visitors. To date, the manager has relied solely on positive word of mouth, publicity, and public relations to draw in new customers. Given the social and business circles in which his potential target market moves, Baldwin considers these to be the most appropriate forms of marketing communication. The only real concern for Waituiwa Lodge has been the criticism of at least one New Zealand lobby group that the company is yet another example of local land passing into "foreign" hands, and that New

Zealanders are prevented from using the retreat and excluded from its financial returns. However, this unwelcome attention has been fairly short-lived.

Identify the likely characteristics of the market segment being targeted by the company. Why are most target customers likely to be foreigners rather than New Zealanders? Suggest what expectations target customers are likely to have regarding the quality, reliability, and range of services. What are the implications for Waituiwa Lodge? How difficult is it for Waituiwa Lodge to undertake market research? Elaborate.

8. Lombardi's Italian Grill

Monica Lombardi, the owner and manager of Lombardi's Italian Grill, is reviewing the slow growth of her restaurant. She's also thinking about the future and wondering if she should change her strategy. In particular, she is wondering if she should join a fast-food or family restaurant franchise chain. Several are located near her, but there are many franchisors without local restaurants. After doing some research on the Internet, she has learned that with help from the franchisors, some of these places gross $500,000 to $1 million a year. Of course, she would have to follow someone else's strategy and thereby lose her independence, which she doesn't like to think about. But those sales figures do sound good, and she has also heard that the return to the owner-manager (including salary) can be over $150,000 per year. She has also considered putting a Web page for Lombardi's Italian Grill on the Internet but is not sure how that will help.

Lombardi's Italian Grill is a fairly large restaurant—about 3,000 square feet—located in the center of a small shopping center completed early in 2005. Lombardi's sells mainly full-course "home-cooked" Italian-style dinners (no bar) at moderate prices. In addition to Lombardi's restaurant, other businesses in the shopping center include a supermarket, a hair salon, a liquor store, a video rental store, and a vacant space that used to be a hardware store. The hardware store failed when a Home Depot located nearby. Monica has learned that a pizzeria is considering locating there soon. She wonders how that competition will affect her. Ample parking space is available at the shopping center, which is located in a residential section of a growing suburb in the East, along a heavily traveled major traffic route.

Monica graduated from a local high school and a nearby university and has lived in this town with her husband and two children for many years. She has been self-employed in the restaurant business since her graduation from college in 1988. Her most recent venture before opening Lombardi's was a large restaurant that she operated successfully with her brother from 1996 to 2002. In 2002, Monica sold out her share because of illness. Following her recovery, she was anxious for something to do and opened the present restaurant in April 2005. Monica feels her plans for the business and her opening were well thought out. When she was ready to start her new restaurant, she looked at several possible locations before finally deciding on the present one. Monica explained: "I looked everywhere, but here I particularly noticed the heavy traffic when I first looked at it. This is the crossroads for three major interstate highways. So obviously the potential is here."

Having decided on the location, Monica signed a 10-year lease with option to renew for 10 more years, and then eagerly attacked the problem of outfitting the almost empty store space in the newly constructed building. She tiled the floor, put in walls of surfwood, installed plumbing and electrical fixtures and an extra washroom, and purchased the necessary restaurant equipment. All this cost $120,000—which came from her own cash savings. She then spent an additional $1,500 for glassware, $2,000 for an initial food stock, and $2,125 to advertise Lombardi's Italian Grill's opening in the local newspaper. The paper serves the whole metro area, so the $2,125 bought only three quarterpage ads. These expenditures also came from her personal savings. Next she hired five waitresses at $275 a week and one chef at $550 a week. Then, with a $24,000 cash reserve for the business, she was ready to open. Reflecting her sound business sense, Monica knew she would need a substantial cash reserve to fall back on until the business got on its feet. She expected this to take about one year. She had no expectations of getting rich overnight. (Her husband, a high school teacher, was willing to support the family until the restaurant caught on.)

The restaurant opened in April and by August had a weekly gross revenue of only $2,400. Monica was a little discouraged with this, but she was still able to meet all her operating expenses without investing any new money in the business. By September business was still slow, and Monica had to invest an additional $3,000 in the business just to survive.

Business had not improved in November, and Monica stepped up her advertising—hoping this would help. In December, she spent $1,200 of her cash reserve for radio advertising—10 late-evening spots on a news program at a station that aims at middle-income America. Monica also spent $1,600 more during the next several weeks for some metro newspaper ads.

By April 2006, the situation had begun to improve, and by June her weekly gross was up to between $3,100 and $3,300. By March 2007, the weekly gross had risen to about $4,200. Monica increased the working hours of her staff six to seven hours a week and added another cook to handle the increasing number of customers. Monica was more optimistic for the future because she was finally doing a little better than breaking even. Her full-time involvement seemed to be paying off. She had not put any new money into the business since summer 2006 and expected business to continue to rise. She had not yet taken any salary for herself, even though she had built up a small surplus of about $9,000. Instead, she planned to put in a bigger air-conditioning system at a cost of $5,000 and was also planning to use what salary she might have taken for herself to hire two new waitresses to handle the growing volume of business. And she saw that if business increased much more she would have to add another cook.

Evaluate Monica's past and present marketing strategy. What should she do now? Should she seriously consider joining some franchise chain?

9. Sweetest Dreams Inn

Mai Phan is trying to decide whether he should make some minor changes in the way he operates his Sweetest Dreams Inn motel or if he should join either the Days Inn or Holiday Inn motel chains. Some decision must be made soon because his present operation is losing money. But joining either of the chains will require fairly substantial changes, including new capital investment if he goes with Holiday Inn.

Phan bought the recently completed 60-room motel two years ago after leaving a successful career as a production manager for a large producer of industrial machinery. He was looking for an interesting opportunity that would be less demanding than the production manager job. The Sweetest Dreams Inn is located at the edge of a very small town near a rapidly expanding resort area and about one-half mile off an interstate highway. It is 10 miles from the tourist area, with several nationally franchised full-service resort motels suitable for "destination" vacations. There is a Best Western, a Ramada Inn, and a Hilton Inn, as well as many mom-and-pop and limited-service, lower-priced motels—and some quaint bed-and-breakfast facilities—in the tourist area. The interstate highway near the Sweetest Dreams Inn carries a great deal of traffic, since the resort area is between several major metropolitan areas. No development has taken place around the turnoff from the interstate highway. The only promotion for the tourist area along the interstate highway is two large signs near the turnoffs. They show the popular name for the area and that the area is only 10 miles to the west. These signs are maintained by the tourist area's Tourist Bureau. In addition, the state transportation department maintains several small signs showing (by symbols) that near this turnoff one can find gas, food, and lodging. Phan does not have any signs advertising Sweetest Dreams Inn except the two on his property. He has been relying on people finding his motel as they go toward the resort area.

Initially, Phan was very pleased with his purchase. He had traveled a lot himself and stayed in many different hotels and motels—so he had some definite ideas about what travelers wanted. He felt that a relatively plain but modern room with a comfortable bed, standard bath facilities, and free cable TV would appeal to most customers. Further, Phan thought a swimming pool or any other nonrevenue-producing additions were not necessary. And he felt a restaurant would be a greater management problem than the benefits it would offer. However, after many customers commented about the lack of convenient breakfast facilities, Phan served a free continental breakfast of coffee, juice, and rolls in a room next to the registration desk.

Day-to-day operations went fairly smoothly in the first two years, in part because Phan and his wife handled registration and office duties as well as general management. During the first year of operation, occupancy began to stabilize around 55 percent of capacity. But according to industry figures, this was far below the average of 68 percent for his classification—motels without restaurants.

After two years of operation, Phan was concerned because his occupancy rates continued to be below average. He decided to look for ways to increase both occupancy rate and profitability and still maintain his independence.

Phan wanted to avoid direct competition with the full-service resort motels. He stressed a price appeal in his signs and brochures and was quite proud of the fact that he had been able to avoid all the "unnecessary expenses" of the full-service resort motels. As a result, Phan was able to offer lodging at a very modest price—about 40 percent below the full-service hotels and comparable to the lowest-priced resort area motels. The customers who stayed at Sweetest Dreams Inn said they found it quite acceptable. But he was troubled by what seemed to be a large number of people driving into his parking lot, looking around, and not coming in to register.

Phan was particularly interested in the results of a recent study by the regional tourist bureau. This study revealed the following information about area vacationers:

1. 68 percent of the visitors to the area are young couples and older couples without children.
2. 40 percent of the visitors plan their vacations and reserve rooms more than 60 days in advance.
3. 66 percent of the visitors stay more than three days in the area and at the same location.
4. 78 percent of the visitors indicated that recreational facilities were important in their choice of accommodations.
5. 13 percent of the visitors had family incomes of less than $27,000 per year.
6. 38 percent of the visitors indicated that it was their first visit to the area.

After much thought, Phan began to seriously consider affiliating with a national motel chain in hopes of attracting more customers and maybe protecting his motel from the increasing competition. There were constant rumors that more motels were being planned for the area. After some investigating, he focused on two national chain possibilities: Days Inn and Holiday Inn. Neither had affiliates in the area even though they each have about 2,000 units nationwide.

Days Inn of America, Inc., is an Atlanta-based chain of economy lodgings. It has been growing rapidly and is willing to take on new franchisees. A major advantage of Days Inn is that it would not require a major capital investment by Phan. The firm is targeting people interested in lower-priced motels, in particular, senior citizens, the military, school sports teams, educators, and business travelers. In contrast, Holiday Inn would probably require Phan to upgrade some of his facilities, including adding a swimming pool. The total new capital investment would be between $300,000 and $500,000, depending on how fancy he got. But then Phan would be able to charge higher prices, perhaps $75 per day on the average rather than the $45 per day per room he's charging now.

The major advantages of going with either of these national chains would be their central reservation systems and their national names. Both companies offer nationwide, toll-free reservation lines, which produce about 40 percent of all bookings in affiliated motels. Both companies also offer websites (www.daysinn.com and www.holidayinn.com) that help find a specific hotel by destination, rate, amenities, quality rating, and availability.

A major difference between the two national chains is their method of promotion. Days Inn uses little TV advertising and less print advertising than Holiday Inn. Instead, Days Inn emphasizes sales promotions. In one campaign, for example, Blue Bonnet margarine users could exchange proof-of-purchase seals for a free night at a Days Inn. This tie-in led to the Days Inn system *selling* an additional 10,000 rooms. Further, Days Inn operates a September Days Club for travelers 50 and over who receive such benefits as discount rates and a quarterly travel magazine.

Days Inn also has other membership programs, including its InnCentives loyalty club for frequent business and leisure travelers. Other programs targeted to business travelers include two Corporate Rate programs and its new Days Business Place hotels. Not to be outdone, Holiday Inn has a membership program called Priority Club Worldwide.

Both firms charge 8 percent of gross room revenues for belonging to their chain—to cover the costs of the reservation service and national promotion. This amount is payable monthly. In addition, franchise members must agree to maintain their facilities and make repairs and improvements as required. Failure to maintain facilities can result in losing the franchise. Periodic inspections are conducted as part of supervising the whole chain and helping the members operate more effectively.

Evaluate Mai Phan's present strategy. What should he do? Explain.

10. Taffe's Ice Land

Ty Taffe, the manager of Taffe's Ice Land, is trying to decide what strategies to use to increase profits.

Taffe's Ice Land is an ice-skating rink with a conventional hockey rink surface (85 feet × 200 feet). It is the only indoor ice rink in a northern U.S. city of about 450,000. The city's recreation department operates some outdoor rinks in the winter, but they don't offer regular ice skating programs because of weather variability.

Ty runs a successful hockey program that is more than breaking even—but this is about all he can expect if he only offers hockey. To try to increase his profits, Ty is trying to expand and improve his public skating program. With such a program, he could have as many as 700 people in a public session at one time, instead of limiting the use of the ice to 12 to 24 hockey players per hour. While the receipts from hockey can be as high as $200 an hour (plus concession sales), the receipts from a two-hour public skating session—charging $5 per person— could yield up to $3,500 for a two-hour period (plus much higher concession sales). The potential revenue from such large public skating sessions could make Taffe's Ice Land a really profitable operation. But, unfortunately, just scheduling public sessions doesn't mean that a large number will come. In fact, only a few prime times seem likely: Friday and Saturday evenings and Saturday and Sunday afternoons.

Ty has included 14 public skating sessions in his ice schedule, but so far they haven't attracted as many people as he hoped. In total, they only generate a little more revenue than if the times were sold for hockey use. Offsetting this extra revenue are extra costs. More staff people are needed to handle a public skating session—guards, a ticket seller, skate rental, and more concession help. So the net revenue from either use is about the same. He could cancel some of the less attractive public sessions—like the noon-time daily sessions, which have very low attendance—and make the average attendance figures look a lot better. But he feels that if he is going to offer public skating he must have a reasonable selection of times. He does recognize, however, that the different public skating sessions do seem to attract different people and really different kinds of people.

The Saturday and Sunday afternoon public skating sessions have been the most successful, with an average of 200 people attending during the winter season. Typically, this is a "kidsitting" session. More than half of the patrons are young children who have been dropped off by their parents for several hours, but there are also some family groups.

In general, the kids and the families have a good time—and a fairly loyal group comes every Saturday and/or Sunday during the winter season. In the spring and fall, however, attendance drops about in half, depending on how nice the weather is. (Ty schedules no public sessions in the summer, focusing instead on hockey clinics and figure skating.)

The Friday and Saturday evening public sessions are a big disappointment. The sessions run from 8 until 10, a time when he had hoped to attract teenagers and young adult couples. At $5 per person, plus $1.50 for skate rental, this would be an economical date. In fact, Ty has seen quite a few young couples—and some keep coming back. But he also sees a surprising number of 8- to 14-year-olds who have been dropped off by their parents. The younger kids tend to race around the rink playing tag. This affects the whole atmosphere, making it less appealing for dating couples and older patrons.

Ty has been hoping to develop a teenage and young-adult market for a "social activity," adapting the format used by roller-skating rinks. Their public skating sessions feature a variety of couples-only and group games as well as individual skating to dance music. Turning ice-skating sessions into such social activities is not common, however, although industry newsletters suggest that a few ice-rink operators have had success with the roller-skating format. Seemingly, the ice-skating sessions are viewed as active recreation, offering exercise or a sports experience.

Ty installed some soft lights to try to change the evening atmosphere. The music was selected to encourage people to skate to the beat and couples to skate together. Some people complained about the "old" music; but it was "danceable," and some skaters really liked it. For a few sessions, Ty even tried to have some couples-only skates. The couples liked it, but this format was strongly resisted by the young boys who felt that they had paid their money and there was no reason why they should be kicked off the ice. Ty also tried to attract more young people and especially couples by bringing in a local rock radio station disk jockey to broadcast from Taffe's Ice Land—playing music and advertising the Friday and Saturday evening public sessions. Taffe's son even set up Facebook and MySpace pages for Taffe's, but only a few people joined the groups. All of this appeared to have no effect on attendance, which varies from 50 to 100 per two-hour session during the winter.

Ty seriously considered the possibility of limiting the Friday and Saturday evening sessions to people age 14 and over—to try to change the environment. He knew it would take time to change people's attitudes. But when he counted the customers, he realized this would be risky. More than a quarter of his customers on an average weekend night appear to be 13 or under. This means that he would have to make a serious commitment to building the teen and young-adult market. And, so far, his efforts haven't been successful. He has already invested over $3,000 in lighting changes and over $9,000 promoting the ses-

sions over the rock music radio station, with very disappointing results. Although the station's sales rep said the station reached teenagers all over town, an on-air offer for a free skating session did not get a single response!

Some days, Ty feels it's hopeless. Maybe he should accept that most public ice-skating sessions are a mixed bag. Or maybe he should just sell the time to hockey groups. Still he keeps hoping that something can be done to improve weekend evening public skating attendance, because the upside potential is so good. And the Saturday and Sunday afternoon sessions are pretty good money-makers.

Evaluate Taffe's Ice Land's situation. What should Ty Taffe do? Why?

11. The Next Step

Libby Nickerson, owner of The Next Step, is trying to decide what she should do with her retail business and how committed she should be to her current target market.

Libby is 42 years old, and she started her The Next Step retail store in 1990 when she was only 24 years old. She was a nationally ranked runner herself and felt that the growing interest in jogging offered real potential for a store that provided serious runners with the shoes and advice they needed. The jogging boom quickly turned The Next Step into a profitable business selling high-end running shoes—and Libby made a very good return on her investment for the first 10 years. From 1990 until 2000, Libby emphasized Nike shoes, which were well accepted and seen as top quality. Nike's aggressive promotion and quality shoes resulted in a positive image that made it possible to get a $5 to $7 per pair premium for Nike shoes. Good volume and good margins resulted in attractive profits for Libby.

Committing so heavily to Nike seemed like a good idea when its marketing and engineering was the best available. In addition to running shoes, Nike had other athletic shoes Libby could sell. So even though they were not her primary focus, Libby did stock other Nike shoes including walking shoes, shoes for aerobic exercise, basketball shoes, tennis shoes, and cross-trainers. She also added more sportswear to her store and put more emphasis on fashion rather than just function.

Even with this broadened product line, Libby's sales flattened out—and she wasn't sure what to do to get her business back in growth mode. She realized that she was growing older and so were many of her longer-term customers. Many of them were finding that jogging isn't just hard work—it's hard on the body, especially the knees. So, many of her previously loyal runner-customers were switching to other, less demanding exercise programs. However, when she tried to orient her store and product line more toward these people she wasn't as effective in serving the needs of serious runners—still an important source of sales for the store.

She was also facing more competition on all fronts. Many consumers who don't really do any serious exercise buy running shoes as their day-to-day casual shoes. As a result, many department stores, discount stores, and regular shoe stores have put more and more emphasis on athletic shoes in their product assortment. When Libby added other brands and put

more emphasis on fashion, she found that she was in direct competition with a number of other stores, which put more pressure on her to lower prices and cut her profit margins. For example, in Libby's area there are a number of local and online retail chains offering lower-cost and lower-quality versions of similar shoes as well as related fashion apparel. Wal-Mart also expanded its assortment of athletic shoes—and it offers rock-bottom prices. Other chains, like Foot Locker, have focused their promotion and product lines on specific target markets. Still, all of them (including Libby's The Next Step, the local chains, Wal-Mart, and Foot Locker) are scrambling to catch up with rival category killers whose selections are immense.

In the spring of 2006 Libby tried an experiment. She took on a line of high-performance athletic shoes that were made to order. The distinctive feature of these shoes was that the sole was molded to precisely fit the customer's foot. A pair of these custom-made shoes cost about $170, so the market was not large. Further, Libby didn't put much promotional emphasis on this line. However, when a customer came in the store with a serious interest in high-performance shoes, Libby's sales clerks would tell them about the custom shoe alternative and show a sample. When a customer was interested, a mold of the customer's bare foot was made at the store, using an innovative material that hardened in just a few minutes without leaving a sticky mess. Libby sent the mold off to the manufacturer by UPS, and about two weeks later the finished shoes arrived. Customers who tried these shoes were delighted with the result. However, the company that offered them ran into financial trouble and went out of business.

Libby recently learned about another company that is offering a very similar custom shoe program. However, that company requires more promotion investment by retailers and in return provides exclusive sales territories. Another requirement is that the store establish a website promoting the shoes and providing more detail on how the order process works. The Next Step had a pretty basic website, so Libby knew she would have to spend some money to make this happen. All of a retailer's salesclerks are also required to go through a special two-day training program so that they know how to present the benefits of the shoe and do the best job creating the molds. The training program is free, but Libby would have to pay travel, hotel, and food expenses for her salespeople. So before even getting started, the new program would cost her several thousand dollars.

Libby is uncertain about what to do. Although sales have dropped, she is still making a reasonable profit and has a relatively good base of repeat customers, with the serious runners still more than half of her sales and profits. She thinks that the custom shoe alternative is a way to differentiate her store from the mass-merchandisers and to sharpen her focus on the target market of serious runners. On the other hand, that doesn't really solve the problem that the "runners" market seems to be shrinking. It also doesn't address the question of how best to keep a lot of the aging customers she already serves who seem to be shifting away from an emphasis on running. She also worries that she'll lose the loyalty of her repeat customers if she shifts the store further away from her running niche and more toward fashionable athletic shoes or fashionable casual wear. Yet athletic wear—women's, in particular—has come a long way in recent years. Designers like Donna Karan, Calvin Klein, Georgio Armani, and Ralph Lauren are part of the fast-growing women's wear business.

So Libby is trying to decide if there is anything else she can do to better promote her current store and product line, or if she should think about changing her strategy in a more dramatic way. Any change from her current focus would involve retraining her current salespeople and perhaps hiring new salespeople. Adding and maintaining a website isn't an insurmountable challenge, but it is not an area where she has either previous experience or skill.

Clearly, a real shift in emphasis would require that Libby make some hard decisions about her target market and her whole marketing mix. She's got some flexibility—it's not like she's a manufacturer of shoes with a big investment in a factory that can't be changed. On the other hand, she's not certain she's ready for a big change, especially a change that would mean starting over again from scratch. She started The Next Step because she was interested in running and felt she had something special to offer. Now she worries that she's just grasping at straws without a real focus or any obvious competitive advantage. She also knows that she is already much more successful than she ever dreamed when she started her business—and in her heart she wonders if she wasn't just spoiled by growth that came fast and easy at the start.

Evaluate Libby Nickerson's present strategy. Evaluate the alternative strategies she is considering. Is her primary problem her emphasis on running shoes, her emphasis on trying to hang on to her current customers, or is it something else? What should she do? Why?

12. DrRay.com—Custom Vitamins and Supplements

Dr. Ray Nielsen has to decide how to handle a complaint letter from a customer. When he received the letter, he passed it along to Jaime Gonzalez, the firm's customer service manager, to get his recommendation. Now Nielsen has a reply from Gonzalez, and he must decide how to respond to the customer and determine if changes are needed in his company's customer service operations.

Dr. Nielsen has a reputation as a health and nutrition guru. His fame grew after he published two books—both of which were very popular and received a lot of attention in the press. Five years ago, Internet entrepreneur Trisha Benson approached him with the idea of creating a website to sell custom vitamins under Dr. Ray's name.

Nielsen and Benson became partners, and the business enjoyed success in its first four years of operation. Benson handles the website technology, inventory, production, and shipping. Dr. Nielsen is the health expert, creates content provided on the website, and is in charge of marketing and customer service.

The complaint letter and reply from Gonzalez follow:

Dear Dr. Nielsen,

I am a longtime fan of your books and like to visit your website for health tips. As a new grandmother, my health is even more important to me. I want to see my grandchildren graduate from high school, go to college, and have kids of their own.

You have made me a bit of a guru as well. I work out every day. People always ask me how I stay so fit and healthy. Having read both your books, I tell them they should exercise regularly and take vitamins and supplements for long-term health. I always recommend your DrRay.com website and especially the section on your custom vitamins. That is my favorite part of your website. I really like that you take information about me and my medical history—and then recommend custom vitamins and supplements. I also like how you send me packages that each contains a daily dose.

But after my recent experiences, my loyalty to you and your company are now in jeopardy. Here is my story.

Six months ago, I went to the website to reorder my vitamins and supplements. The home page announced a new and improved health survey and custom health program. So, I went through the survey and filled out all the details—it would have been nice if you had saved some of them from my previous survey. At the end of the survey the website offered me a 90-day supply of a custom set of vitamins and supplements selected for my specific needs. The $212 price was about $50 more than my previous 90-day supply, but I trusted your advice so I placed the order.

About two-and-a-half months later, I phoned DrRay.com to place a refill order. The person on the phone was very nice and asked if I wanted to set up automatic refills. I said no because I hate those automatic programs. They remind me of those book clubs that automatically send you books you don't want if you do not reply fast enough. About a week later my order arrived—then two days later another identical order arrived. I did not understand this, but I figured I would eventually use them up and I kept everything (and I was billed for both orders—$424 on my credit card). I should mention there was no e-mail explaining this mystery delivery. I was a little annoyed and sent an e-mail to customer service seeking an explanation. I received an automated response, "Thank you for your inquiry, someone will get back to you within 24 hours." No one ever replied, but I forgot about it.

Then two weeks ago I received an e-mail from DrRay.com telling me my refill order had been shipped and would arrive in a few days. But I did not place a refill order! I did not even need more vitamins because I was still working off the two 90-day supplies that I received three months ago. So I replied by e-mail that I did not want the order and to cancel it. A reply e-mail (from Clara) told me that I had signed up for automatic refill six months ago. I replied that I certainly had not and that I would not pay for the order that was being sent.

A few days later I received a call from Jaime Gonzalez, your director of customer service. He told me that I had originally signed up for automatic refill and that was why I received vitamins. I told him that was impossible, and he told me that unless I checked some box on my original order that this was done automatically, "for my convenience." He said there were also several warnings and that I must have missed those. *Basically, I think he told me this was my fault. I did not like that one bit!!!* Mr. Gonzalez told me the vitamins were on their way, but I could refuse delivery of them. He offered to let me have them for 20 percent off if I simply kept them. Unfortunately, the vitamins were on my doorstep when I arrived home that day. I had to take the vitamins to UPS to get them shipped back to you.

You guys are no longer very good at your business. You might have a great product, but I am now seeing other vitamin companies offering the same products. I have no doubt these other companies offer better customer service. If you want me back as a customer, I would expect a formal apology from Mr. Gonzalez and a free 90-day supply. Otherwise, I figure my business will be welcomed at one of your competitors—and I will be sure all my friends know about my experience at DrRay.com. And I will post a bad review at resellerratings.com, too.

Sincerely,

Joan Holliday

Below is the reply that Jaime Gonzalez sent to Dr. Nielsen concerning Joan Holliday's letter.

Dear Ray,

As per your request, I reviewed Mrs. Holliday's order history. Yes, she is a very good customer who spent almost $800 with us last year. And she is a member of our referral program—and we can count at least seven new customers she has directed to us in the last 18 months.

But I want to clarify some of this particular situation.

- You might recall that our automatic refill program has been a big success. Since we instituted the program a year ago, our customer retention rate has jumped by 10 percent. There are occasional complaints, but given the large number of customers we serve, the complaints are really just a "drop in the bucket."
- When Mrs. Holliday placed her order six months ago there were at least two different warnings about the automatic refill program—customers have to check a box at the bottom of the screen to "opt out" of the program. We all agreed that it was better to make them part of the program automatically, but to give them two chances to remove themselves from automatic delivery.
- I do not know if we replied to her e-mail asking for customer service help.
- I did not tell Mrs. Holliday that this was her fault, but I did tell her that when she signed up there were two chances for her to choose to not be part of the automatic refill program.
- Mrs. Holliday did not get an e-mail notifying her of the first refill order because that system was not yet in place. But this has now been fixed, and the e-mail notifying her when we ship shows that this works.
- I offered her 20 percent off as is our standard policy when we make a mistake. Considering this was her mistake, I thought this was generous.
- If Mrs. Holliday had called and asked, I could have had UPS come out and pick up the package for return to us.

I do not recommend giving her a free 90-day supply. This may simply encourage her to complain again in the future. Besides, this was not our mistake. We may be better off without certain customers—and I think Mrs. Holliday falls into this category.

Feel free to call me if you have any more questions.

Jaime

Assess the customer service operations at DrRay.com. What should Nielsen do about Mrs. Holliday? What changes, if any, should Nielsen make to customer service and ordering operations?

13. File-It Supplies, Inc.*

Patsy Akaka, marketing manager for File-It Supplies, Inc. (FIS), must decide whether she should permit her largest customer to buy some of FIS's commonly used file folders under the customer's brand rather than FIS's own FILEX brand. She is afraid that if she refuses, this customer—Business Center, Inc.—will go to another file folder producer and FIS will lose this business.

---

*Adapted from a case by Professor Hardy, University of Western Ontario.

Business Center, Inc., is a major distributor of office supplies and has already managed to put its own brand on more than 45 high-sales-volume office supply products. It distributes these products—as well as the branded products of many manufacturers—through its nationwide distribution network, which includes 150 retail stores. Now Darrell Manning, vice president of marketing for Business Center, is seeking a line of file folders similar in quality to FIS's FILEX brand, which now has over 60 percent of the market.

This is not the first time that Business Center has asked FIS to produce a file folder line for Business Center. On both previous occasions, Patsy turned down the requests and Business Center continued to buy. In fact, Business Center not only continued to buy the file folders but also the rest of FIS's product lines. And total sales continued to grow as Business Center built new stores. Business Center accounts for about 30 percent of Patsy Akaka's business. And FILEX brand file folders account for about 35 percent of this volume.

In the past FIS consistently refused such dealer-branding requests as a matter of corporate policy. This policy was set some years ago because of a desire (1) to avoid excessive dependence on any one customer and (2) to sell its own brands so that its success is dependent on the quality of its products rather than just a low price. The policy developed from a concern that if it started making products under other customers' brands, those customers could shop around for a low price and the business would be very fickle. At the time the policy was set, Patsy realized that it might cost FIS some business. But it was felt wise, nevertheless, to be better able to control the firm's future.

FIS has been in business 28 years and now has a sales volume of $40 million. Its primary products are file folders, file markers and labels, and a variety of indexing systems. FIS offers such a wide range of size, color, and type that no competitor can match it in its part of the market. About 40 percent of FIS's file folder business is in specialized lines such as files for oversized blueprint and engineer drawings; see-through files for medical markets; and greaseproof and waterproof files for marine, oil field, and other hazardous environmental markets. FIS's competitors are mostly small paper converters. But excess capacity in the industry is substantial, and these converters are always hungry for orders and willing to cut prices. Further, the raw materials for the FILEX line of file folders are readily available.

FIS's distribution system consists of 10 regional stationery suppliers (40 percent of total sales), Business Center, Inc. (30 percent), and more than 40 local stationers who have wholesale and retail operations (30 percent). The 10 regional stationers each have about six branches, while the local stationers each have one wholesale and three or four retail locations. The regional suppliers sell directly to large corporations and to some retailers. In contrast, Business Center's main volume comes from sales to local businesses and walk-in customers at its 150 retail stores.

Patsy has a real concern about the future of the local stationers' business. Some are seriously discussing the formation of buying groups to obtain volume discounts from vendors and thus compete more effectively with Business Center's 150 retail stores, the large regionals, and the superstore chains, which are spreading rapidly. These chains—for example, Staples, Office World, Office Max, and Office Depot—operate stores of 16,000 to 20,000 square feet (i.e., large stores compared to the usual office supply stores) and let customers wheel through high-stacked shelves to supermarket-like checkout counters. These chains stress convenience, wide selection, and much lower prices than the typical office supply retailers. They buy directly from manufacturers, such as FIS, bypassing wholesalers like Business Center. It is likely that the growing pressure from these chains is causing Business Center to renew its proposal to buy a file line with its own name. For example, Staples offers its own dealer brand of files and many other types of products.

None of Patsy's other accounts is nearly as effective in retailing as Business Center, which has developed a good reputation in every major city in the country. Business Center's profits have been the highest in the industry. Further, its brands are almost as well known as those of some key producers—and its expansion plans are aggressive. And now, these plans are being pressured by the fast-growing superstores, which are already knocking out many local stationers.

Patsy is sure that FIS's brands are well entrenched in the market, despite the fact that most available money has been devoted to new-product development rather than promotion of existing brands. But Patsy is concerned that if Business Center brands its own file folders it will sell them at a discount and may even bring the whole market price level down. Across all the lines of file folders, Patsy is averaging a 35 percent gross margin, but the commonly used file folders sought by Business Center are averaging only a 20 percent gross margin. And cutting this margin further does not look very attractive to Patsy.

Patsy is not sure whether Business Center will continue to sell FIS's FILEX brand of folders along with Business Center's own file folders if Business Center is able to find a source of supply. Business Center's history has been to sell its own brand and a major brand side by side, especially if the major brand offers high quality and has strong brand recognition.

Patsy is having a really hard time deciding what to do about the existing branding policy. FIS has excess capacity and could easily handle the Business Center business. And she fears that if she turns down this business, Business Center will just go elsewhere and its own brand will cut into FIS's existing sales at Business Center stores. Further, what makes Business Center's offer especially attractive is that FIS's variable manufacturing costs would be quite low in relation to any price charged to Business Center—that is, there are substantial economies of scale, so the extra business could be very profitable—if Patsy doesn't consider the possible impact on the FILEX line. This Business Center business will be easy to get, but it will require a major change in policy, which Patsy will have to sell to Ramon Torres, FIS's president. This may not be easy. Ramon is primarily interested in developing new and better products so the company can avoid the "commodity end of the business."

Evaluate FIS's current strategy. What should Patsy Akaka do about Business Center's offer? Explain.

14. Express Multimedia

Seth Greenberg, manager of Express Multimedia, is looking for ways to increase profits. But he's turning cautious after the poor results of his last effort, during the previous Christmas season. Express Multimedia (EM) is located along a busy crosstown street about two miles from the downtown of a metropolitan area of 1 million and near a large university. It sells a wide variety of products used for its different types of multimedia presentations. Its lines include high-quality video and digital cameras, color scanners for use with computers, flat-panel monitors, teleprompters and projection equipment, including video-beam overhead projectors, and electronic projectors that produce large-screen versions of computer output. Most of the sales of this specialized equipment are made to area school boards for classroom use, to industry for use in research and sales, and to the university for use in research and instruction.

Express Multimedia also offers a good selection of production-quality video media, specialized supplies (such as the large-format acetates used with backlit signs), video and audio editing equipment, and a specialized video editing service. Instead of just duplicating videos on a mass production basis, Express Multimedia gives each video editing job individual attention—to add an audio track or incorporate computer graphics as requested by a customer. This service is really appreciated by local firms that need help producing high-quality DVDs—for example, for training or sales applications.

To encourage the school and industrial trade, Express Multimedia offers a graphics consultation service. If a customer wants to create a video or computerized presentation, professional advice is readily available. In support of this free service, Express Multimedia carries a full line of computer software for multimedia presentations and graphics work.

Express Multimedia has four full-time store clerks and two outside sales reps. The sales reps call on business firms, attend trade shows, make presentations for schools, and help both current and potential customers in their use and choice of multimedia materials. Most purchases are delivered by the sales reps or the store's delivery truck. Many repeat orders come in by phone or mail, but e-mail and electronic file exchange have become common.

The people who make most of the over-the-counter purchases are (1) serious amateurs and (2) some professionals who prepare videos or computerized presentation materials on a fee basis. Express Multimedia gives price discounts of up to 25 percent off the suggested retail price to customers who buy more than $2,000 worth of goods per year. Most regular customers qualify for the discount.

In recent years, many amateur photo buffs have purchased digital cameras to capture family pictures. Frequently, the buyer is a computer user who wants to use the computer as a digital darkroom—and the cameras now available make this easy. Express Multimedia has not previously offered the lower-priced and lower-quality digital models such buyers commonly want. But Seth knew that lots of such digital cameras were bought and felt that there ought to be a good opportunity to expand sales during the Christmas gift-giving season. Therefore, he planned a special pre-Christmas sale of two of the most popular brands of digital cameras and discounted the prices to competitive discount store levels—about $129 for one and $189 for the other. To promote the sale, he posted large signs in the store windows and ran ads in a Christmas gift-suggestion edition of the local newspaper. This edition appeared each Wednesday during the four weeks before Christmas. At these prices and with this promotion, Seth hoped to sell at least 100 cameras. However, when the Christmas returns were in, total sales were five cameras. Seth was extremely disappointed with these results—especially because trade experts suggested that sales of digital cameras in those price and quality ranges were up 300 percent over last year—during the Christmas selling season.

Evaluate what Express Multimedia is doing and what happened with the special promotion. What should Seth Greenberg do to increase sales and profits?

15. The Trujillo Group

Carla Trujillo, owner of The Trujillo Group, is deciding whether to take on a new line. She is very concerned, because although she wants more lines she feels that something is wrong with her latest possibility.

Carla graduated from a large midwestern university in 2004 with a B.S. in business. She worked selling cell phones for a year. Then Carla decided to go into business for herself and formed The Trujillo Group. Looking for opportunities, Carla placed several ads in her local newspaper in Columbus, Ohio, announcing that she was interested in becoming a sales representative in the area. She was quite pleased to receive a number of responses. Eventually, she became the sales representative in the Columbus area for three local computer software producers: Accto Company, which produces accounting-related software; Saleco, Inc., a producer of sales management software; and Invo, Inc., a producer of inventory control software. All of these companies were relatively small and were represented in other areas by other sales representatives like Carla. The companies often sent her leads when customers from her area expressed interest at a trade show or through the company's website.

Carla's main job was to call on possible customers. Once she made a sale, she would fax the signed license agreement to the respective producer, who would then UPS the programs directly to the customer or provide a key code for a website download. The producer would bill the customer, and Carla would receive a commission varying from 5 to 10 percent of the dollar value of the sale. Carla was expected to pay her own expenses. And the producers would handle any user questions, either by using 800 numbers for out-of-town calls or by e-mail queries to a technical support group.

Carla called on anyone in the Columbus area who might use the products she sold. At first, her job was relatively easy, and sales came quickly because she had little competition. Many national companies offer similar products, but at that time they were not well represented in the Columbus area. Most small businesses needed someone to demonstrate what the software could do.

In 2006, Carla sold $250,000 worth of Accto software, earning a 10 percent commission; $100,000 worth of Saleco software, also earning a 10 percent commission; and $200,000 worth of Invo software, earning a 7 percent commission. She was encouraged with her progress and looked forward to expanding sales in the future. She was especially optimistic because she had achieved these sales volumes without overtaxing herself. In fact, she felt she was operating at about 60 percent of her capacity and could easily take on new lines. So she began looking for other products she could sell in the Columbus area. A local software company has recently approached Carla about selling its newly developed software, which is basically a network security product. It is designed to secretly track all of the keystrokes and mouse clicks of each employee as he or she uses the computer—so that an employer can identify inappropriate uses of its computers or confidential data. Carla isn't too enthusiastic about this offer because the commission is only 2 percent on potential annual sales of about $150,000—and she also doesn't like the idea of selling a product that might undermine the privacy of employees who are not doing anything wrong.

Now Carla is faced with another decision. The owner of the MetalCoat Company, also in Columbus, has made what looks like an attractive offer. She called on MetalCoat to see if the firm might be interested in buying her accounting software. The owner didn't want the software, but he was very impressed with Carla. After two long discussions, he asked if she would like to help MetalCoat solve its current problem. MetalCoat is having trouble with marketing, and the owner would like Carla to take over the whole marketing effort.

MetalCoat produces solvents used to make coatings for metal products. It sells mainly to industrial customers in the mid-Ohio area and faces many competitors selling essentially the same products and charging the same low prices.

MetalCoat is a small manufacturer. Last year's sales were $500,000. It could handle at least four times this sales volume with ease and is willing to expand to increase sales—its main objective in the short run. MetalCoat's owner is offering Carla a 12 percent commission on all sales if she will take charge of its pricing, advertising, and sales efforts. Carla is flattered by the offer, but she is a little worried because it is a different type of product and she would have to learn a lot about it. The job also might require a great deal more traveling than she is doing now. For one thing, she would have to call on new potential customers in mid-Ohio, and she might have to travel up to 200 miles around Columbus to expand the solvent business. Further, she realizes that she is being asked to do more than just sell. But she did have marketing courses in college and thinks the new opportunity might be challenging.

Evaluate Carla Trujillo's current strategy and how the proposed solvent line fits in with what she is doing now. What should she do? Why?

16. Bunyan Lumber

Austin Duval, owner of Bunyan Lumber Company, feels his business is threatened by a tough new competitor. And now Austin must decide quickly about an offer that may save his business.

Austin has been a sales rep for lumber mills for about 20 years. He started selling in a clothing store but gave it up after two years to work in a lumberyard because the future looked much better in the building materials industry. After drifting from one job to another, Austin finally settled down and worked his way up to manager of a large wholesale building materials distribution warehouse in Richmond, Virginia. In 1995, he formed Bunyan Lumber Company and went into business for himself, selling carload lots of lumber to lumberyards in southeastern Virginia.

Austin works with five large lumber mills on the West Coast. They notify him when a carload of lumber is available to be shipped, specifying the grade, condition, and number of each size board in the shipment. Austin isn't the only person selling for these mills—but he is the only one in his area. He isn't required to take any particular number of carloads per month—but once he tells a mill he wants a particular shipment, title passes to him and he has to sell it to someone. Austin's main function is to find a buyer, buy the lumber from the mill as it's being shipped, and have the railroad divert the car to the buyer.

Having been in this business for 20 years, Austin knows all of the lumberyard buyers in his area very well and is on good working terms with them. He does most of his business over the telephone or by e-mail from his small office, but he tries to see each of the buyers about once a month. He has been marking up the lumber between 4 and 6 percent—the standard markup, depending on the grades and mix in each carload—and has been able to make a good living for himself and his family. The going prices are widely publicized in trade publications and are listed on the Internet, so the buyers can easily check to be sure Austin's prices are competitive.

In the last few years, a number of Austin's lumberyard customers have gone out of business—and others have lost sales. The main problem is competition from several national home-improvement chains that have moved into Austin's market area. These chains buy lumber in large quantities direct from a mill, and their low prices, available inventory, and one-stop shopping are taking some customers away from the traditional lumberyards. Some customers think the quality of the lumber is not quite as good at the big chains, and some contractors stick with the lumberyards out of loyalty or because they get better service, including rush deliveries when they're needed. Then came the mortgage crisis and the residential housing market really slowed down, though not as bad in Richmond as in other parts of the country. Fortunately for Austin, the commercial market remained pretty strong and he had good relationships there—or Austin's profits would have taken an even bigger hit.

Six months ago though, things got even worse. An aggressive young salesman set up in the same business, covering about the same area but representing different lumber mills. This new salesman charges about the same prices as Austin but undersells him once or twice a week in order to get the sale. On several occasions he even set up what was basically an e-mail-based auction to quickly sell excess wood that was not moving fast enough. Many lumber buyers—feeling the price competition from the big chains and realizing that they are dealing with a homogeneous product—seem to be willing to buy from the lowest-cost source. This has hurt Austin financially and personally—because even some of his old friends are willing to buy from the new competitor if the price is lower. The near-term outlook seems dark, since Austin doubts that there is enough business to support two firms like his, especially if the markup gets shaved any closer. Now they seem to be splitting the shrinking business about equally, as the newcomer keeps shaving his markup.

A week ago, Austin was called on by Rhonda Bruder of Tall Tree Door and Window Co., a large manufacturer of windows, raised-panel doors, and accessories. Tall Tree doesn't sell to the big chains and instead distributes its quality line only through independent lumberyards. Rhonda knows that Austin is well acquainted with the local lumberyards and wants him to become Tall Tree's exclusive distributor (sales rep) of residential windows and accessories in his area. Rhonda gave Austin several brochures on Tall Tree's product lines. She also explained Tall Tree's new support program, which will help train and support Austin and interested lumberyards on how to sell the higher markup accessories. Later, in a lengthy e-mail, Rhonda explained how this program will help Austin and interested lumberyards differentiate themselves in this very competitive market.

Most residential windows of specified grades are basically "commodities" that are sold on the basis of price and availability, although some premium and very low end windows are sold also. The national home-improvement chains usually stock and sell only the standard sizes. Most independent lumberyards do not stock windows because there are so many possible sizes. Instead, the lumberyards custom order from the stock sizes each factory offers. Stock sizes are not set by industry standards; they vary from factory to factory, and some offer more sizes. Most factories can deliver these custom orders in two to six weeks, which is usually adequate to satisfy contractors who buy and install them according to architectural plans. This part of the residential window business is well established, and most lumberyards buy from several different window manufacturers—to ensure sources of supply in case of strikes, plant fires, and so on. How the business is split depends on price and the personality and persuasiveness of the sales reps. And given that prices are usually similar, the sales rep–customer relationship can be quite important.

Tall Tree gives more choice than just about any other supplier. It offers many variations in ⅛-inch increments—to cater to remodelers who must adjust to many situations. Tall Tree has even set up a special system on an Internet website. The lumberyard can connect to the website, enter the specs for a window online, and within seconds get a price quote and estimated delivery time.

One reason Rhonda has approached Austin is because of Austin's many years in the business. But the other reason is that Tall Tree is aggressively trying to expand—relying on its made-to-order windows, a full line of accessories, and a newly developed factory support system to help differentiate it from the many other window manufacturers.

To give Austin a quick big picture of the opportunity she is offering, Rhonda explained the window market as follows:

1. For commercial construction, the usual building code ventilation requirements are satisfied with mechanical ventilation. So the windows do not have to operate to permit natural ventilation. They are usually made with heavy-grade aluminum framing. Typically, a distributor furnishes and installs the windows. As part of its service, the distributor provides considerable technical support, including engineered drawings and diagrams to the owners, architects, and/or contractors.

2. For residential construction, on the other hand, windows must be operable to provide ventilation. Residential windows are usually made of wood, frequently with light-gauge aluminum or vinyl on the exterior. The national chains get some volume with standard-size windows, but lumberyards are the most common source of supply for contractors in Austin's area. These lumberyards do not provide any technical support or engineered drawings. A few residential window manufacturers do have their own sales centers in selected geographic areas, which provide a full range of support and engineering services, but none are anywhere near Austin's area.

Tall Tree feels a big opportunity exists in the commercial building repair and rehabilitation market (sometimes called the retrofit market) for a crossover of residential windows to commercial applications—and it has designed some accessories and a factory support program to help lumberyards get this "commercial" business. For applications such as nursing homes and dormitories (which must meet commercial codes), the wood interior of a residential window is desired, but the owners and architects are accustomed to commercial grades and building systems. And in some older facilities, the windows may have to provide supplemental ventilation for a deficient mechanical system. So what is needed is a combination of the residential *operable* window with a heavy-gauge commercial exterior frame that is easy to specify and install. And this is what Tall Tree is offering with a combination of its basic windows and easily adjustable accessory frames. Two other residential window manufacturers offer a similar solution, but neither has pushed its products aggressively and neither offers technical support to lumberyards or trains sales reps like Austin to do the necessary job. Rhonda feels this could be a unique opportunity for Austin.

The sales commission on residential windows would be about 5 percent of sales. Tall Tree would do the billing and collecting. By getting just 20 to 30 percent of his lumberyards' residential window business, Austin could earn about a third of his current income. But the real upside would come in the long-term by increasing his residential window share. Austin is confident that the housing market will turn around soon and when it does he will be well-positioned for growth. To do this, he will have to help the lumberyards get a lot more (and more profitable) business by invading the commercial market with residential windows and the bigger markup accessories needed for this market. Austin will also earn a 20 percent commission on the accessories, adding to his profit potential.

Austin is somewhat excited about the opportunity because the retrofit market is growing. And owners and architects are seeking ways of reducing costs (which Tall Tree's approach does—over usual commercial approaches). He also likes the idea of developing a new line to offset the slow-growing market for new construction housing. But he is also concerned that a lot of sales effort will be needed to introduce this new idea. He is not afraid of work, but he is concerned about his financial survival.

Austin thinks he has three choices:

1. Take Rhonda's offer and sell both window and lumber products.
2. Take the offer and drop lumber sales.
3. Stay strictly with lumber and forget the offer.

Rhonda is expecting an answer within one week, so Austin has to decide soon.

Evaluate Austin Duval's current strategy and how the present offer fits in. What should he do now? Why?

17. Oh So Pure Water, Inc.

Ali Khan (A.K.) established his company, Oh So Pure Water, Inc. (OSP), to market a product designed to purify drinking water. The product, branded as the PURITY II Naturalizer Water Unit, is produced by Environmental Control, Inc., a corporation that focuses primarily on water purification and filtering products for industrial markets.

Oh So Pure Water is a small but growing business. A.K. started the business with an initial capital of only $20,000, which came from his savings and loans from several relatives. A.K. manages the company himself. He has a secretary and six full-time salespeople. In addition, he employs two college students part-time; they make telephone calls to prospect for customers and set up appointments for a salesperson to demonstrate the unit in the consumer's home. By holding spending to a minimum, A.K. has kept the firm's monthly operating budget at only $4,500—and most of that goes for rent, his secretary's salary, and other necessities like computer supplies and telephone bills.

The PURITY II system uses a reverse osmosis purification process. Reverse osmosis is the most effective technology known for improving drinking water. The device is certified by the Environmental Protection Agency to reduce levels of most foreign substances, including flouride, mercury, rust, sediment, arsenic, lead, phosphate, bacteria, and most insecticides.

Each PURITY II unit consists of a high-quality 1-micron sediment removal cartridge, a carbon filter, a sediment filter, a housing, a faucet, and mounting hardware. The compact system fits under a kitchen sink or a wet bar sink. An OSP salesperson can typically install the PURITY II in about a half hour. Installation involves attaching the unit to the cold water supply line, drilling a hole in the sink, and fastening the special faucet. It works equally well with water from a municipal system or well water, and it can purify up to 15 gallons daily. OSP sells the PURITY II to consumers for $395, which includes installation.

The system has no movable parts or electrical connections, and it has no internal metal parts that will corrode or rust. However, the system does use a set of filters that must be replaced after about two years. OSP sells the replacement filters for $80. Taking into consideration the cost of the filters, the system provides drinking water at a cost of approximately $.05 per gallon for the average family.

There are two major benefits from using the PURITY II system. First, water treated by this system tastes better. Blind taste tests confirm that most consumers can tell the difference between water treated with the PURITY II and ordinary tap water. Consequently, the unit improves the taste of coffee, tea, frozen juices, ice cubes, mixed drinks, soup, and vegetables cooked in water. Perhaps more important, the PURITY II's ability to remove potentially harmful foreign matter makes the product of special interest to the growing number of people who are concerned about health and the safety of the water they consume. For example, there is growing controversy surrounding public fluoridation of drinking water—and many consumers are looking for filters that remove fluoride.

The number of people with health and safety concerns is growing. In spite of increased efforts to protect the environment and water supplies, there are still many problems. Hundreds of new chemical compounds—ranging from insecticides to industrial chemicals to commercial cleaning agents—are put into use each year. Some of the residue from chemicals and toxic waste eventually enters water supply sources. Further, floods and hurricanes have damaged or completely shut down water treatment facilities in some cities. Problems like these have led to rumors of possible epidemics of such dread diseases as cholera and typhoid—and more than one city has recently experienced near-panic buying of bottled water.

Given these problems and the need for pure water, A.K. believes that the market potential for the PURITY II system is very large. Residences, both single-family homes and apartments, are one obvious target. The unit is also suitable for use in boats and recreational vehicles; in fact, the PURITY II is standard equipment on several upscale RVs. And it can be used in taverns and restaurants, in institutions such as schools and hospitals, and in commercial and industrial buildings.

There are several competing ways for customers to solve the problem of getting pure water. Some purchase bottled water. Companies such as Ozarka deliver water monthly for an average price of $.60 per gallon. The best type of bottled water is distilled water; it is absolutely pure because it is produced by the process of evaporation. However, it may be *too pure*. The distilling process removes needed elements such as calcium and phosphate—and there is some evidence that removing these trace elements contributes to heart disease. In fact, some health-action groups recommend that consumers not drink distilled water.

A second way to obtain pure water is to use some system to treat tap water. PURITY II is one such system. Another system uses an ion exchange process that replaces ions of harmful substances like iron and mercury with ions that are not harmful. Ion exchange is somewhat less expensive than the PURITY II process, but it is not well suited for residential use because bacteria can build up before the water is used. In addition, there are a number of other filtering and softening systems. In general, these are less expensive and less reliable than the PURITY II. For example, water softeners remove minerals but do not remove bacteria or germs.

A.K.'s first year with his young company has gone quite well. Customers who have purchased the system like it, and there appear to be several ways to expand the business and increase profits. For example, so far he has had little time to make sales calls on potential commercial and institutional users or residential builders. He also sees other possibilities such as expanding his promotion effort or targeting consumers in a broader geographic area.

At present, OSP distributes the PURITY II in the 13-county gulf coast region of Texas. Because of the Robinson-Patman Act, the manufacturer cannot grant an exclusive distributorship. However, OSP is currently the only PURITY II distributor in this region. In addition, OSP has the right of first refusal to set up distributorships in other areas of Texas. The manufacturer has indicated that it might even give OSP distribution rights in a large section of northern Mexico.

The agreement with the manufacturer allows OSP to distribute the product to retailers, including hardware stores and plumbing supply dealers. A.K. has not yet pursued this channel, but a PURITY II distributor in Florida reported some limited success selling the system to retailers at a wholesale price of $275. Retailers for this type of product typically expect a markup of about 33 percent of their selling price.

Environmental Control, Inc., ships the PURITY II units directly from its warehouse to the OSP office via UPS. The manufacturer's $200 per unit selling price includes the cost of shipping. OSP only needs to keep a few units on hand because the manufacturer accepts faxed orders and then ships immediately—so delivery never takes more than a few days. Further, the units are small enough to inventory in the back room of the OSP sales office. Several of the easy-to-handle units will fit in the trunk of a salesperson's car.

A.K. is thinking about recruiting additional salespeople. Finding capable people has not been a problem so far. However, there has already been some turnover, and one of the current salespeople is complaining that the compensation is not high enough. A.K. pays salespeople on a straight commission basis. A salesperson who develops his or her own prospects gets $100 per sale; the commission is $80 per unit on sales leads generated by the company's telemarketing people. For most salespeople, the mix of sales is about half and half. OSP pays the students who make the telephone contacts $4 per appointment set up and $10 per unit sold from an appointment. A growing number of leads are coming from the company's website, largely due to search ads placed on Google and Yahoo!

An average OSP salesperson easily sells 20 units per month. However, A.K. believes that a really effective and well-prepared salesperson can sell much more, perhaps 40 units per month.

OSP and its salespeople get good promotion support from Environmental Control, Inc. For example, Environmental Control supplies sales training manuals and sales presentation flip charts. The materials are also well done, in part because Environment Control's promotion manager previously worked for Electrolux vacuum cleaners, which are sold in a similar way. The company also supplies print copy for magazine and newspaper advertising and tapes of commercials for radio and television. Thus, all OSP has to do is buy media space or time. In addition, Environmental Control furnishes each salesperson with a portable demonstration unit, and the company recently gave OSP three units to be placed in models of condominium apartments.

A.K. has worked long hours to get his company going, but he realizes that he has to find time to think about how his strategy is working and to plan for the future.

Evaluate Ali Khan's current marketing strategy for Oh So Pure Water. How do you think he's doing so far, and what should he do next? Why?

18. Whisper Valley Volunteer Fire Department

Corey Broom raced out the front door of the Target store where he worked as soon as his beeper sounded. In his pickup truck he heard the call on his special radio scanner, "Highway 18 Fire Department, there is a grass fire at the old Larson place. That's a mile down the old dirt road just past the Wilson house." The directions might appear cryptic to someone who had not grown up around Whisper Valley, but it was all Corey needed to know. Upon arriving at the fire, Corey quickly pulled on his fire-retardant bunker pants and boots. He left his Nomex hood, helmet, and fire pants in the back of his truck—he would not need them for this fire.

Less than 10 minutes from the time the call was placed, Corey and 20 other members of the Whisper Valley Volunteer Fire Department (WVVFD) arrived at the old Larson place. They were able to put out the fire in less than half an hour, but not before a football-field-size patch of grass was scorched. Their quick response saved the neighbor's barn and kept the fire from spreading to a nearby forest. A third straight year of drought has the crew on high alert.

Corey threw his gear in the back of his truck and headed back to finish his shift at Target. He had worked there as a department manager for two years, ever since he graduated from the local state college with a marketing degree. As he drove, Corey thought about what WVVFD Chief Megan Martinez recently asked him to do. Over the last few years, the fire department had more to do but fewer people to do it with. So Chief Martinez asked Corey to draw up a marketing plan to recruit new volunteers.

Corey had already started to gather information for the marketing plan. From an online search he found that WVVFD was one of an estimated 30,000 volunteer fire departments in the United States and that these departments had almost a million volunteers. Corey was surprised that more than 75 percent of all U.S. firefighters were volunteers. Whisper Valley, a small city of just over 100,000 and hours from a big city, only had volunteer firefighters.

There are 48 firefighters currently in the WVVFD—down from 55 five years ago. While there was a surge of interest in the year following the terrorist attacks in 2001, only a few of those volunteers remain. Over time, WVVFD has found that about half of new recruits quit before their three-year anniversary. Those that remain usually stay with the department until they can't keep up with the job's physical demands. Megan Martinez has been chief for the last three years. She replaced long-time Chief Clyde Owen, who retired after being with WVVFD for more than 40 years—the last 10 as chief.

The current volunteers include 44 men and four women; more than half of the force is over 40 years old, and Corey is one of only five members younger than 30. Almost all of them started volunteering while still in their 20s or early 30s. The crew represents all walks of life, and their ranks include a lawyer, a real estate salesperson, a college professor, a carpenter, a stay-at-home mom, and a few guys from the local factory. Many entered firefighting for the thrill of it or because they hoped the experience might help them land a paid firefighting job in a bigger city. But most of the crew stay with it because they feel good about giving back to their community, view it as a hobby, and enjoy the camaraderie with the other firefighters.

Being a volunteer firefighter is much different than Corey thought it would be when he started. Last year he counted

238 hours volunteering for WVVFD, but less than a third of that was actually responding to emergencies. And fewer than half of the emergencies were actual fires. He spent about a quarter of this time in required training and drills. He had to be trained for the many different possible calls, including car accidents, hazardous chemical spills, and terrorist attacks. Another 20 percent of his time was spent in meetings and a similar amount helping with fund-raising. Depending upon financial needs, WVVFD holds at least four fund-raising events a year—some years six or eight. These include annual activities like a chili cook-off, pancake breakfast, and booth at the county fair—and as-needed events like pie auctions, turkey shoots, and basketball tournaments.

The biggest requirement to be a volunteer firefighter is the willingness to make the time commitment. Corey's time commitment and allocation of hours is typical of all the firefighters at WVVFD. Volunteers have to be able to attend at least 80 percent of the twice monthly drills—scheduled on the second and fourth Tuesdays of every month. Firefighters also have to live or work near the city of Whisper Valley so they can quickly respond to an emergency. They also have to be at least 18 years old and have a valid driver's license. There is a physical ability test to make sure that firefighters can stand the rigors of the job. While one doesn't have to be a weightlifter, the job requires volunteers to be in good physical shape.

WVVFD has never really had a marketing strategy or any formal promotion efforts. Most of Corey's fellow volunteers heard about WVVFD through word of mouth. People are always curious when a volunteer firefighter runs out the door from work or suddenly leaves a party. These occasions give volunteers a chance to tell others about what they do. Sometimes those questions bring someone out to see drills and to apply to become a volunteer. One of Corey's high school friends was a volunteer and he encouraged Corey to join up while Corey was in his junior year of college. But still, awareness of volunteer firefighting in the Whisper Valley area is still very low. When Corey tells friends about his volunteer work, most are surprised and think the town has full-time paid staff fighting fires.

Corey thinks his marketing strategy should focus mostly on promotion. From his studies he remembers the AIDA model and integrated marketing communications. But he also wonders if his plan should focus only on gaining new recruits or if current volunteers might also be the target of new promotion. Corey also considers how and what he should communicate to his target market. He knows he will have limited funding for his efforts.

Evaluate the promotion objectives Corey Broom should include in his plan. What promotion methods should he use to achieve those objectives?

19. OurPerfectWedding.com

Claire Wallace is happy with her life but disappointed that the idea she had for starting her own business hasn't taken off as expected. Within a few weeks she either has to renew the contract for her Internet website or decide not to put any more time and money into her idea. She knows that it doesn't make sense to renew the contract if she can't come up with a plan to make her website-based business profitable—and she doesn't like to plan. She's a "doer," not a planner.

Claire's business, OurPerfectWedding.com, started as an idea 18 months ago as she was planning her own wedding. She attended a bridal fair at the convention center in Raleigh, North Carolina, to get ideas for a wedding dress, check out catering companies and florists, and in general learn more about the various services available to newlyweds. While there, she and her fiancé went from one retailer's booth to another to sign up for their wedding gift registries. Almost every major retailer in the city—ranging from the Home Depot warehouse to the Belk's department store to the specialty shops that handle imported crystal glassware—offered a gift registry. Some had computers set up to provide access to their online registries. Being listed in all of the registries improved the odds that her wedding gifts would be items she wanted and could use—and it saved time and hassle for gift-givers. On the way back from the fair, Claire and her fiancé discussed the idea that it would be a lot easier to register gift preferences once on a central Internet site than to provide lots of different stores with bits and pieces of information. A list at a website would also make it easier for gift-givers, at least those who were computer users.

When Claire got home, she did an Internet search and found several sites that focused on weddings. The biggest seemed to be www.weddingchannel.com. It had features for couples who were getting married, including a national gift registry. The site featured products from a number of companies, especially large national retail chains; however, there was a search feature to locate people who provide wedding-related services in a local ZIP code area. Claire thought that the sites she found looked quite good, but that they were not as helpful as a site could be with a more local focus.

The more Claire and her fiancé discussed the idea of a website offering local wedding-related services, the more it looked like an interesting opportunity. Except for the annual bridal fair, there was no other obvious local place for consumers to get information about planning a wedding and buying wedding-related services. And for local retailers, florists, catering companies, insurance agents, home builders, and many other types of firms, there was no other central place to target promotion to newlyweds. Further, the amount of money spent on weddings and wedding gifts is very substantial, and right before and after getting married many young couples make many important purchase decisions for everything from life insurance to pots and pans. Spending on the wedding itself can easily exceed the cost of a year of college.

Claire was no stranger to the Internet. She worked as a website designer for a small firm whose one and only client was IBM. That IBM was the only client was intentional rather than accidental. A year earlier IBM had decided that it wanted to outsource certain aspects of its website development work and have it handled by an outside contractor. After negotiating a three-year contract to do IBM's work, several IBM employees quit their jobs and started the business. IBM was a good client, and all indications were that IBM could give the firm as much work as it could handle as it hired new people and prospected for additional accounts over the next few years. Claire especially liked the creative aspects of designing the "look" of a website, and technical specialists handled a lot of the subtle details.

Before joining this new company, Claire had several marketing-related jobs—but none had been the glamorous ad agency job she dreamed of in college as an advertising major. Her first job as a college graduate was with an ad agency, but she was in a backroom operation handling a lot of the arrangements for printing and mailing large-scale direct-mail promotions. In spite of promises that it was a path to other jobs at the agency, the pay was bad, the work was always pressured, and every aspect of what she had to do was boring. After six punishing months, she quit and went looking for something else.

When a number of job applications didn't turn up something quickly, she took a part-time job doing telemarketing calls for a mortgage refinance company. Claire's boss told her that she was doing a great job reeling in prospects—but she hated disturbing people at night and just didn't like making sales pitches. Fortunately for her, that pain didn't last long. A neighbor in Claire's apartment complex got Claire an interview for a receptionist position at an ad agency. That, at least, got her foot in the door. Her job description wasn't very interesting, but in a small agency she had the opportunity to learn a lot about all aspects of the business—ranging from working on client proposals and media plans to creative sessions for new campaigns. In fact, it was from a technician at that agency that she learned to work with the graphics software used to create ad layouts and website pages. When the website design job came open at the new firm, her boss gave her a glowing recommendation, and in two days she was off on her new career.

Although Claire's jobs had not been high-profile positions, they did give her some experience in sales promotion, personal selling, and advertising. Those skills were complemented by the technical computer skills of her fiancé (now husband), who made a living as a database programmer for a large software consulting firm. Taking everything as a whole, they thought that they could get a wedding-related website up and running and make it profitable.

There were several different facets to the original plan for OurPerfectWedding.com. One facet focused on recruiting local advertisers and "sponsors" who would pay to be listed at the website and be allocated a Web page (which Claire would design) describing their services, giving contact information, and links to their own websites. Another facet focused on services for people who were planning to be married. In addition to an online wedding gift registry, sections of the website provided information about typical wedding costs, planning checklists, details about how to get a required marriage license, and other helpful information (including a discussion forum with comments about the strengths and weaknesses of various local suppliers). Claire also started a blog that helped foster more feedback from customers. A man and woman could sign up for the service online and could pay the modest $20 "membership" fee for a year by credit card. Friends, family, and invited guests could visit the website at no charge and get information about wedding preferences, local hotels, discounts on local car rentals, and even printable maps to all of the churches and synagogues in the area.

When Claire told friends about her plan, they all thought it sounded like a great idea. In fact, each time she discussed it someone came up with another idea for a locally oriented feature to add to the website. Several friends said that they had tried national websites but that the information was often too general. But generating more new ideas was not the problem. The problem was generating revenue. Claire had already contracted for space from an Internet service provider and created some of the initial content for the website, but she only had four paying sponsors, two of whom happened to be family friends.

Claire started by creating a colorful flyer describing the website and sent it to most of the firms that had participated in the bridal fair. When no one sent back the reply coupon for more information, Claire started to make calls (mainly during her lunch hour at her full-time job). Some stores seemed intrigued by the concept, but no one seemed ready to sign up. One reason was that they all seemed surprised at the cost to participate and get ad space at the website—$2,400 a year (about the same as a $1/16$-page display ad in the Raleigh Yellow Pages). Another problem was that no one wanted to be the first to sign up. As one florist shop owner put it, "If you pull this off and other florists sign up, then come back and I will too."

Getting couples to sign up went slowly too. Claire paid for four display ads in local Sunday newspapers in the society section, sent information sheets about the website to clergy in the area, listed the website with about 25 Internet search engines, and sent carefully crafted press releases announcing the service to almost every publication in the area. One article that resulted from a press release got some attention, and for a few weeks there was a flurry of e-mail inquiries about her Web page. But after that it slowed to a trickle again. More recently she tried to use Google AdWords which placed ads next to Google search results when someone from the greater Raleigh area searched on the keyword *wedding*. She got a few more hits from this and wondered if she should increase the number of keywords—and wondered what the best keywords could be.

Claire's diagnosis of the problem was simple. Most people thought it was a great idea, but few couples knew where to look on the Internet for such a service. Similarly, potential advertisers—many of them small local businesses—were not accustomed to the idea of paying for Internet advertising. They didn't know if the cost was reasonable or if her site would be effective in generating business.

Claire's life as a married person was going great and her job as a Web page designer kept her very busy. Her free time outside of work was always in short supply because the young crowd at her office always had some scheme for how to keep entertained. So she wasn't about to quit her job to devote full time to her business idea. Further, she thought that once it got rolling she would only have to devote 10 hours a week to it to earn an extra $30,000 a year. She didn't have delusions of becoming a "dot-com millionaire." She just wanted a good locally oriented business.

However, it still wasn't clear how to get it rolling. After a year of trying on and off, she only had four paying ad sponsors, and one of them had already notified her that he didn't plan to sign up again because it wasn't clear that the website had generated any direct leads or sales. Further, it looked like anything she could do to attract more "members" would end up being expensive and inefficient.

Claire thinks the idea has real potential, and she's willing to do the work. But she's not certain if she can make it pay off.

She has to decide soon, however, because the bill for the Internet service provider is sitting on her desk.

What is Claire's strategy? What should she do? If she were to move forward, what strategy would you recommend? Does her financial goal seem realistic? Why?

20. Recreation Supplies Unlimited

Mike Anderson, owner of Recreation Supplies Unlimited, is worried about his business' future. He has tried various strategies for two years now, and he's still barely breaking even.

Two years ago, Mike bought the inventory, supplies, equipment, and business of Recreation Supplies Unlimited, located on the edge of Minneapolis, Minnesota. The business is in an older building along a major highway leading out of town, several miles from any body of water. The previous owner had sales of about $500,000 a year but was just breaking even. For this reason—plus the desire to retire to Arizona—the owner sold to Mike for roughly the value of the inventory.

Recreation Supplies Unlimited had been selling two well-known brands of small pleasure boats, a leading outboard motor, two brands of snowmobiles and jet-skis, and a line of trailer and pickup-truck campers. The total inventory was valued at $250,000—and Mike used all of his own savings and borrowed some from two friends to buy the inventory and the business. At the same time, he took over the lease on the building—so he was able to begin operations immediately.

Mike had never operated a business of his own before, but he was sure that he would be able to do well. He had worked in a variety of jobs—as a used-car salesman, an auto repairman, and a jack-of-all-trades in the maintenance departments of several local businesses.

Soon after starting his business, Mike hired his friend, Tallulah Windsor. She had worked with Mike selling cars and had experience as a receptionist and in customer service. Together, they handle all selling and setup work on new sales and do maintenance work as needed. Sometimes the two are extremely busy—at the peaks of each sport season. Then both sales and maintenance keep them going up to 16 hours a day. At these times it's difficult to have both new and repaired equipment available as soon as customers want it. At other times, however, Mike and Tallulah have almost nothing to do.

Mike usually charges the prices suggested by the various manufacturers, except at the end of a weather season when he is willing to make deals to clear the inventory. He is annoyed that some of his competitors sell mainly on a price basis—offering 10 to 30 percent off a manufacturer's suggested list prices—even at the beginning of a season! Mike doesn't want to get into that kind of business, however. He hopes to build a loyal following based on friendship and personal service. Further, he doesn't think he really has to cut prices because all of his lines are exclusive for his store. No stores within a five-mile radius carry any of his brands, although nearby retailers offer many brands of similar products. Right now, the Internet does not provide much competition, but he fears future price competition from online boat shows.

To try to build a favorable image for his company, Mike occasionally places ads in local papers and buys some radio spots. The basic theme of this advertising is that Recreation Supplies Unlimited is a friendly, service-oriented place to buy the equipment needed for the current season. Sometimes he mentions the brand names he carries, but generally Mike tries to build an image for concerned, friendly service—both in new sales and repairs—stressing "We do it right the first time." He chose this approach because, although he has exclusives on the brands he carries, there generally are 10 to 15 different manufacturers' products being sold in the area in each product category—and most of the products are quite similar. Mike feels that this similarity among competing products almost forces him to try to differentiate himself on the basis of his own store's services.

The first year's operation wasn't profitable. In fact, after paying minimal salaries to Tallulah and himself, the business just about broke even. Mike made no return on his $250,000 investment.

In hopes of improving profitability, Mike jumped at a chance to add a line of lawn mowers, tractors, and trimmers as he was starting into his second year of business. This line was offered by a well-known equipment manufacturer who wanted to expand into the Minneapolis area. The equipment is similar to that offered by other lawn equipment manufacturers. The manufacturer's willingness to do some local advertising and to provide some point-of-purchase displays appealed to Mike. And he also liked the idea that customers probably would want this equipment sometime earlier than boats and other summer items. So he thought he could handle this business without interfering with his other peak selling seasons.

It's two years since Mike bought Recreation Supplies Unlimited—and he's still only breaking even. Sales have increased a little, but costs have gone up too because he had to hire some part-time help. The lawn equipment helped to expand sales—as he had expected—but unfortunately, it did not increase profits as he had hoped. Mike needed part-time helpers to handle this business—in part because the manufacturer's advertising had generated a lot of sales inquiries. Relatively few inquiries resulted in sales, however, because many people seemed to be shopping for deals. So Mike may have even lost money handling the new line. But he hesitates to give it up because he doesn't want to lose that sales volume, and the manufacturer's sales rep has been most encouraging, assuring Mike that things will get better and that his company will be glad to continue its promotion support during the coming year.

Mike is now considering the offer of a mountain bike producer that has not been represented in the area. The bikes have become very popular with students and serious bikers in the last several years. The manufacturer's sales rep says industry sales are still growing (but not as fast as in the past) and probably will grow for many more years. The sales rep has praised Mike's service orientation and says this could help him sell lots of bikes because many mountain bikers are serious about buying a quality bike and then keeping it serviced. He says Mike's business approach would be a natural fit with bike customers' needs and attitudes. As a special inducement to get Mike to take on the line, the sales rep says Mike will not have to pay for the initial inventory of bikes, accessories, and repair parts for 90 days. And, of course, the company will supply the usual promotion aids and a special advertising allowance of $10,000 to help introduce the line to Minneapolis. Mike kind of likes the idea of carrying mountain bikes because he has one himself and knows that they do require some service year-round. But he also knows that the proposed bikes are very similar in price and quality to the ones now being offered by the bike shops in town. These bike shops are service- rather than price-oriented, and Mike feels that they are doing a good job on service—so he is concerned with how he could be "different."

Evaluate Mike Anderson's overall strategy(ies) and the mountain bike proposal. What should he do now?

21. Advanced Materials, Inc.

Advanced Materials, Inc., is a multinational producer of various chemicals and plastics with plants in the United States, England, France, and Germany. It is run from its headquarters in New Jersey.

Colin Kramer is marketing manager of Advanced Materials' plastics business. Colin is reconsidering his promotion approach. He is evaluating what kind of promotion—and how much—should be directed to car producers and to other major plastics customers worldwide. Currently, Colin has one salesperson who devotes most of his time to the car industry. This man is based in the Detroit area and focuses on GM, Ford, and Chrysler—as well as the various firms that mold plastics to produce parts to supply the car industry. This approach worked well when relatively little plastic was used in each car *and* the auto producers did all of the designing themselves and then sent out specifications for very price-oriented competitive bidding. But now the whole product planning and buying system is changing—and of course foreign producers with facilities in the United States are much more important.

How the present system works can be illustrated in terms of the team approach Ford used on its project to design the Flex, the full-size crossover introduced as a 2009 model. For the Flex, representatives from all the various functions—planning, design, engineering, purchasing, marketing, and manufacturing—work together. In fact, representatives from key suppliers were involved from the outset. The whole team takes final responsibility for a car. Because all of the departments are involved from the start, problems are resolved as the project moves on—before they cause a crisis. Manufacturing, for example, can suggest changes in design that will result in higher productivity or better quality, which is especially important at a time with Ford's initial quality ratings are beating those of Honda and Toyota.

The old approach was different. It involved a five-year process of creating a new vehicle in sequential steps. Under the old system, product planners would come up with a general concept and then expect the design team to give it artistic form. Next engineering would develop the specifications and pass them on to manufacturing and suppliers. There was little communication between the groups and no overall project responsibility.

In the Flex project, Ford engineers followed the Japanese lead and did some reverse engineering of their own. They dismantled several competitors' cars, piece by piece, looking for ideas they could copy or improve. This helped them learn how the parts were assembled and how they were designed. Eventually, Ford incorporated or modified some of the best features into its design of the Flex. For example, the Flex uses a new design to seal the doors and eliminate wind noise.

In addition to reverse engineering, Ford researchers conducted a series of market studies. This led to positioning the Flex as an "anti-minivan." That positioning resulted in a decision to eliminate the sliding side doors and instead to use traditional hinged doors. That cut costs, but the savings were used for dress-up features, like 19-inch aluminum wheels and a special new seat design that reduces movement in the seat and gives the car an even smoother drive. The Flex's optional refrigerator/freezer is another example of a feature that did well in concept tests.

Ford also asked assembly-line workers for suggestions before the car was redesigned and then incorporated their ideas into the new car. Most bolts have the same-size head, for example, so workers don't have to switch from one wrench to another.

Finally, Ford included its best suppliers as part of the planning effort. Instead of turning to a supplier after the car's design was completed, Ford invited them to participate in product planning. For example, Microsoft's Sync system provides the Flex with voice control of the entertainment system.

Most other vehicles are now developed with an approach similar to this. GM, for example, used a very similar team approach to redesign its new Malibu. And major firms in many other industries are using similar approaches. A major outgrowth of this effort has been a trend by these producers to develop closer working relationships with a smaller number of suppliers. To some extent, this is a direct outgrowth of the decision to try to reduce unnecessary costs by using the same components for different vehicles. For example, the powertrain for the Flex is the same as is used in Ford's Edge.

Many of the suppliers selected for the Flex project had not only the facilities, but also the technical and professional managerial staff who could understand—and become part of—the program management approach. Ford expected these major suppliers to join in its total quality management push and to be able to provide just-in-time delivery systems. Ford dropped suppliers whose primary sales technique was to entertain buyers and then submit bids on standard specifications.

Because many firms have moved to these team-oriented approaches and developed closer working relationships with a subset of their previous suppliers, Colin is trying to determine if Advanced Materials' present effort is still appropriate.

Colin's strategy has focused primarily on responding to inquiries and bringing in Advanced Materials' technical people as the situation seems to require. Potential customers with technical questions are sometimes referred to other noncompeting customers already using the materials or to an Advanced Materials plant—to be sure that all questions are answered. But basically, all producer-customers are treated more or less alike. The sales reps make calls and try to find good business wherever they can.

Each Advanced Materials sales rep usually has a geographic area. If an area like Detroit needs more than one rep, each may specialize in one or several similar industries. But Advanced Materials uses the same basic approach—call on present users of plastic products and try to find opportunities for getting a share (or bigger share) of existing purchases or new applications. The sales reps are supposed to be primarily order getters rather than technical specialists. Technical help can be brought in when the customer wants it, or sometimes the sales rep simply sets up a conference call between Advanced Materials' technical experts, the buyer, and the users at the buyer's facility.

Colin sees that some of his major competitors are becoming more aggressive. They are seeking to affect specifications and product design from the start rather than after a product design is completed. This takes a lot more effort and resources, but Colin thinks it may get better results. A major problem he sees, however, is that he may have to drastically change the nature of Advanced Materials' promotion. Instead of focusing primarily on buyers and responding to questions, it may be necessary to try to contact *all* the multiple buying influences and not only answer their questions but help them understand what questions to raise—to find solutions. Such a process may even require more technically trained sales reps. In fact, it may require that people from Advanced Materials' other departments—engineering, design, manufacturing, R&D, and distribution—get actively involved in discussions with their counterparts in customer firms. Further, use of e-mail and a website might make ongoing contacts faster and easier.

While Colin doesn't want to miss the boat if changes are needed, he also doesn't want to go off the deep end. After all, many of the firm's customers don't seem to want Advanced Materials to do anything very different from what it's been doing. In fact, some say that they're very satisfied with their current supply arrangements and really have no interest in investing in a close relationship with a single supplier. Even with the Flex project, Ford wasn't 100 percent dedicated to the team approach. For example, when Ford's research showed that the target market viewed quiet and comfortable seats as an especially important factor in purchases, Ford didn't turn to a supplier for help but rather assigned a team of its own design engineers to develop and test them in-house. Now some of what was learned on the Flex project is going to be used in redesigning other models.

Contrast the previous approach to designing and producing cars to Flex's program management approach, especially as it might affect suppliers' promotion efforts. Given that many other major producers have moved in the program management direction, what promotion effort should Colin Kramer develop for Advanced Materials? Should every producer in every geographic area be treated alike, regardless of size? Explain.

22. Bright Light Innovations: The Starlight Stove*

The top management team of Bright Light Innovations is preparing to meet and review their market situation. The team is a combination of students and faculty from Colorado State University's (CSU) Colleges of Business and Engineering: Dr. Bryan Wilson, Paul Hudnut, Ajay Jha, Sachin Joshi, Katie Lucchesi, Dan Mastbergen, Ryan Palmer, and Chaun Sims. They are excited about the Starlight Stove product they have developed—and passionate about the opportunity that it provides to improve the quality of life for some of the world's poorest people. They know they have a great technology, but they need a marketing plan to bring this product to market.

Every day, over 2.4 billion people—more than one-third of the world's population—burn solid biomass fuel (wood, charcoal, dung, and coal) for cooking and heating. These fuels are usually burned indoors in open pits or traditional cook stoves. About two-thirds of the people using this fuel also have no electricity, so the open fires often burn into the night to provide light. These fires create indoor air pollution that is a leading contributor to respiratory diseases in these countries. U.N. Secretary General Kofi Annan has called for greater energy efficiency and noted that "indoor air pollution has become one of the top 10 causes of mortality and premature death." It is estimated that this source of pollution contributes each year to the deaths of 1 million children under the age of 5, and it is a leading cause of miscarriage and women's health problems.

Hoping to address these consumers' needs for safe cooking and electricity, CSU's Engines and Energy Conversion Laboratory developed the Starlight Stove. The Starlight Stove's improved technology requires 50 to 70 percent less biomass fuel than traditional stoves. It also has a thermoelectric generator that converts heat from the stove into electricity that can power a small lightbulb or be stored in a rechargeable battery for later use. The technology has been refined, and the team believes it is ready to go to market.

There are other competing enclosed cook stoves, but none produce electricity. Solar panels can provide electricity, but they are expensive—costing $360 each. Micro-hydropower allows households to convert the power from streams and rivers into electricity, but homes must be close to a river and water flow in many areas of the country is seasonal. These technologies—solar panels and hydropower—are understood by many consumers and are already in use in some areas. The Starlight Stove, on the other hand, offers a new technology, and that may slow its adoption.

The management team decided on Nepal as the initial target market for the Starlight Stove. Several factors made this

*This case is based on a business plan written by Ajay Jha, Sachin Joshi, Katie Lucchesi, Dan Mastbergen, Ryan Palmer, and Chaun Sims.

market particularly attractive. The climate is relatively cold and only 11 percent of the households have access to electricity, so the heat and electricity production of the stove are particularly beneficial. Eighty-eight percent of the population uses firewood as their main source of energy. In addition, deforestation creates environmental problems in Nepal because it contributes to erosion and flooding. So the social benefits of the Starlight Stove will be particularly appealing to the Nepalese government and aid organizations.

There are approximately 9.2 million households in Nepal, but the gross national income per capita is only about $290, with most adults making between $1 and $3 per day. Nepal is largely rural, with only 14 percent of the population living in urban areas. The country is divided into 75 districts. Each district is further divided into about 60 village development committees (a sort of local government) consisting of about 450 households. The similar characteristics of northern India—immediately south of Nepal—make it a logical follow-up market.

The Starlight Stove offers several benefits to this population. For example, the longer hours with light—thanks to the electricity—and less time required to collect wood or other fuel could allow families to earn money by weaving, farming, or producing other crafts. Family productivity could increase 20 percent or more per day. Or the added hours with light might allow children to gain an education. If the product were manufactured locally, it could provide jobs for the population and help them learn the benefits of technology.

With obvious benefits for such a large number of people, the Bright Light Innovations team could look to donations to subsidize the Starlight Stove for the Nepalese people. But the team has concerns about this traditional form of aid. Financing in the form of grants, government relief, or donations is unreliable. If it is not renewed, projects wallow or die. Further, grants often fail to teach disadvantaged people skills and responsibility. So the team wants to create a sustainable venture that provides benefits for all—and has set up Bright Light Innovations as a for-profit business.

The management team has to make a number of marketing decisions. For example, it has to decide how to price the Starlight Stove. It estimates that the stove will cost about $60 to manufacture after setting up a plant in Nepal and expects that microfinancing organizations will provide loans for families. If units are sold for $80, the loan can be financed at 20 percent interest for three years with payments of $0.68 per week (microfinancing institutions typically collect on a weekly, or sometimes daily, basis). The team thinks that it will be easy to find a microfinancing institution to provide these loans. But the team is still unsure about whether this price will provide adequate margins for distributors.

The team also has to decide how to promote the stove to a population where less than half the adults can read. However, the team does have contacts with some business leaders, government officials, and nongovernmental organizations that may be able to provide advice and help.

What should be the marketing strategy of the Bright Light Innovations team for the Starlight Stove? Why?

23. West Side Furniture

Lupita Ventura, owner of West Side Furniture, is discouraged with her salespeople and is even thinking about hiring some new blood. Ventura has been running West Side Furniture for 10 years and has slowly built the sales to $3.5 million a year. Her store is located on the outskirts of a growing city of 275,000 population. This is basically a factory city, and she has deliberately selected blue-collar workers as her target market.

She carries some higher-priced furniture lines but emphasizes budget combinations and easy credit terms.

Ventura is concerned that she may have reached the limit of her sales growth—her sales have not been increasing during the last two years even though total furniture sales have been increasing in the city as new people move in. Her local cable TV spots and newspaper advertising seem to attract her

Table 1

In Shopping for Furniture I Found (Find) That	Demographic Groups			
	Group A	Group B	Group C	Group D
I looked at furniture in many stores before I made a purchase.	78%	72%	52%	50%
I went (am going) to only one store and bought (buy) what I found (find) there.	2	5	10	11
To make my purchase I went (am going) back to one of the stores I shopped in previously.	63	59	27	20
I looked (am looking) at furniture in no more than three stores and made (will make) my purchase in one of these.	20	25	40	45
I like a lot of help in selecting the right furniture.	27	33	62	69
I like a very friendly salesperson.	23	28	69	67

Table 2 The Sample Design

Demographic Status
Upper class (Group A); 13% of sample This group consists of managers, proprietors, or executives of large businesses; professionals, including doctors, lawyers, engineers, college professors, and school administrators; and research personnel and sales personnel, including managers, executives, and upper-income salespeople above level of clerks. *Family income over $60,000*
Middle class (Group B); 37% of sample Group B consists of white-collar workers, including clerical, secretarial, salesclerks, bookkeepers, etc. It also includes school teachers, social workers, semiprofessionals, proprietors or managers of small businesses, industrial foremen, and other supervisory personnel. *Family income between $35,000 and $70,000*
Lower middle class (Group C); 36% of sample Skilled workers and semiskilled technicians are in this category, along with custodians, elevator operators, telephone linemen, factory operatives, construction workers, and some domestic and personal service employees. *Family income between $20,000 and $45,000. No one in this group has above a high school education.*
Lower class (Group D); 14% of sample Nonskilled employees, day laborers. It also includes some factory operatives and domestic and service people. *Family income under $28,000.* *None has completed high school; some have only grade school education.*

target market, but many of these people come in, shop around, and leave. Some of them come back—but most do not. She thinks her product selections are very suitable for her target market and is concerned that her salespeople don't close more sales with potential customers. Several times, she has discussed this matter with her 10 salespeople. Her staff feels they should treat customers the way they personally want to be treated. They argue that their role is to answer questions and be helpful when asked—not to make suggestions or help customers make decisions. They think this would be too "hard sell."

Ventura says their behavior is interpreted as indifference by the customers attracted to the store by her advertising. She has tried to convince her salespeople that customers must be treated on an individual basis and that some customers need more help in looking and deciding than others. Moreover, Ventura is convinced that some customers would

appreciate more help and suggestions than the salespeople themselves might want. To support her views, she showed her staff the data from a study of furniture store customers (see Tables 1 and 2) that she found on the Internet website for a furniture trade association. She tried to explain the differences in demographic groups and pointed out that her store was definitely trying to aim at specific people. She argued that they (the salespeople) should cater to the needs and attitudes of their customers and think less about how they would like to be treated themselves. Further, Ventura announced that she is considering changing the sales compensation plan or hiring new blood if the present employees can't do a better job. Currently, the sales reps are paid $26,000 per year plus a 5 percent commission on sales.

Contrast Lupita Ventura's strategy and thoughts about her salespeople with their apparent view of her strategy and especially their role in it. What should she do now? Explain.

24. Lone Star Wire, Inc.

Casey Pavlicek, marketing manager of consumer products for Lone Star Wire, Inc., is trying to set a price for her most promising new product—a space-saving shoe rack suitable for small homes or apartments.

Lone Star Wire, Inc.—located in Ft. Worth, Texas—is a custom producer of industrial wire products. The company has a lot of experience bending wire into many shapes and also can chrome- or gold-plate finished products. The company was started 16 years ago and has slowly built its sales volume to $3.6 million a year. Just one year ago, Pavlicek was appointed marketing manager of the consumer products division. It is her responsibility to develop this division as a producer and

marketer of the company's own branded products—as distinguished from custom orders, which the industrial division produces for others.

Pavlicek has been working on a number of different product ideas for almost a year now and has developed several designs for DVD holders, racks for soft-drink cans, plate holders, doll stands, collapsible book ends, and other such products. Her most promising product is a shoe rack for crowded homes and apartments. The wire rack attaches to the inside of a closet door and holds eight pairs of shoes.

The rack is very similar to one the industrial division produced for a number of years for another company. That

plants as they became less efficient to operate. Best Way expanded capacity of the remaining two plants (especially warehouse facilities) so they could operate more profitably with maximum use of existing processing equipment.

Shortly after Chuck's retirement, Carly reviewed the company's situation with her managers. She pointed to narrowing profit margins, debts contracted for new plants and equipment, and an increasingly competitive environment. Even considering the temporary labor-saving competitive advantage of the new cooker system, there seemed to be no way to improve the status quo unless the firm could sell direct—as they do in the local market—thereby eliminating the food brokers' 5 percent commission on sales. This was the plan decided on, and Randy Cook was given the new sales job. An inside salesperson was retained to handle incoming orders and do some telemarketing to smaller accounts.

Randy, the only full-time outside sales rep for the firm, lives in Devil River Valley. Other top managers do some selling but not much. Being a nephew of Chuck, Randy is also a member of the board of directors. He is well qualified in technical matters and has a college degree in food chemistry. Although Randy formerly did call on some important customers with the brokers' sales reps, he is not well-known in the industry or even by Best Way's usual customers.

It is now five months later. Randy is not doing very well. He has made several selling trips, placed hundreds of telephone calls, and maintained constant e-mail contacts with prospective customers—all with discouraging results. He is unwilling to continue sales efforts on his own. There seems to be too many potential customers for one person to reach. And much negotiating, wining, and dining seems to be needed—certainly more than he can or wants to do.

Randy insists that Best Way hire a sales force to continue the present way of operating. Sales are down in comparison both to expectations and to the previous year's results. Some regular supermarket chain customers have stopped buying—though basic consumer demand has not changed. Further, buyers for some supermarket chains that might be potential new customers have demanded quantity guarantees much larger than Best Way can supply. Expanding supply would be difficult in the short run—because the firm typically must contract with growers to ensure supplies of the type and quality they normally offer.

Chuck, still the controlling stockholder, has asked for a special meeting of the board in two weeks to discuss the present situation.

Evaluate Best Way's past and current strategy planning. What should Carly Ross-Whitman tell Chuck Ross? What should Best Way do now?

27. Superior Molding, Inc.

Sarah Stringer is trying to decide whether to leave her present job to buy into another business and be part of top management.

Sarah is now a sales rep for a plastics components manufacturer. She calls mostly on large industrial accounts—such as refrigerator manufacturers—who might need large quantities of custom-made products like door liners. She is on a straight salary of $45,000 per year, plus expenses and a company car. She expects some salary increases but doesn't see much long-run opportunity with this company.

As a result, she is seriously considering changing jobs and investing $60,000 in Superior Molding, Inc., an established Chicago (Illinois) thermoplastic molder (manufacturer). Danny Breen, the present owner, is nearing retirement and has not trained anyone to take over the business. He has agreed to sell the business to Tommy Nakamura, a lawyer, who has invited Sarah to invest and become the sales manager. Tommy has agreed to match Sarah's current salary plus expenses, plus a bonus of 2 percent of profits. However, she must invest to become part of the new company. She will get a 5 percent interest in the business for the necessary $60,000 investment—all of her savings.

Superior Molding, Inc., is well established and last year had sales of $3.2 million but zero profits (after paying Danny a salary of $80,000). In terms of sales, cost of materials was 46 percent; direct labor, 13 percent; indirect factory labor, 15 percent; factory overhead, 13 percent; and sales overhead and general expenses, 13 percent. The company has not been making any profit for several years—but it has been continually adding new computer-controlled machines to replace those made obsolete by technological developments. The machinery is

well maintained and modern, but most of it is similar to that used by its many competitors. Most of the machines in the industry are standard. Special products are made by using specially made dies with these machines.

Sales have been split about two-thirds custom-molded products (that is, made to the specification of other producers or merchandising concerns) and the balance proprietary items (such as housewares and game items, like poker chips).

The housewares are copies of items developed by others and indicate neither originality nor style. Danny is in charge of selling the proprietary items, which are distributed through any available wholesale channels. The custom-molded products are sold through two full-time sales reps—who receive a 10 percent commission on individual orders up to $30,000 and then 3 percent above that level—and also by three manufacturers' reps who get the same commissions.

The company seems to be in fairly good financial condition, at least as far as book value is concerned. The $60,000 investment will buy almost $88,000 in assets—and ongoing operations should pay off the seven-year note (see Table 1). Tommy thinks that with new management the company has a good chance to make big profits. He expects to make some economies in the production process—because he feels most production operations can be improved. He plans to keep custom-molding sales at approximately the present $2 million level. His new strategy will try to increase the proprietary sales volume from $1.2 million to $3 million a year. Sarah is expected to be a big help here because of her sales experience. This will bring the firm up to about capacity level—but it will mean adding additional employees and costs. The major advantage of expanding sales will be spreading overhead.

Table 1 Superior Molding, Inc., Statement of Financial Conditions, December 31, 2006

Assets			Liabilities and Net Worth		
Cash		$ 19,500	Liabilities:		
Accounts receivable		82,500	Accounts payable		$ 105,000
Building	$337,500		Notes payable—7 years (machinery)		291,000
Less: depreciation	112,500				
		225,000			
Machinery	2,100,000		Net worth:		
Less: depreciation	675,000		Capital stock		1,350,000
		1,425,000	Retained earnings		6,000
Total assets		$1,752,000	Total liabilities and net worth		$1,752,000

Some of the products proposed by Tommy for expanding proprietary sales are listed below.

New products for consideration:

Safety helmets for cyclists.

Water bottles for cyclists and in-line skaters.

Waterproof cases for digital cameras.

Toolboxes.

Closet organizer/storage boxes for toys.

Short legs for furniture.

Step-on garbage cans without liners.

Exterior house shutters and siding.

Importing and distributing foreign housewares.

Superior Molding faces heavy competition from many other similar companies including firms that have outsourced production to China and Eastern Europe where labor costs are much lower. Further, most retailers expect a wide margin, sometimes 50 to 60 percent of the retail selling price. Even so, manufacturing costs are low enough so Superior Molding can spend some money for promotion while still keeping the price competitive. Apparently, many customers are willing to pay for novel new products—if they see them in stores. And Sarah isn't worried too much by tough competition. She sees plenty of that in her present job. And she does like the idea of being an "owner and sales manager."

Evaluate Superior Molding's situation and Tommy Nakamura's strategy. What should Sarah Stringer do? Why?

28. Precision Cutting Tools, Inc.

Nikos Pelekanos, president and marketing manager of Precision Cutting Tools, Inc., is deciding what strategy, or strategies, to pursue.

Precision Cutting Tools (PCT) is a manufacturer of industrial cutting tools. These tools include such items as lathe blades, drill press bits, and various other cutting edges used in the operation of large metal cutting, boring, or stamping machines. Nikos takes great pride in the fact that his company—whose $5,700,000 sales in 2008 is small by industry standards—is recognized as a producer of a top-quality line of cutting tools.

Competition in the cutting-tool industry is intense. PCT competes not only with the original machine manufacturers, but also with many other larger domestic and foreign manufacturers offering cutting tools as one of their many different product lines. This has had the effect, over the years, of standardizing the price, specifications, and, in turn, the quality of the competing products of all manufacturers. It has also led to fairly low prices on standard items.

About a year ago, Nikos was tiring of the financial pressure of competing with larger companies enjoying economies of scale. At the same time, he noted that more and more potential cutting-tool customers were turning to small tool-and-die shops that used computer-controlled equipment to meet specialized needs that could not be met by the mass production firms. Nikos thought perhaps he should consider some basic strategy changes. Although he was unwilling to become strictly a custom producer, he thought that the recent trend toward buying customized cutting edges suggested new markets might be developing—markets too small for the large, multiproductline companies to serve profitably but large enough to earn a good profit for a flexible company of PCT's size.

Nikos hired a marketing research company, MResearchPro, to study the feasibility of serving these markets. The initial results were encouraging. It was estimated that PCT might increase sales by 65 percent and profits by 90 percent by serving the emerging markets. The research showed that there are many large users of standard cutting tools who buy directly from large cutting-tool manufacturers (domestic or foreign) or wholesalers who represent these manufacturers. This is the bulk of the cutting-tool business (in terms of units sold and sales dollars). But there are also many smaller users all over the

United States who buy in small but regular quantities. And some of these needs are becoming more specialized. That is, a special cutting tool may make a machine and/or worker much more productive, perhaps eliminating several steps with time-consuming setups. This is the area that the research company sees as potentially attractive.

Next, Nikos had the sales manager hire two technically oriented market researchers (at a total cost of $85,000 each per year, including travel expenses) to maintain continuous contact with potential cutting-tool customers. The researchers were supposed to identify any present or future needs that might exist in enough cases to make it possible to profitably produce a specialized product. The researchers were not to take orders or sell PCT's products to the potential customers. Nikos felt that only through this policy could these researchers talk to the right people.

The initial feedback from the market researchers was most encouraging. Many firms (large and small) had special needs—although it often was necessary to talk to the shop foreman or individual machine operators to find these needs. Most operators were making do with the tools available. Either they didn't know customizing was possible or doubted that their supervisors would do anything about it if they suggested that a more specialized tool could increase productivity. But these operators were encouraging because they said that it would be easier to persuade supervisors to order specialized tools if the tools were already produced and in stock than if they had to be custom made. So Nikos decided to continually add high-quality products to meet the ever-changing, specialized needs of users of cutting tools and edges.

PCT's potential customers for specialized tools are located all over the United States. The average sale per customer is likely to be less than $500, but the sale will be repeated several times within a year. Because of the widespread market and the small order size, Nikos doesn't think that selling direct—as is done by small custom shops—is practical. At the present time, PCT sells 90 percent of its regular output through a large industrial wholesaler—Summit Mill Supply—which serves the area east of the Mississippi River and carries a very complete line of industrial supplies (to "meet every industrial need"). Summit carries over 10,000 items. Some sales come from customers who know exactly what they want and just place orders directly by fax or at the firm's website. But most of the selling is by Summit's sales reps, who work from an electronic catalog on a laptop computer. Summit, although very large and well-known, is having trouble moving cutting tools. It's losing sales of cutting tools in some cities to newer wholesalers specializing in the cutting-tool industry. The new wholesalers are able to give more technical help to potential customers and therefore better service. Summit's president is convinced that the newer, less-experienced concerns will either realize that a substantial profit margin can't be maintained along with their aggressive strategies, or they will eventually go broke trying to overspecialize.

From Nikos' standpoint, the present wholesaler has a good reputation and has served PCT well in the past. Summit has been of great help in holding down Nikos' inventory costs—by increasing the inventory in Summit's 35 branch locations. Although Nikos has received several complaints about the lack of technical assistance given by Summit's sales reps—as well as their lack of knowledge about PCT's new special products—he feels that the present wholesaler is providing the best service it can. All its sales reps have been told about the new products at a special training session, and new pages have been added to the electronic catalog on their laptops. So regarding the complaints, Nikos says, "The usual things you hear when you're in business."

Nikos thinks there are more urgent problems than a few complaints. Profits are declining, and sales of the new cutting tools are not nearly as high as forecast—even though all research reports indicate that the company's new products meet the intended markets' needs perfectly. The high costs involved in producing small quantities of special products and in adding the market research team—together with lower-than-expected sales—have significantly reduced PCT's profits. Nikos is wondering whether it is wise to continue to try to cater to the needs of many specific target markets when the results are this discouraging. He also is considering increasing advertising expenditures including some search engine advertising in the hope that customers will pull the new products through the channel.

Evaluate PCT's situation and Nikos Pelekanos' present strategy. What should he do now?

29. Specialized Castings, Inc.

Kelly Lantern, marketing manager for Specialized Castings, Inc., is trying to figure out how to explain to her boss why a proposed new product line doesn't make sense for them. Kelly is sure it's wrong for Specialized Castings, but isn't able to explain why.

Specialized Castings, Inc., is a producer of malleable iron castings for automobile and aircraft manufacturers and a variety of other users of castings. Last year's sales of castings amounted to over $70 million.

Specialized Castings also produces about 30 percent of all the original equipment bumper jacks installed in new U.S.-made automobiles each year. This is a very price-competitive business, but Specialized Castings has been able to obtain its large market share with frequent personal contact between the company's executives and its customers—supported by very close cooperation between the company's engineering department and its customers' buyers. This has been extremely important because the wide variety of models and model changes frequently requires alterations in the specifications of the bumper jacks. All of Specialized Castings' bumper jacks are sold directly to the automobile manufacturers. No attempt has been made to sell bumper jacks to final consumers through hardware and automotive channels—although they are available through the manufacturers' automobile dealers.

Delrae Booker, Specialized Castings' production manager, now wants to begin producing hydraulic garage jacks for sale through auto-parts wholesalers to auto-parts retailers. Delrae saw a variety of hydraulic garage jacks at a recent automotive show and knew immediately that his plant could produce these products. This especially interested him because of the possibility of using excess capacity. Further, he says "jacks are jacks," and the company would merely be broadening its product line by introducing hydraulic garage jacks. (Note: Hydraulic garage jacks are larger than bumper jacks and are intended for use in or around a garage. They are too big to carry in a car's trunk.)

As Delrae became more enthusiastic about the idea, he found that Specialized Castings' engineering department already had a patented design that appeared to be at least comparable to the products now offered on the market. Further, Delrae says that the company would be able to produce a product that is better made than the competitive products (i.e., smoother castings)—although he agrees that most customers probably wouldn't notice the difference. The production department estimates that the cost of producing a hydraulic garage jack comparable to those currently offered by competitors would be about $48 per unit.

Kelly has just received an e-mail from Marco Piasante, the company president, explaining the production department's enthusiasm for broadening Specialized Castings' present jack line into hydraulic jacks. Marco seems enthusiastic about the idea too, noting that it would be a way to make fuller use of the company's resources and increase its sales. Marco's e-mail asks for Kelly's reaction, but Marco already seems sold on the idea.

Given Marco's enthusiasm, Kelly isn't sure how to respond. She's trying to develop a good explanation of why she isn't excited about the proposal. The firm's six sales reps are already overworked with their current accounts. And Kelly couldn't possibly promote this new line herself—she's already helping other reps make calls and serving as sales manager. So it would be necessary to hire someone to promote the line. And this sales manager would probably have to recruit manufacturers' agents (who probably will want 10 to 15 percent commission on sales) to sell to automotive wholesalers who would stock the jack and sell to the auto parts retailers. The wholesalers will probably expect trade discounts of about 20 percent, trade show exhibits, some national advertising, and sales promotion help (catalog sheets, mailers, and point-of-purchase displays). Further, Kelly sees that Specialized Castings' billing and collection system will have to be expanded because many more customers will be involved. It will also be necessary to keep track of agent commissions and accounts receivable.

Auto-parts retailers are currently selling similar hydraulic garage jacks for about $99. Kelly has learned that such retailers typically expect a trade discount of about 35 percent off of the suggested list price for their auto parts.

All things considered, Kelly feels that the proposed hydraulic jack line is not very closely related to the company's present emphasis. She has already indicated her lack of enthusiasm to Delrae, but this made little difference in Delrae's thinking. Now it's clear that Kelly will have to convince the president or she will soon be responsible for selling hydraulic jacks.

Contrast Specialized Castings, Inc.'s current strategy and the proposed strategy. What should Kelly Lantern say to Marco Piasante to persuade him to change his mind? Or should she just plan to sell hydraulic jacks? Explain.

30. Eden Prairie Mills, Ltd.*

Jeanne Leroux, marketing manager of Eden Prairie Mills, Ltd.—a Canadian company—is being urged to approve the creation of a separate marketing plan for Quebec. This would be a major policy change because Eden Prairie Mills' international parent is trying to move toward a global strategy for the whole firm and Leroux has been supporting Canada-wide planning.

Leroux has been the marketing manager of Eden Prairie Mills, Ltd., for the last four years—since she arrived from international headquarters in Minneapolis. Eden Prairie Mills, Ltd., headquartered in Toronto, is a subsidiary of a large U.S.-based consumer packaged food company with worldwide sales of more than $2.8 billion in 2005. Its Canadian sales are just over $450 million, with the Quebec and Ontario markets accounting for 69 percent of the company's Canadian sales.

The company's product line includes such items as cake mixes, puddings, pie fillings, pancakes, prepared foods, and frozen dinners. The company has successfully introduced at least six new products every year for the last five years. Products from Eden Prairie Mills are known for their high quality and enjoy much brand preference throughout Canada, including the Province of Quebec.

The company's sales have risen every year since Leroux took over as marketing manager. In fact, the company's market share has increased steadily in each of the product categories in which it competes. The Quebec market has closely followed the national trend except that, in the past two years, total sales growth in that market began to lag.

According to Leroux, a big advantage of Eden Prairie Mills over its competitors is the ability to coordinate all phases of the food business from Toronto. For this reason, Leroux meets at least once a month with her product managers—to discuss developments in local markets that might affect marketing plans. While each manager is free to make suggestions and even to suggest major changes, Leroux has the responsibility of giving final approval for all plans.

One of the product managers, Lise Gauthier, expressed great concern at the last monthly meeting about the poor performance of some of the company's products in the Quebec market. While a broad range of possible reasons—ranging from inflation and the threat of job losses to politics—were reviewed to try to explain the situation, Gauthier insisted that it was due to a basic lack of understanding of that market. She felt not enough managerial time and money had been spent on the Quebec market—in part because of the current emphasis on developing all-Canada plans on the way to having one global strategy.

Gauthier felt the current marketing approach to the Quebec market should be reevaluated because an inappropriate

---

*This case was adapted from one written by Professor Roberta Tamilia, University of Windsor, Canada.

Table 1 Per Capita Consumption Index, Province of Quebec (Canada = 100)*

Cake mixes	107	Soft drinks	126
Pancakes	87	Pie fillings	118
Puddings	114	Frozen dinners	79
Salad dressings	85	Prepared packaged foods	83
Molasses	132	Cookies	123

*An index shows the relative consumption as compared to a standard. In this table, the standard is all of Canada. The data shows that per capita consumption of cake mixes is 7% higher in Quebec and pancake consumption 13% lower compared to all of Canada.

marketing plan may be responsible for the sales slowdown. After all, she said, "80 percent of the market is French-speaking. It's in the best interest of the company to treat that market as being separate and distinct from the rest of Canada."

Gauthier supported her position by showing that Quebec's per capita consumption of many product categories (in which the firm competes) is above the national average (see Table 1). Research projects conducted by Eden Prairie Mills also support the "separate and distinct" argument. Over the years, the firm has found many French–English differences in brand attitudes, lifestyles, usage rates, and so on.

Gauthier argued that the company should develop a unique Quebec marketing plan for some or all of its brands. She specifically suggested that the French-language advertising plan for a particular brand be developed independently of the plan for English Canada.

Currently, the Toronto agency assigned to the brand just translates its English-language ads for the French market. Leroux pointed out that the present advertising approach assured Eden Prairie Mills of a uniform brand image across Canada. Gauthier said she knew what the agency is doing, and that straight translation into Canadian-French may not communicate the same brand image. The discussion that followed suggested that a different brand image might be needed in the French market if the company wanted to stop the brand's decline in sales.

The managers also discussed the food distribution system in Quebec. The major supermarket chains have their lowest market share in that province. Independents are strongest there—the mom-and-pop food stores fast disappearing outside Quebec remain alive and well in the province. Traditionally, these stores have stocked a higher proportion (than supermarkets) of their shelf space with national brands, an advantage for Eden Prairie Mills.

Finally, various issues related to discount policies, pricing structure, sales promotion, and cooperative advertising were discussed. All of these suggested that things were different in Quebec and that future marketing plans should reflect these differences to a greater extent than they do now.

After the meeting, Leroux stayed in her office to think about the situation. Although she agreed with the basic idea that the Quebec market was in many ways different, she wasn't sure how far the company should go in recognizing this fact. She knew that regional differences in food tastes and brand purchases existed not only in Quebec but in other parts of Canada as well. But people are people, after all, with far more similarities than differences, so a Canadian and eventually a global strategy makes some sense too.

Leroux was afraid that giving special status to one region might conflict with top management's objective of achieving standardization whenever possible—one global strategy for Canada, on the way to one worldwide global strategy. She was also worried about the long-term effect of such a policy change on costs, organizational structure, and brand image. Still, enough product managers had expressed their concern over the years about the Quebec market to make her wonder if she shouldn't modify the current approach. Perhaps they could experiment with a few brands—and just in Quebec. She could cite the language difference as the reason for trying Quebec rather than any of the other provinces. But Leroux realizes that any change of policy could be seen as the beginning of more change, and what would Minneapolis think? Could she explain it successfully there?

Evaluate Eden Prairie Mills, Ltd.'s present strategy. What should Jeanne Leroux do now? Explain.

31. At-Home Health Services, Inc.

Kathy Beck, executive director of At-Home Health Services, Inc., is trying to clarify her strategies. She's sure some changes are needed, but she's less sure about how *much* change is needed and/or whether it can be handled by her people.

At-Home Health Services, Inc. (AHHS), is a nonprofit organization that has been operating—with varying degrees of success—for 25 years, offering nursing services in clients' homes. Some of its funding comes from the local United Way—to provide emergency nursing services for those who can't afford to pay. The balance of the revenues—about 90 percent of the $2.2 million annual budget—comes from charges made directly to the client or to third-party payers, including insurance companies, health maintenance organizations (HMOs), and the federal government, for Medicare or Medicaid services.

Kathy has been executive director of AHHS for two years. She has developed a well-functioning organization able to meet most requests for service that come from local doctors and from the discharge officers at local hospitals. Some business also comes by self-referral—the client finds the AHHS name in the Yellow Pages of the local phone directory.

The last two years have been a rebuilding time—because the previous director had personnel problems. This led to a weakening of the agency's image with the local referring agencies. Now the image is more positive. But Kathy is not completely satisfied with the situation. By definition, At-Home Health Services is a nonprofit organization. But it still must cover all its costs: payroll, rent payments, phone expenses, and so on, including Kathy's own salary. She can see that while

AHHS is growing slightly and is now breaking even, it doesn't have much of a cash cushion to fall back on if (1) the demand for AHHS nursing services declines, (2) the government changes its rules about paying for AHHS's kind of nursing services, either cutting back what it will pay for or reducing the amount it will pay for specific services, or (3) new competitors enter the market. In fact, the last possibility concerns Kathy greatly. Some hospitals, squeezed for revenue, are expanding into home health care—especially nursing services as patients are being released earlier from hospitals because of payment limits set by government guidelines. For-profit organizations (e.g., Kelly Home Care Services) are expanding around the country to provide a complete line of home health care services, including nursing services of the kind offered by AHHS. These for-profit organizations appear to be efficiently run, offering good service at competitive and sometimes even lower prices than some nonprofit organizations. And they seem to be doing this at a profit, which suggests that it would be possible for these for-profit companies to lower their prices if nonprofit organizations try to compete on price.

Kathy is considering whether she should ask her board of directors to let her offer a complete line of home health care services—that is, move beyond just nursing services into what she calls "care and comfort" services.

Currently, AHHS is primarily concerned with providing professional nursing care in the home. But AHHS nurses are much too expensive for routine home health care activities—helping fix meals, bathing and dressing patients, and other care and comfort activities. The full cost of a nurse to AHHS, including benefits and overhead, is about $65 per hour. But a registered nurse is not needed for care and comfort services. All that is required is someone who is honest, can get along with all kinds of people, and is willing to do this kind of work. Generally, any mature person can be trained fairly quickly to do the job—following the instructions and under the general supervision of a physician, a nurse, or family members. The full cost of aides is $9 to $16 per hour for short visits and as low as $75 per 24 hours for a live-in aide who has room and board supplied by the client.

The demand for all kinds of home health care services seems to be growing. With more dual-career families and more single-parent households, there isn't anyone in the family to take over home health care when the need arises—due to emergencies or long-term disabilities. Further, hospitals send patients home earlier than in the past. And with people living longer, there are more single-survivor family situations where there is no one nearby to take care of the needs of these older people. But often some family members—or third-party payers such as the government or insurers—are willing to pay for some home health care services. Kathy now occasionally recommends other agencies or suggests one or another of three women who have been doing care and comfort work on their own, part-time. But with growing demand, Kathy wonders if AHHS should get into this business, hiring aides as needed.

Kathy is concerned that a new, full-service home health care organization may come into her market and be a single source for both nursing services and less-skilled home care and comfort services. This has happened already in two nearby but somewhat larger cities. Kathy fears that this might be more appealing than AHHS to the local hospitals and other referrers. In other words, she can see the possibility of losing nursing

service business if AHHS does not begin to offer a complete home health care service. This would cause real problems for AHHS—because overhead costs are more or less fixed. A loss in revenue of as little as 10 percent would require some cutbacks—perhaps laying off some nurses or secretaries, giving up part of the office, and so on.

Another reason for expanding beyond nursing services—using paraprofessionals and relatively unskilled personnel—is to offer a better service to present customers *and* make more effective use of the computer systems and organization structure that she has developed over the last two years. Kathy estimates that the administrative and office capabilities could handle twice as many clients without straining the system. It would be necessary to add some clerical help—if the expansion were quite large. But this increase in overhead would be minor compared to the present proportion of total revenue that goes to covering overhead. In other words, additional clients or more work for some current clients could increase revenue and ensure the survival of AHHS, provide a cushion to cover the normal fluctuations in demand, and ensure more job security for the administrative personnel.

Further, Kathy thinks that if AHHS were successful in expanding its services—and therefore could generate some surplus—it could extend services to those who aren't now able to pay. Kathy says one of the worst parts of her job is refusing service to clients whose third-party benefits have run out or for whatever reason can no longer afford to pay. She is uncomfortable about having to cut off service, but she must schedule her nurses to provide revenue-producing services if she's going to meet the payroll every two weeks. By expanding to provide more services, she might be able to keep serving more of these nonpaying clients. This possibility excites Kathy because her nurse's training has instilled a deep desire to serve people in need, whether they can pay or not. This continual pressure to cut off service because people can't pay has been at the root of many disagreements and even arguments between the nurses serving the clients and Kathy, as executive director and representative of the board of directors.

Kathy knows that expanding into care and comfort services won't be easy. Some decisions would be needed about relative pay levels for nurses, paraprofessionals, and aides. AHHS would also have to set prices for these different services and tell current customers and referral agencies about the expanded services.

These problems aren't bothering Kathy too much, however—she thinks she can handle them. She is sure that care and comfort services are in demand and could be supplied at competitive prices.

Her primary concern is whether this is the right thing for At-Home Health Services—basically a nursing organization—to do. AHHS's whole history has been oriented to supplying *nurses'* services. Nurses are dedicated professionals who bring high standards to any job they undertake. The question is whether AHHS should offer less-professional services. Inevitably, some of the aides will not be as dedicated as the nurses might like them to be. And this could reflect unfavorably on the nurse image. At a minimum, she would need to set up some sort of training program for the aides. As Kathy worries about the future of AHHS, and her own future, it seems that there are no easy answers.

Evaluate AHHS's present strategy. What should Kathy Beck do? Explain.

32. Lever, Ltd.*

Chen Li is product manager for Guard Deodorant Soap. He was just transferred to Lever, Ltd., a Canadian subsidiary of Lever Group, Inc., from world headquarters in New York. Chen is anxious to make a good impression because he is hoping to transfer to Lever's London office. He is working on developing and securing management approval of next year's marketing plan for Guard. His first job is submitting a draft marketing plan to Aly Keystone, his recently appointed group product manager, who is responsible for several such plans from product managers like Chen.

Chen's marketing plan is the single most important document he will produce on this assignment. This annual marketing plan does three main things:

1. It reviews the brand's performance in the past year, assesses the competitive situation, and highlights problems and opportunities for the brand.
2. It spells out marketing strategies and the plan for the coming year.
3. Finally, and most importantly, the marketing plan sets out the brand's sales objectives and advertising/promotion budget requirements.

In preparing this marketing plan, Chen gathered the information in Table 1.

---

*Adapted from a case prepared by Daniel Aronchick, who at the time of its preparation was marketing manager at Thomas J. Lipton, Limited.

Chen was somewhat surprised at the significant regional differences in the bar soap market:

1. The underdevelopment of the deodorant bar segment in Quebec, with a corresponding overdevelopment of the beauty bar segment. But some past research suggested that this is due to cultural factors—English-speaking people have been more interested than others in cleaning, deodorizing, and disinfecting. A similar pattern is seen in most European countries, where the adoption of deodorant soaps has been slower than in North America. For similar reasons, the perfumed soap share is highest in French-speaking Quebec.
2. The overdevelopment of synthetic bars (Zest, Dial) in the Prairies (Manitoba/Saskatchewan and Alberta). These bars, primarily in the deodorant segment, lather better in the hard water of the Prairies. Nonsynthetic bars lather very poorly in hard-water areas and leave a soap film.
3. The overdevelopment of the "all-other" segment in Quebec. This segment, consisting of smaller brands, fares better in Quebec, where 43 percent of the grocery trade is done by independent stores. Conversely, large chain grocery stores dominate in Ontario and the Prairies.

Chen's brand, Guard, is a highly perfumed deodorant bar. His business is relatively weak in the key Ontario market. To confirm this share data, Chen calculated consumption of Guard per thousand people in each region (see Table 2).

Table 1 Past 12-Month Share of Bar Soap Market (percent)

	Maritimes	Quebec	Ontario	Manitoba/Saskatchewan	Alberta	British Columbia
Deodorant segment						
Zest	21.3%	14.2%	24.5%	31.2%	30.4%	25.5%
Dial	10.4	5.1	12.8	16.1	17.2	14.3
Lifebuoy	4.2	3.1	1.2	6.4	5.8	4.2
Guard	2.1	5.6	1.0	4.2	4.2	2.1
Beauty bar segment						
Camay	6.2	12.3	7.0	4.1	4.0	5.1
Lux	6.1	11.2	7.7	5.0	6.9	5.0
Dove	5.5	8.0	6.6	6.3	6.2	4.2
Lower-priced bars						
Ivory	11.2	6.5	12.4	5.3	5.2	9.0
Sunlight	6.1	3.2	8.2	4.2	4.1	8.0
All others (including stores' own brands)	26.9	30.8	18.6	17.2	16.0	22.6
Total bar soap market	100.0%	100.0%	100.0%	100.0%	100.0%	100.0%

Table 2   Standard Cases of 3-Ounce Bars Consumed per 1,000 People in 12 Months

	Maritimes	Quebec	Ontario	Manitoba/ Saskatchewan	Alberta	British Columbia
Guard	4.1	10.9	1.9	8.1	4.1	6.2
Sales index	66	175	31	131	131	100

These differences are especially interesting since per capita sales of all bar soap products are roughly equal in all provinces.

A consumer attitude and usage research study was conducted approximately a year ago. This study revealed that consumer "top-of-mind" awareness of the Guard brand differed greatly across Canada. This was true despite the even—by population—expenditure of advertising funds in past years. Also, trial of Guard was low in the Maritimes, Ontario, and British Columbia (see Table 3).

The attitude portion of the research revealed that consumers who had heard of Guard were aware that its deodorant protection came mainly from a high fragrance level. This was the main selling point in the copy, and it was well communicated by Guard's advertising. The other important finding was that consumers who had tried Guard were satisfied with the product. About 70 percent of those trying Guard had repurchased the product at least twice.

Chen has also discovered that bar soap competition is especially intense in Ontario. It is Canada's largest market, and many competitors want a share of it. The chain stores are also quite aggressive in promotion and pricing—offering specials, in-store coupons, and so on. They want to move goods. And because of this, two key Ontario chains have put Guard on their pending delisting sheets. These chains, which control about half the grocery volume in Ontario, are dissatisfied with how slowly Guard is moving off the shelves.

Now Chen feels he is ready to set a key part of the brand's marketing plan for next year: how to allocate the advertising/ sales promotion budget by region.

Guard's present advertising/sales promotion budget is 20 percent of sales. With forecast sales of $4 million, this would amount to an $800,000 expenditure. Traditionally such funds have been allocated in proportion to population (see Table 4).

Chen feels he should spend more heavily in Ontario where the grocery chain delisting problem exists. Last year, 36 percent of Guard's budget was allocated to Ontario, which accounted for only 12 percent of Guard's sales. Chen wants to increase Ontario spending to 48 percent of the total budget by taking funds evenly from all other areas. Chen expects this will increase business in the key Ontario market, which has

over a third of Canada's population, because it is a big increase and will help Guard "outshout" the many other competitors who are promoting heavily.

Chen presented this idea to Keystone, his newly appointed group product manager. Keystone strongly disagrees. She has also been reviewing Guard's business and feels that promotion funds have historically been misallocated. It is her strong belief that, to use her words, "A brand should spend where its business is." Keystone believes that the first priority in allocating funds regionally is to support the areas of strength. She suggested to Chen that there may be more business to be had in the brand's strong areas, Quebec and the Prairies, than in chasing sales in Ontario. The needs and attitudes toward Guard, as well as competitive pressures, may vary a lot among the provinces. Therefore, Keystone suggested that spending for Guard in the coming year be proportional to the brand's sales by region rather than to regional population.

Chen is convinced this is wrong, particularly in light of the Ontario situation. He asked Keystone how the Ontario market should be handled. She said that the conservative way to build business in Ontario is to invest incremental promotion funds. However, before these incremental funds are invested, a test of this Ontario investment proposition should be conducted. Keystone recommended that some of the Ontario money should be used to conduct an investment-spending market test in a small area or town in Ontario for 12 months. This will enable Chen to see if the incremental spending results in higher sales and profits—profits large enough to justify higher spending. In other words, an investment payout should be assured before spending any extra money in Ontario. Similarly, Keystone would do the same kind of test in Quebec—to see if more money should go there.

After several e-mails back and forth, Chen feels this approach would be a waste of time and unduly cautious, given the importance of the Ontario market and the likely delistings in two key chains.

Evaluate the present strategy for Guard and Chen's and Keystone's proposed strategies. How should the promotion money be allocated? Should investment-spending market tests be run first? Why? Explain.

Table 3   Usage Results (in percent)

	Maritimes	Quebec	Ontario	Manitoba/ Saskatchewan	Alberta	British Columbia
Respondents aware of Guard	20%	58%	28%	30%	32%	16%
Respondents ever trying Guard	3	18	2	8	6	4

Table 4 Allocation of Advertising/Sales Promotion Budget, by Population

	Maritimes	Quebec	Ontario	Manitoba/ Saskatchewan	Alberta	British Columbia	Canada
Percent of population	10%	27%	36%	8%	8%	11%	100%
Possible allocation of budget based on population (in 000s)	$80	$216	$288	$64	$64	$88	$800
Percent of Guard business at present	7%	51%	12%	11%	11%	8%	100%

33. Mulligan & Starling

The partners of Mulligan & Starling are having a serious discussion about what the firm should do in the near future.

Mulligan & Starling (M&S) is a medium-size regional certified public accounting firm based in Grand Rapids, Michigan, with branch offices in Lansing and Detroit. Mulligan & Starling has nine partners and a professional staff of approximately 105 accountants. Gross service billings for the fiscal year ending June 30, 2008, were $6.9 million. Financial data for 2008, 2007, and 2006 are presented in Table 1.

M&S's professional services include auditing, tax preparation, bookkeeping, and some general management consulting. Its client base includes municipal governments (cities, villages, and townships), manufacturing companies, professional organizations (attorneys, doctors, and dentists), and various other small businesses. A good share of revenue comes from the firm's municipal practice. Table 1 gives M&S's gross revenue by service area and client industry for 2008, 2007, and 2006.

At the monthly partners' meeting held in July 2008, James Mulligan, the firm's managing partner (CEO), expressed concern about the future of the firm's municipal practice. James' presentation to his partners follows:

Although our firm is considered to be a leader in municipal auditing in our geographic area, I am concerned that as municipals attempt to cut their operating costs, they will solicit competitive bids from other public accounting firms to perform their annual audits. Three of the four largest accounting firms in the world have local offices in our area. Because they concentrate their practice in the manufacturing industry—which typically has December 31 fiscal year-ends—they have "available" staff during the summer months.

Therefore, they can afford to low-ball competitive bids to keep their staffs busy and benefit from on-the-job training provided by municipal clientele. I am concerned that we may begin to lose clients in our most established and profitable practice area.*

Rene Starling, a senior partner in the firm and the partner in charge of the firm's municipal practice, was the first to respond to James' concern.

*Organizations with December fiscal year-ends require audit work to be performed during the fall and in January and February. Those with June 30 fiscal year-ends require auditing during the summer months.

Table 1 Fiscal Year Ending June 30

	2008	2007	2006
Gross billings	$6,900,000	$6,400,000	$5,800,000
Gross billings by service area:			
Auditing	3,100,000	3,200,000	2,750,000
Tax preparation	1,990,000	1,830,000	1,780,000
Bookkeeping	1,090,000	745,000	660,000
Other	720,000	625,000	610,000
Gross billings by client industry:			
Municipal	3,214,000	3,300,000	2,908,000
Manufacturing	2,089,000	1,880,000	1,706,000
Professional	1,355,000	1,140,000	1,108,000
Other	242,000	80,000	78,000

James, we all recognize the potential threat of being underbid for our municipal work by our large accounting competitors. However, M&S is a leader in municipal auditing in Michigan, and we have much more local experience than our competitors. Furthermore, it is a fact that we offer a superior level of service to our clients—which goes beyond the services normally expected during an audit to include consulting on financial and other operating issues. Many of our less sophisticated clients depend on our nonaudit consulting assistance. Therefore, I believe, we have been successful in differentiating our services from our competitors. In many recent situations, M&S was selected over a field of as many as 10 competitors even though our proposed prices were much higher than those of our competitors.

The partners at the meeting agreed with Rene's comments. However, even though M&S had many success stories regarding their ability to retain their municipal clients—despite being underbid—they had lost three large municipal clients during the past year. Rene was asked to comment on the loss of those clients. She explained that the lost clients are larger municipalities with a lot of in-house financial expertise and therefore less dependent on M&S's consulting assistance. As a result, M&S's service differentiation went largely unnoticed. Rene explained that the larger, more sophisticated municipals regard audits as a necessary evil and usually select the low-cost reputable bidder.

James then requested ideas and discussion from the other partners at the meeting. One partner, Frazier Long, suggested that M&S should protect itself by diversifying. Specifically, he felt a substantial practice development effort should be directed toward manufacturing. He reasoned that since manufacturing work would occur during M&S's off-season, M&S could afford to price very low to gain new manufacturing clients. This strategy would also help to counter (and possibly discourage) low-ball pricing for municipals by the three large accounting firms mentioned earlier.

Another partner, Lin Tan, suggested that "if we have consulting skills, we ought to promote them more, instead of hoping that the clients will notice and come to appreciate us. Further, maybe we ought to be more aggressive in calling on smaller potential clients."

Another partner, Will Ruiz, agreed with Tan, but wanted to go further. He suggested that they recognize that there are at least two types of municipal customers and that two (at least) different strategies be implemented, including lower prices for auditing only for larger municipal customers and/or higher prices for smaller customers who are buying consulting too. This caused a big uproar from some who said this would lead to price cutting of professional services and M&S didn't want to be price cutters: "One price for all is the professional way."

However, another partner, Megan Cullen, agreed with Will and suggested they go even further—pricing consulting services separately. In fact, she suggested that the partners consider setting up a separate department for consulting—like the large accounting firms have done. This can be a very profitable business. But it is a different kind of business and eventually may require different kinds of people and a different organization. For now, however, it may be desirable to appoint a manager for consulting services—with a budget—to be sure it gets proper attention. This suggestion too caused serious disagreement. Partners pointed out that having a separate consulting arm had led to major conflicts, especially in some larger accounting firms. The initial problems were internal. The consultants often brought in more profit than the auditors, but the auditors controlled the partnership and the successful consultants didn't always feel that they got their share of the rewards. But there had also been serious external problems and charges of unethical behavior based on the concern that big accounting firms had a conflict of interest when they did audits on publicly traded companies that they in turn relied on for consulting income. Because of problems in this area, the Securities Exchange Commission created new guidelines that have changed how the big four accounting firms handle consulting. On the other hand, several partners argued that this was really an opportunity for M&S because their firm handled very few companies listed with the SEC, and the conflict of interest issues didn't even apply with municipal clients.

James thanked everyone for their comments and encouraged them to debate these issues in smaller groups and to share ideas by e-mail before coming to a one-day retreat (in two weeks) to continue this discussion and come to some conclusions.

Evaluate M&S's situation. What strategy(ies) should the partners select? Why?

34. Innovative Aluminum Products, Inc.*

Diego Puerta, newly hired VP of marketing for Innovative Aluminum Products, Inc. (IAP), is reviewing the firm's international distribution arrangements because they don't seem to be very well thought out. He is not sure if anything is wrong, but he feels that the company should follow a global strategy rather than continuing its current policies.

IAP, based in Atlanta, Georgia, produces finished aluminum products, such as aluminum ladders, umbrella-type clothes racks, scaffolding, and patio tables and chairs that fold flat. Sales in 2008 reached $25 million, primarily to U.S. customers.

In 2004, IAP decided to try selling in select foreign markets. The sales manager, Lisa Wingate, believed the growing affluence of European workers would help the company's products gain market acceptance quickly.

Lisa's first step in investigating foreign markets was to join a trade mission to Europe, a tour organized by the U.S. Department of Commerce. This trade mission visited Italy, Germany, Denmark, Holland, France, and England. During

*Adapted from a case written by Professor Hardy, University of Western Ontario, Canada.

this trip, Lisa was officially introduced to leading buyers for department store chains, import houses, wholesalers, and buying groups. The two-week trip convinced Lisa that there was ample buying power to make exporting a profitable opportunity.

On her return to Atlanta, Lisa's next step was to obtain credit references for the firms she considered potential distributors. To those who were judged creditworthy, she sent letters expressing interest and samples, brochures, prices, and other relevant information.

The first orders were from a French wholesaler. Sales in this market totaled $70,000 in 2005. Similar success was achieved in Germany and England. Italy, on the other hand, did not produce any sales. Lisa felt the semiluxury nature of the company's products and the lower incomes in Italy encouraged a "making do" attitude rather than purchase of goods and services that would make life easier.

In the United States, IAP distributes through fairly aggressive and well-organized merchant hardware distributors and buying groups, such as cooperative and voluntary hardware chains, which have taken over much of the strategy planning for cooperating producers and retailers. In its foreign markets, however, there is no recognizable pattern. Channel systems vary from country to country. To avoid channel conflict, IAP has only one account in each country. The chosen distributor is the exclusive distributor.

In France, IAP distributes through a wholesaler based in Paris. This wholesaler has five salespeople covering the country. The firm specializes in small housewares and has contacts with leading buying groups, wholesalers, and department stores. Lisa is impressed with the firm's aggressiveness and knowledge of merchandising techniques.

In Germany, IAP sells to a Hamburg-based buying group for hardware wholesalers throughout the country. Lisa felt this group would provide excellent coverage of the market because of its extensive distribution network.

In Denmark, IAP's line is sold to a buying group representing a chain of hardware retailers. This group recently expanded to include retailers in Sweden, Finland, and Norway. Together this group purchases goods for about 500 hardware retailers. The buying power of Scandinavians is quite high, and it is expected that IAP's products will prove very successful there.

In the United Kingdom, IAP uses an importer-distributor, who both buys on his own account and acts as a sales agent. The distributor approached IAP after finding the company from an online search. This firm sells to department stores and hardware wholesalers. This firm has not done very well overall, but it has done very well with IAP's line of patio tables and chairs.

Australia is handled by an importer who operates a chain of discount houses. It heard about IAP from a U.K. contact. After extensive e-mailing, this firm discovered it could land aluminum patio furniture in Melbourne at prices competitive with Chinese imports. So it started ordering because it wanted to cut prices in a high-priced garden furniture market.

The Argentina market is handled by an American who lives in Buenos Aires but came to the United States in search of new lines. IAP attributes success in Argentina to the efforts of this aggressive and capable agent. He has built a sizable trade in aluminum ladders.

In Trinidad and Jamaica, IAP's products are handled by traders who carry such diversified lines as insurance, apples, plums, and fish. They have been successful in selling aluminum ladders. This business grew out of inquiries sent to the U.S. Department of Commerce and in researching its website (www.commerce.gov), which Lisa followed up by phone.

Lisa's export policies for IAP are as follows:

1. *Product:* No product modifications will be made in selling to foreign customers. This may be considered later after a substantial sales volume develops.

2. *Place:* New distributors will be contacted through foreign trade shows. Lisa considers large distributors desirable. She feels, however, that they are not as receptive as smaller distributors to a new, unestablished product line. Therefore, she prefers to appoint small distributors. Larger distributors may be appointed after the company has gained a strong consumer franchise in a country.

3. *Promotion:* The firm does no advertising in foreign markets. Brochures and sales literature already being used in the United States are supplied to foreign distributors, who are encouraged to adapt them or create new materials as required. IAP will continue to promote its products by participating in overseas trade shows. These are handled by the sales manager. All inquiries are forwarded to the firm's distributor in that country.

4. *Price:* The company does not publish suggested list prices. Distributors add their own markup to their landed costs. Supply prices will be kept as low as possible. This is accomplished by (*a*) removing advertising expenses and other strictly domestic overhead charges from price calculations, (*b*) finding the most economical packages for shipping (smallest volume per unit), and (*c*) bargaining with carriers to obtain the lowest shipping rates possible.

5. *Financing:* IAP sees no need to provide financial help to distributors. The company views its major contribution as providing good products at the lowest possible prices.

6. *Marketing and planning assistance:* Lisa feels that foreign distributors know their own markets best. Therefore, they are best equipped to plan for themselves.

7. *Selection of foreign markets:* The evaluation of foreign market opportunities for the company's products is based primarily on income and lifestyle patterns. For example, Lisa fails to see any market in North Africa for IAP's products, which she thinks are of a semiluxury nature. She thinks that cheaper products such as wood ladders (often homemade) are preferred to prefabricated aluminum ladders in regions such as North Africa and Southern Europe. Argentina, on the other hand, she thinks is a more highly industrialized market with luxury tastes. Thus, Lisa sees IAP's products as better suited for more highly industrialized and affluent societies.

Evaluate IAP's present foreign markets strategies. Should it develop a global strategy? What strategy or strategies should Diego Puerta (the new VP of marketing) develop? Explain.

35. Mama Rossi's Pizza

Karen Linke, manager of the Mama Rossi's Pizza store in Flint, Michigan, is trying to develop a plan for the "sick" store she just took over.

Mama Rossi's Pizza is an owner-managed pizza take-out and delivery business with three stores located in Ann Arbor, Southfield, and Flint, Michigan. Mama Rossi's business comes from telephone, fax, or walk-in orders. Each Mama Rossi's store prepares its own pizzas. In addition to pizzas, Mama Rossi's also sells and delivers a limited selection of soft drinks.

Mama Rossi's Ann Arbor store has been very successful. Much of the store's success may be due to being close to the University of Michigan campus. Most of these students live within 5 miles of Mama Rossi's Ann Arbor store.

The Southfield store has been moderately successful. It serves mostly residential customers in the Southfield area, a largely residential suburb of Detroit. Recently, the store advertised—using direct-mail flyers—to several office buildings within 3 miles of the store. The flyers described Mama Rossi's willingness and ability to cater large orders for office parties, business luncheons, and so on. The promotion was quite successful. With this new program and Mama Rossi's solid residential base of customers in Southfield, improved profitability at the Southfield location seems assured.

Mama Rossi's Flint location has had mixed results during the last three years. The Flint store has been obtaining only about half of its orders from residential delivery requests. The Flint store's new manager, Karen, believes the problem with residential pizza delivery in Flint is due to the location of residential neighborhoods in the area. Flint has several large industrial plants (mostly auto industry related) located throughout the city. Small, mostly factory-worker neighborhoods are distributed in between the various plant sites. As a result, Mama Rossi's store location can serve only two or three of these neighbor-

hoods on one delivery run. Competition is also relevant. Mama Rossi's has several aggressive competitors who advertise heavily, distribute cents-off coupons, and offer 2-for-1 deals. This aggressive competition is probably why Mama Rossi's residential sales leveled off in the last year or so. And this competitive pressure seems likely to continue as some of this competition comes from aggressive national chains that are fighting for market share and squeezing little firms like Mama Rossi's. For now, anyway, Karen feels she knows how to meet this competition and hold on to the present residential sales level.

Most of the Flint store's upside potential seems to be in serving the large industrial plants. Many of these plants work two or three shifts, five days a week. During each work shift, workers are allowed one half-hour lunch break—which usually occurs at 11 A.M., 8 P.M., or 2:30 A.M., depending on the shift.

Generally, a customer will phone or fax from a plant about 30 minutes before a scheduled lunch break and order several (5 to 10) pizzas for a work group. Mama Rossi's may receive many orders of this size from the same plant (i.e., from different groups of workers). The plant business is very profitable for several reasons. First, a large number of pizzas can be delivered at the same time to the same location, saving transportation costs.

Second, plant orders usually involve many different toppings (double cheese, pepperoni, mushrooms, hamburger) on each pizza. This results in $11 to $14 revenue per pizza. The delivery drivers also like delivering plant orders because the tips are usually $1 to $2 per pizza.

Despite the profitability of the plant orders, several factors make it difficult to serve the plant market. Mama Rossi's store is located 5 to 8 minutes from most of the plant sites, so Mama Rossi's staff must prepare the orders within 20 to 25 minutes after it receives the telephone order. Often, inadequate staff

Table 1 Practical Capacities and Sales Potential of Current Equipment and Personnel

	11 A.M. Break	8 P.M. Break	2:30 A.M. Break	Daily Totals
Current capacity (pizzas)	48	48	48	144
Average selling price per unit	$ 12.50	$ 12.50	$ 12.50	$ 12.50
Sales potential	$600	$600	$600	$1,800
Variable cost (approximately 40 percent of selling price)*	240	240	240	720
Contribution margin of pizzas	360	360	360	1,080
Beverage sales (2 medium-sized beverages per pizza ordered at 75¢ a piece)†	72	72	72	216
Cost of beverages (30% per beverage)	22	22	22	66
Contribution margin of beverages	50	50	50	150
Total contribution of pizza and beverages	$ 410	$ 410	$ 410	$ 1,230

*The variable cost estimate of 40% of sales includes variable costs of delivery to plant locations.

†Amounts shown are not physical capacities (there is almost unlimited physical capacity), but potential sales volume is constrained by number of pizzas that can be sold.

Table 2 Capacity and Demand for Plant Customer Market

	Estimated Daily Demand	Current Daily Capacity	Proposed Daily Capacity
Pizza units (1 pizza)	320	144	300

and/or oven capacity means it is impossible to get all the orders heated at the same time.

Generally, plant workers will wait as long as 10 minutes past the start of their lunch break before ordering from various vending trucks that arrive at the plant sites during lunch breaks. (Currently, no other pizza delivery stores are in good positions to serve the plant locations and have chosen not to compete.) But there have been a few instances when workers refused to pay for pizzas that were only five minutes late! Worse yet, if the same work group gets a couple of late orders, they are lost as future customers. Karen believes that the inconsistent profitability of the Flint store is partly the result of such lost customers.

In an effort to rebuild the plant delivery business, Karen is considering various methods to ensure prompt customer delivery. She thinks that potential demand during lunch breaks is significantly above Mama Rossi's present capacity. Karen also knows that if she tries to satisfy all phone or fax orders on some peak days, she won't be able to provide prompt service and may lose more plant customers.

Karen has outlined three alternatives that may win back some of the plant business for the Flint store. She has developed these alternatives to discuss with Mama Rossi's owner. Each alternative is briefly described below:

Alternative 1: Determine practical capacities during peak volume periods using existing equipment and personnel. Accept orders only up to that capacity and politely decline orders beyond. This approach will ensure prompt customer service and high product quality. It will also minimize losses resulting from customers' rejection of late deliveries. Financial analysis of this alternative—shown in Table 1—indicates that a potential daily contribution to profit of $1,230 could result if this alternative is implemented successfully. This would be profit before promotion costs, overhead, and net profit (or loss). *Note:* Any alternative will require several thousand dollars to reinform potential plant

customers that Mama Rossi's has improved its service and "wants your business."

Alternative 2: Buy additional equipment (one oven and one delivery car) and hire additional staff to handle peak loads. This approach would ensure timely customer delivery and high product quality as well as provide additional capacity to handle unmet demand. Table 2 is a conservative estimate of potential daily demand for plant orders compared to current capacity and proposed increased capacity. Table 3 gives the cost of acquiring the additional equipment and relevant information related to depreciation and fixed costs.

Using this alternative, the following additional pizza delivery and preparation personnel costs would be required:

	Hours Required	Cost per Hour	Total Additional Daily Cost
Delivery personnel	6	6	$36.00
Preparation personnel	8	6	48.00
			$84.00

The addition of even more equipment and personnel to handle all unmet demand was not considered in this alternative because the current store is not large enough.

Alternative 3: Add additional equipment and personnel as described in alternative 2, but move to a new location that would reduce delivery lead times to 2 to 5 minutes. This move would probably allow Mama Rossi's to handle all unmet demand—because the reduction in delivery time will provide for additional oven time. In fact, Mama Rossi's might have excess capacity using this approach.

A suitable store is available near about the same number of residential customers (including many of the store's current residential customers). The available store is slightly larger than needed. And the rent is higher. Relevant cost information on the proposed store follows:

Additional rental expense of proposed store over current store	$1,600 per year
Cost of moving to new store (one-time cost)	$16,000

Table 3 Cost of Required Additional Assets

	Cost	Estimated Useful Life	Salvage Value	Annual Depreciation*	Daily Depreciation
Delivery car (equipped with pizza warmer)	$11,000	5 years	$1,000	$2,000	$5.71
Pizza oven	$20,000	8 years	$2,000	$2,250	$6.43

*Annual depreciation is calculated on a straight-line basis.

†Daily depreciation assumes a 350-day (plant production) year. All variable expenses related to each piece of equipment (e.g., utilities, gas, oil) are included in the variable cost of a pizza.

Karen presented the three alternatives to Mama Rossi's owner, Pepe Rossi. Pepe was pleased that Karen had done her homework. He decided that Karen should make the final decision on what to do (in part because she had a profit-sharing agreement with Pepe) and offered the following comments and concerns:

1. Pepe agreed that the plant market was extremely sensitive to delivery timing. Product quality and pricing, although important, were of less importance.
2. He agreed that plant demand estimates were conservative. "In fact, they may be 10 to 30 percent low."
3. Pepe expressed concern that under alternative 2, and especially under alternative 3, much of the store's capacity would go unused over 80 percent of the time.

4. He was also concerned that Mama Rossi's store had a bad reputation with plant customers because the prior store manager was not sensitive to timely plant delivery. So Pepe suggested that Karen develop a promotion plan to improve Mama Rossi's reputation in the plants and be sure that everyone knows that Mama Rossi's has improved its delivery service.

Evaluate Karen's possible strategies for the Flint store's plant market. What should Karen do? Why? Suggest possible promotion plans for your preferred strategy.

36. Sorenson Builders*

Paul Sorenson, who seven years ago founded Sorenson Builders in Asheville, North Carolina, is excited that he'll complete his first LEED-certified "green" home this month. The LEED (Leadership in Energy and Environmental Design) rating means that the home uses 30 percent less energy and 20 percent less water than a conventional house; construction waste going into landfills must also be reduced. The house will be the model home to showcase Paul's new development, which includes four more homes that he hopes to complete in the next six months.

Although Paul is excited, he is also nervous. Rising interest rates and an uncertain economy have reduced demand in the local housing market. People who do buy a home are more price-sensitive. That's a problem because building a green house usually increases construction costs—but customers are not always aware of the benefits that come with the higher price tag. So, Paul has to figure out how to find home buyers that are willing to pay a premium for his "green" homes.

Prior to building this home, Paul tried to make environmentally responsible building choices that didn't increase his costs. However, two years ago while at the National Association of Home Builders' convention in Orlando, Florida, Paul visited a booth that described LEED Certification and it appealed to him. He also met a number of new suppliers who were offering sustainable building materials. When Paul returned from the convention in Orlando, Sorenson Builders salesperson Charlotte Reyes told him that more home buyers were asking about environmental and energy-saving features. Paul thought the time was right to commit to building at least a few homes that met higher environmental standards.

Paul kept his eye out for a good piece of property for his project. Before long he found a 3-acre parcel of land about 15 minutes from downtown Asheville. The land had a nice mix of hardwood trees and a small stream, but lacked the panoramic mountain views expected by high-end home buyers in the area. Nevertheless, Paul thought the property would be ideal for a small neighborhood of moderate-size green homes. He purchased the land—and his first green project was under way.

Paul worked closely with a local architect, Lauren Page, who had won several awards from the Green Building Council for her innovative designs. Lauren proposed that each home follow a theme based on a classic Appalachian farmhouse design that would blend well with the rural surroundings and fit the concept of clustered development. Clustered development allows a builder to increase the number of home sites allowed if land is set aside for open space. For example, regulations usually required at least one acre for a rural home site. However, in a clustered development, the county would allow Paul to build five homes on 1.5 acres of his land if he dedicated the remaining 1.5 acres as open space controlled by a conservation easement.

Initially, Paul thought the additional two home sites and preservation of open space would be a huge benefit for his project. However, to get the development permit, he had to provide the county with a special land survey and biological inventory of the site. This extra survey work cost Paul $25,000 more than was normal.

Paul is behind schedule with construction because working with new types of materials has slowed him down. In some cases his workers even had to be trained by factory representatives on the proper installation of materials. In addition, many of the materials in a LEED home—such as low-E windows, blown foam insulation, a high-efficiency furnace and water heater, and Energy Star appliances—have premium prices. As a result, Paul's LEED-certified homes cost about 10 percent more than a conventionally built home of the same size.

However, LEED homes do offer buyers a number of benefits. Toxin-free building materials help combat indoor air pollution—and green homes are less likely to have problems with mold or mildew. Energy and water savings for the homes Paul is building should be $2,000 to $3,000 per year. Plus, buyers can feel good that their homes produce fewer greenhouse gases, reduce dependence on fossil fuels, and send less construction waste to the local landfill.

Paul priced the five homes he is building at $250,000 to $300,000—about 10 percent more than similar non-LEED-certified homes in the area. So far, the homes are getting a few looks, but none has sold and he hasn't had an offer. The feedback that Charlotte Reyes hears is that people like the homes, but think that the price seems to be high; they like the general

*Erik Hardy did the research for an earlier version of this case.

idea of owning a green home and saving money on energy, but they don't focus on the benefits. Perhaps that is because real estate agents in the area have little experience with green building and are used to talking about value in terms of "cost per square foot."

Charlotte Reyes works full-time as a real estate agent—and Sorenson Builders is one of her clients. She receives a 1 percent sales commission for every Sorenson home that is sold. She typically writes the listing that all real estate agents can read on the Multiple Listing Service (MLS) website and also handles the contract to complete a sale. However, with no movement on Paul's new houses and with prime spring selling season coming up fast, Paul has asked Charlotte to meet with him to discuss ways to spark more interest in his development. Paul wants a plan that will bring people out to see his new homes and development—and a way to ensure that they are aware of the benefits he is offering.

Paul wonders what needs to be done to tell customers about the benefits of green building. Some other builders are advertising in local media and developing brochures to leave in a rack outside of their homes—but Paul has not needed to do that before. He wonders if he might be able to generate some inexpensive publicity by working with the local newspaper; it has run several feature stories about the environment but none about green building. He also thinks he needs to do more to convince real estate agents about the benefits of green housing. One idea is to ask someone at the Green Building Council or possibly his architect to put on a seminar, but Paul doesn't know if real estate agents will show up. He also wonders if putting signs in his model home to point out the environmental benefits might be helpful.

When Paul started his project, he thought his green homes would sell themselves, but now he wonders if he isn't ahead of his time.

What do you think of Paul Sorenson's marketing strategy so far? What promotion objectives should Paul set for his marketing strategy? What are the advantages and disadvantages of targeting communications at consumers as compared to real estate agents? What would you recommend as a promotion blend?

Guide to the use of computer-aided problems

Computer-Aided Problem Solving

Marketing managers are problem solvers who must make many decisions. Solving problems and making good decisions usually involves analysis of marketing information. Such information is often expressed in numbers—like costs, revenues, prices, and number of customers or salespeople. Most marketing managers use a computer to keep track of the numbers and speed through calculations. The computer can also make it easier to look at a problem from many different angles—for example, to see how a change in the sales forecast might impact expected sales revenue, costs, and profit.

The computer can only take a manager so far. The manager is the one who puts it all together—and it still takes skill to decide what the information means. The computer-aided problems at the end of the chapters in this text were developed by the authors to help you develop this skill. To work on the problems, you use the computer-aided problem (CAP) software that is available at the text's online learning center (and also included on the *Student CD-ROM to Accompany Essentials of Marketing* that is optionally available with this text).

The problems are short descriptions of decisions faced by marketing managers. Each description includes information to help make the decision. With each problem there are several questions for you to answer. Further, the *Learning Aid for Use with Essentials of Marketing* includes additional questions related to each problem.

Although you will use the computer program to do an analysis, most problems ask you to indicate what decision you would make and why. Thus, in these problems—as in the marketing manager's job—the computer is just a tool to help you make better decisions.

Each problem focuses on one or more of the marketing decision areas discussed in the corresponding chapter. The earlier problems require less marketing knowledge and are simpler in terms of the analysis involved. The later problems build on the principles already covered in the text. The problems can be used in many ways. And the same problem can be analyzed several times for different purposes. Although it is not necessary to do all of the problems or to do them in a particular order, you will probably want to start with the first problem. This practice problem is simpler than the others. In fact, you could do the calculations quite easily without a computer. But this problem will help you see how the program works and how it can help you solve the more complicated problems that come later.

Spreadsheet Analysis of Marketing Problems

Marketing managers often use spreadsheet analysis to evaluate their alternatives—and the program for the computer-aided problems does computerized spreadsheet analysis. In spreadsheet analysis, costs, revenue, and other data related to a marketing problem are organized into a data table—a spreadsheet. The spreadsheet analysis allows you to change the value of one or more of the variables in the data table—to see how each change affects the value of other variables. This is possible because the relationships among the variables are already programmed into the computer. You do not need to do any programming. Let's look at an overly simple example.

You are a marketing manager interested in the total revenue that will result from a particular marketing strategy. You are considering selling your product at $10.00 per unit. You expect to sell 100 units. In our CAP analysis, this problem might be shown in a (very simple) spreadsheet that looks like this:

Variable	Value
Selling price	$10.00
Units sold	100
Total revenue	$1,000.00

There is only one basic relationship in this spreadsheet: Total revenue is equal to the selling price multiplied by the number of units sold. If that relationship has been programmed into the computer (as it is in these problems), you can change the selling price or the number of units you expect to sell, and the program will automatically compute the new value for total revenue.

But now you can ask questions like: What if I raise the price to $10.40 and still sell 100 units? What will happen to total revenue? To get the answer, all you have to do is enter the new price in the spreadsheet, and the program will compute the total revenue for you.

You may also want to do many "what-if" analyses—for example, to see how total revenue changes over a range of prices. Spreadsheet analysis allows you to do this quickly and easily. For instance, if you want to see what happens to total revenue as you vary the price between some minimum value (say, $8.00) and a maximum value (say, $12.00), the program will provide the results table for a what-if analysis showing total revenue for 11 different prices in the range from $8.00 to $12.00.

In a problem like this—with easy numbers and a simple relationship between the variables—the spreadsheet does not do that much work for you. You could do it in your head. But with more complicated problems, the spreadsheet makes it very convenient to more carefully analyze different alternatives or situations.

Using the Program

You don't have to know about computers or using a spreadsheet to use the computer-aided problems program. It was designed to be easy to learn and use. The Help button will give you more detailed information if you need it. But it's best to just try things out to see how it works. A mistake won't hurt anything.

You're likely to find that it's quicker and easier to just use the program than it is to read the instructions. So you may want to go ahead and put the CD-ROM in your own computer and try the practice problem now (or go to the online learning center to use the software there). Check the label on the CD-ROM for instructions about how to start the software. It takes just a few minutes and there's nothing to it.

The Spreadsheet Is Easy to Use

The spreadsheet software is very easy to use and specifically designed for the computer-aided problems. It is developed in Flash, so using this will be the same as using a browser to surf the Internet. However, if you want more general information, you can review the Help file.

As with other browser-based Flash programs, you typically use a mouse to move around in the program and select options. When you move the mouse, the cursor (which appears on your screen as an arrow) also moves. If you move the mouse so that the cursor is over one of the options on the screen and quickly press and release the left button on the mouse, the program will perform the action associated with that option. This process of using the mouse to position the cursor and then quickly pressing and releasing the left button is called "clicking" or "selecting." In these instructions, we'll refer to this often. For example, we'll say things like "click the Results button" or "select a problem from the list."

Let's use the first problem to illustrate how the program works.

Start by Selecting a Problem

When you start the *Essentials of Marketing* CD-ROM software or go to the online learning center website, the first screen displayed is a home page with the title of the book and various options. Click on the label that says CAPs (short for computer-aided problems).

The computer-aided problem page will appear. Click the problem you want to work (in this case, select the first one, "Revenue, Cost, and Profit Relationships").

Note: When you first select a problem, be patient while the program loads. It may take a minute or so. Once the program has loaded, calculations are immediate.

Once you select a problem, the problem description window appears. This is simply a convenient reminder of the problem description found in this text. (The assignment questions for each problem are in this book, so it's useful to have your book with you at the computer when you're working on a problem.)

To the left of the box in which the problem description appears you will see buttons labeled Description, Spreadsheet, Results, Graph, and Calculator. After you've reviewed the problem description, click the Spreadsheet button.

Each spreadsheet consists of one or two columns of numbers. Each column and row is labeled. Look at the row and column labels carefully to see what variable is represented by the value (number) in the spreadsheet. Study the layout of the spreadsheet, and get a feel for how it organizes the information from the problem description. The spreadsheet displays the starting values for the problem. Keep in mind that sometimes the problem description does not provide as much detail about the starting values as is provided in the spreadsheet.

You will see that some of the values in the spreadsheet appear in a highlighted edit box. These are usually values related to the decision variables in the problem you are solving. You can change any value (number) that appears in one of these boxes. When you make a change, the rest of the values (numbers) in that column are recalculated to show how a change in the value of that one variable affects the others. Think about how the numbers relate to each other.

Making changes in values is easy. When the spreadsheet first appears, your cursor appears as a free-floating arrow; however, when you pass the cursor over the box for the value that you want to change, the cursor changes to the shape of an I-beam. When you click on the value in that box, you can change it. Or to move the cursor to a value in a different box, just click on that box.

When you have selected the box with the value (number) you want to change, there are different ways to type in your new number. A good approach is to position the I-beam cursor before the first digit, and while depressing the mouse button drag the cursor across all of the digits in the number. This will highlight the entire number. Then simply type in the new number and the old one will be replaced. Alternatively, you can use other keys to edit the number. For example, you can use the backspace key to erase digits to the left of the I-beam cursor; similarly, you can use the Del key to erase digits to the right of the cursor. Or you can use the arrow keys to move the cursor to the point where you want to change part of a number. Then you just type in your change. You may want to experiment to see which of these editing approaches you like the best.

When you have finished typing the new number, press the Enter key and the other values in the spreadsheet will be recalculated to show the effect of your new value. Similarly, the other numbers will recalculate if you click on a different box after you have entered a number.

When you are typing numbers into the edit boxes, you'll probably find it most convenient to type the numbers and the decimal point with the keys on the main part of the keyboard (rather than those on the cursor control pad). For example, a price of 1,000 dollars and 50 cents would be typed as 1000.50 or just 1000.5—using the number keys on the top row of the keyboard and the period key for the decimal point. *Do not type in the dollar sign or the commas to indicate thousands.* Be careful not to type the letters o or l (lowercase L) instead of the numbers 0 or 1.

Typing percent values is a possible point of confusion, since there are different ways to think about a percent. For example,

"ten and a half" percent might be represented by 10.5 or .105. To avoid confusion, the program always expects you to enter percents using the first approach, which is the way percents are discussed in the problems. Thus, if you want to enter the value for ten and a half percent you would type 10.5.

To help prevent errors, each problem is programmed with a set of permitted values for each boxed field. It may be useful to explain what we mean by "permitted values." For example, if you accidentally type a letter when the computer program expects a number, the entry will turn red and what you typed will not be accepted. Further, the program won't allow you to enter a new value for a variable that is outside of a permitted range of values.

For example, if you try to type −10.00 as the price of a product, the entry will turn red. (It doesn't make sense to set the price as a negative number!) If you make an error, check what range of values is permitted—and then retype a new number that is in the permitted range, and press the Enter key to recompute the spreadsheet. When you have entered a permitted value, the value will no longer appear in red.

Remember that a value on the spreadsheet stays changed until you change it again. Some of the questions that accompany the problems ask you to evaluate results associated with different sets of values. It's good practice to check that you have entered all the correct values on a spreadsheet before interpreting the results.

In addition to changing values (numbers) on the spreadsheet itself, there are other options on the spreadsheet menu bar. Click the Description button to go back and review the problem description—or you can use the drop-down list again to select another problem.

Adding Your Comments and Printing

After you have done an analysis, you may want to print a copy of your results (especially if you are expected to hand in your answers to the questions that accompany the computer-aided problem). In fact, the print feature gives you the opportunity to type your name and answers right on the sheet that is printed. To use this feature, just click the printer icon while the spreadsheet is displayed with the results you want to print. A new window will open with a printable version of your analysis. You will also see an edit box area where you can type in your comments. Each comment can be up to 300 characters, and that should be plenty of space for you to type your answers to a question. Sometimes you will want to print more than one spreadsheet (each with its own comments) to answer the different questions.

Once you are satisfied with any comments you have added, you are ready to print your results. Of course, to be able to print you will need to have a printer properly hooked up to your computer and configured for Windows. *Before you select the Print button, make sure that the printer is turned on and loaded with paper!*

Results of a What-if Analysis

The "Show what-if analysis" button makes it easy for you to study in more detail the effect of changing the value of a particular variable. It systematically changes the value of one variable (which you select) and displays the effect that variable has on two other variables. You could do the same thing manually at the spreadsheet—by entering a value for a variable, checking the effect on other variables, and then repeating the process over and over again. But the manual approach is time-consuming and requires you to keep track of the results after each change. A what-if analysis does all this very quickly and presents the results table summary; you can also print or graph the results table if you wish.

Now let's take a step-by-step look at how you can get the exact what-if analysis that you want. The first step is to decide what variable (value) you want to vary and what result values you want to see in the results table.

You select the variables for your analysis by simply clicking the circle ("radio button") beside the number of interest. Click the radio button beside the value of the variable in an edit box that you want to vary. The radio button for the selected value is filled in. You can only select one variable to vary at a time. So if you want to vary some other variable, simply click on your new selection.

When you select a value to vary, the program computes a default "suggested" minimum value and maximum value for the range over which that variable may vary. The minimum value is usually 20 percent smaller than the value shown on the spreadsheet, and the maximum value is 20 percent larger. These default values are used as the minimum and maximum values to compute the results table for a what-if analysis (when you click the Results button).

You can also select the two variables that you want to display in the results table of the what-if analysis. Typically, you will want to display the results (computed values) for variables that will be affected by the variable you select to vary. Remember the example we used earlier. If you had specified that price was going to vary, you might want to display total revenue—to see how it changes at different price levels.

You select a variable to display in the same way that you select the variable you are going to vary. Simply click on the radio button beside a number on the spreadsheet that is not in an edit box. Then use this approach to select a second variable to be displayed in the results table. If you change your mind, you can click on the radio button for another variable. When you have completed this step, you will see a solid radio button next to the variable you chose to vary and solid radio buttons next to the two variables that you want to display.

Now you can let the computer take over. Click the button to show the what-if analysis and it will appear. Each row in the first column of the results table will show a different value for the variable you wanted to vary. The minimum value will be in the first row. The maximum value will be in the bottom row. Evenly spaced values between the minimum and maximum will be in the middle rows. The other columns show the calculated results for the values you selected to display. Each column of values is labeled at the top to identify the column and row from the spreadsheet. The row portion of the label is a short version of the label from the spreadsheet. The results are based on the values that were in the spreadsheet when you selected the Results button, except for the value you selected to vary.

After the results table is displayed, you have the option to type in your own minimum value and maximum value in the edit boxes below the results table. To do that, just use the same approach you used to enter new values in the spreadsheet. When you enter a new minimum or maximum, the results table will be updated based on the new range of values between the minimum and maximum you entered.

At this point you will want to study the results of your analysis. You can also print a copy of the results table by clicking the Print button. The button bar also shows other possibilities. For example, if you select the Spreadsheet button, the spreadsheet will reappear. The radio buttons will still show the values you selected in the previous analysis. From there you can make additional changes in the values in the spreadsheet, check the results table for a new what-if analysis, or select another problem to work. Or you can look at (and print) a graph of values in the results table for the what-if analysis.

Viewing a Graph of Your Results

You can create a graph of values in the results table by clicking the Graph button. The horizontal axis for the graph will be the variable in the first column of the display. The vertical axis on the left side is based on the first variable you selected to display in the results table. The vertical axis on the right side of the graph is for the second variable. There will be a line on the graph that corresponds to each axis.

What to Do Next

The next section gives additional tips on the program. You will probably want to look through it after you have done some work with the practice problem. For now, however, you're probably tired of reading instructions. So work a problem or two. It's easier and faster to use the program than to read about it. Give it a try, and don't be afraid to experiment. If you have problems, remember that the Help button is available when you need it.

Some Tips on Using the CAP Program

Resetting the Spreadsheet to the Initial Values

The initial spreadsheet for each problem gives the "starting values" for the problem. While working a problem, you will often change one or more of the starting values to a new number. A changed value stays in effect, unless you change it again. This is a handy feature. But after you make several changes, you may not be able to remember the starting values. There is a simple solution—you can click the button to return to the home page, then click the CAPs label again, and reselect the problem you want. The spreadsheet will appear with the original set of starting values.

Checking the Computer's Calculations

Some values appear in the spreadsheet as whole numbers, and others appear with one or more digits to the right of a decimal point. For example, dollar values usually have two digits to the right of the decimal point, indicating how many cents are involved. A value indicating, say, number of customers, however, will appear as a whole number.

When you are doing arithmetic by hand, or with a calculator, you sometimes have to make decisions about how much detail is necessary. For example, if you divide 13 by 3 the answer is 4.33, 4.333, 4.3333, or perhaps 4.33333, depending on how important it is to be precise. Usually we round off the number to keep things manageable. Similarly, computers usually display results after rounding off the numbers. This has the potential to create confusion and seeming inaccuracy when many calculations are involved. If the computer uses a lot of detail in its calculations and then displays intermediate results after rounding off, the numbers may appear to be inconsistent. To illustrate this, let's extend the example. If you multiply 4.33 times 2640, you get 11431.20. But if you multiply 4.333 by 2640, you get 11439.12. To make it easier for you to check relationships between the values on a spreadsheet, the CAP software does not use a lot of hidden detail in calculations. If it rounds off a number to display it in the spreadsheet, the rounded number is used in subsequent calculations. It would be easy for the computer to keep track of all of the detail in its calculations—but that would make it harder for you to check the results yourself. If you check the results on a spreadsheet (perhaps with the calculator provided) and find that your numbers are close but do not match exactly, it is probably because you are making different decisions about rounding than were programmed into the spreadsheet.

The software was designed and tested to be easy to use and error free. In fact, it is programmed to help prevent the user from making typing errors. But it is impossible to anticipate every possible combination of numbers you might enter—and some combinations of numbers can cause problems. For example, a certain combination of numbers might result in an instruction for the computer to divide a number by zero, which is a mathematical impossibility. When a problem of this sort occurs, the word ERROR will appear in the spreadsheet (or in the results table for the what-if analysis) instead of a number. If this happens, you should recheck the numbers in the spreadsheet and redo the analysis—to make certain that the numbers you typed in were what you intended. That should straighten out the problem in almost every case. Yet with any computer program there can be a hidden bug that only surfaces in unusual situations or on certain computers. Thus, if you think you have found a bug, we would like to know so that we can track down the source of the difficulty.

Notes

CHAPTER 1

1. For more on McDonald's see www.mcdonalds.com; "McDonald's Credits Menu Items for Strong Earnings," *AdvertisingAge*, January 26, 2009; "Consumers Skip Starbucks for Plain Ol' Joe," *AdvertisingAge*, January 19, 2009; "McD's Grande Plan: Become Java Giant," *Advertising Age*, January 14, 2008; "Would You Like a Mocha with That," *USA Today*, January 8, 2008; "Mickey D's Goes Uptown; Moves from the Big Mac to the Big Chic," *Investor's Business Daily*, November 14, 2007; "Want a Quiet Cup of Coffee in Germany? Head to McDonald's," *Advertising Age*, September 10, 2007; "McDonald's Sets Wake-Up Call for Breakfast Rush," *Wall Street Journal*, July 27, 2007; "Archrivals Storm Starbucks," *BusinessWeek*, July 18, 2007; "McDonald's Pitches Iced-Coffee Campaign," *Wall Street Journal*, May 1, 2007; "McDonald's 24/7," *BusinessWeek*, February 5, 2007; "For McDonalds It's a Wrap," *Wall Street Journal*, January 30, 2007; "The Marketing Legacy of McDonald's," *Advertising Age*, July 25, 2005; "Fast Fruit? At Wendy's and McDonald's, It's a Main Course," *Wall Street Journal*, February 9, 2005. For more on Starbucks, see www.starbucks.com; "Starbucks Plays Common Joe," *Wall Street Journal*, February 9, 2009; "Starbucks' Dismal Quarter Leads to 'Value' Offerings," *AdvertisingAge*, January 28, 2009; "Coffee Jitters," *Brandweek*, November 10, 2008; "Starbucks' Surprise Success: Oatmeal," *AdvertisingAge*, October 13, 2008; "Starbucks Takes Action as Sales Cool," *USA Today*, January 31, 2008; "Is Starbucks Pushing Prices Too High?" *BusinessWeek Online*, August 2, 2007; "Starbucks: Trouble in Latte Land," *BusinessWeek Online*, November 19, 2007; McDonalds Takes on a Weakened Starbucks," *Wall Street Journal*, January 7, 2008; "Starbucks Is Scalded by Slower U.S. Sales," *Wall Street Journal*, April 24, 2008; "The Buzz from Starbucks Customers," *BusinessWeek*, April 28, 2008; "Schultz's Second Act Jolts Starbucks," *Wall Street Journal*, May 19, 2008; "Starbucks, Yahoo! Make a Match," *Brandweek*, February 20, 2006; "Starbucks Calls China Its Top Growth Focus," *Wall Street Journal*, February 14, 2006; "A Tall Skinny Latte, a Nice, Comfy Chair and, Now, Kid Tunes," *Wall Street Journal*, February 14, 2006; "Starbucks, Kellogg Plot Cereal Killing," *Advertising Age*, February 6, 2006; "Starbucks Plans to Make Debut in Movie Business," *Wall Street Journal*, January 12, 2006; "Fill 'Er Up—with Latte," *Wall Street Journal*, January 6, 2006; "A Special Effort: Starbucks Is Reaching Out to People with Disabilities—Both as Employees and as Customers," *Wall Street Journal*, November 14, 2005; "Lattes Lure Brits to Coffee," *Wall Street Journal*, October 20, 2005; "This Java Joint Is Jumping," *Brandweek*, October 10, 2005; "Starbucks to Offer Cold Drinks in Convenience Stores in Japan," *Wall Street Journal*, September 27, 2005; "Brewing the Perfect Concept," *Investor's Business Daily*, September 12, 2005; "At Starbucks, a Blend of Coffee and Music Creates a Potent Mix," *Wall Street Journal*, July 19, 2005; "Strong Lattes, Sour Notes," *BusinessWeek*, June 20, 2005; "Coffee on the Double," *Wall Street Journal*, April 12, 2005; "New Bean Counters: Banks Share Space with Coffee Shops," *Wall Street Journal*, March 22, 2005; "Starbucks Perking in Music Business as It Expands Its CD-Burning Outlets," *Investor's Business Daily*, February 17, 2005.

2. Eric H. Shaw, "A Review of Empirical Studies of Aggregate Marketing Costs and Productivity in the United States," *Journal of the Academy of Marketing Science*, Fall, 1990; Christopher H. Lovelock and Charles B. Weinberg, *Marketing for Public and Nonprofit Managers* (New York: John Wiley & Sons, 1984).

3. Gregory D. Upah and Richard E. Wokutch, "Assessing Social Impacts of New Products: An Attempt to Operationalize the Macromarketing Concept," *Journal of Public Policy and Marketing* 4 (1985).

4. An American Marketing Association committee recently defined marketing as "the activity, set of institutions, and processes for creating, communicating, delivering, and exchanging offerings that have value for customers, clients, partners, and society at large." The definition of marketing can be a source of debate, see "AMA's Definition of Marketing Stirs Debate," *B to B*, February 11, 2008; see also David Glen Mick, "The End(s) of Marketing and the Neglect of Moral Responsibility by the American Marketing Association," *Journal of Public Policy & Marketing*, Fall 2007; Debra Jones Ringold and Barton Weitz, "The American Marketing Association Definition of Marketing: Moving from Lagging to Leading Indicator," *Journal of Public Policy & Marketing*, Fall 2007; George M. Zinkhan and Brian C. Williams, "The New American Marketing Association Definition of Marketing: An Alternative Assessment," *Journal of Public Policy & Marketing*, Fall 2007; Gregory T. Gundlach, "The American Marketing Association's 2004 Definition of Marketing: Perspectives on Its Implications for Scholarship and the Role and Responsibility of Marketing in Society," *Journal of Public Policy & Marketing*, Fall 2007; Jagdish N. Sheth and Can Uslay, "Implications of the Revised Definition of Marketing: From Exchange to Value Creation," *Journal of Public Policy & Marketing*, Fall 2007; William L. Wilkie and Elizabeth S. Moore, "What Does the Definition of Marketing Tell Us About Ourselves?" *Journal of Public Policy & Marketing*, Fall 2007.

5. George Fisk, "Editor's Working Definition of Macromarketing," *Journal of Macromarketing* 2, no. 1 (1982); Shelby D. Hunt and John J. Burnett, "The Macromarketing/Micromarketing Dichotomy: A Taxonomical Model," *Journal of Marketing*, Summer 1982.

6. William McInnes, "A Conceptual Approach to Marketing," in *Theory in Marketing*, second series, ed. Reavis Cox, Wroe Alderson, and Stanley J. Shapiro (Homewood, IL: Richard D. Irwin, 1964).

7. Roderick J. Brodie, Heidi Winklhofer, Nicole E. Coviello, and Wesley J. Johnston, "Is E-Marketing Coming of Age? An Examination of the Penetration of E-Marketing and Firm Performance," *Journal of Interactive Marketing*, Spring 2007; Thorsten Posselt and Eitan Gerstner, "Pre-Sale vs. Post-Sale E-Satisfaction: Impact on Repurchase Intention and Overall Satisfaction," *Journal of Interactive Marketing*, Autumn 2005; Fang Wu, Vijay Mahajan, and Sridhar Balasubramanian, "An Analysis of E-Business Adoption and Its Impact on Business Performance," *Journal of the Academy of Marketing Science*, Fall 2003; Peter R. Dickson, "Understanding the Trade Winds: the Global Evolution of Production, Consumption, and the Internet," *Journal of Consumer Research*, June 2000; Xueming Luo and Christian Homburg, "Neglected Outcomes of Customer Satisfaction," *Journal of Marketing*, April 2007.

8. Marian Friestad and Peter Wright, "The Next Generation: Research for Twenty-First-Century Public Policy on Children and Advertising," *Journal of Public Policy & Marketing*, Fall 2005; Kevin D. Bradford, Gregory T. Gundlach, and William L. Wilkie, "Countermarketing in the Courts: The Case of Marketing Channels and Firearms Diversion," *Journal of Public Policy & Marketing*, Fall 2005; Gary T. Ford and John E. Calfee, "Food Politics: How the Food Industry Influences Nutrition and Health/The Obesity Myth: Why America's Obsession with Weight Is Hazardous to Your Health/Fat Land: How Americans Became the Fattest People in the World," *Journal of Public Policy & Marketing*, Spring 2005; Graham Hooley, Tony Cox, John Fahy, David Shipley et al. "Market Orientation in the Transition Economies of Central Europe: Tests of the Narver and Slater Market Orientation Scales," *Journal of Business Research*, December 2000; Saeed Samiee, "Globalization, Privatization, and Free Market Economy," *Journal of*

the Academy of Marketing Science, Summer 2001; Robert A. Peterson and Ashutosh Prasad, "A General Theory of Competition: Resources, Competencies, Productivity, Economic Growth," *Journal of the Academy of Marketing Science*, Fall 2001.

9. "Rustic Wisdom: Unilever to Take Project Shakti Global," *Economic Times*, January 19, 2009; "Strategic Innovation: Hindustan Lever Ltd.," *Fast Company*, December 19, 2007; "Shakti—Changing Lives in Rural India," http://hll.com/citizen_lever/project_shakti.asp; P. Indu, Komal Chary, and Vivek Gupta, "Reviving Hindustan Lever Limited," ICFAI Center for Management Research, Case Study # 306-410-1, 2006; V. Kasturi Rangan and Rhithari Rajan, "Unilever in India: Hindustan Lever's Project Shakti—Marketing FMCG to the Rural Consumer," Harvard Business School, Case # 9-505-056, 2006; "Shakti: Growing the Market while Changing Lives in Rural India," Case Weatherhead School of Management Case # 000362, 2005; C. K. Prahalad, *The Fortune at the Bottom of the Pyramid* (Philadelphia: Wharton School Publishing, 2005); "Access to Electricity: White Paper on ABB's Initiative for Access to Electricity," April 2005, www. abb.com; "India—Water Supply and Sanitation: Bridging the Gap between Infrastructure and Service Executive Summary," The World Bank, siteresources.worldbank.org/INTINDIA/Resources/Bridging_the_Gap_Exec_Sum.pdf.

10. Kathleen Seiders and Ross D. Petty, "Taming the Obesity Beast: Children, Marketing, and Public Policy Considerations," *Journal of Public Policy & Marketing*, Fall 2007; Victor V. Cordell, "Effects of Public Policy on Marketing," *Journal of Macromarketing*, Spring 1993; James M. Carman and Robert G. Harris, "Public Regulation of Marketing Activity, Part III: A Typology of Regulatory Failures and Implications for Marketing and Public Policy," *Journal of Macromarketing*, Spring 1986.

11. Malte Brettel, Andreas Engelen, Florian Heinemann, and Pakpachong Vadhanasindhu, "Antecedents of Market Orientation: A Cross-Cultural Comparison," *Journal of International Marketing*, (2) 2008; Ahmet H. Kirca, Satish Jayachandran and William O. Bearden, "Market Orientation: A Meta-Analytic Review and Assessment of Its Antecedents and Impact on Performance," *Journal of Marketing*, April 2005; Ranjay Gulati and James B. Oldroyd, "The Quest for Customer Focus," *Harvard Business Review*, April 2005; Dave Webb, Cynthia Webster, and Areti Krepapa, "An Exploration of the Meaning and Outcomes of a Customer-Defined Market Orientation," *Journal of Business Research*, May 2000; Jagdish N. Sheth, Rajendra S. Sisodia, and Arun Sharma, "The Antecedents and Consequences of Customer-Centric Marketing," *Journal of the Academy of Marketing Science*, Winter 2000; Karen Norman Kennedy, Jerry R. Goolsby, and Eric J. Arnould, "Implementing a Customer Orientation: Extension of Theory and Application," *Journal of Marketing*, October 2003; See also Charles R. Weiser, "Championing the Customer," *Harvard Business Review*, November–December 1995; Stanley F. Slater and John C. Narver, "Market Orientation and the Learning Organization," *Journal of Marketing*, July 1995; R. W. Ruekert, "Developing a Market Orientation: An Organizational Strategy Perspective," *International Journal of Research in Marketing*, August 1992; Bernard J. Jaworski and Ajay K. Kohli, "Market Orientation: Antecedents and Consequences," *Journal of Marketing*, July 1993; Franklin S. Houston, "The Marketing Concept: What It Is and What It Is Not," *Journal of Marketing*, April 1986.

12. For more on the marketing concept in the banking industry, see "Legal and Illegal, Welcome," *Wall Street Journal*, November 10, 2007; "Even Cozier Deals on Campus," *BusinessWeek*, October 1, 2007; "The Return of Ma & Pa Banker," *Fortune*, May 14, 2007; "Seeing if Banks Are Any Nicer," *Wall Street Journal*, March 29, 2007; "Banks Court a New Client: The Low-Income Earner," *Wall Street Journal*, March 16, 2007; "Big Banks on Campus," *Wall Street Journal*, September 6, 2006; "Banks Offer Card Perks Only to Clients," *USA Today*, July 31, 2006.

13. "Would You Recommend Us?" *BusinessWeek*, January 30, 2006; "Pyromarketing: Up in Flames," *Point*, December 2005; "Progressive Businesses," *Brandweek*, November 28, 2005; "Get Creative! How

to Build Innovative Companies," *BusinessWeek*, August 1, 2005; "In Search of the Next i-Pod," *Brandweek*, June 20, 2005; "Cult Brands," *BusinessWeek*, August 2, 2004; "Inventing to Order," *BusinessWeek*, July 5, 2004; "When the Factory Is a Theme Park," *BusinessWeek*, May 3, 2004; "Go for the Outrageous," *Investor's Business Daily*, January 3, 2004; "Will Jeff Immelt's New Push Pay Off for GE? Helping Customers Beyond the Call of Duty," *BusinessWeek*, October 13, 2003; "Remedies for an Economic Hangover," *Fortune*, June 25, 2001; "The Best Little Grocery Store in America," *Inc.*, June 2001; "Fanatics!" *Inc.*, April 2001; "Why Some Customers Are More Equal Than Others," *Fortune*, September 19, 1994; See also Murali Chandrashekaran, Kristin Rotte, Stephen S. Tax, and Rajdeep Grewal, "Satisfaction Strength and Customer Loyalty," *Journal of Marketing Research*, February 2007; Xie Chunyan, Richard P. Bagozzi, and Sigurd V. Troye, "Trying to Prosume: Toward a Theory of Consumers as Co-creators of Value," *Journal of the Academy of Marketing Science*, Spring 2008; Min Soonhong, John T. Mentzer, and Robert T. Ladd, "A Market Orientation in Supply Chain Management," *Journal of the Academy of Marketing Science*, Winter 2007; Wolfgang Ulaga and Andreas Eggert, "Value-Based Differentiation in Business Relationships: Gaining and Sustaining Key Supplier Status," *Journal of Marketing*, January 2006; Christian Homburg, Nicole Koschate, and Wayne D. Hoyer, "Do Satisfied Customers Really Pay More? A Study of the Relationship Between Customer Satisfaction and Willingness to Pay," *Journal of Marketing*, April 2005; Youn-Rex Yuxing Du, Wagner A. Kamakura and Carl F. Mela, "Size and Share of Customer Wallet," *Journal of Marketing*, April 2007; Roger Baxter and Sheelagh Matear, James C. Anderson, James A. Narus, and Wouter van Rossum, "Customer Value Propositions in Business Markets," *Harvard Business Review*, March 2006; Ronald L. Hess, Jr., Shankar Ganesan, and Noreen M. Klein, "Service Failure and Recovery: the Impact of Relationship Factors on Customer Satisfaction," *Journal of the Academy of Marketing Science*, Spring 2003; Mihaly Csikszentmihalyi, "The Costs and Benefits of Consuming," *Journal of Consumer Research*, September 2000; Jaishankar Ganesh, Mark J. Arnold, and Kristy E. Reynolds, "Understanding the Customer Base of Service Providers: an Examination of the Differences Between Switchers and Stayers," *Journal of Marketing*, July 2000; George S. Day, "Managing Market Relationships," *Journal of the Academy of Marketing Science*, Winter 2000; Deepak Sirdeshmukh, Jagdip Singh, and Barry Sabol, "Consumer Trust, Value, and Loyalty in Relational Exchanges," *Journal of Marketing*, January 2002; Stanley F. Slater and John C. Narver, "Market Orientation, Customer Value, and Superior Performance," *Business Horizons*, March–April 1994; Sharon E. Beatty, "Keeping Customers," *Journal of Marketing*, April 1994.

14. See www.curves.com; "Gary Heavin Is on a Mission from God," *Inc.*, October 2006; "How to Grow a Chain That's Already Everywhere," *Business 2.0*, March 2005; "A Slim Gym's Fat Success," *Time* (Inside Business Bonus Section), May 5, 2003.

15. Stacy Landreth Grau and Judith Anne Garretson Folse, "Cause-Related Marketing (CRM)," *Journal of Advertising*, Winter 2007; "Helping Nonprofits Find Hidden Gold," *Business 2.0*, December 2005; "Uncle Sam Wants You in the Worst Way," *BusinessWeek*, August 11, 2005; "Advertising . . . Nonprofit Organizations Are Going Commercial," *The New York Times*, February 20, 2004; "When Nonprofits Go After Profits," *BusinessWeek*, June 26, 2000; "Modern Marketing Helps Sell Life as a Nun," *Wall Street Journal*, May 11, 1999. See also Glenn B. Voss and Zannie Giraud Voss, "Strategic Orientation and Firm Performance in an Artistic Environment," *Journal of Marketing*, January 2000; Dennis B. Arnett, Steve D. German, and Shelby D. Hunt, "The Identity Salience Model of Relationship Marketing Success: the Case of Nonprofit Marketing," *Journal of Marketing*, April 2003; "Public Policy, Technology, and Ethics: Marketing Decisions for NASA's Space Shuttle," *Journal of Marketing*, Summer 1984.

16. "NYC Promotes Free Water," *Brandweek*, July 9, 2007.

17. "Companies Try Keeping Ice Cream Frozen, Emissions Down," *Wall Street Journal*, May 4, 2005; "The Black Market vs. the Ozone,"

BusinessWeek, July 7, 1997; "CFC-Span: Refrigerant's Reign Nears an End," *USA Today,* August 22, 1994; "Air-Conditioner Firms Put Chill on Plans to Phase Out Use of Chlorofluorocarbons," *Wall Street Journal,* May 10, 1993. See also Xueming Luo and C. B. Bhattacharya, "Corporate Social Responsibility, Customer Satisfaction, and Market Value," *Journal of Marketing,* October 2006; Alan R. Andreasen, "Social Marketing: Its Definition and Domain," *Journal of Public Policy & Marketing,* Spring 1994.

18. "Wrestling with Your Conscience," *Time,* November 15, 1999; "Wal-Mart Provides Many an Introduction to Sport Shooting," *Wall Street Journal,* April 15, 1999; "GreenMountain.com Makes Pitch for Clean Energy," *Wall Street Journal,* May 1, 2000. For more on overseas sweatshops, see "Sweatshops: Finally, Airing the Dirty Linen," *BusinessWeek,* June 23, 2003.

19. C. B. Bhattacharya and Sankar Sen, "Doing Better at Doing Good: When, Why and How Customers Respond to Corporate Social Initiatives," *California Management Review,* Fall 2004; Grahame R. Dowling, "Corporate Reputations: Should You Compete on Yours?" *California Management Review,* Spring 2004; Edward J. O'Boyle and Lyndon E. Dawson, Jr., "The American Marketing Association Code of Ethics: Instructions for Marketers," *Journal of Business Ethics,* December 1992; Ellen J. Kennedy and Leigh Lawton, "Ethics and Services Marketing," *Journal of Business Ethics,* October 1993.

20. Andrew V. Abela and Patrick E. Murphy, "Marketing with Integrity: Ethics and the Service-dominant Logic for Marketing," *Journal of the Academy of Marketing Science,* Spring 2008; Lawrence B. Chonko and Shelby D. Hunt, "Ethics and Marketing Management: a Retrospective and Prospective Commentary," *Journal of Business Research,* December 2000; Barry J. Babin, James S. Boles, and Donald P. Robin, "Representing the Perceived Ethical Work Climate Among Marketing Employees," *Journal of the Academy of Marketing Science,* Summer 2000; Jeffrey G. Blodgett, Long-Chuan Lu, Gregory M. Rose, and Scott J. Vitell, "Ethical Sensitivity to Stakeholder Interests: a Cross-Cultural Comparison," *Journal of the Academy of Marketing Science,* Spring 2001; George G. Brenkert, "Ethical Challenges of Social Marketing," *Journal of Public Policy & Marketing,* Spring 2002.

21. "Too Much Corporate Power?" *BusinessWeek,* September 11, 2000; "Ad Nauseam," *Advertising Age,* July 10, 2000. See also C. B. Bhattacharya and Daniel Korschun, "Stakeholder Marketing: Beyond The Four Ps and the Customer," *Journal of Public Policy & Marketing,* Spring 2008; Stephen J. Arnold and Monika Narang Luthra, "Market Entry Effects of Large Format Retailers: a Stakeholder Analysis," *International Journal of Retail & Distribution Management,* (4) 2000.

CHAPTER 2

1. See www.cirquedusoleil.com; "Super Pregame Show," *Miami-Herald.com,* January 10, 2007; "Cirque du Success," *U.S. News and World Report,* November 20, 2006; "The *Onliness* of Strong Brands," *BusinessWeek.com,* November 16, 2006; "Crazy for 'Delirium,'" *Billboard,* July 15, 2006; "The Disney of the New Age," *Maclean's,* June 26, 2006; "Cirque du Balancing Act," *Fortune,* June 12, 2006; "How Cirque du Soleil Uses Email to Sell Out Shows at Local Cities," *MarketingSherpa.com,* June 1, 2006; W. Chan Kim and Renée Mauborgne, *Blue Ocean Strategy* (Boston: Harvard Business School Press, 2005); "Join the Circus," *Fast Company,* July 1, 2005; "Lord of the Rings," *Economist,* February 5, 2005; "Best Launch: Zumanity," *Marketing Magazine,* November 11, 2004; "Big Top Television," *Marketing Magazine,* August 9–16, 2004; "Mario D'Amico—Cirque du Soleil," *Reveries,* July 2002.

2. George S. Day, "Is It Real? Can We Win? Is It Worth Doing?" *Harvard Business Review,* December 2007; John G. Singer, "What Strategy Is Not," *MIT Sloan Management Review,* Winter 2008; Rebecca J. Slotegraaf and Peter R. Dickson, "The Paradox of a Marketing Planning Capability," *Journal of the Academy of Marketing Science,* Fall 2004; Kwaku Atuahene-Gima and Janet Y. Murray, "Antecedents

and Outcomes of Marketing Strategy Comprehensiveness," *Journal of Marketing,* October 2004; Gail J. McGovern, David Court, John A. Quelch and Blair Crawford, "Bringing Customers into the Boardroom," *Harvard Business Review,* November 2004; Charles H. Noble, Rajiv K. Sinha, and Ajith Kumar, "Market Orientation and Alternative Strategic Orientations: a Longitudinal Assessment of Performance Implications," *Journal of Marketing,* October 2002; Mary Anne Raymond and Hiram C. Barksdale, "Corporate Strategic Planning and Corporate Marketing: Toward an Interface," *Business Horizons,* September–October 1989; George S. Day, "Marketing's Contribution to the Strategy Dialogue," *Journal of the Academy of Marketing Science,* Fall 1992; P. Rajan Varadarajan and Terry Clark, "Delineating the Scope of Corporate, Business, and Marketing Strategy," *Journal of Business Research,* October–November 1994.

3. See www.learningco.com; "Broderbund: Identify a Need, Turn a Profit," *Fortune,* November 30, 1992.

4. "Carrying Your Groceries in Eco-Style," *Wall Street Journal,* March 20, 2008; "Supermarkets Copy Whole Foods' Shopping List," *USA Today,* June 29, 2006; "Whole Foods Fare's Pricey?" *Wall Street Journal,* January 13, 2006; "Whole Foods Market on Growth Spurt," *Wall Street Journal,* December 14, 2005; "Pricier Gourmet Sodas Grab Attention," *Wall Street Journal,* December 8, 2005; "Eating Too Fast at Whole Foods," *BusinessWeek,* October 24, 2005; "Marketers of the Year 2005: John Mackey; For Shoppers, It's Love," *Brandweek,* "Zigging while Wal-Mart Zags," *Investor's Business Daily,* June 20, 2005; "Metropolitan Magnet," *Wall Street Journal,* May 11, 2005; "A Whole New Ballgame in Grocery Shopping," *USA Today,* March 9, 2005.

5. "What Customers Want," *Fortune,* July 7, 2003; "The Unprofitable Customers," *Wall Street Journal Reports,* October 28, 2002; "Will This Customer Sink Your Stock," *Fortune,* September 30, 2002; "Keep 'Em Coming Back," *BusinessWeek E-Biz,* May 15, 2000. See also Paul D. Berger, Naras Eechambadi, Morris George, Donald R. Lehmann, Ross Rizley, and Rajkumar Venkatesan, "From Customer Lifetime Value to Shareholder Value: Theory, Empirical Evidence, and Issues for Future Research," *Journal of Service Research,* May 2006; Peter S. Fader, Bruce G. S. Hardie, and Kinshuk Jerath, "Estimating CLV Using Aggregated Data: The Tuscan Lifestyles Case Revisited," *Journal of Interactive Marketing,* Summer 2007; Sunil Gupta, Dominique Hanssens, Bruce Hardie, William Kahn, V. Kumar, Nathaniel Lin, and Nalini Ravishanker S. Sriram, "Modeling Customer Lifetime Value," *Journal of Service Research,* May 2006; Rajkumar Venkatesan and V. Kumar, "A Customer Lifetime Value Framework for Customer Selection and Resource Allocation Strategy," *Journal of Marketing,* October 2004; Edward C. Malthouse and Robert C. Blattberg, "Can We Predict Customer Lifetime Value?" *Journal of Interactive Marketing,* Winter 2004; Heinz K. Stahl, Kurt Matzler, and Hans H. Hinterhuber, "Linking Customer Lifetime Value with Shareholder Value," *Industrial Marketing Management,* May 2003; Charlotte H. Mason, "Tuscan Lifestyles: Assessing Customer Lifetime Value," *Journal of Interactive Marketing,* Autumn 2003; Vikas Mittal, "Driving Customer Equity: How Customer Lifetime Value Is Reshaping Corporate Strategy," *Journal of Marketing,* April 2001.

6. For information on Silverman's new business, see www.preschoolians.com. For more on Toddler University see "Genesco Names New Executive of Children's Footwear Division," *Press Release,* Genesco, July 15, 1994; "Toddler University Ends Up in Westport," *Westport News,* March 8, 1991; "Whiz Kid," *Connecticut,* August 1989; "The Young and the Restless," *Children's Business,* May 1989.

7. Orville C. Walker, Jr., and Robert W. Ruekert, "Marketing's Role in the Implementation of Business Strategies: A Critical Review and Conceptual Framework," *Journal of Marketing,* July 1987; Thomas V. Bonoma, "A Model of Marketing Implementation," *1984 AMA Educators' Proceedings* (Chicago: American Marketing Association, 1984); Kevin Romer and Doris C. Van Doren, "Implementing Marketing in a High-Tech Business," *Industrial Marketing Management,* August 1993.

8. V. Kumar and Morris George, "Measuring and Maximizing Customer Equity: a Critical Analysis," *Journal of the Academy of Marketing Science*, Summer 2007; Thorsten Wiesel, Bernd Skiera, and Julin Villanueva, "Customer Equity: An Integral Part of Financial Reporting," *Journal of Marketing*, March 2008; Werner Reinartz, Jacquelyn S. Thomas, and Ganaël Bascoul, "Investigating Cross-buying and Customer Loyalty," *Journal of Interactive Marketing*, Winter 2008; Robert P. Leone, Vithala R. Rao, Kevin Lane Keller, Anita Man Luo, Leigh McAlister, and Rajendra Srivastava, "Linking Brand Equity to Customer Equity," *Journal of Service Research*, May 2006; Florian v Wangenheim and Tomás Bayón, "The Chain from Customer Satisfaction via Word-of-mouth Referrals to New Customer Acquisition," *Journal of the Academy of Marketing Science*, Summer 2007; Roland T. Rust, Katherine N. Lemon, and Valarie A. Zeithaml, "Return on Marketing: Using Customer Equity to Focus Marketing Strategy," *Journal of Marketing*, January 2004; Jacquelyn S. Thomas, Werner Reinartz, and V. Kumar, "Getting the Most Out of All Your Customers," *Harvard Business Review*, July 2004; Michael D. Johnson, Andreas Herrmann, and Frank Huber, "The Evolution of Loyalty Intentions," *Journal of Marketing*, April 2006; Peter C. Verhoef, "Understanding the Effect of Customer Relationship Management Efforts on Customer Retention and Customer Share Development," *Journal of Marketing*, October 2003; Roland T. Rust, Valarie A. Zeithaml, and Katherine N. Lemon, "Customer-Centered Brand Management," *Harvard Business Review*, September 2004.

9. "How Timex Plans to Upgrade Its Image, *Wall Street Journal*, June 21, 2007; "Unwatched Masses," *San Diego Union-Tribune*, February 20, 2006; "The Times They Are a-Changing," *Wall Street Journal*, January 18, 2006; "Watches Shift into Automatic," *Wall Street Journal*, November 12, 2005; "The Clock Is Ticking for Aging Timex," *Advertising Age*, October 17, 2005; "Timex Seeks New Faces to Capture 18–34 Range," *DM News*, September 19, 2005; "A Workout Pro Close at Hand," *BusinessWeek*, August 15, 2005; "Microsoft's Latest, Strapped to a Wrist," *New York Times*, January 8, 2004; "It's Comeback Time for Luxury Watches," *New York Times*, January 6, 2004; "Now, Even Your Watch Can Help You Carry Your Computer Files," *Wall Street Journal*, September 25, 2003; "Bill Has Designs on Your Wrist," *BusinessWeek*, January 20, 2003; "Timex Pursues Hip, Younger Set in Ads for Its New iControl Watch," *Wall Street Journal*, May 19, 2000.

10. Richard A. D'Aveni, "Mapping Your Competitive Position," *Harvard Business Review*, February 2008; George S. Day and Robin Wensley, "Assessing Advantage: A Framework for Diagnosing Competitive Superiority," *Journal of Marketing*, April 1988; Michael E. Porter, *Competitive Advantage—Creating and Sustaining Superior Performance* (New York: Free Press, MacMillan, 1986); Mark B. Houston, "Competing for the Future: Breakthrough Strategies for Seizing Control of Your Industry and Creating the Markets of Tomorrow," *Journal of the Academy of Marketing Science*, Winter 1996; Kevin P. Coyne, "Sustainable Competitive Advantage—What It Is, What It Isn't," *Business Horizons*, January–February 1986.

11. See www.soapworks.com; "Taking on Procter & Gamble," *Inc.*, October 2000.

12. Ruth N. Bolton, Katherine N. Lemon, and Peter C. Verhoef, "Expanding Business-to-Business Customer Relationships: Modeling the Customer's Upgrade Decision," *Journal of Marketing*, January 2008; Stephen J. Arnold, "Lessons Learned from the World's Best Retailers," *International Journal of Retail & Distribution Management*, (11) 2002; Ashesh Mukherjee and Wayne D. Hoyer, "The Effect of Novel Attributes on Product Evaluation," *Journal of Consumer Research*, December 2001; Douglas W. Vorhies and Neil A. Morgan, "A Configuration Theory Assessment of Marketing Organization Fit with Business Strategy and Its Relationship with Marketing Performance," *Journal of Marketing*, January 2003; Jean L. Johnson, Ruby Pui-Wan Lee, Amit Saini, and Bianca Grohmann, "Market-Focused Strategic Flexibility: Conceptual Advances and an Integrative Model," *Journal of the Academy of Marketing Science*, Winter 2003; Ian C. MacMillan and Rita G. McGrath, "Discovering New Points of Differentiation," *Harvard Business Review*, July–August 1997.

13. For more on Coleman, see "The Grill of Their Dreams," *Business 2.0*, February 2002; "Growing to Match Its Brand Name," *Fortune*, June 13, 1994. See also Peter C. Verhoef, "Understanding the Effect of Customer Relationship Management Efforts on Customer Retention and Customer Share Development," *Journal of Marketing*, October 2003; Youjae Yi and Hoseong Jeon, "Effects of Loyalty Programs on Value Perception, Program Loyalty, and Brand Loyalty," *Journal of the Academy of Marketing Science*, Summer 2003.

14. For more on E-Z-Go, see "Wanna Drag? Now Golf Carts Are in the Race," *Wall Street Journal*, March 6, 2007; "Off-Roading, Golf-Cart Style," *Wall Street Journal*, June 14, 2001. For more on Dunkin' Donuts, see "Dunkin' Donuts Whips Up a Recipe for Expansion," *Wall Street Journal*, May 3, 2007; "Dunkin' Donuts Tries to Go Upscale, but Not Too Far," *Wall Street Journal*, April 8, 2006. See also Michael S. Garver, "Best Practices in Identifying Customer-Driven Improvement Opportunities," *Industrial Marketing Management*, August 2003; John H. Roberts, "Developing New Rules for New Markets," *Journal of the Academy of Marketing Science*, Winter 2000.

15. For more on Campbell, see "Campbell's Lowering Sodium in Almost 50 Soups," *USA Today*, February 18, 2008. For more on ski resorts, see "Seeking Growth, Ski Areas Target Minorities," *Wall Street Journal*, December 22, 2004; "Bikers Give Ski Resorts Summer Time Lift," *Wall Street Journal*, July 7, 1994. For more on Nike, see *2007 Annual Report*, Nike; "When Nike Met iPod," *Wall Street Journal*, May 24, 2006; "Nike Puts Its Swoosh on MP3 Players, Walkie-Talkies, Heart Monitors," *Wall Street Journal*, May 10, 2000. See also Sarah J. Marsh and Gregory N. Stock, "Building Dynamic Capabilities in New Product Development Through Intertemporal Integration," *Journal of Product Innovation Management*, March 2003; George C. Kingston and Beebe Nelson, "Leading Product Innovation: Accelerating Growth in a Product-Based Business," *Journal of Product Innovation Management*, November 2001.

16. For more on McDonald's and its hotel diversification effort, see "Would You Like a Bed with Your Burger?" *Ad Age Global*, February 2001; "The Golden Arches: Burgers, Fries and 4-Star Rooms," *Wall Street Journal*, November 17, 2000.

17. For more on Purafil, see "Small Businesses Find International Success," *USA Today*, June 30, 2000.

18. For more on JLG, see www.jlg.com; "JLG Industries Acquisition Gives a Big Lift to Oshkosh Truck Sales," *Investor's Business Daily*, October 31, 2007; "The Secret of U.S. Exports: Great Products," *Fortune*, January 10, 2000.

19. For more on international marketing in China, see James McGregor, *One Billion Customers: Lessons from the Front Lines of Doing Business in China* (Free Press, 2005); "Doing Business in China Is Complex," *USA Today*, November 21, 2005; "One Billion Opportunities?" *Wall Street Journal*, October 18, 2005; "Let a Thousand Brands Bloom," *BusinessWeek*, October 17, 2005; "Relaxed Marketing Rules in China Open the Door for More Sales," *Investor's Business Daily*, October 7, 2005; "Localizing the Brand," *Inc.*, October 2005; "Chinese Dragon, Hidden Treasure: The Peril and Promise of Selling in China," *Selling Power*, June 2005; "Nestle Stumbles in China's Evolving Market," *Wall Street Journal*, December 8, 2004; "Outsiders Get Smarter about China's Tastes," *Wall Street Journal*, August 5, 2004; "Getting a Foothold in China," *Wall Street Journal*, August 3, 2004; "Cracking China's Market: Adapting to Chinese Customs, Cultural Changes . . .," *Wall Street Journal*, January 9, 2003. See also Naresh K. Malhotra, Francis M. Ulgado, and James Agarwal, "Internationalization and Entry Modes: A Multitheoretical Framework and Research Propositions," *Journal of International Marketing*, 2003; Peter N. Golder, "Insights from Senior Executives about Innovation in International Markets," *Journal of Product Innovation Management*, September 2000; Shaoming Zou and S. Tamer Cavusgil, "The GMS: A Broad Conceptualization of Global Marketing Strategy and its Effect on Firm

Performance," *Journal of Marketing*, October 2002; Susan P. Douglas, "Exploring New Worlds: the Challenge of Global Marketing," *Journal of Marketing*, January 2001.

CHAPTER 3

1. See www.amazon.com; "Why It's So Hard to Get a Read on Amazon," *BusinessWeek*, April 20, 2009; "Amazon Error Removes Gay, Health Books from Search," *Wall Street Journal*, April 14, 2009; "Amazon Packages Green Site," *Investor's Business Daily*, February 25, 2009; "Amazon.com's Third-Party Sales Balloon," *Investor's Business Daily*, April 8, 2009; "Amazon Gets in Used-Game Business," *Wall Street Journal*, March 6, 2009; "When Service Means Survival: How Amazon Aims to Keep You Clicking," *BusinessWeek*, March 2, 2009; "The World's Most Innovative Companies," *Fast Company*, March 2009; "Bezos: How Frugality Drives Innovation," *BusinessWeek*, April 28, 2008; "Slow Slog for Amazon's Digital Media," *Wall Street Journal*, April 23, 2008; "How Much Is an Amazon.com Customer Worth?" *New York Times*, January 5, 2008; "Amazon Won't Go Down with the Ship," *USA Today*, July 30, 2007; "How Amazon's Dream Alliance with Toys 'R' Us Went So Sour," *Wall Street Journal*, January 23, 2006; "Keeping Amazon in Check," *Point* (Supplement to *Advertising Age*), June 2005. For more on Kindle, see "How the E-Book Will Change the Way We Read and Write," *Wall Street Journal Reports*, April 20, 2009; "Sony, Google Mount Challenge to Amazon over Digital Books," *Wall Street Journal*, March 19, 2009; "Amazon Faces Suit over Kindle Device," *Wall Street Journal*, March 18, 2009; "Kindle 2: The Delight Is in the Details," *BusinessWeek*, March 9, 2009; "IPod Touch, iPhone Join Kindle's Book Club," *USA Today*, March 4, 2009; "Amazon's Kindle 2 Improves the Good, Leaves Out the Bad," *Wall Street Journal*, February 26, 2009; "Amazon Electronic Reader Kindle 2 Is a Nifty, if Costly, Second Act," *USA Today*, February 24, 2009; "Amazon Kindle 2 E-Book Reader Thinner, Faster—Not Cheaper," *Investor's Business Daily*, February 10, 2009; "Kindle's New, but Price Is Old," *USA Today*, February 10, 2009; "Amazon Raises an E-Book Specter," *Wall Street Journal*, February 9, 2009; "Tech & You," *BusinessWeek*, December 3, 2007; "Reading E-Books Is Fundamental," *USA Today*, November 29, 2007; "IPod of E-Book Readers? Amazon Taps Apple Strategy," *Wall Street Journal*, November 20, 2007.

2. See Peter F. Drucker, *Management: Tasks, Responsibilities, Practices, and Plans* (New York: Harper & Row, 1973); Sev K. Keil, "The Impact of Business Objectives and the Time Horizon of Performance Evaluation on Pricing Behavior," *International Journal of Research in Marketing*, June 2001; Kenneth E. Clow, "Marketing Strategy: The Challenge of the External Environment," *Journal of the Academy of Marketing Science*, Summer 2000.

3. Lance Leuthesser and Chiranjeev Kohli, "Corporate Identity: The Role of Mission Statements," *Business Horizons*, May–June 1997; Christopher K. Bart, "Sex, Lies, and Mission Statements," *Business Horizons*, November–December 1997.

4. "Why Inflation Is Not Inevitable," *Fortune*, September 12, 1988.

5. For more on Starbucks, see Chapter 1, endnote 1.

6. For more on the BlackBerry patent case, see "In Blackberry Case, Big Winner Faces His Own Accusers," *Wall Street Journal*, August 23, 2006; "Blackberry Deal: Patently Absurd," *Newsweek*, March 13, 2006; "RIM to Pay NTP $612.5 Million to Settle BlackBerry Patent Suit," *Wall Street Journal*, March 4, 2006; "BlackBerry Gambles Patent Office Will Be on Its Side in Court," *Wall Street Journal*, January 17, 2006; "Pay Up—or You're Done For," *Fortune*, December 12, 2005. For more on patents, see "The Patent Epidemic," *BusinessWeek*, January 9, 2006; "Patent Applications So Abundant That Examiners Can't Catch Up," *USA Today*, September 21, 2005; "Brothers of Invention: Design-Arounds Surge as More Companies Imitate Rivals Patented Products," *Wall Street Journal*, April 19, 2004; "Businesses Battle over Intellectual Property," *USA Today*, August 2, 2000.

7. For more on the Xbox 360, see "Microsoft's Gamble with Xbox Business Has Turned Corner," *Investor's Business Daily*, March 5, 2008; "EA's Net Drops 31% as Shortage of Xboxes Weakens Game Sales," *Wall Street Journal*, February 3, 2006; "For Every Xbox, a Big Fat Loss," *BusinessWeek*, December 5, 2005; "New Xbox Aim for Microsoft: Profitability," *Wall Street Journal*, May 24, 2005.

8. "Don't Call It Blockbuster Video Now," *Advertising Age*, March 31, 2008; "Netflix Dazzles as Competition Thins," *Investor's Business Daily*, February 28, 2008; "Netflix, Blockbuster Make Users Happy, Investors Unhappy," *Investor's Business Daily*, July 30, 2007; "Blockbuster Unveils Online-Only Rentals to Undercut Netflix," *Investor's Business Daily*, June 13, 2007; "Netflix to Rent High-Def DVDs Pronto," *Investor's Business Daily*, February 27, 2006; "Multiplex under Seige," *Wall Street Journal*, December 24, 2005; "Blockbuster Takes on the Entire Block," *Fortune*, March 21, 2005; "Blockbuster Erases Its Late Fees—Sort of," *Advertising Age*, January 17, 2005; "Blockbuster Brings Heavy Ammunition to Its Netflix Battle," *Investor's Business Daily*, January 11, 2005; "Blockbuster Jabs Back at Its Rivals . . . Tries New Services," *USA Today*, June 22, 2004.

9. Timothy B. Heath, Gangseog Ryu, Subimal Chatterjee, Michael S. McCarthy et al., "Asymmetric Competition in Choice and the Leveraging of Competitive Disadvantages," *Journal of Consumer Research*, December 2000; Kao, (Cambridge, MA: Harvard Business School Press, 1984); Bruce R. Klemz, "Managerial Assessment of Potential Entrants: Processes and Pitfalls," *International Journal of Research in Marketing*, June 2001. For more on P&G's diaper competition in United States see "Value Positioning Becomes a Priority," *Advertising Age*, February 23, 2004; "Rivals Take P&G to Court to Challenge Ads," *Wall Street Journal*, June 17, 2003.; "Dueling Diapers," *Fortune*, February 17, 2003. For a different competitor analysis in the cosmetics market, see "Face-Off: An Unlikely Rival Challenges L'Oreal in Beauty Market," *Wall Street Journal*, January 9, 2003; "L'Oreal's Global Makeover," *Fortune*, September 30, 2002.

10. "P&G Wins Lawsuit, Loses Market," *Advertising Age*, September 18, 1989. For more on corporate spying and competitive intelligence, see "Snooping on a Shoestring," *Business 2.0*, May 2003; "More U.S. Trade Secrets Walk Out Door with Foreign Spies," *USA Today*, February 13, 2003; "The Case of the Corporate Spy," *BusinessWeek*, November 26, 2001. For more on the Oracle/Microsoft case, see "Oracle-Style Investigations Common, Experts Say," *USA Today*, June 29, 2000; "How Piles of Trash Became Latest Focus in Bitter Software Feud," *Wall Street Journal*, June 29, 2000. See also Shaker A. Zahra, "Unethical Practices in Competitive Analysis: Patterns, Causes and Effects," *Journal of Business Ethics*, January 1994.

11. For more on economic environment, see Rajdeep Grewal, "Building Organizational Capabilities for Managing Economic Crisis: The Role of Market Orientation and Strategic Flexibility," *Journal of Marketing*, April 2001.

12. For more on technological environment, see Brian T. Ratchford, Debabrata Talukdar and L. E. E. Myung-Soo, "The Impact of the Internet on Consumers' Use of Information Sources for Automobiles: A Re-Inquiry," *Journal of Consumer Research*, June 2007; Anand V. Bodapati, "Recommendation Systems with Purchase Data," *Journal of Marketing Research*, February 2008; Siva Viswanathan, Jason Kuruzovich, Sanjay Gosain and Ritu Agarwal, "Online Infomediaries and Price Discrimination: Evidence from the Automotive Retailing Sector," *Journal of Marketing*, July 2007; Jo Brown, Amanda J. Broderick, and Nick Lee, "Word of Mouth Communication within Online Communities: Conceptualizing the Online Social Network," *Journal of Interactive Marketing*, Summer 2007; P. Rajan Varadarajan and Manjit S Yadav, "Marketing Strategy and the Internet: an Organizing Framework," *Journal of the Academy of Marketing Science*, Fall 2002; Guilherme D. Pires and Janet Aisbett, "The Relationship Between Technology Adoption and Strategy in Business-to-Business Markets: the Case of E-Commerce," *Industrial Marketing Management*, May 2003.

13. "Technology: A Tech To-Do List," *Wall Street Journal Reports,* November 17, 2003; "Advances in Car Technology Bring High-Class Headaches," *USA Today,* November 12, 2003; Noel Capon and Rashi Glazer, "Marketing and Technology: a Strategic Coalignment," *Journal of Marketing,* July 1987. For more on privacy, see Chapter 13, endnote 15 and Chapter 18, endnote 12.

14. For more on GM, see "Which Is More American?" *USA Today,* March 22, 2007. See also "When It Comes to Toys, Buying American Is Tough," *USA Today,* October 5, 2007; "Toy Makers Make It Hard to Miss What's U.S.-Made," *Wall Street Journal,* September 19, 2007; "Made in USA? Now, Customers Get to Choose," *Wall Street Journal,* August 9, 2006; "Cash and Controversy," *Inc.,* May 2007. See also "Craftsman: Made in USA (Sort of)," *BusinessWeek,* July 4, 2005; "How China Will Change Your Business," *Inc.,* March 2005; "The China Price," *BusinessWeek,* December 6, 2004. See also Durairaj Maheswaran and Cathy Yi Chen, "Nation Equity: Incidental Emotions in Country-of-Origin Effects," *Journal of Consumer Research,* October 2006; Jody Evans, Felix T. Mavondo and Kerrie Bridson, "Psychic Distance: Antecedents, Retail Strategy Implications, and Performance Outcomes," *Journal of International Marketing,* (2) 2008; George Balabanis and Adamantios Diamantopoulos, "Domestic Country Bias, Country-of-Origin Effects, and Consumer Ethnocentrism: a Multidimensional Unfolding Approach," *Journal of the Academy of Marketing Science,* Winter 2004; Zeynep Gurhan-Canli and Durairaj Maheswaran, "Determinants of Country-of-Origin Evaluations," *Journal of Consumer Research,* June 2000; Kent L. Granzin and John J. Painter, "Motivational Influences on 'Buy Domestic' Purchasing: Marketing Management Implications from a Study of Two Nations," *Journal of International Marketing,* (2) 2001; Gopalkrishnan R. Iyer, "Anticompetitive Practices in Japan: Their Impact on the Performance of Foreign Firms," *Journal of Marketing,* October 1997.

15. For more on Lands' End example, see "German Shoppers May Get Sale Freedom," *Wall Street Journal,* January 23, 2002; "Border Crossings," *Wall Street Journal Reports,* November 22, 1999. For another example, see "Corn Flakes Clash Shows the Glitches in European Union," *Wall Street Journal,* November 1, 2005. For more on EU, see "Squeezed by the Euro," *BusinessWeek,* June 6, 2005; "EU Expansion Brings USA Opportunities," *USA Today,* April 27, 2004; "Mega Europe," *BusinessWeek,* November 25, 2002; "Europe's Borders Fade and People and Goods Can Move More Freely," *Wall Street Journal,* May 18, 1993. See also Andrew Paddison, "Retailing in the European Union: Structures, Competition and Performance," *International Journal of Retail & Distribution Management,* (6) 2003.

16. For more on NAFTA, see www.nafta.org; "Central American Free Trade Agreement Faces Obstacles," *USA Today,* May 12, 2005. "Refighting NAFTA," *BusinessWeek,* March 31, 2008; "10 Years Ago, NAFTA Was Born," *USA Today,* December 31, 2003; "Was NAFTA Worth It? A Tale of What Free Trade Can and Cannot Do," *BusinessWeek,* December 22, 2003; "Border Crossing? No Problema," *BusinessWeek Small Biz,* July 16, 2001; "NAFTA Scorecard: So Far, So Good," *BusinessWeek,* July 9, 2001; "In the Wake of NAFTA, a Family Firm Sees Business Go South," *Wall Street Journal,* February 23, 1999.

17. For more on Beech-Nut, see "What Led Beech-Nut Down the Road to Disgrace," *BusinessWeek,* February 22, 1988. See also Kersi D. Antia, Mark E. Bergen, Shantanu Dutta, and Robert J. Fisher, "How Does Enforcement Deter Gray Market Incidence?" *Journal of Marketing,* January 2006; Debra M. Desrochers, Gregory T. Gundlach, and Albert A. Foer, "Analysis of Antitrust Challenges to Category Captain Arrangements," *Journal of Public Policy & Marketing,* Fall 2003; "Stock Now, Pay Later," *Forbes,* October 27, 2003; "EU Court Sends a Tough Antitrust Message," *Wall Street Journal,* October 24, 2003; "Big Drug Wholesaler Fights Charges of Fakes, Price Fixing," *Wall Street Journal,* October 7, 2003; "The EU vs. Microsoft: A Rugged Endgame," *BusinessWeek,* August 25, 2003; "Europe Decides to

Fine Nintendo," *Wall Street Journal,* October 25, 2002; "Sotheby's Taubman Is Sentenced to Jail Time, Fined $7.5 Million," *Wall Street Journal,* April 23, 2002; "Hard Profits: A Cement Titan in Mexico Thrives by Selling to Poor," *Wall Street Journal,* April 22, 2002; David A. Balto, "Emerging Antitrust Issues in Electronic Commerce," *Journal of Public Policy & Marketing,* Fall 2000; "Europe: A Different Take on Antitrust," *BusinessWeek,* June 25, 2001; "In ArcherDaniels Saga, Now the Executives Face Trial," *Wall Street Journal,* July 9, 1998. See also Mary W. Sullivan, "The Role of Marketing in Antitrust," *Journal of Public Policy & Marketing,* Fall 2002; Jeff Langenderfer and Steven W. Kopp, "Which Way to the Revolution? The Consequences of Database Protection as a New Form of Intellectual Property," *Journal of Public Policy & Marketing,* Spring 2003; David E. M. Sappington and Donald K. Stockdale Jr, "The Federal Communications Commission's Competition Policy and Marketing's Information Technology Revolution," *Journal of Public Policy & Marketing,* Spring 2003. See also Louis W. Stern and Thomas L. Eovaldi, *Legal Aspects of Marketing Strategy: Antitrust and Consumer Protection Issues* (Englewood Cliffs, NJ: Prentice-Hall, 1984).

18. For more on auto safety, see "The Number of Small-Car Owners Is Growing Even Though More Drivers Die in Small Cars," *USA Today,* August 20, 2007; "Cars Are Getting Bossy when It Comes to Safety," *USA Today,* May 24, 2007; "Surfing the Freeway: Cars Get PCs," *Wall Street Journal,* January 26, 2006; "Safety Features' Cost Turns Off Buyers," *Wall Street Journal,* December 6, 2005; "Crash Test Smarties," *Business 2.0,* October 2005; "How U.S. Shifted Gears to Find Small Cars Can Be Safe, Too," *Wall Street Journal,* September 26, 2005; "New Sticker Shock for Car Buyers," *Wall Street Journal,* May 18, 2005. For more on CPSC, see "More Paper Tiger than Watchdog?" *BusinessWeek,* September 3, 2007, p. 45; "Product-Safety Cops Handcuffed," *Wall Street Journal,* December 18, 2007. For an overview of the food, toy, and pet product recalls of 2007, see "The New China Price," *Fortune,* November 12, 2007; "Spate of Recalls Boosts Potency of User Reviews," *Advertising Age,* October 29, 2007; "China's Brands: Damaged Goods," *BusinessWeek,* September 24, 2007; "China Rushes Upmarket," *BusinessWeek,* September 17, 2007; "China's Recall Woes Bad for Wal-Mart," *Brandweek,* September 10, 2007; "Not Made in China," *BusinessWeek,* July 30, 2007; "China-Product Scare Hits Home, Too," *Wall Street Journal,* July 20, 2007; "Made in China," *USA Today,* July 3, 2007; "Product Recalls Scare Some Away, Forever," *Brandweek,* June 11, 2007. For more on just the food recalls, see "Private Food Standards Gain Favor: Wal-Mart, McDonald's Adopt European Safety Guidelines," *Wall Street Journal,* March 11, 2008; "FDA to Get Slight Increase in Food-Safety Funding," *USA Today,* December 19, 2007; "How Safe Is the Food Supply?" *BusinessWeek,* May 21, 2007; "U.S. Food Imports Outrun FDA Resources," *USA Today,* March 19, 2007. For more on just the toy recalls, see "States Alter Rules of Game on Safety for Toy Makers," *Wall Street Journal,* March 25, 2008; "Protests Spur Stores to Seek Substitute for Vinyl in Toys," *Wall Street Journal,* February 12, 2008; "Toys Recalled in the U.S. Are Still for Sale in China," *Wall Street Journal,* January 3, 2008; "After the Recalls, Two Toy Stories," *Wall Street Journal,* December 21, 2007; "Retailers Face the Test of Testing," *Wall Street Journal,* November 26, 2007; "Products Recalled for Lead Still Being Sold on the Web," *Investor's Business Daily,* November 13, 2007; "Feds Focus on Lead in Kids' Jewelry," *USA Today,* September 6, 2007; "Mattel's Stellar Reputation Tainted," *USA Today,* August 15, 2007; "Recall of More China-Made Toys Unnerves Parents," *USA Today,* August 3, 2007; "Toy Magnets Attract Sales, and Suits," *New York Times,* July 15, 2007; "Lead Toxins Take a Global Round Trip," *Wall Street Journal,* July 12, 2007. For more on just the pet food recalls, see "Some Pet Foods Still Not on Shelves," *USA Today,* March 25, 2008; "Selling Pet Owners Peace of Mind," *BusinessWeek,* May 28, 2007; "Who Was Watching Suppliers?" *USA Today,* May 10, 2007; "101 Brand Names, 1 Manufacturer," *Wall Street Journal,* May 9, 2007.

19. www.consumerist.com; "Consumers Have Allies on the Web, *The New York Times,* February 3, 2007; "Marketing Law: A Marketer's

Guide to Alphabet Soup," *Business Marketing*, January 1990; Ray O. Werner, "Marketing and the Supreme Court in Transition, 1982–1984," *Journal of Marketing*, Summer 1985; Ray O. Werner, "Marketing and the United States Supreme Court, 1975–1981," *Journal of Marketing*, Spring 1982; Dorothy Cohen, "Trademark Strategy," *Journal of Marketing*, January 1986.

20. Based on U.S. Census data including *Statistical Abstract of the United States 2008*, Tables 1298, pp. 824–27, available online at www.census.gov/statab; U.S. Census Bureau "International Data Base" available online at www.census.gov/ipc/www/idb/; Population Reference Bureau data, including *2007 World Pop Data Sheet*, available online at www.prb.org/pubs/wpds2007; World Bank data, available online at www.worldbank.org/countries/; CIA data, including *CIA Factbook 2008*, available online at www.odci.gov/cia/publications/factbook2008. Also based on GlobalEDGE data from Michigan State University at http://globaledge.msu.edu. See also "Can Greed Save Africa?" *BusinessWeek*, December 10, 2007; "China's Grappling with One Helluva Problem," *USA Today*, September 18, 2007; "In Estonia, Paying Women to Have Babies Is Paying Off," *Wall Street Journal*, October 20, 2006; "A Red Tag Sale for China," *Brandweek*, September 4, 2006; "Russia: Shoppers Gone Wild," *BusinessWeek*, February 20, 2006; "India Rising," *Newsweek*, March 6, 2006; "The Battle for the Face of China," *Fortune*, December 12, 2005; "The Rise of Central Europe," *BusinessWeek*, December 12, 2005; "India's Bumpy Ride," *Fortune*, October 31, 2005; "China & India," *BusinessWeek* (special issue), August 22, 2005; "Global Aging: Now, the Geezer Glut," *BusinessWeek*, January 31, 2005; "Techs Awaken to the Muslim Market," *Wall Street Journal*, July 29, 2004; "To Put It in Perspective," *American Demographics*, June 2003; "When Globalization Suffers, the Poor Take the Heat," *BusinessWeek*, April 21, 2003; "Global Baby Bust: Economic, Social Implications Are Profound as Birthrates Drop in Almost Every Nation," *Wall Street Journal*, January 24, 2003; Tarun Khanna and Krishna Palepu, "Why Focused Strategies May Be Wrong for Emerging Markets," *Harvard Business Review*, July–August 1997; Tamer S. Cavusgil, "Measuring the Potential of Emerging Markets: An Indexing Approach," *Business Horizons*, January–February 1997.

21. Based on World Bank GNI and GDP data and available online at www.worldbank.org/countries.

22. Based on CIA data, including *CIA Factbook 2008*, available online at www.odci.gov/cia/publications/factbook2008. See also "The Lowdown on Literacy," *American Demographics*, June 1994; Madhubalan Viswanathan, Jose Antonio Rosa, and James Edwin Harris, "Decision Making and Coping of Functionally Illiterate Consumers and Some Implications for Marketing Management," *Journal of Marketing*, January 2005; Natalie Ross Adkins, Julie L. Ozanne, Dawn Iacobucci, and Eric Arnould, "The Low Literate Consumer," *Journal of Consumer Research*, June 2005.

23. Based on U.S. Census data including U.S. Bureau of the Census, *Statistical Abstract of the United States 2008*, pp. 17 and 19 and available at www.census.gov/statab; "Is Florida Over?" *Wall Street Journal*, September 29, 2007; "The Coming Crunch," *Wall Street Journal*, October 13, 2006; "Fastest Growth Found in Red States," *USA Today*, December 22, 2004; "Manifest Destiny 3.0," *American Demographics*, September 2004; "America's Gray Area Dilemma," *American Demographics*, July/August 2004; *Census 2000 Special Reports: Demographic Trends in the 20th Century CENSR-4* and "The Next 25 Years," *American Demographics* (Marketing Tools Sourcebook 2004); "Moving West Is No Longer the Norm," *USA Today*, August 6, 2003; "Decade of Change for USA," *USA Today*, June 5, 2002. Also based on data from Population Reference Bureau at www.prb.org>www.prb.org.

24. Based on U.S. Census data including U.S. Bureau of the Census, *Statistical Abstract of the United States 2008*, pp. 24–29, and *Census 2000 Special Reports: Demographic Trends in the 20th Century CENSR-4*; "Population Boom Spawns Super Cities," *USA Today*,

July 11, 2005; "The Cloning of Austin, TX," *American Demographics*, July–August 2004; "Small-Town USA Goes Micropolitan," *USA Today*, June 28, 2004; "Minorities Reshape Suburbs," *USA Today*, July 9, 2001; "Counting Change," *Advertising Age*, May 14, 2001; "U.S. Cities Buck Trend with Boom Downtown," *USA Today*, May 7, 2001.

25. Based on U.S. Census data including U.S. Bureau of the Census, *Statistical Abstract of the United States 2008*, pp. 10 and 14, and available online at www.census.gov/statab and *Census 2000 Special Reports: Demographic Trends in the 20th Century CENSR-4*; "Love Those Boomers," *BusinessWeek*, October 24, 2005; "When We're All 64," *Wall Street Journal Reports*, September 26, 2005; "Half of Boomers Hit the 50 Mark, but Spending Not Likely to Slow Down," *Advertising Age*, July 4, 2005; "The Next 25 Years," *American Demographics*, April 2003; "The Boomer Attitude," *American Demographics*, October 2002; "Chasing Youth," *American Demographics*, October 2002. See also "Tech Giants Target Older Buyers—and Their Cash," *USA Today*, November 30, 2007; "Banks Work to Bond with Seniors," *USA Today*, December 13, 2005; "2046, a Boomer Odyssey," *USA Today*, October 28, 2005; "Old. Smart. Productive," *BusinessWeek*, June 27, 2005; "Marketing Surprise: Older Consumers Buy Stuff, Too," *Wall Street Journal*, April 6, 2004; Patti Williams and Aimee Drolet, "Age-Related Differences in Responses to Emotional Advertisements," *Journal of Consumer Research*, December 2005; Linda L. Price, Eric J. Arnould, and Carolyn Folkman Curasi, "Older Consumers' Disposition of Special Possessions," *Journal of Consumer Research*, September 2000.

26. Frank R. Bacon, Jr., and Thomas W. Butler, Jr., *Planned Innovation*, rev. ed. (Ann Arbor: Institute of Science and Technology, University of Michigan, 1980).

27. Jonathan Lash and Fred Wellington, "Competitive Advantage on a Warming Planet," *Harvard Business Review*, March 2007; "50 Ways to Green Your Business," *Fast Company*, December 19, 2007; "Business 3.0," *Fast Company*, December 19, 2007; "A Consumer's Guide to Going Green," *Wall Street Journal*, November 12, 2007; "Green Power," *CNNMoney.com*, September 26, 2007; "Sony Likes the Yield from Its Junk," *BusinessWeek*, September 17, 2007; "Where Computers Go When They Die," *Wall Street Journal*, April 11, 2007; "10 Ways to Go Green," www.bestoday.com.au/wind/archives/00107810_ways_to_go_green.php.

28. "Ahead of the Pack," *Wall Street Journal*, March 24, 2008; "50 Ways to Green Your Business," *Fast Company*, December 19, 2007; www.greenbiz.com/news/.

29. Paul F. Anderson, "Marketing, Strategic Planning and the Theory of the Firm," *Journal of Marketing*, Spring 1982; George S. Day, "Analytical Approaches to Strategic Market Planning," in *Review of Marketing 1981*, ed. Ben M. Enis and Kenneth J. Roering (Chicago: American Marketing Association, 1981); Ronnie Silverblatt and Pradeep Korgaonkar, "Strategic Market Planning in a Turbulent Business Environment," *Journal of Business Research*, August 1987.

30. Keith B. Murray and Edward T. Popper, "Competing under Regulatory Uncertainty: A U.S. Perspective on Advertising in the Emerging European Market," *Journal of Macromarketing*, Fall 1992; "Inside Russia—Business Most Unusual," *UPS International Update*, Spring 1994; "Freighted with Difficulties," *Wall Street Journal*, December 10, 1993; "Russia Snickers after Mars Invades," *Wall Street Journal*, July 13, 1993; Michael G. Harvey and James T. Rothe, "The Foreign Corrupt Practices Act: The Good, the Bad and the Future," in *1983 American Marketing Association Educators' Proceedings*, ed. P. E. Murphy et al. (Chicago: American Marketing Association, 1983).

31. "Sensitive Export: Seeking New Markets for Tampons, P&G Faces Cultural Barriers," *Wall Street Journal*, December 8, 2000; "Pizza Queen of Japan Turns Web Auctioneer," *Wall Street Journal*, March 6, 2000; Kamran Kashani, "Beware the Pitfalls of Global Marketing," *Harvard Business Review*, September–October 1989.

CHAPTER 4

1. "Wii Fit's Sales Likely Healthy," *Investor's Business Daily*, May 19, 2008; "For Wii Lovers, Something Worth Sweating Over," *Wall Street Journal*, May 14, 2008; "Nintendo Wii Has More Uses Than Just as Game," *Voice of America*, February 8, 2008; "As Wii Changes Gaming, Video Arcades Pull Back," *International Herald Tribune*, February 7, 2008; "To Wii or Not to Wii," *CNNMoney.com*, November 9, 2007; "Nintendo Is Ad Age's Marketer of the Year," *Advertising Age*, October 15, 2007; "Nintendo: Calling All Players," *BusinessWeek*, October 10, 2007; "Wii Did It," *Brandweek*, October 8, 2007; "Chips, Dip, and Nintendo Wii," *Advertising Age*, August 27, 2007; "Best Global Brands," *BusinessWeek*, August 6, 2007; "Wii Toys for More Than Boys," *Forbes*, July 17, 2007; "Can the Wii Save Your Life?" *Forbes*, July 12, 2007; "Wii's Success Spurs a Reset on Approach to Casual Gamers," *Investor's Business Daily*, July 11, 2007; "Cooler Ways to Slay Your Opponent," *Wall Street Journal*, July 5, 2007; "Wii Will Rock You," *Fortune*, June 11, 2007; "Nintendo Hits the Sweet Spot," *BusinessWeek*, April 26, 2007; "Wii and DS Turn Also-Ran Nintendo into Winner in Videogames Business," *Wall Street Journal*, April 19, 2007; "Nintendo Storms the Gaming World," *BusinessWeek*, January 26, 2007; "In the Game Wars, Nintendo's All Charged Up," *BusinessWeek*, July 28, 2006; "Nintendo's Brand New Game," *BusinessWeek*, June 22, 2006; "Nintendo DS Lite," *Time*, June 14, 2006; "Survived the '60s? You May Want to Try This Nintendo Game," *Wall Street Journal*, March 23, 2006; "Nintendo's New Look," *Forbes*, February 7, 2006; "The Golden Age of Home Video Games: From the Reign of Atari to the Rise of Nintendo," Harvard Business Review, 2004; "Nintendo Shifts Direction," *CNNMoney.com*, May 11, 2004.

2. See www.hallmark.com.; *2007 Annual Report*, Hallmark; "Caring Enough about Loyalty," *Brandweek*, August 9, 2004; "Hallmark Cards' Joyce C. Hall," *Investor's Business Daily*, October 14, 2003; "Hallmark Hits the Mark," *USA Today*, June 14, 2001.

3. Glen L. Urban and John R. Hauser, "Listening In to Find and Explore New Combinations of Customer Needs," *Journal of Marketing*, April 2004; Terri C. Albert, "Need-Based Segmentation and Customized Communication Strategies in a Complex-Commodity Industry: a Supply Chain Study," *Industrial Marketing Management*, May 2003; Rajendra K. Srivastava, Mark I. Alpert, and Allan D. Shocker, "A Customer-Oriented Approach for Determining Market Structures," *Journal of Marketing*, Spring 1984.

4. For more on Nvidia, see "Chipmaker Nvidia Makes a Big Leap into Smart Phones," *Investor's Business Daily*, February 13, 2008; "Intel vs. Nvidia Moves into a New Phase," *Investor's Business Daily*, September 25, 2007; "Nvidia Takes on Intel over Graphics Chips," *Wall Street Journal*, September 24, 2007; "Nvidia's New Thrust Competes with Intel in High-End Markets," *Investor's Business Daily*, June 21, 2007; "Intel, Nvidia Both Partners and Rivals," *Investor's Business Daily*, August 21, 2007; "Nvidia's Powerful Chip Moves Closer to Reality," *Wall Street Journal*, November 9, 2006; "Nvidia Raises the Graphics Bar with a New High-End Chip Line," *Investor's Business Daily*, November 9, 2006; "ATI Has Been Off Its Game," *Wall Street Journal*, July 6, 2006; "Perseverance May Pay Off for Chipmaker," *USA Today*, June 27, 2005; "Nvidia Packs New Chip with Speed," *Wall Street Journal*, June 22, 2005; "Nvidia Swings into Hollywood," *Business 2.0*, July 2004; "ATI Is Enlisted to Design Chips for Xbox Console," *Wall Street Journal*, August 15, 2003; "Little Niches That Grew," *BusinessWeek*, June 18, 2001.

5. For more on Herman Miller, see www.hermanmiller.com; "Herman Miller Is Sitting Pretty," *Fortune*, November 27, 2006; "A Cult Chair Gets a Makeover," *Wall Street Journal*, September 17, 2002; "The Net as a Lifeline," *BusinessWeek E.Biz*, October 29, 2001; "Reinventing Herman Miller," *BusinessWeek E.Biz*, April 3, 2000.

6. Sally Dibb and Lyndon Simkin, "Market Segmentation: Diagnosing and Treating the Barriers," *Industrial Marketing Management*, November 2001; Terry Elrod and Russell S. Winer, "An Empirical Evaluation of Aggregation Approaches for Developing Market Segments," *Journal of Marketing*, Fall 1982; Frederick W. Winter, "A Cost-Benefit Approach to Market Segmentation," *Journal of Marketing*, Fall 1979.

7. See www.kaepa.com.; "Tapping into Cheerleading," *Adweek's Marketing Week*, March 2, 1992.

8. Thomas Reutterer, Andreas Mild, Martin Natter, and Alfred Taudes, "A Dynamic Segmentation Approach for Targeting and Customizing Direct Marketing Campaigns," *Journal of Interactive Marketing*, Summer 2006; S. Tamer Cavusgil, Tunga Kiyak, and Sengun Yeniyurt, "Complementary Approaches to Preliminary Foreign Market Opportunity Assessment: Country Clustering and Country Ranking," *Industrial Marketing Management*, October 2004; Malaika Brengman, Maggie Geuens, Bert Weijters, Scott M. Smith, and William R. Swinyard, "Segmenting Internet Shoppers Based on Their Web-Usage-Related Lifestyle: a Cross-Cultural Validation," *Journal of Business Research*, January 2005; Amit Bhatnagar and Sanjoy Ghose, "Segmenting Consumers Based on the Benefits and Risks of Internet Shopping," *Journal of Business Research*, December 2004; Ruth N. Bolton and Matthew B. Myers, "Price-Based Global Market Segmentation for Services," *Journal of Marketing*, July 2003; Philip A. Dover, "Segmentation and Positioning for Strategic Marketing Decisions," *Journal of the Academy of Marketing Science*, Summer 2000; Joel S. Dubow, "Occasion-based vs. User-based Benefit Segmentation, A Case Study," *Journal of Advertising Research*, March–April 1992; Peter R. Dickson and James L. Ginter, "Market Segmentation, Product Differentiation, and Marketing Strategy," *Journal of Marketing*, April 1987; Russell I. Haley, "Benefit Segmentation—20 Years Later," *Journal of Consumer Marketing*, (2) 1984.

9. "Marketers Find 'Tweens' Too Hot to Ignore," *USA Today*, July 10, 2001; "Yamada Card Gives Credit to Struggling Brazilians," *Wall Street Journal*, March 27, 2001; "Grown-Up Drinks for Tender Taste Buds," *BusinessWeek*, March 5, 2001; "Soda Pop That Packs a Punch," *Newsweek*, February 19, 2001; Dean M. Krugman, Margaret A. Morrison, and Yongjun Sung, "Cigarette Advertising in Popular Youth and Adult Magazines: A Ten-Year Perspective," *Journal of Public Policy & Marketing*, Fall 2006; Suzeanne Benet, Robert E. Pitts, and Michael LaTour, "The Appropriateness of Fear Appeal Use for Health Care Marketing to the Elderly: Is It OK to Scare Granny?" *Journal of Business Ethics*, January 1993; Richard W. Pollay, S. Siddarth, Michael Siegel, Anne Haddix et al., "The Last Straw? Cigarette Advertising and Realized Market Shares Among Youths and Adults, 1979–1993," *Journal of Marketing*, April 1996.

10. Stephen D. Ross, "Segmenting Sports Fans Using Brand Associations: A Cluster Analysis," *Sports Marketing Quarterly*, (1) 2007; Rjan Sambandam, "Cluster Analysis Gets Complicated," *Marketing Research*, Spring 2003; "Girish Punj and David W. Stewart, "Cluster Analysis in Marketing Research: Review and Suggestions for Application," *Journal of Marketing Research*, May 1983.

11. See www.cdw.com; "Tech Reseller CDW: No Slowdown," *Investor's Business Daily*, February 1, 2008; "Growth Computes for Tech Resellers," *Investor's Business Daily*, February 14, 2007; "CDW Taps Resellers as It Eyes Comeback in Business Spending," *Investor's Business Daily*, May 18, 2004; "CDW Wins Gov't Contracts with Direct Sales," *BtoB*, May 3, 2004; "Return of the Middleman," *Business 2.0*, March 2003.

12. Timothy Bohling, Douglas Bowman, Steve Lavalle, Vikas Mittal, Das Narayandas, Girish Ramani, and Rajan Varadarajan, "CRM Implementation: Effectiveness Issues and Insights," *Journal of Service Research*, May 2006; H. Wilson, M. Clark, and B. Smith, "Justifying CRM Projects in a Business-to-Business Context: The Potential of the Benefits Dependency Network," *Industrial Marketing Management*, June 2007; Katherine N. Lemon, Tiffany Barnett White, and Russell S. Winer, "Dynamic Customer Relationship Management: Incorporating Future Considerations into the Service

Retention Decision," *Journal of Marketing*, January 2002. For more on privacy, see Chapter 13, endnote 15 and Chapter 18, endnote 12.

13. Charles Blankson, Stavros P. Kalafatis, Julian Ming-Sung Cheng, and Costas Hadjicharalambous, "Impact of Positioning Strategies on Corporate Performance," *Journal of Advertising Research*, March 2008; Girish Punj and Junyean Moon, "Positioning Options for Achieving Brand Association: a Psychological Categorization Framework," *Journal of Business Research*, April 2002; Kalpesh Kaushik Desai and S. Ratneshwar, "Consumer Perceptions of Product Variants Positioned on Atypical Attributes," *Journal of the Academy of Marketing Science*, Winter 2003; David A. Aaker and J. Gary Shansby, "Positioning Your Product," *Business Horizons*, May/June, 1982; Al Ries and Jack Trout, *Positioning: The Battle for Your Mind* (New York: McGraw-Hill, 1981). For some examples of positioning, see "Hulking Hummer Steers Nimbly around Critics," *Wall Street Journal*, November 15, 2005; "Beauty's New Regimen: a Note from the Doctor," *Advertising Age*, July 25, 2005; "Sparkler on the Other Hand," *Brandweek*, April 19, 2004; "Getting Corian Out of the Kitchen," *Wall Street Journal*, December 12, 2000.

CHAPTER 5

1. "The iPhone Gold Rush," *New York Times*, April 5, 2009; "Some Favorite Apps That Make the iPhone Worth the Price," *Wall Street Journal*, March 26, 2009; "The Real Potential of Apple's iPhone," *BusinessWeek*, January 26, 2009; "What Makes Apple Golden?" *Fortune*, March 17, 2008; "The iPhone in the Gray Flannel Suit," *BusinessWeek*, March 17, 2008; "Apple Positions iPhone as Rival to the Blackberry," *Wall Street Journal*, March 7, 2008; "Apple Dials Up iPhone Improvements," *Investor's Business Daily*, March 7, 2008; "From Admirable to Addlebrained," *USA Today*, December 31, 2007; "For Apple iPhone, Japan Could Be the Next Big Test," *Wall Street Journal*, December 19, 2007; "All Eyes on Apple," *Fast Company*, December 2007; "The iPhone on Training Wheels," *Fortune*, November 26, 2007; "The Elegant iPod Touch," *BusinessWeek*, October 1, 2007; "Hold the Phone: New iPod Has iPhone Qualities," *USA Today*, September 13, 2007; "Why Some Apple Fans Won't Buy the iPhone," *Wall Street Journal*, September 12, 2007; "Steve Jobs Offers Rare Apology, Credit for iPhone," *Wall Street Journal*, September 7, 2007; "Apple Slashes iPhone Price and Dials Up an iPhone-Like iPod," *Investor's Business Daily*, September 6, 2007; "Welcome to Apple World," *BusinessWeek*, July 9, 2007; "Testing Out the iPhone," *Wall Street Journal*, June 27, 2007; "From the Start, iPhone Is iFun," *USA Today*, June 27, 2007; "iPhone Mania Nears Fever Pitch," *USA Today*, June 20, 2007; "Apple Buffs Marketing Savvy to a High Shine," *USA Today*, March 9, 2007; "Apple's iPhone: Is It Worth It?" *Wall Street Journal*, January 10, 2007; "Apple Unveils All-in-One iPhone," *USA Today*, January 10, 2007; "Apple Rolls Out $69 iPods, New Showtime Downloads," *USA Today*, February 8, 2006; "More Music-Playing Phones Are Coming," *Wall Street Journal*, February 8, 2006; "The Bug in Microsoft's Ear," *BusinessWeek*, February 6, 2006; "Preloaded iPods Prompt Legal Ponderings," *USA Today*, January 24, 2006; "What's That Ringing in iPod's Ears?" *BusinessWeek*, January 16, 2006; "Album Sales Slump as Downloads Rise," *USA Today*, January 5, 2006; "How Apple Does It," *Time*, October 24, 2005; Will Viewing Habits Switch with Video iPod Programs?" *Brandweek*, October 17, 2005; "iPod's Latest Siblings," *Wall Street Journal*, September 8, 2005; "Apple Tries a New Tack: Lower Prices," *Wall Street Journal*, January 12, 2005; "Apple Transcends Lifestyle Brand," *Advertising Age* (AdAge Marketer of the Year), December 15, 2003; "Music That You Don't Have to Steal," *Wall Street Journal*, April 30, 2003.

2. Based on U.S. Census data, including U.S. Bureau of the Census, *Statistical Abstract of the United States 2009*, and "Table F-1. Income Limits for Each Fifth and Top 5 Percent of Families (All Races): 1947 to 2007," "Table F-2. Share of Aggregate Income Received by Each Fifth and Top 5 Percent of Families (All Races): 1947 to 2007,"

and "Table F-7. Regions—Families (All Races) by Median and Mean Income: 1953 to 2007" (all three tables at www.census.gov/hhes/income/hitinc). For more on income, see "Struggling to Stay Middle Class," *News & Observer* (Raleigh, NC), April 10, 2008; "Generation Gap? About $200,000," *USA Today*, May 21, 2007; "Mo' Money, Mo' Buyin': As the Wealthy Splurge, Overall Spending Jumps," *Advertising Age*, January 15, 2007; "Luxuries of Past Become Necessities," *USA Today*, December 15, 2006; "A-Hunting We Will Go—After Time at the Spa," *USA Today*, December 1, 2005; "McMansions on Wheels," *BusinessWeek*, October 17, 2005; "As Consumers Find Other Ways to Splurge, Apparel Hits a Snag," *Wall Street Journal*, February 4, 2005; "New Luxury Goods Set Super-Wealthy Apart from Pack," *Wall Street Journal*, December 14, 2004; "Waking Up from the American Dream," *BusinessWeek*, December 1, 2003;" Economic Inequality Grew in 90's Boom, Fed Reports," *The New York Times*, January 23, 2003. For more on poverty, see www.census.gov/hhes/poverty; "Goals for Black America Not Met," *USA Today*, February 28, 2008; "Poverty Drops as Nation's Income Hits 5-Year High," *USA Today*, August 29, 2007; "The Poverty Business," *BusinessWeek*, May 21, 2007, pp. 56–67; "Black Poverty's Human Face," *BusinessWeek*, September 19, 2005; "The Other America," *Newsweek*, September 19, 2005.

3. Ravindra Chitturi, Rajagopal Raghunathan, and Vijay Mahajan, "Delight by Design: The Role of Hedonic Versus Utilitarian Benefits," *Journal of Marketing*, June 2008; Kristina D. Frankenberger, "Consumer Psychology for Marketing," *Journal of the Academy of Marketing Science*, Summer 1996; K. H. Chung, *Motivational Theories and Practices* (Columbus, OH: Grid, 1977); A. H. Maslow, *Motivation and Personality* (New York: Harper & Row, 1970).

4. See www.oxo.com; "Features Drive Kitchen Gadget Evolution," *DSN Retailing Today*, May 19, 2003; "What Works for One Works for All," *BusinessWeek*, April 20, 1992.

5. See Marcus Cunha Jr, Chris Janiszewski and Juliano Laran, "Protection of Prior Learning in Complex Consumer Learning Environments," *Journal of Consumer Research*, April 2008; Les Carlson, Russell N. Laczniak, and Ann Walsh, "Socializing Children about Television: an Intergenerational Study," *Journal of the Academy of Marketing Science*, Summer 2001; Elizabeth Cowley and Andrew A. Mitchell, "The Moderating Effect of Product Knowledge on the Learning and Organization of Product Information," *Journal of Consumer Research*, December 2003; Stacy L. Wood and John G. Lynch Jr, "Prior Knowledge and Complacency in New Product Learning," *Journal of Consumer Research*, December 2002; Naomi Mandel and Eric J. Johnson, "When Web Pages Influence Choice: Effects of Visual Primes on Experts and Novices," *Journal of Consumer Research*, September 2002; Elizabeth S. Moore and Richard J. Lutz, "Children, Advertising, and Product Experiences: a Multimethod Inquiry," *Journal of Consumer Research*, June 2000; Julie A. Ruth, Frederic F. Brunel, and Cele C. Otnes, "Linking Thoughts to Feelings: Investigating Cognitive Appraisals and Consumption Emotions in a Mixed-Emotions Context," *Journal of the Academy of Marketing Science*, Winter 2002; Stijn M. J. Van Osselaer and Chris Janiszewski, "Two Ways of Learning Brand Associations," *Journal of Consumer Research*, September 2001; William E. Baker, "When Can Affective Conditioning and Mere Exposure Directly Influence Brand Choice?" *Journal of Advertising*, Winter 1999; M. C. Macklin, "Preschoolers' Learning of Brand Names from Visual Cues," *Journal of Consumer Research*, December 1996; Jaideep Sengupta, Ronald C. Goodstein, and David S. Boninger, "All Cues Are Not Created Equal: Obtaining Attitude Persistence Under Low-Involvement Conditions," *Journal of Consumer Research*, March 1997; John Kim, Jeen-Su Lim, and Mukesh Bhargava, "The Role of Affect in Attitude Formation: A Classical Conditioning Approach," *Journal of the Academy of Marketing Science*, Spring 1998; Hairong Li, Terry Daugherty, and Frank Biocca, "The Role of Virtual Experience in Consumer Learning," *Journal of Consumer Psychology*, 2003; Thomas W. Gruen, Talai Osmonbekov, and Andrew J. Czaplewski, "eWOM: The Impact Of Customer-to-Customer Online

Know-How Exchange on Customer Value and Loyalty," *Journal of Business Research*, April 2006; James C. Ward and Amy L. Ostrom, "The Internet as Information Minefield: An Analysis of the Source and Content of Brand Information Yielded by Net Searches," *Journal of Business Research*, November 2003.

6. "Secrets of That New-Car Smell," *Car and Driver*, November 2003; "Battling the Inferior-Interior Complex," *Wall Street Journal*, December 3, 2001. See also Anna S. Mattila and Jochen Wirtz, "Congruency of Scent and Music as a Driver of In-Store Evaluations and Behavior," *Journal of Retailing*, Summer 2001.

7. "Sweet Success," *Brandweek*, May 12, 2003.

8. "Nike Makes Shoes from Trash, Nokia Envisions Remade Cell Phones," *Greenbiz.com*, February 15, 2008; "Nothing But Green Skies," *Inc.*, November 2007; "UPS: Getting Big Brown Machines to Go Green," *Investor's Business Daily*, November 26, 2007; "Subway's Diet: Less Oil, More Recycling," *Wall Street Journal*, November 21, 2007.

9. "Will the British Warm Up to Iced Tea? Some Big Marketers Are Counting on It," *Wall Street Journal*, August 22, 1994. See also "Starbucks Hits a Humorous Note in Pitching Iced Coffee to Brits," *Wall Street Journal*, September 1, 1999. See also Rohini Ahluwalia, "Examination of Psychological Processes Underlying Resistance to Persuasion," *Journal of Consumer Research*, September 2000; J. Joseph Cronin Jr, Michael K Brady, and G. T. M. Hult, "Assessing the Effects of Quality, Value, and Customer Satisfaction on Consumer Behavioral Intentions in Service Environments," *Journal of Retailing*, Summer 2000; Yih Hwai Lee, "Manipulating Ad Message Involvement Through Information Expectancy: Effects on Attitude Evaluation and Confidence," *Journal of Advertising*, Summer 2000.

10. "How Danone Turns Bacteria into Bucks," *BusinessWeek*, November 26, 2007; "Foreign Culture Makes Selling Bacteria a Strain," *Financial Times*, September 24, 2007; "Probiotics Growth Spurt Continues in New Categories," *Brandweek*, June 11, 2007; "Yogurt Cultivating Unprecedented Popularity," *USA Today*, January 23, 2006; "Benefits of Probiotic Drinks: Healthy Bugs," *The Independent* (London), November 7, 2005; "Health: It's Just a Gut Feeling: Millions of Us Drink Yogurts with 'Friendly Bacteria'," *The Independent* (London), March 1, 2005; "Yogurt: The Culture Catches On," *The Boston Globe*, September 13, 2004; *Trading Up Trends, Brands, and Practices, 2004 Research Update*, Boston Consulting Group, May 2004; Actimel Leads the Culture Club," *Brand Strategy*, November 11, 2003; "RKCR/Y&R Unveil the Actimel Challenge," *Campaign*, January 10, 2003.

11. For more on wrinkle-free clothing, see "Botox for Broadcloth," *Wall Street Journal*, October 7, 2002; "'Wrinkle-Free' Shirts Don't Live Up to the Name," *Wall Street Journal*, May 11, 1994. For more on stain-resistant clothing, see "A Tie You Can Wipe Your Mouth With," *Wall Street Journal*, October 14, 2003; "Look, Ma, No Stains," *Time*, December 9, 2002. For more on service quality, see Chapter 8, endnote 4. For more on service expectations, see "Can I Get a Smile with My Burger and Fries?" *Wall Street Journal*, September 23, 2003; "Service—with a Side of Sales," *Wall Street Journal Reports*, October 29, 2001; "Why Service Stinks," *BusinessWeek*, October 23, 2000. See also Chezy Ofir and Itamar Simonson, "The Effect of Stating Expectations on Customer Satisfaction and Shopping Experience," *Journal of Marketing Research*, February 2007; Alain Genestre and Paul Herbig, "Service Expectations and Perceptions Revisited: Adding Product Quality to SERVQUAL," *Journal of Marketing Theory & Practice*, Fall 1996; Valarie A. Zeithaml, Leonard L. Berry, and A. Parasuraman, "The Nature and Determinants of Customer Expectations of Service," *Journal of the Academy of Marketing Science*, Winter 1993; Rashmi Adaval, "How Good Gets Better and Bad Gets Worse: Understanding the Impact of Affect on Evaluations of Known Brands," *Journal of Consumer Research*, December 2003; Alexander Chernev, David Glen Mick, and Michael D. Johnson, "When More Is Less and Less Is More:

The Role of Ideal Point Availability and Assortment in Consumer Choice," *Journal of Consumer Research*, September 2003.

12. Harold H. Kassarjian and Mary Jane Sheffet, "Personality and Consumer Behavior: An Update," in H. Kassarjian and T. Robertson, *Perspectives in Consumer Behavior* (Glenview, IL: Scott, Foresman, 1981); Todd A. Mooradian and James M. Olver, "I Can't Get No Satisfaction: The Impact of Personality and Emotion on Postpurchase Processes," *Psychology & Marketing*, July 1997.

13. "It's Mind Vending . . . in the World of Psychographics," *Time* (Inside Business Bonus Section), October 2003; "Lifestyles Help Shape Innovation," *DSN Retailing Today*, August 4, 2003; "Generation Next," *Advertising Age*, January 15, 2001; "Head Trips," *American Demographics*, October 2000; "Join the Club," *Brandweek*, February 15, 1999; "The Frontier of Psychographics," *American Demographics*, July 1996; W. D. Wells, "Psychographics: A Critical Review," *Journal of Marketing Research*, May 1975.

14. See www.sric-bi.com; "Markets with Attitude," *American Demographics*, July 1994; Lynn R. Kahle, Sharon E. Beatty, and Pamela Homer, "Alternative Measurement Approaches to Consumer Values: The List of Values (LOV) and Values and Life Styles (VALS)," *Journal of Consumer Research*, December 1986.

15. "Families Spend Less on Food as They Pursue House, Car Dreams," *Advertising Age*, February 7, 2005; "Buying Young," *Wall Street Journal*, November 26, 2004; "Targeting Young Adults," *Wall Street Journal*, October 4, 2004; "Farther along the X Axis," *American Demographics*, May 2004; "La-Z-Boy: Up from Naugahyde," *BusinessWeek*, April 12, 2004; "Work & Family," *Wall Street Journal*, March 31, 1997. See also Michel Laroche, Yang Zhiyong, Kim Chankon, and Marie-Odile Richard, "How Culture Matters in Children's Purchase Influence: a Multi-level Investigation," *Journal of the Academy of Marketing Science*, Spring 2007; Richard G. Netemeyer, Thomas Brashear-Alejandro, and James S. Boles, "A Cross-National Model of Job-Related Outcomes of Work Role and Family Role Variables: a Retail Sales Context," *Journal of the Academy of Marketing Science*, Winter 2004; Patrick E. Murphy and William A. Staples, "A Modernized Family Life Cycle," *Journal of Consumer Research*, June 1979.

16. Based on U.S. Census data and "The American Consumer 2006," *Advertising Age*, January 2, 2006; "The State of Our Unions," *USA Today*, February 26, 2004; "Do Us Part," *American Demographics*, September 2002; "The Ex-Files," *American Demographics*, February 2001. See also James A. Roberts, Chris Manolis, and John F. Tanner Jr, "Family Structure, Materialism, and Compulsive Buying: a Reinquiry and Extension," *Journal of the Academy of Marketing Science*, Summer 2003.

17. Based on U.S. Census data and "Trying to Connect with Generation Y," *Wall Street Journal*, October 13, 2005; "American Express Tries to Find Its Place with a Younger Crowd," *Wall Street Journal*, September 22, 2005; "Wireless Services Get Wakeup Call from Youth," *Advertising Age*, June 6, 2005; "Teens Shift Gears," *Display and Design Ideas*, October 2004, pp 32–34; "Firms Aim Prepaid Credit Cards at Young Consumers," *USA Today*, August 4, 2004; "Nextel Chases Teen Market," *Wall Street Journal*, April 13, 2004; "Verizon Wireless Upsells Youth via Instant Texting," *Advertising Age*, March 1, 2004; "Hooking Up with Gen Y," *Business 2.0*, October 2003; "More Parents Are Leaving School Shopping to the Kids," *USA Today*, August 11, 2003; "Kids, Tweens & Teens," *Advertising Age*, February 17, 2003.

18. Based on U.S. Census data and "Why Grown Kids Come Home," *USA Today*, January 11, 2005; "Mom and Dad, I'm Home—Again," *BusinessWeek*, November 3, 2003; "Free at Last!" *Newsweek*, October 13, 2003; "Bringing Up Adultolescents," *Newsweek*, March 25, 2002.

19. For more on kids' influence in purchase decisions, see L. A. Flurry and Alvin C. Burns, "Children's Influence in Purchase Decisions: a Social Power Theory Approach," *Journal of Business*

Research, May 2005; "Kiddies' Wired Wish Lists," *Wall Street Journal*, December 19, 2007; "Inconvenient Youths," *Wall Street Journal*, September 29, 2007; "This Is the Car We Want, Mommy," *Wall Street Journal*, November 9, 2006; "Honey, I Shrunk the Toilet Paper," *Brandweek*, March 13, 2006; "Walkie-Talkie Phones Hit the Family Market," *Wall Street Journal*, February 23, 2006; "Marketing to Kids: More Than Child's Play," *Poultry*, June–July 2005; "Kids," *Advertising Age*, February 21, 2005; "Advertising Huggies and Pampers Are Seeking to Extend Their Brands ...," *The New York Times*, January 18, 2005; "K-C Pampers Tots with Toiletries," *Advertising Age*, December 13, 2004; "Toymakers Launch Videogame Consoles Aimed at Preschoolers," *Wall Street Journal*, September 8, 2004; "Marketing to Kids, Tweens, & Teens," *Advertising Age*, March 29, 2004; "Hey Kid, Buy This!" *BusinessWeek*, June 30, 1997. See also Sharon E. Beatty and Salil Talpade, "Adolescent Influence in Family Decision Making: A Replication with Extension," *Journal of Consumer Research*, September 1994; Ugur Yavas, Emin Babakus, and Nejdet Delener, "Family Purchasing Roles in Saudi Arabia: Perspectives from Saudi Wives," *Journal of Business Research*, September 1994; Ellen R. Foxman, Patriya S. Tansuhaj, and Karin M. Ekstrom, "Adolescents' Influence in Family Purchase Decisions: A Socialization Perspective," *Journal of Business Research*, March 1989; C. Lackman and J. M. Lanasa, "Family Decision-Making Theory: An Overview and Assessment," *Psychology & Marketing*, March/April 1993. For more on women's influence in purchase decisions, see U.S. Census data, including "Women in the United States: A Profile, March 2000," at www.census.gov/population/www/socdemo/women; "A Guide to Who Holds the Purse Strings," *Wall Street Journal*, June 22, 2000; "How to Market to Women," *Advertising Age*, June 12, 2000.

20. "Consumers Enjoy Lap of Luxury," *Investor's Business Daily*, October 27, 2003; "Downsized Luxury," *Wall Street Journal*, October 14, 2003; "The Japanese Paradox," *Wall Street Journal*, September 23, 2003; "Luxury for the Masses," *Brandweek*, June 25, 2001. See also Cornelia Pechmann and Susan J. Knight, "An Experimental Investigation of the Joint Effects of Advertising and Peers on Adolescents' Beliefs and Intentions about Cigarette Consumption," *Journal of Consumer Research*, June 2002; Albert M. Muniz Jr and Thomas C. O'Guinn, "Brand Community," *Journal of Consumer Research*, March 2001; Gary Cross, "Valves of Desire: a Historian's Perspective on Parents, Children, and Marketing," *Journal of Consumer Research*, December 2002; Terry L. Childers and Akshay R. Rao, "The Influence of Familial and Peer-based Reference Groups on Consumer Decisions," *Journal of Consumer Research*, September 1992; David B. Wooten and Americus Reed Ii, "Playing It Safe: Susceptibility to Normative Influence and Protective Self-Presentation," *Journal of Consumer Research*, December 2004.

21. For more on opinion leaders and word-of-mouth publicity, see Chapter 13, endnote 23. See also "In Search of True Marketplace Influencers," *Advertising Age*, December 5, 2005; "In Era of Consumer Control, Marketers Crave the Potency of Word-of-Mouth," *Advertising Age*, November 28, 2005; "Blogs Cause Word of Mouth Business to Spread Quickly," *Brandweek*, October 3, 2005; "How to Calculate Word-of-Mouth," *Advertising Age*, July 26, 2004; "The Net of Influence," *Business 2.0*, March 2004; "Word of Mouth in the Digital Age: Marketers Win when Friends Hit 'Send,'" *Brandweek*, October 2, 2000. See also Dee T. Allsop, Bryce R. Bassett, and James A. Hoskins, "Word-of-Mouth Research: Principles and Applications," *Journal of Advertising Research*, December 2007; Ed Keller, "Unleashing the Power of Word of Mouth: Creating Brand Advocacy to Drive Growth," *Journal of Advertising Research*, December 2007; Girish N. Punj and Robert Moore, "Smart Versus Knowledgeable Online Recommendation Agents," *Journal of Interactive Marketing*, Fall 2007; Judith A. Chevalier and Dina Mayzlin, "The Effect of Word of Mouth on Sales: Online Book Reviews," *Journal of Marketing Research*, August 2006; Paul Dwyer, "Measuring the Value of Electronic Word of Mouth and Its Impact in Consumer Communities," *Journal of Interactive Marketing*, Spring 2007; Thomas W. Gruen, Talai Osmonbekov,

and Andrew J. Czaplewski, "Customer-to-Customer Exchange: Its MOA Antecedents and Its Impact on Value Creation and Loyalty," *Journal of the Academy of Marketing Science*, Winter 2007; Michael A. Belch, Kathleen A. Krentler, and Laura A. Willis-Flurry, "Teen Internet Mavens: Influence in Family Decision Making," *Journal of Business Research*, May 2005; Ellen Garbarino and Michal Strahilevitz, "Gender Differences in the Perceived Risk of Buying Online and the Effects of Receiving a Site Recommendation," *Journal of Business Research*, July 2004; Fred Thorsten Hennig-Thurau, Kevin P. Gwinner, Gianfranco Walsh, and Dwayne D. Gremler, "Electronic Word-of-Mouth via Consumer-Opinion Platforms: What Motivates Consumers to Articulate Themselves on the Internet?" *Journal of Interactive Marketing*, Winter 2004; Ronald A. Clark and Ronald E. Goldsmith, "Market Mavens: Psychological Influences," *Psychology & Marketing*, April 2005; Barbara Bickart and Robert M. Schindler, "Internet Forums as Influential Sources of Consumer Information," *Journal of Interactive Marketing*, Summer 2001.

22. "Art of Noise," *Brandweek*, November 1, 1999.

23. Based on "The American Consumer 2006," *Advertising Age*, January 2, 2006; *The Multicultural Economy 2004, America's Minority Buying Power*, Selig Center for Economic Growth, University of Georgia, and U.S. Census data, including *Census 2000 Special Reports: Demographic Trends in the 20th Century CENSR-4*. For an overview of ethnic populations in the United States, see "Nation's Minority Numbers Top 100M," *USA Today*, May 17, 2007; "Immigrants Courted as Good Customers," *USA Today*, May 11, 2006; "Special Report: Culture Mosaic," *Advertising Age*, March 13, 2006; *Racial and Ethnic Diversity* (Ithaca, NY: New Strategist, 2000); "Airlines See Potential in Travel by Immigrants," *USA Today*, December 27, 2005; "Give Me Your Tired, Your Poor, Your Beloved Products," *Business 2.0*, October 2005; "Embracing Illegals," *BusinessWeek*, July 18, 2005; "Sears Tries Multicultural Style," *USA Today*, November 16, 2004; "The Art of Cultural Correctness," *American Demographics*, November 2004; "Zooming In on Diversity," *American Demographics*, July/August 2004; "Census Projects Growing Diversity," *USA Today*, March 18, 2004; "The New Face of Beauty?" *Brandweek*, January 19, 2004; "Ads for Ethnic Hair Care Show a New Face," *Wall Street Journal*, July 21, 2003; "Multicultural Marketing," *Advertising Age*, July 7, 2003; "Ethnic Marketing," *DSN Retailing Today*, March 24, 2003; Geng Cui, "Marketing to Ethnic Minority Consumers: An Historical Journey (1932–1997)," *Journal of Macromarketing*, June 2001, Vol. 21, 1; Marilyn Halter, *Shopping for Identity: The Marketing of Ethnicity* (Schocken Books, 2000). For more on the white population, see U.S. Census data, including *The White Population: August 2001*. For more on the African-American market, see U.S. Census data, including *The Black Population in the United States: April 2003* at www.census.gov/population/www/socdemo/race; "Has This Group Been Left Behind?" *Brandweek*, March 14, 2005; "Offerings Hope to Extend the Oprah Effect," *Advertising Age*, March 7, 2005; "Revival," *American Demographics*, October 2003; "Color Bind," *American Demographics*, September 2003; "Card Crafter Uses Creativity to Carve Out Niche," *USA Today*, March 19, 2003; "The New Demographics of Black Americans," *BusinessWeek*, December 4, 2000; Carol M. Motley, "Aunt Jemima, Uncle Ben, and Rastus: Blacks in Advertising, Yesterday, Today, and Tomorrow," *Journal of Marketing*, April 1995. For more on the Hispanic market, see U.S. Census data, including *The Hispanic Population in the United States: March 2002* at www.census.gov/population/www/socdemo/race; "At Goya, It's All in la Familia," *USA Today*, March 24, 2008; "Hispanic Marketing Report," *Adweek Media* (Special Report), March 3, 2008; "Hispanic Fact Book," *Advertising Age* (Special Report), July 23, 2007; "Get Connected with Latinos in Nuevo America," *Advertising Age*, May 14, 2007; "How Nextel Quickly Expanded Its Hispanic Sales," *AdAge.com*, May 25, 2005; "IKEA, Circuit City Stores Go Bilingual," *Advertising Age*, January 3, 2005; "Hispanic Fact Pack," *Advertising Age*, 2004 and 2005 editions; "Hispanic Nation," *BusinessWeek*, March 15, 2004; "P&G's Hispanic

Accent," *BusinessWeek Online*, March 15, 2004; "How Wells Fargo Banks on Hispanics," *BusinessWeek Online*, March 15, 2004; "Marketing to Hispanics," *Advertising Age*, September 15, 2003; "39 Million Make Hispanics Largest Minority Group," *USA Today*, June 19, 2003; "Advertisers Point and Click to Find Hispanic Audiences," *Adweek*, April 7, 2003; "Fresh from the Border," *Time* (Inside Business). April 2003; "Advertisers Tap into Hispanic Gold Mine," *USA Today*, February 21, 2003. For more on the Asian-American market, see U.S. Census data, including *The Asian and PI Population in the United States: March 2002* at www.census.gov/population/www/socdemo/race; "The Invisible Market," *Brandweek*, January 30, 2006; "Banks Market to Asian Communities," *USA Today*, September 22, 2004; "For Asians in U.S. Mini-Chinatowns Sprout in Suburbia," *Wall Street Journal*, April 28, 2004; p. A6; "The Asian American Blind Spot," *American Demographics*, July 2001; "U.S. Asian Population Grew and Diversified, Census Shows," *Wall Street Journal*, May 15, 2001; Sonya A. Grier, Anne M. Brumbaugh, and Corliss G. Thornton, "Crossover Dreams: Consumer Responses to Ethnic-Oriented Products," *Journal of Marketing*, April 2006; David Luna and Laura A. Peracchio, "Advertising to Bilingual Consumers: The Impact of Code Switching on Persuasion," *Journal of Consumer Research*, March 2005; Shi Zhang and Bernd H. Schmitt, "Activating Sound and Meaning: The Role of Language Proficiency in Bilingual Consumer Environments," *Journal of Consumer Research*, June 2004; Ainsworth Anthony Bailey, "A Year in the Life of the African-American Male in Advertising: A Content Analysis," *Journal of Advertising*, Spring 2006; D. Anthony Platha and Thomas H. Stevenson, "Financial Services Consumption Behavior across Hispanic American Consumers," *Journal of Business Research*, August 2005. See also Lucette B. Comer and J. A. F. Nicholls, "Communication Between Hispanic Salespeople and Their Customers: A First Look," *The Journal of Personal Selling & Sales Management*, Summer 2000.

24. "Women in Italy Like to Clean but Shun the Quick and Easy," *Wall Street Journal*, April 25, 2006. See also Eric J. Arnould and Craig J. Thompson, "Consumer Culture Theory (CCT): Twenty Years of Research," *Journal of Consumer Research*, March 2005; John L. Graham, "How Culture Works," *Journal of Marketing*, April 1996; Gary D. Gregory and James M. Munch, "Cultural Values in International Advertising: An Examination of Familial Norms and Roles in Mexico," *Psychology & Marketing*, March 1997; Grant McCracken, "Culture and Consumption: A Theoretical Account of the Structure and Movement of the Cultural Meaning of Consumer Goods," *Journal of Consumer Research*, June 1986.

25. "No More Shoppus Interruptus," *American Demographics*, May 2001; "No Buy? Then Bye-Bye," *BusinessWeek E.Biz*, April 16, 2001; "E-Tailing," *BusinessWeek E.Biz*, May 15, 2000. See also Markus Giesler, "Consumer Gift Systems," *Journal of Consumer Research*, August 2006; Jennifer Chang Coupland, Dawn Iacobucci, and Eric Arnould, "Invisible Brands: An Ethnography of Households and the Brands in Their Kitchen Pantries," *Journal of Consumer Research*, June 2005; S. Christian Wheeler, Richard E. Petty, and George Y. Bizer, "Self-Schema Matching and Attitude Change: Situational and Dispositional Determinants of Message Elaboration," *Journal of Consumer Research*, March 2005; Steven Bellman, Eric J. Johnson, Gerald L. Lohse, and Naomi Mandel, "Designing Marketplaces of the Artificial with Consumers in Mind: Four Approaches to Understanding Consumer Behavior in Electronic Environments," *Journal of Interactive Marketing*, Winter 2006; Pratibha A. Dabholkar and Richard P. Bagozzi, "An Attitudinal Model of Technology Based Self-Service: Moderating Effects of Consumer Traits and Situational Factors," *Journal of the Academy of Marketing Science*, Summer 2002; Russell W. Belk, "Situational Variables and Consumer Behavior," *Journal of Consumer Research*, (2) 1975; John F. Sherry, Jr., "Gift Giving in Anthropological Perspective," *Journal of Consumer Research*, September 1983.

26. Adapted and updated from James H. Myers and William H. Reynolds, *Consumer Behavior and Marketing Management* (Boston: Houghton Mifflin, 1967). See also Mary Frances Luce, Jianmin Jia, and Gregory W. Fischer, "How Much Do You Like It? Within-Alternative Conflict and Subjective Confidence in Consumer Judgments," *Journal of Consumer Research*, December 2003; Ann E. Schlosser, David Glen Mick, and John Deighton, "Experiencing Products in the Virtual World: The Role of Goal and Imagery in Influencing Attitudes versus Purchase Intentions," *Journal of Consumer Research*, September 2003; Jennifer Edson Escalas, Marian Chapman Moore, and Julie Edell Britton, "Fishing for Feelings? Hooking Viewers Helps!" *Journal of Consumer Psychology*, (1) 2004; Anna Lund Jepsen, "Factors Affecting Consumer Use of the Internet for Information Search," *Journal of Interactive Marketing*, Summer 2007; Kineta H. Hung and Stella Yiyan Li, "The Influence of eWOM on Virtual Consumer Communities: Social Capital, Consumer Learning, and Behavioral Outcomes," *Journal of Advertising Research*, December 2007; "How and What Do Consumers Maximize?" *Psychology & Marketing*, September 2003; Ronald E. Goldsmith, "A Theory of Shopping," *Journal of the Academy of Marketing Science*, Fall 2000; Judith Lynne Zaichkowsky, "Consumer Behavior: Yesterday, Today, and Tomorrow," *Business Horizons*, May–June 1991; Dan Ariely, "Controlling the Information Flow: Effects on Consumers' Decision Making and Preferences," *Journal of Consumer Research*, September 2000; Amitav Chakravarti and Chris Janiszewski, "The Influence of Macro-Level Motives on Consideration Set Composition in Novel Purchase Situations," *Journal of Consumer Research*, September 2003; Mary Frances Luce, Jianmin Jia, and Gregory W. Fischer, "How Much Do You Like It? Within-Alternative Conflict and Subjective Confidence in Consumer Judgments," *Journal of Consumer Research*, December 2003; Ravi Dhar and Steven J. Sherman, "The Effect of Common and Unique Features in Consumer Choice," *Journal of Consumer Research*, December 1996; Victor V. Cordell, "Consumer Knowledge Measures as Predictors in Product Evaluation," *Psychology & Marketing*, May 1997; John V. Petrof and Naoufel Daghfous, "Evoked Set: Myth or Reality?" *Business Horizons*, May–June 1996; Wayne D. Hoyer, "An Examination of Consumer Decision Making for a Common Repeat Purchase Product," *Journal of Consumer Research*, December 1984; James R. Bettman, *An Information Processing Theory of Consumer Choice* (Reading, MA: Addison-Wesley Publishing, 1979); Richard W. Olshavsky and Donald H. Granbois, "Consumer Decision Making: Fact or Fiction?" *Journal of Consumer Research*, September 1979.

27. Craig J. Thompson, "Consumer Risk Perceptions in a Community of Reflexive Doubt," *Journal of Consumer Research*, September 2005; Alice M. Tybout, Brian Sternthal, Prashant Malaviya, Georgios A. Bakamitsos, Se-Bum Park, Dawn Iacobucci, and Frank Kardes, "Information Accessibility as a Moderator of Judgments: The Role of Content versus Retrieval Ease," *Journal of Consumer Research*, June 2005; Nitika Garg, J. Jeffrey Inman, Vikas Mittal, Dawn Iacobucci and Stephen Nowlis, "Incidental and Task-Related Affect: A Re-Inquiry and Extension of the Influence of Affect on Choice," *Journal of Consumer Research*, June 2005; Susan Jung Grant, Prashant Malaviya, and Brian Sternthal, "The Influence of Negation on Product Evaluations," *Journal of Consumer Research*, December 2004; Laura L. Pingol and Anthony D. Miyazaki, "Information Source Usage and Purchase Satisfaction: Implications for Product-Focused Print Media," *Journal of Advertising Research*, March 2005; Stijn M. J. Van Osselaer, Joseph W. Alba, and Puneet Manchanda, "Irrelevant Information and Mediated Intertemporal Choice," *Journal of Consumer Psychology*, 2004; Judi Strebel, Tulin Erdem, and Joffre Swait, "Consumer Search in High Technology Markets: Exploring the Use of Traditional Information Channels," *Journal of Consumer Psychology*, (1) 2004; Ram D. Gopal, Bhavik Pathak, Arvind K. Tripathi, and Fang Yin, "From Fatwallet to eBay: An Investigation of Online Deal-Forums and Sales Promotions," *Journal of Retailing*, June 2006; Fuan Li, Paul W. Miniard, and Michael J. Barone, "The Facilitating Influence of Consumer Knowledge on the Effectiveness of Daily Value Reference Information," *Journal of the Academy of Marketing Science*, Summer 2000; Robin A. Coulter, Linda L. Price, and Lawrence Feick, "Rethinking the

Origins of Involvement and Brand Commitment: Insights from Post-socialist Central Europe," *Journal of Consumer Research,* September 2003; Gal Zauberman, "The Intertemporal Dynamics of Consumer Lock-In," *Journal of Consumer Research,* December 2003; Brian T. Ratchford, "The Economics of Consumer Knowledge," *Journal of Consumer Research,* March 2001; Cele Otnes, Tina M. Lowrey, and L. J. Shrum, "Toward an Understanding of Consumer Ambivalence," *Journal of Consumer Research,* June 1997; Ronald E. Goldsmith, "Consumer Involvement: Concepts and Research," *Journal of the Academy of Marketing Science,* Summer 1996; Jeffrey B. Schmidt and Richard A. Spreng, "A Proposed Model of External Consumer Information Search," *Journal of the Academy of Marketing Science,* Summer 1996; Raj Arora, "Consumer Involvement—What It Offers to Advertising Strategy," *International Journal of Advertising* 4, no. 2 (1985); J. Brock Smith and Julia M. Bristor, "Uncertainty Orientation: Explaining Differences in Purchase Involvement and External Search," *Psychology & Marketing,* November/December 1994.

28. Jeffrey V. Rayport, "Demand-Side Innovation: Where IT Meets Marketing," *InformationWeek,* February 1, 2007; "Web Stores Tap Product Reviews," *Wall Street Journal,* September 11, 2007; J. Jeffrey Inman and Marcel Zeelenberg, "Regret in Repeat Purchase versus Switching Decisions: the Attenuating Role of Decision Justifiability," *Journal of Consumer Research,* June 2002; Michael Tsiros and Vikas Mittal, "Regret: A Model of its Antecedents and Consequences in Consumer Decision Making," *Journal of Consumer Research,* March 2000; Thomas A. Burnham, Judy K. Frels, and Vijay Mahajan, "Consumer Switching Costs: a Typology, Antecedents, and Consequences," *Journal of the Academy of Marketing Science,* Spring 2003; Ziv Carmon, Klaus Wertenbroch, and Marcel Zeelenberg, "Option Attachment: When Deliberating Makes Choosing Feel Like Losing," *Journal of Consumer Research,* June 2003; Alan D. J. Cooke, Tom Meyvis, and Alan Schwartz, "Avoiding Future Regret in Purchase-Timing Decisions," *Journal of Consumer Research,* March 2001; Anna S. Mattila, "The Impact of Cognitive Inertia on Postconsumption Evaluation Processes," *Journal of the Academy of Marketing Science,* Summer 2003; William Cunnings and Mark Venkatesan, "Cognitive Dissonance and Consumer Behavior: A Review of the Evidence," *Journal of Marketing Research,* August 1976.

29. Adapted from E. M. Rogers, *Diffusion of Innovation* (New York: Free Press, 2003). For other sampling examples, see "McDonald's Gives Free Samples of Chicken Selects," *USA Today,* February 16, 2005; "Test Drives Get a New Spin," *Wall Street Journal,* February 3, 2005; "Unilever Pitch to Hispanics: Taste Ragu, Register to Vote," *Wall Street Journal,* March 25, 2004; "Mr., Mrs., Meet Mr. Clean," *Wall Street Journal,* January 30, 2003; "J&J Supports Marathon Runners at Point of Pain," *Brandweek,* December 2, 2002; "Taking the Free Out of Free Samples," *Wall Street Journal,* September 25, 2002; "Marketers Revel with Spring Breakers," *USA Today,* March 12, 2002; "When Free Samples Become Saviors," *Wall Street Journal,* August 14, 2001; "Small Wonder," *Wall Street Journal,* June 25, 2001; "Use of Samples in Drug Industry Raises Concern," *Wall Street Journal,* July 19, 2000; "Try It. You'll Like It," *Wall Street Journal,* September 27, 1999; See also Donald Lehmann and Mercedes Esteban-Bravo, "When Giving Some Away Makes Sense to Jump-start the Diffusion Process," *Marketing Letters,* October 2006; Michael A. Jones, David L. Mothersbaugh, and Sharon E. Beatty, "Switching Barriers and Repurchase Intentions in Services," *Journal of Retailing,* Summer 2000; Kevin Mason, Thomas Jensen, Scot Burton, and Dave Roach, "The Accuracy of Brand and Attribute Judgments: the Role of Information Relevancy, Product Experience, and Attribute-Relationship Schemata," *Journal of the Academy of Marketing Science,* Summer 2001; Stephen J. Hoch, "Product Experience Is Seductive," *Journal of Consumer Research,* December 2002.

30. "PepsiCo Tries to Clarify Pepsi One's Image," *Wall Street Journal,* February 25, 2000.

31. Robert M. March, *The Honourable Customer: Marketing and Selling to the Japanese in the 1990s* (Melbourne, Vic.: Longman Professional, 1990); Robert Gottliebsen, "Japan's Stark Choices," *Business Review Weekly,* October 16, 1992. See also Lawrence Feick, Robin A. Coulter, and Linda L. Price, "Rethinking the Origins of Involvement and Brand Commitment: Insights from Postsocialist Central Europe," *Journal of Consumer Research,* September 2003; Annamma Joy, "Gift Giving in Hong Kong and the Continuum of Social Ties," *Journal of Consumer Research,* September 2001.

32. "Fuel and Freebies," *Wall Street Journal,* June 10, 2002.

CHAPTER 6

1. See www.deere.com and www.metokote.com. See also *2007 Annual Report,* Deere & Company; "John Deere's Big-Wheel Rally," *Investor's Business Daily,* September 24, 2007; "Why Deere Is Weeding Out Dealers Even as Farms Boom," *Wall Street Journal,* August 14, 2007; "Deere's Revolution on Wheels," *BusinessWeek,* July 2, 2007; "Deere," *Fortune,* April 30, 2007; "John Deere Cultivates Its Image," *Advertising Age,* July 25, 2005; "Metokote Develops Customized Systems for Applying High Tech Coatings; More than Just Painting a Part," *Diesel Progress,* April 2003; and "John Deere Golf & Turf One Source," www.deere.com/en_US/golfturf/one_source_partners/; "Deere Uses E-Hubs to Build Relationships with Dealers," *BtoB,* September 9, 2002; "Outsourcing Is More Than Cost Cutting," *Fortune,* October 26, 1998.

2. "Detroit to Suppliers: Quality or Else," *Fortune,* September 30, 1996. See also Thomas H. Stevenson and Frank C. Barnes, "What Industrial Marketers Need to Know Now about ISO 9000 Certification: a Review, Update, and Integration with Marketing," *Industrial Marketing Management,* November 2002; Roger Calantone and Gary Knight, "The Critical Role of Product Quality in the International Performance of Industrial Firms," *Industrial Marketing Management,* November 2000; Sime Curkovic and Robert Handfield, "Use of ISO 9000 and Baldrige Award Criteria in Supplier Quality Evaluation," *International Journal of Purchasing & Materials Management,* Spring 1996.

3. Jae-Eun Chung, Brenda Sternquist, and Zhengyi Chen, "Retailer-Buyer Supplier Relationships: The Japanese Difference," *Journal of Retailing,* December 2006; Masaaki Kotabe and Janet Y. Murray, "Global Sourcing Strategy and Sustainable Competitive Advantage," *Industrial Marketing Management,* January 2004; R. Bruce Money, "Word-of-Mouth Promotion and Switching Behavior in Japanese and American Business-to-Business Service Clients," *Journal of Business Research,* March 2004; "The Push to Streamline Supply Chains," *Fortune,* March 3, 1997; P. F. Johnson, Michiel R. Leenders, and Harold E. Fearon, "Evolving Roles and Responsibilities of Purchasing Organizations," *International Journal of Purchasing & Materials Management,* Winter 1998; Scott Elliott, "Collaborative Advantage: Winning Through Extended Enterprise Supplier Networks," *The Journal of Product Innovation Management,* September 2001.

4. Jörg Brinkmann and Markus Voeth, "An Analysis of Buying Center Decisions Through the Salesforce," *Industrial Marketing Management,* July 2007; Jeffrey E. Lewin and Naveen Donthu, "The Influence of Purchase Situation on Buying Center Structure and Involvement: A Select Meta-Analysis of Organizational Buying Behavior Research," *Journal of Business Research,* October 2005; Jae H. Pae, Namwoon Kim, Jim K. Han, and Leslie Yip, "Managing Intraorganizational Diffusion of Innovations: Impact of Buying Center Dynamics and Environments," *Industrial Marketing Management,* November 2002; Jerome M. Katrichis, "Exploring Departmental Level Interaction Patterns in Organizational Purchasing Decisions," *Industrial Marketing Management,* March 1998; Robert D. McWilliams, Earl Naumann, and Stan Scott, "Determining Buying Center Size," *Industrial Marketing Management,* February 1992; R. Venkatesh, Ajay K. Kohli, and Gerald Zaltman, "Influence Strategies in Buying Centers," *Journal of Marketing,* October 1995.

5. Daniel J. Flint, Robert B. Woodruff, and Sarah Fisher Gardial, "Exploring the Phenomenon of Customers' Desired Value

Change in a Business-to-Business Context," *Journal of Marketing,* October 2002; E. Stephen Grant, "Buyer-Approved Selling: Sales Strategies from the Buyers Side of the Desk," *Journal of the Academy of Marketing Science,* Winter 2004; Minette E. Drumwright, "Socially Responsible Organizational Buying: Environmental Concern As a Noneconomic Buying Criterion," *Journal of Marketing,* July 1994; Lisa M. Ellram, "A Structured Method for Applying Purchasing Cost Management Tools," *International Journal of Purchasing & Materials Management,* Winter 1996; Morgan P. Miles, Linda S. Munilla, and Gregory R. Russell, "Marketing and Environmental Registration/Certification: What Industrial Marketers Should Understand about ISO 14000," *Industrial Marketing Management,* July 1997; M. Bixby Cooper, Cornelia Droge, and Patricia J. Daugherty, "How Buyers and Operations Personnel Evaluate Service," *Industrial Marketing Management* 20, no. 1 (1991).

6. Richard F. Beltramini, "Exploring the Effectiveness of Business Gifts: Replication and Extension," *Journal of Advertising,* Summer 2000; Jeanette J. Arbuthnot, "Identifying Ethical Problems Confronting Small Retail Buyers During the Merchandise Buying Process," *Journal of Business Ethics,* May 1997; Gail K. McCracken and Thomas J. Callahan, "Is There Such a Thing as a Free Lunch?" *International Journal of Purchasing & Materials Management,* Winter 1996; Robert W. Cooper, Garry L. Frank, and Robert A. Kemp, "The Ethical Environment Facing the Profession of Purchasing and Materials Management," *International Journal of Purchasing & Materials Management,* Spring 1997; I. Fredrick Trawick, John E. Swan, Gail W. McGee, and David R. Rink, "Influence of Buyer Ethics and Salesperson Behavior on Intention to Choose a Supplier," *Journal of the Academy of Marketing Science,* Winter 1991; J. A. Badenhorst, "Unethical Behaviour in Procurement: A Perspective on Causes and Solutions," *Journal of Business Ethics,* September 1994.

7. Neeraj Bharadwaj, "Investigating the Decision Criteria Used in Electronic Components Procurement," *Industrial Marketing Management,* May 2004; Jacques Verville and Alannah Halingten, "A Six-Stage Model of the Buying Process for ERP Software," *Industrial Marketing Management,* October 2003; Carol C. Bienstock, "Understanding Buyer Information Acquisition for the Purchase of Logistics Services," *International Journal of Physical Distribution & Logistics Management,* (8) 2002; David Tucker and Laurie Jones, "Leveraging the Power of the Internet for Optimal Supplier Sourcing," *International Journal of Physical Distribution & Logistics Management,* (3) 2000; H. L. Brossard, "Information Sources Used by an Organization During a Complex Decision Process: An Exploratory Study," *Industrial Marketing Management,* January 1998; Michele D. Bunn, "Taxonomy of Buying Decision Approaches," *Journal of Marketing,* January 1993; Mark A. Farrell and Bill Schroder, "Influence Strategies in Organizational Buying Decisions," *Industrial Marketing Management,* July 1996; Richard G. Newman, "Monitoring Price Increases with Economic Data: A Practical Approach," *International Journal of Purchasing & Materials Management,* Fall 1997; Barbara Kline and Janet Wagner, "Information Sources and Retailer Buyer Decision-Making: The Effect of Product-Specific Buying Experience," *Journal of Retailing,* Spring 1994; Ellen Day and Hiram C. Barksdale, Jr., "How Firms Select Professional Services," *Industrial Marketing Management,* May 1992; Edward F. Fern and James R. Brown, "The Industrial/Consumer Marketing Dichotomy: A Case of Insufficient Justification," *Journal of Marketing,* Spring 1984.

8. "Green PC Push by Feds May Seed Wider Adoption," *Computerworld,* January 14, 2008; "Working with the Enemy," *Fast Company,* September 2007; "Eco Wal-Mart Costs Marketers Green," *Advertising Age,* October 1, 2007; "Guide to the Business Case & Benefits of Sustainability Purchasing," *Sustainability Purchasing Network,* March 2007; "The Mayor's Green Procurement Code," *Local Economy,* February 2007; "Innovation Wednesday: Wal-Mart Surpasses Goal to Sell 100 Million Fluorescent Light Bulbs Three Months Early, *Fast*

Company.com, October 3, 2007; "Home Depot to Display an Environmental Label," *The New York Times,* April 17, 2007.

9. "With Promise of Big Savings, Net Bill Paying Could Soon Win Fans among U.S. Businesses," *Investor's Business Daily,* February 26, 2001; "How Baxter, PNC, Pratt & Whitney Make the Internet Work for Them," *Investor's Business Daily,* February 12, 2001; "Look, Ma, No Humans," *BusinessWeek E.Biz,* November 20, 2000; "Hewlett-Packard's Slick Procurement System," *Ecompany,* November 2000; "Setting Standards for Corporate Purchasing on the Internet," *Fortune,* September 8, 1997. See also Werner Delfmann, Sascha Albers, and Martin Gehring, "The Impact of Electronic Commerce on Logistics Service Providers," *International Journal of Physical Distribution & Logistics Management,* (3) 2002; Daniel Knudsen, "Aligning Corporate Strategy and E-procurement Tools," *International Journal of Physical Distribution & Logistics Management,* (8) 2003.

10. For more on Allstates, see "The Role of Search in Business to Business Buying Decisions," *Enquiro Search Solutions,* October 27, 2004. See also "10 Great Websites," *B2B,* September 10, 2007; "Usability Problems Plague B-to-B Sites," *BtoBonline.com,* April 23, 2007. See also Goutam Chakraborty, Prashant Srivastava, and David L. Warren, "Understanding Corporate B2B Web Sites' Effectiveness from North American and European Perspective," *Industrial Marketing Management,* July 2005; Samir Gupta, Jack Cadeaux, and Arch Woodside, "Mapping Network Champion Behavior in B2B Electronic Venturing," *Industrial Marketing Management,* July 2005; Cindy Claycomb, Karthik Iyer, and Richard Germain, "Predicting the Level of B2B E-Commerce in Industrial Organizations," *Industrial Marketing Management,* April 2005; D. Eric Boyd and Robert E. Spekman, "Internet Usage Within B2B Relationships and Its Impact on Value Creation: A Conceptual Model and Research Propositions," *Journal of Business-to-Business Marketing,* (1) 2004; B. Mahadevan, "Making Sense of Emerging Market Structures in B2B E-Commerce," *California Management Review,* Fall 2003; C. M. Sashi and Bay O' Leary, "The Role of Internet Auctions in the Expansion of B2B Markets," *Industrial Marketing Management,* February 2002; Geoff Easton and Luis Araujo, "Evaluating the Impact of B2B E-commerce: a Contingent Approach," *Industrial Marketing Management,* July 2003; Irvine Clarke III and Theresa B. Flaherty, "Web-based B2B Portals," *Industrial Marketing Management,* January 2003; Rajdeep Grewal, "An Investigation into the Antecedents of Organizational Participation in Business-to-Business Electronic Markets," *Journal of Marketing,* July 2001; LiPheng Khoo, Shu B. Tor, and Stephen S. G. Lee, "The Potential of Intelligent Software Agents in the World Wide Web in Automating Part Procurement," *International Journal of Purchasing & Materials Management,* Winter 1998.

11. "Reverse Auctions: A Supplier's Survival Guide," *Inc.,* May 2007; "Always Compare Before a Big Purchase," *USA Today,* April 25, 2005; "Buying Online Yields Net Value," *New York Business,* June, 2004. See also Sandy D. Jap, "The Impact of Online Reverse Auction Design on Buyer-Supplier Relationships," *Journal of Marketing,* January 2007; M. L. Emiliani, "Regulating B2B Online Reverse Auctions Through Voluntary Codes of Conduct," *Industrial Marketing Management,* July 2005; Shawn P. Daly and Prithwiraj Nath, "Reverse Auctions for Relationship Marketers," *Industrial Marketing Management,* February 2005; Richard W. Schrader, Julie Toner Schrader, and Eric P. Eller, "Strategic Implications of Reverse Auctions," *Journal of Business-to-Business Marketing,* (1) 2004; "Buying Online Yields Net Value," *New York Business,* June 2004.

12. "The New Golden Rule of Business," *Fortune,* February 21, 1994; Janet L. Hartley and Thomas Y. Choi, "Supplier Development: Customers as a Catalyst of Process Change," *Business Horizons,* July–August 1996; Theodore P. Stank, Margaret A. Emmelhainz, and Patricia J. Daugherty, "The Impact of Information on Supplier Performance," *Journal of Marketing Theory & Practice,* Fall 1996.

13. "Ford Seeks Big Savings by Overhauling Supply System," *Wall Street Journal,* September 29, 2005; Turning Vendors into Partners," *Inc.,* August 2005; "A 'China Price' for Toyota," *BusinessWeek,*

February 21, 2005; "Ford to Suppliers: Let's Get Cozier," *BusinessWeek*, September 20, 2004; "How Would You Like Your Ford?" *Business-Week*, August 9, 2004; "Wal-Mart's Low-Price Obsession Puts Suppliers through Wringer," *Investor's Business Daily*, January 30, 2004; "Push from Above," *Wall Street Journal*, May 23, 1996; Jan B. Heide, "Plural Governance in Industrial Purchasing," *Journal of Marketing*, October 2003; Shibin Sheng, James R. Brown, Carolyn Y. Nicholson, and Laura Poppo, "Do Exchange Hazards Always Foster Relational Governance? An Empirical Test of the Role of Communication," *International Journal of Research in Marketing*, March 2006; Erin Anderson and Sandy D. Jap, "The Dark Side of Close Relationships," *MIT Sloan Management Review*, Spring 2005.

14. Much of the discussion in this section is based on research reported in Joseph P. Cannon and William D. Perreault, Jr., "Buyer-Seller Relationships in Business Markets," *Journal of Marketing Research*, November 1999. See also Cheng Lu Wang, "Guanxi vs. Relationship Marketing: Exploring Underlying Differences," *Industrial Marketing Management*, January 2007; Jan B. Heide and Kenneth H. Wathne, "Friends, Businesspeople, and Relationship Roles: A Conceptual Framework and a Research Agenda," *Journal of Marketing*, July 2006; Robert W. Palmatier, Rajiv P. Dant, Dhruv Grewal, and Kenneth R. Evans, "Factors Influencing the Effectiveness of Relationship Marketing: A Meta-Analysis," *Journal of Marketing*, October 2006; Kapil R. Tuli, Ajay K. Kohli, and Sundar G. Bharadwaj, "Rethinking Customer Solutions: From Product Bundles to Relational Processes," *Journal of Marketing*, July 2007; Joseph P. Cannon and Christian Homburg, "Buyer-Supplier Relationships and Customer Firm Costs," *Journal of Marketing*, January 2001; Kishore Gopalakrishna Pillai and Arun Sharma, "Mature Relationships: Why Does Relational Orientation Turn into Transaction Orientation?" *Industrial Marketing Management*, November 2003; Kelly Hewett, R. Bruce Money, and Subhash Sharma, "An Exploration of the Moderating Role of Buyer Corporate Culture in Industrial Buyer-Seller Relationships," *Journal of the Academy of Marketing Science*, Summer 2002; Christian Homburg, Harley Krohmer, Joseph P. Cannon, and Ingo Kiedaisch, "Customer Satisfaction in Transnational Buyer-Supplier Relationships," *Journal of International Marketing*, (4) 2002; Christopher R. Moberg, Bob D. Cutler, Andrew Gross, and Thomas W. Speh, "Identifying Antecedents of Information Exchange Within Supply Chains," *International Journal of Physical Distribution & Logistics Management*, (9) 2002; William W. Keep, Stanley C. Hollander, and Roger Dickinson, "Forces Impinging on Long-Term Business-to-Business Relationships in the United States: an Historical Perspective," *Journal of Marketing*, April 1998; Das Narayandas and V. Kasturi Rangan, "Building and Sustaining Buyer-Seller Relationships in Mature Industrial Markets," *Journal of Marketing*, July 2004; Thomas Tellefsen and Gloria Penn Thomas, "The Antecedents and Consequences of Organizational and Personal Commitment in Business Service Relationships," *Industrial Marketing Management*, January 2005; Mary T. Holden and Thomas O'Toole, "A Quantitative Exploration of Communication's Role in Determining the Governance of Manufacturer-Retailer Relationships," *Industrial Marketing Management*, August 2004; Gerrit H. Van Bruggen, Manish Kacker, and Chantal Nieuwlaat, "The Impact of Channel Function Performance on Buyer-Seller Relationships in Marketing Channels," *International Journal of Research in Marketing*, June 2005.

15. "Purchasing's New Muscle," *Fortune*, February 20, 1995.

16. "Early Warnings in the Supply Chain," *Financial Times*, March 24, 2009; "United They'll Stand," *Wall Street Journal*, March 23, 2009.

17. Jeffrey K. Liker and Thomas Y. Choi, "Building Deep Supplier Relationships," *Harvard Business Review*, December 2004.

18. "Buyers and Suppliers Team Up for Greater Savings," *Purchasing*, March 5, 2005.

19. For more on outsourcing, see "The Future of Outsourcing," *BusinessWeek*, January 30, 2006; "Pulling the Plug," *Fortune*, August 8, 2005, pp. 96B-D; "Outsourcing with a Twist," *Wall Street Journal*, January 18, 2005; "Call Centers Phone Home," *Wall Street Journal*, June 9, 2004; "Culture Course—Awareness Training," *Wall Street Journal*, May 25, 2005; "Lost in Translation," *Wall Street Journal*, May 18, 2004; "Lesson in India: Not Every Job Translates Overseas," *Wall Street Journal*, March 3, 2004; "Outsourcing Trend Puts Tech Firm in a Sea of Green," *Investor's Business Daily*, December 10, 2003; "The Rise of India," *BusinessWeek*, December 8, 2003; "Where Your Job Is Going," *Fortune*, November 24, 2003; "All the World's a Call Center," *BusinessWeek*, October 27, 2003; "Offshore Outsourcing: Where the Growth Is," *Investor's Business Daily*, October 27, 2003; "At 2 AM in Manila, It's Time to Break for a Midday Snack," *Wall Street Journal*, October 20, 2003; "Outsourcing Jobs—and Workers—to India," *Wall Street Journal*, October 13, 2003; "Surviving the Onslaught: U.S. Companies Customize, Rethink Strategies to Compete with Products from Abroad," *Wall Street Journal*, October 6, 2003; "India, the Export Launching Pad," *Wall Street Journal*, October 2, 2003; "Ah, That Excellent German Engineering—Straight from Southern Austria," *Wall Street Journal*, September 10, 2003; "Outsourcing Jobs: Is It Bad?" *BusinessWeek*, August 25, 2003; "Move Over, India," *BusinessWeek*, August 11, 2003; "Is Your Job Next?" *BusinessWeek*, February 3, 2003; "U.S. Manufacturing Jobs Fading Away Fast," *USA Today*, December 13, 2002; "Calling Bangalore," *BusinessWeek*, November 25, 2002; "A Killing in the Caymans?" *BusinessWeek*, May 11, 1998. See also Mosad Zineldin and Torbjorn Bredenlow, "Strategic Alliance: Synergies and Challenges: A Case of Strategic Outsourcing Relationship (SOUR)," *International Journal of Physical Distribution & Logistics Management*, (5) 2003; Scott J. Mason, Michael H. Cole, Brian T. Ulrey, and Li Yan, "Improving Electronics Manufacturing Supply Chain Agility Through Outsourcing," *International Journal of Physical Distribution & Logistics Management*, (7) 2002; Richard Peisch, "When Outsourcing Goes Awry," *Harvard Business Review*, May–June 1995; Stanley E. Fawcett, Linda L. Stanley, and Sheldon R. Smith, "Developing a Logistics Capability to Improve the Performance of International Operations," *Journal of Business Logistics*, 1997; P. F. Johnson and Michiel R. Leenders, "Make-or-Buy Alternatives in Plant Disposition Strategies," *International Journal of Purchasing & Materials Management*, Spring 1997; Thomas Kiely, "Business Processes: Consider Outsourcing," *Harvard Business Review*, May–June 1997; Leonard V. Coote, Edward J. Forrest, and Terence W. Tam, "An Investigation into Commitment in Non-Western Industrial Marketing Relationships," *Industrial Marketing Management*, October 2003; Teresa M. McCarthy and Susan L. Golicic, "Implementing Collaborative Forecasting to Improve Supply Chain Performance," *International Journal of Physical Distribution & Logistics Management*, (6) 2002; James Hoyt and Faizul Huq, "From Arms-Length to Collaborative Relationships in the Supply Chain, an Evolutionary Process," *International Journal of Physical Distribution & Logistics Management*, (9) 2000.

20. For other examples of big/small partnerships, see "A Fruitful Relationship," *BusinessWeek E.Biz*, November 20, 2000, pp. EB94–EB96; "Automating an Automaker," *Inc. Tech 2000*, no. 4. See also "Polaroid Corp. Is Selling Its Technique for Limiting Supplier Price Increases," *Wall Street Journal*, February 13, 1985; "Making Honda Parts, Ohio Company Finds, Can Be Road to Ruin," *Wall Street Journal*, October 5, 1990.

21. "A Blaze in Albuquerque Sets Off Major Crisis for Cell-Phone Giants," *Wall Street Journal*, January 29, 2001; "Toyota's Fast Rebound after Fire at Supplier Shows Why It Is Tough," *Wall Street Journal*, May 8, 1997.

22. "US Manufacturing: Dying . . . or Still Going Strong?" *US-China Business Council*, 2006; "Lean and Unseen," *Economist*, July 1, 2006; "Share of World Production Falls as China Surges," *Financial Times*, May 22, 2006; "The Case of the Missing Jobs," *BusinessWeek Online*, April 3, 2006; "A Leaner, More Skilled U.S. Manufacturing Workforce," *Current Issues in Economics and Finance* (New York Federal Reserve Bank), February–March 2006; "Are We Engineering Ourselves Out of Manufacturing Jobs," *Federal Reserve Bank of*

Cleveland, January 1, 2006; "If You Can Make It Here," *The New York Times*, September 4, 2005.

23. See www.naics.com. See also "Classified Information," *American Demographics*, July 1999; "SIC: The System Explained," *Sales and Marketing Management*, April 22, 1985; "Enhancement of SIC System Being Developed," *Marketing News Collegiate Edition*, May 1988.

24. "The Long Road to Wal-Mart," *Wall Street Journal*, September 19, 2005, See also Peter Kaufman, Satish Jayachandran, and Randall L. Rose, "The Role of Relational Embeddedness in Retail Buyers' Selection of New Products," *Journal of Marketing Research*, November 2006.

25. Based on U.S. Census data and "Eyes Wide Open," *Fortune*, September 19, 2005, pp. 316B-D; "How Bikers' Water Backpack Became Soldiers' Essential," *Wall Street Journal*, July 19, 2005; "Targeting the DHS," *Inc.*, May 2005; "Heavy Load Now Lighter with Bleex," *Investor's Business Daily*, December 29, 2004; "Pentagon Sales Give Powerful Jolt to Ultralife's Business," *Investor's Business Daily*, April 6, 2004; "Uncle Sam Is a Tough Customer," *Investor's Business Daily*, October 20, 2003; "Super Soldiers," *BusinessWeek*, July 28, 2003; "For G.I. Joe, Smart Uniforms via Nanotech," *BusinessWeek*, June 9, 2003; "The Humvee of Laptops," *BusinessWeek*, April 21, 2003; "Invented to Save Gas, Kevlar Now Saves Lives," *USA Today*, April 16, 2003; "Raytheon on Target," *Business 2.0*, February 2003.

26. "U.S., Other Nations Step Up Bribery Battle," *Wall Street Journal*, September 12, 2008; For a detailed discussion of business ethics in a number of countries, see *Journal of Business Ethics*, October 1997. See also John B. Ford, Michael S. LaTour, and Tony L. Henthorne, "Cognitive Moral Development and Japanese Procurement Executives: Implications for Industrial Marketers," *Industrial Marketing Management*, November 2000; "How Can a U.S. Company Go International, Avoid the Economic Disaster of a Thai Baht . . . and Pay No Bribes?" *USA Today*, November 17, 1997; Larry R. Smeltzer and Marianne M. Jennings, "Why an International Code of Business Ethics Would Be Good for Business," *Journal of Business Ethics*, January 1998.

CHAPTER 7

1. See www.whitestrips.com; "Crest Provides Tartar Alibi for Quietly Vain Consumers," *Brandweek*, February 24, 2008; "P&G to Launch 5-Minute Tooth Whitener," *Foxnews.com*, February 9, 2007; "P&G Seeks Renewal in Teeth Whitening," *Brandweek*, January 16, 2006; "Broadening the Brand," *Strategy and Innovation*, July-August 2004; "Procter & Gamble's Likely Foray into Oral Care in India, *Indiainfoline.com*, March 11, 2004; "Crest Biting Back with Whiter Strips," *Brandweek*, September 8, 2003; "P&G: New and Improved," *BusinessWeek*, July 7, 2003; "P&G Seeks Rejuvenating Effect for New Crest Line," *Brandweek*, June 16, 2003; "The Cranky Consumer Works on Its Smile," *Wall Street Journal*, January 14, 2003; "How Do You Feel about a $44 Tooth-Bleaching Kit?" *Business 2.0*, October 2001.

2. Venkatesh Shankar and Russell S. Winer, "When Customer Relationship Management Meets Data Mining," *Journal of Interactive Marketing*, Summer 2006; Amy Miller and Jennifer Cioffi, "Measuring Marketing Effectiveness and Value: The Unisys Marketing Dashboard," *Journal of Advertising Research*, September 2004; "Making Marketing Measure Up," *BusinessWeek*, December 13, 2004; "How Verizon Flies by Wire," *CIO Magazine*, November 1, 2004.

3. Gary L. Lilien, Arvind Rangaswamy, Gerrit H. van Bruggen, and Berend Wierenga, "Bridging the Marketing Theory-Practice Gap with Marketing Engineering," *Journal of Business Research*, February 2002; "Virtual Management," *BusinessWeek*, September 21, 1998; John T. Mentzer and Nimish Gandhi, "Expert Systems in Marketing: Guidelines for Development," *Journal of the Academy of Marketing Science*, Winter, 1992; William D. Perreault, Jr., "The Shifting Paradigm in Marketing Research," *Journal of the Academy of Marketing Science*, Fall 1992.

4. See www.lenscrafters.com; "LensCrafters Focuses on China," *Wall Street Journal*, February 6, 2008; "At LensCrafters, Selling Candor and Designer Frames," *The New York Times*, April 14, 2006; "Lens Crafters Hits One Billion in Sales," *Business Wire*, February 3, 1998; "LensCrafters Polishes Image with Style," *Chain Store Age Executive*, October 1996.

5. See www.staples.com; "Supermarkets Slot Space for Staples," *DSN Retailing Today*, March 28, 2005; "Staples Blows into Chicago," *DSN Retailing Today*, March 14, 2005; "Easy Does It: Staples Enjoys Success of Recent Strategies," *DSN Retailing Today*, September 20, 2004; "Office Supplies Chain Pencils in a New Plan," *Investor's Business Daily*, September 14, 2004; "Three-Way Competition Is Here to Stay," *DSN Retailing Today*, November 10, 2003; "Fire Awards: Staples Finest in Office Supplies," *DSN Retailing Today*, September 8, 2003; "Staples: Office-Supplies Chain Beats Economic Blues," *Investor's Business Daily*, September 2, 2003; "Staples: Thinking Outside the Big Box," *BusinessWeek*, August 11, 2002; "When Worlds Collide," *Wall Street Journal Reports*, April 28, 2003; "Looking for Intelligence in Ice Cream," *Fortune*, March 17, 2003; "Advertising: Staples Is Changing Its Slogan to Stress the Ease of Shopping for Office Supplies in Its Stores," *New York Times*, February 27, 2003; "Web Delivers Big Results for Staples," *BtoB*, November 11, 2002; "The Architect of Happy Customers," *Business 2.0*, August 2002; "How to Lower Marketing Costs—and Eliminate Guesswork," *Investor's Business Daily*, November 21, 2001.

6. Larry Selden and Ian C. MacMillan, "Manage Customer Centric Innovation Systematically," *Harvard Business Review*, April 2006; Bruce H. Clark, "Business Intelligence Using Smart Techniques," *Journal of the Academy of Marketing Science*, Fall 2003; Mark Peyrot, Nancy Childs, Doris Van Doren, and Kathleen Allen, "An Empirically Based Model of Competitor Intelligence Use," *Journal of Business Research*, September 2002; Stanley F. Slater and John C. Narver, "Intelligence Generation and Superior Customer Value," *Journal of the Academy of Marketing Science*, Winter 2000; Deborah Utter, "Information-Driven Marketing Decisions: Development of Strategic Information Systems," *Journal of the Academy of Marketing Science*, Spring 1998; James M. Sinkula, "Market Information Processing and Organizational Learning," *Journal of Marketing*, January 1994; Jim Bessen, "Riding the Marketing Information Wave," *Harvard Business Review*, September–October 1993; Lawrence B. Chonko, John F. Tanner, Jr., and Ellen Reid Smith, "The Sales Force's Role in International Marketing Research and Marketing Information Systems," *Journal of Personal Selling and Sales Management*, Winter, 1991.

7. William Boulding, Richard Staelin, Michael Ehret, and Wesley J. Johnston, "A Customer Relationship Management Roadmap: What Is Known, Potential Pitfalls, and Where to Go," *Journal of Marketing*, October 2005; Satish Jayachandran, Subhash Sharma, Peter Kaufman, and Pushkala Raman, "The Role of Relational Information Processes and Technology Use in Customer Relationship Management," *Journal of Marketing*, October 2005; Yong Cao and Thomas S. Gruca, "Reducing Adverse Selection Through Customer Relationship Management," *Journal of Marketing*, October 2005; Darrell K. Rigby and Dianne Ledingham, "CRM Done Right," *Harvard Business Review*, November 2004; Peter M. Chisnall, "The Effective Use of Market Research: A Guide for Management to Grow the Business," *International Journal of Market Research*, 42, no. 2, (Summer 2000); Seymour Sudman and Edward Blair, *Marketing Research: A Problem Solving Approach* (Burr Ridge, IL: Irwin/McGraw-Hill, 1998). See also Christine Moorman, Rohit Deshpande, and Gerald Zaltman, "Factors Affecting Trust in Market Research Relationships," *Journal of Marketing*, January 1993.

8. See www.kiwifreshins.com and www.kiwishoeproducts.com; "Kiwi Goes beyond Shine in Effort to Step up Sales," *Wall Street Journal*, December 20, 2007.

9. "Finding Information on the Internet: A Tutorial," UC Berkeley—Teaching Library Internet Workshops, www.lib.berkeley.

10. For more on focus groups, see "Hypnosis Brings Groups into Focus," *Brandweek*, March 24, 2008; "The Perils of Packaging: Nestle

Aims for Easier Openings," *Wall Street Journal*, November 17, 2005; "Puppet's Got a Brand-New Bag," *Business 2.0*, October 2005; "Focus Groups Should Be Abolished," *Advertising Age*, August 8, 2005; "Where the Stars Design the Cars," *Business 2.0*, July 2005; "Sticky Fingers? How Avery Found an Office Problem to Solve," *Wall Street Journal*, July 13, 2004; "This Volvo Is Not a Guy Thing," *Business-Week*, March 15, 2004; "The New Science of Focus Groups," *American Demographics*, March 2003; "Selling Cellphone with Mixed Messages," *Wall Street Journal*, February 27, 2003; "Web Enhances Market Research," *Advertising Age*, June 18, 2001. See also William J. Mc-Donald, "Focus Group Research Dynamics and Reporting: An Examination of Research Objectives and Moderator Influences," *Journal of the Academy of Marketing Science*, Spring 1993; Thomas Kiely, "Wired Focus Groups," *Harvard Business Review*, January–February 1998; see also James R. Stengel, Andrea L. Dixon, and Chris T. Allen, "Listening Begins at Home," *Harvard Business Review*, November 2003.

11. "The New Focus Groups: Online Networks," *Wall Street Journal*, January 14, 2008; "Expand Your Brand Community Online," *Advertising Age*, January 7, 2008; "Design It before You Buy It," *Wall Street Journal*, August 2, 2007; "P&G Plunges into Social Networking," *Wall Street Journal*, January 8, 2007; "It Takes a Web Village," *BusinessWeek*, September 4, 2006; "Shoot the Focus Group," *BusinessWeek Online*, November 14, 2005; "Take Your Market Research Online," *Fortune Small Business*, May 29, 2005.

12. "Selling Sibelius Isn't Easy," *American Demographics*, The 1994 Directory; "Symphony Strikes a Note for Research as It Prepares to Launch a New Season," *Marketing News*, August 29, 1988.

13. For more on surveys, see "Forget Phone and Mail: Online's the Best Place to Administer Surveys," *Advertising Age*, July 17, 2006; "Electrolux Cleans Up," *BusinessWeek*, February 27, 2006; "Chrysler's Made-Up Customers Get Real Living Space at Agency," *Wall Street Journal*, January 4, 2006; "VW's American Road Trip," *Wall Street Journal*, January 4, 2006; "The Only Question That Matters," *Business 2.0*, September 2005; "Flour Power," *Business 2.0*, June 2004; "A New Style: QB Net . . . Japanese Consumers," *Wall Street Journal Reports*, September 22, 2003; "Marketers Re-evaluate Research," *BtoB*, February 10, 2003; "Today, Brawny Men Help with the Kids and the Housework," *Wall Street Journal*, October 4, 2002; "A Matter of Opinion," *Wall Street Journal Reports*, October 23, 2000; "Online Testing Rated," *Advertising Age*, May 8, 2000; "Market Research for the Internet Has Its Drawbacks," *Wall Street Journal*, March 2, 2000; See also Pierre Chandon, Vicki G. Morwitz, and Werner J. Reinartz, "Do Intentions Really Predict Behavior? Self-Generated Validity Effects in Survey Research," *Journal of Marketing*, April 2005; Stanley E. Griffis, Thomas J. Goldsby, and Martha Cooper, "Web-Based and Mail Surveys: a Comparison of Response, Data, and Cost," *Journal of Business Logistics*, (2) 2003; Terry L. Childers and Steven J. Skinner, "Toward a Conceptualization of Mail Survey Response Behavior," *Psychology & Marketing*, March 1996.

14. Paco Underhill, *Why We Buy* (New York: Simon and Shuster, 1999); Stephen R. Rosenthal and Mark Capper, "Ethnographies in the Front End: Designing for Enhanced Customer Experiences," *Journal of Product Innovation Management*, May 2006.

15. Pierre Berthon, James Mac Hulbert, and Leyland Pitt, "Consuming Technology: Why Marketers Sometimes Get It Wrong," *California Management Review*, Fall 2005. See also "Why Are Tech Gizmos So Hard to Figure Out?" *USA Today*, November 2, 2005; "Poll: Many Like Tech Gizmos but Are Frustrated," *USA Today*, October 31, 2005; "The Fine Art of Usability Testing," *Dev Source*, March 2005; "Living on Internet Time: Product Development at Netscape, Yahoo!, NetDynamics, and Microsoft," *Harvard Business School*, April 21, 1997. See also "IBM.com Looks for Big Improvements from Some Subtle Design Tweaks," *BusinessWeek Online*, April 5, 2001.

16. "Online Ads Targeted—But Safely?" *Investor's Business Daily*, December 11, 2007; "Watching What You See on the Web," *Wall Street Journal*, December 6, 2007; "Internet Firms Get Better at Tar-

geting Ads," *Investor's Business Daily*, December 3, 2007; "Behavioral Targeting: The New Killer App for Research," *Advertising Age*, January 22, 2007; "Technology: Analyze This," *BusinessWeek.com*, BW SmallBiz, Winter 2006.

17. "Red, White, and Blue," *Beverage Industry*, February 2002.

18. For more on types of observation, see "A Virtual View of the Store Aisle," *Wall Street Journal*, October 3, 2007; "Marketers Zooming In on Your Daily Routines," *USA Today*, April 30, 2007; "Seeing Through Buyers' Eyes," *Wall Street Journal*, January 29, 2007; "Health Care Taps Mystery Shoppers," *Wall Street Journal*, August 8, 2006; "The Science of Desire," *BusinessWeek*, June 5, 2006; "K-C Tries Seeing Things from Consumer's POV," *Brandweek*, September 5, 2005; "Studying Messy Habits to Sweep Up a Market," *Wall Street Journal*, July 14, 2005; "P&G Chief's Turnaround Recipe: Find Out What Women Want," *Wall Street Journal*, June 1, 2005; "The World on a String," *Point*, February 2005; "Spying on the Sales Floor," *Wall Street Journal*, December 21, 2004; "Sharpening the Focus," *Brandweek*, November 3, 2003; "Rear Window," *Business 2.0*, August 2003; "Shop, You're on Candid Camera," *USA Today*, November 6, 2002; "Ethnographic Research: Watch Me Now," *American Demographics*, October 2002; "McDonald's Asks Mystery Shoppers What Ails Sales," *Wall Street Journal*, December 17, 2001; "P&G Checks Out Real Life," *Wall Street Journal*, May 17, 2001; "The New Market Research," *Inc.*, July 1998. See also Stephen J. Grove and Raymond P. Fisk, "Observational Data Collection Methods for Services Marketing: An Overview," *Journal of the Academy of Marketing Science*, Summer 1992; Magid M. Abraham and Leonard M. Lodish, "An Implemented System for Improving Promotion Productivity Using Store Scanner Data," *Marketing Science*, Summer 1993.

19. "Will Your Web Business Work? Take It for a Test Drive," *Ecompany*, May 2001; "Ads Awaken to Fathers' New Role in Family Life," *Advertising Age*, January 10, 1994; "AT&T's Secret MultiMedia Trials Offer Clues to Capturing Interactive Audiences," *Wall Street Journal*, July 28, 1993; "Experimenting in the U.K.: Phone, Cable Deals Let U.S. Test Future," *USA Today*, June 28, 1993. See also Raymond R. Burke, "Virtual Shopping: Breakthrough in Marketing Research," *Harvard Business Review*, March–April 1996; Glen L. Urban, Bruce D. Weinberg, and John R. Hauser, "Premarket Forecasting of Really-New Products," *Journal of Marketing*, January 1996.

20. For more on Nielsen's people meters, see "Made to Measure," *Fortune*, March 3, 2008; "Couch to Supermarket: Connecting Dots," *Wall Street Journal*, February 11, 2008; "TNS Aims to Take Bite Out of Nielsen," *Wall Street Journal*, January 31, 2008; "Where's the Ratings, Dude?" *Wall Street Journal*, March 7, 2005; "Nielsen's Search for Hispanics Is a Delicate Job," *Wall Street Journal*, October 11, 2004; "For Nielsen, Fixing Old Ratings System Causes New Static," *Wall Street Journal*, September 16, 2004; "Outdoor Ads, Here's Looking at You," *Wall Street Journal*, July 12, 2004; "Nielsen's Feud with TV Networks Shows Scarcity of Marketing Data," *Wall Street Journal*, September 29, 2003; "Confessions of a Nielsen Household," *American Demographics*, May 2001. See also Peter J. Danaher and Terence W. Beed, "A Coincidental Survey of People Meter Panelists: Comparing What People Say with What They Do," *Journal of Advertising Research*, January–February 1993.

21. "Pen Proving to Be Mighty for Brands, Consumers," *Brandweek*, May 7, 2007; "More than Squeaking by: WD-40 CEO Garry Ridge Repackages a Core Product," *Wall Street Journal*, May 23, 2006; "WD-40 Is Well-Oiled for Growth," *BusinessWeek*, April 18, 2006; "P&G Provides Product Launchpad, a Buzz Network of Moms," *Advertising Age*, March 20, 2006; "Loosening the Wheels of Innovation," *Quirk's Marketing Research Review*, March 2006.

22. "Marketing Research on a Shoestring," *Fortune*, May 29, 2005; "Listen Up: Your Customers Are Talking About You Online," *MarketingProfs.com*, May 24, 2005 "Why Market Research Matters," *Fortune*, August 31, 2004; "On Target," *Entrepreneur*, August 2004; "Borrowing from the Big Boys," *MarketingProfs.com*, June 17, 2003.

23. For more detail on data analysis techniques, see Joe Hair, Rolph Anderson, Ron Tatham, and William Black, *Multivariate Data Analysis* (New York: Prentice-Hall, 2005) or other marketing research texts. See also "Ice Cream Shop Gets Scoop on Locales," *Investor's Business Daily*, February 17, 2006; "Is Your Business in the Right Spot?" *Business 2.0*, May 2004; Michael D. Johnson and Elania J. Hudson, "On the Perceived Usefulness of Scaling Techniques in Market Analysis," *Psychology & Marketing*, October 1996; Milton D. Rosenau, "Graphing Statistics and Data: Creating Better Charts," *Journal of Product Innovation Management*, March 1997.

24. "Careful What You Ask For," *American Demographics*, July 1998. See also John G. Keane, "Questionable Statistics," *American Demographics*, June 1985. Detailed treatment of confidence intervals is beyond the scope of this text, but it is covered in most marketing research texts, such as Donald R. Lehmann and Russ Winer, *Analysis for Marketing Planning* (Burr Ridge, IL: Irwin/McGraw-Hill, 2005).

25. For a discussion of ethical issues in marketing research, see "What Makes Tesco, Kroger More Than Just Rivals?" *Wall Street Journal*, December 24, 2007; "Intimate Shopping: Should Everyone Know What You Bought Today?" *The New York Times*, December 23, 2007; "Ma Bell, the Web's New Gatekeeper?" *BusinessWeek*, November 19, 2007; "Firm Mines Offline Data to Target Online Ads," *Wall Street Journal*, October 17, 2007; "Name, Please: Surveyor Quietly Sells Student Information to Youth Marketer," *Wall Street Journal*, December 13, 2001; "How 'Tactical Research' Muddied Diaper Debate: a Case," *Wall Street Journal*, May 17, 1994. See also Rita Marie Cain, "Supreme Court Expands Federal Power to Regulate the Availability and Use of Data," *Journal of the Academy of Marketing Science*, Fall 2001; Malcolm Kirkup and Marylyn Carrigan, "Video Surveillance Research in Retailing: Ethical Issues," *International Journal of Retail & Distribution Management*, (11) 2000; Brian Carroll, "Price of Privacy: Selling Consumer Databases in Bankruptcy," *Journal of Interactive Marketing*, Summer 2002; Eve M. Caudill and Patrick E. Murphy, "Consumer Online Privacy: Legal and Ethical Issues," *Journal of Public Policy & Marketing*, Spring 2000; John R. Sparks and Shelby D. Hunt, "Marketing Researcher Ethical Sensitivity: Conceptualization, Measurement, and Exploratory Investigation," *Journal of Marketing*, April 1998; Naresh K. Malhotra, and Gina L. Miller, "An Integrated Model for Ethical Decisions in Marketing Research," *Journal of Business Ethics*, February 1998.

26. "China Market Research Strategies," *China Business Review*, May-June 2004.

27. "More Companies Are Offshoring R&D," *Investor's Business Daily*, November 21, 2005; "Chinese Puzzle: Spotty Consumer Data," *Wall Street Journal*, October 15, 2003. See also Thomas Tsu Wee Tan and Tan Jee Lui, "Globalization and Trends in International Marketing Research in Asia," *Journal of Business Research*, October 2002; Masaaki Kotabe, "Using Euromonitor Database in International Marketing Research," *Journal of the Academy of Marketing Science*, Spring 2002.

CHAPTER 8

1. "Under Armour Reboots," *Fortune*, February 2, 2009; "The CMO Interview: Steve Battista, Under Armour," *Advertising Age*, January 12, 2009; "Under Armour Hopes to Outrun Nike," *Advertising Age*, April 28, 2008; "Under Armour: Putting Thoughts Back 'Into the Box,'" CNBC.com; "Do These Clothes Help You Work Out?" *BusinessWeek*, March 24, 2008; "Under Armour, Nike Plot Cross-Trainer Comeback," *Advertising Age*, December 3, 2007; "Room to Run for Under Armour," *Wall Street Journal*, October 23, 2007; "No Sugar and Spice Here," *Advertising Age*, June 18, 2007; "Under Armour May Be Overstretched," *BusinessWeek*, April 30, 2007; "Under Armour: Thrown for a Loss," *BusinessWeek*, February 1, 2007; "Under Armour," *Apparel Magazine*, February 2007; "Motion Commotion," *Time*, September 11, 2006; "Perspiration Inspiration," *BusinessWeek*, June 5, 2006; "Rag Trade Rivalry," *Forbes*, June 5, 2006; "Under Armour, A Brawny Tee House? No Sweat," *BusinessWeek Online*, May 25, 2006; "Under Armour Hits the Ground Running," *SGB*, May 2006; "Under Armour Finds Sports Shoe Fits Its Philosophy," *USA Today*, April 14, 2006; "Hot and Cool," *Government Executive*, October 15, 2005; "Protect this House," *Fast Company*, August 2005; "Under Armour Shows Feminine Side," *Women's Wear Daily*, February 24, 2005; "Under Armour's Apparel Appeal," *Brandweek*, February 21, 2005; *2007 Annual Report*, Under Armour; *2007 Annual Report*, Army and Air Force Exchange Service; "Kevin Plank," *Brandweek*, April 12, 2004; "Tight Skivvies," *Time*, January 5, 2003.

2. R. Kenneth Teas and Sanjeev Agarwal, "The Effects of Extrinsic Product Cues on Consumers' Perceptions of Quality, Sacrifice, and Value," *Journal of the Academy of Marketing Science*, Spring 2000; Amna Kirmani and Akshay R. Rao, "No Pain, No Gain: a Critical Review of the Literature on Signaling Unobservable Product Quality," *Journal of Marketing*, April 2000; Neil A. Morgan and Douglas W. Vorhies, "Product Quality Alignment and Business Unit Performance," *The Journal of Product Innovation Management*, November 2001; Joseph M. Juran, "Made In U.S.A.: A Renaissance in Quality," *Harvard Business Review*, July–August 1993.

3. Example inspired by other case studies: Robert Solomon and Kathleen Higgins, *Case Study: Cement for Sale*, Center for the Study of Ethics, Utah Valley State College; C.B. Fledderman (1999), *Denver Runway Concrete*, Engineering Ethics, Prentice Hall.

4. For more on service expectations, see Chapter 5, endnote 11. For more on service quality, see "The Payoff for Trying Harder," *Business 2.0*, July 2002; "Avis to Try Even Harder with Ads Touting High Quality of Service," *Wall Street Journal*, February 18, 2000. For more on air service, see "Paved Paradise: The New Airport Parking Lots," *Wall Street Journal*, November 12, 2003; "Flat-Out Winners," *BusinessWeek*, October 27, 2003. See also Roland T. Rust and Chung Tuck Siong, "Marketing Models of Service and Relationships," *Marketing Science*, November–December 2006; Frances X. Frei, "The Four Things a Service Business Must Get Right," *Harvard Business Review*, April 2008; Paul P. Maglio and Jim Spohrer, "Fundamentals of Service Science," *Journal of the Academy of Marketing Science*, Spring 2008; Shannon Anderson, Lisa Klein Pearo, and Sally K. Widener, "Drivers of Service Satisfaction: Linking Customer Satisfaction to the Service Concept and Customer Characteristics," *Journal of Service Research*, November 2008; Neeli Bendapudi and Robert P. Leone, "Psychological Implications of Customer Participation in Co-Production," *Journal of Marketing*, January 2003; Leonard L. Berry, Kathleen Seiders, and Dhruv Grewal, "Understanding Service Convenience," *Journal of Marketing*, July 2002; James Reardon, Chip Miller, Ronald Hasty, and Blaise J. Waguespack, "A Comparison of Alternative Theories of Services Marketing," *Journal of Marketing Theory & Practice*, Fall 1996; James C. Anderson and James A. Narus, "Capturing the Value of Supplementary Services," *Harvard Business Review*, January–February 1995; Matthew L. Meuter, Mary Jo Bitner, Amy L. Ostrom, and Stephen W. Brown, "Choosing Among Alternative Service Delivery Modes: An Investigation of Customer Trial of Self-Service Technologies," *Journal of Marketing*, April 2005; D. Todd Donavan, Tom J. Brown, and John C. Mowen, "Internal Benefits of Service-Worker Customer Orientation: Job Satisfaction, Commitment, and Organizational Citizenship Behaviors," *Journal of Marketing*, January 2004; Stephen L. Vargo and Robert F. Lusch, "Evolving to a New Dominant Logic for Marketing," *Journal of Marketing*, January 2004; Ruth N. Bolton, George S. Day, John Deighton, Das Narayandas, Evert Gummesson, Shelby D. Hunt, C. K. Prahalad, Roland T. Rust, and Steven M. Shugan, "Invited Commentaries on "Evolving to a New Dominant Logic for Marketing"," *Journal of Marketing*, January 2004; Robert D. Winsor, Jagdish N. Sheth, and Chris Manolis, "Differentiating Goods and Services Retailing Using Form and Possession Utilities," *Journal of Business Research*, March 2004; Jeffrey F. Rayport,

Bernard J. Jaworski, and Ellie J. Kyung, "Best Face Forward: Improving Companies' Service Interfaces with Customers," *Journal of Interactive Marketing*, Autumn 2005; Michel Laroche, Linda C. Ueltschy, Shuzo Abe, Mark Cleveland, and Peter P. Yannopoulos, "Service Quality Perceptions and Customer Satisfaction: Evaluating the Role of Culture," *Journal of International Marketing*, 2004; Dawn Jing Lei, Roger Pruppers, Hans Ouwersloot, and Jos Lemmink, "Service Intensiveness and Brand Extension Evaluations," *Journal of Service Research*, February 2004; Tom DeWitt and Michael K. Brady, "Rethinking Service Recovery Strategies," *Journal of Service Research*, November 2003; Leonard L. Berry, Venkatesh Shankar, Janet Turner Parish, Susan Cadwallader, and Thomas Dotzel, "Creating New Markets Through Service Innovation," *MIT Sloan Management Review*, Winter 2006.

5. For more on Listerine PocketPaks, see "The Strip Club," *Business 2.0*, June 2003; "Marketer of the Year: PocketPaks, a Breath of Minty Fresh Air," *Brandweek*, October 14, 2002, pp. M42–M46. For more on brand extensions, see "A Little Less Salt, a Lot More Sales: Campbell's Line Extension," *Advertising Age*, March 10, 2008; "Like Our Sunglasses? Try Our Vodka!" *Wall Street Journal*, November 8, 2007; "P&G Rekindles an Old Flame: New Febreze Candles," *Wall Street Journal*, June 5, 2007; Alokparna Basu Monga and Deborah Roedder John, "Cultural Differences in Brand Extension Evaluation: The Influence of Analytic versus Holistic Thinking," *Journal of Consumer Research*, December 2007; Franziska Vlckner and Henrik Sattler, "Drivers of Brand Extension Success," *Journal of Marketing*, April 2006; Chris Pullig, Carolyn J. Simmons, and Richard G. Netemeyer, "Brand Dilution: When Do New Brands Hurt Existing Brands?" *Journal of Marketing*, April 2006; Tülin Erdem, Joffre Swait, and Ana Valenzuela, "Brands as Signals: A Cross-Country Validation Study," *Journal of Marketing*, January 2006; Eric Yorkston and Geeta Menon, "A Sound Idea: Phonetic Effects of Brand Names on Consumer Judgments," *Journal of Consumer Research*, June 2004; Mike Bendixen, Kalala A. Bukasa, and Russell Abratt, "Brand Equity in the Business-to-Business Market," *Industrial Marketing Management*, July 2004; Pamela W. Henderson, Joseph A. Cote, Siew Meng Leong, and Bernd Schmitt, "Building Strong Brands in Asia: Selecting the Visual Components of Image to Maximize Brand Strength," *International Journal of Research in Marketing*, December 2003; Yih Hwai Lee and Kim Soon Ang, "Brand Name Suggestiveness: A Chinese Language Perspective," *International Journal of Research in Marketing*, December 2003; Thomas J. Madden, Frank Fehle, and Susan Fournier, "Brands Matter: An Empirical Demonstration of the Creation of Shareholder Value Through Branding," *Journal of the Academy of Marketing Science*, Spring 2006; Thomas J. Reynolds and Carol B. Phillips, "In Search of True Brand Equity Metrics: All Market Share Ain't Created Equal," *Journal of Advertising Research*, June 2005; Girish N. Punj and Clayton L. Hillyer, "A Cognitive Model of Customer-Based Brand Equity for Frequently Purchased Products: Conceptual Framework and Empirical Results," *Journal of Consumer Psychology*, (1) 2004; Richard G. Netemeyer, Balaji Krishnan, Chris Pullig, Guangping Wang, Mehmet Yagci, Dwane Dean, Joe Ricks, and Ferdinand Wirth, "Developing and Validating Measures of Facets of Customer-Based Brand Equity," *Journal of Business Research*, February 2004. For more on brand equity and brand value, see "Built for the Long Haul," *BusinessWeek*, January 30, 2006; "Ranking Corporate Reputations," *Wall Street Journal*, December 6, 2005; "Hershey's Trumps Donald, McDonald's, and Martha," *Brandweek*, November 28, 2005; "High Tech High Loyalty," *Brandweek*, October 31, 2005, pp. 22–24; "Welch's Juices Equity with Fresh-Fruit Line," *Brandweek*, August 22, 2005; "Mattress Maker Spreads the Word through Aggressive Marketing," *Investor's Business Daily*, July 1, 2005; Mega Brands," *Advertising Age*, July 2005; "Sharp Pursues Big-Screen Ambitions," *Wall Street Journal*, June 9, 2005; "Hard Lesson Learned: Premium and No-Frills Don't Mix," *Wall Street Journal*, November 3, 2003; "Nonprofits Can Provide a Brand Name That Sells," *Wall Street Journal*, September 23, 2003. For more on brand naming, see "New Names for Old Companies," *Business 2.0*, November 2005; "Lost Verizon: Survey Urges Brand Names

to Get Real," *Brandweek*, September 5, 2005; "Tech Sector Ponders: What's in a Name?" *Advertising Age*, May 9, 2005; "The New Science of Naming," *Business 2.0*, December 2004. See also Arjun Chaudhuri and Morris B. Holbrook, "The Chain of Effects from Brand Trust and Brand Affect to Brand Performance: the Role of Brand Loyalty," *Journal of Marketing*, April 2001; Russell Casey, "Designing Brand Identity: A Complete Guide to Creating, Building, and Maintaining Strong Brands," *Journal of the Academy of Marketing Science*, Winter 2004; Subramanian Balachander and Sanjoy Ghose, "Reciprocal Spillover Effects: a Strategic Benefit of Brand Extensions," *Journal of Marketing*, January 2003; Elizabeth S. Moore, William L. Wilkie, and Richard J. Lutz, "Passing the Torch: Intergenerational Influences as a Source of Brand Equity," *Journal of Marketing*, April 2002; John A. Quelch and David Kenny, "Extend Profits, Not Product Lines," *Harvard Business Review*, September 1994–October 1994; Linda B. Samuels and Samuels Jeffery M, "Famous Marks Now Federally Protected Against Dilution," *Journal of Public Policy & Marketing*, Fall 1996; Pamela W. Henderson and Joseph A. Cote, "Guidelines for Selecting or Modifying Logos," *Journal of Marketing*, April 1998.

6. "What's New with the Chinese Consumer," *The McKinsey Quarterly*, October 2008.

7. "Lost in Translation," *Business 2.0*, August 2004; "Global Products Require Name-Finders," *Wall Street Journal*, April 11, 1996; Martin S. Roth, "Effects of Global Market Conditions on Brand Image Customization and Brand Performance," *Journal of Advertising*, Winter 1995.

8. See www.yahoo.com. See also "Nielsen//NetRatings Reports the Fastest Growing Web Sites Year-over-Year Among Top Internet Properties: Apple, Google, and Amazon Take the Lead," Nielsen/NetRatings Press Release, December 20, 2005; "Yahoo: Exporting an *Uber*-Brand," *BusinessWeek Online*, April 4, 2005; "Coterie of Early Hires Made Yahoo! A Hit but an Insular Place," *Wall Street Journal*, March 9, 2001; "Voulez-vous Yahoo Avec Moi?" *Fortune*, October 16, 2000; "The Two Grown-Ups behind Yahoo!'s Surge," *Wall Street Journal*, April 10, 1998.

9. See www.hermanmiller.com. See also Peter Lawrence and Leigh McAllister, "Marketing Meets Design: Core Necessities for Successful New Product Development," *Journal of Product Innovation Management*, March 2005; Helen Perks, Rachel Cooper, and Cassie Jones, "Characterizing the Role of Design in New Product Development: An Empirically Derived Taxonomy," *Journal of Product Innovation Management*, March 2005; K. Scott Swan, Masaaki Kotabe, and Brent B. Allred, "Exploring Robust Design Capabilities, Their Role in Creating Global Products, and Their Relationship to Firm Performance," *Journal of Product Innovation Management*, March 2005; Lan Luo; Kannan, Babak Besharati, and Shapour Azarm, "Design of Robust New Products under Variability: Marketing Meets Design," *Journal of Product Innovation Management*, March 2005; Julie H. Hertenstein, Marjorie B. Platt, and Robert W. Veryzer, "The Impact of Industrial Design Effectiveness on Corporate Financial Performance," *Journal of Product Innovation Management*, January 2005; Mariëlle E. H. Creusen and Jan P. L. Schoormans, "The Different Roles of Product Appearance in Consumer Choice," *Journal of Product Innovation Management*, January 2005. See also "Masters of Design," *Fast Company*, June 2004; Artemis March, "Usability: The New Dimension of Product Design," *Harvard Business Review*, September–October 1994.

10. "TiVo's Time Ticks Away, DirecTV Programs Attack," *Brandweek*, October 10, 2005; "Road to Foreign Franchises Is Paved with New Problems," *Wall Street Journal*, May 14, 2001; "Tiger Fight Sees Kellogg, ExxonMobil Clash in Court," *Ad Age Global*, November 2000; "Wrestling, Wildlife Fund Battle over WWF Site," *USA Today*, October 25, 2000; "More Firms Flash New Badge," *USA Today*, October 4, 2000; "Name Lawsuit Prompts AppleSoup to Become Flycode," *USA Today*, September 11, 2000. See also Karen Gantt, "Revisiting the Scope of Lanham Act Protection," *Journal of the Academy of Marketing Science*, Winter 2004; Maureen Morrin and Jacob Jacoby,

"Trademark Dilution: Empirical Measures for an Elusive Concept," *Journal of Public Policy & Marketing*, Fall 2000; F. C. Hong, Anthony Pecotich, and Clifford J. Schultz II, "Brand Name Translation: Language Constraints, Product Attributes, and Consumer Perceptions in East and Southeast Asia," *Journal of International Marketing*, (2) 2002; Lee B. Burgunder, "Trademark Protection of Product Characteristics: A Predictive Model," *Journal of Public Policy & Marketing*, Fall 1997.

11. For more on piracy, see "The Economic Effect of Counterfeiting and Piracy," Executive Summary, Organization for Economic Co-Operation and Development, 2007; "Deaf to Music Piracy," *BusinessWeek*, September 10, 2007; "A Small Firm Takes on Chinese Pirates," *Wall Street Journal*, July 5, 2007; "Smart Tech Fights Fakes," *Business 2.0*, March 2007; "Fed Up with Fakes," *BusinessWeek*, October 9, 2006; "Fakes Are a Real Headache," *Telegraph.Co.UK*, July 15, 2006; "A Question of Value: Zippo Case Sparks Clash," *Wall Street Journal*, June 2, 2006; "Here's How to Make It Stop," *Inc.*, June 2006; "Not Exactly Counterfeit," *Fortune*, May 1, 2006; "Fighting Fakes," *Inc.*, February 2006; "Fighting Bogus Goods to Protect the Brand," *Brandweek*, January 2, 2006; Ashutosh Prasad and Vijay Mahajan, "How Many Pirates Should a Software Firm Tolerate?: An Analysis of Piracy Protection on the Diffusion of Software," *International Journal of Research in Marketing*, December 2003; "Holograms Tell Fake from Fendi," *Wall Street Journal*, February 22, 2006; "Bagging Fakers and Sellers," *Wall Street Journal*, January 31, 2006; "As Luxury Industry Goes Global, Knock-Off Merchants Follow," *Wall Street Journal*, January 31, 2006; "As Pfizer Battles Fakes in China, Nation's Police Are Uneasy Allies," *Wall Street Journal*, January 24, 2006; "Pirated DVDs among Hottest Items on Shelves in Iraq," *USA Today*, January 20, 2006; "Software Shift to Subscriptions, Services Helps to Deter Piracy," *Investor's Business Daily*, December 5, 2005; "Firestorm Rages over Lockdown on Digital Music," *USA Today*, November 14, 2005; "Cybercrime," *USA Today*, November 3, 2005, Sect. A&B; "Bootlegs Go Corporate," *Wall Street Journal*, September 27, 2005; "Newest Export from China: Pirated Pay TV," *Wall Street Journal*, September 2, 2005; "Now, Complaints of Brand Name Piracy Go Both Ways," *Wall Street Journal*, July 11, 2005; "Companies Fight Hard vs. Fakes but Problems Are Getting Worse," *Investor's Business Daily*, July 7, 2005; "Fakes!" *BusinessWeek*, February 7, 2005. See also Laurence Jacobs, A. Coskun Samli, and Tom Jedlik, "The Nightmare of International Product Piracy: Exploring Defensive Strategies," *Industrial Marketing Management*, August 2001; Janeen E. Olsen and Kent L. Granzin, "Using Channels Constructs to Explain Dealers' Willingness to Help Manufacturers Combat Counterfeiting," *Journal of Business Research*, June 1993.

12. For more on licensing, see "Food Marketers Hope Veggies Look Fun to Kids," *USA Today*, July 15, 2005; "Testing Limits of Licensing: SpongeBob-Motif Holiday Inn," *Wall Street Journal*, October 9, 2003; "Making Tracks beyond Tires," *Brandweek*, September 15, 2003; "Candy Cosmetics: Licensing's Sweet Spot," *DSN Retailing Today*, August 4, 2003; "The Creative License," *Brandweek*, June 9, 2003; "Procter & Gamble Deals License Several Brand Names," *USA Today*, April 18, 2003.

13. For more on branding organic products, see "When Buying Organic Makes Sense—and When It Doesn't," *Wall Street Journal*, January 26, 2006; "The Organic Myth," *BusinessWeek*, October 16, 2006; "Private Food Labels also Seeking Organic Growth," *Brandweek*, November 7, 2005; "Soap Can Proudly Display Certified 'Organic' Label," *USA Today*, August 25, 2005; "Health-Food Maker Hain Faces Rivals," *Wall Street Journal*, August 13, 2003; "Big Brand Logos Pop Up in Organic Aisle," *Wall Street Journal*, July 29, 2003; "USDA Enters Debate on Organic Label Law," *The New York Times*, February 26, 2003; "Food Industry Gags at Proposed Label Rule for Trans Fat," *Wall Street Journal*, December 27, 2002; "Curbs Are Eased on Food Makers' Health Claims," *Wall Street Journal*, December 19, 2002; "In Natural Foods, a Big Name's No Big Help," *Wall Street Journal*, June 7, 2002. See also Amitabh Mungale, "Managing Product

Families," *Journal of Product Innovation Management*, January 1998; Gloria Barczak, "Product Management," *Journal of Product Innovation Management*, September 1997.

14. S. Chan Choi and Anne T. Coughlan, "Private Label Positioning: Quality versus Feature Differentiation from the National Brand," *Journal of Retailing*, June 2006; David E. Sprott and Terence A. Shimp, "Using Product Sampling to Augment the Perceived Quality of Store Brands," *Journal of Retailing*, Winter 2004.

15. "A Swift Kick to the Privates," *Brandweek*, September 3, 2007; "From Cheap Stand-in to Shelf Star," *Wall Street Journal*, August 29, 2007; "Saving Private Labels," *Brandweek*, May 8, 2006; "Here's Mr. Macy," *Fortune*, November 28, 2005; "Private Label Brands Expand Public Image," *Brandweek*, February 2, 2004; "Brand Killers, *Fortune*, August 11, 2003; "And the Coolest New PC Is Made by . . . Best Buy?" *Business 2.0*; "Going Private (Label), *Wall Street Journal*, June 12, 2003; "7–Eleven Cracks Open a Private-Label Brew," *Wall Street Journal*, May 2, 2003; "White Clouds Could Bring Rain on P&G," *Advertising Age*, July 2, 2001; See also Maureen Morrin, Jonathan Lee, and Greg M. Allenby, "Determinants of Trademark Dilution," *Journal of "Consumer Research*, August 2006; Bart J. Bronnenberg, Sanjay K. Dhar, and Jean-Pierre Dub, "Consumer Packaged Goods in the United States: National Brands, Local Branding," *Journal of Marketing Research*, February 2007; Donna F. Davis, Susan L. Golicic, and Adam J. Marquardt, "Branding a B2B Service: Does a Brand Differentiate a Logistics Service Provider?" *Industrial Marketing Management*, February 2008; S. Sriram, Subramanian Balachander, and Manohar U. Kalwani, "Monitoring the Dynamics of Brand Equity Using Store-Level Data," *Journal of Marketing*, April 2007; Lien Lamey, Barbara Deleersnyder, Marnik G. Dekimpe, and Jan-Benedict E. M. Steenkamp, "How Business Cycles Contribute to Private-Label Success: Evidence from the United States and Europe," *Journal of Marketing*, January 2007; Judith A. Garretson, Dan Fisher, and Scot Burton, "Antecedents of Private Label Attitude and National Brand Promotion Attitude: Similarities and Differences," *Journal of Retailing*, Summer 2002; Piyush Kumar, "The Impact of Cobranding on Customer Evaluation of Brand Counterextensions," *Journal of Marketing*, July 2005; Anders Bengtsson and Per Servais, "Co-Branding On Industrial Markets," *Industrial Marketing Management*, October 2005.

16. For more on Soup at Hand, see "Demand for Convenient Foods Continues to Rise," *Brandweek*, November 18, 2002. For another example, milk packaging, see "Dean Foods: Dairy Processor Looks to Milk Other Products," *Investor's Business Daily*, March 28, 2003; "Dean Foods: Dairy Firm Milks New Products for Growth, though Cows Still Account for Most Sales," *Investor's Business Daily*, September 18, 2002; "Milk Chug Sweetens Double Chocolate Push," *Brandweek*, February 25, 2002; "Many-Flavored Milk Competes with Sodas," *USA Today*, January 26, 2001.

17. "Coke, Pepsi, A-B Attracted to Metal," *Brandweek*, December 17, 2007; "Can Wine in a Sippy Box Lure Back French Drinkers," *Wall Street Journal*, August 24, 2007; "As Costs Rise, Whirlpool Makes a Dent in Dings," *Wall Street Journal*, July 30, 2007; "Selling Detergent Bottles' Big Shrink," *Wall Street Journal*, May 21, 2007; "Cure for the Common Cold in the Beverage Aisles?" *Brandweek*, October 3, 2005; "Thinking Outside of the Clamshell," *Business 2.0*, July 2005; "Packaging as Entertainment," *Business 2.0*, June 2005; "Going Home with the Customers," *Newsweek*, May 23, 2005; "Put Some Pizzazz in Your Packaging," *Brandweek*, January 17, 2005; "Beef's New Bag," *USA Today*, June 21, 2004; "Thinking Outside the Can," *Brandweek*, October 13, 2003; "Are Your Competitors Packing?" *Business 2.0*, July 2003; "Salad in Sealed Bags Isn't So Simple, It Seems," *The New York Times*, January 14, 2003. See also Brian Wansink and Koert van Ittersum, "Bottoms Up! The Influence of Elongation on Pouring and Consumption Volume," *Journal of Consumer Research*, December 2003.

18. Anthony D. Cox, Dena Cox, and Gregory Zimet, "Understanding Consumer Responses to Product Risk Information," *Journal*

of *Marketing*, January 2006; "Bar Codes: Beyond the Checkout Counter," *BusinessWeek*, April 8, 1985; Ronald C. Goodstein, "UPC Scanner Pricing Systems: Are They Accurate?" *Journal of Marketing*, April 1994.

19. "Canon Unveils 'Generation Green' Brand," *GreenBiz.com*, January 8, 2008; "Tesco to 'Carbon Label' Its Products," *Financial Times*, January 19, 2007; "Carbon Confusion," *BusinessWeek.com*, March 6, 2008.

20. For more on food labeling, see "The Whole Truth about Whole Grain," *Wall Street Journal*, February 16, 2006; "Major Changes Set for Food Labels," *Wall Street Journal*, December 28, 2005; "FDA Says Food Labels Can Tout Tomatoes' Benefits on Cancer," *Wall Street Journal*, November 10, 2005; "Read It and Weep? Big Mac Wrapper to Show Fat, Calories," *Wall Street Journal*, October 26, 2005; "FDA Re-examines 'Serving Sizes,' May Change Misleading Labels," *Wall Street Journal*, November 20, 2003; "A 'Fat-Free' Product That's 100% Fat: How Food Labels Legally Mislead," *Wall Street Journal*, July 15, 2003. See also Lauren G. Block and Laura A. Peracchio, "The Calcium Quandary: How Consumers Use Nutrition Labels," *Journal of Public Policy & Marketing*, Fall 2006; Siva K. Balasubramanian and Catherine Cole, "Consumers' Search and Use of Nutrition Information: the Challenge and Promise of the Nutrition Labeling and Education Act," *Journal of Marketing*, July 2002; Bruce A. Silverglade, "The Nutrition Labeling and Education Act—Progress to Date and Challenges for the Future," *Journal of Public Policy & Marketing*, Spring 1996; Sandra J. Burke, Sandra J. Milberg, and Wendy W. Moe, "Displaying Common but Previously Neglected Health Claims on Product Labels: Understanding Competitive Advantages, Deception, and Education," *Journal of Public Policy & Marketing*, Fall 1997; Christine Moorman, "A Quasi Experiment to Assess the Consumer and Informational Determinants of Nutrition Information Processing Activities: The Case of the Nutrition Labeling and Education Act," *Journal of Public Policy & Marketing*, Spring 1996.

21. For more on package volume, see "Pay the Same, Get Less as Package Volume Falls," *USA Today*, March 17, 2003; "Taking the Value Out of Value-Sized," *Wall Street Journal*, August 14, 2002; "Critics Call Cuts in Package Size Deceptive Move," *Wall Street Journal*, February 5, 1991. For more on food claims, see "Snacks: Does This Bag Make Me Look Fat?" *USA Today*, February 20, 2008; "Do Food Claims Help Consumers or Baffle Them?" *Wall Street Journal*, May 27, 2005; Paula Fitzgerald, Bone Corey, and Robert J. Corey, "Ethical Dilemmas in Packaging: Beliefs of Packaging Professionals," *Journal of Macromarketing*, Spring 1992.

22. For more on Hyundai warranty, see "BMW, Mercedes—and Hyundai?" *BusinessWeek*, December 5, 2005; "Hyundai Makes Safety a Primary Selling Point," *Advertising Age*, May 2, 2005; "Extended Warranty Heats Up Auto Sales," *Advertising Age*, November 1, 2004. For more on warranties and service guarantees, see "Little Tikes Proves Durable with Low-Tech Plastic Toys," *USA Today*, December 15, 2005; "Faulty Chip Mars Many Camera Models," *Wall Street Journal*, October 27, 2005; "Or Your Money Back," *Inc.*, September 2005; "Building a Luxury Retail Business on the Web," *Wall Street Journal*, July 12, 2005; "Certified Used Cars Come under Fire," *Wall Street Journal*, July 12, 2005; "Wal-Mart Expands Warranty Business to Its Stores," *Wall Street Journal*, October 29, 2005; "Sheraton Plans to Pay Guests for Bad Service," *Wall Street Journal*, September 6, 2002; "Guaranteed to Last a Whole 90 Days," *Wall Street Journal*, July 16, 2002; "Best Buy Co.: Retailer's 'Guaranteed' Strategy for Growth," *Investor's Business Daily*, May 21, 2002. See also Monika Kukar-Kinney, Rockney G. Walters, and Scott B. MacKenzie, "Consumer Responses to Characteristics of Price-Matching Guarantees: The Moderating Role of Price Consciousness," *Journal of Retailing*, June 2007; Jennifer Hamilton and Ross D. Petty, "The European Union's Consumer Guarantees Directive," *Journal of Public Policy & Marketing*, Fall 2001; M. E. Blair and Daniel E. Innis, "The Effects of Product Knowledge on the Evaluation of Warranteed Brands," *Psychology & Marketing*, August 1996; Ellen M. Moore and F. Kelly Shuptrine, "Warranties: Continued Readability Problems After the 1975 Magnuson-Moss Warranty Act," *Journal of Consumer Affairs*, Summer 1993.

23. Edward M. Tauber, "Why Do People Shop?" *Journal of Marketing*, October 1972; Christopher H. Lovelock, "Classifying Services to Gain Strategic Marketing Insights," *Journal of Marketing*, Summer 1983; Tom Boyt and Michael Harvey, "Classification of Industrial Services," *Industrial Marketing Management*, July 1997.

24. Dennis W. Rook, "The Buying Impulse," *Journal of Consumer Research*, September 1987; Cathy J. Cobb and Wayne D. Hoyer, "Planned versus Impulse Purchase Behavior," *Journal of Retailing*, Winter 1986.

25. For example, see "Russian Maneuvers Are Making Palladium Ever More Precious," *Wall Street Journal*, March 6, 2000. See also William S. Bishop, John L. Graham, and Michael H. Jones, "Volatility of Derived Demand in Industrial Markets and Its Management Implications," *Journal of Marketing*, Fall 1984.

26. William B. Wagner and Patricia K. Hall, "Equipment Lease Accounting in Industrial Marketing Strategy," *Industrial Marketing Management* 20, no. 4 (1991); Robert S. Eckley, "Caterpillar's Ordeal: Foreign Competition in Capital Goods," *Business Horizons*, March–April 1989; M. Manley, "To Buy or Not to Buy," *Inc.*, November 1987.

27. P. Matthyssens and W. Faes, "OEM Buying Process for New Components: Purchasing and Marketing Implications," *Industrial Marketing Management*, August 1985; Paul A. Herbig and Frederick Palumbo, "Serving the Aftermarket in Japan and the United States," *Industrial Marketing Management*, November 1993.

28. Ruth H. Krieger and Jack R. Meredith, "Emergency and Routine MRO Part Buying," *Industrial Marketing Management*, November 1985; Warren A. French et al., "MRO Parts Service in the Machine Tool Industry," *Industrial Marketing Management*, November 1985. See also "The Web's New Plumbers," *Ecompany*, March 2001.

CHAPTER 9

1. See www.irobot.com; "The Robot Revolution May Finally Be Here," *US News & World Report*, April 9, 2008; "2008 CRM Service Awards: Elite—iRobot," *CRM Magazine*, April 2008; "The World's Most Innovative Companies," *Fast Company*, March 2008; "IRobot Boots Up 2 New Models," *Investor's Business Daily*, September 28, 2007; "IRobot's Military Business on a Roll," *Investor's Business Daily*, August 22, 2007; "Maker Eyes Mainstream with Its Cleanup Robot," *Investor's Business Daily*, August 22, 2007; "Cleaning Up with Customer Evangelists," *BtoB*, August 13, 2007; "Keep Up with the Jetsons: iRobot's New Scooba," *Fortune*, February 20, 2006; "Robotic Orb Can Scrubba, Dub, Dub," *Raleigh News and Observer*, December 25, 2005; "What Can Scooba Do? Wash the Floor for You," *USA Today*, December 8, 2005; "Danger, Will Robinson! Dust Balls Ahead!" *Investor's Business Daily*, November 1, 2005; "Companies Tap into Consumer Passion," *Business 2.0*, October 2005; "A Robot That Could Hit the Wall," *BusinessWeek Online*, September 5, 2005; "The Best Product Design of 2005 Winners," *BusinessWeek*, July 4, 2005; "Death to Cool . . . iRobot," *Inc.*, July 2005; "How the Roomba Was Realized," *BusinessWeek*, October 6, 2003.

2. Rosanna Garcia, Fleura Bardhi, and Colette Friedrich, "Overcoming Consumer Resistance to Innovation," *MIT Sloan Management Review*, Summer 2007; Shih Chuan-Fong and Alladi Venkatesh, "Beyond Adoption: Development and Application of a Use-Diffusion Model," *Journal of Marketing*, January 2004; Darren W. Dahl and Steve Hoeffler, "Visualizing the Self: Exploring the Potential Benefits and Drawbacks for New Product Evaluation," *Journal of Product Innovation Management*, July 2004; Youngme Moon, "Break Free from the Product Life Cycle," *Harvard Business Review*, May 2005; Alina B. Sorescu, Rajesh K. Chandy, and Jaideep C. Prabhu, "Sources and Financial Consequences of Radical Innovation: Insights from

Pharmaceuticals," *Journal of Marketing*, October 2003; Ulrike de Brentani, "Innovative versus Incremental New Business Services: Different Keys for Achieving Success," *The Journal of Product Innovation Management*, May 2001; Marion Debruyne, Rudy Moenaert, Abbie Griffin, Susan Hart et al., "The Impact of New Product Launch Strategies on Competitive Reaction in Industrial Markets," *The Journal of Product Innovation Management*, March 2002; X. Michael Song, C. Anthony Di Benedetto, and Lisa Z. Song, "Pioneering Advantage in New Service Development: A Multi-Country Study of Managerial Perceptions," *The Journal of Product Innovation Management*, September 2000; Christopher M. McDermott and Gina Colarelli O'Connor, "Managing Radical Innovation: An Overview of Emergent Strategy Issues," *Journal of Product Innovation Management*, November 2002; Ronald W. Niedrich and Scott D. Swain, "The Influence of Pioneer Status and Experience Order on Consumer Brand Preference: A Mediated-Effects Model," *Journal of the Academy of Marketing Science*, Fall 2003; Rajesh K. Chandy and Gerard J. Tellis, "The Incumbent's Curse? Incumbency, Size, and Radical Product Innovation," *Journal of Marketing*, July 2000; Robert W. Veryzer, "Key Factors Affecting Customer Evaluation of Discontinuous New Products," *Journal of Product Innovation Management*, March 1998; Neil A. Morgan, "Managing Imitation Strategies: How Later Entrants Seize Market Share from Pioneers," *Journal of Marketing*, October 1995; David M. Szymanski, Lisa C. Troy, and Sundar G. Bharadwaj, "Order of Entry and Business Performance: An Empirical Synthesis and Reexamination," *Journal of Marketing*, October 1995; George Day, "The Product Life Cycle: Analysis and Applications Issues," *Journal of Marketing*, Fall 1981; Igal Ayal, "International Product Life Cycle: A Reassessment and Product Policy Implications," *Journal of Marketing*, Fall 1981.

3. "Countering Tech Copycats," *Investor's Business Daily*, October 31, 2005; "Behind TiVo, iPod, and Xbox: An Industry Struggles for Profits," *Wall Street Journal*, October 14, 2004; "Flash Memory Firms, Disk Drive Industry in Escalating Rivalry," *Investor's Business Daily*, October 13, 2005. See also Jorge Alberto Sousa De Vasconcellos, "Key Success Factors in Marketing Mature Products," *Industrial Marketing Management* 20, no. 4 (1991); Paul C.N. Michell, Peter Quinn, and Edward Percival, "Marketing Strategies for Mature Industrial Products," *Industrial Marketing Management* 20, no. 3 (1991); Peter N. Golder and Gerard J. Tellis, "Pioneer Advantage: Marketing Logic or Marketing Legend?" *Journal of Marketing Research*, May 1993.

4. "Milk Industry's Pitch in Asia: Try the Ginger or Rose Flavor," *Wall Street Journal*, August 9, 2005.

5. "Video Slips as DVD Market Matures," *USA Today*, January 4, 2006; "DVD's Success Steals the Show," *USA Today*, January 8, 2004; "DVD: It Pays to Spend a Little More," *USA Today*, December 3, 2003; "Backseat Movies: Car DVD Entertainment Systems . . .," *BusinessWeek*, May 26, 2003; "High-Definition Discs Aim to Outshine DVDs," *Investor's Business Daily*, May 6, 2003; "Safe at Home and All Plugged In," *USA Today*, January 8, 2002; "Blockbuster Tests Postvideo Future," *Wall Street Journal*, June 18, 2001; "Sales of DVD Players Boom, but Makers Record Little Profit," *Investor's Business Daily*, January 22, 2001.

6. "PC Makers Race to Market with Low-Cost Netbooks," *Wall Street Journal*, April 8, 2008; "Wanted: One CEO for One Laptop per Child," *BusinessWeek*, March 17, 2008; "Cheaper by the Laptop," *Newsweek*, March 10, 2008; "Intel's Amazon Ambitions," *Fast Company*, February 2008; "A Little Laptop with Big Ambitions: How a Computer for the Poor Got Stomped by Tech Giants," *Wall Street Journal*, November 24, 2007; "Ratcheting Up Enterprises with a Social Vision," *Investor's Business Daily*, September 4, 2007; "This PC Wants to Save the World," *Fortune*, October 30, 2006; "In Search of a PC for the People," *BusinessWeek*, June 12, 2006; "I'd Like to Teach the World to Type," *Fortune*, November 28, 2005; "The $100 Laptop Moves Closer to Reality," *Wall Street Journal*, November 14, 2005.

7. For more on EV1, see "An Electric Car Propelled by Star Power?" *BusinessWeek*, December 9, 1996; "GM Energizes EV1 Launch with $8 Mil Ad Blitz," *Advertising Age*, December 2, 1996; "A Big Charge for Electric Vehicles," *BusinessWeek*, November 18, 1996. For another example involving the portable digital music market, see "Late Starts Can Be Great Starts," *Investor's Business Daily*, February 13, 2006; "An iPod Casualty: The Rio Digital-Music Player," *Wall Street Journal*, September 1, 2005; "When Being First Doesn't Make You No. 1," *Wall Street Journal*, August 12, 2004. See also Sungwook Min, Manohar U. Kalwani, and William T. Robinson, "Market Pioneer and Early Follower Survival Risks: A Contingency Analysis of Really New versus Incrementally New Product-Markets," *Journal of Marketing*, January 2006.

8. For more on Zara, see "Pace-Setting Zara Seeks More Speed to Fight Its Rising Cheap-Chic Rivals," *Wall Street Journal*, February 20, 2008; "The Old World's New Vigor," *BusinessWeek*, May 14, 2007; "Solid Foundation Braces Spain," *Wall Street Journal*, January 31, 2007; "Fashion Conquistador," *BusinessWeek*, September 4, 2006; "Respond to Trends Early or Miss the Opportunity," *Investor's Business Daily*, July 25, 2005; "At Gucci, Mr. Polet's New Design Upends Rules for High Fashion," *Wall Street Journal*, August 9, 2005; "Making Fashion Faster," *Wall Street Journal*, February 24, 2004; "Just-in-Time Fashion," *Wall Street Journal*, May 18, 2001; "Zara Has a Made-to-Order Plan for Success," *Fortune*, September 4, 2000.

9. "Runway to Rack: Finding Looks that Will Sell," *Wall Street Journal*, March 6, 2008; "Work Wear: Designers Who Get It," *Wall Street Journal*, February 14, 2008; "How Fashion Makes Its Way from the Runway to the Rack," *Wall Street Journal*, February 8, 2007; "Dismissed as a Fad, Uggs Sheepskin Boots Step Out, Find Traction," *Investor's Business Daily*, December 13, 2007; "A New Stretch for Fashion," *Wall Street Journal*, February 23, 2006; "Uggs Again? What Last Year's 'It' Gift Does for an Encore," *Wall Street Journal*, December 9, 2005; "Nice (Horizontal) Pants!" *Business 2.0*, December 2005; "Men Say Bling It On," *Wall Street Journal*, November 30, 2005; "Escaping the Fashion Trap," *Wall Street Journal*, October 15, 2005; "Thinking Outside the Shoe Box," *Business 2.0*, September 2005; "Brace Yourself: Wristbands . . .," *USA Today*, July 8, 2005; "Mattel Creates a Living Barbie to Revive Sales," *Wall Street Journal*, June 22, 2005. See also Craig J. Thompson and Diana L. Haytko, "Speaking of Fashion: Consumers' Uses of Fashion Discourses and the Appropriation of Countervailing Cultural Meanings," *Journal of Consumer Research*, June 1997.

10. For more on the recent battle between Blu-Ray and HD-DVD, see "Toshiba Surrenders in Next-Gen DVD Battle," *Investor's Business Daily*, February 20, 2008; "As Toshiba Surrenders, What's Next for DVDs?" *Wall Street Journal*, February 19, 2008; "Is Tug of War over High-Def DVD Format Over?" *USA Today*, February 15, 2008; "In Blu-Ray Coup, Sony Has Opening but Hurdles, Too," *Wall Street Journal*, January 17, 2008; "Next-Gen DVDs: Advantage, Sony," *BusinessWeek*, December 17, 2007; "The Beta-VHS Battle Offers Some Insights into Coming DVD War," *Wall Street Journal*, January 25, 2006.

11. "Big Brands (Small Companies)," *BusinessWeek Small Biz*, August 13, 2001.

12. "Oreo, Ritz Join Nabisco's Low-Fat Feast," *Advertising Age*, April 4, 1994; "They're Not Crying in Their Crackers at Nabisco," *BusinessWeek*, August 30, 1993; "Nabisco Unleashes a New Batch of Teddies," *Adweek's Marketing Week*, September 24, 1990.

13. "Going Global by Going Green," *Wall Street Journal*, February 26, 2008.

14. For more on Tide, see "Mover & Shaker," *Brandweek*, June 18, 2007; "The Endurance Test," *Advertising Age*, November 14, 2005, pp. 3, 38–39; "Testing New-Style Stain Removers," *Wall Street Journal*, July 5, 2005; "Life on the Go Means Eating on the Run, and a Lot of Spilling," *Wall Street Journal*, June 7, 2005; "Detergent Tablets of the '70s Make a Comeback," *USA Today*, July 27, 2000; "Boom in Liquid Detergents Has P&G Scrambling," *Wall Street Journal*, September 25, 1997; "Ultra-Clean—Retail Cheers Still More P&G Concentrates,"

Advertising Age, August 22, 1994; "Detergent Industry Spins into New Cycle," *Wall Street Journal*, January 5, 1993; "P&G Unleashes Flood of New Tide Products," *Advertising Age*, June 16, 1986. See also "The Hard Life of Orphan Brands," *Wall Street Journal*, April 13, 2001; "Orphan Relief," *Advertising Age*, March 19, 2001.

15. "Making Old Brands New," *American Demographics*, December 1997; "Classic Roller Skates Return as Safety Fears Dull Blades," *Wall Street Journal*, October 24, 1997; "Dusting Off the *Britannica*," *BusinessWeek*, October 20, 1997; "At DuPont, Time to Both Sow and Reap," *BusinessWeek*, September 29, 1997; "A Boring Brand Can Be Beautiful," *Fortune*, November 18, 1991; "Teflon Is 50 Years Old, but DuPont Is Still Finding New Uses for Invention," *Wall Street Journal*, April 7, 1988; Stephen W. Miller, "Managing Imitation Strategies: How Later Entrants Seize Markets from Pioneers," *Journal of the Academy of Marketing Science*, Summer 1996.

16. "The Power of Shape Shifters," *Fast Company*, December 2007; "Wish List," *Fast Company*, December 2007; "Personal Technology," *USA Today*, November 28, 2007; "The Best of 2006: Products," *BusinessWeek*, December 18, 2006; "Annual Design Awards 2006," *BusinessWeek*, July 10, 2006; "Bottom Line Design Awards," *Business 2.0*, April 2006;

17. For more on new-product definition, see "Electronic Code of Federal Regulations: Title 16 (Commercial Practices), Part 502 (Introductory Offers) at http://ecfr.gpoaccess.gov/.

18. "Reposition: Simplifying the Customer's Brandscape," *Brandweek*, October 2, 2000; "Consumers to GM: You Talking to Me?" *BusinessWeek*, June 19, 2000; "How Growth Destroys Differentiation," *Brandweek*, April 24, 2000; "P&G, Seeing Shoppers Were Being Confused, Overhauls Marketing," *Wall Street Journal*, January 15, 1997; "Make It Simple," *BusinessWeek*, September 9, 1996; "Diaper Firms Fight to Stay on the Bottom," *Wall Street Journal*, March 23, 1993.

19. "Ignore the Consumer," *Point*, September 2005; "Too Many Choices," *Wall Street Journal*, April 20, 2001; "New Products," *Ad Age International*, April 13, 1998; "The Ghastliest Product Launches," *Fortune*, March 16, 1998; "Flops: Too Many New Products Fail. Here's Why—and How to Do Better," *BusinessWeek*, August 16, 1993; Brian D. Ottum and William L. Moore, "The Role of Market Information in New Product Success/Failure," *Journal of Product Innovation Management*, July 1997.

20. "Flavor Experiment for KitKat Leaves Nestle with a Bad Taste," *Wall Street Journal*, July 6, 2006; "Makers of Chicken Tonight Find Many Cooks Say, 'Not Tonight,'" *Wall Street Journal*, May 17, 1994; "Failure of Its Oven Lovin' Cookie Dough Shows Pillsbury Pitfalls of New Products," *Wall Street Journal*, June 17, 1993; Sharad Sarin and Gour M. Kapur, "Lessons from New Product Failures: Five Case Studies," *Industrial Marketing Management*, November 1990.

21. "Design Software Helps Give Life to ZMP's Robots," *Investor's Business Daily*, August 9, 2005; "This Is Not a BMW Plant," *Fortune*, April 18, 2005; "Helping Designers Go Digital," *Investor's Business Daily*, January 24, 2005; "Not Your Grandfather's Assembly Line," *Fortune*, July 12, 2004; "Design Tools Move into the Fast Lane," *BusinessWeek*, June 2, 2003; "Digital Workflow Speeds Time to Shelf," *Brand Packaging*, March–April 2001; "How Fast Can This Baby Go?" *BusinessWeek*, April 10, 2000. See also Muammer Ozer, "Process Implications of the Use of the Internet in New Product Development: a Conceptual Analysis," *Industrial Marketing Management*, August 2003; J. Daniel Sherman, William E. Souder, and Svenn A. Jenssen, "Differential Effects of the Primary Forms of Cross Functional Integration on Product Development Cycle Time," *The Journal of Product Innovation Management*, July 2000; Daniel J. Flint, "Compressing New Product Success-to-Success Cycle Time: Deep Customer Value Understanding and Idea Generation," *Industrial Marketing Management*, July 2002; Cornelia Droge, Jayanth Jayaram, and Shawnee K. Vickery, "The Ability to Minimize the Timing of New Product Development

and Introduction: an Examination of Antecedent Factors in the North American Automobile Supplier Industry," *Journal of Product Innovation Management*, January 2000; Kathleen M. Eisenhardt and Shona L. Brown, "Time Pacing: Competing in Markets That Won't Stand Still," *Harvard Business Review*, March–April 1998; For more on P&G's efforts to bring products to market faster, see "Brands in a Bind," *BusinessWeek*, August 28, 2000; "Warm and Fuzzy Won't Save Procter & Gamble," *BusinessWeek*, June 26, 2000.

22. "Why the Kids Are Dissing Leapfrog," *Business 2.0*, November 2005; "LED Technology," *NecDigest*, August 2005, pp. 10, 48–53; "Let There Be L.E.D.s," *The New York Times*, January 8, 2004; "Building a Better R&D Mousetrap," *Business 2.0*, September 2003; "Critical Curds: At Kraft, Making Cheese Fun Is Serious Business," *Wall Street Journal*, May 31, 2002; "Stuck on You: P&G's New Outlast Lipstick Is Nothing to Pout About," *Wall Street Journal*, May 9, 2002; "Bleeding Cash: Pfizer Youth Pill Ate Up $71 Million before It Flopped," *Wall Street Journal*, May 2, 2002; "How Burger King Got Burned in Quest to Make the Perfect Fry," *Wall Street Journal*, January 16, 2001. See also Ashish Sood and Gerard J. Tellis, "Technological Evolution and Radical Innovation," *Journal of Marketing*, July 2005; Debra Zahay, Abbie Griffin, and Elisa Fredericks, "Sources, Uses, and Forms of Data in the New Product Development Process," *Industrial Marketing Management*, October 2004; Janice Griffiths-Hemans and Rajiv Grover, "Setting the Stage for Creative New Products: Investigating the Idea Fruition Process," *Journal of the Academy of Marketing Science*, Winter 2006; John E. Ettlie and Mohan Subramaniam, "Changing Strategies and Tactics for New Product Development," *Journal of Product Innovation Management*, March 2004; Lisa C. Troy, David M. Szymanskis, and P. Rajan Varadarajan, "Generating New Product Ideas: an Initial Investigation of the Role of Market Information and Organizational Characteristics," *Journal of the Academy of Marketing Science*, Winter 2001; Rajesh Sethi, "New Product Quality and Product Development Teams," *Journal of Marketing*, April 2000; Mark A. A. M. Leenders and Berend Wierenga, "The Effectiveness of Different Mechanisms for Integrating Marketing and R&D," *Journal of Product Innovation Management*, July 2002; George J. Avlonitis, Susan J. Hart, and Nikolaos X. Tzokas, "An Analysis of Product Deletion Scenarios," *Journal of Product Innovation Management*, January 2000; Elliot Maltz, William E. Souder, and Ajith Kumar, "Influencing R&D/Marketing Integration and the Use of Market Information by R&D Managers: Intended and Unintended Effects of Managerial Actions," *Journal of Business Research*, April 2001; Robert Polk, Richard E. Plank, and David A. Reid, "Technical Risk and New Product Success: An Empirical Test in High Technology Business Markets," *Industrial Marketing Management*, November 1996; Jeffrey B. Schmidt and Roger J. Calantone, "Are Really New Product Development Projects Harder to Shut Down?" *Journal of Product Innovation Management*, March 1998; Cheryl Nakata and K. Sivakumar, "National Culture and New Product Development: An Integrative Review," *Journal of Marketing*, January 1996; Gary S. Lynn, Joseph G. Morone, and Albert S. Paulson, "Marketing and Discontinuous Innovation: The Probe and Learn Process," *California Management Review*, Spring 1996; X. M. Song and Mitzi M. Montoya-Weiss, "Critical Development Activities for Really New versus Incremental Products," *Journal of Product Innovation Management*, March 1998.

23. "Where Do the Best Ideas Come From? The Unlikeliest Sources," *Advertising Age*, July 14, 2008; "Breakthrough Thinking from Inside the Box," *Harvard Business Review*, December 2007; "Blooming Great Business Ideas," *Investor's Business Daily*, July 16, 2007; "Turn Customer Input into Innovation," *Harvard Business Review*, January 2002; "Geeks in Toyland," *Wired*, February 2006; Judy A. Siguaw, Penny M. Simpson, and Cathy A. Enz, "Conceptualizing Innovation Orientation: A Framework for Study and Integration of Innovation Research," *Journal of Product Innovation Management*, November 2006.

24. Martin Schreier and Reinhard Prugl, "Extending Lead-User Theory: Antecedents and Consequences of Consumers' Lead Userness," *Journal of Product Innovation Management*, July 2008; Lance A. Bettencourt and Anthony W. Ulwick, "The Customer-Centered Innovation Map," *Harvard Business Review*, May 2008; "Mosh Pits of Creativity," *BusinessWeek*, November 7, 2005; "Employers See Gold Mining Employees for Ideas," *Brandweek*, October 10, 2005; "Managing Google's Idea Factory," *BusinessWeek*, October 3, 2005; "Staples Lets Customers Do the Designing," *Fortune*, April 18, 2005; "Outsourcing Innovation," *BusinessWeek*, March 21, 2005; "This Volvo Is Not a Guy Thing," *BusinessWeek*, March 15, 2004; "Pickups Get Women's Touch," *USA Today*, June 13, 2001 p. 1B; "Where Great Ideas Come From," *Inc.*, April 1998. See also Edward F. McDonough III, Kenneth B. Kahn, and Gloria Barczak, "An Investigation of the Use of Global, Virtual, and Collocated New Product Development Teams," *Journal of Product Innovation Management*, March 2001; Ari-Pekka Hameri and Jukka Nihtila, "Distributed New Product Development Project Based on Internet and World Wide Web: A Case Study," *Journal of Product Innovation Management*, March 1997.

25. "It Was a Hit in Buenos Aires—So Why Not Boise?" *Business-Week*, September 7, 1998. See also Rudy K. Moenaert, Filip Caeldries, Annouk Lievens, and Elke Wauters, "Communication Flows in International Product Innovation Teams," *Journal of Product Innovation Management*, September 2000; Vittorio Chiesa, "Global R&D Project Management and Organization: a Taxonomy," *Journal of Product Innovation Management*, September 2000; John J. Cristiano, Jeffrey K. Liker, and Chelsea C. White III, "Customer-Driven Product Development Through Quality Function Deployment in the U.S. and Japan," *Journal of Product Innovation Management*, July 2000.

26. Alexandra Harney, *The China Price: The True Cost of Chinese Competitive Advantage* (Penguin Group USA, March 2008); "The Toxic Ten," *Portfolio.com*, March 2008; "China's Pollution Nightmare Is Now Everyone's Pollution Nightmare," *csmonitor.com*, March 19, 2008; "Cost of Pollution in China," World Bank report at http://go.worldbank.org/FFCJVBTP40; "The Price of China's Pollution, and Its Environmental Catch-22," *chinadaily.com* at bbs.chinadaily.com.cn, December 6, 2007; "WB: Air Pollution Costs 3.8% of China GDP," *chinadaily.com*, November 19, 2007; "Toxic Cost of China's Success," *timesonline.com.uk*.

27. "Shielding the Shield Makers," *Wall Street Journal*, November 26, 2003; "Gun Makers to Push Use of Gun Locks," *Wall Street Journal*, May 9, 2001; "U.S. Recalls Millions of Evenflo 'Joyride' Infant Seats, Carriers," *Wall Street Journal*, May 2, 2001; "Stand Up and Fight," *BusinessWeek*, September 11, 2000; "Why One Jury Dealt a Big Blow to Chrysler in Minivan-Latch Case," *Wall Street Journal*, November 19, 1997; "How a Jury Decided that a Coffee Spill Is Worth $2.9 Million," *Wall Street Journal*, September 1, 1994; Jennifer J. Argo and Kelley J. Main, "MetaAnalyses of the Effectiveness of Warning Labels," *Journal of Public Policy & Marketing*, Fall 2004; Paul A. Herbig and James E. Golden, "Innovation and Product Liability," *Industrial Marketing Management*, July 1994; Robert N. Mayer and Debra L. Scammon, "Caution: Weak Product Warnings May Be Hazardous to Corporate Health," *Journal of Business Research*, June 1992.

28. "Want Shelf Space at the Supermarket? Ante Up," *BusinessWeek*, August 7, 1989; "Grocer 'Fee' Hampers New-Product Launches," *Advertising Age*, August 3, 1987.

29. Susumu Ogawa and Frank T. Piller, "Reducing the Risks of New Product Development," *MIT Sloan Management Review*, Winter 2006; Joseph M. Bonner, Robert W. Ruekert, and Orville C. Walker, Jr. "Upper Management Control of New Product Development Projects and Project Performance," *Journal of Product Innovation Management*, May 2002; Harold Z. Daniel, Donald J. Hempel, and Narasimhan Srinivasan, "A Model of Value Assessment in Collaborative R&D Programs," *Industrial Marketing Management*, November 2002; Sundar Bharadwaj and Anil Menon, "Making Innovations Happen in Organizations: Individual Creativity Mechanisms, Organizational Creativity Mechanisms or Both?" *Journal of Product Innovation Management*, November 2000; Preston G. Smith, "Mastering Virtual Teams: Strat-

egies, Tools, and Techniques That Succeed," *Journal of Product Innovation Management*, March 2001; Gregory D. Githens, "Customer Centered Products: Creating Successful Products Through Smart Requirements Management," *Journal of Product Innovation Management*, September 2001; Keith Goffin, "Evaluating Customer Support During New Product Development—An Exploratory Study," *Journal of Product Innovation Management*, January 1998; Paul S. Adler, Avi Mandelbaum, Vien Nguyen, and Elizabeth Schwerer, "Getting the Most Out of Your Product Development Process," *Harvard Business Review*, March–April 1996.

30. "Torture Testing," *Fortune*, October 2, 2000; "Industry's Amazing New Instant Prototypes," *Fortune*, January 12, 1998; "Secrets of Product Testing," *Fortune*, November 28, 1994; "A Smarter Way to Manufacture," *BusinessWeek*, April 30, 1990.

31. "Oops! Marketers Blunder Their Way Through the 'Herb Decade,'" *Advertising Age*, February 13, 1989.

32. Albert L. Page and Gary R. Schirr, "Growth and Development of a Body of Knowledge: 16 Years of New Product Development Research, 1989–2004," *Journal of Product Innovation Management*, May 2008; Gloria Barczak, Kenneth B. Kahn, and Roberta Moss, "An Exploratory Investigation of NPD Practices in Nonprofit Organizations," *Journal of Product Innovation Management*, November 2006; Mette Praest Knudsen, "The Relative Importance of Interfirm Relationships and Knowledge Transfer for New Product Development Success," *Journal of Product Innovation Management*, March 2007; Angela Paladino, "Investigating the Drivers of Innovation and New Product Success: A Comparison of Strategic Orientations," *Journal of Product Innovation Management*, November 2007; Kwaku Atuahene-Gima and Janet Y. Murray, "Exploratory and Exploitative Learning in New Product Development: A Social Capital Perspective on New Technology Ventures in China," *Journal of International Marketing*, (2) 2007; Khaled Aboulnasr, Om Narasimhan, Edward Blair, and Rajesh Chandy, "Competitive Response to Radical Product Innovations," *Journal of Marketing*, May 2008; Stephen J. Carson, "When to Give Up Control of Outsourced New Product Development," *Journal of Marketing*, January 2007; Eyal Biyalogorsky, William Boulding, and Richard Staelin, "Stuck in the Past: Why Managers Persist with New Product Failures," *Journal of Marketing*, April 2006; Shankar Ganesan, Alan J. Malter and Aric Rindfleisch, "Does Distance Still Matter? Geographic Proximity and New Product Development," *Journal of Marketing*, October 2005; Subin Im and John P. Workman Jr, "Market Orientation, Creativity, and New Product Performance in High-Technology Firms," *Journal of Marketing*, April 2004; Steven C. Michael and Tracy Pun Palandjian, "Organizational Learning and New Product Introductions," *Journal of Product Innovation Management*, July 2004; Erwin Danneels and Elko J. Kleinschmidt, "Product Innovativeness from the Firm's Perspective: Its Dimensions and Their Relation with Project Selection and Performance," *Journal of Product Innovation Management*, November 2001; R. Jeffrey Thieme, Michael Song, and Geon-Cheol Shin, "Project Management Characteristics and New Product Survival," *Journal of Product Innovation Management*, March 2003; John P. Workman, Jr., "Marketing's Limited Role in New Product Development in One Computer Systems Firm," *Journal of Marketing Research*, November 1993.

33. See www.3m.com; "Counterintuitive Discovery of the Month," *CopernicusMarketing.com*, March 2008; "Scrutinizing Six Sigma," *BusinessWeek*, July 2, 2007; "At 3M, a Struggle between Efficiency and Creativity," *IN* (Supplement to *BusinessWeek*), June 2007; "Pushing Past Post-Its by Allowing Top Scientists to Peek over Horizon . . .," *Business 2.0*, November 2005; "3M: Reading Between the Lines," *BusinessWeek Online*, August 1, 2005; "3M Aims to Make 'Vikuiti' a Household Name," in TV Screens," *Minneapolis Star Tribune*, July 18, 2005; "3M Innovation Will Juice Power Lines," *Wall Street Journal*, October 6, 2004; "3M's Rising Star," *BusinessWeek*, April 12, 2004; "How Leader at 3M Got His Employees to Back Big Changes," *Wall Street Journal*, April 23, 2002; "3M: A Lab for

Growth?" *BusinessWeek*, January 21, 2002; "How 3M, by Tiptoeing into Foreign Markets, Became a Big Exporter," *Wall Street Journal*, March 29, 1991. See also Ali E. Akgün, Gary S. Lynn, and John C. Byrne, "Antecedents and Consequences of Unlearning in New Product Development Teams," *Journal of Product Innovation Management*, January 2006.

34. "Care, Feeding, and Building of a Billion-Dollar Brand," *Advertising Age*, February 23, 2004; "Brands at Work," *Brandweek*, April 13, 1998; "Auto Marketing & Brand Management," *Advertising Age*, April 6, 1998; "P&G Redefines the Brand Manager," *Advertising Age*, October 13, 1997. See also Sanjay K. Dhar, Stephen J. Hoch, and Nanda Kumar, "Effective Category Management Depends on the Role of the Category," *Journal of Retailing*, Summer 2001; Don Frey, "Learning the Ropes: My Life as a Product Champion," *Harvard Business Review*, September–October 1991; Stephen K. Markham, "New Products Management," *Journal of Product Innovation Management*, July 1997.

35. The restaurant case is adapted from Marie Gaudard, Roland Coates, and Liz Freeman, "Accelerating Improvement," *Quality Progress*, October 1991. For more on quality management and control, see "By Focusing on Customers, Firms Can Boost Shareholder Value," *Investor's Business Daily*, October 11, 2002; "Quality Isn't Just for Widgets," *BusinessWeek*, July 22, 2002; "Nicknamed 'Nag,' She's Just Doing Her Job," *Wall Street Journal*, May 14, 2002; "The Net as a Lifeline," *BusinessWeek E.Biz*, October 29, 2001; "The Lure of Six Sigma Quality: It Gets Everyone Thinking Alike," *Investor's Business Daily*, November 7, 2001; "How to Bring Out Better Products Faster," *Fortune*, November 23, 1998; Elizabeth Gelfand Miller, Barbara E. Kahn, and Mary Frances Luce, "Consumer Wait Management Strategies for Negative Service Events: A Coping Approach," *Journal of Consumer Research*, February 2008; Carmen Antón, Carmen Camarero, and Mirtha Carrero, "The Mediating Effect of Satisfaction on Consumers' Switching Intention," *Psychology & Marketing*, June 2007; Roland T. Rust, Anthony J. Zahorik, and Timothy L. Keiningham, "Return on Quality (ROQ): Making Service Quality Financially Accountable," *Journal of Marketing*, April 1995. See also Mark R. Colgate and Peter J. Danaher, "Implementing a Customer Relationship Strategy: the Asymetric Impact of Poor versus Excellent Execution," *Journal of the Academy of Marketing Science*, Summer 2000; Jagdip Singh, "Performance Productivity and Quality of Frontline Employees in Service Organizations," *Journal of Marketing*, April 2000; Simon J. Bell and Bulent Menguc, "The Employee-Organization Relationship, Organizational Citizenship Behaviors, and Superior Service Quality," *Journal of Retailing*, Summer 2002; Roland T. Rust, Christine Moorman, and Peter R. Dickson, "Getting Return on Quality: Revenue Expansion, Cost Reduction, or Both?" *Journal of Marketing*, October 2002; Pratibha A. Dabholkar, C. David Shepherd, and Dayle I. Thorpe, "A Comprehensive Framework for Service Quality: an Investigation of Critical Conceptual and Measurement Issues Through a Longitudinal Study," *Journal of Retailing*, Summer 2000; Scott S. Elliott, "Managing by Measuring: How to Improve Your Organization's Performance Through Effective Benchmarking," *Journal of Product Innovation Management*, July 2000.

36. For Whole Foods example of empowerment, see Chapter 2, endnote 4. See also "Hotels Train Employees to Think Fast," *USA Today*, November 29, 2006; "Takin' Off the Ritz—a Tad," *Wall Street Journal*, June 23, 2006; "Hotels Take 'Know Your Customer' to New Level," *Wall Street Journal*, February 7, 2006; "Listener Runner-up: W Hotels," *Fast Company*, October 2005; "Companies Give Front-Line Employees More Power," *USA Today*, June 27, 2005; "Thinking Outside the Cereal Box," *BusinessWeek*, July 28, 2003; "Pentair Fixes Its Own Mess," *Fortune*, September 30, 2002; "Glass Act: How a Window Maker Rebuilt Itself," *Fortune*, November 13, 2000. See also Douglas W. Vorhies and Neil A. Morgan, "Benchmarking Marketing Capabilities for Sustainable Competitive Advantage," *Journal of Marketing*, January 2005; Roland T. Rust, Tim Ambler, Gregory S. Carpenter, V. Kumar, and Rajendra K. Srivastava, "Measuring

Marketing Productivity: Current Knowledge and Future Directions," *Journal of Marketing*, October 2004; Anthony J. Capraro and Robert D. Yearout, "Selecting Quality Initiatives to Pursue: Integrating Demand Effects into the Evaluation and Selection of Potential Quality Initiatives," *Journal of Marketing Theory & Practice*, Summer 2004; Frederick E. Webster Jr, Alan J. Malter, and Shankar Ganesan, "The Decline and Dispersion of Marketing Competence," *MIT Sloan Management Review*, Summer 2005; Dawn R. DeeterSchmelz and Rosemary P. Ramsey, "An Investigation of Team Information Processing in Service Teams: Exploring the Link Between Teams and Customers," *Journal of the Academy of Marketing Science*, Fall 2003; Emin Babakus, Ugur Yavas, Osman M. Karatepe, and Turgay Avci, "The Effect of Management Commitment to Service Quality on Employees' Affective and Performance Outcomes," *Journal of the Academy of Marketing Science*, Summer 2003; Roland T. Rust, Anthony J. Zahorik, and Timothy L. Keiningham, *Return on Quality* (Chicago: Probus, 1994); J. J. Cronin and Steven A. Taylor, "SERVPERF versus SERVQUAL: Reconciling Performance-Based and Perceptions-Minus-Expectations Measurement of Service Quality," *Journal of Marketing*, January 1994; Shirley Taylor, "Waiting for Service: The Relationship Between Delays and Evaluations of Service," *Journal of Marketing*, April 1994; Mary J. Bitner, Bernard H. Booms, and Lois A. Mohr, "Critical Service Encounters: The Employee's Viewpoint," *Journal of Marketing*, October 1994; Robert Simons, "Control in an Age of Empowerment," *Harvard Business Review*, March–April 1995.

CHAPTER 10

1. See www.dell.com; "Direct Seller Dell Now Offers the Full Middleman Route," *Investor's Business Daily*, April 14, 2009; "No Longer Solely a Direct Seller, Dell Embraces Resellers," *Investor's Business Daily*, April 1, 2008; "Dell Treads Carefully into Selling PCs in Stores," *Wall Street Journal*, January 3, 2008; "Former Direct-Only Seller Dell Adds Best Buy," *Investor's Business Daily*, December 7, 2007; "Dell's U.S. Sales Fall, Profits Disappear," *USA Today*, November 30, 2007; "Where Dell Sells with Brick and Mortar," *BusinessWeek*, October 8, 2007; "Direct-Selling PC Specialist Dell Hooks Up with Retailer in China," *Investor's Business Daily*, September 25, 2007; "The Back Roads to IT Growth," *BusinessWeek*, August 6, 2007; "Dell Pushes Reset Button on Its Image," *Wall Street Journal*, July 10, 2007; "Hmm, Hell Can Freeze Over—Dell to Sell PCs at Retail," *Investor's Business Daily*, May 25, 2007; "Dell Reverses, Steps into Wal-Mart," *USA Today*; "Uh . . . Maybe I Should Drive," *Fortune*, April 30, 2007; "Where Dell Went Wrong," *BusinessWeek*, February 19, 2007; "Grudge Match in China," *BusinessWeek*, April 2, 2007; "Can Dell Succeed in an Encore?" *Wall Street Journal*, February 5, 2007; "Dell in the Penalty Box," *Fortune*, September 18, 2006; "Dark Days at Dell," *BusinessWeek*, September 4, 2006; "Consumer Demand and Growth in Laptops Leave Dell Behind," *Wall Street Journal*, August 30, 2006; "It's Dell vs. the Dell Way," *BusinessWeek*, March 6, 2006; "Computer King Dell Beats Views on Strong Server, Foreign Sales," *Investor's Business Daily*, February 17, 2006; "Dell's Midlife Crisis," *Fortune*, November 28, 2005; "Dell May Have to Reboot in China," *BusinessWeek*, November 7, 2005; "Dell Finds Itself in Blog Hell," *BusinessWeek*, September 5, 2005; "Dell Doesn't Want You to Buy Its Computers," *Advertising Age*, August 12, 2005; "Dell: The Action Hero of Product Support," *BusinessWeek*, August 1, 2005; "For Dell, Success in China Tells Tale of Maturing Market," *Wall Street Journal*, July 5, 2005; "Can the PC King Excel in Services?" *BusinessWeek*, May 30, 2005; "The Education of Michael Dell," *Fortune*, March 7, 2005; "Steamrolled by the Dell Machine," *Newsweek*, February 21, 2005; "Where Dell Is Going Next," *Fortune*, October 18, 2004; "Now Dell Is Rolling Out Its First Plasma TVs, Other Consumer Items," *Wall Street Journal*, October 14, 2004; "Dell Outfoxes Its Rivals," *BusinessWeek*, September 6, 2004; "Still Giving 'em Dell," *Business 2.0*, May 2004; "What You Don't Know about Dell," *BusinessWeek*, November 3, 2003; "How IBM,

Dell Managed to Build Crushing Tech Dominance," *USA Today*, May 21, 2003; "Dell Gets Greener," *BusinessWeek*, May 5, 2002; "The Dell Way," *Business 2.0*, February 2003; "How to Thrive in a Sick Economy," *Business 2.0*, January 2003; "The Upper Hand in Handhelds?" *BusinessWeek*, December 23, 2002; "Dell Slashes Prices and Still Turns a Profit; Credit It to Planning," *Investor's Business Daily*, September 30, 2002; "Dell Does Domination," *Fortune*, January 21, 2002; "The Net as a Lifeline," *BusinessWeek E.Biz*, October 29, 2001; "Dell, the Conqueror," *BusinessWeek*, September 24, 2001; "The Mother of All Price Wars," *BusinessWeek*, July 20, 2001; "Dell Builds an Electronics Superstore on the Web," *Wall Street Journal*, March 3, 1999; Joan Magretta, "The Power of Virtual Integration: An Interview with Dell Computer's Michael Dell," *Harvard Business Review*, March–April 1998.

2. For more on Glaceau, see "Are Sodas Losing Their Fizz?" *Investor's Business Daily*, November 19, 2007; "Coke Unit Adds Some Muscle to Water Line," *USA Today*, October 31, 2007; "Coke Plan Riles Glaceau's Old Network," *Wall Street Journal*, September 14, 2007; "A Unique Marketing Bond," *USA Today*, July 30, 2007; "Hydropower, the Coca-Cola Way," *Brandweek*, June 4, 2007; "Coca-Cola Is in Deal Talks with Glaceau," *Wall Street Journal*, April 25, 2007; "Note to Coke: Glaceau Biz Plan Is Heating Up," *Brandweek*, August 7, 2006; "Move Over, Coke: How a Small Beverage Maker Managed to Win Shelf Space . . .," *Wall Street Journal Reports*, January 30, 2006; "Pepsi Picks Water Fight with Surging Glaceau," *Advertising Age*, October 17, 2005.

3. S. Chan Choi, "Expanding to Direct Channel: Market Coverages as Entry Barrier," *Journal of Interactive Marketing*, Winter 2003; David Shipley, Colin Egan, and Scott Edgett, "Meeting Source Selection Criteria: Direct versus Distributor Channels," *Industrial Marketing Management* 20, no. 4 (1991).

4. For more on Avon, see "Is Avon's Latest Scent Sweet Smell of Success?" *Wall Street Journal*, October 15, 2007; "New Rules in China Have Direct Sellers Eyeing Big Returns," *Investor's Business Daily*, April 30, 2007; "Avon's Calling, but China Opens Door Only a Crack," I, February 26, 2007; "China's New Rules Open Door to Amway, Avon, Others," *USA Today*, December 1, 2005; "Avon Works Out the Wrinkles," *Wall Street Journal*, August 31, 2005; "Avon Gets Its (Supply Chain) Makeover," *Fortune*, November 1, 2004; "Avon Calls, Vietnam Answers," *Wall Street Journal*, April 22, 2004; "Avon Tries Knocking on Dorm Doors," *Wall Street Journal*, March 28, 2003; "Sears Says Stores Won't Sell Makeup, a Setback for Avon's New Line," *Wall Street Journal*, July 11, 2001. For other examples of direct channels, see "Party Time: Home Events See Sales," *USA Today*, October 5, 2005; "Catwalk to Coffee Table," *Wall Street Journal*, November 7, 2003; "India's Retailing Makeover," *Wall Street Journal*, October 28, 2003; "Amway in China: Once Barred, Now Booming," *Wall Street Journal*, March 12, 2003; "Knock, Knock: In Brazil, an Army of Underemployed Goes Door-to-Door," *Wall Street Journal*, February 19, 2003. See also Ruud T. Frambach, Henk C. A. Roest, and Trichy V. Krishnan, "The Impact of Consumer Internet Experience on Channel Preference and Usage Intentions across the Different Stages of the Buying Process," *Journal of Interactive Marketing*, Spring 2007; Mitzi M. Montoya-Weiss, Glenn B. Voss and Dhruv Grewal, "Determinants of Online Channel Use and Overall Satisfaction with a Relational, Multichannel Service Provider," *Journal of the Academy of Marketing Science*, Fall 2003; Inge Geyskens, Katrijn Gielens, and Marnik G. Dekimpe, "The Market Valuation of Internet Channel Additions," *Journal of Marketing*, April 2002.

5. Edward L. Nash, *Direct Marketing* (New York: McGraw-Hill, 1986).

6. For an example of Levi Strauss's new indirect channels via discount stores, see "Levi's Signature Spreads Its Wings," *DSN Retailing Today*, April 25, 2005; "Levi's Officially Goes Mass as Signature Lands at Kmart," *DSN Retailing Today*, August 16, 2004; "Jean Therapy, $23 a Pop," *BusinessWeek*, June 28, 2004; "In Bow to Retailers' New Clout, Levi Strauss Makes Alterations," *Wall Street Journal*, June 17, 2004; "Lessons from a Faded Levi Strauss," *BusinessWeek*, December 15, 2003; "At Levi Strauss, Trouble Comes from All Angles," *Wall Street Journal*, October 13, 2003; "Wal-Mart Adds Touch of Hip to Fashion Choices," *USA Today*, July 22, 2003; "Levi's Won't Fly Signature Ads," *Brandweek*, June 16, 2003; "Mass Levi's, Class Levi's," *Wall Street Journal*, October 31, 2002. For two examples of unsuccessful attempts at indirect channels, see "Ovens Are Cooling at Krispy Kreme as Woes Multiply," *Wall Street Journal*, September 3, 2004; "A Deal with Target Put Lid on Revival at Tupperware," *Wall Street Journal*, February 14, 2004. For a discussion of indirect channel systems, see Richard Parker and G. R. Funkhouser, "The Consumer As an Active Member of the Channel: Implications for Relationship Marketing," *Journal of Marketing Theory & Practice*, Spring 1997; Lou E. Pelton, David Strutton, and James R. Lumpkin, *Marketing Channels: A Relationship Management Approach* (Burr Ridge, IL: Irwin/McGraw-Hill, 2002). See also Bert Rosenbloom and Trina L. Larsen, "How Foreign Firms View Their U.S. Distributors," *Industrial Marketing Management*, May 1992; Frank Lynn, "The Changing Economics of Industrial Distribution," *Industrial Marketing Management*, November 1992. For more on intermediaries and their functions, see Richard Greene, "Wholesaling," *Forbes*, January 2, 1984; W. Benoy et al., "How Industrial Distributors View Distributor-Supplier Partnership Arrangements," *Industrial Marketing Management*, January 1995.

7. For a classic discussion of the discrepancy concepts, see Wroe Alderson, "Factors Governing the Development of Marketing Channels," in *Marketing Channels for Manufactured Goods*, ed. Richard M. Clewett (Homewood, IL: Richard D. Irwin, 1954).

8. For some examples of how channels change to adjust discrepancies, see "Selling Literature Like Dog Food Gives Club Buyer Real Bite," *Wall Street Journal*, April 10, 2002. See also Robert Tamilia, Sylvain Senecal, and Gilles Corriveau, "Conventional Channels of Distribution and Electronic Intermediaries: a Functional Analysis," *Journal of Marketing Channels*, (3, 4) 2002; Robert A. Mittelstaedt and Robert E. Stassen, "Structural Changes in the Phonograph Record Industry and Its Channels of Distribution, 1946–1966," *Journal of Macromarketing*, Spring 1994; Arun Sharma and Luis V. Dominguez, "Channel Evolution: A Framework for Analysis," *Journal of the Academy of Marketing Science*, Winter 1992.

9. Arne Nygaard and Robert Dahlstrom, "Role Stress and Effectiveness in Horizontal Alliances," *Journal of Marketing*, April 2002; M. B. Sarkar, Raj Echambadi, S. Tamer Cavusgil, and Preet S. Aulakh, "The Influence of Complementarity, Compatibility, and Relationship Capital on Alliance Performance," *Journal of the Academy of Marketing Science*, Fall 2001; Jakki J. Mohr, Robert J. Fisher, and John R. Nevin, "Collaborative Communication in Interfirm Relationships: Moderating Effects of Integration and Control," *Journal of Marketing*, July 1996; Joseph P. Cannon, "Contracts, Norms, and Plural Form Governance," *Journal of the Academy of Marketing Science*, Spring 2000.

10. "What's Wrong with Selling Used CDs?" *BusinessWeek*, July 26, 1993.

11. Nirmalya Kumar, "Living with Channel Conflict," *CMO*, October 2004; Gregory M. Rose and Aviv Shoham, "Interorganizational Task and Emotional Conflict with International Channels of Distribution," *Journal of Business Research*, September 2004.

12. "Get Great Results from Salespeople by Finding What Really Moves Them," *Investor's Business Daily*, July 2, 2001.

13. Shailendra Gajanan, Suman Basuroy, and Srinath Beldona, "Category Management, Product Assortment, and Consumer Welfare," *Marketing Letters*, July 2007; Kenneth H. Wathne and Jan B. Heide, "Relationship Governance in a Supply Chain Network," *Journal of Marketing*, January 2004; David I. Gilliland, "Designing Channel Incentives to Overcome Reseller Rejection," *Industrial Marketing Management*, February 2004; James R. Brown, Anthony T. Cobb and Robert F. Lusch, "The Roles Played by Interorganizational Contracts and Justice in Marketing Channel Relationships," *Journal of Business Research*, February 2006; Keysuk Kim and Changho Oh, "On Distributor Commitment in Marketing Channels for Industrial Products: Contrast Between the United States and Japan," *Journal of International Marketing*, (1) 2002; Pierre Berthon, Leyland F. Pitt, Michael T. Ewing, and Gunnar Bakkeland, "Norms and Power in Marketing Relationships: Alternative Theories and Empirical Evidence," *Journal of Business Research*, September 2003; Rajiv Mehta, Alan J. Dubinsky, and Rolph E. Anderson, "Marketing Channel Management and the Sales Manager," *Industrial Marketing Management*, August 2002; Zhan G. Li and Rajiv P. Dant, "An Exploratory Study of Exclusive Dealing in Channel Relationships," *Journal of the Academy of Marketing Science*, Summer 1997.

14. "Big Grocer Pulls Unilever Items Over Pricing," *Advertising Age*, February 11, 2009.

15. See Janice M. Payan and Richard G. McFarland, "Decomposing Influence Strategies: Argument Structure and Dependence as Determinants of the Effectiveness of Influence Strategies in Gaining Channel Member Compliance," *Journal of Marketing*, July 2005; G. Peter Dapiran and Sandra Hogarth-Scott, "Are Co-operation and Trust Being Confused with Power? An Analysis of Food Retailing in Australia and the UK," *International Journal of Retail & Distribution Management*, (4) 2003; David I. Gilliland and Daniel C. Bello, "Two Sides to Attitudinal Commitment: the Effect of Calculative and Loyalty Commitment on Enforcement Mechanisms in Distribution Channels," *Journal of the Academy of Marketing Science*, Winter 2002; Jan B. Heide, "Interorganizational Governance in Marketing Channels," *Journal of Marketing*, January 1994; Jean L. Johnson et al., "The Exercise of Interfirm Power and Its Repercussions in U.S.-Japanese Channel Relationships," *Journal of Marketing*, April 1993.

16. For some examples of vertical integration, see "Mothers Work: Oh Baby, Business at This Retailer Is Booming," *Investor's Business Daily*, December 2, 2002; "Mothers Work: Giving the Lady What She Wants," *Fortune*, October 30, 2000, pp. T208BB–HH; "Moving On Up: Agricultural Firms Are Looking for New Growth Model . . . Vertical Integration," *Wall Street Journal Reports*, October 25, 2004; "Tiger's New Threads," *Wall Street Journal*, March 26, 2004.

17. "A Movie Theater as Comfy as Our Sofa," *Wall Street Journal*, April 24, 2008; "Transforming the Movie-Rental Model," *Advertising Age*, January 7, 2008; LG, Netflix to Offer Downloaded Movies on TV," *Wall Street Journal*, January 3, 2008; "Curtain Falls on Movie Download 1.0," *Investor's Business Daily*, December 12, 2007; "Netflix to Rent High-Def DVDs Pronto," *Investor's Business Daily*, February 27, 2006; "Coming Soon . . . Movies as You Like Them, and on the Same Day!" *USA Today*, January 12, 2006; "Multiplex under Seige," *Wall Street Journal*, December 24, 2005; "Wal-Mart Gives Up Online DVD Rentals, Will Promote Netflix," *Investor's Business Daily*, May 20, 2005; "Blockbuster Takes on the Entire Block," *Fortune*, March 21, 2005; "Showtime for Netflix," *Business 2.0*, March 2005; "Blockbuster Erases Its Late Fees—Sort of," *Advertising Age*, January 17, 2005; "TiVo Strikes Deal with Netflix for Online Delivery of Movies," *Wall Street Journal*, October 1, 2004; "Blockbuster Jabs Back at Its Rivals . . . Tries New Services," *USA Today*, June 22, 2004.

18. "Kimberly-Clark Keeps Costco in Diapers, Absorbing Costs Itself," *Wall Street Journal*, September 7, 2000. For another example, see "Made to Measure: Invisible Supplier Has Penney's Shirts All Buttoned Up," *Wall Street Journal*, September 11, 2003.

19. Junhong Chu, Pradeep K. Chintagunta, and Naufel J. Vilcassim, "Assessing the Economic Value of Distribution Channels: An Application to the Personal Computer Industry," *Journal of Marketing Research*, February 2007; Kevin L. Webb, "Managing Channels of Distribution in the Age of Electronic Commerce," *Industrial Marketing Management*, February 2002; Charles A. Ingene and Mark E. Parry, "Is Channel Coordination All It Is Cracked up to Be?" *Journal of Retailing*, Winter 2000; Kenneth H. Wathne and Jan B. Heide, "Opportunism in Interfirm Relationships: Forms, Outcomes, and Solutions," *Journal*

of Marketing, October 2000; Kersi D. Antia and Gary L. Frazier, "The Severity of Contract Enforcement in Interfirm Channel Relationships," *Journal of Marketing*, October 2001; Aric Rindfleisch and Jan B. Heide, "Transaction Cost Analysis: Past, Present, and Future Applications," *Journal of Marketing*, October 1997.

20. "A Talk with the Man Who Got Rayovac All Charged Up," *BusinessWeek*, February 21, 2000.

21. See www.esprit.com; "Esprit, a 1980s Fashion Icon, Struggles to Find a U.S. Fit," *Wall Street Journal*, October 28, 2005; "Esprit in the Spirit for Retail Expansion," *Brandweek*, June 20, 2005; "Esprit Tries to Shed Its Youth Image," *Wall Street Journal*, September 3, 2004; "Can Esprit Be Hip Again?" *Wall Street Journal*, June 17, 2002. See also Carol J. Johnson, Robert E. Krapfel, Jr., and Curtis M. Grimm, "A Contingency Model of Supplier-Reseller Satisfaction Perceptions in Distribution Channels," *Journal of Marketing Channels*, (1, 2) 2001; Inge Geyskens and Jan-Benedict E. M. Steenkamp, "Economic and Social Satisfaction: Measurement and Relevance to Marketing Channel Relationships," *Journal of Retailing*, Spring 2000; Gary L. Frazier and Walfried M. Lassar, "Determinants of Distribution Intensity," *Journal of Marketing*, October 1996.

22. "Antitrust Issues and Marketing Channel Strategy" and "Case 1—Continental T.V., Inc., et al. v. GTE Sylvania, Inc.," in Louis W. Stern and Thomas L. Eovaldi, *Legal Aspects of Marketing Strategy* (Englewood Cliffs, NJ: Prentice-Hall, 1984). See also Debra M. Desrochers, Gregory T. Gundlach, and Albert A. Foer, "Analysis of Antitrust Challenges to Category Captain Arrangements," *Journal of Public Policy & Marketing*, Fall 2003. For some examples of exclusive deals, see "Blue Nile: Online Jewelry Seller Looks to Be a Cut Above the Competition," *Investor's Business Daily*, December 15, 2005; "When Exclusivity Means Illegality," *Wall Street Journal*, January 6, 2005; "Bringing Chic to Sheets," *Wall Street Journal*, September 8, 2004.

23. For more on Reebok, see "Reebok's Direct Sales Spark a Retail Revolt," *Adweek's Marketing Week*, December 2, 1991. See also Rajkumar Venkatesan, V. Kumar, and Nalini Ravishanker, "Multichannel Shopping: Causes and Consequences," *Journal of Marketing*, April 2007; Scott A. Neslin, Dhruv Grewal, Robert Leghorn, Venkatesh Shankar, Marije L. Teerling, Jacquelyn S. Thomas, and Peter C. Verhoef, "Challenges and Opportunities in Multichannel Customer Management," *Journal of Service Research*, May 2006; Sertan Kabadayi, Nermin Eyuboglu, and Gloria P. Thomas, "The Performance Implications of Designing Multiple Channels to Fit with Strategy and Environment," *Journal of Marketing*, October 2007; Arun Sharma and Anuj Mehrotra, "Choosing an Optimal Channel Mix in Multichannel Environments," *Industrial Marketing Management*, January 2007; Bert Rosenbloom, "Multi-channel Strategy in Business-to-Business Markets: Prospects and Problems," *Industrial Marketing Management*, January 2007; Asim Ansari, Carl F. Mela, and Scott A. Neslin, "Customer Channel Migration," *Journal of Marketing Research*, February 2008; Jule B. Gassenheimer, Gary L. Hunter, and Judy A. Siguaw, "An Evolving Theory of Hybrid Distribution: Taming a Hostile Supply Network," *Industrial Marketing Management*, May 2007; Peter C. Verhoef, Scott A. Neslin, and Björn Vroomen, "Multichannel Customer Management: Understanding the Research-Shopper Phenomenon," *International Journal of Research in Marketing*, June 2007; Jacquelyn S. Thomas and Ursula Y. Sullivan, "Managing Marketing Communications with Multichannel Customers," *Journal of Marketing*, October 2005; David W. Wallace, Joan L. Giese, and Jean L. Johnson, "Customer Retailer Loyalty in the Context of Multiple Channel Strategies," *Journal of Retailing*, Winter 2004; Stephanie M. Noble, David A. Griffith, and Marc G. Weinberger, "Consumer Derived Utilitarian Value and Channel Utilization in a Multi-Channel Retail Context," *Journal of Business Research*, December 2005; Sridhar Balasubramanian, Rajagopal Raghunathan, and Vijay Mahajan, "Consumers in a Multichannel Environment: Product Utility, Process Utility, and Channel Choice," *Journal of Interactive Marketing*, Spring 2005; Ruby Roy Dholakia, Miao Zhao, and Nikhilesh

Dholakia, "Multichannel Retailing: A Case Study of Early Experiences," *Journal of Interactive Marketing*, Spring 2005; Debra L. Scammon and Mary Jane Sheffet, "Legal Issues in Channels Modification Decisions: The Question of Refusals to Deal," *Journal of Public Policy and Marketing*, (5) 1986.

24. Gregory T. Gundlach and Patrick E. Murphy, "Ethical and Legal Foundations of Relational Marketing Exchanges," *Journal of Marketing,* October 1993; Craig B. Barkacs, "Multilevel Marketing and Antifraud Statutes: Legal Enterprises or Pyramid Schemes?" *Journal of the Academy of Marketing Science*, Spring 1997; Robert A. Robicheaux and James E. Coleman, "The Structure of Marketing Channel Relationships," *Journal of the Academy of Marketing Science*, Winter 1994; Brett A. Boyle and F. Robert Dwyer, "Power, Bureaucracy, Influence and Performance: Their Relationships in Industrial Distribution Channels," *Journal of Business Research*, March 1995.

25. R. Glenn Richey, Haozhe Chen, Stefan E. Genchev, and Patricia J. Daugherty, "Developing Effective Reverse Logistics Programs," *Industrial Marketing Management*, November 2005; Joseph D. Blackburn, V. Daniel R. Guide Jr, Gilvan C. Souza and Luk N. Van Wassenhove, "Reverse Supply Chains for Commercial Returns," *California Management Review*, Winter 2004; Roland Geyer and Tim Jackson, "Supply Loops and Their Constraints: The Industrial Ecology of Recycling and Reuse," *California Management Review*, Winter 2004; H. Scott Matthews, "Thinking Outside 'the Box': Designing a Packaging Take-Back System," *California Management Review*, Winter 2004. For more on return policies, see "Some Retailers Tighten Return Policies," *USA Today*, February 1, 2008; "Returning Your Goods Isn't a Cakewalk," *Wall Street Journal*, February 22, 2007; "After That Item Arrives Broken, How Easy Can You Return It?" *Investor's Business Daily*, May 22, 2006; "Stores Toughen Return Policies," *USA Today*, December 27, 2005; "Taking Back That Bathrobe Gets Harder," *Wall Street Journal*, December 15, 2005. See also Andy A. Tsay, "Risk Sensitivity in Distribution Channel Partnerships: Implications for Manufacturer Return Policies," *Journal of Retailing*, Summer 2002.

26. "Hyper-Green Products Go Cradle to Cradle," *MSNBC.com*, October 12, 2007; "Can One Green Deliver the Other," *Harvard Business Review*, 2005; "HP Wants Your Old PCs Back," *Businessweek.com*, April 10, 2006.

27. See Rene B. M. de Koster, Marisa P. de Brito, and Masja A. van de Vendel, "Return Handling: an Exploratory Study with Nine Retailer Warehouses," *International Journal of Retail & Distribution Management*, (8) 2002; Ronald S. Tibben-Lembke, "Life after Death: Reverse Logistics and the Product Life Cycle," *International Journal of Physical Distribution & Logistics Management*, (3) 2002; Chad W. Autry, Patricia J. Daugherty, and R. Glenn Richey, "The Challenge of Reverse Logistics in Catalog Retailing," *International Journal of Physical Distribution & Logistics Management*, (1) 2001; Dale S. Rogers and Ronald TibbenLembke, "An Examination of Reverse Logistics Practices," *Journal of Business Logistics*, (2) 2001.

28. Joseph Johnson and Gerard J. Tellis, "Drivers of Success for Market Entry into China and India," *Journal of Marketing*, May 2008; Mohammed Y. A. Rawwas, Kazuhiko Konishi, Shoji Kamise, and Jamal Al-Khatib, "Japanese Distribution System: The Impact of Newly Designed Collaborations on Wholesalers' Performance," *Industrial Marketing Management*, January 2008.

CHAPTER 11

1. "Tea Time: Coke Buys 40% of Honest Tea," *USA Today*, February 6, 2008; "So Many New Soft Drinks, So Little Time," *USA Today*, March 14, 2007; "Queen of Pop," *Business Week*, August 7, 2006; "Coke Tries to Pop Back in Vital Japan Market," *Wall Street Journal*, July 11, 2006; "Afghan Coke a Taste of Things to Come," *Financial Times*, December 6, 2005.

2. See www.transora.com and www.fmi.org/media/bg/ecr1; "How to Make a Frozen Lasagna (with Just $250 Million)," *Fortune*, April 30, 2001; "Delivering the Goods," *Fortune*, November 28, 1994; "Making the Middleman an Endangered Species," *BusinessWeek*, June 6, 1994; "The Nitty-Gritty of ECR Systems: How One Company Makes It Pay," *Advertising Age*, May 2, 1994; "Behind the Tumult at P&G," *Fortune*, March 7, 1994; See also Daniel Corsten and Nirmalya Kumar, "Do Suppliers Benefit from Collaborative Relationships with Large Retailers? An Empirical Investigation of Efficient Consumer Response Adoption," *Journal of Marketing*, July 2005; Stefan Borchert, "Implementation Hurdles of ECR Partnerships—the German Food Sector as an ECR Case Study," *International Journal of Retail & Distribution Management*, (6) 2002.

3. "Compaq Stumbles as PCs Weather New Blow," *Wall Street Journal*, March 9, 1998; "At What Profit Price?" *Brandweek*, June 23, 1997; "Delivering the Goods," *Fortune*, November 28, 1994; See also Alexander E. Ellinger, Scott B. Keller and John D. Hansen, "Bridging the Divide Between Logistics and Marketing: Facilitating Collaborative Behavior," *Journal of Business Logistics*, #2 2006; Kofi Q. Dadzie, Cristian Chelariu and Evelyn Winston, "Customer Service in the Internet-Enabled Logistics Supply Chain: Website Design Antecedents and Loyalty Effects," *Journal of Business Logistics*, 2005; Elliot Rabinovich and Philip T. Evers, "Product Fulfillment in Supply Chains Supporting Internet-Retailing Operations," *Journal of Business Logistics*, 2003; Daniel Corsten and Thomas Gruen, "Stock-Outs Cause Walkouts," *Harvard Business Review*, May 2004; Chris Dubelaar, Garland Chow and Paul D. Larson, "Relationships Between Inventory, Sales and Service in a Retail Chain Store Operation," *International Journal of Physical Distribution & Logistics Management*, (2) 2001; Lloyd M. Rinehart, M. Bixby Cooper, and George D. Wagenheim, "Furthering the Integration of Marketing and Logistics Through Customer Service in the Channel," *Journal of the Academy of Marketing Science*, Winter 1989; Edward A. Morash and John Ozment, "Toward Management of Transportation Service Quality," *The Logistics and Transportation Review*, June 1994; William D. Perreault, Jr., and Frederick A. Russ, "Physical Distribution Service in Industrial Purchase Decisions," *Journal of Marketing*, April 1976.

4. "Wal-Mart's H-P Elves," Wall Street Journal, December 15, 2005; "A More Profitable Harvest," Business 2.0, May 2005; "66,207,896 Bottles of Beer on the Wall," Business 2.0, January/February, 2004; "Logistics Gets a Little Respect," *BusinessWeek E.Biz*, November 20, 2000; "One Smart Cookie," *BusinessWeek E.Biz*, November 20, 2000; "A Cereal Maker Hitches Its Wagons to the Web," *BusinessWeek E.Biz*, September 18, 2000; "Costs Too High? Bring in the Logistics Experts," *Fortune*, November 10, 1997. See also G. Tomas M. Hult, Kenneth K. Boyer, and David J. Ketchen, Jr, "Quality, Operational Logistics Strategy, and Repurchase Intentions: A Profile Deviation Analysis," *Journal of Business Logistics*, (2) 2007; Thierry Sauvage, "The Relationship Between Technology and Logistics Third Party Providers," *International Journal of Physical Distribution & Logistics Management*, (3) 2003; Donald J. Bowersox, David J. Closs, and Theodore P. Stank, "Ten Mega-Trends That Will Revolutionize Supply Chain Logistics," *Journal of Business Logistics*, (2)2000; James R. Stock, "Marketing Myopia Revisited: Lessons for Logistics," *International Journal of Physical Distribution & Logistics Management*, (1) 2002; Mark Goh and Charlene Ling, "Logistics Development in China," *International Journal of Physical Distribution & Logistics Management*, (9) 2003; James H. Bookbinder and Chris S. Tan, "Comparison of Asian and European Logistics Systems," *International Journal of Physical Distribution & Logistics Management*, (1) 2003.

5. See Forrest E. Harding, "Logistics Service Provider Quality: Private Measurement, Evaluation, and Improvement," *Journal of Business Logistics*, 1998; Carol C. Bienstock, John T. Mentzer, and Monroe M. Bird, "Measuring Physical Distribution Service Quality," *Journal of the Academy of Marketing Science*, Winter 1997.

6. "More Green from Green Beans," *Business 2.0*, August 2004. Mikko Karkkainen, Timo Ala-Risku, and Jan Holmstrom, "Increasing Customer Value and Decreasing Distribution Costs with

Merge-In-Transit," *International Journal of Physical Distribution & Logistics Management*, (1) 2003; Marc J. Schniederjans and Qing Cao, "An Alternative Analysis of Inventory Costs of JIT and EOQ Purchasing," *International Journal of Physical Distribution & Logistics Management*, (2) 2001; Amy Z. Zeng and Christian Rossetti, "Developing a Framework for Evaluating the Logistics Costs in Global Sourcing Processes: an Implementation and Insights," *International Journal of Physical Distribution & Logistics Management*, (9) 2003.

7. "California Fires Fuel Squabbles about Readiness," *Wall Street Journal*, October 24, 2007; Ozlem Ergun, Pinar Keskiocak, and Julie Swann, "Humanitarian Relief Logistics," *OR/MS Today*, December 2007; "Good Logistics Offer Better Relief," *Financial Times*, December 16, 2005; "Disasters Demand Supply Chain Software, Research Shows." *eWeek*, October 5, 2005; "The Only Lifeline Was the WalMart," *Fortune*, October 3, 2005; "For FedEx, It Was Time to Deliver," *Fortune*, October 3, 2005; "Can Wal-Mart Wear a White Hat?" *BusinessWeek Online*, September 22, 2005; "They Don't Teach This in B-School," *BusinessWeek*, September 19, 2005, pp. 46–48: "At Wal-Mart, Emergency Plan Has Big Payoff," *Wall Street Journal*, September 12, 2005; "Wal-Mart Praised for Hurricane Katrina Response Efforts," *NewsMax.com*, September 6, 2005; "A Logistics Nightmare," *Traffic World*, January 10, 2005; "How to Deliver on the Promises," *Financial Times*, January 7, 2005; "Geography and Logistics Confound Relief," *MSNBC.com*, January 3, 2005; *Logistics and the Effective Delivery of Humanitarian Relief* (The Fritz Institute, 2005); "Emergency Relief Logistics—A Faster Way across the Global Divide," *Logistics Quarterly*, Summer 2001; Anisya Thomas and Lynn Fritz, "Disaster Relief, Inc," *Harvard Business Review*, November 2006.

8. For more on JIT, see "Retailers Rely More on Fast Deliveries," *Wall Street Journal*, January 14, 2004; "Uncertain Economy Hinders Highly Precise Supply System," *The New York Times*, March 15, 2003; "Port Tie-Up Shows Vulnerability," *USA Today*, October 9, 2002; "Deadline Scramble: A New Hazard for Recovery, Last-Minute Pace of Orders," *Wall Street Journal*, June 25, 2002; "Parts Shortages Hamper Electronics Makers," *Wall Street Journal*, July 7, 2000. See also Richard E. White and John N. Pearson, "JIT, System Integration and Customer Service," *International Journal of Physical Distribution & Logistics Management*, (5) 2001; Richard Germain, Cornelia Droge, and Nancy Spears, "The Implications of Just-in-Time for Logistics Organization Management and Performance," *Journal of Business Logistics*, 1996; Faye W. Gilbert, Joyce A. Young, and Charles R. O'Neal, "Buyer-Seller Relationships in Just-in-Time Purchasing Environments," *Journal of Business Research*, February 1994.

9. "A New Industrial Revolution," *Wall Street Journal*, April 28, 2008; "Global Scramble for Goods Gives Corporate Buyers a Lift," *Wall Street Journal*, October 2, 2007.

10. See Martin Christopher and John Gattorna, "Supply Chain Cost Management and Value-Based Pricing," *Industrial Marketing Management*, February 2005; G. Tomas M. Hult, "Global Supply Chain Management: An Integration of Scholarly Thoughts," *Industrial Marketing Management*, January 2004; Daniel J. Flint, "Strategic Marketing in Global Supply Chains: Four Challenges," *Industrial Marketing Management*, January 2004; Daniel C. Bello, Ritu Lohtia, and Vinita Sangtani, "An Institutional Analysis of Supply Chain Innovations in Global Marketing Channels," *Industrial Marketing Management*, January 2004; Daekwan Kim, S. Tamer Cavusgil, and Roger J. Calantone, "Information System Innovations and Supply Chain Management: Channel Relationships and Firm Performance," *Journal of the Academy of Marketing Science*, Winter 2006; Brian J. Gibson, John T. Mentzer, and Robert L. Cook, "Supply Chain Management: the Pursuit of a Consensus Definition," *Journal of Business Logistics*, 2005; Theodore P. Stank, Beth R. Davis, and Brian S. Fugate, "A Strategic Framework for Supply Chain Oriented Logistics," *Journal of Business Logistics*, 2005; Terry L. Esper, Thomas D. Jensen, Fernanda L. Turnipseed, and Scot Burton, "The Last Mile: An Examination of Effects of Online Retail Delivery Strategies on Consumers," *Journal*

of Business Logistics, 2003; Dale S. Rogers and Rudolf Leuschner, "Supply Chain Management: Retrospective and Prospective," *Journal of Marketing Theory & Practice*, Fall 2004; Taylor R. Randall, Ruskin M. Morgan, and Alysse R. Morton, "Efficient versus Responsive Supply Chain Choice: an Empirical Examination of Influential Factors," *Journal of Product Innovation Management*, November 2003; Christopher R. Moberg and Thomas W. Speh, "Evaluating the Relationship Between Questionable Business Practices and the Strength of Supply Chain Relationships," *Journal of Business Logistics*, (2) 2003; Subroto Roy, K. Sivakumar, and Ian F. Wilkinson, "Innovation Generation in Supply Chain Relationships: a Conceptual Model and Research Propositions," *Journal of the Academy of Marketing Science*, Winter 2004; Katarina Kempainen and Ari P. J. Vepsalainen, "Trends in Industrial Supply Chains and Networks," *International Journal of Physical Distribution & Logistics Management*, (8) 2003; Rakesh Niraj, "Customer Profitability in a Supply Chain," *Journal of Marketing*, July 2001.

11. For an excellent example of EDI, see "To Sell Goods to WalMart, Get on the Net," *Wall Street Journal*, November 21, 2003. See also Cornelia Droge and Richard Germain, "The Relationship of Electronic Data Interchange with Inventory and Financial Performance," *Journal of Business Logistics*, (2) 2000.

12. "A Smart Cookie at Pepperidge," *Fortune*, December 22, 1986.

13. "A New Push Against Sweatshops," *Time*, October 7, 2005; "Cops of the Global Village, *Fortune*, June 27, 2005; "Stamping Out Sweatshops," *BusinessWeek Online*, May 23, 2005; "Nike Opens Its Books on Sweatshop Audits," *BusinessWeek Online*, April 27, 2000; "Nike Names Names," *BusinessWeek Online*, April 13, 2005; "Corporate Social Responsibility—Companies in the News Nike," see www.mallenbaker.net/csr/CSRfiles/nike.html.

14. David Grant, Douglas Lambert, James R. Stock, and Lisa M. Ellram, *Fundamentals of Logistics* (Burr Ridge, IL: Irwin/McGraw-Hill, 2005).

15. For more on transportation security, see "Four Words Rarely Seen on Unsafe Imported Foods: United States Refused Entry," *USA Today*, October 10, 2007; "Technology Roots Out Cargo Risks," *Investor's Business Daily*, October 4, 2005; "Keeping Cargo Safe from Terror," *Wall Street Journal*, July 29, 2005; "In Terrorism Fight, Government Finds a Surprising Ally: FedEx," *Wall Street Journal*, May 26, 2005; "Sensors on Containers May Offer Safer Shipping," *Wall Street Journal*, March 31, 2005; "Protecting America's Ports," *Fortune*, November 10, 2003; "FedEx Takes Direct Approach to Terrorism," *Wall Street Journal*, October 9, 2003; "Safe Harbors?" *Wall Street Journal*, April 21, 2003; "Companies Must Add Rising Security Costs to Bottom Line," *USA Today*, March 28, 2003; "Shippers Get Caught in Customs' Net," *BusinessWeek*, March 24, 2003; "Transportation Deregulation, JIT, and Inventory Levels," *Logistics and Transportation Review*, June 1991; James C. Nelson, "Politics and Economics in Transport Regulation and Deregulation—A Century Perspective of the ICC's Role," *Logistics and Transportation Review*, March 1987.

16. For a more detailed comparison of mode characteristics, see Robert Dahlstrom, Kevin M. McNeilly, and Thomas W. Speh, "Buyer-Seller Relationships in the Procurement of Logistical Services," *Journal of the Academy of Marketing Science*, Spring 1996.

17. "New Rail-Building Era Dawns," *Wall Street Journal*, February 13, 2008; "Next Stop: The 21st Century," *Business 2.0*, September 2003; "Back on Track: Left for Dead, Railroads Revive by Watching Clock," *Wall Street Journal*, July 25, 2003; "Trains: Industry Report," *Investor's Business Daily*, May 7, 2001.

18. "Truckers Question Traffic-Relief Efforts," *USA Today*, December 27, 2007; "Shipping Hubs Spring Up Inland," *USA Today*, December 17, 2007; "Waterways Could Be Key to Freeing Up Freeways," *USA Today*, October 11, 2007; "Costs of Trucking Seen Rising under New Safety Rules," *Wall Street Journal*, November 12, 2003; "Trucker Rewards Customers for Good Behavior," *Wall Street Journal*,

September 9, 2003; "Trucking: Rig and Roll," *Wall Street Journal*, October 23, 2000; "Trucking Gets Sophisticated," *Fortune*, July 24, 2000.

19. For more on overnight carriers, see "UPS Battles Traffic Jams to Gain Ground in India," *Wall Street Journal*, January 25, 2008; "Why FedEx Is Gaining Ground," *Business 2.0*, October 2003; "FedEx Recasts Itself on the Ground," *Wall Street Journal*, September 4, 2003; "UPS, FedEx Wage Handheld Combat," *Investor's Business Daily*, May 19, 2003.

20. K. Raguraman and Claire Chan, "The Development of SeaAir Intermodal Transportation: An Assessment of Global Trends," *Logistics and Transportation Review*, December 1994; "Yule Log Jam," *Fortune*, December 13, 2004; "Monsters of the High Seas," *BusinessWeek*, October 13, 2003.

21. "Western Grocer Modernizes Passage to Indian Markets," *Wall Street Journal*, November 28, 2007; "Widening Aisles for Indian Shoppers," *BusinessWeek*, April 30, 2007; "Road to Indian Market Full of Potholes for German Retailer, *Deutsche Welle*, November 5, 2006.

22. "DHL Completes More Eco-Friendly Ship Voyage as Industry Comes Under Fire," *GreenBiz.com*, February 15, 2008; *State of Green Business 2008*, Greener World Media (2008), *GreenBiz.com*. See also *2007 Annual Report*, Du Pont; *2007 Annual Report*, Matlack; *2007 Annual Report*, Shell; *2007 Annual Report*, FedEx; *2007 Annual Report*, UPS; "FedEx and Brown Are Going Green," *BusinessWeek*, August 11, 2003; "Conservation Power," *BusinessWeek*, September 16, 1991. See also Lawrence Christensen, "The Environment and Its Impact on the Supply Chain," *International Journal of Retail & Distribution Management*, (11) 2002.

23. For more on Tostitos Gold example, see "Buyers Seek Hard-to-Find Tostitos Gold," *USA Today*, February 9, 2003; "Relevance Is Operative Word in Catfight or Chip-Dip Ads," *Advertising Age*, January 27, 2003; "Frito-Lay Leverages National Championship Game as Major Marketing Platform for New Tostitos Gold Tortilla Chips," *PR Newswire*, December 30, 2002; Anita Haley, "Brand Revolution," www.fmi.org. See also J. Mahajan et al., "An Exploratory Investigation of the Interdependence Between Marketing and Operations Functions in Service Firms," *International Journal of Research in Marketing*, January 1994; Edward U. Bond III, Beth A. Walker, Michael D. Hutt, and Peter H. Reingen, "Reputational Effectiveness in Cross-Functional Working Relationships," *Journal of Product Innovation Management*, January 2004.

24. "Hospital Cost Cutters Push Use of Scanners to Track Inventories," *Wall Street Journal*, June 10, 1997. See also Charu Chandra and Sameer Kumar, "Taxonomy of Inventory Policies for Supply-Chain Effectiveness," *International Journal of Retail & Distribution Management*, (4) 2001; Walter Zinn, John T. Mentzer, and Keely L. Croxton, "Customer-Based Measures of Inventory Availability," *Journal of Business Logistics*, (2) 2002; Timothy L. Urban, "The Interdependence of Inventory Management and Retail Shelf Management," *International Journal of Physical Distribution & Logistics Management*, (1) 2002; Matthew B. Myers, Patricia J. Daugherty, and Chad W. Autry, "The Effectiveness of Automatic Inventory Replenishment in Supply Chain Operations: Antecedents and Outcomes," *Journal of Retailing*, Winter 2000.

25. "The Supersizing of Warehouses," *The New York Times*, February 4, 2004; "New Warehouses Take On a Luxe Look," *Wall Street Journal*, June 18, 2003; Chad W. Autry, Stanley E. Griffis, Thomas J. Goldsby, and L. Michelle Bobbitt, "Warehouse Management Systems: Resource Commitment, Capabilities, and Organizational Performance," *Journal of Business Logistics*, 2005.

26. "RFID Systems Move beyond Stockroom as Technology Finds Lots of New Uses," *Investor's Business Daily*, April 4, 2008; "Wireless Grapes," *Fortune*, March 6, 2006; "RFID Technology Getting Static in New Hampshire," *Brandweek*, January 23, 2006; "LoJack Steals Street's Heart with CrimeBusting Devices," *Investor's Business Daily*,

September 7, 2005; "IBM, Smart Tags Helping Toyota Customize Its Cars," *Investor's Business Daily*, August 15, 2005; "Who Made My Cheese? Tags Track Parmesan's Age, Origin," *Wall Street Journal*, July 7, 2005; "Frequency of the Future," *DSN Retailing Today*, (1Q) 2005; "Electronic Tags Should Help Drug Makers Identify Fakes," *Investor's Business Daily*, November 29, 2004; "Suppliers Struggle with Wal-Mart ID-Tag Plan," *Wall Street Journal*, November 18, 2004; "RFID: Robot for Infinite Decluttering?" *USA Today*, October 6, 2004; "What's So Great about RFID Tags," *Investor's Business Daily*, August 16, 2004; "Down, but Far from Out: RFID Technology Is Off to a Disappointing Start, but Retailers Are Convinced," *Wall Street Journal Reports*, January 12, 2004; "Wal-Mart Keeps the Change," *Fortune*, November 10, 2003.

27. "Frito-Lay," *Short Cases from the CSCMP Toolbox*, 2005.

28. "Wal-Mart's Need for Speed," *Wall Street Journal*, September 26, 2005. See also Kum Khiong Yang, "Managing a Single Warehouse, Multiple Retailer Distribution Center," *Journal of Business Logistics*, (2) 2000; Chin Chia Jane, "Storage Location Assignment in a Distribution Center," *International Journal of Physical Distribution & Logistics Management*, (1) 2000; "Distribution Center Doubles Output with Paperless System," *Modern Materials Handling/Scan Tech News*, September 1994.

CHAPTER 12

1. "Best Buy Confronts Newer Nemesis," *Wall Street Journal*, March 17, 2009; "Big Box Retailer Goes Little," *Wall Street Journal*, February 12, 2009; "Best Buy, Other Retailers Tap Tech to Boost Sales," *BusinessWeek*, February 8, 2009; "Fifth Avenue Duel: Best Buy vs. Circuit City," *USA Today*, December 20, 2007; "Best Buy Smashes Analysts' Q3 Views," *Investor's Business Daily*, December 19, 2007; "More Clicks at the Bricks," *BusinessWeek*, December 17, 2007; "Best Buy Moves to More Mobile Selections," *Wall Street Journal*, July 12, 2007; "Best Buy, Wal-Mart Take on RadioShack in Cell Phone Retail," *Investor's Business Daily*, April 5, 2007; "Best Buy Gets in Touch with Its Feminine Side," *USA Today*, December 21, 2006; "Best Buy Looking beyond Big Digital TV-Driven Growth," *Investor's Business Daily*, September 14, 2006; "Talking Shop," *Fortune*, August 21, 2006; "Can Best Buy Get Geekier?" *Business 2.0*, June 2006; "Best Buy's Giant Gamble," *Fortune*, April 3, 2006; "Geek Squad Is Popular at Best Buy," *Wall Street Journal*, December 14, 2005; "Best Buy Launches Six Niche Sites," *Advertising Age*, November 28, 2005; "Best Buy Sees Growth by Studying Shoppers," *Investor's Business Daily*, July 5, 2005; "Best Buy Taps Rapp to Weed Out Angels, Devils," *Advertising Age*, May 16, 2005; "Slimming Down Stores: Big-Box Retailer Best Buy Experiments with Boutiques," *Wall Street Journal*, April 29, 2005; "Customer-Centric Model Future Focus at Best Buy," *DSN Retailing Today*, April 25, 2005; "Why Some Marketers Turn Away Customers," *Advertising Age*, February 14, 2005; "Electronics Retailers Woo Women," *Advertising Age*, November 15, 2004; "Minding the Store: Analyzing Customers, Best Buy Decides Not All Are Welcome," *Wall Street Journal*, November 8, 2004; "5 Rules for Finding the Next Dell," *Fortune*, July 12, 2004; "Best Buy's Selling Machine," *Business 2.0*, July 2004; "New Retail Offering: Geeks on Call," *Wall Street Journal*, May 20, 2004; "The Unprofitable Customer," *Wall Street Journal*, October 28, 2003.

2. See www.census.gov/mrts/www/data/html/nsal05.html; U.S. Bureau of the Census, *Statistical Abstract of the United States 2008* (Washington, DC: U.S. Government Printing Office, 2007); *2002 Economic Census—Retail Trade, Subject Series, Establishment and Firm Size* (Washington, DC: U.S. Government Printing Office, 2005); "Where Consumers Shop Changes, but When They Do It Stays the Same," *Advertising Age*, November 21, 2005; "Retail: Upscale Experience, Downscale Prices," *Wall Street Journal Reports*, November 21, 2005; "Annual Industry Report, Top 150," *DSN Retailing Today*, July, 2005; "A Store Made for Right Now: You Shop until It's Dropped,"

The New York Times, February 17, 2004; "Just Take the Money!" *Time* (*Inside Business Bonus Section*), July 2003; "Islands in the Mall: Pushcarts as Revenue Streams," *The New York Times*, January 22, 2003; "The 40 People and Events That Have Shaped Mass Market Retailing," *DSN Retailing Today*, August 2002; "Retail Reckoning," *BusinessWeek*, December 10, 2001; Vincent R. Nijs, Shuba Srinivasan, and Koen Pauwels, "Retail-Price Drivers and Retailer Profits," *Marketing Science*, July–August 2007; Velitchka D. Kaltcheva and Barton A. Weitz, "When Should a Retailer Create an Exciting Store Environment?" *Journal of Marketing*, January 2006; Kathleen Seiders, Glenn B. Voss, Dhruv Grewal, and Andrea L. Godfrey, "Do Satisfied Customers Buy More? Examining Moderating Influences in a Retailing Context," *Journal of Marketing*, October 2005; Ruth N. Bolton and Venkatesh Shankar, "An Empirically Derived Taxonomy of Retailer Pricing and Promotion Strategies," *Journal of Retailing*, Winter 2003; Arthur W. Allaway, David Berkowitz, and Giles D'Souza, "Spatial Diffusion of a New Loyalty Program Through a Retail Market," *Journal of Retailing*, Fall 2003; Katherine B. Hartman and Rosann L. Spiro, "Recapturing Store Image in Customer-Based Store Equity: A Construct Conceptualization," *Journal of Business Research*, August 2005; Mark J. Arnold, Kristy E. Reynolds, Nicole Ponder, and Jason E. Lueg, "Customer Delight in a Retail Context: Investigating Delightful and Terrible Shopping Experiences," *Journal of Business Research*, August 2005; Sevgin A. Eroglu, Karen Machleit, and Terri Feldman Barr, "Perceived Retail Crowding and Shopping Satisfaction: The Role of Shopping Values," *Journal of Business Research*, August 2005; Kiran Karande and John R. Lombard, "Location Strategies of Broad-Line Retailers: an Empirical Investigation," *Journal of Business Research*, May 2005.

3. For more on discount (dollar) stores, see "More Shoppers Head to Discount Stores," *USA Today*, February 8, 2008; "Can the Dollar Stores Rebound?" *Wall Street Journal*, September 21, 2005; "Behind the Dollar-Store Boom: A Nation of Bargain Hunters," *Wall Street Journal*, December 13, 2004; "Out-Discounting the Discounter," *BusinessWeek*, May 10, 2004; "Family Dollar Stores: Growth Means Respect for Discount Retailer," *Investor's Business Daily*, February 22, 2002; "Cheap Thrills for Shoppers," *Newsweek*, April 16, 2001; "Beyond the Database: Sales and Service on a First-Name Basis," *Colloguy*, No. 1, 1997; "Neiman Marcus, Saks Wage Expensive Battle for Upscale Shoppers," *Wall Street Journal*, November 21, 1996; See also Kristy E. Reynolds and Mark J. Arnold, "Customer Loyalty to the Salesperson and the Store: Examining Relationship Customers in an Upscale Retail Context," *Journal of Personal Selling & Sales Management*, Spring 2000; Alain d'Astous, "Irritating Aspects of the Shopping Environment," *Journal of Business Research*, August 2000.

4. "As Malls Think Small, Boutiques Get Their Big Chance," *Wall Street Journal*, June 24, 2005; "Urban Rarity: Stores Offering Spiffy Service," *Wall Street Journal*, July 25, 1996; "Airports: New Destination for Specialty Retailers," *USA Today*, January 11, 1996; Sharon E. Beatty, Morris Mayer, James E. Coleman, Kristy E. Reynolds, and Jungki Lee, "Customer-Sales Associate Retail Relationships," *Journal of Retailing*, Fall 1996.

5. See www.census.gov; U.S. Bureau of the Census, *2002 Economic Census Retail Trade, Subject Series, Establishment and Firm Size*. For more on department stores, see "Big Retailers Seek Teens (and Parents)," *USA Today*, April 14, 2008; "J.C. Penney Gets the Net," *BusinessWeek*, May 7, 2007; "Departments of Energy," *Brandweek*, February 26, 2007; "And on This Floor, a Comeback," *USA Today*, February 21, 2007; "Chasing Mr. and Mrs. Middle Market, J.C. Penney, Kohl's Open 85 New Stores," *Wall Street Journal*, October 6, 2006; "J.C. Penney Sells with an Attitude," *USA Today*, March 3, 2006; "Changes in Store for Department Stores?" *USA Today*, January 21, 2005; "The Department Store Rises Again," *Business 2.0*, August 2004.

6. David Appel, "The Supermarket: Early Development of an Institutional Innovation," *Journal of Retailing*, Spring 1972.

7. See www.census.gov and www.fmi.org/facts_figs/?fuseaction+superfact; "Do-It-Yourself Supermarket Checkout," *Wall Street Journal*, April 5, 2007; "Inventory Management 2002: Data, Detail, & Discipline in Supermarkets," *Chain Store Age*, December 2002; "Grocery Shoppers Can Be Own Cashiers," *USA Today*, March 9, 1998; "The Taste of the Nation," *USA Today*, March 9, 1998. See also Brian T. Ratchford, "Has the Productivity of Retail Food Stores Really Declined?" *Journal of Retailing*, Fall 2003; Mohammed A. AlSudairy and N. K. H. Tang, "Information Technology in Saudi Arabia's Supermarket Chains," *International Journal of Retail & Distribution Management*, (8) 2000.

8. For more on Wal-Mart's Neighborhood Markets, see "Neighborhood Market Caps Year with Round of New Market Entries," *DSN Retailing Today*, January 27, 2003; "For America's Big Retailers, Small Is Beautiful, Sometimes," *The New York Times*, January 22, 2003; "Wal-Mart Is Eating Everyone's Lunch," *BusinessWeek*, April 15, 2002.

9. For more on Target as mass-merchandiser, see "Target Applies GM Merchandising to Food," *Food Retailing Today*, November 10, 2003; "Target: The Challenges and Rewards of Being the No. 2 Discount Retailer," *DSN Retailing Today*, April 7, 2003; "Is Target's Wardrobe in Wal-Mart's Sights?" *AM Apparel Merchandising*, April 7, 2003; "Target: The Cool Factor Fizzles," *BusinessWeek*, February 24, 2003; "Marketer of the Year: On Target," *Advertising Age*, December 11, 2000.

10. For more on supercenters, see "Wal-Mart, the Category King," *DSN Retailing Today*, June 9, 2003; "Price War in Aisle 3," *Wall Street Journal*, May 27, 2003; "Supershoppers," *American Demographics*, May 2003; "Wal-Mart, Target Gain Supercenter Share," *Food Retailing Today*, February 24, 2003; "Supercenters Take Lead in Food Retailing," *Food Retailing Today*, May 6, 2002.

11. For more on warehouse clubs, see "Costco's Well-Off Customers Still Shopping," *Investor's Business Daily*, April 8, 2008; "Ruling Is Setback for Costco on Beer and Wine Sales," *Wall Street Journal*, January 30, 2008; "Costco Starts a Barroom Brawl," *BusinessWeek*, December 31, 2007; "Turning Shopping Trips into Treasure Hunts," *Wall Street Journal*, August 27, 2007; "The Tiger in Costco's Tank," *Fast Company*, July–August 1007; "Sam's Club Reaching Out for Non-Business Consumers," *USA Today*, November 22, 2006; "Why Costco Is So Damn Addictive," *Fortune*, October 30, 2006; "The Smart Way to Buy in Bulk," *Wall Street Journal*, March 4, 2006; "Warehouses Go Luxe," *Wall Street Journal*, November 11, 2005, p. B1ff; "Small Business Focus Pays Off for Sam's," *Food Retailing Today*, October 11, 2004; "Costco Wins Loyalty with Bulky Bargains," *USA Today*, September 24, 2004; "Rising Sales, Falling Prices: Wal-Mart and Warehouse Clubs Claim Bulk of Discounters' Revenue," *Investor's Business Daily*, September 13, 2004; "Costco: Retailer Sets Itself Apart from the Crowd," *Investor's Business Daily*, July 21, 2004; "The Only Company Wal-Mart Fears," *Fortune*, November 24, 2003.

12. For more on category killers, see "Big Boxes Aim to Speed Up Shopping," *Wall Street Journal*, June 27, 2007; "Big-Box Stores Squeeze into Big Apple: Home Depot, Others . . .," *USA Today*, October 19, 2004; "Office Depot Shifts Store Expansion to M2 Format," *DSN Retailing Today*, July 19, 2004, pp. 4, 21; "Toys 'R' Us: Taking the Family of Brands to New Heights," *DSN Retailing Today*, October 2003; "Category Killers Go from Lethal to Lame in the Space of a Decade," *Wall Street Journal*, March 9, 2000.

13. For more on 7-Eleven in the United States, see "Know What Customers Want," *Inc.*, August 2005; "7-Eleven Getting Boost from Wal-Mart's Rise," *Investor's Business Daily*, June 20, 2005; "Convenience Stores Change Gears," *USA Today*, June 13, 2005; "It's a Wrap: 7-Eleven Delivers Freshness," *DSN Retailing Today*, April 11, 2005; For more on 7-Eleven in Japan, see "From Convenience Store to Online Behemoth?" *BusinessWeek*, April 10, 2000; "Japan Goes Web Crazy," *Fortune*, February 7, 2000.

14. For more on vending and wireless, see "Soda? IPod? Vending Machines Diversity," *USA Today*, September 4, 2007; Self-Serve Movie Rental Kiosks a Surprise Hit with Consumers," *Investor's Business Daily*, May 31, 2007; "Buying an iPod from a Vending Machine," *Wall Street Journal*, September 1, 2005; "Getting Your Drugs from a Vending Machine," *Wall Street Journal*, June 21, 2005; "Want a Soda? Call the Machine," *Investor's Business Daily*, November 13, 2002; "Speedpass Use Shows Demand for Wireless Payments," *Investor's Business Daily*, April 19, 2002.

15. "Cutting the Stack of Catalogs," *BusinessWeek*, December 31, 2007; "This Isn't the Holiday Catalog You Remember," *Advertising Age*, October 29, 2007; "Catalogs, Catalogs, Everywhere," *Business-Week*, December 4, 2006; "New QVC Catalog Is a Beauty," *DM News*, September 19, 2005; "Catalog Sellers Also E-Tailers," *Investor's Business Daily*, September 12, 2005; "Mail Order Survives, Thrives," *Investor's Business Daily*, February 22, 2005; "Major Retailers to Stuff Mailboxes with Catalogs," *USA Today*, November 11, 2003; "New Page in E-Retailing: Catalogs," *Wall Street Journal*, November 30, 2000; "Catalogers Expand in Asia," *USA Today*, October 18, 1996. See also Charla Mathwick, Naresh K. Malhotra, and Edward Rigdon, "The Effect of Dynamic Retail Experiences on Experiential Perceptions of Value: An Internet and Catalog Comparison," *Journal of Retailing*, Spring 2002; C. R. Jasper and P. N. R. Lan, "Apparel Catalog Patronage: Demographic, Lifestyle, and Motivational Factors," *Psychology & Marketing*, July–August 1992.

16. "A Sales Channel They Can't Resist," *Business 2.0*, September 2005; "Getting Ready for Prime Time," *Inc.*, November 2003; "Is There a Future for the TV Mall?" *Brandweek*, March 25, 1996; "QVC Draws Wares from Everywhere," *USA Today*, November 1, 1994; "Battling for Buck$," *Profiles*, November 1994.

17. Chris Anderson, *The Long Tail* (New York: Hyperion, 2006); "The Long Tail," *Wired*, October 2004; Eri Brynjolfsson, Yu "Jeffrey" Hu, and Michael D. Smith, "From Niches to Riches: Anatomy of a Long Tail," *Sloan Management Review*, Summer 2006, p. 67.

18. "Ring Up E-Commerce Gains with a True Multichannel Strategy," *Advertising Age*, March 10, 2008; "Retailing: What's Working Online," *The McKinsey Quarterly*, (3) 2005; "Very Merry Holidays for Online Retailers," *Investor's Business Daily*, December 30, 2005; "Target Finds Way to Beat Wal-Mart: Online," *Advertising Age*, November 14, 2005; "Online Stores Keep Delivery Fees Low," *Wall Street Journal*, October 26, 2005; "Networks Hope Remote-Control Shopping Clicks," *USA Today*, May 25, 2005; "A Wider Net Catches Shoppers," *Investor's Business Daily*, May 24, 2005; "Target: FineTuning the Right Formula for Success," *DSN Retailing Today*, April 11, 2005; "E-Biz Strikes Again," *BusinessWeek*, May 10, 2004; Joel E. Collier and Carol C. Bienstock, "How Do Customers Judge Quality in an E-tailer?" *MIT Sloan Management Review*, Fall 2006; "Converting Web Site Visitors into Buyers: How Web Site Investment Increases Consumer Trusting Beliefs and Online Purchase Intentions," *Journal of Marketing*, April 2006; Yakov Bart, Venkatesh Shankar, Fareena Sultan, and Glen L. Urban, "Are the Drivers and Role of Online Trust the Same for All Web Sites and Consumers? A Large-Scale Exploratory Empirical Study," *Journal of Marketing*, October 2005; Fabio Ancarani and Venkates Shankar, "Price Levels and Price Dispersion Within and Across Multiple Retailer Types: Further Evidence and Extension," *Journal of the Academy of Marketing Science*, Spring 2004; Michael Lewis, "The Effect of Shipping Fees on Customer Acquisition, Customer Retention, and Purchase Quantities," *Journal of Retailing*, March 2006; Manjit S. Yadav and P. Rajan Varadarajan, "Understanding Product Migration to the Electronic Marketplace: A Conceptual Framework," *Journal of Retailing*, 2005; Heiner Evanschitzkya, Gopalkrishnan R. Iyer, Josef Hessea, and Dieter Ahlerta, "E-Satisfaction: A Re-Examination," *Journal of Retailing*, Fall 2004; Khai Sheang Lee and Soo Jiuan Tan, "E-Retailing versus Physical Retailing: A Theoretical Model and Empirical Test of Consumer Choice," *Journal of Business Research*, November 2003.

19. Chip E. Miller, "The Effects of Competition on Retail Structure: an Examination of Intratype, Intertype, and Intercategory Competition," *Journal of Marketing*, October 1999; "New Options for Saving at the Pump," *Wall Street Journal*, August 16, 2005; "Your New Banker?" *BusinessWeek*, February 7, 2005; "Snak 'n' Shop," *Wall Street Journal*, July 13, 2004; "A Quart of Milk, a Dozen Eggs, and a 2.6-GHz Laptop," *Business 2.0*, October 2003; "Jordan's Puts Imax in Its Furniture Picture," *Wall Street Journal*, October 4, 2002; "Latest Supermarket Special—Gasoline," *Wall Street Journal*, April 30, 2001; "Levi's Doesn't Fancy Selling with Cukes," *Wall Street Journal*, April 10, 2001; "Barnes & Noble Finds Grinch Effect in Games Strategy," *Wall Street Journal*, December 20, 2000; "Savoring Chocolate," *Advertising Age*, September 4, 2000; "In Aisle 10, Soup, Tea—and Bikinis?" *Wall Street Journal*, June 28, 2000; Jack M. Cadeaux, "Industry Product Volatility and Retailer Assortments," *Journal of Macromarketing*, Fall 1992; Ronald Savitt, "The 'Wheel of Retailing' and Retail Product Management," *European Journal of Marketing* 18, no. 6/7 (1984).

20. "How Did Sears Blow This Gasket?" *BusinessWeek*, June 29, 1992; "An Open Letter to Sears Customers," *USA Today*, June 25, 1992. See also John Paul Fraedrich, "The Ethical Behavior of Retail Managers," *Journal of Business Ethics*, March 1993.

21. "What Price Virtue? At Some Retailers, 'Fair Trade' Carries a Very High Cost," *Wall Street Journal*, June 8, 2004.

22. See www.census.gov; U.S. Bureau of the Census, "Table 1: Sales Size of Establishments for the United States: 2002," *2002 Economic Census Retail Trade, Subject Series, Establishment and Firm Size*; "Retailers Grab Power, Control Marketplace," *Marketing News*, January 16, 1989. See also Kusum L. Ailawadi, "The Retail Power Performance Conundrum: What Have We Learned?" *Journal of Retailing*, Fall 2001; Dale D. Achabal, John M. Heineke, and Shelby H. McIntyre, "Issues and Perspectives on Retail Productivity," *Journal of Retailing*, Fall 1984; Charles A. Ingene, "Scale Economies in American Retailing: A Cross-Industry Comparison," *Journal of Macromarketing* 4, no. 2 (1984).

23. For an excellent example of AutoZone as successful chain, see "Rallying the Troops to Get Back in the Profit Zone," *DSN Retailing Today*, September 6, 2004; "An Auto-Parts Store Your Mother Could Love," *Fortune*, November 10, 2003; "Auto Accessories Still in the Fast Lane," *DSN Retailing Today*, May 5, 2003; "AutoZone: The Hottest Growth Concept in Retailing," *DSN Retailing Today*, November 11, 2002; "In Corporate America It's Clean Up Time," *Fortune*, September 16, 2002. See also "European Inns Take the Hilton Route," *Wall Street Journal*, April 23, 2001; "Forging Ahead with Custom Contracts," *Foodservice Equipment & Supplies Specialist*, June 1994; "CLOUT! More and More, Retail Giants Rule the Marketplace," *BusinessWeek*, December 21, 1992. See also Gary K. Rhoads, William R. Swinyard, Michael D. Geurts, and William D. Price, "Retailing as a Career: A Comparative Study of Marketers," *Journal of Retailing*, Spring 2002; Marilyn Lavin, 'Not in My Neighborhood': Resistance to Chain Drugstores," *International Journal of Retail & Distribution Management*, (6) 2003.

24. "Do You Have What It Takes? *Wall Street Journal Reports*, September 19, 2005; "How to Grow a Chain That's Already Everywhere," *Business 2.0*, March 2005; "When Franchisees Lose Part of Their Independence," *The New York Times*, February 3, 2005. See also Surinder Tikoo, "Franchiser Influence Strategy Use and Franchisee Experience and Dependence," *Journal of Retailing*, Fall 2002; Patrick J. Kaufmann and Rajiv P. Dant, "The Pricing of Franchise Rights," *Journal of Retailing*, Winter 2001; Madhav Pappu and David Strutton, "Toward an Understanding of Strategic Inter-Organizational Relationships in Franchise Channels," *Journal of Marketing Channels*, (1,2) 2001; Rajiv P. Dant and Patrick J. Kaufmann, "Structural and Strategic Dynamics in Franchising," *Journal of Retailing*, (2) 2003; Robert Dahlstrom, "Franchising: Contemporary Issues and Research," *Journal of Public Policy & Marketing*, Spring 1996.

25. "How China Eats a Sandwich: Opening Subway Franchises . . .," *Fortune*, March 21, 2005, pp. F210B-D; "Tesco: California Dreaming?" *BusinessWeek*, February 27, 2006; "Tesco Jumps the Pond," *Wall Street Journal*, February 10, 2006; "China's New Entrepreneurs: McDonald's and KFC Race to Recruit More Franchisees . . .," *Wall Street Journal*, January 25, 2005; "China: Let the Retail Wars Begin," *BusinessWeek*, January 17, 2005; "Carrefour Chief Gets Ultimatum," *Wall Street Journal*, July 9, 2004; "Global Retailing," *DSN Retailing Today*, July 5, 2004; "Bare-Bones Shopping ... Germany," *Wall Street Journal Reports*, May 10, 2004; "The Next Wal-Mart?" *BusinessWeek*, April 26, 2004; "China's Rush to Convenience," *Wall Street Journal*, November 3, 2003; "Making the Cuts," *Wall Street Journal Reports*, September 22, 2003; "Big German Retailer Metro AG Brings Superstores to Vietnam," *Wall Street Journal*, August 13, 2002; "Western Stores Woo Chinese Wallets," *Wall Street Journal*, November 26, 2002; "To Russia, with Love: The Multinationals' Song," *BusinessWeek*, September 16, 2002; "U.S. Superstores Find Japanese Are a Hard Sell," *Wall Street Journal*, February 14, 2000. See also Valerie Severin, Jordan J. Louviere, and Adam Finn, "The Stability of Retail Shopping Choices over Time and Across Countries," *Journal of Retailing*, Summer 2001; Jozefina Simova, Colin M. Clarke-Hill, and Terry Robinson, "A Longitudinal Study of Changes in Retail Formats and Merchandise Assortment in Clothing Retailing in the Czech Republic in the Period 1994–1999," *International Journal of Retail & Distribution Management*, (6) 2003; Arieh Goldman, "The Transfer of Retail Formats into Developing Economies: the Example of China," *Journal of Retailing*, Summer 2001; Nicholas Alexander and Marcelo de Lira e Silva "Emerging Markets and the Internationalisation of Retailing: the Brazilian Experience," *International Journal of Retail & Distribution Management*, (6) 2002.

26. "Wal-Mart: Looking Overseas for Growth," *CNNMoney.com*, October 24, 2007; "A Dollar Store's Rich Allure in India," *Wall Street Journal*, January 23, 2007; "Wal-Mart: Struggling in Germany," *BusinessWeek*, April 11, 2005; "Japan Isn't Buying The Wal-Mart Idea," *BusinessWeek*, February 28, 2005.

27. See www.friedas.com; "How Lower-Tech Gear Beat Web 'Exchanges' at Their Own Game," *Wall Street Journal*, March 16, 2001; "Family Firms Confront Calamities of Transfer," *USA Today*, August 29, 2000; "Business, Too Close to Home," *Time*, July 17, 2000; "The Kiwi to My Success," *Hemispheres*, July 1999; "Searching for the Next Kiwi: Frieda's Branded Produce," *Brandweek*, May 2, 1994; "Strange Fruits," *Inc.*, November 1989; "The Produce Marketer," *Savvy*, June 1988.

28. "Why the Web Can't Kill the Middleman," *Ecompany*, April 2001; "Not Dead Yet," *Inc. Tech*, (1), 2001; "Electronics Distributors Are Reporting Record Profits," *Wall Street Journal*, July 13, 2000; "Chow (On)Line," *BusinessWeek E.Biz*, June 5, 2000; "Why Online Distributors—Once Written Off—May Thrive," *Fortune*, September 6, 1999. See also Susan Mudambi and Raj Aggarwal, "Industrial Distributors: Can They Survive in the New Economy?" *Industrial Marketing Management*, May 2003; Das Narayandas, Mary Caravella, and John Deighton, "The Impact of Internet Exchanges on Business-to-Business Distribution," *Journal of the Academy of Marketing Science*, Fall 2002; Amrik S. Sohal, Damien J. Power, and Mile Terziovski, "Integrated Supply Chain Management from the Wholesaler's Perspective: Two Australian Case Studies," *International Journal of Physical Distribution & Logistics Management*, (1) 2002.

29. "Cold War: Amana Refrigeration Fights Tiny Distributor," *Wall Street Journal*, February 26, 1992. For another example, see "Quickie-Divorce Curbs Sought By Manufacturers' Distributors," *Wall Street Journal*, July 13, 1987; "Merger of Two Bakers Teaches Distributors a Costly Lesson (3 parts)," *Wall Street Journal*, September 14, 1987; October 19, 1987; November 11, 1987.

30. See www.census.gov; U.S. Bureau of the Census, "Table 1a: Summary Statistics for the United States: 2002," *2002 Economic Census Wholesale Trade, Geographic Area Series, United States* (Washington, DC: U.S. Government Printing Office, 2005).

31. See www.fastenal.com; "Fastenal: Need to Fix Up a Building? This Firm's Got Your One-Stop Shop," *Investor's Business Daily*, November 28, 2005; "Fastenal: In This Sluggish Market, You Gotta Have Faith," *Investor's Business Daily*, August 13, 2001.

32. "Revolution in Japanese Retailing," *Fortune*, February 7, 1994; Arieh Goldman, "Evaluating the Performance of the Japanese Distribution System," *Journal of Retailing*, Spring 1992; "Japan Begins to Open the Door to Foreigners, a Little," *Brandweek*, August 2, 1993.

33. See www.rell.com; "Richardson Electronics Ltd.: Maker of Ancient Tech Finds a Way to Prosper," *Investor's Business Daily*, June 27, 2000; *2005 Richardson Electronics*.

34. See www.inmac.com and www.grainger.com; "B2B: Yesterday's Darling," *Wall Street Journal*, October 23, 2000; "W.W. Grainger's Web Investments: Money Well Spent? Don't Ask Street," *Investor's Business Daily*, September 19, 2000.

35. For more on manufacturers' agents being squeezed, see "Philips to End Long Relations with North American Reps—Will Build Internal Sales Force Instead," *EBN*, November 10, 2003; "Wal-Mart Draws Fire: Reps, Brokers Protest Being Shut Out by New Policy," *Advertising Age*, January 13, 1992. For more discussion on wholesaling abroad, see "Japan Rises to P&G's No. 3 Market," *Advertising Age*, December 10, 1990; "Papa-Mama Stores in Japan Wield Power to Hold Back Imports," *Wall Street Journal*, November 14, 1988. See also Daniel C. Bello and Ritu Lohtia, "The Export Channel Design: The Use of Foreign Distributors and Agents," *Journal of the Academy of Marketing Science*, Spring 1995; D. Steven White, "Behind the Success and Failure of U.S. Export Intermediaries: Transactions, Agents and Resources," *Journal of the Academy of Marketing Science*, Summer 2001.

36. "Will That Be Cash, Credit—or Fingertip?" *USA Today*, December 2, 2005; "A Speedier Superstore," *Business 2.0*, December 2005; "Putting a Finger on Biometrics," *Convenience Store Decisions*, August 2005; "The Grocery Store of the Future," *Business 2.0*, March 2005; "The World of Business in 2020," *Business 2.0*, April 2004; "Delivering the Goods," *Wall Street Journal Reports*, February 11, 2002; "What's Ahead for Retailing," *Wall Street Journal*, June 25, 2001; "Digital ID Cards," *Wall Street Journal*, June 25, 2001; See also Enrico Colla, "International Expansion and Strategies of Discount Grocery Retailers: The Winning Models," *International Journal of Retail & Distribution Management*, (1) 2003; Robert A. Peterson and Sridhar Balasubramanian, "Retailing in the 21st Century: Reflections and Prologue to Research," *Journal of Retailing*, Spring 2002; Elliot Rabinovich and Philip T. Evers, "Product Fulfillment in Supply Chains Supporting Internet-Retailing Operations," *Journal of Business Logistics*, (2) 2003; *International Journal of Physical Distribution & Logistics Management*, (9) 2001; Stacy L. Wood, "Future Fantasies: a Social Change Perspective of Retailing in the 21st Century," *Journal of Retailing*, Spring 2002.

CHAPTER 13

1. See www.geico.com; "Umbrella Coverage for Preventing Your Ruin," *The New York Times*, March 18, 2008; "Clan of the Caveman," *Fast Company*, December 19, 2007; "Geico," *Advertising Age*, October 15, 2007; "Leapin' Lizards," *Brandweek*, October 8, 2007; "Cavemen (TV Series)," *Wikipedia*, April 21, 2007; "Will the Cavemen's Evolution Boost Geico? *Fortune*, April 2, 2007; "The Caveman: Evolution of a Character," *Adweek*, March 12, 2007; "Trio of TV Ad Campaigns Succeeds in Wooing Different Target Audience," *Television Week*, March 12, 2007; "How a Gecko Shook Up Insurance Ads," *Wall Street Journal*, January 2, 2007; "When Geckos Aren't Enough," *BusinessWeek*, October 16, 2006; "10 Breakaway Brands," *Fortune*, September 8, 2006; "Loving the Lizard," *Adweek*, October 24, 2005; "Buffet Wants to Know: Do Geico Ads Get Job Done?" *USA Today*, January 24, 2005.

2. "How Southwest Airlines Sold $1.5 Million in Tickets by Posting Four Press Releases Online," *Marketing Sherpa*, October 27, 2004.

3. "Old-Fashioned PR Gives General Mills Advertising Bargains," *Wall Street Journal*, March 20, 1997. See also "Helping Dating Sites Stand Out in Crowds: Matchmaker Learns to Attract Tons of Publicity," *Investor's Business Daily*, April 21, 2008; "The Benefits of Plugging a Big Company's Products," *Wall Street Journal*, May 8, 2007; "How a Small Boutique Gets $25 Moccasins on Celebrities' Feet," *Wall Street Journal*, November 19, 2004; "Aflac Duck's Paddle to Stardom: Creativity on the Cheap," *Wall Street Journal*, July 30, 2004; Siva K. Balasubramanian, "Beyond Advertising and Publicity: Hybrid Messages and Public Policy Issues," *Journal of Advertising*, December 1994; Thomas H. Bivins, "Ethical Implications of the Relationship of Purpose to Role and Function in Public Relations," *Journal of Business Ethics*, January 1989.

4. "President's Tumble Off a Segway Seems a Tiny Bit Suspicious," *USA Today*, June 18, 2003; "Watch Your Step: Segways Ahead," *USA Today*, June 17, 2003.

5. "MarketingSherpa's Viral Marketing Hall of Fame 2007: Top 10 Efforts to Inspire You," *MarketingSherpa.com*, April 25, 2007.

6. For an example of integrated campaign, see "Tylenol Hits the Gym for Launch," *Advertising Age*, May 26, 2003. See also David A. Griffith, Aruna Chandra, and John K. Ryans, Jr. "Examining the Intricacies of Promotion Standardization: Factors Influencing Advertising Message and Packaging," *Journal of International Marketing*, (3) 2003; Kim Bartel Sheehan and Caitlin Doherty, "Re-Weaving the Web: Integrating Print and Online Communications," *Journal of Interactive Marketing*, Spring 2001; Kathleen J. Kelly, "Integrated Marketing Communication: Putting It Together & Making It Work," *Journal of the Academy of Marketing Science*, Winter 1997.

7. "Reckitt Thrives in an Unloved Niche," *Wall Street Journal*, May 24, 2005.

8. "In a Shift, Marketers Beef Up Ad Spending Inside Stores," *Wall Street Journal*, September 21, 2005.

9. "Wi-Fis, PDAs, Blogs, Smart Phones, PVRs, Hmm . . . Overload?" *Investor's Business Daily*, November 7, 2005; "Survey Shows Consumers Befuddled by Technology," *Advertising Age*, July 12, 2004; "Ever Heard of a DVD Recorder? Many Americans Haven't, a New Survey Shows," *Investor's Business Daily*, May 4, 2004; "High-Tech Branding: Pushing Digital PCS," *Brandweek*, August 4, 1997; "Brand Builders: Delivery Guy Chic," *Brandweek*, June 30, 1997; "Eye-Catching Logos All Too Often Leave Fuzzy Images in Minds of Consumers," *Wall Street Journal*, December 5, 1991. See also George S. Low and Jakki J. Mohr, "Factors Affecting the Use of Information in the Evaluation of Marketing Communications Productivity," *Journal of the Academy of Marketing Science*, Winter 2001; David I. Gilliland and Wesley J. Johnston, "Toward a Model of Business-to-Business Marketing Communications Effects," *Industrial Marketing Management*, January 1997; Louisa Ha and Barry R. Litman, "Does Advertising Clutter Have Diminishing and Negative Returns?" *Journal of Advertising*, Spring 1997; Barbara B. Stern, "A Revised Communication Model for Advertising: Multiple Dimensions of the Source, the Message, and the Recipient," *Journal of Advertising*, June 1994.

10. "Capturing a Piece of the Global Market," *Brandweek*, June 20, 2005; "Global Branding: Same, But Different," *Brandweek*, April 9, 2001; "When You Translate 'Got Milk' for Latinos, What Do You Get?" *Wall Street Journal*, June 3, 1999; "Cash, Cache, Cachet: All 3 Seem to Matter When You Buy a PC," *Wall Street Journal*, December 18, 1998; "Hey, #!@*% Amigo, Can You Translate the Word 'Gaffe'?" *Wall Street Journal*, July 8, 1996; "Lost in Translation: How to 'Empower Women' in Chinese," *Wall Street Journal*, September 13, 1994.

11. For more on video publicity releases, see "The Corruption of TV Health News," *BusinessWeek*, February 28, 2000; "Collagen Corp.'s Video Uses News Format," *Wall Street Journal*," March 29, 1994; Thomas H. Bivins, "Public Relations, Professionalism, and the Public Interest," *Journal of Business Ethics*, February 1993; Siva K. Balasubramanian, "Beyond Advertising and Publicity: Hybrid Messages and Public Policy Issues," *Journal of Advertising*, December 1994. For more on celebrity endorsements, see "Yao Gives Reebok an Assist in China," *Wall Street Journal*, September 28, 2007; "Queen of the Product Pitch: Martha Stewart . . . ," *BusinessWeek*, April 30, 2007; "Culture of Celebrity," *Advertising Age*, February 20, 2006; "Nike Relaunches Kobe Bryant after Two Years of Prep Work," *Wall Street Journal*, November 11, 2005; "Michelle Wie Wins a Deal Helping Nike Target Women Golfers," *Wall Street Journal*, October 5, 2005; "Playing the Hip-Hop Name Drop," *Brandweek*, July 25, 2005; "Athletes on the Outs in Ads," *USA Today*, July 5, 2005; "Nascar Courts Minorities," *Wall Street Journal*, March 3, 2005; "Wow! Yao!" *BusinessWeek*, October 25, 2004; "Dale Jr. Zooms to Front of Pack in Endorsements," *USA Today*, February 13, 2004. See also Therese A. Louie and Carl Obermiller, "Consumer Response to a Firm's Endorser (Dis)association Decisions," *Journal of Advertising*, Winter 2002; Marla Royne Stafford, Thomas F. Stafford, and Ellen Day, "A Contingency Approach: the Effects of Spokesperson Type and Service Type on Service Advertising Perceptions," *Journal of Advertising*, Summer 2002; Dwane Hal Dean and Abhijit Biswas, "Third Party Organization Endorsement of Products: an Advertising Cue Affecting Consumer Prepurchase Evaluation of Goods and Services," *Journal of Advertising*, Winter 2001; Ronald E. Goldsmith, Barbara A. Lafferty, and Stephen J. Newell, "The Impact of Corporate Credibility and Celebrity Credibility on Consumer Reaction to Advertisements and Brands," *Journal of Advertising*, Fall 2000.

12. "Depending on Direct: Discipline Grows to $161B," *Advertising Age*, October 24, 2005; "Direct Gets Respect: Budgets Swell as Marketers Seek Accountability," *Advertising Age*, August 30, 2004, pp. 1, 21; "Direct Marketing," *BtoB*, October 13, 2003; "DMA Benchmarks Response Rates," *BtoB*, July 14, 2003; "Direct Marketing Gets Cannes Do Spirit," *USA Today*, June 17, 2002; "Escalade Got Game," *Advertising Age*, June 11, 2001. For an electronic direct mail example, see "Web Slice," *Brandweek*, May 26, 1997. See also Sally J. McMillan and Jang-Sun Hwang, "Measures of Perceived Interactivity: an Exploration of the Role of Direction of Communication, User Control, and Time in Shaping Perceptions of Interactivity," *Journal of Advertising*, Fall 2002; Carrie M. Heilman, Frederick Kaefer, and Samuel D. Ramenofsky, "Determining the Appropriate Amount of Data for Classifying Consumers for Direct Marketing Purposes," *Journal of Interactive Marketing*, Summer 2003; Mark J. Arnold and Shelley R. Tapp, "The Effects of Direct Marketing Techniques on Performance: an Application to Arts Organizations," *Journal of Interactive Marketing*, Summer 2001; Patrick Barwise and Colin Strong, "Permission-Based Mobile Advertising," *Journal of Interactive Marketing*, Winter 2002; Charles R. Taylor, George R. Franke, and Michael L. Maynard, "Attitudes Toward Direct Marketing and its Regulation: a Comparison of the United States and Japan," *Journal of Public Policy & Marketing*, Fall 2000.

13. "Behind-the-Scenes Discoveries from HP's Email Segmentation Tests," *Marketing Sherpa*, September 29, 2005; "Personal Touch Opens Up Hewlett-Packard's Portal Strategy," *inside 1to1*, July 11, 2005; "HP Continues Cost Savings with Vertical E-Newsletters," *BtoB*, July 1, 2004.

14. "54% of Permission E-mailers Are Filtered as Spammers: Including AOL News, Wal-Mart, IBM, and the Feds," *Marketing Sherpa*, June 9, 2005.

15. For more on privacy, see Chapter 18, endnote 12. For more on regulation of spam, junk mail, and telemarketing calls, see "Paper War," *Time*, January 2006; "Record Fine Levied against Telemarketer," *Wall Street Journal*, December 14, 2005; "Splogs Roil Web, and Some Blame Google," *Wall Street Journal*, October 19, 2005; "A New Battle over No-Call Lists," *Wall Street Journal*, September 28, 2005; "Silence of the Spams," *Brandweek*, October 20, 2003; "America Hangs Up on Telemarketers," *Fortune*, October 13, 2003; "FTC Told to Enforce

Do-Not-Call List," *USA Today*, October 8, 2003; "A Stab at Stemming Spam," *BusinessWeek*, October 6, 2003; "The Do-Not-Call Law Won't Stop the Calls," *BusinessWeek*, September 29, 2003; Keith Anderson, "The Costs and Benefits of Do-Not-Call Regulations: A Comment on Beard and Abernethy's 'Consumer Prices and the Federal Trade Commision's 'Do-Not Call' Program," *Journal of Public Policy & Marketing*, T. Randolph Beard and Avery M. Abernethy, "Costs and Benefits of the Federal Trade Commission's Do-Not-Call Regulations: A Second Look and Reply to Anderson," *Journal of Public Policy & Marketing*, Spring 2007.

16. "Web Stores Tap Product Reviews," *Wall Street Journal*, September 11, 2007; "Look Who's Talking," *Wall Street Journal*, June 25, 2007; James C. Ward and Amy L. Ostrom, "Complaining to the Masses: The Role of Protest Framing in Customer-Created Complaint Web Sites," *Journal of Consumer Research*, August 2006; Shahana Sen and Dawn Lerman, "Why Are You Telling Me This? An Examination into Negative Consumer Reviews on the Web," *Journal of Interactive Marketing*, Fall 2007; V. Kumar, J. Andrew Petersen and Robert P. Leone, "How Valuable Is Word of Mouth?" *Harvard Business Review*, October 2007.

17. Monica Perry and Charles D. Bodkin, "Fortune 500 Manufacturer Websites: Innovative Marketing Strategies or Cyberbrochures?" *Industrial Marketing Management*, February 2002; Nicole Coviello, Roger Milley, and Barbara Marcolin, "Understanding IT-Enabled Interactivity in Contemporary Marketing," *Journal of Interactive Marketing*, Autumn 2001; Donna L. Hoffman and Thomas P. Novak, "Marketing in Hypermedia Computer-Mediated Environments: Conceptual Foundations," *Journal of Marketing*, July 1996.

18. For more on direct-to-consumer drug advertising, see "Under Scrutiny, Drug Makers Rethink Ad Campaigns," *Investor's Business Daily*, October 24, 2005; "Being Bold at Bristol-Myers Squibb," *Point*, October 2005; "PR Seems to Be the Rx to Get Around DTC Rules," *Advertising Age*, September 26, 2005; "Big Pharma Finds Way into Doctors' Pockets," *Advertising Age*, September 19, 2005; "Drugmakers Are Changing Channels," *BusinessWeek*, August 15, 2005; "FDA to Review Drug Marketing to Consumers," *Wall Street Journal*, August 2, 2005; "Direct-to-Consumer Advertising Takes Direct Hit from FDA," *Investor's Business Daily*, May 31, 2005. See also Steven W. Kopp and Mary J. Sheffet, "The Effect of Direct-to-Consumer Advertising of Prescription Drugs on Retail Gross Margins: Empirical Evidence and Public Policy Implications," *Journal of Public Policy & Marketing*, Fall 1997.

19. "Decker Scores with Sweepstakes to Promote Days Inn," *USA Today*, November 6, 1997; "Biore: The Nose Knew at Lilith Fair," *Brandweek*, September 15, 1997; "Brand Builders: Progresso Warriors," *Brandweek*, June 23, 1997; "Advertisers Often Cheer the Loudest," *USA Today*, March 27, 1997; "Crossing the Border," *Brandweek*, December 16, 1996.

20. "The New B-to-B Fundamentals," *Target Marketing*, October 2003, at www.targetonline.com; "The Changing Face of B-to-B Sales & Marketing," October 20, 2003, http://news.thomasnet.com/IMT/archives/.

21. "Blogs in Business," *Marketing* (UK), March 1, 2006, pp. 35–36; "The Blog in the Corporate Machine," *Economist*, February 11, 2006; "When Blogs Go Bad," *Inc.*, November 2005; "Slowly, Marketers Learn How to Let Go and Let Blog: Losing Some Control of the Brand Starts to Pay Off," *Advertising Age*, October 31, 2005; "Get Connected: Leverage Blogs as Biz Tool," *Marketing News*, September 1, 2005; "Blogging Becomes a Corporate Job: Digital 'Handshake'?" *Wall Street Journal*, May 31, 2005; "Six Tips for Corporate Bloggers," *BusinessWeek Online*, May 2, 2005. See also Huang Chun-Yao, Shen Yong-Zheng, Lin Hong-Xiang, and Chang Shin-Shin, "Bloggers' Motivations and Behaviors: A Model," *Journal of Advertising Research*, December 2007.

22. *Retail Customer Dissatisfaction Study—2006*, Verde Group—Baker Retail Initiative at Wharton, 2006.

23. For more on BzzAgent, see "BzzAgent Seeks to Turn Word of Mouth into a Saleable Medium," *Advertising Age*, February 13, 2006; "Small Firms Turn to Marketing Buzz Agents," *Wall Street Journal*, December 27, 2005. For more on opinion leaders, word-of-mouth publicity, and buzz marketing, see Chapter 5, endnote 21. See also "In China, Add a Caterpillar to the Dog and Pony Show," *Wall Street Journal*, December 10, 2007; "Talk Is Cheap," *Wall Street Journal*, November 26, 2007; "Threadless: From Clicks to Bricks," *BusinessWeek*, November 26, 2007; "Nescafe Brews Buzz via Blogs," *Wall Street Journal*, November 23, 2007; "Word-of-Mouth Worth $1 Billion," *Advertising Age*, November 19, 2007; "You've Played the Videogame, Now Buy the Car," *Wall Street Journal*, October 24, 2007; "GM Floods Net with Malibu Ads," *USA Today*, October 22, 2007; "Fad Marketing's Balancing Act," *BusinessWeek*, August 6, 2007; "Word of Mouth Helps Guard Grain," *USA Today*, July 5, 2007; "The Wizards of Buzz," *Wall Street Journal*, February 10, 2007; "Cold Stone Aims to Be Hip in Japan," *Wall Street Journal*, December 14, 2006; "Selling TV Like Tupperware," *Wall Street Journal*, June 29, 2006; "I Sold It Through the Grapevine," *BusinessWeek*, May 29, 2006; "Word Games," *Brandweek*, April 24, 2006; "BzzAgent Seeks to Turn Word of Mouth into a Saleable Medium," *Advertising Age*, February 13, 2006; "Rules of the Game," *Point*, December 2005; "Buzz Tactics …: Play to Passions of Adults, Use Events, Experts Urge," *Advertising Age*, November 28, 2005; "Leader of the Packs," *BusinessWeek*, October 31, 2005; "What's in a Word?" *Brandweek*, October 24, 2005; "Mitsubishi Zips Past the Scrap Heap," *BusinessWeek*, October 24, 2005; "What's the Buzz? If You're Smart, It's about Your Product," *USA Today*, July 25, 2005; "From a Whisper to a Scream," *Investor's Business Daily*, June 13, 2005; "Word-of-Mouth Marketing Gets People Buzzing," *BtoB*, June 13, 2005; "Word on the Street," *Adweek*, May 16, 2005; "Marketers of the Next Generation: Microsoft's Gamer Shrouded Halo 2 …," *Brandweek*, April 11, 2005; "Getting Buzz Marketers to Fess Up," *Wall Street Journal*, February 9, 2005; "Clif Bar's Solo Climb," *Business 2.0*, December 2004; "Tall Tales," *Adweek*, October 11, 2004, pp. 28–29, 34; "The Rebirth of Cool," *Business 2.0*, September 2004. "Buzz Giant Poster Boy," *American Demographics*, June 2004. See also De Liu, Xianjun Geng, and Andrew B. Whinston, "Optimal Design of Consumer Contests," *Journal of Marketing*, October 2007; Kelly D. Martin and N. Craig Smith, "Commercializing Social Interaction: The Ethics of Stealth Marketing," *Journal of Public Policy & Marketing*, Spring 2008; George R. Milne, Shalini Bahl, and Andrew Rohm, "Toward a Framework for Assessing Covert Marketing Practices," *Journal of Public Policy & Marketing*, Spring 2008; Aviv Shoham and Ayalla Ruvio, "Opinion Leaders and Followers: A Replication and Extension," *Psychology & Marketing*, March 2008; Jyh-Shen Chiou and Cathy Cheng, "Should a Company Have Message Boards on its Web Sites?" *Journal of Interactive Marketing*, Summer 2003; Raji Srinivasan, Gary L. Lilien, and Arvind Rangaswamy, "Technological Opportunism and Radical Technology Adoption: an Application to E-Business," *Journal of Marketing*, July 2002; Suman Basuroy, Subimal Chatterjee, and S. Abraham Ravid, "How Critical Are Critical Reviews? The Box Office Effects of Film Critics, Star Power, and Budgets," *Journal of Marketing*, October 2003; Jeffrey G. Blodgett, Donald H. Granbois, and Rockney G. Walters, "The Effects of Perceived Justice on Complainants' Negative Word-of-Mouth Behavior and Repatronage Intentions," *Journal of Retailing*, Winter 1993; Paula Fitzgerald Bone, "Word-of-Mouth Effects on Short-Term and Long-Term Product Judgments," *Journal of Business Research*, March 1995.

24. Hokey Min and William P. Galle, "E-Purchasing: Profiles of Adopters and Nonadopters," *Industrial Marketing Management*, April 2003; Yikuan Lee and Gina Colarelli O'Connor, "The Impact of Communication Strategy on Launching New Products: the Moderating Role of Product Innovativeness," *Journal of Product Innovation Management*, January 2003; David R. Fell, Eric N. Hansen, and Boris W. Becker, "Measuring Innovativeness for the Adoption of Industrial Products," *Industrial Marketing Management*, May 2003; Subin Im, Barry L. Bayus, and Charlotte H. Mason, "An Empirical Study of Innate Consumer Innovativeness, Personal Characteristics, and New-Product Adoption Behavior," *Journal of the Academy of Marketing Science,* Winter 2003; Eric Waarts, Yvonne M. van Everdingen, and Jos van Hillegersberg, "The Dynamics of Factors Affecting the Adoption of Innovations," *Journal of Product Innovation Management,* November 2002; S. Ram and Hyung-Shik Jung, "Innovativeness in Product Usage: A Comparison of Early Adopters and Early Majority," *Psychology & Marketing,* January–February 1994; Robert J. Fisher and Linda L. Price, "An Investigation into the Social Context of Early Adoption Behavior," *Journal of Consumer Research,* December 1992; Everett M. Rogers and F. Floyd Shoemaker, *Communication of Innovations: A Cross-Cultural Approach* (New York: Free Press, 1971).

25. "All-in-One Dinner Kits Gain Popularity," *Food Retailing Today,* May 5, 2003; "Marketers of the Year: This One's a Stove Topper," *Brandweek,* October 14, 2002.

26. Kusum L. Ailawadi, Paul W. Farris, and Mark E. Parry, "Share and Growth Are Not Good Predictors of the Advertising and Promotion/Sales Ratio," *Journal of Marketing,* January 1994.

27. Kissan Joseph and Vernon J. Richardson, "Free Cash Flow, Agency Costs, and the Affordability Method of Advertising Budgeting," *Journal of Marketing,* January 2002; John A. Weber, "Managing the Marketing Budget in a Cost-Constrained Environment," *Industrial Marketing Management,* November 2002; Deborah Utter, "Marketing on a Budget," *Journal of the Academy of Marketing Science,* Summer 2000; Kim P. Corfman and Donald R. Lehmann, "The Prisoner's Dilemma and the Role of Information in Setting Advertising Budgets," *Journal of Advertising,* June 1994; C. L. Hung and Douglas West, "Advertising Budgeting Methods in Canada, the UK and the USA," *International Journal of Advertising* 10, no. 3 (1991); Pierre Filiatrault and Jean-Charles Chebat, "How Service Firms Set Their Marketing Budgets," *Industrial Marketing Management,* February 1990; James E. Lynch and Graham J. Hooley, "Industrial Advertising Budget Approaches in the U.K.," *Industrial Marketing Management* 18, no. 4 (1989); Douglas J. Dalrymple and Hans B. Thorelli, "Sales Force Budgeting," *Business Horizons,* July–August 1984; Peter J. Danaher and Roland T. Rust, "Determining the Optimal Level of Media Spending," *Journal of Advertising Research,* January–February 1994.

CHAPTER 14

1. Based on author interviews with Ferguson management. See also www.ferguson.com; "Customer Focused," *US Business Review,* May 2005.

2. "Where Yellow's a Faux Pas and White Is Death," *Wall Street Journal,* December 6, 2007; "Doing Business Abroad? Simple Faux Pas Can Sink You," *USA Today,* August 24, 2007; "The Samurai Sell: Lexus Dealers Bow to Move Swank Cars," *Wall Street Journal,* July 9, 2007; "Teaching Americans How to Behave Abroad," *Wall Street Journal,* April 11, 2006; "Why the Chinese Hate to Use Voice Mail," *Wall Street Journal,* December 1, 2005; "Mind Your Manners," *Inc.,* September 2005; "Avoid Costly Missteps in Overseas Business," *Investor's Business Daily,* June 27, 2005; "The Seoul Answer to Selling," *Going Global* (supplement to *Inc.*), March 1994; "AIG Sells Insurance in Shanghai, Testing Service Firms' Role," *Wall Street Journal,* July 21, 1993; "Hungarians Seeking to Find a New Way Find Instead Amway," *Wall Street Journal,* January 15, 1993; Paul A. Herbig and Hugh E. Kramer, "Do's and Don'ts of Cross-Cultural Negotiations," *Industrial Marketing Management,* November 1992; Alan J. Dubinsky et al., "Differences in Motivational Perceptions among U.S., Japanese, and Korean Sales Personnel," *Journal of Business Research,* June 1994; Carl R. Ruthstrom and Ken Matejka, "The Meanings of 'YES' in the Far East," *Industrial Marketing Management,* August 1990.

3. "Shhh!" *Forbes,* November 24, 2003; "Deliver More Value to Earn Loyalty," *Selling,* May 2003; "Hush: Improving NVH through Improved Material," *Automotive Design and Production,* July 2003.

4. Andris A. Zoltners, Prabhakant Sinha, and Sally E. Lorimer, "Match Your Sales Force Structure to Your Business Life Cycle," *Harvard Business Review,* July–August 2006; George R. Franke and Jeong-Eun Park, "Salesperson Adaptive Selling Behavior and Customer Orientation: A Meta-Analysis," *Journal of Marketing Research,* November 2006; Diane Coutu, "Leveraging the Psychology of the Salesperson," *Harvard Business Review,* July–August 2006; David Mayer and Herbert M. Greenberg, "What Makes a Good Salesman," *Harvard Business Review,* July–August 2006; Christian Pfeil, Thorsten Posselt, and Nils Maschke, "Incentives for Sales Agents after the Advent of the Internet," *Marketing Letters,* January 2008; Dawn R. Deeter-Schmelz, Daniel J. Goebel, and Karen Norman, "What Are the Characteristics of an Effective Sales Manager? An Exploratory Study Comparing Salesperson and Sales Manager Perspectives," *Journal of Personal Selling & Sales Management,* Winter 2008; Jerome A. Colletti and Mary S. Fiss, "The Ultimately Accountable Job: Leading Today's Sales Organization," *Harvard Business Review,* July–August 2006; Robert W. Palmatier, Lisa K. Scheer, and Jan-Benedict E. M. Steenkamp, "Customer Loyalty to Whom? Managing the Benefits and Risks of Salesperson-Owned Loyalty," *Journal of Marketing Research,* May 2007; Judy A. Siguaw, Sheryl E. Kimes, and Jule B. Gassenheimer, "B2B Sales Force Productivity: Applications of Revenue Management Strategies to Sales Management," *Industrial Marketing Management,* October 2003; William C. Moncrief, Greg W. Marshall, and Felicia G. Lassk, "A Contemporary Taxonomy of Sales Positions," *Journal of Personal Selling & Sales Management,* Winter 2006; Eli Jones, Steven P. Brown, Andris A. Zoltners, and Barton A. Weitz, "The Changing Environment of Selling and Sales Management," *Journal of Personal Selling & Sales Management,* Spring 2005; Simon J. Bell and James A. Luddington, "Coping with Customer Complaints," *Journal of Service Research,* February 2006; Julie T. Johnson, Hiram C. Barksdale, Jr., and James S. Boles, "The Strategic Role of the Salesperson in Reducing Customer Defection in Business Relationships," *Journal of Personal Selling & Sales Management,* Spring 2001; Sandy D. Jap, "The Strategic Role of the Salesforce in Developing Customer Satisfaction Across the Relationship Lifecycle," *Journal of Personal Selling & Sales Management,* Spring 2001; William M. Strahle, Rosann L. Spiro, and Frank Acito, "Marketing and Sales: Strategic Alignment and Functional Implementation," *Journal of Personal Selling & Sales Management,* Winter 1996; John E. Swan, Cathy Goodwin, Michael A. Mayo, and Lynne D. Richardson, "Customer Identities: Customers as Commercial Friends, Customer Coworkers or Business Acquaintances," *Journal of Personal Selling & Sales Management,* Winter 2001; Michael J. Dorsch, Les Carlson, Mary Anne Raymond, and Robert Ranson, "Customer Equity Management and Strategic Choices for Sales Managers," *Journal of Personal Selling & Sales Management,* Spring 2001; Thomas W. Leigh, Ellen Bolman Pullins, and Lucette B. Comer, "The Top Ten Sales Articles of the 20th Century," *Journal of Personal Selling & Sales Management,* Summer 2001; Thomas Tellefsen and Nermin Eyuboglu, "The Impact of a Salesperson's In-House Conflicts and Influence Attempts on Buyer Commitment," *Journal of Personal Selling & Sales Management,* November 2002.

5. "Bank of (Middle) America," *Fast Company,* March 2003; "A French Bank Hits the Road," *BusinessWeek,* November 17, 2003; "NationsBank Asks Tellers to Branch Out," *Raleigh News & Observer,* September 12, 1993. See also "Forget 'May I Help You?'" *Wall Street Journal,* July 8, 2003; "Service—with a Side of Sales," *Wall Street Journal Reports,* October 29, 2001; Rita Marie Cain, "Federal Do Not Call Registry Is Here Stay: What's Next for Direct Marketing Regulation?" *Journal of Interactive Marketing,* Winter 2005.

6. "The Customer Strikes Back," *Brandweek,* April 26, 2008; "Customer Service Champs," *BusinessWeek,* March 3, 2008; "Consumer Vigilantes," *BusinessWeek,* February 21, 2008; "Comcast Takes Its Whacks on Service," *USA Today,* December 3, 2007; "Comcast Must Die," *Advertising Age,* November 19, 2007, p. 1; "Woman Fined for Hammer Fit at Comcast," *USA Today,* October 19, 2007; "Dell Learns to Listen," *BusinessWeek,* October 17, 2007;

"Consumers Take Their Fights to the Web," *abcnews.com*, August 31, 2007; "One Tough Customer," *Brandweek*, March 19, 2007, pp. 18–24; "Customer Service Champs," *BusinessWeek*, March 5, 2007, pp. 52–64; "Price Points: Good Customer Service Costs Money," *Wall Street Journal*, October 30, 2006, p. R7; "Dell Draws Flak from PC Fans on New Desktop," *Wall Street Journal*, September 21, 2006; "Satisfaction Not Guaranteed," *BusinessWeek*, June 19, 2006; "Dell: In the Bloghouse," *BusinessWeek*, August 25, 2005; "The Customer Vigilante Files," *Church of the Customer Blog*, November 25, 2003.

7. Glen Urban and John Hauser, "Now Is the Time to Advocate for Your Customers," *Listening In to Find Unmet Customer Needs and Solutions*, Center for eBusiness@MIT, MIT Sloan School of Management; "The Man Who Wanted a Live Operator," *Inc.*, February 2006; "Finding the Best Cell Phone Service Requires a Bit of Research," *Investor's Business Daily*, December 6, 2005; "TMobile's Novel Sell: Great Cell Service," *Advertising Age*, November 28, 2005; "Service with a Smile. Really. How Technology Ruined Customer Service . . .," *Inc.*, October 2005; "For Happier Customers, Call HR," *Fortune*, November 28, 2005; "Help (May Be) on the Way," *Wall Street Journal Reports*, March 21, 2005; "Customer Service via Machine," *Investor's Business Daily*, February 14, 2005; "They're Off to See the Wizards," *The New York Times*, January 27, 2005; "This Call Is Being Monitored," *Business 2.0*, July 2004; "Pop-Up Sales Clerks: Web Sites Try the Hard Sell," *Wall Street Journal*, April 15, 2004; "Giving Buyers Better Information," *Investor's Business Daily*, February 2, 2004; "Whatever Happened to Customer Service?" *USA Today*, September 26, 2003; "Where the Customer Service Rep Is King," *Business 2.0*, June 2003; "The Annoying New Face of Customer Service," *Wall Street Journal*, January 21, 2003; "Specialized Training Can Improve Sales Force Focus," *Investor's Business Daily*, January 16, 2003; "Joe Galli's Army," *Fortune*, December 30, 2002; "Operator, I Demand an Automated Menu," *Wall Street Journal*, July 30, 2002; "Best Call Centers Stress Training, Track Results to Gauge Success," *Investor's Business Daily*, October 17, 2001. For more about major account selling see George S. Yip and Audrey J. M. Bink, "Managing Global Accounts," *Harvard Business Review*, September 2007; Paolo Guenzi, Catherine Pardo, and Laurent Georges, "Relational selling strategy and key account managers' relational behaviors: An Exploratory Study," *Industrial Marketing Management*, January 2007; Michael G. Harvey, Milorad M. Novicevic, Thomas Hench, and Matthew Myers, "Global Account Management: a Supply-Side Managerial View," *Industrial Marketing Management*, October 2003; Roberta J. Schultz and Kenneth R. Evans, "Strategic Collaborative Communication by Key Account Representatives," *Journal of Personal Selling & Sales Management*, Winter 2002; Sanjit Sengupta, Robert E. Krapfel, and Michael A. Pusateri, "An Empirical Investigation of Key Account Salesperson Effectiveness," *The Journal of Personal Selling & Sales Management*, Fall 2000; Mark A. Moon and Susan F. Gupta, "Examining the Formation of Selling Centers: A Conceptual Framework," *Journal of Personal Selling & Sales Management*, Spring 1997.

8. "How to Remake Your Sales Force," *Fortune*, May 4, 1992; "Apparel Makers Play Bigger Part on Sales Floor," *Wall Street Journal*, March 2, 1988.

9. "The Task at Hand," *Beverage World*, December 15, 2003; "Sales Force Effectiveness through E-Learning," *Pharmaceutical Executive*, October 2003; "The Biggest Mouth in Silicon Valley," *Business 2.0*, September 2003; "Software That's Actually Useful," *Sales & Marketing Management*, August 2003; Scott M. Widmier, Donald W. Jackson, Jr., and Deborah Brown McCabe, "Infusing Technology into Personal Selling," *Journal of Personal Selling & Sales Management*, November 2002; "Salespeople Say Automation Software Still Lacking," *Investor's Business Daily*, January 18, 2001.

10. Gary K. Hunter and William D. Perreault, "Making Sales Technology Effective," *Journal of Marketing*, January 2007; Michael Ahearne, Douglas E. Hughes, and Niels Schillewaert, "Why Sales Reps Should Welcome Information Technology: Measuring the Impact of CRM-based IT on Sales Effectiveness," *International Journal of Research in Marketing*, December 2007; Earl D. Honeycutt Jr, Tanya Thelen, Shawn T. Thelen, and Sharon K. Hodge, "Impediments to Sales Force Automation," *Industrial Marketing Management*, May 2005; Stephan F. Gohmann, Jian Guan, Robert M. Barker, and David J. Faulds, "Perceptions of Sales Force Automation: Differences Between Sales Force and Management," *Industrial Marketing Management*, May 2005; Deva Rangarajan, Eli Jones and Wynne Chin, "Impact of Sales Force Automation on Technology-Related Stress, Effort, and Technology Usage Among Salespeople," *Industrial Marketing Management*, May 2005; George J. Avlonitis and Nikolaos G. Panagopoulos, "Antecedents and Consequences of CRM Technology Acceptance in the Sales Force," *Industrial Marketing Management*, May 2005; Alan J. Bush, Jarvis B. Moore, and Rich Rocco, "Understanding Sales Force Automation Outcomes: A Managerial Perspective," *Industrial Marketing Management*, May 2005; Richard E. Buehrer, Sylvain Senecal, and Ellen Bolman Pullins, "Sales Force Technology Usage—Reasons, Barriers, and Support: An Exploratory Investigation," *Industrial Marketing Management*, May 2005; Leroy Robinson Jr, Greg W. Marshall, and Miriam B. Stamps, "An Empirical Investigation of Technology Acceptance in a Field Sales Force Setting," *Industrial Marketing Management*, May 2005; Devon S. Johnson and Sundar Bharadwaj, "Digitization of Selling Activity and Sales Force Performance: An Empirical Investigation," *Journal of the Academy of Marketing Science*, Winter 2005; Thomas G. Brashear, Danny N. Bellenger, James S. Boles, and Hiram C. Barksdale, Jr, "An Exploratory Study of the Relative Effectiveness of Different Types of Sales Force Mentors," *Journal of Personal Selling & Sales Management*, Winter 2006; Gary L. Hunter, "Information Overload: Guidance for Identifying When Information Becomes Detrimental to Sales Force Performance," *Journal of Personal Selling & Sales Management*, Spring 2004; Amy J. Morgan and Scott A. Inks, "Technology and the Sales Force: Increasing Acceptance of Sales Force Automation," *Industrial Marketing Management*, July 2001; Mary E. Shoemaker, "A Framework for Examining IT-Enabled Market Relationships," *Journal of Personal Selling & Sales Management*, Spring 2001; Robert C. Erffmeyer and Dale A. Johnson, "An Exploratory Study of Sales Force Automation Practices: Expectations and Realities," *Journal of Personal Selling & Sales Management*, Spring 2001; Cheri Speier and Viswanath Venkatesh, "The Hidden Minefields in the Adoption of Sales Force Automation Technologies," *Journal of Marketing*, July 2002; Eli Jones, Suresh Sundaram, and Wynne Chin, "Factors Leading to Sales Force Automation Use: a Longitudinal Analysis," *Journal of Personal Selling & Sales Management*, November 2002.

11. "Selling Salesmanship," *Business 2.0*, December 2002; "The Art of the Sale," *Wall Street Journal*, January 11, 2001.

12. See www.achievement.com/sales; M. Asri Jantan, Earl D. Honeycutt, Shawn T. Thelen, and Ashraf M. Atria, "Managerial Perceptions of Sales Training and Performance," *Industrial Marketing Management*, October 2004; Karen E. Flaherty and James M. Pappas, "Job Selection Among Salespeople: A Bounded Rationality Perspective," *Industrial Marketing Management*, May 2004; Anand Krishnamoorthy, Sanjog Misra, and Ashutosh Prasad, "Scheduling Sales Force Training: Theory and Evidence," *International Journal of Research in Marketing*, December 2005; Ashraf M. Attia, Earl D. Honeycutt, Jr., and Mark P. Leach, "A Three-Stage Model for Assessing and Improving Sales Force Training and Development," *Journal of Personal Selling & Sales Management*, Summer 2005; Mark P. Leach, Annie H. Liu, and Wesley J. Johnston, "The Role of Self-Regulation Training in Developing the Motivation Management Capabilities of Salespeople," *Journal of Personal Selling & Sales Management*, Summer 2005; William L. Cron, Greg W. Marshall, Jagdip Singh, Rosann L. Spiro, and Harish Sujan, "Salesperson Selection, Training, and Development: Trends, Implications, and Research Opportunities," *Journal of Personal Selling & Sales Management*, Spring 2005; G. Martin Izzo and Scott J. Vitell, "Exploring the Effects of Professional Education on Salespeople:

The Case of Autonomous Agents," *Journal of Marketing Theory & Practice*, Fall 2003; Brian P. Matthews and Tom Redman, "Recruiting the Wrong Salespeople: Are the Job Ads to Blame?" *Industrial Marketing Management*, October 2001; R. Edward Bashaw, Thomas N. Ingram, and Bruce D. Keillor, "Improving Sales Training Cycle Times for New Trainees: an Exploratory Study," *Industrial Marketing Management*, July 2002; Ellen Bolman Pullins and Leslie M. Fine, "How the Performance of Mentoring Activities Affects the Mentor's Job Outcomes," *Journal of Personal Selling & Sales Management*, Fall 2002; Phillip H. Wilson, David Strutton, and, M. Theodore Farris II, "Investigating the Perceptual Aspect of Sales Training," *Journal of Personal Selling & Sales Management*, Spring 2002; Earl D. Honeycutt, Jr., Kiran Karande, Ashraf Attia, and Steven D. Maurer, "An Utility Based Framework for Evaluating the Financial Impact of Sales Force Training Programs," *Journal of Personal Selling & Sales Management*, Summer 2001; Ellen B. Pullins, Leslie M. Fine, and Wendy L. Warren, "Identifying Peer Mentors in the Sales Force: An Exploratory Investigation of Willingness and Ability," *Journal of the Academy of Marketing Science*, Spring 1996.

13. William H. Murphy, Peter A. Dacin, and Neil M. Ford, "Sales Contest Effectiveness: An Examination of Sales Contest Design Preferences of Field Sales Forces," *Journal of the Academy of Marketing Science*, Spring 2004; Steven P. Brown, Kenneth R. Evans, Murali K. Mantrala, and Goutam Challagalla, "Adapting Motivation, Control, and Compensation Research to a New Environment," *Journal of Personal Selling & Sales Management*, Spring 2005; Charles H. Schwepker, Jr., and David J. Good, "Marketing Control and Sales Force Customer Orientation," *Journal of Personal Selling & Sales Management*, Summer 2004; Jeong Eun Park and George D. Deitz, "The Effect of Working Relationship Quality on Salesperson Performance and Job Satisfaction: Adaptive Selling Behavior in Korean Automobile Sales Representatives," *Journal of Business Research*, February 2006; J. K. Sager, H. D. Strutton, and D. A. Johnson, "Core Self-Evaluations and Salespeople," *Psychology & Marketing*, February 2006; Ken Grant, David W. Cravens, George S. Low, and William C. Moncrief, "The Role of Satisfaction with Territory Design on the Motivation, Attitudes, and Work Outcomes of Salespeople," *Journal of the Academy of Marketing Science*, Spring 2001; Balaji C. Krishnan, Richard G. Netemeyer, and James S. Boles, "Self-Efficacy, Competitiveness, and Efforts as Antecedents of Salesperson Performance," *Journal of Personal Selling & Sales Management*, Fall 2002; Guangping Wang and Richard G. Netemeyer, "The Effects of Job Autonomy, Customer Demandingness, and Trait Competitiveness on Salesperson Learning, Self-Efficacy, and Performance," *Journal of the Academy of Marketing Science*, Summer 2002; Joseph O. Rentz, C. David Shepherd, Armen Tashchian, Pratibha A. Dabholkar, and Robert T. Ladd, "A Measure of Selling Skill: Scale Development and Validation," *Journal of Personal Selling & Sales Management*, Winter 2002.

14. Sridhar N. Ramaswami and Jagdip Singh, "Antecedents and Consequences of Merit Pay Fairness for Industrial Salespeople," *Journal of Marketing*, October 2003; Sunil Erevelles, Indranil Dutta, and Carolyn Galantine, "Sales Force Compensation Plans Incorporating Multidimensional Sales Effort and Salesperson Efficiency," *Journal of Personal Selling & Sales Management*, Spring 2004; "The Sales Commission Dilemma," *Inc.*, May 2003; "Creating Incentives Down in Ranks: Marriott Ties Pay to Guest Replies," *Investor's Business Daily*, July 6, 2001; "Get Great Results from Salespeople by Finding What Really Moves Them," *Investor's Business Daily*, July 2, 2001; "Medical Gear Sales Force Works on Commission," *Investor's Business Daily*, July 25, 2000; R. Venkatesh, Goutam Challagalla, and Ajay K. Kohli, "Heterogeneity in Sales Districts: Beyond Individual-Level Predictors of Satisfaction and Performance," *Journal of the Academy of Marketing Science*, Summer 2001; Ellen Bolman Pullins, "An Exploratory Investigation of the Relationship of Sales Force Compensation and Intrinsic Motivation," *Industrial Marketing Management*, July 2001; Sridhar N. Ramaswami and Jagdip Singh, "Antecedents and Consequences of Merit Pay Fairness for Industrial Salespeople," *Journal of Marketing*,

October 2003; Goutam Ghallagalla, "Supervisory Orientations and Salesperson Work Outcomes: the Moderating Effect of Salesperson Location," *Journal of Personal Selling & Sales Management*, Summer 2000; Kissan Joseph and Manohar U. Kalwani, "The Role of Bonus Pay in Salesforce Compensation Plans," *Industrial Marketing Management*, March 1998.

15. "New Software's Payoff? Happier Salespeople," *Investor's Business Daily*, May 23, 2000.

16. Eric G. Harris, John C. Mowen, and Tom J. Brown, "Reexamining Salesperson Goal Orientations: Personal Influencers, Customer Orientation, and Work Satisfaction," *Journal of the Academy of Marketing Science*, Winter 2005; Dominique Rouziès, Erin Anderson, Ajay K. Kohli, Ronald E. Michaels, Barton A. Weitz, and Andris A. Zoltners, "Sales and Marketing Integration: A Proposed Framework," *Journal of Personal Selling & Sales Management*, Spring 2005; Eric Fang, Kenneth R. Evans, and Shaoming Zou, "The Moderating Effect of Goal-Setting Characteristics on the Sales Control Systems Job Performance Relationship," *Journal of Business Research*, September 2005; Kenneth B. Kahn, Richard C. Reizenstein, and Joseph O. Rentz, "Sales-Distribution Interfunctional Climate and Relationship Effectiveness," *Journal of Business Research*, October 2004; Rolph E. Anderson and Wen-yeh Huang, "Empowering Salespeople: Personal, Managerial, and Organizational Perspectives," *Psychology & Marketing*, February 2006; Thomas G. Brashear, James S. Boles, Danny N. Bellenger, and Charles M. Brooks, "An Empirical Test of Trust-Building Processes and Outcomes in Sales Manager-Salesperson Relationships," *Journal of the Academy of Marketing Science*, Spring 2003; Andrea L. Dixon, Rosann L. Spiro, and Lukas P. Forbes, "Attributions and Behavioral Intentions of Inexperienced Salespersons to Failure: an Empirical Investigation," *Journal of the Academy of Marketing Science*, Fall 2003; Mark C. Johlke, Dale F. Duhan, Roy D. Howell, and Robert W. Wilkes, "An Integrated Model of Sales Managers' Communication Practices," *Journal of the Academy of Marketing Science*, Spring 2000; Dominique Rouzies and Anne Macquin, "An Exploratory Investigation of the Impact of Culture on Sales Force Management Control Systems in Europe," *Journal of Personal Selling & Sales Management*, Winter 2002–2003; Scott B. MacKenzie, Philip M. Podsakoff, and Gregory A. Rich, "Transformational and Transactional Leadership and Salesperson Performance," *Journal of the Academy of Marketing Science*, Spring 2001; Cengiz Yilmaz and Shelby D. Hunt, "Salesperson Cooperation: the Influence of Relational, Task, Organizational, and Personal Factors," *Journal of the Academy of Marketing Science*, Fall 2001; Richard L. Oliver and Erin Anderson, "An Empirical Test of the Consequences of Behavior and Outcome-Based Sales Control Systems," *Journal of Marketing*, October 1994; Steven P. Brown and Robert A. Peterson, "The Effect of Effort on Sales Performance and Job Satisfaction," *Journal of Marketing*, April 1994; Frederick A. Russ, Kevin M. McNeilly, and James M. Comer, "Leadership, Decision Making and Performance of Sales Managers: A Multi-Level Approach," *Journal of Personal Selling & Sales Management*, Summer 1996; Douglas N. Behrman and William D. Perreault, Jr., "A Role Stress Model of the Performance and Satisfaction of Industrial Salespersons," *Journal of Marketing*, Fall 1984.

17. "Chief Executives Are Increasingly Chief Salesmen," *Wall Street Journal*, August 6, 1991; Joe F. Alexander, Patrick L. Schul, and Emin Babakus, "Analyzing Interpersonal Communications in Industrial Marketing Negotiations," *Journal of the Academy of Marketing Science*, Spring 1991.

18. "Managing Technology: Selling Software," *Wall Street Journal*, March 19, 2007.

19. Eli Jones, Andrea L. Dixon, Lawrence B. Chonko, and Joseph P. Cannon, "Key Accounts and Team Selling: A Review, Framework, and Research Agenda," *Journal of Personal Selling & Sales Management*, Spring 2005; Dennis B. Arnett, Barry A. Macy, and James B. Wilcox, "The Role of Core Selling Teams in Supplier-Buyer Relationships," *Journal of Personal Selling & Sales Management*, Winter 2005; Kirk

Smith, Eli Jones, and Edward Blair, "Managing Salesperson Motivation in a Territory Realignment," *Journal of Personal Selling & Sales Management*, Fall 2000; Andris A. Zoltners, "Sales Territory Alignment: An Overlooked Productivity Tool," *Journal of Personal Selling & Sales Management*, Summer 2000; Ken Grant, "The Role of Satisfaction with Territory Design on the Motivation, Attitudes, and Work Outcomes of Salespeople," *Journal of the Academy of Marketing Science*, Spring 2001.

20. "How to Get Your Company Where You Want It," *American Salesman*, December 2003; "When Should I Give Up on a Sales Prospect?" *Inc.*, May 1998. See also Sean Dwyer, John Hill, and Warren Martin, "An Empirical Investigation of Critical Success Factors in the Personal Selling Process for Homogenous Goods," *Journal of Personal Selling & Sales Management*, Summer 2000; Doris C. Van Doren and Thomas A. Stickney, "How to Develop a Database for Sales Leads," *Industrial Marketing Management*, August 1990.

21. "Novartis' Marketing Doctor," *BusinessWeek*, March 5, 2001.

22. For more on sales presentation approaches, see Richard G. McFarland, Goutam N. Challagalla, and Tasadduq A. Shervani, "Influence Tactics for Effective Adaptive Selling," *Journal of Marketing*, October 2006; Death of a Pushy Salesman," *BusinessWeek*, July 3, 2006; "Firing Up Your Cold Calls," *Business 2.0*, December 2005; "Trapped in the Sales Presentation from Hell," *Information Week*, November 10, 2003; "Advise and Conquer," *Brandweek*, May 14, 2001; "Rick Francolini, TV Guide," *Brandweek*, October 25, 1999; "The 60-Second Sales Pitch," *Inc.*, October 1994. See also Daniel M. Eveleth and Linda Morris, "Adaptive Selling in a Call Center Environment: a Qualitative Investigation," *Journal of Interactive Marketing*, Winter 2002; Thomas W. Leigh and John O. Summers, "An Initial Evaluation of Industrial Buyers' Impressions of Salespersons' Nonverbal Cues," *Journal of Personal Selling & Sales Management*, Winter 2002; Kalyani Menon and Laurette Dube, "Ensuring Greater Satisfaction by Engineering Salesperson Response to Customer Emotions," *Journal of Retailing*, Fall 2000; Susan K. DelVecchio, James E. Zemanek, Roger P. McIntyre, and Reid P. Claxton, "Buyers' Perceptions of Salesperson Tactical Approaches," *Journal of Personal Selling & Sales Management*, Winter 2002–2003; Alfred M. Pelham, "An Exploratory Model and Initial Test of the Influence of Firm Level Consulting-Oriented Sales Force Programs on Sales Force Performance," *Journal of Personal Selling & Sales Management*, Spring 2002; Annie H. Liu and Mark P. Leach, "Developing Loyal Customers with a Value-Adding Sales Force: Examining Customer Satisfaction and the Perceived Credibility of Consultative Salespeople," *Journal of Personal Selling & Sales Management*, Spring 2001; Richard S. Jacobs, Kenneth R. Evans, Robert E. Kleine III, and Timothy D. Landry, "Disclosure and its Reciprocity as Predictors of Key Outcomes of an Initial Sales Encounter," *Journal of Personal Selling & Sales Management*, Winter 2001; Gary L. Frankwick, Stephen S. Porter, and Lawrence A. Crosby, "Dynamics of Relationship Selling: a Longitudinal Examination of Changes in Salesperson-Customer Relationship Status," *Journal of Personal Selling & Sales Management*, Spring 2001; Willemijn van Dolen, Jos Lemmink, Ko de Ruyter, and Ad de Jong, "Customer-Sales Employee Encounters: a Dyadic Perspective," *Journal of Retailing*, Winter 2002; Nancy M. Puccinelli, "Putting Your Best Face Forward: The Impact of Customer Mood on Salesperson Evaluation," *Journal of Consumer Psychology*, 2006; Thomas E. DeCarlo, "The Effects of Sales Message and Suspicion of Ulterior Motives on Salesperson Evaluation," *Journal of Consumer Psychology*, 2005; Amy Sallee and Karen Flaherty, "Enhancing Salesperson Trust: An Examination of Managerial Values, Empowerment, and the Moderating Influence of SBU Strategy," *Journal of Personal Selling & Sales Management*, Fall 2003; Geok Theng Lau and Hsueh Wei Chin, "Trustworthiness of Salespeople in the Business-to-Business Market: The Five C's," *Journal of Business-to-Business Marketing*, 2003; Tará Burnthorne, Jon Carr, Brian T. Gregory, and Sean Dwyer, "The Influence of Psychological Climate on the Salesperson Customer Orientation–Salesperson Performance

Relationship," *Journal of Marketing Theory & Practice*, Spring 2005; J. David Lichtenthal and Stephen A. Goodwin, "Product Attributes for Business Markets: Implications for Selling and Sales Management," *Psychology & Marketing*, March 2006; C. David Shepherd, Sarah F. Gardial, Michael G. Johnson, and Joseph O. Rentz, "Cognitive Insights into the Highly Skilled or Expert Salesperson," *Psychology & Marketing*, February 2006.

23. Thomas N. Ingram, Raymond W. LaForge, and Charles H. Schwepker, Jr., "Salesperson Ethical Decision Making: The Impact of Sales Leadership and Sales Management Control Strategy," *Journal of Personal Selling & Sales Management*, Fall 2007; Jay Prakash Mulki, Fernando Jaramillo, and William B. Locander, "Effects of Ethical Climate and Supervisory Trust on Salesperson's Job Attitudes and Intentions to Quit," *Journal of Personal Selling & Sales Management*, Winter 2006; Lawrence B. Chonko, Thomas R. Wotruba, and Terry W. Loe, "Direct Selling Ethics at the Top: An Industry Audit and Status Report," *Journal of Personal Selling & Sales Management*, Spring 2002; Lawrence B. Chonko, John F. Tanner, and William A. Weeks, "Ethics in Salesperson Decision Making: A Synthesis of Research Approaches and an Extension of the Scenario Method," *Journal of Personal Selling & Sales Management*, Winter 1996; Eugene Sivadas, Susan Bardi Kleiser, James Kellaris, and Robert Dahlstrom, "Moral Philosophy, Ethical Evaluations, and Sales Manager Hiring Intentions," *Journal of Personal Selling & Sales Management*, Winter 2002–2003; John Cherry and John Fraedrich, "Perceived Risk, Moral Philosophy and Marketing Ethics: Mediating Influences on Sales Managers' Ethical Decision-Making," *Journal of Business Research*, December 2002. For more on pharmaceutical company selling tactics, see "Side Effects: As Drug-Sales Teams Multiply, Doctors Start to Tune Them Out," *Wall Street Journal*, June 13, 2003; "New Prescription: Its Rivals in Funk, Novartis Finds a Way to Thrive," *Wall Street Journal*, August 23, 2002; "Swallow This: How Drug Makers Use Pharmacies to Push Pricey Pills," *Wall Street Journal*, May 1, 2002; "Sorry, Doc, No Dinners-to-Go," *Wall Street Journal*, April 23, 2002; "More than Ads, Drug Makers Rely on Sales Reps," *Wall Street Journal*, March 14, 2002; "Pushing Pills: Drug Firms' Incentives to Pharmacists in India Fuel Mounting Abuse," *Wall Street Journal*, August 16, 2001; "Doctors Step Out; Drug Salesmen Step In," *USA Today*, July 5, 2001; "Sales Pitch: Drug Firms Use Perks to Push Pills," *USA Today*, May 16, 2001. For more on Oracle's selling tactics, see "Learning to Be a Great Host," *Business 2.0*, May 2003; "Oracle Puts Priority on Customer Service," *Wall Street Journal*, January 21, 2003; "Out of Control," *Business 2.0*, August 2002.

CHAPTER 15

1. "Subway Goes Mobile," *Response*, March 2008; "Subway Can't Stop Jonesing for Jared," *Advertising Age*, February 18, 2008; "Subway Gets Eaters Active with Reactrix," *Brandweek*, December 17, 2007; "Family Guy Teams with Subway for In-Store Promo," *Promo*, November 20, 2007; "Subway Seeks to Slice Domino's, Pizza Hut Pie," *Brandweek*, April 9, 2007; "Friday's, Subway Tailor Meals for Health-Conscious," *USA Today*, March 1, 2007; "Finding Just Enough of That Sticky Stuff," *Brandweek*, January 29, 2007: "Subway Corporate Grabs for Advertising Control: Franchisees Wary of Power Play," April 24, 2006, *AdAge.com*; "Subway Begins Playing Games," *Chain Leader*, February 2006; "Subway Teams with Discovery Kids to Reach Children," *Nation's Restaurant News*, January 9, 2006; "It's Lunchtime and Jared from Subway Is on the Phone," Associated Press State & Local Wire, December 27, 2005; "Subway Announces 3-Year Little League Baseball and Softball Sponsorship, Reflects Chain's Dual Focus on Good Nutrition and Physical Activity," *PR Newswire US*, August 20, 2005; "Subway Targets Teen Appetites," *Connecticut Post*, May 17, 2005; "Subway Lets Local Tastes Guide New Products," *Advertising Age*, May 16, 2005; "Subway Will Shed Fallon Worldwide," *Wall Street Journal*, May 25, 2004; "Subway to Sell Kids Pak Meal that Focuses on Health," *USA Today*, September 26, 2003; "Subway Orders Weightier Campaign," *Wall Street Journal*,

August 21, 2003; "Creative: Ordinary People," *Adweek*, August 11, 2003; "FastFood Firms' Big Budgets Don't Buy Consumer Loyalty," *Wall Street Journal*, July 24, 2003; "Fallon Takes Home Subway after All-Star Shootout," *Adweek*, July 21, 2003; "Marketers of the Year: Subway, in Search of Fresh Ideas," *Brandweek*, October 15, 2001.

2. Manfred Schwaiger, Carsten Rennhak, Charles R. Taylor, and Hugh M. Cannon, "Can Comparative Advertising Be Effective in Germany? A Tale of Two Campaigns," *Journal of Advertising Research*, March 2007; Carolyn A. Lin, "Cultural Values Reflected in Chinese and American Television Advertising," *Journal of Advertising*, Winter 2001; Christophe Collard, Michael Pustay, Christophe Roquilly, and Asghar Zardkoohi, "Competitive Cross-Couponing: a Comparison of French and U.S. Perspectives," *Journal of Public Policy & Marketing*, Spring 2001; Charles R. Taylor, Gordon E. Miracle, and R. D. Wilson, "The Impact of Information Level on the Effectiveness of U.S. and Korean Television Commercials," *Journal of Advertising*, Spring 1997; Ronald E. Taylor, Mariea G. Hoy, and Eric Haley, "How French Advertising Professionals Develop Creative Strategy," *Journal of Advertising*, Spring 1996; Nan Zhou and Mervin Y. T. Chen, "A Content Analysis of Men and Women in Canadian Consumer Magazine Advertising: Today's Portrayal, Yesterday's Image?" *Journal of Business Ethics*, April 1997; Yong Zhang and Betsy D. Gelb, "Matching Advertising Appeals to Culture: The Influence of Products' Use Conditions," *Journal of Advertising*, Fall 1996.

3. "Global Marketers: Top 100," *Advertising Age* (Special Issue), December 8, 2008; "Magna Expects 4.5% Decline in U.S. Spending in '09," at www.adage.com/print?article_id=133085.

4. For more on advertising to sales ratios, see "2008 Advertising to Sales Ratios for 200 Largest Ad Spending Industries," at http://adage.com/datacenter/datapopup.php?article_id=130981. For more on advertising to sales ratios for individual companies, see "U.S. Company Revenue per 2007 Ad Dollar," at http://adage.com/datacenter/datapopup.php?article_id= 127916.

5. "Annual 2009," *Advertising Age* (Special Issue), December 29, 2008; "Annual 2008," *Advertising Age* (Special Issue), December 31, 2007; various "Insider's Reports" by Robert Coen of Universal McCann; and "100 Leading National Advertisers," *Advertising Age* (Special Report), June 25, 2007; all available online at www.adage.com.

6. Exact data on this industry are elusive, but see "Datacenter," *Advertising Age*, August 25, 2008.

7. "Viral Hall of Fame 2006: #1: Peerflix Paparazzi," *Marketing Sherpa*, http://marketingsherpa.com/vas2006/1.html. See also www.tacobell.com.

8. For more on Dryel, see "Putting Home Dry-Cleaning Products to the Test," *Wall Street Journal*, January 12, 2006; "The Dirt on At-Home Dry Cleaning," *Wall Street Journal*, September 15, 2000; See also "Industry Wrestles with Comparative Ads," *Advertising Age*, October 27, 2003; "Sour Dough: Pizza Hut v. Papa John's," *Brandweek*, May 21, 2001; "Irate Firms Take Comparisons to Court," *Wall Street Journal*, December 22, 1999; "Survey: Comparative Ads Can Dent Car's Credibility," *Advertising Age*, May 4, 1998. For more on AT&T, MCI, and Sprint's comparative ads, see "Best Phone Discounts Go to Hardest Bargainers," *Wall Street Journal*, February 13, 1997; "Fighting for Customers Gets Louder," *USA Today*, January 9, 1995. For other examples of comparative advertising, see "Allergy Drugs Wage a Bitter War of the Noses," *Wall Street Journal*, May 23, 1996; "New Drug Ads Give Doctors Heartburn," *Wall Street Journal*, April 25, 1996. See also Peter J. Danaher, André Bonfrer, and Sanjay Dhar, "The Effect of Competitive Advertising Interference on Sales for Packaged Goods," *Journal of Marketing Research*, May 2008; Debora Viana Thompson and Rebecca W. Hamilton, "The Effects of Information Processing Mode on Consumers' Responses to Comparative Advertising," *Journal of Consumer Research*, March 2006; Robert D. Jewell, H. Rao Unnava, David Glen Mick, and Merrie L. Brucks, "When Competitive Interference Can Be Beneficial," *Journal of Consumer Research*, September 2003; Michael J. Barone, Kay M. Palan, and Paul W. Miniard, "Brand

Usage and Gender as Moderators of the Potential Deception Associated with Partial Comparative Advertising," *Journal of Advertising*, Spring 2004; Gerd Bohner, Sabine Einwiller, Hans-Peter Herb, and Frank Siebler, "When Small Means Comfortable: Relations Between Product Attributes in Two-Sided Advertising," *Journal of Consumer Psychology*, 2003; Paschalina Ziamou and S. Ratneshwar, "Innovations in Product Functionality: When and Why Are Explicit Comparisons Effective?" *Journal of Marketing*, April 2003; Patrick Meirick, "Cognitive Responses to Negative and Comparative Political Advertising," *Journal of Advertising*, Spring 2002; Bruce E. Pinkleton, Nam-Hyun Um, and Erica Weintraub Austin, "An Exploration of the Effects of Negative Political Advertising on Political Decision Making," *Journal of Advertising*, Spring 2002; Diana L. Haytko, "Great Advertising Campaigns: Goals and Accomplishments," *Journal of Marketing*, April 1995; Carolyn Tripp, "Services Advertising: An Overview and Summary of Research, 1980–1995," *Journal of Advertising*, Winter 1997; Thomas E. Barry, "Comparative Advertising: What Have We Learned in Two Decades?" *Journal of Advertising Research*, March–April 1993.

9. "Feature: Cause Marketing," *Advertising Age*, June 13, 2005; "The Selling of Breast Cancer," *Business 2.0*, February 2003; "Seeking Cause and Effect," *Brandweek*, November 11, 2002; "Brands Step Up to Battle Breast Cancer," *USA Today*, September 5, 2001; "Spiffing up the Corporate Image," *Fortune*, July 21, 1986: See also Amitav Chakravarti and Chris Janiszewski, "The Influence of Generic Advertising on Brand Preferences," *Journal of Consumer Research*, March 2004; T. Bettina Cornwell, Donald P. Roy, and Edward A. Steinard II, "Exploring Managers' Perceptions of the Impact of Sponsorship on Brand Equity," *Journal of Advertising*, Summer 2001; Michael J. Barone, Anthony D. Miyazaki, and Kimberly A. Taylor, "The Influence of Cause-Related Marketing on Consumer Choice: Does One Good Turn Deserve Another?" *Journal of the Academy of Marketing Science*, Spring 2000; Minette E. Drumwright, "Company Advertising with a Social Dimension: The Role of Noneconomic Criteria," *Journal of Marketing*, October 1996.

10. For more on Got Milk campaign (and others), see "Got Milk? (Got Mess)," *Brandweek*, April 19, 2004. For more on Wendy's, see "The Year in 2003—Review," *Nation's Restaurant News*, December 22, 2003. For more on Cadillac, see "Cadillac Steers Dealers toward Unified Messages," *Brandweek*, October 6, 2003. See also Steffen Jorgensen, Simon Pierre Sigue, and Georges Zaccour, "Dynamic Cooperative Advertising in a Channel," *Journal of Retailing*, Spring 2000.

11. For more on co-op ads, see "Nestle Warns Stores: Prove It or Lose Out," *Advertising Age*, September 13, 2004, pp. 1, 52; "Appeals Court Rules against Pork Council," *Advertising Age*, October 27, 2003; "Big Blue Offers Solutions with $60 Mil Co-op Effort," *Advertising Age*, April 30, 2001; "Revlon Plans Another Makeover," *Wall Street Journal*, November 21, 2000; "Joint Marketing with Retailers Spreads," *Wall Street Journal*, October 24, 1996; "H&R Block, Excedrin Discover Joint Promotions Can Be Painless," *Wall Street Journal*, February 28, 1991; John P. Murry and Jan B. Heide, "Managing Promotion Program Participation Within Manufacturer-Retailer Relationships," *Journal of Marketing*, January 1998.

12. "The Results Issue," *Brandweek*, July 23, 2007; "Brands in the 'Hood," *Point*, December 2005; "TV's New Parallel Universe," *BusinessWeek*, November 14, 2005. "As Podcasts Boom, Big Media Rushes to Stake a Claim," *Wall Street Journal*, October 10, 2005; "Advertisers Forced to Think Way Outside the Box," *USA Today*, June 20, 2005; "Non-Traditional Media Gain Ground, Consumers," *USA Today*, March 14, 2005. For more on videogame medium, see Victoria Mallinckrodt and Dick Mizerski, "The Effects of Playing an Advergame on Young Children's Perceptions, Preferences, and Requests," *Journal of Advertising*, Summer 2007; Mira Lee and Ronald J. Faber, "Effects of Product Placement in On-Line Games on Brand Memory," *Journal of Advertising*, Winter 2007; "You've Played the Videogame, Now Buy the Car," *Wall Street Journal*, October 24, 2007; "GM Floods Net with Malibu Ads," *USA Today*, October 22,

2007; "Guess What's Hiding in Your Videogame," *Wall Street Journal*, July 26, 2005. For more on cell phone medium, see Shintaro Okazaki, Akihiro Katsukura, and Mamoru Nishiyama, "How Mobile Advertising Works: The Role of Trust in Improving Attitudes and Recall," *Journal of Advertising Research*, June 2007; Mark Ferris, "Insights on Mobile Advertising, Promotion, and Research," *Journal of Advertising Research*, March 2007. "Shop by Phone Gets New Meaning," *USA Today*, December 19, 2007; "As Eyeballs, Dollars Converge, Mobile Marketing Will Explode," *Advertising Age*, December 3, 2007; "Retailers Come Calling, Literally, for the Holidays," *Wall Street Journal*, November 16, 2007. For more on in-store medium, see "In a Shift, Marketers Beef Up Ad Spending Inside Stores," *Wall Street Journal*, September 21, 2005; "Is Wal-Mart TV a Smart Buy or a Defensive One?" *Advertising Age*, September 19, 2005, pp. 3, 49. For more on the Yellow Pages medium, see "Print Yellow Pages Are Still Profitable," *Wall Street Journal*, May 22, 2000. For more on the outdoor medium, see "Neighbors Hope to Pull Plug on Signs," *USA Today*, September 5, 2007; "In Billboard War, Digital Signs Spark a Truce," *Wall Street Journal*, February 3, 2007; "Going Outside, Beyond the Billboard," *Wall Street Journal*, July 21, 2005. See also Charles R. Taylor, George R. Franke, and Bang Hae-Kyong, "Use and Effectiveness of Billboards," *Journal of Advertising*, Winter 2006; Charles R. Taylor and John C. Taylor, "Regulatory Issues in Ourdoor Advertising: A Content Analysis of Billboards," *Journal of Public Policy & Marketing*, Spring 1994. For more on the radio medium, see "The New Radio Revolution: From Satellite to Podcasts . . .," *BusinessWeek*, March 14, 2005; "Sending Fans a Clear Signal," *Brandweek*, January 31, 2005; Daniel M. Haygood, "A Status Report on Podcast Advertising," *Journal of Advertising Research*, December 2007. For more on the newspaper medium, see "Read All about It: How Newspapers Got into Such a Fix, and Where They Go from Here," *Wall Street Journal*, December 29, 2007; "Hatching Newsstand Revivals," *Investor's Business Daily*, October 30, 2006; "As Market Shifts, Newspapers Try to Lure New, Young Readers," *Wall Street Journal*, March 22, 2006; "Special Report: Newspapers," *Advertising Age*, April 29, 2002. For more on the magazine medium, see "Mags Grow Online but Still Dwarfed by Web Bigs," *Advertising Age*, March 3, 2008; "Magazine Editors Buck Marketers," *Wall Street Journal*, October 17, 2005. For more on the television and cable medium, see Kenneth C. Wilbur, "How the Digital Video Recorder (DVR) Changes Traditional Television Advertising," *Journal of Advertising*, Spring 2008; Ye Hu, Leonard M. Lodish, and Abba M. Krieger, "An Analysis of Real World TV Advertising Tests: A 15-Year Update," *Journal of Advertising Research*, September 2007; Siva K. Balasubramanian, James A. Karrh, and Hemant Patwardhan, "Audience Response to Product Placements," *Journal of Advertising*, Fall 2006; Elizabeth Cowley and Chris Barron, "When Product Placement Goes Wrong," *Journal of Advertising*, Spring 2008; "As 30-Second Spot Fades, What Advertisers Will Do Next," *Wall Street Journal*, January 3, 2006; "TV Ad Rules Are Challenged by Pod Busters," *Wall Street Journal*, November 21, 2005; "How to Watch TV," *Wall Street Journal*, November 9, 2005; "Hey, Advertisers, TiVo Is Your Friend," *BusinessWeek*, October 17, 2005; "New Ways to Drive Home the Message," *Newsweek*, May 30, 2005; "Cable's Big Bet on Hyper-Targeting," *BusinessWeek*, July 4, 2005; "Pay Per View Comes Full Circle," *Wall Street Journal*, April 1, 2005; "Can Mad Ave. Make Zap-Proof Ads?" *BusinessWeek*, February 2, 2004; Fareena Sultan and Andrew Rohm, "The Coming Era of Brand in the Hand Marketing," *MIT Sloan Management Review*, Fall 2005; James R. Coyle and Esther Thorson, "The Effects of Progressive Levels of Interactivity and Vividness in Web Marketing Sites," *Journal of Advertising*, Fall 2001; Mandeep Singh, Siva K. Balasubramanian, and Goutam Chakraborty, "A Comparative Analysis of Three Communication Formats: Advertising, Infomercial, and Direct Experience," *Journal of Advertising*, Winter 2000.

13. "Staid U.S. Marketers Try Racier Ads," *Wall Street Journal*, July 31, 2003; "A Leap for Advertising," *Adweek*, June 16, 2003; "Sex-Themed Ads Often Don't Travel Well," *Wall Street Journal*, March 31, 2000; "Underwear Ads Caught in Bind over Sex Appeal," *Advertising Age*, July 8, 1996;

14. "Looking for Mr. Plumber," *MediaWeek*, June 27, 1994; "Those Really Big Shows Are Often Disappointing to Those Who Advertise," *Wall Street Journal*, June 14, 1994.

15. V. Kumar, Rajkumar Venkatesan, and Werner Reinartz, "Knowing What to Sell, When, and to Whom," *Harvard Business Review*, March 2006; Jacquelyn S. Thomas, Werner Reinartz, and V. Kumar, "Getting the Most Out of All Your Customers," *Harvard Business Review*, July–August 2004.

16. For more on ATM ads, see "Ads on Automated Teller Machines Multiply as Technology Improves," *Investor's Business Daily*, October 5, 2000. For more on Nascar ads, see "America's Fastest Growing Sport," *Fortune*, September 5, 2005; "Sponsored by . . . SomethingAde," *Business 2.0*, October 2004; "Hotel Rides with Race Fans," *USA Today*, November 4, 2003; "The Changing Face of Nascar," *USA Today* (Bonus Section E), August 29, 2003; "Space for Rent," *Brandweek*, June 2, 2003. See also Carolyn J. Simmons and Karen L. Becker-Olsen, "Achieving Marketing Objectives Through Social Sponsorships," *Journal of Marketing*, October 2006; Jan Drengner, Hansjoerg Gaus, and Steffen Jahn, "Does Flow Influence the Brand Image in Event Marketing?" *Journal of Advertising Research*, March 2008; Angeline G. Close, R. Zachary Finney, Russell Z. Lacey, and Julie Z. Sneath, "Engaging the Consumer through Event Marketing: Linking Attendees with the Sponsor, Community, and Brand," *Journal of Advertising Research*, December 2006; Stephen W. Pruitt, T. Bettina Cornwell, and John M. Clark, "The NASCAR Phenomenon: Auto Racing Sponsorships and Shareholder Wealth," *Journal of Advertising Research*, September 2004; Nora J. Rifon, Sejung Marina Choi, Carrie S. Trimble, and Hairong Li, "Congruence Effects in Sponsorship," *Journal of Advertising*, Spring 2004; Shelly Rodgers, "The Effects of Sponsor Relevance on Consumer Reactions to Internet Sponsorships," *Journal of Advertising*, Winter 2004.

17. "Pet Sounds: Purina Hopes to Boost Its Brand Loyalty with Podcasts," *Wall Street Journal*, June 29, 2005, p. B2A.

18. "Cell Phone Ads That Consumers Love," *Harvard Business School Working Knowledge*, February 28, 2005; Rama Yelkur, Chuck Tomkovick, and Patty Traczyk, "Super Bowl Advertising Effectiveness: Hollywood Finds the Games Golden," *Journal of Advertising Research*, March 2004.

19. "Guerrilla Marketing 2007," *Brandweek*, November 26, 2007; "Ads Keep Spreading, but Are Consumers Immune?" *Advertising Age*, November 19, 2007; "What's In-Store? Lots of TV Ads," *Brandweek*, November 19, 2007; "Bills Make Room for Advertising," *Wall Street Journal*, October 16, 2007; "EcoHangers: A Clean, Green Brand Strategy," *Brandweek*, October 8, 2007; "Checking Out CBS in the Checkout Line," *Wall Street Journal*, September 7, 2007; "Shout a Message from the Rooftops to the World," *USA Today*, June 5, 2007; "Caught in the Clutter Crossfire: Your Brand," *Advertising Age*, April 2, 2007; "The Newest Ad Frontier: Airport Security Lines," *Advertising Age*, March 5, 2007; "Trash Trucks: A New Hot Spot for Ads," *Advertising Age*, February 5, 2007; "How a Gecko Shook Up Insurance Ads," *Wall Street Journal*, January 2, 2007; "Want to Stand Out? Make a Splash with Mini Billboards," *Inc.*, December 2006; "Product Placement— You Can't Escape It," *USA Today*, October 11, 2006; "Sky's the Limit for Advertisers," *USA Today*, August 10, 2006; "Look—Up in the Sky! Product Placement!" *Wall Street Journal*, April 18, 2006; "Rated M for Mad Ave," *BusinessWeek Online*, February 27, 2006; "Ads, Ads, Everywhere," *ABC News Online*, January 19, 2006; "Advertisers Find a Captive Audience: Travelers on Planes," *Wall Street Journal*, December 20, 2005; "Film Fans Can Expect More Advertising on Big Screen," *USA Today*, December 6, 2005; "Subject: Email Ads Grow Up," *Wall Street Journal*, November 23, 2005; "Advertising: Anywhere, Anytime," *Wall Street Journal*, November 21, 2005; "Art Meets Ads: Can Sculpture Sell Moisturizer?" *Wall Street Journal*, October 25, 2005; "Best Appliance in a Supporting Role . . .," *Wall Street Journal*, September 22, 2005; "Tired of On-Air Promos? Nets Fan Out to Gain Buzz," *Advertising Age*, September 19, 2005; "PepsiCo's Mountain Dew Backs Film," *Wall Street Journal*, September 12, 2005; "Product Placement Grows as Nets Worry about Glut," *Adweek*, August 22, 2005; "With Ads Everywhere, U.S. Culture Is Reshaped," *The Detroit News*, May 8, 2005; www.detnews.com and www.keyad.com; "Advertising on Truck Mud Flaps Comes to an Interstate near You," *PR Newswire*, January 6, 2005; "Get Me Rewrite! Miller Calls the TV Shots," *Wall Street Journal*, October 13, 2004; "The Robot Wore Converses," *Wall Street Journal*, September 2, 2004; "Trump to Brands: You're Hired," *Wall Street Journal*, September 2, 2004; "Water Works: How Fiji Brand Got Hip to Sip," *Wall Street Journal*, August 16, 2004; "Also Starring (Your Product Name Here)," *USA Today*, August 12, 2004; "Too Much of a Good Thing?" *Brandweek*, August 9, 2004; "For More Advertisers, the Medium Is the Text Message," *Wall Street Journal*, August 2, 2004; "Hubcap Ads Put New Spin on Marketing," *USA Today*, July 19, 2004; Ross D. Petty and J. Craig Andrews, "Covert Marketing Unmasked: A Legal and Regulatory Guide for Practices That Mask Marketing Messages," *Journal of Public Policy & Marketing*, Spring 2008.

20. "Nielsen Online Reports Topline U.S. Data for March 2008," *News Release*, Nielsen Online, April 14, 2008; "IBM Consumer Survey Shows Decline of TV as Primary Media Device," *Press Release*, IBM Corp., August 22, 2007; "IDC Finds Online Consumers Spend Almost Twice as Much Time Using the Internet as Watching TV," *IDC Press Release*, www.idc.com; "Internet's Influence on In-Store Purchasing Behavior Is Rising, According to CMO Council/Yahoo! Survey," *Market Wire*, October 2005. See also Jeffrey F. Rayport, "Demand-Side Innovation: Where IT Meets Marketing," *InformationWeek*, February 1, 2007.

21. "Flowers That Pop," *Fortune*, December 3, 2003.

22. "Average Search CPC Data by Category for March 2008," *Search Engine Watch*, April 7, 2008. See also "Agencies Know the Score on Web Tracking," *Wall Street Journal*, April 21, 2008; "So Many Ads, So Few Clicks," *BusinessWeek*, November 12, 2007; "Competing for Clients, and Paying by the Click," *The New York Times*, October 15, 2007; "The New Benefits of Web-Search Queries," *Wall Street Journal*, February 6, 2007; "Web Numbers: What's Real?" *BusinessWeek*, October 23, 2006. See also "Click Fraud: The Dark Side of Online Advertising," *BusinessWeek*, October 2, 2006.

23. "Ad Networks, Confusion Grow on Web," *Wall Street Journal*, April 16, 2008; "Online Ads Getting Down to Business," *Investor's Business Daily*, January 16, 2008; "Outlook Bright for Online Advertising," *BtoB*, January 14, 2008; "Can't Skip This: Consumers Acclimating to Internet Ads," *Brandweek*, December 31, 2007; "Industry Turns Page on Page View Stats," *Brandweek*, June 4, 2007; "Behind the Curtain: How Google Determines the Ranks and Rates of Its Sponsored Links," *SFGate.com*, March 5, 2006; "Internet's Ad Gains Bringing Bad News to Newspapers, TV," *Investor's Business Daily*, November 18, 2005; "Car Makers Hone Their Pitch Online," *Wall Street Journal*, October 14, 2005; "Innovation: The Future of Advertising," *Fortune*, August 8, 2005; "I-Intelligence," *Advertising Age*, July 11, 2005; "Measuring Up," *Brandweek*, June 6, 2005; "In Click Fraud, Web Outfits Have a Costly Problem," *Wall Street Journal*, April 6, 2005; "Web Search Sites See Clicks Add Up to Big Ad Dollars," *The New York Times*, February 4, 2005. See also Juran Kim and Sally J. McMillan, "Evaluation of Internet Advertising Research," *Journal of Advertising*, Spring 2008; Kelli S. Burns and Richard J. Lutz, "The Function of Format: Consumer Responses to Six On-line Advertising Formats," *Journal of Advertising*, Spring 2006; Robert S. Moore, Claire Allison Stammerjohan, and Robin A. Coulter, "Banner Advertiser-Web Site Context Congruity and Color Effects on Attention and Attitudes," *Journal of Advertising*, Summer 2005; Nigel Hollis, "Ten Years of Learning on How Online Advertising Builds Brands," *Journal of Advertising Research*, June 2005; Ritu Lohtia, Naveen Donthu, and Edmund K. Hershberger, "The Impact of Content and Design Elements on Banner Advertising Click-through Rates," *Journal of Advertising Research*, December 2003; David R. Fortin and Ruby Roy Dholakia, "Interactivity and Vividness Effects on Social Presence and Involvement with a Web-Based Advertisement," *Journal of Business Research*, March 2005; Chan Yun Yoo and Kihan Kim, "Processing of Animation in Online Banner Advertising: The Roles of Cognitive and Emotional Responses," *Journal of Interactive Marketing*, Autumn 2005; Kim Bartel Sheehan, "Re-Weaving the Web: Integrating Print and Online Communications," *Journal of Interactive Marketing*, Spring 2001.

24. "Febreze Sniffs Out New Target: Dorm of Dwellers," *Advertising Age*, October 29, 2007.

25. For an example of creative campaign, see "Toyota Makes a Sharp Turn on the Web," *Wall Street Journal*, March 7, 2008; "Hey, No Whopper on the Menu?" *Wall Street Journal*, February 8, 2008; "Did Telling a Whopper Sell the Whopper?" *Advertising Age*, January 14, 2008; "From Admirable to Addlebrained," *USA Today*, December 31, 2007; "Marketers Get More Creative with TV Ads," *USA Today*, November 12, 2007; "Tide's Washday Miracle: Not Doing Laundry," *Advertising Age*, November 12, 2007; "Starbucks, PepsiCo Bring Subopera to Shanghai," *Wall Street Journal*, November 1, 2007; "Madison Avenue Wants You! (or at Least Your Videos)," *USA Today*, June 21, 2007; "Best of Show: Five Interactive Efforts that Got the Industry Talking . . . ," *IQ*, January 22, 2007; "Kleenex Invites Everyone to a Tearjerker," *Brandweek*, January 22, 2007; "Ads Reach for Reality," *Wall Street Journal*, December 21, 2005; Burger King's Subservient Chicken at www.subservientchicken.com; "Keepers of the Flame: A BK Roundtable," *Brandweek*, March 28, 2005; "Agency of the Year, Crispin Ups Ante," *Advertising Age*, January 10, 2005. For some creative and controversial ads, see "Marketers of the Year," *Brandweek*, October 20, 2003; "How to Sell a Strange Idea," *Adweek*, July 14, 2003; "Downloading the Future of TV Advertising," *Business 2.0*, July 2003; "Cheers and Jeers," *Adweek*, June 30, 2003; "Ikea's 'Lamp' Wins Cannes," *Advertising Age*, June 23, 2003; "A Leap for Advertising," *Adweek*, June 16, 2003; "The Lowest Moments in Advertising," *Adweek*, June 9, 2003; "Best Awards," *Advertising Age*, May 26, 2003. See also Josephine L. C. M. Woltman Elpers, Ashesh Mukherjee, and Wayne D. Hoyer, "Humor in Television Advertising: A Moment-to-Moment Analysis," *Journal of Consumer Research*, December 2004; Anand Kumar and Shanker Krishnan, "Memory Interference in Advertising: A Replication and Extension," *Journal of Consumer Research*, March 2004; Carl Obermiller, Eric Spangenberg, and Douglas L. MacLachlan, "Ad Skepticism," *Journal of Advertising*, Fall 2005, p. 7; Edward F. McQuarrie and Barbara J. Phillips, "Indirect Persuasion in Advertising," *Journal of Advertising*, Summer 2005; Kathryn A. Braun-LaTour, Michael S. LaTour, Jacqueline E. Pickrell, and Elizabeth F. Loftus, "How and When Advertising Can Influence Memory for Consumer Experience," *Journal of Advertising*, Winter 2004; Darrel D. Muehling and David E. Sprott, "The Power of Reflection," *Journal of Advertising*, Fall 2004; William E. Baker, Heather Honea, and Cristel Antonia Russell, "Do Not Wait to Reveal the Brand Name," *Journal of Advertising*, Fall 2004; Brett A. S. Martin, Bodo Lang, and Stephanie Wong, "Conclusion Explicitness in Advertising," *Journal of Advertising*, Winter 2004; Thomas W. Cline, Moses B. Altsech, and James J. Kellaris, "When Does Humor Enhance or Inhibit Ad Responses?" *Journal of Advertising*, Fall 2003; Joan Meyers-Levy and Durairaj Maheswaran, "Exploring Message Framing Outcomes When Systematic, Heuristic, or Both Types of Processing Occur," *Journal of Consumer Psychology*, (1) 2004; David W. Stewart and Ingrid M. Martin, "Advertising Disclosures: Clear and Conspicuous or Understood and Used?" *Journal of Public Policy & Marketing*, Fall 2004; Mark I. Alpert, Judy I. Alpert, and Elliot N. Maltz, "Purchase Occasion Influence on the Role of Music in Advertising," *Journal of Business Research*, March 2005; Barbara J. Phillips and Edward F. McQuarrie, "The Development, Change, and Transformation of Rhetorical Style in Magazine Advertisements 1954–1999," *Journal of Advertising*, Winter 2002.

26. "Mac and PC's Overseas Adventures," *Wall Street Journal*, March 1, 2007; "One Size Doesn't Fit All," *Wall Street Journal*, October 1, 2003; "Exxon Centralizes New Global Campaign," *Wall Street Journal*, July 11, 2001; "McCann Finds Global a Tough Sell in Japan," *Wall Street Journal*, June 19, 1997. See also Fahad S. Al-Olayan, "A Content Analysis of Magazine Advertisements from the United States and the Arab World," *Journal of Advertising*, Fall 2000; Theodore Levitt, "The Globalization of Markets," *Harvard Business Review*, May–June 1983; Kamran Kashani, "Beware the Pitfalls of Global Marketing," *Harvard Business Review*, September–October 1989.

27. See "Agency Report," *Advertising Age* (Special Report), May 5, 2008. See also "Madison Ave. Lights Up," *Fortune*, December 12, 2005; "Ending Advertising's Spiral," *Business 2.0*, September 2005; "Agencies Are from Mars, Clients Are from Venus," *Point*, July 2005; "The Fall of a Madison Avenue Icon," *Adweek*, July 25, 2005; "The Big Four Holding On," *Point*, July 2005; "How You Size Up the Competition," *Adweek*, May 2, 2005; "Bigger and Bigger," *Fortune*, November 29, 2004; "China's Edgy Advertising," *Wall Street Journal*, October 27, 2003; "How Tiny German Shop Landed McDonald's," *Wall Street Journal*, August 6, 2003; "Still in the Hunt," *BusinessWeek*, July 7, 2003; "WPP's Sorrell Bests Publicis in Cordiant Bid," *Wall Street Journal*, June 18, 2003; "Are Holding Companies Obsolete?" *Adweek*, June 9, 2003; "Integrated Agencies," *Advertising Age*, May 19, 2003; "Agency Report: Top 100 National Agencies," *Adweek*, April 7, 2003. See also Gerard Prendergast, Yizheng Shi, and Douglas West, "Organizational Buying and Advertising Agency-Client Relationships in China," *Journal of Advertising*, Summer 2001; George C. Hozier, Jr., and John D. Schatzberg, "Advertising Agency Terminations and Reviews: Stock Returns and Firm Performance," *Journal of Business Research*, November 2000.

28. "Commission Returns (with Twist)," *Advertising Age*, November 5, 2007; "Ad-Industry Secret Comes to Light," *Wall Street Journal*, September 23, 2005; "It's Pretty Grim (Hint) over There," *Advertising Age*, September 19, 2005; "The Scramble on Mad. Ave.," *Fortune*, August 8, 2005; "Taken for a Ride," *Brandweek*, November 1, 2004; "Agencies Face New Accountability," *Wall Street Journal*, October 2, 2003; "Interpublic May Become More Open," *Wall Street Journal*, September 10, 2003; "Kraft Rethinks Agency Pay, Brand Duties," *Adweek*, August 18, 2003; "GM Overhauls Compensation," *Advertising Age*, March 17, 2003. See also Hao Zhao, "Incentive-Based Compensation to Advertising Agencies: A Principal-Agent Approach," *International Journal of Research in Marketing*, September 2005; Diana L. Haytko, "Firm-to-Firm and Interpersonal Relationships: Perspectives from Advertising Agency Account Managers," *Journal of the Academy of Marketing Science*, Summer 2004; John Sutherland, Lisa Duke, and Avery Abernethy, "A Model of Marketing Information Flow," *Journal of Advertising*, Winter 2004; Judy Harris and Kimberly A. Taylor, "The Case for Greater Agency Involvement in Strategic Partnerships," *Journal of Advertising Research*, December 2003; Mukund S. Kulkarni, Premal P. Vora, and Terence A. Brown, "Firing Advertising Agencies," *Journal of Advertising*, Fall 2003.

29. "Web vs. TV: Research Aims to Gauge Ads," *Wall Street Journal*, March 19, 2008; "AFLAC CMO Says: Shut the Duck Up," *Advertising Age*, February 19, 2007; "Ad Effectiveness Takes Pounding," *Advertising Age*, August 17, 2006; "Counting the Eyeballs," *BusinessWeek*, January 16, 2006; "Econometrics Buzzes Ad World as a Way of Measuring Results," *Wall Street Journal*, August 16, 2005; "Putting a Value on Marketing Dollars," *Wall Street Journal*, July 27, 2005; "Call to Action Ads Give Clients Results They Can Measure," *Wall Street Journal*, March 22, 2005; "How to Measure Product Placement," *Adweek*, January 17, 2005; "Making Marketing Measure Up," *BusinessWeek*, December 13, 2004; "At Last a Way to Measure Ads," *Wall Street Journal Reports*, June 16, 2003; "The Top 5 Rules of the Ad Game," *BusinessWeek*, January 20, 2003; "Consumers May Notice the Ads, but Will They Buy the Product?" *Investor's Business Daily*, December 19, 2002; "Does Creativity Count?" *Brandweek*, December 11, 2000. See also John E. Hogan, Katherine N. Lemon, and Barak Libai, "Quantifying the Ripple: Word-of-Mouth and Advertising Effectiveness," *Journal of Advertising Research*, September 2004; Margaret H. Blair and Allan R. Kuse, "Better Practices in Advertising Can Change a Cost of Doing Business to Wise Investments in the Business," *Journal of Advertising Research*, March 2004; Subodh Bhat, Michael Bevans, and Sanjit Sengupta, "Measuring Users' Web Activity to Evaluate and Enhance Advertising Effectiveness," *Journal of Advertising*, Fall 2002; Ann Marie Barry, "How Advertising Works: The Role of Research," *Journal of the Academy of Marketing Science*, Winter 2001; Els Gijsbrechts, Katia Campo, and Tom Goossens, "The Impact of Store Flyers on Store Traffic and Store Sales: A Geo-Marketing Approach," *Journal of Retailing*, (1) 2003; Fuyuan Shen, "Banner Advertisement Pricing, Measurement, and Pretesting Practices: Perspectives from Interactive Agencies," *Journal of Advertising*, Fall 2002; DeAnna S. Kempf and Russell N. Laczniak, "Advertising's Influence on Subsequent Product Trial Processing," *Journal of Advertising*, Fall 2001; Gerald J. Tellis and Doyle L. Weiss, "Does TV Advertising Really Affect Sales? The Role of Measures, Models, and Data Aggregation," *Journal of Advertising*, Fall 1995; John H. Holmes, "When Ads Work," *Journal of the Academy of Marketing Science*, Winter 1997; Karen Whitehill King, John D. Pehrson, and Leonard N. Reid, "Pretesting TV Commercials: Methods, Measures, and Changing Agency Roles," *Journal of Advertising*, September 1993; Erik du Plessis, "Recognition versus Recall," *Journal of Advertising Research*, May–June 1994.

30. "Catching the Eye of China's Elite," *BusinessWeek*, February 11, 2008; "In Korea, Ads Become Must-See TV," *Wall Street Journal*, December 13, 2007; "For Reality Shows in China, Rules Have Never Been Tighter," *Advertising Age*, October 8, 2007; "A Sign of Things to Come?" *Advertising Age*, October 1, 2007; "Beijing Mystery: What's Happening to the Billboards," *Wall Street Journal*, June 25, 2007; "Pigs Get the Ax in China TV Ads, in Nod to Muslims," *Wall Street Journal*, January 25, 2007; "China Blocks News Corp. Plan for TV Channel," *Wall Street Journal*, August 25, 2005; "China Demands Concrete Proof of Ad Claims," *Wall Street Journal*, July 8, 2005; "Treaty May Stub Out Cigarette Ads in China," *Wall Street Journal*, December 2, 2003; "U.K. TV Can Pose Tricky Hurdles," *Wall Street Journal*, June 27, 2003. See also Young Sook Moon and George R. Franke, "Cultural Influences on Agency Practitioners' Ethical Perceptions: a Comparison of Korea and the U.S.," *Journal of Advertising*, Spring 2000; Kim Bartel Sheehan, "Balancing Acts: an Analysis of Food and Drug Administration Letters about Direct-to-Consumer Advertising Violations," *Journal of Public Policy & Marketing*, Fall 2003; J. Howard Beales III, "The Federal Trade Commission's Use of Unfairness Authority: Its Rise, Fall, and Resurrection," *Journal of Public Policy & Marketing*, Fall 2003; Alexander Simonson, "The Impact of Advertising Law on Business and Public Policy," *Journal of Marketing*, October 1994; Ross D. Petty, "Advertising Law in the United States and European Union," *Journal of Public Policy & Marketing*, Spring 1997; Steve Lysonski and Michael F. Duffy, "The New Zealand Fair Trading Act of 1986: Deceptive Advertising," *Journal of Consumer Affairs*, Summer 1992.

31. For more on regulatory battle between Splenda and Equal, see "How Sweet It Isn't," *Wall Street Journal*, April 6, 2007; "What Works: Finding the Sweet Spot," *Business 2.0*, November 2005; "Sweetness and Fight," *Newsweek*, November 7, 2005; "Splenda Suit Points Up Dangers of Ad Claim Cases," *Adweek*, August 1, 2005. For more on KFC, see "Hey, Fast Food: We Love You Just the Way You Are," *Brandweek*, November 24, 2003; "FTC Examines Health Claims in KFC's Ads," *Wall Street Journal*, November 19, 2003; "Garfield's Ad Review: KFC Serves Big, Fat Bucket of Nonsense in 'Healthy' Spots," *Advertising Age*, November 3, 2003. See also "Regulators Take Another Look at Product Placement," *Brandweek*, October 10, 2005; "As 'Safer Smokes' Multiply, States Probe Marketing Claims," *Wall Street Journal*, May 18, 2004; "Lawsuit Alleges Alcohol Industry Targets Underage Drinkers," *Wall Street Journal*, November 28, 2003; "P&G Is Settling Disputes on Ads as Suits Pile Up," *Wall Street Journal*,

November 26, 2003; "Beer Ads on TV, College Sports: Explosive Mix?" *Wall Street Journal*, November 12, 2003; "Watchdog Group Hits TV Product Placement," *Advertising Age*, October 6, 2003. See also Boris W. Becker, "The Tangled Web They Weave: Truth, Falsity, & Advertisers," *Journal of Advertising*, Summer 1996; Elizabeth K. LaFleur, R. E. Reidenbach, Donald P. Robin, and P. J. Forrest, "An Exploration of Rule Configuration Effects on the Ethical Decision Processes of Advertising Professionals," *Journal of the Academy of Marketing Science*, Winter 1996; Barbara B. Stern, "'Crafty Advertisers': Literary Versus Literal Deceptiveness," *Journal of Public Policy & Marketing*, Spring 1992; Joel J. Davis, "Ethics in Advertising Decisionmaking: Implications for Reducing the Incidence of Deceptive Advertising," *Journal of Consumer Affairs*, Winter 1994. For more on advertising to kids, see Chapter 18, endnote 13.

32. "Guides for the Use of Environmental Marketing Claims," Federal Trade Commission (FTC.gov), 1992; "Marketers Not Consumers Need an Environmental Education," *Advertising Age*, April 28, 2008.

33. Kathy R. Fitzpatrick, "The Legal Challenge of Integrated Marketing Communication (IMC)," *Journal of Advertising*, Winter 2005; Ivan L. Preston, "Regulatory Positions Toward Advertising Puffery of the Uniform Commercial Code and the Federal Trade Commission," *Journal of Public Policy & Marketing*, Fall 1997; Claude R. Martin, Jr., "Ethical Advertising Research Standards: Three Case Studies," *Journal of Advertising*, September 1994; George M. Zinkhan, "Advertising Ethics: Emerging Methods and Trends," *Journal of Advertising*, September 1994.

34. "The Goody-Bag Game," *Wall Street Journal*, December 7, 2005; "High Noon in Aisle Five," *Inc.*, January 2004; "P&G Breaks Out of Its Slump," *USA Today*, October 14, 2003; "Ads Mmm, Junk Mail," *Newsweek*, August 18, 2003; "Road Shows Take Brands to the People," *Wall Street Journal*, May 14, 2003; "Offbeat Marketing Sells," *Investor's Business Daily*, March 27, 2002.

35. "Too Many Choices," *Wall Street Journal*, April 20, 2001; "Reposition: Simplifying the Customer's Brandscape," *Brandweek*, October 2, 2000. See also Page Moreau, Aradhna Krishna, and Bari Harlam, "The Manufacturer-Retailer-Consumer Triad: Differing Perceptions Regarding Price Promotions," *Journal of Retailing*, Winter 2001; Devon DelVecchio, David H. Henard, and Traci H. Freling, "The Effect of Sales Promotion on Post-Promotion Brand Preference: A Meta-Analysis," *Journal of Retailing*, September 2006; Kusum L. Ailawadi, Bari A. Harlam, Jacques César, and David Trounce, "Promotion Profitability for a Retailer: The Role of Promotion, Brand, Category, and Store Characteristics," *Journal of Marketing Research*, November 2006; Kusum L. Ailawadi, Karen Gedenk, Christian Lutzky, and Scott A. Neslin, "Decomposition of the Sales Impact of Promotion-Induced Stockpiling," *Journal of Marketing Research*, August 2007.

36. For more on Pampers example, see "P&G Promotion Is Too Successful, Angering Buyers," *Wall Street Journal*, April 2, 2002. For another example, see "Shopper Turns Lots of Pudding into Free Miles," *Wall Street Journal*, January 24, 2000; "The Pudding Guy Flies Again (and Again) Over Latin America," *Wall Street Journal*, March 16, 2000.

37. George E. Belch and Michael E. Belch, *Advertising and Promotion, an Integrated Marketing Communication Perspective* (Burr Ridge, IL: McGraw-Hill, 2004); Priya Raghubir, J. Jeffrey Inman, and Hans Grande, "The Three Faces of Consumer Promotions," *California Management Review*, Summer 2004.

38. "Cut It Out: U.S. Stores May Kill Coupon Clutter," *Advertising Age*, November 7, 2005, pp. 4, 57; "Designated Shopper," *Brandweek*, February 4, 2002; "Cybercoupons," *Discount Store News*, March 9, 1998; "The Scoop on Coupons," *Brandweek*, March 17, 1997; "Many Companies Are Starting to Wean Shoppers Off Coupons," *Wall Street Journal*, January 22, 1997; "Internet Coupons offer H.O.T! Deals," *USA Today*, December 13, 1996.

39. "The Show Goes On: Online Trade Shows," *Wall Street Journal Reports*, April 28, 2003; "The Cyber-Show Must Go On," *Trade Media*, May 7, 2001; "Getting the Most from a Trade Show Booth," *Investor's Business Daily*, April 25, 2000. See also Li Ling-yee, "Relationship Learning at Trade Shows: Its Antecedents and Consequences," *Industrial Marketing Management*, February 2006; Timothy M. Smith, Srinath Gopalakrishna, and Paul M. Smith, "The Complementary Effect of Trade Shows on Personal Selling," *International Journal of Research in Marketing*, March 2004; Marnik G. Dekimpe, Pierre Francois, Srinath Gopalakrishna, Gary L. Lilien, and Christophe Van den Bulte, "Generalizing About Trade Show Effectiveness: A Cross-National Comparison," *Journal of Marketing*, October 1997; Scott Barlass, "How to Get the Most Out of Trade Shows," *Journal of Product Innovation Management*, September 1997; Srinath Gopalakrishna, Gary L. Lilien, Jerome D. Williams, and Ian K. Sequeira, "Do Trade Shows Pay Off?" *Journal of Marketing*, July 1995; "Trade Promotion Rises," *Advertising Age*, April 3, 2000.

40. "Creating Incentives Down in Ranks: Marriott Ties Pay to Guest Replies," *Investor's Business Daily*, July 6, 2001; "Get Great Results from Salespeople by Finding What Really Moves Them," *Investor's Business Daily*, July 2, 2001.

CHAPTER 16

1. "Flip Video," *Wikipedia*, retrieved May 2, 2009; "Sony Turns Focus to Low-Cost Video Camera," *Wall Street Journal*, April 17, 2009; "The World's Most Innovative Companies," *Fast Company*, March 2009; "Consumers Flip for Mini Camcorders," *Fortune*, January 27, 2009; "Gadget of the Stars," *Newsweek*, December 15, 2008; "Flip Video Rolls Out New HD Mini Camcorder: The Mino HD," *CNET*, November 11, 2008; "The Lebowski Flip Mino: If You Will It, Dude, It Is No Dream," *CNET*, October 14, 2008; "Moving Pictures," *Economist*, September 6, 2008; "Flip Video's Mighty Mino," *CNET News*, June 3, 2008; "Camcorder Brings Zen to the Shoot," *New York Times*, March 20, 2008; "Pure Digital Launches Higher-Capacity Video Camera," *TWICE*, October 8, 2007; "An Easier Way to Make and Share Videos," *Wall Street Journal*, September 12, 2007; "Smile—You're Always On Camera," *Forbes*, June 18, 2007; "A Sweet and Simple Camcorder," *BusinessWeek*, May 23, 2007; "The History of Home Movies," *Internet Video Magazine*, 2007; "The Video Camera Revised," *Wall Street Journal*, May 3, 2006; "Pure Digital's Point & Shoot Video Camera," *Engadget.com*, May 2, 2006; "The History of Video Cameras," *Internet Video Magazine*, 2006; "Single-Use Digital Video Cams Now Available in CVS," *Engadget.com*, June 6, 2005.

2. "Car Makers Cut Free Maintenance," *Wall Street Journal*, July 7, 2005; "Detroit's Latest Offer: Pay More, Get Less," *Wall Street Journal*, July 24, 2002; "Did You Overpay for Your Car? States Sue Dealers over Fees," *Wall Street Journal*, June 20, 2002; "Sticker Shock: Detroit's Hidden Price Hikes," *Wall Street Journal*, April 10, 2002; "Adding Options Helps Car Firms Increase Prices," *Wall Street Journal*, December 27, 1993; "Car Makers Seek to Mask Price Increases," *Wall Street Journal*, August 16, 1989. For another example involving the cruise industry, see "A Sea of Extra Charges," *USA Today*, March 14, 2003; "All Your Onboard Fun Is Included*," *Wall Street Journal*, December 27, 2001. For another example involving the car rental industry, see "Car-Rental Agencies Talk of Realistic Total Pricing," *The New York Times*, February 10, 2004; See also Srabana Dasgupta, S. Siddarth, and Jorge Silva-Risso, "To Lease or to Buy? A Structural Model of a Consumer's Vehicle and Contract Choice Decisions," *Journal of Marketing Research*, August 2007; Hope Jensen Schau, Michael F. Smith, and Per Ivar Schau, "The Healthcare Network Economy: The Role of Internet Information Transfer and Implications for Pricing," *Industrial Marketing Management*, February 2005; Ashutosh Dixit, Karin Braunsberger, George M. Zinkhan, and Yue Pan, "Information Technology—Enhanced Pricing Strategies: Managerial and Public Policy Implications," *Journal of Business Research*, September 2005; Robert M. Schindler, Maureen Morrin, and Nada Nasr Bechwati, "Shipping Charges and Shipping-Charge Skepticism: Implications for Direct Marketers' Pricing Formats," *Journal of Interactive Marketing*, Winter 2005; Rajneesh Suri, Srinivasan Swaminathan, and Kent B. Monroe, "Price Communications in Online and Print Coupons: An Empirical Investigation," *Journal of Interactive Marketing*, Autumn 2004; Michael R. Baye, John Morgan, and Patrick Scholten, "Temporal Price Dispersion: Evidence from an Online Consumer Electronics Market," *Journal of Interactive Marketing*, Autumn 2004; Xing Pan, Brian T. Ratchford, and Venkatesh Shankar, "Price Dispersion on the Internet: A Review and Directions for Future Research," *Journal of Interactive Marketing*, Autumn 2004.

3. Alfred Rappaport, "Executive Incentives versus Corporate Growth," *Harvard Business Review*, July–August 1978; David M. Szymanski, Sundar G. Bharadwaj, and P. Rajan Varadarajan, "An Analysis of the Market Share-Profitability Relationship," *Journal of Marketing*, July 1993.

4. "Decision on Lipitor Sets Express Scripts Apart from Its Field," *Investor's Business Daily*, November 7, 2005; "EU Court Backs Resale of Drugs," *Wall Street Journal*, April 2, 2004; "The Telecom Follies," *Wall Street Journal*, March 26, 2004; "It's Time to Look at Rx Pricing," *Modern Healthcare*, March 15, 2004; "The New Drug War," *Fortune*, March 8, 2004; "Rethinking Restructuring," *Public Utilities Fortnightly*, February 2004; "The Economy: Steel Prices Jump, Spurring Protests from Customers," *Wall Street Journal*, January 23, 2004.

5. For more on the dot-com bust, see "Applying Old Pricing Lessons to a New Investing World," *Wall Street Journal*, May 21, 2001; Stephen E. Frank, *Net Worth* (2001); "E-Assets for Sale," *BusinessWeek E.Biz*, May 14, 2001; "Last Guys Finish First," *Ecompany*, May 2001; "After the Wild Ride," *BusinessWeek E.Biz*, April 16, 2001; "Study: Net Start-Ups Ignored Economics 101," *Investor's Business Daily*, March 2, 2001; "12 Months When the Dot Turned into a Dark Period," *Investor's Business Daily*, January 2, 2001; "We're Heading into Something Big—but What?" *USA Today*, December 29, 2000; "What Detonated Dot-Bombs?" *USA Today*, December 4, 2000; "Dot-Bombs," *Brandweek*, November 27, 2000. See also Lisa E. Bolton and Joseph W. Alba, "Price Fairness: Good and Service Differences and the Role of Vendor Costs," *Journal of Consumer Research*, August 2006; Lan Xia, Kent B. Monroe, and Jennifer L. Cox, "The Price Is Unfair! A Conceptual Framework of Price Fairness Perceptions," *Journal of Marketing*, October 2004; K. Sivakumar, "Price-Tier Competition: Distinguishing Between Intertier Competition and Intratier Competition," *Journal of Business Research*, December 2003.

6. "Aluminum Firms Offer Wider Discounts but Price Cuts Stop at Some Distributors," *Wall Street Journal*, November 16, 1984. For another example of administered pricing, see "Why a Grand Plan to Cut CD Prices Went off the Track," *Wall Street Journal*, June 4, 2004.

7. Moritz Fleischmann, Joseph M. Hall, and David F. Pyke, "Smart Pricing," *MIT Sloan Management Review*, Winter 2004; Man-Mohan S. Sodhi and Navdeep S. Sodhi, "Six Sigma Pricing," *Harvard Business Review*, May 2005; Eric Anderson and Duncan Simester, "Mind Your Pricing Cues," *Harvard Business Review*, September 2003; Kissan Joseph, "On the Optimality of Delegating Pricing Authority to the Sales Force," *Journal of Marketing*, January 2001; Michael V. Marn and Robert L. Rosiello, "Managing Price, Gaining Profit," *Harvard Business Review*, September–October 1992; Subhash C. Jain and Michael B. Laric, "A Framework for Strategic Industrial Pricing," *Industrial Marketing Management*, (8) 1979; Peter R. Dickson and Joel E. Urbany, "Retailer Reactions to Competitive Price Changes," *Journal of Retailing*, Spring 1994; Gerard J. Tellis, "Beyond the Many Faces of Price: An Integration of Pricing Strategies," *Journal of Marketing*, October 1986.

8. For more on Priceline, see "Priceline 2.0," *Brandweek*, March 6, 2006; "Priceline Offers Two Approaches to Distinguish Itself from Herd," *Investor's Business Daily*, May 27, 2005; "A Humbler, Happier Priceline," *BusinessWeek*, August 11, 2003; "Inside Jay Walker's House of Cards," *Fortune*, November 13, 2000; "Letting the Masses Name Their Price," *BusinessWeek E.Biz*, September 18, 2000. See

also "The Discount Cards That Don't Save You Money," *Wall Street Journal*, January 21, 2003; "Beating Retailers at the Discount Game," *Wall Street Journal*, November 27, 2002; "Lessons from a Grocer," *Investor's Business Daily*, April 3, 2002. For more on other online travel sites, see "Discount Travel Web Sites Offering Last-Minute Deals," *Investor's Business Daily*, December 21, 2005; "Meet the Aggregators: A New Bread of Online Travel Web Sites ...," *Brandweek*, May 30, 2005; "Scoring a Travel Discount Gets Easier," *Wall Street Journal*, November 4, 2003; "The Travel Agent Bosses Love," *BusinessWeek*, October 27, 2003. See also Sucharita Chandran and Vicki G. Morwitz, "Effects of Participative Pricing on Consumers' Cognitions and Actions: A Goal Theoretic Perspective," *Journal of Consumer Research*, September 2005.

9. For more on EBay and its flexible pricing, see "EBay's Bid for Buyers Draws Mixed Reviews," *Wall Street Journal*, April 16, 2008; "Online Auction King eBay Also Big in Classifieds," *Investor's Business Daily*, April 7, 2008; "EBay Bids for Staying Power in a Changing Digital World," *USA Today*, March 31, 2008; "EBay Aligns with Sells in New Fee Structure," *Wall Street Journal*, January 30, 2008; "eBay's Chaos Theory," *Fast Company*, November 2007; "EBay's Aim: Be Lifestyle for Europe," *Investor's Business Daily*, November 15, 2007; "EBay Makes a Bid to Lure Lapsed Buyers," *Wall Street Journal*, October 12, 2007; "eBay's Bid for Celebrity Cachet," *BusinessWeek*, March 12, 2007; "EBay Bids for Younger Auction Crowd at Social-Network Sites," *Wall Street Journal*, March 1, 2007; "EBay's Bid to Go beyond Auctions Isn't Selling Well," *Wall Street Journal*, December 20, 2006; "Out-eBaying eBay in Korea," *BusinessWeek*, July 17, 2006; "What Happens When an eBay Steal Is a Fake," *Wall Street Journal*, June 29, 2006; "EBay's Bid for Impatient Shoppers," *BusinessWeek*, April 17, 2006; "EBay Ups U.S. Fees and Cuts China Fees," *Investor's Business Daily*, February 10, 2006; "The Big Guns' Next Target: eBay," *Business 2.0*, January–February 2006; "FT MONEY: eBay," *Financial Times*, December 31, 2005; "Who'll Give Me $50 for This Purse from Nana?" *Wall Street Journal*, December 28, 2005; "Getting an Oil Change off eBay," *Wall Street Journal*, November 17, 2005; "Skype Plus eBay Equals Conversational Markets," *Financial Times*, September 21, 2005; "EBay Bidding to Give Voice to Customers," *Investor's Business Daily*, September 13, 2005; "Buyers Kick Virtual Tires on eBay Motors Auction Site," *USA Today*, August 26, 2005. See also Tat Y. Chan, Vrinda Kadiyali, and Young-Hoon Park, "Willingness to Pay and Competition in Online Auctions," *Journal of Marketing Research*, May 2007; Matthew J. C. Walley and David R. Fortin, "Behavioral Outcomes from Online Auctions: Reserve Price, Reserve Disclosure, and Initial Bidding Influences in the Decision Process," *Journal of Business Research*, October 2004; Markus Voeth and Uta Herbst, "Supply-Chain Pricing: A New Perspective on Pricing in Industrial Markets," *Industrial Marketing Management*, January 2006; Howard Forman and James M. Hunt, "Managing the Influence of Internal and External Determinants on International Industrial Pricing Strategies," *Industrial Marketing Management*, February 2005; Eric Matson, "Customizing Prices," *Harvard Business Review*, November–December 1995; Michael H. Morris, "Separate Prices as a Marketing Tool," *Industrial Marketing Management*, May 1987; P. Ronald Stephenson, William L. Cron, and Gary L. Frazier, "Delegating Pricing Authority to the Sales Force: The Effects on Sales and Profit Performance," *Journal of Marketing*, Spring 1979.

10. "Haggling Starts to Go the Way of the Tail Fin," *BusinessWeek*, October 29, 2007; "Online Stores Charge Different Prices Based on Shoppers' Surfing Habits," *USA Today*, June 2, 2005; "No-Haggle Pricing Climbs Higher, Finds Fans among Affluent, Educated," *Advertising Age*, August 1, 2005. For more on Amazon offering different prices to different customers, see "Price? For You, $2; For the Rich Guy, $5," *Investor's Business Daily*, September 29, 2000. For more on Winn-Dixie example, see "Squeezin' the Charmin," *Fortune*, January 16, 1989; "Grocers Join Winn-Dixie," *Advertising Age*, November 7, 1988; "Grocery Chains Pressure Suppliers for Uniform Prices," *Wall Street Journal*, October 21, 1988. For more on car haggling, see

"CarMax: Psst, Wanna Buy a Used Car, Hassle-Free?" *Investor's Business Daily*, January 30, 2002. See also "Pay-as-You-Go M.D.: The Doctor Is In, but Insurance Is Out," *Wall Street Journal*, November 6, 2003; "Medical Care: Can We Talk Price?" *Wall Street Journal*, February 8, 2002.

11. "What's a Fair Price for Drugs?" *BusinessWeek*, April 30, 2001; "AIDS Gaffes in Africa Come Back to Haunt Drug Industry at Home," *Wall Street Journal*, April 23, 2001; "Vaccine's Price Drives a Debate about Its Use," *Wall Street Journal*, February 16, 2000. See also Richard A. Spinello, "Ethics, Pricing and the Pharmaceutical Industry," *Journal of Business Ethics*, August 1992; Nicholas H. Lurie and Joydeep Srivastava, "Price-Matching Guarantees and Consumer Evaluations of Price Information," *Journal of Consumer Psychology*, 2005; Bruce McWilliams and Eitan Gerstner, "Offering Low Price Guarantees to Improve Customer Retention," *Journal of Retailing*, June 2006; Sujay Dutta and Abhijit Biswas, "Effects of Low Price Guarantees on Consumer Post-Purchase Search Intention: The Moderating Roles of Value Consciousness and Penalty Level," *Journal of Retailing*, 4, 2005.

12. For information about pricing in the early years of cell phones, see "Mobile Warfare," *Time*, May 26, 1997; "Motorola Goes for the Hard Cell," *BusinessWeek*, September 23, 1996; "Why Motorola Has Nonworking Numbers," *BusinessWeek*, July 22, 1996; "Cell-Phone Service May Be Getting Cheaper," *Wall Street Journal*, January 11, 1996.

13. "New Features Coming for Blu-ray Format," *USA Today*, March 19, 2008; "Sony's PS3 Gets Boost from Its Blu-ray Drive," *Wall Street Journal*, March 12, 2008; "Game-Ad Boom Looms as Sony Opens Up PS3," *Advertising Age*, February 25, 2008; "Getting Back into the Game," *Investor's Business Daily*, December 18, 2006.

14. Check out foreign exchange rates at www.imf.org and www.federalreserve.gov and www.x-rates.com. See also "Small U.S. Firms Make Big Global Sales," *USA Today*, April 7, 2008; "Trade Winds," *Inc.*, November 2003; "Same Cars Can Cost Oodles Less in Canada," *USA Today*, May 6, 2003; "Ship Those Boxes; Check the Euro!" *Wall Street Journal*, February 7, 2003; "Revealing Price Disparities, the Euro Aids Bargain-Hunters," *Wall Street Journal*, January 30, 2002; "One Dollar Is Worth One Dollar, but That Wasn't Always So," *Wall Street Journal*, January 13, 1998. See also Ashok K. Lalwani and Kent B. Monroe, "A Reexamination of Frequency Depth Effects in Consumer Price Judgments," *Journal of Consumer Research*, December 2005; Luc Wathieu, A. V. Muthukrishnan, and Bart J. Bronnenberg, "The Asymmetric Effect of Discount Retraction on Subsequent Choice," *Journal of Consumer Research*, December 2004; Chris Janiszewski and Marcus Cunha, Jr., "The Influence of Price Discount Framing on the Evaluation of a Product Bundle," *Journal of Consumer Research*, March 2004; Keith S. Coulter and Robin A. Coulter, "Size Does Matter: The Effects of Magnitude Representation Congruency on Price Perceptions and Purchase Likelihood," *Journal of Consumer Psychology*, 1, 2005; V. Kumar, Vibhas Madan, and Srini S. Srinivasan, "Price Discounts or Coupon Promotions: Does It Matter?" *Journal of Business Research*, September 2004; David Smagalla, "Does Promotional Pricing Grow Future Business?" *MIT Sloan Management Review*, Summer 2004; Priya Raghubir and Joydeep Srivastava, "Effect of Face Value on Product Valuation in Foreign Currencies," *Journal of Consumer Research*, December 2002; Matthew B. Myers and Michael Harvey, "The Value of Pricing Control in Export Channels: a Governance Perspective," *Journal of International Marketing*, (4) 2001.

15. "Now Hoarding: Airlines Are Giving Frequent Fliers More Ways to Cash In," *Wall Street Journal*, December 9, 2005; "Who Really Reaps Mileage Rewards?" *Advertising Age*, June 20, 2005; "Why Your Free Trip to Maui Is Hobbling the Airline Industry," *Wall Street Journal*, February 4, 2004; "Fliers' Dilemma: Save Now or Later?" *BusinessWeek*, October 13, 2003: See also "Search Engines Start Rewards Programs," *Wall Street Journal*, February 23, 2006; "A New Wrinkle in Rewards Programs," *Wall Street Journal*, March 2, 2005;

"Pizza Hut Adds Videos, Loyalty Cards to Recipe," *Brandweek*, September 29, 2003; "Plastic's New Pitch: Something for Nothing," *Wall Street Journal*, July 31 2003; "Frequent Flier to Rental Driver Has Its Price," *The New York Times*, January 14, 2003; "The Holy Grail: Getting Miles for Your Mortgage," *Wall Street Journal*, December 5, 2002. See also Andy A. Tsay, "Managing Retail Channel Overstock: Markdown Money and Return Policies," *Journal of Retailing*, Winter 2001; David E. Sprott, Kenneth C. Manning, and Anthony D. Miyazaki, "Grocery Price Setting and Quantity Surcharges," *Journal of Marketing*, July 2003; Douglas D. Davis and Charles A. Holt, "List Prices and Discounts: The Interrelationship Between Consumer Shopping Patterns and Profitable Marketing Strategies," *Psychology & Marketing*, July 1996; David W. Arnesen, C. P. Fleenor, and Rex S. Toh, "The Ethical Dimensions of Airline Frequent Flier Programs," *Business Horizons*, January–February 1997; K. J. Blois, "Discounts in Business Marketing Management," *Industrial Marketing Management*, April 1994; James B. Wilcox et al., "Price Quantity Discounts: Some Implications for Buyers and Sellers," *Journal of Marketing*, July 1987; Mark T. Spriggs and John R. Nevin, "The Legal Status of Trade and Functional Price Discounts," *Journal of Public Policy & Marketing*, Spring 1994.

16. "Grocery Stores Cut Out the Weekly Special," *Wall Street Journal*, July 20, 2005. For more on P&G's everyday low pricing, see "P&G, Others Try New Uses for Coupon-Heavy Media," *Advertising Age*, September 22, 1997; "Move to Drop Coupons Puts Procter & Gamble in Sticky PR Situation," *Wall Street Journal*, April 17, 1997; "Zeroing In on Zero Coupons," *Brandweek*, June 3, 1996; "Company Makes Big Cuts to Stay Fit," *USA Today*, July 16, 1993. See also Kusum L. Ailawadi, Donald R. Lehmann, and Scott A. Neslin, "Market Response to a Major Policy Change in the Marketing Mix: Learning from Procter & Gamble's Value Pricing Strategy," *Journal of Marketing*, January 2001; Monika Kukar-Kinney and Rockney G. Walters, "Consumer Perceptions of Refund Depth and Competitive Scope in Price-Matching Guarantees: Effects on Store Patronage," *Journal of Retailing*, Fall 2003.

17. For more on slotting fees, see "Kraft Speeds New Product Launch Times," *Advertising Age*, November 18, 2002; "The Hidden Cost of Shelf Space," *BusinessWeek*, April 15, 2002. See also Ramarao Desiraju, "New Product Introductions, Slotting Allowances, and Retailer Discretion," *Journal of Retailing*, Fall 2001; David Balto, "Recent Legal and Regulatory Developments in Slotting Allowances and Category Management," *Journal of Public Policy & Marketing*, Fall 2002; William L. Wilkie, Debra M. Desrochers and Gregory T. Gundlach, "Marketing Research and Public Policy: the Case of Slotting Fees," *Journal of Public Policy & Marketing*, Fall 2002.

18. For more on coupons, see "Clipped Profits?" *Wall Street Journal Reports*, December 13, 2004; "The Latest Craze in Coupon-Clipping: Free Trial Offers for Prescription Drugs," *Wall Street Journal*, April 16, 2002; "Penny-Pinchers' Paradise," *BusinessWeek E.Biz*, January 22, 2001; "E-Tailers Missing the Mark with Flood of Web Coupons," *Advertising Age*, September 25, 2000; Gail Ayala Taylor, "Coupon Response in Services," *Journal of Retailing*, Spring 2001.

19. "The Real Problem with Rebates," *Primedia*, January 11, 2006; "The Great Rebate Runaround," *BusinessWeek*, December 5, 2005; "Would You Like Some E-Mail with That Pizza? Papa John's, Blackberry Tie-in," *Advertising Age*, July 11, 2005, pp. 3, 37; "Many Consumers Never Cash in Rebates," *Newsday*, January 23, 2005; "Use Them or Lose Them: Rebates Key to Driving Tech Sales," *Business Wire*, December 27, 2004; "Retailers Simplify the Rebate Process," *Boston Globe*, November 7, 2004; "Livewire: When Rebates Yield Headaches Instead of Cash," *Forbes*, June 25, 2003; "Let's Make a (Tough) Deal," *Newsweek*, June 23, 2003; "Ford Tames the Rebate Monster," *BusinessWeek*, May 5, 2003; "Rejected! Rebates Get Harder to Collect," *Wall Street Journal*, June 11, 2002.

20. "Easy Does It All," *Business 2.0*, August 2005; "America's Pricing Paradox," *Wall Street Journal*, May 16, 2003; "Ideas & Innovations:

How to Thrive When Prices Fall," *Fortune*, May 12, 2003; "Why Some Companies Can Levy Premium Prices and Others Not," *Investor's Business Daily*, April 15, 2003; "Survival Strategies: After Cost Cutting, Companies Turn toward Price Rises," *Wall Street Journal*, September 18, 2002; "Stepping Up: Middle Market Shrinks as Americans Migrate toward the High End," *Wall Street Journal*, March 29, 2002; "Two-Tier Marketing," *BusinessWeek*, March 17, 1997; "Value Marketing," *BusinessWeek*, November 11, 1991.

21. "Freeze-Dried Berries Heat Up Cereal Duel," *Wall Street Journal*, May 15, 2003; "Garfield's Ad Review: A Few Spoons of Truth Tossed into Special K Red Berries Spot," *Advertising Age*, May 12, 2003.

22. For an excellent discussion of laws related to pricing, see Louis W. Stern and Thomas L. Eovaldi, *Legal Aspects of Marketing Strategy: Antitrust and Consumer Protection Issues* (Englewood Cliffs, NJ: Prentice-Hall, 1984). See also Joseph P. Guiltinan and Gregory T. Gundlach, "Aggressive and Predatory Pricing: A Framework for Analysis," *Journal of Marketing*, July 1996.

23. For more on steel tariff, see "Steel Bends but Doesn't Break," *Investor's Business Daily*, May 3, 2004; "Administration Weighs New Protection for Steel," *The New York Times*, December 12, 2003; "The Genie Is Out of the Bottle," *Wall Street Journal*, December 8, 2003; "US-China Trade Tensions Rise," *Christian Science Monitor*, December 2, 2003; "The Steel Tariff's Costs," *Wall Street Journal*, February 25, 2003. For more on China dumping, see "How China Will Change Your Business," *Inc.*, March 2005; "The China Price," *BusinessWeek*, December 6, 2004; "Dumping: China Strikes Back," *BusinessWeek*, July 5, 2004; "Wielding a Heavy Weapon against China," *BusinessWeek*, June 21, 2004; "Chinese Furniture Faces U.S. Tariffs," *Wall Street Journal*, June 17, 2004.

24. Patrick J. Kaufmann, N. Craig Smith, and Gwendolyn K. Ortmeyer, "Deception in Retailer High-Low Pricing: A 'Rule of Reason' Approach," *Journal of Retailing*, Summer 1994.

25. For more on airline pricing, see Ashutosh Dixit, Gregory T. Gundlach, Naresh K. Malhotra, and Fred C. Allvine, "Aggressive and Predatory Pricing: Insights and Empirical Examination in the Airline Industry," *Journal of Public Policy & Marketing*, Fall 2006; "Is American-United Rivalry Too Friendly?" *USA Today*, June 27, 2001; "Predatory Pricing: Cleared for Takeoff," *BusinessWeek*, May 14, 2001; "American Airlines Secures Antitrust Win," *Wall Street Journal*, April 30, 2001; "Caveat Predator?" *BusinessWeek*, May 22, 2000. For more on credit card pricing, see "House of Cards?" *Time*, October 23, 2000; "Breaking Up the Old Card Game," *BusinessWeek*, June 12, 2000; "Antitrust Suit Targeting MasterCard and Visa Puts the Pair at Odds," *Wall Street Journal*, June 12, 2000. For more on CD pricing, see "Prices of CDs Likely to Drop, Thanks to FTC," *Wall Street Journal*, May 11, 2000. For more on De Beers, see "De Beers to Pay $10 Million Fine, Ending 10-Year, Price-Fixing Suit," *Wall Street Journal*, July 14, 2004; "De Beers Is in Talks to Settle Price-Fixing Charge . . . Could Finally Give Cartel a Retail Presence in U.S.," *Wall Street Journal*, February 24, 2004. For more on ADM, see "Questions Linger on Price of Seeds," *The New York Times*, January 6, 2004; "In Archer-Daniels Saga, Now the Executives Face Trial," *Wall Street Journal*, July 9, 1998; "The ADM Scandal: Betrayal," *Fortune*, February 3, 1997. See also "In FCC Auctions of Airwaves, Gabelli Was behind the Scenes," *Wall Street Journal*, December 27, 2005; "Samsung Fined $300 Million in Price Fix Case," *Investor's Business Daily*, October 14, 2005; "Sweet Deals or Strong-Arm Tactics? AMD Allege That Intel Gave Customers Discounts to Keep Rivals Out . . .," *BusinessWeek*, July 11, 2005; "Probing Price Tags," *Wall Street Journal*, May 13, 2005; "How Driving Prices Lower Can Violate Antitrust Statutes," *Wall Street Journal*, January 27, 2004; "Online Booksellers Abound in Japan, But Legal Price Fixing Poses Challenge," *Wall Street Journal*, July 31, 2000; "P&G Calls the Cops as It Strives to Expand Sales in Latin America," *Wall Street Journal*, March 20, 1998; "Independent Bookstores Are Suing Borders Group and Barnes & Noble," *Wall Street Journal*, March 19,

1998; "Cargill Agrees to Pay $24 Million to Settle Price-Fixing Suit," *Wall Street Journal*, March 11, 2004. See also Alexander James Nicholls, "Strategic Options in Fair Trade Retailing," *International Journal of Retail & Distribution Management*, (1) 2002.

26. "A New Twist for Light Bulbs that Conserve Energy," *USA Today*, April 22, 2008; "Ban on Incandescent Lamps Discussed by Finnish Parliament," *Helsingin Sanomat*, retrieved May 5, 2008; "Tesco to Sell Energy Saving Bulbs for a Penny," *Supermarket & Retailer*, March 18, 2008; "Venture Capitalists Tout Green Lighting," *Wall Street Journal*, March 17, 2008; "The Right Light," *Electric Perspectives*, March–April 2008; "The Shape of Light to Come? Not Everyone's Buying It," *USA Today*, February 28, 2008; "The Next Big Idea," *Retailing Today*, December 2007–January 2008; "Father of the Compact Fluorescent Bulb Looks Back," *CNETNews.com*, August 16, 2007; "LED Prices Expected to Fall," *Purchasing*, August 16, 2007; "Deviant Shops: Increase in Power Tariff under Study," *PakTribune.com*, August 10, 2007; "Bad-Guy Bulbs," *Electrical Wholesaling*, July 2007; "More Retailers Go for Green—the Eco Kind," *USA Today*, April 17, 2007; "Cheaper LEDs to Light a Green Path?" *CNETNews.com*, April 9, 2007; "Building a Better Light Bulb: At $10 to $20 Each, Buyers May Balk at New Technology," *Washington Post*, June 2, 1992.

27. "Century-Old Ban Lifted on Minimum Retail Pricing," *The New York Times*, June 29, 2007.

28. Richard L. Pinkerton and Deborah J. Kemp, "The Industrial Buyer and the Robinson-Patman Act," *International Journal of Purchasing & Materials Management*, Winter 1996.

29. "Firms Must Prove Injury from Price Bias to Qualify for Damages, High Court Says," *Wall Street Journal*, May 19, 1981.

30. "Booksellers Say Five Publishers Play Favorites," *Wall Street Journal*, May 27, 1994; Joseph P. Vaccaro and Derek W. F. Coward, "Managerial and Legal Implications of Price Haggling: A Sales Manager's Dilemma," *Journal of Personal Selling & Sales Management*, Summer 1993; John R. Davidson, "FTC, Robinson-Patman and Co-operative Promotion Activities," *Journal of Marketing*, January 1968; L. X. Tarpey, Sr., "Buyer Liability under the RobinsonPatman Act: A Current Appraisal," *Journal of Marketing*, January 1972.

CHAPTER 17

1. "Sony's Newest Display Is a Culture Shift," *Wall Street Journal*, May 8, 2008; "A Clearer Picture for Flat-Panel TVs," *BusinessWeek*, April 24, 2008; "U.S. Upstart Takes on TV Giants in Price War," *Wall Street Journal*, April 15, 2008; "Sony Teams with Sharp in Flat-Panel LCD Plant," *Investor's Business Daily*, February 27, 2008; "TV Makers Aren't Turned Off by Slump," *Wall Street Journal*, January 29, 2008; "Panasonic, Sony, Philips Laud Digital Countdown," *Brandweek*, January 14, 2008; "Middle of Nowhere," *Brandweek*, January 7, 2008; "That Giant Sucking Sound May Be Your New TV," *Wall Street Journal*, December 12, 2007; "High-Tech TVs Are Popular but Puzzling," *USA Today*, December 12, 2007; "Laser TV Seems Back on Course," *Investor's Business Daily*, December 7, 2007; "The Picture Gets Fuzzy for TV Deals," *Wall Street Journal*, December 6, 2007; "Wide World of HDTV," *USA Today*, November 26, 2007; "TV Sellers Are Thinking Big," *Wall Street Journal*, November 20, 2007; "Sharp Takes a Gamble on New TV Plant in Mexico," *USA Today*, November 6, 2007; "Sharp Grabs LCD-TV Sales Lead," *Wall Street Journal*, November 2, 2007; "Flat-Panel TV World Crowns Unexpected New King: Vizio," *USA Today*, August 21, 2007; "Attack of the No-Name HDTV Brands," *Brandweek*, June 18, 2007; "Flat-TV Makers Target Commercial Market," *Nikkei Weekly*, May 28, 2007; "A Dutchman Could Jolt the Flat-Panel Biz," *BusinessWeek*, May 21, 2007; "Flat-Panel TVs Display Effects of Globalization," *USA Today*, May 8, 2007; "How Wal-Mart's TV Prices Crushed Rivals," *BusinessWeek*, April 23, 2007; "Flat Panels, Thin Margins," *BusinessWeek*, February 26, 2007; "The World Is Flat," *Money Magazine*,

January 18, 2007; "Plasma vs. LCD: The Battle Heats Up," *Business-Week*, January 17, 2007; "You Want a Flat-Panel TV. When Should You Buy?" *USA Today*, January 5, 2007; "Flat-Panel TV Jam," *Wall Street Journal*, January 3, 2007; "Hefty Discounting of Flat-Panel TVs Pinches Retailers," *Wall Street Journal*, December 12, 2006; "As Flat-Panel TV Sales Soar, Unlikely Retailers Step In," *Wall Street Journal*, September 21, 2006; "How to Shop for Flat-Panel TVs," *Investor's Business Daily*, June 3, 2006; "Flat-Panel TVs, Long Touted, Finally Are Becoming the Norm," *Wall Street Journal*, April 15, 2006; "War of the Screens," *BusinessWeek*, September 12, 2005; "Prices of Flat-Panel TVs, Monitors Could Drop More," *USA Today*, June 28, 2005; "Flat-Panel TVs You Can Afford," *Wall Street Journal*, June 1, 2005; "Your Next TV," *BusinessWeek*, April 4, 2005; "Cheaper Flat-Panel TVs—from PC Makers," *Wall Street Journal*, December 23, 2004; "Texas Instruments Inside?" *BusinessWeek*, December 6, 2004; "Flat TV Prices Are Falling, but . . . Not Low Enough … Blame Retailers' Margins," *Wall Street Journal*, November 3, 2004; "Once a Footnote, Flat Screens Grow into Huge Industry," *Wall Street Journal*, August 30, 2004; "I Want My Flat TV. Now! . . . Supply Shortfall," *Wall Street Journal*, May 27, 2004; "Flat-Panel Sets Enhance Visibility of Samsung," *The New York Times*, January 8, 2004; "In a Sleek Flat Set, Plasma's Price Plunges," *The New York Times*, January 8, 2004; "For Digital TVs, the Future Is Now," *USA Today*, December 3, 2003; "The Skinny on Flat Screens," *Wall Street Journal*, November 26, 2003.

2. Kusum L. Ailawadi and Bari Harlam, "An Empirical Analysis of the Determinants of Retail Margins: The Role of Store-Brand Share," *Journal of Marketing*, January 2004; Ritu Lohtia, Ramesh Subramaniam, and Rati Lohtia, "Are Pricing Practices in Japanese Channels of Distribution Finally Changing?" *Journal of Marketing Channels*, (1,2) 2001; Marvin A. Jolson, "A Diagrammatic Model for Merchandising Calculations," *Journal of Retailing*, Summer 1975; C. Davis Fogg and Kent H. Kohnken, "Price-Cost Planning," *Journal of Marketing*, April 1978.

3. "The Little Extras That Count (Up)," *Wall Street Journal*, July 12, 2001; "Battle-Tested Rules of Online Retail," *Ecompany*, April 2001; "The Return of Pricing Power," *BusinessWeek*, May 8, 2000; "The Power of Smart Pricing," *BusinessWeek*, April 10, 2000. See also Mary L. Hatten, "Don't Get Caught with Your Prices Down: Pricing in Inflationary Times," *Business Horizons*, March 1982; Douglas G. Brooks, "Cost Oriented Pricing: A Realistic Solution to a Complicated Problem," *Journal of Marketing*, April 1975; Steven M. Shugan, "Retail Product-Line Pricing Strategy When Costs and Products Change," *Journal of Retailing*, 77, no. 1 (Spring 2001).

4. G. Dean Kortge, "Inverted Breakeven Analysis for Profitable Marketing Decisions," *Industrial Marketing Management*, October 1984; Thomas L. Powers, "Breakeven Analysis with Semifixed Costs," *Industrial Marketing Management*, February 1987.

5. Approaches for estimating price-quantity relationships are reviewed in Kent B. Monroe, *Pricing: Making Profitable Decisions* (New York: McGraw-Hill, 2003). For specific examples, see Gordon A. Wyner, Lois H. Benedetti, and Bart M. Trapp, "Measuring the Quantity and Mix of Product Demand," *Journal of Marketing*, Winter 1984. See also Michael F. Smith and Indrajit Sinha, "The Impact of Price and Extra Product Promotions on Store Preference," *International Journal of Retail & Distribution Management*, (2) 2000; Michael H. Morris and Mary L. Joyce, "How Marketers Evaluate Price Sensitivity," *Industrial Marketing Management*, May 1988; David E. Griffith and Roland T. Rust, "The Price of Competitiveness in Competitive Pricing," *Journal of the Academy of Marketing Science*, Spring 1997; Frank D. Jones, "A Survey Technique to Measure Demand under Various Pricing Strategies," *Journal of Marketing*, July 1975; Robert J. Dolan, "How Do You Know When the Price Is Right?" *Harvard Business Review*, September–October 1995; S. C. Choi, "Price Competition in a Duopoly Common Retailer Channel," *Journal of Retailing*, Summer 1996.

6. "Getting Skewered by Shrimp Prices," *Wall Street Journal*, October 16, 2003; "Secret in the Dairy Aisle: Milk Is a Cash Cow," *Wall Street Journal*, July 28, 2003; "New Status Symbol: Overpaying for Your Minivan," *Wall Street Journal*, July 23, 2003; "The Paradox of Value," *Brandweek*, June 5, 2000; Watts Wacker and Jim Taylor, *The Visionary's Handbook: Nine Paradoxes That Will Shape the Future of Your Business* (HarperCollins, 2000). See also Narayan Janakiraman, Robert J. Meyer, and Andrea C. Morales, "Spillover Effects: How Consumers Respond to Unexpected Changes in Price and Quality," *Journal of Consumer Research*, October 2006; Shuba Srinivasan, Koen Pauwels, and Vincent Nijs, "Demand-Based Pricing versus Past-Price Dependence: A Cost-Benefit Analysis," *Journal of Marketing*, March 2008; Marc Vanhuele, Gilles Laurent, and Xavier Drèze, "Consumers' Immediate Memory for Prices," *Journal of Consumer Research*, August 2006; Manoj Thomas and Geeta Menon, "When Internal Reference Prices and Price Expectations Diverge: The Role of Confidence," *Journal of Marketing Research*, August 2007; Kirk L. Wakefield and J. Jeffrey Inman, "Situational Price Sensitivity: The Role of Consumption Occasion, Social Context and Income," *Journal of Retailing*, Winter 2003; Kristin Diehl, Laura J. Kornish, and John G. Lynch, Jr., "Smart Agents: When Lower Search Costs for Quality Information Increase Price Sensitivity," *Journal of Consumer Research*, June 2003; Amir Heiman, Bruce McWilliams, Jinhua Zhao, and David Zilberman, "Valuation and Management of Money-Back Guarantee Options," *Journal of Retailing*, Fall 2002; Dhruv Grewal, Kent B. Monroe, and R. Krishnan, "The Effects of Price-Comparison Advertising on Buyers' Perceptions of Acquisition Value, Transaction Value, and Behavioral Intentions," *Journal of Marketing*, April 1998; John T. Gourville, "Pennies-a-Day: The Effect of Temporal Reframing on Transaction Evaluation," *Journal of Consumer Research*, March 1998; Joel E. Urbany, Rosemary Kalapurakal, and Peter R. Dickson, "Price Search in the Retail Grocery Market," *Journal of Marketing*, April 1996; Venkatesh Shankar and Lakshman Krishnamurthi, "Relating Price Sensitivity to Retailer Promotional Variables and Pricing Policy: An Empirical Analysis," *Journal of Retailing*, Fall 1996; Chakravarthi Narasimhan, Scott A. Neslin, and Subrata K. Sen, "Promotional Elasticities and Category Characteristics," *Journal of Marketing*, April 1996; K. Sivakumar and S. P. Raj, "Quality Tier Competition: How Price Change Influences Brand Choice and Category Choice," *Journal of Marketing*, July 1997.

7. "Seeking Perfect Prices, CEO Tears Up the Rules," *Wall Street Journal*, March 27, 2007.

8. Thomas T. Nagle and Reed R. Holder, *The Strategy and Tactics of Pricing* (Englewood Cliffs, NJ: Prentice-Hall, 2002); "Fram Pays Up Now," *Brandweek*, July 20, 1998; "New Long-Life Bulbs May Lose Brilliance in a Crowded Market," *Wall Street Journal*, June 2, 1992; Andreas Hinterhuber, "Towards Value-Based Pricing—An Integrative Framework for Decision Making," *Industrial Marketing Management*, November 2004; Benson P. Shapiro and Barbara P. Jackson, "Industrial Pricing to Meet Customer Needs," *Harvard Business Review*, November–December 1978; "The Race to the $10 Light Bulb," *BusinessWeek*, May 19, 1980. See also Michael H. Morris and Donald A. Fuller, "Pricing an Industrial Service," *Industrial Marketing Management*, May 1989.

9. For more on eBay, see Chapter 16, endnote 9. See also "Copart: Auctioneer's Web Move Puts It in Fast Lane," *Investor's Business Daily*, June 16, 2004; "Renaissance in Cyberspace," *Wall Street Journal*, November 20, 2003; "Sold! to Save the Farm," *Wall Street Journal*, August 29, 2003; "Online Liquidators Help Firm Shed Unsold Goods," *Investor's Business Daily*, August 13, 2002; "Good-Bye to Fixed Pricing?" *BusinessWeek*, May 4, 1998. See also Larry R. Smeltzer and Amelia S. Carr, "Electronic Reverse Auctions: Promises, Risks and Conditions for Success," *Industrial Marketing Management*, August 2003; Sandy D. Jap, "An Exploratory Study of the Introduction of Online Reverse Auctions," *Journal of Marketing*, July 2003.

10. "The Price Is Really Right," *BusinessWeek*, March 31, 2003; "New Software Manages Price Cuts," *Investor's Business Daily*, March 31, 2003; "The Power of Optimal Pricing," *Business 2.0*, September 2002; "Priced to Move: Retailers Try to Get Leg Up on Markdowns with New Software," *Wall Street Journal*, August 7, 2001; "The Price Is Right," *Inc.*, July 2001. See also Ashutosh Dixit, Thomas W. Whipple, George M. Zinkhan, and Edward Gailey, "A Taxonomy of Information Technology-Enhanced Pricing Strategies," *Journal of Business Research*, April 2008; Devon DelVecchio, H. Shanker Krishnan, and Daniel C. Smith, "Cents or Percent? The Effects of Promotion Framing on Price Expectations and Choice," *Journal of Marketing*, July 2007; Kelly L. Haws and William O. Bearden, "Dynamic Pricing and Consumer Fairness Perceptions," *Journal of Consumer Research*, October 2006; Tridib Mazumdar, S. P. Raj, and Indrajit Sinha, "Reference Price Research: Review and Propositions," *Journal of Marketing*, October 2005; Michael J. Barone, Kenneth C. Manning, and Paul W. Miniard, "Consumer Response to Retailers' Use of Partially Comparative Pricing," *Journal of Marketing*, July 2004; Chezy Ofir, "Reexamining Latitude of Price Acceptability and Price Thresholds: Predicting Basic Consumer Reaction to Price," *Journal of Consumer Research*, March 2004; Aradhna Krishna, Mary Wagner, Carolyn Yoon, and Rashmi Adaval, "Effects of Extreme-Priced Products on Consumer Reservation Prices," *Journal of Consumer Psychology*, 2006; Sangkil Moon, Gary J. Russell, and Sri Devi Duvvuri, "Profiling the Reference Price Consumer," *Journal of Retailing*, March 2006; John T. Gourville and Youngme Moon, "Managing Price Expectations Through Product Overlap," *Journal of Retailing*, Spring 2004; Marc Vanhuele and Xavier Dreze, "Measuring the Price Knowledge Shoppers Bring to the Store," *Journal of Marketing*, October 2002; Rashmi Adaval and Kent B. Monroe, "Automatic Construction and Use of Contextual Information for Product and Price Evaluations," *Journal of Consumer Research*, March 2002; Sangman Han, Sunil Gupta, and Donald R. Lehmann, "Consumer Price Sensitivity and Price Thresholds," *Journal of Retailing*, Winter 2001; David Ackerman and Gerard Tellis, "Can Culture Affect Prices? A Cross-Cultural Study of Shopping and Retail Prices," *Journal of Retailing*, Spring 2001; David M. Hardesty and William O. Bearden, "Consumer Evaluations of Different Promotion Types and Price Presentations: the Moderating Role of Promotional Benefit Level," *Journal of Retailing*, (1) 2003; Rajesh Chandrashekaran and Dhruv Grewal, "Assimilation of Advertised Reference Prices: the Moderating Role of Involvement," *Journal of Retailing*, (1) 2003; Thomas Jensen, Jeremy Kees, Scot Burton, and Fernanda Lucarelli Turnipseed, "Advertised Reference Prices in an Internet Environment: Effects on Consumer Price Perceptions and Channel Search Intentions," *Journal of Interactive Marketing*, Spring 2003; Joel E. Urbany, Peter R. Dickson, and Alan G. Sawyer, "Insights into Crossand Within-Store Price Search: Retailer Estimates vs. Consumer Self-Reports," *Journal of Retailing*, Summer 2000; Merrie Brucks, Valarie A. Zeithaml, and Gillian Naylor, "Price and Brand Name as Indicators of Quality Dimensions for Consumer Durables," *Journal of the Academy of Marketing Science*, Summer 2000; Joydeep Srivastava and Nicholas Lurie, "A Consumer Perspective on Price-Matching Refund Policies: Effect on Price Perceptions and Search Behavior," *Journal of Consumer Research*, September 2001; Ronald W. Niedrich, Subhash Sharma, and Douglas H. Wedell, "Reference Price and Price Perceptions: a Comparison of Alternative Models," *Journal of Consumer Research*, December 2001; Erica Mina Okada, "Trade-Ins, Mental Accounting, and Product Replacement Decisions," *Journal of Consumer Research*, March 2001; Aradhna Krishna, Richard Briesch, Donald R. Lehmann, and Hong Yuan, "A Meta-Analysis of the Impact of Price Presentation on Perceived Savings," *Journal of Retailing*, Summer 2002; Valerie A. Taylor and William O. Bearden, "The Effects of Price on Brand Extension Evaluations: the Moderating Role of Extension Similarity," *Journal of the Academy of Marketing Science*, Spring 2002; James K. Binkley and John Bejnarowicz, "Consumer Price Awareness in Food Shopping: the Case of Quantity Surcharges," *Journal of Retailing*, (1) 2003; Lesa E. Bolton, Luk Warlop,

and Joseph W. Alba, "Consumer Perceptions of Price (Un)fairness," *Journal of Consumer Research*, March 2003; Amir Heiman, Bruce McWilliams, and David Zilberman, "Demonstrations and Money-Back Guarantees: Market Mechanisms to Reduce Uncertainty," *Journal of Business Research*, October 2001; Edward A. Blair, Judy Harris, and Kent B. Monroe, "Effects of Shopping Information on Consumers' Responses to Comparative Price Claims," *Journal of Retailing*, Fall 2002; Hooman Estelami, "The Impact of Research Design on Consumer Price Recall Accuracy: An Integrative Review," *Journal of the Academy of Marketing Science*, Winter 2001; Richard A. Briesch, Lakshman Krishnamurthi, Tridib Mazumdar, and S. P. Raj, "A Comparative Analysis of Reference Price Models," *Journal of Consumer Research*, September 1997.

11. For a classic example applied to a high-price item, see "Sale of Mink Coats Strays a Fur Piece from the Expected," *Wall Street Journal*, March 21, 1980.

12. Franziska Völckner and Julian Hofmann, "The Price-perceived Quality Relationship: A Meta-analytic Review and Assessment of Its Determinants," *Marketing Letters*, October 2007; K. Douglas Hoffman, L. W. Turley, and Scott W. Kelley, "Pricing Retail Services," *Journal of Business Research*, December 2002; Steven M. Shugan and Ramarao Desiraju, "Retail Product Line Pricing Strategy When Costs and Products Change," *Journal of Retailing*, Spring 2001; Noel M. Noel and Nessim Hanna, "Benchmarking Consumer Perceptions of Product Quality with Price: An Exploration," *Psychology & Marketing*, September 1996; Niraj Dawar and Philip Parker, "Marketing Universals: Consumers' Use of Brand Name, Price, Physical Appearance, and Retailer Reputation as Signals of Product Quality," *Journal of Marketing*, April 1994; Tung-Zong Chang and Albert R. Wildt, "Impact of Product Information on the Use of Price as a Quality Cue," *Psychology & Marketing*, January 1996; B. P. Shapiro, "The Psychology of Pricing," *Harvard Business Review*, July–August 1968; Lutz Hildebrandt, "The Analysis of Price Competition Between Corporate Brands," *International Journal of Research in Marketing*, June 2001.

13. Keith S. Coulter and Robin A. Coulter, "Distortion of Price Discount Perceptions: The Right Digit Effect," *Journal of Consumer Research*, August 2007; Lee C. Simmons and Robert M. Schindler, "Cultural Superstitions and the Price Endings Used in Chinese Advertising," *Journal of International Marketing*, (2) 2003; Robert M. Schindler and Thomas M. Kibarian, "Image Communicated by the Use of 99 Endings in Advertised Prices," *Journal of Advertising*, Winter 2001; Robert M. Schindler and Patrick N. Kirby, "Patterns of Rightmost Digits Used in Advertised Prices: Implications for Nine-Ending Effects," *Journal of Consumer Research*, September 1997; Mark Stiving and Russell S. Winer, "An Empirical Analysis of Price Endings with Scanner Data," *Journal of Consumer Research*, June 1997; Robert M. Schindler and Alan R. Wiman, "Effects of Odd Pricing on Price Recall," *Journal of Business Research*, November 1989.

14. "For Landlords, Jewelry Stores Are Big Gems," *Wall Street Journal*, May 20, 2005; "Diamond Store in the Rough: Opening of De Beers Boutique …," *Wall Street Journal*, May 20, 2005; "Reaching Out to Younger Crowd Works for Tiffany," *USA Today*, February 26, 2004; "Tiffany & Co. Branches Out under an Alias," *Wall Street Journal*, July 23, 2003; "The Cocoon Cracks Open," *Brandweek*, April 28, 2003; "Goodbye, Mr. Goodbar: Chocolate Gets Snob Appeal," *Wall Street Journal*, February 13, 2003; "Luxury Marketing," *Advertising Age*, March 11, 2002; "Keeping the Cachet," *Wall Street Journal*, April 23, 2001; "Luxury Sites Get Scrappy," *Wall Street Journal*, December 4, 2000; "Online Luxury Has Limits," *BusinessWeek E.Biz*, September 18, 2000; "Luxury Marketing," *Advertising Age*, August 14, 2000; "The Galloping Gourmet Chocolate," *Brandweek*, July 31, 2000. See also Xing Pan, Brian T. Ratchford, and Venkatesh Shankar, "Can Price Dispersion in Online Markets Be Explained by Differences in E-Tailer Service Quality?" *Journal of the Academy of Marketing Science*, Fall 2002; Kusum L. Ailawadi, Donald R. Lehmann, and Scott A. Neslin,

"Revenue Premium as an Outcome Measure of Brand Equity," *Journal of Marketing*, October 2003; "Life on Easy Street," *American Demographics*, April 1997; G. Dean Kortge and Patrick A. Okonkwo, "Perceived Value Approach to Pricing," *Industrial Marketing Management*, May 1993.

15. "The Economics of Giving It Away," *Wall Street Journal*, January 31, 2009; "Would You Pay Money to See Your Favorite Site Ad-Free?" *AdvertisingAge*, December 8, 2008; "Free! Why $0.00 Is the Future of Business," *Wired Magazine*, March 2008; "Free Love" *Trendwatching.com*, March 2008; "Danger of Free," *ReadWriteWeb*, January 16, 2008.

16. For more on Gillette's complementary pricing, see "How Many Blades Is Enough?" *Fortune*, October 31, 2005; "Gillette's Smooth Bet: Men, Will Pay More for Five-Blade Razor," *Wall Street Journal*, September 15, 2005; "Can Gillette Regain Its Edge?" *BusinessWeek*, January 26, 2004. See also "Google, Sun Agree to Bundle Programs," *Investor's Business Daily*, October 5, 2005; "Adobe Turns Page with New Software Line," *Investor's Business Daily*, November 13, 2003; "The Allure of Bundling," *Wall Street Journal*, October 7, 2003; "Computer Deals Hit New Lows," *Wall Street Journal*, August 13, 2003. For more on phone bundling, see "Internet Phone Calls Could Squeeze Prices," *Investor's Business Daily*, December 12, 2003; "Circuit Breaker: Battered Telecoms Face New Challenge: Internet Calling," *Wall Street Journal*, October 9, 2003; "BellSouth Hooks Up with DirecTV," *Wall Street Journal*, August 27, 2003; "Honey, I Shrunk the Phone Bill," *BusinessWeek*, June 9, 2003; "Cellphone Giveaways Get an Upgrade," *Wall Street Journal*, May 20, 2003; "A Nickel Here, a Buck There Add Up to Big Local Bills," *USA Today*, February 28, 2003; "Phone, Cable Cos. Use Bundling to Keep Users from Switching," *Investor's Business Daily*, December 13, 2002. For more on airline food unbundling, see "Dining Out at 32,000 Feet," *Wall Street Journal*, June 3, 2003; "Food Flights," *USA Today*, January 17, 2003. See also Alexander Chernev, "Differentiation and Parity in Assortment Pricing," *Journal of Consumer Research*, August 2006; Bram Foubert and Els Gijsbrechts, "Shopper Response to Bundle Promotions for Packaged Goods," *Journal of Marketing Research*, November 2007; R. Venkatesh and Rabikar Chatterjee, "Bundling, Unbundling, and Pricing of Multiform Products: The Case of Magazine Content," *Journal of Interactive Marketing*, Spring 2006; Andrea Ovans, "Make a Bundle Bundling," *Harvard Business Review*, November–December 1997; Preyas S. Desai and Kannan Srinivasan, "Aggregate Versus Product-Specific Pricing: Implications for Franchise and Traditional Channels," *Journal of Retailing*, Winter 1996; Manjit S. Yadav and Kent B. Monroe, "How Buyers Perceive Savings in a Bundle Price: An Examination of a Bundle's Transaction Value," *Journal of Marketing Research*, August 1993; Dorothy Paun, "When to Bundle or Unbundle Products," *Industrial Marketing Management*, February 1993.

17. Mary Anne Raymond, John F. Tanner, Jr., and Jonghoon Kim, "Cost Complexity of Pricing Decisions for Exporters in Developing and Emerging Markets," *Journal of International Marketing*, (3) 2001; Peter E. Connor and Robert K. Hopkins, "Cost Plus What? The Importance of Accurate Profit Calculations in Cost-Plus Agreements," *International Journal of Purchasing & Materials Management*, Spring 1997; Daniel T. Ostas, "Ethics of Contract Pricing," *Journal of Business Ethics*, February 1992; J. Steve Davis, "Ethical Problems in Competitive Bidding: The Paradyne Case," *Business and Professional Ethics Journal*, 7, no. 2 (1988); David T. Levy, "Guaranteed Pricing in Industrial Purchases: Making Use of Markets in Contractual Relations," *Industrial Marketing Management*, October 1994; Akintola Akintoye and Martin Skitmore, "Pricing Approaches in the Construction Industry," *Industrial Marketing Management*, November 1992.

CHAPTER 18

1. For more on consumer choice, see Ross D. Petty, "Limiting Product Choice: Innovation, Market Evolution, and Antitrust," *Journal of Public Policy & Marketing*, Fall 2002; Mitch Griffin, Barry J. Babin, and Doan Modianos, "Shopping Values of Russian Consumers: The Impact of Habituation in a Developing Economy," *Journal of Retailing*, Spring 2000; Suk-ching Ho, "The Emergence of Consumer Power in China," *Business Horizons*, September–October 1997; Matthew B. Myers, "New and Improved: The Story of Mass Marketing in America," *Journal of the Academy of Marketing Science*, Summer 1997; Terry Clark, "Moving Mountains to Market: Reflections on Restructuring the Russian Economy," *Business Horizons*, March–April 1994. See also "From Sour Grapes to Online Whine," *USA Today*, April 7, 2000; "Service with a What?" *BusinessWeek*, September 8, 1997; "Oh, What a Feeling," *Newsweek*, July 28, 1997; "Attention, Wal-Mart Shoppers: You Want Fries with That?" *Wall Street Journal*, July 25, 1997; "Buyers Get No Satisfaction," *USA Today*, July 22, 1997. For more on Tesco, see "British Invasion Hits Grocery Stores," *USA Today*, April 7, 2008; "Tesco Reinvents the 7-Eleven," *Fortune*, November 26, 2007; "Tesco Studies Hard for U.S. Debut," *Wall Street Journal*, June 28, 2007; "Two Big Bets Against the Buck," *BusinessWeek*, June 26, 2006; "No. 1 Retailer in Britain Uses 'Clubcard' to Thwart Wal-Mart," *Wall Street Journal*, June 6, 2006; "Can Brits Reinvent the Convenience Store?" *Business 2.0*, May 2006; "Tesco Aims to Crack U.S. with Convenience Stores," *Advertising Age*, February 27, 2006; "Tesco: California Dreaming?" *BusinessWeek*, February 27, 2006; "Tesco Jumps the Pond," *Wall Street Journal*, February 10, 2006; "Teaching the Big Box New Tricks," *Fortune*, November 14, 2005, pp. 208B-F; "With Help of Clever Trolley, Tesco Speeds Online Orders," *Investor's Business Daily*, December 8, 2004; "British Supermarket Giant Cooks Up Plans to Go Global," *Wall Street Journal*, July 5, 2001; "British Grocer Tesco Thrives Filling Web Orders from Its Stores' Aisles," *Wall Street Journal*, October 16, 2000; "Tesco: A Fresh Approach to Online Groceries," *BusinessWeek E.Biz*, September 18, 2000; For more on online shopping for groceries in the United States, see "Click Here for Groceries," *Health*, October 2005; "FreshDirect Cooks Up New Web Retail Angle," *DSN Retailing Today*, October 11, 2004; "Online Grocers: Ready to Deliver?" *Brandweek*, May 3, 2004; "The Big Cheese of Online Grocers," *Business 2.0*, January–February 2004; "Virtual Bounty: Groceries to Go," *Brandweek*, November 24, 2003; "Services: Online Grocers," *Newsweek*, August 4, 2003; "Amazon, Mail-Order Retailers Reheat Online Food Sales," *Wall Street Journal*, June 23, 2003; "What's for Dinner?" *Time*, May 19, 2003; "Online Grocers: Finally Delivering the Lettuce," *BusinessWeek*, April 28, 2003; "Back from the Dead: Buying Groceries Online," *Wall Street Journal*, February 25, 2003; "Webvan May Be Long Gone, but the Concept's Living On," *Investor's Business Daily*, November 5, 2001. For more on Webvan's failed effort, see "Traditional Grocers Feel Vindicated by Webvan's Failure," *Wall Street Journal*, July 11, 2001. See also "Information Gridlock: Fate, Fortune Ride on Flow of Critical Data," *USA Today*, July 2, 1996; Michael B. Mazis, "Marketing and Public Policy: Prospects for the Future," *Journal of Public Policy & Marketing*, Spring 1997; Cornelia Droge et al., "The Consumption Culture and Its Critiques: A Framework for Analysis," *Journal of Macromarketing*, Fall 1993. For more on obesity concerns, see "General Mills Sees Wealth via Health," *Wall Street Journal*, February 25, 2008; "Inside Drugmakers' War on Fat," *BusinessWeek*, March 17, 2008; "Get Healthy—or Else," *BusinessWeek*, February 26, 2007; "Obesity of China's Kids Stuns Officials," *USA Today*, January 9, 2007; "More Americans Clean Their Plates of 'Bad' Food," *USA Today*, December 13, 2006; "New York Transfat Ban Could Spread," *Wall Street Journal*, December 6, 2006; "A Soda Maker, Touting Health, Moves to Sugar," *Wall Street Journal*, December 5, 2006; "The Big Opportunity," *Business 2.0*, June 2006; "Flak over Fast Food Nation," *Wall Street Journal*, May 18, 2006; "The Not-So-Skinny: U.S. Population Weighs in as the World's Most Obese," *Advertising Age*, May 15, 2006; "Does Advertising Make Us Fat? Yes!" *Brandweek*, February 20, 2006; "Some Weighty Issues Face Firms that Eye New Obesity Drugs," *Investor's Business Daily*, February 6, 2006; "Helping Your Kids Slim Down,"

BusinessWeek, January 9, 2006; "Tony the Tiger on Death Row?" *Advertising Age*, December 12, 2005, pp. 1, 30; "Panel Faults Food Packaging for Kid Obesity," *Wall Street Journal*, December 7, 2005; "Why Kraft Decided to Ban Some Food Ads to Children," *Wall Street Journal*, October 31, 2005; "You Want Nutrition Info with That?" *USA Today*, October 26, 2005; "Slimmer Kids, Fatter Profits," *BusinessWeek*, September 5, 2005; "Food Fight's New Fronts: Viral Marketing, Games," *Advertising Age*, July 18, 2005, pp. 3, 35; "Food Makers Propose Tougher Guidelines for Children's Ads," *Wall Street Journal*, July 13, 2005; "Obesity Surges among Affluent," *USA Today*, May 3, 2005; "For the Health-Unconscious, Era of Mammoth Burger Is Here," *Wall Street Journal*, January 27, 2005; "New Obesity Boom in Arab Countries Has Old Ancestry," *Wall Street Journal*, December 29, 2004; "Let Them Eat Cake—If They Want To," *BusinessWeek*, February 23, 2004; "Downsize This!" *Wall Street Journal*, January 27, 2004; "Why We're Losing the War against Obesity," *American Demographics*, January 2004; "Today's Kids Are Helping Themselves," *USA Today*, November 20, 2003; "Junk Food Super-Sizing Europeans," *USA Today*, November 18, 2003; *USA Today*, November 3, 2003; "Pizza Hut to Serve Up Slices of Healthier Pie," *USA Today*, October 15, 2003; "Americans Start to Shape Up, Eat Healthier," *Wall Street Journal*, October 14, 2003; "Obesity Predicted for 40% of America," *USA Today*, October 14, 2003; "A Real Food Fight Breaks Out in Schools," *Investor's Business Daily*, September 22, 2003; "Guess What F Is For? Fat," *Time*, September 15, 2003; "Obesity Suit against McDonald's Is Dismissed by Federal Judge," *Wall Street Journal*, September 5, 2003; "Frito-Lay Puts Smart-Snack Label on Baked Chips," *Wall Street Journal*, August 6, 2003; "Judge Drops Lawsuit against McDonald's," *USA Today*, January 23, 2003; "That Veggie Wrap You Just Chowed Down Is More Fattening than a Ham Sandwich," *Wall Street Journal*, January 14, 2003; "Obesity: A World-Wide Woe," *Wall Street Journal*, July 1, 2002; "Is Food the Next Tobacco?" *Wall Street Journal*, June 13, 2002. See also Debra M. Desrochers and Debra J. Holt, "Children's Exposure to Television Advertising: Implications for Childhood Obesity," *Journal of Public Policy & Marketing*, Fall 2007; Elizabeth S. Moore and Victoria J. Rideout, "The Online Marketing of Food to Children: Is It Just Fun and Games?" *Journal of Public Policy & Marketing*, Fall 2007; Kathleen Seiders and Leonard L. Berry, "Should Business Care About Obesity?" *MIT Sloan Management Review*, Winter 2007; Jaideep Sengupta and Rongrong Zhou, "Understanding Impulsive Eaters' Choice Behaviors: The Motivational Influences of Regulatory Focus," *Journal of Marketing Research*, May 2007; Kelly Geyskens, Mario Pandelaere, Siegfried Dewitte, and Luk Warlop, "The Backdoor to Overconsumption: The Effect of Associating 'Low-Fat' Food with Health References," *Journal of Public Policy & Marketing*, Spring 2007; Pierre Chandon and Brian Wansink, "Is Obesity Caused by Calorie Underestimation? A Psychophysical Model of Meal Size Estimation," *Journal of Marketing Research*, February 2007; Sonya A. Grier, Janell Mensinger, Shirley H. Huang, Shiriki K. Kumanyika, and Nicolas Stettler, "Fast-Food Marketing and Children's Fast-Food Consumption: Exploring Parents' Influences in an Ethnically Diverse Sample," *Journal of Public Policy & Marketing*, Fall 2007; Marvin E. Goldberg and Kunter Gunasti, "Creating an Environment in Which Youths Are Encouraged to Eat a Healthier Diet," *Journal of Public Policy & Marketing*, Fall 2007; Stephanie Dellande, Mary C. Gilly, and John L. Graham, "Gaining Compliance and Losing Weight: The Role of the Service Provider in Health Care Services," *Journal of Marketing*, July 2004; Rosellina Ferraro, Baba shiv Shiv, James R. Bettman, Dawn Iacobucci, and Barbara Kahn, "Let Us Eat and Drink, for Tomorrow We Shall Die: Effects of Mortality Salience and Self-Esteem on Self-Regulation in Consumer Choice," *Journal of Consumer Research*, June 2005; Melissa Grills Robinson, Paul N. Bloom, and Nicholas H. Lurie, "Combating Obesity in the Courts: Will Lawsuits Against McDonald's Work?" *Journal of Public Policy & Marketing*, Fall 2005; Kathleen Seiders and Ross D. Petty, "Obesity and the Role of Food Marketing: A Policy Analysis of Issues and Remedies,"

Journal of Public Policy & Marketing, Fall 2004; Brian Wansink and Mike Huckabee, "De-Marketing Obesity," *California Management Review*, Summer 2005.

2. *The American Customer Satisfaction Index*, www.theacsi.org, and "Now Are You Satisfied? The 1998 American Customer Satisfaction Index," *Fortune*, February 16, 1998. See also "Would You Recommend Us?" *BusinessWeek*, January 30, 2006; Terrence H. Witkowski and Mary F. Wolfinbarger, "Comparative Service Quality: German and American Ratings Across Service Settings," *Journal of Business Research*, November 2002; Eugene W. Anderson and Linda Court Salisbury, "The Formation of Market-Level Expectations and its Covariates," *Journal of Consumer Research*, June, 2003; Claes Fornell, Michael D. Johnson, Eugene W. Anderson, Jaesung Cha, and Barbara E. Bryant, "The American Customer Satisfaction Index: Nature, Purpose, and Findings," *Journal of Marketing*, October 1996; Eugene W. Anderson, Claes Fornell, and Donald R. Lehmann, "Customer Satisfaction, Market Share, and Profitability: Findings from Sweden," *Journal of Marketing*, July 1994; John F. Gaski and Michael J. Etzel, "The Index of Consumer Sentiment Toward Marketing," *Journal of Marketing*, July 1986; "The Limits of Customer Satisfaction," *Brandweek*, March 3, 1997; Hiram C. Barksdale et al., "A Cross-National Survey of Consumer Attitudes Toward Marketing Practices, Consumerism, and Government Regulations," *Columbia Journal of World Business*, Summer 1982; Hiram C. Barksdale and William D. Perreault, Jr., "Can Consumers Be Satisfied?" *MSU Business Topics*, Spring 1980.

3. "Expanding J.D.'s Power," *BusinessWeek*, November 22, 2004; "Consumer Complaints Soared in 2002," *Wall Street Journal*, November 25, 2003; "Will Jeff Immelt's New Push Pay Off for GE?" *BusinessWeek*, October 13, 2003; "Whatever Happened to Customer Service?" *USA Today*, September 26, 2003; "Ma'am, Please: Never Call Us Again," *Brandweek*, September 22, 2003; "J.D. Power for the People," *USA Today*, August 28, 2003; "Web-Portal Satisfaction Rises," *Wall Street Journal*, August 20, 2003; "My Cookies Are Crumbled: The Art of Consumer Griping," *Wall Street Journal*, August 27, 2002. See also Judy Strauss and Donna J. Hill, "Consumer Complaints by E-Mail: An Exploratory Investigation of Corporate Responses and Customer Reactions," *Journal of Interactive Marketing*, Winter 2001; James G. Maxham III and Richard G. Netemeyer, "Modeling Customer Perceptions of Complaint Handling over Time: The Effects of Perceived Justice on Satisfaction and Intent," *Journal of Retailing*, Winter 2002; James G. Maxham III, and Richard G. Netemeyer, "A Longitudinal Study of Complaining Customers' Evaluations of Multiple Service Failures and Recovery Efforts," *Journal of Marketing*, October 2002; James G. Maxham III, and Richard G. Netemyer, "Firms Reap What They Sow: The Effects of Shared Values and Perceived Organizational Justice on Customers' Evaluations of Complaint Handling," *Journal of Marketing*, January 2003; Roger Bougie, Rik Pieters, and Marcel Zeelenberg, "Angry Customers Don't Come Back, They Get Back: The Experience and Behavioral Implications of Anger and Dissatisfaction in Services," *Journal of the Academy of Marketing Science*, Fall 2003; Amy K. Smith and Ruth N. Bolton, "The Effect of Customers' Emotional Responses to Service Failures on Their Recovery Effort Evaluations and Satisfaction Judgements," *Journal of the Academy of Marketing Science*, Winter 2002; Michael Brady, "Improving Your Measurement of Customer Satisfaction: A Guide to Creating, Conducting, Analyzing, and Reporting Customer Satisfaction Measurement Programs," *Journal of the Academy of Marketing Science*, Spring 2000; David M. Szymanski, "Customer Satisfaction: A Meta-Analysis of the Empirical Evidence," *Journal of the Academy of Marketing Science*, Winter 2001; Thorsten Hennig-Thurau and Alexander Klee, "The Impact of Customer Satisfaction and Relationship Quality on Customer Retention: A Critical Reassessment and Model Development," *Psychology & Marketing*, December 1997; Scott W. Hansen, Thomas L. Powers, and John E. Swan, "Modeling Industrial Buyer Complaints: Implications for Satisfying and Saving Customers," *Journal of Marketing Theory & Practice*, Fall 1997; Paul G. Patterson, Lester W. Johnson, and Richard A. Spreng, "Modeling the Determinants of Customer Satisfaction for Business-to-Business Professional Services," *Journal of the Academy of Marketing Science*, Winter 1997; Stephen S. Tax, Stephen W. Brown, and Murali Chandrashekaran, "Customer Evaluations of Service Complaint Experiences: Implications for Relationship Marketing," *Journal of Marketing*, April 1998; F. Gouillart and F. Sturdivant, "Spend a Day in the Life of Your Customers," *Harvard Business Review*, January–February 1994.

4. Claes Fornell, Sunil Mithas, Forrest V. Morgeson Iii, and M. S. Krishnan, "Customer Satisfaction and Stock Prices: High Returns, Low Risk," *Journal of Marketing*, January 2006; Neil A. Morgan, Eugene W. Anderson, and Vikas Mittal, "Understanding Firms' Customer Satisfaction Information Usage," *Journal of Marketing*, July 2005; Eugene W. Anderson, Claes Fornell, and Sanal K. Mazvancheryl, "Customer Satisfaction and Shareholder Value," *Journal of Marketing*, October 2004; Michael Tsirod, Vikas Mittal, and William T. Ross, Jr., "The Role of Attributions in Customer Satisfaction: A Reexamination," *Journal of Consumer Research*, September 2004; Scott R. Colwell, "The Future of Marketing: Practical Strategies for Marketers in the Post-Internet Age," *Journal of the Academy of Marketing Science*, Winter 2003; Kevin J. Clancy and Robert S. Shulman, *Marketing Myths That Are Killing Business: The Cure for Death Wish Marketing* (New York: McGraw-Hill, 1994); Regina E. Herzlinger, "Can Public Trust in Nonprofits and Governments Be Restored?" *Harvard Business Review*, March–April 1996; Michael S. Minor, "Relentless: The Japanese Way of Marketing," *Journal of the Academy of Marketing Science*, Spring 1998; Charles C. Snow, "Twenty-First-Century Organizations: Implications for a New Marketing Paradigm," *Journal of the Academy of Marketing Science*, Winter 1997; Frederick F. Reichheld, "Learning from Customer Defections," *Harvard Business Review*, March–April 1996. For a classic discussion of the problem and mechanics of measuring the efficiency of marketing, see Reavis Cox, *Distribution in a High-Level Economy* (Englewood Cliffs, NJ: Prentice-Hall, 1965).

5. For more on criticisms of advertising, see David C. Vladeck, "Truth and Consequences: the Perils of Half-Truths and Unsubstantiated Health Claims for Dietary Supplements," *Journal of Public Policy & Marketing*, Spring 2000; Barbara J. Phillips, "In Defense of Advertising: A Social Perspective," *Journal of Business Ethics*, February 1997; Charles Trappey, "A Meta-Analysis of Consumer Choice and Subliminal Advertising," *Psychology & Marketing*, August 1996; Karl A. Boedecker, Fred W. Morgan, and Linda B. Wright, "The Evolution of First Amendment Protection for Commercial Speech," *Journal of Marketing*, January 1995; Thomas C. O'Guinn and L. J. Shrum, "The Role of Television in the Construction of Consumer Reality," *Journal of Consumer Research*, March 1997. See also Robert B. Archibald, Clyde A. Haulman, and Carlisle E. Moody, Jr., "Quality, Price, Advertising, and Published Quality Ratings," *Journal of Consumer Research*, March 1983.

6. Thomas O. Jones and W. E. Sasser, "Why Satisfied Customers Defect," *Harvard Business Review*, November–December 1995; "The Satisfaction Trap," *Harvard Business Review*, March–April 1996.

7. "Angry NFL Slams ABC's 'Desperate Housewives' Promo," *Wall Street Journal*, November 17, 2004; "FDA Tells Pfizer to Pull Viagra Ads about 'Wild Thing,'" *Wall Street Journal*, November 16, 2004; "First, FCC Scrutiny, Are Ad Probes Next?" *Brandweek*, March 1, 2004; "Can Money Buy Happiness?" *Adweek*, February 3, 2003; James E. Burroughs and Aric Rindfleisch, "Materialism and Well-Being: a Conflicting Values Perspective," *Journal of Consumer Research*, December 2002; John Watson, Steven Lysonski, Tamara Gillan, and Leslie Raymore, "Cultural Values and Important Processions: a Cross-Cultural Analysis," *Journal of Business Research*, November 2002; Roy F. Baumeister, "Yielding to Temptation: Self-Control Failure, Impulsive Purchasing, and Consumer Behavior," *Journal of Consumer Research*, March 2002; Donald F. Dixon, "The Economics of Conspicuous Consumption: Theory and Thought Since 1700," *Journal of Macromarketing*, 21, no. 1 (June 2001); Guliz Ger, "Human

Development and Humane Consumption: Well-Being Beyond the 'Good Life,'" *Journal of Public Policy & Marketing*, Spring 1997; Ronald P. Hill and Sandi Macan, "Consumer Survival on Welfare with an Emphasis on Medicaid and the Food Stamp Program," *Journal of Public Policy & Marketing*, Spring 1996; Dennis J. Cahill, "The Refinement of America: Persons, Houses, Cities," *Journal of Marketing*, October 1994. See also Michael J. Barone, Randall L. Rose, Kenneth C. Manning, and Paul W. Miniard, "Another Look at the Impact of Reference Information on Consumer Impressions of Nutrition Information," *Journal of Public Policy & Marketing*, Spring 1996; Thomas A. Hemphill, "Legislating Corporate Social Responsibility," *Business Horizons*, March–April 1997; Priscilla A. La Barbera and Zeynep Gurhan, "The Role of Materialism, Religiosity, and Demographics in Subjective Well-Being," *Psychology & Marketing*, January 1997; Dennis J. Cahill, "Consumption and the World of Goods," *Journal of Marketing*, April 1994; Jacqueline K. Eastman, Bill Fredenberger, David Campbell, and Stephen Calvert, "The Relationship Between Status Consumption and Materialism: A Cross-Cultural Comparison of Chinese, Mexican and American Students," *Journal of Marketing Theory & Practice*, Winter 1997; James A. Muncy and Jacqueline K. Eastman, "Materialism and Consumer Ethics: An Exploratory Study," *Journal of Business Ethics*, January 1998; Donald P. Robin and R. Eric Reidenbach, "Identifying Critical Problems for Mutual Cooperation Between the Public and Private Sectors: A Marketing Perspective," *Journal of the Academy of Marketing Science*, Fall 1986. See also Terrence H. Witkowski, "The Early American Style: A History of Marketing and Consumer Values," *Psychology & Marketing*, March 1998; Arnold J. Toynbee, *America and World Revolution* (New York: Oxford University Press, 1966); John Kenneth Galbraith, *Economics and the Public Purpose* (Boston: Houghton Mifflin, 1973).

8. Peter R. Dickson, Paul W. Farris, and Willem J. M. I. Verbeke, "Dynamic Strategic Thinking," *Journal of the Academy of Marketing Science*, Summer 2001; Gloria Barczak, "Analysis for Marketing Planning," *Journal of Product Innovation Management*, September 1997; William A. Sahlman, "How to Write a Great Business Plan," *Harvard Business Review*, July–August 1997; Paul Boughton, "The 1-Day Marketing Plan: Organizing and Completing the Plan That Works," *Journal of the Academy of Marketing Science*, Summer 1996; William Sandy, "Avoid the Breakdowns Between Planning and Implementation," *Journal of Business Strategy*, September–October 1991; Michael MacInnis and Louise A. Heslop, "Market Planning in a High-Tech Environment," *Industrial Marketing Management*, May 1990; David Strutton, "Marketing Strategies: New Approaches, New Techniques," *Journal of the Academy of Marketing Science*, Summer 1997; Rita G. McGrath and Ian C. MacMillan, "Discovery-Driven Planning," *Harvard Business Review*, July 1995–August 1995; Jeffrey Elton and Justin Roe, "Bringing Discipline to Project Management," *Harvard Business Review*, March–April 1998; Andrew Campbell and Marcus Alexander, "What's Wrong with Strategy?" *Harvard Business Review*, November–December 1997.

9. For more on global social responsibility, see Chapter 1, endnote 9; and Chapter 9, endnote 6. See also "Smaller, Smarter," *Wall Street Journal*, February 11, 2008; "Her Signal Is Loud and Clear," *Investor's Business Daily*, December 26, 2007; "Behind One Effort to Tap into India's Water Market," *Wall Street Journal*, August 14, 2007; *IN* (Whole Issue), March 2007; J. Craig Andrews, Richard G. Netemeyer, Scot Burton, D. Paul Moberg, and Ann Christiansen, "Understanding Adolescent Intentions to Smoke: An Examination of Relationships Among Social Influence, Prior Trial Behavior, and Antitobacco Campaign Advertising," *Journal of Marketing*, July 2004; Jill Gabrielle Klein, N. Craig Smith, and Andrew John, "Why We Boycott: Consumer Motivations for Boycott Participation," *Journal of Marketing*, July 2004; Robert V. Kozinets and Jay M. Handelman, "Adversaries of Consumption: Consumer Movements, Activism, and Ideology," *Journal of Consumer Research*, December 2004; Eric J. Arnould and Jakki J. Mohr, "Dynamic Transformations for Base-of-the-Pyramid Market Clusters," *Journal of the Academy of Marketing Science*, Summer

2005; Jagdip Singh, Jean E. Kilgore, Rama K. Jayanti, Kokil Agarwal, and Ramadesikan R. Gandarvakottai, "What Goes Around Comes Around: Understanding Trust—Value Dilemmas of Market Relationships," *Journal of Public Policy & Marketing*, Spring 2005; Julie M. Donohue and Ernst R. Berndt, "Effects of Direct-to-Consumer Advertising on Medication Choice: The Case of Antidepressants," *Journal of Public Policy & Marketing*, Fall 2004; Ajit M. Menon, Aparna D. Deshpande, Matthew Perri Iii, and George M. Zinkhan, "Consumers' Attention to the Brief Summary in Print Direct-to-Consumer Advertisements: Perceived Usefulness in Patient—Physician Discussions," *Journal of Public Policy & Marketing*, Fall 2003; Donald A. Fuller and Jacquelyn A. Ottman, "Moderating Unintended Pollution: The Role of Sustainable Product Design," *Journal of Business Research*, November 2004; Marie-Louise Fry and Michael Jay Polonsky, "Examining the Unintended Consequences of Marketing," *Journal of Business Research*, November 2004; Joann Peck and Barbara Loken, "When Will Larger-Sized Female Models in Advertisements Be Viewed Positively? The Moderating Effects of Instructional Frame, Gender, and Need for Cognition," *Psychology & Marketing*, June 2004; Renato J. Orsato, "Competitive Environmental Strategies: When Does It Pay to be Green?" *California Management Review*, Winter 2006; Jill Meredith Ginsberg and Paul N. Bloom, "Choosing the Right Green Marketing Strategy," *MIT Sloan Management Review*, Fall 2004.

10. For other environmental issues, see "War on the Water Front," *Time*, December 19, 2005; "Whole Fuels," *Business 2.0*, December 2005; "Is It Too Easy Being Green?" *Wall Street Journal*, October 19, 2005; "Turning Waste into Watts," *Business 2.0*, October 2005; "Getting More Miles to the Gallon—Fast," *BusinessWeek*, September 26, 2005; "It's Easier Being Green," *BusinessWeek*, September 19, 2005; "Automakers Jack Up MPG PDG," *USA Today*, September 16, 2005; "New Incentives for Being Green," *Wall Street Journal*, August 4, 2005; "The Great Windfall," *Business 2.0*, August 2005; "China: Wasteful Ways," *BusinessWeek*, April 11, 2005; "Eco Trends," *BusinessWeek*, March 21, 2005; "Beyond Recycling: Manufacturers Embrace C2C Design," *Wall Street Journal*, March 3, 2005; "Old Cellphones Pile Up by the Millions," *Wall Street Journal*, September 23, 2004; "The Race to Save a Rainforest," *BusinessWeek*, November 24, 2003; "Cellphone Makers Connect for Recycling Program," *USA Today*, October 22, 2003; "The Information Age's Toxic Garbage," *BusinessWeek*, October 6, 2003; "Offsetting Environmental Damage by Planes," The *New York Times*, February 18, 2003; "Behind Roses' Beauty, Poor and Ill Workers," The *New York Times*, February 13, 2003; "Industrial Evolution," *BusinessWeek*, April 8, 2002; "Green Sales Pitch Isn't Moving Many Products," *Wall Street Journal*, March 6, 2002; "Brazilian Mahogany: Too Much in Demand," *Wall Street Journal*, November 14, 2001; "How Much Power Do You Use?" *Wall Street Journal*, August 16, 2001; "Choice of Evils: As a Tropical Scourge Makes a Comeback, So, Too, Does DDT," *Wall Street Journal*, July 26, 2001; "It May Be Time to Toss Old Ideas on Recycling," *USA Today*, July 2, 2001; "As BP Goes Green, the Fur Is Flying," *Wall Street Journal*, April 16, 2001; "Once Is Not Enough," *BusinessWeek*, April 16, 2001; "EarthShell Saw Big Macs and Big Bucks—Got Big Woes," *Wall Street Journal*, April 10, 2001; "Recycling Redefined," *Wall Street Journal*, March 6, 2001; "More Gas-Powered Autos on 'Green' List," *USA Today*, February 9, 2001; "Nonprofits—and Landfills—Deluged with Old PCs," *Investor's Business Daily*, November 27, 2000; "Conservation: Been There, Doing That," *BusinessWeek*, November 27, 2000; "Recycler's Nightmare: Beer in Plastic," *Wall Street Journal*, November 16, 1999; "As Old Pallets Pile Up, Critics Hammer Them as a New Eco-Menace," *Wall Street Journal*, April 1, 1998. See also Lynette Knowles Mathur and Ike Mathur, "An Analysis of the Wealth Effects of Green Marketing Strategies," *Journal of Business Research*, November 2000; Subhabrata Bobby Banerjee, Easwar S. Iyer, and Rajiv K. Kashyap, "Corporate Environmentalism: Antecedents and Influence of Industry Type," *Journal of Marketing*, April 2003; Anil Menon and Ajay Menon, "Enviropreneurial Marketing Strategy: The Emergence of Corporate Environmentalism as Market

Strategy," *Journal of Marketing*, January 1997; William E. Kilbourne, "Green Advertising: Salvation or Oxymoron?" *Journal of Advertising*, Summer 1995.

11. "False 'Green' Ads Draw Global Scrutiny," *Wall Street Journal*, January 30, 2008; "The Six Sins of Greenwashing," TerraChoice Environmental Marketing, Inc., November 2007, www.terrachoice.com; "Most Americans and Canadians Say 'Green' Labeling Just a Marketing Tactic," *GreenBiz.com*, October 2, 2007; Gregory C. Unruh, "The Biosphere Rules," *Harvard Business Review*, February 2008.

12. For more on privacy, see Chapter 13, endnote 15. See also "Company to Offer Tracking by Phone," *Investor's Business Daily*, November 16, 2005; "Security's New World Order," *Investor's Business Daily*, November 7, 2005; "'Working Late' Won't Work Anymore," *BusinessWeek*, October 31, 2005; "New Services Guard against ID Theft," *Wall Street Journal*, October 6, 2005; "Prying Eyes Are Everywhere," *USA Today*, April 14, 2005; "America Online, RSA Wage Token Effort to Improve Security," *Investor's Business Daily*, September 22, 2004; "You're on Candid Cellphone!" *Wall Street Journal*, September 30, 2003; "Stalk Market: New Battleground in Web Privacy War, Ads that Snoop," *Wall Street Journal*, August 27, 2003; "Online Shopper Still Fear Security Issues," *Investor's Business Daily*, June 3, 2003; "Privacy in an Age of Terror," *BusinessWeek*, November 5, 2001; "Internet Insecurity," *Time*, July 2, 2001; "Privacy Options Are a Blur," *USA Today*, April 10, 2001; "The Battle Over Web Privacy," *Wall Street Journal*, March 21, 2001. See also George R. Milne and Mary J. Culnan, "Strategies for Reducing Online Privacy Risks: Why Consumers Read (or Don't Read) Online Privacy Notices," *Journal of Interactive Marketing*, Summer 2004; Curt J. Dommeyer and Barbara L. Gross, "What Consumers Know and What They Do: An Investigation of Consumer Knowledge, Awareness, and Use of Privacy Protection Strategies," *Journal of Interactive Marketing*, Spring 2003; John A. McCarty, "Data Privacy in the Information Age," *Journal of Public Policy & Marketing*, Fall 2002; George R. Milne and Andrew J. Rohm, "Consumer Privacy and Name Removal Across Direct Marketing Channels: Exploring Opt-In and Opt-Out Alternatives," *Journal of Public Policy & Marketing*, Fall 2000; Joseph E. Phelps, Giles D'Souza, and Glen J. Nowak, "Antecedents and Consequences of Consumer Privacy Concerns: an Empirical Investigation," *Journal of Interactive Marketing*, Autumn 2001; Ellen R. Foxman and Paula Kilcoyne, "Information Technology, Marketing Practice, and Consumer Privacy: Ethical Issues," *Journal of Public Policy & Marketing*, Spring 1993; Robert E. Thomas and Virginia G. Maurer, "Database Marketing Practice: Protecting Consumer Privacy," *Journal of Public Policy & Marketing*, Spring 1997; Marren J. Roy, "Regulation of Automatic Dialing and Announcing Devices Upheld," *Journal of the Academy of Marketing Science*, Summer 1997.

13. "School Buses Latest Victim of Ad Creep," *Brandweek*, February 4, 2008; "Channel One: New Owner, Old Issues," *Advertising Age*, November 26, 2007; "Food Marketers Pledge No More Kids Ads in the European Union," *Advertising Age*, December 17, 2007; "Babes in Brandland," *Brandweek*, October 15, 2007; "Kellogg Move Bodes Ill for Ads to Kids," *Advertising Age*, June 18, 2007; "Food Manufacturers Tell Kids to Eat Their Fruits and Veggies," *Investor's Business Daily*, June 4, 2007; "Movement to Ban School Junk Food," *USA Today*, April 26, 2007; "No Sugarcoating This: Kids Besieged by Food Ads," *USA Today*, March 29, 2007; "Food Companies Vow to Tighten Limits on Kids' Ads," *Wall Street Journal*, November 15, 2006; "Disney Pulls Characters from Junk Food," *Wall Street Journal*, October 17, 2006; "Beverage Firms Yield to Pressure on School Sales," *Wall Street Journal*, May 4, 2006; "Bob Takes a Hit," *Brandweek*, January 23, 2006; "Advertisers Catch the School Bus," *USA Today*, December 27, 2005; "CARU's Medicine Hard to Swallow," *Advertising Age*, November 28, 2005; "MealPay Tracks Kids' Eating," *USA Today*, October 4, 2005; "McDonald's Kicks Off School PE Program," *USA Today*, September 13, 2005; "Fast Food Surrounds Metropolitan Schools," *USA Today*, August 24, 2005; "Health Movement Has School Cafeterias in a Food Fight," *USA Today*, August 22, 2005; "Soda Marketers Will Cut Back

Sales to Schools," *Wall Street Journal*, August 17, 2005; "Divided, Companies Fight for Right to Plug Kids' Food," *Wall Street Journal*, January 26, 2005; "Got Bottles? Schools Sell More Milk Outside Box," *Wall Street Journal*, December 29, 2004; "Stonyfield Heads Back to School," *Advertising Age*, September 20, 2004; "Seals and Deals," *Wall Street Journal*, July 20, 2004; "A Lesson in Selling Healthy Snacks," *Investor's Business Daily*, May 24, 2004; "Junk-Food Games," *Wall Street Journal*, May 3, 2004; "Is Marketing to Kids Ethical?" *Brandweek*, April 5, 2004; "How Young Is Too Young?" *Brandweek*, April 5, 2004; "Coming Up Next . . . Calls for Tighter Restrictions on Kids' Ads," *Wall Street Journal*, March 15, 2004; "The Good News: No More Coke in School. The Bad News: Snapple Is Replacing It," *Wall Street Journal*, January 13, 2004; "Coke's Guidelines for Soft Drinks in Schools Faces Some Criticism," *Wall Street Journal*, November 17, 2003; "New in School Vending Machines: Yogurt, Soy," *Wall Street Journal*, October 15, 2003; "A Real Food Fight Breaks Out in Schools," *Investor's Business Daily*, September 22, 2003; "Head of the Class: Don't Spare the Brand," *Brandweek*, March 10, 2003; "Cafeteria Food Fight," *Wall Street Journal*, June 14, 2002; "Coke Finds Its Exclusive School Contracts Aren't So Easily Given Up," *Wall Street Journal*, June 26, 2001; "Web-Filter Data from Schools Put Up for Sale," *Wall Street Journal*, January 26, 2001; "On Many Campuses, Big Brewers Play a Role in New Alcohol Policies," *Wall Street Journal*, November 2, 2000; "Pepsi Hits High Note with Schools," *Advertising Age*, October 9, 2000; "If It's Marketing, Can It Also Be Education?" *Fortune*, October 2, 2000; "AOL to Announce This Week the Launch of Free Online Service Aimed at Schools," *Wall Street Journal*, May 16, 2000; "Mouse-Trapping the Student Market," *American Demographics*, May 2000; "Grad Students Match Wits in Marketing Competition," *Wall Street Journal*, February 9, 2000; "Pitching Saturns to Your Classmates—for Credit," *Wall Street Journal*, January 31, 2000; "Marketers on Campus: A New Bag of Tricks," *Wall Street Journal*, January 31, 2000; "Tobacco Money Sparks a New Fight," *Wall Street Journal*, December 10, 1999; "Schools for Sale," *Advertising Age*, October 25, 1999; "Big Cards on Campus," *BusinessWeek*, September 20, 1999; "Cola Contracts Lose Fizz in Schools," *USA Today*, August 18, 1999; "Ads in Schools: Lesson in Failure?" *Advertising Age*, June 7, 1999; "Classrooms for Sale," *Time*, April 19, 1999; "Big Car on Campus?" *BusinessWeek*, August 31, 1998; "Are We Selling Our Students?" *Raleigh News & Observer*, August 2, 1998; "This School Was Sponsored by . . .," *Parenting*, March 1998; "Channel One Taps Principals as Promoters," *Wall Street Journal*, September 15, 1997; "School's Back, and So Are the Marketers," *Wall Street Journal*, September 15, 1997; "Hey Kid, Buy This!" *BusinessWeek*, June 30, 1997; "This Class Brought to You by . . .," *USA Today*, January 3, 1997; "New Ad Vehicles: Police Car, School Bus, Garbage Truck," *Wall Street Journal*, February 20, 1996. See also Judith A. Garretson and Scot Burton, "The Role of Spokescharacters as Advertisement and Package Cues in Integrated Marketing Communications," *Journal of Marketing*, October 2005; Sabrina M. Neeley and David W. Schumann, "Using Animated Spokes-Characters in Advertising to Young Children," *Journal of Advertising*, Fall 2004.

14. For more on online fraud, see "At Online Stores, Sniffing Out Crooks Is a Matter of Survival," *Wall Street Journal*, August 4, 2005; "Problem for Cops on eBay Beat: Crooks Keep Getting Smarter," *Wall Street Journal*, August 3, 2004; "Scammed! Web Merchants Use New Tools to Keep Buyers from Ripping Them Off," *Wall Street Journal Reports*, January 27, 2003; "E-Commerce Report: Crime Is Soaring in Cyberspace," *The New York Times*, January 27, 2003; "Credit-Card Scams Bedevil E-Stores," *Wall Street Journal*, September 19, 2000; "Fraud on the Internet," *BusinessWeek E.Biz*, April 3, 2000; "Online Scambusters," *BusinessWeek E.Biz*, April 3, 2000; "Card Sharps," *BusinessWeek E.Biz*, April 3, 2000. For more on in-store fraud, see "Stores Battle Employee Theft," *Raleigh News & Observer*, October 15, 2000; "As Thievery by Insiders Overtakes Shoplifting, Retailers Crack Down," *Wall Street Journal*, September 8, 2000; "Electronic Tags Are Beeping Everywhere," *Wall Street Journal*, April 20, 1998; "A Time to Steal," *Brandweek*, February 16, 1998.

15. For more on socially responsible and ethical behavior, see "Alcohol Makers Tread Tricky Path in Marketing to College Students," *USA Today*, November 17, 2005; "Rx from Marlboro Man: Device That Delivers Drugs, Not Smoke," *Wall Street Journal*, October 27, 2005; "The Debate over Doing Good," *BusinessWeek*, August 15, 2005; "Cops of the Global Village," *Fortune*, June 27, 2005; "At Some Retailers, 'Fair Trade' Carries a Very High Cost," *Wall Street Journal*, June 8, 2004; "Drug Ills? Follow the Money," *Brandweek*, February 7, 2005, pp. 24–28; "Car Seats for Eight-Year-Olds," *Wall Street Journal*, January 27, 2005; "Money and Morals at GE," *Fortune*, November 15, 2004; "Nestle Markets Baby Formula to Hispanic Mothers in U.S.," *Wall Street Journal*, March 4, 2004; "Teaching the Wrong Lesson," *Business 2.0*, November 2003; "Food Sellers Push Animal Welfare," *USA Today*, August 13, 2003; "In the Name of Responsibility," *Brandweek*, May 12, 2003; "For MBAs, Soul-Searching 101," *BusinessWeek*, September 16, 2002; "Wanted: Ethical Employer," *Wall Street Journal*, July 9, 2002; "I Take Thee . . . Back to the Store," *Wall Street Journal*, May 30, 2002. See also John C. Kozup, Elizabeth H. Creyer, and Scot Burton, "Making Healthful Food Choices: the Influence of Health Claims and Nutrition Information on Consumers' Evaluations of Packaged Food Products and Restaurant Menu Items," *Journal of Marketing*, April 2003; Sankar Sen, Zeynep Gurhan-Canli, and Vicki Morwitz, "Withholding Consumption: a Social Dilemma Perspective on Consumer Boycotts," *Journal of Consumer Research*, December 2001; Steve Hoeffler and Kevin Lane Keller, "Building Brand Equity Through Corporate Societal Marketing," *Journal of Public Policy & Marketing*, Spring 2002; Dwane Hal Dean, "Associating the Cooperation with a Charitable Event Through Sponsorship: Measuring the Effects on Corporate Community Relations," *Journal of Advertising*, Winter 2002; Richard Pearce and Maria Hansson, "Retailing and Risk Society: Genetically Modified Food," *International Journal of Retail & Distribution Management*, (11) 2000; W. P. Cunningham, "The Golden Rule as Universal Ethical Norm," *Journal of Business Ethics*, January 1998; "Ethnic Pricing' Means Unfair Air Fares," *Wall Street Journal*, December 5, 1997; William P. Cordeiro, "Suggested Management Responses to Ethical Issues Raised by Technological Change," *Journal of Business Ethics*, September 1997; Eli P. I. Cox, Michael S. Wogalter, Sara L. Stokes, and Elizabeth J. T. Murff, "Do Product Warnings Increase Safe Behavior? A Meta-Analysis," *Journal of Public Policy & Marketing*, Fall 1997; "On the Net, Anything Goes," *Newsweek*, July 7, 1997; "Levi's As Ye Sew, So Shall Ye Reap," *Fortune*, May 12, 1997; "48% of Workers Admit to Unethical or Illegal Acts," *USA Today*, April 4, 1997; H. R. Dodge, Elizabeth A. Edwards, and Sam Fullerton, "Consumer Transgressions in the Marketplace: Consumers' Perspectives," *Psychology & Marketing*, December 1996; David W. Stewart, "Internet Marketing, Business Models, and Public Policy," *Journal of Public Policy & Marketing*, Fall 2000; Albert A. Foer, "E-commerce Meets Antitrust: A Primer," *Journal of Public Policy & Marketing*, Spring 2001; "Ethics for Hire," *BusinessWeek*, July 15, 1996; "How a Drug Firm Paid for University Study, Then Undermined It," *Wall Street Journal*, April 25, 1996; James A. Roberts, "Will the Real Socially Responsible Consumer Please Step Forward?" *Business Horizons*, January–February 1996; John Priddle, "Marketing Ethics, Macromarketing, and the Managerial Perspective Reconsidered," *Journal of Macromarketing*, Fall 1994; Bernard Avishai, "What is Business's Social Compact?" *Harvard Business Review*, January–February 1994; Paul N. Bloom, George R. Milne, and Robert Adler, "Avoiding Misuse of New Information Technologies: Legal and Societal Considerations," *Journal of Marketing*, January 1994; James A. Muncy and Scott J. Vitell, "Consumer Ethics: An Investigation of the Ethical Beliefs of the Final Consumer," *Journal of Business Research*, June 1992; Gene R. Laczniak and Patrick E. Murphy, "Fostering Ethical Marketing Decisions," *Journal of Business Ethics*, April 1991.

Illustration Credits

CHAPTER 1

Exhibits: Exhibit 1–1, adapted from William McInnes, "A Conceptual Approach to Marketing," in *Theory in Marketing*, 2d ser., ed. Reavis Cox, Wroe Alderson, and Stanley J. Shapiro (Homewood, IL: Richard D. Irwin, 1964), pp. 51–67. Exhibit 1–2, model suggested by Professor A. A. Brogowicz, Western Michigan University. Exhibit 1–4, adapted from R. F. Vizza, T. E. Chambers, and E. J. Cook, *Adoption of the Marketing Concept—Fact or Fiction* (New York: Sales Executive Club, Inc., 1967), pp. 13–15. Exhibit 1–5, this exhibit is different from, but stimulated by, a graph that appears on the Satisfaction Management Systems, Inc., website, www.satmansys.com. Exhibit 1–7, adapted from discussions of an American Marketing Association Strategic Planning Committee.

Photos/ads: P. 2–3, Courtesy McDonald's USA, LLC. P. 4, ©Bob Allen. P. 5, Courtesy Nationwide Mutual Insurance Company; Agency: TM Advertising/Dallas, TX. P. 8, AP Photo/Kent Gilbert. P. 8, ©Evans Vestal Ward. P. 11, These materials have been reproduced with the permission of eBay, Inc. COPYRIGHT ©2006 EBAY INC. ALL RIGHTS RESERVED. P. 11, Ad courtesy of CARQUEST AUTO Parts, General Parts, Inc. P. 12, Courtesy Ten Thousand Villages. P. 15, No credit. P. 22, Courtesy World Wildlife Fund/Adena; Agency: Contrapunto S.A./Madrid. P. 23, New York City Department of Health/DCF Advertising. P. 24, Courtesy Network BBDO/Johannesburg, South Africa.

CHAPTER 2

Exhibits: Exhibit 2–9, Igor Ansoff, *Corporate Strategy* (New York; McGraw-Hill, 1965).

Photos/ads: P. 30–31, Adrian Dennis/AFP/Getty Images. P. 37, Courtesy British Airways North America. P. 38, Both Courtesy Toddler University. P. 41, All Courtesy of Campbell Soup Company. P. 45, Courtesy Timex Corporation; Agency: Arnold Communications/New York. P. 48, Courtesy Johnson & Johnson. P. 49, ©William D. Perreault, Jr., Ph.D. P. 51, Courtesy McCann Erickson Advertising Ltd./London. P. 51, Courtesy Crocs, Inc. P. 52, Courtesy Unilever P.L.C. P. 52, ©1999 Barry Lewis/Network.

CHAPTER 3

Exhibits: Exhibit 3–5, table based on U.S. Census data including *Statistical Abstract of the United States 2008* (Washington, DC: U.S. Government Printing Office), Tables 1298, pp. 824–27, available online at www.census.gov/statab; U.S. Census Bureau "International Data Base" available online at www.census.gov/ipc/www/ibd/; Population Reference Bureau data, including *2007 World Pop Data Sheet*, available online at www.prb.org/pubs/wpds2007; World Bank data, available online at www.worldbank.org/countries/; CIA data, including *CIA Factbook 2008*, available online at www.odci.gov/cia/publications/factbook2008. Exhibit 3–6, map developed by the authors based on U.S. Census data including *Statistical Abstract of the United States 2008* (Washington, DC: U.S. Government Printing Office), Tables 12 and 14, pp. 17 and 19; available online at www.census.gov/statab; Exhibit 3–7, graph developed by the authors based on U.S. Census data including *Statistical Abstract of the United States 2008* (Washington, DC: U.S. Government Printing Office), Table 10, p. 14 (for 2020 figures); Table 10, p. 14 (for 2010 figures); Table 7, p. 10 (for 2000 figures); available online at www.census.gov/statab; Exhibit 3–10, adapted from M. G. Allen, "Strategic Problems Facing Today's Corpo-

rate Planner," speech given at the Academy of Management, 36th Annual Meeting, Kansas City, Missouri, 1976. Chapter 3

Photos/ads: P. 56, Rex Tystedt/Time Life Pictures/Getty Images. P. 60, Courtesy 3M; Agency: Grey Worldwide Johannesburg. P. 62, ©2008 General Mills, Inc. P. 62, Courtesy Nucor Corporation. P. 63, Reprinted with permission from the Minwax Company/Upper Saddle River, N.J. ©2006 Minwax Company. All Rights Reserved. P. 63, Courtesy Royal Appliance Mfg. Co. P. 64, Agency: John St./Toronto; Art Director: Nellie Kim; Copywriter: Chris Hirsch; Photographer: Mark Zibert. P. 68, Courtesy BBDO Dusseldorf; Creative Director: Ton Hollander; Copy-Writer: Markus Steinkemper; Photographer: Uwe Düttmann; Account Representative: Sebastian Schlosser. P. 69, Courtesy Outcast Public Relations. P. 70, Courtesy Adero, Inc. P. 71, Mucinex®is a registered trademark of Adams Respiratory Operations, Inc. P. 74, These materials have been reproduced with the permission of eBay, Inc. COPYRIGHT ©2008 EBAY INC. ALL RIGHTS RESERVED. P. 76, Kevin Lee/CopixFotoagentur. P. 78, Courtesy CNBC. P. 84, Con Agra Foods Specialty Potato Products; Agency: Strahan Advertising. P. 84, Courtesy Click 2 Asia.

CHAPTER 4

Exhibits: Exhibit 4–11, Russell I. Haley, "Benefit Segmentation: A Decision-Oriented Research Tool," *Journal of Marketing*, July 1968, p. 33.

Photos/ads: P. 89, Yoshikazu Tsuno/AFP/Getty Images. P. 92, Courtesy Glaces Thiriet SAS. P. 92, Courtesy Kahala Management LLC; Blimpie Franchise Systems. P. 93, Courtesy Nestlé S.A. P. 97, Courtesy GlaxoSmithKline. P. 97, ©The Procter & Gamble Company. Used by permission. P. 97, Photo courtesy of Del Pharmaceuticals. P. 99, ©William D. Perreault, Jr., Ph.D. P. 100, Courtesy Playtex Products, Inc. P. 100, Creative Director/Copywriter: Emily Smeraldo; Art Director: Wayne Kan & Jonathan Lee; School: School of Visual Arts, New York; Instructors: Richard Pels & Paul Jarvis. P. 104, ©M. Hruby. P. 106, Courtesy Fleishman-Hillard for AT&T; Agency: BBDO North America/New York.

CHAPTER 5

Exhibits: Exhibit 5–3, adapted from C. Glenn Walters, *Consumer Behavior*, 3d ed. (Homewood, IL: Richard D. Irwin, 1979). Exhibit 5–6, Joseph T. Plummer, "The Concept and Application of Life-Style Segmentation," *Journal of Marketing*, January 1974, pp. 33–37; Exhibit 5–7, adapted from Patrick E. Murphy and William A. Staples, "A Modern Family Life Cycle," *Journal of Consumer Research*, June 1979, p. 17.

Photos/ads: P. 112–113, Carl De Souza/AFP/Getty Images. P. 116, Courtesy The Diamond Trading Company; Agency: J. Walter Thompson U.S.A., Inc. P. 117, Courtesy GEICO. P. 117, Courtesy of ConAgra Foods. P. 120, Agency: Richter 7; Art Director: Ryan Anderson; Copywriter: Gary Sume. P. 121, Courtesy of The Beef Checkoff Program. P. 121, Courtesy Cartridge World North America. P. 125, Courtesy Hunt Adkins; Art Director: Mark Fairbanks; Copywriter: Rob Franks. P. 126, ©Matthew Staver. P. 127, Courtesy Two by Four/Chicago; Photo courtesy Tim Tadder. P. 129, Courtesy Univision Communications, Inc.; Photography: Kevin Banna ©2007. P. 131, Courtesy Expedia, Inc. P. 131, Courtesy A.T. Cross Company. P. 134, Courtesy The Coca-Cola Company. P. 135, AP Photo/Mandatory Credit: Christopher Morris/VII. P. 135, AP Photo/Saleh Rifai.

CHAPTER 6

Exhibits: Exhibit 6–5, adapted from Rowland T. Moriarty, Jr., and Robert E. Spekman, "An Empirical Investigation of the Information Sources Used during the Industrial Buying Process, *Journal of Marketing Research*, May 1984, pp. 137–47. Exhibit 6–7, graph developed by the authors based on U. S. Census data including "Table 5: Industry Statistics for Subsectors by Employment Size: 2002" from *2002 Economic Census - Manufacturing, Subject Series, General Summary* (Washington, DC: U.S. Government Printing Office, 2005) and available online at http://www.census.gov. Exhibit 6–8, available online at http://www.naics.com.

Photos/ads: P. 139, Compliments of John Deere. P. 142, Kyocera Mita America, Inc. P. 142, Courtesy Michelin North America. P. 143, Courtesy IBM Corporation. P. 144, Both ©Roger Ball Photography. P. 145, Courtesy AirTran Airways, Agency: Cramer-Krasselt. P. 147, Courtesy Eastman Chemical. P. 150, Courtesy The California Department of Transportation. P. 151, Courtesy AFLAC, Inc. P. 153, Courtesy CDW. P. 156, All photos: Courtesy of Alcoa. P. 158, Courtesy Hertz Corporation. P. 159, Courtesy Haier America. P. 159, Courtesy Lowe's Companies. P. 161, Reprinted Courtesy of Caterpillar Inc. P. 161, Courtesy Eye Safety Systems, Inc.

CHAPTER 7

Photos/ads: P. 165, ©The Procter & Gamble Company. Used by permission. P. 168, Courtesy of MapInfo. P. 170, Courtesy JRP Marketing Research Services. P. 170, Courtesy infosurv. P. 175, Courtesy Acxiom Corporate Marketing; Photographer: Dero Sanford. P. 175, Courtesy Catalina Marketing. P. 177, Courtesy Focus Vision Worldwide, ™Inc. P. 177, Courtesy Focus World International. P. 179, Both Courtesy Southwest Airlines. P. 181, Courtesy Ocean Spray Cranberries, Inc.; Photo: ©Margaret Lampert. P. 185, Source: Survey Sampling International 2008. P. 185, Courtesy i,think, Inc. P. 187, Courtesy P. Robert & Partners. P. 187, Courtesy InterfaceASIA.

CHAPTER 8

Exhibits: Exhibit 8–3, P. 198, Courtesy New Balance Athletic Shoe, Inc. P. 198 , Courtesy Cisco Systems, Inc. P. 198, Courtesy Starbucks Corporation. P. 198, Courtesy Volkswagen of America. P. 198, Courtesy Michelin North America. P. 198, Courtesy Intel Corporation. P. 198, Courtesy Boys & Girls Clubs of America. P. 198, ©2006 Hertz System, Inc. and Hertz is registered service mark and trademark of Hertz System, Inc. P. 198, ©Cable News Network. P. 198, Courtesy POM Wonderful. P. 198, Courtesy Dole Food Company, Inc. P. 198, Created by Larry Ewing and The Gimp. P. 198, [eBay Mark] is a trademark of eBay Inc. P. 198, Courtesy United Parcel Service, Inc.

Photos/ads: P. 191, ©Brendan Mattingly. P. 194, Courtesy Garrity Industries. P. 194, Courtesy Hertz Corporation. P. 196, Reproduced with permission from the Prudential Insurance Company of America. All rights reserved. P. 196, Courtesy of VFIS. P. 196, Advertisement provided courtesy of Frito-Lay North America, Inc. P. 196, Courtesy Robert Falls & Co. Public Relations. P. 199, Courtesy Unilever, United States, Inc. P. 199, Courtesy The Dow Chemical Company. P. 202, ©William D. Perreault, Jr., Ph.D. P. 203, Courtesy Societe Alimentaire de Guidel/France. P. 203, Courtesy Del Monte Fresh Produce N.A., Inc. P. 204, ©William D. Perreault, Jr., Ph.D. P. 205, Courtesy Stonyfield Farm. P. 206, ©William D. Perreault, Jr., Ph.D. P. 207, Courtesy Bristol-Myers Squibb Co. P. 207, Courtesy LensCrafters, Inc. P. 210, Courtesy Joint Juice, Inc. P. 210, Courtesy of BSH Home Appliances Corporation. P. 211, Both ads: Courtesy Bush Brothers & Company.

CHAPTER 9

Exhibits: Exhibit 9–4, adapted from Frank R. Bacon, Jr., and Thomas W. Butler, *Planned Innovation* (Ann Arbor: University of Michigan Institute of Science and Technology, 1980). Exhibit 9–5, adapted from Philip Kotler, "What Consumerism Means for Marketers," *Harvard Business Review*, May–June 1972, pp. 55–56; Exhibit 9–7, Marie Gaudard, Roland Coates, and Liz Freeman, "Accelerating Improvement," *Quality Progress*, October 1991, pp. 81–88. Exhibit 9–8, Marie Gaudard, Roland Coates, and Liz Freeman, "Accelerating Improvement," *Quality Progress*, October 1991, pp. 81–88.

Photos/ads: P. 218–219, Courtesy iRobot Corporation. P. 222, Courtesy Magellan GPS. P. 223, Courtesy Colgate-Palmolive Company. P. 223, ©The Procter & Gamble Company. Used by permission. Photographer: Dasha Wright. P. 224, Courtesy Kaz, Inc. P. 225, Courtesy Fuseproject; RacePoint Group, Inc. P. 226, Courtesy Zara International, Inc. P. 229, Courtesy DuPont Textiles & Interiors' LYCRA®; Agency: Saatchi & Saatchi/Zurich. P. 229, ©The Procter & Gamble Company. Used by permission. P. 229, ©The Procter & Gamble Company. Used by permission. P. 230, Courtesy Bic Corporation. P. 234, AP Photo/Paul Sakuma. P. 236, Courtesy Microsoft Corporation. P. 236, Courtesy Weyerhaeuser Company. Pg. 240, Courtesy CSA International. Pg. 240, ©American Honda Motor Co., Inc.

CHAPTER 10

Exhibits: Exhibit 10–2, adapted from D. J. Bowersox and E. J. McCarthy, "Strategic Development of Planned Vertical Marketing Systems," in *Vertical Marketing Systems*, ed. Louis Bucklin (Glenview, IL: Scott, Foresman, 1970).

Photos/ads: P. 247, Photo by Joe Raedle/Getty Images. P. 250, ©The Procter & Gamble Company. Used by permission. P. 250, Courtesy Colgate-Palmolive Company. P. 251, Courtesy Oakley United States of America. P. 251, Courtesy Unilever, P.L.C. P.251, Courtesy Unilever, P.L.C. P. 251, Courtesy Unilever, P.L.C.; Photographer: Bill Prentice. P. 252, Courtesy Energy Brands, Inc. P. 253, ©William D. Perreault, Jr., Ph.D. P. 255, AP Photo/Ben Margot. P. 256, Courtesy Peterson Manufacturing Company. P. 256, Courtesy Electrolux North America. P. 259, Courtesy Apple, Inc. P. 261, Courtesy Mothers Work, Inc. P. 261, Courtesy Stihl Incorporated. P. 262, Courtesy Dunkin Brands, Inc. P. 267, Agency: Alice BBDO, Istanbul; Art Director: Kutlay Sindirgi; Copy Writer: Ali Goral; Creative Director: Ozan Varisli; Photographer: Rainer Stratman; Illustrator: Ralph Hillert.

CHAPTER 11

Exhibits: Exhibit 11–4, adapted from B. J. LaLonde and P. H. Zinzer, *Customer Service: Meaning and Measurement* (Chicago: National Council of Physical Distribution Management, 1976); and D. Phillip Locklin, *Transportation for Management* (Homewood, IL: Richard D. Irwin, 1972). Exhibit 11–7, adapted from Louis W. Stern and Adel I. El-Ansary, *Marketing Channels* (Englewood Cliffs, NJ: Prentice Hall, 1977), p. 150.

Photos/ads: P. 271, AP Photo/Peter Morgan. P. 274, Courtesy Fahlgren Advertising; Mike Sanford/Copywriter, Dave Rogers/Art Director. P. 274, Courtesy United Parcel Services of America, Inc. P. 276, Courtesy Sauder Woodworking Company. P. 278, Courtesy Manitowac Crane Group. P. 279, Both ads Courtesy Marsh. P. 281, ©Allan Hunter Shoemake Photography, Inc. P. 281, ©Steve Smith. P. 282, Courtesy SABMiller plc./One Red Eye. P. 283, Courtesy of API. P. 284, AP Photo/Luis E. Ascui. P. 285, Courtesy Cash & Carry International GmbH. P. 286, ©William D. Perreault, Jr., Ph.d. P. 287, Courtesy Menasha Corporation. P. 287, Courtesy U.S. Environmental Protection Agency. P. 289, Courtesy Zappos.com.

CHAPTER 12

Exhibits: Exhibit 12–4 graph developed by the authors based on U.S. Census data including, "Table 1a: Summary Statistics for the United States 2002," from *2002 Economic Census—Wholesale Trade Geographic Area Series, United States* (Washington, DC: U.S. Government Printing Office, 2005) and available online at http://www.census.gov.

CHAPTER 13

CHAPTER 14

CHAPTER 15

CHAPTER 16

CHAPTER 17

CHAPTER 18

APPENDIX B

APPENDIX C

Author Index

Company Index

Subject Index

Glossary

Accessories Short-lived capital items—tools and equipment used in production or office activities.

Accumulating Collecting products from many small producers.

Administered channel systems Various channel members informally agree to cooperate with each other.

Administered prices Consciously set prices aimed at reaching the firm's objectives.

Adoption curve Shows when different groups accept ideas.

Adoption process The steps individuals go through on the way to accepting or rejecting a new idea.

Advertising Any *paid* form of nonpersonal presentation of ideas, goods, or services by an identified sponsor.

Advertising agencies Specialists in planning and handling mass-selling details for advertisers.

Advertising allowances Price reductions to firms in the channel to encourage them to advertise or otherwise promote the firm's products locally.

Advertising managers Managers of their company's mass-selling effort in television, newspapers, magazines, and other media.

Agent wholesalers Wholesalers who do not own (take title to) the products they sell.

AIDA model Consists of four promotion jobs: (1) to get *Attention,* (2) to hold *Interest,* (3) to arouse *Desire,* and (4) to obtain *Action.*

Allowance (accounting term) Occurs when a customer is not satisfied with a purchase for some reason and the seller gives a price reduction on the original invoice (bill), but the customer keeps the goods or services.

Allowances Reductions in price given to final consumers, customers, or channel members for doing something or accepting less of something.

Assorting Putting together a variety of products to give a target market what it wants.

Attitude A person's point of view toward something.

Auction companies Agent wholesalers that provide a place where buyers and sellers can come together and complete a transaction.

Automatic vending Selling and delivering products through vending machines.

Average cost (per unit) The total cost divided by the related quantity.

Average-cost pricing Adding a reasonable markup to the average cost of a product.

Average fixed cost (per unit) The total fixed cost divided by the related quantity.

Average variable cost (per unit) The total variable cost divided by the related quantity.

Bait pricing Setting some very low prices to attract customers but trying to sell more expensive models or brands once the customer is in the store.

Balance sheet An accounting statement that shows a company's assets, liabilities, and net worth.

Basic list prices The prices that final customers or users are normally asked to pay for products.

Basic sales tasks *Order-getting, order-taking,* and *supporting.*

Battle of the brands The competition between dealer brands and manufacturer brands.

Belief A person's opinion about something.

Bid pricing Offering a specific price for each possible job rather than setting a price that applies for all customers.

Brand equity The value of a brand's overall strength in the market.

Brand familiarity How well customers recognize and accept a company's brand.

Brand insistence Customers insist on a firm's branded product and are willing to search for it.

Brand managers Manage specific products, often taking over the jobs formerly handled by an advertising manager—sometimes called *product managers.*

Brand name A word, letter, or a group of words or letters.

Brand nonrecognition Final customers don't recognize a brand at all—even though intermediaries may use the brand name for identification and inventory control.

Brand preference Target customers usually choose the brand over other brands, perhaps because of habit or favorable past experience.

Brand recognition Customers remember the brand.

Brand rejection Potential customers won't buy a brand—unless its image is changed.

Branding The use of a name, term, symbol, or design—or a combination of these—to identify a product.

Break-even analysis An approach to determine whether the firm will be able to break even—that is, cover all its costs—with a particular price.

Break-even point (BEP) The sales quantity where the firm's total cost will just equal its total revenue.

Breakthrough opportunities Opportunities that help innovators develop hard-to-copy marketing strategies that will be very profitable for a long time.

Brokers Agent wholesalers who specialize in bringing buyers and sellers together.

Bulk-breaking Dividing larger quantities into smaller quantities as products get closer to the final market.

Business and organizational customers Any buyers who buy for resale or to produce other goods and services.

Business products Products meant for use in producing other products.

Buying center All the people who participate in or influence a purchase.

Buying function Looking for and evaluating goods and services.

Capital item A long-lasting product that can be used and depreciated for many years.

Cash-and-carry wholesalers Like service wholesalers, except that the customer must pay cash.

Cash discounts Reductions in the price to encourage buyers to pay their bills quickly.

Catalog wholesalers Sell out of catalogs that may be distributed widely to smaller industrial customers or retailers that might not be called on by other wholesalers.

Channel captain A manager who helps direct the activities of a whole channel and tries to avoid, or solve, channel conflicts.

Channel of distribution Any series of firms or individuals who participate in the flow of products from producer to final user or consumer.

Close The salesperson's request for an order.

Clustering techniques Approaches used to try to find similar patterns within sets of data.

Collaborators Firms that provide one or more of the marketing functions other than buying or selling.

Combination export manager A blend of manufacturers' agent and selling agent—handling the entire export function for several producers of similar but noncompeting lines.

Combined target market approach Combining two or more submarkets into one larger target market as a basis for one strategy.

Combiners Firms that try to increase the size of their target markets by combining two or more segments.

Command economy Government officials decide what and how much is to be produced and distributed by whom, when, to whom, and why.

Communication process A source trying to reach a receiver with a message.

Comparative advertising Advertising that makes specific brand comparisons using actual product names.

Competitive advantage A firm has a marketing mix that the target market sees as better than a competitor's mix.

Competitive advertising Advertising that tries to develop selective demand for a specific brand rather than a product category.

Competitive barriers The conditions that may make it difficult, or even impossible, for a firm to compete in a market.

Competitive bids Terms of sale offered by different suppliers in response to the buyer's purchase specifications.

Competitive environment The number and types of competitors the marketing manager must face, and how they may behave.

Competitive rivals A firm's closest competitors.

Competitor analysis An organized approach for evaluating the strengths and weaknesses of current or potential competitors' marketing strategies.

Complementary product pricing Setting prices on several related products as a group.

Components Processed expense items that become part of a finished product.

Concept testing Getting reactions from customers about how well a new product idea fits their needs.

Confidence intervals The range on either side of an estimate from a sample that is likely to contain the true value for the whole population.

Consultative selling approach A type of sales presentation in which the salesperson develops a good understanding of the individual customer's needs before trying to close the sale.

Consumer panel A group of consumers who provide information on a continuing basis.

Consumer Product Safety Act A 1972 law that set up the Consumer Product Safety Commission to encourage more awareness of safety in product design and better quality control.

Consumer products Products meant for the final consumer.

Consumer surplus The difference to consumers between the value of a purchase and the price they pay.

Containerization Grouping individual items into an economical shipping quantity and sealing them in protective containers for transit to the final destination.

Continuous improvement A commitment to constantly make things better one step at a time.

Contractual channel systems Various channel members agree by contract to cooperate with each other.

Convenience (food) stores A convenience-oriented variation of the conventional limited-line food stores.

Convenience products Products a consumer needs but isn't willing to spend much time or effort shopping for.

Cooperative advertising Producers sharing in the cost of ads with wholesalers or retailers.

Cooperative chains Retailer-sponsored groups, formed by independent retailers, to run their own buying organizations and conduct joint promotion efforts.

Copy thrust What the words and illustrations of an ad should communicate.

Corporate chain A firm that owns and manages more than one store—and often it's many.

Corporate channel systems Corporate ownership all along the channel.

Corrective advertising Ads to correct deceptive advertising.

Cost of sales Total value (at cost) of the sales during the period.

Cues Products, signs, ads, and other stimuli in the environment.

Cultural and social environment Affects how and why people live and behave as they do.

Culture The whole set of beliefs, attitudes, and ways of doing things of a reasonably homogeneous set of people.

Cumulative quantity discounts Reductions in price for larger purchases over a given period, such as a year.

Customer equity The expected earnings stream (profitability) of a firm's current and prospective customers over some period of time.

Customer relationship management (CRM) An approach where the seller fine-tunes the marketing effort with information from a detailed customer database.

Customer satisfaction The extent to which a firm fulfills a consumer's needs, desires, and expectations.

Customer service A personal communication between a seller and a customer who wants the seller to resolve a problem with a purchase—is often the key to building repeat business.

Customer service level How rapidly and dependably a firm can deliver what customers want.

Customer service reps Supporting salespeople who work with customers to resolve problems that arise with a purchase, usually after the purchase has been made.

Customer value The difference between the benefits a customer sees from a market offering and the costs of obtaining those benefits.

Data warehouse A place where databases are stored so that they are available when needed.

Dealer brands Brands created by intermediaries—sometimes referred to as *private brands*.

Decision support system (DSS) A computer program that makes it easy for marketing managers to get and use information *as they are making decisions*.

Decoding The receiver in the communication process translating the message.

Demand-backward pricing Setting an acceptable final consumer price and working backward to what a producer can charge.

Demand curve A graph of the relationship between price and quantity demanded in a market, assuming all other things stay the same.

Department stores Larger stores that are organized into many separate departments and offer many product lines.

Derived demand Demand for business products derives from the demand for final consumer products.

Determining dimensions The dimensions that actually affect the customer's purchase of a *specific* product or brand in a *product-market*.

Differentiation The marketing mix is distinct from and better than what's available from a competitor.

Direct investment A parent firm has a division (or owns a separate subsidiary firm) in a foreign market.

Direct marketing Direct communication between a seller and an individual customer using a promotion method other than face-to-face personal selling.

Direct type advertising Competitive advertising that aims for immediate buying action.

Discount houses Stores that sell hard goods (cameras, TVs, appliances) at substantial price cuts to customers who go to discounter's low-rent store, pay cash, and take care of any service or repair problems themselves.

Discounts Reductions from list price given by a seller to buyers, who either give up some marketing function or provide the function themselves.

Discrepancy of assortment The difference between the lines a typical producer makes and the assortment final consumers or users want.

Discrepancy of quantity The difference between the quantity of products it is economical for a producer to make and the quantity final users or consumers normally want.

Discretionary income What is left of income after paying taxes and paying for necessities.

Dissonance Tension caused by uncertainty about the rightness of a decision.

Distribution center A special kind of warehouse designed to speed the flow of goods and avoid unnecessary storing costs.

Diversification Moving into totally different lines of business—perhaps entirely unfamiliar products, markets, or even levels in the production-marketing system.

Door-to-door selling Going directly to the consumer's home.

Drive A strong stimulus that encourages action to reduce a need.

Drop-shippers Wholesalers that own (take title to) the products they sell but do not actually handle, stock, or deliver them.

Dumping Pricing a product sold in a foreign market below the cost of producing it or at a price lower than in its domestic market.

Early adopters The second group in the adoption curve to adopt a new product; these people are usually well respected by their peers and often are opinion leaders.

Early majority A group in the adoption curve that avoids risk and waits to consider a new idea until many early adopters try it and like it.

E-commerce Exchanges between individuals or organizations—and activities that facilitate those exchanges—based on applications of information technology.

Economic and technological environment Affects the way firms, and the whole economy, use resources.

Economic buyers People who know all the facts and logically compare choices to get the greatest satisfaction from spending their time and money.

Economic needs Needs concerned with making the best use of a consumer's time and money—as the consumer judges it.

Economic system The way an economy organizes to use scarce resources to produce goods and services and distribute them for consumption by various people and groups in the society.

Economies of scale As a company produces larger numbers of a particular product, the cost of each unit of the product goes down.

Elastic demand If prices are dropped, the quantity demanded will stretch enough to increase total revenue.

Elastic supply The quantity supplied does stretch more if the price is raised.

Electronic data interchange (EDI) An approach that puts information in a standardized format easily shared between different computer systems.

Emergency products Products that are purchased immediately when the need is great.

Empowerment Giving employees the authority to correct a problem without first checking with management.

Empty nesters People whose children are grown and who are now able to spend their money in other ways.

Encoding The source in the communication process deciding what it wants to say and translating it into words or symbols that will have the same meaning to the receiver.

Equilibrium point The quantity and the price sellers are willing to offer are equal to the quantity and price that buyers are willing to accept.

Everyday low pricing Setting a low list price rather than relying on frequent sales, discounts, or allowances.

Exclusive distribution Selling through only one intermediary in a particular geographic area.

Expectation An outcome or event that a person anticipates or looks forward to.

Expense item A product whose total cost is treated as a business expense in the period it's purchased.

Expenses All the remaining costs that are subtracted from the gross margin to get the net profit.

Experimental method A research approach in which researchers compare the responses of two or more groups that are similar except on the characteristic being tested.

Export agents Manufacturers' agents who specialize in export trade.

Export brokers Brokers who specialize in bringing together buyers and sellers from different countries.

Exporting Selling some of what the firm produces to foreign markets.

Extensive problem solving The type of problem solving consumers use for a completely new or important need—when they put much effort into deciding how to satisfy it.

Factor A variable that shows the relation of some other variable to the item being forecast.

Factor method An approach to forecast sales by finding a relation between the company's sales and some other factor (or factors).

Fad An idea that is fashionable only to certain groups who are enthusiastic about it—but these groups are so fickle that a fad is even more short-lived than a regular fashion.

Family brand A brand name that is used for several products.

Farm products Products grown by farmers, such as oranges, sugar cane, and cattle.

Fashion Currently accepted or popular style.

Federal Fair Packaging and Labeling Act A 1966 law requiring that consumer goods be clearly labeled in easy-to-understand terms.

Federal Trade Commission (FTC) Federal government agency that polices antimonopoly laws.

Financing Provides the necessary cash and credit to produce, transport, store, promote, sell, and buy products.

Fishbone diagram A visual aid that helps organize cause and effect relationships for "things gone wrong."

Fixed-cost (FC) contribution per unit The selling price per unit minus the variable cost per unit.

Flexible-price policy Offering the same product and quantities to different customers at different prices.

F.O.B. A transportation term meaning free on board some vehicle at some point.

Focus group interview An interview of 6 to 10 people in an informal group setting.

Foreign Corrupt Practices Act A law passed by the U.S. Congress in 1977 that prohibits U.S. firms from paying bribes to foreign officials.

Franchise operation A franchisor develops a good marketing strategy, and the retail franchise holders carry out the strategy in their own units.

Freight-absorption pricing Absorbing freight cost so that a firm's delivered price meets the nearest competitor's.

Full-line pricing Setting prices for a whole line of products.

General merchandise wholesalers Service wholesalers that carry a wide variety of nonperishable items such as hardware, electrical supplies, furniture, drugs, cosmetics, and automobile equipment.

General stores Early retailers who carried anything they could sell in reasonable volume.

Generic market A market with *broadly* similar needs—and sellers offering various and *often diverse* ways of satisfying those needs.

Generic products Products that have no brand at all other than identification of their contents and the manufacturer or intermediary.

Gross domestic product (GDP) The total market value of all goods and services provided in a country's economy in a year by both residents and nonresidents of that country.

Gross margin (gross profit) The money left to cover the expenses of selling the products and operating the business.

Gross sales The total amount charged to all customers during some time period.

Heterogeneous shopping products Shopping products the customer sees as different and wants to inspect for quality and suitability.

Homogeneous shopping products Shopping products the customer sees as basically the same and wants at the lowest price.

Hypermarkets Very large stores that try to carry not only food and drug items but all goods and services that the consumer purchases *routinely* (also called *supercenters*).

Hypotheses Educated guesses about the relationships between things or about what will happen in the future.

Ideal market exposure When a product is available widely enough to satisfy target customers' needs but not exceed them.

Implementation Putting marketing plans into operation.

Import agents Manufacturers' agents who specialize in import trade.

Import brokers Brokers who specialize in bringing together buyers and sellers from different countries.

Impulse products Products that are bought quickly as *unplanned* purchases because of a strongly felt need.

Indirect type advertising Competitive advertising that points out product advantages—to affect future buying decisions.

Individual brands Separate brand names used for each product.

Individual product A particular product within a product line.

Inelastic demand Although the quantity demanded increases if the price is decreased, the quantity demanded will not stretch enough to avoid a decrease in total revenue.

Inelastic supply The quantity supplied does not stretch much (if at all) if the price is raised.

Innovation The development and spread of new ideas, goods, and services.

Innovators The first group to adopt new products.

Installations Important capital items such as buildings, land rights, and major equipment.

Institutional advertising Advertising that tries to promote an organization's image, reputation, or ideas rather than a specific product.

Integrated marketing communications The intentional coordination of every communication from a firm to a target customer to convey a consistent and complete message.

Intensive distribution Selling a product through all responsible and suitable wholesalers or retailers who will stock or sell the product.

Intermediary Someone who specializes in trade rather than production.

Internet A system for linking computers around the world.

Intranet A system for linking computers within a company.

Introductory price dealing Temporary price cuts to speed new products into a market and get customers to try them.

Inventory The amount of goods being stored.

ISO 9000 A way for a supplier to document its quality procedures according to internationally recognized standards.

Job description A written statement of what a salesperson is expected to do.

Joint venture In international marketing, a domestic firm entering into a partnership with a foreign firm.

Jury of executive opinion Forecasting by combining the opinions of experienced executives, perhaps from marketing, production, finance, purchasing, and top management.

Just-in-time delivery Reliably getting products there *just* before the customer needs them.

Laggards Prefer to do things the way they have been done in the past and are very suspicious of new ideas; sometimes called *nonadopters*—see *adoption curve*.

Lanham Act A 1946 law that spells out what kinds of marks (including brand names) can be protected and the exact method of protecting them.

Late majority A group of adopters who are cautious about new ideas—see *adoption curve*.

Law of diminishing demand If the price of a product is raised, a smaller quantity will be demanded—and if the price of a product is lowered, a greater quantity will be demanded.

Leader pricing Setting some very low prices—real bargains—to get customers into retail stores.

Learning A change in a person's thought processes caused by prior experience.

Licensed brand A well-known brand that sellers pay a fee to use.

Licensing Selling the right to use some process, trademark, patent, or other right for a fee or royalty.

Lifestyle analysis The analysis of a person's day-to-day pattern of living as expressed in that person's Activities, Interests, and Opinions—sometimes referred to as *AIOs* or *psychographics*.

Limited-function wholesalers Merchant wholesalers that provide only *some* wholesaling functions.

Limited-line stores Stores that specialize in certain lines of related products rather than a wide assortment—sometimes called *single-line stores*.

Limited problem solving When a consumer is willing to put *some* effort into deciding the best way to satisfy a need.

Logistics The transporting, storing, and handling of goods in ways that match target customers' needs with a firm's marketing mix—both within individual firms and along a channel of distribution (i.e., another name for *physical distribution*).

Low-involvement purchases Purchases that have little importance or relevance for the customer.

Macro-marketing A social process that directs an economy's flow of goods and services from producers to consumers in a way that effectively matches supply and demand and accomplishes the objectives of society.

Magnuson-Moss Act A 1975 law requiring that producers provide a clearly written warranty if they choose to offer any warranty.

Major accounts sales force Salespeople who sell directly to large accounts such as major retail chain stores.

Management contracting The seller provides only management skills—others own the production and distribution facilities.

Manufacturer brands Brands created by producers.

Manufacturers' agents Agent wholesalers who sell similar products for several noncompeting producers for a commission on what is actually sold.

Manufacturers' sales branches Separate warehouses that producers set up away from their factories.

Marginal analysis Evaluating the change in total revenue and total cost from selling one more unit to find the most profitable price and quantity.

Markdown A retail price reduction that is required because customers won't buy some item at the originally marked-up price.

Markdown ratio A tool used by many retailers to measure the efficiency of various departments and their whole business.

Market A group of potential customers with similar needs who are willing to exchange something of value with sellers offering various goods or services—that is, ways of satisfying those needs.

Market development Trying to increase sales by selling present products in new markets.

Market-directed economy The individual decisions of the many producers and consumers make the macro-level decisions for the whole economy.

Market growth A stage of the product life cycle when industry sales grow fast—but industry profits rise and then start falling.

Market information function The collection, analysis, and distribution of all the information needed to plan, carry out, and control marketing activities.

Market introduction A stage of the product life cycle when sales are low as a new idea is first introduced to a market.

Market maturity A stage of the product life cycle when industry sales level off and competition gets tougher.

Market penetration Trying to increase sales of a firm's present products in its present markets—probably through a more aggressive marketing mix.

Market potential What a whole market segment might buy.

Market segment A relatively homogeneous group of customers who will respond to a marketing mix in a similar way.

Market segmentation A two-step process of (1) *naming* broad product-markets and (2) *segmenting* these broad product-markets in order to select target markets and develop suitable marketing mixes.

Marketing The performance of activities that seek to accomplish an organization's objectives by anticipating customer or client needs and directing a flow of need-satisfying goods and services from producer to customer or client.

Marketing company era A time when, in addition to short-run marketing planning, marketing people develop long-range plans—sometimes five or more years ahead—and the whole company effort is guided by the marketing concept.

Marketing concept The idea that an organization should aim *all* its efforts at satisfying its *customers*—at a *profit*.

Marketing dashboard Displaying up-to-the-minute marketing data in an easy-to-read format.

Marketing department era A time when all marketing activities are brought under the control of one department to improve short-run policy planning and to try to integrate the firm's activities.

Marketing ethics The moral standards that guide marketing decisions and actions.

Marketing information system (MIS) An organized way of continually gathering, accessing, and analyzing information that marketing managers need to make ongoing decisions.

Marketing management process The process of (1) *planning* marketing activities, (2) directing the *implementation* of the plans, and (3) *controlling* these plans.

Marketing mix The controllable variables that the company puts together to satisfy a target group.

Marketing model A statement of relationships among marketing variables.

Marketing orientation Trying to carry out the marketing concept.

Marketing plan A written statement of a marketing strategy *and* the time-related details for carrying out the strategy.

Marketing program Blends all of the firm's marketing plans into one big plan.

Marketing research Procedures to develop and analyze new information to help marketing managers make decisions.

Marketing research process A five-step application of the scientific method that includes (1) defining the problem, (2) analyzing the situation, (3) getting problem-specific data, (4) interpreting the data, and (5) solving the problem.

Marketing strategy Specifies a target market and a related marketing mix.

Markup A dollar amount added to the cost of products to get the selling price.

Markup chain The sequence of markups firms use at different levels in a channel—determining the price structure in the whole channel.

Markup (percent) The percentage of selling price that is added to the cost to get the selling price.

Mass marketing The typical production-oriented approach that vaguely aims at everyone with the same marketing mix.

Mass-merchandisers Large, self-service stores with many departments that emphasize soft goods (housewares, clothing, and fabrics) and staples (like health and beauty aids) and selling on lower margins to get faster turnover.

Mass-merchandising concept The idea that retailers should offer low prices to get faster turnover and greater sales volume by appealing to larger numbers.

Mass selling Communicating with large numbers of potential customers at the same time.

Merchant wholesalers Wholesalers who own (take title to) the products they sell.

Message channel The carrier of the message.

Metropolitan Statistical Area (MSA) An integrated economic and social unit with a large population nucleus.

Micro-macro dilemma What is good for some producers and consumers may not be good for society as a whole.

Mission statement Sets out the organization's basic purpose for being.

Missionary salespeople Supporting salespeople who work for producers by calling on intermediaries and their customers.

Modified rebuy The in-between process where some review of the buying situation is done—though not as much as in new-task buying or as little as in straight rebuys.

Monopolistic competition A market situation that develops when a market has (1) different (heterogeneous) products and (2) sellers who feel they do have some competition in this market.

Multichannel distribution When a producer uses several competing channels to reach the same target market—perhaps using several intermediaries in addition to selling directly.

Multiple buying influence Several people share in making a purchase decision—perhaps even top management.

Multiple target market approach Segmenting the market and choosing two or more segments, then treating each as a separate target market needing a different marketing mix.

Nationalism An emphasis on a country's interests before everything else.

Natural products Products that occur in nature—such as timber, iron ore, oil, and coal.

Needs The basic forces that motivate a person to do something.

Negotiated contract buying Agreeing to a contract that allows for changes in the purchase arrangements.

Negotiated price A price that is set based on bargaining between the buyer and seller.

Net An invoice term meaning that payment for the face value of the invoice is due immediately—also see *cash discounts*.

Net profit What the company earns from its operations during a particular period.

Net sales The actual sales dollars the company receives.

New product A product that is new *in any way* for the company concerned.

New-task buying When an organization has a new need and the buyer wants a great deal of information.

New unsought products Products offering really new ideas that potential customers don't know about yet.

Noise Any distraction that reduces the effectiveness of the communication process.

Nonadopters Prefer to do things the way they have been done in the past and are very suspicious of new ideas; sometimes called *laggards*—see *adoption curve*.

Noncumulative quantity discounts Reductions in price when a customer purchases a larger quantity on an *individual order*.

Nonprice competition Aggressive action on one or more of the Ps other than Price.

North American Free Trade Agreement (NAFTA) Lays out a plan to reshape the rules of trade among the United States, Canada, and Mexico.

North American Industry Classification System (NAICS) codes Codes used to identify groups of firms in similar lines of business.

Odd-even pricing Setting prices that end in certain numbers.

Oligopoly A special market situation that develops when a market has (1) essentially homogeneous products, (2) relatively few sellers, and (3) fairly inelastic industry demand curves.

One-price policy Offering the same price to all customers who purchase products under essentially the same conditions and in the same quantities.

Open to buy A buyer has budgeted funds that he can spend during the current time period.

Operating ratios Ratios of items on the operating statement to net sales.

Operating statement A simple summary of the financial results of a company's operations over a specified period of time.

Operational decisions Short-run decisions to help implement strategies.

Opinion leader A person who influences others.

Order getters Salespeople concerned with establishing relationships with new customers and developing new business.

Order-getting Seeking possible buyers with a well-organized sales presentation designed to sell a good, service, or idea.

Order takers Salespeople who sell to regular or established customers, complete most sales transactions, and maintain relationships with their customers.

Order-taking The routine completion of sales made regularly to target customers.

Outsource When the buying organization chooses to contract with an outside firm to produce goods or services rather then producing them internally.

Packaging Promoting, protecting and enhancing the product.

Pareto chart A graph that shows the number of times a problem cause occurs, with problem causes ordered from most frequent to least frequent.

Penetration pricing policy Trying to sell the whole market at one low price.

Perception How we gather and interpret information from the world around us.

Personal needs An individual's need for personal satisfaction unrelated to what others think or do.

Personal selling Direct spoken communication between sellers and potential customers, usually in person but sometimes over the telephone or even via a video conference over the Internet.

Phony list prices Misleading prices that customers are shown to suggest that the price they are to pay has been discounted from list.

Physical distribution (PD) The transporting, storing, and handling of goods in ways that match target customers' needs with a firm's marketing mix—both within individual firms and along a channel of distribution (i.e., another name for *logistics*).

Physical distribution (PD) concept All transporting, storing, and product-handling activities of a business and a whole channel system should be coordinated as one system that seeks to minimize the cost of distribution for a given customer service level.

Physiological needs Biological needs such as the need for food, drink, rest, and sex.

Piggyback service Loading truck trailers or flatbed trailers carrying containers on railcars to provide both speed and flexibility.

Pioneering advertising Advertising that tries to develop primary demand for a product category rather than demand for a specific brand.

Place Making goods and services available in the right quantities and locations—when customers want them.

Population In marketing research, the total group you are interested in.

Positioning An approach that refers to how customers think about proposed or present brands in a market.

Prepared sales presentation A memorized presentation that is not adapted to each individual customer.

Prestige pricing Setting a rather high price to suggest high quality or high status.

Price The amount of money that is charged for "something" of value.

Price discrimination Injuring competition by selling the same products to different buyers at different prices.

Price fixing Competitors illegally getting together to raise, lower, or stabilize prices.

Price lining Setting a few price levels for a product line and then marking all items at these prices.

Primary data Information specifically collected to solve a current problem.

Primary demand Demand for the general product idea, not just the company's own brand.

Private brands Brands created by intermediaries—sometimes referred to as *dealer brands*.

Private warehouses Storing facilities owned or leased by companies for their own use.

Product The need-satisfying offering of a firm.

Product advertising Advertising that tries to sell a specific product.

Product assortment The set of all product lines and individual products that a firm sells.

Product-bundle pricing Setting one price for a set of products.

Product development Offering new or improved products for present markets.

Product liability The legal obligation of sellers to pay damages to individuals who are injured by defective or unsafe products.

Product life cycle The stages a new product idea goes through from beginning to end.

Product line A set of individual products that are closely related.

Product managers Manage specific products, often taking over the jobs formerly handled by an advertising manager—sometimes called *brand managers*.

Product-market A market with *very* similar needs—and sellers offering various *close substitute* ways of satisfying those needs.

Production Actually *making* goods or *performing* services.

Production era A time when a company focuses on production of a few specific products—perhaps because few of these products are available in the market.

Production orientation Making whatever products are easy to produce and *then* trying to sell them.

Professional services Specialized services that support a firm's operations.

Profit maximization objective An objective to get as much profit as possible.

Promotion Communicating information between seller and potential buyer or others in the channel to influence attitudes and behavior.

Prospecting Following all the leads in the target market to identify potential customers.

Psychographics The analysis of a person's day-to-day pattern of living as expressed in that person's Activities, Interests, and Opinions—sometimes referred to as *AIOs* or *lifestyle analysis*.

Psychological pricing Setting prices that have special appeal to target customers.

Public relations Communication with noncustomers—including labor, public interest groups, stockholders, and the government.

Public warehouses Independent storing facilities.

Publicity Any *unpaid* form of nonpersonal presentation of ideas, goods, or services.

Pulling Using promotion to get consumers to ask intermediaries for the product.

Purchase discount A reduction of the original invoice amount for some business reason.

Purchasing managers Buying specialists for their employers.

Purchasing specifications A written (or electronic) description of what the firm wants to buy.

Pure competition A market situation that develops when a market has (1) homogeneous (similar) products, (2) many buyers and sellers who have full knowledge of the market, and (3) ease of entry for buyers and sellers.

Pure subsistence economy Each family unit produces everything it consumes.

Push money (or prize money) allowances Allowances (sometimes called *PMs* or *spiffs*) given to retailers by manufacturers or wholesalers to pass on to the retailers' salesclerks for aggressively selling certain items.

Pushing Using normal promotion effort—personal selling, advertising, and sales promotion—to help sell the whole marketing mix to possible channel members.

Qualifying dimensions The dimensions that are relevant to including a customer type in a product-market.

Qualitative research Seeks in-depth, open-ended responses, not yes or no answers.

Quality A product's ability to satisfy a customer's needs or requirements.

Quantitative research Seeks structured responses that can be summarized in numbers—like percentages, averages, or other statistics.

Quantity discounts Discounts offered to encourage customers to buy in larger amounts.

Rack jobbers Merchant wholesalers that specialize in hard-to-handle assortments of products that a retailer doesn't want to manage—and they often display the products on their own wire racks.

Raw materials Unprocessed expense items—such as logs, iron ore, and wheat—that are moved to the next production process with little handling.

Rebates Refunds to consumers after a purchase.

Receiver The target of a message in the communication process, usually a potential customer.

Reference group The people to whom an individual looks when forming attitudes about a particular topic.

Reference price The price a consumer expects to pay.

Regrouping activities Adjusting the quantities or assortments of products handled at each level in a channel of distribution.

Regularly unsought products Products that stay unsought but not unbought forever.

Reinforcement Occurs in the learning process when the consumer's response is followed by satisfaction—that is, reduction in the drive.

Reminder advertising Advertising to keep the product's name before the public.

Requisition A request to buy something.

Research proposal A plan that specifies what marketing research information will be obtained and how.

Resident buyers Independent buying agents who work in central markets for several retailer or wholesaler customers based in outlying areas or other countries.

Response An effort to satisfy a drive.

Response rate The percent of people contacted in a research sample who complete the questionnaire.

Retailing All of the activities involved in the sale of products to final consumers.

Return When a customer sends back purchased products.

Return on assets (ROA) The ratio of net profit (after taxes) to the assets used to make the net profit—multiplied by 100 to get rid of decimals.

Return on investment (ROI) Ratio of net profit (after taxes) to the investment used to make the net profit—multiplied by 100 to get rid of decimals.

Reverse channels Channels used to retrieve products that customers no longer want.

Risk taking Bearing the uncertainties that are part of the marketing process.

Robinson-Patman Act A 1936 law that makes illegal any price discrimination if it injures competition.

Routinized response behavior When consumers regularly select a particular way of satisfying a need when it occurs.

Safety needs Needs concerned with protection and physical well-being.

Sale price A temporary discount from the list price.

Sales analysis A detailed breakdown of a company's sales records.

Sales decline A stage of the product life cycle when new products replace the old.

Sales era A time when a company emphasizes selling because of increased competition.

Sales forecast An estimate of how much an industry or firm hopes to sell to a market segment.

Sales managers Managers concerned with managing personal selling.

Sales-oriented objective An objective to get some level of unit sales, dollar sales, or share of market—without referring to profit.

Sales presentation A salesperson's effort to make a sale or address a customer's problem.

Sales promotion Those promotion activities—other than advertising, publicity, and personal selling—that stimulate interest, trial, or purchase by final customers or others in the channel.

Sales promotion managers Managers of their company's sales promotion effort.

Sales quota The specific sales or profit objective a salesperson is expected to achieve.

Sales territory A geographic area that is the responsibility of one salesperson or several working together.

Sample A part of the relevant population.

Scientific method A decision-making approach that focuses on being objective and orderly in *testing* ideas before accepting them.

Scrambled merchandising Retailers carrying any product lines that they think they can sell profitably.

Search engine A computer program that helps a marketing manager find information that is needed.

Seasonal discounts Discounts offered to encourage buyers to buy earlier than present demand requires.

Secondary data Information that has been collected or published already.

Segmenters Aim at one or more homogeneous segments and try to develop a different marketing mix for each segment.

Segmenting An aggregating process that clusters people with similar needs into a market segment.

Selective demand Demand for a company's own brand rather than a product category.

Selective distribution Selling through only those intermediaries who will give the product special attention.

Selective exposure Our eyes and minds seek out and notice only information that interests us.

Selective perception People screen out or modify ideas, messages, and information that conflict with previously learned attitudes and beliefs.

Selective retention People remember only what they want to remember.

Selling agents Agent wholesalers who take over the whole marketing job of producers, not just the selling function.

Selling formula approach A sales presentation that starts with a prepared presentation outline—much like the prepared approach—and leads the customer through some logical steps to a final close.

Selling function Promoting the product.

Senior citizen group People over 65.

Service mark Those words, symbols, or marks that are legally registered for use by a single company to refer to a service offering.

Service wholesalers Merchant wholesalers that provide all the wholesaling functions.

Shopping products Products that a customer feels are worth the time and effort to compare with competing products.

Simple trade era A time when families traded or sold their surplus output to local distributors.

Single-line (or general-line) wholesalers Service wholesalers that carry a narrower line of merchandise than general merchandise wholesalers.

Single-line stores Stores that specialize in certain lines of related products rather than a wide assortment—sometimes called *limited-line stores*.

Single target market approach Segmenting the market and picking one of the homogeneous segments as the firm's target market.

Situation analysis An informal study of what information is already available in the problem area.

Skimming price policy Trying to sell the top of the market—the top of the demand curve—at a high price before aiming at more price-sensitive customers.

Social class A group of people who have approximately equal social position as viewed by others in the society.

Social needs Needs concerned with love, friendship, status, and esteem—things that involve a person's interaction with others.

Social responsibility A firm's obligation to improve its positive effects on society and reduce its negative effects.

Sorting Separating products into grades and qualities desired by different target markets.

Source The sender of a message.

Specialty products Consumer products that the customer really wants and makes a special effort to find.

Specialty shop A type of conventional limited-line store—usually small and with a distinct personality.

Specialty wholesalers Service wholesalers that carry a very narrow range of products and offer more information and service than other service wholesalers.

Standardization and grading Sorting products according to size and quality.

Staples Products that are bought often, routinely, and without much thought.

Statistical packages Easy-to-use computer programs that analyze data.

Status quo objectives "Don't-rock-the-*pricing*-boat" objectives.

Stocking allowances Allowances given to wholesalers or retailers to get shelf space for a product—sometimes called *slotting allowances*.

Stockturn rate The number of times the average inventory is sold during a year.

Storing The marketing function of holding goods.

Storing function Holding goods until customers need them.

Straight rebuy A routine repurchase that may have been made many times before.

Strategic business unit (SBU) An organizational unit (within a larger company) that focuses its efforts on some product-markets and is treated as a separate profit center.

Strategic (management) planning The managerial process of developing and maintaining a match between an organization's resources and its market opportunities.

Substitutes Products that offer the buyer a choice.

Supercenters Very large stores that try to carry not only food and drug items, but all goods and services that the consumer purchases routinely (also called *hypermarkets*).

Supermarkets Large stores specializing in groceries—with self-service and wide assortments.

Supplies Expense items that do not become part of a finished product.

Supply chain The complete set of firms and facilities and logistics activities that are involved in procuring materials, transforming them into intermediate and finished products, and distributing them to customers.

Supply curve The quantity of products that will be supplied at various possible prices.

Supporting salespeople Salespeople who help the order-oriented salespeople but don't try to get orders themselves.

Sustainability The idea that it's important to meet present needs without compromising the ability of future generations to meet their own needs.

S.W.O.T. analysis Identifies and lists the firm's strengths and weaknesses and its opportunities and threats.

Target market A fairly homogeneous (similar) group of customers to whom a company wishes to appeal.

Target marketing A marketing mix is tailored to fit some specific target customers.

Target return objective A specific level of profit as an objective.

Task method An approach to developing a budget—basing the budget on the job to be done.

Team selling Different sales reps working together on a specific account.

Technical specialists Supporting salespeople who provide technical assistance to order-oriented salespeople.

Technology The application of science to convert an economy's resources to output.

Telemarketing Using the telephone to call on customers or prospects.

Telephone and direct-mail retailing Allows consumers to shop at home—usually placing orders by mail or a toll-free long-distance telephone call and charging the purchase to a credit card.

Total cost The sum of total fixed and total variable costs.

Total cost approach Evaluating each possible PD system and identifying *all* of the costs of each alternative.

Total fixed cost The sum of those costs that are fixed in total—no matter how much is produced.

Total quality management (TQM) The philosophy that everyone in the organization is concerned about quality, throughout all of the firm's activities, to better serve customer needs.

Total variable cost The sum of those changing expenses that are closely related to output—such as expenses for parts, wages, packaging materials, outgoing freight, and sales commissions.

Trade (functional) discount A list price reduction given to channel members for the job they are going to do.

Trade-in allowance A price reduction given for used products when similar new products are bought.

Trademark Those words, symbols, or marks that are legally registered for use by a single company.

Traditional channel systems A channel in which the various channel members make little or no effort to cooperate with each other.

Transporting The marketing function of moving goods.

Transporting function The movement of goods from one place to another.

Trend extension Extends past experience to predict the future.

Truck wholesalers Wholesalers that specialize in delivering products that they stock in their own trucks.

2/10, net 30 Allows a 2 percent discount off the face value of the invoice if the invoice is paid within 10 days.

Unfair trade practice acts Put a lower limit on prices, especially at the wholesale and retail levels.

Uniform delivered pricing Making an average freight charge to all buyers.

Universal functions of marketing Buying, selling, transporting, storing, standardizing and grading, financing, risk taking, and market information.

Universal product code (UPC) Special identifying marks for each product readable by electronic scanners.

Unsought products Products that potential customers don't yet want or know they can buy.

Validity The extent to which data measures what it is intended to measure.

Value in use pricing Setting prices that will capture some of what customers will save by substituting the firm's product for the one currently being used.

Value pricing Setting a fair price level for a marketing mix that really gives the target market superior customer value.

Vendor analysis Formal rating of suppliers on all relevant areas of performance.

Vertical integration Acquiring firms at different levels of channel activity.

Vertical marketing systems Channel systems in which the whole channel focuses on the same target market at the end of the channel.

Voluntary chains Wholesaler-sponsored groups that work with independent retailers.

Wants Needs that are learned during a person's life.

Warranty What the seller promises about its product.

Wheel of retailing theory New types of retailers enter the market as low-status, low-margin, low-price operators and then, if successful, evolve into more conventional retailers offering more services with higher operating costs and higher prices.

Wheeler Lea Amendment Law that bans unfair or deceptive acts in commerce.

Wholesalers Firms whose main function is providing *wholesaling activities*.

Wholesaling The *activities* of those persons or establishments that sell to retailers and other merchants, or to industrial, institutional, and commercial users, but who do not sell in large amounts to final consumers.

Zone pricing Making an average freight charge to all buyers within specific geographic areas.